International Journal on Advances in Software

2017 vol. 10 nr. 3&4

Printed from e-media with permission by:

Curran Associates, Inc.
57 Morehouse Lane
Red Hook, NY 12571

Some format issues inherent in the e-media version may also appear in this print version.

Printed by Curran Associates, Inc. (2018)

International Academy, Research, and Industry Association (IARIA)
412 Derby Way
Wilmington, DE 19810

Phone: (408) 893-6407
Fax: (408) 527-6351

petre@iaria.org

Additional copies of this publication are available from:

Curran Associates, Inc.
57 Morehouse Lane
Red Hook, NY 12571 USA
Phone: 845-758-0400
Fax: 845-758-2633
Email: curran@proceedings.com
Web: www.proceedings.com

The *International Journal on Advances in Software* is published by IARIA.
ISSN: 1942-2628
journals site: http://www.iariajournals.org
contact: petre@iaria.org

International Journal on Advances in Software
Volume 10, Number 3 & 4, 2017

Antonio Bucchiarone, Fondazione Bruno Kessler, Italy
Georg Buchgeher, Software Competence Center Hagenberg GmbH, Austria
Dumitru Burdescu, University of Craiova, Romania
Martine Cadot, University of Nancy / LORIA, France
Isabel Candal-Vicente, Universidad del Este, Puerto Rico
Juan-Vicente Capella-Hernández, Universitat Politècnica de València, Spain
Jose Carlos Metrolho, Polytechnic Institute of Castelo Branco, Portugal
Alain Casali, Aix-Marseille University, France
Yaser Chaaban, Leibniz University of Hanover, Germany
Savvas A. Chatzichristofis, Democritus University of Thrace, Greece
Antonin Chazalet, Orange, France
Jiann-Liang Chen, National Dong Hwa University, China
Shiping Chen, CSIRO ICT Centre, Australia
Wen-Shiung Chen, National Chi Nan University, Taiwan
Zhe Chen, College of Computer Science and Technology, Nanjing University of Aeronautics and Astronautics, China PR
Po-Hsun Cheng, National Kaohsiung Normal University, Taiwan
Yoonsik Cheon, The University of Texas at El Paso, USA
Lau Cheuk Lung, INE/UFSC, Brazil
Robert Chew, Lien Centre for Social Innovation, Singapore
Andrew Connor, Auckland University of Technology, New Zealand
Rebeca Cortázar, University of Deusto, Spain
Noël Crespi, Institut Telecom, Telecom SudParis, France
Carlos E. Cuesta, Rey Juan Carlos University, Spain
Duilio Curcio, University of Calabria, Italy
Mirela Danubianu, "Stefan cel Mare" University of Suceava, Romania
Paulo Asterio de Castro Guerra, Tapijara Programação de Sistemas Ltda. - Lambari, Brazil
Cláudio de Souza Baptista, University of Campina Grande, Brazil
Maria del Pilar Angeles, Universidad Nacional Autonónoma de México, México
Rafael del Vado Vírseda, Universidad Complutense de Madrid, Spain
Giovanni Denaro, University of Milano-Bicocca, Italy
Nirmit Desai, IBM Research, India
Vincenzo Deufemia, Università di Salerno, Italy
Leandro Dias da Silva, Universidade Federal de Alagoas, Brazil
Javier Diaz, Rutgers University, USA
Nicholas John Dingle, University of Manchester, UK
Roland Dodd, CQUniversity, Australia
Aijuan Dong, Hood College, USA
Suzana Dragicevic, Simon Fraser University- Burnaby, Canada
Cédric du Mouza, CNAM, France
Ann Dunkin, Palo Alto Unified School District, USA
Jana Dvorakova, Comenius University, Slovakia
Lars Ebrecht, German Aerospace Center (DLR), Germany
Hans-Dieter Ehrich, Technische Universität Braunschweig, Germany
Jorge Ejarque, Barcelona Supercomputing Center, Spain
Atilla Elçi, Aksaray University, Turkey

International Journal on Advances in Software
Volume 10, Numbers 3 & 4, 2017

CONTENTS

International Journal on Advances in Software, vol 10 no 3 & 4, year 2017, http://www.iariajournals.org/software/

An Approach to Provide User Guidance in Special Purpose Machines and its Evaluation

Valentin Plenk*, Sascha Lang†, Florian Wogenstein‡
Institute of Information Systems at Hof University, Hof, Germany
Email: *valentin.plenk@iisys.de, †sascha.lang@iisys.de, ‡florian.wogenstein@iisys.de

Abstract—**This paper proposes to make complex production machines more user-friendly. Improved machines help the operator in case of an error message or a process event by displaying recommendations, such as "at the last 10 occurrences of this event the operators performed the following keystrokes". The messages are generated from statistical data on former user-interaction and previous process-events. The data represents the knowledge of all the machine operators. The data is gathered by logging user-interaction and process-events during regular operation of the production machine. This approach allows to store the operators' expert knowledge in the production machine without human intervention.**

Keywords–machine-learning; human machine interfaces; special-purpose machines; production machines

I. Introduction

State of the art appliances (e.g., photocopiers) are equipped with user interfaces that help the operator fix problems (e.g., paper jam). The implementation of the software driving the interface contains structured knowledge about error scenarios and step by step instructions on how to deal with them.

While this approach leads to very well usable appliances, its proliferation is hampered by the engineering effort required for the definition of the error scenarios. This effort is only economically reasonable if it can be refinanced over a large number of appliances. In the context of production machines, particularily special purpose machines, where the usual lot size is in a range below 10 similar machines per annum [2], a different approach is needed.

To deal with that problem the authors propose to use machine-learning algorithms to generate situation-specific user guidance information from former user interactions and previous process events.

Similar applications of machine learning algorithms are commonly used to enhance user interfaces in smartphones or other IT-systems [3] [4]. In the production-machine sector, however, the application of machine learning algorithms is apparently limited to applications dealing with pattern detection in process data or distingushing different datasets [5] [6] [7] [8]. In these papers the authors use the output of the algorithms to detect errors or problems with production quality. This information is then presented to the production-machine operator requesting him to deal with the situation. While this approach undoubtedly helps to make processes more stable, it also demands ever more expertise of the operators.

Challiol et al. [9] describe an application striving to display content dependent on the users context. While addressing a completely different application domain this is similar to our approach in terms of matching context to content. The context matching algorithm proposed in [10] is quite abstract as is its performance evaluation presented in [11].

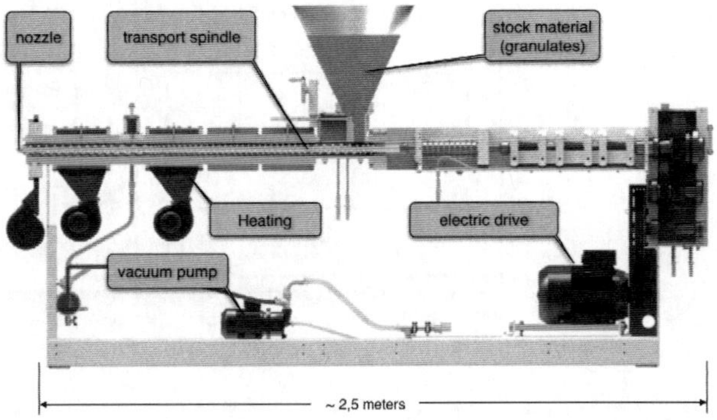

Figure 1. Working principle of an extruder
(courtesy: Hans Weber Maschinenfabrik, Kronach, Germany)

All the papers cited above assume the content to be available, while we propose to automatically generate the content of the recommendations. The algorithms presented in Section V build a knowledge base that can be edited, i.e., the recommendations can be presented to an experienced operator who can modify or delete them. This is a marked difference to most machine learning algorithms whose knowledge base cannot be edited.

In this paper we extend our previous work. Our initial approach presented in [1] transformed the raw data into an event sequence. In [12] we added a second group of algorithms working with the raw data and performed tests to compare the performance of both algorithm types. In this paper we present a more detailed evaluation of our algorithms. Section VII-C introduces a bigger dataset which we processed differently based on feedback from our test users.

Section II describes the application context and the system architecture. Section III explains the fundamental idea of the knowledge base. In Section IV we detail strategies for data preprocessing. The main component, i.e., the recommendation algorithms, is presented in Section V. Section VI briefly presents the GUI of the system. In Section VII we describe an mostly automatic way to score the quality of the recommendations generated by our algorithm. Section VIII summarizes the different scores achieved by the different algorithms and reviews the computing exigencies of the algorithms. Section IX briefly summarizes our findings so far and then gives an outlook on our work schedule for the future.

II. Test Environment

The test scenario for the development of the system is a plastics extruder (see Figure 1). The basic purpose of this machine is to melt and transport plastic granulates by means of a threaded spindle towards a nozzle. The main process

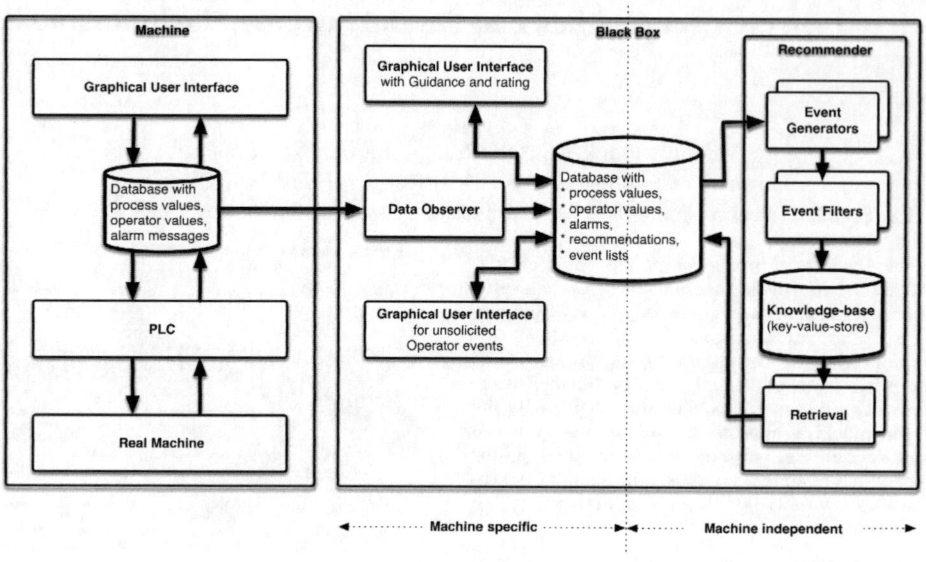

Figure 2. Structure of the system

parameters are the speed of the spindle, the temperature of the extruded material and the pressure of the material at the nozzle. We have equipped three production machines with our systems. All three extruders are manufactured by Hans Weber Maschinenfabrik GmbH. They provide the machine specific part of our system (see Figure 2). The machines are operated by our other project partners: Two of them by H.N. Zapf GmbH & Co. KG and one by Rehau AG & Co. KG. These two partners provide us with data and feedback from the users.

Figure 2 shows the structure of the system. The box on the left represents the existing machine consisting of the actual machine, a PLC-controller for the real-time control and a graphical user interface (GUI). The GUI communicates with the PLC by means of a database containing all PLC-variables and all alarms raised by the PLC. This is a fairly standard architecture.

Our addition is shown in the right box. The Black Box is basically a PC running several software components:

The DataObserver reads the data in the machine database, transforms it to our internal format and stores it in a second database. This component is machine specific and needs read-only access to the PLC variables.

The database is the interface between the machine specific parts and the machine independent part. It stores the PLC-variables and the PLC-alarms written by the DataObserver as well as the output of the Event Generators and the Recommender. The two main tables in the database are shown in Tables I and II. The PLC-variable table contains all the process and operator values of the machine's PLC. Each variable is stored in its own column. The DataObserver adds a new row every 10 seconds. The second table stores alarms which are raised by the machine.

The Recommender is machine-independent. It is the key component of the system. It builds a knowledge base from the logged PLC-variables and generates recommendations when it detects a new alarm message in the database.

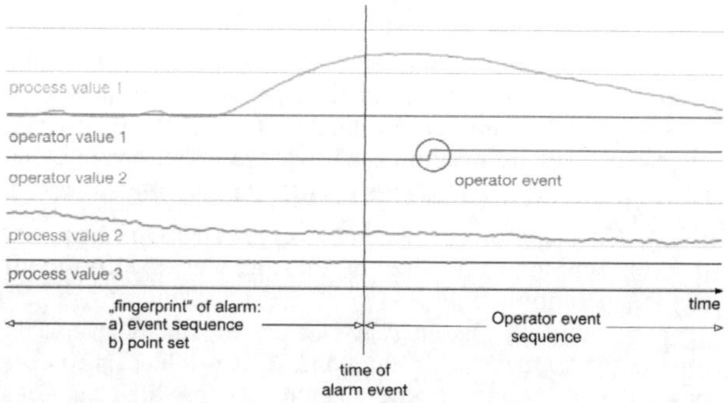

Figure 3. Principle of user guidance generation

The GUI is used to translate the recommendations into operator instructions that reflect the wording on standard GUI of the machine. It displays a recommendation and allows the operator to evaluate the quality of the recommendation.

III. Proposed Approach

The basic idea of our approach is to extract operator knowledge from the continuous stream of PLC-variables logged during the operation of the machine. We want our algorithms to be as generic as possible and to work without deeper understanding of the machine. However, we need information to recommend actions to the machine operator: Which columns in the PLC variable database (Table I) correspond to values affected by the process, e.g., actual temperature, and which are controlled by the operator, e.g., temperature set-point. We call the first set of variables process values and the second set operator values. The rows of the database hold consecutive values for these variables.

With this information we propose to generate user guidance as shown in Figure 3: The alarm messages in the alarm database are used to tag discrete parts of the endless stream of data logged in the PLC-variable database. The alarm tag and the data before the occurrence of the alarm are regarded as a fingerprint that identifies the alarm. This fingerprint consists of process and operator variables. The data after the occurrence of the alarm also consists of process and operator values. The actions performed by the operator will change some of these operator values. By detecting these changes we build a sequence of operator events. This sequence represents the actions of the operator corresponding to a fingerprint.

With fingerprints and corresponding operator sequences we build a key value store representing the operators' expert knowledge. The fingerprint is the key and the operator sequence the value. These key-value pairs are generated by monitoring the continuous stream of data logged during the operation of the machine. When the machine raises an alarm the algorithms generate a key for that new problem. Now the key-value pairs in the knowledge base are searched for the best matching elements. The best matches are then provided as a recommendation to solve the problem. The fingerprint and the operator sequence performed by the operator is then stored in the knowledge base as a new key value pair.

In Section V we describe two generally different approaches for the processing of the fingerprints: One set of algorithms directly uses the process and operator variables. The other set converts the data in the fingerprint into an event sequence. Events are generated for the parts of a time series where the data changes. Several events for one or several columns constitute an event sequence.

IV. Generation of Events

The curves for process value 2 and process value 3 presented in Figure 3 show little variance over time. By generating events for the points in time where a variable changes we can suppress bits of data with no or low variance.

We distinguish between process events and operator events. The process events are generated from process values, the operator events from operator values.

For process events we have developed two different algorithms. The selection of the appropriate algorithm for each process value needs to be done by a person with sufficient knowledge about the process and the machine.

We encode all events as string values containing the name of the PLC variable and either a numerical value or a class name. This encoding is not as efficient as a binary coding but it allows us to interpret the event lists during our tests.

A. Operator Events

Operator events represent human interaction with the machine. These events are identified by checking columns containing operator values.

We developed two algorithms to generate these operator event sequences.

The first type compares all consecutive rows within an alarm situation. For each column whose value changes it generates an event when the new value stays constant for at least three rows. We need this restriction because some operator inputs are made by a hand wheel. To detect the final value we wait until the operator has not made a change for 30 seconds. If we use this method we can get multiple steps for one operator value.

The second method lakes all operator values in the moment the alarm starts and compares them with the values they have at the end of the alarm. If one value has changed it will then be part of our operator sequence.

In consultation with our project partners we use the second type for dataset 4. As a further improvement we replace the absolute value with a relative value and come up with recommendations like "Change drive speed by +5 rpm" instead of telling "Set the drive to 15 rpm".

In both cases these events represent operator interactions. They are coded as string values, e.g., `Loop2_SP_170`, containing the name of the PLC variable and the (relative) value of the setpoint adjusted by the operator.

B. Process Events

For process variables we distinguish two types of variables: The first group of variables has an associated setpoint. The second group does not have such a setpoint, but we are able to create our own setpoint.

For both classifications we chose to use literals instead of numbers for our classes. Thus, we can easily distinguish between operator events and process events when reviewing the data.

TABLE I. Example of the database with PLC-Variables

PointID	AIn1_1	AOut1_1	AIn1_2	AIn2_1	AOut2_1	Loop1_1_PV	Loop1_1_SP	Loop1_1_OP	...
2016-09-27 07:42:37	87.488	87	65.169	95.985	95	22.5	120	0	...
2016-09-27 07:42:47	87.47	88	65.638	95.973	95	22.6	120	0	...
2016-09-27 07:42:57	87.03	87	65.461	96.027	96	22.6	120	0	...
2016-09-27 07:43:07	88.378	88	64.559	96.011	96	22.7	120	0	...
2016-09-27 07:43:17	85.695	86	64.93	96.008	96	22.8	120	0	...
2016-09-27 07:43:27	87.792	88	65.272	95.968	95	22.8	120	0	...
2016-09-27 07:43:37	87.615	88	65.589	96.004	95	22.7	120	0	...
2016-09-27 07:43:47	86.761	87	65.272	95.946	96	22.8	120	0	...
2016-09-27 07:43:57	87.446	87	65.191	95.997	96	22.8	120	0	...
2016-09-27 07:44:07	87.213	87	65.182	95.969	96	22.8	120	0	...
2016-09-27 07:44:17	86.472	86	64.172	95.973	96	22.8	120	0	...
2016-09-27 07:44:27	86.634	86	65.349	95.893	96	22.7	120	0	...
2016-09-27 07:44:37	87.291	87	64.776	96	96	22.6	120	0	...
2016-09-27 07:44:47	87.58	87	65.428	96.023	96	22.5	120	0	...
2016-09-27 07:44:57	86.966	87	65.522	95.981	96	22.6	120	0	...
...									

1) Process Values with Setpoint: We need a pair of process and operator variable. The latter contains the setpoint. We calculate the deviation from the setpoint of the variable

$$Var_{rel} = \left| \frac{Var_{Process}}{Var_{Setpoint}} \cdot 100\% \right| \quad (1)$$

Then, we sort Var_{rel} into one of the classes shown in Table III and generate an event every time the process value enters a new class. These events are also coded as string values, e.g., `Loop_1_2_PV_X`.

2) Process Values relative to Moving Average: For process variables without corresponding setpoint, we calculate the arithmetic mean over the last n values. With this as the setpoint we treat the variable as described in Section IV-B1.

For our fingerprint, we have arbitrarily chosen to use the five minutes before an alarm occurred. So, we have 30 datasets per alarm. To create a suitable moving average we have to take much more then 30 datasets. At the moment, we again arbitrarily chose to use 360 values, which equals one hour. Both the time which is used for the fingerprint and the amount of values used for the moving average need further investigation whether they are reasonable values or not.

V. Recommendation Generation

In case the machine needs operator assistance, i.e., it raised an alarm by adding a new row in the error message table, our guidance generation algorithm is triggered. The fingerprint of the current situation is used as a search key for the knowledge base.

Section V-A describes a set of algorithms that convert the data in the fingerprint into an event sequence and then searches for this sequence. In Section V-B, we introduce algorithms that directly use the N-dimensional point set of process and operator variables in the fingerprint as a key.

A. Recommendation Generation using Event Sequences

1) Map: In [1], we used a content addressable memory, i.e., a Java map, to store the knowledge base. We build the knowledge base by iterating through all past occurrences of alarms. For each fingerprint we calculate the event sequence and use it as key and the corresponding operator event sequence as the value. Each key-value pair is then stored in the map. For multiple entries, we store the frequency of the respective sequence in the past.

To generate a recommendation, we simply generate the event sequence corresponding to the fingerprint of the current alarm and query the map for this key. For map entries with several values for one key, we return several recommendations and their frequency in the past. In case this key is not in the map, we cannot generate a recommendation.

TABLE II. Example of the database with machine alarms

MainNr	SubNr	Start	End
212	0	2016-09-27 07:42:37	2016.09-27 07:45:47
213	0	2016-09-27 07:42:47	2016.09-27 07:48:57
214	0	2016-09-27 07:42:47	2016.09-27 10:50:36
215	0	2016-09-27 07:42:47	2016.09-27 07:46:47
216	0	2016-09-27 07:42:47	2016.09-27 07:46:57
221	0	2016-09-27 07:42:57	2016.09-27 07:46:07
224	0	2016-09-27 07:43:17	2016.09-27 07:49:17
126	0	2016-09-27 07:46:17	2016.09-29 00:48:02
		...	

TABLE III. Classes for process variables

Var_{rel}	$\leq 1.77\%$	$\leq 3.16\%$	$\leq 5.62\%$	$\leq 10.0\%$	$\leq 17.78\%$
Class	A	B	C	D	E
Var_{rel}	$\leq 31.62\%$	$\leq 56.23\%$	$\leq 100.0\%$	$\leq 177.8\%$	$> 177.8\%$
Class	F	G	H	I	X

2) Map with Statistical Event Filtering: The map presented in Section V-A1 will only find a recommendation if the search key exactly matches one of the stored keys. If the event sequences contain spurious events, e.g., caused by noise, we cannot find a match. So, we created an algorithm to suppress the irrelevant events.

We use a statistical approach identifying unimportant events to remove them from the process event sequence. The filtered event list is then processed as described in Section V-A1.

The filtering is done in two steps. First, we iterate through the event sequences of all stored fingerprints for one alarm and count how often an event is contained in the set of event sequences. In the next step, we remove all events with a frequency below a defined threshold from the event sequences. So far our tests indicate that 0.5 is a reasonable choice.

3) String matching: The map algorithm presented in Section V-A1 requires the key in the query to be absolutely identical to one key in the map. Thus, it is very sensitive to changes in the key, i.e., the event-sequence. We alleviate this rigorous selection criterion by storing all keys and the corresponding values in a vector. We then loop through all the elements and compare the sequence of the query to the sequence stored in the vector. We return the value as a recommendation that is most similar to the key in the query.

We evaluate the similarity with two distance measurements for string values: the Levenshtein distance and the Jaccard distance, as described in [13]. For the comparison, we treat each event in the sequence as one letter.

a) Levenshtein distance: For two strings of length a and b the Levenshtein distance is defined as:

$$d_l = \begin{cases} \text{if } a = b, & 0 \\ \text{otherwise,} & min\left\{d_{lv}\left(a, b_{1:|b|-1}\right) + 1\,,\right. \\ & d_{lv}\left(a_{1:|a|-1}, b\right) + 1, \\ & \left. d_{lv}\left(a_{1:|a|-1}, b_{1:|b|-1}\right) + 1\right\} \end{cases} \quad (2)$$

b) Jaccard distance: For the sets A and B each containing all letters of the strings a and b, the Jaccard distance is defined as:

$$d_j\left(A, B\right) = 1 - J\left(A, B\right) = 1 - \frac{|A \cap B|}{|A \cup B|} \quad (3)$$

with $0 \leq d_j(A, B) \leq 1$.

c) Some Examples: Table IV gives some examples by comparing four different event sequences. Smaller numbers in the distance columns indicate more similar sequences. The values in the Jaccard and the Levenshtein columns use different scales and are only comparable inside their respective column.

The first row shows the distances between two event sequences having one event switched. The Jaccard distance has the lowest possible value of 0, whereas the Levenshtein distance returns 2 by a maximum possible value of 3.

In the second example, only one event differs from another element. Here the Jaccard distance returns 0.5 whereas the Levenshtein distance returns 1.

The third row shows an example with one switched event and one different event. Jaccard judges them with a distance of 0.5 whereas Levenshtein returns 3. Although they are not completely different Levenshtein returns its maximum value.

The last three rows show the performance on completely different event sequences. Both distance measurements confirm this dissimilarity.

In conclusion, the Jaccard distance is more robust if some event sequences are switched. If both have a completely different order but the same elements, they will be treated as similar. Whereas the Levenshtein distance will treat them as totally dissimilar in the worst case.

B. Recommendation using point sets

The approach described in Section V-A3 allows for disturbance by not requiring a complete match between search key and stored key. We can take this idea one step further by regarding the data points in the fingerprint as a set of n-dimensional points. For one timestamp every process and operator value is one dimension.

As in Section V-A3, we store the point sets, i.e., the keys, and the corresponding operator events, i.e., the values, in a vector. We then loop through all the elements and compare the sequence of the query to the sequence stored in the vector. We return the value as a recommendation that is most similar to the key in the query. The procedures to find the most similar point set are described in the following sections.

1) Distance measurements for points: Bacher et al. [14] propose several ways to compare two points in space.

a) Minkowski-Metric: For two points a and b with the dimension i the Minkowski-Metric is defined as:

$$d_m(a,b) = \left[\sum_i |a_i - b_i|^r\right]^{\frac{1}{q}} \tag{4}$$

If we modify the two parameters q and r, we get different distance measurements. In particular, we use:

- $q = \infty$ and $r = \infty$: Chebychev- or Maximum-distance
- $q = 1$ and $r = 1$: Manhattan-distance
- $q = 2$ and $r = 2$: Euclidean-distance
- $q = 1$ and $r = 2$: Squared Euclidean-distance

TABLE IV. COMPARISON BETWEEN JACCARD AND LEVENSHTEIN DISTANCE

EventSequence 1 (query)	EventSequence 2 (key)	Jaccard	Levenshtein
T_1_A#T_3_C#AIn1_B	T_1_A#Ain1_B#T_3_C	0	2
T_1_A#T_3_C#AIn1_B	T_1_B#T_3_C#AIn1_B	0.5	1
T_1_A#Ain1_B#T_3_C	T_1_B#T_3_C#AIn1_B	0.5	3
T_1_A#T_3_C#AIn1_B	T_2_A#AIn2_C#T_4_D	1	3
T_1_A#Ain1_B#T_3_C	T_2_A#AIn2_C#T_4_D	1	3
T_1_B#T_3_C#AIn1_B	T_2_A#AIn2_C#T_4_D	1	3

b) Jaccard-Metric: The Jaccard similarity can be used for sets, as described in Section V-A3. It can also be used for points. Let a and b be two n-dimensional data points. With i being one of the dimensions the Jaccard distance for two points is defined as:

$$d_{jp}(a,b) = 1 - \frac{\sum_i a_i + \sum_i b_i - 2\sum_i \min(a_i, b_i)}{\sum_i a_i + \sum_i b_i - \sum_i \min(a_i, b_i)} \tag{5}$$

c) Canberrra-Metric: The Canberra metric for two points a and b with i being a dimension it is defined as:

$$d_c(a,b) = \sum_i \frac{|a_i - b_i|}{a_i + b_i} \tag{6}$$

Identical differences in the nominator result in a higher weighting for small values of the denominator.

2) Distance measurements for point sets: In this section, we discuss distances for point sets. The Hausdorff distance as well as the Linkage measurements make use of point distances presented in Section V-B1. Jaccard, Dice and Sokal-Sneath distances on the other hand do not use them.

a) Hausdorff-Distance: The Hausdorff-distance defines a similarity between two not empty sets A and B.

Let a be an element of set A and b an element of B. And d being a distance defined in Section V-B1, the distance between a and B is defined as:

$$D_H(a,B) = \min_{b \in B} d(a,b) \tag{7}$$

With this definition, the Hausdorff-distance between two sets A and B can be expressed as:

$$d_h(A,B) = \max\left\{\max_{a \in A} D(a,B), \max_{b \in B} D(b,A)\right\} \tag{8}$$

b) Single-, Complete- and Average-Linkage: These metrics determine the distance from one point of one set to all the other points of the second set.

The Single-Linkage method only uses the smallest distance between two points of both sets. The Complete-Linkage on the other hand uses the longest.

The Average-Linkage method calculates the arithmetic mean of all point-to-point distances. This mean is taken as the result.

Let A and B be two point-sets. Together with a and b being points in A and B and d being a distance defined in V-B1, the Single-Linkage can be written as:

$$D_{SL}(A,B) = \min_{a \in A, b \in B} d(a,b) \tag{9}$$

With the same notation, the Complete-Linkage can be written as:

$$D_{CL}(A,B) = \max_{a \in A, b \in B} d(a,b) \tag{10}$$

Let $|A|$ be the number of points contained in set A and $|B|$ the number of points in set B, then the Average-Linkage is defined as:

$$D_{AL}(A,B) = \frac{1}{|A||B|} \sum_{a \in A, b \in B} d(a,b) \tag{11}$$

VI. Guidance Display

As soon as the Recommender has found operator sequences that fit the current fingerprint the GUI decodes the operator event sequence and displays the recommendations as shown in Figure 4.

On the left hand a list of currently raised alarm messages is shown. The list on the top right shows the recommendations found for the current fingerprint belonging to this alarm. Underneath this lists the selected recommendation is displayed with detailed actions that the operator has to take.

The recommendations can be scored by the operator. In future this will help our algorithms to create better results.

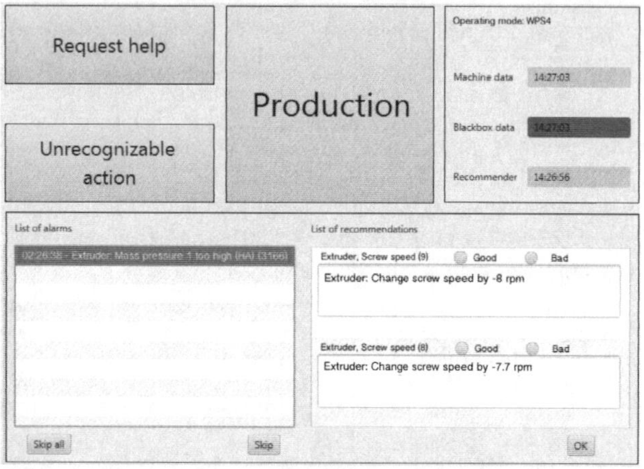

Figure 4. An example user guidance display

VII. Quality of Recommendations

In the previous section we described a system for generating user guidance. Since this system has been designed to interact with the operator during production it is not well suited for comparative testing of different algorithms and parameter sets lest we disrupt production or frustrate the operator. Instead in this section, we use a "batch-mode"to automatically evaluate our algorithms.

The batch-mode basically iterates through a long time series of PLC-variables and alarms. It triggers the recommender for each alarm encountered during the iterations and requests a recommendation. This recommendation is compared to the operator sequence stored in the time series. This sequence is taken as the expected recommendation or "truth" for this particular alarm. If the recommendation is equal to the operator sequence in the test-set the test is positive and C_{pos} is incremented. If a different sequence is returned or the algorithm returns nothing the test fails and C_{neg} is incremented. With these two parameters we can calculate the Quality Q_{alg} for the algorithm:

$$Q_{alg} = \frac{C_{pos}}{C_{neg} + C_{pos}} \cdot 100\% \tag{12}$$

We need to train the recommender algorithms before feeding them alarms. We generate the training data by dividing the dataset into four subsets with an equal number of alarms. One of these sets is taken as the test-set. The others are combined into a training set. Thus, we can run four tests on each of our algorithms by using the test-sets as training data. The remaining sets of alarms and data are used to train the algorithms.

TABLE V. Dataset 1: The five most frequently raised alarms

Alarm number	Alarm count	With op-sequence	Different op-sequences
1101	171	57	12
1012	107	86	19
12	106	53	19
22	106	49	16
2	59	30	10

The expression in Equation (12) ranges between $0 \leq Q_{alg} \leq 100\%$. However, a closer look at the test-sets reveals cases where an operator sequence only occurs in the test set and not in the training set. Thus, the algorithm cannot learn this recommendation and is not able to detect it correctly. Some other keys have more than one associated value. In these cases the algorithm is not able to decide which operator sequence is the right one. Consequently the maximum possible score is less than 100%.

For our evaluation, we use the data gathered during 5 minutes before the alarm to generate the fingerprint. The operator sequence is generated for the duration of the alarm, i.e., for the period of time in which the alarm condition is true.

A. Dataset 1 – Simulation

As a first dataset, we use a slightly extended version of the data, we used in [1]. This dataset was obtained by operating a simulation model of the production machine. It contains $N_{Rows} = 1,150,063$ rows and $N_{Alarms} = 1,254$ alarms.

As in [1], we focus on alarm 1101. There are 171 instances of this alarm in the dataset. For 57 of these instances, we could generate the 12 different operator sequences shown in Table VI. The remaining 114 occurrences of the alarm do not contain operator sequences because the simulation was not always operated properly.

8 of these operator sequences corresponding to 10 occurrences of alarm 1101 are only contained in one of the four subsets. Thus these sets are either part of the training data or of the test data. Therefore, we reduce the maximum possible score from 57 to 47.

For the event based algorithms, we found 3 ambiguous event sequences. Table XI shows all event sequences. The ambiguous event sequences have more than one corresponding operator sequence. We consider ambiguous sequences as unlearnable. Our algorithm will always recommend the sequence

TABLE VI. Dataset 1: Operator sequences

Frequency	Operator Sequence	Learnable
36	Loop1_3_SP_170	yes
7	Loop1_2_SP_170#Loop1_3_SP_170	yes
4	Loop1_4_SP_170	yes
2	Loop1_3_SP_250	no
1	Loop1_3_SP_225	no
1	AOUT1_1_OutValue_10	no
1	AOUT1_1_OutValue_29	no
1	AOUT1_1_OutValue_50	no
1	AOUT1_2_OutValue_9	no
1	Loop1_7_SP_250	no
1	Loop1_2_SP_250#Loop1_3_SP_250	no
1	Loop1_3_SP_170#Loop1_4_SP_170	no

with the highest frequency. Therefore, we subtract the number of the other sequences from the maximum possible. In our case this reduces the maximum possible by 10 to 37.

For event sequence based algorithms we get a maximum possible score of

$$Q_{alg_{1evmax}} = \frac{37}{57} \cdot 100\% \approx 65\% \tag{13}$$

For the point based algorithms, we get a maximum score of

$$Q_{alg_{1Pmax}} = \frac{47}{57} \cdot 100\% \approx 82\% \tag{14}$$

B. Dataset 2 – Converted Data from real Machine

The second set of process- and operator values was taken from a production machine. This dataset is identical to the dataset we introduced in [12].

The database of that machine does not yet conform to our interface standard and thus did not log the alarms. We resorted to generating our own alarms based on process experts' definitions for lower and upper bounds of process values. The first occurrence of a value being outside the bounds was the starting time for an alarm. The stopping time was taken the moment the value was back inside the bounds.

The resulting database contains $N_{Rows} = 1,223,992$ rows describing the machine state and $N_{Alarms} = 5,667$ alarms. Table VII shows the five most frequent alarms in the dataset. With the machine logging the data every 10 seconds, we have a runtime of $\approx 3,400$ hours. This means, we have 1.7 alarms per hour. According to H.N. Zapf GmbH & Co. KG, the project partner operating the machine, this number seems to be very high.

Not all alarms, we generated from the machine were useful for our test. Some alarms were not followed by operator events. We assume that these alarms are artifacts of our data preparation algorithm. Other alarms obviously occurred at the end of a production shift and consequently led to the recommendation to shut down the machine. We chose alarm 225 for our evaluation.

Alarm 225 occurred 1949 times. For 277 instances of this alarm, we could create a fingerprint and an operator sequence.

We assume that this difference is partly due to our self-generated alarms and partly due to spurious and short alarms that disappear without user intervention.

For these 277 instances of alarm 225, we generated the 22 operator sequences shown in Table VIII.

13 of these operator sequences corresponding to 46 event sequences occur in only one of the four subsets. Consequently, we reduce the theoretical maximum by 46. Furthermore, we found 33 ambiguous event sequences shown in Table XII. We subtract all but one of these ambiguous sequences except for

TABLE VII. DATASET 2: THE FIVE MOST FREQUENTLY RAISED ALARMS

Alarm number	Alarm count	With op-sequence	Different op-equences
225	1949	277	22
423	1059	70	43
122	763	243	93
123	503	149	69
214	238	142	81
213	109	76	60

TABLE VIII. DATASET 2: OPERATOR SEQUENCES FOR ALARM 225

Frequency	Operator Sequence	Learnable
54	AOut1_1_85#	yes
53	AOut1_1_84#	yes
30	AOut1_1_83#	yes
30	AOut1_1_86#	yes
20	AOut1_1_81#	yes
17	AOut1_1_82#	yes
16	AOut1_1_77#	no
14	AOut1_1_87#	yes
11	AOut1_1_80#	yes
9	AOut1_1_76#	no
7	AOut1_1_78#	no
5	AOut1_1_79#	no
2	AOut1_1_88#	yes
1	AOut1_1_0#AOut2_1_6#	no
1	AOut1_1_83#AOut2_1_64#	no
1	AOut1_1_83#AOut2_1_98#	no
1	AOut1_1_84#AOut2_1_98#	no
1	AOut1_1_85#AOut2_1_98#	no
1	AOut1_1_87#AOut2_1_73#	no
1	AOut1_1_89#	no
1	AOut1_1_91#Loop2_2_SP_230#	no
1	AOut2_1_99#	no

those that are already marked as not learnable because they are appearing in only one subset. So, we have to subtract further 47 alarms.

For event based algorithms, we get a maximum score of:

$$Q_{alg_{2evmax}} = \frac{184}{277} \cdot 100\% \approx 66\% \tag{15}$$

For the point based algorithms, we get a maximum score of:

$$Q_{alg_{2Pmax}} = \frac{231}{277} \cdot 100\% \approx 83\% \tag{16}$$

C. Dataset 4 – Real Data

Dataset 4 was gathered on a new production machine equipped with our system. The machine became fully productive a few weeks ago, so we now have $N_{Rows} = 1,062,541$ of data corresponding to a run time of $\approx 2,951$ hours. During this time period, we found $N_{Alarms} = 10.431$ alarms.

We could also conduct some interviews with operators regarding the recommendations generated from the earlier version of that dataset presented as dataset 3 in [12].

As a result of this discussion we now distinguish between set-up operation and production. For now we focus on production because the set-up operations are deemed too sensitive to environmental influences not included in the process data. We found $N_{Alarms} = 1446$ alarms during operation.

Further investigation of our recommendations showed that the gap between some alarms is less or equal to ten seconds. To get operator sequences for these instances we decided to combine two or more alarms if the gap between them is 10 seconds or less. We also removed alarms with a duration of less than 10 seconds.

This gives us total of $N_{Alarms} = 358$ alarms. For 194 of these alarms we can generate an operator sequence. Table IX lists the recommendations that occur more than once.

1) Dataset 4a – including "no operation": Previously we ignored alarms without an operator event sequence. Our interview partners assured us however, that sometimes the appropriate operator action is to just wait for the alarm to clear

TABLE IX. DATASET 4: OPERATOR SEQUENCES

Frequency	Operator Sequence	Learnable
164	*no operator action*	yes
4	Meltpump.Output.Value_-1.0#	yes
4	Meltpump.Output.Value_-9.0#	yes
4	Meltpump.Output.Value_-4.0#	yes
4	Meltpump.Output.Value_-2.0#	yes
3	Meltpump.Output.Value_-0.1#	yes
3	Meltpump.Output.Value_-3.0#	yes
3	Meltpump.Output.Value_-0.5#	yes
3	Meltpump.Output.Value_-5.0#	yes
3	Meltpump.Output.Value_-10.0#	no
3	Tool.Temp1.SP_5.0#	no
2	Meltpump.Output.Value_-0.3#	yes
2	Meltpump.Output.Value_-0.2#	yes
2	Meltpump.Output.Value_12.0#	yes
2	Meltpump.Output.Value_4.0#	yes
2	Meltpump.Output.Value_-0.4#	yes
2	Meltpump.Output.Value_-5.8#	yes
2	Tool.Temp2.SP_5.0#	yes
2	Extruder.Temp3.SP_5.0# Extruder.Temp4.SP_5.0# Tool.Temp0.SP_5.0#	yes
2	Tool.Temp3.SP_-5.0#	no
2	Meltpump.Output.Value_-7.0#	no
2	Meltpump.Output.Value_-20.0#	no
2	Tool.Temp1.SP_10.0#	no

itself. Therefore, we include a "do nothing"-recommendation for alarms without operator event sequences.

Thus, we get get a maximum score for the point set based algorithms:

$$Q_{alg_{4_aPmax}} = \frac{208}{358} \cdot 100\% \approx 58\% \tag{17}$$

And for the event sequence based ones:

$$Q_{alg_{4_aevmax}} = \frac{198}{358} \cdot 100\% \approx 55\% \tag{18}$$

2) Dataset 4b – excluding "no operation": The 164 alarms without operator event sequences constitute nearly half of our alarms. Thus any algorithms recommending "do nothing" will achieve a high score. For a more detailed study of the other recommendations we remove these alarms from the test sets. This gives us a total of $N_{Alarms} = 195$ alarms. The learnable operator sequences are the same as in Table IX, only the first line with the empty recommendation is not in the dataset any more

If we determine which operator sequences are learnable we get a maximum score for the point set based algorithms:

$$Q_{alg_{4_bPmax}} = \frac{44}{195} \cdot 100\% \approx 23\% \tag{19}$$

And for the event sequence based ones:

$$Q_{alg_{4_bevmax}} = \frac{38}{195} \cdot 100\% \approx 19\% \tag{20}$$

VIII. COMPARISON OF THE ALGORITHMS

After processing the three datasets through all of our algorithms, we calculated the score for each dataset according to Equation (12). Table X shows the results of our tests. As discussed in Section VII the resulting values for Q_{alg} are not comparable between the datasets because of unlearnable and ambiguous operator event sequences.

Equations (13) to (20) give the maximum possible score for each dataset. With this score, we can normalize the results as

$$Q_{alg_{rel}} = \frac{Q_{alg}}{Q_{alg_{max}}} \cdot 100\% \tag{21}$$

To put the performance into perspective, we calculate the performance of a simple approach that always recommends the most frequent user sequence in the knowledge base. Such an approach will propose a correct operator sequence for all the alarms associated with the most frequent operator sequence:

$$Q_{simple} = \frac{100\%}{N_{OpSeq}} \cdot N_{mostFreqOpSeq} \tag{22}$$

i.e.,

$$Q_{simple_1} = \frac{100\%}{57} \cdot 36 \approx 63\% \tag{23}$$

$$Q_{simple_2} = \frac{100\%}{277} \cdot 54 \approx 19\% \tag{24}$$

$$Q_{simple_{4_a}} = \frac{100\%}{208} \cdot 164 \approx 79\% \tag{25}$$

$$Q_{simple_{4_b}} = \frac{100\%}{44} \cdot 4 \approx 9\% \tag{26}$$

Figure 5 shows the normalized performance of the different algorithms on the three datasets and for reference the normalized scores of the simple approach.

The mapping algorithm introduced in [1] and V-A1 scored $\approx 63\%$ on dataset 1. On dataset 2 it performed less with only $\approx 12\%$. On dataset 4a it only gives a few correct recommendations. On dataset 4b, however, it did not give any correct recommendations. We attribute this lack of performance to the fact that we have only a few identical event sequences. Only operator sequences which are mapped at least two times to identical event sequences can be discovered by the simple mapping algorithm. In dataset 4a we found 38 operator sequences which could be discovered by the simple mapping, in dataset 4b instead it was only one operator sequence. In total it scores less than the simple approach on all datasets based on real data.

With $\approx 42\%$ on dataset 2 the statistical filter performs better than the simple approach and is almost on par with the point based algorithms. It also shows good performance on dataset 4a together with the Levenshtein String Matching algorithm. However, in this case it is outperformed by the simple algorithm. With 16.7 % on dataset 4b it shows the best performance of all tested algorithms.

The point based algorithms score better on dataset 1 with almost 90% and mostly $> 40\%$ on dataset 2. Dataset 4a, however, proves difficult with $\approx 30 \ldots 37\%$. On dataset 4b the best results are near the simple algorithm or just a few percent above.

A. Computing exigencies

1) Memory requirements: The recommendation algorithms need to store keys and values for all past occurences of an alarm.

In our test environment, we used a table with $N_{Columns} = 51$ data columns in dataset 2 and 3 and $N_{Columns} = 250$ in dataset 1.

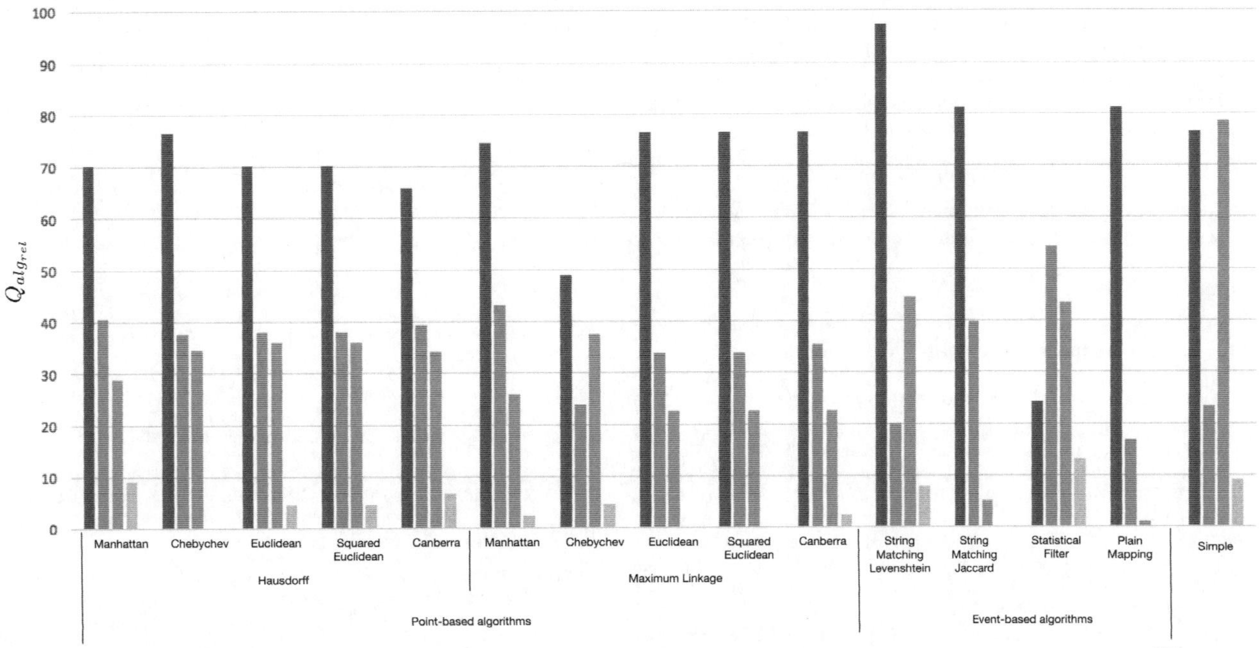

Figure 5. Normalized results for various recommender algorithms (left bars: Dataset 1, second bars: Dataset 2, third bars: Dataset 4a, right bars: Dataset 4b)

For every fingerprint, we use $N_{Rows} = 30$ rows, i.e., $N_{Rows} = 30$ datapoints per set.

For the dataset 1, we used alarm 225 with 276 occurences and split the data into four test sets. The test data for each test set contained approximately $N_{Alarms} = 210$ point sets.

The point based algorithms store $N_{Rows} \cdot N_{Columns}$ double variables as keys and a small number of operator events as values. Thus, in our worst case one fingerprint uses $30 \cdot 250 \cdot 8\,\text{byte} \approx 60\,\text{kbyte}$ of memory for the point set algorithms.

In $1\,\text{Gbyte}$ of memory, we can store data for ≈ 16.000 alarms. At a rate of $2\frac{\text{Alarms}}{\text{h}}$, which is considered a very high rate, this corresponds to $\approx 8000\text{h}$ of operation. A standard computer should have enough memory for two years of operation.

With an efficient coding of the events the event based algorithms will use considerably less memory for the fingerprint.

B. Processing times

Once the data is stored, the algorithms have to iterate through the stored keys to identify the proper record.

To determine the distance between two sets, we have to compare each data point from one set with each data point from the other set. For point based algorithms this results in N_{Rows}^2 comparisons. Every dimension has to be considered in the distance measurements, so overall a comparison of two sets will take $N_{Rows}^2 \cdot N_{Columns}$ floating point operations. To find a new recommendation the new point set has to be compared to all respective point sets in the stored data resulting in $N_{Rows}^2 \cdot N_{Columns} \cdot N_{Alarms}$ floating point operations.

For our test one recommendation will take round about $30^2 \cdot 250 \cdot 276 \cdot \frac{3}{4} \approx 46$ million floating point operations.

A standard computer should need significantly less than $1\,\text{sec}$ to produce a recommendation.

Event based algorithms do not have to compare all points but just the events generated from the points. The processing for the event generation is run only once prior to the iteration through the stored keys and therefore does not significantly increase the total processing time.

IX. Conclusion and Future Work

We presented a system to extract knowledge from data logged during the operatiom of a production machine. Three systems have been linked to actual production machines and have started to collect data.

Based on the scoring introduced in [12] we have shown that our recommender algorithms outperform a simple algorithm by a factor of 2 on some datasets. On the real data in our latest dataset they lack performance.

That being said, we want to point out that all algorithms need the operator sequences, we generate from the logged data. On dataset 4b we found 195 alarms with 159 different operator sequences. This shows that our approach is able to extract operator-knowledge from the logged data. Table IX shows that we still only have a few cases for each operator sequence. We hope that with more data we will also find more cases for these operator sequences, not just more different operator sequences.

Alarm conditions in the real data sometimes overlap each other, e.g., a warning for exceeding a first temperature level (high-alarm) and a second more urgent warning for exeeding a second higher temperature level (high-high-alarm). In these cases we generate several, usually identical, operator sequences and consequently generate multiple recommendations that might confuse the operator. Therefore, we plan to generate operator sequences without considering the alarms.

This approach will also permit us to identify situations that need operator action without the machine raising an alarm. This may help us to incite operators to fix potential problems before the machine detects them. Maybe, we can even indicate problems that the machine itself can not identify.

ACKNOWLEDGMENT

We thank our industry partners Hans Weber Maschinenfabrik GmbH, H.N. Zapf GmbH & Co. KG and Rehau AG & Co. KG for giving us access to their machines and feedback on our software.

This work is funded by Hof University's research center for car infotainment and man-machine-interfaces.

REFERENCES

[1] V. Plenk, "Improving special purpose machine user-interfaces by machine-learning algorithms," in Proceedings of CENTRIC 2016 : The Ninth International Conference on Advances in Human-oriented and Personalized Mechanisms, Technologies, and Services, Rome, August 2016, pp. 24 – 28.

[2] V. Plenk, "A benchmark for embedded software processes used by special-purpose machine manufacturers," in Proceedings of the Third international Conference on Software Engineering Advances. Los Alamonitos: CPS, 2008, pp. 166 – 171.

[3] H. J. C. et al., "Learning styles diagnosis based on user interface behaviors for the customization of learning interfaces in an intelligent tutoring system," in Proceedings of the 8th International Conference on Intelligent Tutoring Systems (ITS 2006). Jhongli, Taiwan: Springer, June 26-30 2006, pp. 513 – 524.

[4] B. D. Davison and H. Hirsh, "Predicting sequences of user actions," in AAAI Technical Report WS-98-07, 1998, pp. 5 – 12.

[5] P. K. Wonga, J. Zhonga, Z. Yanga, and C. M. Vong, "Sparse bayesian extreme learning committee machine for engine simultaneous fault diagnosis," in Neurocomputing, 2016, pp. 331 – 343.

[6] K. Zidek, A. Hosovsky, and J. Dubjak, "Diagnostics of surface errors by embedded vision system and its classification by machine learning algorithms," in Key Engineering Materials, 2015, pp. 459 – 466.

[7] J. Luo, C.-M. Vong, and P.-K. Wong, "Sparse bayesian extreme learning machine for multi-classification," in IIEEE Transactions on Neural Networks and Learning Systems, 2014, pp. 836 – 843.

[8] A. Ziaja, I. Antoniadou, T. Barszcz, W. J. Staszewski, and K. Worden, "Fault detection in rolling element bearings using wavelet-based variance analysis and novelty detection," Journal of Vibration and Control, vol. 22, no. 2, February 2016, pp. 396–411.

[9] C. Challiol, A. Fortier, S. Gordillo, and G. Rossi, "A Flexible Architecture for Context-Aware Physical Hypermedia," in 18th International Workshop on: Database and Expert Systems Applications, 2007. DEXA '07., September 2007.

[10] S. Sigg, S. Haseloff, and K. David, "Context Prediction by Alignment Methods," in Proceedings of the 4th International Conference on Mobile Systems, Applications, and Services (MobiSys 2006), June 2006.

[11] S. Sigg, D. Gordon, G. von Zengen, M. Beigl, S. Haseloff, and K. David, "Investigation of Context Prediction Accuracy for Different Context Abstraction Levels," IEEE Transactions on Mobile Computing, vol. 11, no. 6, June 2012, pp. 1047 – 1059.

[12] V. Plenk, S. Lang, and F. Wogenstein, "Scoring of machine-learning algorithms for providing user guidance in special purpose machines," in Proceedings of CENTRIC 2017: The Tenth International Conference on Advances in Human-oriented and Personalized Mechanisms, Technologies, and Services, Athens, October 2017.

[13] M. P. J. van der Loo, "The stringdist Package for Approximate String Matching," The R Journal, vol. Vol. 6/1, 2014, pp. 111 – 122.

[14] J. Bacher, A. Pöge, and K. Wenzig, Clusteranalyse - Anwendungsorientierte Einführung in Klassifikationsverfahren. München: Oldenbourg, 2010.

[15] J. Lunze, Ereignisdiskrete Systeme. München: Oldenbourg, 2006.

APPENDIX A

TABLE X. RESULTS OF OUR TESTS (NON NORMALIZED)

	Dataset 1			Dataset 2		
Algorithm	C_{pos}	C_{neg}	Q_{alg_1}	C_{pos}	C_{neg}	Q_{alg_2}
Plain Mapping	30	6 (21) [1]	52.6	31	67 (179)[1]	11.2
Statistical Filter	9	37 (11) [1]	15.8	100	133 (44)[1]	36.1
String Matching + Jaccard	30	6 (21) [1]	52.6	73	104 (100) [1]	26.5
String Maching + Levenshtein	36	21	63.2	37	240	13.6
Hausdorff + Manhattan	33	24	57.9	94	183	33.9
Hausdorff + Chebychev	36	21	63.2	87	190	31.4
Hausdorff + Euclidean	33	24	57.9	88	189	31.8
Hausdorff + Squared Euclidean	33	24	57.9	88	189	31.8
Hausdorff + Canberra	31	26	15.8	91	186	32.9
Average Linkage + Manhattan	32	25	56.1	83	194	30
Average Linkage + Chebychev	26	31	45.6	80	197	28.9
Average Linkage + Euclidean	26	31	45.6	83	194	30
Average Linkage + Squared Euclidean	32	25	56.1	83	194	30
Average Linkage + Canberra	32	25	56.1	84	193	30.3
Single Linkage + Manhattan	21	36	36.8	93	184	33.6
Single Linkage + Chebychev	21	36	36.8	81	196	29.2
Single Linkage + Euclidean	21	36	36.8	84	193	30.3
Single Linkage + Squared Euclidean	21	36	36.8	84	193	30.3
Single Linkage + Canberra	21	36	36.8	78	199	28.2
Maximum Linkage + Manhattan	35	22	61.4	100	177	36.1
Maximum Linkage + Chebychev	23	34	40.4	55	222	19.9
Maximum Linkage + Euclidean	36	21	63.2	78	199	28.2
Maximum Linkage + Squared Euclidean	36	21	63.2	78	199	28.2
Maximum Linkage + Canberra	36	21	63.2	82	195	29.6

	Dataset 4 a			Dataset 4 b		
Algorithm	C_{pos}	C_{neg}	Q_{alg4_a}	C_{pos}	C_{neg}	Q_{alg4_b}
Plain Mapping	2	2 (354) [1]	0.6	0	0 (195)[1]	0
Statistical Filter	86	203 (69) [1]	24.0	5	147 (43)[1]	2.6
String Matching + Jaccard	10	7 (341) [1]	2.8	0	3 (192) [1]	0
String Maching + Levenshtein	88	270	24.6	3	192	1.5
Hausdorff + Manhattan	60	298	16.8	4	191	2.0
Hausdorff + Chebychev	72	286	20.1	0	195	0
Hausdorff + Euclidean	75	283	21.0	2	193	1.0
Hausdorff + Squared Euclidean	75	283	21.0	2	193	1.0
Hausdorff + Canberra	71	287	19.8	3	192	1.5
Average Linkage + Manhattan	44	314	12.3	2	193	1.0
Average Linkage + Chebychev	45	313	12.6	0	195	0
Average Linkage + Euclidean	48	310	13.4	0	195	0
Average Linkage + Squared Euclidean	50	308	14.0	1	194	0.5
Average Linkage + Canberra	87	271	24.3	0	195	0
Single Linkage + Manhattan	45	313	12.6	3	192	1.5
Single Linkage + Chebychev	57	301	15.9	3	192	1.5
Single Linkage + Euclidean	48	310	13.4	1	194	0.5
Single Linkage + Squared Euclidean	48	310	13.4	1	194	0.5
Single Linkage + Canberra	85	273	23.7	1	194	0.5
Maximum Linkage + Manhattan	54	304	15.1	1	194	0.5
Maximum Linkage + Chebychev	78	280	21.8	2	193	1.0
Maximum Linkage + Euclidean	47	311	13.1	0	195	0
Maximum Linkage + Squared Euclidean	47	311	13.1	0	195	0
Maximum Linkage + Canberra	57	301	15.9	1	195	0

[1]The first value is the number of wrong recommendations. The value in parentheses is the amount of cases in which the algorithm is unable to find a recommendation. For scoring both numbers are added, i.e., $C_{neg} = Val + (Val)$.

TABLE XI. DATASET 1: EVENT SEQUENCES AND OPERATOR SEQUENCES

EventSequence	Operator Sequence	Frequency	Learnable
Empty[1]	Loop1_3_SP_225	1	no
	Loop1_3_SP_250	2	no
	AOUT1_1_OutValue_29	1	no
	Loop1_3_SP_170	2	yes
	Loop1_2_SP_170#Loop1_3_SP_170	1	yes
	Loop1_2_SP_250#Loop1_3_SP_250	1	no
	AOUT1_1_OutValue_10	1	no
Loop1_4_PV_B#Loop1_4_PV_X	Loop1_4_SP_170	1	yes
Loop1_3_SP_0.0	Loop1_3_SP_170	28	yes
	Loop1_2_SP_170#Loop1_3_SP_170	6	yes
Loop1_4_PV_H#Loop1_4_SP_50.0# Loop1_4_PV_G#Loop1_4_PV_F	Loop1_4_SP_170	1	yes
Loop1_4_SP_0.0	Loop1_4_SP_170	2	yes
Loop1_2_SP_0.0#Loop1_4_SP_0.0	Loop1_3_SP_170#Loop1_4_SP_170	1	no
	Loop1_3_SP_170	2	yes
Loop1_3_SP_10.0	Loop1_3_SP_170	1	yes
Loop1_4_PV_H#Loop1_5_PV_H# Loop1_6_PV_H#Loop1_7_SP_50.0	Loop1_7_SP_250	1	no
Loop1_3_SP_60.0	Loop1_3_SP_170	3	yes
AIN2_1_Value_G#MP1_Value_G#MT1_Value_F# MP1_Value_F#AIN2_1_Value_F#MP1_Value_B# MT1_Value_E#MP1_Value_C	AOUT1_2_OutValue_9	1	no
MP1_Value_E#MP1_BandMin_E#MP1_BandMax_E# Loop1_6_PV_E#Loop1_6_PV_F#Loop1_6_PV_E# Loop1_6_PV_D#Loop1_6_PV_C#Loop1_6_PV_B# Loop1_6_PV_A#MP1_BandMax_F#MP1_Value_H# MP1_BandMax_H#MP1_BandMin_F	AOUT1_1_OutValue_50	1	no

[1]In our simulation empty event sequences can occur when an alarm is generated by changing the alarm condition. This happens during testing or demonstration.

TABLE XII. DATASET 2: AMBIGIOUS EVENT SEQUENCES

Event-Sequence	Operator-Sequence	Frequency	Learnable	Event-Sequence	Operator-Sequence	Frequency	Learnable
1	AOut1_1_84#	2	yes	18	AOut1_1_86#	2	yes
	AOut1_1_82#	1	yes		AOut1_1_87#	1	yes
2	AOut1_1_86#	3	yes	19	AOut1_1_85#	5	yes
	AOut1_1_87#	1	yes		AOut1_1_85#AOut2_1_98#	1	no
	AOut1_1_85#	1	yes		AOut1_1_84#	1	yes
3	AOut1_1_86#	2	yes	20	AOut1_1_82#	1	yes
	AOut1_1_87#	1	yes		AOut1_1_81#	1	yes
4	AOut1_1_84#	5	yes	21	AOut1_1_85#	1	yes
	AOut1_1_85#	4	yes		AOut1_1_87#	1	yes
5	AOut1_1_83#	2	yes	22	AOut1_1_87#	3	yes
	AOut1_1_85#	2	yes		AOut1_1_85#	1	yes
	AOut1_1_84#	1	yes		AOut1_1_86#	1	yes
6	AOut1_1_80#	2	yes	23	AOut1_1_83#	1	yes
	AOut1_1_79#	1	no		AOut1_1_81#	1	yes
7	AOut1_1_87#	1	yes	24	AOut1_1_81#	2	yes
	AOut1_1_86#	1	yes		AOut1_1_80#	1	yes
8	AOut1_1_85#	1	yes	25	AOut1_1_85#	1	yes
	AOut1_1_84#	1	yes		AOut1_1_86#	1	yes
9	AOut1_1_83#	1	yes	26	AOut1_1_80#	3	yes
	AOut1_1_84#	1	yes		AOut1_1_81#	1	yes
10	AOut1_1_84#	2	yes	27	AOut1_1_84#	1	yes
	AOut1_1_83#	1	yes		AOut1_1_85#	1	yes
11	AOut1_1_82#	1	yes	28	AOut1_1_77#	3	no
	AOut1_1_83#	2	yes		AOut1_1_78#	1	no
12	AOut1_1_86#	2	yes	29	AOut1_1_85#	1	yes
	AOut1_1_88#	1	yes		AOut1_1_86#	1	yes
	AOut1_1_87#	1	yes		AOut1_1_84#	2	yes
13	AOut1_1_87#	1	yes	30	AOut1_1_82#	1	yes
	AOut1_1_86#	1	yes		AOut1_1_81#	1	yes
14	AOut1_1_86#	2	yes	31	AOut1_1_85#	1	yes
	AOut1_1_87#	1	yes		AOut1_1_86#	1	yes
15	AOut1_1_85#	2	yes	32	AOut1_1_83#	1	yes
	AOut1_1_86#	2	yes		AOut1_1_85#	1	yes
16	AOut1_1_84#	1	yes	33	AOut1_1_84#	1	yes
	AOut1_1_83#	1	yes		AOut1_1_83#	1	yes
	AOut1_1_85#	1	yes		AOut1_1_85#	2	yes
	AOut1_1_82#	1	yes				
17	AOut1_1_83#	1	yes				
	AOut1_1_85#	7	yes				
	AOut1_1_84#	3	yes				

An Evolutionary Intelligent Algorithm Approach for the Doctor Scheduling Problem

Abir Alharbi and Kholood AlQahtani

Mathematics Department, King Saud University, Riyadh, Saudi Arabia

e-mail:

abir@ksu.edu.sa , 432201096@student.ksu.edu.sa

Abstract- **In this paper, we present an automated intelligent nature inspired algorithm solution to the scheduling problem for doctors in Pediatric Department of Prince Sultan Military Medical City in Riyadh Saudi Arabia. The genetic algorithm approach is utilized, which is an adaptive heuristic search algorithm based on the evolutionary ideas of natural selection and on genetics. A cost bit matrix of which each cell indicates any violation of the required constraints to make an acceptable doctor schedule, and this novel cost bit matrix is used as an objective function for the genetic algorithm. The experimental results showed that our genetic algorithm approach generates an automated intelligent doctor schedule faster and with less violated constrains than the traditional manual methods and other hill climbing search techniques.**

Keywords- Doctor Scheduling Problem; Genetic Algorithms; Cost bit matrix; Hard constrains; Soft constrains.

I. INTRODUCTION

Time Scheduling assigns an appropriate number of workers to the specified jobs during each day of work. Many fields require scheduling such as job, production, railway, personnel scheduling and many more. Personnel scheduling plays an important task in institutions, it balances the workload of the personnel, departments, and effects the productivity of the whole institution. Personnel scheduling involves assigning of personnel to time slots and possible different locations known as time scheduling. It is made to maximize the work done in the institution and guarantee the increasing productivity or (to increase productivity). In hospitals, personnel scheduling is applied to assign doctors or nurses to their respective departments and making sure all shifts are covered.

A hospital providing a round-the-clock service divides its daily work into consecutive shifts, and a shift is a period of time in which a group of employees are in-service. A doctor is assigned to a set of shifts which satisfies several constraints that may be set up by staffing requirements, rules by the administration, and labor contract clauses. In a doctor scheduling problem (DSP) each doctor is assigned to the set of shifts and rest days in a timetable called a doctor roster.

The objective of DSP is to satisfy doctors' requests as much as possible while fulfilling the employers' requirements. In DSP there are many constraints and there can be several different instances with separate set of constraints. In this study, we focus on the cyclic Doctor scheduling problem described through the following three components and constrains:

(l) The personal preference of each doctor to work on particular days and shifts,
(2) The minimal coverage constraints of the minimal required number of doctors per shift and per day,
(3) The case-specific constraints specified by personal time requirements, specific workplace conditions, etc.

DSP consists of creating weekly or monthly schedules for a number of doctors by assigning one out of a number of possible shift patterns to each doctor. These schedules must satisfy working contracts and meet the requirements for the number of doctors of different grades for each shift, while being seen to be fair by the staff concerned. In a hospital, there are various kinds of employers like doctors, nurses, attendants, etc. and they must be assigned to shifts to do their work. In this study, we concentrated mainly on the doctor shifts.

DSP was proven to be NP-hard even with only a subset of real world constraints [4]. DSP can be modeled as a partial constraints satisfaction problem. Numerous studies have been done in the recent years, meta-heuristics such as Tabu search [23], genetic algorithm (GA) [3], [1], [18], constraint logic programming [2], and simulated annealing [13] have been proven to be effective in obtaining good solutions for doctor or nurse scheduling problem. The idea behind using genetic algorithm to solve DSP is to breed the fittest solutions in a specific generation. GA works with a population of "individuals", each representing a possible solution to a given problem. Each individual is assigned a "fitness score" according to how good a solution is to the problem. Individuals with higher fitness scores are given opportunities to "reproduce" by "cross breeding" with other individuals in the population. Genetic Algorithms (GAs) are powerful general-purpose optimization tools which model the principles of evolution [15]. They are often capable of finding globally optimal solutions even in the most complex of search spaces [11]. They operate on a population of coded solutions which are selected according to their quality then used as the basis for a new generation of solutions found by combining (crossover) and (mutating) current individuals. The strength of GAs comes from the fact that the technique is robust and can deal successfully with a wide range of problem areas, including those which are difficult for other methods to solve. In this paper, we apply a GA approach with a cost bit matrix that penalizes the solution of the DSP if it violates constrains, and eventually finds the optimum doctor's schedule.

In Section II, we will present some of best practices that are available in the literature on solutions of DSP. In Section III, we will briefly introduce the GA and its parameter settings, also our DSP setup and its objective function, which is designed from the customized cost bit matrix. Moreover, in Section IV, the GA results are discussed and compared to other methods. Finally, conclusions and future work are discussed in Section V.

II. LITRATURE REVIEW

In the literature, many research works are done on DSP or the similar Nurse scheduling problem (NSP). Miller et al. [16], and Warner et al. [23], used linear programming to formulate the Nursing Schedule Problem as the selection of a timetable that minimizes an objective function, which balanced the trade-off between staffing coverage and nurses' preferences. Abdannadher et al. [2] applied a Constraint Logic Program (CLP) framework, and Li et al. [14] employed Bayesian optimization algorithm. Aickelin et al. [3], applied an indirect genetic algorithm to NSP. Existing research work has been proposing diverse models and methodologies to improve nurse and doctor scheduling problems. Most of the current proposed solutions either make use of random based optimization algorithms such as Silver et al. [19], where a lot of research work related to Medical Informatics has done, and presented deep discussions about the role of data warehouse management system to handle hospital and nurse management information. Moreover, multidimensional analysis techniques under different parameters were used to extract the required data and information.

An approach that has been implemented successfully in many of the American hospitals, is based on two data mining techniques called; patient rule introduction method (PRMI) and weighted items sets (WLS). They were used to analyze large quantities of data in Villiers et al. [22], where data mining techniques for solving clinical data warehouse functionality was applied, and they proposed a flexible clinical data mining system (CDMS) using SAS statistical software. In addition, they conducted research in two stages. In first stage, controlled environment was provided for CDMS access based systems and transformed it into analytical clinical data, and in the later stage, operations were tested. Cheng et al. [7] describes the design and implementation of a constraint-based nurse rostering system using a redundant modeling approach, to reduce search time. An effective way to increase constraint propagation through cooperation among different models for the same problem, was also proposed. Kundu et al. [13] described the use of GA for solving nursing schedule problem. They used two different models, a Simulated Annealing approach, and a Simulated Annealing combined with GA approach. They compared nurse performance at various levels, and have considered soft and hard constraints.

Juhos et al. [12] described a novel representation and ordering model that was aided by an evolutionary algorithm, to solve the graph k-coloring problem setup of NSP. Its strength lies in reducing the number of neighbors that need to be checked for validity. An empirical comparison was made with two other algorithms on a popular selection of problem instances and on a suite of instances in the phase transition. The new representation in combination with a heuristic mutation operator showed promising results. Culberson and Gent [9] denned the 'frozen development' of coloring random graphs and identified two nodes in a graph as frozen if they were the same color in all legal colorings. This was analogous to studies of the development of a backbone or spine in SAT (the Stainability problem). In other works, the graph coloring techniques and greedy algorithm were used for NSP, such as by Ratnayaka et. al. [17], where they used an enhanced greedy optimization algorithm with data warehousing for an automated nurse scheduling system, and by Gideon [10], where a thesis on a nurse scheduling methods and solutions were presented. In reference [18] a GA is used to solve nurse scheduling problem for private hospitals in the Philippines. This study considered preferences of nurses in terms of work schedule while meeting the objective of the hospital management of minimizing total salary cost, and used different operators for the genetic algorithm in solving the NSP, they claim that their method could save 12% staffing expenses monthly as compared to existing manual schedules.

GAs are used to solve other scheduling problems such as timetables problem in schools [8], where they compared a GA-based approach with various versions of Simulated Annealing and Tabu search, and in the experiments GAs produced better timetables than Simulated Annealing, but slightly worse timetables than Tabu search. The railway scheduling problem was also considered in [21] which implies the optimization of trains on a railway line that is occupied (or not) by other trains with fixed timetables. The timetable for the new trains is obtained with GA, which includes a guided process to build the initial population. The proposed GA is tested on real instances obtained from the Spanish Manager of Railway Infrastructure (ADIF). The results point out that GA is an appropriate method to explore the search space of this complex problems and can lead to good solutions in a short amount of time.

In this paper, we apply a GA with a cost bit matrix that penalizes the solution of the DSP if the constrains are violated, and hence finds an automated schedule that optimizes the doctors' roasters and satisfies all the constraints. Our novel cost bit matrix is specially designed for the constrains requested by the hospital and it is used as the objective function in the evolutionary genetic algorithm, this new automated technique has not been reported before in the literature on the DSP.

III. Genetic Algorithms

Genetic Algorithms (GAs) are adaptive heuristic search algorithms based on the evolutionary ideas of natural selection and genetics [20]. The basic concepts of the GA were designed to simulate those processes in natural evolution system, and survival of the fittest [15]. GA are a powerful tool to solve optimization problems with multiple variables [11]. GA were applied to several scheduling problems [1], [6], [21]. GA are a search algorithm to simulate the process of natural selection. GA start with the set of potential solutions called population and evolves toward more optimal solutions. The solutions are evaluated by a fitness function. The fitness value represents the quality measure of a solution so that the algorithm can use it to select ones with better genetic material for producing new solutions and further generations. The selection chooses superior solutions in every generation and assures that inferior solutions extinct. The crossover operator chooses two solutions from current population and generates a new solution based on their genetic material. Selection and crossover operators will expand good features of superior individuals through the entire population. They will also direct the search process towards a local optimum [20]. The mutation operator changes the value of some genes in a solution and help to search other parts of problem space. The main disadvantage of GA is the requirement for a large computation time.

A. Doctor Scheduling Problem

Hospital care units must provide twenty-four-hour coverage at levels to match patient demand while adhering to organizational policies designed to protect the health and welfare of patients and staff. The already difficult scheduling problem is further compounded by a shortage of doctors. The schedule must determine the day-to-day shift assignments of each doctor for a specified period in a way that satisfies the given requirements as much as possible, taking into account the wishes of doctors as closely as possible. In most studies of DSP, the restrictions are categorized as Hard Constraints and Soft Constraints. Hard constraints are the constraints, which must be satisfied to get feasible solution for use in practice, and Soft constraints are the constraints, which are used to evaluate the quality of the solution. So, soft constraints are not compulsory but are desired to be satisfied as much as possible. Hard constraints should always be satisfied in any working schedule so that there will be no breaches. Any schedule that does not satisfy all the hard constraints cannot be a feasible one. Possible examples include restrictions on the number of doctors for each shift; the maximum number of shifts in a week, a month, etc. On the contrary, soft constraints can be violated but as minimal as possible. In other words, the soft constraints are expected to be satisfied, but violation does not make it an infeasible solution. The doctors are divided into three categories: consultants (C), senior (S) and junior doctors (J) working in the same department. In this project we are concerned with scheduling shifts for junior doctors in the pediatric department wards for one month only. A major problem with any scheduling problem is the allocation of resources in an effective way, and not violating the constraints, which affects the quality of the solution. We confined the constraints as follows:

(a) Hard constraints

(i) There are constraints on the number of doctors for each working shift per day. The number of doctors for morning (m), evening (e), and night shift (n) should be between the minimum and maximum values.

(ii) There are constraints for the working patterns. Morning after night shift, evening after night, morning after evening shift and three consecutive night shifts are restricted combination of working patterns.

(b) Soft constraints

There are constraints for the total number of off-days (o), night, morning and evening shifts during the certain period of days for each doctor.

In this paper, we shall present an automated scheduling solution for Pediatric Department of Prince Sultan Military Medical City (PSMMC) in Riyadh, Saudi Arabia. Monthly doctors' rosters are made manually before the end of each month, Figure 1, shows the original hospital roasters for the month of February 2016. Even though making monthly rosters manually required significant effort and time, it did not resolve all conflicts in the doctors' schedules specially in the time of emergency interventions or in times of sudden timetables' changes. In fact, sometimes making slight changes in one doctor's timetable meant creating a lot of tedious adjustments to the rest of the doctors' timetables working in the same ward. Proposing an automated software that can handle making all doctors roasters according to the constraints and at the same time be flexible enough to produce a new schedule quickly in case of needed sudden change, is very desirable by the hospital.

B. The Cost Function

We must define a customized objective or cost function so that when we optimize it, it will obtain optimal time schedules for all doctors in the department. Let N be the number of doctors, and D the number of days. Then, DSP may be represented as an optimization problem to find a schedule matrix X of size NxD, so that each element of the matrix, x_{ij}, expresses shifts for the doctor i working on day j, and takes one of the four shift values (m, e, n, or o): m=morning, n=night e=evening, and o= off days. We calculate the fitness of each suggested schedule table by using our customized cost bit matrix through the following procedure:

(a) To evaluate the violation of hard constraint (i), we define mt, et, nt as the total number of doctors for morning, evening, and night shift on a day. If any of these numbers are not between the minimum and maximum number of doctors for each shift (mmin, mmax, emin, emax, nmin, nmax), provided by the hospital, then the cost C_1 will be incremented by l.

(b) To evaluate the violation of hard constraint (ii), working patterns are examined. Any violation of the working patterns specified (such as m after n, e after n, m after e, or consecutive n, n, n) will increment the cost C_2 by l.

(c) To evaluate the violation of soft constraint, we define M, E, N, O as the total number of the corresponding shifts, morning, evening and night and off-days for a doctor during a period of days. Mreq, Ereq, Nreq, and Oreq are set as the required number of mornings, evenings, nights shift and off-days for all doctors during a period of days. If any of these numbers M, E, N, O does not meet, Mreq, Ereq, Nreq, and Oreq respectively, then the cost C_3 will be incremented by 1.

Hence, our cost function will consist of the three parts representing each cost: C_1, C_2 and C_3 as follows:

$$f= C_1w_1 + C_2w_2+ C_3w_3 \quad (1)$$

where w_1, w_2 and w_3 are weight values set for each C_1, C_2 and C_3, respectively emphasizing our priority in the satisfaction of constraints, and are determined by trial and error to find the best combination of weights.

Our goal is to minimize the cost function f given in (1) and hence find an optimal doctor schedule satisfying all hard and soft constrains. The simplest method to find the solution is a brute force approach (manually) evaluating all possible doctor schedules and finding the feasible one with the minimum cost among them. Manual methods guarantee finding a feasible schedule with the minimum cost, however, if the number of doctors increases, this approach is intractable. Moreover, it is not easy to adjust manually a timetable for one doctor's shift due to an emergency or sudden time schedule change, without needing to make many changes in the other involved doctors' timetables as well. This is considered as a class of NP-hard problem for which many methods have been applied and no unique solution exists [5], [24]. Hence, an automated algorithm that produces an optimal schedule for N doctors in D day in minutes and with no constraints violated is needed. Here, we propose to use genetic algorithm to design such an automated algorithm, and therefore present an optimal solution to the DSP in an abbreviated time, via our novel cost bit matrix construction of doctors' time schedules.

C. GA Paramreters for Selction and Crossover

For the first week of Febraury, the Hospital divides doctors into three groups. Each group has one senior and three to four junior doctors based on the department daily requirement, which requires availability of ten junior and three senior doctors on that week, as seen in Table I . So they setup three groups: A, B, and C for doctors to cover the days of the week and the doctors shared the same daily schedule. For our approach with genetic algorithms, we did not need to use groups for the doctors instead we worked on producing an independent schedule for each junior doctor.

The initial population for the GA is made of different possible schedules for doctors' shifts, such as each member of the population is a NxD matrix, generated randomly assigning each doctor to one of the four daily shifts and assuring a day-off on each week, Table II shows a sample of a week schedule for 10 junior doctors (10x7 matrix), in the population. The costs of each member schedule in the population is calculated by the cost function given in (1). We will start with z = 60 members in the initial population set in random.

The method of selection in this study, is the roulette wheel selection method, which is the most common type of selection methods [11]. Two schedules, P1 and P2, are chosen randomly based on their cost and are used to produce an offspring. One schedule can be selected for a parent more than once. The crossover between the two chosen parents' genome is done at a single point randomly chosen with probability 0.8 to produce the new generation offspring. Additionally, the mutation rate is set to 0.01.

The remaining initial parameters are set as given by the PSMMC hospital for February 2016:

- N=24, D=29
- mmin=8, mmax=10, emin=6, emax=10, nmin=6, nmax=10
- soft constrains for each week were: Mreq=Ereq=Nreq=2, and Oreq=1.

The method was activated to reach an optimum cost according to (1) (f = 0, i.e., no violations to both soft and hard constrains on the proposed optimum schedule) using MATLAB genetic algorithm toolbox with Intel Core ™ i5-250M 2.5 Ghz CPU and 4GB. The GA goes through the following steps:

Step 1: Initialize the population randomly (with z individuals or NxD schedules) and calculate the fitness function for each member of the initial population using the cost bit matrix (f) defined by in (1).

Step 2: Select the elite members of the population, which will go through crossover and mutation based on their high fitness scores (satisfying most hospital constrains with the minimum number of violations).

Step 3: Choose parents for crossover, and with the crossover rate, generate offspring, in which the ranking mechanism is used for selection of chromosomes.

Step 4: Apply the mutation, on selected offspring, according to mutation rate.

Step 5: Select the members of the new generation consisting of: the parents in the old generation and the produced new offspring in Step 4, according to their fitness values.

Step 6: Repeat the procedure in Step 2 through Step 5 until the maximum number of generations is reached, or the objective function is optimized, and the threshold is met.

TABLE I. SAMPLE OF HOSPITAL SCHEDULE GROUPS FOR JUNIOR AND SENIOR DOCTORS

Group	Doctors
A	J1, J5, J4 and S1
B	J3, J2, J6, J10 and S2 .
C	J7, J8, J9 and S3

TABLE II. SAMPLE HOSPITAL SCHEDULE FOR 10 DOCTORS AND DURATION 7 DAYS: MONDAY-SUNDAY)

Doctor	M	T	W	TH	F	S	SU
J1	m	e	n	o	m	m	n
J2	e	m	m	n	o	m	n
J3	n	n	o	m	e	e	e
J4	m	m	e	e	n	o	m
J5	e	o	e	n	m	n	e
J6	m	e	n	o	m	m	n
J7	e	m	m	n	o	m	n
J8	n	n	o	m	e	n	e
J9	m	m	e	e	n	o	m
J10	e	o	e	n	m	n	e

IV. GA RESULTS

The GA started with a population size of z=60 individuals, with the size of each genome NxD matrix (24 doctors for 29 days). The algorithm terminated when the maximum number of generations was reached at 300, or when the increase in fitness of the best individual over five successive generations fell below a certain threshold, set at 2 × 10^{-6}. Our fitness function *f* is set to the cost function:

$$f = 5C_1 + 5C_2 + C_3,$$

which penalizes schedule tables violating the constrains according to the assigned weights. The weights were chosen according to several attempts of trial and error on different weight values, and it was concluded that any values chosen for w_1 and w_2 as penalties for violating C_1 and C_2 should be equal, but w_3 must be set to a lesser value since it is hard to avoid violating C_3 [1]. The GA ran throughout generations to find the best genome in this population. The best genome is the doctor schedule table, which violates the least number of constrains. After all 300 generations (repeated 50 times), the genetic algorithm found the optimum genome; hence, it found the best doctor schedule table, which violates the least number of soft constrains. Our proposed GA applied on the cost bit matrix have given excellent results on solving this doctor schedule problem in both time efficiency and accuracy. Figure 2 shows the plots of the best fitness value reached (with only 3 soft constrains violations over 4 weeks for all 24 doctors) and the mean fitness value over the generations. Moreover, Figure 3 shows the average distance between all individuals during the GA generations. The best doctor schedule produced from the GA is given in Table VI, and it can be seen through the plot of the best individual with 695 variables in Figure 4.

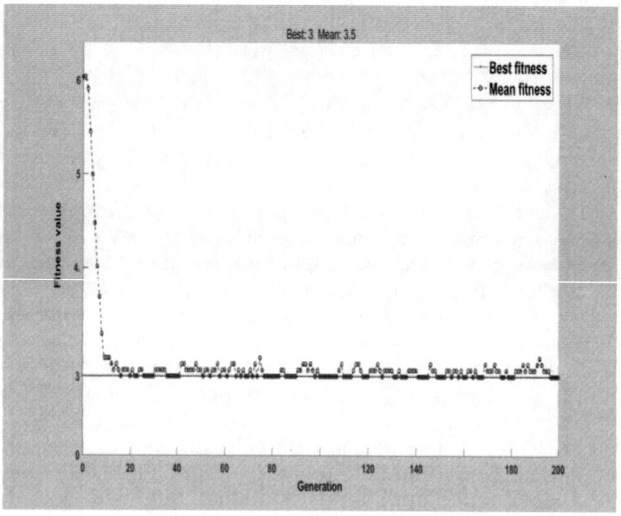

Figure 2. The best and mean fitness value over the generations for 4 week.

The proposed GA results are compared to the hospital manual roaster tables derived from Figure 1 and Table V, which shows the incident matrix for the 24 doctors in PSMMC for the month of February 2016. For comparison purposes our data was also used to find the best doctor schedule with two other methods published in the literature Kundu et al. [13] using a Simulated Annealing and Genetic

Algorithm combination method. Also, we compared our results with the hill climbing technique described by Wojciech et al. in [24].

A hill climbing (HC) algorithm, which is a fast-local search algorithm, despite being a simple search method, showed a satisfactory performance for small size instance while, it could not cope with medium and large size instances. HC is driven by a greedy procedure. It processes interventions one by one trying to assign them to teams as early as possible. Above that, it iterates over the intervention urgency classes and several possible sorting strategies. At the top level, different permutations of intervention priorities are considered. Finally, the algorithm tries to improve the current partial solution by applying a hill climbing metaheuristic and by abandoning some interventions. In simple words, it depends on the trade-off between the weights in the scoring procedure and the distribution of intervention priorities. Where Perm(x) is a certain permutation function of priorities {G1, G2, G3, G4} given in Table III. In order to analyze all possible orderings of priority classes, the whole algorithm is executed for six different permutations Perm: (G1, G2, G3, G4), (G1, G3, G2, G4), (G2, G1, G3, G4), (G2, G3, G1, G4), (G3, G1, G2, G4) and (G3, G2, G1,G4). Eventually, the final solution is the best obtained. Notice that the last priority never changes, because the scoring function is defined in such a way that it does not take into account the finish time of interventions of priority 4.

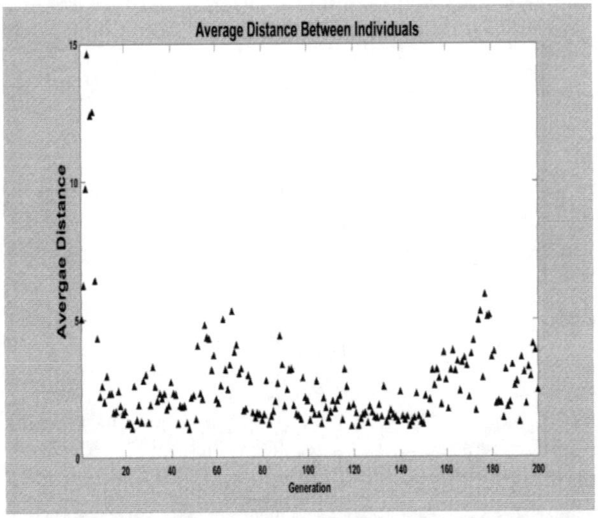

Figure 3. The average distance between the individuals competing for best schedule

Table IV shows a comparison of the performance results of the four methods. Here f_{opt} is the average optimum solution from 50 trials in each method. As we can see, all methods solved all the given problem instances and the results did not violate any of the hard constraints in all periods. Moreover, The GA approach generated schedules with optimal cost in all periods, compared to the manual schedules, the hill climbing technique and the GA with simulated annealing approach. The average execution time T over all periods of the GA is around 3.37 minutes, which is much faster than all other methods. Figure 5 plots the cost function of each method for comparison purposes over the 4 weeks. As can be seen in the plot our GA with a cost bit matrix is very effective compared to the other methods based on time and minimum constrains violation.

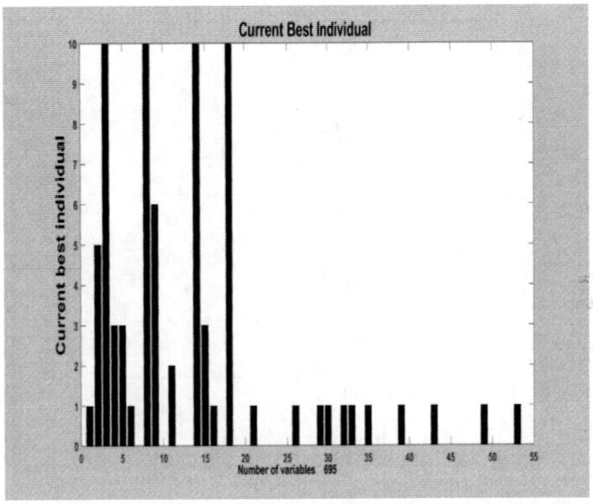

Figure 4. The Current best individual for DSP with 695 variables.

TABLE III. GROUPS AFTER APPLYING HILL CLIMBING, DISTRIBUTION OF R DOCTORS IN 6 WARDS

Group	Doctors
G1	$R1_3$, $R3_4$, $R4_2$, $R4_3$, $R3_1$
G2	$R4_1$, $R4_4$, $R3_3$, $R3_2$
G3	$R1_4$, $R1_2$, $R1_1$, $R2_1$, SUB_3
G4	$R1_5$, $R2_5$, SUB_4, $R2_6$, $R2_4$

A	B	C	D	E	F
$R3_1$	$R4_1$	SUB_1	$R2_4$	$R1_5$	$R1_1$
$R4_2$	$R3_2$	$R2_1$	SUB_2	$R2_5$	$R1_2$
$R4_3$	$R3_3$	$R2_2$	$R1_3$	$R2_6$	SUB_3
$R3_4$	$R4_4$	$R2_3$	$R2_7$	SUB_4	$R1_4$

TABLE IV. COMPARISONS OF GA AND OTHER METHODS ON PSMMC HOSPITAL DOCTOR SCHEDULE

period	Method	f_{opt}	T (min)
1 week	GA	2	2.6
	Hill Climbing	3	3.9
	Manual	7	
	GA and simulated annealing	3	3.5
2 Weeks	GA	2	3.2
	Hill Climbing	6	4
	Manual	9	
	GA and simulated annealing	5	3.9
3 weeks	GA	3	3.75
	Hill Climbing	5	4
	Manual	12	
	GA and simulated annealing	6	4.5
4 weeks	GA	3	3.96
	Hill Climbing	5	5
	Manual	10	
	GA and simulated annealing	4	4.5

V. CONCLUSION AND FUTURE WORK

In this paper, we proposed a Genetic Algorithm approach with a cost bit matrix to solve a Doctor Schedule Problem in PSMMC hospital. We designed a cost bit matrix which resulted in pruning of the search space and that was the main cause of reduction in execution time. In addition, the result of pruning increased the possibility to find feasible solution, which made our algorithm find solutions satisfying all the constraints. This automated GA approach generated a doctor roaster faster in time and better in quality with the least constraints violations than the manual method and the other considered computational methods. Although we have presented this work in terms of doctor scheduling, it should be noted that the main idea of the approach could be applied to many other scheduling problems. Our future plans include producing a software program coded by our proposed GA method with a user manual and friendly interface that can be used in hospitals to help them design schedules according to their constrains for their doctors and nurses. The software will allow the hospital management to enter the number of doctors, days, days off, night shifts, constrains, … etc., with simple inputs and less time, and hence produce an automated optimum doctor or nurse schedule in a few minutes and avoid manual schedule making, and tedious work when faced with the need for sudden modifications in these schedules.

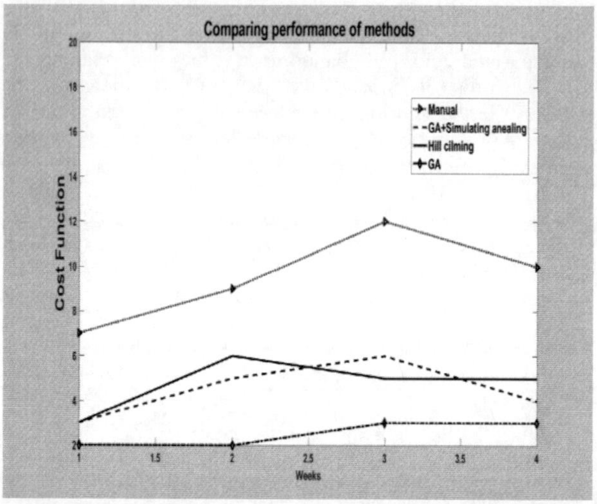

Figure 5. Comparison of performance (f_{opt}) of the four methods on PSMMC hospital doctor schedule

ACKNOWLEDGMENT

This research project was supported by a grant from the "Research Centre of the Female Scientific and Medical Colleges", Deanship of Scientific Research, King Saud University.

REFERENCES

[1] A. Alharbi and K. AlQahtani, "A Genetic Algorithm solution for the Doctor Scheduling Problem", ADVCOMP 5/COMARA: Computational Mathematics in Real-life Applications The Tenth International Conference on Advanced Engineering Computing and Applications in Sciences, October 9 - 13, (2016)-Venice, Italy.

[2] S. Abdennadher and H. Schienker, "Nurse Scheduling using Constraint Logic Programming", Proc. AAAI '99/IAAI '99, (1999), pp. 838-843.

[3] U. Aickelin and K.A. Dowsland, "An indirect Genetic Algorithm for a Nurse-Scheduling", Computers & Operations Research, vol. 31, no. 5, (2004) April, pp. 761-778.

[4] U. Aickelin and K.A. Dowsland, "Exploiting Problem structure roistering problem", Journal of Scheduling, vol. 3, (2000), pp. 139-153.

[5] G. Baskaran, A. Bargiela and R. Qu, "Hierarchical Method for Nurse Rostering Based on Granular Pre-Processing of Constraints," The 23rd EUROPEAN Conference on Modelling and Simulation, Madrid, 9-12 June 2009, pp. 855-861.

[6] A. Brezulianu, F. Monica, and F. Lucian, "A Genetic Algorithm Approach for a Constrained Employee Scheduling Problem as Applied to Employees at Mall Type Shops", IJAST, vol. 14, (2010), pp. 1-14.

[7] B. M. W Cheng, J. H. M Lee, and J. C. K Wu," A constraint-based Nurse Rostering system using a Redundant modeling Approach", IEEE Transactions on Information Technology in Biomedicine, (1997), pp. 44 - 54.

[8] A. Colorni, M. Dorigo, and V. Maniezzo, "A Genetic Algorithm To Solve The Timetable Problem", computational optimization and applications Journal (1994),

[9] J. Culberson and Gent, "Frozen development in graph colouring", Theoretical Computer Science. (2001), 265, 1-2, pp.227-264

[10] A. Gideon, "A Nurse Scheduling Using Graph Coloring", Master thesis submitted, Mathematics Department, Kwame Nkrumah University, Ghana, (2013).

[11] D. E. Goldberg, "Genetic Algorithms in Search, Optimization and Machine Learning", Addison Wesley (1989) .

[12] J. Istvan, A. Toth, and J. I. van Hemert, "Binary Merge Model Representation of the Graph Colouring Problem", Evolutionary Computation in Combinatorial Optimization (2004), pp. 124-130.

[13] S. Kundu, M. Mahato, B. Mahanty, and S. Acharyya, "Comparative Performance of Simulated Annealing and Genetic Algorithm in Solving Nurse Scheduling Problem", Proc. Int'l Multi Conference of Engineers and Computer Scientists 2008, (2008) January, pp. 1-5.

[14] J. Li and U. Aickelin, "A Bayesian Optimization Algorithm for the Nurse Scheduling", Evolutionary Computation, (2003). In: CEC '03.

[15] Z. Michalewicz, "Genetic Algorithms+Data Structures= Evolution Programs", 3rd edition, Springer-Verlag, (1996).

[16] H. E. Miller, W. P. Pierskalla, and G. J. Rath, "Nurse Scheduling using Mathematical Programming", Operations Research, vol. 24, no. 5, (1976), pp. 857-870.

[17] R. Ratnayaka, Z. Wang, S. Anamalamudi and S. Cheng, "Enhanced Greedy Optimization Algorithm with Data Warehousing for Automated Nurse Scheduling System," E-Health Telecommunication Systems and Networks, Vol. 1 No. 4, (2012), pp. 43-48.

[18] R. A. Namoco, and R. G. Salazar, "Solving the Nurse Scheduling Problem of Private Hospitals in the Philippines using Various Operators for Genetic Algorithm", Indian Journal of Science and Technology, (2016), Vol 9(47), pp. 2-17.

[19] M. Silver, T. Sakuta , H. C. Su, S. B. Dolins, and M. J Oshea, "Case Study: How to Apply Data Mining Techniques in a Healthcare Data Warehouse," Journal of Healthcare Information Information Management, (2001) Vol. 15, No. 2, pp. 155-164.

[20] S. N. Sivanandam, S. N. Deepa, "Introduction to Genetic Algorithms", Springer, (2007).

[21] P. Tormos, A. Lova, F. Barber, L. Ingolotti, M. Abril, and M.A. Salido, "A Genetic Algorithm for Railway Scheduling Problems", In: Xhafa F., Abraham A. (eds) Metaheuristics for Scheduling in Industrial and Manufacturing Applications. Studies in Computational Intelligence, (2008) vol 128. Springer, Berlin, Heidelberg.

[22] P. Villiers, "Clinical Data Warehouse Functionality," SAS Institute Inc., New Caledonia, (1998).

[23] D. M. Warner and J. Prawda, "A Mathematical Programming Model for Scheduling Nursing Personnel in a Hospital", Management Science, vol. 19 (4-Part-1), (1972) December, pp. 411-422.

[24] J. Wojciech and W. Szymon, "Efficient Greedy Algorithm with Hill Climbing for Technicians and Interventions Scheduling Problem", Roadef chalange, France, (2007).

Department of Paediatrics									
Paediatric ICU Team									
Division Mobile: 0504585767				Feb 2016					
		1-6 PICU On- call Team A 08:00-08:00			3-1 PICU service Team B 08:00 – 16:00			PRRT & Transportation 08:00-08:00 Team C	
Date	Day	Consultant	Fellow / Registrar	Resident	Consultant	Fellow	Registrar/Resident	Consultant	Fellow /Registrar
1	Mon	Chehab	Rizwan	ELGAWHARAH	Mohaimeed	Rizwan	NOUR S	Mohaimeed	Rizwan
2	Tues	Chehab	Warwar	QASSIM	Mohaimeed	Rizwan	NOUR S	Mohaimeed	Rizwan
3	Wed	Chehab	Yacoub	M. ASIRI	Mohaimeed	Rizwan	NOUR S	Mohaimeed	Rizwan
4	Thu	Mohaimeed	Inayat	GRACE	Mohaimeed	Inayat	GRACE	Mohaimeed	Inayat
5	Fri	Mohaimeed	Rizwan	TAGHREED	Mohaimeed	Rizwan	TAGHREED	Mohaimeed	Rizwan
6	Sat	Mohaimeed	Ahmed	ELGAWHARAH	Mohaimeed	Ahmed	ELGAWHARAH	Mohaimeed	Ahmed
7	Sun	Thabet	Warwar	AMAL	Bafaqih	Warwar	MALIK	Bafaqih	Warwar
8	Mon	Thabet	Yacoub	NADA ALHARBI	Bafaqih	Warwar	MALIK	Bafaqih	Warwar
9	Tues	Thabet	Inayat	RAED	Bafaqih	Warwar	MALIK	Bafaqih	Warwar
10	Wed	Thabet	Rizwan	BODOUR	Bafaqih	Warwar	MALIK	Bafaqih	Warwar
11	Thu	Bafaqih	Yaser	MUJAHID	Bafaqih	Yaser	MUJAHID	Bafaqih	Yaser
12	Fri	Bafaqih	Warwar	NADA	Bafaqih	Warwar	NADA	Bafaqih	Warwar
13	Sat	Bafaqih	Yacoub	ESRAA M	Bafaqih	Yacoub	ESRAA M	Bafaqih	Yacoub
14	Sun	Mohaimeed	Inayat	EBTISAM	Chehab	Inayat	HAMDAN	Chehab	Inayat
15	Mon	Mohaimeed	Rizwan	TAGHREED	Chehab	Inayat	HAMDAN	Chehab	Inayat
16	Tues	Mohaimeed	Yaser	NADA	Chehab	Inayat	HAMDAN	Chehab	Inayat
17	Wed	Mohaimeed	Yacoub	QASSIM	Chehab	Inayat	HAMDAN	Chehab	Inayat
18	Thu	Thabet	Ahmed	ESRAA M	Thabet	Ahmed	ESRAA M	Thabet	Ahmed
19	Fri	Thabet	Inayat	MUJAHID	Thabet	Inayat	MUJAHID	Thabet	Inayat
20	Sat	Thabet	Warwar	SARAH F	Thabet	Warwar	SARAH F	Thabet	Warwar
21	Sun	Bafaqih	Rizwan	RAED	Thabet	Yaser	Abdullah S	Thabet	Yaser
22	Mon	Bafaqih	Ahmed	TAGHREED	Thabet	Yaser	Abdullah S	Thabet	Yaser
23	Tues	Bafaqih	Inayat	AMAL	Thabet	Yaser	Abdullah S	Thabet	Yaser
24	Wed	Bafaqih	Warwar	QASSIM	Thabet	Yaser	Abdullah S	Thabet	Yaser
25	Thu	Chehab	Rizwan	NADA ALHARBI	Chehab	Rizwan	FATIMAH	Chehab	Rizwan
26	Fri	Chehab	Yacoub	EBTISAM	Chehab	Yacoub	HALA	Chehab	Yacoub
27	Sat	Chehab	Yaser	MUJAHID	Chehab	Yaser	NADA ALHARBI	Chehab	Yaser
28	Sun	Chehab	Inayat	QASSIM	Mohaimeed	Ahmed	Yosef	Mohaimeed	Ahmed
29	Mon	Chehab	Warwar	M. ASIRI	Mohaimeed	Ahmed	Yosef	Mohaimeed	Ahmed

Figure 1. Example of a Hospital Manual Doctor schedule PSMMC hospital

TABLE V. THE HOSPITAL INCIDENT MATRIX FOR DOCTORS WORKING IN SAME GROUP AND IN 6 WARD FOR N=24.

	$R3_1$	$R4_1$	$R1_1$	$R1_5$	$R2_4$	SUB_1	$R3_2$	$R4_2$	$R1_2$	$R2_1$	$R2_5$	SUB_2	$R3_3$	$R4_3$	$R1_3$	$R2_2$	$R2_6$	SUB_3	$R3_4$	$R4_4$	$R1_4$	$R2_3$	$R2_7$	SUB_4
$R3_1$	0	1	1	1	1	1	0	0	0	0	0	0	0	0	0	0	0	0	0	0	0	0	0	0
$R4_1$	1	0	1	1	1	1	0	0	0	0	0	0	0	0	0	0	0	0	0	0	0	0	0	0
$R1_1$	1	1	0	1	1	1	0	0	0	0	0	0	0	0	0	0	0	0	0	0	0	0	0	0
$R1_5$	1	1	1	0	1	1	0	0	0	0	0	0	0	0	0	0	0	0	0	0	0	0	0	0
$R2_4$	1	1	1	1	0	1	0	0	0	0	0	0	0	0	0	0	0	0	0	0	0	0	0	0
SUB_1	1	1	1	1	1	0	0	0	0	0	0	0	0	0	0	0	0	0	0	0	0	0	0	0
$R3_2$	0	0	0	0	0	0	0	1	1	1	1	1	0	0	0	0	0	0	0	0	0	0	0	0
$R4_2$	0	0	0	0	0	0	1	0	1	1	1	1	0	0	0	0	0	0	0	0	0	0	0	0
$R1_2$	0	0	0	0	0	0	1	1	0	1	1	1	0	0	0	0	0	0	0	0	0	0	0	0
$R2_1$	0	0	0	0	0	0	1	1	1	0	1	1	0	0	0	0	0	0	0	0	0	0	0	0
$R2_5$	0	0	0	0	0	0	1	1	1	1	0	1	0	0	0	0	0	0	0	0	0	0	0	0
SUB_2	0	0	0	0	0	0	1	1	1	1	1	0	0	0	0	0	0	0	0	0	0	0	0	0
$R3_3$	0	0	0	0	0	0	0	0	0	0	0	0	0	1	1	1	1	1	0	0	0	0	0	0
$R4_3$	0	0	0	0	0	0	0	0	0	0	0	0	1	0	1	1	1	1	0	0	0	0	0	0
$R1_3$	0	0	0	0	0	0	0	0	0	0	0	0	1	1	0	1	1	1	0	0	0	0	0	0
$R2_2$	0	0	0	0	0	0	0	0	0	0	0	0	1	1	1	0	1	1	0	0	0	0	0	0
$R2_6$	0	0	0	0	0	0	0	0	0	0	0	0	1	1	1	1	0	1	0	0	0	0	0	0
SUB_3	0	0	0	0	0	0	0	0	0	0	0	0	1	1	1	1	1	0	0	0	0	0	0	0
$R3_4$	0	0	0	0	0	0	0	0	0	0	0	0	0	0	0	0	0	0	0	1	1	1	1	1
$R4_4$	0	0	0	0	0	0	0	0	0	0	0	0	0	0	0	0	0	0	1	0	1	1	1	1
$R1_4$	0	0	0	0	0	0	0	0	0	0	0	0	0	0	0	0	0	0	1	1	0	1	1	1
$R2_3$	0	0	0	0	0	0	0	0	0	0	0	0	0	0	0	0	0	0	1	1	1	0	1	1
$R2_7$	0	0	0	0	0	0	0	0	0	0	0	0	0	0	0	0	0	0	1	1	1	1	0	1
SUB_4	0	0	0	0	0	0	0	0	0	0	0	0	0	0	0	0	0	0	1	1	1	1	1	0

TABLE VI. THE GENETIC ALGORITHM BEST DOCTOR SCHEDULE N=24, D=29 FOR PSMMC HOSPITAL DOCTOR SCHEDULE

Days/ Junior doctors	1	2	3	4	5	6	7	8	9	10	11	12	13	14	15	16	17	18	19	20	21	22	23	24	25	26	27	28	29
J1	m	e	n	o	m	m	n	m	e	n	o	m	m	n	m	e	n	o	m	m	n	m	e	n	o	m	m	n	m
J2	e	m	m	n	o	m	n	e	m	m	n	o	m	n	e	m	m	n	o	m	n	e	m	m	n	o	m	n	e
J 3	n	n	o	m	e	e	e	n	n	o	m	e	e	e	n	n	o	m	e	e	e	n	n	o	m	e	e	e	n
J 4	m	m	e	e	n	o	m	m	m	e	e	n	o	m	m	m	e	e	n	o	m	m	m	e	e	n	o	m	m
J 5	e	e	e	n	m	n	o	e	e	e	n	m	n	o	e	e	e	n	m	n	o	e	e	e	n	m	n	o	e
J 6	m	e	n	o	m	m	n	m	e	n	o	m	m	n	m	e	n	o	m	m	n	m	e	n	o	m	m	n	m
J 7	e	m	m	n	o	m	n	e	m	m	n	o	m	n	e	m	m	n	o	m	n	e	m	m	n	o	m	n	e
J 8	n	n	o	m	e	e	e	n	n	o	m	e	e	e	n	n	o	m	e	e	e	n	n	o	m	e	e	e	n
J 9	m	m	e	e	n	o	m	m	m	e	e	n	o	m	m	m	e	e	n	o	m	m	m	e	e	n	o	m	m
J 10	e	e	e	n	m	n	o	e	e	e	n	m	n	o	e	e	e	n	m	n	o	e	e	e	n	m	n	o	e
J 11	m	e	n	o	m	m	n	m	e	n	o	m	m	n	m	e	n	o	m	m	n	m	e	n	o	m	m	n	m
J 12	e	m	m	n	o	m	n	e	m	m	n	o	m	n	e	m	m	n	o	m	n	e	m	m	n	o	m	n	e
J 13	n	n	o	m	e	e	e	n	n	o	m	e	e	e	n	n	o	m	e	e	e	n	n	o	m	e	e	e	n
J 14	m	m	e	e	n	o	m	m	m	e	e	n	o	m	m	m	e	e	n	o	m	m	m	e	e	n	o	m	m
J 15	e	e	e	n	m	n	o	e	e	e	n	m	n	o	e	e	e	n	m	n	o	e	e	e	n	m	n	o	e
J 16	m	e	n	o	m	m	n	m	e	n	o	m	m	n	m	e	n	o	m	m	n	m	e	n	o	m	m	n	m
J 17	e	m	m	n	o	m	n	e	m	m	n	o	m	n	e	m	m	n	o	m	n	e	m	m	n	o	m	n	e
J 18	n	n	o	m	e	e	e	n	n	o	m	e	e	e	n	n	o	m	e	e	e	n	n	o	m	e	e	e	n
J 19	m	m	e	e	n	o	m	m	m	e	e	n	o	m	m	m	e	e	n	o	m	m	m	e	e	n	o	m	m
J 20	e	e	e	n	m	n	o	e	e	e	n	m	n	o	e	e	e	n	m	n	o	e	e	e	n	m	n	o	e
J 21	m	e	n	o	m	m	n	m	e	n	o	m	m	n	m	e	n	o	m	m	n	m	e	n	o	m	m	n	m
J 22	e	m	m	n	o	m	n	e	m	m	n	o	m	n	e	m	m	n	o	m	n	e	m	m	n	o	m	n	e
J 23	n	n	o	m	e	e	e	n	n	o	m	e	e	e	n	n	o	m	e	e	e	n	n	o	m	e	e	e	n
J 24	m	m	e	e	n	o	m	n	m	e	e	n	o	m	n	m	e	e	n	o	m	m	m	e	e	n	o	m	m

International Journal on Advances in Software, vol 10 no 3 & 4, year 2017, http://www.iariajournals.org/software/

Control Mechanisms for Managed Evolution of Automotive Software Product Line Architectures

Christoph Knieke, Marco Körner, Andreas Rausch,
Mirco Schindler, Arthur Strasser, and Martin Vogel
TU Clausthal, Department of Computer Science, Software Systems Engineering
Clausthal-Zellerfeld, Germany
Email: {christoph.knieke|marco.koerner|andreas.rausch|
mirco.schindler|arthur.strasser|m.vogel}@tu-clausthal.de

Abstract—**The high time and cost pressure in the automotive market encourages reuse of components and software in different vehicle projects leading to a high degree of variability within the software. Often, a product line approach is used to handle variability. However, the increasing complexity and degree of variability of automotive software systems hinders the capabilities for reusability and extensibility of these systems to an increasing degree. After several product generations, software erosion is growing steadily, resulting in an increasing effort of reusing software components, and planning of further development. Here, we propose control mechanisms for a managed evolution of automotive software product line architectures. We introduce a description language and its meta model for the specification of the software product line architecture and the software architecture of the corresponding products. Based on the description language we propose an approach for architecture conformance checking to identify architecture violations as a means to prevent architecture erosion. We demonstrate our methodology on a real world case study, a brake servo unit (BSU) software system from automotive software engineering. To show the benefits of our approach, we define several metrics on architecture and software level and apply the metrics on the BSU example.**

Keywords–Architecture Conformance Checking; Architecture Description Language; Software Product Lines; Automotive Software Engineering.

I. Introduction

This paper is a substantial extension of the work presented at the ADAPTIVE 2017 conference [1]. In the development of electronic control unit (ECU) software for vehicles, the reduction of development costs and the increase of quality are essential objectives. A significant measure to achieve these goals is the reuse of software components [2]. The reuse is mainly achieved by a product-wide development for different vehicle variants: Different configurations of driver assistance systems, comfort functions, or powertrains can be variably combined, creating an individual and unique product. Furthermore, for each new vehicle generation, the software of preceding generations of the vehicle is reused or adopted [3].

However, the possibilities for reuse and extensibility of existing functions can not be fully exploited in many cases. Rather, it can be observed that due to the increase in so-called "accidental" complexity [3] (see Section VI-B), the reusability and further developability reaches its limits. One reason for this is the lack of a product-line-oriented overall planning, based on the concepts of software product line engineering already established in other domains. A central factor here is the planning based on a product line architecture (PLA), on the specification of which the individual products are derived. The PLA describes the structure of all realizable products. Each product that is developed has an individual product architecture (PA) whose structure should be mapped onto the PLA.

An important challenge with regard to the architecture is to minimize architecture erosion as illustrated in the following. In [4], architecture erosion is defined as "*the phenomenon that occurs when the implemented architecture of a software system diverges from its intended architecture.*" As shown in Figure 1 a PLA is designed initially and develops over time [5]. It makes no difference whether the PLA is explicitly planned or exists only implicitly in the minds of the participants. In the further development, it must be ensured that the product architecture remains compliant with the product line architecture. However, due to the high time and cost pressure in the automotive sector, it is not possible for every further development to be controlled via the product line. Rather, some product-specific adjustments have to be made. This can lead (intentionally or unintentionally) to a product architecture that differs in comparison to the product line architecture: the architecture erodes. In the long-term, this leads to reduced reusability and extensibility of the software artifacts.

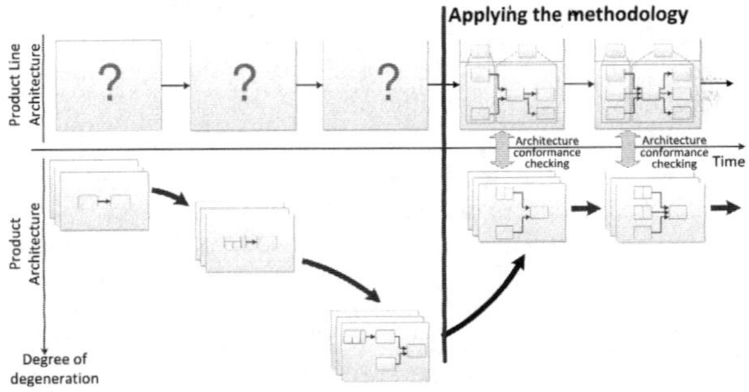

Figure 1. Avoiding architecture erosion by applying our methodology

To prevent architecture erosion, we propose control mechanisms for a managed evolution of automotive software product line architectures in this paper. We refer to the results shown in a preceding paper [5] to create a PLA as a prerequisite for our approach by applying strategies for architecture recovery and discovery. First, we introduce a description language and its meta model for the specification of the software product line architecture and the software architecture of the corresponding products. Based on the description language we propose an approach for architecture conformance checking to identify architecture violations as a means to prevent architecture erosion (indicated on the right side of Figure 1). Due to the size of the product line architecture, an automated consistency check is necessary, which is an essential part of our approach to counteract architecture erosion.

The application of the software product line development must take into account the special properties, boundary conditions and requirements that exist in the automotive environment [6]. Therefore, a method adapted to the automotive environment is required and is presented in this paper.

An important aspect is the design and planning of further developments of the product line architecture. When designing the product line architecture, the architecture must be based on architecture principles appropriate for the automotive domain, aiming at reusability and further development [3]. Since a wide range of products can be affected by the further development of the product line architecture, changes must be carefully planned: High demands are placed on the reliability of the systems, but the reliability is endangered by extensive adaptations.

The major objectives of our approach can be summarized as follows:

1) Maintaining stability of the PLA and minimizing product architecture erosion even if extensive further development of the system takes place.
2) Achieving high scalability, and a high degree of usage of the modules.

The first objective primarily addresses the software architecture: The PLA should be based on appropriate design principles that allow further developments with a minimal adjustment effort of the PLA. At the same time, the erosion of product architecture is to be minimized.

The second objective focuses on the software components: These should be kept scalable so that they can be used for as many variants as possible. Nevertheless, the software components should be able to be reused over time in subsequent product generations. However, the high variability within the components increases the complexity of the components and thus makes reuse more difficult.

The paper is structured as follows: Section II gives an overview on the related work. In Section III we propose a methodology for managed evolution of automotive software product line architectures. Section IV introduces an architecture description language for the specification of the product line architecture and the product architecture. Based on this description language Section V proposes an approach for architecture conformance checking. In Section VI, we apply our approach on a real world example, a brake servo unit, from automotive software engineering. The results of a corresponding field study are evaluated and discussed in Section VII. Section VIII concludes.

II. RELATED WORK

To the best of our knowledge, no continuous overall development cycle for automotive software product line architectures exists. Several aspects of our process are already covered in literature:

A. Reference Architectures

The purpose of the reference architecture is to provide guidance for future developments. In addition, the reference architecture incorporates the vision and strategy for the future. The work in [7] examines current reference architectures and the driving forces behind development of them to come to a collective conclusion on what a reference architecture should truly be. Furthermore, in [7], reference architectures are assumed to be the basis for the instantiation of product line architectures (so-called family architectures, see [7]).

Nakagawa et. al. discuss the differences between reference architectures and product line architectures by highlighting basic questions like definitions, benefits, and motivation for using each one, when and how they should be used, built, and evolved, as well as stakeholders involved and benefited by each one [8]. Furthermore, they define a reference model of reference architectures [9], and propose a methodology to design product line architectures based on reference architectures [10][11].

B. Software Erosion

In [4], de Silva and Balasubramaniam provide a survey of technologies and techniques either to prevent architecture erosion or to detect and restore architectures that have been eroded. However, each approach discussed in [4] refers to architecture erosion for a single PA, whereas architecture erosion in software product lines are out of the scope of the paper. Furthermore, as discussed in [4], none of the available methods singly provides an effective and comprehensive solution for controlling architecture erosion.

Van Gurp and Bosch [12] illustrate how design erosion works by presenting the evolution of the design of a small software system. The paper concludes that even an optimal design strategy for the design phase does not lead to an optimal design. The reason for this are unforeseen requirement changes in later evolution cycles. These changes may cause design decisions taken earlier to be less optimal.

The work in [13] describes an approach to flexible architecture erosion detection for model-driven development approaches. Consistency constraints expressed by architectural aspects called architectural rules are specified as formulas on a common ontology, and models are mapped to instances of that ontology. A knowledge representation and reasoning system is then utilized to check whether these architectural rules are satisfied for a given set of models. Three case studies are presented demonstrating that architecture erosion can be minimized effectively by the approach.

C. Software Product Line Architectures

As discussed in [5] an overall automotive product line architecture is often missing due to software sharing. Thus, architecture recovery and discovery has to be applied by concepts of software product line extraction [5]. The aim of software product line extraction is to identify all the valid points of variation and the associated functional requirements of component diagrams. The work in [14] shows an approach to extract a product line from a user documentation. The Product Line UML-based Software Engineering (PLUS) approach permits variability analysis based on use case scenarios and the specification of variable properties in a feature model [15]. In [16], variability of a system characteristic is described in a feature model as variable features that can be mapped to use cases. In contrast to our approach, these approaches are based on functional requirements whereas our approach is focused on products.

In numerous publications, Bosch et. al. address the field of product line architecture, software architecture erosion, and reuse of software artifacts: The work in [17] proposes a method that brings together two aspects of software architecture: the design of software architecture and software product lines. Deelstra et al. [18] provide a framework of terminology and concepts regarding product derivation. They have identified that companies employ widely different approaches for software product line based development and that these approaches evolve over time. The work in [19] discusses six maturity levels that they have identified for software product line approaches. In [20], a methodical and structured approach of architecture restoration in the specific case of the brake servo unit (BSU) is applied. Software product lines from existing BSU variants are extracted by explicit projection of the architecture variability and decomposition of the original architecture.

The work in [21] gives a systematic survey and analysis of existing approaches supporting multi product lines and a general discussion of capabilities supporting multi product lines in various domains and organizations. They define a multi product line (MPL) as a set of several self-contained but still interdependent product lines that together represent a large-scale or ultra-large-scale system. The different product lines in an MPL can exist independently but typically use shared resources to meet the overall system requirements. According to this definition, a vehicle system is also an MPL assuming that each product line is responsible for a particular subsystem. However, in the following, we only regard classic product lines, since the dependencies between the individual product lines in vehicle systems are very low, unlike MPL.

D. Software Product Line Architecture Evolution

Thiel and Hein [22] propose product lines as an approach to automotive system development because product lines facilitate the reuse of core assets. The approach of Thiel and Hein enables the modeling of product line variability and describes how to manage variability throughout core asset development. Furthermore, they sketch the interaction between the feature and architecture models to utilize variability.

Holdschick [23] addresses the challenges in the evolution of model-based software product lines in the automotive domain. The author argues that a variant model created initially quickly becomes obsolete because of the permanent evolution of software functionalities in the automotive area. Thus, Holdschick proposes a concept how to handle evolution in variant-rich model-based software systems. The approach provides an overview of which changes relevant to variability could occur in the functional model and where the challenges are when reproducing them in the variant model.

Automotive manufacturers have to cope with the erosion of their ECU software. The work in [3] proposes a systematic approach for managed and continuous evolution of dependable automotive software systems. It is described how complexity of automotive software systems can be managed by creating modular and stable architectures based on well-defined requirements. Both architecture and requirements have to be managed in relation. Furthermore, to face the lack of flexibility of existing hieratic automotive software systems development approaches, they are focusing on four driving factors: systems engineering and agile function development, feature and function driven team development, agile management principles, and a seamless tooling infrastructure supporting continuously and iteratively evolving automotive software systems in a flexible manner.

To counteract erosion it is necessary to keep software components modular. But modularity is also a necessary attribute for reuse. Several approaches deal with the topic reuse of software components in the development of automotive products [2][24]. In [2], a framework is proposed, which focuses on modularization and management of a function repository. Another practical experience describes the introduction of a product line for a gasoline system from scratch [24]. However, in both approaches a long-term minimization of erosion is not considered.

A previous version of our approach is described in [5] focusing on the key ideas of the management cycle for product line architecture evolution. Furthermore, an approach for repairing an eroded software consisting of a set of product architectures by applying strategies for recovery and discovery of the product line architecture is proposed.

III. Overall Development Cycle

Our methodology for managed evolution of automotive software product line architectures is depicted in Figure 2. The left part of Figure 2 depicts the recovery and discovery activity introduced in a previous paper [5]. This activity is performed once before the long term evolution cycle (right side of Figure 2) can start. The latter consists of two levels of development: The cycle on the top of Figure 2 constitutes the development activities for product line development, whereas the second cycle is required for product specific development. Not only both levels of development are executed in parallel but even the activities within a cycle may be performed concurrently. The circular arrow within the two cycles indicates the dependencies of an activity regarding the artifacts of the previous activity. Nevertheless, individual activities may be performed in parallel, e.g., the planned implementations can be realized from activity `PL-Plan`, while a new PLA is developed in parallel (activity `PL-Design`). The large arrows between the two development levels indicate transitions requiring an external decision-making process, e.g., the decision to start a new product development or prototyping, respectively.

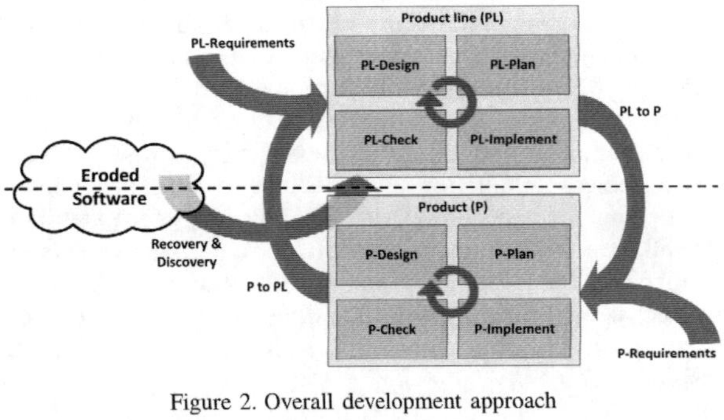

Figure 2. Overall development approach

In the following three subsections, we will explain the basic activities of our approach in detail by referring to the terms depicted in Figure 2. Table I gives a brief overview on the

TABLE I. Explanation of the activities in Figure 2.

Activity	*Input*	*Objective*	*Output*
PL-Design	Software system / component requirements and documentation from product development.	Further development of PLA with consideration of design principles. Application of measuring techniques to assess quality of PLA.	New PLA (called "PLA vision").
PL-Plan	PLA vision.	Planning of a set of iterations of further development toward the PLA vision taking all affected projects into account.	Development plan including the planned order of module implementations and the planned related projects.
PL-Implement	Development plan for product line.	Implementation including testing as specified by the development plan for product line development.	Implemented module versions.
PL-Check	Architecture rules and set of implemented modules to be checked.	Minimization of product architecture erosion by architecture conformance checking based on architecture rules.	Check results.
P-Design	Project plan and product specific requirements.	Designing product architecture and performing architecture adaptations taking product specific requirements into account. Compliance checking with PLA to minimize erosion.	Planned product architecture.
P-Plan	Product architecture.	Definition of iterations to be performed on product level toward the planned product architecture.	Development plan for product development.
P-Implement	Development plan for product development.	Product specific implementations including testing as specified by the development plan for product development.	Implemented module versions.
P-Check	Architecture rules and set of implemented modules to be checked.	Architecture conformance checking between PLA and PA.	Check results.
PL to P	Development plan for product line.	Defining a project plan by selecting a project from the the product line.	Project plan.
P to PL	Developed product.	Providing product related information of developed product for integration into product line development.	Product documentation and implementation artifacts of developed products.
PL-Requirements	Requirements.	Specification and validation of software system and software component requirements by requirements engineering.	Software system and software component requirements.
P-Requirements	Requirements in particular from calibration engineers.	Specification of special requirements for a certain vehicle product including vehicle related parameter settings.	Vehicle related requirements.
Recovery & Discovery	Source artifacts (developed products).	Recovery of the implemented PLA from the source artifacts (developed products) and discovery of the intended PLA.	Implemented and intended PLA.

objectives of each of the 13 activities, including inputs and outputs.

We distinguish between the terms 'project' and 'product' in the following: A project includes a set of versioned software components, so-called modules. These modules contain variability so that a project can be used for different vehicles. On the other hand, a product is a fully executable software status for a certain vehicle based on a project in conjunction with vehicle related parameter settings.

A. *Planning and Evolving Automotive Software Product Line Architectures*

(`PL-Requirements`) Software system requirements and software component requirements from requirements engineering serve as input to the management cycle of the PLA. Errors occurring during the phase of requirements elicitation and specification have turned out to be major reasons for the failure of IT projects [25]. In particular, errors occur in case the requirements are specified erroneous or the requirements have inconsistencies and incompleteness. Errors during the phase of requirements elicitation and specification can be avoided by choosing an appropriate specification language enabling the validation of the requirements. In [26], e.g., activity diagrams are considered for the validation of system requirements by directly executable models including an approach for symbolic execution and thus enabling validation of several products simultaneously.

(`P to PL`) Artifacts of the developed product from the product cycle in Figure 2 serve as further input to the management cycle of the PLA: The product documentation contains architectural adaptations and change proposals, which can be integrated in the PLA. Furthermore, the modified modules in their new implementation are committed to the management cycle of the PLA for integration in product line.

(`PL-Design`) Next, we consider the design of the PLA. Generally, a software system architecture defines the basic organization of a system by structuring different architectural elements and relationships between them. The specification of "good" software system architecture is crucial for the success of the system to be developed. By our definition, a "good" architecture is a modular architecture that is built according to the following: (a) design principles for high cohesion, (b) design principles for abstraction and information hiding, and (c) design principles for loose coupling. In [3], we propose methods and techniques for a good architecture design. Based on these methods and techniques a new PLA is defined (called PLA vision) taking the new requirements (`PL-Requirements`) and product related information (`P to PL`) into account. To assess the quality of the designed PLA, it is necessary to measure complexity and to describe the results numerically. In particular, we consider properties such as cohesion, coupling, reusability and variability in order to draw conclusions about the quality of the PLA.

(`PL-Plan`) As further development of the PLA will effect a high number of products, the changes have to be planned carefully in order to avoid errors within the corresponding products and to avoid architecture erosion. Thus, the planning phase has to define a set of iterations of further development towards the PLA vision. All allowed changes are planned as a schedule containing the type of change and timestamp. It is planned, in which order the implementation of corresponding modules should take place. It should be emphasized that there are many parallel product developments, which must be taken into account when planning. Next, either affected projects and modules are determined or a pilot project is selected.

Some further developments can lead to extensive architectural changes. In this case the effects of the architectural changes on the associated projects have to be closely examined. For this purpose further development projects can be defined as prototype projects for certain iterations of the PLA. These projects are then tested within the product cycle.

B. Automotive Product Development and Prototyping

(`PL-Implement`) The former planning activity has determined the schedule for PLA adaptations and product releases. Thus, on the implementation level, new versions of the software are planned, too. Vehicle functions are modeled using a set of modules, specifying the discrete and continuous behavior of the corresponding function. As required by ISO 26262 [27], each module needs to be tested separately. Established techniques for model-based testing necessitate a requirements specification, from which a test model can be derived. In practice, requirements are specified by natural language and on the level of whole vehicle functions instead of modules so that test models on module level can not be derived directly. Therefore, in [28], a systematic model-based, test-driven approach is proposed to design a specification on the level of modules, which is directly testable. The idea of test-driven development is to write a test case first for any new code that is written [29]. Then the implementation is improved to pass the test case. Based on the approach in [28] we use the tool Time Partition Testing (TPT) because it suits particularly well due to the ability to describe continuous behavior [30]. The modules may be developed in ASCET or MATLAB/Simulink.

(`P-Requirements`) Releasing a fully executable software status for a certain vehicle product requires a specification of vehicle related parameter settings. Furthermore, special requirements for a specific product may exist necessitating further development of certain implementation artifacts. Building an executable software status for a certain vehicle product is realized by the cycle at the bottom of Figure 2. In contrast, the product line cycle in Figure 2 includes the development of sets of software artifacts of all planned projects.

(`PL to P`) Automotive software product development and prototyping starts with selecting a product from the product line. Therefore, the project plan is transferred containing module descriptions and descriptions of the logical product architecture integration plan with associated module versions.

(`P-Plan`) The product planning defines the iterations to be performed. An iteration consists of selected product architecture elements and planned implementations. An iteration is part of a sequence of iterations.

(`P-Implement`) An iteration is completed when all planned elements of an iteration are implemented according to the test-driven approach of [28].

C. Architecture Conformance Checking

Architecture erodes when the implemented architecture of a software system diverges from its intended architecture. Software architecture erosion can reduce the quality of software systems significantly. Thus, detecting software architecture erosion is an important task during the development and maintenance of automotive software systems. Even in our model-driven approach where implementation artifacts are constructed w.r.t. a given architecture the intended architecture and its realization may diverge. Hence, monitoring architecture conformance is crucial to limit architecture erosion.

Each planned product refers to a set of implementation artifacts, called modules. These modules constitute the product architecture. The aim of `PL-Check` and `P-Check` is the minimization of product architecture erosion. In [13], a method is described to keep the erosion of the software to a minimum: Consistency constraints expressed by architectural aspects called architectural rules are specified as formulas on a common ontology, and models are mapped to instances of that ontology. Based on this approach we are extracting rules from a PLA to minimize the erosion of the product architecture. During the development of implementation artifacts the rules can be accessed via a query mechanism and be used to check the consistency of the product architecture. Those rules can, e.g., contain structural information about the software like allowed communications. In [13], the rules are expressed as logical formulas, which can be evaluated automatically to the compliance to the PLA.

(`PL-Check`) After each iteration planned in activity `PL-Plan` all related product architectures have to be checked. As `P-Check` refers to one product only, the check is performed after all related implementation artifacts of the product are developed.

(`P-Design`) The creation of a new product starts with a basically planned product architecture commonly derived from the product line. For the development of the product, new functionalities have to be realized and thus necessary adaptations to the planned product architecture are made. In order to keep the erosion to a minimum we have to ensure the compliance to the architecture design principles of the PLA. Therefore, we check consistency of the planned product architecture by applying architecture rules from the PLA.

However, in the case of prototyping it may be desired that the planned product architecture differs from PLA specifications. Thus, as a consequence, the architecture rules are violated. As pointed out in Section III-A, product related information is returned to the management cycle of the PLA after product delivery. If the development of a product required a differing product architecture w.r.t. the PLA, this could advance the erosion. Necessary changes must be communicated to `PL-Design` and `PL-Plan` s.t. the changes can be evaluated and adopted. As changes to the PLA can have severe influences on all the other architectures the changes are not applied immediately but considered for further development.

IV. Architecture Description Language

The software architecture serves as input for the subsequent development steps, e.g., for implementation and test. In this architecture, the software building blocks of the cars embedded system are documented. Thereby, the implementation step follows the model-based development approach, where code is generated from architecture models using tools of the industrial partner. To model these architectures in the industrial projects we introduced the EMAB (Einheitliche Modulare Architektur Beschreibung) architecture description language. The EMAB is applied for the architecture extraction and the managed evolution approach presented in this paper. In addition, the EMAB includes all aspects to describe the static structure of the project partners electronic control unit system domains.

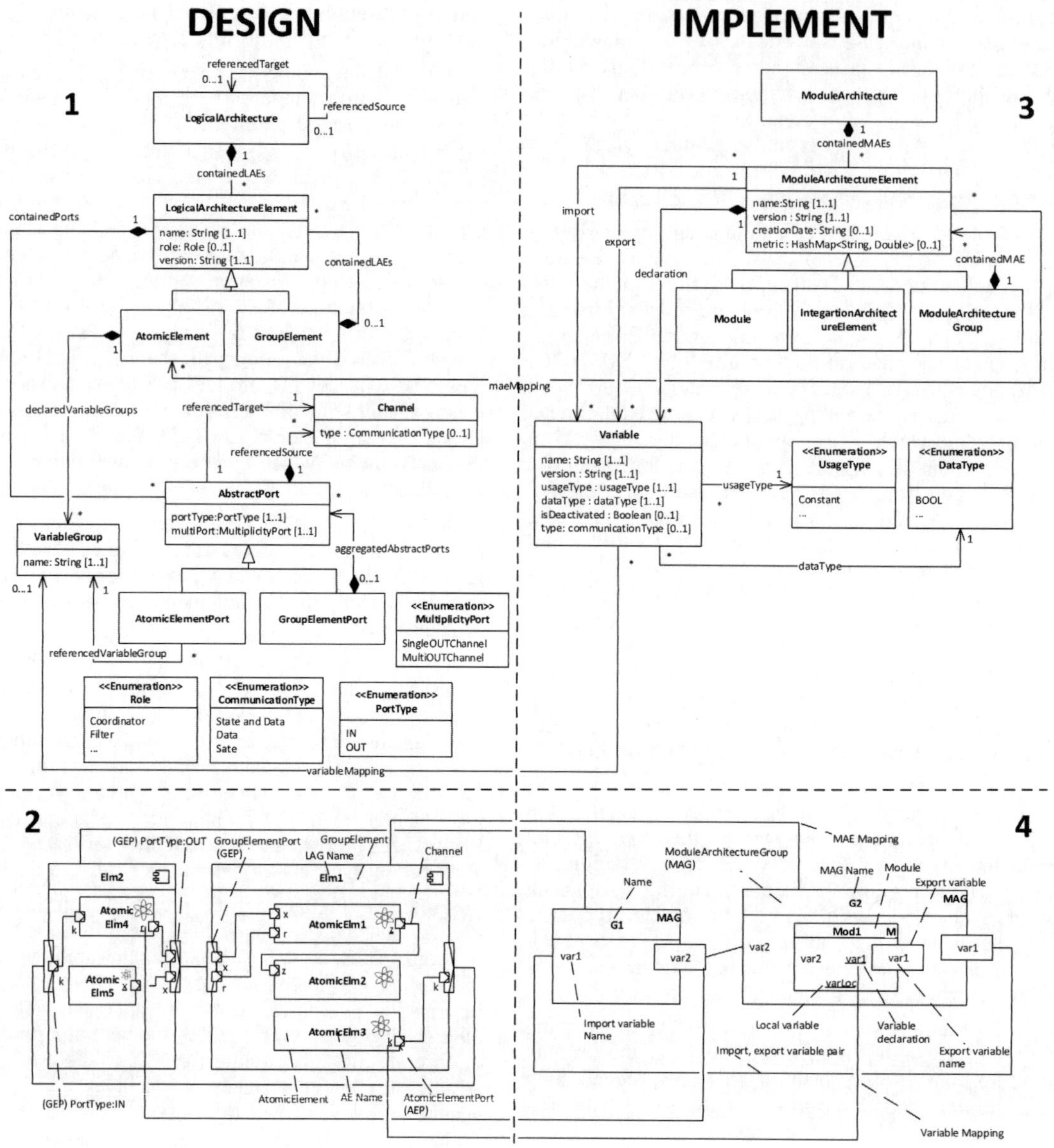

Figure 3. EMAB: The meta model (1,3) and the two views as instances of the meta model (2,4).

EMAB is used to describe two layered architectures consisting of the logical architecture layer called DESIGN and the technical software architecture layer called IMPLEMENT. Both are defined by the syntax and semantics of the EMAB meta model elements. For each layer, the EMAB also defines the appropriate block diagram based views for architecture description. In our approach, the two layers DESIGN and IMPLEMENT refer to activities `PL-Design/P-Design` and `PL-Implement/P-Implement`, respectively.

The following subsections IV-A, IV-B illustrate the details of the EMAB syntax and appropriate semantics of the DESIGN layer and IMPLEMENT layer and their appropriate views. Figure 3 shows the meta model to illustrate the description language syntax (top) and also shows an exemplary instance of the meta model to illustrate the syntax of the views (bottom). Each layer and view are identified by one of the four quadrants in Figure 3.

A. Meta Model and View of the DESIGN Layer

Logical Architecture Element: The first quadrant of Figure 3 shows the syntax of the logical architecture comprising the building blocks. The `LogicalArchitecture` contains a set of `LogicalArchitectureElements` (LAEs). The LAE is defined by at least the `name` attribute, the `version` attribute and optionally by the `role` attribute. The meta model contains the roles `Coordinator`, `Support`, `Filter`, which are used for several architecture concepts.

There are two types of LAEs: Decomposable GroupElement and not decomposable AtomicElement architecture building blocks. The GroupElement is used to describe a hierarchy of building blocks. A GroupElement can be decomposed into smaller LAEs.

The second quadrant of Figure 3 shows the DESIGN view by a meta model instance example of the logical architecture. The diagram represents a logical architecture consisting of two GroupElement building blocks and five AtomicElement building blocks. The block named Elm1 represents a GroupElement and the building block AtomicElm1 represents an AtomicElement. The hierarchy is shown by nesting of the AtomicElement block AtomicElm1 in the GroupElement block Elm1.

Interface of a LAE: The interface of a building block is defined by ports. There are two kinds of ports: Decomposable ports called GroupElementPort (GEP) and not decomposable ports called AtomicElementPort (AEP). GEPs can be used only by GroupElement building blocks whereas AEP ports can be used by both, GroupElement and AtomicElement, building blocks. A GEP of the outer GroupElement block enables the composition of ports of nested inner LAEs. Thereby, several ports of a GroupElement building block can be grouped to one port. The type of information that is used to pass by a port to extern is defined by a VariableGroup. A VariableGroup represents the functional information that abstracts existing interfaces of the IMPLEMENT layer.

The syntax to describe ports of a building block is depicted in the first quadrant of Figure 3. Therefore, the LAE has a containment association aggregatedAbstractPorts to any number of AbstractPorts. The AbstractPort element has to define at least the attribute portType, which is an enumeration type of IN, OUT. GEP and AEP have an inherit association to AbstractPort. Though, an AbstractPort can be associated to zero or one GEP. The AEP has a containment association referencedVariableGroup to any number of VariableGroups. A VariableGroup must be associated to exactly one AtomicElement and can be associated by any number of AEPs.

The second quadrant of Figure 3 shows the block diagram notation of instances of AEP and GEP meta model elements. The right border of the GroupElement block Elm2 has a rectangular block that consists of several smaller squares-shaped blocks. The rectangular block represents a GEP element and the smaller square-shaped blocks represent AEP elements. The GEP composes the two out ports of the AtomicElements AtomicElm4 and AtomicElm5. Thereby, to represent that a AEP owned by the inner AtomicElement is composed by the GEP of the outer GroupElement, the following must be modeled: For each AEP of an inner AtomicElement that has to be composed, a second AEP is described that is contained by the GEP. Both, the AEP contained by the inner AtomicElement and the AEP contained by the GEP must reference the same VariableGroup and must be connected to each other. For example, the two connected OUT AbstractPorts that reference the VariableGroup x in the Elm2 block represent the composed OUT AEP of the AtomicElement AtomicElm5. This modeling step is used to enable a more detailed visualization of the composition of different kinds of information. Connections are modeled by the Channel meta model element, which is introduced in the following.

Channel: The communication in the development of control systems is modeled by data flow. The data flow represents functional information of the communication. Each data flow has a source, a target and forms a point to point connection for a source, target pair. The point to point connection is called Channel. In the industrial projects several kinds of functional information (e.g., states, functional data) have been identified. These represent the types of the Channel.

The Channel meta model element is shown in the first quadrant of Figure 3. This element has an optional attribute type to define the functional information, which can be one of the three CommunicationType items. The items of this enumeration type are State and Data, Data, and State. The Channel has at least one association referencedSource to a source AbstractPort and at least one association referencedTarget to a target AbstractPort.

The connections, which are instances of the Channel meta model element, are depicted in the second quadrant of Figure 3. For example, the connections of ports, which have associations to VariableGroups x, r of AtomicElm1, AtomicElm4, and AtomicElm5, specify the communication of these AtomicElements. These connections comprise the ports of the GroupElements Elm1 and Elm2, as each AtomicElement is contained in a different GroupElement. Therefore, ports of the inner AtomicElements are connected to ports of the outer GroupElements to model the communication path along with the connections of the GroupElements.

B. Meta Model and View of the IMPLEMENT Layer

Module Architecture Element: The building block of the software system is described by the ModuleArchitectureElements (MAE). These building blocks are used to form a module architecture, which describes the structure of the software system. Each MAE is managed in a versioning system and is identified by its name and its version. Moreover, each MAE has a time stamp to identify the last time of modification and a quality degree regarding modularity measuring. The following kinds of MAEs are distinguished:

- Not decomposable building blocks called Module representing code artifacts.
- Building blocks that can be composed are called ModuleArchitectureGroup (MAG) to describe hierarchical structures.
- The IntegratedArchitectureElement that is used to describe building blocks of software subsystems developed by software suppliers.

The third quadrant of Figure 3 shows the syntax of the meta model for the description of the IMPLEMENT layer of the module architecture. The ModuleArchitecture is the root of the architecture that has a containment association containedMAEs to any number of MAEs. The MAE has at least the attributes name, version and has the optional attributes creationDate, metric. The MAG, the IntegratedArchitectureElement and the Module have an inheritance association to MAE. The MAE has the association containedMAE to any number of MAEs. A MAE can be associated via containedMAE by exactly one MAG.

The fourth quadrant of Figure 3 shows the block diagram syntax as meta model instance example of the view of the IMPLEMENT layer. The diagram represents an instance of the meta model module architecture that contains two MAG instances named G1, G2. Moreover, in the block G2, another block named M1 is nested. M1 represents an instance of the meta model Module element.

Interface - Variable: The interface of a MAE is defined by the set of all import and export variables that can be compared to the imports/exports of an ANSI C header file. Only Module declares its signals called Variables that are used for communication to other MAEs. A Variable is globally known and has a system global unique identifier that is identified by its name and its version and has at least a DataType (e.g., byte) and at least the UsageType. The UsageType is used to describe whether the data of a Variable is constant at run time or not. Moreover, some Variables are used in some software systems but in others not. Therefore, the flag isDeactivated is used to define the presence of a variable declaration. The flag is retrieved at compile time to remove variable declarations from code. Several kinds of variable types for communication have been identified from the functional point of view. For this purpose, a variable can have one of the following CommunicationTypes: State and Data, Data, and State. Another special feature of the MAG is that its interface can only be defined by its inner MAE interfaces. For example, an export interface v1 of a MAG can only be defined when the MAG has an inner MAE that declares variable v1 and exports this variable.

The syntax of the meta model to describe the MAE interface is depicted in the third quadrant of Figure 3. The MAE has several associations to describe the interface. First, the MAE has an association import to a number of Variables. Each import can be associated by a Variable to a number of MAEs. Second, the MAE has an association export to a number of Variables. Each export Variable can be associated by exactly one MAE. Third, the MAE has an association declaration to any number of Variables. Each declaration can be associated by exactly one MAE. For each declared Variable, at least attributes name, version, dataType, usageType have to be defined. The other attributes isDeactiveable und type are optional.

In the fourth quadrant of Figure 3 each diagram element represents an instance of the appropriate meta model element. In the case of the interfaces, the diagram shows three declared variables varLoc, var1, var2. Import variables are shown on the left border side within each block. For example, the MAG G2 has the import variable var2. Export variables are shown on the right border side of each block. Module Mod1 has the export variable var1. Moreover, var1 is declared by Mod1, which is shown by the underlined name of the variable. If a variable is only declared but not used as an interface, then it is used only local by the module. For example, varLoc is used by Mod1 locally.

Communication: The communication in software control systems is modeled as data flow in structures that represent directed graphs. For example, executable models in Mathlab Simulink or ASCET, represent this kind of data flow based graphs. The ModuleArchitecture is used to describe the communication implicitly by a pair of MAE interfaces. An interface pair has to describe a variable that is shared by the pair of an import interface and an export interface of two MAE. These two MAEs describe the same variable for communication from one MAE to another MAE. One MAE must declare the variable as an export interface. The other MAE must have the same variable as an import interface.

The syntax of the meta model to describe the communication is shown in the third quadrant of Figure 3. The communication is described implicitly by two MAE. One MAE must have an association import to a Variable. The other MAE must have an association export to the same Variable as the other MAE.

The fourth quadrant of Figure 3 shows an example model of the view where the communication of G2 and G1 is described by a connection of the export var1 block of G2 to import var1 of G1. Thereby, a connection is shown only in the case where the pair of import interface and export interface belong two inner MAEs of common outer MAE as root architecture element.

Mapping of the implement layer and the design layer: The structure of the logical architecture description of the DESIGN layer must be fulfilled by the module architecture of the IMPLEMENT layer. The EMAB description is called consistent, if the DESIGN layer is fulfilled by the IMPLEMENT layer. Therefore, each AtomicElement and each VariableGroup must have equivalent Variable elements and MAE elements in the IMPLEMENT layers.

The first quadrant and third quadrant of Figure 3 show the syntax of the meta model for the Variable mapping and the MAE mapping. The mapping is necessary to describe equivalent elements of the two layers. The MAE element from the first quadrant has the association maeMapping to any number of AtomicElements. The Variable has the association variableMapping to zero or one VariableGroup. Each VariableGroup is associated by any number of Variables and each AtomicElement to any number of MAEs.

Figure 3 shows the syntax of the view where an instance of a mapping is represented by a connection. The export interface var1 of block G2 and the VariableGroup k are mapped by a connection, which represents an instance of the variableMapping. The connection between block G2 and block Elm1 represents an instance of the maeMapping.

C. Valid Descriptions

From the technical point of view, the EMAB models are stored as XML files. During the export or import the file validity against the XML schema is checked. But not every model that is valid against the XML schema, is also a valid architecture description. Therefore, in the following several rules are introduced for each layer in detail. These rules must be fulfilled to ensure the validity of the description of the two architecture layers. In the following all necessary rules ensuring that EMAB models from the technical point of view are valid XML files are specified in prose. Each rule can be implemented using some constraint language. Figure 7 (see Section V) shows an example of some conformance checking

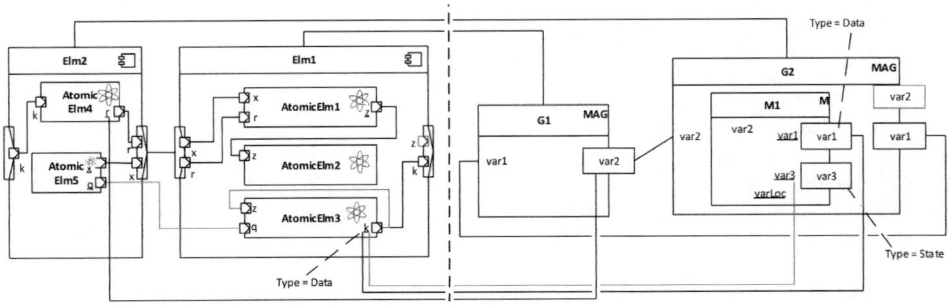

Figure 4. Example of invalid EMAB descriptions

rule that is implemented in the object constraint language (OCL).

Design layer rules: The EMAB description of the logical architecture is valid, if the following rules are fulfilled:

1) A `Channel` can connect two ports of two LAEs, only if both LAEs are children of the same `Group-Element` father.
2) A `Channel` can connect two ports of two LAEs, only if both ports of the two LAEs have a reference to the same `VariableGroup`.
3) A `Channel` connects exactly a `IN` port, `OUT` port pair with each other.
4) Ports of the outer `GroupElement` must be connected to ports of the inner LAEs.
5) A `Channel` connects exactly two ports.
6) A `Channel` must have an association `referencedSource` to the `OUT` port and must have an association `referencedTarget` to the `IN` port.
7) A `VariableGroup` can only be associated by exactly one `OUT` port.
8) Only an `AbstractPort` of `Multiplicity-Port` type `MultiOUTChannel` can be associated by more then one `referencedSource`.

On the left side of Figure 4 a further developed block diagram of Figure 3 is shown. The logical architecture in the diagram violates rules 1, 2, 4. The diagram elements that violate a rule are shown in red. For example, the port of `AtomicElm3` in `GroupElement Elm1` is directly connected by a channel to the port of the inner `AtomicElm3` of `GroupElement Elm2`. This is a violation against rule 1. Rule 4 is also violated, because `Elm2` has an `OUT` port that is unconnected. Moreover, at the block `AtomicElm3` two ports are connected that have associations to different `VariableGroups`.

Implement layer rules: The EMAB description of the module architecture is valid, if the following rules are fulfilled:

1) An export variable of an outer MAG must have an appropriate export variable of a inner MAE. Both MAE have associations to the same variable declaration.
2) A MAE may declare a `Variable`, if it is a `Module` or an `IntegratedArchitectureElement`.
3) A MAE may have the association `import` to a `Variable v1`, when there already exists a `Variable v1` that is associated as `export` by a MAE.
4) A `Variable` that is associated as `import` by an outer MAG, must have an inner MAE that has an `import` association to the same `Variable`.
5) A `Variable v1` can be associated as export by an MAE `m`, when the `Variable v1` is declared by the MAE `m`.

On the right side of Figure 4 an extended module architecture block diagram of Figure 3 is shown. The architecture in the diagram violates implement layer rule 1. Elements in the block diagram that violate a rule are shaped in red. For example, the outer block `G2` has an association to `Variable var2` but `G2` has no inner MAE with has the appropriate `export` interface.

Mapping rule: The EMAB description for mapping the module architecture to the logical architecture is valid, if the following rules are fulfilled:

1) A `Variable v1` may have an association `VariableMapping` to a `VariableGroup vg1`, only if the `VariableGroup vg1` and the `Variable v1` are of the same `CommunicationType`.

The block diagram of Figure 4 contains mapping elements. One of these mappings is shaped in red, because mapping rule 1 is violated. Rule 1 is violated, as `var3` of `CommunicationType State` and `var1` of `CommunicationType Data` have a different `CommunicationType` and are mapped by a connection.

In contrast to these technically originated rules, the conformance checking rules ensure the validity of some domain specific layered architectural concept (see Section V).

V. Architecture Conformance Checking

In the Section IV-C the syntax and general low-level semantic checking of an EMAB model instance is performed. This section focuses on the individual product and the corresponding product line. Conformance checking and its objectives were shortly introduced in Section III-C, now we center the technical aspects. The architectural concepts defined by the dedicated architecture and represented by its architectural rules are the input for this architecture conformance checking activity together with the implemented modules, respectively the realized parts of the systems. Output of a check is a set of violations, so a list of pointers where the implementation does not fulfill the defined architecture.

As it is known from the field of architectural concepts and design patterns, these can be defined generally but it is not uncommon, that a software architecture contains more than one concept or pattern. Thereby the patterns can be adapted or modified to meet special requirements in a different level of specialization. Furthermore, the number of concepts and its variations are increasing stately in practice. On the other hand, it might happen that realized concepts are dropped during the ongoing evolution steps. Hence, this activity has to be managed and supported by tools to support architects and developers, and for making concepts explicit.

In the following subsections the fundamentals are described individually and explained with the help of a simple example. Next, the individual checking activities, which are part of our methodology, are illustrated in detail.

A. The "Checking" Views

As explained in Section IV and shown in Figure 3, we provide different views towards visualizing the architecture of a product and a product line. LAEs have to be referred to implementation artifacts for product development. Therefore, the EMAB meta model determines that the MAE can reference at most one LAE using the `mapArchitectureElement` to determine the appropriate module elements of a logical element.

The DESIGN layer focuses on the logical architecture. In the block diagram in Figure 5 a very simple example is given with three instances of a LAE, two `AtomicElements` and one `GroupElement`. Whereby the `LAE3` declares the `VariableGroup X` and references it by an AEP as an `OUT` port type. The `LAE2` defines an AEP as an `IN` port type, which references the same `VariableGroup X`. Nevertheless, a `Channel` is specified within our simple example connecting this two ports. This is the typical view, in which a high-level architecture is specified on the PLA as well as on the PA level.

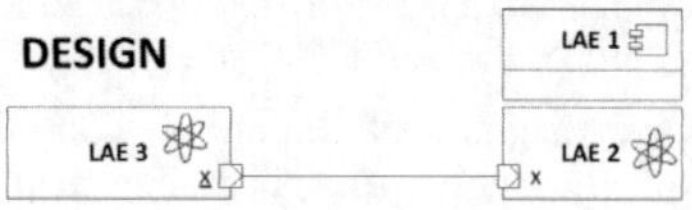

Figure 5. DESIGN view as part of the meta model instance

The IMPLEMENT view shown in Figure 6 represents the MAEs instances as blocks and their connection as concrete connections. Moreover, each MAE is referencing one LAE visualized by dashed connections between a module element block and logical element block. Regarding the development process this is, e.g., the typical view a concrete realization of a product is developed.

One simple conformance checking activity is the review of valid connections between MAEs towards the constraints specialized by the product line architecture. During development it might happen that a communication between two elements is implemented, which is not allowed with respect to the logical architecture. Because of the mapping between LAE and MAE this violations can be detected automatically and visualized.

Figure 7 shows the CHECK view for our simple example, checking the conformance rule on connections of the DESIGN layer's logical architecture elements and IMPLEMENT layer's module architecture elements. In this case the rule can be specified by an *object constraint language* (OCL) rule. This OCL rule is drawn at the top of Figure 7 and is fulfilled as

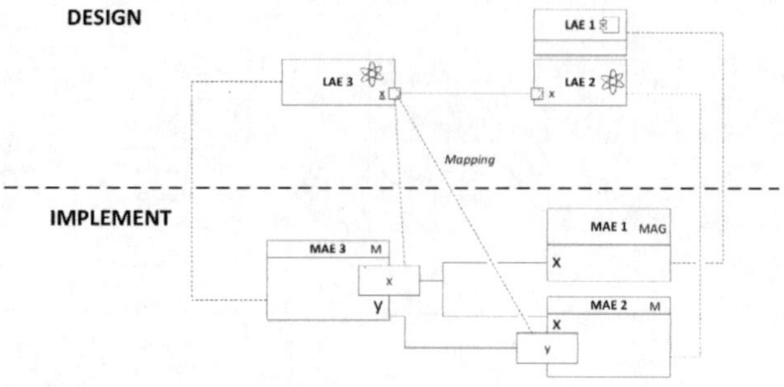

Figure 6. IMPLEMENT view as part of the meta model instance

the specified connection between the two module architecture elements corresponds to the connection between the mapped logical architecture elements.

As illustrated in Figure 7 only one of the three existing communication channels existing in the realization is permitted. Two of them (marked with the red X) are architecture violations. The connection between `MAE3` and `MAE1` is not allowed because of the mapping to `LAE3`, respectively `LAE1`, this communication is not specified. Therefore it is not valid to establish a communication between these elements in a concrete implementation.

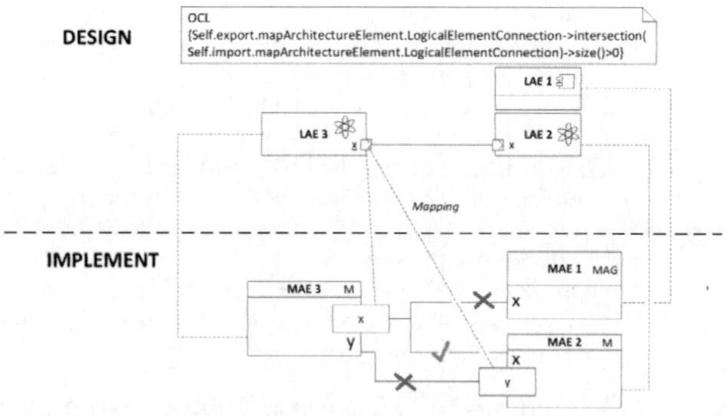

Figure 7. CHECK view as part of the meta model instance

The violation between `MAE3` and `MAE2` results of how the communication between these elements is established over variable `Y`. In the design it is specified that the variable is exported by `LAE3`, which is mapped to `MAE3` and this element is importing and not exporting variable `Y`. Hence, this results in a violation, as the realization is not conform to the specified architecture.

This simple example illustrates how the checking activity is performed in general. In the next subsections this general approach is discussed in detail corresponding to the concrete activities defined by our overall development cycle.

B. The "Checking" Activities

In this subsection the specific checking activities are described in detail. The checking takes place between a DESIGN and an IMPLEMENT instance in general and is performed on a model-to-model checking level due to the high degree of code generation from models in the automotive domain.

As illustrated in Figure 2 we defined two explicit checking activities, one on the product line level, and one on the product level.

1) Activity PL-Check: This activity contains of two scenarios, first the conformance checking of the realized elements on the product line level, these are elements, which are realized for reuse in nearly every product. Second, the holistic conformance checking taking the PLA and all products, which are existing and derived from this product line architecture, into account.

The first case is equivalent to the checking activity on product level and is described in detail in the following subsection. In the other case special challenges exit contingent on the characteristics of a product line itself. As outlined a product line architecture specifies a set of concepts, which are represented as architectural rules. The goal of the holistic conformance checking on PLA level is to check if all existing products are fulfilling these requirements. What leads to violations on this level? - Because of the high number of parallel existing product variants, which are developed individually from different teams with different know-how available using development paradigms. Nevertheless, each product has its own additional requirements. Theses are reasons why given presets by the PLA architecture are violated during development.

But also the planned extensions can lead to inconsistencies. In these cases it is very important to make the effects of architectural changes visible to get a feeling of it and to act in an adequate way. A simple example for this are the different versions of modules existing in parallel. Each architecture element of the product line development and of the product development is kept in a repository, which provides a version control capability. Predecessor relations are defined in case of modifications of an existing version. The repository also enables the selection of elements for product line development or product development. As defined in the meta model in Figure 3 an `AtomicElement` can be realized by more than one `Module`, e.g., by the same `Module` in different versions, respectively. This can lead to architectural violations if the architecture of a MAE changes during development and older versions of the same MAE are in use in other products. So as a result, a module is only applicable for a particular architecture in a concrete version. On the other hand, if the logical architecture is changing, than it could happen that not all versions of a MAE meet the requirements. The checking activity makes this visible by the set of violations.

2) Activity P-Check: Referring to our development cycle (see Figure 2) the realization of new functions or even a new product is triggered by activity `PL to P`, which defines a project plan by selecting a concrete project and set of MAEs. In addition, a concrete product can have some special requirements, especially when we have a prototype realization with the aim to evaluate a new complex function. Such requirements, which are inserted by activity `P-Requirement`, are considered in the `Design` activity and realized by `P-Implement`.

The aim of the activity `Check` is to check whether all the specifications of the product line architecture have been adhered and if the additional developments at product level fulfill the requirements of the planned product architecture.

During development, it might happen that some specifications defined by the product line and the product architecture are violated, maybe the architecture is not realizable due to technical reasons, for example. To prevent architecture erosion a checking step as introduced in subsection V-A is performed on the product level during the development cycles.

Input is the concrete realization of a product and further developed architecture of the concrete product. Specialized or additional added architecture rules are derived from this architecture. If an inconsistency between implementation and architecture exists, there are two ways to deal with these violations: Modifying the architecture or modifying the realization. It is the aim of the checking activity to make violations visible and to support this decision making process. If the developer was perhaps not familiar with the architecture for example, and this is the reason for the violations, it can still be fixed at the product level so that no erosion can occur.

However, if it is decided that there will be an adaptation to the architecture, this may have a major impact, as the concepts of the product line architecture may no longer be fulfilled. On the other hand, this also offers the opportunity to transfer evaluated and tested modifications into the product line to roll them out to all or nearly all other products.

3) Effects of the Checking Activities: The potential effects of the checking activities to other activities are visualized in Figure 8 (cases 1-3, red arrows). In every case the effects belong to the detected violations between architecture and realization and to eliminate them the architecture and/or implementation has to be adapted.

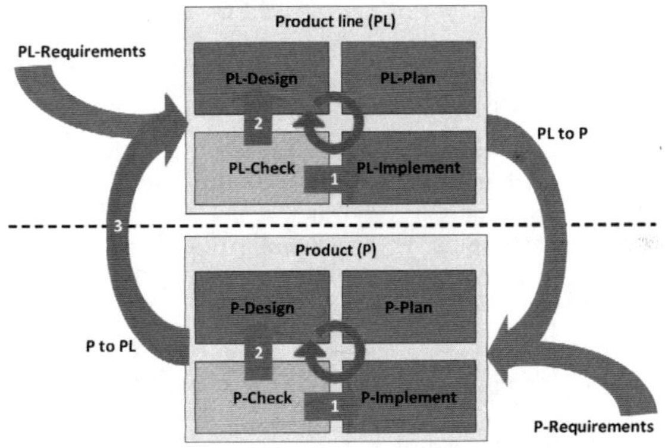

Figure 8. Potential effects of the checking activities

Case (1) describes the adaption of the implementation, this effects the `Implement` activities both on product line (`PL-Implement`) and product (`P-Implement`) level. This case arises if the detected violation is declared as an implementation fault and the architecture should be realized as specified.

Case (2) effects the `Design` activities as well on product line (`PL-Design`) as on product (`P-Design`) level. The detected violation results in an adaption of the architecture not the implementation. This typically occurs if an architectural constraint is not realizable on technical level respectively it was realized in a "better" way, so it was decided to bring the implemented concept to the architecture level.

Case (3) is similar to case (2) but can effect all products of a product line. As mention it is very common to elaborate new functionalities especially complex functions, which might influence the software architecture. After testing, evaluating and approving it in a single prototype product, the violations on the product level can be resolved by case (1) or (2). But if there are major changes, it might happen that the architecture of the prototype does not fulfill all requirements of the product line architecture. In this case the effects of these changes have to be discussed on product line level. This can result in an adaption of the whole product line, if it seems reasonable to integrate the new developed concepts of the prototype in the product line architecture to improve the existing products. In the other case, if it is not reasonable to modify the product line architecture, the product that was originally derived from the product line will be marked as a special product variant. So deviation of a product architecture from a product line architecture is handled in a managed way.

The results from the checking activity support the synchronization between product and product line, because it is pointed out, where the product architectures differ from the guidelines defined by the product line architecture. Therefore, we have to keep in mind that in practice more than one product variant is in development: there are many that are developed in parallel, which leads to architectural changes, and, without syncing these variants in a managed process, the changes will force the erosion of the product architecture as well as the product line architecture.

C. The "Checking" Tool Support

Due to the high number of product lines existing in parallel and the high number of derived and realized product variants it is not economical to implement such a checking activity without a suitable tool support. Thereby the following use cases have to be supported:

1) Creation of architecture rules,
2) selecting the implemented artifacts,
3) selecting the right rules,
4) performing the check and
5) visualizing the checking results to determine further actions.

For performing the checking activity we use an approach based on a logical fact base, as described in [13], [31].

In Figure 9 the checking process is visualized. First the implemented artifacts that should be checked, have to be selected as module architecture instance. This model instance is transformed to a logical representation. In parallel, the architect derives and/or selects the architectural rules, which are representing the architectural concepts specified by the corresponding logical architecture instance. Today this rule creation step is a human centered process and not automated.

After transferring the software artifacts into a logical fact base and describing the architectural concepts by first-order logic statements, queries can be executed on the fact base to validate the rules. This results in a list of violations or in the best case the implementation fulfills all architecture rules, so the implementation is conform to the specified logical architecture.

Now it is the task of the developer respectively the software architect to handle the violations. This is similar with the rule creation, the second step, which is performed and based on the experience of a human to resolve possible architectural violations.

We define the *Checking* activity as a separate activity for two reasons. On the one hand, it is a process composed of several steps and, on the other hand, the checking is a snapshot based step. So, related to a development process, it makes sense to have an explicit activity triggered by launching new snapshots of a system.

Focusing the tool support, an important open issue is the creation of architectural rules, but also the extraction of architectural concepts introduced by the developers best practice and making them explicit. Consequently, we have some ongoing research in this field. One approach is to concentrate on the implemented artifacts and extracting architectural concepts from it with the help of machine learning techniques to compare them with the given logical architecture to support the decision making process described in the previous subsection.

VI. Real World Example: Brake Servo Unit (BSU)

In this section, we present an example of a software system we developed in cooperation with Volkswagen. The main task of this system is to ensure a sufficient vacuum within the brake booster that is needed to amplify the driver's braking force. At first, we describe the context the system is embedded in and a view onto the system's structure. We show how the system has evolved. After the presentation of the mapping of the evolution onto our approach, we give results and a discussion.

A. System Structure and Context of BSU

In vehicles, a vacuum brake booster (brake servo unit/BSU) is mounted between the brake pedal and the hydraulic brake cylinder. It consists of two chambers separated through a movable diaphragm. If the driver is not braking, the air is evacuated from both chambers. When he pushes on the brake pedal a valve opens and atmospheric pressure air flows into one chamber. Due to the differential air pressure within the BSU the diaphragm starts to move towards the vacuum chamber creating a force. This force is used to amplify the driver's braking force.

The vacuum can be generated using different techniques. The BSU is either attached to the intake manifold using its internal lower pressure or to an electrically or mechanically driven vacuum pump. Using the intake manifold as vacuum generator can be problematic. Special operating modes of other vehicle's subsystems can increase the intake manifold pressure so much that its internal vacuum is not sufficient to evacuate the BSU when needed.

The software system realizes a set of feedback controllers to reduce the disturbances caused by other systems or to switch on the vacuum pump, respectively. Since it makes no sense to use all controllers at the same time it is necessary to coordinate their activation. Besides the controlling of BSU vacuum and the coordination of controllers, the software has to provide valid pressure information all the time. For this purpose the software selects from several sensors the one that provides the best quality of pressure information. The logical view of the designed architecture is presented in Figure 10.

The BSU hardware system is part of a wide range of products within the huge family of cars. Since the diversity of

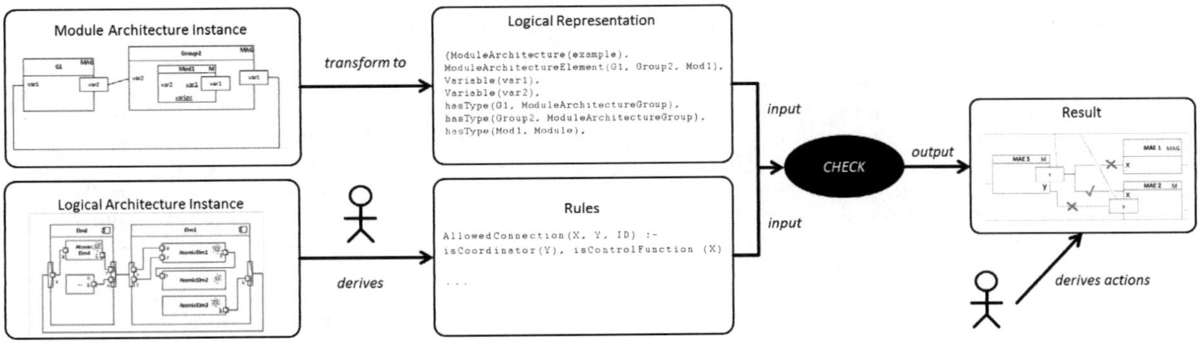

Figure 9. Tool supported checking process

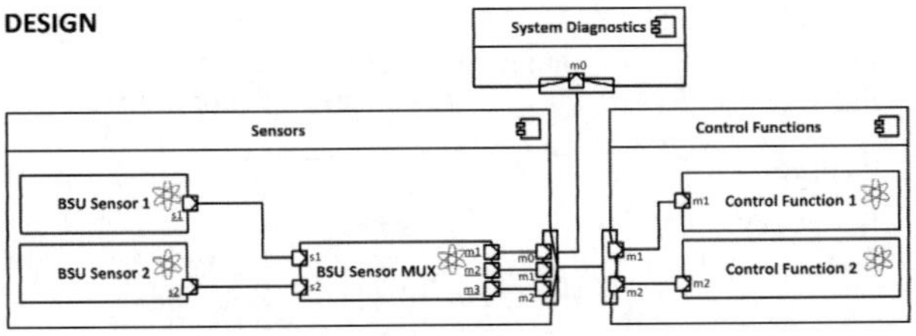

Figure 10. Logical view of the software architecture of BSU

the used hardware components like sensors and actuators that are mounted to the braking system and features that influence the BSU software one important goal of the architecture development was to support variability. The BSU software system is decomposed into two major parts: `Sensors` and `Control Functions`. The decomposition of the `Sensors` component into parts for every sensor type each allows a one to one mapping from features to components. To realize variability in an efficient way, standardized interfaces are used for communication. A coordinating component `BSU Sensor MUX` just has to provide a sufficient amount of ports for the interaction with the sensors and control functions.

The `Control Functions` component is decomposed using a similar technique. Every control function is realized by a specific component. These components provide standardized interfaces for communication with subsequent vehicle functions, which must follow the BSU commands, e.g., disable the start-stop system (not depicted in Figure 10).

B. Evolution of BSU

As it was customary in the automotive domain, BSU's hardware and software have been implemented by various suppliers in the past. The requirements for the functionalities of the system were the same for all suppliers, but there were differences in the type of implementation by the respective suppliers. During the further development of the system over many years, new requirements had to be continuously implemented. Examples of this are the support of various engine variants such as otto, diesel and electric engines. As the range of functions increased, the essential complexity grew; however, the accidental complexity [32] has increased disproportionately. The growth of accidental complexity results from a "bad" architecture with strong coupling and a low cohesion, which have evolved over the time. Despite extensive further development of the system, the original structure of the software was not adequately adapted. Overall, the monolithic structure of the software remained. The software consisted of a single software module, which, however, was internally characterized by increasing accidental complexity. The variability was realized completely by annotations. Thereby, the system's maintainability and expandability has been complicated additionally.

In recent years, many automotive manufacturers have begun to develop software primarily in-house to save costs and to secure important know-how. However, the hardware components are still being developed by the supplier companies in general. Against this background, Volkswagen decided to develop the BSU in-house in the future. Together with our institute, Volkswagen developed its own software for the BSU in 2012 on the basis of the existing system. Configurability, extensibility and comprehensibility were defined as essential quality targets. In addition, new architecture and design concepts have been introduced to meet these quality objectives in the long term and permanently.

After successful introduction of the system into series production, the software system was continuously developed after 2012. In all, the BSU system was reused in more than 140 project versions, some of them with adaptations. There were, e.g., the introduction of five additional control functions that were necessary because of changes to the system environment. This includes, in particular, the introduction of new components such as actuators, which were essentially driven by the electrification of the powertrain. In the following sections, we will present our methodology by means of the BSU's further development and discuss the results. However, due to the obligation of secrecy, we can not name real-world functions. Instead, we will abstract from real control functions, actuators, and sensors in the following sections.

C. Application of our Approach to BSU Further Development

In this section, we will outline the evolution of BSU further development, described in the previous section, mapped to the overall development cycle visualized in Figure 2. As mentioned in Section VI-B, the development started in 2012 and continues until today. We will pick out the milestones of this evolution process and explain in detail, how our approach supports the management of development. Therefore, we will describe the further development of the BSU chronologically.

The architecture of the BSU at this point is equivalent to Figure 10.

The first considerable development activities leading to architectural evolution results from two new control functions. These new control functions are specified as product line requirements (`PL-Requirement`). In the following activity `PL-Design`, the new requirements including all open requirements and feedbacks from the ongoing product development activities submitted by activity `P to PL`, are took into account by the designing of the new PLA (called "PLA vision"). The resulting PLA includes two new components, whereby each component represents one of the new control functions.

After assessing and determining the new PLA vision, the `PL-Plan` activity starts. It was decided to realize the new PLA vision in two iterations, per iteration cycle, one of the new components should be implemented completely. Regarding to the development plan in activity `PL-Implement` the first component was implemented. `PL-Check` activity is triggered after the new component is fully implemented. In this activity, the conformance of the implementation is checked against the planned architecture (PLA vision), as illustrated in Section IV. An example for an architectural rule, which was checked, is defined informally as follows: `"Each BSU Sensor has to communicate to Control Functions by the BSU Sensor MUX"`. This rule can be easily derived from the logical view shown in Figure 10. The outcome of the checks was positive so the next iteration was started.

Parallel to the implementation of the second defined component some concrete products are selected to integrate the new developed control function in real products (activity `PL to P`). It was decided to setup a new pilot product additionally. The pilot got a special requirement by a `P-Requirement` activity. The proving by prototypes or pilots is a common approach in the automotive domain. Due to the specification of the special requirement, which includes a new control function with a coordinating feature, a prototyping approach was used to realize this requirement. This simply means that we have a main control function and a backup control function, if the main function is not available the backup function should be used.

The solution of the `P-Design` activity was a solution that fulfills all requirements. It was decided to add a new component representing the new control function and to establish an additional coordinator component. The coordinator has the responsibility of the controlling of main and backup functions and realizing the coordinating feature.

In the `P-Plan` activity the iterations to be performed had to be defined and scheduled. The outcome was a development plan with two iteration steps. In the first step, the new control function and the coordinator component should be implemented. And in a second step, all existing control functions had to be adapted, because they had to be defeatable to perform as main or backup function.

According to the development plan, the `P-Implement` activity was performed. After each iteration step, a conformance check was done (`P-Check`). In our case study we detected a violation of an architectural rule. Consequently, it was evaluated and discussed, if the solution of the violation results in adapting the implementation or in adapting the architectural rule itself - or in simple words, is there a crummy implementation or an insufficient architecture (cf. Section V-B). In terms of internal classification we cannot go in detail at this point.

After evaluating the product realization all adaptations and changes of architecture and implementation are forwarded to the product line architecture level by a `P to PL` activity. These are inputs for the next `PL-Design` activity, thereby it had to be decided, which changes should be integrated into the product line architecture and its implementation or otherwise, which had to be declared as a "special" solution. In our case the coordinator concept was established in the product line. This leads, e.g., to the new architectural rule: `"Each Control Function must have a communication connection to the Coordinator"`, which is now mandatory for all products derived from this product line. The final architecture is visualized in Figure 11 including all newly developed control functions, the `Coordinator` component, and the additional connections between the control functions and the `Coordinator` for the controlling of activation.

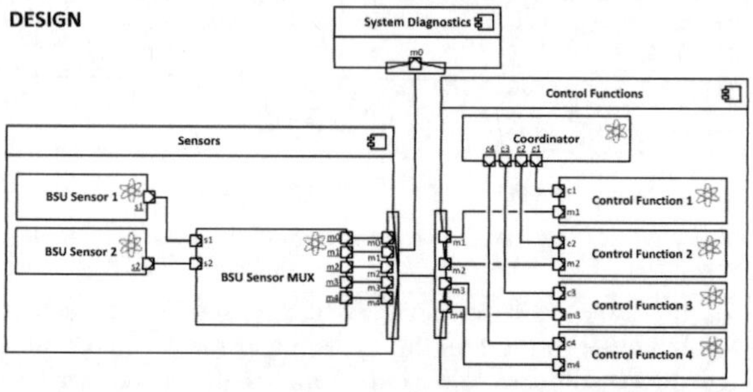

Figure 11. Logical view of the software architecture of BSU including the coordinator concept and the three new control functions (in 2012)

In summary, the architecture of the BSU is largely stable after the introduction of the coordinator concept until today.

Overall we state that our approach can deal with many parallel activities at product line and product level. This becomes apparent by the controlling character of the synchronization points both in the development cycle on product line and product level by activities `PL-Check` and `P-Check` and between the product line and product level by activities `PL to P` and `P to PL`. In this way, it was possible to detect architecture erosion in an early state and to take adequate countermeasures. Furthermore, we can take care of a planned generalization on the one hand and a planned specialization or exceptional case handling on the other hand. This is evidenced by the coordinator concept: A concept designed and fully realized and proved by a pilot product and than transferred into the product line architecture and finally fully integrated within the next development iterations in the product line architecture and all products belonging to this architecture.

VII. Evaluation and Discussion

In this section we present and discuss the results of a field study of a five year BSU software development and evaluate, if the main objectives introduced in Section I are fulfilled.

A. General Results of the Quantitative Analysis

To evaluate our methodology, we present the quantitative analysis for the BSU software development that is realized

TABLE II. RESULT OF THE QUANTITATIVE ANALYSIS FOR THE BSU SOFTWARE FOR THE INTERVAL OF 5 YEARS.

	Count	*Number of versions*	*Average number of versions*	*Min. number of versions*	*Max. number of versions*
LAE	15	15	15/15 = 1	1	1
MAE	15	57	57/15 $\approx$ 4	1	6
Projects	21	146	146/21 $\approx$ 7	1	12

TABLE III. FURTHER RESULTS OF THE QUANTITATIVE ANALYSIS FOR THE BSU SOFTWARE.

	Number of versions used in projects	*Cumulated number of versions used over all project versions*	*Average degree of reuse of each version*	*Number of used design configurations*
MAE	46	1611	1611/46 $\approx$ 35	n/a
Projects	n/a	n/a	n/a	14

and maintained in cooperation with our project partner over a period of 5 years. In the following, we focus on the applicability of the product line and product development activities. Two criteria are important to evaluate. First, the amount and kinds of modifications on architecture elements calling this *complexity controlling*. Second, the amount and kinds of design configurations calling this *variant controlling*.

Table II shows the result of the quantitative analysis. The data record for the quantitative analysis refers to the development of the BSU software and the product realizations consisting of the BSU software and further vehicle functions. The record contains the version control graph of the past 5 years of BSU software development, called *repository* in the following. Each node is a version of an architecture element or realized product. Edges connect two subsequent versions. Table II shows the number of logical architecture element (LAE) versions, of module architecture element (MAE) versions, and of project versions from the record. Modifications were triggered by the realization of BSU software `PL-Requirements` or by the realization of products due to `P-Requirements`.

Table II shows the count of 15 LAE referring to modifications at the DESIGN layer and the count of 15 MAE referring to modifications at the IMPLEMENT layer. The kind of modifications refers to the connection structure and to the architecture element structure of the appropriate MAE. Each LAE is available in exactly one version in the repository. Thereby, the current state of the logical architecture is represented, which is unmodified since the beginning of the record. Unfortunately, the data of prior development stages of the BSU software logical architecture is not considered by the record due to data protection reasons. In total, 57 versions for MAE exist. A module element of the module architecture was modified in minimum 1 time, in maximum 6 times, and in average 4 times. Thereby, each version of the MAE is mapped in this case to exactly one version of the appropriate LAE.

Line "Projects" in Table II refers to the product development of the BSU software and shows that 21 projects containing the BSU software exist. A project defines a set of architecture element versions from logical architecture and from module architecture used to realize a product. In the following, we call the set of versions of architecture elements *design configuration*. Each time a project is modified, a new version of that project is committed to be used for subsequently realize the product. The project modifications resulting in a new version commit always refers to changes of the design configuration. In total, the project version number is 146. The average number of versions is 7, the minimum number is 1, and the maximum number is 12.

The data in Table III shows two quantitative aspects. First, the number of BSU software architecture element versions used in projects is 46 and the cumulated number of BSU software architecture element versions used in all project versions is 1611. Hence, the average degree of reuse of each version of MAE is 35. Second, the number of different design configurations of all project version concerning the BSU software is 14. This induces the fact that 14 architecture structure variants of the BSU software architecture (logical and module) are used in projects to realize products in the past 5 years.

Complexity controlling: Complexity in BSU software is induced by modifications on architecture elements of the logical architecture and the module architecture, which are triggered to realize the two kinds of requirements described by the record. To handle complexity, each modification must be controlled for violations on architecture elements and on violations referring quality properties.

Our methodology aims to control violations of quality properties in the `Design` activity and of violations of architecture rules in the `Check` activity. The `Design` activity provides the modified DESIGN layer in each iteration and the `Implement` activity provides the modified IMPLEMENT layer in each iteration. The BSU software modifications are applied to realize requirements resulting in a product dependent BSU software or in a new product independent realization of the BSU software. Therefore, `PL-Requirements` corresponding to new features triggers the controlling of BSU software modifications during the product line development activities, using the versions of logical architecture at the DESIGN layer and of versions of module architecture at the IMPLEMENT layer. New project related requirements corresponding to `P-Requirements` triggers the product development activities to control all modifications considering project related versions and architecture related versions corresponding to the appropriate layers and of the EMAB meta model.

After applying the methodology two important results are observed: First, no violations on architecture quality properties at the DESIGN layer were found. Second, after checking the modifications of the BSU software applying inter alia the rule described by the EMAB meta model in Section IV, only one minor violation between the layers of the BSU software was found. This evaluation result shows that nearly all modifications of BSU software in the past 5 years preserved the architecture conformance of the IMPLEMENT layer to the DESIGN layer. Moreover, the structure of the DESIGN layer is well realized considering the quality properties.

Variant controlling: The term variant in the case of BSU software describes a software architecture variant reused to realize a software product. Thereby, each project version refers to exactly one design configuration to define architecture elements for reuse that are contained in the software architecture variant. Modifications of the logical and module architecture can introduce violations on expected derivable structure variants. To handle such violations the control of variants must be applied to the modifications. The control of such architecture rule violations is applied during the `Check` activity of the product line development considering the versions corresponding to the IMPLEMENT layer and to the DESIGN layer. After applying our methodology, no violations are found in the past 5 years of development. This corresponds to the result of complexity evaluation where conformance of the EMAB layers is confirmed.

B. Evaluation with Regard to the Main Objectives of our Approach

We will evaluate, if the main objectives introduced in Section I are fulfilled by the BSU example. These objectives are:

1) Maintaining stability of the PLA and minimizing product architecture erosion even if extensive further development of the system takes place.
2) Achieving high scalability, and a high degree of usage of the modules.

The first objective focuses on the software architecture issues whereas the second objective regards the software components. Obviously, the following four sub-objectives can be derived by the two major objects:

1) Stability of a product line architecture
2) Erosion indicator
3) Usage of a module
4) Scalability of a module

1) Definitions of Evaluation Criteria: We will explain each sub-objective in detail and by proposing metrics to evaluate the sub-objectives.

General notations:

- $PLA_t :=$ active PLA at point t
- $P_{t,x} :=$ project variant at point t, which is corresponding to the PLA_t with the same t. This is feasible because only one PLA is active at a point t in the case study. No point t exists where two PLAs are active.
- $p_{t,x} :=$ an explicit version of a project $P_{t,y}$ at point t.
- $|P_{t,x}| :=$ number of explicit versions of a project variant $P_{t,x}$ at point t.
- $M_{t,x} :=$ module / realization artifact at point t, which is corresponding to the PLA_t with the same t.
- $m_{t,x} :=$ an explicit version of a module $M_{t,y}$ at point t.
- $|M_{t,x}| :=$ number of explicit versions of a module $M_{t,x}$ at point t.
- $\Phi_{PLA_t,P} := \{P_{t,1}, P_{t,2}, ..., P_{t,n}$, is defined as the set of all projects existing at point t and derived from the given PLA.
- $\Phi_{PLA_t,M} := \{M_{t,1}, M_{t,2}, ..., M_{t,m}\}$, is defined as the set of all modules existing at point t and derived from the given PLA.
- $\Phi_{PLA_t} := \Phi_{PLA_t,P} \cup \Phi_{PLA_t,M} = \{P_{t,1}, P_{t,2}, ..., P_{t,n}, M_{t,1}, M_{t,2}, ..., M_{t,m}\}$, is defined as the set of all projects and modules existing at point t and derived from the given PLA.

Stability of a product line architecture:
is described by the amount of changes between two PLAs. The stability $Stab$ and the number of project versions existing during the period a PLA is active, NAP, are defined as follows:

$$Stab(PLA_t) = \frac{w(PLA_{\Delta t-1,t})}{\frac{w(PLA_{t-1})+w(PLA_t)}{2}} \tag{1}$$

with weight $w(PLA_t) = |N_{PLA_t}| + |E_{PLA_t}|$, whereby $N_{PLA_t} :=$ set of nodes of PLA_t and $E_{PLA_t} :=$ set if edges of PLA_t.

The delta-graph $w(PLA_{\Delta t-1,t})$, which is containing the changed elements, is defined by the edges that are added or deleted comparing PLA_{t-1} and the following PLA_t and all nodes connected by these edges.

In addition $Stab\,(PLA_t) \rightarrow [0, 2(|N_{PLA_t}| + 1)]$, whereby a high value indicates comprehensive changes and a low value small diversities. The assumption is that the value should not be higher than 1, but this had to be validated.

$$NAP(PLA_t) = \sum_{x=1}^{|\Phi_{PLA_t,P}|} |P_{t,x}| \tag{2}$$

Erosion indicator
The erosion of a PLA is indicated by the number of violations of project versions. Therefore the mean number of violations MV is defined as,

$$MV\,(PLA_t, P_t) = \frac{v(PLA_t, P_t)}{|P_{t,x}|} \tag{3}$$

with

$$v(PLA_t, P_t) = \sum_{x=1}^{|P_{t,x}|} v(PLA_t, p_{t,x}) \tag{4}$$

and $v(PLA_t, p_{t,x})$ is defined as the number of violations of $p_{t,x}$ in PLA_t.

Usage of a module
The usage of a Module $M_{t,x}$ is defined as how many project variants P_t at point t use a version of $M_{t,x}$. Therefore we define τ as,

$$\tau(p_{t,x}, m_{t,y}) = \begin{cases} 1 & \text{, iff project } p_{t,x} \text{ uses module version } m_{t,y} \\ 0 & \text{, otherwise} \end{cases} \tag{5}$$

The same applies for $\tau(P_{t,x}, M_{t,y})$, in this case it means that any version of a Module M_t is used in any version of a project P_t.

Furthermore we define τ for a set of projects of a PLA as,

$$\tau(\Phi_{PLA_t,P}, m_{t,y}) = \begin{cases} 1 & \text{, iff a } p_{t,x} \text{ exists that uses } m_{t,y} \\ 0 & \text{, otherwise} \end{cases} \tag{6}$$

So the usage u is defined as,

$$u(\Phi_{PLA_{t,P}}, M_t) = \frac{\sum_{x=1}^{|\Phi_{PLA_{t,P}}|} \tau(P_{t,x}, M_t)}{|\Phi_{PLA_{t,P}}|} \quad (7)$$

In addition $u(\Phi_{PLA_{t,P}}, M_t) \rightarrow [0, 1]$, where a value near one means a high penetration of module M_t and a low value corresponds to a minor usage of the module.

Scalability of a module
The scalability $Scal$of a module describes the parallel usage of different versions of a module M_t and it is defined as,

$$Scal(\Phi_{PLA_{t,P}}, M_t) = \sum_{y=1}^{|M_{t,x}|} \tau(\Phi_{PLA_{t,P}}, m_{t,y}) \quad (8)$$

The value for the scalability of a module should be one. It is not profitable have a high value, because this means that the variability of a module is realized by different versions of a module, which results in a high maintainability effort. As well as a scalability value of zero is not preferable, because this indicates the non-use of a module.

2) Evaluation of the Defined Criteria: Next we apply our metrics to the BSU example. The discrete timestamps for t are the following five values $t = \{2012, 2013, 2014, 2015, 2016\}$ for the year 2012-2016.

Table IV shows the evolution of the BSU over the period 2012-2016 and is the basis for the following evaluations. Column *MAE vers.* contains the version number of the MAE. Version "1" is the first version of a MAE indicating a new development of a MAE. The total number of MAE versions is 57.

Stability of a product line architecture:

For the calculation of stability we consider the PLA of 2012 and 2013. The PLA for the year 2013 is shown in Figure 12. Figure 11 in the previous section shows the PLA for 2012. In order to calculate the stability, we have constructed a simple graph with the nodes and edges for both PLAs in Figure 13. Hierarchical components such as `Sensors` are also represented by nodes. Channels become edges in the graph. Multiple channels between two nodes are combined into one edge.

The graph for the PLA from 2012 is depicted on the left side in Figure 13. The weight w is calculated from the sum of nodes and edges and is 24 for PLA_{2012}. On the right side the graph for the PLA from 2013 is shown. There is a new node, `Control Function 5`, and two additional connections. However, there are also adjustments of the channels up to the `BSU Sensor MUX`. All changes are indicated by the dashed lines. In the middle of Figure 13, the delta graph is shown. All added and modified edges with the associated nodes are included there.

Below we calculate the stability for the years 2013-2016. Since the stability always calculates the change to the previous version, there is no calculation for 2012. As there was no further development of the PLA in 2014 and 2016, the stability is 0 in both years. Even in the years with adaptations of the

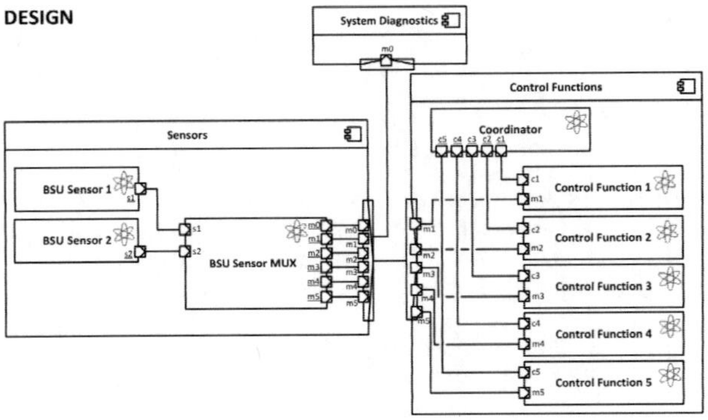

Figure 12. PLA of the BSU in 2013

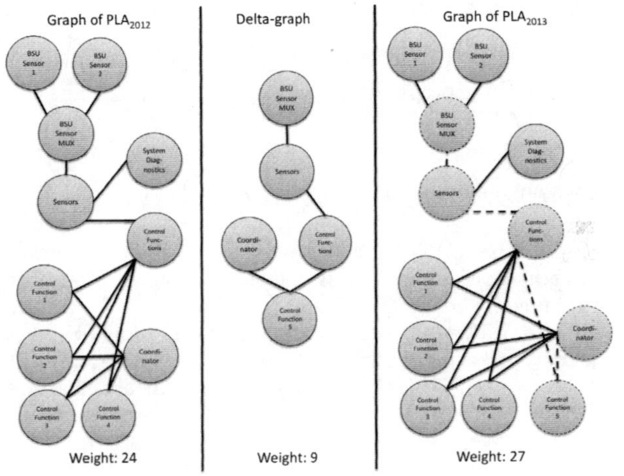

Figure 13. Building the delta-graph (graph in the middle) of PLA_{2012} (left) and $PLA_{2013}(right)$

PLA, a relatively small change effort results, which leads to a low weight of the delta-graph. Overall, a high stability of the PLA can be observed over the period.

$$Stab(PLA_{2013}) = \frac{w(PLA_{\Delta 2012,2013})}{\frac{w(PLA_{2012})+w(PLA_{2013})}{2}} = \frac{9}{\frac{24+27}{2}} \approx 0,35$$

$$Stab(PLA_{2014}) = \frac{w(PLA_{\Delta 2013,2014})}{\frac{w(PLA_{2013})+w(PLA_{2014})}{2}} = \frac{0}{\frac{27+27}{2}} = 0$$

$$Stab(PLA_{2015}) = \frac{w(PLA_{\Delta 2014,2015})}{\frac{w(PLA_{2014})+w(PLA_{2015})}{2}} = \frac{15}{\frac{27+36}{2}} \approx 0,48$$

$$Stab(PLA_{2016}) = \frac{w(PLA_{\Delta 2015,2016})}{\frac{w(PLA_{2015})+w(PLA_{2015})}{2}} = \frac{0}{\frac{36+36}{2}} = 0$$

In order to evaluate the stability of the product line architecture, we also want to relate $Stab$ to the quantity of project versions (NAP). After counting the versions of the projects from 2012 to 2016, we get the following values:
$NAP(PLA_{2012}) = 9$, $NAP(PLA_{2013}) = 9$,
$NAP(PLA_{2014}) = 32$, $NAP(PLA_{2015}) = 58$,
$NAP(PLA_{2016}) = 38$.

The values point to a high degree of further development, especially from 2014 onwards. Nevertheless, the values for $Stab$ are relatively low so that the overall stability of the PLA can be assessed as high.

TABLE IV. EVOLUTION OF THE BSU SOFTWARE FROM 2012 TILL 2016.

2012			2013			2014			2015			2016		
MAE vers.	*MAE name*	*Creation date*	*MAE vers.*	*MAE name*	*Creation date*	*MAE vers.*	*MAE name*	*Creation date*	*MAE vers.*	*MAE name*	*Creation date*	*MAE vers.*	*MAE name*	*Creation date*
1	BSU-A	23.04.2012	2	BSU-F	22.02.2013	1	BSU-N	11.06.2014	6	BSU-A	16.01.2015	3	BSU-O	05.01.2016
1	BSU-B	24.04.2012	3	BSU-A	12.03.2013	3	BSU-D	18.06.2014	5	BSU-C	22.01.2015	6	BSU-C	25.04.2016
1	BSU-C	07.05.2012	2	BSU-D	15.03.2013	3	BSU-B	30.06.2014	4	BSU-H	11.03.2015	3	BSU-M	25.04.2016
1	BSU-D	07.05.2012	2	BSU-H	15.03.2013	3	BSU-G	30.06.2014	4	BSU-G	21.04.2015	7	BSU-C	28.04.2016
1	BSU-E	07.05.2012	2	BSU-I	15.03.2013	4	BSU-C	01.07.2014	5	BSU-H	22.04.2015	8	BSU-C	30.04.2016
1	BSU-F	07.05.2012	1	BSU-K	25.03.2013	5	BSU-A	01.07.2014	7	BSU-A	23.04.2015	9	BSU-C	11.05.2016
1	BSU-G	07.05.2012	4	BSU-A	28.08.2013	3	BSU-E	02.07.2014	1	BSU-L	26.05.2015	10	BSU-C	12.05.2016
1	BSU-H	07.05.2012				3	BSU-F	02.07.2014	1	BSU-M	27.05.2015	11	BSU-C	14.05.2016
1	BSU-I	09.05.2012				2	BSU-J	03.07.2014	8	BSU-A	02.06.2015			
1	BSU-J	10.05.2012				3	BSU-H	03.07.2014	1	BSU-O	11.09.2015			
2	BSU-E	19.07.2012				2	BSU-K	03.07.2014	2	BSU-M	05.10.2015			
2	BSU-A	10.08.2012				3	BSU-I	03.07.2014	2	BSU-O	04.12.2015			
2	BSU-B	05.09.2012				4	BSU-E	28.11.2014						
2	BSU-G	05.09.2012				3	BSU-K	08.12.2014						
2	BSU-C	11.09.2012												
3	BSU-C	26.09.2012												
Number of versions: 16			Number of versions: 7			Number of versions: 14			Number of versions: 12			Number of versions: 8		

Erosion indicator

For a given PLA, architecture rules are derived as a means to check conformity. In this context, the degree of erosion is measured by counting the number of violations of architecture rules for a PLA per year. Ideally, this value should be kept as small as possible. Only one violation was detected in 2014. Accordingly $MV\ (PLA_{2014}, P_{2014}) = 1$. In all other cases, $MV = 0$.

Usage of a module

In Table V we specify the result of the usage calculation. Some modules were developed after 2012. No value could be calculated for the corresponding fields where the module did not yet exist. Therefore, these fields are marked with n/a. It is noticeable that module BSU-N is never used in the period under consideration. Many fields have the value 1, which means a complete usage. For the modules created in 2015 (BSU-L, BSU-M, BSU-O), the usage is initially low but improves in 2016. With module BSU-B, the usage deteriorates over the period of time. The causes of this should be investigated.

TABLE V. USAGE OF A MODULE

MAE name	*2012*	*2013*	*2014*	*2015*	*2016*
BSU-A	1	1	1	1	1
BSU-B	1	1	0.8	0.2	0.1
BSU-C	1	1	1	0.7	0.8
BSU-D	1	1	1	0.7	0.8
BSU-E	1	1	1	0.7	0.8
BSU-F	1	1	1	0.7	0.8
BSU-G	1	1	1	1	1
BSU-H	1	1	1	1	1
BSU-I	1	1	1	0.6	0.7
BSU-J	1	1	1	1	1
BSU-K	n/a	1	0.5	0.7	0.8
BSU-L	n/a	n/a	n/a	0.4	0.8
BSU-M	n/a	n/a	n/a	0.6	0.8
BSU-N	0	0	0	0	0
BSU-O	n/a	n/a	n/a	0.3	0.8

Figure 14 illustrates the course of the usage. Modules showing the same course of the usage are summarized.

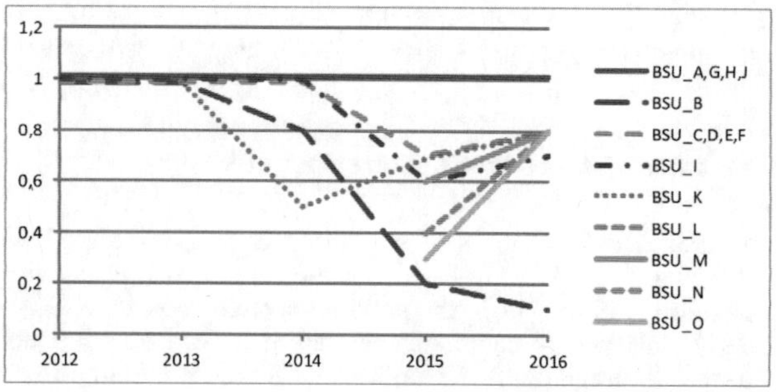

Figure 14. Usage of BSU modules A-O

Scalability of a module

In Table VI we show the calculated values of scalability. The value 1 represents the optimum value and is therefore represented by a green background color. Values greater than 1 indicate a negative scalability and are therefore shown as yellow (value = 2) or red (value > 2). A value of 0 is also generally seen as negative (BSU-N) because a version of the module exists, but is not used in any project.

The development of the scalability of 2012-2016 is shown in Figure 15. The number of respective values is counted here. In 2014 and 2015 there is a deterioration in scalability. In 2016, the scalability of the modules improves again significantly.

TABLE VI. SCALABILITY OF A MODULE

MAE name	*2012*	*2013*	*2014*	*2015*	*2016*
BSU-A	2	3	3	4	1
BSU-B	2	1	1	2	1
BSU-C	1	2	2	2	4
BSU-D	1	2	2	2	1
BSU-E	2	1	2	2	1
BSU-F	1	2	2	2	1
BSU-G	2	1	2	3	1
BSU-H	1	2	2	4	1
BSU-I	1	2	2	2	1
BSU-J	1	1	2	2	1
BSU-K	n/a	1	2	2	1
BSU-L	n/a	n/a	n/a	1	1
BSU-M	n/a	n/a	n/a	2	3
BSU-N	0	0	0	0	0
BSU-O	n/a	n/a	n/a	2	2

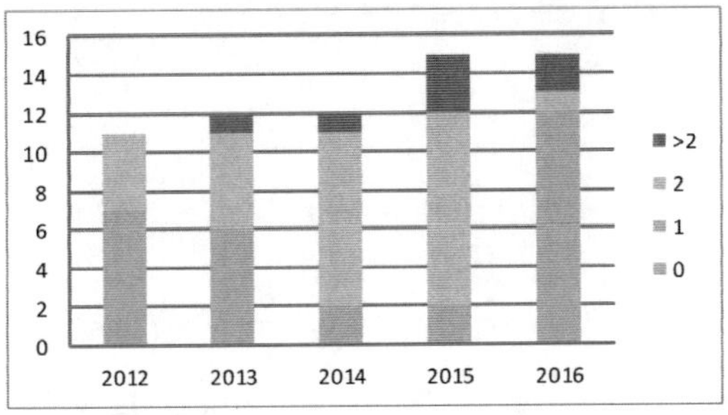

Figure 15. Number of modules with scalability 0, 1, 2, and >2

VIII. CONCLUSION AND FUTURE WORK

We proposed a holistic approach for a long-term manageable and plannable software product line architecture for automotive software systems. Our approach aims at a long-term minimization of architecture erosion, and thereby guarantee a constant high degree of reusability. Thus, we propose concepts like architecture compliance checking with specific adaptations to the automotive domain. The focus is on scalability, to manage a huge number of variants in real world automotive systems.

We introduced the description language EMAB and its meta model for the specification of the software product line architecture and the software architecture of the corresponding products. The EMAB is applied for the architecture extraction and the managed evolution approach presented in this paper.

In contrast to the validation checking of an EMAB model instance, where a syntax and general low-level semantic checking is performed, we proposed an approach for architecture conformance checking to identify architecture violations as a means to prevent architecture erosion. The architectural concepts defined by the dedicated architecture and represented by its architectural rules are the input for this architecture conformance checking activity together with the implemented modules, respectively the realized parts of the systems. Output of a check is a set of violations, so a list of pointers where the implementation does not fulfill the defined architecture.

We demonstrated our methodology on a real world case study, a brake servo unit (BSU) software system from automotive software engineering. In the case study, we could show that we have met the two main objectives defined in Section I:

1) Maintaining stability of the PLA and minimizing product architecture erosion even if extensive further development of the system takes place.
2) Achieving high scalability, and a high degree of usage of the modules.

As a result, with regard to objective (1), we could limit architecture erosion to a minimum: Only one minor violation occurred in a period of five years. All further developments have followed the originally planned architectural principles and thus resulted in a high stability of the PLA. Moreover, with regard to objective (2) we were surprised at the high number of usage of the modules: Most modules were used in all projects existing at that time. Only the scalability deteriorated in 2014 and 2015. But in 2016, the value has improved considerably again.

As a further observation a high degree of reuse could be observed: Each module was reused on average in 35 projects. Even the high number of potential variants could be managed with the approach.

As a future work, we aim at realizing a tool-chain enabling the architecture description of the different architectures (PLA, PA, including versioning), the measure and evaluation of quality attributes, as well as the integration of the ArCh-Framework [13]. Appropriate abstraction techniques are crucial to cope with the huge set of adjustable parameters within the ECU software and to manage variability. Thus, we are currently developing a concept including a prototypical tool environment that enables the description and visualization of variability.

REFERENCES

[1] C. Knieke, M. Körner, A. Rausch, M. Schindler, A. Strasser, and M. Vogel, "A Holistic Approach for Managed Evolution of Automotive Software Product Line Architectures," in Special Track: Managed Adaptive Automotive Product Line Development (MAAPL), along with ADAPTIVE 2017. IARIA XPS Press, 2017, pp. 43–52.

[2] B. Hardung, T. Kölzow, and A. Krüger, "Reuse of Software in Distributed Embedded Automotive Systems," in Proceedings of the 4th ACM international conference on Embedded software. ACM, 2004, pp. 203–210.

[3] A. Rausch, O. Brox, A. Grewe, M. Ibe, S. Jauns-Seyfried, C. Knieke, M. Körner, S. Küpper, M. Mauritz, H. Peters, A. Strasser, M. Vogel, and N. Weiss, "Managed and Continuous Evolution of Dependable Automotive Software Systems," in Proceedings of the 10th Symposium on Automotive Powertrain Control Systems, 2014, pp. 15–51.

[4] L. de Silva and D. Balasubramaniam, "Controlling Software Architecture Erosion: A Survey," Journal of Systems and Software, vol. 85, no. 1, Jan. 2012, pp. 132–151.

[5] B. Cool, C. Knieke, A. Rausch, M. Schindler, A. Strasser, M. Vogel, O. Brox, and S. Jauns-Seyfried, "From Product Architectures to a Managed Automotive Software Product Line Architecture," in Proceedings of the 31st Annual ACM Symposium on Applied Computing, ser. SAC'16. New York, NY, USA: ACM, 2016, pp. 1350–1353.

[6] A. Pretschner, M. Broy, I. H. Krüger, and T. Stauner, "Software Engineering for Automotive Systems: A Roadmap," in 2007 Future of Software Engineering, ser. FOSE '07. IEEE Computer Society, 2007, pp. 55–71.

[7] R. Cloutier, G. Muller, D. Verma, R. Nilchiani, E. Hole, and M. Bone, "The Concept of Reference Architectures," Systems Engineering, vol. 13, no. 1, Feb. 2010, pp. 14–27.

[8] E. Y. Nakagawa, P. O. Antonino, and M. Becker, "Reference Architecture and Product Line Architecture: A Subtle but Critical Difference," in Proceedings of the 5th European Conference on Software Architecture, ser. ECSA'11. Berlin, Heidelberg: Springer-Verlag, 2011, pp. 207–211.

[9] E. Y. Nakagawa, F. Oquendo, and M. Becker, "RAModel: A Reference Model for Reference Architectures," in Proceedings of the 2012 Joint Working IEEE/IFIP Conference on Software Architecture and European Conference on Software Architecture, ser. WICSA-ECSA '12. Washington, DC, USA: IEEE Computer Society, 2012, pp. 297–301.

[10] E. Y. Nakagawa, M. Becker, and J. C. Maldonado, "Towards a Process to Design Product Line Architectures Based on Reference Architectures," in Proceedings of the 17th International Software Product Line Conference, ser. SPLC '13. New York, NY, USA: ACM, 2013, pp. 157–161.

[11] E. Y. Nakagawa, M. Guessi, J. C. Maldonado, D. Feitosa, and F. Oquendo, "Consolidating a Process for the Design, Representation, and Evaluation of Reference Architectures," in Proceedings of the 2014 IEEE/IFIP Conference on Software Architecture, ser. WICSA '14. Washington, DC, USA: IEEE Computer Society, 2014, pp. 143–152.

[12] J. van Gurp and J. Bosch, "Design Erosion: Problems & Causes," Journal of Systems and Software, vol. Volume 61, 2002, pp. 105–119.

[13] S. Herold and A. Rausch, "Complementing Model-Driven Development for the Detection of Software Architecture Erosion," in 5th Modelling in Software Engineering (MiSE 2013) Workshop at Intern. Conf. on Softw. Eng. (ICSE 2013), 2013.

[14] I. John and J. Dörr, "Elicitation of Requirements from User Documentation," in Ninth International Workshop on Requirements Engineering: Foundation for Software Quality. REFSQ '03, 2003.

[15] H. Gomaa, Designing Software Product Lines with UML: From Use Cases to Pattern-Based Software Architectures. Addison-Wesley Professional, 2004.

[16] P. Clements and L. Northrop, Software Product Lines: Practices and Patterns. Addison Wesley, 2001.

[17] J. Bosch, Design and use of software architectures: Adopting and evolving a product-line approach. Pearson Education, 2000.

[18] S. Deelstra, M. Sinnema, and J. Bosch, "Product derivation in software product families: a case study," Journal of Systems and Software, vol. 74, no. 2, 2005, pp. 173–194.

[19] J. Bosch, "Maturity and Evolution in Software Product Lines: Approaches, Artefacts and Organization," in Proceedings of the Second International Conference on Software Product Lines, ser. SPLC 2. London, UK, UK: Springer-Verlag, 2002, pp. 257–271.

[20] A. Strasser, B. Cool, C. Gernert, C. Knieke, M. Körner, D. Niebuhr, H. Peters, A. Rausch, O. Brox, S. Jauns-Seyfried, H. Jelden, S. Klie, and M. Krämer, "Mastering Erosion of Software Architecture in Automotive Software Product Lines," in SOFSEM 2014: Theory and Practice of Computer Science, ser. LNCS, V. Geffert, B. Preneel, B. Rovan, J. Stuller, and A. M. Tjoa, Eds., vol. 8327. Springer, 2014, pp. 491–502.

[21] G. Holl, P. Grünbacher, and R. Rabiser, "A Systematic Review and an Expert Survey on Capabilities Supporting Multi Product Lines," Inf. Softw. Technol., vol. 54, no. 8, Aug. 2012, pp. 828–852.

[22] S. Thiel and A. Hein, "Modeling and Using Product Line Variability in Automotive Systems," IEEE Softw., vol. 19, no. 4, Jul. 2002, pp. 66–72.

[23] H. Holdschick, "Challenges in the Evolution of Model-based Software Product Lines in the Automotive Domain," in Proceedings of the 4th International Workshop on Feature-Oriented Software Development, ser. FOSD '12. ACM, 2012, pp. 70–73.

[24] M. Steger, C. Tischer, B. Boss, A. Müller, O. Pertler, W. Stolz, and S. Ferber, "Introducing PLA at Bosch Gasoline Systems: Experiences and Practices," in Software Product Lines. Springer, 2004, pp. 34–50.

[25] The Standish Group International, Inc., "CHAOS Chronicles 2003 report," West Yarmouth, MA, 2003.

[26] C. Knieke and M. Huhn, "Semantic Foundation and Validation of Live Activity Diagrams," Nordic Journal of Computing, vol. 15, no. 2, 2015, pp. 112–140.

[27] International Organization for Standardization, "ISO/DIS 26262: Road vehicles – functional safety," 2009.

[28] H. Peters, C. Knieke, O. Brox, S. Jauns-Seyfried, M. Krämer, and A. Schulze, "A Test-driven Approach for Model-based Development of Powertrain Functions," in Agile Processes in Software Engineering and Extreme Programming. 15th International Conference on Agile Software Development, XP 2014, G. Cantone and M. Marchesi, Eds. Berlin, Heidelberg: Springer-Verlag, 2014, pp. 294–301.

[29] K. Beck, Test Driven Development. By Example. Addison-Wesley Longman, 2002.

[30] E. Lehmann, "Time Partition Testing – Systematischer Test des kontinuierlichen Verhaltens von eingebetteten Systemen," Ph.D. dissertation, Fakultät IV – Elektrotechnik und Informatik, TU Berlin, 2004.

[31] M. Mues, "Taint Analysis - Language Independent Security Analysis for Injection Attacks," Master's Thesis, TU Clausthal, Institute for Applied Software Systems Engineering, 2016.

[32] F. P. Brooks, Jr., "No silver bullet essence and accidents of software engineering," Computer, vol. 20, no. 4, Apr. 1987, pp. 10–19.

Content Structures, Organization, and Processes for Localized Content Management

Hans-Werner Sehring
Namics
Hamburg, Germany
e-mail: hans-werner.sehring@namics.com

***Abstract*—Content management systems are in widespread use for document production. In particular, we see the pervasive application of web content management systems for web sites. These systems serve both authors that produce content and web site users that perceive content in the form of documents. Today, one focus lies on the consideration of the context of the web site user. Context is considered in order to serve users' information needs best. Many applications, e.g., marketing sites, focus on making the user experience most enjoyable. To this end, content is directed at the users' environmental and cultural background. This includes, first and foremost, the native language of the user. Practically, all respective web sites are offered in multiple languages and, therefore, multilingual content management is very common today. Content and its structure need to be prepared by authors for the different contexts, languages in this case. Contemporary content management system products, though, each follow different approaches to model context. There is no single agreed-upon approach because the different ways of modeling context put an emphasis on different content management properties. This paper discusses different aspects of multilingual content management and publication. The Minimalistic Meta Modeling Language is well suited for context-aware content management. This paper demonstrates how this modeling language can be used to master the requirements of multilingual content management within the framework of a common meta model. This allows content modeling without consideration of CMS product properties. This way, it takes away constraints from content modeling and it removes dependencies to content management system products.**

Keywords-content management; web site management; multilingual content management; multilinguality; localization; internationalization; context-awareness.

I. Introduction

Web sites are operated by nearly all organizations and enterprises, and they are created for various purposes. The management of such sites has evolved to *content management* that separates web site content, structure, and layout from each other. This way, content can be published on different media and on different channels. Certain parameters can influence the production of documents from content, e.g., the viewing device used by the user or her or his current context.

Consequently, most web sites are produced by a *content management system* (CMS), a web CMS in this case. Currently, web sites increasingly exhibit consideration of content that is tailored to the context of the content's percipient. They do so either to provide content with maximal value to the visitor, in order to inform a user in the most suitable way, to convey a message best, to present a company or a brand in the most appealing way, etc.

The most basic contextual property, to this end, is the native language of the consumer. Content should be presented to the user in this language. At least, textual content is translated. More advanced approaches take the culture and the habits of a user into account.

(Written) Language has an impact on layout. E.g., there need to be web page layouts for languages written from left to right and for ones written from the right to the left. On top of that, the writing direction has an impact on, e.g., the placement of navigation and search elements on a web page.

The relationship between translations of content can be viewed as contextualization as pointed out in an initial paper on the topic [1]. A translation is content to be managed in the context of the original content it has been derived from.

Some time ago, multilingual web appearances and print publications were identified as a major challenge for organizations [2]. In practice today, the problem is addressed by various approaches in different CMS products. However, there is no systematic consideration of these approaches and the characteristics of the resulting solutions. This leads to the content management approach taken to be dependent on the CMS product chosen for a particular web site appearance.

This paper reviews approaches to multilingual content management. The Minimalistic Meta Modeling Language allows abstract representations of these approaches and comparing their implications on content management tasks.

The rest of this paper is organized as follows. Section II defines requirements for multilingual web sites and the CMSs producing them. Section III describes related approaches to multilingual web site production. Section IV briefly introduces the Minimalistic Meta Modeling Language. Section V discusses the application of this language for multilingual content management. The conclusions and acknowledgement close the paper.

II. Localized Content Management Requirements

The general approach to multilingual web site production is similar for most approaches. It is a two-phase process.

Its foundation is language- and country-independent content, or at least content storage organized in a way that allows content to be localized easily. To this end, an initial *internationalization* (often abbreviated as I18n) step removes all cultural assumptions from content.

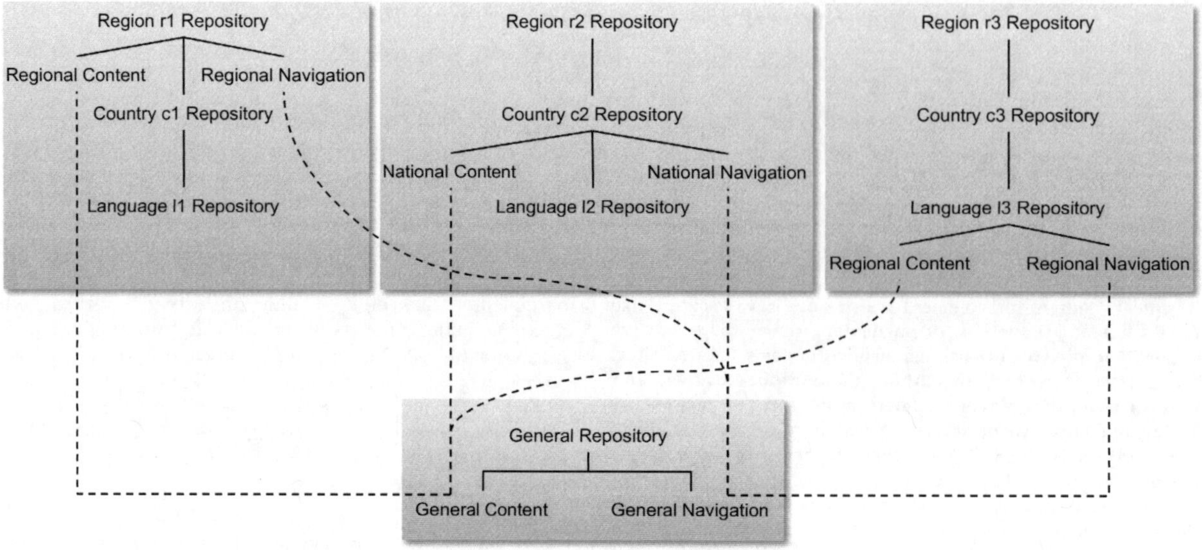

Figure 1. Example of a content repository organization for multilingual content with content distribution on different levels.

On that basis, a *localization* (L10n) procedure adapts content for a specific country, region, or language.

There are many considerations that have to be taken into account to enable this basic process. On top of the linguistic and cultural tasks of localization, there are business considerations and technical issues about the management of content, its structure, and organization (its physical structure) [3]. Choices are made based on the required content management strategy.

Content management processes for localization have to be defined. As part of those, the process of rendering localized content into publishable documents needs to be aligned with the actual content organization.

In this paper, we concentrate on the technical issues of multilingual content management and representation.

A. Basic Multilingual Content Management Strategies

There are three typical strategies for the management of multilingual and multicultural content [4]:

1) Central control over the content: Content is distributed by a central authority and it is translated to different target languages, but it is typically not adapted in other ways. I.e., there are no structural changes, and the layouts are not adapted to local preferences.

2) Decentralized management of multiple local sites without coordination: The local sites typically use a localized design. This approach does not ensure homogeneous quality in all localized appearances, there is no means to enforce content to be current in all local repositories, and there is no way to grant a globally recognizable web site standard, e.g., a corporate design.

3) A hybrid approach of the first two: It allows dealing with global, regional, and local content. Global content is produced centrally and translated for global use. Regional content is localized from centrally provided content, but is also adapted to and used in a regional context. Local content is produced locally in the local language in addition to global and regional content.

Because of the possibly combined advantages, many organizations favor the third approach. It requires tool support that is discussed in the subsequent subsections.

In practice, there are basically two CMS setups that correspond to centralized and decentralized content management: a central multi-tenant CMS that allows hosting multiple sites and relating these to each other, and isolated local CMSs that exchange content while providing their own web site structure and layout. The subsequent subsections of this section discuss these two approaches.

Fig. 1 shows an overview over different exemplary content repositories organized according to the two ways of multisite content management. Each repository represents one CMS instance or one content collection inside a CMS together with its structure, layouts, etc.

The three repositories at the top of Fig. 1 show content localization at different levels in content trees of multisite CMSs. In this example, each CMS hosts collections for regional, national, and language-specific content. These are just three arbitrary levels of content collections. The solid lines in the figure denote relationships between collections where the lower one is derived from the upper one.

The *General Repository* at the bottom represents the pool of internationalized content that is used for content distribution from a central content pool. The dashed lines represent content passed from one repository to another.

The sample repositories in Fig. 1 contain content (text, images, etc.), as well as navigation nodes and structure. These parts of the repositories are only shown where needed.

Maintaining content consistency across different localized versions is time consuming and error prone. There are two primary ways of content distribution and localization: manual and semiautomatic [3]. These apply to both approaches, centralized as well as decentralized CMSs.

B. Multilingual Content Structures

Content needs a defined structure in order to be processed by content management systems. There are two basic forms of content organization for the support of the aforementioned multilingual content management strategies: related content variants and independent content collections.

1) Related content variants: Professional CMSs allow defining content collections and relating them to each other. A typical pattern is a master-variant model, where a *variant* can be derived from every piece of content. The original content then plays the role of a *master*. Typically the master is internationalized content in a certain language, and the variants are the translations. The structures of master and variants are identical or at least similar.

2) Independent content collections: In a decentralized approach, CMSs maintain local content and structures that are connected logically only. Localization may be performed by translation of internationalized content that is provided in a central content pool, by adding new local content, and by omitting centrally provided content from a local repository.

C. Content Localization Processes

The two ways of organizing content, either as related variants or as independent content collections, allow different localization processes. The most important ones are the translation of content from an internationalized form into a localized variant, and the transmission of content from a central content pool to a national, regional, or local content collection.

1) Translation of content using a master-variant model: Whenever the master content changes, some actions on the localized variants are induced. In terms of Fig. 1, e.g., when content in a regional repository is modified then localizations in the national repositories are updated.

Whenever master content is changed and variants are not yet translated, as well as in cases where the master is extended with additional content, e.g., new substructures, the variants have to be considered outdated. In these cases a repository may provide *default* or *fallback* values to the variants. In the simplest case the master content is taken as the fallback. Often the English version of a web site is chosen as a master, so that new content that is not yet localized shows up in English on the various sites.

Fallbacks are problematic for composite documents, e.g., images embedded in a text [5]. When an image is updated, this may, e.g., result in an English image contained in a French text. An application-specific fallback logic may be needed for composites.

Additionally, changes to the master may result in translation workflows being started. Such a workflow either demands that new or changed content is translated manually, or it employs automatic translation tools to create localized content. There are various degrees of *machine translation*, ranging from machine-aided human translation, over human-aided machine translation to fully automated translation [6].

It is current practice to minimize manual translation effort by using a *Translation Memory System* (TMS) that is employed for terminology management and to record all existing translations [7]. To enable these to work with a CMS, there are content interchange formats like the *XML Localisation Interchange File Format* (XLIFF) [8] and *Translation Memory eXchange* (TMX) [9] for output and input of multilingual content.

During automatic localization there are easy translation tasks like adaptations of number formats, measurement units, currencies, etc. From a cultural viewpoint, there is no general answer to the question whether a document's content can be changed while retaining its structure, though [10]. In general, only the translation of content according to a centrally given structure is achievable.

There are approaches to automatic translation that employ semantic models of content, e.g., ontology-based [11]. These are mainly subject to research.

In any case, it is crucial for editors to learn how to prepare content in a way that is suitable for localization [12].

2) Shipping of content between independent repositories: For the translation processes mentioned above, content needs to be exchanged between a CMS and a TMS using some external format that allows identifying related content when content is transferred back to the CMS.

When following a content strategy that employs independent content collections, content regularly needs to be transferred between repositories as part of the localization process. In terms of Fig. 1, e.g., internationalized content in the general repository is distributed to regional repositories.

For content collections inside one CMS, content transfer might just consist of internal references. If separate CMS instances need to exchange content, some external content format is required.

As indicated in Fig. 1, the repositories might form a hierarchical network of content pools, ranging from global over regional down to local repositories. Though these hierarchies result from the master-variant relationships (see Section B.1)), content shipping should take hierarchy levels into consideration (see the dashed lines in Fig. 1).

D. Content Presentation

Content is rendered into documents that are used for publication, e.g., HTML documents for web sites or XML documents for typesetting programs. Documents in various languages are produced from multilingual content.

Typically, predefined layouts are used for document creation. The way documents are created depends on the content structure, i.e., related content or independent content collections.

Related content is typically based on identical or at least similar structures. Rendering layouts for multilingual content have to be defined using a uniform structure. Consequently, a uniform layout or a set of layout variants is typically provided centrally. It is possible to provide local variations, but this requires thorough knowledge of the content structure and its variants. While predefined layouts limit the degree to which presentations can be adapted to local preferences they support quality assurance. E.g., international enterprises with localized web sites typically wish to have their corporate identity and design (CI/CD) to be reflected in every local appearance.

The scenario where independent content collections are employed gives single CMS instances complete freedom concerning the visualization of content. Together with every decentralized repository, localized layouts can be defined. While this allows the highest degree of localization, it makes quality assurance harder. There is no enforced commonality between the local layouts.

III. RELATED WORK

We briefly discuss related approaches to multilingual content management and commercial CMS products.

A. Modeling Approaches

Typically, the management of multilingual web sites relies on a CMS. There are approaches to solve multilingual content management on the level of HTML files, though.

MultiLingual XHTML (MLHTML) [13] is an extension to HTML. It was designed to include content for different languages in the same page file. An XSL style sheet is used to transform it to a plain HTML page for a given language. The approach is well suited for static sites without a CMS in the background and for large sets of existing static HTML pages. It requires web sites to have the same structure and the same layout across all languages, though.

B. Content Management System Products

Professional CMS products support multilingual content management. To name some examples, Adobe Experience Manager (AEM), CoreMedia CMS, and Sitecore Experience Platform all follow a master-variant approach to multisite management. They provide functionality to create a deep copy of a master site. The content entities from the copy are automatically related to the corresponding master entities.

All products allow local editing of content copies, and changes to the master lead to notifications sent to editors. CoreMedia also allows editing the content's structure. Sitecore manages navigation structures locally.

Some products add workflow tasks for the translation of all content entities. Workflows may drive automatic or manual translation processes. Some of the products provide workflows for external translations using XLIFF.

The master site serves as a fallback for missing localized content. To this end, AEM and CoreMedia allow to freely choose the master. Sitecore prefers US English for master content and it additionally provides fallback chains to, e.g., have a series of fallback languages before using the master.

IV. M3L

The *Minimalistic Meta Modeling Language* (*M3L*, pronounced "mel") is a modeling language that is applicable to a range of modeling tasks. It proved particularly useful for context-aware content modeling [14].

```
model           ::= ⟨def-list⟩
def-list        ::= ⟨def⟩ [⟨def-list⟩]
def             ::= ⟨ref⟩ "is" ⟨id-list⟩
                    ( "{"⟨def-list⟩"}" [⟨production-rule⟩]
                    | ⟨production-rule⟩
                    | ";"
                    )
ref             ::= ⟨id⟩ ["from" ⟨ref⟩]
id-list         ::= ("a" | "an" | "the") ⟨ref⟩ ["," ⟨id-list⟩]
production-rule ::= ( "|=" ⟨def⟩
                    | "|-" {⟨ref⟩ | string | "the" "name" }
                    ) ";"
```

Figure 2. Simplified grammer of the M3L.

In order to be able to discuss multilingual content management with M3L in the subsequent section, we briefly introduce the M3L modeling constructs.

M3L offers a rather minimalistic syntax that is described by the slightly simplified grammar (in EBNF) shown in Fig. 2. It is only simplified for readability and still complete.

The production for identifiers (*id*) is omitted here. It is a typical lexical rule that defines identifiers as character sequences. Identifiers may—in contrast to typical formal languages—be composed of any character sequence. Quotation is used to define identifiers containing whitespace, brackets, or other reserved symbols. The same holds for string literals (*string*).

The descriptive power of M3L lies in the fact that the formal semantics is rather abstract. There is no fixed domain semantics connected to M3L definitions. The exact semantics of M3L evaluation will not be discussed in this paper. For more details see [14].

A. Concept Definitions and References

A M3L model consists of a series of definitions (⟨*def*⟩ in the grammar definition above). Each definition starts with a previously unused identifier that is introduced by the definition and may end with a semicolon. For an example, see Fig. 3 line 1.

We call the entity referenced by such an identifier a *concept*. Its constituents are presented in the following.

The keyword `is` introduces an optional reference to a base concept. An inheritance relationship as known from object-oriented modeling is established between the base concept and the newly defined *derived concept*. This relationship leads to the concepts defined in the context (see below) of the base concept to be visible in the derived concept. Furthermore, the refined concept can be used wherever the base concept is expected (similar to subtype polymorphism).

As can be seen in the grammar, the keyword `is` always has to be followed by either `a`, `an`, or `the`. The keywords `a` and `an` are synonyms for indicating that a classification allows multiple sub concepts of the base concept. Lines 2 and 3 of Fig. 3 show an example.

There may be more than one base concept. Base concepts can be enumerated in a comma-separated list (Fig. 3 line 4).

```
001 NewConcept;
002 NewConcept is an ExistingConcept;
003 NewerConcept is an ExistingConcept;
004 NewConcept is an ExistingConcept, an AnotherExistingConcept;
005 TheOnlySubConcept is the SingletonConcept;

006 NewConcept;
007 NewConcept is an ExistingConcept;
008 NewConcept is an AnotherExistingConcept;

009 Person { name is a String; }
010 Peter is a Person { "Peter Smith" is the name; }
011 Employee { salary is a Number; }
012 Programmer is an Employee;
013 PeterTheEmployee is a Peter, a Programmer { 30000 is the salary; }

014 salary from Employee;

015 Person { sex; status; }
016 MarriedFemalePerson is a Person { female is the sex; married is the status; } |= Wife;
017 MarriedMalePerson is a Person { male is the sex; married is the status; } |= Husband;

018 Person { name is a String; } |- "<person>" name "</person>";
```

Figure 3. Code example of M3L statements.

The keyword `the` indicates a closed refinement: there may be only one refinement of the base concept (the currently defined one), e.g., line 5 of Fig. 3.

Any further refinement of the base concept(s) leads to the redefinition ("unbinding") of the existing refinements.

Statements about already existing concepts lead to their redefinition. E.g., the statements in lines 6-8 in Fig. 3 lead to the same definition of the concept *NewConcept* as the above variant.

Every statement defining a concept is also an expression that evaluates to a concept. Definition statements evaluate to the defined concept; e.g., line 6 of Fig. 3 has no effect on concept definitions, but it evaluates to *NewConcept* as defined in lines 1-4. Further evaluation rules follow from the remaining M3L constructs.

B. Content and Context Definitions

Concept definitions as introduced in the preceding section are valid in a *context*. Definitions like the ones seen so far add concepts to the topmost of a tree of contexts. Curly brackets open a new context. Lines 9-13 if Fig. 3 show an example.

In this example, we assume that concepts *String* and *Number* are already defined. The subconcepts created in context are unique specializations in that context only. In practice, the concept *30000* should also be given. If not, it will be introduced locally in the context of *PeterTheEmployee*, preventing reuse of the identical number.

M3L has visibility rules that correlate to contexts. Each context defines a scope in which definition identifiers are valid. Concepts from outer contexts are visible in inner scopes. E.g., in the above example the concept *String* is visible in *Person* because it is defined in the topmost scope. *salary* is visible in *PeterTheEmployee* because it is defined in *Employee* and the context is inherited. *salary* is not valid in the topmost context and in *Peter*. Contexts with those names may be defined later on, though.

Tying a context to a concept can be interpreted in different ways, e.g., as contextualization or as aggregation.

Contexts can be referenced using the projection operator `from` in order to use concepts across contexts. Fig. 3, line 14 shows an example where the salary of employee is selected.

C. Narrowing and Production Rules

M3L allows assigning one *semantic production rule* to each concept. Production rules fire when an instance comes into existence that matches the definition of the left-hand side of the rule. They replace the new concept by the concept referenced by the right-hand part of the rule.

In the example of Fig. 3 line 16, whenever a *MarriedFemalePerson* shall be created then a *Wife* is created instead.

Production rules are usually used in conjunction with M3L's *narrowing* of concepts. Before a production rule is applied, a concept is narrowed down as much as possible. Narrowing is a kind of matchmaking process to apply the most specific definition possible.

If a base concept fulfills all definitions—base concepts and constituents of the context—of a derived concept, then the base concept is taken as an equivalent of that derived concept. If a production rule is defined for the derived concept, this rule is used in place of all production rules defined for any super concept.

The code in lines 15-17 of Fig. 3 shows an example of combined narrowing and semantic production rules. Fig. 4 illustrates the narrowing of concepts resulting from these definitions. Whenever an "instance" (a derived concept) of *Person* is created, it is checked whether it actually matches one of the more specific definitions. A married female *Person* is replaced by *Wife*, a married male *Person* by *Husband*, every other *Person* is kept as it is.

In addition to the semantic production rules that create new concepts, M3L also has *syntactic production rules* like the one in line 18 of Fig. 2.

`Person {`
` male is the sex;`
`}`
	→	`Person {`
		` male is the sex;`
		`}`

`Person {`
` female is the sex;`
` married is the status;`
`}`
	→	`Wife;`

`Person {`
` male is the sex;`
` married is the status;`
`}`
	→	`Husband;`

Figure 4. Illustration of the semantic production rules from Fig. 3.

Syntactic production rules evaluate to a string. The rules consist of a list of string literals and concept references whose production rules are applied recursively.

An additional keyword sequence `the name` (see grammar in Fig. 2) refers to the name of the concept to which the current rule belongs. This dynamic reference is required because syntactic production rules of a concept are chosen after narrowing in the same way as semantic production rules. In the example in Fig. 3 this means that the shown syntactic production rule may not only be applied to *Person*s, but also to refinements like *PeterTheEmployee*.

The syntactic rules are also used as grammar rules to generate recognizers that create concepts from strings.

If no rule is given, then the default syntactic production rule evaluates a concept to its name.

V. M3L FOR MULTILINGUAL CONTENT

To demonstrate how the M3L can be used to model multilingual content, we use a M3L representation of a setup like that from Fig. 1 as an example. Concepts for local repositories are derived from those of a central repository, this way relating content, content structure, navigation hierarchies, and document layouts. We briefly touch workflows and content interchange formats.

A. Content Models

We use M3L concepts to model content repositories and local collections as shown in Fig. 1 as well as to model content itself. Contextualization represents content structure. Relationships between repositories or collections are established by concept derivation.

In the course of the example, we concentrate on the navigation structure of a hypothetical website. In contrast to the actual content, this frees us from content modeling details that are not relevant for the discussion. The arguments to be discussed are the same in both cases.

We use contextualization for the navigation hierarchy. An example is shown in Fig. 5, lines 1-8. *ContentRepository*, *Content*, *Navigation*, and *NavItem* may be given concepts here. They are used to model repositories and collections, single content items, navigation hierarchies, and navigation entries, respectively.

In this example, the general repository is defined as a M3L concept holding concepts for centrally provided internationalized content. It encloses further concepts representing two main parts of the repository, the main content (*GeneralContent*) and the navigation structure (*GeneralNavigation*).

The navigation part hosts a central navigation structure with a main navigation node *Products+Services*. This one has subordinate navigation items *Consumer Products*, *Professional Products*, and *Support*.

The following models use derivation to relate translations of navigation items to those in the general repository.

We present two modeling alternatives to translate the navigation hierarchy. In the first alternative, outlined in Fig. 5, lines 9-16, editors translate each navigation item one by one. This way, the structure is kept as it is. We do so by deriving a sub concept, here *GermanNavigation*, from the general navigation. In this "copy" of the general navigation we can locally "replace" the navigation items by translations.

We provide exactly one translation (`is the`) per navigation item in the specific region context. Other translations can still be given in the context of other local repositories.

Changes in the general repository are propagated to local ones in such a model. E.g., when a new navigation item is added globally, it is inherited in the local repositories. Such an item will not be translated automatically, but the overall navigation structure stays up-to-date. The inherited concept provides a default value in this case.

As a second alternative, shown in Fig. 5 lines 17-24, we create a navigation structure locally. We populate it by picking single instances from the general repository. This way we detach the local structures from the global structure. The other properties, e.g., the pages assigned to a navigation node, are inherited, though.

The repository base is a new, "empty" one since *GermanNavigation* is derived from just *Navigation*, not *GeneralNavigation*. The inserted navigation items are derived from those from the global repository, though.

In such a detached repository, possible changes in the central repository are not propagated, but have to be reapplied locally. This can be performed either completely manually, or by means of a workflow (see below).

When structures are changed during localization, there are various possibilities for structural differences. The model in lines 25-37 of Fig. 5 gives two examples (without translation) for a company's web site in countries with smaller markets and, therefore, a smaller offering.

```
GeneralRepository is a ContentRepository {
 GeneralContent is a Content { … }
 GeneralNavigation is a Navigation {
  "Products+Services" is a NavItem {
   "Consumer Products" is a NavItem;
   "Professional Products" is a NavItem;
   Support is a NavItem;
} } }

GermanRepository1 is a GeneralRepository {
 GermanContent is the GeneralContent { … }
 GermanNavigation is the GeneralNavigation {
  Produkte+Dienste is the Products+Services {
   Verbraucher is the "Consumer Products";
   Profis is the "Professional Products";
   Kundendienst is the Support;
} } }

GermanRepository2 is a Repository {
 GermanContent is a Content { … }
 GermanNavigation is a Navigation {
  Produkte+Dienste is a Products+Services from GeneralNavigation from GeneralRepository {
   Verbraucher is a "Consumer Products" from GeneralNavigation from GeneralRepository;
   Profis is a "Professional Products" from GeneralNavigation from GeneralRepository;
   Kundendienst is a Support from GeneralNavigation from GeneralRepository;
} } }

NicheMarkets is a ContentRepository {
 SmallCountry1 is a GeneralRepository {
  Country1Content is the GeneralContent { … }
  Country1Nav is the GeneralNavigation {
   Products is the Products+Services {
    "Consumer Products";
    "Professional Products";
 } } }
 SmallCountry2 is a GeneralRepository {
  Country2Content is the GeneralContent { … }
  Country2Nav is the GeneralNavigation {
   Products is the Products+Services;
} } }
```

Figure 5. Sample multilingual content model definitions using the M3L.

In the first example, *SmallCountry1*, a subset (two out of the three) of navigation items is inserted into the navigation tree below *Products*, the navigation item that generally appears as *Products+Services*. The second example, *SmallCountry2*, shows a flatter structure with no sub navigation items under *Products*.

Content and its structure are localized the same way as the navigation structure. Content typically is composed of multiple basic pieces of content, forming trees similar to the navigation hierarchies.

B. Layout Descriptions

Content is managed with the goal of finally being published. To this end, layouts are defined that are used to render content in documents.

Such documents can be published on certain *channels*. Channels are, in content management terms, media of a certain kind combined with means of document distribution. Examples are web sites, print publications, public kiosks, and mobile applications. Different channels require different presentations and include different sets of content.

Along with content also the layouts used for its publication can be localized when documents are produced using M3L's syntactic productions attached to localized concepts.

Fig. 6 shows an example of M3L code for localized layouts. Adding to the example of the repositories shown in Fig. 5, it presents two further repositories for Greek and French content.

In addition to the management of content alone, here a base concept *GeneralLayout* is given. This concept represents an additional part of content repositories holding layout descriptions (not shown in Fig. 1).

Inside this part of the repository, typical graphical elements like pages, text components, image components, etc. of the respective publication channel can be found. For this example, assume *Page* to be a given concept for web pages that aggregate content in one HTML file.

The main technical purpose of refinements of this concept is to define syntactic production rules that describe how documents are created from content. In the example of web pages, these rules create HTML and CSS code.

```
001 GreekRepository is a GeneralRepository {
002  GreekContent is the GeneralContent { … }
003  GreekNaviation is the GeneralNavigation {
004   NavItem is the NavItem { LatinTitle is a Title; }
005   …
006  }
007  GreekLayout is the GeneralLayout {
008   GreekPage is a Page
009   |- … "<html>" … "<body>" … GreekNavigation … "</body></html>";
010   GreekNavigation
011   |- "<ol class=\"greeknavigationbartoplevel\">"
012        "<li class=\"greeknavigationitem\">" NavItem "</li><ol>";
013   NavItem from GreekNavigation
014   |- "<ol class=\"greeknavigationbar\">"
015        "<li class=\"greeknavigationitem\">" the name
016         "<span class=\"latintranscription\">" LatinTitle "</span>"
017          NavItem "</li></ol>";
018   NavItem from Navigation
019   |- "";
020  }
021 }
022 FrenchRepository is a GeneralRepository {
023  FrenchContent is the GeneralContent { … }
024  FrenchNavigation is the GeneralNavigation { … }
025  FrenchLayout is the GeneralLayout {
026   FrenchPage is a Page {…}
027   |- … "<html>" … "<body>" … FrenchNavigation … "</body></html>";
028   FrenchNavigation
029   |- "<ol class=\"frenchnavigationbartoplevel\">"
030        "<li class=\"frenchnavigationitem\">" NavItem "</li><ol>";
031   NavItem from FrenchNavigation
032   |- "<ol class=\"frenchnavigationbar\">"
033        "<li class=\"frenchnavigationitem\">" the name
034          NavItem "</li></ol>";
035   NavItem from Navigation
036   |- "";
037  }
038 }
```

Figure 6. Sample multilingual layout definitions using the M3L.

For the course of the example we assume distinct layouts to be given for the two repositories. In Fig. 6, lines 7 to 20 sketch a fragment of a web page on the Greek web site, and the lines 25 to 37 show code for a French web page. In HTML it is typical to represent navigation hierarchies as nested ordered lists (ol) with list items (li) for leaf nodes.

Note that there are no references from the content or the navigation to the layouts. This way, multiple layouts can be defined for the same content, thus allowing *multi-channel publishing*.

All pages of our hypothetical web sites shall contain the whole navigation hierarchy of the web site they belong to. Therefore, the syntactic production rule for pages references the whole navigation part of the repository as the respective hierarchy's root.

The syntactic rule of *Navigation* outputs HTML code for the navigation root. As part of the production it addresses *NavItem*. This reference evaluates to the set of all contained (refinements of) *NavItems*. This leads to all syntactic representations of the concrete *NavItem* refinements to be concatenated in the output.

NavItems emit code for one navigation entry each. This includes their (localized) name. The hierarchy is traversed by recursion through the reference to the nested *NavItem* refinements.

In the case of leaf navigation items, there is no refinement of *NavItem*. For these, the reference evaluates to *NavItem* as defined in *Navigation*, not any of the refinements in the context of the localized repositories. We add a rule to the "plain" *NavItem* to terminate recursion (lines 18/19 and 35/36 in Fig. 6). Otherwise, lines 17 and 34 would print "NavItem" as the default production rule would be used.

In the example, the two sets of web pages mainly differ in some CSS classes that are attributed to HTML elements. To illustrate possible structural differences, Greek navigation items that are assumedly labeled in Greek writing contain an additional transcription using Latin letters.

In fact, this structural difference even has an impact on the content (the navigation, in our example). The Latin transcription needs to be maintained by content editors. Therefore, according content *LatinTitle* is defined in the context of every Greek navigation item by refining *NavItem* in that context.

With this redefinition Greek, navigation items also print the Latin transcription as part of the syntactic production rule for the layout (line 16 of Fig. 6).

```
001 WorkflowTask is a … { Agent is a …; }

002 TranslationWorkflowTask is a WorkflowTask {
003  ContentToTranslate is a String;
004  ResultingContent is a String;
005  Translator is the Agent;
006 } |= TranslatedContent;

007 NewsContent is a … {
008  Title is a String;
009  Text is a String;
010 }
011 GeneralNews is a NewsContent, an InternationalizedContent
012 |= TranslationWorkflowTask {
013  Title is a ContentToTranslate;
014  Text is a ContentToTranslate;
015  … Translator;
016 }
017 |- … (code exporting content, e.g. XLIFF, for the given translator)
018 News is a NewsContent, a TranslatedContent {
019  Title is the Title from TranslatedContent from Translator;
020  Text is the Text from TranslatedContent from Translator;
021 }
022 |- … (rule for importing content from, e.g., XLIFF)
```

Figure 7. Code example of basic M3L concepts for workflow definitions.

The example shown in Fig. 6 exhibits a lot of duplicate code. Note that in practical cases there will be reuse of layouts by providing standard layouts on the level of *GeneralRepository* or some additional intermediate repositories, rather than defining everything inside the local repositories. Such an intermediate repository might be, e.g., a repository for all languages using Latin writing.

The termination rule stating that *NavItem* renders an empty string may even be defined in the context of *GeneralRepository*, thus holding for every repository.

C. *Workflows*

Translation tasks in a CMS are often driven by workflows. Introducing a complete workflow management system is beyond the scope of this paper. We provide a sketch of an approach based on M3L structures.

A workflow consists of workflow tasks, e.g., represented by derivations of a *WorkflowTask* as shown in Fig. 7, line 1.

A translation workflow task derived from it may look like shown in Fig. 7, lines 2-6.

For the sake of simplicity, we assume content to consist of *Strings* in this example. In practice, it may be structured.

We create workflows by deriving specific workflow tasks and by connecting them using semantic production rules. There are rules for content that initializing workflow tasks and rules for workflow tasks creating a subsequent step.

In the case of interactive workflow tasks, syntactic rules create representations for exchange with external processors.

The example in lines 7-17 of Fig. 7 shows a definition of content of type *GeneralNews*. Whenever new content that is derived from *GeneralNews* is created, its semantic rule is inherited and thus a *TranslationWorkflowTask* is created. *InternationalizedContent* contains content that needs to be localized and, therefore, starts a translation workflow task and initializes it with the *Title* and *Text* as content that needs translation. Inside a translation workflow task, *ContentToTranslate* flags content as requiring translation.

As a parameter directing the translation process, Fig. 7 shows a *Translator* in the context *TranslationWorkflowTask*. In practice, it may be evaluated by the following workflow execution.

The workflow tasks' syntactic production rules produce an external representation that can be passed to, e.g., a TMS.

When a result from such a translation service is received, a *TranslatedContent* is produced from it. We need this concept to distinguish it from *InternationalizedContent* so that is not subject to further workflow enactments.

In this example, the workflow yields the translated *NewsContent*. In order to create the concepts from translated external content, refinements like *News* in the example of Fig. 7 (lines 18-22) declare the mapping of an external representation to a M3L concept by a semantic rule.

D. *Content Exchange*

When sharing content with external parties, as discussed above, as well as in manual translation processes, content needs to be shipped between the different parties.

Inside one organization, communication can be established using M3L's structures directly. In order to interchange content with external organizations, we use an external format for input and output. This can be defined using M3L's syntactic production rules. Fig. 8 shows a sketch of an example.

In lines 1-4 of Fig. 8, the *Text* component of content of type *NewsContent* (compare Fig. 7) is externalized in XLIFF by means of the syntactic rule of *ExternalizableNews*. The resulting file can be sent to a translator, and the result can be parsed in to form an *ExternalizableNews* again.

```
001 ExternalizableNews is NewsContent
002 |- "<xliff …> … <source>"
003    Text
004    "</source> … </xliff>";
005 News is an ExternalizableNews;
006 GeneralNews is an ExternalizableNews;
```

Figure 8. Code example for a content interchage format.

In addition to Fig. 7, we also define *GeneralNews* and *News* as refinements of *ExternalizableNews* in order to inherit the syntactic rule (lines 5 and 6 of Fig. 8), replacing the sketch shown there.

With these definitions, *GeneralNews* can be exported in XLIFF using the syntactic rule for the production of XML. *News* can be imported from XLIFF using the syntactic rule to recognize XML.

VI. Summary and Outlook

This section recaps the paper and discusses future work.

A. Summary

Multilingual content management is in widespread use, and various requirements for the management of localized variants of global content exist. This paper discusses an approach to multilingual content management using context.

The Minimalistic Meta Modeling Language (M3L) is a general-purpose modeling language that has proven particularly useful for context-aware content management. In this paper we demonstrate how to employ M3L to model multilingual content management in a product-agnostic way. This way, properties of content management systems can be discussed independent of implementations.

B. Outlook

M3L can be executed by evaluating M3L statements. However, this kind of execution is not an adequate approach for building running systems. CMS products, on the other hand, are of practical importance. Therefore, in the future we want generate product configurations out of M3L statements.

To this end, software artifacts (e.g., configuration files and source code files) can be created using syntactic rules the way HTML is generated in the examples above. Alternatively, product-specific model compilers for content models [15] can possibly be adapted to M3L.

By means of generation, heterogeneous systems can be achieved by generating code for different CMS products from the same content model. This way, local repositories are free to choose an implementation technology.

The workflows for content localization need further work, in particular those incorporating external translators.

So far, internationalized content immediately creates a workflow task. In practice, sets of concepts are translated together. Therefore, a practical workflow needs to be enacted at a defined point in time on a selected content set.

Acknowledgment

The author wishes to express gratitude to his employer, Namics, for enabling him to follow his scientific ambitions.

The insights presented here are taken from numerous practical projects. Thanks to all the colleagues as well as the business and technology partners that helped understanding problems and developing ideas for their solution.

The anonymous reviewers of the original conference paper as well as those of this article are acknowledged for their valuable input that helped improving it.

References

[1] H.-W. Sehring, "Localized Content Management with the Minimalistic Meta Modeling Language," Proc. The Ninth International Conference on Creative Content Technologies (CONTENT 2017), pp. 8-13, Feb. 2017.

[2] S. Mescan, "Why Content Management Should Be Part of Every Organization's Global Strategy," Information Management Journal, vol. 38, no. 4, pp. 54-57, Jul./Aug. 2004.

[3] S. Huang and S. Tilley, "Issues of Content and Structure for a Multilingual Web Site," Proc. 19th Annual International Conference on Computer Documentation (SIGDOC '01), ACM New York, NY, USA, pp. 103-110, Oct. 2001.

[4] R. Lockwood, "Have Brand & Will Travell," Language International, vol. 12, no. 2, pp. 14-16, 2000.

[5] J.-M. Lecarpentier, C. Bazin, and H. Le Crosnier, "Multilingual Composite Document Management Framework For The Internet: an FRBR approach," Proc. 10th ACM Symposium on Document Engineering (DocEng '10), ACM New York, NY, USA, pp. 13-16, Sep. 2010.

[6] W. J. Hutchins and H. L. Somers, An Introduction to Machine Translation. Academic Press, 1992.

[7] E. Macklovitch and G. Russell, "What's Been Forgotten in Translation Memory," Proc. The 4th Conference of the Association for Machine Translation in the Americas on Envisioning Machine Translation in the Information Future (AMTA '00), pp. 137-146, Oct. 2000.

[8] Organization for the Advancement of Structured Information Standards (OASIS). XLIFF Version 2.0. [Online]. Available from: http://docs.oasis-open.org/xliff/xliff-core/v2.0/xliff-core-v2.0.html

[9] Globalization & Localization Association (GALA). TMX 1.4b Specification. [Online]. Available from: https://www.gala-global.org/node/59010

[10] P. Sandrini, "Website Localization and Translation," Proc. EU High Level Scientific Conferences, Marie Curie Euroconferences, MuTra: Challenges of Multidimensional Translation, pp. 131-138, May 2005.

[11] D. Jones, A. O'Connor, Y. M. Abgaz, and D. Lewis, "A Semantic Model for Integrated Content Management, Localisation and Language Technology Processing," Proc. 2nd International Conference on Multilingual Semantic Web (MSW'11), vol. 775, pp. 38-49, 2011.

[12] R. Miller, "Multilingual Content Management: Found in Translation," EContent, vol. 29, no. 6, pp. 22-27, Jul. 2006.

[13] P. Tonella, F. Ricca, E. Pianta, and C. Girardi, "Restructuring Multilingual Web Sites," Proc. International Conference on Software Maintenance, pp. 290-299, Oct. 2002.

[14] H.-W. Sehring, "Content Modeling Based on Concepts in Contexts," Proc. The Third International Conference on Creative Content Technologies (CONTENT 2011), pp. 18-23, Sep. 2011.

[15] H.-W. Sehring, S. Bossung, and J.W. Schmidt, "Content is Capricious: A Case for Dynamic System Generation," Proc. 10th East European Conference, ADBIS 2006, pp. 430-445, September 2006.

Allen's Interval Algebra and Smart-type Environments

Dineshen Chuckravanen, Jacqueline W. Daykin
Department of Computer Science
Aberystwyth University
(Mauritius Branch Campus)
Mauritius
dic4@aber.ac.uk,jwd6@aber.ac.uk

Karen Hunsdale
Department of Applied Management
Winchester Business School
University of Winchester
UK
karen.hunsdale@winchester.ac.uk

Amar Seeam
Department of Computer Science
Middlesex University
(Mauritius Branch Campus)
Mauritius
a.seeam@mdx.ac.uk

***Abstract*—Allen's interval algebra is a calculus for temporal reasoning that was introduced in 1983. Reasoning with qualitative time in Allen's full interval algebra is nondeterministic polynomial time (NP) complete. Research since 1995 identified maximal tractable subclasses of this algebra via exhaustive computer search and also other *ad-hoc* methods. In 2003, the full classification of complexity for satisfiability problems over constraints in Allen's interval algebra was established algebraically. Recent research proposed scheduling based on the Fishburn-Shepp correlation inequality for posets. This article first reviews Allen's calculus and surrounding computational issues in temporal reasoning. We then go on to describe three potential temporal-related application areas as candidates for scheduling using the Fishburn-Shepp inequality. We also illustrate through concrete examples, and conclude the importance of Fishburn-Shepp inequality for the suggested application areas that are the development of smart homes, intelligent conversational agents and in physiology with emphasis during time-trial physical exercise. The Fishburn-Shepp inequality will enable the development of smart type devices, which will in turn help us to have a better standard of living.**

Keywords*—*Allen's interval algebra; artificial intelligence; qualitative temporal reasoning; scheduling; smart-type reasoning.

I. Introduction

The study of problems involving temporal information or constraints can yield ornate patterns and structures [1]. Temporal reasoning is a mature research endeavor and arises naturally in numerous diverse applications of artificial intelligence, such as: planning and scheduling [2], natural language processing [3], diagnostic expert systems [4], behavioural psychology [5], circuit design [6], software tools for comprehending the state of patients in intensive care units from their temporal information [7], business intelligence [8], and timegraphs, that is graphs partitioned into a set of chains supporting search, which originated in the context of story comprehension [9].

Allen [10] introduced an algebra of binary relations on intervals (of time), for representing and reasoning about time. These binary relations, for example *before*, *during*, *meets*, describe *qualitative* temporal information, which we will be concerned with here. The problem of satisfiability for a set of interval variables with specified relations between them is that of deciding whether there exists an assignment of intervals on the real line for the interval variables, such that all of the specified relations between the intervals are satisfied. When the temporal constraints are chosen from the full form of Allen's algebra, this formulation of satisfiability problem is known to be NP-complete. However, reasoning restricted to certain fragments of Allen's algebra is generally equivalent to related well-known problems such as the interval graph and interval order recognition problems [11], which in turn find application in molecular biology [12][13][14].

The scope of this paper is to explore applications of Allen's interval algebra in the context of smart environments. Further, we combine theory from correlation inequalities with temporal reasoning concepts targeted towards smart-type scheduling applications. The inequality of interest is the Fishburn-Shepp inequality.

This paper is structured as follows: Section II, we describe various applications in temporal reasoning that include applications in smart homes, applications in intelligent conversational agents, and also applications in exercise physiology, followed by Section III, which describes conclusions and future work.

A. Allen's Interval Algebra

Allen's [10] calculus for reasoning about time is based on the concept of *time intervals* together with *binary relations* on them. In this approach, time is considered to be an infinite dense ordered set, such as the rationals $\mathbf{R}$, and a *time interval* X is an ordered pair of time points (X^-, X^+) such that $X^- < X^+$.

Given two time intervals, their relative positions can be described by exactly one of the members of the set $\mathbf{B}$ of 13 basic interval relations, which are depicted in Table I; note that the relations $X^- < X^+$ and $Y^- < Y^+$ are always valid, hence omitted from the table. These basic relations describe relations between *definite* intervals of time. On the other hand, *indefinite* intervals, whose exact relation may be uncertain, are described by a set of all the basic relations that may apply.

The universe of Allen's interval algebra consists of all the binary relations on time intervals, which can be expressed as disjunctions of the basic interval relations. These disjunctions are written as sets of basic relations, leading to a total of $2^{13} = 8192$ binary relations, including the *null relation* $\emptyset$ (also

TABLE I. THE SET $\mathbf{B}$ OF THE THIRTEEN BASIC QUALITATIVE RELATIONS DEFINED BY ALLEN [15].

Basic Interval Relation	Symbol	Endpoint Relations
X precedes (before) Y	p $(\prec)$	$X^+ < Y^-$
Y preceded-by (after) X	$p^\smile$ $(\succ)$	
X meets Y	m	$X^+ = Y^-$
Y met-by X	$m^\smile$	
X overlaps Y	o	$X^- < Y^- < X^+ < Y^+$
Y overlapped-by X	$o^\smile$	
X during Y	d	$X^- > Y^-,\ X^+ < Y^+$
Y includes X	$d^\smile$	
X starts Y	s	$X^- = Y^-,\ X^+ < Y^+$
Y started-by X	$s^\smile$	
X finishes Y	f	$X^- > Y^-,\ X^+ = Y^+$
Y finished-by X	$f^\smile$	
X equals Y	$\equiv$	$X^- = Y^-,\ X^+ = Y^+$

denoted by $\bot$) and the *universal relation* $\mathbf{B}$ (also denoted by $\top$). The set of all binary relations $2^{\mathbf{B}}$ is denoted by $\mathcal{A}$; every temporal relation in $\mathcal{A}$ can be defined by a conjunction of disjunctions of endpoint relations of the form $X < Y, X = Y$ and their negations.

The operations on the relations defined in Allen's algebra are: unary *converse* (denoted by $^\smile$), binary *intersection* (denoted by $\bigcap$) and binary *composition* (denoted by $\circ$), which are defined as follows:

$$\begin{aligned}
\forall\, X,Y: &\quad Xr^\smile Y \leftrightarrow YrX \\
\forall\, X,Y: &\quad X(r\textstyle\bigcap s)Y \leftrightarrow XrY \bigwedge XsY \\
\forall\, X,Y: &\quad X(r\circ s)Y \leftrightarrow \exists Z:(XrZ \bigwedge ZsY),
\end{aligned}$$

where X, Y, Z are intervals, and r, s are interval relations. Allen [10] gives a composition table for the basic relations.

Fundamental *reasoning problems* in Allen's framework have been studied by a number of authors, including Golumbic and Shamir [16][17], Ladkin and Maddux [18], van Beek [19] and Vilain and Kautz [20].

A *graph* is an ordered pair $G = (V, E)$ comprising a set V of *vertices* together with a set E of *edges*, which are 2-element subsets of V; if these subsets comprise ordered pairs of vertices then the graph is said to be *directed*. The following example illustrates a directed constraint graph expressing indefinite qualitative temporal information.

Example 1.1:

Consider the following CSP (constraint satisfaction problem) where the constraints are the relations of Allen's interval algebra, and each J_i, say job to be scheduled, is a time interval of the form (X^-, X^+).

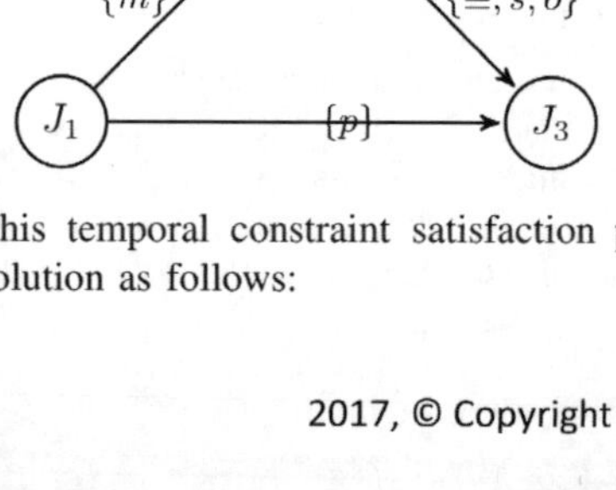

This temporal constraint satisfaction problem has a unique solution as follows:

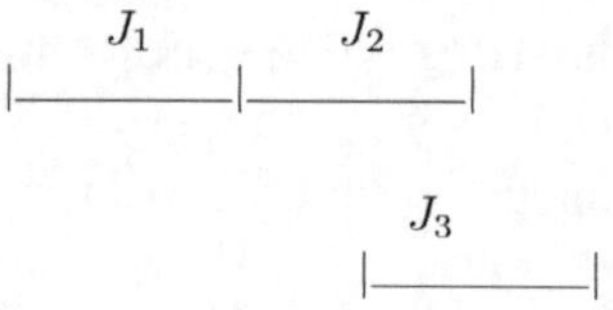

In contrast, the following CSP has no solution.

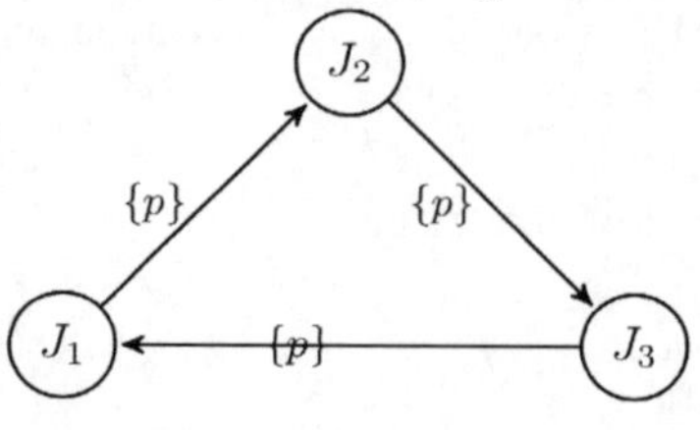

B. Subclasses of Allen's Interval Algebra

In this section we consider restricted temporal reasoning problems in which the relations are chosen from specified subsets of the set of all temporal relations on intervals, $\mathcal{A}$. Note that there are $2^{|\mathcal{A}|}$ such subsets, that is 2^{8192}, or approximately 10^{2466} – clearly a massive combinatorial issue.

For every subset $\Gamma \subseteq \mathcal{A}$ of temporal relations, the corresponding restricted satisfiability problem ISAT(Γ) is equivalent to CSP(Γ) - hence the complexity of ISAT(Γ) can be obtained via the complexity of CSP(Γ).

We now consider some well-known tractable subclasses of Allen's algebra.

Example 1.2 (The continuous endpoint class, $\mathcal{C}$):

This class includes all temporal relations, which may be defined using conjunctions of clauses of endpoint relations of the form $x = y$, $x \leq y$ and $x \neq y$, such that (1) there are only unit clauses, and (2) for each unit clause $x \neq y$, the clause form also contains a unit clause of the form $x \leq y$ or $y \leq x$.

It contains 83 relations, including $\{d,\ o,\ s\}$, $\{s^\smile,\ o^\smile,\ \equiv,\ f\}$, and $\{d^\smile,\ f^\smile,\ o,\ m,\ p\}$, (as well as the null relation, $\bot$). For example, the relation $\{d,\ o,\ s\}$ is defined by the following conjunction of endpoint relations (see Table I):

$$\begin{aligned}
&\{(X^- \leq X^+),\ (X^- \neq X^+),\ (Y^- \leq Y^+),\ (Y^- \neq Y^+),\\
&(X^- \leq Y^+),\ (X^- \neq Y^+),\ (Y^- \leq X^+),\ (X^+ \neq Y^-),\\
&(X^+ \leq Y^+),\ (X^+ \neq Y^+)\}.
\end{aligned}$$

The continuous endpoint class was first described and shown to be tractable by Vilain, Kautz and van Beek [21], and subsequently described by Ligozat in terms of "convex relations" with respect to a lattice representation [22]. This subclass has the computational advantage that the path-consistency method solves ISI($\mathcal{C}$) [23], [24], [21].

Example 1.3 (The pointisable class, $\mathcal{P}$):

This slight generalization of class $\mathcal{C}$ is defined in the same way as $\mathcal{C}$, but without the condition (2). It contains 188 relations, including all relations in $\mathcal{C}$ together with (non-convex) relations such as $\{d,\ o\}$, $\{d^\smile,\ o^\smile,\ f^\smile,\ f\}$, and $\{d^\smile,\ f^\smile,\ o,\ p\}$.

This class of temporal relations was first described and shown to be tractable by Ladkin and Maddux [18] and studied by van Beek and Cohen [24]. Although path-consistency is not sufficient for solving ISI($\mathcal{P}$) [23], it is for deciding ISAT($\mathcal{P}$) [18], [20]. Van Beek [23], [25] and van Beek and Cohen [24] give algorithms for solving ISI($\mathcal{P}$) in $O(n^4)$ time; van Beek specifies an algorithm for deciding ISAT($\mathcal{P}$) in $O(n^2)$ time [25].

Example 1.4 (The ORD-Horn class, $\mathcal{H}$):

This class is a strict superset of $\mathcal{P}$, defined using conjunctions of *disjunctions* of the endpoint relations in $\mathcal{P}$, and where each disjunction contains at most one relation, which is not of the form $x \neq y$. That is, the relations permit an ORD-clause form containing only clauses with at most one positive literal. It contains 868 relations, including all those in $\mathcal{P}$ together with relations such as $\{f^{\smile}, s, o\}$, whose endpoint relations are given by the set:

$$\{(X^- \leq X^+), (X^- \neq X^+), (Y^- \leq Y^+), (Y^- \neq Y^+), (X^- \leq Y^-), (X^- \leq Y^+), (X^- \neq Y^+), (Y^- \leq X^+), (X^+ \neq Y^-), (X^+ \leq Y^+), (X^- \neq Y^- \vee X^+ \neq Y^+)\}.$$

Nebel and Bürckert [15] identified this, via machine enumeration, to be the first known maximal tractable subclass, and, the unique greatest tractable subclass amongst those that contain all 13 basic relations – comprising over 10% of the full algebra. Further, they established that the path-consistency method is sufficient for deciding ISAT($\mathcal{H}$), implying its wider applicability [15].

Ligozat [26] showed that any subalgebra which contains all basic relations, and a relation, which is not ORD-Horn, will contain at least two of four "corner" relations: $\{d^{\smile}, s^{\smile}, o^{\smile}, f, d\}$, $\{o^{\smile}, s^{\smile}, d^{\smile}, f^{\smile}, o\}$ and their converses.

Example 1.5 (Starting point and ending point algebras):

Drakengren and Jonsson [27] discovered a large family of maximal tractable subclasses, "starting point" and "ending point" algebras, denoted $S(b), S^*, E(b), E^*$ - the parameter b is chosen from specified basic relations. The six algebras $S(b)$ & $E(b)$ contain 2312 elements each, and $S^\star$ & $E^\star$ contain 1445 elements each. For brevity we only define $S(b)$; for $E(b)$, $S^\star$ and $E^\star$ see [27].

Let $r_s = \{\succ, d, o^{\smile}, m^{\smile}, f\}$, and let $r_e = \{\prec, d, o, m, s\}$. Then, for $b \in \{\succ, d, o^{\smile}\}$, define $S(b)$ to be the set of relations r such that:

$$\begin{aligned} \{b, b^{\smile}\} &\subseteq r \\ \{b\} &\subseteq r \subseteq r_s \cup \{\equiv, s, s^{\smile}\} \\ \{b^{\smile}\} &\subseteq r \subseteq r_s^{\smile} \cup \{\equiv, s, s^{\smile}\} \\ r &\subseteq \{\equiv, s, s^{\smile}\}. \end{aligned}$$

The algebras allow for metric constraints on interval starting or ending points.

Initially, various computer-assisted exhaustive searches led to a classification of complexity within parts of Allen's algebra [27], [28], [29]. For further progress, it was understood that theoretical studies of the structure of Allen's algebra would be necessary, since using these methods to obtain a classification would require dealing with more than 10^{50} individual cases - clearly not feasible.

We proceed to consider an algebraic approach to the characterisation of tractable subclasses of relations.

C. Algebraic Closure Properties of Constraints

Jeavons *et al.* [30] developed a theory of *algebraic closure properties of constraint relations*, which can be used to distinguish between sets of relations, which give rise to tractable CSPs and those which give rise to NP-complete CSPs. In this theory the significant algebraic properties of a relation are the operations under which it is *closed*: in the sense of the following definition.

Definition 1.1: [30] Let R be an n-ary relation over a domain D, and let $\varphi : D^k \to D$ be a k-ary operation on D. The relation R is said to be *closed under* φ if, for all $t_1, t_2, \ldots, t_k \in R$, $\varphi(t_1, t_2, \ldots, t_k) \in R$, where $\varphi(t_1, t_2, \ldots, t_k) =$ $\langle \varphi(t_1[1], t_2[1], \ldots, t_k[1]), \varphi(t_1[2], t_2[2], \ldots, t_k[2]), \ldots, \varphi(t_1[n], t_2[n], \ldots, t_k[n]) \rangle$.

The algebraic approach to tractability refers to special properties of operations including: *idempotent, constant, unary, projection, semiprojection, majority, affine, or ACI (associative, commutative & idempotent)* - details in [30].

Further theoretical advances followed. In 2003, Krokhin *et al.* [31] completed the analysis of complexity for satisfiability problems expressed in Allen's algebra by showing that all known maximal subclasses were the only forms of tractability within this interval algebra: Allen's algebra contains exactly eighteen maximal tractable subalgebras and that reasoning within any subset not included in one of these is NP-complete.

Their purely analytical method makes extensive use of the operations defined in the algebra (converse, intersection and composition), while exploiting the fact that tractability of a subalgebra is a pertinent hereditary property in Allen's algebra. Importantly, both the result and the algebraic method can be used to classify the complexity in other temporal and spatial formalisms.

See [32] for a fuller account of this survey of temporal reasoning. The discussion of complexity and related computational issues leads naturally to the next section involving heuristics.

D. Posets and the Fishburn-Shepp Inequality

We now consider novel research proposed in [32], namely, to specify heuristics for scheduling based on representing a collection of intervals of time with constraints as a poset, and applying the Fishburn-Shepp inequality to guide a scheduling algorithm. In [32], applications are sought for this approach: we address this first step here by describing potential applications, which are also related to smart-type reasoning. First, we commence with overviews of the scheduling problem and the Fishburn-Shepp inequality.

Generally, a *schedule* of tasks (or simply schedule) is the assignment of tasks to specific time intervals of resources, such that no two tasks occupy any resource simultaneously – additionally, a requirement can be that the capacity of resources is not exceeded by the tasks. A schedule is *optimal* if it minimizes a given optimality criterion. However, our ultimate interest is in providing an algorithm to solve, or schedule, temporal constraint satisfaction problems; since we also consider indefinite qualitative temporal information, the solution may assign events simultaneously to intervals.

Let Q be a finite *poset* (partially ordered set) with n elements and C be a chain $1 < 2 < \cdots < c$. For (Q, C), a map $\omega : Q \rightarrow C$ is *strict order-preserving* if, for all $x, y \in Q$, $x < y$ implies $\omega(x) < \omega(y)$. Let $\lambda : Q \rightarrow \{1 < 2 < \cdots < n\}$ be a *linear extension* of Q, that is, an order-preserving injection.

A poset Q is equivalently a *directed acyclic graph (DAG)*, $G = (V, E)$; for temporal reasoning, the vertices represent time intervals, and edges between vertices are labeled with relations in Allen's algebra, which satisfy the partial ordering. For scheduling problems, a linear extension λ of Q (or G) can be used to schedule tasks: λ must respect interval constraints, that is relations between comparable elements. Algorithmically, a linear extension of a DAG, G, can be determined in linear time by performing a depth-first search of G; while G (Q) can be represented by an adjacency matrix.

The Fishburn-Shepp inequality [33] [34] is an inequality for the number of extensions of partial orders to linear orders, expressed as follows. Suppose that x, y and z are incomparable elements of a finite poset, then

$$P(x < y)P(x < z) < P((x < y) \wedge (x < z)) \quad (1)$$

where $P(*)$ is the probability that a linear extension has the property *. By re-expressing this in terms of conditional probability, $P(x < z) < P((x < z) \mid (x < y))$, we see that $P(x < z)$ strictly increases by adding the condition $x < y$. The problem posed in [32] concerns applying the Fishburn-Shepp inequality to efficiently find a favourable schedule under specified criteria, where a naive scheduling algorithm is also given together with an illustrative example. However, our focus here is in introducing application scenarios.

II. Applications in Temporal Reasoning

A. Applications in Smart Homes

Buildings consume a considerable amount of energy. Managing that energy is challenging, though is achievable through building control and energy management systems. These systems will typically monitor, measure, manage and control services for the lighting, Heating, Ventilation and Air Conditioning (HVAC), security, and safety of the building. They also permit a degree of scheduling, albeit they are often limited by static programming and may have no awareness incorporated of external events. For example, a building's HVAC system

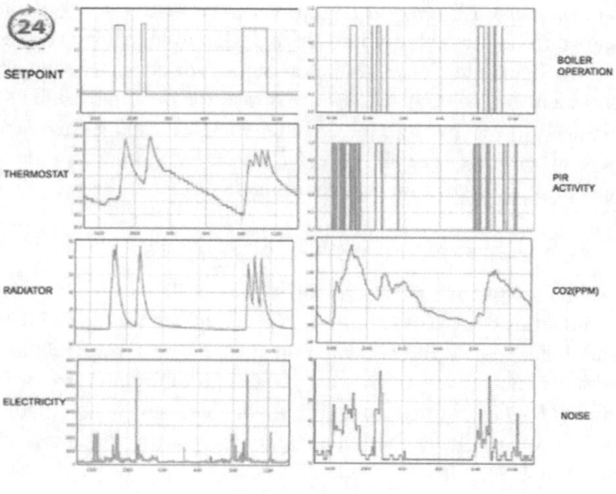

Fig. 1. Smart Home Temporal Data captured over 24 hours.

may heat rooms that are unoccupied as the setpoint has been programmed to be a certain temperature for a specified interval of the day (Figure 1). Clearly this is quite inefficient, and though motion detectors can play a role in actuating lights during periods of room occupancy, maintaining a comfortable indoor climate using similar sensors to detect people cannot provide the same benefits. Furthermore, the indoor climate is impacted by outdoor thermodynamic processes, as well as internal heat gains, which can be unaccountable (e.g., people, mobile equipment, etc). However, most modern non-residential building's energy management systems will be configured to turn building services on and off throughout the day using a pre-programmed schedule (e.g., a repeating daily pattern of heating use) and can also employ intelligent start-up controllers with external temperature compensation to delay the turning on of heating for example. Modern heating controllers (i.e., programmable thermostats) in homes can also have setpoints configured in a daily schedule (e.g., 6-8am: increase setpoint to 20°C, representing a waking-up phase; 9am - 4pm: heating deactivated or set to a maximum (e.g., 15°C); and from 5pm - 6pm: 21°C, representing a heating-up phase to anticipate arrival of an occupant from a workplace, and so forth).

Aside from heating control, homes can now also employ smart home systems to perform some degree of energy management and appliance automation. These systems are becoming more commonplace, particularly as the Internet of Things (IoT) paradigm is gaining more traction, whereby humans are bypassed, and machine to machine communication takes place (e.g., Smart Homes communicating with Smart Grids [35]) [36]. This gives rise to smart automation and reasoning where decision making can take place and determine when home appliances can be scheduled, particularly in the case of peak-load shaving [37] or demand response optimization [38]. In these cases, consumption patterns can be shifted to times of lower cost electricity. Appliance scheduling can be further classified by, for instance, their minimum required periods of operations, whether or not their operations can be interrupted, and if a human occupant is involved (i.e., in climate control scenarios). For instance, washing machines will have varying periods of operation depending on the program (wash, spin, dry) and cannot (typically) be interrupted if scheduled. Heating or cooling systems will have optimum start-up times to turn on in anticipation of occupants requiring the temperature of the house to be at a preset setpoint upon arrival. The Internet of Things has even enabled this particular scenario to be influenced by the distance an occupant is from the home or building, whereby the driving time is estimated via tracking of a Global Positioning System (GPS signal) [39]. In [40], driving patterns were analysed, and a programmable thermostat augmented with GPS control enabled energy savings of 7%.

The emerging Internet of Things in this respect will be responsible for huge volumes of temporal pattern data as shown in Figure 1 (i.e., timestamped sequences of events, be it a change in temperature, or a light being turned on and off, or the duration of activity of an entertainment system, etc [41]), thus also incorporating quantitative temporal information. In the smart home, the ability to detect user behaviour or house activities from this kind of temporal pattern data can provide a better understanding of how to identify patterns of energy use and thus determine when or how to gain energy savings. Naturally, the accumulative savings factor is increased many-fold in the smart city concept. Temporal pattern event detection inspired by Allen's relations has proved useful in smart environments: for anomaly detection in assisted living applications [42], and in activity monitoring [43]. In these examples, intervals represent the sensed data (cooking would imply the stove being on while an inhabitant is present in the kitchen [44] [45]). Such kinds of recognition are useful for determining normal behaviour of elderly occupants, and thus, for instance, detecting any onsets of dementia [46].

Clearly, efficient, or ideally optimized, scheduling of events can lead to enhanced savings of time and energy – it is with this goal that we propose applying the Fishburn-Shepp inequality, possibly to a specified subset of events in a larger complex system. Regarding this goal we consider Example 8 from [32] and illustrate applying it to a potential smart-type environment.

Example 2.1 (adapted from Example 8 in [32]): Consider a set of time intervals of events (alternatively jobs as in [32]), $\mathcal{E} = \{E_1, E_2, E_3, E_4, E_5, E_6\}$ with a partial order $\leq$ defined by $(X^- < Y^-) \wedge (X^+ \leq Y^+)$, which requires scheduling – note the partial order defines a subclass of Allen's interval algebra. Suppose that $\mathcal{E}$ is the poset / DAG shown below, where the edges have been labeled with satisfying temporal relations, and there are two triples of incomparable elements: $\{E_2, E_3, E_5\}$ and $\{E_2, E_3, E_6\}$. Then

$P(E_2 < E_3) \wedge (E_2 < E_5)) = 6/30$, $P((E_3 < E_2) \wedge (E_3 < E_5)) = 6/30$, and $P((E_5 < E_2) \wedge (E_5 < E_3)) = 18/30$;

$P((E_2 < E_3) \wedge (E_2 < E_6)) = 12/30$, $P((E_3 < E_2) \wedge (E_3 < E_6)) = 12/30$, and $P((E_6 < E_2) \wedge (E_6 < E_3)) = 6/30$.

The largest set of linear extensions corresponding to the first triple is when $(E_5 < E_2) \wedge (E_5 < E_3)$ and for the second triple is (w.l.o.g.) when $(E_2 < E_3) \wedge (E_2 < E_6)$. Their intersection has 6 linear extensions and we arbitrarily choose $E_1 < E_5 < E_2 < E_6 < E_3 < E_4$ as a schedule – so, although any linear extension would suffice we are selecting one which appears more "suitable" to satisfy: this illustrates the heuristic – the proposed algorithm is described in [32].

A parallel solution to this temporal constraint satisfaction problem from [32] is: $E_1 = (10, 20)$, $E_5 = (5, 10)$, $E_2 = (12, 23)$, $E_6 = (20, 22)$, $E_3 = (15, 20)$ and $E_4 = (18, 23)$. We will proceed to make this somewhat abstract schedule more concrete in a smart scenario.

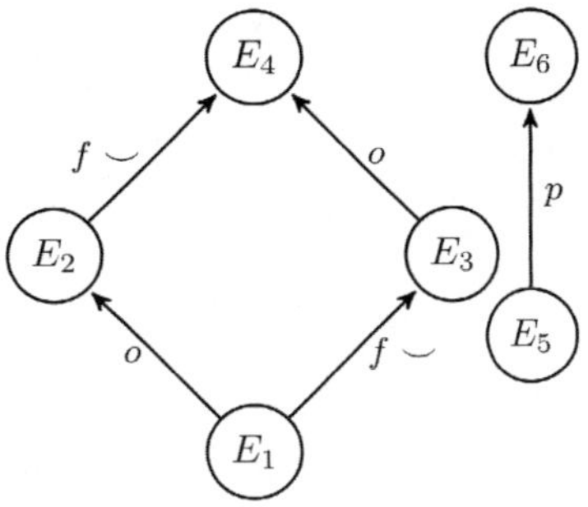

Suppose that the time intervals corresponding to the duration of events are interpreted in an integrated smart working and home environment as follows.

- E_1 denotes working in a flexible mode such as driving between locations and using mobile devices.
- E_2 denotes commuting home.
- E_3 denotes smart HVAC-type home ventilation.
- E_4 denotes activating and running a home appliance such as an oven.
- E_5 denotes robotic mowing of the lawn.
- E_6 denotes automated watering of the mowed lawn.

The temporal relations for this example are clarified as follows:

- E_1 *overlaps* E_2 as the employee could optimize work flow to organize driving home while completing their work assignment.
- E_2 *finishes* $\smile$ E_4 (E_2 *finished-by* E_4) as the GPS system tracking the employee's return home will synchronize with the oven timer so that the meal is cooked when the employee arrives.
- E_1 *finishes* $\smile$ E_3 (E_1 *finished-by* E_3) as the GPS tracker will also synchronize with the ventilation system so that the house is aired appropriately.
- E_3 *overlaps* E_4 as the ventilation should be completed before the meal is ready as the HVAC heating or air conditioning is likely to be activated with the residents' meal.
- E_5 *precedes* E_6 as the [electric & electronic] robot must return to a storage area before the watering starts.

Then an alternative "suitable" schedule (from the set of 6 linear extensions) can be specified as: $E_1 < E_5 < E_2 < E_3 < E_4 < E_6$. A solution using a 24-hour clock is given by: $E_1 = (09:00, 17:00)$, $E_5 = (10:00, 11:00)$, $E_2 = (16:15, 17:30)$, $E_3 = (15:30, 17:00)$, $E_4 = (16:30, 17:30)$ and $E_6 = (23:00, 24:00)$. Note that the noisy lawn mowing occurs after the resident has gone to work, while the garden is watered during an off-peak water consumption period and also when there is no sun.

We demonstrate another abstract type example of a "suitable" schedule for this poset, again with $(E_5 < E_2) \wedge (E_5 < E_3)$, but this time choosing $(E_3 < E_2) \wedge (E_3 < E_6)$. Then a linear extension is $E_5 < E_1 < E_3 < E_6 < E_2 < E_4$. A solution is $E_5 = (5, 10), E_1 = (10, 20), E_3 = (14, 20), E_6 = (15, 25), E_2 = (16, 50), E_4 = (18, 50)$. Note that each edge on this chain satisfies the partial order $\leq$. We conclude this section with:

Question, does this heuristic based on the Fishburn-Shepp inequality make finding a solution to a temporal constraint satisfaction problem easier?

B. Applications in Intelligent Conversational Agents

Intelligent conversational agents (CA) enable natural language interaction with their human participant. Following an input string, the CA works through its knowledge-base in search of an appropriate output string. The knowledge-base consists of natural language sentences based on a specific domain. Through the use of semantic processing using a lexical database with grouped sets of cognitive synonyms, word similarity is determined, with thus the highest semantically similar ranked string returned to the user as output.

Scripts consist of contexts that relate to a specific theme or topic of conversation. Each context contains one or more rules, which possess a number of prototype natural language sentences. An example of a scripted natural language rule is shown below, where s is a natural language sentence and r is a response statement.

<Rule-01>

s: I am having problems accessing my email account.
r: I'm sorry to hear that. Have you tried contacting IT support?

One such CA, as proposed by O'Shea *et al.* ([47] [48] [49]), uses semantics as a means to measure sentence similarity. The semantic-based CA is organized into contexts consisting of a number of similarly related rules. Through the use of a sentence similarity measure, a match is determined between the user's utterance and the scripted natural language sentences. Similarity ratings are measured in the range from 0 to 1, in which a value of 0 denotes no semantic similarity, and 1 denotes an identical sentence pair. The highest ranked sentence is 'fired' and its associated response is sent as output. The following algorithm describes the application:

1. Natural language dialogue is received as input from the user.

2. Semantic-based CA receives natural language dialogue from the user, which is sent to the sentence similarity measure.

3. Semantic-based CA receives natural language sentences from the scripts files, which are sent to the sentence similarity measure.

4. Sentence similarity measure calculates a firing strength for each sentence pair, which is returned and processed by the semantic-based CA.

5. The highest ranked sentence is fired and its associated response is sent as output.

The use of CAs can be applied to educational settings to better support teaching and learning and provide alternative learning environments. Computing underpins almost all areas of the modern world and many new opportunities in science and engineering could not have been realized without it. Thus, computer scientists have the potential to revolutionize societies, develop economic wealth and change peoples' lives. Employers need to ensure that the future generations have the skills required, which is only achieved through effective teaching and learning practices at our schools. If we do not engage at this level, we are unlikely to produce the number of computer scientists required to satisfy the demands of industry. However, teachers need support from the science community and industry to increase the number of students (especially girls) leaving school confident in coding, algorithmic thinking and computer science.

In order to develop knowledge exchanges, evidence is needed to assess its provision and accessibility. This would lead to studies discussing effective pedagogy and research into developing alternative approaches for engagement. However, opportunities may exist using alternative approaches, including artificial intelligence (AI). Artificial intelligence within teaching and learning is an opportunity to seek novel ways to deliver curriculum content. This may come in the form of a CA using intelligent adaptive learning methodologies. Such CAs or learning companions can accompany students asking questions, providing encouragement, offering suggestions and connections to resources, and help talk through difficulties as a teacher would demonstrate in class. Over time, the companion would 'learn' what you know, what interests you, and what kind of learner you are. Such research would raise ethical questions to the use of AI applications alongside human educators; however is it a challenge that will impact profoundly on the nature of teaching and learning? There is enormous potential for such research that remains undiscovered along with its associated benefits. AI will empower teachers, which will better inform them on how to manage the learning of their students.

The use of CAs using intelligent learning methodologies may also provide a means to support different types of conversations and thus, learning styles. The premise for such CAs is to guide students through the questioning process as opposed to simply providing an answer. Students will gain independence by answering questions for themselves through appropriate dialogue. This appropriate dialogue can be modelled using Allens interval algebra: the intervals of speech could satisfy the basic relation p, if one speaks before the other, or the relation o if their speech overlaps, and so on. In terms of scheduling a set of speech events with specified relations, that is constructing a linear extension by applying the Fishburn-Shepp inequality, we envisage an application for the learning impaired, which schedules the events sequentially to reduce confusion from simultaneous speech. This could then be integrated with the CA technology.

C. Applications in Physiology

In exercise physiology, the study of complex rhythms arising from the peripheral systems (for example, the cardiovascular system) and the central nervous system of the human body is important to optimize athletic performance while using a suitable type of pacing. Pacing plays an important part during athletic competition so that the metabolic resources are used effectively to complete the physical activity in the minimum time possible, as well as to maintain enough metabolic resources to complete that task [50].

Moreover, according to the Central Governor Model (CGM) [51], there is a central regulator that paces the peripheral systems during physical activity to reach the endpoint of that physical activity without physiological system failure. This central governor model of fatigue is a complex integrative control model, which involves the continuous interaction, in a deterministic way, among all the physiological systems, and that of the central system. There has been good evidence that the brain decreases its neural drive to protect the body from irreversible damage. The brain subconsciously controls the status of all systems of the body and it continuously calculates the metabolic costs to continue at the current pace as well as it compares that to the existing physical state. Based on this important information the brain adjusts the optimum pace so that the physical task can be completed in the most efficient way while simultaneously maintaining the overall homeostasis of the body by sustaining physical and mental capacity reserves. The brain protects the body through the regulation of power output during any form of physical exercise (especially long distance running or cycling exercise) with the ultimate aim of maintaining the body's homeostasis and protecting life.

Fig. 2 shows the CGM model of exercise regulation [52], which proposes that it is the brain that regulates exercise performance by changing continuously the number of motor units that are recruited in the exercising limbs. This change occurs in response to conscious and subconscious feedbacks that are present before and during the physical activity.

The goal of this central controller is to ensure that one always exercises with reserve and terminates the physical exercise bout without catastrophic failure of the body systems. The brain employs the feelings of fatigue to control the exercise intensity and duration of maintaining that exercise intensity so that these factors are always within the exercisers' physiological capacity. Therefore, Allen's interval algebra basic relations (precedes, meets, overlaps etc.) can be used to express those time intervals of switching among different pacing in a particular endurance physical activity for instance. The switching times between different pacing strategy themselves depend on many physiological factors (that have relation with

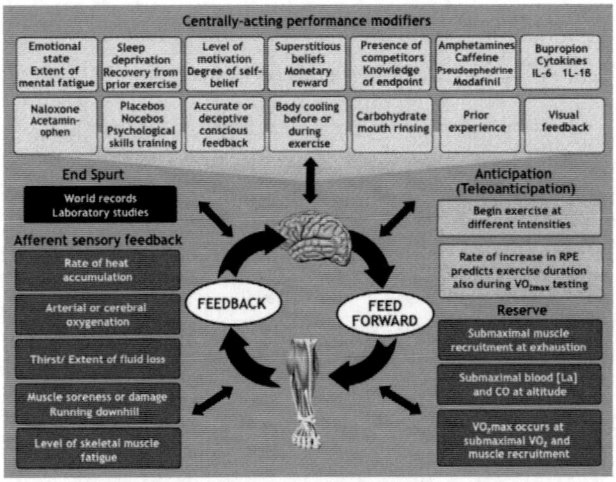

Fig. 2. The Central Governor Model of Exercise Regulation [52]

time of experiencing that factor) including exogenous factors such as surrounding temperature (change in temperature), change in air pressure especially running at higher altitudes and endogenous factors such as one's metabolic energy reserve (that are different at different times), accumulation of lactic acid (low or high depending on the duration of the exercise and the physiological processes' time to discard it), fluid loss through sweating depends on body heat, which changes through time, level of muscle damage as well as level of skeletal muscle fatigue change through time.

In this context, the decision making process involved when an athlete changes his or her pacing strategy during a particular race (and especially during endurance exercise) seems quite complex. However, the change in the decision making process could be simply explained by the basic relations in Allen's interval algebra. Consider the following scenario, shown in Fig. 3, where an athlete or runner needs to complete a 20-km race. An experienced runner will subconsciously be aware of the amount of energy resources they will need during the race so that they can effectively complete the race without catastrophic failure. During the race, there are both exogenous and endogenous factors, which will influence the optimal performance of the runner, and therefore she or he has to make important decisions as to when, or when not, to change their pacing during the race so that they can complete the race in the minimum time possible. For instance, there may be three major changes in the patterns of the running speed, power output, or pacing strategies that the runner could adopt for a long distance race such as the 20-km race [53]. Initially, on the first stage of the race, he or she will accelerate from a resting standing (or crouching) position to reach a constant optimal speed as determined by the runner's physical ability; meanwhile their heart rate (HR) will accelerate as well as their volume of oxygen consumption (VO2). In the second stage, they will maintain the same constant running speed for most of the race while their heart rate will be quite steady; moreover, the volume of oxygen consumption will be kept practically

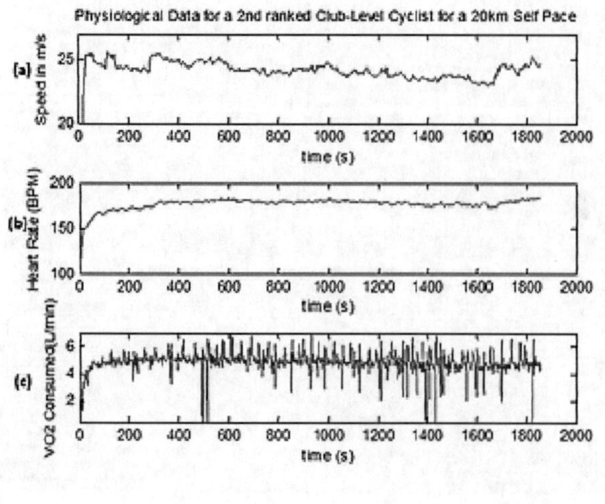

Fig. 3. Physiological data for a 2nd ranked club level cyclist for a 20km self pace under laboratory conditions under ambient body temperature

constant throughout the race. Finally, in the third stage of the race, the runner will accelerate or sprint in order to complete the race, which will at the same time, increase their heart rate as well as the rate of volume of oxygen consumption.

This represents one possible scenario that may occur during a race, which illustrates that Allen's temporal relations can be exploited to more clearly express the complex decision-making processes related to the human body during physical exertion, and hence allow for scheduling the pacing strategy adopted by a runner during a particular race. In fact, the Allen's interval algebra can be applied in smart-type devices, which in turn can help an athlete or sportsman in their decision-making process in real time. For instance, these smart-type devices can integrate various biomarkers computed from measured biosignals or physiological data (such as heart rate, pulse rate, sweating rate, volume of oxygen consumption) of the human body under physical activity (for example, running or cycling). These intelligent devices will help the users or the athletes in making important decisions by providing them useful biofeedbacks and will notify them whether they need to slow down to avoid catastrophic physiological systems failure, or they can just continue with same pace or speed.

III. CONCLUSION AND FUTURE WORK

This paper has brought together our previous findings with support for further and future developments. The management for appropriate dialogue using CAs or learning companions has been highlighted with the potential to support and enhance teaching and learning. This would be applied through the use of novel AI technologies and the application of intelligent conversational approaches using scheduling.

Previous research in temporal pattern reasoning surrounding smart homes has largely focused on activity recognition of inhabitants, and gaining an understanding from sensor data retrieved from indoor environments (such as electricity, temperature, light, or motion). The Internet of Things, however, will provide further dimensions of data from people (wearable sensors, tracking of GPS, etc.). This kind of outdoor data will provide additional context to the smart home and enable it to make better and more informed decisions as to how to actuate and control building services.

For example, returning to the case of augmented heating control using GPS - an occupant leaves the house and goes for a short jog (automatically disabling the heating as they leave) - as they run their own body temperature rises. The wearable sensors will be monitoring their temperature and their GPS coordinates. As they return and approach their home, the augmented heating control with the GPS system will turn on the heating, but will also take into account the occupant's current body temperature, and accordingly apply the appropriate heating control strategy (i.e., reducing the return-to-home setpoint from a previously higher setting and actuation time). In this case, the quantitative temporal information between arrival and heating activation will be lengthened as the temperature setpoint requirement will be reduced. This is just one of a myriad of possibilities that can be realized from the abundance of potential sensor data generated from the Internet of Things. We believe the relation between indoor and outdoor sensing (as well as any other sensing source for that matter) and reasoning strategies requires further exploration, and as part of our future research strategy we will investigate smart home event and action temporal reasoning from multiple data streams beyond enclosed indoor scenarios. In particular, smart-type scheduling is a key factor in energy-related issues.

We envisage enhanced synergy in the smart-environment by integrating intelligent CAs. Useful responses to even simple sentences such as *Where are my keys?* can have impact on human energy and stress levels and allow for more efficient use of time.

To date, physiological research into pacing strategies has focused on the amount of energy resources that are available for a runner to complete a long distance race. Also, pacing is crucial for improving human performance in time-trial physical exercise. Therefore, we propose that the future area in, which the exercise physiology field should endeavour to concentrate more on, is the optimal time in switching between the different types of pacing strategies, so that a race is completed successfully and in the minimum time possible without body systems' homeostatic failure. In order to achieve this, the various changes in pacing, namely, increasing pace, constant pace or decreasing pace, depends on each individual's resource capacity and endurance for each type of pacing so as to achieve the target or complete a physical endurance activity in the least possible time.

Therefore, we suggest that the decision-making process underlying the choice of the various pacing strategies can be informed through the application of Allen's time interval algebra, and the resulting scheduling can be easily controlled and applied to promote and improve world elite athletic performance. For example, the impact of facilitating the decision-making process of an elite athlete is enormous as he or she will feel more comfortable to tap into their inner optimized physical potentials, and hence boost overall confidence, which may contribute further to greater physical performances.

REFERENCES

[1] D. Chuckravanen, J. W. Daykin, K. Hunsdale, and A. Seeam, "Temporal patterns: Smart-type reasoning and applications," *in Proc. Patterns*, pp. 88–92, 2017.

[2] J. F. Allen, "Temporal reasoning and planning," in *Reasoning about Plans, J.F Allen, H.A. Kautz, R.N. Pelavin and J.D. Tenenberg (eds.)*. Morgan Kaufman, 1991, pp. 1–67.

[3] F. Song and R. Cohen, "The interpretation of temporal relations in narrative," *National Conference on Artificial Intelligence (AAAI-88)*, 1988.

[4] K. Nökel, *Temporally distributed symptoms in technical diagnosis*. Springer Science & Business Media, 1991, vol. 517.

[5] C. H. Coombs and J. Smith, "On the detection of structure in attitudes and developmental processes." *Psychological processes*, vol. 80, no. 5, p. 337, 1973.

[6] S. A. Ward and R. H. Halstead, *Computation structures*. MIT press, 1990.

[7] J. Juarez, M. Campos, A. Morales, J. Palma, and R. Marin, "Applications of temporal reasoning to intensive care units," *Journal of Healthcare Engineering*, vol. 1, no. 4, pp. 615–636, 2010.

[8] H.-U. Krieger, B. Kiefer, and T. Declerck, "A framework for temporal representation and reasoning in business intelligence applications." in *AAAI Spring Symposium: AI Meets Business Rules and Process Management*, 2008, pp. 59–70.

[9] A. Gerevini, L. Schubert, and S. Schaeffer, "Temporal reasoning in timegraph i–ii," *ACM SIGART Bulletin*, vol. 4, no. 3, pp. 21–25, 1993.

[10] J. F. Allen., "Maintaining knowledge about temporal intervals," *Commun.*, vol. 26, no. 11, pp. 832–843, 1983.

[11] I. Pe'er and R. Shamir, "Satisfiability problems on intervals and unit intervals," *Theoretical Computer Science*, vol. 175, no. 2, pp. 349–372, 1997.

[12] M. C. Golumbic, H. Kaplan, and R. Shamir, "On the complexity of dna physical mapping," *Advances in Applied Mathematics*, vol. 15, no. 3, pp. 251–261, 1994.

[13] R. M. Karp, "Mapping the genome: some combinatorial problems arising in molecular biology," in *Proceedings of the twenty-fifth annual ACM symposium on Theory of computing*. ACM, 1993, pp. 278–285.

[14] I. Mandoiu and A. Zelikovsky, *Bioinformatics algorithms: techniques and applications*. John Wiley & Sons, 2008, vol. 3.

[15] B. Nebel and H.-J. Bürckert, "Reasoning about temporal relations: a maximal tractable subclass of allen's interval algebra," *Journal of the ACM (JACM)*, vol. 42, no. 1, pp. 43–66, 1995.

[16] M. C. Golumbic and R. Shamir, "Algorithms and complexity for reasoning about time," in *AAAI*, 1992, pp. 741–747.

[17] G. Martin Charles and R. Shamir, "Complexity and algorithms for reasoning about time: A graph-theoretic approach," *Journal of the ACM (JACM)*, vol. 40, no. 5, pp. 1108–1133, 1993.

[18] P. B. Ladkin and R. D. Maddux, *On binary constraint networks*. Kestrel Institute Palo Alto, CA, 1988.

[19] P. Van Beek, "Reasoning about qualitative temporal information," *Artificial intelligence*, vol. 58, no. 1-3, pp. 297–326, 1992.

[20] M. B. Vilain and H. A. Kautz, "Constraint propagation algorithms for temporal reasoning." in *Aaai*, vol. 86, 1986, pp. 377–382.

[21] H. Kautz, "Constraint propagation algorithms for temporal reasoning: A revised report," *Readings in Qualitative Reasoning About Physical Systems*, p. 373, 2013.

[22] G. Ligozat, "Figures for thought: Temporal reasoning with pictures," AAAI, Tech. Rep. WS-97-11, 1997.

[23] P. van Beek, "Approximation algorithms for temporal reasoning," in *11th International Joint Conference on Artificial Intelligence (IJCAI'89)*, 1989, pp. 1291–1296.

[24] P. Van Beek, "Exact and approximate reasoning about qualitative temporal relations," Ph.D. dissertation, Citeseer, 1990.

[25] ——, "Reasoning about qualitative temporal information," in *AAAI'90*, 1990, pp. 728–734.

[26] G. Ligozat, ""Corner" relations in Allen's algebra," *Constraints*, vol. 3(2-3), pp. 165–177, 1998.

[27] T. Drakengren and P. Jonsson, "Eight maximal tractable subclasses of allen's algebra with metric time," *J. Artif. Intell. Res.(JAIR)*, vol. 7, pp. 25–45, 1997.

[28] ——, "Twenty-one large tractable subclasses of allen's algebra," *Artificial Intelligence*, vol. 93, no. 1-2, pp. 297–319, 1997.

[29] ——, "A complete classification of tractability in Allen's algebra relative to subsets of basic relations," *Artif. Intell.*, vol. 106, no. 2, pp. 205–219, 1998.

[30] P. Jeavons, D. A. Cohen, and M. Gyssens, "Closure properties of constraints," *J. ACM*, vol. 44, no. 4, pp. 527–548, 1997.

[31] A. Krokhin, P. Jeavons, and P. Jonsson, "Reasoning about temporal relations: The tractable subalgebras of Allen's interval algebra," *J. ACM.*, vol. 50(5), pp. 591–640, 2003.

[32] J. W. Daykin, M. Miller, and J. Ryan, "Trends in temporal reasoning: Constraints, graphs and posets," in *International Conference on Mathematical Aspects of Computer and Information Sciences*. Springer, 2015, pp. 290–304.

[33] P. C. Fishburn, "A correlational inequality for linear extensions of a poset," *Order*, vol. 1, no. 2, pp. 127–137, 1984.

[34] L. A. Shepp *et al.*, "The xyz conjecture and the fkg inequality," *The Annals of Probability*, vol. 10, no. 3, pp. 824–827, 1982.

[35] K. M. Tsui and S.-C. Chan, "Demand response optimization for smart home scheduling under real-time pricing," *IEEE Transactions on Smart Grid*, vol. 3, no. 4, pp. 1812–1821, 2012.

[36] X. Bellekens, A. Seeam, K. Nieradzinska, C. Tachtatzis, A. Cleary, R. Atkinson, and I. Andonovic, "Cyber-physical-security model for safety-critical iot infrastructures," in *Wireless World Research Forum (WWRF)*, 2015.

[37] G. T. Costanzo, J. Kheir, and G. Zhu, "Peak-load shaving in smart homes via online scheduling," in *2011 IEEE International Symposium on Industrial Electronics*. IEEE, 2011, pp. 1347–1352.

[38] J. Zhu, F. Lauri, A. Koukam, and V. Hilaire, "Scheduling optimization of smart homes based on demand response," in *IFIP International Conference on Artificial Intelligence Applications and Innovations*. Springer, 2015, pp. 223–236.

[39] A. B. John Krumm, "Learning time-based presence probabilities," in *Pervasive 2011*. Springer Verlag, June 2011. [Online]. Available: https://www.microsoft.com/en-us/research/publication/learning-time-based-presence-probabilities[retrieved2/2017].

[40] M. Gupta, S. S. Intille, and K. Larson, "Adding gps-control to traditional thermostats: An exploration of potential energy savings and design challenges," in *International Conference on Pervasive Computing*. Springer, 2009, pp. 95–114.

[41] A. Mohammed, A. Seeam, X. Bellekens, K. Nieradzinska, and V. Ramsurrun, "Gesture based iot light control for smart clothing," in *Emerging Technologies and Innovative Business Practices for the Transformation of Societies (EmergiTech), IEEE International Conference on*. IEEE, 2016, pp. 139–142.

[42] V. Jakkula and D. J. Cook, "Anomaly detection using temporal data mining in a smart home environment," *Methods of information in medicine*, vol. 47, no. 1, pp. 70–75, 2008.

[43] J. Ullberg, A. Loutfi, and F. Pecora, "Towards continuous activity monitoring with temporal constraints," in *Proc. of the 4th Workshop on Planning and Plan Execution for Real-World Systems at ICAPS09*, 2009, pp. 3833–3860.

[44] F. Palumbo, J. Ullberg, A. Štimec, F. Furfari, L. Karlsson, and S. Coradeschi, "Sensor network infrastructure for a home care monitoring system," *Sensors*, vol. 14, no. 3, pp. 3833–3860, 2014.

[45] X. Bellekens, K. Nieradzinska, A. Bellekens, P. Seeam, A. Hamilton, and A. Seeam, "A study on situational awareness security and privacy of wearable health monitoring devices," *International Journal On Cyber Situational Awareness (IJCSA)*, vol. 1, no. 1, 2016.

[46] P. C. e. a. Roy, "A possibilistic approach for activity recognition in smart homes for cognitive assistance to alzheimers patients," in *Activity Recognition in Pervasive Intelligent Environments*. Springer, 2011, pp. 33–58.

[47] K. O'shea, Z. Bandar, and K. Crockett, "Towards a new generation of conversational agents using sentence similarity," in *Advances in Electrical Engineering and Computational Science*, L. N. in Electrical Engineering, Ed. Sio-Long Ao and Len Gelman, Ed. Netherlands: Springer, 2009, vol. 39, pp. 505–514.

[48] K. O'shea, Z. Bandar, and K. A. Crockett, "Application of a semantic-based conversational agent to student debt management," in *World Congress on Computational Intelligence*, I. International, Ed. Conference on Fuzzy Systems, Barcelona: 978-1-4244-6917-8, 2010, pp. 760–766.

[49] K. O'shea, "An approach to conversational agent design using sentence similarity measures," *International Journal of Artificial Intelligence*, pp. 558–568, 2012.

[50] H. Ulmer, "Concept of an extracellular regulation of muscular metabolic rate during heavy exercise in humans by psychophysiological feedback," *Experimentia*, vol. 52, pp. 416–420, 1996.

[51] E. Lambert, A. St Clair Gibson, and T. Noakes, "Complex systems model of fatigue: integrative homeostatic control of peripheral physiological systems during exercise in humans," *B J Sports Med*, vol. 39, pp. 52–62, 2004.

[52] T. Noakes, "Fatigue is a brain-derived emotion that regulates the exercise behavior to ensure the protection of whole body homeostasis," *Frontiers in Physiology*, vol. 3, no. 82, pp. 1–13, 2012.

[53] D. Chuckravanen and S. Rajbhandari, "Management of metabolic resources for a 20-km cycling time-trial using different types of pacing," *Journal of Human Sport and Exercise*, vol. 10, no. 1, pp. 95–103, 2015.

Watermarking Technique for Images Captured with Cameras Using Color–Difference-Modulated Light

Kazutake Uehira and Hiroshi Unno
Kanagawa Institute of Technology
Atsugi, Japan
e-mail: uehira@nw.kanagawa-it.ac.jp

Abstract— **We propose a new optically written watermarking technique that can protect the portrait rights of real objects. It produces a watermarking pattern in the illumination light by modulating color differences. The illumination light that contains such watermarking is projected onto an object. An image of the object taken by a camera contains the same watermarking, which can be extracted by image processing. Therefore, this technique can protect the portrait rights of real objects. We discovered three findings through simulation where binary data were embedded as watermarking and we evaluated the accuracy with which the binary data were read out. The first was that the accuracy when color differences were modulated was higher than that when brightness was modulated. The second was that errors in reading out embedded binary data particularly tended to occur in dark areas, yellow areas, and areas that contained fine textures. The third was that we could satisfy both the invisibility and readability requirements of embedded data by using appropriate amplitudes of modulation.**

Keywords-Watermarking patterns; information embedding; portrait rights.

I. INTRODUCTION

We recently proposed a digital watermarking technique that used illumination light whose color differences were modulated as a technique to embed information in a captured image of a real object [1] and we demonstrated its feasibility. This paper presents the detailed results obtained from research, application conditions, and advantages with other methods.

Digital watermarking technology had originally been studied as a copyright protection technology for digital content. Copyright protection of digital content has become increasingly important as it has been progressively more distributed throughout various media because it consists of digital data that can easily be copied, which are exactly like that in the original. Digital watermarking is an effective way of protecting copyrights from being illegally copied and various techniques of digital watermarking for digital content have been developed [2]–[9].

Out of all the techniques to process various kinds of content, those for images have been studied and developed the most. Digital watermarking of image content is embedded in digital images in various ways. Embedded watermarking is invisible when the images are displayed in most of these ways. Although it is invisible, it can be read out by applying digital processing to image data.

Digital watermarking has also been used in printed images, where digital watermarking is embedded in the digital data before the images are printed [10]–[13]. This is to prevent the images from being copied from printed images by digital cameras or scanners. The watermarking in this case is read out from the image data produced by digital cameras or scanners.

However, whether digital watermarking is in the digital data of an image, in a displayed image on an electronic display or in a printed image, conventional digital watermarking rests on the premise that people who want to protect the copyrights of their digital content, i.e., content creators or content providers, have the original digital data and they can embed watermarking in the original digital data by digital processing.

However, this premise does not apply to some cases. Let us assume that a person took a picture of a painting at a museum with a digital camera. Since recent digital cameras are highly advanced, captured images have very high levels of quality and if the painting is invaluable as a portrait, e.g., an artwork that has been painted by a famous artist, the captured image of such an irreplaceable painting may be extremely expensive. Therefore, the portrait rights of well-known paintings should be protected. However, images captured with digital cameras do not have watermarking in this case because they have been captured by visitors to museums who are not interested in protecting portrait rights; therefore, they are susceptible to illegal use.

The portrait rights or copyrights of such images should be protected. We previously proposed a technology that could prevent the images of objects from being used in such cases [14], [15]. It used illumination that contained invisible watermarking. As the illumination contained the watermarking, the images of photographs of objects that were illuminated by such illumination also contained watermarking. We demonstrated the feasibility of this technique and demonstrated that this technique could also be applied to objects with curved surfaces [16]. We produced watermarking by spatially modulating the brightness of the illumination.

Accuracy in reading embedded information from the captured image of a real object is one of the most important evaluation indexes. Sufficient accuracy has not been obtained for various kinds of images when the amplitude of modulation has been small by using watermarking produced by modulating the brightness of illumination because the invisibility of watermarking in the degree of modulation

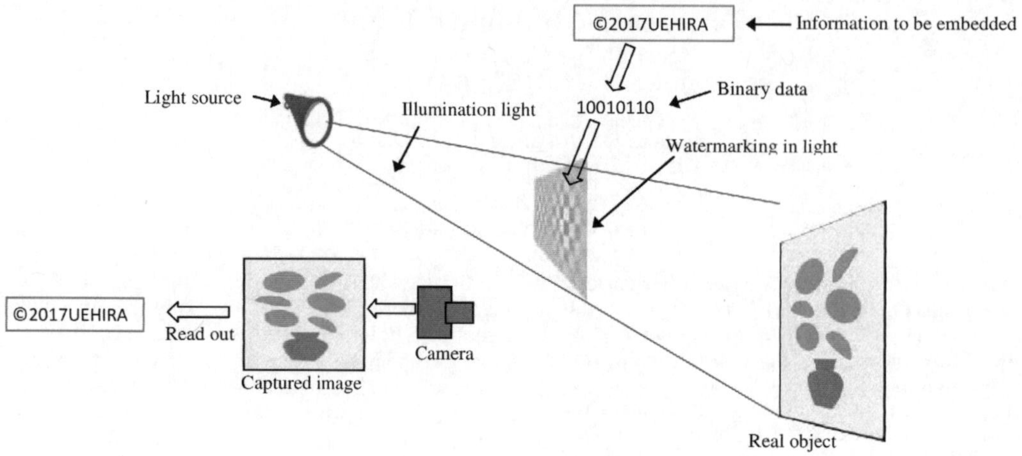

Figure 1. Basic concept underlying proposed technology

needs to be as small as possible. We studied a technique of watermarking using color difference-modulated light in this study to improve accuracy in reading embedded information. Uchida et al. used color difference signals to produce watermarking in digital images [17]. This was different from their method that produced watermarking with lighting that illuminated real objects; on the other hand, they electronically generated it directly in the digital images.

This paper is structured as follows. Section II explains the optical watermarking we propose and have studied thus far. Section III presents a new technique we used in this study that used color difference. Section Ⅳ describes simulations we conducted to evaluate the readability of the watermarking from captured images with the new technique. Section Ⅴ presents the results obtained from an experiment and discusses them. Section Ⅵ concludes the paper.

II. EMBEDDING WATERMARKING IN ILLUMINATION AND RELATED WORK

Figure 1 outlines the basic concept underlying our watermarking technique using illumination light to embed a watermark. An object is illuminated by projected light that

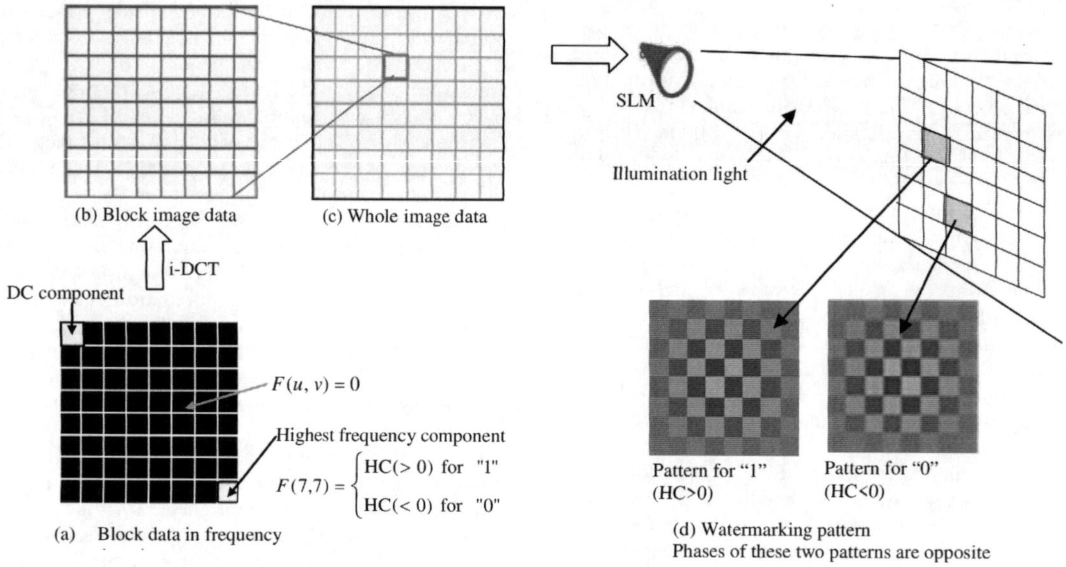

Figure 2. Procedure for producing optical watermarking

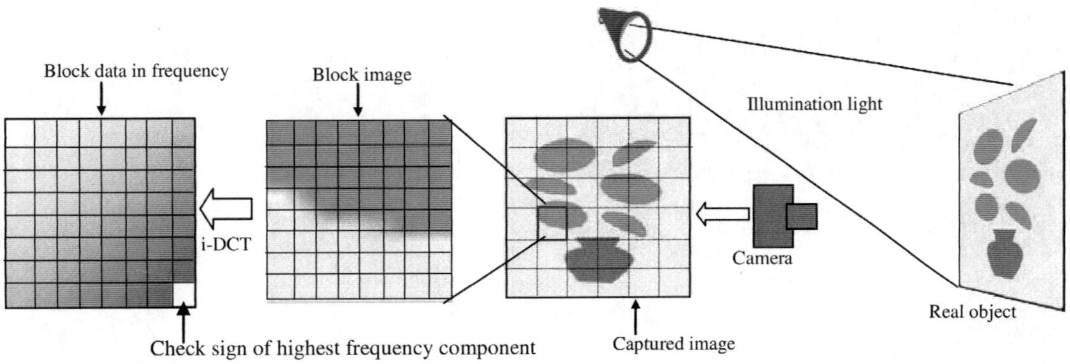

Figure 3. Procedure for reading out embedded information from captured image

contains an invisible watermark. A photograph taken of the object illuminated in this way would also contain the watermark. The watermark can be extracted in the same way as that used in conventional watermarking techniques for digital content.

There are various ways of possibly producing optical watermarking. Figure 2 illustrates the procedure for producing optical watermarking in our previous studies. A watermarking pattern was produced by modulating the brightness of the illumination light. First, we produced a watermark pattern as image data. The whole image area that corresponds to the illumination area in Fig. 2 is divided into numerous blocks. Each block has 8 x 8 pixels. First, each block datum is expressed in the frequency domain. Each block only has a DC component and a highest frequency component (HC) in both the x and y directions. The DC components in all blocks have the same value and they provide the brightness of illumination. The absolute value of HCs is the magnitude of modulation in brightness. We express one-bit binary data to be embedded by the sign of the HCs, i.e., if an HC is positive, it is expressed as "1" and if it is negative, it is expressed as "0". After the HCs for all blocks have been set, data in the frequency domain are converted to those in the space domain as image data by inverse discreet cosine transformation (i-DCT), and they are then input to a space light modulator (SLM) and changed to illumination light that illuminates real objects, such as paintings. We could use a commercial projector as an SLM for this purpose. Fig. 2 (d) shows the watermarking pattern in the light. These two patterns are for the "1" and "0" of binary data and the phases of these two are opposite.

The image of the object captured with a camera, $I(x,y)$, is given as a product of the reflectance of the object surface, $R(x,y)$, and the luminance of the projected light, $L(x,y)$, as:

$$I(x,y) = kR(x,y)\{L(x,y) + L_0\}, \quad (1)$$

where L_0 is bias luminance, such as that produced by room light and k is a constant.

The captured image also has a high-frequency pattern produced by modulating brightness because, as derived in Eq. (1), it is given by the product of the reflectance of the object surface and the luminance of the illumination light that contains the high-frequency pattern. This means the captured image also contain watermarking.

The watermarking pattern in the light and in the captured image cannot be seen by the human visual system because it is modulated at the highest frequency and the amplitude of modulation is small.

Figure 3 illustrates the procedure for reading out embedded information from a captured image. A captured image is divided into blocks in similar ways as that in the original, and then the pixel data in each block are converted into data in the frequency domain by discreet cosine transformation (DCT). Finally, the embedded data are read out by checking the sign of the HC for each block.

A technique based on a similar concept has been proposed by Zhou et al. [18] in related work. They temporally modulated the brightness of light by using a digital light processing (DLP) display. Although this was the same in terms of invisibly embedding information in projected light, luminance was temporally modulated it could not be applied to our purposes because our technology was targeted at shooting still images. Moreover, a method of using near infrared light has been studied [19] from the viewpoint of invisibly embedding information in light. Although this technique exploited the differences between sensory perceptions of humans and devices, it had the disadvantage that embedded information was eliminated by using an infrared cut filter.

III. OPTICAL WATERMARKING USING COLOR–DIFFERENCE MODULATION

We evaluated a method of producing watermarking in this study by modulating color differences instead of brightness. Luminance, i.e., chroma-blue and chroma-red (YCbCr) signals, was used to produce the watermarking. The basic procedure for producing the watermarking was the same as that in our previous study where we produced watermarking by modulating the brightness, Y. First, we produced the

(a) Image A (b) Image B

(c) Image C (d) Image D

Figure 4. Images used as objects in simulation.

original data of the color difference, Cb, as the frequency domain data for each block, then converted them into a block image in the space domain by i-DCT, and combined all block images into one image. The Y and Cr components were constant. After the YCbCr were converted into a red, green, and blue (RGB) signal, the RGB signal was input to a projector, and the watermarking pattern was projected onto the object.

A captured image was first converted into a YCbCr signal, and then the Cb component was divided into blocks and converted into data in the frequency domain by using DCT. Finally, the embedded data were read out by checking the sign of the HC of the Cb for each block in the same way as the method outlined in Fig. 3.

IV. SIMULATION

We evaluated the technique that used color difference modulation, which was explained in Section Ⅲ, by simulating the procedure in Fig. 3. The image data, $I(x,y)$, of an object that was captured with a camera were obtained using Eq. (1).

We used standard images as objects that had 512x512 pixels, as shown in Fig. 4, i.e., we used RGB pixel values of standards images as the reflectance of the object surface, $R(x,y)$, in Eq. (1).

We first generated the initial data of Cb in the frequency domain for $L(x,y)$ in Eq.(1), as shown in Fig. 2 (a). The data were generated for each block that had 8 x 8 components. Therefore, the $L(x,y)$ used in this simulation is given as:

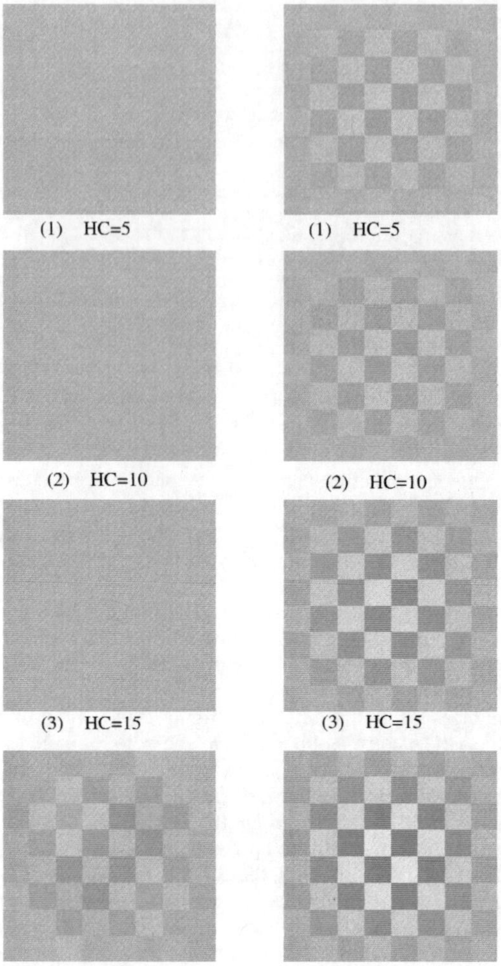

(1) HC=5 (1) HC=5

(2) HC=10 (2) HC=10

(3) HC=15 (3) HC=15

(4) HC=20 (4) HC=20

(a) Modulating Cb (b) Modulating Y

Figure 5. Luminance distribution images of projected light L(x,y) These are magnified images of block

$$L(x,y) = \frac{1}{4}\sum_{u=0}^{7}\sum_{v=0}^{7} C(u)C(v)F(u,v) \times \cos\frac{(2m+1)u\pi}{16}\cos\frac{(2n+1)v\pi}{16}, \quad (2)$$

where m and n are the pixel coordinates within the block and are given as:

$$m = \mathrm{mod}(512, y) \text{ and} \quad (3)$$
$$n = \mathrm{mod}(512, x) . \quad (4)$$

Here, mod (i,j) represents the remainder when i is divided by

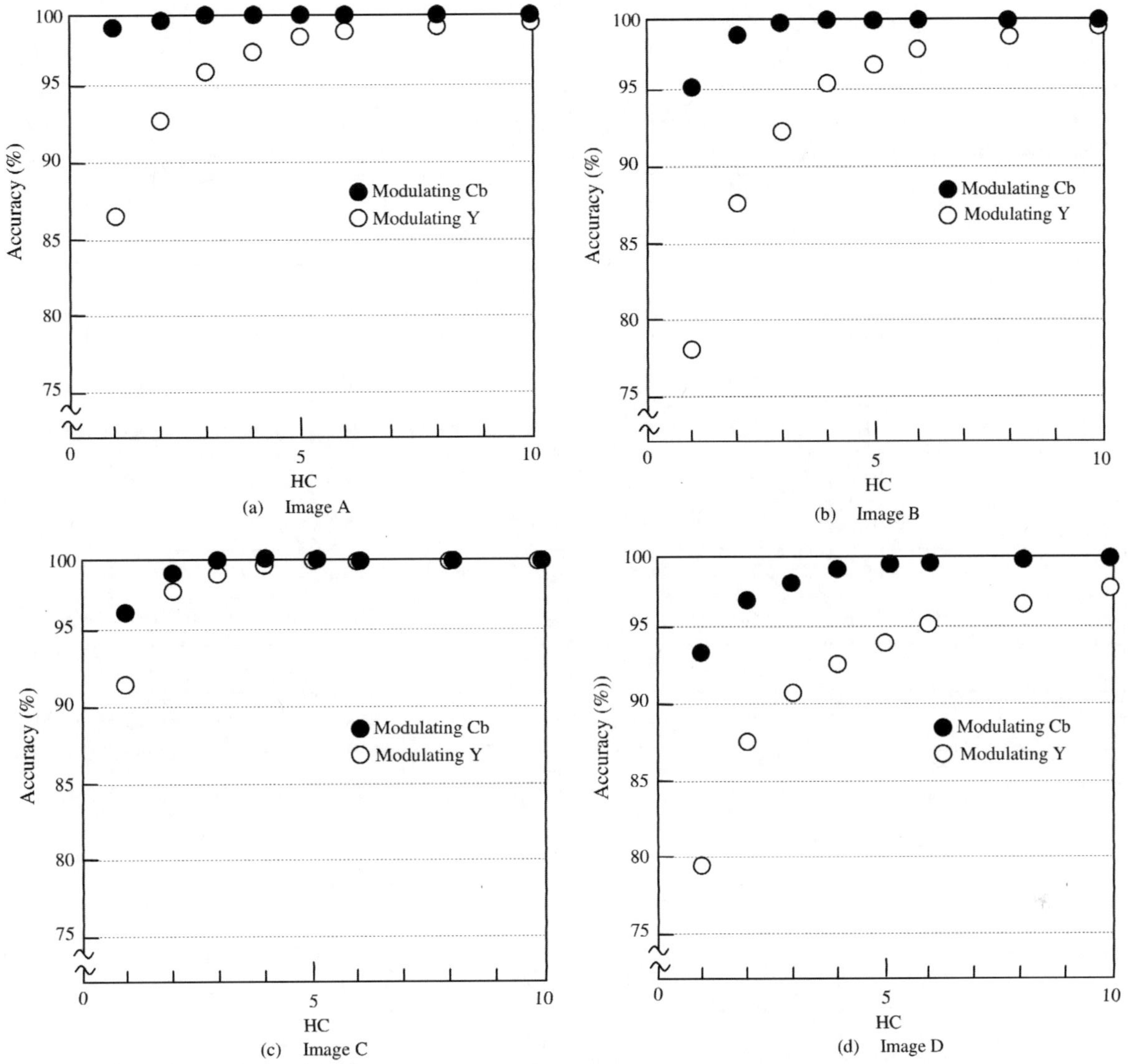

Figure 6. Accuracy in reading out binary data.
Accuracy indicates percentage of data correctly read out from 4096 binary data.

j. $F(u,v)$ in Eq. (2) is given as:

$$F(u,v) = \begin{cases} 200 & \text{for} \quad u,v = 0 \\ HC & \text{for} \quad u,v = 7 \\ 0 & \text{for} \quad u,v \neq 0 \text{ or } 7 \end{cases} \tag{5}$$

The number of blocks of the initial data in the frequency domain was set to 64 x 64 (=4096) to make the number of pixels of $L(x,y)$ equal the number of pixels of $R(x,y)$, i.e., 512 x 512. The signs of the highest frequency component (HC) for each block were determined depending on whether to embed "1" or "0" in that block. The same number of "1" and "0" were randomly embedded. The magnitude of HC in the original data was changed from one to 20 as an experimental parameter, while Y, Cr, and L_0 were set to correspond to constant values of 200, 0, and 40. These values were the gray levels of image data whose maximum was 255. We embedded a watermarking pattern for reference by using our previous method, where we modulated Y. Here, Cb and Cr were set to zero, and L_0 was set to 40. Figure 5 has images of $L(y,x)$ when HC was 5, 10, 15 and 20. These images are magnified images of a block.

After $I(x,y)$ was derived with Eq. (1) and it was converted into YCbCr format data, it was divided into 4096 (64 x 64)

TABLE I ACCURACY IN READING OUT BINARY DATA

Magnitude of HC	Accuracy in reading out binary data (%)							
	Image A		Image B		Image C		Image D	
	Modulating Cb	Modulating Y	Cb	Y	Cb	Y	Cb	Y
HC=1	99.1	86.8	95.2	78.4	95.9	91.6	79.6	93.6
2	99.9	92.5	99.1	87.8	99.6	97.9	87.5	97.0
3	**100.0**	95.6	99.7	92.5	99.9	99.3	90.7	98.2
4	**100.0**	97.5	99.9	95.6	99.9	99.6	92.7	99.0
5	**100.0**	98.4	99.9	97.0	99.9	99.7	94.3	99.3
6	**100.0**	98.7	99.9	97.9	**100.0**	99.9	95.2	99.4
8	**100.0**	99.3	**100.0**	99.1	**100.0**	99.9	96.8	99.8
10	**100.0**	99.4	**100.0**	99.7	**100.0**	**100.0**	97.8	99.9
12	**100.0**	99.5	**100.0**	99.9	**100.0**	**100.0**	98.6	99.9
14	**100.0**	99.6	**100.0**	99.9	**100.0**	**100.0**	98.9	**100.0**
16	**100.0**	99.6	**100.0**	99.9	**100.0**	**100.0**	99.1	**100.0**
18	**100.0**	99.7	**100.0**	99.9	**100.0**	**100.0**	99.2	**100.0**
20	**100.0**	99.8	**100.0**	99.9	**100.0**	**100.0**	99.3	**100.0**

blocks, each whose 8 x 8 pixels and Cb components were converted into data in the frequency domain by the DCT for each block.

Embedded data were read out by checking the sign of the highest frequency component of the Cb for each block. The accuracy with which data were read out was evaluated based on the percentage of data that were correctly read out from 4096 binary data.

V. RESULTS AND DISCUSSION

Figure 6 and Table I indicate the accuracy with which the binary data were read out. The results reveal that the accuracy when Cb was modulated is higher than that when Y was modulated for all four images. When Cb was modulated, the accuracy for Image A was over 99 % even at the HC of one, and it reached 100% when HC was three. It was over 99% for HC over two for Images B and C. That for Image D was over 99% for HC over four. The accuracies for all these four images reached 100% at HCs of 6–14. In contrast, the accuracy when Y was modulated was smaller by over 10% than that when Cb was modulated for the HC of one. They became 100% for HCs over 10.

It can be seen from Fig. 6 and Table I that the accuracy differs depending on images. Figure 7 indicates where the readout errors occurred in each image when color differences were modulated and presents the results when HC was set to one. The areas in red in the images are blocks in which errors had occurred. It can be seen from Fig. 7 that errors particularly tended to occur in dark, yellow, and other areas that contained fine textures. This is because the reflectance there was low and the high frequency component became so small that the sign was reversed under the influence of a slight amount of noise. It is also reasonable for errors to have tended to occur in finely textured areas because such areas contained large high frequency components and functioned as noise for watermarking. The main reason the errors occurred in yellow areas is that the Cb component of YCbCr was very small for these areas because yellow does not contain blue components.

Figure 8 is a reference that shows blocks where readout errors occurred in images when watermarking was generated by modulating brightness Y. It can be seen that there are many errors that occurred on the pattern edge. Not many such errors can be seen when Cb was modulated, as indicated in Fig. 7. Blocks marked A to D, which are

(a) Image A

(b) Image B

(c) Image C

(d) Image D

Figure 7. Blocks where readout error occurred when HC was set to one.
Red squares indicate blocks where readout error occurred.

surrounded by dashed circles in Fig. 8, are examples on pattern edges where errors occurred. The magnitude of the highest frequency component, F(7,7), in these blocks in the original image that was not modulated are summarized in Table II , where it can be seen that the highest frequency component for Y is larger than that for Cb. Therefore, when watermarking was generated by modulating Y, the influence of the high frequency component of the object image was more strongly received in the positive/negative determination of the highest frequency component of the modulated image. This is the main reason the accuracy when Cb was modulated was higher than that when Y was modulated.

It is possible that these two methods can improve the accuracy with which the embedded data are read out by taking into consideration the results in Fig. 6, Fig. 7, and Table I . The first method involves embedding watermarking by avoiding error-prone areas, such as dark and yellow areas.

TABLE II EXAMPLES OF VALUE OF HIGHEST FREQUENCY COMPONENT OF BLOCK ON PATTERN EDGE

	Y	Cb
A	-1.29	0.41
B	0.75	0.64
C	-0.29	0.08
D	0.80	0.08

(a) Image A

(b) Image B

(c) Image C

(d) Image D

Figure 8. Blocks where readout errors occurred when luminance was modulated (HC= 1). Red squares indicate blocks where readout errors occurred.

The second entails the use of error correction techniques, where many of these are used in the fields of communication. We used majority voting as an error correction method in our previous study [14], where we also used brightness modulation. It embedded the same 1-bit data into three blocks that were sufficiently separated from one another and when embedded data were read out, we decided whether to use majority voting if their readout data differed. Accuracy reached 100% even it was less than 90%. This technique of modulating color differences can be very accurate by combining it with error correction technologies.

Figure 5 indicates that modulating Cb is superior to modulating Y in terms of invisibility. Consequently, the technique of modulating Cb is better than that of modulating Y for both the readability and invisiblity requirements of embedded watermarking. Figure 9 presents the captured images simulated by using Eq. (1) when HC was set to five. We could not see any watermarking patterns in the images. These results indicate that we could satisfy both the invisibility and readability requirements of embedded data by using appropriate HC ranges.

(a) Image A

(b) Image B

(c) Image C

(d) Image D

Figure 9.Captured images simulated using Eq. 1 when HC was set to five

VI. CONCLUSION AND FUTURE WORK

We developed a technique that could embed an invisible watermarking pattern into captured images of real objects using illumination that contained the pattern. We embedded the pattern into the illumination by modulating color differences.

We discovered four main findings through simulation in this study. The first was that the accuracy when modulating Cb was higher than that when modulating Y. The second was that errors in reading out embedded binary data particularly tended to occur in dark, yellow, and other areas that contained fine textures. The third was that we could satisfy both the invisibility and readability requirements of embedded data by using appropriate HC ranges. The fourth was that we found that this technique of modulating color differences could be a very accurate method when combined with error correction technology.

We intend to examine detailed conditions on the invisibility of watermarks in the future. Future research will also involve quantitatively finding what effects there are when error correction is added to the technique proposed in this research. Moreover, we will examine the effects of image compression on the accuracy with which embedded information could be read out because the captured image has been handled in compressed form in many cases.

ACKNOWLEDGMENTS

This study has been supported by a Japan Society for the Promotion of Science (JSPS) Research Institute Grant: No. 16H02820.

REFERENCES

[1] K. Uehira and H. Unno, "Optical Watermark Pattern Technique using Color–Difference Modulation," Proceedings of PATTERNS 2017, 2017.

[2] I. J. Cox, J. Kilian, F. T. Leighton, and T. Shamoon, "Secure spread spectrum watermarking for multimedia," IEEE Trans. Image Process., Vol. 6, No. 12, pp. 1673–1687, 1997.

[3] M. D. Swanson, M. Kobayashi, and A. H. Tewfik, "Multimedia data-embedding and watermarking technologies," Proc. IEEE, Vol. 86, No. 6, pp. 1064–1087, 1998.

[4] M. Hartung and M. Kutter, "Multimedia watermarking techniques," Proc IEEE, Vol. 87, No.7, pp. 1079–1107, 1999.

[5] G. C. Langelaar, I. Setyawan, and R. L. Lagendij, "Watermarking digital image and video data," IEEE Signal Processing Magazine, Vol. 17, No.5, pp. 20–46, 2000.

[6] J. Haitsma and T. Kalker, "A Watermarking Scheme for Digital Cinema," ICIP2001, Vol. 2, pp. 487–489, 2001.

[7] Digital cinema system specification V1.2, Digital Cinema Initiatives, Mar. 2008.

[8] S. Goshi, H. Nakamura, H. Ito, R. Fujii, M. Suzuki, S. Takai, and Y. Tani, "A New Watermark Surviving after Re-shooting the Images Displayed on a Screen," KES2005, LNAI3682, pp. 1099–1107, 2005.

[9] K. Okihara, Y. Inazumi, and H. Kinoshita, "A Watermark Method that Improves the Relationship Between the Number of Embedded Bits and Image Degradation," IEIJ, Vol. 58, No. 10, pp. 1465–1467, 2004.

[10] T. Mizumoto and K. Matsui, "Robustness investigation of DCT digital watermark for printing and scanning," Trans. IEICE (A), Vol. J85-A, No. 4, pp. 451–459, 2002.

[11] M. Ejima and A. Miyazaki, "Digital watermark technique for hard copy image," Trans. IEICE (A), Vol. J82-A, No. 7, pp. 1156–1159, 1999.

[12] Y. Horiuchi and M. Muneyasu, "Information Embedding to the Printing Images Based on DCT," Proc. of ITC-CSCC2004, No. 7F3P50-1-4, 2004.

[13] Z. Liu, "New trends and challenges in digital watermarking technology: Application for printed materials" in Multimedia Watermarking Techniques and Applications, B. Furht and D. Kirovski, pp. 289–305, Auerbach Publications, 2006

[14] K. Uehira and M. Suzuki, "Digital watermarking technique using brightness-modulated light," Proceedings of the IEEE ICME2008, pp. 257–260, 2008.

[15] Y. Ishikawa, K. Uehira, and K. Yanaka, "Practical Evaluation of Illumination Watermarking Technique Using Orthogonal Tranforms," Journal of Display Technology, Vol. 6, No. 9, pp. 351–358, 2010.

[16] M. Komori and K. Uehira, "Optical watermarking technology for protecting portrait rights of three-dimensional shaped real objects using one-dimensional high-frequency patterns," Journal of Electronic Imaging, Vol. 22, No. 3, pp. 033004-1 to 033004-7, 2013.

[17] Y. Goto and O. Uchida, "Recognizable digital watermarking for printed materials embedding in hue component," Proceedings of the IIEEJ Image Electronics and Visual Computing Workshop 2010, 2P-9, 2010.

[18] L. Zhou, S. Fukushima, and T. Naemura, "Dynamically Reconfigurable Framework for Pixel-level Visible Light Communication Projector," Proc. of SPIE Vol. 8979 89790J-1, 2014.

[19] T. Yamada, S. Gohshi, and I. Echizen, "Re-shooting prevention based on difference between sensory perceptions of humans and devices," Proc. of the 17th International Conference on Image Processing, pp. 993–996, 2010.

Method to Use Low-priced Data-glove Effectively Based on Medical Knowledge for Hand Motion Pattern

Kenji Funahashi
Department of Computer Science
Nagoya Institute of Technology
Nagoya 466–8555 Japan
Email: kenji@nitech.ac.jp

Yutaro Mori[1] Hiromasa Takahashi[2]
Nagoya Institute of Technology
([1]present: NEC Solution Innovators, Ltd.)
([2]present: Chubu Electric Power Co.,Inc.)
[1]Email: moriyu@center.nitech.ac.jp
[2]Email: hiromasa@center.nitech.ac.jp

Yuji Iwahori
Department of Computer Science
Chubu University
Kasugai, Aichi 487-8501 Japan
Email: iwahori@cs.chubu.ac.jp

***Abstract*—A data glove is one of the major interfaces used in the field of virtual reality. In order to get detailed data about the finger joint angles, we must use a data glove with many sensors. However, a data glove with many sensors is expensive and a low-priced data glove does not have enough sensors to capture all the hand data correctly. We propose a method to obtain all finger joint angles by estimating the pattern of hand motion from the low-priced data glove sensor values. In our experiment system, we assumed some representative hand motion patterns as grasping behavior based on medical knowledge. We also assumed that other hand motions can be represented by synthetic motion of the representative patterns. In this paper, we used the data glove with sensors covering two joints of each finger. And we also estimate the finger joint angles when using the data glove that sensors cover only the middle angle of each finger.**

Keywords–Data-glove; Hand motion estimation; Finger joint angles estimation; Medical knowledge.

I. INTRODUCTION

Virtual Reality (VR) is a rapidly growing research field in recent years. VR technologies give us various advantages. There are simulators to practice an operation and to fly a plane as examples of VR technologies. These simulators enable us to avoid the risk and to save on cost. VR researches that targets to households also have been attracted. A data glove is one of the major interfaces, which are used in the field of VR. It measures curvatures of fingers using bend sensors. In our laboratory, we propose a method to get plausible user hand motion pattern from the low-cost glove [1]. In our first work, we use 5DT Data Glove (see Figure 1) whose sensors cover two joints of each finger. Then, we estimate finger joint angles when using the data glove DG5 VHand (see Figure 2) whose sensors cover only the middle angle of each finger.

The rest of the paper is structured as follows. In Section II, we present a state of the art of data gloves. In Section III, we describe a method how to estimate finger joint angels. In Section IV, we describe about representative hand motion patterns based on medical knowledge. In Section V, we apply this method to the data-glove whose sensor positons are limited. In Section VI, the experimental results are shown. In Section VII, we consider the difference between users' hand shapes. In Section VIII, the experimental results for hand shape are shown. Finally, we conclude in Section IX.

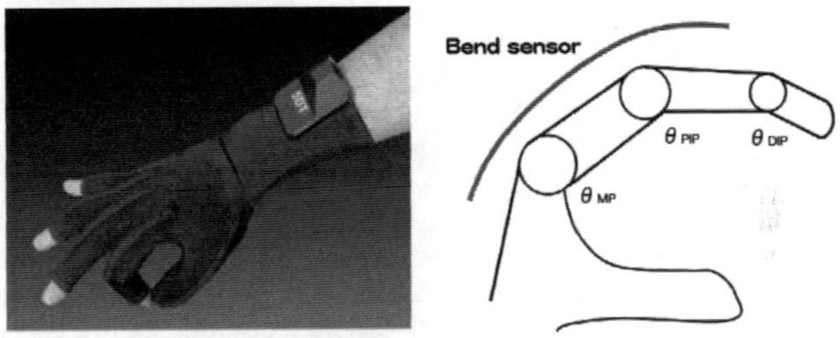

Figure 1. 5DT Data Glove 5 Ultra

Figure 2. DG5 VHand

II. STATE OF THE ART

In order to obtain accurate hand motions, it is necessary to use a data glove, i.e. Immersion CyberGlove, which has many sensors, but it is expensive. It is preferable that an interface is small scale and low cost. Various types of researches about data glove have been conducted [2][3][4][5]. On the other hand, there is a low cost data glove, which measures an angle for each finger through one sensor. But it cannot get detailed data directly. For example, the 5DT Data Glove 5 Ultra and DG5 VHand have a single sensor on each finger, so they have five sensors in the whole hand (see Figures 1 and 2). However, there are three finger joints for each finger, a single sensor can not measure all of these three angles directly.

Our proposed novel method estimates the kind of hand motion patterns using each relation among angles of fingers

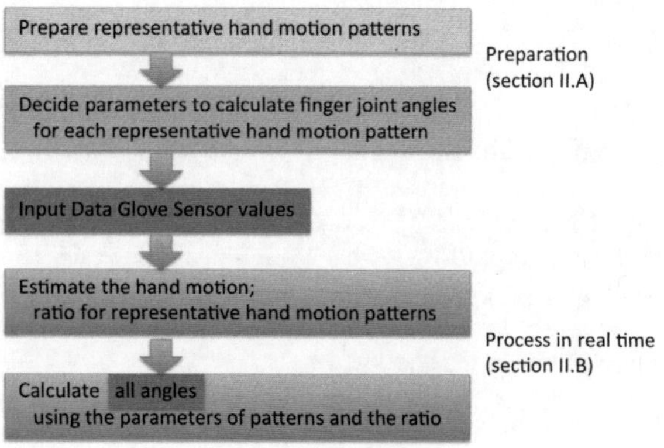

Figure 3. Overview of method

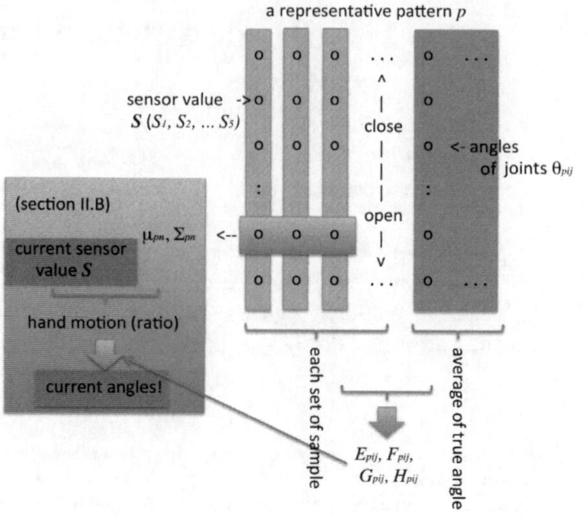

Figure 4. Detail of method

during operation. Then, it estimates all finger joint angles by estimating the types of hand motion patterns from the correlation between each finger angle in the hand motion pattern. We assume some representative hand motion patterns based on medical knowledge [6], and consider that other hand motions can be represented as a synthetic motion of the representative hand motion patterns. In addition, we calculate the ratio of each representative motion pattern. Moreover, estimating each finger angle using the result, we express any hand motion patterns other than the representative hand motions.

III. Estimation of Finger Joint Angles

In Section III, we describe an estimation method of finger joint angles using 5DT data glove, which is developed in our laboratory (see Figure 3).

A. Representative Hand Motion Patterns

To estimate finger joint angles, this method limits user's hand motion to grasping motion. First of all, we had set the three representative hand motions as grip, pinch and nip.

Furthermore, we assume that a human's grasping motion can be represented as a synthetic motion of representative hand motion patterns. To derive three finger joint angles from a single sensor value, we use the following method (see Figure 4). We sample many sets of the sensor values with the low-priced data glove when some subjects open their hand first and then close it to each representative hand motion patterns. Also, we sample the sets of the true angles of finger joints for the same representative patterns, provided that we use true angles obtained from a data glove, which has a lot of sensors. We use Immersion CyberGlove as data glove with a lot of sensors. Then, the sensor values and the true angles of finger joints at the same time are associated. We show an example of correspondence in Figure 5.

We derive the following numerical formulas using this correspondence.

$$\theta_{pi1} = \frac{2}{3}\theta_{pi2} \quad (1)$$

$$\theta_{pi2} = E_{pi2}S_i^3 + F_{pi2}S_i^2 + G_{pi2}S_i + H_{pi2} \quad (2)$$

$$\theta_{pi3} = E_{pi3}S_i^3 + F_{pi3}S_i^2 + G_{pi3}S_i + H_{pi3} \quad (3)$$

where pattern p is one of representative hand motion patterns. Angles θ_{pi1}, θ_{pi2} and θ_{pi3} express the DIP, PIP, and MP joint angle of the finger i for the pattern p. The DIP, PIP, and MP joint mean the first, second and third joint of a finger respectively. The S_i is sensor value of finger i. And E_{pij}, F_{pij}, G_{pij} and H_{pij} are constant parameters for the pattern p, finger i and joint j. These parameters, E_{pij} to H_{pij}, are calculated by pre-experiment. Besides, DIP joint angle is obtained by proportional connection with PIP joint angle (equation (1)) [7]. Joint angles of finger i of pattern p are obtained by these numerical formulas.

B. Hand Motion Estimation and Angles Estimation

To represent user's hand motion as synthetic motion of representative hand motion patterns, we need to know how similar the user's hand motion is and to which representative hand motion patterns. Then, we set the following formula based on the probability density function of the multivariate normal distribution for n points in the five dimensional feature amount space.

$$L_{pn} = exp\{-\frac{1}{2}(\boldsymbol{S} - \boldsymbol{\mu}_{pn})^T \boldsymbol{\Sigma}_{pn}^{-1}(\boldsymbol{S} - \boldsymbol{\mu}_{pn})\} \quad (4)$$

where $\boldsymbol{S}$ is the sensor value vector. And $\boldsymbol{\mu}_{pn}$ and $\boldsymbol{\Sigma}_{pn}$ represent mean vector of sensor sample values, and variance-covariance matrix of sample point n (an integer satisfying $1 \leq n \leq$ a number of samples) in representative hand motion pattern p. Besides, $\boldsymbol{\mu}_{pn}$ and $\boldsymbol{\Sigma}_{pn}$ are obtained by pre-experiment for an average user. If the sensor values are obtained actually

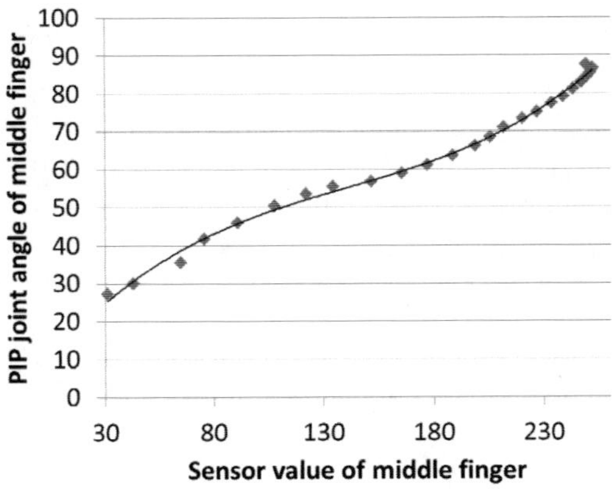

Figure 5. Example of correspondence

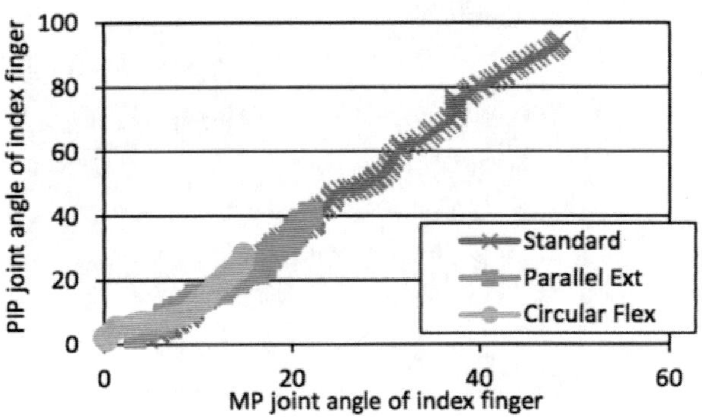

Figure 7. Example of MP and PIP Joint Angle of Index Finger

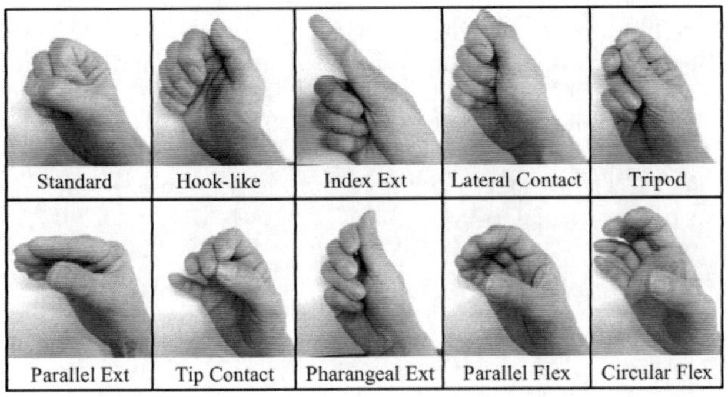

Figure 6. Candidates of representative motions

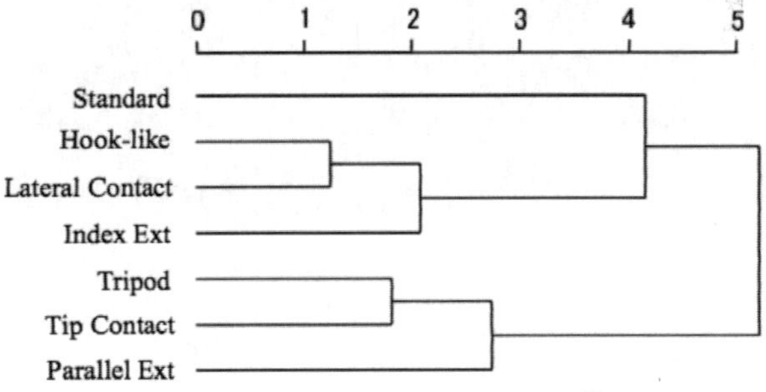

Figure 8. Dendrogram of the Candidata 1

from the glove, we select the maximum value according to the following formula.

$$L_p = \underset{n}{max}\{L_{pn}(\boldsymbol{S} : \boldsymbol{\mu}_{pn}, \boldsymbol{\Sigma}_{pn})\} \quad (5)$$

Thus, we get the likelihood on representative hand motion pattern p in current sensor values. After that, we decide the ratio r_p of hand motion pattern p according to the following formula.

$$r_p = \frac{L_p}{\Sigma_{p=1}^{P} L_p} \quad (6)$$

where P is the total number of representative hand motions, which takes the value of four. As stated above, we can obtain θ_{pij} and r_p. At last, each angle θ_{ij} of current hand posture is derived by the following formula.

$$\theta_{ij} = \sum_{p=1}^{P} r_p \cdot \theta_{pij} \quad (7)$$

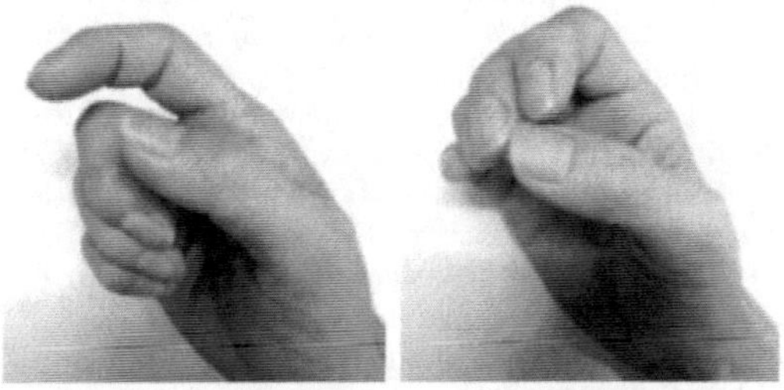

Figure 9. Average Hand Motions (left: MC_2, right: MC_3)

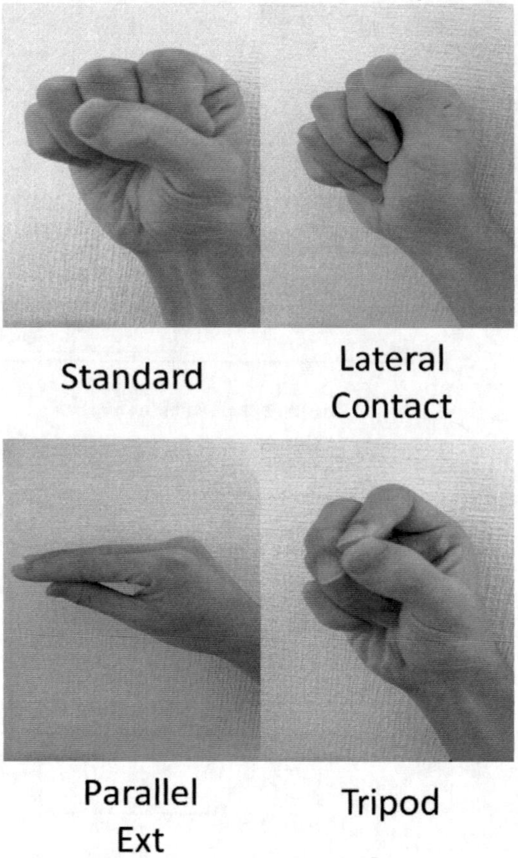

Figure 10. Representative hand motion patterns

IV. Reconsider Representative Hand Motions

In Section IV, we reconsider the representative hand motion patterns based on medical knowledge.

A. Candidate Selection

We reconsider them through the research on the grasping behavior of human hand [8]. They had observed daily grasping forms in experimental condition and classified them into 14 types to help reference in clinical. We select 10 candidates as representative hand motion from these 14 types, because they change enough sensor values of a data-glove respectively (Figure 6). And we obtained the transitions of each finger joint angle of the 10 motions from open hand to each form using data-glove, which has many sensor (CyberGlove). It was also confirmed that Parallel Flex and Circular Flex can be represented in a part of Standard (Figure 7), and Phalangeal Ext can be represented in a part of Lateral Contact. Therefore, we selected 7 motions as representative ones of candidate No.1.

B. Candidate Reduction

If one of the representative hand motions is similar to another one, it may not occur good estimation. If the number of the motions of candidate 1 can be reduced with enough result, we can remove the redundant computation. So, we sampled the sensor values for the candidate 1 and standardize them (mean 0 and variance 1). Then we performed hierarchical cluster analysis for them using the ward method to create a dendrogram about the candidate 1 (Figure 8). The hand motions were classified into 4 classes based on the cutting point 2.5 as a middle distance. The classes are defined as following; C_1: Standard, C_2: Hook-like, Lateral Contact, Index Ext, C_3: Tripod, Tip Contact, and C_4: Parallel Ext. Thereby Standard, Lateral Contact, Tripod and Parallel Ext were selected as candidate No.2 according to the score. Furthermore we constructed average hand motions MC_2 and MC_3 for the classes C_2 and C_3 respectively (Figure 9), and obtained candidate No.3.

TABLE I. JOINT ANGLE ERROR (INPUT: REPRESENTATIVE ONE) [DEGREE]

	thumb	index	middle	ring	little	average
Candidate 1	8.3	5.7	3.9	3.4	6.5	5.6
Candidate 2	5.9	2.5	3.2	4.9	3.0	3.9
Candidate 3	7.2	4.2	3.2	4.5	4.2	4.7

TABLE II. JOINT ANGLE ERROR (INPUT: EXCEPT REPRESENTATIVE ONE) [DEGREE]

	thumb	index	middle	ring	little	average
Candidate 1	8.5	9.4	9.1	6.5	18.5	10.4
Candidate 2	9.4	9.6	9.6	6.5	17.55	10.5
Candidate 3	8.2	8.7	8.7	7.4	12.22	9.0

C. Confirmation Experiment

We had experiment for the three candidates using the 5DT Data Glove 5 Ultra, which has a bend sensor for each finger. When the input data are the representative motions in this experiment, the averages of estimated ratio r_p are; candidate 1: 0.83, candidate 2: 0.86, and candidate 3: 0.95. We can also confirm the average of candidate 3 is higher than the average 0.92 of conventional system with first representative hand motions as grip, pinch and nip. Table I shows the average of the errors of DIP, PIP and MP between estimated finger joint angles and obtained angles by CyberGlove. The input data is Tripod motion for candidate 1 and 2, and MC_2 for candidate 3. Table II shows the error when the input motion data is not representative one for each candidate, that is, the input data is MC_2 motion for candidate 1 and 2, and Tripod for candidate 3. We confirmed that the error of candidate 3 is smallest for the average of both results, and it can deal with any hand motions other than the representative ones. Therefore, we found that candidate No.3 is the most suitable for representative hand motions, and candidate No.2 is the second suitable one.

V. Data-glove whose Sensor Positions are Limited

In Section V, we describe an estimation method of finger joint angles using DG5 data glove whose sensor positions are limited only to PIP joints.

A. MP Angle for Representative Hand Motion Pattern

Although we mentioned above a set of representative hand motion patterns is selected as candidate No.3, the pattern Parallel Ext is almost the motion related only to MP joints. When doing the Parallel Ext pattern, the sensor values hardly change. We tentatively use three other patterns as representative hand motion patterns except Parallel Ext from the candidate No.2 (Figure 10) for now.

For the 5DT data glove whose sensors cover PIP and MP joints, the DIP angle is related to PIP directly, as mentioned in the Section III. It means the sensor values contain all of their information. However, using DG5 whose sensors are only on PIP, the motion of MP does not change the sensor value. Of course, we assume that the hand motion is a grasping one, so the MP angle of a finger is related to the PIP angle of the same finger. Then we can assume that the MP of a finger is related to the PIPs of all fingers.

We consider a new estimation model to obtain angles for representative hand motion patterns using multiple regression analysis. First, we make a estimation equation with explanatory variable is a set of sensor values, and response variable is each MP joint angle, as follows.

$$\theta_{pi3} = \sum_{f=1}^{5} C_{pif3} S_f + I_{pi3} \tag{8}$$

where θ_{pi3} is MP joint angle of finger i of representative pattern p, S_f is sensor value of finger f, and C_{pif3} and I_{pi3} are constant.

Now, a subject opens his hand first and then closes it to each representative pattern with DG5 data glove, the set of sensor value $S_f(time)$ of finger f at $time$ is sampled. Then, the subject moves his hand as each same pattern with CyberGlove, which has many sensors, the set of angle value $\theta_{pi3}(time)$ is sampled as true one.

Here, we should get the constant C_{pif3} and I_{pi3}. The residual sum of squares Q is represented as in (9).

$$Q = \sum_{time} \left\{ \theta_{pi3}(time) - \left(\sum_{f=1}^{5} C_{pif3} S_f(time) + I_{pi3} \right) \right\}^2 \tag{9}$$

Focusing on coefficient C_{pi13} where $f = 1$;

$$\begin{aligned} Q = \sum_{time} \Bigg\{ & \left(S_1(time) C_{pi13}\right)^2 \\ & + 2S_1(time) C_{pi13} \left(\sum_{f=2}^{5} C_{pif3} S_f(time) + I_{pi3} \right) \\ & - 2\theta_{pi3}(time) S_1(time) C_{pi13} \\ & + \left(\sum_{f=2}^{5} C_{pif3} S_f(time) + I_{pi3} \right)^2 \\ & - 2\theta_{pi3}(time) \left(\sum_{f=2}^{5} C_{pif3} S_f(time) + I_{pi3} \right) \\ & + \left(\theta_{pi3}(time)\right)^2 \Bigg\} \end{aligned} \tag{10}$$

Using the partial differentiations with C_{pi13};

$$\begin{aligned} \frac{\partial Q}{\partial C_{pi13}} = 2 \sum_{time} S_1(time) \Bigg\{ & \sum_{f=1}^{5} C_{pif3} S_f(time) \\ & + I_{pi3} - \theta_{pi3}(time) \Bigg\} \end{aligned} \tag{11}$$

Using the partial differentiations also with C_{pif3} and I_{pi3};

$$\begin{aligned} \frac{\partial Q}{\partial C_{pif3}} = 2 \sum_{time} S_f(time) \Bigg\{ & \sum_{f'=1}^{5} C_{pif'3} S_{f'}(time) \\ & + I_{pi3} - \theta_{pi3}(time) \Bigg\} \end{aligned} \tag{12}$$

$$\begin{aligned} \frac{\partial Q}{\partial I_{pi3}} = 2 \sum_{time} \Bigg\{ & I_{pi3} + \sum_{f=1}^{5} C_{pif3} S_f(time) \\ & - \theta_{pi3}(time) \Bigg\} \end{aligned} \tag{13}$$

The constant C_{pif3} and I_{pi3} to be obtained make Q represented as the minimum of the equation from (9). And the C_{pif3} and I_{pi3} that make Q minimum satisfy following equation.

$$\frac{\partial Q}{\partial C_{pif3}} = \frac{\partial Q}{\partial I_{pi3}} = 0 \tag{14}$$

Solving this, coefficient C_{pif3} and constant I_{pi3} are obtained to estimate MP joint angle for representative pattern with (8). The angles of PIP are obtained directly from the sensor value with (2), and the angles of DIP are also obtained only from PIP with (1).

B. Hand Motion Estimation with Pseudo-Inverse Matrix

When the variance of sensor values is zero at the sample point n of representative hand motion pattern, the variance-covariance matrix will be abnormal at the sample point n. It means the inverse matrix of variance-covariance matrix of sensor values $\boldsymbol{\Sigma}_{pn}^{-1}$ can not be obtained, and the likelihood for the sample data of representative pattern p can not be obtained with (4).

So, we use Moore-Penrose pseudo-inverse matrix to solve it. The variance-covariance 5×5 matrix of sensor values $\boldsymbol{\Sigma}_{pn}^{-1}$, which is abnormal at the sample point n is represented as next equation with $5 \times r$ matrix $\boldsymbol{A}_{pn}$ and $r \times 5$ matrix $\boldsymbol{B}_{pn}$ where $\mathrm{rank}\left(\boldsymbol{\Sigma}_{pn}\right) = r$;

$$\boldsymbol{\Sigma}_{pn} = \boldsymbol{A}_{pn} \boldsymbol{B}_{pn} \tag{15}$$

Here the Moore-Penrose pseudo-inverse matrix $\boldsymbol{\Sigma}_{pn}^{+}$ for $\boldsymbol{\Sigma}_{pn}$ is described as:

$$\begin{aligned} \boldsymbol{\Sigma}_{pn}^{+} &= \boldsymbol{B}_{pn}^{T} \left(\boldsymbol{A}_{pn}^{T} \boldsymbol{\Sigma}_{pn} \boldsymbol{B}_{pn}^{T} \right)^{-1} \boldsymbol{A}_{pn}^{T} \\ &= \boldsymbol{B}_{pn}^{T} \left(\boldsymbol{B}_{pn} \boldsymbol{B}_{pn}^{T} \right)^{-1} \left(\boldsymbol{A}_{pn}^{T} \boldsymbol{A}_{pn} \right)^{-1} \boldsymbol{A}_{pn}^{T} \end{aligned} \tag{16}$$

Using this Moore-Penrose pseudo-inverse matrix $\boldsymbol{\Sigma}_{pn}^{+}$ for (4) instead of the inverse matrix of variance-covariance matrix of

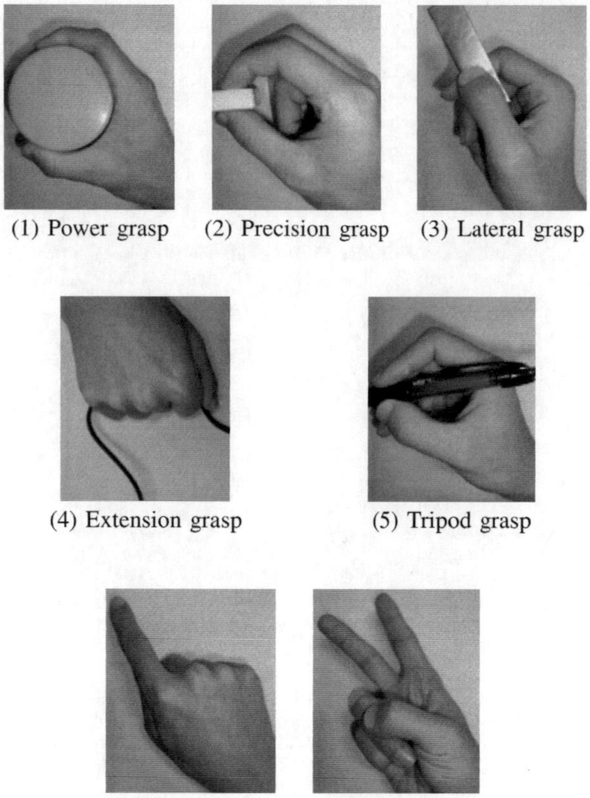

(1) Power grasp (2) Precision grasp (3) Lateral grasp

(4) Extension grasp (5) Tripod grasp

(6) Index pointing (7) Basic gestures

Figure 11. Hand motions needed for ADL

sensor values Σ_{pn}^{-1} at the sample point n where inverse matrix can not be defined, the likelihood is obtained and the ratio of each hand motion pattern is determined with (5) and (6), respectively. Now, we can use a low-priced data glove whose sensors cover only the middle angle of each finger to estimate all finger joint angles of current hand posture with (7).

VI. Experiment and Result

We performed an experiment to confirm the effectiveness of the method described above. The experiment system was constructed using the DG5 Data Glove whose sensor positions are limited only on middle joints. Other hand motions that were different from representative patterns were tested. The minimum of Activities of Daily Living (ADL) needs the following hand motions (see Figure 11) [9].

1) Power grasps (used in 35% ADLs)
2) Precision grasps (30% ADLs)
3) Lateral grasps (20% ADLs)
4) Extension grasps (10% ADLs),
5) Tripod grasps,
6) Index pointing, and
7) Basic gestures.

We tested five motions; 1)–5).

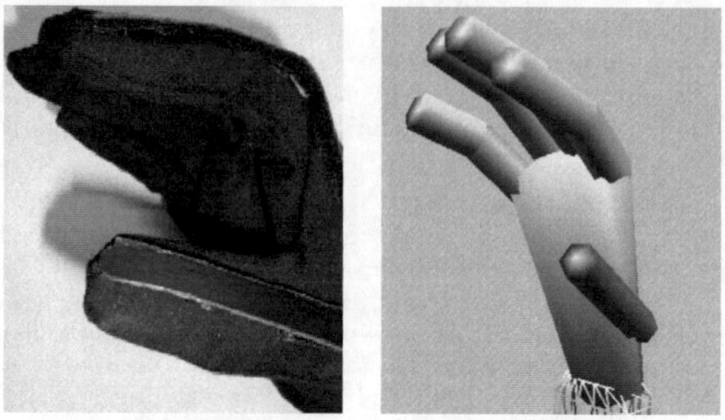

Figure 12. Result CG for Power grasp

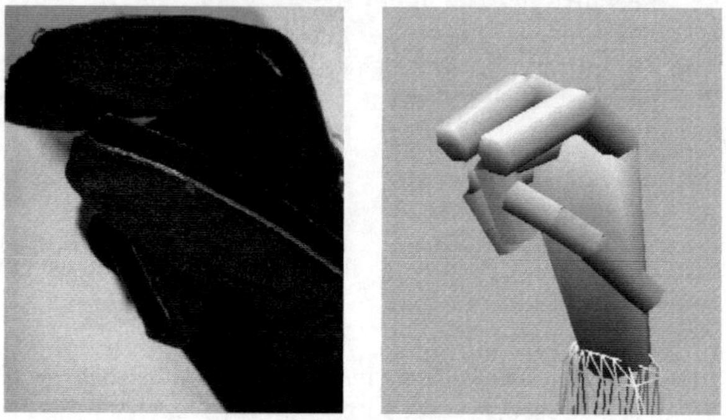

Figure 13. Result CG for Precision grasp

The subjects opened their hands and then closed them to each test pattern 1)–5) with DG5 data glove. The average of estimated joint angles were compared with the true angles obtained from CyberGlove, which had many bend sensors.

Table III shows the average error of finger joint angles. Each error is around 10 degrees. The result using the 5DT data glove whose sensors cover two joints of each finger also had about 10 degrees error [6]. This means that the lower-priced data glove can obtain joint angles accurately enough.

Actual hand posture images and the CG images generated from estimated joint angles are shown in Figures 12 and 13. The MP joints that were not covered with bend sensors are estimated from the sensors on PIP joints.

VII. Difference of Hand Shape

In the method stated in previous sections, parameters are needed to be precomposed for each user. However, using an

TABLE III. ERROR OF FINGER JOINT ANGLES [DEGREE]

	thumb	index	middle	ring	little	average
Power G.	7.3	12.0	10.5	12.5	10.0	10.5
Precision G.	8.1	9.2	7.2	7.0	6.8	7.7
Lateral G.	9.4	6.0	8.8	7.5	10.5	8.4
Extension G.	9.8	8.1	11.0	11.3	9.0	9.9
Tripod G.	8.5	8.5	7.2	11.6	10.9	9.3
average	8.6	8.7	8.9	10.0	9.4	9.2

expensive glove to obtain the true angles of finger joints is not suitable from perspective of utilization in ordinary home. Furthermore, parameters to calculate angles are obtained by a lot of trials of hand motions. They are troublesome for general user. In this section, we try to determine the parameters automatically for motion and angles estimation.

A. Estimation Accuracy between Different Users

We investigated estimation accuracy between different users. With the cooperation of three research participants, we had an experiment. In this experiment we asked each participant to grasp a plastic bottle ($500ml$) with equipped data glove. The reason to choose this grasping motion was user's hand motion is little by little different every time even if user thinks that one performs the same hand motion. And we defined the hand size of user as H_{size}, which is decided by the distance from the wrist to the top of the middle finger (Figure 14). The H_{size} of each participant is shown in Table IV. The sample person is who provided each parameter for estimation in pre-experiment. And the parameters for estimation were obtained by the sample person's hand. When each participant grasped the plastic bottle, their finger joint angles were estimated by these parameters of sample person. We measured finger joint angles when their hand was touching completely with the plastic bottle. And we investigated the average of the errors between estimated finger joint angles and obtained angles by CyberClove. Table V shows the results. These results indicate that estimation accuracy using parameters of the person whose hand size is different becomes worse. We expected that joint angle errors of the sample person was minimum because sample person's parameters were used for estimation. However the average error of participant 2 was minimum in Table V. We concluded that the reason was the sensor values were not uniform but also scattering when user moved one's hand. However, only because of these numerical values, the results can not be judged whether they are significant or not. Then we had statistical hypothesis testing to confirm these results are significant. At this time, we adopted Student's t-test. We had Student's t-test to the average of joint angle errors of the sample person and other participants. Test statistic t_0 is obtained from the following formula.

$$t_0 = \frac{|\bar{X} - \bar{Y}|}{\sqrt{U_e(\frac{1}{m} + \frac{1}{n})}} \tag{17}$$

where $\bar{X}$ and $\bar{Y}$ are the average of joint angle errors, m and n represent the sample size of two groups. And U_e is obtained from the following formula.

$$U_e = \frac{(m-1)U_x + (n-1)U_y}{m+n-2} \tag{18}$$

where U_x and U_y are unbiased variance. As stated above, test statistic t_0 can be obtained and t_0 follows t-distribution. P-values obtained from Student's t-test are shown in Table VI. The $P(T{\leq}t)$ represents significance probability. In this paper, we decide that significance level α is 0.05. So, it is statistical significance if $P(T{\leq}t)$ is smaller than 0.05. Looking at Table VI, the $P(T{\leq}t)$ in all categories are smaller than 0.05. They indicate that there are statistical significance in estimation accuracy between the sample person and other participants. We confirmed necessity of determining parameters for each user.

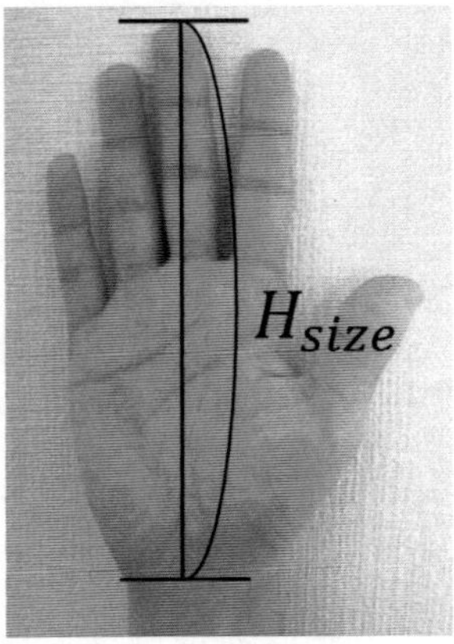

Figure 14. Definition of hand size

TABLE IV. H_{size} OF EACH PARTICIPANT $[cm]$

	H_{size}	standard deviation
participant 1	17.0	-
participant 2	18.1	-
participant 3	20.5	-
sample person	17.7	-
average of Japanese male [10]	18.3	0.8
average of Japanese female [10]	16.9	0.7

B. Hand Size Estimation

We assume that parameters to calculate finger joint angles are determined by knowledge of user's H_{size}. To evaluate user's H_{size}, we try to use the sensor values when user performs one hand motion. When deciding hand motion for estimation of hand size, it is important that a hand motion is simple. If it is obscurity motion, there is difficulty in performing hand motion. Then, we consider the total value of five sensors when user closes hand (=S_{total}). We obtained S_{total} and each H_{size} from each research participant. The correspondence between H_{size} and S_{total} is shown in Figure 15. Then we conclude the following formula.

$$H_{size} = aS_{total} + b \tag{19}$$

where a, b are constant parameters. Using this formula, user's H_{size} can be obtained by performing the simple hand motion.

TABLE V. JOINT ANGLE ERROR OF GRASPING PLASTIC BOTTLE [DEGREE]

	Thumb	Index	Middle	Ring	Little	avg.
sample	7.6	17.9	11.2	16.2	14.8	13.6
participant 1	31.1	17.7	26.4	5.0	5.1	17.1
participant 2	15.3	17.7	11.6	11.7	5.0	12.3
participant 3	30.2	10.5	27.2	17.7	17.7	20.7

TABLE VI. P-VALUES OF STUDENT'S T-TEST

	$P(T{\leq}t)$
participant 1	6.8×10^{-6}
participant 2	1.0×10^{-2}
participant 3	9.6×10^{-4}

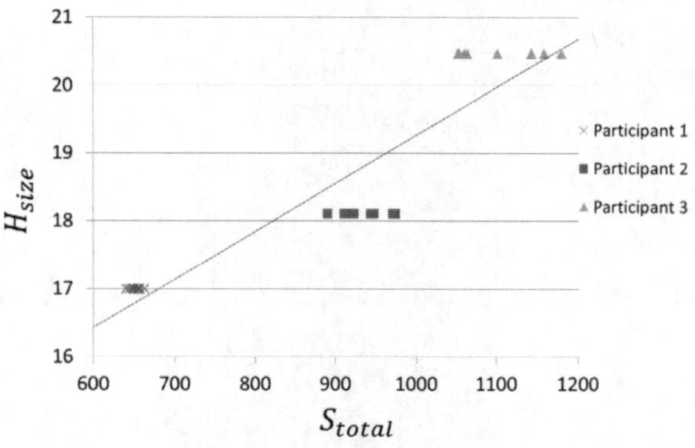

Figure 15. Relation between H_{size} and S_{total}

C. Determination of Estimation Parameters

We would like to determine the estimation parameters of new user whose H_{size} is h_u. The size h_u is obtained by (19). If two of the three participants are A and B, each hand size is h_A and h_B respectively ($h_A > h_B$), the parameters for h_u user are defined as below.

$$E_{upij} = \frac{(h_u - h_B)E_{Apij} + (h_A - h_u)E_{Bpij}}{h_A - h_B} \quad (20)$$

$$F_{upij} = \frac{(h_u - h_B)F_{Apij} + (h_A - h_u)F_{Bpij}}{h_A - h_B} \quad (21)$$

$$G_{upij} = \frac{(h_u - h_B)G_{Apij} + (h_A - h_u)G_{Bpij}}{h_A - h_B} \quad (22)$$

$$H_{upij} = \frac{(h_u - h_B)H_{Apij} + (h_A - h_u)H_{Bpij}}{h_A - h_B} \quad (23)$$

Of course the parameters E_{Apij} to H_{Apij} and E_{Bpij} to H_{Bpij} for h_A and h_B participants are calculated previously using expensive data glove (parameters for another participant are also calculated). Then numerical formula for estimation of finger joint angles of the user is decided as follows.

$$\theta_{upij} = E_{upij}S_i^3 + F_{upij}S_i^2 + G_{upij}S_i + H_{upij} \quad (24)$$

Also, we decide the $\boldsymbol{\mu}_{upn}$ according to the following formula.

$$\boldsymbol{\mu}_{upn} = \frac{(h_u - h_B)\boldsymbol{\mu}_{Apn} + (h_A - h_u)\boldsymbol{\mu}_{Bpn}}{h_A - h_B} \quad (25)$$

where $\boldsymbol{\mu}_{upn}$, $\boldsymbol{\mu}_{Apn}$, and $\boldsymbol{\mu}_{Bpn}$ represent vector of sensor sample values of user, A, and B. The $\boldsymbol{\mu}_{upn}$ is used when using (4). Using a weighted average of hand size, each parameter for estimation can be determined.

D. Equivalency of Variance-Covariance Matrix

When using (4) to estimate hand motion, it is difficult to calculate the all parameters $\boldsymbol{\Sigma}_{pn}^{-1}$ directly for each user. So, we investigated equivalency of variance-covariance matrix between different users by using Box's M Test. First of all, we got the sensor values when each participant performed representative hand motions. Each representative hand motion is performed n times. Table VII shows an example of the sensor values at the time t in motion p. Next, the average of

TABLE VII. EXAMPLE OF SENSOR VALUE FOR MOTION p AT THE TIME t

trial	Thumb	Index	Middle	Ring	Little
1	s_{11}	s_{21}	s_{31}	s_{41}	s_{51}
2	s_{12}	s_{22}	s_{32}	s_{42}	s_{52}
3	s_{13}	s_{23}	s_{33}	s_{43}	s_{53}
$\vdots$	$\vdots$	$\vdots$	$\vdots$	$\vdots$	$\vdots$
n	s_{1n}	s_{2n}	s_{3n}	s_{4n}	s_{5n}

the sensor values $\overline{s_i}$ for finger i is obtained by the following formula.

$$\overline{s_i} = \frac{1}{n}\sum_{j=1}^{n} s_{ij} \quad (26)$$

At this time, covariance of finger x and y, represented as V_{xy}, is obtained by (27). And variance-covariance matrix $\boldsymbol{V}$ is defined as (28).

$$V_{xy} = \frac{1}{n}\sum_{k=1}^{n}(s_{xk} - \overline{s_x})(s_{yk} - \overline{s_y}) \quad (27)$$

$$\boldsymbol{V} = \begin{bmatrix} V_{11} & V_{12} & \dots & V_{15} \\ V_{21} & V_{22} & \dots & V_{25} \\ \vdots & \vdots & \ddots & \vdots \\ V_{51} & V_{52} & \dots & V_{55} \end{bmatrix} \quad (28)$$

Then we decide V' according to the following natural logarithm (29).

$$V' = \ln\frac{|\boldsymbol{V}_{AB}|^{\nu_1+\nu_2}}{|\boldsymbol{V}_A|^{\nu_1}|\boldsymbol{V}_B|^{\nu_2}} \quad (29)$$

$$\nu_1 = n_A - 1 \quad (30)$$

$$\nu_2 = n_B - 1 \quad (31)$$

where $\boldsymbol{V}_A$ and $\boldsymbol{V}_B$ represent mean variance-covariance matrix of participant A and B. The number of times n of participant A is different from B generally, each number is defined as n_A and n_B respectively. In this paper, each participant performs hand motion 10 times. And $\boldsymbol{V}_{AB}$ is the matrix obtained from the following formula.

$$\boldsymbol{V}_{AB} = \frac{\nu_1\boldsymbol{V}_A + \nu_2\boldsymbol{V}_B}{\nu_1 + \nu_2} \quad (32)$$

Also, we decide k according to the following formula.

$$k = 1 - \left(\frac{1}{\nu_1} + \frac{1}{\nu_2} - \frac{1}{\nu_1 + \nu_2}\right)\cdot\frac{2q^2 + 3q - 1}{6(q+1)} \quad (33)$$

where q represents the number of explanatory variables. Now q is number of Thumb, Index, Middle, Ring, and Little finger, 5. Finally, we obtain test statistic χ_0^2 from the following formula.

$$\chi_0^2 = kV' \quad (34)$$

The χ_0^2 follows chi-squared distribution. We describe the χ_0^2 of each motion/user in Table VIII. We decide significance level α as 0.001. The $\chi^2(\alpha = 0.001)$ is 37.70. So, if the χ_0^2 is smaller than 37.70, there is not significantly different in variance-covariance matripants as $\boldsymbol{\Sigma}_{pn}$. Finally we can obtain the finger joint angles of new user.

TABLE VIII. χ_0^2 OF EACH RESEARCH PARTICIPANT

	participant 1, 2	participant 2, 3	pariticpant 1, 3
Standard	22.44	28.64	28.84
Lateral Contact	29.34	36.22	20.87
Tripod	31.60	35.51	29.89
Parallel Ext	33.69	35.54	32.41

TABLE IX. ESTIMATED H_{size} OF PARTICIPANTS $[cm]$

	True H_{size}	Estimated H_{size}	Error
Participant 4	17.6	18.0	0.4
Participant 5	19.1	19.9	0.8

VIII. Experiment and Result for Hand Shape

We had an experiment to confirm the effectiveness of the method for hand shape.

A. Experiment Environment

We used 5DT data glove with representative hand motion set No.2 for two experiment systems, system A and system B. And two research participants 4 and 5 performed several hand motions.

1) System A: The system A estimates user's finger joint angles using same parameters for all users. These parameters were obtained by the hand of participant 2 because his hand size is mostly the same as average Japanese male's one.

2) System B: The system B estimates user's finger joint angles using parameters obtained by the user's own hand. User closes hand first, then each parameter is determined using H_{size}.

B. Estimation Results

Table IX shows estimated H_{size} of two participants. An estimation error of participant 4 is 0.37, and the error of participant 5 is 0.79. The method can estimate user's H_{size} almost correctly. We confirmed the effectiveness of the H_{size} estimation method described in Section VII-B.

Tables X to XIII show the average of the errors of the finger joint angles between estimated finger joint angles and obtained angles by CyberGlove. Besides, "Plastic bottle" represents the hand motion as same as in Section VII-A.

These results indicate that the estimation accuracy of the system B is better than the system A. We had Student's t-test to these averages of the errors of each finger joint angles. Tables XIV and XV show the differences of the estimation accuracy between the system A and B, and p-values obtained from Student's t-test. It is statistical significance if the $P(T \leq t)$ is smaller than 0.05. They show that there is statistical significance about the hand motion of which estimation accuracy were improved. There is not statistical significance about Parallel Ext, but the estimation accuracy was not improved. Totally the system B is better than the system A, it means calibrated parameters for each user is effectiveness, and hand size estimation is needed.

IX. Conclusion

In this paper, we described a useful method using a low-priced data-glove based on hand motion patterns. It estimates all finger joint angles using the data glove that sensors cover two joints of each finger, and also only the middle angle of each finger. A data glove is one of the major interfaces, which are used in the field of VR. It measures curvatures of fingers using bend sensor. However, in order to obtain accurate hand motions, it is necessary to use an expensive data glove, which has many sensors. On the other hand, there is a low cost data glove, which measures an angle for each finger through one sensor. It cannot get detailed data directly. Our method estimates plausible user hand motion patterns using each relation among angles of fingers during the operation of the low-cost glove first. Then, it estimates all finger joint angles by estimating the types of hand motion patterns from the correlation between each finger angle in the hand motion pattern. We assumed some representative hand motion patterns, and considered that other hand motions could be represented as synthetic motion of these. In the method for the glove whose sensors cover only the middle angle, the ratio of each representative motion pattern is calculated using Moore-Penrose pseudo-inverse matrix, and all finger angles are estimated using multiple regression analysis. The difference between users' hand shape was considered and confirmed using the glove whose sensors cover two joint angles. With the low priced data-glove being useful, it is expected that VR systems that target households will become more popular. In the future, we should reconsider the representative hand motion patterns because we removed Parallel Ext from our

TABLE X. JOINT ANGLE ERROR OF PARTICIPANT 4 IN SYSTEM A [DEGREE]

	Thumb	Index	Middle	Ring	Little	avg.
Standard	8.8	11.2	11.1	11.5	10.1	10.5
Lateral Contact	10.8	13.1	13.6	15.1	7.3	12.0
Tripod	18.6	10.6	13.5	11.5	17.5	14.4
Parallel Ext	10.4	13.4	8.8	9.0	10.3	10.4
Plastic bottle	15.2	10.7	15.3	20.2	9.9	14.3

TABLE XI. JOINT ANGLE ERROR OF PARTICIPANT 4 IN SYSTEM B [DEGREE]

	Thumb	Index	Middle	Ring	Little	avg.
Standard	6.5	6.3	3.6	15.0	18.4	10.0
Lateral Contact	12.0	11.7	11.4	11.4	8.7	11.0
Tripod	18.3	7.5	12.7	8.4	15.8	12.5
Parallel Ext	13.8	11.4	9.6	9.2	9.8	10.8
Plastic bottle	15.8	3.6	14.0	14.2	8.9	11.3

TABLE XII. JOINT ANGLE ERROR OF PARTICIPANT 5 IN SYSTEM A [DEGREE]

	Thumb	Index	Middle	Ring	Little	avg.
Standard	12.3	12.8	12.7	14.2	13.8	13.2
Lateral Contact	11.5	21.5	16.4	21.2	19.2	18.0
Tripod	10.2	8.2	12.8	22.9	17.6	14.3
Parallel Ext	24.0	9.2	4.3	7.6	13.6	11.7
Plastic bottle	23.2	13.6	16.2	31.0	20.8	21.0

TABLE XIII. JOINT ANGLE ERROR OF PARTICIPANT 5 IN SYSTEM B [DEGREE]

	Thumb	Index	Middle	Ring	Little	avg.
Standard	13.1	8.5	6.9	8.8	12.5	10.0
Lateral Contact	9.3	14.1	13.1	11.4	16.8	12.9
Tripod	9.4	7.7	18.8	19.0	17.5	14.5
Parallel Ext	13.0	8.8	16.0	10.8	13.5	12.4
Plastic bottle	26.1	10.3	20.8	13.4	11.0	16.3

TABLE XIV. DIFFERENCE BETWEEN SYSTEM A AND B OF PARTICIPANT 4

	participant 4	
	difference	$P(T \leq t)$
Standard	-0.6	3.3×10^{-2}
Lateral Contact	-1.0	2.7×10^{-2}
Tripod	-1.8	3.9×10^{-2}
Parallel Ext	+0.4	1.6×10^{-1}
Plastic bottle	-3.0	6.7×10^{-3}
average	-1.2	-

TABLE XV. DIFFERENCE BETWEEN SYSTEM A AND B OF PARTICIPANT 5

	participant 5	
	difference	$P(T \leq t)$
Standard	-3.2	3.4×10^{-2}
Lateral Contact	-5.0	1.7×10^{-2}
Tripod	+0.2	4.0×10^{-2}
Parallel Ext	+0.7	8.1×10^{-1}
Plastic bottle	-4.6	1.0×10^{-2}
average	-2.4	-

first research based on medical knowledge. We should also expand the target hand motion patterns to various ones that are not only grasping patterns.

ACKNOWLEDGMENT

The authors would like to thank our colleagues in our laboratory for useful discussions.

REFERENCES

[1] K. Funahashi, Y. Mori, H. Takahashi, and Y. Iwahori, "A Data Adjustment Method of Low-priced Data-glove based on Hand Motion Pattern," in *Proceedings of the PATTERNS 2017 (ComputationWorld)*, 2017, pp. 97–102.

[2] P. Temoche, E. Ramirez, and O. Rodrigues., "A Low-cost Data Glove for Virtual Reality," in *Proceedings of the XI International Congress of Numerical Methods in Engineering and Applied Sciences (CIMENICS)*, 2012, pp. TCG31–36.

[3] F. Camastra and D. Felice, "LVQ-based Hand Gesture Recognition using a Data Glove," in *Proceedings of the Neural Nets and Surroundings Smart Innovation, Systems and Technologies*, vol. 19, 2013, pp. 159–168.

[4] N. Tongrod, T. Kerdcharoen, N. Watthanawisuth, and A. Tuantranont, "A Low-Cost Data-Glove for Human Computer Interaction Based on Ink-Jet Printed Sensors and ZigBee Networks," in *Proceedings of the International Symposium on Wearable Computers (ISWC)*, 2010, pp. 1–2.

[5] Y. Mori, K. Kawashima, Y. Yoshida, and K. Funahashi, "A Study for Vision Based Data Glove with Back Image of Hand," in *Proceedings of the ICAT2015*, 2015, (USB Flash Drive, no page number).

[6] H. Takahashi and K. Funahashi, "A Data Adjustment Method of Low-priced Data-glove based on Representative Hand Motion Using Medical Knowledge," in *Proceedings of the ICAT2013*, 2013, (USB Flash Drive, no page number).

[7] G. Elkoura, "Handrix: Animating the Human hand," in *Proceedings of the ACM SIGGRAPH/Eurographics Symposium on Computer Animation*, 2003, pp. 110–119.

[8] N. Kamakura, H. Matsuo, M. Ishii, and Y. Mitsuboshi, F. Miura, "Patterns of Static Prehension in Normal Hands," *Am J Occup Ther 34*, pp. 437–445, 1980.

[9] C. Capriani, "Objectives, criteria and methods for the design of the SmartHand transradial prosthesis," in *Proceedings of the Robotica 2010*, vol. 28, 2010, pp. 919–927.

[10] M. Kawauchi, "AIST Measurements Hand Data of Japanese," in *https://www.dh.aist.go.jp/database/hand/ 2012*. (in Japanese, last access: 5/Nov/2017)

Implementing a Framework for QoS Measurement in SOA

A Uniform Approach Based on a QoS Meta Model

Andreas Hausotter, Arne Koschel
University of Applied Sciences & Arts Hannover
Faculty IV, Department of Computer Science,
Hannover, Germany
email: Andreas.Hausotter@hs-hannover.de
email: Arne.Koschel@hs-hannover.de

Johannes Busch, Markus Petzsch, Malte Zuch
University of Applied Sciences & Arts Hannover
Faculty IV, Department of Computer Science,
Hannover, Germany
email: Johannes.Busch@stud.hs-hannover.de
email: Markus.Petzsch@stud.hs-hannover.de
email: Malte.Zuch@hs-hannover.de

Abstract—**The globalized markets now offer customers a variety of products and services as never before. This enormous selection reduces the loyalty of the customers to the companies. Today, products and services are highly interchangeable. This requires a strategic rethinking of the companies from a product-centric perspective to a customer-centric perspective. Therefore, businesses need to change their operational processes in a flexible and agile manner to maintain their competitive edge. A Service-oriented Architecture (SOA) may help to meet these need. Particularly in the insurance industry, this is an established key technology. Old monolithic software architectures have already been successfully transformed to 'traditional' SOAs. This could even be a good basis for future upgrades to micro-service architectures. But, before this upgrade is accomplishable, it is necessary to analyze and measure the already established SOA. As the application landscape of enterprises is inherently heterogeneous and highly distributed, it is a great challenge to provide services with a certain quality. A measurement system can help to capture the relevant QoS parameters of a software architecture. This is, particularly the case, when services are requested externally via the web. Therefore, quality of service (QoS) measurement and analysis is a crucial issue in Service-oriented Architectures. As the key contribution of this paper, we present a generic SOA Quality Model (SOA QM) based on the measurement standard ISO/IEC 15939, a SOA Information Model (SOA IM), and an architectural concept of a QoS System. The SOA IM is an XML-based specification for the measurement to be performed. The QoS System provides an execution platform for the SOA IM, based on a Complex Event Processing (CEP) approach and guarantees minimal impact on the SOA environment. The concepts are explained in detail using a standard process of the German insurance domain. Moreover, implementation details for our concept are given, including an overview of the general deployment of such a technology.**

Keywords*—*Service-oriented Architecture (SOA); Quality of Service (QoS); Measurement Process; Complex Event Processing (CEP).

I. INTRODUCTION

Distributed IT-systems are commonly used in today's companies to fulfill the needs of agility and scalability of their business processes to manage the highly variable demand of the market. Typical scenarios are real time logistics and delivery, just in time supply chain management and in general, handling services in real time to fit market demands.

The latter is commonly used within the finance and insurance industry during their internal computation of risk and money management and for their external customer services, like proposal calculations (including the current market conditions). Especially the external customer services must have a high quality in terms of time behavior. Google has shown that a latency of 100 ms up to 400 ms causes an impact of -0.2 % up to -0.6 % concerning the daily usage of web services by the customers [2]. The integration of those services to run business processes in a stable way, fulfilling the varying demand of the market, is commonly realized with Service-Oriented Architectures (SOA).

These architectures integrate services within distributed systems to run business processes with a high capability in terms of agility. Especially the distribution of the services over several systems allows scaling with the market demands.

Distributing and handling several services is a common concern of the insurance industry. But an increasing distribution and more complex business processes will only gain more agility with SOA, if the distribution of the services over several systems is realized in a reasonable way. For getting the required control of the distribution of those services, a measurement system is required. Measuring the general quality of service (QoS) in distributed systems is part of the motivation of this work and is explained in detail in the next subsection. The subsection thereafter will show our contribution to the general problem of measuring QoS in SOA within the application scenario of the insurance industry. This scenario is detailed in Section III.

A. Motivation

In many cases it is not possible to forecast, how much computing power and bandwidth the infrastructure needs to host the allocated services within the distributed computing system. Beside these design decisions of the infrastructure, there is a further problem in allocating the services to the right locations within the distributed system. This allocation will influence how much bandwidth and calculation power is available for the services and how many services will share identical resources during the same time. So, if several services will use the same part of the infrastructure, this could lead to increasing latencies over the whole system, resulting in an unfavorable time behavior for the users. Especially, if some services are requested with intense demands of the market, latencies could rise in an unpredictable manner.

This research is partly related to major German insurance companies, where latency considerations are particularly important. In this regard, research and prototype development can be tested by a quality of service (QoS) measurement system on a practice-relevant application case. In this case, the insurance companies' partners provide a typical service-oriented software architecture (SOA) for running business processes. In this context, insurance companies have to guarantee short response times of their services. Other quality of service parameters such as the measurement of reliability, resource consumption or error rate would also be possible. In the context of the practical application case, here the focus is on the measurement of the response time as it is particularly significant in the insurance industry.

Such a scenario is typical for the German insurance industry. At the end of the year, millions of users are able to switch their insurance contracts and will request therefore designated online services. The general demand is not foreseeable and the intense interaction between the insurance industry and the finance industry requires a high quality of those services. Especially, the historically low interest rates in today's market provokes, fast changing business models and the need for a fast adoption to new business processes.

Moreover, the ability to offer services of high quality to fulfill the external user demands and the internal interaction within the finance industry is very much required. To fulfill these demands, distributed systems with SOA will benefit from an across broader measurement of the quality of those services, particularly in terms of latency. Such a measurement system is the contribution of this work and is explained in the following subsection.

B. Contribution

The need for a new development of a flexible measurement system is influenced by the limitations of common solutions. As a result, the scenario of this work is based on a German insurance companies SOA, which already uses Dynatrace as a measurement solution [3].

Since the partner from the insurance industry is currently restructuring and modernizing his business processes and therefore, he needs a more flexible and generic approach to integrate an external measurement system for monitoring and analyzing the time behavior of his services. Additionally, a more detailed analyzer component was required to process the measured data.

So on the one hand, the approach has to be integrated in a generic way with minimal interaction points within the SOA of the partner from the insurance industry to guarantee a simple integration during the continuous development process. But on the other hand, the solution should offer a flexible and detailed analyzer component.

This article will present our currently ongoing applied research work. It extends our previous work from, mentioned in [1]. Since as a whole it is still 'work in progress', here we will mostly focus on measurement concepts and an adequate measurement model here.

The concrete presentation of the results and the evaluation would be beyond the scope of this work. Therefore, it will take place directly in the next publication, which will be in the direct context of this work. This following publication is currently in the process of submission to the conference 'The Tenth International Conference on Advanced Service Computing - SERVICE COMPUTATION 2018' and will appear there as soon as the acceptance is completed. In that case, the evaluation of the measuring system will be explicitly discussed there. Here in this work the preparatory presentation of the concept of the QoS measuring system takes place.

This work is the extension of our previous publication 'Agent based Framework for QoS Measurement applied in SOA' [1]. In this regard, we provide much more concrete technical details for our current prototype implementation. Based on the previous publication, this work here shows in detail how the required QoS parameter (the response time) is measured.

In particular, we will present more details on service call sequences and measurement within our framework (cf. Section VI-C). In addition, more implementation details on software, hardware and deployment of our prototype are presented in the whole Section VI. Detailed QoS measurement results will be presented in future work.

The required solution was defined by the following:

- generic approach to generate the measurement system,
- automatic integration of the measurement system into the existing SOA,
- lose couplings within the existing SOA,
- flexible agent based approach,
- technology independent approach using standards (XML),
- individual and customizable analyzer component.

As stated above, besides technical concepts, we will also present some details mainly from our utilized application scenario, which is based upon the ideas from the 'Check 24' process. Within this process, different offerings for the same kind of insurance are compared. These offerings typically origin from several insurance companies. For example, there are different offerings for car insurances. Based on certain input parameters, the end user eventually gets different insurance offers by this process. The proposal service used by 'Check 24' is a common service throughout the German insurance sector and is implemented by various insurance companies.

This service can be called externally by applications such as 'Check 24' through a common interface given by a so called 'BiPro specification'. BiPro is widely used throughout the German insurance sector and the availability of these services has a significant impact on competitiveness. Internally the proposal service is, for example, used in the process 'Angebot erstellen' ('create proposal') of the general German 'Versicherungsanwendungsarchitektur (VAA)' (cf. [4]). The VAA describes a set of standardized insurance processes working within a generalized 'insurance application architecture'. Our project partner has implemented a similar process for its own agent's respective customer portal.

The remainder of this paper is structured as follows: In Section II we discuss some related work. Section III describes our application scenario in some detail. In Section IV and Section V our general Quality of Service (QoS) measurement model and overall concepts are described. Section VI looks at implementation details of our prototypic work. Finally, Section VII concludes this paper and gives some outlook to future work.

II. PRIOR AND RELATED WORK

In prior work, we already discussed several aspects of the combination of SOA, Business Process Management (BPM), Workflow Management Systems (WfMS), Business Rules Management (BRM), and Business Activity Monitoring (BAM) [5][6][7] as well as Distributed Event Monitoring and Distributed Event-Condition-Action (ECA) rule processing [8][9]. Building on this experience, we now address the area of QoS measurement for combined BRM, BPM, and SOA environments within the (German) insurance domain context.

Work related to our research falls into several categories. We will discuss these categories in sequence.

General work on (event) monitoring has a long history (cf. [10][11] or the ACM DEBS conference series for overviews). Monitoring techniques in such (distributed) event based systems are well understood, thus such work can well contribute general monitoring principles to the work presented here. This also includes commercial solutions, such as the Dynatrace [3] system or open source monitoring software, like for example, the NAGIOS [12] solution. In these systems, there is however, no focus on QoS measurement within SOAs. Also, they usually do not take application domain specific requirements into account (as we do with the insurance domain).

Active DBMS (ADBMS) offer some elements for use in our work (see [13][14] for overviews). Event monitoring techniques in ADBMSs are partially useful, but concentrate mostly on monitoring ADBMS internal events, and tend to neglect external and heterogeneous event sources. A major contribution of ADBMSs is their very well defined and proven semantics for definition and execution of Event-Condition-Action (ECA) rules. This leads to general classifications for parameters and options in ADBMS core functionality [14]. We may capture options that are relevant to event monitoring within parts of our general event model. QoS aspects are handled within ADBMS, for example, within the context of database transactions. However, since ADBMSs mostly do not concentrate on heterogeneity (and distribution), let alone SOAs, our work extends research into such directions.

The closest relationship to our research work is which directly combines the aspects QoS and SOA. Since 2002, several articles fall into this category. However, in almost all known articles, the SOA part focuses on WS-* technologies. This is in contrast to our work, which takes the operational environment of our insurance industry partners into account.

Examples of WS-* related QoS work include QoS-based dynamic service bind [15][16], related WS-* standards such as WS-Policy [17], and general research questions for QoS in SOA environments [18].

Design aspects and models for QoS and SOA are addressed in [15][19][20][21][22], SOA performance including QoS in [23], and monitoring for SOA is discussed in articles like [24][25][26][27].

While the above articles discuss several aspects of QoS work including performance monitoring in SOA style environments, none of them takes a standards based insurance domain into account. In contrast, however, we do so by grounding our work on typical insurance services and processes – the Check 24 service and the German 'Versicherungsanwendungsarchitektur (VAA)' (cf. [4]) – as well as in the German-speaking countries (cf. [30]) frequently utilized ISO/IEC 9126 standard for our adjusted SOA quality model.

III. APPLICATION SCENARIO

Customers are using online platforms to compare the conditions and proposals offered by different companies. The online platform check24.com allows customers to compare different insurance proposals. Therefore, the insurance companies need to respond to those requests to be aware of potential customers on such platforms. The underlying scenario for this work is a service for calculating individual proposals for such online platforms. This scenario is automatically requested by the online customer information platform and needs to respond in a timely manner. The business process, for calculating the proposal, follows four steps:

- check input parameters for plausibility,
- call all additional relevant services to get required data,
- calculate the proposal based on internal business rules,
- deliver the proposal to the requesting online platform.

The partner from the insurance industry has already developed a distributed system to create and run such business processes. This system uses the approach of SOA and integrates various SOA-style services located across several locations.

Measuring the time behavior is a feasible approach to maintain the overall system and scale it to changing market demands to fulfill the required quality of such services (QoS). The distributed system is designed with the concept illustrated in Fig. 1.

The system part alpha is the enterprise service bus (ESB) of the system, which is responsible to integrate the business processes with further applications and services. These business processes are parameterized by specific business rules, stored in a business rule database.

The communication with this business rule database is realized via web service calls. In general, alpha is the central communication component of the system.

The system part beta is the current process engine to run the business processes and is connected via JMS with alpha. These

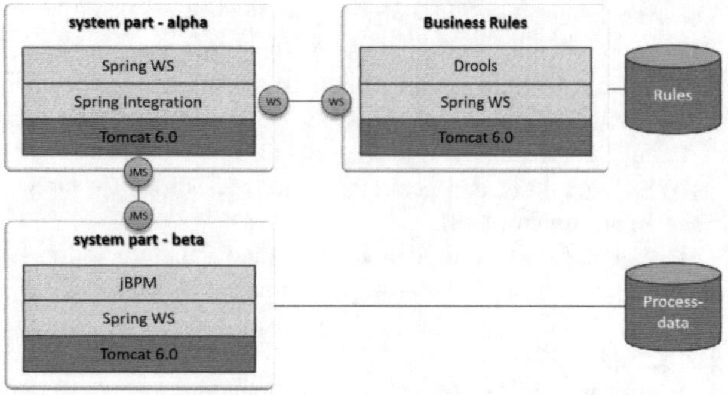

Figure 1: The application scenario

business processes are influenced by the stored business rules and the business process data, which are stored in a separated database.

This distributed system defines the scenario where several services are parameterized, called and integrated (via alpha) over several locations. The generic and XML-based measurement concept of this work will use this scenario to measure QoS-Parameters, especially the time behavior of services. The specific measurement model is described in the next section.

IV. MEASUREMENT MODEL

The assessment of the QoS in Service-oriented Architectures is based on a *SOA Quality Model (SOA QM)*, which combines characteristics and sub-characteristics in a multilevel hierarchy. For this purpose, we adjusted the ISO/IEC-Standard 9126 to meet the SOA-specific requirements. Fig. 2 illustrates the characteristics, sub-characteristics and relationships between these concepts. In our research work, we will focus on the *Time Behavior*, which contributes to *Efficiency*.

Although ISO/IEC 9126 was revised by the ISO/IEC-Standard 25010 (*Systems and software engineering – Systems and software Quality Requirements and Evaluation (SQuaRE) – System and software quality models*, cf. [28][29]) we use ISO/IEC 9126 as a starting point because of its high degree of awareness in German-speaking countries (cf. [30]). Moreover, the German version of the ISO/IEC 25000 series has been prepared by the German Institute for Standardization (DIN) but is not yet available (cf. [31]).

Instead of applying the quality metrics division of SQuaRE (i.e., ISO/IEC 2503x), our approach is based on the comprehensive ISO/IEC-Standard 15939 (cf. [28]). The basic model, as found in similar form in the contribution of Garcia et al. ([32]), has been aligned and extended by quality requirements, quality models, and some system components. In the following subsections, we describe the main concepts of our *SOA Measurement Information Model (SOA MM)* as shown in Fig. 4.

A. Information Need and Information Product

The determination of the QoS in a SOA is always demand-driven, since both the specification ('*What* and *how* should be measured?'), execution of the measurement itself and the subsequent interpretation of the results can cause a significant organizational and technical effort.

So, first of all, the *Information Need* with objectives, potential risks and expected problems has to be defined and documented properly. In terms of the application scenario presented in Section III, the objective is to assess the performance of the business process for calculating the offer in order to identify and resolve problems in time.

B. Core measurement process

The *Information Product* is the result of the execution of the *Core Measurement Process* as depicted in Fig. 3 (cf. [33]). The *Information Need* provides the input for the sub-process *Plan the Measurement Process* (planning stage) and sub-process *Perform the Measurement Process* (execution stage) generates the output, i.e., the Information Product. The process goal is to satisfy the Information Need. All concepts presented below directly or indirectly contribute to the Information Product.

C. Concepts of the planning stage

SOA Services are investigated concerning their QoS, is the main focus of this research work. For this purpose, *Quality Attributes* are measured. In this context, the *Measurable Concept* outlines in an abstract way, *how* the attributes values are determined to satisfy the required Information Needs. In doing so, it references one or more sub-characteristics of the SOA QM.

For the application scenario described in Section III, the process performance is to be determined first and then evaluated. The corresponding Measurable Concept is the calculation of the processing time. To do this, instantiation of a process and termination of the process instance are to be determined. The process identification represents the Quality Attribute to be measured, and the sub-characteristic, referenced by the Measurable Concept, is the Time Behavior.

In order to implement the Measurable Concept and to perform measurements of attributes, first of all *Measures* are to be specified. A Measure assigns each Quality Attribute a value on a *Scale* of a particular *Type*. The ISO/IEC-Standard 15939 provides 3 different types of Measures, namely Base Measures, Derived Measures, and Indicators respectively.

A *Base Measure* specifies by its *Measurement Method* how the value of a Quality Attribute is to be determined. It is always atomic and therefore independent on other Measures.

A *Derived Measure* uses one or more Basic Measures or other Derived Measures, whilst the *Measurement Function* specifies the calculation method and thus the combination of the Measures used.

For the application scenario illustrated in Section III, the Basic Measures process instantiation t_{inst} and process instance termination t_{term} are specified. The identification of the processes instance $piID$ represents the Quality Attribute measured by t_{inst} and t_{term}. As the Measurement Method, we select the time of the start and end event respectively. The

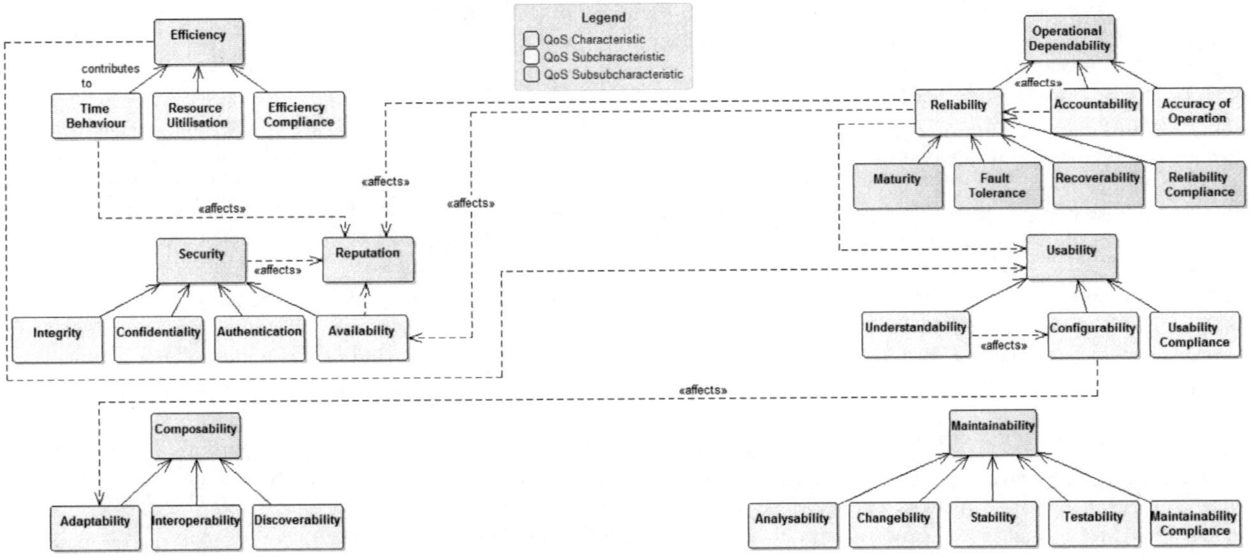

Figure 2: SOA Quality Model

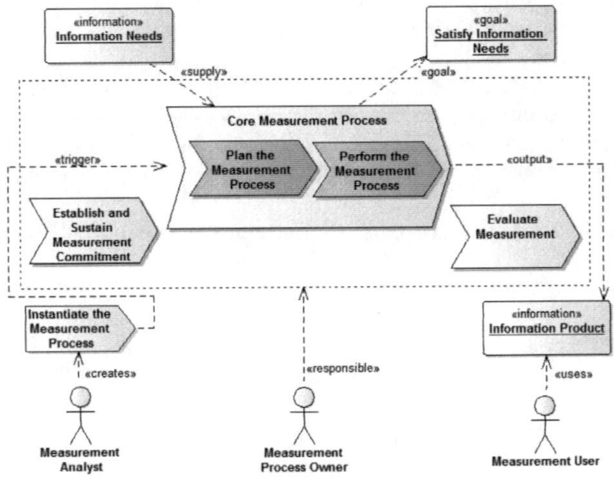

Figure 3: Process for determining the QoS (cf. [33])

Derived Measure processing time of the instance T_{Proc} will be calculated by the Measurement Function

$$T_{Proc}(piID) = \Delta t = t_{term}(piID) - t_{inst}(piID) \quad (1)$$

Another Derived Measure R calculates the percentage of the process instances within a given time period. Than there is a check, if the processing time T_{Proc} exceeds twice the standard deviation. R will be calculated by the Measurement Function

$$R = \frac{m}{n} \cdot 100 \quad (2)$$

where n is the number of all process instances in the given time period and m the number of process instances with $T_{Proc} \geq 2 \cdot \sigma$. The standard deviation σ is given by the formula

$$\sigma = \sqrt{\frac{1}{n} \cdot \sum_{1 \leq i \leq n} (T^i_{Proc} - \overline{T_{Proc}})^2} \quad (3)$$

Finally, an *Indicator* is a qualitative evaluation of Quality Attributes, which directly addresses the issue raised in the Information Needs. Indicators always use a nominal scale with qualifying values and thus show if necessary action is needed for further root cause analysis. An Indicator is derived from other Quality Measures, i.e., Base and Derived Measures, and Indicators. The combination of the Quality Measures used and the method of calculation is based on an *Analysis Model* in conjunction with *Decision Criteria* using thresholds and target values.

For the application scenario illustrated in Section III, the indicator adequacy of the processing time of all process instances in a given time period $SLoT_{Proc}(R)$ is based on the Derived Measure R according to Table I:

TABLE I. ADEQUACY OF THE PROCESSING TIME

R	$SLoT_{Proc}$
$0\% \leq R < 3\%$	high
$3\% \leq R < 5\%$	medium
$5\% \leq R < 100\%$	low

D. Concepts of the execution stage

After the concepts of the planning stage have been presented, now we explain the execution phase in brief (subprocess *Perform the Measurement Process*, depicted in Fig. 3). Section V will discuss their conceptual implementation in more detail.

The actual measuring procedure, i.e., the execution of the instructions for determining the value of a Quality Attribute, is called *Measurement*. Hereby, *Measurement Results* are created, collected in a container, namely *Data*, which is inserted into a *Data Store*.

The measurement system comprises different supporting software components, which are conceptually presented in Section V. The *QoS Measurement* performs the instructions specified in the Measurement Method or Measurement Function respectively, to generate the Measurement Results for further processing. The *QoS Analyser* performs the statistical analysis and evaluation of the collected data and creates the Information Product. The *QoS Reporting* makes the Information Product available to the *Measurement User* (cf. Fig. 3).

E. QoS Measurement Information Model

We designed a domain-specific language to specify the values of the concepts introduced above according to the Information Need. This specification document is referred to as *QoS Information Model (QoS IM)*. The aim of this approach is to automate the measurement process by the generation of artifacts required by the QoS system to execute a measurement.

The QoS IM consists of an abstract and a concrete section. In the abstract section, the concepts of the Planning Stage and partly the Execution Stage are specified. In the concrete section, the implementation specific definitions are explained. Since our QoS-System is based on a complex event processing (CEP) approach, the specification of events, agents and rules is subject of this section.

A sophisticated XML Schema was developed to realize the domain-specific language. We opted for XML as a universally accepted standard that is highly flexible, platform and vendor independent and supported by a wide variety of tools. In a follow-up project an XText-based tool will be developed that generates the (XML) QoS IM from a (XText) source code.

Its semantic model is shown in Fig. 4. The following rules for modeling apply:

- Concepts are mapped to XML elements (graphically represented by UML classes).
- Details of a concept are mapped to XML attributes of the owning element (graphically represented by UML instance variables).
- If possible, relationships between concepts are mapped to element hierarchies (graphically represented by UML associations).
- Otherwise, they are mapped to constraints (i.e., keyrefs) (graphically represented by UML dependencies).

V. Measurement Concept

In Section IV, a QoS IM based upon a SOA QM is described. To execute a specific QoS IM (and thus sub-process 'Perform the Measurement Process') an execution platform is needed. This platform and the underlying QoS architecture are given in this section. First reasons for choosing this specific architecture are discussed shortly. Furthermore, an overview is shown, detailing in the central agent concept and CEP.

A. Design decisions

As described above, the goal of the measurement concept is to provide the execution platform for a specific QoS IM. Therefore, basic design criteria for the measurement concept are derived from the QoS IM. Furthermore, quality criteria are given, which also have to be considered in the architecture design. These criteria are:

- measurement of Quality Attributes as described by QoS IM,
- flexibility of measurement and computation,
- low impact (modification, performance, etc.) onto SOA components.

The proposed Measurement Concept is based upon a general architecture given in [34]. The basic idea is to separate the measurement (e.g., sensors, agents, etc.) and 'analysis and statistics' functionality into different modules. This separation opens the opportunity to cater each module to their specific functional and quality requirements.

Overall, the given general architecture already fulfills the requirement to measure Quality Attributes and provide the needed evaluations to produce Measurement Results and Information Products.

The measurement module has to provide the QoS System with information about the observed service. To provide the needed flexibility a sensor has to be placed into it. To keep the impact onto the SOA at a low level, an agent based approach was chosen. Agents capsule the needed parsing and computation and thus can be easily integrated into arbitrary SOA modules. Furthermore, minimizing the performance impact (through threading, non-blocking, etc.) can be integrated into the agents.

The 'analysis and statistics' module does not have these strict requirements on performance impact. Flexibility of computation and measurement execution is the main quality requirement. Thus, a platform approach was chosen. Basically, artifacts generated through the QoS IM are placed into the QoS Platform and executed.

B. Overall system architecture

On a high level, the QoS System splits the QoS Measurement Agents and further processing (QoS Platform) into different components. This approach allows to easily split these components into different processes to comply with the quality requirements. While the Measurement Agents (encapsulating the agent concept) represents the client component, the server component is represented by the QoS Platform and contains the CEP engine and further analysis processing. Fig. 5 shows a high level overview of important components and their relationships.

The general purpose of the Measurement Agents is to emit specific events based on the defined Base Measures. As described in Section IV events are emitted, e.g., for process instance instantiation/termination. In general, concepts

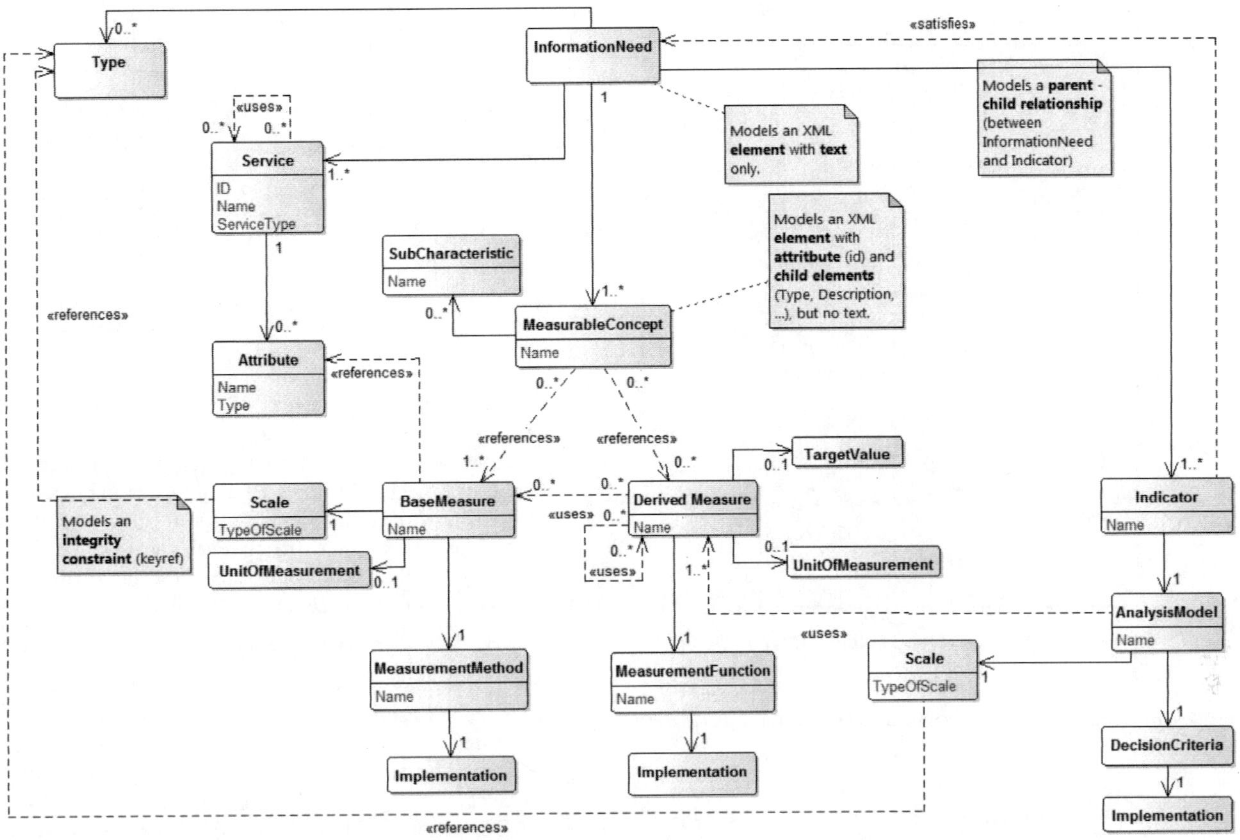

Figure 4: QoS Measurement Information Model (QoS MIM)

for agent implementation can be categorized by agent location and time of execution (cf. [35] and [36]). To measure a specific process instance, agents can be placed into corresponding SOA service calls. Thus, Measurement Agents are only logically placed into the QoS System component. One and currently used approach is to use the concept of interceptors, which offers a low modification impact and can deliver precise Measurement Results.

The QoS Platform consist of several components, most notably the QoS Measurement and QoS Analyzer. In general, the purposes of these modules are to collect, clean and compute the emitted events and provide further analysis of stored Measurement Results (specifically stored as complex events).

Before any event is given to the Measurement Method, it will be handled by the control module. Purpose of this module is event routing, general cleaning steps and an optional filter step. Cleaning (or formatting) events in the analyzer is needed because Measurement Agents are placed in the monitored system, thus shall minimize their performance impact. The Measurement Method is implemented as a CEP rule executed by the engine and emits complex events for further near real-time processing and long term analysis.

The QoS Analyzer module provides a basis for statistical analysis and evaluations. Every complex event is stored into a Data Store implemented as a relational database. The different analysis and evaluations defined by Derived Measures and Indicators are implemented through SQL and plain Java. Furthermore, the module provides an interface to the computed Information Product. As of now, this interface is not further defined. A comprehensive way to define a QoS specific interface is given in [37]. It is defined upon the ISO/IEC 25010 quality standard and specifically includes the ability to describe relationships between QoS attributes. This corresponds with our presented QoS IM approach.

C. Applying the described measurement concept

In Fig. 6, the given measurement concept (QoS Platform) is applied onto the application scenario, thus providing the missing link between the QoS IM and the insurance based application scenario. In this example, a simplified scenario is used consisting only of an external 'Check24' mock-up service (representing a simple consumer), the central ESB and the proposal service (which represents the producer). The task of the measurement model and thus the concept is to measure the

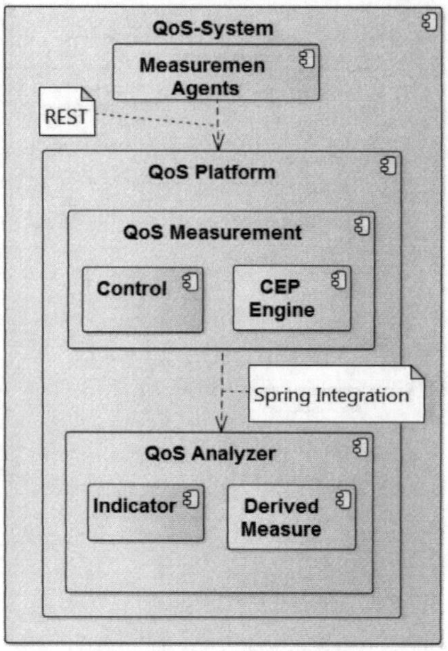

Figure 5: The QoS architecture

processing time of this service and to compute the Information Product for further evaluations.

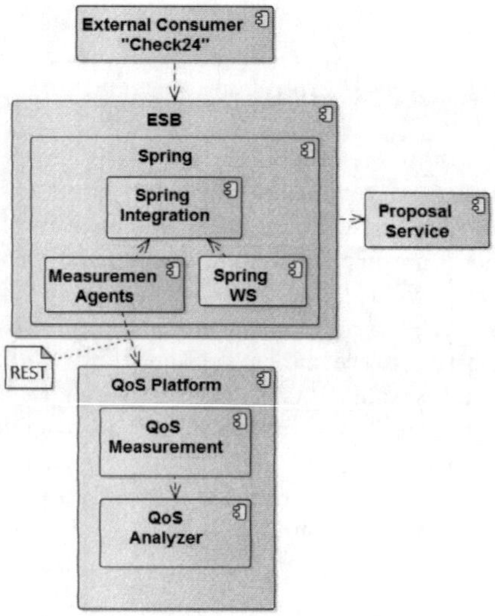

Figure 6: Applied QoS architecture

To measure this service the Measurement Agents, defined through base measures, are placed directly into the ESB. This offers a measurement independent of service location and different load balancing scenarios. To minimize the integration effort, functionality given by Spring Integration is extensively used (especially the interceptors for message queues). In this simplified example, base measures (and thus the agents) only determine service call start / end times and announces these

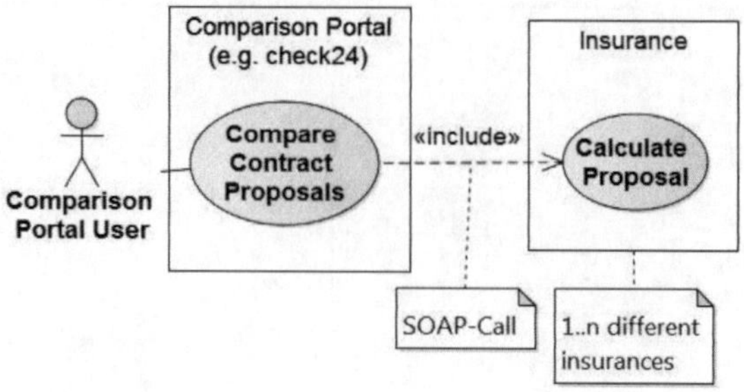

Figure 7: Use case diagram for Proposal Service

to the QoS Platform. Furthermore, the agents try to minimize their performance impact by using non-blocking techniques and performing only necessary parsing steps (e.g., service call IDs, etc.). These will be shown in detail in further publications.

As described above, the QoS Platform performs further cleaning and processing steps to compute the QoS IM Indicators ($SLoT_{Proc}(T_{Proc})$) and provides these to downstream systems (e.g., reporting, presentation, load balancing, etc.).

VI. IMPLEMENTATION DETAILS

Based on the above conceptual groundwork, this section contains a deeper insight into several implementation areas of the QoS System. First, a description of the measured services is given, providing further information about the application scenario. Second, the process of applying a specific QoS IM is shown. After that a detailed walk through of a QoS Event call is presented, describing the different stages and components that are passed through. Furthermore, the distribution of the components is shown, which culminates into a testable runtime environment.

A. *Proposal Service*

In Section III, the overall application scenario is described. Detailing on this a use case diagram is given in Fig. 7. When a user (such as a customer) requests a proposal for a new insurance contract, some information (birthday, coverage, etc.) has to be given to complete the request. Furthermore, certain parameters can be adjusted to gain better results.

After initial parameter checks (validity, completeness, etc.), requests are passed to different companies by SOAP web service calls containing all entered information. Responses (computed proposals) are only considered when they arrive in a timely manner to provide acceptable user experience. This imposes a hard boundary for the QoS Measurement because it has a considerable business impact in case of failures. If a customer decides to sign a new contract, further business processes (e.g., prepare an insurance offer) are started.

To evaluate the general approach and the QoS Platform, a Proposal Service is needed. Using an actual service of the insurance company wasn't possible due to the potential business impact. Also the implementation of a comprehensive business logic was considered to be too complex and thus abandoned. On the other hand, only special information (e.g.,

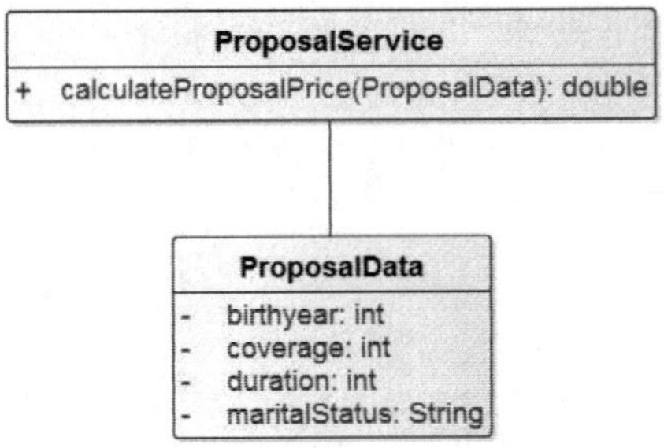

Figure 8: Interface of the (Mock) Proposal Service

correlation id) of the SOA (SOAP call) is needed to determine the Indicator. The Proposal request and result data isn't considered. Therefore, we decided to develop a Mock Service, which also provides the opportunity to customize the desired load behaviour.

The interface of the Mock Proposal Service is given in Fig. 8. It consists of a method returning the monthly cost of the contract to the customer. To calculate the costs, different information is required. For reasons of simplicity, the number of parameters was reduced to four attributes of a customer, in particular her/his birth year, insurance coverage, duration of the contract, and the marital status. Furthermore, these parameters are used in the Mock Service to control the load behaviour.

B. Relationship between IM and QoS platform

In Fig. 9, the general process for applying a specific IM by the QoS Platform is shown. It is divided into different phases. Not all phases have to be executed on each change of the IM.

The first step is to develop an IM for a specific Information Need. As described before, an IM consists of abstract and concrete parts. To satisfy the Information Need, an Indicator and thus different Derived and Basic Measures have to be defined. This represents the first phase. In addition to the abstract part, every Measure and Indicator contains a concrete part. The specification of these parts represents the second phase. In order to develop concrete parts, specific technologies and frameworks have to be chosen, which have to be provided by the QoS Platform or added to it if missing.

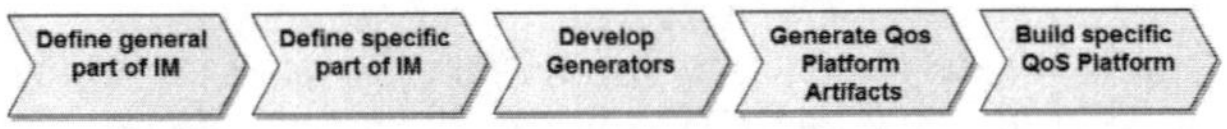

Figure 9: General Process of applying a specific IM

The goal of next phase is to develop the different Generators. This can be skipped if fitting Generators are already developed. The QoS Platform is designed around the concepts of extensibility and modularization. The same ideas were significant when designing the QoS Generator. In general, it provides a parser step to build an optimized in-memory model of an IM. Following this step the Generators are executed. They use the concrete and abstract parts to generate usable artifacts (e.g., Java classes, SQL queries, etc.). A deeper insight into the QoS Generator itself and the concrete parts will be provided in future articles.

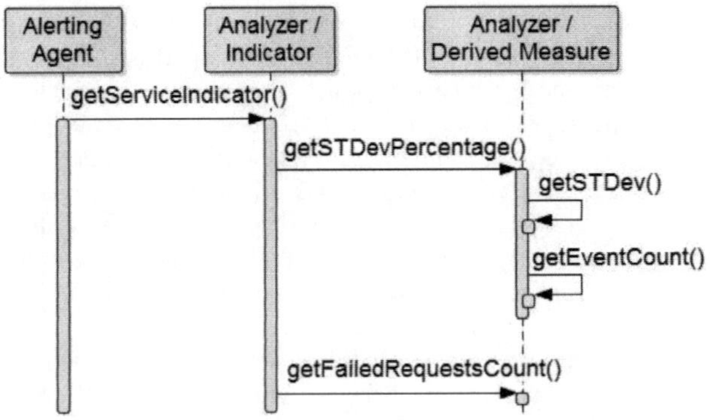

Figure 10: Determining an Indicator

After the generation phase, the goal of the last phase is to build a specific QoS Platform by the integration of artifacts. This is done by developing the necessary bridges and transformations between an artifact and the interfaces (e.g., Event interface) of the platform. Furthermore, the integration of the agents into the SOA is part of this stage. After the last phase is completed, the QoS System can be deployed.

C. Computing an Indicator

The computation of an Indicator is split into two phases. Each phase is initiated by a particular system and refers to different sections of the QoS IM. Furthermore, a specific stage is executed by diverse modules of the QoS System.

The first phase to compute an Indicator is shown in Fig. 11. It details the creation of base events and the persistence of the resulting complex events for long term analysis. This step is executed by the Measurement Agents and QoS Measurement modules and focuses on short term computations.

The computation of an Indicator starts with a call of the corresponding domain service (process, business, or basic service) initiated by a service consumer. As shown in Fig. 11 currently the client is a JMeter based test client, which issues a SOAP call against the Proposal Service. This call is routed by the ESB to a corresponding service handler by passing through several (Spring based) message queues. A QoS Agent is attached to the ProposalRequestChannel as a message queue interceptor which is shown by the handleMessage(request) method call. All requests are parsed inside an Agent and relevant data (e.g., service call id, timestamp, etc.) are combined into raw event data package. A call of the QoS Measurement endpoint of the QoS Platform completes the task of an Agent.

Inside the Measurement module, a new QoS Event is created by formatting (and optionally filtering) the raw event data. Subsequently, this new event is inserted into the CEP Engine. Only if corresponding start and end QoS Events are inserted, the CEP rule is fired and a defined Measurement Method is executed. The method execution results in a complex event /

QoS Event which is send to the QoS Analyzer module. After persisting the event by the module, the first part is completed.

The second phase to compute an Indicator is given in Fig. 10. It includes the computation of further Derived Measures and concludes with the calculation of an Indicator. This step is executed by the QoS Analyzer module and focuses on long term analyses. Actually, this phase is executed only if it is requested by a downstream system (e.g., a system for alerting). For this, the downstream system sends a REST call to the Analyzer module of the Platform.

To get the current Indicator value, several Derived Measures have to be computed first. This is performed by the Derived Measure module. For this application scenario, the Indicator depends on several Measures based upon the standard deviation and number of 'failed' requests.

First, the percentage of requests with a duration above the doubled standard deviation is computed as shown by the getSTDevPercentage() method call. It is done by a combination of Java code and other Derived Measures. The Measures (e.g., getEventCount() method call) are computed by SQL queries against the Data Store. The percentage value is then computed by Java code. The getFailedRequestsCount() method call includes a SQL query. All long term analysis is performed by SQL queries and designed to be based on a specific time frame. The Indicator itself is determined via a Java based decision table which is created by the QoS Generator. The different computation approaches offer the required flexibility for various types of Indicators.

D. Deployment

Fig. 12 shows the current distribution of nodes and components within the QoS-aware SOA. The ESB and the Proposal Service are representing the core of the system. They are deployed in a combined .war file into a Tomcat web application server. Furthermore, it contains the Spring framework dependencies and a company-specific enterprise framework. The Measurement Agents are part of the Framework.jar. Also several configuration files are part of the .war, handling message routing, database access and further functions. The Service Schema .jar file bundles required schemas and classes to allow SOAP communication.

The Proposal Service (e.g., the Service handler and domain logic) itself is part of the ESB Service .jar file. All necessary configurations for an Agent to intercept a service request are part of this file. The corresponding database schema (e.g., for business objects, process and service call relevant data) is deployed into a DB2 database. A JMeter client was used during development and will be applied for further load testing. The Config.xml contains the SOAP request call and further JMeter configuration. The QoS Platform is deployed as a .war file into another Tomcat application server, separating the measured system from the analysis modules.

Table II summarizes our software versions in use. Especially the versions of the OpenSuse virtual machines are based on requirements of our partners from the insurance industry to achieve certain compatibility. The JMeter virtual machine is only relevant for functional testing. Thus, matching versions are irrelevant.

TABLE II. USED SOFTWARE PRODUCTS

Virtual Machine	Software versions
JMeter Ubuntu VM	Apache JMeter: 3.2, Oracle Java: 1.8.0.131, Ubuntu: 14.04.5 LTS
ESB OpenSuse VM	Apache Tomcat: 6.0.44, Oracle Java: 1.6.0.45, OpenSuse: 13.2
DB2 OpenSuse VM	DB2: 10.5.0.5, OpenSuse: 13.2
QoS Platform Ubuntu VM	Apache Tomcat: 6.0.45, Oracle Java: 1.6.0.45, Ubuntu: 14.04.5 LTS

For development and initial testing, the QoS-aware SOA is deployed into virtual machines for several reasons. First, this deployment provides an easy handover procedure with the partner companies. Second, a 'clean' environment for development could be achieved, which helps especially with the database and ESB parts. Third, the distribution of these VMs on a more sophisticated hardware platform is easier. This is the next step and will be followed with more complex tests and first measurements in our ongoing work.

VII. CONCLUSION AND FUTURE WORK

The presented approach for monitoring a distributed SOA environment is a promising path to take: Our SOA QM is aiming to follow the ISO/IEC-Standard 15939 (cf. [33]), which enables a wide range of use cases. The Measurement Concept outlines an execution platform for the specific QoS IM, which should cause minimal impact on the SOA environment. The separation of Measurement Agents and QoS-Analyzer allows lightweight agents on the one hand and a very capable analyzer component on the other hand.

Our ongoing work of applying the QoS System to an application scenario is very much relevant to our partner in the insurance industry (the 'Check 24 process'). It will provide evidence of the practical usability of the created framework. In the present article, the framework and the corresponding platform are applied onto a basic, business relevant scenario (the Proposal Service). Furthermore, it is planned to apply these techniques to the more complex process 'Angebot erstellen' ('create individual proposal') of the VAA, thus implementing a more complex scenario.

It is expected that the monitoring system will help to discover potential bottlenecks in the current system design of our partner's distributed services and therefore creating high value in the process of solving these issues.

In future work, the actual measurement and analysis of the results will be done. It is also planned to apply these results onto cloud based environments. Moreover, a further sub-division or extraction from the current coarse granular SOA services into more fine-grained micro-services 'where it makes sense', (e.g., to allow for a better scalability of individual micro-services) will be investigated by us in future work.

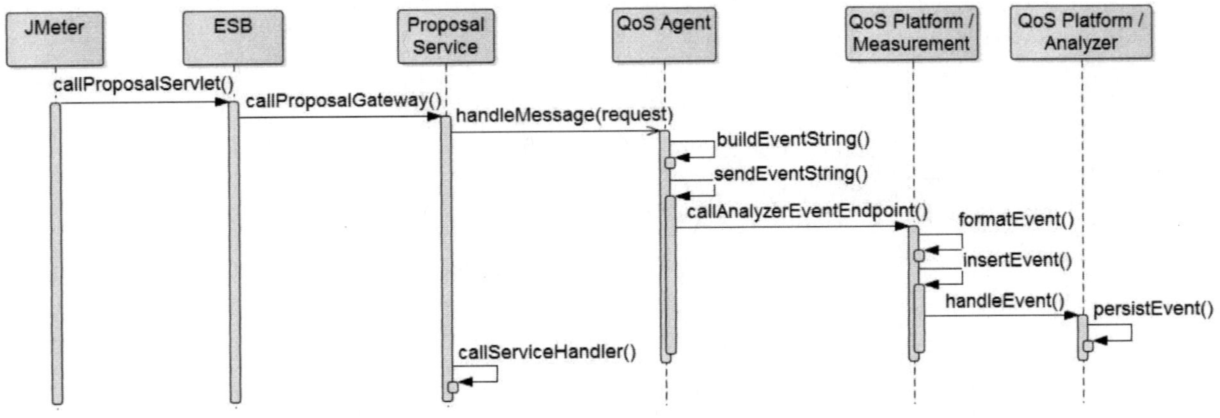

Figure 11: Integration and sequence of a QoS Event call

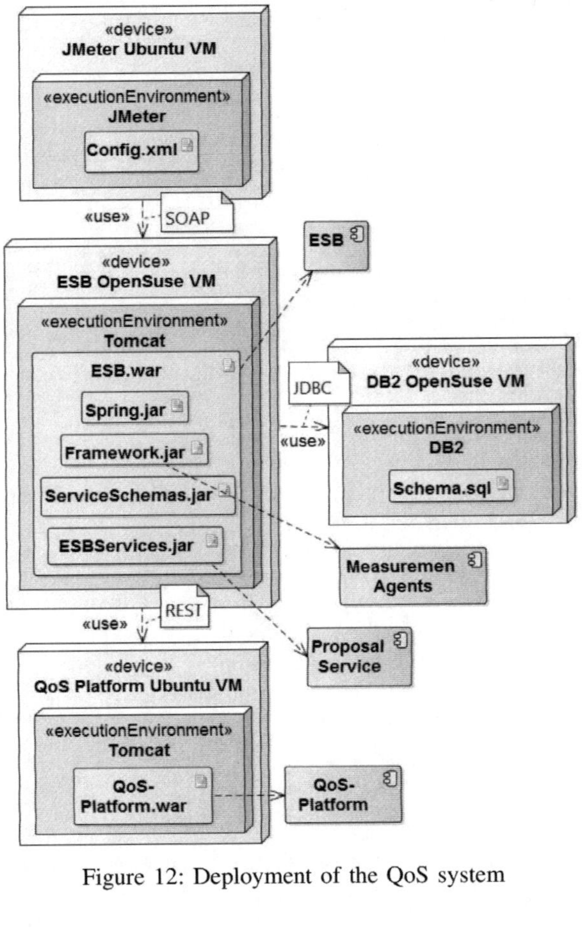

Figure 12: Deployment of the QoS system

REFERENCES

[1] A. Hausotter, A. Koschel, J. Busch, M. Petzsch, and Malte Zuch, "Agent based Framework for QoS Measurement Applied in SOA," in: The Ninth International Conferences on Advanced Service Computing (Service Computation), IARIA, Athens, Greece, pp. 16-23, 2017.

[2] J. Brutlag, "Speed Matters for Google Web Search," Google Inc., Mountain View, 2009, [Online]. URL: http://services.google.com/fh/files/blogs/google_delayexp.pdf [accessed: 2016-12-26].

[3] Dynatrace LLC, "Dynatrace Application Monitoring," [Online]. URL: https://www.dynatrace.com/de/products/application-monitoring.html [accessed: 2016-12-26].

[4] GDV (Gesamtverband der Deutschen Versicherungswirtschaft e.V. – General Association o.t. German Insurance Industry), "Die Anwendungsarchitektur der Versicherungswirtschaft: Das Objektorientierte Fachliche Referenzmodell (The application architecture of the German insurance business – The functional object-oriented reference model", VAA Final Edt. Vers. 2.0, 2001, [Online]. URL: http://www.gdv-online.de/vaa/vaafe_html/dokument/ofrm.pdf [accessed: 2017-01-11].

[5] C. Gäth et al., "Always Stay Agile! – Towards Service-oriented Integration of Business Process and Business Rules Management," in: The Sixth International Conferences on Advanced Service Computing (Service Computation), IARIA, Venice, Italy, 2014, pp. 40-43.

[6] A. Hausotter, C. Kleiner, A. Koschel, D. Zhang, and H. Gehrken, "Always Stay Flexible! WfMS-independent Business Process Controlling in SOA," in: IEEE EDOCW 2011: Workshops Proc. of the 15th IEEE Intl. Enterprise Distributed Object Computing Conference, IEEE: Helsinki, Finnland, 2011, pp. 184-193.

[7] T. Bergemann, A. Hausotter, and A. Koschel, "Keeping Workflow-Enabled Enterprises Flexible: WfMS Abstraction and Advanced Task Management," in: 4th Int. Conference on Grid and Pervasive Computing Conference (GPC), 2009, pp. 19-26.

[8] A. Koschel and R. Kramer, "Configurable Event Triggered Services for CORBA-based Systems," Proc. 2nd Intl. Enterprise Distributed Object Computing Workshop (EDOC'98), San Diego, U.S.A, 1998, pp. 1-13.

[9] M. Schaaf, I. Astrova, A. Koschel, and S. Gatziu, "The OM4SPACE Activity Service - A semantically well-defined cloud-based event notification middleware," in: IARIA Intl. Journal On Advances in Software, 7(3,4), 2014, pp. 697-709.

[10] B. Schroeder, "On-Line Monitoring: A Tutorial," IEEE Computer, 28(6), pp. 72-80, 1995.

[11] S. Schwiderski, "Monitoring the Behavior of Distributed Systems," PhD thesis, Selwyn College, University of Cambridge, University of Cambridge, Computer Lab, Cambridge, United Kingdom, 1996.

[12] Nagios.ORG, "Nagios Core Editions," [Online]. URL: https://www.nagios.org/ [accessed: 2016-12-26].

[13] N. W. Paton (ed.), "Active Rules for Databases," Springer, New York, 1999.

[14] ACT-NET Consortium, "The Active DBMS Manifesto," ACM SIGMOD Record, 25(3), 1996.

[15] M. Garcia-Valls, P. Basanta-Val, M. Marcos, and E. Estévez, "A bi-dimensional QoS model for SOA and real-time middleware," in: Intl. Journal of Computer Systems Science and Engineering, CLR Publishing, 2013, pp. 315-326.

[16] V. Krishnamurthy and C. Babu, "Pattern Based Adaptation for Service Oriented Applications," in: ACM SIGSOFT Softw. Eng. Notes 37, 2012(1), 2012, pp. 1-6.

[17] T. Frotscher, G. Starke (ed.), and S. Tilkov (ed.), "Der Webservices-Architekturstack," in: SOA-Expertenwissen, Heidelberg, dpunkt.verlag, 2007, pp. 489-506.

[18] F. Curbera, R. Khalaf, and N. Mukhi, "Quality of Service in SOA Environments. An Overview and Research Agenda," in: it - Information Technology 50, 2008(2), 2008, pp. 99-107.

[19] G. Wang, A. Chen, C. Wang, C. Fung, and S. Uczekaj, "Integrated Quality of Service (QoS) Management in Service-Oriented Enterprise Architectures," in: Proceedings of the 8th IEEE Intl. Enterprise Distributed Object Computing Conference (EDOC'04), Washington DC, USA, IEEE, 2004, pp. 21-32.

[20] S.W. Choi, J.S. Her, and S.D. Kim, "QoS Metrics for Evaluating Services from the Perspective of Service Providers," in: Proc. of the IEEE International Conference on e-Business Engineering, Washington DC, USA : IEEE Computer Society (ICEBE'07), 2007, pp. 622-625.

[21] M. Varela, L. Skorin-Kapov, F. Guyard, and M. Fiedler, "Meta-Modeling QoE", PIK-Praxis der Informationsverarbeitung und Kommunikation, 2014, Vol. 37(4), pp. 265-274.

[22] Z. Balfagih and M.F. Hassan, "Quality Model for Web Services from Multi-stakeholders' Perspective," in: Proceedings of the 2009 International Conference on Information Management and Engineering, Washington DC, USA : IEEE Computer Society (ICIME'09), 2009, pp. 287-291.

[23] R.W. Maule and W.C. Lewis, "Performance and QoS in Service-Based Systems", Proc. of the 2011 IEEE World Congress on Services, IEEE Computer Society, 2011, pp. 556-563.

[24] F. Rosenberg, C. Platzer, and S. Dustdar, "Bootstrapping Performance and Dependability Attributes of Web Services," in: Proc. International Conference on Web Services (ICWS'06), 2006, pp. 205-212.

[25] M. Schmid, J. Schaefer, and R. Kroeger, "Ein MDSD-Ansatz zum QoS-Monitoring von Diensten in Serviceorientierten Architekturen," in: PIK Praxis der Informationsverarbeitung und Kommunikation, 31 (2008) 4, 2008, pp. 232-238.

[26] B. Wetzstein et al., "Monitoring and Analyzing Influential Factors of Business Process Performance," in: Proc. IEEE Intl. Enterprise Distributed Object Computing Conf. (EDOC'09), 2009, pp. 141-150.

[27] S.M.S. da Cruz, R.M. Costa, M. Manhaes, and J. Zavaleta, "Monitoring SOA-based Applications with Business Provenance", Proc. of the 28th Annual ACM Symposium on Applied Computing (ACM SAC), ACM, 2013, pp. 1927-1932.

[28] ISO - International Organization for Standardization (ed.), "ISO/IEC 25010:2011 - Systems and software engineering – Systems and software Quality Requirements and Evaluation (SQuaRE) – System and software quality models", 2011.

[29] M. Azuma, "SQuaRE: the next generation of the ISO/IEC 9126 and 14598 international standards series on software product quality, " in: Proc. of European Software Control and Metrics (ESCOM), 2001, pp. 337-346.

[30] H. Balzert, "Lehrbuch der Softwaretechnik: Softwaremanagement", Springer Spektrum, Heidelberg, 2008.

[31] DIN NIA, "ISO/IEC 25000 System und Software-Engineering - Qualitätskriterien und Bewertung von System- und Softwareprodukten (SQuaRE - Leitfaden für SQuaRE," [Online]. URL: http://www.din.de/de/mitwirken/normenausschuesse/nia/normen/wdc-beuth:din21:204260933 [accessed: 2017-01-01].

[32] F. Garcia et al., "Towards a consistent terminology for software measurement," in: Information and Software Technology, vol. 48, 2006, No. 8, pp. 631-644.

[33] ISO - International Organization for Standardization (ed.), "ISO/IEC 15939:2007 - Systems and software engineering - Measurement process," 2007.

[34] A. Wahl, A. Al-Moayed, and B. Hollunder, "An Architecture to Measure QoS Compliance in SOA Infrastructures," Service Computation, 2010, pp. 27-33.

[35] E. Oberortner, S. Sobernig, U. Zdun, and S. Dustdar, "Monitoring Performance-Related QoS Properties in Service-Oriented Systems: A Pattern-Based Architectural Decision Model," EuroPLoP, 2011, pp. 1-37.

[36] E. Oberortner, U. Zdun, and S. Dustdar, "Patterns for Measuring Performance-related QoS Properties in Service-oriented Systems," Pattern Languages of Programs Conference, 2010, pp. 1-21.

[37] L. Lavazza, S. Morasca and D. Tosi, "Enriching Specifications to Represent Quality in Web Services in a Comprehensive Way," IEEE Symposium on Service-Oriented System Engineering, 2015, pp. 203-208.

Solution Languages: Easing Pattern Composition in Different Domains

Michael Falkenthal, Johanna Barzen, Uwe Breitenbücher, and Frank Leymann
Institute of Architecture of Application Systems
University of Stuttgart
Stuttgart, Germany
Email: {lastname}@iaas.uni-stuttgart.de

Abstract—**Patterns and pattern languages are a pervasive means to capture proven solutions for frequently recurring problems. However, there is often a lack of concrete guidance to apply them to concrete use cases at hand. Since patterns capture the essence of many solutions, which have practically proven to solve a problem properly, the knowledge about applying them to concrete individual problems at hand is lost during the authoring process. This is because information about how to apply a pattern in particular fields, technologies, or environmental contexts is typically lost due to the abstract nature of the solution of a pattern. In our previous works, we presented (i) the concept of linking concrete solutions to patterns in order to ease the pattern application and (ii) how these concrete solutions can be organized into so-called Solution Languages. In this work, we build upon these concepts and show the feasibility of Solution Languages via their application in different domains. Finally, we show how Solution Languages can be authored via a wiki-based prototype.**

Keywords–Pattern Language; Solution Language; Pattern Application; Solution Selection; Digital Humanities.

I. Introduction

In many domains, expertise and proven knowledge about how to solve frequently recurring problems are captured into patterns. Besides the conceptual solution knowledge captured into patterns also concrete realizations can ease and guide the elaboration of overall solutions. In this work we build upon our concept of *Solution Languages* [1] to show its general feasibility by application scenarios in different domains. Thereby, we provide evidence for the generality of Solution Languages by means of applications in IT domains and, exemplarily, in the non-IT domain of the digital humanities.

Originated by Christopher Alexander et al. [2] in the domain of building architecture, the pattern concept was also heavily applied in many disciplines in computer science. Patterns were authored, e.g., to support object-oriented design [3], for designing software architectures [4], for human-computer interaction [5], to integrate enterprise applications [6], for documenting collaborative projects [7], to support application provisioning [8] or to foster the understanding of new emerging fields like the Internet of Things [9] [10]. Triggered by the successful application of the pattern concept in computer science, it also gains momentum in non-IT disciplines such as creative learning [11] as well as disaster prevention and surviving [12]. Recently, collaborative research led to the application of patterns to the domain of *digital humanities* [13].

In general, patterns capture domain knowledge as *nuggets of advice*, which can be easily read and understood. They are interrelated with each other to form pattern languages, which ease and guide the navigation through the domain knowledge. This is often supported by links between patterns that carry specific semantics that help to find relevant other patterns based on a currently selected one [14]. In previous work, we showed that this principle can be leveraged to organize patterns on different levels of abstraction into pattern languages [15]. *Refinement links* can be used to establish navigation paths through a set of patterns, which lead a user from abstract and generic patterns to more specific ones that, e.g., provide technology-specific implementation details about the problem – often presented as implementation examples. We further showed that also concrete solutions, i.e., concrete artifacts that implement a solution described by a pattern, can be stored in a solution repository and linked to patterns [16] [17]. Thus, we were able to show that pattern-based problem solving is not only limited to the conceptual level, but rather can be guided via pattern refinement towards technology-specific designs and, finally, the selection and reuse of concrete solutions.

However, this approach still lacks guidance for navigation through the set of concrete solutions. Currently, navigation is only enabled on the level of pattern languages, while it is not possible to navigate from one concrete solution to others, due to missing navigation structures. This hinders the reuse of available concrete solutions especially in situations when many different and technology-specific concrete implementations of patterns have to be combined. As a result, it is neither easily understandable which concrete solutions can be combined to realize an aggregated solution, nor which working steps actually have to be done to conduct an aggregation. Thus, an approach is missing that allows to systematically document such knowledge in an easily accessible, structured, and human-readable way.

Therefore, we present the concept of *Solution Languages*, which introduces navigable semantic links between concrete solutions. A Solution Language organizes concrete solution artifacts analogously to pattern languages organize patterns. Their purpose is to ease and guide the navigation through the set of concrete solutions linked to patterns of a pattern language and, thus, ease the actual implementation of patterns via the reuse of already present concrete solutions. Thereby, knowledge about how to aggregate two concrete solutions is documented on the semantic link connecting them. This concept results in navigable networks of concrete solution artifacts, which can be aggregated to ease the implementation of overall solutions. It connects the perspective design with concrete implementations resulting in a novel approach for pattern-based software engineering.

The remainder of this paper is structured as following: as in our previous work [1], we provide background information and give a more detailed motivation in Section II. Then, we introduce the concept of Solution Languages and a means to add knowledge about solution aggregation in Section III. Besides the application in the domain of cloud application architecture, we extend the validation of our approach by an application scenarios in the domain of cloud application management. Further, we discuss how the presented concept of Solution Languages can be applied in domains apart from information technology (IT) in the domain of costumes in films in Section IV. We show the technical feasibility of Solution Languages by a prototype based on wiki-technology and by implementing the presented use cases of cloud application architecture and cloud application management in Section V. We discuss related work in Section VI and, finally, conclude this work in Section VII by an outlook to future work.

II. Background and Motivation

Patterns document proven solutions for recurring problems. They are human-readable documentations of domain expertise. Thereby, their main purpose is to make knowledge about how to effectively solve problems easily accessible to readers. According to Meszaros and Doble [18], they are typically written and structured using a common format that predefines sections such as the *Problem*, which is solved by a pattern, the *Context* in which a pattern can be applied, the *Forces* that affect the elaboration of concrete solutions, the *Solution*, which is a description of how to solve the exposed problem, and a *Name* indicating the essence of a pattern's solution.

Patterns are typically not isolated from each other but are linked with each other to enable the navigation from one pattern to other ones, which are getting relevant once it is applied. In this manner, a navigable network of patterns is established — a *pattern language* [19]. Often, a pattern language is established by referring other patterns in the running text of a pattern by mentioning them. This applies, especially, to pattern languages that are published as a monograph. Using wikis as platforms for authoring and laying out a library of patterns has further enabled to establish semantic links between patterns [7] [20]. This allows to enrich a pattern language to clearly indicate different navigation possibilities by different link types. Such link types can state, e.g., *AND*, *OR*, and *XOR* semantics, describing that after the application of a pattern other patterns are typically also applied, that there are additional patterns, which can be alternatively applied, or that there is an exclusive choice of further patterns that can be applied afterwards, respectively [7]. Further, they can tell a reader, for example, that a pattern is dealing with the equivalent problem of another pattern, but gives solution advice on a more fine-grained level in terms of additional implementation- and technology-specific knowledge [15]. Thus, the navigation through and even between pattern languages can be eased significantly.

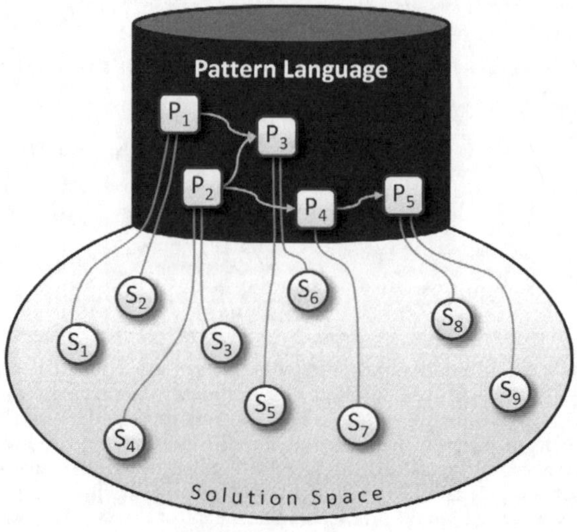

Figure 1. Missing Navigation Support through the Space of Concrete Solutions connected to a Pattern Language

Since patterns and pattern languages capture the essence and expertise from many concrete solutions of recurring problems, implementation details, such as technology-specific or environmental constraints, which affect the actual application of a pattern for specific problems at hand, are abstracted away during the pattern authoring process [21] [22]. As a result, this abstraction ensures that only the *conceptual core ideas* of how to solve a problem in a context are captured into a pattern, which makes the pattern applicable to many similar concrete use cases that may occur. In the course of this, the application of patterns for specific use cases gets unnecessarily hard because concrete solutions, i.e., implementations of a pattern, are lost during this authoring process. Thus, we showed that connecting concrete solutions to patterns in order to make them reusable when a pattern has to be applied is a valuable concept to save time consuming efforts [16] [17]. This concept is depicted in Fig. 1, where a pattern language is illustrated as a graph of connected patterns at the top. Based on the conceptual solution knowledge, the pattern language opens a solution space, illustrated as an ellipse below the pattern language, which is the space of all possible implementations of the pattern language. Concrete solutions that implement individual patterns of the pattern language are, consequently, located in the solution space and are illustrated as circles. They are linked with the pattern they implement, which enables to directly reuse them once a pattern is selected from the pattern language in order to be applied.

However, while navigation through conceptual solutions is provided by pattern languages in terms of links between patterns, such navigation capabilities are currently not present on the level of concrete solutions due to the absence of links between the concrete solutions. Thus, if a concrete solution is selected, there is no guidance to navigate through the set of all available and further relevant concrete solutions.

Navigation is only possible on the conceptual level of patterns by navigation structures of the pattern language. This is time consuming if experts have their conceptual solution already in mind and want to quickly traverse through available concrete solutions in order to examine if they can reuse some of them for implementing their use case at hand. Further, if a set of concrete solutions is already present that provides implementation building blocks for, e.g., a specific technology, it is often necessary to quickly navigate between them in order to understand their dependencies for reusing them. This is specifically the case if concrete solutions cannot be reused directly but need to be adapted to a specific use case, especially if they have to be used in combination. Then, they still can provide a valuable basis for starting adaptions instead of recreating a concrete solution from scratch. Finally, if some concrete solutions have proven to be typically used in combination it is valuable to document this information to ease their reuse. While this could be done on the level of a pattern language, we argue that this is bad practice because implementation details would mix up with the conceptual character of the pattern language. This would require to update a pattern language whenever implementation insights have to be documented. It can get cumbersome, if concrete solutions are collected over a long period of time and technology shifts lead to new implementations and approaches on how to aggregate them, while the more general pattern language stays the same.

Therefore, to summarize the above discussed deficits, there is (i) a lack of organization and structuring at the level of concrete solutions, which (ii) leads to time consuming efforts for traversing concrete solutions, and that (iii) prevents the documentation of proven combinations of concrete solutions.

III. Solution Languages: A Means to Structure, Organize, and Compose Concrete Solutions

To overcome the discussed deficits, we introduce the concept of *Solution Languages*. The core idea of Solution Languages is to transfer the capabilities of a pattern language to the level of concrete solutions having the goal of easing and guiding the application of patterns via reusing concrete solutions in mind. Specifically, the following capabilities have to be enabled on the level of concrete solutions: (R_1) navigation between concrete solutions, (R_2) navigation guidance to find relevant further concrete solutions, and (R_3) documentation capabilities for managing knowledge about dependencies between concrete solutions, e.g., how to aggregate different concrete solutions to elaborate comprehensive solutions based on multiple patterns.

A. Ease and Guide Traversing of Concrete Solutions

In our previous work we have shown how concrete solutions can be linked with patterns in order to ease pattern application [16] [17]. While this is indicated in Fig. 1 by the links between the patterns and the concrete solutions in the solution space, the systematic structuring and organization of the concrete solutions is still an open issue (cf. Section II).

Thus, to realize the requirements (R_1) and (R_2), a Solution Language establishes links between concrete solutions, which are annotated by specific semantics that support a user to decide if a further concrete solution is relevant to solve his or her problem at hand. This is especially important, if multiple patterns have to be applied and, thus, also multiple linked concrete solutions have to be combined. Thereby, the semantics of a link can indicate that concrete solutions connected to different patterns *can be aggregated* with each other, that individual concrete solutions are *variants* that implement the same pattern, or if exactly one of more *alternative* concrete solutions can be used in combination with another one.

Depending on the needs of users also additional link semantics can be added to a Solution Language. To give one example, semantic links can be introduced that specifically indicate that selected concrete solutions *must not be aggregated*. This is useful in cases when concrete solutions can be technically aggregated on the one hand, but on the other hand implement non-functional attributes that prevent to create a proper aggregated solution. Such situations might occur, e.g., in the field of cloud computing, where applications can be distributed across different cloud providers around the world. Then, this is also implemented by the concrete solutions that are building blocks of such applications. Different concrete solutions can force that individual parts of an application are deployed in different regions of the world. In some cases, law, local regulations, or compliance policies of a company can restrict the distribution of components of an application to specific countries [23]. In such situations, it is very valuable to document these restrictions on the level of concrete solutions via the latter mentioned link type. This can prevent users from unnecessarily navigating to concrete solutions that are irrelevant in such use cases. Nevertheless, the concrete solutions that are not allowed to be used in a specific scenario can be kept in a Solution Language, e.g., for later reuse if preventing factors change or as a basis for adaptions that make them compliant.

While (R_1) and (R_2) can be realized by means of semantically typed links between concrete solutions as introduced above, (R_3) requires to introduce the concept of a *Concrete Solution Aggregation Descriptor (CSAD)*. A CSAD allows to annotate a link between concrete solutions by additional documentation that describes how concrete solutions can be aggregated in a human-readable way. This can be, e.g., a specific description of the working steps required to aggregate the concrete solutions connected by the annotated link. Beyond that, a CSAD can also contain any additionally feasible documentation, such as a sketch of the artifact resulting from the aggregation, which supports the user. The actual content of a CSAD is highly specific for the domain of the concrete solutions. The aggregation of concrete solutions that are programming code can, for example, often be described by adjustments of configurations, by manual steps to be performed in a specific integrated development environment (IDE), or by means of additional code snippets required for the aggregation. In other domains, such as the non-technical domain of costumes in films, the required documentation to aggregate concrete solutions looks quite different and can be, for example, a manual about how to combine different pieces of clothing, which in this case are concrete solutions, in order to achieve a desired impression

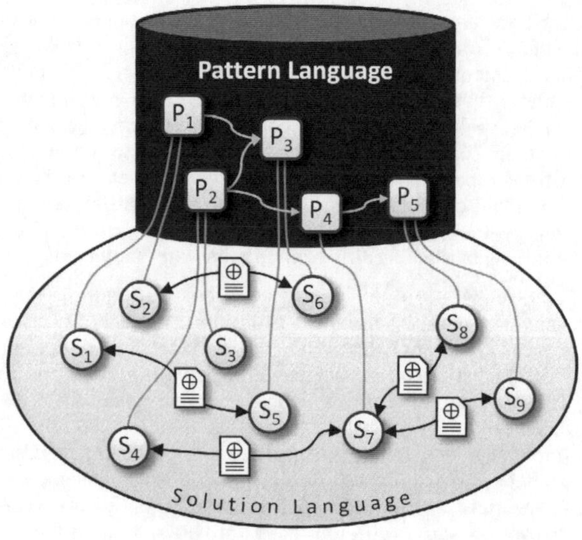

Figure 2. A Solution Language structures the Solution Space of a Pattern Language and enables navigation through relevant Concrete Solutions

of a character in a movie. Thus, a CSAD can be leveraged to systematically document concrete implementation knowledge about how to create aggregated overall solutions.

As a result, CSADs are the means to add arbitrary documentation to a Solution Language about how to aggregate concrete solutions. Hence, a Solution Language can be iteratively extended over time to preserve the expert knowledge of a domain on the implementation level the same way as pattern languages do on the conceptual level. Especially in situations when technologies are getting outdated and experts, which are required to maintain systems implemented in such technologies are getting only scarcely available, Solution Languages can be valuable instruments that preserve technology-specific implementation expertise and documentation. Since concrete solutions are also connected to the patterns they implement, conceptual as well as implementation knowledge can be kept easily accessible and inherently connected.

The overall concept of a Solution Language is illustrated in Fig. 2. There, concrete solutions are linked to the patterns they implement. This enables a user to navigate from patterns to concrete implementations that can be reused, as described in our earlier work [16] [17]. Additionally, the concrete solutions are also linked with each other in order to allow navigation on the level of concrete solutions. For the sake of simplicity and clarity, Fig. 2 focusses on links that represent *can be aggregated with* semantics, thus, we omitted other link types. Nevertheless, the relations between the concrete solutions can capture arbitrary semantics, such as those discussed above. The semantic links between concrete solutions and the fact that they are also linked to the patterns, which they implement, enables to enter the Solution Language at a certain concrete solution and allows to navigate among only the relevant concrete solutions that are of interest for a concrete use case at hand. For example, if concrete solutions are available that implement patterns in different technologies, then they typically cannot be aggregated. Thus, entering the Solution language at a certain concrete solution and then navigating among only those concrete solutions that are implemented using the same technology, using semantic links indicating this coherence (e.g., *can be aggregated with*), can reduce the effort to elaborate an overall composite solution significantly. Finally, Fig. 2 depicts CSADs attached to links between concrete solutions in the form of documents. These enrich the semantic links and provide additional arbitrary documentation on how to aggregate the linked concrete solutions. This way, a Solution Language delegates the principles of pattern languages to the level of concrete solutions, which helps to structure and organize the set of available concrete solutions. While a pattern language guides a user through a set of abstract and conceptual solutions in the form of patterns, a Solution Language provides similar guidance for combining concrete solutions to overall artifacts, all provided by semantic links between concrete solutions and additional documentation about how to aggregate them. Navigation support between concrete implementations of patterns cannot be given by a pattern language itself, because one pattern can be implemented in many different ways, even in ones that did not exist at the time of authoring the pattern language. Thus, the elucidated guidance is required on the solution level due to the fact that a multitude of different and technology-specific concrete solutions can implement the concepts provided by a pattern language.

B. Mapping Solution Paths from Pattern Languages to Solution Languages

Since pattern languages organize and structure patterns to a navigable network, they can be used to select several patterns to solve a concrete problem at hand by providing conceptual solutions. A user typically tries to find a proper entry point to the pattern language by selecting a pattern that solves his or her problem at least partially. Starting from this pattern, he or she navigates to further patterns in order to select a complete set of patterns that solve the entire problem at hand in combination. This way, several patterns are selected along paths through the pattern language. Thus, the selected patterns are also called a *solution path* through the pattern language [15] [24]. Figure 3 shows such a solution path by the selected patterns P_2, P_4, and P_5. If several solution paths proof to be successful for recurring use cases, this can be documented into the pattern language to present stories that provide use case-specific entry points to the pattern language [25]. Further, if several concrete solutions are often aggregated by means of the same CSAD, then this can reveal that there might be a candidate of a composite pattern that can be added to the pattern language by abstracting the underlying solution principles. This might be supported and automated by data mining techniques in specific domains [26].

Due to the fact that concrete solutions are linked with the patterns they implement, solution paths through a pattern language can support to find suitable entry points to the

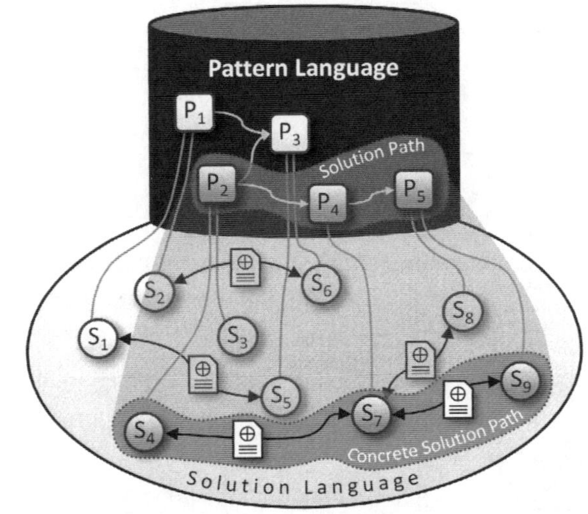

Figure 3. Solution Path from a Pattern Language projected to a Solution Language

corresponding Solution Language. Accordingly, a user can navigate from P_2 to the concrete solution S_4. From there, the Solution Language provides navigation support to find further concrete solutions that can be aggregated with S_4. If concrete solutions are available for all patterns contained in the solution path, and if these can be aggregated with each other, then the solution path can be mapped to a *concrete solution path* in the Solution Language. This is illustrated in Fig. 3 by the highlighted path from S_4 via S_7 to S_9 through the Solution Language. Concrete solution paths allow to translate design decisions that are taken on the conceptual level of the pattern language to reusable concrete solutions that are organized into the Solution Language. The mapping of the solution path to a corresponding set of concrete solutions of the Solution Language can, consequently, provide knowledge about how to elaborate an aggregated solution of the selected patterns by CSADs of the Solution Language, which can significantly speed up the elaboration of an overall composite concrete solution.

IV. Application of Solution Languages

In the following, we show the feasibility of the Solution Languages concept on the basis of application scenarios in domains in which we have already investigated and researched pattern languages. These are the IT domains *Cloud Application Architecture* and *Cloud Application Management* as well as the non-IT domain of *Costumes in Films*. The latter scenario demonstrates that the concept of Solution Languages is not tied to IT but can be rather applied to other domains, too.

A. Application in the Domain of Cloud Architecture

The first application scenario deals with designing application architectures that natively support cloud computing characteristics and technologies. In this context, the pattern language of Fehling et al. [27] provides knowledge about tailoring applications to leverage the capabilities of cloud environments such as Amazon Web Services (AWS) [28]. One important capability in terms of cloud computing is the automatic and elastic scaling of compute resources. To enable this, the pattern language provides the patterns *Elastic Load Balancer* and *Stateless Component*. *Elastic Load Balancer* describes how the workload of an application can be distributed among multiple instances of the application. If the workload increases, additional instances are added to keep the application responsive. Once the workload decreases unnecessary instances are decommissioned to save processing power and expenses. Thereby, the actual workload, i.e., requests from clients, is spread among the different application instances by means of a so-called load balancer component, which maintains and manages the available endpoints of the instances. The *Elastic Load Balancer* pattern links to the *Stateless Component* pattern, which describes how components that contain the business logic of an application can manage their state externally, e.g., in an additional database. This behavior enables to scale them elastically because recently created instances can fetch state from the external datastore and write changes back to it. As a result, state synchronization among the different application instances is handled via the database and no further synchronization and state replication mechanisms are required. Both patterns are depicted at the top of Fig. 4, whereby a directed edge connects them indicating the pattern language structure expressing that once *Elastic Load Balancer* is used then also *Stateless Component* is ordinarily used.

Realizations of these patterns can be connected to them, as depicted in the figure by S_1 and S_2. These concrete solutions implement the patterns by means of AWS CloudFormation [29] snippets, which allows to describe collections of AWS-resources by means of a java script object notation (JSON)-based configuration language. Such configurations can be uploaded to AWS CloudFormation, which then automatically provisions new instances of the described resources. An excerpt of the CloudFormation snippet that describes a load balancer is shown on the left of Fig. 4. The *MyLoadBalancer* configuration defines properties of the load balancer, concretely the port and protocol, which are required to receive and forward workload. The corresponding CloudFormation snippet, which implements the concrete solution S_2 is shown on the right. So-called *Amazon Machine Images (AMI)* allow to package all information required to create and start virtual servers in the AWS cloud. Therefore, the *MyLaunchCfg* snippet of S_2 contains a reference to the AMI *ami-statelessComponent*, which is able to create and start a new virtual server that hosts an instance of a stateless component. The link between S_1 and S_2 illustrates that they *can be aggregated* in order to obtain an overall composite solution, which results in a complete configuration that allows the load balancer instance to distribute workload over instances of virtual servers hosting the stateless component.

If a user wants to aggregate both snippets, he or she can study the CSAD attached to the link between both concrete solutions, which is outlined in the middle of the

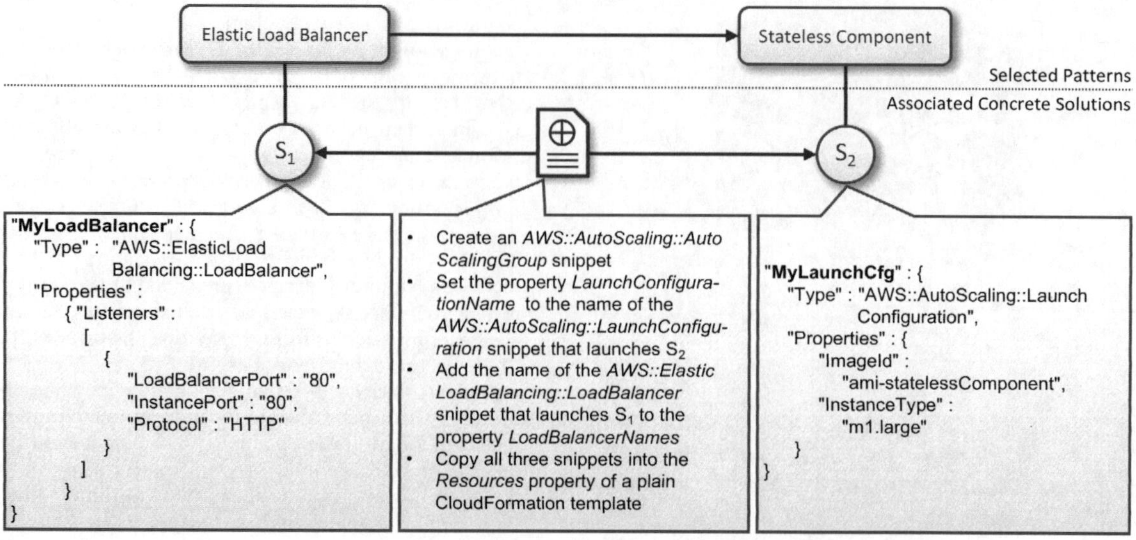

Figure 4. Concrete Solution Aggregation Descriptor documenting how to aggregate concrete solutions in the form of two CloudFormation snippets

figure. The CSAD provides detailed information about the actual working steps that have to be performed in order to combine both CloudFormation snippets. Therefore, the CSAD describes that both snippets have to be aggregated via a so-called *AutoScalingGroup*, which is itself also a CloudFormation snippet. The AutoScalingGroup references both, the *MyLoadBalancer* and the *MyLaunchCfg* snippets via the properties *LaunchConfigurationName* and *LoadBalancerNames*. Finally, all three snippets have to be integrated into the property *Resources* of a plain CloudFormation template. By documenting all this information into the Solution Language, (i) the link from concrete solutions in form of CloudFormation snippets to the patterns they implement, (ii) the semantic link between these concrete solutions indicating that they *can be aggregated*, and (iii) the detailed documentation about how to perform the aggregation can significantly ease the application of the two patterns to elaborate an overall combined solution.

B. Application in the Domain of Cloud Management

In this section, we apply the concept of Solution Languages to the domain of cloud application management. Considering that we build upon the application scenario described in the previous section. Thereby, we show how patterns from the pattern language by Fehling et al. [27] can also be used to deal with the question about how to systematically describe and model the interplay of the components of an application to enable the automated provisioning of new application instances via standard-compliant provisioning engines. Hence, in combination with the previous one, this use case shows that Solution Languages can be created and maintained addressing completely different aspects of a domain captured into overall and comprehensive pattern languages. Such a pattern language is the above introduced one by Fehling et al. [27], which covers different viewpoints of the field of cloud computing and, thus, acts as an entry point to Solution Languages providing and organizing completely different solution artifacts. Thereby, we specifically focus on the provisioning of cloud applications based on the OASIS cloud standard *Topology and Orchestration Specification for Cloud Applications* (TOSCA) [30].

Thus, in the following, we firstly explain the patterns of this application scenario to understand the cloud management specific issues to be tackled. Secondly, we give a brief description of the main concepts provided by TOSCA, which are required to understand the concrete solutions we use in this scenario. Finally, we show how CSADs can be used either to provide descriptions for manually aggregating concrete solutions or, respectively, also to automate the aggregation to overall composite solutions.

The application scenario is depicted in Fig. 5. There, the three patterns *Stateless Component*, *Elastic Infrastructure*, and *Key Value Store* are illustrated. While the pattern *Stateless Component* describes that the state of an application should be kept externally from its processing components, the pattern *Key Value Store* provides the conceptual solution of a datastore, which is specifically designed to store and retrieve data via identifying keys. For instance, if an application has to handle workload, which requires user sessions such as shopping carts of a web store, the user sessions constitute the state of the interaction with the user. Although components of the application have to process this state it should not be kept in the actual processing components as discussed above but moved to an external store, which can be a *Key Value Store* while the unique session ids of the user sessions can be used to select and manipulate the data. Thus, both *Stateless Component* and *Key Value Store* provide conceptual solutions, which have to be combined to an overall solution in order to create an application,

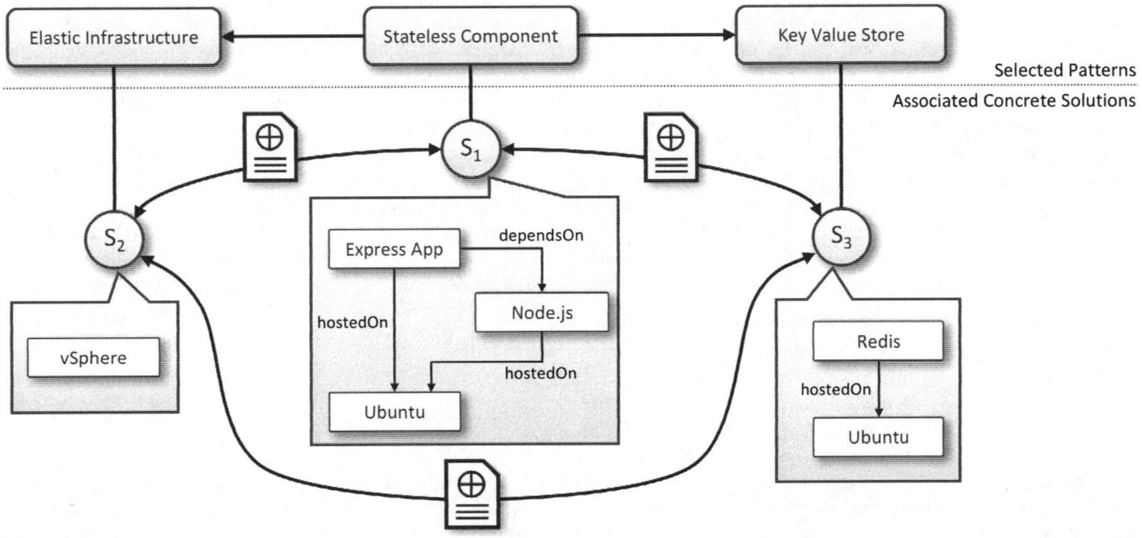

Figure 5. Solution Language comprising of Service Templates

which on the one hand can handle state and, on the other hand, can assure that processing components are stateless. However, to run such an application also a hosting environment is required. In the domain of cloud computing, where automation is important, hosting environments commonly follow the concept of an *Elastic Infrastructure*, which enables the automated provisioning and decommissioning of compute resources in the form of virtual machines. So, besides public cloud offerings, such as Amazon Elastic Compute Cloud [31] or Microsoft Azure Virtual Machines [32], also private cloud technologies, such as VMWare vSphere [33] or OpenStack [34], provide an application programming interface (API) allowing to access these offerings programmatically. Thus, from the perspective of cloud management *Elastic Infrastructure* provides a conceptual solution for elastically hosting cloud applications.

The conceptual knowledge provided by these three patterns can be complemented by an implementation-specific Solution Language capturing concrete solutions, which can be aggregated for the complete provisioning of applications. In this scenario, we leverage the expressiveness of TOSCA to populate the Solution Language as indicated in Fig. 5 by means of TOSCA *service templates*. A service template is the core entity of TOSCA to describe the *topology* of an application, i.e., its structure in terms of its components and the relations between them. Components are called *node templates* and relations *relationship templates*, which both can be abstracted into *node types* and *relationship types*, respectively, to enable their reuse in different service templates [35]. Besides these structural description also all required software executables (*deployment artifacts*) and management logic (*implementation artifacts*) to install, configure, start, stop, and terminate the application are contained. Thus, a service template can be grasped as a blue print of the application, which can be automatically instantiated to create new running instances of an application. Such service templates can be processed by TOSCA-compliant provisioning engines, such as OpenTOSCA [8] [36]. Thereby, the provisioning engine parses the modeled application topology and triggers all actions in terms of API-calls and executions of management logic to create a new application instance in the specified hosting environment.

A Solution Language comprising of service templates as concrete solutions is depicted in Fig. 4 by the concrete solutions S_1, S_2, and S_3. S_1 provides a realization of the *Stateless Component* pattern by means of a service template that describes the topology of an Express [37] application, which is a web framework based on Node.js [38].

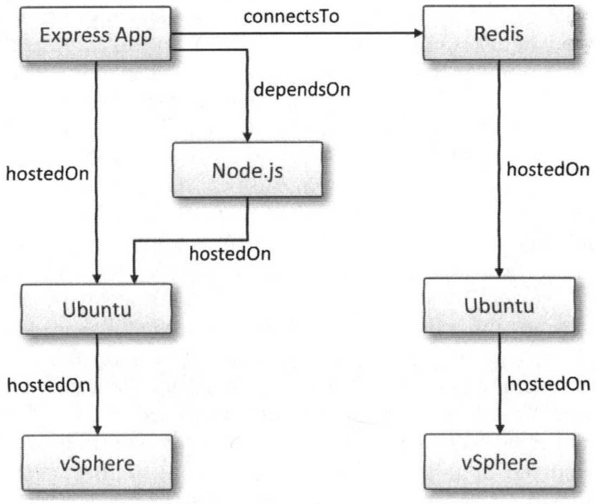

Figure 6. Aggregated Service Template

This reflects in the *dependsOn* relation between the Express App and the Node.js component in the depicted topology. Accordingly, both components are *hostedOn* an Ubuntu [39] operating system. A concrete solution of the *Key Value Store* pattern is provided by the concrete solution S_3 via a service template containing a node template that is capable of installing Redis [40], which is an open source key value store, onto an Ubuntu operating system. Finally, to bring up an entire application, S_2 provides an implementation of the *Elastic Infrastructure* pattern by means of a service template wrapping the API of a vSphere infrastructure.

The CSADs attached to the links between these concrete solutions can either be descriptions about how to manually combine these service templates in order to get an overall solution that can be provisioned, or they can also comprise of programs, which allow to automatically aggregate the different service templates. In the first case, the CSAD between S_1 and S_2 explains that the Ubuntu node template of S_1 has to be linked via a *hostedOn* relation with the vSphere node template of S_2 in order to be provisioned in a proper cloud environment based on the vSphere technology. Likewise, the Ubuntu node template of S_2 has to be wired with a vSphere node template. Further, the CSAD between S_1 and S_3 explains that the Express App node template of S_1 has to be linked via a *connectsTo* relation with the Redis node template of S_3. This can be done, for example, through a TOSCA-compliant modeling tool such as Eclipse Winery [41] but also directly in the respective TOSCA-files. Thus, the CSADs can provide different descriptions respective to available tooling.

However, in the second case, the CSADs can also link to programmatic solutions that allow the aggregation of different service templates. The TOSCA concepts of *requirements* and *capabilities* can be used to specify constrained requirements that have to be resolved and fulfilled by a TOSCA provisioning engine to generate provisionable service templates [42]. Using these concepts, on the one hand, the node templates Ubuntu of S_1 and S_3 can be associated with requirements stating that a hosting environment is required, which can provision and run Ubuntu. On the other hand, the vSphere node template of S_2 can expose the very same as a capability. Then, a TOSCA-compliant provisioning engine can aggregate S_1 and S_2 as well as S_3 and S_2 to resolve the defined requirements providing complete application stacks for provisioning and hosting. However, the resulting stacks, finally, have to be wired. Thus, to connect them the node template Express App, which implements the *Stateless Component* pattern, can be associated with a requirement stating that a *Key Value Store* is required to manage its state. Further, the Redis node template can, respectively, expose a capability fulfilling this requirement in order to enable the automatic aggregation of both service templates into an overall one [43] [42]. This results in a service template in which the aggregated topologies of S_1 and S_3 are connected via a *connectsTo* relationship between the node templates Express App and Redis. In this case, the aggregation is done automatically via the TOSCA completion mechanisms based on requirements and capabilities [43] [42]. Note that also the deployment and implementation artifacts of all node templates are packed into the overall service template to keep the newly created service template provisionable. The resulting aggregated application topology is depicted in Section IV-B and represents the service template based on the different concrete solutions linked to the patterns *Stateless Component*, *Key Value Store*, and *Elastic Infrastructure*. This service template can then be used as a starting point to add arbitrary business logic in the Express App to be processed as a stateless component. The application scenario has shown that CSADs can either be used to provide human-readable manuals about how to aggregate concrete solutions but also that CSADs can be provided as corresponding automation logic that enables the automation of aggregating concrete solutions to comprehensive ones.

C. *Application in the Domain of Costumes in Films*

In addition to the domain of IT, Solution Languages are also promising for rather different domains of pattern languages, as we want to prove by applying these concepts to the domain of costume languages in films [21]. Costume languages capture the knowledge of proven solutions about how to communicate a certain stereotype, its character traits or transformations, as well as geographical and historical setting of a film by the costumes worn by roles [21]. As depicted in Fig. 7, an example of a costume pattern is the *Sheriff*: a pattern describing all significant elements — like the shirt, the trousers, the ammunition belt and the wild west vest, the neckerchief, the boots and spurs, the cowboy hat and the sheriffs star — to communicate the stereotype of a sheriff in a western genre movie to the audience [44].

However, not only entire outfits are captured as costume patterns. Also proven principles describing, e.g., how to specifically wear or modify certain costumes or parts of them to indicate different character traits or how conditions of a costume can transport specific moods of a character are also captured into costume patterns. Therefore, as illustrated on the right of the pattern language in Fig. 7, another possible pattern is the pattern *Active Character* capturing actions and modifications to make a character look more active in the sense of being more energetic. Each of the depicted costume patterns has multiple concrete solutions connected to it representing concrete costumes in films. The Sheriff costume pattern, e.g., is linked to the concrete costumes worn by sheriffs in different western films, such as *John T. Chance* (John Wayne) in *Rio Bravo* (1959) or *Burnett* (Frank Wolf) in *Il grande silenzio* (1968), as indicated by S_1 and S_3 in Fig. 7. Moreover, concrete solutions of the *Active Character* pattern are, e.g., *Jake Lonergan* (Daniel Craig) in *Cowboys and Aliens* (2011) or *John T. Chance* (John Wayne) in *Rio Bravo* (1959). To create different arrangements of these patterns for specific scenes in films a costume designer can hark back to these captured concrete solutions to get an idea about the required costume and its style.

Other than the IT domain, which deals with concrete solutions that are intangible in the sense that they are often programming code or other forms of digital artifacts, in the domain of costumes in films, the concrete solutions are tangible artifacts. Thus, they could be kept in a wardrobe

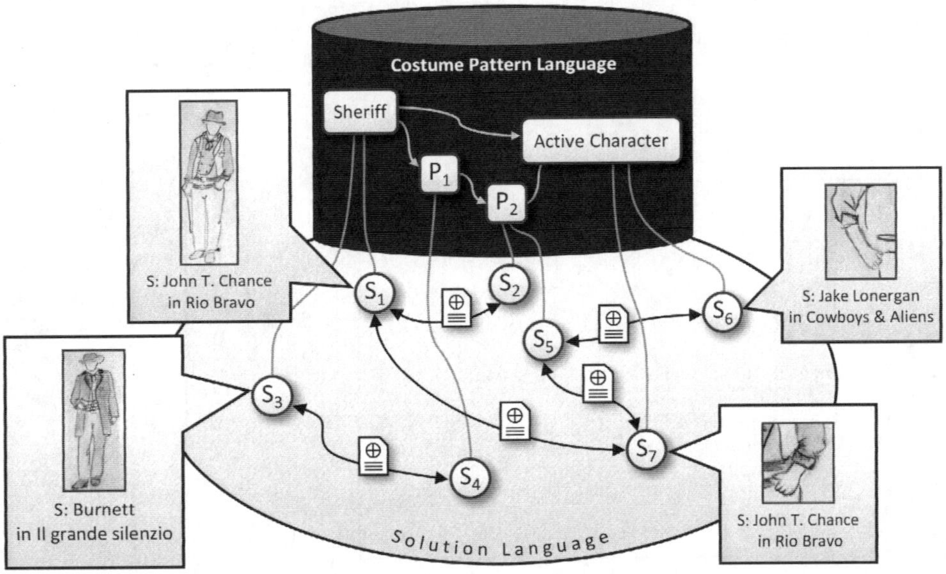

Figure 7. Example of a Costume Pattern Language linked to its Solution Language

of the costume designer at a specific film set or could also be provided by a costume rental. While the aggregation of intangible solutions can often be automated [16] [17] as described above, e.g., by merging code snippets to an aggregated solution, the aggregation of tangible solutions, such as concrete costumes, often has to be done manually. However, also in the case of tangible solutions, the concept of Solution Languages can be used for documenting knowledge about how to combine concrete solutions. Such knowledge is typically not systematically captured yet because of a missing methodical approach. Therefore, CSADs can be used to overcome this problem by documenting procedures and manuals describing the working steps to combine solutions.

In case of costumes in films [21], a Solution Language linking together all concrete costumes as concrete solutions of a costume pattern can be authored that allows to reuse already existing costumes for dressing actors. Thereby, a CSAD can describe, for example, how characters have to be dressed in order to create an intended effect. This information can be used by costume designers to create suitable costumes as required for particular scenes in a film. While Fig. 7 illustrates the general coherence between costumes as concrete solutions and costume patterns, in the following we describe a CSAD in the domain of costumes in films exemplarily.

When aiming to give the impression to the audience via the costume that a sheriff is particularly active in a specific scene, the *Sheriff* pattern has to be combined with the *Active Character* pattern. Further, concrete solutions are selected, which are linked with each other indicating that they can be combined as depicted in Fig. 8. Also a CSAD is attached to the relation between both concrete solutions containing all relevant information for combining them to achieve the desired impression by rolling up the sleeves of the sheriff's shirt. The CSAD specifically describes the actions to be performed by a costume designer in order to combine the concrete solutions under consideration. The CSAD depicted in Fig. 8 briefly illustrates this and shows how the concrete solution S_1 of the *Sheriff* pattern and the concrete solution S_2 of the *Active Character* pattern can be combined. The resulting modified costume, i.e., the combination of S_1 and S_2 is depicted on the right as a new combined concrete solution S_{new}. Note that this combined concrete solution can indicate further solution principles, which might worth to be captured into an additional pattern if created many times for different scenes and films.

V. Prototype

To proof the technical feasibility of the presented approach of Solution Languages, we implemented a prototype on the basis of *PatternPedia* [20]. PatternPedia is a wiki that is built upon the MediaWiki [45] technology and the Semantic MediaWiki extensions [46]. We implemented the application scenario about cloud architectures presented in the previous section. Therefore, we captured the cloud computing patterns in form of wiki pages into PatternPedia and added links between them accordingly to the pattern language of Fehling et al. [27]. We also added the concrete solutions in the form of AWS CloudFormation snippets to PatternPedia so that each AWS CloudFormation snippet is represented by a separate wiki page that references a file containing the corresponding JSON-code. Then, we linked the wiki pages of the concrete solutions with wiki pages representing the patterns they implement to enable the navigation from abstract solution principles captured in patterns to technology-specific implementations in the form of concrete

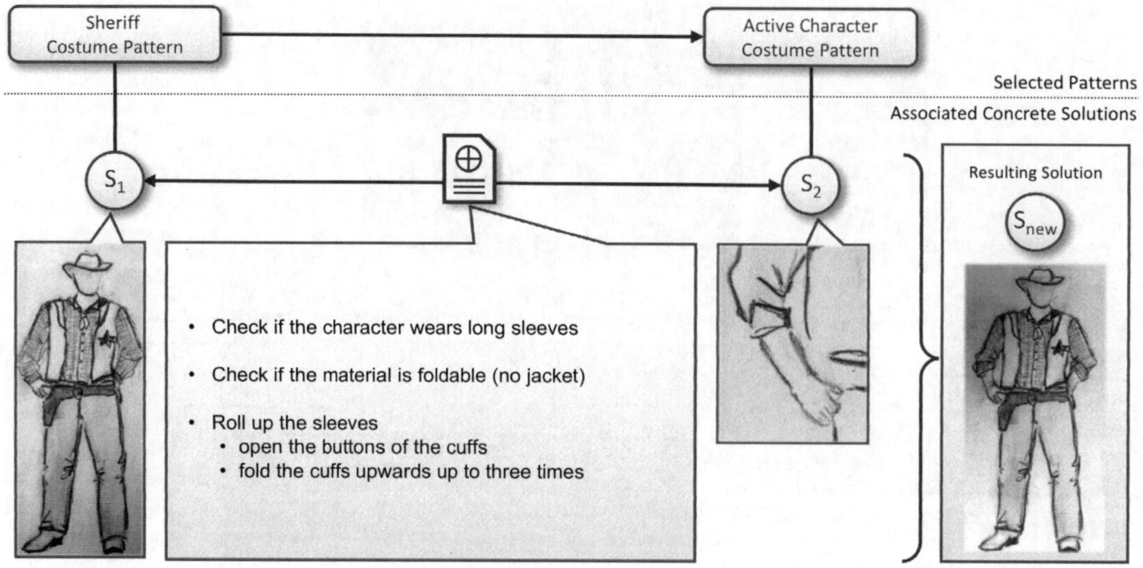

Figure 8. Concrete Solution Aggregation Descriptor documenting how to aggregate concrete solutions in the domain of costumes in films

solutions. So, we were able to navigate from patterns to concrete solutions and select them for reuse once a pattern has to be applied. To establish a Solution Language we declared a new property *can be aggregated with* using the Semantic MediaWiki extensions. Properties can be used to define arbitrary semantics, which can be added to wiki pages. The defined property accepts one parameter as a value, which we used to reference wiki pages that represent concrete solutions. This way, concrete solutions can be semantically linked with each other by adding the property into the markdown of their wiki pages and providing the link to the wiki page of the concrete solution, which the *can be aggregated with* semantics holds.

To annotate the link between two specific concrete solutions with information required for their aggregation, we added a CSAD as a separate wiki page containing a detailed description of the working steps required for aggregating them. Finally, we used the query functionality of the Semantic MediaWiki extensions to attach the CSAD to the semantic link between two concrete solutions. We utilized the parser function *#ask* of the Semantic MediaWiki extensions to query the two concrete solutions that are semantically linked with each other via the *can be aggregated with* property. This allowed us to also navigate from one concrete solution to other relevant concrete solutions based on the information of the semantic links, by also providing information about how to aggregate both concrete solutions to an overall one in a human-readable way.

Similarly, we also realized the second application scenario about cloud management via PatternPedia. The concrete solutions in this scenario, however, are represented by so-called TOSCA cloud service archives (CSAR). These archives are used to bundle service templates as well as all related deployment and implementation artifacts in a self-contained way and were linked with the wiki-pages representing them as concrete solutions. We further linked them with each other and added CSADs to describe how the several service templates can be combined as described in Section IV. Finally, we also added links to an instance of Eclipse Winery [41], which is a TOSCA-compliant modeling tool capable of merging different service templates automatically. Thus, Winery provides the automation of CSADs as conceptually described in the application scenario.

VI. Related Work

The term pattern language was introduced by Alexander et al. [2]. They use this term metaphorically to express that design patterns are typically not just isolated junks of knowledge, but are rather used and valuable in combination. At this, the metaphor implies that patterns are related to each other like words in sentences. While each word does only sparsely provide any information only the combination to whole sentences creates an overall statement. So, also patterns only unfold their generative power once they are applied in combination, while they are structured and organized into pattern languages in order to reveal their combinability to human readers.

Mullet [14] discusses how pattern catalogues in the field of human-computer interaction design can be enhanced to pattern languages to ease the application of patterns in combination. He reveals the qualities of pattern languages by discussing structuring elements in the form of different semantics of pattern relations. Further, the possibility to connect artifacts to patterns, such as detailed implementation documentation or also concrete implementations is identified as future research.

Zdun [24] formalizes pattern language in the form of pattern language grammars. Using this approach, he tackles the problem of selecting patterns from a pattern language. He reflects design decisions by annotating effects on quality attributes to a pattern language grammar. Relationships between patterns express semantics, e.g., that a pattern *requires* another pattern, a pattern is an *alternative* to another one, or that a pattern is a *variant* of another pattern. Thus, he describes concepts of pattern languages, which are transferred in this work to the level of concrete solutions and Solution Languages.

Reiners et al. [47] present a requirements catalogue to support the collaborative formulation of patterns. These requirements can be used as a basis to implement pattern repositories. While the requirements mainly address the authoring and structuring of pattern languages, they can also be used as a basis to detail the discussion about how to design and implement repositories to author Solution Languages. Pattern Repositories [7] [20] [48] have proven to support the authoring of patterns. They enable to navigate through pattern languages by linking patterns with each other. Some (c.f. [7] [20]) also enable to enrich links between patterns by semantics to further ease the navigation. Also, conceptual approaches exist that allow to connect a pattern repository with a solution repository, which can be the foundation to implement the concepts introduces in this work. These concepts and repository prototypes can be combined with our approach to develop sophisticated solution repositories.

Barzen and Leymann [21] present a general approach to support the identification and authoring of patterns based on concrete solutions. Their approach is based on research in the domain of costumes in films, where they formalize costume languages as pattern languages. Costumes are concrete solutions that solve specific design problems of costume designers. They enable to hark back to concrete solutions a pattern is evolved from by keeping them connected. They also introduce the terminus Solution Language as an ontology that describes types of clothes and their relations in the form of metadata, as well as instances of these types. This completely differs from the concept of a Solution Language as described in this work.

Fehling et al. [22] present a method for identifying, authoring and applying patterns. The method is decomposed into three phases, whereby, in the pattern application phase, they describe how abstract solutions of patterns can be refined towards concrete implementations. To reduce the efforts to spend for implementing patterns, they apply the concept of concrete solutions by means of code repositories that contain reference implementations of patterns. While our approach is designed and detailed for organizing concrete solutions the argumentation in their work is mainly driven by considerations about patterns and pattern languages. Thus, the method does not introduce how to systematically combine semantics and documentation in order to organize concrete solutions for reuse, which is the principal contribution of our work.

VII. Conclusion and Future Work

In this work, we presented the concept of Solution Languages that allows to structure and organize concrete solutions, which are implementations of patterns. We showed how Solution Languages can be created and how they can support the navigation through the solution space of pattern languages based on semantic links, all targeting to ease and guide pattern application. We further presented the concept of Concrete Solution Aggregation Descriptors, which allows to add arbitrary human-readable documentation to links between concrete solutions. Besides these concepts, we showed that concrete solutions addressing different aspects of a pattern language can be organized into Solution Languages and linked to their respective patterns. Finally, the generality of the presented concepts is shown via comprehensive application scenarios in the domains of cloud application architecture, cloud management, and costumes in films. While the first two show the plurality of concrete solutions and Solution Languages, especially, the application to the domain of costumes in films provide evidence that Solution Languages are not bound to the domain of IT but can also be used to ease and guide the application and combination of concrete solutions in general.

In future work, we are going to conduct research on how to analyze Solution Languages in order to derive new pattern candidates based on Concrete Solution Aggregation Descriptors annotated to links between concrete solutions, but also on the question if a Solution Language can indicate new patterns in a pattern language, for instance, in the case if links between concrete solutions are missing or if aggregation documentation cannot be clearly authored. We are also going to apply the concept of Solution Languages to domains besides cloud computing, e.g., to the emerging field of the Internet of Things. Finally, we are going to develop an algorithm in order to automate the selection of suitable concrete solution paths on the basis of a selected sequence of patterns and additional user constraints. This automation approach for selectiing concrete solutions will also make it possible to evaluate the concept of solution languages experimentally via runtime mesasurements.

Acknowledgment

This work is partially funded by the BMWi project SePiA.Pro (01MD16013F) as part of the Smart Service World.

References

[1] M. Falkenthal and F. Leymann, "Easing Pattern Application by Means of Solution Languages," in Proceedings of the 9th International Conferences on Pervasive Patterns and Applications. Xpert Publishing Services (XPS), 2017, pp. 58–64.

[2] C. Alexander, S. Ishikawa, and M. Silverstein, A pattern language: towns, buildings, construction. New York: Oxford University Press, 1977.

[3] E. Gamma, R. Helm, R. Johnson, and J. Vlissides, "Design Patterns: Abstraction and reuse of objectoriented design," in European Conference on Object-Oriented Programming, 1993, pp. 406–431.

[4] F. Buschmann, R. Meunier, H. Rohnert, P. Sommerlad, and P. Stal, Pattern-oriented software architecture: A system of patterns, 1996, vol. 1.

[5] M. van Welie and G. C. van der Veer, "Pattern Languages in Interaction Design : Structure and Organization," in Human-Computer Interaction '03: IFIP TC13 International Conference on Human-Computer Interaction. IOS Press, 2003, pp. 527–534.

[6] G. Hohpe and B. Woolf, Enterprise Integration Patterns: Designing, Building, And Deploying Messaging Systems. Addison-Wesley, 2004.

[7] R. Reiners, "An Evolving Pattern Library for Collaborative Project Documentation," PhD Thesis, RWTH Aachen University, 2013.

[8] C. Endres, U. Breitenbücher, M. Falkenthal, O. Kopp, F. Leymann, and J. Wettinger, "Declarative vs. Imperative: Two Modeling Patterns for the Automated Deployment of Applications," in Proceedings of the 9th International Conferences on Pervasive Patterns and Applications. Xpert Publishing Services (XPS), 2017, pp. 22–27.

[9] L. Reinurt, U. Breitenbücher, M. Falkenthal, F. Leymann, and A. Riegg, "Internet of things patterns," in Proceedings of the 21th European Conference on Pattern Languages of Programs, 2016.

[10] L. Reinfurt, U. Breitenbücher, M. Falkenthal, F. Leymann, and A. Riegg, "Internet of Things Patterns for Devices," in Proceedings of the 9th International Conferences on Pervasive Patterns and Applications. Xpert Publishing Services (XPS), 2017, pp. 117–126.

[11] T. Iba and T. Miyake, "Learning patterns: a pattern language for creative learners II," in Proceedings of the 1st Asian Conference on Pattern Languages of Programs (AsianPLoP 2010). ACM Press, 2010, pp. I–41—-I–58.

[12] T. Furukawazono, I. Studies, S. Seshimo, I. Studies, D. Muramatsu, and T. Iba, "Survival Language : A Pattern Language for Surviving Earthquakes," in Proceedings of the 20th Conference on Pattern Languages of Programs. ACM, 2013, p. Article No. 30.

[13] J. Barzen et al., "The vision for MUSE4Music," Computer Science - Research and Development, vol. 22, no. 74, 2016, pp. 1–6.

[14] K. Mullet, "Structuring pattern languages to facilitate design. chi2002 patterns in practice: A workshop for ui designers," 2002. [Online]. Available: https://www.semanticscholar.org/paper/Structuring-Pattern-Languages-to-Facilitate-Design-Mullet/2fa5e4c25eea30687605115649191cd009a8f33c

[15] M. Falkenthal et al., "Leveraging pattern application via pattern refinement," in Proceedings of the International Conference on Pursuit of Pattern Languages for Societal Change. epubli GmbH, pp. 38–61.

[16] M. Falkenthal, J. Barzen, U. Breitenbuecher, C. Fehling, and F. Leymann, "From Pattern Languages to Solution Implementations," in Proceedings of the 6th International Conferences on Pervasive Patterns and Applications, 2014, pp. 12–21.

[17] M. Falkenthal, J. Barzen, U. Breitenbücher, C. Fehling, and F. Leymann, "Efficient Pattern Application : Validating the Concept of Solution Implementations in Different Domains," International Journal On Advances in Software, vol. 7, no. 3&4, 2014, pp. 710–726.

[18] G. Meszaros and J. Doble, "A Pattern Language for Pattern Writing," in Pattern Languages of Program Design 3. Addison-Wesley, 1997, ch. A Pattern Language for Pattern Writing, pp. 529–574.

[19] C. Alexander, S. Ishikawa, and M. Silverstein, A Pattern Language: Towns, Buildings, Construction. Oxford University Press, Aug. 1977.

[20] C. Fehling, J. Barzen, M. Falkenthal, and F. Leymann, "PatternPedia Collaborative Pattern Identification and Authoring," in Pursuit of Pattern Languages for Societal Change - The Workshop 2014: Designing Lively Scenarios With the Pattern Approach of Christopher Alexander. epubli GmbH, 2015, pp. 252–284.

[21] J. Barzen and F. Leymann, "Costume Languages as Pattern Languages," in Pursuit of Pattern Languages for Societal Change - The Workshop 2014: Designing Lively Scenarios With the Pattern Approach of Christopher Alexander, 2015, pp. 88–117.

[22] C. Fehling, J. Barzen, U. Breitenbücher, and F. Leymann, "A Process for Pattern Identification, Authoring, and Application," in Proceedings of the 19th European Conference on Pattern Languages of Programs, 2015, article no. 4.

[23] U. Breitenbücher et al., "Policy-Aware Provisioning and Management of Cloud Applications," International Journal On Advances in Security, vol. 7, no. 1 & 2, 2014, pp. 15–36.

[24] U. Zdun, "Systematic pattern selection using pattern language grammars and design space analysis," Software: Practice and Experience, vol. 37, no. 9, jul 2007, pp. 983–1016.

[25] F. Buschmann, K. Henney, and D. C. Schmidt, Pattern-Oriented Software Architecture: On Patterns and Pattern Languages. Wiley & Sons, 2007, vol. 5.

[26] M. Falkenthal et al., "Pattern research in the digital humanities: how data mining techniques support the identification of costume patterns," Computer Science - Research and Development, vol. 22, no. 74, 2016.

[27] C. Fehling, F. Leymann, R. Retter, W. Schupeck, and P. Arbitter, Cloud Computing Patterns: Fundamentals to Design, Build, and Manage Cloud Applications. Springer, 2014.

[28] Amazon, "Amazon Web Services," 2017. [Online]. Available: http://aws.amazon.com/

[29] ——, "Amazon Cloud Formation," 2017. [Online]. Available: https://aws.amazon.com/cloudformation

[30] OASIS, Topology and Orchestration Specification for Cloud Applications (TOSCA) Version 1.0, Organization for the Advancement of Structured Information Standards (OASIS), 2013.

[31] Amazon, "Amazon Elastic Compute Cloud," 2017. [Online]. Available: https://aws.amazon.com/ec2

[32] Microsoft, "Microsoft Azure Virtual Machines," 2017. [Online]. Available: https://azure.microsoft.com/en-us/services/virtual-machines

[33] VMWare, Inc, "Vmware vsphere," 2017. [Online]. Available: https://www.vmware.com/products/vsphere.html

[34] OpenStack Project, "Openstack," 2017. [Online]. Available: https://www.openstack.org

[35] T. Binz, G. Breiter, F. Leymann, and T. Spatzier, "Portable Cloud Services Using TOSCA," IEEE Internet Computing, vol. 16, no. 03, May 2012, pp. 80–85.

[36] T. Binz, U. Breitenbücher, F. Haupt, O. Kopp, F. Leymann, A. Nowak, and S. Wagner, "OpenTOSCA - A Runtime for TOSCA-based Cloud Applications," in Proceedings of the 11th International Conference on Service-Oriented Computing (ICSOC 2013). Springer, Dec. 2013, pp. 692–695.

[37] Node.js Foundation, "Express," 2017. [Online]. Available: https://expressjs.com

[38] ——, "Node.js," 2017. [Online]. Available: https://nodejs.org/en

[39] Canonical Ltd, "Ubuntu," 2017. [Online]. Available: https://www.ubuntu.com

[40] redislabs, "Redis," 2017. [Online]. Available: https://redis.io

[41] O. Kopp, T. Binz, U. Breitenbücher, and F. Leymann, "Winery – A Modeling Tool for TOSCA-based Cloud Applications," in Proceedings of the 11th International Conference on Service-Oriented Computing (ICSOC 2013). Springer, Dec. 2013, pp. 700–704.

[42] M. Zimmermann, U. Breitenbücher, M. Falkenthal, F. Leymann, and K. Saatkamp, "Standards-based Function Shipping How to use TOSCA for Shipping and Executing Data Analytics Software in Remote Manufacturing Environments," in Proceedings of the 21st International Enterprise Distributed Object Computing Conference. IEEE, 2017, in press.

[43] P. Hirmer, U. Breitenbücher, T. Binz, and F. Leymann, "Automatic Topology Completion of TOSCA-based Cloud Applications," in Lecture Notes in Informatics - Informatik 2014, 2014, pp. 247–258.

[44] D. Schumm, J. Barzen, F. Leymann, and L. Ellrich, "A Pattern Language for Costumes in Films," in Proceedings of the 17th European Conference on Pattern Languages of Programs, 2012, article no. 7.

[45] Wikimedia Foundation, "MediaWiki," 2017. [Online]. Available: https://www.mediawiki.org/

[46] M. Krötzsch, "Semantic MediaWiki," 2017. [Online]. Available: https://www.semantic-mediawiki.org/

[47] R. Reiners, M. Falkenthal, D. Jugel, and A. Zimmermann, "Requirements for a Collaborative Formulation Process of Evolutionary Patterns," in Proceedings of the 18th European Conference on Pattern Languages of Programs, 2013, article no. 16.

[48] U. van Heesch, "Open Pattern Repository," 2009. [Online]. Available: http://www.cs.rug.nl/search/ArchPatn/OpenPatternRepository

All links were last accessed on December, 1st 2017.

Binary Space Partitioning for Parallel and Distributed Closest-Pairs Query Processing

George Mavrommatis, Panagiotis Moutafis, and Michael Vassilakopoulos

Data Structuring & Engineering Lab
Dept. of Electrical & Computer Eng.
University of Thessaly
Volos, Greece
Email: {gmav, pmoutafis, mvasilako}@uth.gr

***Abstract*—The (k) Closest-Pair(s) Query, kCPQ, consists in finding the (k) closest pair(s) of objects between two spatial datasets. Up to date, only few solutions have appeared that process the kCPQ in parallel and distributed frameworks. Currently, Apache Spark is the state of the art of parallel and distributed frameworks, having several advantages compared to other popular ones, like Hadoop MapReduce. A major step towards answering a query is proper partitioning, a task that is of even greater importance in distributed environments. In this work, we present algorithms for processing the kCPQ in Apache Spark that split the datasets into strips across an axis. Two variations of the Binary Space Partitioning (BSP) technique are used to partition the data, based on two different criteria: equal size and equal width of the child strips. These schemes are compared to a third strategy (previously developed by us), namely splitting into a predefined number of strips. We have performed an extensive set of experiments to evaluate the efficiency and scalability of the algorithm and the performance of the different partitioning schemes by using large real-world datasets. Results show that splitting into strips by means of BSP achieves better performance. This is mainly due to the fact that selecting the number of points within each strip as the preset criterion, instead of the number of strips, provides more flexibility in fine tuning the system.**

Index Terms*—Closest-Pairs Query; Spatial Query Processing; Apache Spark; Binary Space Partitioning.

I. Introduction

The (k) Closest-Pair(s) Query (kCPQ) consists in finding the (k) closest pair(s) of objects between two spatial datasets. Up to date, only few solutions have appeared that process the kCPQ in parallel and distributed frameworks. Currently, Apache Spark is the leader of such frameworks, having several advantages compared to other popular ones, like Hadoop MapReduce. In [1], for the first time in the literature, we presented an algorithm for answering the kCPQ in this framework. In this paper, by extending the method of [1], we present new algorithms for answering the kCPQ in Apache Spark, along with an extended experimental comparison of their performance.

Geographic information systems (GIS) [2] have been around for several decades. They provide the means for storing, querying, analyzing and sharing geographic information and have proven valuable in many modern application domains (e.g., disaster management, mapping, urban planning, transportation planning, environmental impact analysis, etc.).

Spatial databases [3] are specialized databases that support storage and querying of multidimensional data (usually, points, line-segments, regions, polygons, volumes). They are core elements of GIS. Processing of spatial queries can become very demanding if the volume of data on which such a query is applied is large, or if the number of the combinations of data objects that need to be examined for answering such a query is large.

Some typical spatial queries are: the point query, range query, spatial join, and nearest neighbor query [4]. Spatial Join queries find all pairs of spatial objects from two spatial data sets that satisfy a spatial predicate, like intersects, contains, is enclosed by, etc. Nearest neighbor queries locate the spatial object(s) that is (are) nearest to a query object. The kCPQ discovers the (K) closest pair(s) of object(s) (usually ordered by distance), between two spatial datasets. It combines join and nearest neighbor queries: like a join query, all pairs (combinations) of objects from the two datasets are candidates for the result, and like a nearest neighbor query, the (K) smallest distance(s) is (are) the basis for inclusion in the result (and the final ordering) [5], [6]. The kCPQ can be very demanding if the datasets involved are large, since all the combinations of pairs of objects from the two datasets are candidates for the result.

For example, we can use two spatial datasets that represent the archaeological sites and popular beaches of Greece. A kCPQ (K=10) can discover the 10 closest pairs of archaeological sites and beaches (in increasing order of their distances). The result of this query can be used for planning tourist trips in Greece that combine travelers interest for history / civilization and leisure / enjoyment.

Parallel and distributed computing using shared-nothing clusters on large volumes of data has been very popular during last years. Hadoop MapReduce [7] is an open-source software framework for storing data and running applications on such clusters. MapReduce is file-intensive and computing nodes intercommunicate only through sorts and shuffles. Therefore, MapReduce is suitable mostly for non-iterative batch processing jobs.

Apache Spark [8] is another, more recent, open-source cluster-computing framework with an application programming interface based on Resilient Distributed Datasets (RDDs), read-only multisets of data items distributed over the cluster of machines [9]. It was developed to overcome limitations of the MapReduce paradigm. Through RDDs a form of distributed shared memory is provided and the implementation of iterative algorithms is facilitated.

Recently, the utilization of main memory in processing kCPQs on big datasets in centralized systems has been explored [10], [11]. In [1], considering ideas and methods presented in [10], [11] we presented a Spark based algorithm for computing kCPQs. Moreover, we presented an experimental analysis of the performance of this algorithm, based on large real-world datasets. In this paper, we extend [1] by developing three alternative algorithms. The first algorithm is a simple modification of the method of [1] that is based on single sampling for partitioning data. The other two algorithms are based on more elaborate partitioning techniques. Moreover, through an extensive experimental evaluation, we compare the performance of the three algorithms. Contrary to [1], where we performed experiments using 4 data nodes only, in this paper, we perform experiments using 4, as well as, 8 data nodes, to study the scalability of the presented techniques.

The rest of the paper is organized as follows. In Section II, we review related frameworks and work (extending the material presented in [1]); in Section III, we present Spark basics, we define the query that we study and present the algorithm of [1]; in Section IV we present two different data portioning schemes that lead to alternative algorithms for kCPQ; in Section V, we present experimentation set-up and the results of extensive experiments we performed for studying the efficiency of the presented methods. Finally, in the last section, we present our conclusions and our plans for future work.

II. Related Work

In [12] Spark is used to compute top-k similarity join in large multidimensional data. Data are being partitioned into buckets so that points that are close to each other are grouped into the same bucket, with high probability. Partitioning is made by means of locality-sensitive hashing and hamming distance computation between every two elements. The method uses Cartesian product, as provided by Spark, to create all possible buckets couples and computes local top-k over each node, then collects the results and combines them to the final solution. Divide & Conquer strategy and pruning is performed at local level.

In [13] Spark is used to perform several computational geometry operations such as Geometry Union, Convex Hull, Closest and Farthest pair, Spatial Range, Join and Aggregation on both small, medium and large data sets. Computation of Farthest Pair is performed by brute force and Closest Pair is reported difficult and time costly to be solved the same way, being efficient solely for small data sets. In order to overcome the problem, computation is being performed in two steps. The first step works per partition and computes the closest point in each subset, plus the points that may still be candidates (found by sorting the x-axis of the points per partition). Local computation is performed by a Divide and Conquer method that splits the local dataset recursively. The second step creates one single partition containing the closest points that were found in step one and all the candidates and once again performs the same Divide and Conquer approach. As authors report "there is a huge jump in execution time for the "large" dataset suggesting algorithm's effectiveness probably decreases as size increase" and "the increase in computational resources is offset by the communication cost in the latter case". The latter case refers to the "large" dataset of the experiments, which is about 100MB.

Extensions of Hadoop MapReduce supporting large-scale spatial data processing include Parallel-Secondo [14], Hadoop-GIS [15] and SpatialHadoop [16]. In [17], a general plane-sweep approach for processing kCPQs in SpatialHadoop and a more sophisticated version that first computes an upper bound of the distance of the K-th closest pair from sampled data points have been presented.

Extensions of Apache Spark supporting large-scale spatial data processing include the following:

- GeoSpark [18], an in-memory cluster computing framework for processing large-scale spatial data. The project is still under development. It uses Spark as its base layer and adds two more layers, the Spatial RDD (SRDD) Layer and Spatial Query Processing Layer, thus providing Spark with in-house spatial capabilities. The SRDD layer consists of three newly defined RDDs, PointRDD, RectangleRDD and PolygonRDD. SRDDs support geometrical operations, like Overlap and Minimum Bounding Rectangle. SRDDs are automatically partitioned by using the uniform grid technique, where the global grid file is splitted into a number of equal geographical size grid cells. Elements that intersect with two or more grid cells are being duplicated. GeoSpark provides spatial indexes like Quad-Tree and R-Tree on a per partition base. The Spatial Query Processing Layer includes spatial range query, spatial join query, spatial KNN query. GeoSpark relies heavily on the JTS topology suite and therefore conforms to the specifications published by the Open Geospatial Consortium. Experiments, reported by the paper, show that GeoSpark outperforms its Hadoop-based counterparts (e.g., SpatialHadoop). Mainly because caches the datasets in memory, a functionality that is natively built in the underlying Spark platform.
- SpatialSpark [19], that supports indexed spatial joins and range queries. Same as with GeoSpark it utilizes the JTS suite (written in Java). As reported by the authors, JTS seems to be faster than GEOS, a C/C++ port of a subset of JTS and selected functions. Authors report that in some cases of data intensive applications SpatialSpark performs worse on multiple computing nodes than on a single node, thus showing low scalability. This fact is attributed to pos-

sible bottlenecks due to communication overheads among computing nodes a factor that is related to the number of partitions, thus rising an interesting research question: "optimizing the number of partitions which represents the tradeoffs between the degrees of parallelisms (the higher the better) and the communication overheads (the lower the better)".

- LocationSpark [20], an ambitious project, built as a library on top of Spark. It requires no modifications to Spark and provides spatial query APIs on top of the standard operators. It provides Dynamic Spatial Query Execution and operations (Range, kNN, Insert, Delete, Update, Spatial-Join, kNN-Join, Spatio-Textual). The system builds two indexes, a global (grid, quadtree and a Spatial-Bloom Filter) and a local per-worker, user-decided index (grid, rtree, etc). Global index is constructed by sampling the data. Spatial indexes are aiming to tackle unbalanced data partitioning. Additionally, the system contains a query scheduler, aiming to tackle query skew. As reported in the paper, LocationSpark can outperform GeoSpark by one order of magnitude.
- Spatial In-Memory Big data Analytics (SIMBA) [21] that is perhaps the most mature framework. It extends the Spark SQL engine to support spatial queries and analytics through SQL and the DataFrame API. Simba partitions data in a manner that they are of proper and balanced size and gathers records that locate close to the same partition. It builds a local index per partition and a global index by aggregating information from local indexes. It supports range and kNN queries, kNN and distance joins. As being reported in the paper, Simba outperforms SpatialHadoop, HadoopGIS, SpatialSpark and GeoSpark by a few or more orders of magnitude. In the case of distance join queries, Simba runs about 1.2-1.5 times faster than its closest counterparts GeoSpark and SpatialSpark.

The kCPQ has been actively studied in centralized environments, when both [5], [6], [22]–[24], one [25], or none [10], [11] of the two spatial datasets are indexed. Two improvements of the classic plane-sweep algorithm and a new plane-sweep algorithm, called Reverse Run Plane Sweep, were proposed in [10] for processing kCPQs when the two datasets are not indexed and reside in main-memory. In [11], it is assumed that the (big) spatial datasets reside on secondary storage and are progressively transferred in main memory, by dividing them in strips, for processing utilizing the methods of [10].

In this paper, we utilize ideas presented in [10], [11] to develop an algorithm for processing kCPQs in Spark, by separating data in strips and utilizing a plane-sweep approach within each strip.

III. KCPQ IN A PARALLEL AND DISTRIBUTED CONTEXT

Hadoop MapReduce processing is based on pairs of Map and Reduce phases. It is an excellent solution for one-step computations on massive datasets, but it not very efficient for problems that require multi-step computations. The output of each step is stored in the distributed file system, so that it can be used as input for the next, or one of the following steps. Replication and disk storage contribute to slowing down the overall computation. Apache Spark (or more simply, Spark) is an alternative to Hadoop MapReduce. Its not intended to replace Hadoop MapReduce, but to extend it and allow the development of solutions for different big data problems and requirements.

Spark, the distributed in-memory computation framework has reached a significant level of maturity, being already at version 2.2.0, which has been recently released. Spark is written in Scala, a relatively new functional programming language but it supports multiple programming languages, with special focus on Scala, Java, Python, and R. It allows a user application to cache data in memory, in a flexible manner that lets the application to decide what data should be cached and at what point in the processing flow. This is a major step forward from the classic Hadoop MapReduce procedure that uses disk I/O extensively. Spark uses an advanced job execution scheme based on creation of a directed acyclic graph (DAG) of stages. In contrast to MapReduce that in many cases constrains the programmer to split a complex algorithm into jobs executed sequentially, Spark uses a lazy evaluation scheme that allows previous knowledge of the full processing path, thus making it easier to optimize the execution. This functionality makes Spark ideal for iterative algorithms implementation. The Spark API relies on two important abstractions, namely SparkContext and Resilient Distributed Datasets (RDDs). An application interacts with Spark by means of these two abstractions. Data are being represented as RDDs in the Spark context, and are distributed among Workers of the cluster. Spark provides several methods defined in the RDD class or other subclasses of RDD. These methods operate on the RDD and finally on the underlying data. They are classified in two categories: transformations that create a new RDD and actions that return values to the Driver program. Transformations are lazy, which means that Spark does not perform any computation when they are called in an application. Actual computation is triggered by action methods. As already mentioned, this scheme provides Spark with the power to optimize RDD operations. Although Spark uses a shared-nothing architecture, it also supports the concept of shared variables that are being materialized as broadcasts and accumulators. By using broadcast variables, Spark sends data to each node, thus enabling all Workers to share a piece of information. Broadcast variables may be useful in cases of problems in the field of combinatorial optimization. For example, in NP-hard graph problems such as the maximum clique number, knowing a good lower bound of the maximum clique helps pruning the search space and speeding up the computation. A similar notion holds for the kCPQ. If we know a good upper bound for the k-th smaller distance and transmit it to all Workers, this will lead to discarding a large volume of computation among pairs of points that their distance is greater than the upper bound.

In the following, we present the basics for kCPQ processing in Spark. Let two datasets P and Q of spatial objects, a positive natural number K and a distance function between pairs of data objects formed from P and Q (members of the Cartesian Product of P and Q). The kCPQ discovers k pairs of data objects formed from P and Q that have the k smallest distances between them among all pairs of data objects that can be formed from P and Q.

Since distances between objects may not be unique, note that if multiple pairs of objects have the same k-th distance value between them, more than one sets of k different pairs of objects can form the result of this query. The presented algorithm can be easily tailored to report all such sets of pairs.

An important step, towards answering a query in a parallel and distributed environment, is proper partitioning of the datasets. Data partitioning improves the query performance in two ways [26]:

1) partitioning the data into smaller units enables processing of a query in parallel and
2) I/O can be significantly reduced by only scanning a few partitions that contain relevant data to answer the query.

In the case of the kCPQ, (b) is not applicable; in order to answer the query, we have to search pairs of points from the whole dataset. Therefore, in the case of kCPQ, the most severe obstacle, one has to face, in datasets partitioning, is data skewness. In most real-world cases, data is not uniformly distributed in a dataset. Using partitioning techniques such as uniform grid [27] very often leads to partitions that contain much more objects than others, a fact that in a parallel system may prevent proper load balancing and therefore delay the computation of the final result. There are many alternative strategies that can be found in the literature aiming to deal with the skewness problem. Most of them require the construction of a spatial data structure, which allows the queries about spatial relationships of objects to be answered. The simplest spatial data structure is the uniform grid, but, as already said, it very often leads to bad performance in the case of non-uniformly distributed data. This observation has led to more elaborate partition schemes, many of them being generalizations of binary search trees.

A quad-tree [28] is a non-uniform subdivision of area where a region is split into four quadrants by two axis-aligned dividing lines. The decomposition proceeds until a certain property is met, i.e., each quadrant contains less than a predefined number of points.

An R-tree [29] is a hierarchical data structure derived from the B-tree [30]. Data objects are represented by their enclosing MBRs, which are grouped into larger nodes hierarchically until the root node of the tree. Each leaf node contains the actual objects, and can store a certain, predefined number of objects.

In most cases within the context parallel and distributed frameworks, the creation of these hierarchical data structures is based on reading a random sample from the input file and using this sample to partition the whole space.

In order to efficiently compute the k closest pairs query in the Spark context, there are three main tasks, our algorithm has to deal with:

1) Find a good bound for the kCPQ and broadcast it to Workers. This will lead to good pruning criteria, on both Driver and Workers contexts.
2) Partition the data, by setting a proper indexing, and check all pairs of partitions so that all eligible pairs of points from P and Q will be considered, thus preventing any loss of the optimal solution.
3) Use a fast algorithm to compute kCPQ in the Workers context, collect the results and select the top k, having the smallest distance.

The method for answering the kCPQ, as presented in [1] consists of four steps that cover all the above mentioned tasks.

A. Lower Bound Computation

We initially compute an upper *bound* for the k-th closest pair. We use the Spark-provided function *sample* to create two RDDs containing samples from each one of the two datasets. We use a sample ratio of $f = 0.001$ on each dataset.

In order to obtain a good upper bound, we partition the sampled RDDs in a manner so that points with close x-axis values fall into the same partition.

Partitioning each of the two sampled datasets into n strips of unequal width is done by calculating the border (separation) x-axis points, separately for each sampled dataset. Both samples are collected to the Driver and their x-values are extracted and stored in two sorted arrays sP and sQ. The predefined number n and the sizes of the two arrays obtain the indices of each array that contain the separation x-points $PSep$ and $QSep$. Value $stepP$ is $sP.size/n$ and value $stepQ$ is $sQ.size/n$. The two arrays $PSep$ and $QSep$ are merged into a sorted array $PQSep = PSep ++ QSep$ that contains the separation x-axis points applicable on both sampled RDDs. This array is passed to Spark and all points in both the sampled RDDs are being assigned the proper keys.

A *join* is performed between the two keyed RDDs, creating an RDD of type $(Int, (Point, Point))$ that is mapped to an RDD$[Double, (Point, Point)]$ where the Double presents the distance (Euclidean in our case) of every pair of points in the joined RDD. By using the $takeOrdered$ function of Spark, we select the k pairs with smaller distance. The k-th distance is our upper *bound*. This means that in the following steps we do not need to seek for pairs that have their distance greater than this *bound* and consequently we do not need to examine pairs that have their x-axis (y-axis can also be used) distance greater than *bound*.

B. Datasets Partitioning

After the bound computation from samples, both datasets are separately divided into a, user defined, number of n strips. Partitioning each of the two datasets into strips of unequal width is done by calculating the border (separation) points from samples, separately for each dataset by the same procedure shown in the previous step.

Sampling with a ratio m is used here. In [1] the sample size was set to $dataset.size/n$ where n is the number of desired partitions. Each point from the sample is mapped to its x-axis coordinate and all 1D points are collected to the Master node as an Array $A[m]$. Sorting is performed on the array and the number of predefined strips n determines the $step = m/n$ on the indices of the array that contain the separation x-points. The actual x-values, depicted in Fig. 1, are $X1 = A[step], X2 = A[2 * step], \ldots, Xn = A[(n-1) * step]$.

Each subinterval contains approximately m/n points and therefore the projection of this upon the whole dataset creates strips with approx. equal size of points. The separation points, shown in gray in Fig. 1, are being used on the whole dataset, to split it into n strips. The partitioning is being done a function $xPartitionSpace$, which assembles the envelopes of the strips

$$Env[minX : X1, minY : maxY],$$
$$Env[X1, X2, minY : maxY], \ldots,$$
$$Env[Xn - 1 : maxX, minY : maxY]$$

The function returns an array of type (Int, Env), by assigning consecutive integers to each partition presented as Envelope. Actual partitioning is done by passing a function to Spark with parameter the array of Envelopes and each Worker scans the dataset and assigns the proper key to each point.

C. Classification of Strips

The third step of the algorithm presented in [1] uses $bound$, the distance of the k-th closest pair, which was computed from the sample as described in step 1, to classify all pairs of strips from the two datasets into two categories, *Eligible* and *non-Eligible*.

This is accomplished by first finding the relative position between each pair of strips. The criterion used to derive the relative position is based on the relation of the minimum and maximum value of the x-coordinates of the strips. In Fig. 2 all possible cases are being depicted.

In the case of overlapping pairs, as it happens with W and B, the expression $(W.x1 < B.x2 \,\&\&\, W.x2 > B.x1)$ evaluates to *true*.

If it evaluates to *false*, then there are two cases, either strip is on the left of W (strip A), and $W.x1 > A.x2$, or strip is on the right of W (strip C) and $W.x2 < C.x1$.

Eligible and *non-Eligible* categories are defined as follows:

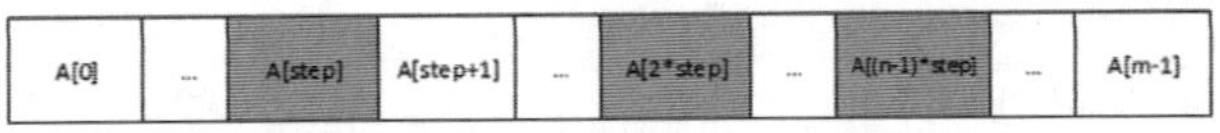

Fig. 1. Selection of splitting points in [1]

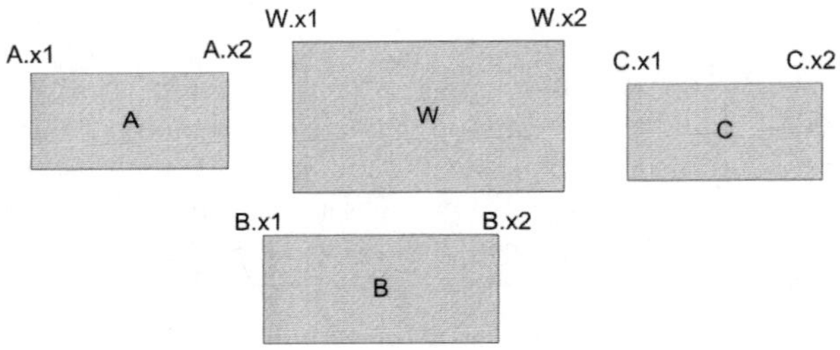

Fig. 2. Relative position of strips

1) *Eligible* pairs consist of all pairs of strips containing points that may contribute to the final query answer. The eligible pairs may be:
   a) Pairs that overlap. As seen in Fig. 3, strip P1 from P overlaps with strips Q1 and Q2 from Q.
   b) Pairs that do not overlap, but have their x-axis distance smaller than $bound$. In Fig. 3 the x-distance between P1 and Q3 is $d1 < bound$.
2) *non-Eligible* pairs consist of all pairs of strips that do not overlap and have their x-axis distance greater than $bound$. The contained points cannot contribute to the final query answer. Such a pair is P1 and Q4, two strips that have their x-distance $d2 > bound$, as shown in Fig. 3. The same holds for every consecutive Q-strip after Q4.

In the case of non-overlapping but yet eligible pairs (case 1-a, above), not all points from both strips need to be considered in the forthcoming step, since pruning can be performed to reduce both strips to these points that their x-axis distance from each other is smaller than $bound$.

For example, in the case of pair P1, Q3, we use the $filter$ function of Spark to reduce Q3 to these points (Q3.x, Q3.y) such that $Q3.x - P1.max < bound$ and also reduce P1 to these points (P1.x, P1.y) such that $Q3.xmin - P1.x < bound$.

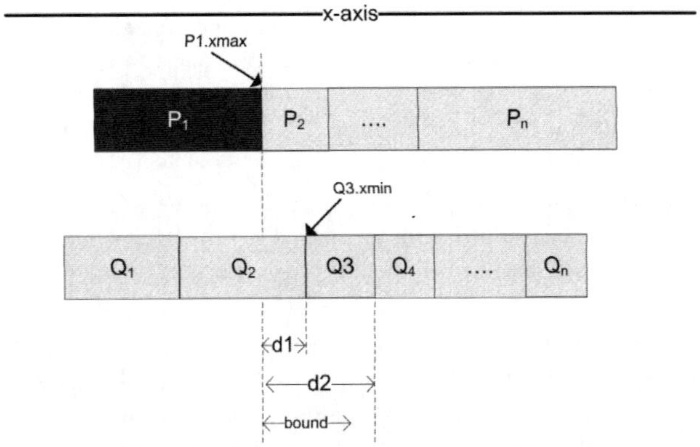

Fig. 3. Eligible strips and filtering of non overlapping strips

D. kCPQ computation

Having located all the eligible pairs, we create two new RDDs, with all possible pairs of strips containing points that may contribute to the answer of the query. This is done by duplicating, as needed, the points from strips of each dataset that have to be accounted with points from strips from the other dataset (a union) and assigning proper keys.

In the final step, a Plane-sweep algorithm is applied within each eligible (and filtered) pair of strips from P and Q for calculating k Closest Pairs and storing the result in a, separately for each partition, maximum binary heap (max-Heap). Previously, the *bound* (computed in step 1) has been broadcasted to all workers to use it as stop condition for the plane sweep algorithm. Taking the first (sorted on distance) k tuples with the smaller distances, yields the final (and exact) solution.

IV. Binary Space Partitioning for the kCPQ

As already described, the method of [1] uses a lightweight partitioning scheme that splits the datasets into strips. In the current work we are maintaining the fundamental concept of partitioning into strips, but implement two additional partitioning schemes, influenced by the Quad-tree and R-tree principles. Since the partitioning derives from Quad-tree and R-tree, we call them Q-split and R-split partitionings, respectively.

A. Outline of the partitioning procedure

As in the original method, partitioning of datasets is performed along an axis, which in our case is the x-axis. Both Q-split and R-split partitions use a Binary Search Tree (BST) to store the splitting points. A *class BST* extends Scala collection *mutable.Map* and is used to implement the Binary Search Tree. Each Node of the BST is defined as a Scala class of type *class Node(key, value, left: Node, right: Node).*

Parameter key is of type Double and is the actual splitting x-coordinate. Parameter $value$, in our case is of type (Int, Double) where the Int in $value$ is showing the level of decomposition and the Double is the splitting x-point. Parameter $value$ can store any kind of information and we intend to use it in further experimentation, for example, one can store sizes of every child area and use it to make decisions regarding the computation. The BST class is equipped with a function $compare$ that is used to compare the keys of the points to be added.

Every new node is being added by a function + that recursively scans the BST, locates its correct position and adds it to the tree.

By sampling the dataset with ratio f, we map the points to their x-coordinates and collect the results to the Driver program, in an array DS. The "middle" point selection depends on the criterion used to partition the array and afterwards the dataset.

In the case of R-split, $middle$ is selected as the point that leaves equal number of points on the two sub-intervals, while in the case of Q-split $middle$ is the point that splits the interval into two sub-intervals with the same x-axis width. This means that in the first case $middle$ is an actual x-point from the dataset, while in the latter it may be not since it is computed as the median of each interval.

Each dataset is partitioned separately, as happens in [1]. In both partitioning schemes, we set two parameters $PCapacity$ and $QCapacity$, which represent the maximum number of points that a node can store. In contrast to [1], no additional sampling is performed, as partitioning is done by using the samples taken for upper bound computation.

B. R-split

We perform Quicksort on array DS (the full sample) and locate the first splitting point of the array, named $middle$. In the case of R-split, initial value of $middle$ is set as the quotient $DS.length/2$. The value of $capacity$, idx (an integer counting the level of decomposition), TR (an empty BST), DS (the array with x-points from sample) and the splitting point $middle$ are passed to a function $partitionEqualSize$ that uses recursion to create and return the BST with the splitting points. The pseudo code snippet in Fig. 4 outlines the procedure.

C. Q-split

The initial value of $middle$ is computed as the median of the maximum and minimum x-values of each dataset. For example, in the case of dataset P, middle is the quotient $(P.maxX+P.minX)/2$. Function $partitionEqualwidth$ is similar to $partitionEqualSize$, with two differences. Line 12 is replaced with $ml = (FPLeft.maxX+FPLeft.minX)/2$ and Line 16 is $mr = (FPRight.maxX + FPRight.minX)/2$

```
1:  function PARTITIONEQUALSIZE(capacity, idx, TR, DS, middle): BST
2:      function PS(capacity,idx, TR, DS, middle): Int
3:          id = idx + 1
4:          TR += middle -> (id, middle)
5:          FPLeft = DS.filter(x => x < middle)
6:          FPRight = DS.filter(x => x >= middle)
7:          FPLeftSize = FPLeft.length
8:          FPRightSize = FPRight.length
9:          FL = FPLeftSize / f                    ▷ f is the sampling ratio
10:         FR = FPRightSize / f
11:         if (FL > capacity) then
12:             ml = FPLeft(FPLeftSize / 2)
13:             id = ps(capacity,id, TR, FPLeft, ml)
14:         end if
15:         if (FR > capacity) then
16:             mr = FPRight(FPRightSize / 2)
17:             id = ps(capacity, id, TR, FPRight, mr)
18:         end if
19:         return id
20:     end function
21:     ps(capacity, idx, TR, DS, middle)
22:     return TR
23: end function
```

Fig. 4. R-SPLIT outline.

In both R-split and Q-split, the splitting points are retrieved from the BST by using an inorder traversal, being utilized by means of a properly designed iterator.

V. Experimental Evaluation

To evaluate the performance of our methods, we used three large real 2d datasets from OpenStreetMap [16]: WATER resources consisting of 5,836,360 line segments, PARKS (or green areas) consisting of 11,504,035 polygons and BUILDINGS of the world consisting of 114,736,611 polygons. To create sets of points, we used the centers of the Minimum Bounding Rectangles (MBRs) of the line-segments from WATER and the centroids of polygons from PARK and BUILDINGS.

All experiments were conducted on a cluster of 9 nodes. Each node has 4 vCPUs running at 2.1GHz, with a total of 16GB of main memory per node, running Ubuntu Linux 16.04 operating system. Spark 2.1.1 running on Hadoop 2.7.2 Distributed File System (HDFS) was used as our parallel computing system. The block size of HDFS was 128 MB. Of the 9 computing nodes, one was running the NameNodes for Hadoop and Master for Spark, while the remaining eight (8 nodes x 4 vCPUs = 32 vCPUs) were used as HDFS DataNodes and Spark Worker nodes. Java openjdk ver. 1.8.0 and Scala code runner ver. 2.11 were used.

In all experiments, the data sets P and Q are in the form of text files formatted in columns with a separator (in our case a tab), one point per line (x, y coordinates). We also make the assumption that the two data files have already been stored in the HDFS, at an earlier phase without being subject to any kind of processing (e.g., sorting, indexing, and so forth). The datasets are read by using the $textFile$ function of Spark. Each dataset is presented as an RDD[$Point$], where $Point$ is of type Tuple2[Double, Double]. In all experiments the number of closest pairs is set to k = 10.

A. Speedup of method in [1]

First we measure the total computing time for 4 and 8 computing nodes in the case of BUILDINGS x PARKS (Fig. 5) and PARKS x WATER (Fig. 6) of the method presented in [1], varying the number of the preset partitions.

We measured total execution time (i.e., response time) in seconds (sec) that expresses the overall CPU, I/O and communication time needed for the execution of each query.

Let $T4$ be the execution time for four nodes and $T8$ be the execution time for eight nodes. The speedup is defined by $T4/T8$. We observe that execution time decreases more rapidly in the cases of larger number of partitions. This is expected since a larger number of partitions leads to more Spark jobs being more efficiently managed when a larger number of computing nodes is available. In the case of BUILDINGS x PARKS, best speedup (1.7) is measured at 32 partitions. Best response time is measured with 16 partitions, where the speedup is about 1.6. In the case of PARKS x WATER, best speedup (1.84) is measured at 64 partitions. Best response time comes when number of partitions is set to 32, and the speedup is 1.3

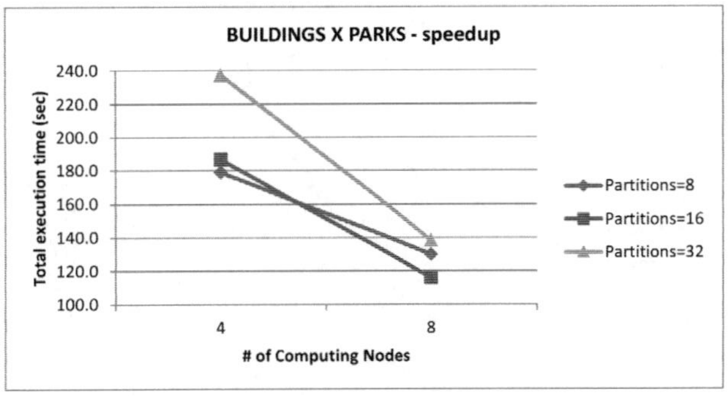

Fig. 5. kCPQ(BUILDINGS x PARKS), Nodes =4, 8

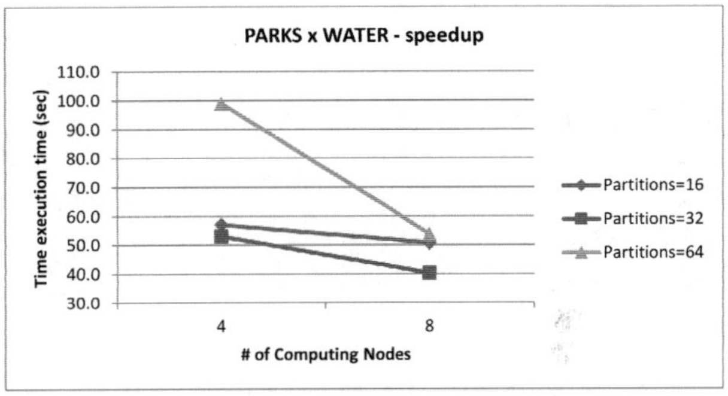

Fig. 6. kCPQ(BUILDINGS x PARKS), Nodes =4, 8

B. Original method in [1] vs improved (single sampling)

The second experiment deals with the improvement we have made to the algorithm in [1] and mentioned beforehand. By refactoring the code, we have removed the second sampling that is used by the original method in order to partition the datasets. Instead, we use the sample already taken for the upper bound computation. The results are being presented in Fig. 7 and Fig. 8.

It was observed that a sample ratio of $f = 0.001$ is adequate to efficiently partition the datasets. In general, the system runs faster, mostly in the case of larger datasets where a relatively small fixed number of partitions are used. This is reasonable, since in the original method the sample size is computed as the quotient of dataset size and number of partitions; therefore as partitions number decreases it results in an increase of the sample size and therefore an increase in upper bound computation time.

We use this strategy (a single sampling per dataset) in all following experiments, and use only one very small sample, with ratio 0.001 for computing both upper bound and partitioning x-axis points.

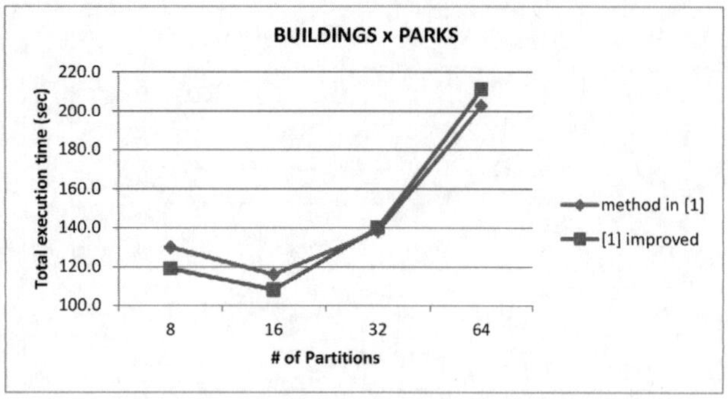

Fig. 7. BUILDINGS x PARKS. Method [1] vs method [1] improved

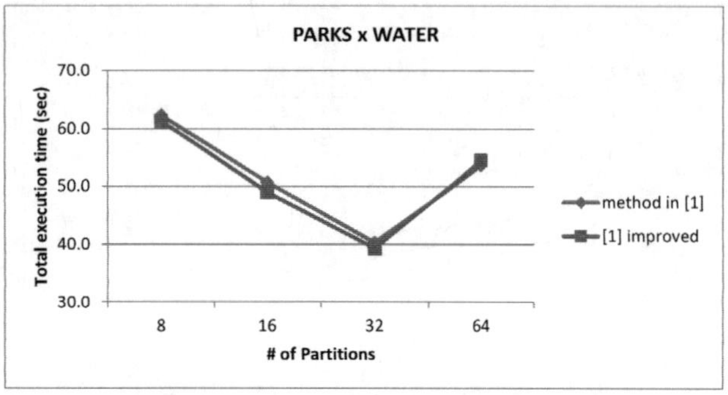

Fig. 8. PARKS x WATER. Method [1] vs method [1] improved

C. *R-split and Q-split performance*

In the third experiment we test the performance of the method in the case of both R-split and Q-split. We have run several experiments with various combinations of capacity for each dataset. Table I presents the results of the experiment regarding R-split for BUILDINGS x PARKS and PARKS x WATER datasets. As it can be observed, the new partitioning scheme provides much more freedom in fine tuning the system, since we now don't need to preset the number of partitions, but rather set capacities and have the system compute the number of partitions that meet the settings.

In Fig. 9 and Fig. 10 we compare the results measured for the improved version of [1], as described above, with the best obtained by using the R-split, subject to the same number of partitions between the two methods. It can be deduced that an R-split achieves better running times compared to both the original and the improved version of method presented in [1] especially when dealing with larger datasets.

Table II presents the results of the experiment regarding Q-split for BUILDINGS x PARKS and PARKS x WATER datasets. In contrast to R-split, using Q-split leads to a, more or less, worse performance in almost every case when compared to both R-split and the improved method in [1]. Another observation is that Q-split leads to a number of derived partitions that varies more widely than in the case of R-split, where the number of partitions is mostly constant.

TABLE I. R-SPLIT RESULTS FOR THE KCPQ

Capacity (millions of points)		**Derived partitions #**		**Eligible pairs #**	**Time (sec)**
BUILDINGS	PARKS	BUILDINGS	PARKS		
23	2.3	8	8	15	111.3
14.5	1.5	8	8	15	104
14.5	1.4	8	16	23	126
14	1.4	16	16	31	104.3
12	1.4	16	16	31	101.3
10	1.4	16	16	31	96
10	0.75	16	16	31	98
10	0.7	16	32	47	138
8	1.4	16	16	31	99
8	0.75	16	16	31	95.7
8	0.7	16	32	47	138.7
6	1.4	32	16	47	104.3
6	0.7	32	32	63-64	125
4	1.4	32	16	47	109
2	1.4	64	16	79	131.3
2	0.35	64	64	127-128	199.3
Capacity (millions of points)		**Derived partitions #**		**Eligible pairs #**	**Time (sec)**
BUILDINGS	PARKS	BUILDINGS	PARKS		
1.4	0.7	16	16	31	49.7
1.4	0.35	16	32	47	39
2.8	1.4	8	8	15	61
0.7	0.35	32	32	63	40.3
0.7	0.7	32	16	47	40.7
0.35	0.175	64	64	127-128	53

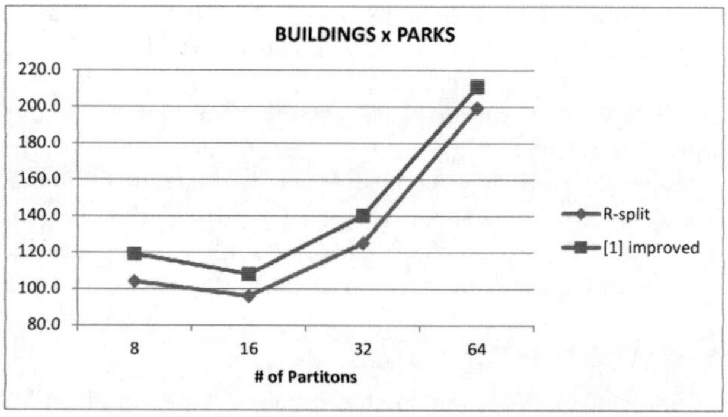

Fig. 9. BUILDINGS x PARKS. R-split vs method [1] improved

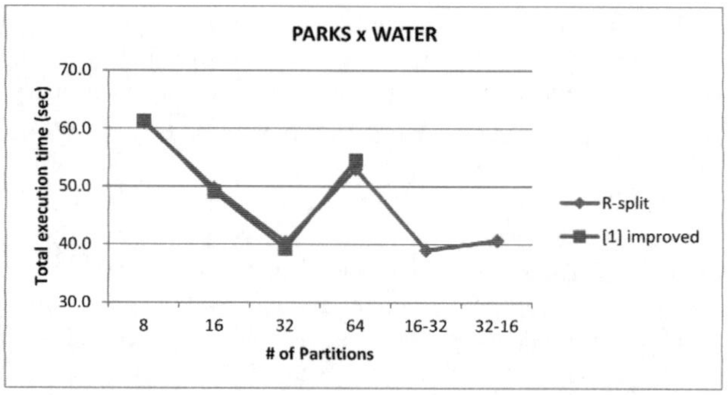

Fig. 10. PARKS x Water. R-split vs method [1] improved

TABLE II. Q-SPLIT RESULTS FOR THE KCPQ

Capacity (millions of points)		Derived partitions #		Eligible	Time
BUILDINGS	PARKS	BUILDINGS	PARKS	pairs #	(sec)
23	2.3	8	8	17	141.7
14.5	1.5	15	11-14	25-28	122.3
14.5	1.4	14-15	12-15	25-29	121.3
14	1.4	15-16	14-15	29-30	118.3
12	1.4	16	15-16	30-31	120
10	1.4	18-19	14-15	32-33	116.7
10	0.75	18-19	22-24	41-42	132.3
10	0.7	19	24	42	135.7
8	1.4	22	15	36	118.3
8	0.75	22-23	22-24	44-45	127.3
8	0.7	22-23	24-25	45-47	136
6	1.4	28	14	41	116
6	0.7	28	23-27	50-54	127.7
4	1.4	46	14-15	59-60	130.7
2	1.4	84-86	14-15	98-99	205.3
2	0.35	86-87	47-48	134	230
Capacity (millions of points)		**Derived partitions #**		**Eligible**	**Time**
BUILDINGS	PARKS	BUILDINGS	PARKS	**pairs #**	**(sec)**
1.4	0.7	14-15	15-16	28-30	35
1.4	0.35	14-15	26-27	40-41	39.3
2.8	1.4	8	8-9	16-15-15	59.7
0.7	0.35	24-25	27-28	50-52	41
0.7	0.7	24-25	16-17	39-41	33.3
0.35	0.175	48-49	55-56	102-104	49

D. R-split and Q-split performance

The fourth experiment is aiming to check the quality of R-split and Q-split partitions. As it can be seen, R-split partitioning results in strips with uniformly allocated number of points (Fig. 11 and Fig. 12). Furthermore, the selection of a small sample with ratio 0.001 is proved to be sufficient for this purpose.

On the other hand, a Q-split partition results in strips with unequal number of points (Fig. 13 and Fig. 14).

E. Dataset points replication

The fifth experiment is aiming to enlighten the differences measured in execution times regarding different $PCapacity$

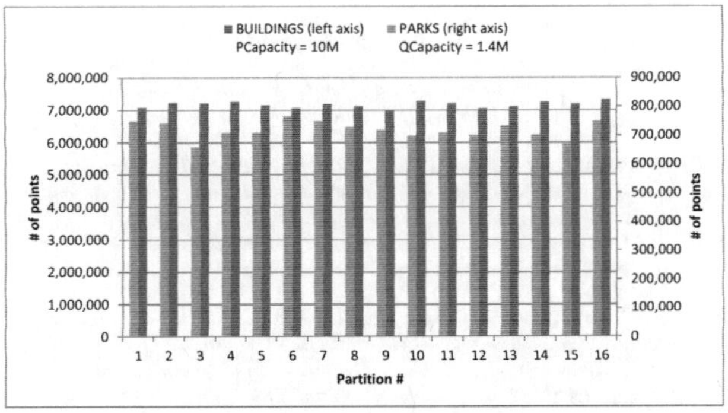

Fig. 11. R-split: # of points per partition. Capacity = (10M, 1.4M)

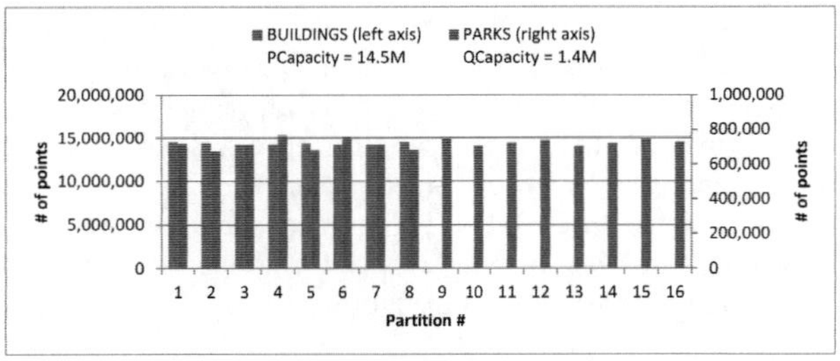

Fig. 12. R-split: # of points per partition. Capacity = (14.5M, 1.4M)

and $QCapacity$ settings, for both R-split and Q-split partitions.

As already mentioned, after locating all the eligible pairs of strips, two RDDs are derived containing all possible pairs of strips with points that may contribute to the answer of the query. These RDDs are created as a union of properly keyed points from strips of each dataset that have to be accounted with points from strips from the other dataset.

In the (usual) case a strip from P has to be combined to more than one strip from Q, then P is being duplicated (and filtered in the case of non overlapping strips) as needed and proper keys are being assigned. This means that the derived RDDs upon which the actual computation is being performed contain replicated points from both datasets.

In Fig. 15 and Fig. 16 we present the derived datasets in two different cases of partitioning by using R-split and Q-split

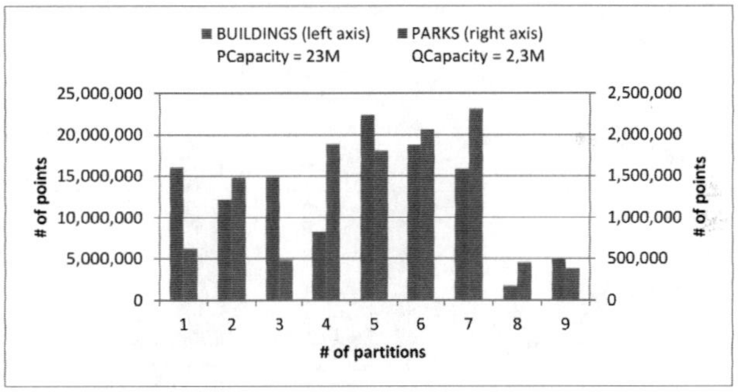

Fig. 13. Q-split: # of points per partition. Capacity = (23M, 2.3M)

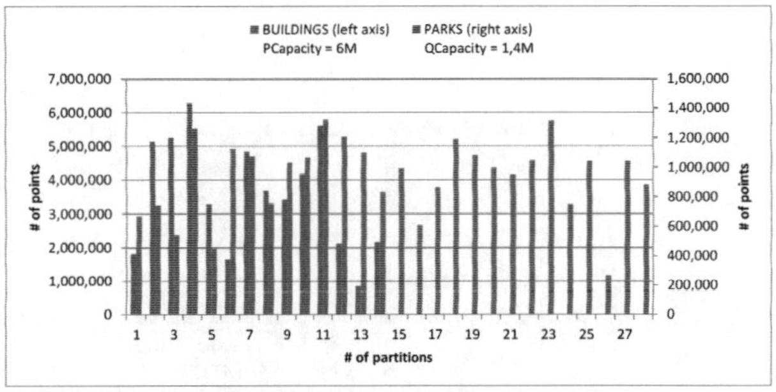

Fig. 14. Q-split: # of points per partition. Capacity = (6M, 1.4M)

respectively. In both figures, the first pair of columns presents the sizes of the original datasets and the rest two pairs present the sizes of the derived datasets (that are actually used for kCPQ computation) for two pairs of capacity settings. Using larger capacities leads to a smaller number of partitions (as shown in Table I and Table II) but this leads to an increased number of eligible points, a fact that influences the total execution time (also shown in figures).

F. Testing with larger datasets

In order to test our method on even larger pairs of datasets, we used CLUS_LAKES[1], a new big quasi-real dataset derived from a real one. To create this dataset, for each point of LAKES, p, 15 new points gathered around p (i.e., the center of the cluster) are generated according to a Gaussian distribution with mean = 0.0 and standard deviation = 0.2. The dataset CLUS_LAKES contains around 126M of points. We computed the kCPQ on the pair P = BUILDINGS and Q = CLUS_LAKES for several combinations of PCapacity and QCapacity and the total execution time (averaged) is shown in Table III (R-split has been used for the partitioning of the whole datasets).

VI. Conclusion and Future Plans

In this paper, extending [1], we have presented a method for the kCPQ computation in Spark. This method splits data into strips and computes closest pairs by plane sweep within each strip. Since proper partitioning is of great essence, especially in the context of parallel and distributed environments, we have particularized this method by presenting and implementing three different partitioning schemes that split the datasets into strips.

[1]Kindly provided by Antonio Corral and Francisco García-García, University of Almeria, Spain.

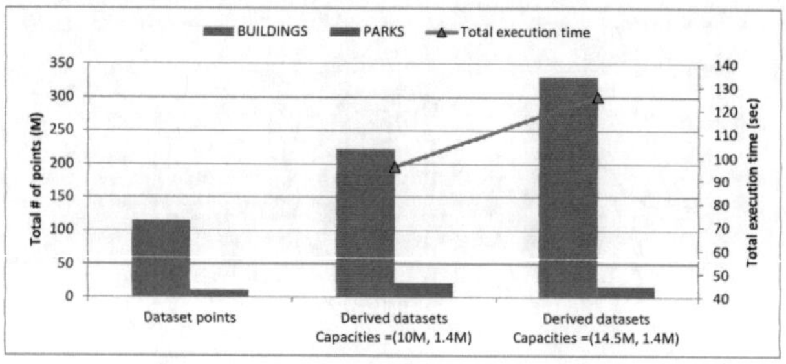

Fig. 15. R-split: Replicated points and execution time

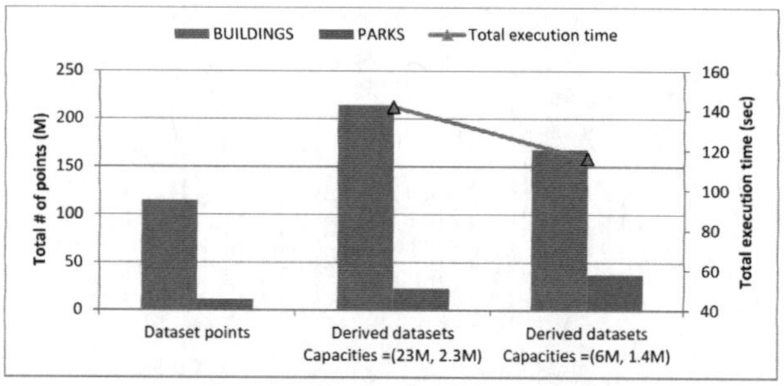

Fig. 16. Q-split: Replicated points and execution time

TABLE III. R-SPLIT RESULTS FOR THE KCPQ(BUILDINGS X CLUS_LAKES)

R-split					
Capacity (millions of points)		**Derived partitions #**		**Eligible pairs #**	**Time (sec)**
BUILD-INGS	CLUS_LAKES	BUILD-INGS	CLUS_LAKES		
2	2	64	64	127-129	433.7
6	6	32	32	63	316.0
6	8	32	16	47	287.7
8	6	16	32	48	548.7
8	8	16	16	31	385.0

By conducting experiments on large real datasets we have explored the performance of our method and the performance of the partitioning schemes. Splitting into strips by means of Binary Space Partitioning techniques is proven to provide flexibility in tuning the system, thus resulting to faster execution time. R-split (divide datasets into parts with equal sizes) was shown to work better than Q-split (divide datasets into parts of equal width).

In a very recently published paper [31] we have presented SliceNBound, an algorithm for the kCPQ and Distance Join Query (DJQ), influenced by the ideas presented in the current paper. Simba [21] does not support KCPQs, but does support DJQs, so a comparison had been performed between the methods [31] and [21] on DJQ. In the future, we plan to compare the methods for kCPQ presented in current paper with kCPQ implemented in Simba and other spatial oriented, Spark based, platforms. We also plan to further elaborate this method and investigate partitioning schemes for Spark to reduce the need for examining combinations of data that reside in different strips and also reduce the network communication traffic. Furthermore, we plan to research for a faster and stricter upper bound computation, since we have observed that this bound strongly influences the total running time of the query.

References

[1] G. Mavrommatis, P. Moutafis, and M. Vassilakopoulos, "Closest-Pairs Query Processing in Apache Spark," in *Proceedings of the 8th International Conference on Cloud Computing, GRIDs and Virtualization (CLOUD COMPUTING 2017), Athens, Greece, February 19-23*, 2017, pp. 26–31, ISBN: 978-1-61208-529-6, ISSN: 2308-4294.

[2] S. Shekhar and H. Xiong, Eds., *Encyclopedia of GIS*. Springer, 2008.

[3] P. Rigaux, M. Scholl, and A. Voisard, *Spatial databases - with applications to GIS*. Elsevier, 2002.

[4] A. Corral and M. Vassilakopoulos, "Query processing in spatial databases," in *Encyclopedia of Database Technologies and Applications*. Idea Group, 2005, pp. 511–516.

[5] A. Corral, Y. Manolopoulos, Y. Theodoridis, and M. Vassilakopoulos, "Closest pair queries in spatial databases," in *Proceedings of the 2000 ACM SIGMOD International Conference on Management of Data, Dallas, TX, USA, May 16-18*, 2000, pp. 189–200.

[6] ——, "Algorithms for processing k-closest-pair queries in spatial databases," *Data Knowl. Eng.*, vol. 49, no. 1, pp. 67–104, 2004.

[7] J. Dean and S. Ghemawat, "Mapreduce: simplified data processing on large clusters," *Commun. ACM*, vol. 51, no. 1, pp. 107–113, 2008.

[8] M. Zaharia, M. Chowdhury, M. J. Franklin, S. Shenker, and I. Stoica, "Spark: Cluster computing with working sets," in *Proceedings of the 2Nd USENIX Conference on Hot Topics in Cloud Computing, Boston, MA, USA, June 22-25*, 2010, pp. 10–10.

[9] M. Zaharia, M. Chowdhury, T. Das, A. Dave, J. Ma, M. McCauley, M. J. Franklin, S. Shenker, and I. Stoica, "Resilient distributed datasets: A fault-tolerant abstraction for in-memory cluster computing," in *Proceedings of the 9th USENIX Conference on Networked Systems Design and Implementation, San Jose, CA, USA, April 25-27*, 2012, pp. 2–2.

[10] G. Roumelis, M. Vassilakopoulos, A. Corral, and Y. Manolopoulos, "A new plane-sweep algorithm for the k-closest-pairs query," in *SOFSEM 2014: Theory and Practice of Computer Science - Proceedings of the 40th International Conference on Current Trends in Theory and Practice of Computer Science, Nový Smokovec, Slovakia, January 26-29*, 2014, pp. 478–490.

[11] G. Roumelis, A. Corral, M. Vassilakopoulos, and Y. Manolopoulos, "New plane-sweep algorithms for distance-based join queries in spatial databases," *GeoInformatica*, vol. 20, no. 4, pp. 571–628, 2016.

[12] D. Chen, C. Shen, J. Feng, and J. Le, "An efficient parallel top-k similarity join for massive multidimensional data using spark," *International Journal of Database Theory and Application*, vol. 8, no. 3, pp. 57–68, 2015.

[13] D. N. Rao and D. S. Rao, "Computational geometry leveraged by apache spark," *Journal of Innovation in Electronics and Communication Engineering*, vol. 5, no. 2, pp. 15–31, 2015, ISSN: 2249-9946, Online ISSN: 2455-3514.

[14] J. Lu and R. H. Güting, "Parallel secondo: Boosting database engines with hadoop," in *Proceedings of the 18th IEEE International Conference on Parallel and Distributed Systems, ICPADS 2012, Singapore, December 17-19*, 2012, pp. 738–743.

[15] A. Aji, F. Wang, H. Vo, R. Lee, Q. Liu, X. Zhang, and J. H. Saltz, "Hadoop-gis: A high performance spatial data warehousing system over mapreduce," *PVLDB*, vol. 6, no. 11, pp. 1009–1020, 2013.

[16] A. Eldawy and M. F. Mokbel, "Spatialhadoop: A mapreduce framework for spatial data," in *Proceedings of the 31st IEEE International Conference on Data Engineering, ICDE 2015, Seoul, South Korea, April 13-17*, 2015, pp. 1352–1363.

[17] F. García-García, A. Corral, L. Iribarne, M. Vassilakopoulos, and Y. Manolopoulos, "Enhancing spatialhadoop with closest pair queries," in *Advances in Databases and Information Systems - Proceedings of the 20th East European Conference, ADBIS 2016, Prague, Czech Republic, August 28-31*, 2016, pp. 212–225.

[18] J. Yu, J. Wu, and M. Sarwat, "Geospark: a cluster computing framework for processing large-scale spatial data," in *Proceedings of the 23rd SIGSPATIAL International Conference on Advances in Geographic Information Systems, Bellevue, WA, USA, November 3-6*, 2015, pp. 70:1–70:4.

[19] S. You, J. Zhang, and L. Gruenwald, "Large-scale spatial join query processing in cloud," in *Proceedings of the 31st IEEE International Conference on Data Engineering Workshops, ICDE Workshops 2015, Seoul, South Korea, April 13-17*, 2015, pp. 34–41.

[20] M. Tang, Y. Yu, Q. M. Malluhi, M. Ouzzani, and W. G. Aref, "Locationspark: A distributed in-memory data management system for big spatial data," *PVLDB*, vol. 9, no. 13, pp. 1565–1568, 2016.

[21] D. Xie, F. Li, B. Yao, G. Li, L. Zhou, and M. Guo, "Simba: Efficient in-memory spatial analytics," in *Proceedings of the 2016 International Conference on Management of Data, SIGMOD Conference 2016, San Francisco, CA, USA, June 26-July 01*, 2016, pp. 1071–1085.

[22] G. R. Hjaltason and H. Samet, "Incremental distance join algorithms for spatial databases," in *Proceedings of the ACM SIGMOD International Conference on Management of Data, Seattle, Washington, USA, June 2-4*, 1998, pp. 237–248.

[23] H. Shin, B. Moon, and S. Lee, "Adaptive and incremental processing for distance join queries," *IEEE Trans. Knowl. Data Eng.*, vol. 15, no. 6, pp. 1561–1578, 2003.

[24] C. Yang and K. Lin, "An index structure for improving closest pairs and related join queries in spatial databases," in *Proceedings of the International Database Engineering & Applications Symposium, IDEAS'02, Edmonton, Canada, July 17-19*, 2002, pp. 140–149.

[25] G. Gutierrez and P. Sáez, "The k closest pairs in spatial databases - when only one set is indexed," *GeoInformatica*, vol. 17, no. 4, pp. 543–565, 2013.

[26] A. Aji, H. Vo, and F. Wang, "Effective spatial data partitioning for scalable query processing," *CoRR*, vol. abs/1509.00910, 2015.

[27] A. Eldawy, L. Alarabi, and M. F. Mokbel, "Spatial partitioning techniques in spatial hadoop," *PVLDB*, vol. 8, no. 12, pp. 1602–1605, 2015.

[28] H. Samet, C. A. Shatter, R. C. Nelson, Y. Huang, K. Fujimura, and A. Rosenteld, "Recent developments in linear quadtree-based geographic information systems," *Image Vision Comput.*, vol. 5, no. 3, pp. 187–197, 1987.

[29] A. Guttman, "R-trees: A dynamic index structure for spatial searching," in *SIGMOD'84, Proceedings of Annual Meeting, Boston, Massachusetts, June 18-21*, 1984, pp. 47–57.

[30] S. T. Leutenegger, J. M. Edgington, and M. A. López, "STR: A simple and efficient algorithm for r-tree packing," in *Proceedings of the Thirteenth International Conference on Data Engineering, Birmingham, U.K., April 7-11*, 1997, pp. 497–506.

[31] G. Mavrommatis, P. Moutafis, M. Vassilakopoulos, F. García-García, and A. Corral, "Slicenbound: Solving closest pairs and distance join queries in apache spark," in *Advances in Databases and Information Systems - Proceedings of the 21st European Conference, ADBIS 2017, Nicosia, Cyprus, September 24-27*, 2017, pp. 199–213, ISBN: 978-3-319-66916-8, ISSN: 0302-9743.

Programming Spreadsheets in Natural Language: Design of a Natural Language User Interface

Alexander Wachtel, Felix Eurich, Walter F. Tichy

Karlsruhe Institute of Technology, Karlsruhe, Germany
Email: alexander.wachtel@kit.edu, felix.eurich@student.kit.edu, walter.tichy@kit.edu

***Abstract*—In this paper, we present the idea to use the natural language as the user interface for programming tasks. Programming languages assist with repetitive tasks that involve the use of conditionals, loops and statements. However, users can easily describe tasks in their natural language. We aim to develop a *Natural Language User Interface* that enables users to describe algorithms, including statements, loops, and conditionals. For this, we extend our current spreadsheet system to support control flows. Although far from perfect, this research might lead to fundamental changes in computer use. With natural language, programming would become available to everyone. We believe that it is a reasonable approach for end-user software engineering and will, therefore, overcome the present bottleneck of IT proficients.**

Keywords–Natural Language Processing; End-User Development; Natural Language Interfaces; Human Computer Interaction; Programming In Natural Language; Dialog Systems.

I. Introduction

Since their invention, digital computers have been programmed using specialized, artificial notations, called programming languages. Programming requires years of training. However, only a tiny fraction of human computer users can actually work with those notations. With natural language and end-user development methods, programming would become available to everyone and enable end-users to program their systems or extend it without any knowledge of programming languages. This vision forms the basis for our natural language user interface [1]. Already in 1987, Tichy discussed that AI techniques are useful for software engineering, pointing out the potential of natural language processing [2] and natural-language help systems [3].

According to Liberman [4], the main question in the End-User Development area of research is how to allow non-programming users, who have no access to source code, to program a computer system or extend the functionality of an existing system. Similar to programming languages, our natural language contains all necessary prerequisites to describe an algorithm. However, although you already have the required ability in its core, you have to go through a lengthy learning process in order to master a programming language. Our idea is that, in the future, it will no longer be necessary. The goal is to create a way for the computer to deal directly with natural language. Therefore its necessary to identify and use these similarities between our natural language and the programming language. In general, the system adapts to us and we don't have to go the tedious way through a programming language anymore. Through this paradigm shift natural language would enable almost anyone to program and would thus cause a fundamental shift in the way computers are used. Rather than being a mere consumer of programs written by others, each user could write his or her own programs [5]. However, programming in natural language remains an open challenge [6].

We are working on the *Natural Language User Interface (NLUI)* that expects natural language input, interprets it in the context of programming and delivers a valid output for this via the dialog system (see Figure 1).

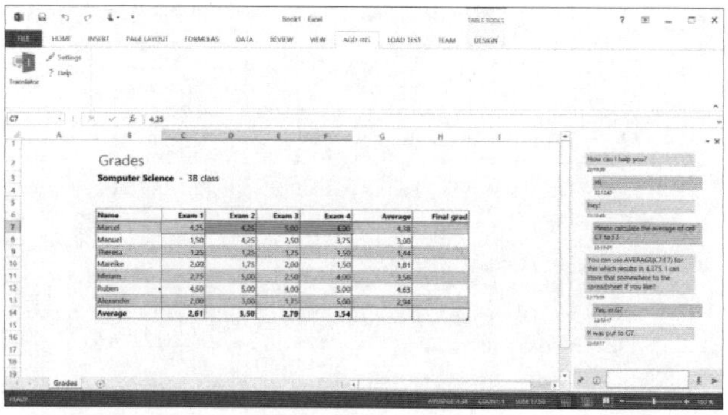

Figure 1. User Interface of the natural language dialog system

In our prototype, we decided to address spreadsheets for several reasons:

- a lot of open data available [7]
- easy to manipulate data
- well-known and well-distributed

In general, spreadsheets have been used for at least 7000 years [8]. Myers [9] and Scaffidi [10] compared the number of end users and professional programmers in the United States. Nearly 90 million people use computers at work and 50 million of them use spreadsheets. In a self-assessment 12 million considered themselves as programmers, but only 3 million people are professional programmers. The created spreadsheets are not only the traditional tabular representation of relational data that convey information space efficiently, but also allow a continuous revision and formula-based data manipulation. It is estimated that users create hundreds of millions of spreadsheets each year [11].

Our paper is structured as following: Section II presents related work in the research areas of programming in natural language, End-User Programming and natural language dialog systems. Section III describes our work on NLUI: pilot study, dialog system, data representation, analysis of data, and finally, control flows. Section IV evaluates latest prototype in an user study. Finally, Section V presents a conclusion of our topic and future work.

II. RELATED WORK

The idea of programming in natural language was first proposed by Sammet in 1966 [12], but enormous difficulties have resulted in disappointingly slow progress. One of the difficulties is that natural language programming requires a domain-aware counterpart that asks for clarification, thereby overcoming the chief disadvantages of natural language, namely ambiguity and imprecision. In recent years, significant advances in natural language techniques have been made, leading, for instance, to IBM's Watson [13] computer winning against the two world champions in a quiz game called Jeopardy!, where general knowledge is presented in the form of answers and the candidates must phrase the belonging questions, Apple's Siri routinely answering wide-ranging, spoken queries, and automated translation services such as Google's becoming usable [14][6]. In 1979, Ballard et al. [15][16][17] introduced their Natural Language Computer (NLC) that enables users to program simple arithmetic calculations using natural language. Although NLC resolves references as well, there is no dialog system. Metafor introduced by Liu et al. [18] has a different orientation. Based on user stories the system tries to derive program structures to support software design. A different approach regarding software design via natural language is taken by RECAA [19]. RECAA can automatically derive UML models from the text and also keep model and specification consistent through an automatic feedback component. A limited domain end-to-end programming is introduced by Le. SmartSynth [20] allows synthesizing smartphone automation scripts from natural language description. However, there is no dialog interaction besides the results output and error messages.

Initially, Cypher [21] used unstructured text for their research. But later found out that the unstructured approach caused too many false interpretations. Their approach, called sloppy programming, uses a specific grammar, based on an existing set of scripts and allows users to enter something simple and natural. Controlled natural language (CNL) is similar, in that it is simple and natural enough, yet it restricts the grammar, and requires the user to learn the restrictions from examples and by feedback. Gordon [22][23] works on scenario-based programming directly in a controlled natural language. They also believes that a natural language interface to an intuitive programming language may play a major role in programming. [24] translates use-case templates written a CNL to process algebra. Similar to our work, they have implemented the prototype in a Microsoft Word plug-in. It checks adherence of use-case specifications to a CNL grammar and translates them into process algebra. Understanding of natural language by a computer system is a complicated problem and has been studied widely [25]. Command & control systems [26] [27] can retrieve answers that may be given in natural language, or sometimes in more appropriate forms. Smarter applications can take into account the moving speed of the mobile phone and provide a more relevant answer. These Activities like schedule dinner in a restaurant, however, are not programming. Such natural language interactions [28] can be carried out using voice or natural text interfaces. Vadas et al. [29] create runnable programs code from unrestricted natural language. It is inspired by [18] and uses deep semantics derived by a parser for combinatory categorical grammars (CCG). As with NaturalJava, the user must know the target programming language. Furthermore, Mihalcea et al. [30] handles effectively some aspects of procedural programming, e.g., steps and loops.

Paternò [31] introduces the motivations behind end-user programming defined by Liberman [4] and discusses its basic concepts, and reviews the current state of art. Various approaches are discussed and classified in terms of their main features and the technologies and platforms for, which they have been developed. In 2006, Myers [9] provides an overview of the research in the area of End-User Programming. As he summarized, many different systems for End-User Development have already been realized [32][33][34]. However, there is no system such as our prototype that can be controlled with natural language. During a study in 2006, Ko [32] identifies six learning barriers in End-User Programming: design, selection, coordination, use, understanding and information barriers. In 2008, Dorner [35] describes and classifies End-User Development approaches taken from the literature, which are suitable approaches for different groups of end-users. Implementing the right mixture of these approaches leads to embedded design environments, having a gentle slope of complexity. Such environments enable differently skilled end-users to perform system adaptations on their own. Sestoft [36] increases expressiveness and emphasizing execution speed of the functions thus defined by supporting recursive and higher-order functions, and fast execution by a careful choice of data representation and compiler technology. Cunha [37] realizes techniques for model-driven spreadsheet engineering that employs bidirectional transformations to maintain spreadsheet models and synchronized instances. Begel [38] introduces voice recognition to the software development process. His approach uses program analysis to dictate code in natural language, thereby enabling the creation of a program editor that supports voice-based programming.

NLyze [39], an Add-In for Microsoft Excel that has been developed by Gulwani, Microsoft Research, at the same time as our system. It enables end-users to manipulate spreadsheet data by using natural language. It uses a separate domain-specific language for logical interpretation of the user input. Instead of recognizing the tables automatically, it uses canonical tables, which should be marked by the end-user. Another Gulwani's tool QuickCode [40] deals with the production of the program code in spreadsheets through input-output examples provided by the end-user [34]. It automates string processing in spreadsheets using input-output examples and splits the manipulations in spreadsheet by entering examples. The focus of his work is on the synthesizing of programs that consist of text operations. Furthermore, many dialog systems have already been developed. Commercially successful systems, such as Apple's Siri, actually based on active ontology [41], and Google's Voice Search [42][43] cover many domains. Reference resolution makes the systems act natural. However, there is no dialog interaction. The Mercury system [44] designed by the MIT research group is a telephone hotline for automated booking of airline tickets. Mercury guides the user through a mixed initiative dialog towards the selection of a suitable flight based on date, time and preferred airline. Furthermore, Allen [45] describes a system called PLOW developed at Stanford University. As a collaborative task agent PLOW can learn to perform certain tasks, such as extracting specific information from the internet, by demonstration, explanation, and dialog.

III. Natural Language User Interface

In 1979, Ballard et al. [15][16][17] introduced the Natural Language Computer (NLC) that enables end-users to program simple arithmetic calculations using natural language. This section describes different research steps of our work on NLUI prototype.

A. Pilot Study

Initially, we needed to see how real users would interact with spreadsheets in natural language. For this purpose, we recruited subjects and asked them to describe how to solve problems with the aid of a spreadsheet. Spreadsheets with data were provided together with the problems. The subjects were asked to imagine explaining to a human partner how to solve a given problem and to write down what they would say. Even though there were no suggestions to ask the imaginary partner for help, many participants did just that. The problems to be solved were selected from the first four chapters of the textbook Excel 2013 Step by Step [46]. The study consists of 35 questions, six of, which are mathematical problems (i.e., calculation of sum and average, rounding decimal values, copying an existing formula to other cells, conditional functions) and six are data and document manipulation tasks (i.e., inserting and sorting of columns, creating tables and diagrams, labeling cells). Other questions dealt with experience with spreadsheets and familiarity with certain functions.

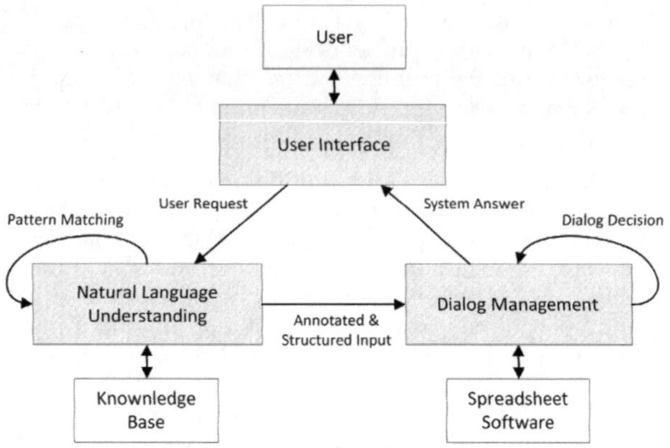

Figure 2. Architecture Overview.

B. Dialog System

Motivated by our pilot study on the natural language prototype, it became clear that a dialog between humans and the computer is required. Suendermann [47] states that in a natural-language dialog system, language perception, and speech production interact with a number of other components. A dialog system is able to communicate with a software system in another language, called meta-language. In general, a dialog system consists of a series of three units, a speech analysis unit for the perception of the natural language input, a dialog management unit for controlling the dialog process, and a speech synthesis unit.

In 2015, first prototype of an assistant has been presented that uses natural language understanding and a dialog management system to allow inexperienced users to manipulate spreadsheets with natural language [48]. The system requests missing information and is able to resolve ambiguities by providing alternatives to choose from. Furthermore, the dialog system must resolve references to previous results, allowing the construction of complex expressions step-by-step. The system architecture consists of a user interface responsible for human interaction, as well as a natural language understanding and a dialog management unit (see Figure 2). In a first step, the natural language understanding unit (NLU) performs essential language analysis relying on a basic vocabulary specifically built to cover the system's domain. Synonyms are substituted using a handcrafted synonym database. Mathematical terms and numerical values as well as references to regions within the spreadsheet are tagged. In the following step, the system groups elements representing a sentence or clause to enable subsequent analysis to perform their work sentence by sentence. With all these adjustments the given example yields a single sentence illustrated in Figure 3 is mapped to a tree structure.

$$\text{Please}_{(Request)}\ \text{calculate}_{(Calculation)}\ \text{the}_{(Article)}\ \text{sum}_{(Operator)}\ \text{of}_{(Possession)}\ \text{column}_{(Positioning)}\ \text{FinalExam}_{(ReferenceTableColumn)}\ \text{divided}_{(Operator)}\ \text{by}_{(Specification)}\ 11_{(Number)}$$

Figure 3. Example of an annotated user input.

Following this, the semantic meaning of any annotated sentence is derived. For this purpose patterns were designed with each pattern consisting of a sequence of keywords and placeholders. The latter can either take a single column, row, cell, number, or arbitrary elements of any type. All patterns are compared with each clause matching the keyword. As part of the given example the pattern *sum* matches the first clause, with keywords *add* and *to*, and placeholders *any* (see Figure 4). The placeholders are filled with the respective elements (*4* and *A1*). By successively matching additional patterns within the placeholder elements, more complex sentences can be transformed into a semantic representation. It builds a tree structure consisting of operators and operands which makes it easy to determine whether a valid arithmetic expression has been provided (see Figure 5). Entirely identified patterns are mapped onto spreadsheet formulas, with the respective placeholders serving as operands, while others have to be processed by the dialog management unit. Incompletely matched patterns are handled by the DMU.

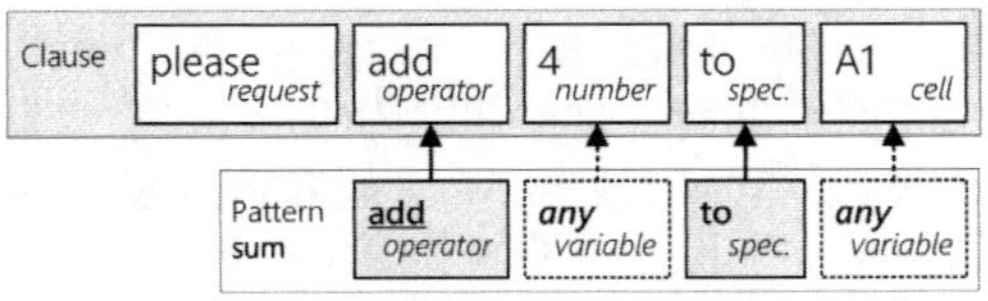

Figure 4. Examplary pattern matching

The purpose of the dialog management unit (DMU) is to deal with the tree structure that has been created by the NLU unit, resolve references, create a valid spreadsheet formula and generate a human-like response to the user input.

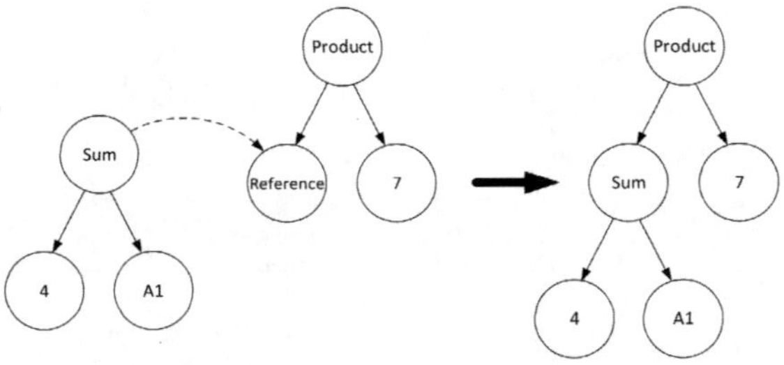

Figure 5. Reference resolution to the previous calculation

Figure 6 shows the process of each user input through three dialog system interpretation stages: contextual, general and fallback. The contextual interpretation runs if the system expects an user answer for missing information or for statement of insert the formula into the spreadsheet. It is always executed before the general interpretation and tries to find a match to the previously posed question within the current user input. For this purpose a set of values from the current conversational context stores all information that might help with dialog decisions. The current context together with any information on previous dialog iterations is presented by a history that keeps track during prolonged conversations with multiple iterations.

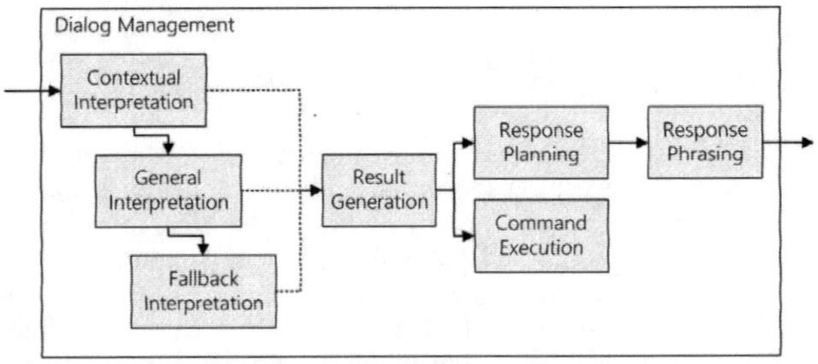

Figure 6. Dialog Management Unit.

Each time a new request is entered by the user, the history is extended by a new context representing the new input. If the user input is not directly related to an earlier iteration, the general interpretation module tries to interpret the entire NLU data structure concerning mathematical operations. If no mathematical topic could be identified, a rudimental fallback interpretation module tries to decide whether the user posed a question or stated a request. Based on the result a universal output is generated that attempts to guide the user towards a well-interpreted input. The main task of the general interpretation is to interpret the roughly structured NLU data structure and to generate a well-formed representation. Since the NLU result might consist of multiple possible ways of understanding the input, this step should be performed independently for each interpretation.

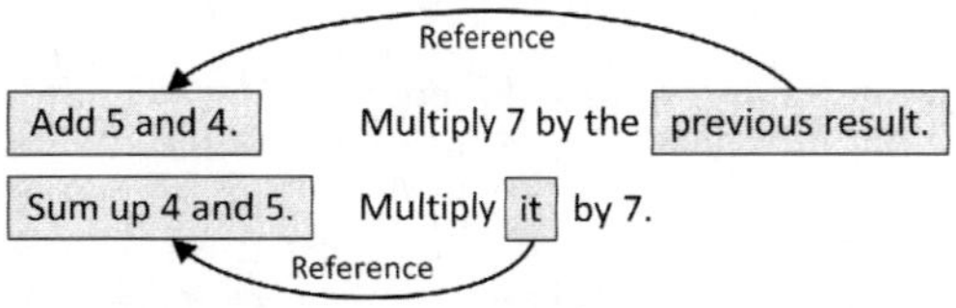

Figure 7. Resolution of references.

Furthermore, the interpretation process deals with resolving references to other clauses inside one sentence or to the topics of previous inputs. In a conversation between humans words like *this*, *that* or *it* usually refer to the most recent subject (see Figure 7). The systems approach works in a similar way and tries to replace a reference by information that fits the conversational context. In order to prevent extensive ambiguities, only elements that turned out to represent a valid formula are taken into account. If multiple results are interpreted as valid, the user has to choose the required calculation.

Besides the interpretations stages, the DMU performs generation of a result and command execution. Furthermore, it responses to the user input as a human-like dialog system. If the operation tree structure found in the current context contains one or more valid operations, the module hands all those over to the response generation module, which will then generate a suitable answer. The response planning module handles the generation of a set of abstract response segments that will be phrased in natural language. In this connection a response phrasing database is used to support the automated phrasing process. A single sentence is represented by a response segment that abstractly specified all required parameters. Those parameters will be later integrated at a certain position in the response. As seen in Figure 8, each segment consists of one or more rules indicated by '*'. A rule consists of one or more alternative phrases that are picked randomly. The same applies for vocabulary entries representing a single word that are indicated by '#'.

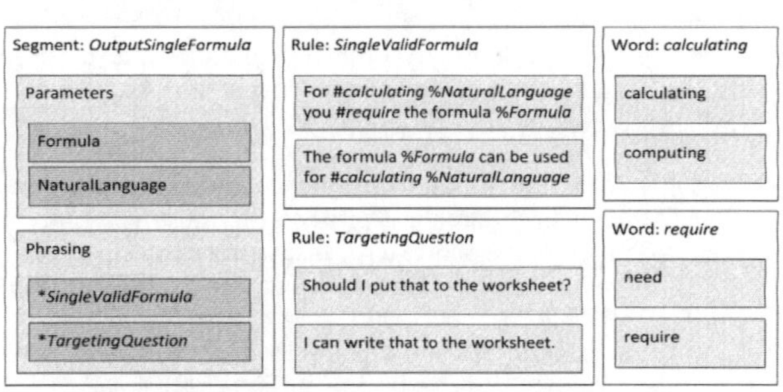

Figure 8. Response Phrasing Database.

Finally, the response phrasing module takes care of generating a string from prepared segments. In case of one valid result without target specification our system choose the segment *OutputSingleFormula*. This segment uses the formula and its natural language expression as parameters and applies the two rules *SingleValidFormula* and *TargetingQuestion*.

The rules choose randomly the vocabulary entries *calculating* and *need*:

For calculating the sum of column FinalGrade divided by 11 you need the formula (SUM(Grades[FinalGrade])/11). Should I put that to the worksheet?

The evaluation of the prototype exceeded expectations. 80% of 170 tasks have been solved successfully. The system helped users to solve tasks and received positive feedback from nearly two thirds of the users. Inspired by the Turing Test [49], the authors asked 17 independent spreadsheet users to formulate requests for particular calculation tasks. Each task was answered by both, the prototype and a human, independently. Afterwards, the participants were encouraged to identify the computer generated response. This however turned out to be surprisingly hard to decide. With 34 decisions made in total, 47.1% falsely identified the dialog system answer as human.

C. Data & Knowledge Representation

In early 2016, the natural language dialog system has been extended with a natural language dialog system based on active ontologies, which enables the user to create and manipulate excel sheets without having to know the complex formula language of excel [50]. Our system is able to resolve references, detect and help resolve ambiguous statements and ask for missing information if necessary. While already quite powerful, this system was not able to handle conditions properly or understand statements involving loops or instructions affecting multiple cells. In this paper, we will present an approach on how to attack these weaknesses.

By adding additional information to an ontology, such as a rule evaluation system and a fact store, it becomes an execution environment instead of just being a representation of knowledge. Sensor nodes register certain events and store them in the fact store. An evaluation mechanism tests the new facts against the existing rules and performs the associated action if one or more rules apply to the stored facts.

In our system, each rule is represented by a separate node in the active ontology. By connecting nodes the developer decides, which type of facts are relevant to which node. In [50], we presented four different types of nodes:

1) Selection-Nodes: These nodes gather all information of their children and pass on the most fitting according to some score, e.g., Instruction node in Figure 9.
2) Gather-Nodes: These nodes gather the information of all children nodes and only create a new fact if all necessary children facts exist, e.g., Binary operation node or Unary operation in Figure 9.
3) Pass-Nodes: These nodes bundle all obtained information of their children into 1 new fact.
4) Sensor-Nodes: These nodes are the "leaves" of the ontology and react directly to the user input.

Each node-type can be seen as one possible evaluation mechanism. While with these types a developer is able to cover most parts of standard domains of dialog systems one can think of far more complex ones. This is where our new system comes into play. By allowing the developer to use his own evaluation mechanisms, we created an infinite amount of new possibilities what our system is capable of.

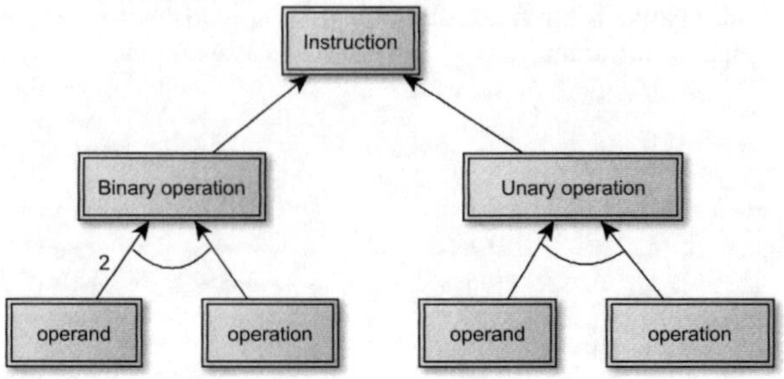

Figure 9. Example of an Active Ontology for mathematical tasks.

Our system consists mainly of two active ontologies: Natural Language Understanding ontology, to interpret the user input, and Natural Language Generation (NLG) ontology, to generate answers (see Figure 10).

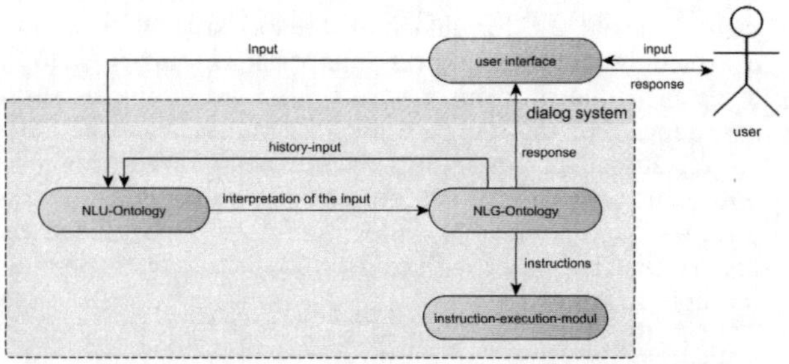

Figure 10. Overview of the active ontology-based dialog system.

The active ontologies recognize several mathematical operations by searching the input, and then recursively building an entire instruction. This instruction is the input to the second active ontology that, based on the type and content of the built instructions, generates a response. When a node gets triggered it builds an answer based on patterns stored in its children. Thus, the answer can be built recursively from reusable predefined patterns. The response generator carries out the process of speech generation in six basic tasks according to Reiter [51]:

- *Content determination*: the basic planning of what should be communicated in the output
- *Discourse planing*: process of imposing the order and structure over the set of messages
- *Sentence aggregation*: grouping of information that should be processed in the response sentence

- *Lexicalization*: choice of words for the sentence
- *Referring expression generation*: insertion of anaphoras to shorten the output
- *Linguistic realization*: bringing the selected words and phrases in a grammatically correct form

Our system roughly follows these steps to generate the answers. Sentence aggregation is almost irrelevant for our use case since the answers of the system are most likely just one or two sentences. The content determination is covered by the use of the input of the NLU ontology. This way the system always knows that information should be communicated in the coming answer. Discourse planning and lexicalization are implicitly stored in the structure and the content of the NLG ontology. The structure of the ontology defines the structure of the generated output and the saved words in the nodes provide this output with the necessary vocabulary. Since the content of the answer is already very specific and very short, referring expressions can be inserted in the sentence structure and do not need to be added in a separate processing step. The structure of the NLG ontology also guarantees a grammatically valid output.

D. Analysis of Data

Interactive Spreadsheet Processing Module (ISPM) [52] is an active dialog management system that uses machine learning techniques for context interpretation within spreadsheets and connects natural language to the data in the spreadsheets. First, the rows of a spreadsheet are divided into different classes and the table's schema is made searchable for the dialog system (see Figure 11).

	A	B	C	
1	**Table 1: persons**			CAPTION
2	**name**			SUPER HEADER
3	**first name**	**last name**	**age**	HEADER
4	**group A**			GROUP HEADER
5	Sloane	Morgan	37	DATA
6	Dustin	Brewer	33	DATA
7	Valentine	Yates	38	DATA
8	Michael	Gregori	50	DATA
9	**group B**			GROUP HEADER
10	Ina	Hoffman	40	DATA
11	Oliver	Hopkins	27	DATA
12	Damon	Vasquez	22	DATA
13	Mark	Richards	25	DATA

Figure 11. A spreadsheet table annotated with row labels.

In the case of a user input, it searches for headers, data values from the table and key phrases for operations. Implicit cell references like "people of age 18" are then resolved to explicit references using the schema. Using the ISPM, end-users are able to search for values in the schema of the table and to address the data in spreadsheets implicitly, e.g., *What is the average age of people in group A?* (see Figure 12).

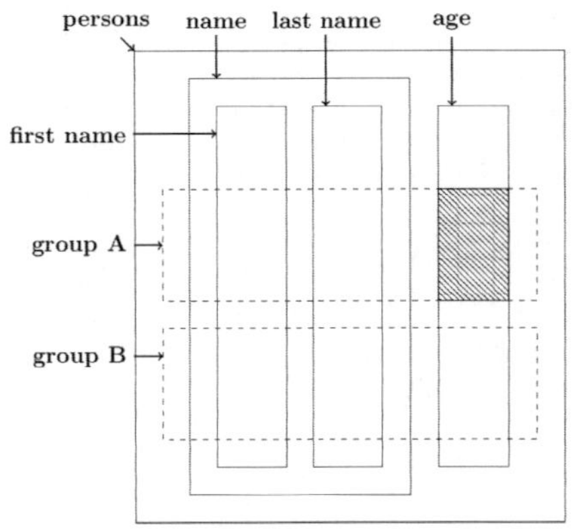

Figure 12. Context detection of user input.

Furthermore, the system enables users to select (88% successfully solved), sort (88%), group (75%) and aggregate (63%) the spreadsheet data by using natural language for end-user software engineering.

E. Action Sets

In 2017, we introduced an interface for natural language dialog system and the Microsoft Excel API [53]. This interface enables users to describe actions in unrestricted natural language interactively and run these actions in the technical domain like Microsoft Excel. We implemented a hybrid system that supports natural language interactions similar as a chat bot and gesture control to follow the users showing actions. For this purpose and also to avoid the lack of inconsistent code documentation, we dynamically export the provided documentation for coding in Visual Studio and provide it in the xml-format to the hybrid system. Users can use already existing actions and provide new action sets to the hybrid system at runtime. For our first prototype of the hybrid system, we concentrate on extending for handling graphs and charts. Evaluated by a user study the hybrid system can successfully resolve more that 80 % of the given user tasks.

Due to the potential complexity and dimensions, the hybrid system extends the consisting natural language approach that manages the interaction through the dialog system and introduces a new graphical user interface providing a better overview and more interaction choices. During runtime, users can switch at any time between these systems. Each interaction increases the associated probability that is used for an assumption about interactions. On each interaction, the dialog system presents the user a limited amount of options, chosen regarding to its probability. To simplify the process for the user only interactions with the last object are available, so no reference is needed. After each interaction the user is asked, if more interactions are welcome, and if so another iteration will be started. If there are no new interaction, the recent set of actions can be saved using an arbitrary name. To avoid duplicate action sets, the module compares the current one with saved sets. If it is duplicate, the user is informed, but still able to save it under new name.

Using the graphical user interface users have access to all options of each object. We defined action sets as arbitrary sets of API calls learned and executed during runtime (see Figure 13). The system can learn a new action set during runtime from the user via two options: the established dialog system and a graphical user interface. Both systems have the same basic functionality, although the dialog system reduces the options for interactions in each iteration. The dialog system target group are unexperienced users who need more advice from the system and who are quicker using natural language. Advanced users can pick the next interaction freely or users who are quicker by clicking the system are provided a graphical user interface. In case of user input Please, draw a chart, the system tries to detect some implicit steps and asks user for data and chart type to execute this command.

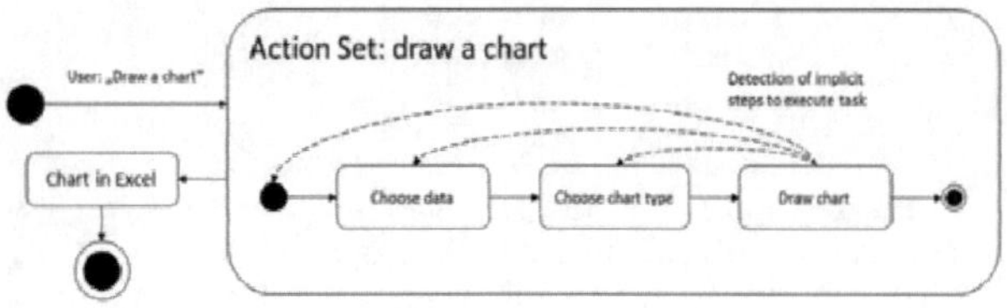

Figure 13. Action set for a simple use input.

F. Control flows

Also in 2017, two new modules have been developed to extend the current system for support of control flows [1]. The first module is capable of handling conditional instructions and the second is able to understand statements that contain loops.

1) Conditional Statements: Conditional instructions are often hard to understand due to their complex grammatical and contextual structure. Also references are complicated to resolve in this kind of sentences. The advantage of conditions is that they have a small set of key-words (such as if, in case of, etc.) that indicate that the user uses a conditional statement. In domain of spreadsheet manipulation to be able to understand, the condition has to result in a boolean operation. These two facts enable us to develop a specialized service dealing with conditional statements. We react to the keywords and try to find a boolean value in the user input. If we can not find any boolean operation, the dialog system asks the user directly for it. After user answers, it is just recognizing, which action the user wants to perform. Unconditional statements were already supported in our older system, so we can rely on it to find the proper action. As already noted, *if* gets recognized as a condition keyword. The system already knows that it is dealing with a conditional statement. *A1 is greater than 3* is a boolean operation and may be used as condition. The trivial statement *save 5 in B1* can be easily recognized as unconditional action and handled by our system (see Figure 14).

2) Loop Statements: Dealing with statements that affect more than one cell can be seen as a looped instruction. In that case, the target of the instruction is the loop variable. Knowing this, we can handle it in a similar way we used for conditional statements. In contrast to conditions, loop do not necessarily have to contain clear keywords. Often times these keywords are hidden within the sentence like *for all, for each, as long as*. However, there may also be explicit instruction like *do something three times*.

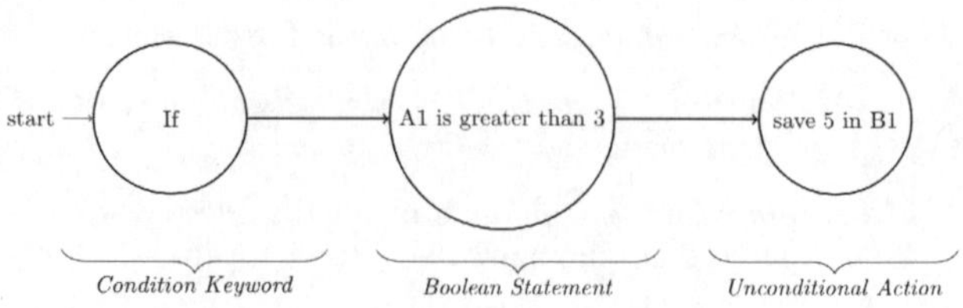

Figure 14. Example for a conditional statement.

Once any of these keywords are recognized, the system has to find the corresponding action and execute it for the given range of cells. In order for our active ontology to be able for recognizing the proper action, we introduced a Looptarget. This is an operator that acts like a normal cell and is able to be recognized by normal actions (such as save, multiply), but at the same time indicates that it can be executed on a range of cells. Once activated by a loop keyword, the loop service reacts to actions containing the regarding targets. In this case, next step is to split input into several instructions for each cell of the given range. This may also be combined with conditional instructions. User input *add 2 to B2 for each cell of column A, which is greater than B2* is correctly handled by our system (see Figure 15).

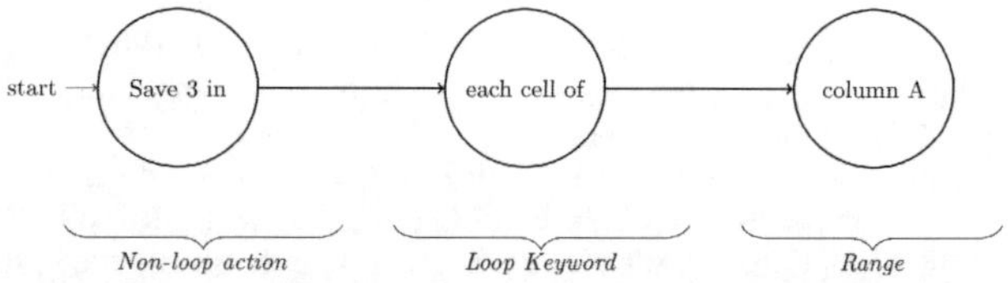

Figure 15. Example for a loop statement.

3) Sample Dialog: To demonstrate the extended features, we present a short dialog between the NLUI and user. For each iteration of the dialog we listed the user input (User), the operation the system executed as consequence of this input (NLU) and the response generated by the system (DMU):

User: Write 30 in all cells of column A

NLU: save(30, A:A)

DMU: Already done. Is there anything else i can do?

User: Subtract 10 from each cell between A1 and A10

NLU: save(A1:A10 - 10, A1:A10)

DMU: Ok, I did that for you.

Can I do something else for you?

User: No

DMU: Alright

...After a break, user turns back to the NLUI

User: For each cell of column A which is greater than 25 add 2 to B2

NLU: conditionalAction(A:A>25, save(B2 + 2, B2))

User: If A3 is greater than A2 write 2 in A3 else in B3

NLU: conditionalAction(A3>A2, save(2, A3), save(2, B3))

DMU: Ok, I did that for you.

User: If A5 is greater than B5

NLU: NoAction

DMU: I see you used a condition.

What do you want to do if the condition is true?

User: Save 4 in B3

NLU: conditionalAction(A5 > B5, save(4, B3))

DMU: Everything done as you wished.

IV. Evaluation

In this section, the system will be evaluated in terms of its ability to recognize control structures. The detailed evaluations of previous versions of the system described in III-A and III-B can be found in [48], III-C in [50], III-D in [52], and finally III-E in [53]. To evaluate the quality of control flows solution described in III-F, we conducted an user study. We asked 12 participants to solve given tasks by using our system and recorded their experience with it. In detail, we asked for each task:

- whether they were able to solve the task,
- if the system was helping them to solve the task,
- if the system output was natural,
- and if the system was able to understand their input.

The participants were Non-native English speakers and the majority of them have never used our system before. Most of them stated that they knew and already used excel before, but not on a regular basis.

Since we already evaluated our system for standard arithmetic tasks, response time as well as scalability in our last paper [50], we specifically designed the tasks to test the discussed control flow features, e.g.:

- Insert the specified value 10 into all cells of a column.
- Multiply all cells in a range (between A1 and A10) that are greater than 2 by 3.
- If the value in cell A3 is greater than A2, they should add 2 to B1, else to B2.

The results show that the users where able to solve more than 60% of the tasks at least partially and found our system as useful in over 60% of the cases (see Figure 16). Additionally nearly 70% of the system outputs were considered as natural by the participants. The participants stated in over 50% of the cases that the system did not understand their input. The improvement of the systems output has to be worked on. Overall, the system's quality was rated at 3.33 out of 5 stars, and except for one participant all participants said that they would use our system.

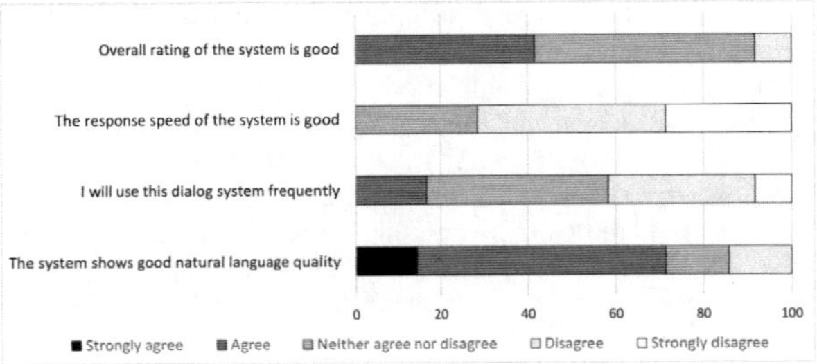

Figure 16. Overall results in %.

While this result demonstrates that our system is far from perfect it also shows that there is added value when using the system especially for inexperienced users. Knowing that nearly half of the unsolved tasks stemmed from the same question and the most common problem were synonym problems, which are easy to fix the results we achieved are auspicious. Since our system will most likely only improve in coming versions due to the growing number of services and the size of our word databases we consider this a promising approach.

V. Conclusion and Future Work

In this paper, we presented the new idea to use the natural language as the user interface. Users can easily describe tasks and delegate it to the system. Often these descriptions contains conditionals, loops and statements (see Section III). To enable the system for end-user development, these parts should be recognized correctly by the system. In the current version of our prototype, the system supports control flows, such as conditionals and loops.

The next goal is to implement valid scripts from natural language input that describes some algorithm like:

- *Find the maximum element of a set:*
  Use an auxiliary variable. Initialize the variable with an arbitrary element of the set. Then, visit all the remaining elements. Whenever an element is larger than the auxiliary variable, store it in the auxiliary variable. In the end, the maximum is in the auxiliary variable.
- *Switching sort of an array:*
  If there are two elements out of order, switch them. Continue doing this until there are no more elements out of order. Out of order means that an element is larger than its right neighbor. The right neighbor of an element x[i] in a vector x is x[i+1].

The challenge is not only the identification of control structures and statements but the recognition of the correct sequence of the given instructions. For considering the relations between user inputs, it is also essential to develop a contextual knowledge. This allows the users to place new statements at any point in the process at runtime and combine several statements into a function, which can be executed at a later time by the system.

In addition to the development of contextual knowledge, the analysis of the input has to be extended by various programming concepts in order to be able to recognize declarations and actions in them. Therefore, the system should (i) enable end-users to give instructions step-by-step, to avoid the complexity in full descriptions and give directly feedback of success (ii) create an abstract meta model for user input during the linguistic analysis and (iii) independently interpret meta model to code sequences that contains loops, conditionals, and statements.

$$Input : A\ sequence\ of\ n\ numbers\ (a_1, ..., a_n)$$

$$\downarrow$$

User Input: the result is a vector. Initially it is empty. Find the minimal element of the set and append it to the vector. Remove the element form the set. Then, repeatedly find the minimum of the remaining elements and move them to the result in order, until there are no more elements in the set.

$$\downarrow$$

Algorithm 1

procedure SELECTIONSORT(input as a set of numbers)
    result $\leftarrow$ *empty set*
    while input IsNotEmpty **do**
        n $\leftarrow$ *length (input) - 1*
        tmpMin $\leftarrow$ *0*
        for $i \leftarrow 0 \rightarrow n$ **do**
            if *input[i]* $<$ *input[tmpMin]* **then**
                $tmpMin \leftarrow i$
        Add input[tmpMin] at the end of result.
        Remove element at index tmpMin from input.

$$\downarrow$$

$$Output : A\ permutation\ (b_1, ..., b_n)\ with\ b_1 \leq b_2, ..., \leq b_n$$

The second step after achieving the recognition of algorithms is to allow object-based modeling with natural language. In this case, the system should be able to assign these algorithms as methods to a class. Concepts such as inheritance and relationships between objects should also be identified on the basis of natural language input. With regard to spreadsheets, there are many areas of application that can make the user's life much easier. If you assign value ranges within a spreadsheet to a class, the data can be linked with knowledge from the real world. Through additional assignment of individual methods, questions like "Which cars were built before 2011 and sold more than 5 million times?" can be answered without having to refer to the different areas of the open spreadsheet. The application ranges and extension possibilities of an interface that allows such a mapping between natural language and programming are almost unlimited. However, we are still in the early stages of this development and present the first developments in this direction.

We are also exploring ways to extend the system functionality with the help of the dialog. The system needs to be extended for handling graphs, and charts. Furthermore, there are some properties of tables, which are not considered in the current system and can potentially lead to problems.

REFERENCES

[1] A. Wachtel, J. Klamroth, and W. F. Tichy, "Natural Language User Interface For Software Engineering Tasks," Tenth International Conference on Advances in Computer-Human Interactions, March 2017.

[2] W. F. Tichy, "What Can Software Engineers Learn from Artificial Intelligence," Computer, Vol 20:11, November 1987.

[3] ——, "NLH/E: A Natural Language Help System," the 11th International Conference on Software Engineering, 1989.

[4] H. Liberman, F. Paternò, M. Klann, and V. Wulf, "End-user development: An emerging paradigm, human-computer interaction series, volume 9," 2006.

[5] W. F. Tichy, M. Landhäußer, and S. J. Körner, "Universal Programmability - How AI Can Help. Artificial Intelligence Synergies in Software Engineering," May 2013.

[6] C. L. Ortiz, "The Road to Natural Conversational Speech Interfaces," IEEE Internet Computing, March 2014.

[7] Eurostat, "European statistics database," 2017, last accessed 2017.11.30. [Online]. Available: http://ec.europa.eu/eurostat/data/database

[8] M. Hurst, "The interpretation of tables in texts," University of Ediburgh, Ph.D., 2000.

[9] B. A. Myers, A. J. Ko, and M. M. Burnett, "Invited Research: Overview End-User Programming," CHI, 2006.

[10] C. Scaffidi, M. Shaw, and B. Myers, "Estimating the numbers of end users and end user programmers," in Visual Languages and Human-Centric Computing, 2005.

[11] R. Abraham, "Header and Unit Inference for Spreadsheets Through Spatial Analyses," in IEEE Symposium on Visual Languages - Human Centric Computing, 2004.

[12] J. E. Sammet, "The Use of English as a Programming Language," Communication of the ACM, March 1966.

[13] D. Ferrucci, "Building Watson: An Overview of the DeepQA Project," Association for the Advancement of Artificial Intelligence, 2010.

[14] H. Liu and H. Liebermann, "Toward a programmatic semantics of natural language," Visual Languages and Human Centric Computing, 2004.

[15] B. W. Ballard and A. W. Biermann, "Programming in natural language: NLC as a prototype," Association for Computing Machinery (ACM), Volume 10, 1979.

[16] A. W. Biermann and B. W. Ballard, "Toward Natural Language Computation," American Journal of Computational Linguistics, Volume 6, Number 2, 1980.

[17] A. W. Biermann, B. W. Ballard, and A. H. Sigmon, "An experimental study of natural language programming," International Journal of Man-Machine Studies, 1983.

[18] H. Liu and H. Lieberman, "Metafor: Visualizing stories as code," 10th international conference on Intelligent user interfaces, 2005.

[19] S. J. . Körner, M. Landhäußer, and W. F. Tichy, "Transferring Research Into the Real World - How to Improve RE with AI in the Automotive Industry," 2014.

[20] V. Le, S. Gulwani, and Z. Su, "SmartSynth: Synthesizing Smartphone Automation Scripts from Natural Language," Proceeding of the 11th annual international conference on Mobile systems, applications, and services (MobiSys), 2013.

[21] A. Cypher, M. Dontcheva, T. Lau, and J. Nichols, "No Code Required: Giving Users Tools to Transform the Web," Morgan Kaufmann Publishers Inc, 2010.

[22] M. Gordon and D. Harel, "Steps towards Scenario-Based Programming with a Natural Language Interface," Lecture Notes in Computer Science, vol 8415. Springer, 2014.

[23] ——, "Evaluating a Natural Language Interface for Behavioral Programming," IEEE Symp. on Visual Languages and Human-Centric Computing, 2012.

[24] G. Cabral and A. Sampaio, "Formal Specification Generation from Requirement Documents," Notes Theor. Comput. Sci. 195, 2008.

[25] T. Winograd, "Understanding natural language," in Cognitive Psychology 3(1), 1972.

[26] M. A. Hearst, "natural search user interfaces," in Commun. ACM 55(11), 2011.

[27] B. Shneiderman, "Designing the User Interface: Strategies for Effective Human-Computer Interaction," Addison-Wesley Longman, 1986.

[28] T. Gellar, "Talking to machines," in Commun. ACM 55(4), 2012.

[29] D. Vadas and J. R. Curran, "Programming with unrestricted natural language," in Proceedings of the Australasian Language Technology Workshop 2005, 2005.

[30] R. Mihalcea, H. Liu, and H. Lieberman, "NLP (Natural Language Processing) for NLP (Natural Language Programming)," CICLing, LNCS, vol. 3878, 2006.

[31] F. Paternò, "End user development: Survey of an emerging field for empowering people," in ISRN Software Engineering, vol. 2013, 2013.

[32] A. J. Ko and B. A. Myers, "Designing the whyline: a debugging interface for asking questions about program behavior," in Proceedings of the SIGCHI conference on Human factors in computing systems. ACM, 2004.

[33] S. Gulwani, W. R. Harris, and R. Singh, "Spreadsheet data manipulation using examples," in ACM, 2012.

[34] A. Cypher, "Watch what I do: programming by demonstration," in MIT Press, 1993.

[35] C. Dorner, M. Spahn, and V. Wulf, "End user development: Approaches towards a flexible software design," in European Conference on Information Systems, 2008.

[36] P. Sestoft and J. Z. Sorensen, "Sheet-defined functions: Implementation and initial evaluation," 2013.

[37] J. Cunha, J. P. Fernandes, and J. Mendes, "Bidirectional Transformation of Model-Driven Spreadsheets," Springer Lecture Notes in Computer Science, 2012.

[38] A. Begel, "Spoken Language Support for Software Development," Ph.D. Thesis, Berkeley, 2005.

[39] S. Gulwani and M. Marron, "NLyze: Interactive programming by natural language for spreadsheet data analysis and manipulation," SIGMOD, 2014.

[40] S. Gulwani, "Automating string processing in spreadsheets using input-output examples," in ACM SIGPLAN, 2011.

[41] D. Guzzoni, "Active: A unified platform for building intelligent web interaction assistants," in IEEE, Web Intelligence and Intelligent Agent Technology Workshops, 2006.

[42] J. R. Bellegarda, "Spoken Language Understanding for Natural Interaction: The Siri Experience," Springer New York, 2014.

[43] J. D. Williams, "Spoken dialogue systems: challenges and opportunities for research," 2009.

[44] S. Seneff, "Response planning and generation in the MERCURY flight reservation system," 2002.

[45] J. Allen, N. Chambers, and G. Ferguson, "PLOW: A Collaborative Task Learning Agent," Association for the Advancement of Artificial Intelligence, 2007.

[46] C. D. Frye, "Microsoft Excel 2013, Step by Step," O'Reilly Media, 2013.

[47] D. Suendermann, "Advances in Commercial Deployment of Spoken Dialog Systems," Springer Science Business Media, 2011.

[48] A. Wachtel, S. Weigelt, and W. F. Tichy, "Initial implementation of natural language turn-based dialog system," International Conference on Intelligent Human Computer Interaction (IHCI), December 2015.

[49] A. M. Turing, "Computing machinery and intelligence," Mind, vol. 59, 1950, pp. 433–460.

[50] A. Wachtel, J. Klamroth, and W. F. Tichy, "A Natural Language Dialog System Based on Active Ontologies," The Ninth International Conference on Advances in Computer-Human Interactions, April 2016.

[51] E. Reiter and R. Dale, "Building applied natural language generation systems," 1997.

[52] A. Wachtel, M. T. Franzen, and W. F. Tichy, "Context Detection In Spreadsheets Based On Automatically Inferred Table Schema," 18th International Conference on Human- Computer Interaction, rated with Best Paper Award, October 2016.

[53] A. Wachtel, J. Paczia, and W. F. Tichy, "An Interactive Action Set Detection In Natural Language Hybrid System," Eleventh International Conference on Interfaces and Human Computer Interaction, July 2017.

Model-based Visualization of Execution Traces and Testing Results

Bernard Stepien, Liam Peyton
School of Engineering and Computer Science
University of Ottawa
Ottawa, Canada
Email: (bernard, lpeyton)@uottawa.ca

Mohamed Alhaj
Computer Engineering Department
Al-Ahliyya Amman University
Amman, Jordan
Email: m.alhaj@ammanu.edu.jo

***Abstract*— Support for model-based visualization of execution traces in testing tools is limited at best, even though model-based approaches to specifying and visualizing behavior are well known and commonly used in the development of software applications. There has been active research on generating test scripts from formal models of behavior, but most testing tools in industry have little or no support for structuring test results based on behavior models. We present an approach for extending the Testing and Test Control Notation version 3 (TTCN-3) test results message sequence chart feature to address this problem. TTCN-3 is a test specification and test implementation language owned by European Telecommunications Standards Institute (ETSI). This leverages TTCN-3 support of the *with-statement* language construct to allow for custom configuration of the test results display. The approach is illustrated with two examples: testing a communication protocol used for controlling multimedia sessions called Session Initiation Protocol (SIP) and testing an avionics flight management system.**

Keywords-Software modeling; Behavior modeling; Software testing; Automated Testimg; TTCN-3.

I. INTRODUCTION

This paper extends, updates, and provides more detail on earlier research results presented at the International Conference on Trends and Advances in Software Engineering [1].

Support for model-based visualization of execution traces in testing tools is limited at best, even though model-based approaches to specifying and visualizing behavior are well known and commonly used in the development of software applications. There has been active research on generating test scripts from formal models of behavior, but most testing tools in industry have little or no support for structuring test results based on behavior models.

We present an approach for extending the TTCN-3 test results message sequence chart feature to address this problem. This leverages TTCN-3 support of the *with-statement* language construct to allow for custom configuration of the test results display. TTCN-3 is a test specification and test implementation language created by industry and academia experts at the European Telecommunications Standards Institute (ETSI) [2]. TTCN-3 is a powerful scripting language that is employed to test web applications [3], composite applications enabled in SOA [4]. It also has been extended to web penetration testing that involves- SQL injection and XSS attacks [5]. Using separation of concerns modeling principle, TTCN-3 separates the Abstract Test Suite (ATS) from the coding/decoding and communication, and presentation details; providing powerful matching mechanism that separates behavior and the conditions governing the behaviors and there by promoting systematic approach to testing. This separation of concern between ATS and Adapter Test Layer provides full portability of test suites, making them independent of platform implementation [6].

The approach is illustrated with two examples: testing a SIP protocol and testing an avionics flight management system.

Model-based specification of behavior while developing software applications can be done using interaction diagrams in the Unified Modeling Language (UML) [7], message sequence charts (MSC) in the Specification and Description Language (SDL) [8] and use case maps (UCM) in the User Requirements Notation (URN) [9]. The relationship between model-based specifications of behavior and testing is well understood [10]. A UML Testing Profile has been developed to support model driven testing [11] that has been mapped to test languages like Junit [12] and TTCN-3 [13]. Automatic generation of test scripts from models has been an active area of research using UML interaction diagrams [14], UCM [15] and MSC [16].

Figure 1 shows an example of a simple MSC diagram using Pragmadev Studio [17]. Such a diagram enables the software engineer to visualize the behavior of a system even before it has been implemented giving them the possibility to detect design flaws early with model checking [18]. MSC diagrams and UML interaction diagrams are similar, and MSC diagrams can be derived from UCM diagrams [19] [20]. MSC diagrams have been used to address security [21], conformance [22], performance [8] and business processes [9] as well as concurrency and real-time processing [7].

Testing tools that are currently available on the market do not adequately support for structuring test results in relationship to model-based specifications. Test frameworks, like Junit, which are oriented towards unit tests, have no built-in support at all for MSC or similar diagrams. Formally modelled test frameworks, like TTCN-3, are oriented towards integrated component-based system testing and do have basic support for message sequence charts. Unfortunately, the available support is not sufficient when working with complex, structured data. TTCN3; however, does provide advantages over frameworks like Junit, with strong typing, a powerful matching mechanism, and a separation of concerns between the abstract test specification layer and the concrete layer that handles coding/decoding data, which can result in significant code reuse [23].

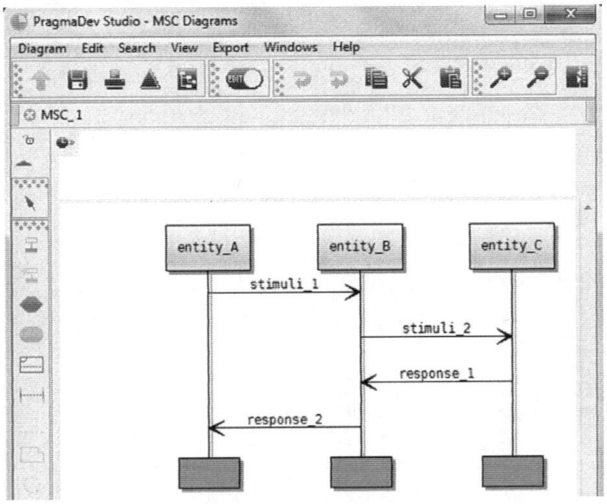

Figure 1. Simple MSC

Figure 2 shows the test results for a particular test script in the TTWorkbench tool from Spirent [24]. It is displayed in the context of an MSC diagram. There is similar support for displaying results in the context of an MSC diagram in all the industry tools that support the TTCN-3 standard, including Testcast from Elvior [25], Tester from PragmaDev [17] and the open source tool Titan that was originally developed at Ericsson [26] [26] before being made available as an Eclipse project. However, the TTworkbench tool is significant because it is the only one that compares the test oracle (the expected response message) against the data received from the system under test (SUT) and flags any mismatches in red.

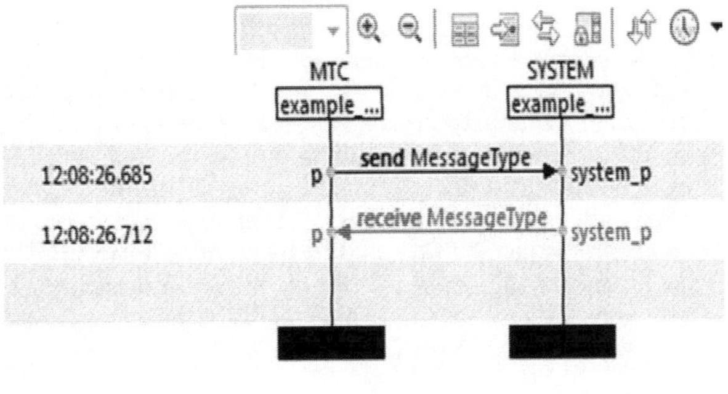

Figure 2. Test results as MSC

While all of these tools are able to display test results in the context of a basic MSC diagram, it is of limited use for visualizing, analyzing and navigating test results in a productive fashion. Typically, the "MessageType" shown in Figure 2 is complex structured data. Displaying only the type of the structured data does not really provide useful information for understanding what has gone wrong.

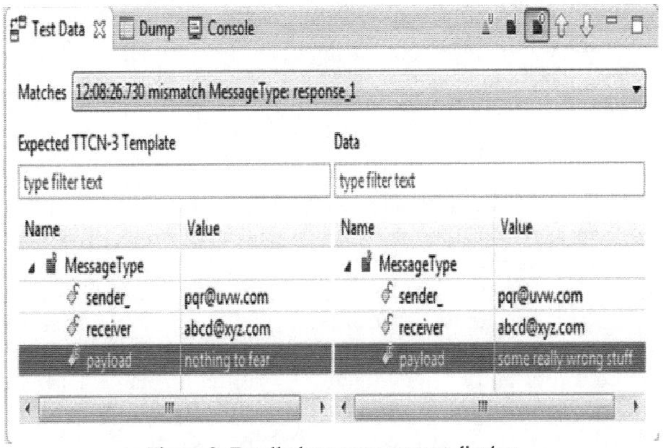

Figure 3. Detailed message content display

To see the actual data, the user has to click on one of the arrows in the diagram and the content or value of the message is shown in a separate window (Figure 3 above). It is difficult to understand the error, without being able to see the step by step details of the data involved in each message that leads to the error. This requires a tedious message by message inspection for each arrow in the MSC diagram. On the other hand, there is too much data in a complex data type to display all the data for each message arrow in Figure 2.

Note that a model MSC and a test result MSC may not be identical. A model MSC may contain alternate behavior as shown in Figure 4, while the test result MSC is by definition only a trace through the model MSC that would traverse only one of the branches of the alternative behavior.

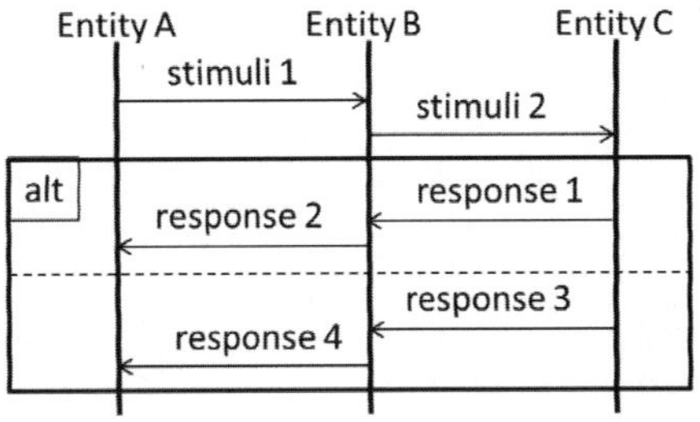

Figure 4. Complex Model MSC

We would like to address this MSC visualization problem by enabling custom configuration of the MSC diagram so that only a specified subset of the data will be displayed in order to provide the tester with an overview of the test results and the flow of data from message to message. That way, only the most critical messages need to be clicked on to view the full details in a separate window. To achieve this goal we found that we can use the TTCN-3 standard extension mechanism, which allows the tester to give instructions to the execution tools without having to change the syntax or the semantics of the TTCN-3 language itself.

The paper is organized as follows: Section II presents the TTCN-3 concept of template; Section III presents the Selecting data fields to display in TTCN-3; Section IV presents two application examples: testing SIP protocol and testing an avionics flight management system; and section V presents the conclusion.

II. TTCN-3 CONCEPT OF TEMPLATE

The central concept of TTCN-3 is the template language construct that enables the specification of both test stimuli and test oracles as structured data in a single template. This, in turn, is used by the TTCN-3 built-in matching mechanism to compare the values of a template to the actual values contained in the response message. This is supported for both message-based and procedure-based communication. More importantly, the template has a precise name and is a building block that can be re-used to specify the value of an individual field, or it can be re-used by another template that specifies a modification to its values. This is a concept of inheritance.

TTCN-3 has a data typing capability mostly because early applications of TTCN-3 were in the telecommunication sector where data typing is common in order that various test events could share parts of data. In this case, these data types would be abstract, independent from any coding/decoding considerations. Abstract data has the advantage of enabling generic matching mechanisms that are applicable to any kind of application. For example, splitting data into fields of a structured data type enables easy referencing to a specific field for all sorts of manipulations.

The data string: "abcd10xyz" could be split into 3 fields of a structured data type with its use after decoding into a variable:

```
type record MyType
{
 charstring field_1,
 integer field_2,
 charstring field_3
}

var MyType myVar :=
{
 field_1 := "abcd",
 field_2 := 10,
 field_3 := "xyz"
};
```

This approach is more efficient than, for example, an assertion statement used in JUnit such as:

```
assertTrue(substring(response_string,
0,4).equals("abcd");
```

An example, to illustrate re-usability of template consists in specifying the templates for the sender and the receiver entities separately:

```
template charstring
entityA_Template:= "abcd@xyz.com";
template charstring
entityB_Template:= "pqr@uvw.com";
```

A stimuli message can then be specified by re-using them as:

```
template MessageType stimuli_1 := {
sender := entityA_Template,
receiver := entityB_Template,
payload := "it was a dark and stormy
night"
}
```

The response template can itself reuse the above entity addresses by merely reversing the roles of (sender and receiver):

```
template MessageType response_1 := {
sender := entityB_Template,
receiver := entityA_Template,
payload := "nothing to fear"
}
```

The TTCN-3 template modification language construct can be used to specify more stimuli or responses for the same pairs of communicating entities:

```
template MessageType stimuli_2
modifies stimuli_1 :=
{
payload := "the sun is shining at
last"
}
```

Templates can then be used either in send or receive statements to describe behaviors in the communication with the SUT. Such behavior can be sequential, alternative or even interleaved behavior and can make use of timers to check for lost messages. The TTCN-3 *receive* statement does more than just receiving data in the sense of traditional general purpose languages (GPL). It compares the data received on a communication port with the content of the template specified. The following abstract specification means that upon sending template *stimuli_1* to the SUT, if we receive and match the response message to the template *response_1* we decide that the test has passed. Instead, if we receive and match instead the *alt_response* template we decide that the test has failed and finally if the timer expires we decide that the test is inconclusive.

```
Timer myTimer(5.0);
myPort.send(stimuli_1);
alt
{
   [] myPort.receive(response_1){
```

```
        setverdict(pass)}
    [] myPort.receive(alt_response){
        setverdict(fail)}
    [] myTimer.timeout {
        Setverdict(inconc)}
}
```

The use of structured data types for describing message content is not new as we already mentioned, but their internal representation in a generic way has the advantage to allow a generic matching mechanism. In other words, instead of specifying multiple assertions, all the fields of the template are checked at once without any additional effort from the test designer.

III. SELECTING DATA FIELDS TO DISPLAY

The central concept of our approach is to use the standard TTCN-3 extension capabilities that can be specified at the abstract layer using the *with-statement* language construct. TTCN-3 extensions were included in the TTCN-3 standard to allow tools to handle various non-abstract aspects of a test such as associated codecs and display test results in the most appropriate way the user desires. While the language is standardized, there is no standardization on how a tool operates and, in particular, how it displays test results.

Most of the TTCN-3 tools provide test results in the form of an XML file. This enables users to customize their own proprietary test results display and to store test results in a file for later consultation. We wanted to avoid having to re-develop the MSC display software and especially the message selection mechanism that displays the detailed structured data table. We also wanted to maintain consistency between the abstract and concrete layers for the TTCN-3 tool. As a result, we decided to modify the TTCN-3 test execution source code to handle the extensions we specified using the *with-statement* language construct. This approach is a first in TTCN-3 tools. We updated the display software source code to display data values as configured by the user using the *with-statement* language construct. This ensured that the existing detailed data features when clicking on the arrows of the MSC were preserved.

Here, we use the template definition itself and its associated *with-statement* in the abstract layer as a way to specify the field values that will be displayed in the MSC diagram during test execution since the template is used by the matching mechanism. The grammar in Bachus Naur Form (BNF) for the TTCN-3 *with-statement* is as follows:

```
455.WithStatement::=WithKeyword
WithAttribList

456.WithKeyword ::= "with"

457.WithAttribList::="{"
MultiWithAttrib "}"

458.MultiWithAttrib::=
{SingleWithAttrib [SemiColon]}

459.SingleWithAttrib ::=
AttribKeyword [OverrideKeyword]
[AttribQualifier]FreeText

460.AttribKeyword::=EncodeKeyword
|VariantKeyword|DisplayKeyword
|ExtensionKeyword|OptionalKeyword

461.EncodeKeyword ::= "encode"

462.VariantKeyword ::= "variant"

463.DisplayKeyword ::= "display"

464.ExtensionKeyword ::= "extension"

465.OverrideKeyword ::= "override"

466.AttribQualifier ::= "("
DefOrFieldRefList ")"

467.DefOrFieldRefList ::=
DefOrFieldRef {"," DefOrFieldRef}

468.DefOrFieldRef ::=
QualifiedIdentifier |((FieldReference
| "[" Minus "]")
[ExtendedFieldReference]) |AllRef

469.QualifiedIdentifier ::=
{Identifier Dot} Identifier

470.AllRef ::= (GroupKeyword
AllKeyword [ExceptKeyword "{"
QualifiedIdentifierList"}"]) |
((TypeDefKeyword |TemplateKeyword
|ConstKeyword |AltstepKeyword
|TestcaseKeyword |FunctionKeyword
|SignatureKeyword |ModuleParKeyword)
AllKeyword [ExceptKeyword"{"
IdentifierList"}"])
```

In the above BNF, we can observe the definition of the *DisplayKeyword* on line 463. Unfortunately, this display construct cannot be used for our purposes. Effectively, what is meant by display is the way a given identifier is displayed. The example below given in the standard is very clear means that the type name "MyService" will be displayed in the test execution results log as "ServiceCall".

```
type record MyService
{
   integer i,
   float f
```

```
}
   with { display "ServiceCall" }
```

In the following example, where we are testing some database content for information about cities that is a well multi-layered data structure with fields and sub-fields, we have used the extension keyword defined in line 464 of the above BNF as follows.

```
template CityResponseType response_1
:= {
    location :=
    {
           city := "ottawa",
           district := "ontario",
           country := "canada"
    },
    statistics :=
    {
           population := 900000,
           average_temperature := 10.3,
           hasUniversity := true
    }
}
with
{extension
"{display_fields
{
    location {city},
    statistics {population}
}}";
}
```

The above TTCN-3 *with-statement* uses the standard TTCN-3 *extension* keyword. It contains a user definition that is represented as a string. The content of this string is not covered by the TTCN-3 syntax but by syntax defined by the user. Thus, it is the responsibility of the user to handle syntax and semantic checking of that string's content. First, within this string, we have defined a keyword called *display_fields* to indicate that the extension specification is about selecting the fields to display. Then, we specify a list of fields and subfields of the data type being used to display. The curly brackets indicate the scope of subfields. In the above example, we specified that we want to see the *city* subfield of the *location* field and the *population* subfield of the *statistics* field. This hierarchy is necessary because various fields may have subfields with identical names.

We have implemented this feature on the Titan [26] open-source TTCN-3 execution tool software since this feature requires modifying the source code of the tool. None of the commercial TTCN-3 tool vendors make their source code available. Two areas of the Tool's source code (see Figure 5) were modified:

- The source code for the GPL executable code generator that will propagate the selected fields to display while generating execution logs.
- The TTCN-3 test case management code that generates the Execution results log used by the MSC display software.

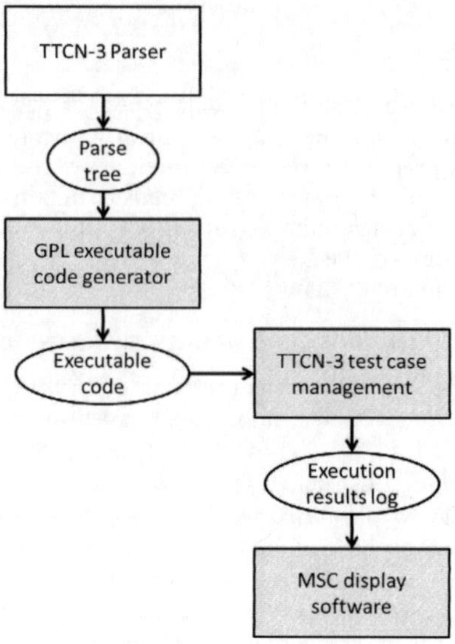

Figure 5. Structure of a TTCN-3 tool

This did not require modification of the TTCN-3 parser since the content of the *with-statement* is user defined, thus not modifying the grammar of the TTCN-3 language. However, the user definition turns up in the parse tree that is used for test execution code generation. It is during this code generation that we take into account this extension for the display specification. Most TTCN-3 test execution is based on execution code generated in a general-purpose language (GPL) like Java for TTworkbench or C++ for Titan and PragmaDev studio and multiple strategies for TestCast. The general principle of the GPL generated code is to transform the abstract TTCN-3 definitions into executable GPL code. For example, in the TITAN tool, the abstract TTCN-3 template definition *response_1* shown previously becomes a series of C++ definitions, one for defining constants and the other to define the template matching mechanism as follows:

```
static const CHARSTRING cs_7(2,
"75"),
cs_2(6, "canada"),
cs_8(6, "france"),
cs_4(8, "new york"),
cs_3(13, "new york city"),
cs_1(7, "ontario"),
cs_0(6, "ottawa"),
cs_6(5, "paris"),
...
```

The above definitions are in turn used to generate the C++ source code for the template definition as follows where, for example, the city field gets assigned the cs_0 constant that represents the string "ottawa":

```
static void post_init_module()
{
TTCN_Location
current_location("../src/NewLoggingSt
udyStruct.ttcn3", 0,
TTCN_Location::LOCATION_UNKNOWN,
"NewLoggingStudyStruct");
current_location.update_lineno(42);

#line 42
"../src/NewLoggingStudyStruct.ttcn3"
template_request__1.city() = cs_0;
template_request__1.district() =
cs_1;
template_request__1.country() = cs_2;
current_location.update_lineno(48);

#line 48
"../src/NewLoggingStudyStruct.ttcn3"
{
LocationType_template& tmp_0 =
template_response__1.location();
tmp_0.city() = cs_0;
tmp_0.district() = cs_1;
tmp_0.country() = cs_2;
}
```

We use the same technique of C++ variable definitions to pass on the value of our field display definitions since at run-time, the parse tree is no longer available. Test results are written in a log file. The TTCN-3 MSC feature reads that same log file to build and display the MSC itself. Here this is illustrated by calling TITAN function *log_event_str()* using the string value of the *display_fields* extension as defined in the template being used as follows:

```
alt_status
AtlasPortType_BASE::receive(const
CityRequestType_template&
value_template, CityRequestType
*value_ptr, const COMPONENT_template&
sender_template, COMPONENT
*sender_ptr)
{
...

TTCN_Logger::log_event_str(":
extension {display_fields { location
{city}, statistics { population,
average_temperature}}}
@NewLoggingStudyStruct.CityRequestTyp
e : "),
my_head->message_0->log(),
TTCN_Logger::end_event_log2str()),
msg_head_count+1);
...
```

In that generated source code, only the *display_fields* string and the data type are shown as strings. The content of the message itself is found in the variable *my_head->message_0*. Here the *log()* method will actually write all the fields with name and value in the log file.

Using the above source code, during the test execution, the Titan tool writes a log file that contains the matching mechanism results, i.e., the field names and instantiated values of the TTCN-3 template but also after the code modifications, the *display_fields* specifications as follows:

```
09:33:49.443373 Receive operation on
port atlasPort succeeded, message
from SUT(3): extension {
display_fields { location {city},
statistics { population,
temperature}}}
  @NewLoggingStudy.CityResponseType :
{ city := "ottawa", district :=
"ontario", country := "canada",
population := 900000,
average_temperature := 10.300000,
hasUniversity := true
} id 1
```

The above data is used by the MSC display tool (Eclipse) and shows two different kinds of information. The first is the content of our *display_fields* definition and the second is the full data that was received and matched. In fact all we had to do was to prepend the field selection logic to the actual log data that remained unchanged. The first will enable the MSC display software to extract the requested fields data and to display it as shown in Figure 13 (at the end of this paper), while the second one is used for the detailed message content table that is obtained traditionally by clicking on the selected arrow of the MSC diagram as shown in Figure 3.

In the open source Titan tool, the execution code is written in C++, but actual Eclipse-based MSC display is written in Java. Thus we had to modify the Java code that displays the MSC as well.

It should be noted that this implementation is valid for the Titan tool only. Each tool vendor has different coding approaches and would require different code generation strategies. Unfortunately, since they do not make their source code available, all we can do is to strongly encourage these tool vendors to implement our MSC display approach.

IV. APPLICATION EXAMPLES

We have worked on two examples, both drawn from industrial applications we were involved with. The first example is a widely used abstract test suite for the SIP protocol that has a very complex structured data type. It illustrates the benefits of our MSC display approach because in this case, it is obvious that it is totally impossible to display all the fields of a SIP message, especially since most of them are optional and would contain no values. The second example is an avionics application that illustrates the overview qualities of our approach when trying to navigate through long sequences of test events. It consists of long sequences of key strokes and screen display results verification.

A. The SIP protocol testing example

The SIP protocol [27] is a very complex text based protocol. For example, an INVITE method message text would be as follows:

```
INVITE sip:user:passwd@127.0.0.1:5060
SIP/2.0
Call-ID: 121231231
Contact:  <sip:auser@127.0.0.1:5060>
Content-Length: 0
CSeq: 666 INVITE
From: "aDisplayName"
<sip:auser@127.0.0.1:5060>
Max-Forwards: 70
To: "aDisplayName"
<sip:user@127.0.0.1:5060>
Via: SIP/2.0/udp 127.0.0.1:5060
```

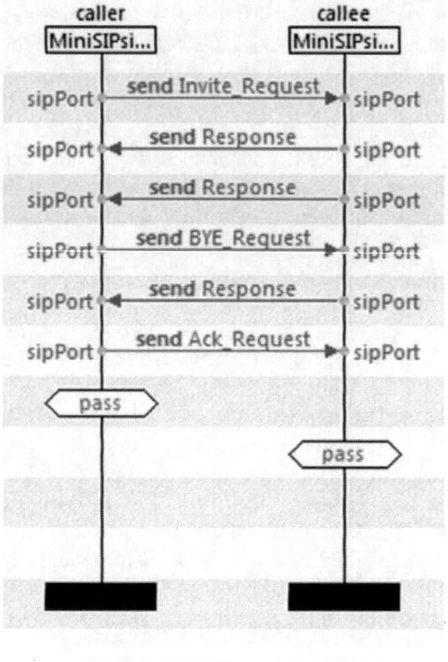

Figure 6. TTCN-3 generated MSC

When testing with TTCN-3, this text message is decoded and assigned to a complex structured data type including a substantial proportion of optional fields. The SIP protocol TTCN-3 test suites are available from ETSI [2]. The resulting MSC diagram would indicate only the message types but with no values as shown in Figure 6.

Name	Value
INVITE_Request	
requestLine	
method	INVITE_E
requestUri	
scheme	sip
userInfo	
userOrTelephoneSubscriber	user
password	passwd
hostPort	
host	127.0.0.1
portField	5060
urlParameters	omit
headers	omit
sipVersion	SIP/2.0
msgHeader	
accept	omit
acceptEncoding	omit
acceptLanguage	omit
alertInfo	omit
allow	omit
authenticationInfo	omit
authorization	omit
callId	
fieldName	CALL_ID_E
callid	121231231
callInfo	omit

Figure 7. Portion of the detailed message content inspection window

Traditional TTCN-3 tools will display all the fields in the detailed message content table, but the large amount of fields renders its inspection tedious. Relevant information may not be contiguous and requires scrolling through several pages of the message content table as shown in Figure 7. The user must click on some fields of interest to see the structured content. However, most real application messages make use of only a fraction of all the available fields. Thus, our approach can easily display this fraction of available fields in the MSC.

SIP application engineers actually use MSCs as models to guide development as shown in Figure 8 for a typical SIP call establishment and tear down. Note the alternative behavior portion of the MSC diagram, "alt", that expresses the fact that the 100 TRYING event is optional. It could happen or not depending on what is the load of the system. It is mainly used to prevent premature timeouts.

Industrial applications we have worked on consisted in several hundreds of messages. The experience of walking through the messages content made us aware of the need for the approach we are suggesting. Thus here, there are no additional activities required to produce the MSC from the model and a straightforward comparison with the test results MSC can be performed.

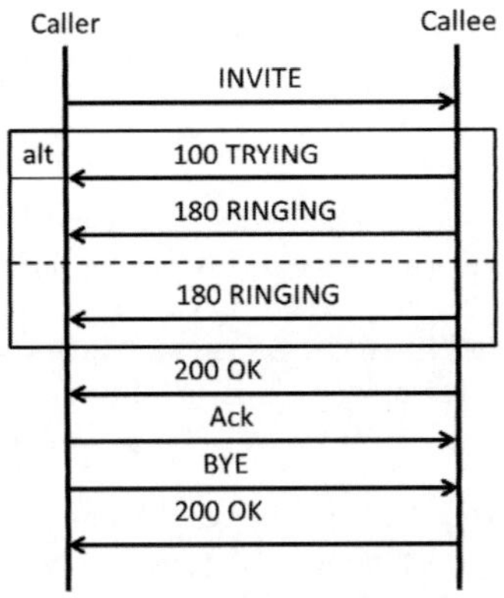

Figure 8. SIP protocol example model MSC

The ETSI definitions for the SIP protocol have used a strategy to try to alleviate the data type display problem in test result MSCs. The approach consists of redefining several times the same structured data type giving different type names like in the following excerpt where there is a type for an INVITE method and the BYE request that are absolutely identical from a field definition point of view but they will display differently on the MSC using data type names only. However, this approach has the disadvantage to hide various other active fields that differentiate the sequences of SIP events that otherwise would look the same.

```
type record INVITE_Request
{
  RequestLine requestLine,
  MessageHeader msgHeader,
  MessageBody messageBody optional,
  Payload payload optional
}
  type record BYE_Request {
  RequestLine requestLine,
  MessageHeader msgHeader,
  MessageBody messageBody optional,
  Payload payload optional
}
```

Where the main field is defined as:

```
type record RequestLine
{
  Method method,
  SipUrl requestUri,
  charstring sipVersion
}
```

And the method type is an enumerated type:

```
type enumerated Method
{
  ACK_E,
  BYE_E,
  CANCEL_E,
  INVITE_E,
  ...
}
```

All of these can be used to specify a template that has all its fields set to any value except for the method as follows:

```
template INVITE_Request
INVITE_Request_r_1 :=
{
   requestLine :=
   {
     method := INVITE_E,
     requestUri := ?,
     sipVersion := SIP_NAME_VERSION
   },
   msgHeader :=
   {

   callId :=
   {
     fieldName := CALL_ID_E,
     callid := ?
   },
     contact := ?,
     cSeq :=
   {
     fieldName := CSEQ_E,
     seqNumber := ?,
     method := "INVITE"
   },
     fromField := ?,
     toField := ?,
   ...
  }
```

We can select the field for the SIP *method* field to display in the test results MSC by adding the *with-statement* to the above template as follows:

```
with
{ extension
"{display_fields
{ requestLine
{ msgHeader
{cSeq {method}
}} }}";
}
```

The resulting test execution MSC using our approach would look like Figure 9 which is easier to recollect with the model shown on Figure 8.

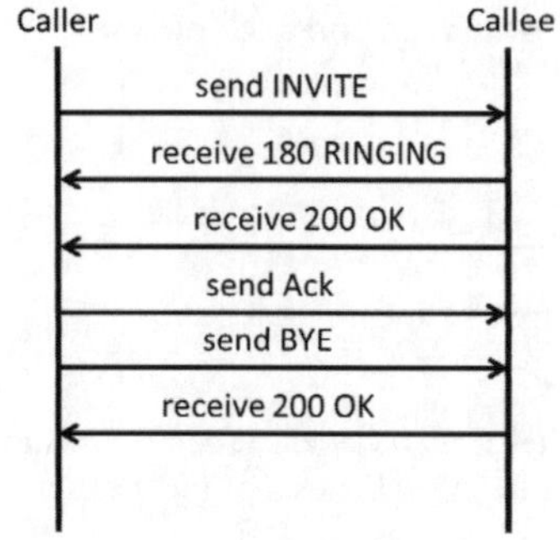

Figure 9. SIP test execution MSC

This approach is particularly effective for SIP response messages because they show the return code and the reason verb in the status line. Here, the SIP test suite designers have not used the type renaming strategy as they did for SIP requests. Thus, all responses will show the *Response* type name only on the traditional MSC. The status line is defined as follows:

```
type record StatusLine {
   charstring sipVersion,
   integer statusCode,
   charstring reasonPhrase
}
```

Which is used in the definition of the response type:

```
type record Response {
   StatusLine statusLine,
   MessageHeader msgHeader,
   MessageBody messageBody optional,
   Payload payload optional
}
```

A typical response message template can then use a *with-statement* that would only specify the *statusCode* and the *reasonPhrase* fields to be displayed.

```
template (value) Response
Response_200_s_1(
   CallId loc_CallId,
   CSeq loc_CSeq,
   From loc_From,
   To loc_To,
   Via loc_Via) := {
   statusLine := {
       sipVersion := SIP_NAME_VERSION,
       statusCode := 200,
       reasonPhrase := "OK"
       },
    msgHeader := {
          callId := loc_CallId,
   ...
   }
with extension
"{display_fields
     { statusLine
    { statusCode,reasonPhrase}}";
```

This will produce exactly the test results MSC that will be a trace through the model MSC shown in Figure 8. Here the additional benefit would consist in declaring a single SIP message definition for SIP requests that would be used by any of the SIP message kinds as follow:

```
type record SIP_Request
{
   RequestLine requestLine,
   MessageHeader msgHeader,
   MessageBody messageBody
   optional,
   Payload payload optional
}
```

B. An Avionics testing example

The idea of selecting data to display on a test results MSC originated in an industrial application that we have worked on for testing the CMC Esterline Flight Management System (FMS) [28]. The FMS shown in Figure 10 enables pilots to enter flight plans and display the flight plan on the FMS screen. A flight plan can be modified as a flight progresses. Flight plans and modifications are entered by typing the information using the alphanumeric key pad that consist of letters of the alphabet, numbers and function keys.

Figure 10. Flight Management System

For test automation purposes, key presses can be simulated by sending messages to a TCP/IP communication port. The content of a screen can be retrieved anytime with a special function invocation that will return a response message on the TCP/IP connection. Thus, we have the behavior of a typical telecommunication system sending and receiving messages with the difference that the response message must be requested explicitly via a screen query message. It is not coming back spontaneously and is subject to response delays that must be handled carefully in case of time outs.

In this case, stimuli messages are simple characters or names of function keys. These messages are by definition very short and can easily be displayed in full on the test results MSC. For such short messages, we have devised a default display option where if there is no with-statement with a display field specification for a given template, the MSC will display all data of this message. This is particularly optimal for short message content like the FMS key presses. The original test results MSC provided by Titan was displayed using useless message type names as shown in Figure 11.

The TTCN-3 abstract test suite has a data type definition for the content of the FMS screen that is returned as a response to the tester. The definition has been simplified due to confidentiality requirements from the industrial partner but this example renders the structural elements. Each line of the screen is defined using the *LineType* data type that has two subfields, the *title* and the *data*. Then, we define a screen type that is composed of two lines. The real application has a total of 26 subfields and illustrates well the fact that the entire screen content cannot be displayed on the test execution results MSC.

```
type record LineType {
      charstring title,
      charstring data
}

type record ScreenType {
      LineType line_1,
      LineType line_2
}
```

Using these data type definitions, we can define a template to match against the screen content and specify in the *with-statement* that we want to display only the data subfield of the second line:

```
    template ScreenType
screen_response_1 := {
      line_1 := {
          title := "waypoint 1",
          data := "CYUL"},
      line_2 := {
          title := "waypoint 2",
          data := "CYYZ"}
  }
    with {extension "display_fields {
              line_2 { data }}"};
```

All of these being used in the test case behavior description as follows:

```
testcase loggingDisplayTC()
  runs on MTCType system SystemType {

    var SUTType sut :=
          SUTType.create("FMS");

    connect(mtc:fmsPort, sut:fmsPort);

    sut.start(FMSbehavior());

    fmsPort.send("C");
    fmsPort.send("Y");
    fmsPort.send("U");
    fmsPort.send("L");
    fmsPort.send("EXEC");
    fmsPort.send("LEGS");

    alt {
          []fmsPort.receive(
                screen_response_1) {
                setverdict(pass);
          }
          [] fmsPort.receive {
                setverdict(fail);
          }
    }

    sut.stop;
    setverdict(pass);
}
```

It is clear from looking at Figure 11 that this MSC is not useful as an overview because it shows only the same message type name for each stimulus while our approach in Figure 14 shows the messages values, which allows the user to explore rapidly the test results before deciding to go for a fully detailed view of the results when for example the matching of the test oracle with the resulting response shows a failure. These values can be compared to those shown in a model such as the UCM diagram in Figure 12.

The UCM diagram of Figure 12 can be transformed into an MSC as described in [19] and shown in Figure 13. The MSC diagram in Figure 13 can then be compared with the test execution results shown in Figure 14.

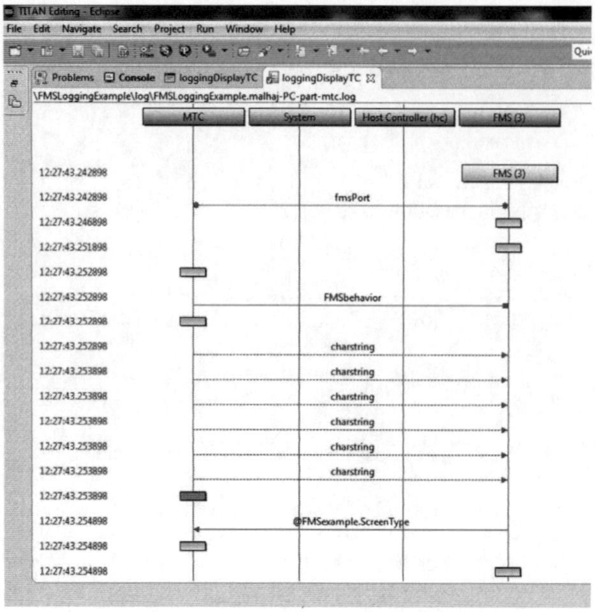

Figure 11. Original TITAN test results MSC display

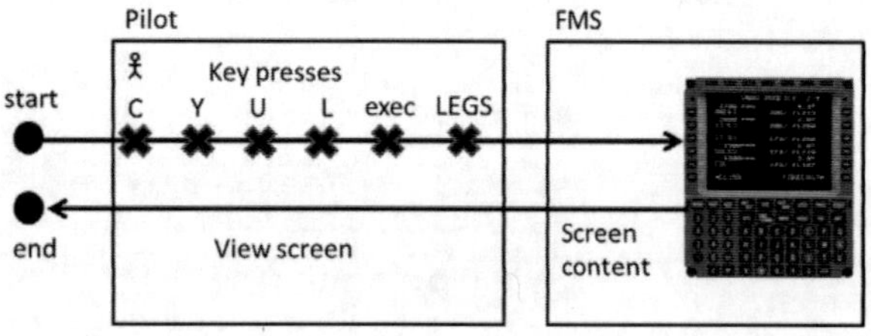

Figure 12. FMS model as UCM

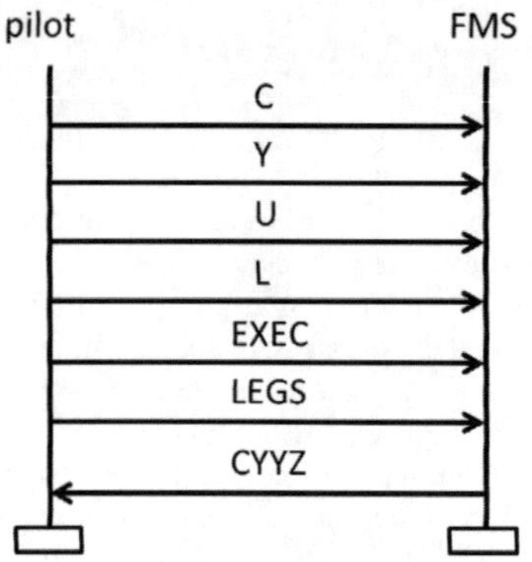

Figure 13. MSC diagram generated from UCM

The response message contains the content of the screen of the FMS. It is mapped to a data structure that contains fields for the various lines of the screen and also subfields to describe the left and the right sides of the screen. The FMS has 26 such fields, a title line, 6 lines structured into 4 subfields and a scratch pad line. Normally a test is designed to verify a given requirement, which consists in verifying that a limited number of fields have changed their values. For example, the result of a sequence of stimuli may have changed the field that displays the destination airport on line 2 in the right part of the screen. This is specified as a display fields request to show only the *line_2* field and the subfield *data*.

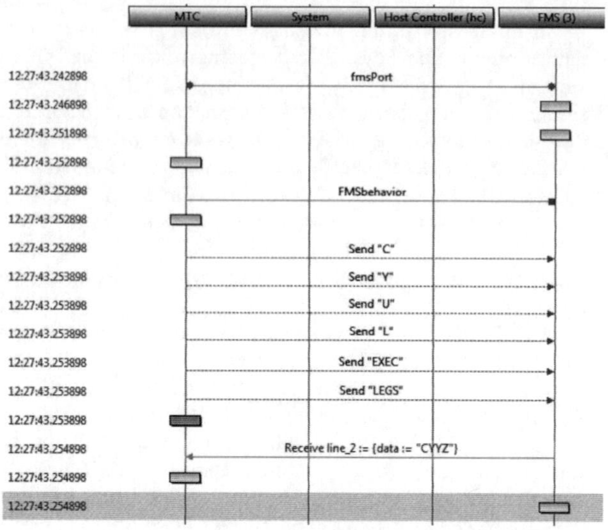

Figure 14. Modified Titan test result MSC

V. CONCLUSION

TTCN-3 tools provide limited support for visualizing test results in the context of MSC diagrams. We have shown how the with-statement language construct in TTCN-3 can be used to flexibly configure the display of data in the context of an MSC diagram without requiring changes to the TTCN-3 parser or grammar. The approach was validated by implementing it in the open-source Titan framework for TTCN-3 and applying it to two real-world examples: a SIP protocol and an avionics flight management system. Our approach successfully provided testers with a better mechanism for visualizing and navigating the complete set of test results in an efficient and effective manner.

ACKNOWLEDGMENT

We would like to thank CRIAQ, MITACS, Isoneo Solutions and CMC Esterline for their financial support of this research.

REFERENCES

[1] B. Stepien, M. Alhaj, and L. Peyton, "Visualizing Execution Models and Testing Results", 3rd Int'l Conference on Trends and Advances in Software Engineering (SOFTENG 2017), Venice, Italy, April 2017

[2] SIP TTCN-3, ETSI (2017) http://www.ttcn-3.org/index.php/downloads/publicts/publicts-etsi/27-publicts-sip

[3] Bernard Stepien, L. P. (2014, 06). Innovation and evolution in integrated web application testing with TTCN-3. International Journal on Software Tools for Technology Transfer, pp. 269-283.

[4] Peyton, L., Stepien, B., & Seguin, P. (2008). Integration Testing of Composite Applications. Waikoloa, HI: IEEE.

[5] Stepien, B., Xiong, P., & Peyton, L. (2011). A Systematic Approach to Web Application Penetration Testing Using TTCN-3. MCETECH (pp. pp. 1–16). Berlin Heidelberg: Springer-Verlag.

[6] Stepien, B. (2015, February 14). Testing and Test Control Notation. Retrieved from TTCN-3 in a Nutshell (2017): http://www.site.uottawa.ca/~bernard/ttcn3_in_a_nutshell.html

[7] S. Jagadish, C. Lawrence, and R.K. Shyamasunder, "cmUML - A UML based Framework for Formal Specification of Concurrent, Reactive Systems", Journal of Object Technology (JOT), Vol. 7, No. 8, pp 188-207, November-December 2008.

[8] A. Mitschele-Thiel, and B. Müller-Clostermann, "Performance engineering of SDL/MSC systems", Computer Networks, 31(17), 1801-1815, 1999.

[9] A. Pourshahid, D. Amyot, L. Peyton, S. Ghanavati, P. Chen, M. Weiss, and AJ Forster, "Business Process Management with the User Requirements Notation", Electronic Commerce Research, Springer, Vol. 9 No. 4, pp 269-316, 2009.

[10] M. Utting, A. Pretschner, and B. Legeard, "A taxonomy of model - based testing approaches" Software Testing, Verification and Reliability 22.5 (2012): 297-312

[11] P. Baker, Z. R. Dai, J. Grabowski, Ø. Haugen, I. Schieferdecker, and C. Williams, "Model-Driven Testing Using the UML Testing Profile", Springer ISBN 978-3-540-72562-6 Springer Berlin Heidelberg New York, Springer-Verlag Berlin Heidelberg, 2008.

[12] Y. Cheon and G. T. Leavens, "A simple and practical approach to unit testing: The JML and JUnit way", In European Conference on Object-Oriented Programming, pp. 231-255. Springer Berlin Heidelberg, June 2002.

[13] ETSI ES 201 873-1 version 4.9.1, The Testing and Test Control Notation version 3 Part 1: TTCN-3 Core Language, last accessed August 2017: http://www.ttcn-3.org/index.php/downloads/standards

[14] E. G. Cartaxo, F. G. Neto, and P. D. Machado, "Test case generation by means of UML sequence diagrams and labeled transition systems", In Systems, Man and Cybernetics, 2007. ISIC. IEEE International Conference on (pp. 1292-1297).

[15] D. Amyot, L. Logrippo, and M. Weiss, "Generation of test purposes from Use Case Maps", Computer Networks, 49(5), 643-660

[16] J. Grabowski, B. Koch, M. Schmitt, and D. Hogrefe, SDL and MSC based test generation for distributed test architectures. In SDL Forum, Vol. 99, pp. 389-404, 1999, June.

[17] PragmaDev, last accessed August, 2017 at http://www.pragmadev.com/

[18] R. Alur and M. Yannakakis, "Model checking of message sequence charts", International Conference on Concurrency Theory. Springer Berlin Heidelberg, pp 114-129, 1999.

[19] A. Miga, D. Amyot, F. Bordeleau, C. Cameron, and M. Woodside, "Deriving Message Sequence Charts from Use Case Maps Scenario Specifications", Tenth SDL Forum (SDL'01), Copenhagen, Denmark, LNCS 2078, 268-287, June 2001.

[20] J. Kealey and D. Amyot, "Enhanced Use Case Map Traversal Semantics", *13th SDL Forum (SDL 2007)*, Paris, France, LNCS 4745, Springer, 133-149, September 2007.

[21] B. Stepien, L. Peyton, and P. Xiong, "Using TTCN-3 as a Modeling Language for Web Penetration Testing", Proceedings of the 2012 IEEE International Conference on Industrial Technology (ICIT 2012), Athens, Greece, IEEE Explore, pp 674 - 681 March 2012.

[22] H. Dan and R. M. Hierons, "Conformance testing from message sequence charts", In Software Testing, Verification and Validation (ICST), IEEE Fourth International Conference, pp. 279-288, March 2011.

[23] B. Stepien, L.Peyton, M. Shang, and T.Vassiliou-Gioles, "An Integrated TTCN-3 Test Framework Architecture for Interconnected Object-based Internet Applications", International Journal of Electronic Business, Inderscience Publishers, Vol. 11, No. 1, pp. 1-23, 2014. DOI: http://dx.doi.org/10.1504/IJEB.2014.057898

[24] TTworkbench, Spirent, last accessed August 2017 at https://www.spirent.com/Products/TTworkbench

[25] Testcast, Elvior, last accessed August 2017 at http://www.elvior.com/testcast/ttcn-3

[26] Titan, last accessed August 2017 at https://projects.eclipse.org/proposals/titan

[27] SIP RFC 3261, https://www.ietf.org/rfc/rfc3261.txt

[28] FMS, href= http://www.esterline.com/avionicssystems/en-us/productsservices/aviation/navigationfmsgps/flightmanagementsystems.aspx

Analysis of Hardware Implementations to Accelerate Convolutional and Recurrent Neuronal Networks

Florian Kästner, Osvaldo Navarro Guzmán, Benedikt Janßen, Javier Hoffmann, Michael Hübner
Chair for Embedded Systems of Information Technology
Ruhr-University Bochum
Email: {Florian.Kaestner;Osvaldo.NavarroGuzman;Benedikt.Janssen;Javier.Hoffmann;Michael.Huebner}@rub.de

Abstract*—Hardware platforms, like FPGAs and ASICs, turned out to be a viable alternative to GPUs for the implementation of deep learning algorithms, especially in applications with strict power and performance constraints. In terms of flexibility, FPGAs are more beneficial, while ASICs can provide a better energy efficiency and higher performance. Deep Learning is a subgroup of machine learning algorithms that has a major impact on modern technology. Among these algorithms, Convolutional Neural Networks (CNN) and Recurrent Neural Networks (RNN) have been of great interest due to their accuracy in comparison to other methods. In this article, we conducted an analysis of the hardware implementation of these two popular network types. Different types of neural networks offer different opportunities to create an optimized hardware implementation due to their specific characteristics. Therefore, we split the analysis into two parts, discussing CNN and RNN implementations separately. Our contribution is an inside view on several hardware approaches and a comparison of their architectural characteristics. We aim to propose hints for their implementations.

Keywords*— *FPGA; Recurrent; Convolutional; Neural Network; ASIC.

I. PREAMBLE

This article targets to collect solutions for hardware implementation of special types of Neural Networks (NNs) presented in [1]. The scope of this is, therefore, the discussion of hardware implementations of convolutional and recurrent neural networks. However, experience has shown that a short recapitulation of basics is beneficial. That is the reason why, this section is dedicated as a short review on the principles of NN.

NNs are a collection of connected units called $neurons$, which are typically organized in $layers$. In a NN each neuron is equipped with a linear and / or non-linear $activation function$, mapping the weighted inputs to the output. The layers can be connect in many different ways. For instance if they are connected in a sequential manner from the input to the output of the network, we are talking about a feedforward NN. The variation of the structure of neurons and their connections allow a wide field of NN types. The internal layers, i.e., not the one receiving the input or generating the output, are called hidden layers. If the network has several hidden layers, then it is said to be a Deep Neural Network. Both, Convolutional Neural Networks (CNNs) and Recurrent Neural Networks (RNNs) are implementations of these Deep Learning Networks (DLN).

II. INTRODUCTION

Over the last 30 years Deep Learning (DL) has become consistently more powerful providing accurate prediction or recognition. The breakthrough in the academic area was achieved in 2012 at the ImageNet Large Scale Visual Recognition Challenge [2] when a convolutional neural network (CNN), a specific type of Deep Neural Network (DNN), firstly won this challenge. After this breakthrough, the popularity and sets of application, not only of CNNs but of DL in general, has grown dramatically. In contrast to traditional machine learning principles the data representation models are trained without the need of handcrafted feature engineering. Within the structure and learning process of DNNs, features are extracted from the input data by itself rather than by humans. This is a mandatory advantage designing machine learned classifications or regressions for highly complex applications like detecting objects, for instance animals or everyday objects, from input images.

The resulting DNNs are capable of representing functions of high complexity with the help of connected simple, mostly hierarchical, components [3]. The supported complexity depends on the amount of layers and neurons or units inside each layer. Due to this structure, NNs can be trained to extract features at different levels of representations.

Two varieties of DNN have especially shown great potential to real life applications, CNNs and RNNs. CNNs are typically used for imagery classification [4], [5]. RNNs are suitable for time-variant problems such as speech recognition [6], due to their recursive structure. While the idea and structure of NNs are not new, their recent success is based on new training methods, namely backpropagation and pretraining. The increasing amount of collected data in combination with the processing power of modern compute platforms enables the exploitation of massive parallelism. Parallelism of data processing is a key principle regarding the training and also the inference phase, when only the feedforward path is active. The data flow driven architecture of DNNs allow coarse and fine grained parallelism. Additionally, distributed learning, batch processing and mini-batch processing increase the model's parallelism possibilities for accelerating the training of DNNs.

Nowadays Graphics Processing Units (GPUs) or clusters of GPUs are usually used to accelerate the training. Thus, highly complex models can be trained with a huge amount of data within days instead of weeks. GPUs are originally designed to accelerate data-flow driven graphic applications with massively parallel multi-core architectures. This architecture is also beneficial accelerating DL. Furthermore, improvements in the software infrastructure have lowered the effort of GPU implementations of DL algorithms. Frameworks like Caffe [7], Theano [8] or Tensorflow [9], in combination with efficient libraries like cuDNN[10] or cuBLAS [11] are designed to simplify the DNN implementation and enable a more efficient usage of GPUs.

However, GPUs have a high power consumption, compared to other processing units. Due to this disadvantage they are not suitable for an integration in most embedded devices, with strong power limitations. While service oriented applications, communicating via Internet and executing DNNs in the cloud, dont suffer due to that fact, applications with high safety criteria like autonomous driving need to have onboard processing of the inference phase of this DNNs to classify or predict. While GPU implementations have good framework-support and provide great performance capabilities, hardware acceleration implementations on Field Programmable Gate Arrays (FPGAs) or Application Specific Integrated Circuits (ASICs) represent an interesting and promising research area. However, currently such implementations are rarely used in industry.

In this paper we extend our previous work presented in [1] focusing on hardware implementations, their analysis and comparison. We further elaborate current trends in deep learning and how these trends could affect the popularity of hardware platforms like FPGAs. The rest of this paper is organized as follows. Section II-A describes the general structure and the improvements of popular and state-of-the-art CNNs. The same is done in Section II-B for RNNs. In Section III, we explain how the current trends could affect the choice of future platforms accelerating DNNs. The major part of this paper focuses on the analysis and comparison of hardware implementations of CNNs in Section IV and RNNs in Section V. The paper ends with a short conclusion in Section VI.

A. Convolutional Neural Networks

CNNs are a type of DNN for processing data that has a grid-like topology [3], [12]. CNNs are widely adopted for practical applications, especially in image processing tasks like object recognition or tracking. The input data of such tasks can be interpreted as a 2D grid of input pixels. The processing of these input pixels is depicted in Figure 1. One major advantage of CNNs is the absence of the need to flatten the input to a single dimension, avoiding information loss like positional relationships. CNNs usually consists of the following components: convolution layer, evaluation of a non-linear activation function, subsampling layer, fully-connected layer and classification or regression layer.

The convolution component extracts features from the input image with a set of adaptive filters called kernels. The convolution computation is done through a dot-product between the elements of the kernel and the input section of same size across the entire input frame and channels. Figure 2 shows a detailed demonstration of the computations applying a 2x2x2 convolution and max pooling on a 3x3x2 input image. Firstly, a multi-dimensional dot product is computed through the convolution layer consisting of 2 kernels. Each of these kernels possess dimension of 2x2x2. The depth of the input data, which can be defined as channels of an input image like Red-Green-Blue(RGB), has to be equal with the depth of the kernels. The resulting dimension of the output of the convolution layer is dependent on the dimension of the kernel and the used stride and padding behavior. Stride controls how the kernel convolves around the input data in a shifting manner. Padding is used to avoid a fast decrease of the output data adding data around the border of the input image. Thus, the height and width of the input image can be remained. The convolution layer in Figure 2 has a stride of one without padding. Therefore, the resulting output owns a dimension of 2x2x2, which can be described as a double-channel image or an output with two feature maps with a size of 2x2. Another possible method is to share one kernel for all channels to create decomposed images. The output of the dot-product is forwarded to an non-linear activation function, typically $sigmoid()$, $ReLU()$ or $tanh()$, which increases the nonlinear properties of the CNN. In practice, the rectified linear unit (ReLU), defined as $f(x) = max(0, x)$, is the most popular activation function used for CNNs due to its sparse activation, efficient computation and benefits regarding back propagation reducing the effect of vanishing gradients. Then, the pooling component, also called subsampling, reduces the spatial dimension of each feature map and keeps relative positional informations. The main purpose of this layer is generalization to avoid overfitting, by reducing the amount of parameters and keeping relative relationships. The most popular type of subsampling is max pooling as applied in Figure 2. In traditional CNNs like ImageNet [13], these three stages alternate several times. At the next stage of the feedforward path one or more Fully-Connected (FC) layers are applied. Typically, all neurons within these layers have full connections to the previous layer, while CNN layers are characterized through local connections and parameter sharing. However, both layers still compute dot products and therefore it is possible to replace fully-connected with convolution layer. At the last stage of a CNN a classification or regression layer is used to extract the desired information and build the quadratic cost function to train the network with the help of logistic or linear regression. The training of CNNs is done via a gradient-based backpropagation algorithm. Since the breakthrough in 2012, many researchers and companies modified the architecture and training methodologies for CNNs improving generalization and precision. The developers of

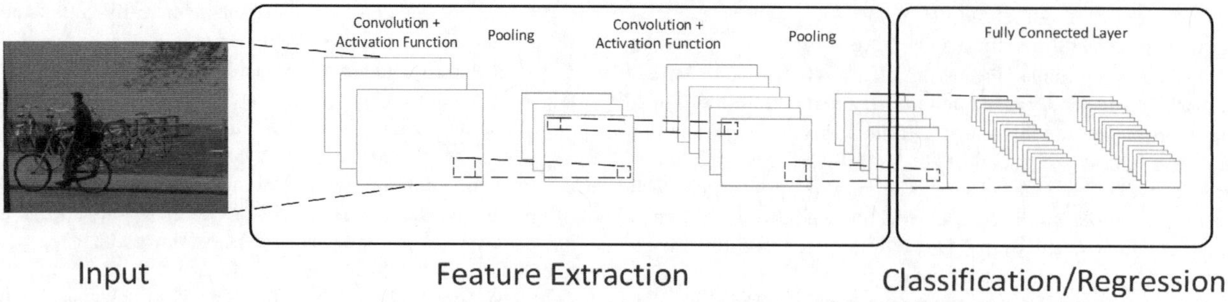

Fig. 1: Common processing flow of a convolutional neural network [3].

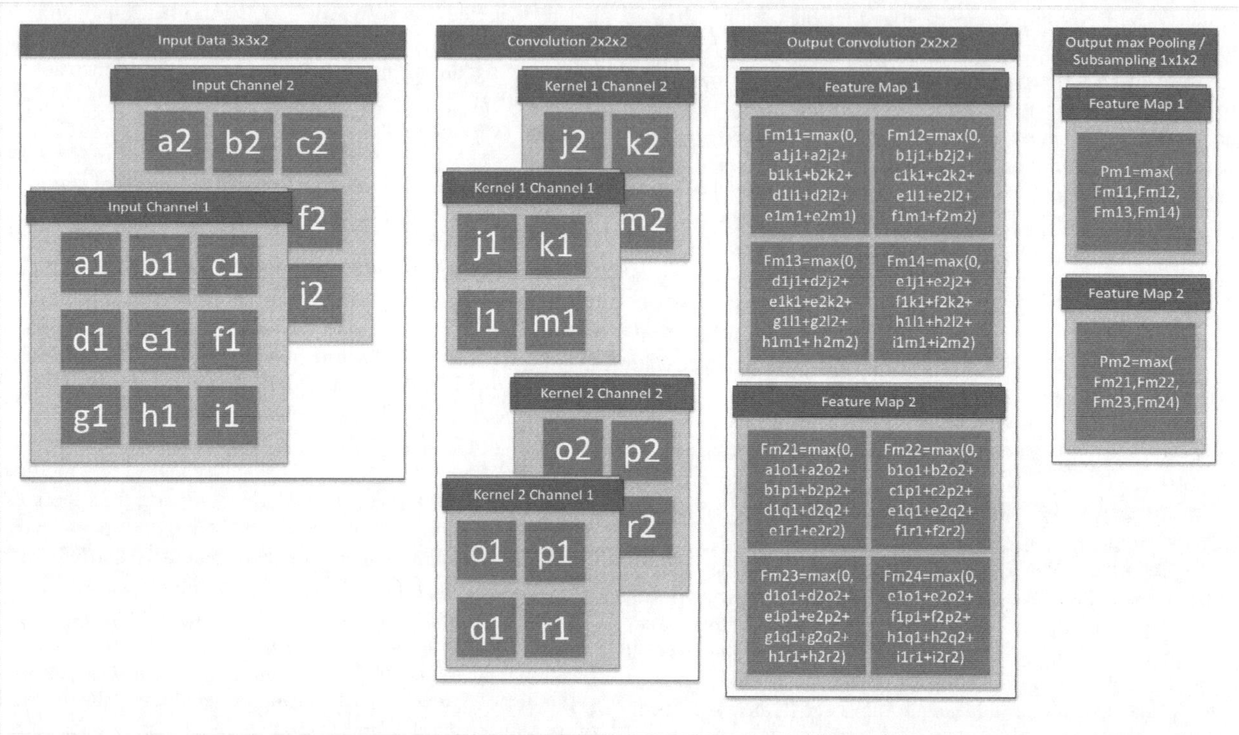

Fig. 2: Demonstration of the computations by applying a 2x2x2 convolution with max pooling on a 3x3x2 input image

VGGNet [14] (2014) proved that keeping CNNs simple and deep is a useful method in order to improve their performance to a certain degree. Karen Simonyan and Andrew Zisserman archieved the lowest error rate with 16 layer CNN using 3x3 kernels with a stride of one and 2x2 max pooling with a stride of two in every layer [14]. Another approach to improve the precision of CNNs was presented by Szegredy et al. [15] in the same year with a similar error rate compared to VGG-16, but with a model size which consists of only 6 million instead of 140 million parameters. The introduction of inception modules leads to the evolution of GoogleNet. The basic idea of GoogleNet is to break with the traditional sequential order of layers. The inception module proposed in [15] consists of a 3x3 max pooling, a 3x3 convolution and a 5x5 convolution executed in parallel. The output of these components are concatenated in the depth dimension. In order to reduce dimensions to 1x1 convolutions to each component are applied. Furthermore, instead of FC layers, average pooling layers are used. Thus, the amount of parameters, mainly arised from the FC layers, has been significantly decreased. As a result the decreasing size of the model and the increasing data parallelization possibility is beneficial for accelerating training and inference phase. However, the current state of the art CNN for object classification, detection and localization is ResNet [16]. These CNN introduced by He et al. 2015 is by far the biggest network of the mainly used ones with a total size of 152 layer and 60 million parameters. Due to the huge size of the network even applying ReLU activation units the vanishing gradient problem is exacerbated. Therefore, the basic idea of ResNet is to sequentially apply shortcuts over convolutional layer. The output of the convolution is then added to the original input. Thus, a slightly different representation of the input data is created. The resulting residual mapping simplifies the backpropagation optimization and allow models to be even deeper.

B. Recurrent Neural Networks

Recurrent neural networks (RNNs) can be utilized for recognition, production or prediction problems [17]. Unlike conventional NNs, they can include temporal information in the processing, as they can handle information relation between sequential data for sequences of arbitrary length. RNNs extend the concept of conventional acyclic feedforward NNs by maintaining a hidden state. This ability is enabled by cycles inside the network, and it is a key feature for tasks such as speech and handwriting recognition [18]. The cycles inside the network are connections from the output of a layer looping back, either to itself, or to a previous layer. The feedback connection enables the network to represent previous information as activation [19]. Thereby, the activation of the hidden state depends on previous activations [20]. In [21], Schmidhuber describes RNNs as more powerful general computers in comparison to acyclic feedforward NN. According to Schmidhuber, RNNs can learn from arbitrary data inputs, as well as create such data as output. Even a mixture of sequential and parallel data can be processed. Similar to other DNNs, RNNs can benefit from a massive parallelism in processing, as offered by todays computing platforms. In comparison to Markov chains, which can also handle dependencies in time between sequential input data, the state space of RNNs is growing slower for growing context windows. In a Markov model the growth of state space is exponential, for RNNs, it is quadratic at most [22].

One of the first approaches for NN to include temporal information, is the work of Hopfield [23]. He describes an early NN that allows temporal dependencies of the neurons state and an encoding of temporal information of data. One of the first approaches in the direction of todays RNNs was done by Jain et al. They developed a partially RNN to learn character strings [24]. According to [24] the architecture of RNN can be anything between a fully interconnected network and a partially interconnected network. In fully interconnected networks, every neuron is connected to every other neuron, as well as to itself via feedback connections. This structure is depicted in Figure 3. However, in contrast to Figure 3, for a fully interconnected RNN, there are no distinct input and output layers.

In the 90s, there have been difficulties to train RNNs for applications whose data includes dependencies over long temporal intervals. The results from Bengio et al. in [25], indicated that it is more likely for the learning process to take into account dependencies with short temporal character, rather than those with long-term dependencies. In [17], Bengio et al. discuss this issue for a better understanding of the problem. They suggest alternative optimization algorithms to gradient-descent, which showed encouraging results. Within their paper, they reveal the vanishing gradient problem and the exploding gradient problem. Pascanu et al. investigated this problem further and proposed a regularization term that hinders the error signal to vanish [26].

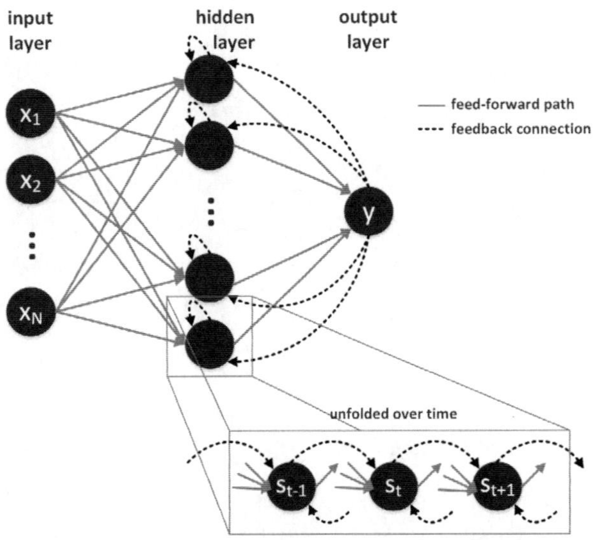

Fig. 3: General architecture of RNNs with optional input and output layer.

The first contribution to a network to overcome the issue of learning long-term dependencies, was made by Hochreiter and Schmidhuber in 1997 [19]. They proposed a new recurrent network architecture, together with a gradient-based learning algorithm, called long short-term memory networks (LSTM). These networks can be categorized as a sub-group of RNNs. The network architecture contains an input layer, a hidden layer, and an output layer. The hidden layer contains so called memory cells and is fully connected. A LSTM cell architecture is depicted in Figure 4.

Another notable approach was presented by Schuster and Paliwal [27]. They proposed bidirectional recurrent neural networks (BRNNs). BRNNs are designed to overcome the issue of choosing the right time for the output delay to include future input data. Therefore, Schuster and Paliwal proposed to split the neuron state to cover positive time direction and the negative time direction. This means that the network structures includes positive and negative delays. Their results show a significant improvement for the classification of phonemes from the TIMIT speech database over other types of RNNs and multi-layer perceptron networks.

More recently, Cho et al. proposed a new type of hidden units, called gated recurrent unit (GRU) [28]. The approach was motivated by the LSTM approach, but instead of three or four gating units in LSTM, depending on the implementation, it uses only two gating units. In [20], Chung et al. show that GRUs can gain advantage over LSTM-based RNNs.

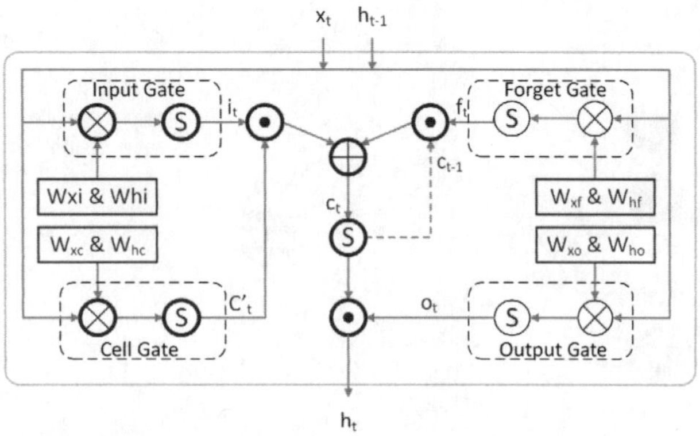

Fig. 4: LSTM architecture with four gated units. The S denotes the Sigmoid function [18].

III. Hardware Acceleration on GPU and FPGA

The advantage in energy efficiency of FPGAs in comparison to other computing platforms is well known [29], [30], [31]. However, in the area of DNNs, GPUs are a more prominent platform for implementations in comparison to FPGAs. This dominance is, among other aspects, based on a higher computing performance and more efficient programmability in e.g., CUDA programming language. The advantage in performance is based on the heavy use of floating-point operations of current DNN implementations. In [32], Nurvitadhi et al. compare the implementation of RNNs on FPGAs, CPUs, GPUs and ASICS. Without the usage of batch processing, the FPGA implementation performs better than its counterpart on CPUs and GPUs. This is due to its customizable hardware architecture. With the usage of batch processing, the implementation on CPUs and GPUs achieve a better performance, however, their utilization is not as optimal, leading to a worse efficiency.

In [33], the authors present their follow-up work. They analyzed the capabilities of upcoming FPGA technology, and the latest developments of DNN, to identify benefits of FPGA-based implementations. For their evaluation, they compared implementations on Intels Arria 10 and Stratix 10 FPGAs to implementations on Nvidias Titan X Pascal GPU. According to the authors, the latest developments in the field of DNNs are reported to be an increase in efficiency, compact data types, and network sparsity. Architectures with more efficient data paths are necessary, as the size of current DNNs is growing, due to a coherence in inference accuracy. Moreover, the data processing can be optimized by exploiting zero values in the network weights and biases, called sparsity. It is necessary to take advantage of zero values by avoiding their computation [33]. Recent publications [33] have shown a significant improvement in representing the data inside DNNs with less bits, while still maintaining a high accuracy.

Modern GPUs are often based on a single-instruction multiple-thread (SIMT) compute model, meaning that multiple threads are processed in parallel, executing the same instructions on different data. This is the case for the compute model of OpenCL, where a single program counter is used for a group of threads, called wavefront [34]. Thus, thread-level divergence is an issue, as only one execution path can be followed at a time. Therefore, a homogeneous processing is beneficial for GPU implementations. Moreover, GPUs usually support a fixed set of native data types. Thus, compact data types with only a few or single bits are less likely beneficial for GPU implementations and can even become a performance disadvantage. Modern FPGAs on the other hand offer an increasing amount of on-chip memory. For instance, Intels Stratix 10 offers up to 28 MB [35], and Xilinx Virtex UltraScale+ offers more than 45 MB [36]. Moreover, their maximum frequency is increasing due to improvements in the production process, as well as new features, such as Intels HyperFlex. In addition, the number of hardwired DSPs cores, equipped with native floating-point support, is increasing. Furthermore, the achievable bandwidth is increasing too, for instance the usage of high-bandwidth memory (HBM) in future FPGA generations.

Based on these properties of GPUs and FPGAs, as well as the trends of current DNN development, the authors of [33] foresee a possible performance benefit for DNN implementations on FPGAs, in addition to the performance/Watt advantage.

Nurvitadhi et al. results indicate that for single-precision floating-point implementations of DNNs, FPGAs still fall behind the performance of GPUs. However, as stated earlier, the results show an advantage for FPGAs when looking at performance/Watt. To evaluate sparsity, the Nurvitadhi et al. evaluated AlexNet with matrices with 85 % sparsity. This means that only 15 % of the elements are non-zero. Due to the shortcomings of GPUs thread-divergence, FPGAs can offer a benefit. In fact, the results show that the Stratix 10 FPGA outperforms the Titan X GPU in matrix multiplication for DNNs with pruning for implementations with a clock frequency of 500 MHz and more. The evaluation of an extreme case of compact data types, binary neural networks with data types of 1bit width, reveal the disadvantage of a fixed set of natively supported data types. The results of Nurvitadhi et al. show that the Stratix 10 FPGA outperforms the Titan X GPU in matrix multiplication for binarized DNNs for all implementations. This is even the case for the implementation on the lower-cost Arria 10.

Another DNN type with compact data types are ternary DNNs, which use a ternary representation of the network weights, e.g., +1, 0, -1. For their evaluation, Nurvitadhi et al. analyzed Ternary ResNet. Their implementation takes advantage not only of compact data types but also sparsity in layers. On average, they report 51 % sparsity of the weights, and 60 % sparsity of the neurons. In their experiments, the FPGA implementation, running at 450 MHz, was able to beat the implementation on the Titan X GPU in terms of performance, as well as performance/Watt.

As indicated by the results of Nurvitadhi et al., in addition to the advantage in performance/Watt, there is a good chance for next-generation FPGA technology to beat GPUs for DNN implementations.

Therefore, within this paper we will analyze implementation details of the two prominent kinds of DNNs, namely CNNs and RNNs, and discuss their properties and benefits.

IV. Analysis of CNN Implementation

As mentioned in Section II-A, CNNs are data flow oriented and offer great possibilities to design hardware accelerators and even coprocessors exploiting fine and coarse grained parallelism. Filtered Connections (FC) and convolution layers can be seen as big matrix multiplications. Within the convolution layer of the example shown in Figure 2, 64 Multiplications and Accumulate Computations (MACs) can be executed in parallel. The amount of operations without data dependencies which are able to be executed in parallel increases, due to the kernel and input data size. However, several challenges arise designing an efficient hardware accelerator for CNNs. Obviously, modern CNNs with a huge amount of layers like ResNet are not suitable to implement it as a whole. Therefore, methods and architectures have to been found facing a trade-off between resource utilization and performance. Furthermore, the biggest challenge focuses on the memory allocation and access, which is the main bottleneck in every architecture.

While image processing cores have already been extensively studied and widely used on FPGAs, to the best of our knowledge Sankaradas et al. firstly designed and implemented a coprocessor able to execute and accelerate the inference phase of an entire CNN [37]. The authors of [37] bypass the bottleneck of memory access and allocation with the help of off-chip memory with a large bandwith. The off-chip memory, including 4 banks of DDR2 SDRAM of 256MB, is connected to a Xilinx Virtex-5 FPGA via PCI. The basic unit of this architecture is a handcrafted 2D convolver using Single Instruction Multiple Data (SIMD) processing elements called Vector Processing Elements (VPEs). These VPEs consist of fixed amount of chained digital signal processing processor (DPS) units optimized for an efficient execution of MAC operations and a First In First Out (FIFO) buffer as can be seen in Figure 5. Furthermore, these VPEs are organized in clusters whereby the output of each VPE tile is added to the previous one with the help of an additional DSP unit. The advantage of dynamic reconfiguration is not used due to the fact that the FPGA is used as a prototyping platform. Thus, the size of the clusters and amount of DSP units inside each VPE is fixed. Although the VPEs are programmable to skip convolutions, the size of the baseline kernel has to be previously determined. Thus, bigger kernels are not suitable for executing convolution on this architecture. The clusters also include subsampling and non-linear activation function primitives performed by look-up tables. The input data is streamed in a sequential manner and no intermediate data is stored on the on-chip memory. To further increase the communication performance, Sankaradas et al reduce the data precision from floating point to fixed point operations of 20 bits. Later studies [38] proved that reducing the data precision in a certain region does not impact the accuracy loss significantly. Sankaradas et al. achieved with the first coprocessor, capable to accelerate a complete CNN on hardware, a performance of $3,37GMAC$ per second with a total power consumption of $11W$. This baseline coprocessor is a very well designed architecture. However, this architecture still does not use the parallelization possibilities properly and seems to be very inefficient applied to a CNN with varying kernel and sampling sizes. On the other side, this static architecture is perfectly suitable applied to simple and homogenous CNNs like VGG.

In contrast to the architecture described in [37] the authors of [39] abandon the option of using external memory and a persistent connection to a local host computer in their hardware accelerator design focusing on mobile embedded applications. Jin et al. use a Xilinx Zynq-7000 device including a dual ARM Cortex-A9 core and an Artix-7 FPGA to implement their architecture consisting of 2 main components, namely a memory router and a collection network. A collection is defined as a group of operator blocks performing arithmetic operations like convolution. Within a single pass through the collection, an output of a 1-to-1 convolution plane is applied. Each collection can be executed in parallel with an interval of 1, which means that every clock cycle, an output datum is produced. To control the data flow between each operator, each collection owns a router. This router is also able to bypass an incoming data stream from neighbored collections. The operators inside each collection are arranged in a sequential manner similar to the VPE described above. The other major component of this architecture is the memory router, which consist of 3 AXI Direct Memory Access (DMA) IP cores. These DMAs, performing the memory access via AXI4-bus coupled with AXI4 Stream, acting as a gateway to the collection. Furthermore, the memory router is able to distribute incoming streams to not occupied collections. Unfortunately, Jin et al. did not describe properly how the streams are built or how the exact operator blocks are designed in order to synchronize kernels and input data. The authors mention that the peak performance of 40Gops/s consuming less than 4W significantly decreases, applying deep CNNs producing deep feature maps according to the huge amount of intermediate data. However, the smart routing technique and reduced number of global connections is a promising method to execute inference phase of CNNs keeping intermediate data in a pipelined stream.

Although the above described architectures are carefully designed and programmable in a certain degree, they are very static and inflexible to introduce changes, which leads to inefficiency implementing different types of CNNs. Redesigning the hardware to improve different stages of different CNNs produces high engineering effort. Therefore, newer approaches and design flows implementing custom CNNs on hardware try to overcome this issue with the help of High Level Synthesis (HLS). HLS is an automated design process producing hardware description at the Register-Transfer-Level (RTL) from a higher level of abstraction, namely the algorithm-level. Thus, Verilog or VHDL code can be automatically generated from

C/C++, SystemC or OpenCL code. Typically, the architectural design of the resulting hardware architecture can be influenced with a set of constraints and directives. This method ensures a fast design space exploration and an easy customization of the hardware to accelerate DNNs. The authors of [40] use Vivado HLS from Xilinx to implement a five-layer CNN on a FPGA including 2 convolutions with 5x5 kernels and 2 average pooling layer. Instead of data streaming combined with smart routing or external memory, Zhou et al. use mainly the on-chip memory of a Virtex7 to store parameters, intermediate and input data. After noticing that the onboard Block RAM (BRAM) has only two ports preventing convolution to be executed in parallel sufficiently, Zhou et al. switch to a sea of registers through a line buffer chain. In combination unrolling the most inner loop of the convolution they were able to execute 25 11bit-MAC operations in parallel. The hardware accelerator is driven with a clock frequency of 150 MHz. Therefore, this design has a theoretical maximum peak performance of $3.75GMACs$. However, this paper shows the advantage of HLS designing custom CNN accelerators due to the easy handling and the hardware generation speedup with state-of-the-art HLS tools.

The authors of [41] use the properties of HLS to effectively perform a Design Space Exploration optimizing FPGA hardware accelerators for CNNs. This research is based on the roofline performance model described in [42] relating the system performance to off-chip memory traffic and the peak performance. The goal of the design space exploration is to achieve a certain computation to communication ratio in order to reach the computational roof of the attainable performance. Due to that goal the authors of [41] first started to optimize the computation of the convolution by generating a series of valid CNN implementations. Thus, specific directives provided by Vivado HLS, namely unrolling and pipelining, are used to generate a series of valid hardware accelerators of CNNs with an equivalent functionality with the help of loop scheduling and loop tile size enumeration. More precisely Zhang et al. investigated in the impact of tile size selections in order to find the computational roof of a convolution with the given loop scheduling. To reduce the amount of memory access, local memory promotion is proposed for keeping the intermediate data on-chip as long as possible. In order to increase the reusability of intermediate data, a polyhedral-based optimization framework is used, identifying all legal loop transformations. As a result Zhang et al. performed a Design Space Exploration of a convolution layer with multiple input channels and feature maps to compute a set of Pareto points. Thus, a hardware implementation can be chosen achieving the best performance in combination with a suitable communication to computation ratio. The synthesized IP-core is coupled to two ping-pong buffers for each input and output AXI4 bus. The off-chip data transfer is managed by two data transfer engines to perform DMA access. In order to gain the needed bandwidth, the amount of AXI4 bus interfaces has been adjusted. However, the multi-layer CNN accelerator suffers due to a chosen global unroll factor. This fact leads to inefficient hardware utilization in heterogeneous CNNs especially by performing the feedforward path of FC layers. The 5 layer CNN hardware accelerator is implemented on a Xilinx Virtex 7 device achieving $61.62GFLOP/s$. The hardware is working with $100MHz$ consuming $18.61W$. Instead of fixed point Zhang et al. only use floating point operations in their design.

To further increase the performance of FPGA based accelerators of CNNs, Li et al. investigated the opportunities to customize every type of layer due to their specific characteristics. Therefore, the authors of [43] try to optimize the memory access method and the level of parallelism depending on the layer type and their properties. While the system architecture and the parallelism space exploration is very similar to the architecture presented in [41], the major difference is the fact that Li et al. treat convolution and FC layers differently in terms of optimizing the level of parallelism and off-chip memory access. The FC layers are handled as big matrix multiplications and divided into small scale matrix multiplications. Furthermore, computing the optimal data parallelism Li et al. took the limitation of the hardware resources, namely DSP and BRAM units, directly into account. Due to the fact that FC layers are very memory-bounded and less computation-bounded caused by their dense interconnections, a batch-based processing method for FC layers has been proposed. The basic idea of this approach is to continuously run the FC feedforward path without waiting for data. Therefore, Li et al. compute a batch size matching the computing pattern for the FC layers in order to increase the operations executed in parallel without increasing the needed bandwidth. Hence, the 8-layer AlexNet hardware implementation on a Virtex 7 device is working concurrently in a pipeline structure achieving $565.94GOP/s$ with an energy consumption of $30.2W$.

While Li et al. used floating point operations, the authors of [44] used a data quantification strategy reducing the bit-width down to 8-bit without increasing the accuracy loss significantly. The data quantification strategy aims to search for radix point positions for each layer for a given bit-width while the CNN is still trained with floating point operations on a GPU. By producing a histogram of the logarithmic values of the feature maps, initial radix point positions are set. Then, a greedy strategy is used to optimize the positions layer by layer. After the best accuracy is achieved with a set of radix point positions, the CNN was fine-tuned converting back to floating point format. However, Guo et al. used a 24 bit-width to store intermediate data avoiding an increasing accuracy loss. Another major benefit of the architecture described in [44] is the fact, that this design is reconfigurable during runtime. The architecture supports kernel sizes of 1x1, 3x3 and 5x5. To configure the accelerator Guo et al. extend their previous work [45] with flexible set of instructions. Furthermore, a compiler is provided for mapping the network descriptor to the instructions. This compiler performs a set of optimizations to achieve a good computation communication ratio with the use of all available hardware resources. The coprocessor was tested with different CNNs such as GoogleNet, VGG-16 or

SquezzeNet achieving $137GOP/s$ on a Xilinx Zynq-7020 device with a power consumption of $3.5W$.

As a novel idea for improving the performance of the system, [46] presents the *Global Summation*, designed to minimize resource consumption on the latest layers in favor of the overall performance. In contrast, [47] presents several techniques to improve the control method of the process, among several improvements, for instance, it is important to mention the input reuse and the concatenation of data. The Input reuse, consists on extending the information to convolution modules even though if the amount of available ports is smaller than that of free convolution modules. Those convolution modules that have access to the port can share the information to those who are idle. The concatenation of data profits of the Q8.8 format. The Q8.8 format uses 16 bits in a 32 bitstream, so that 2 different data words can be transmitted in a unique stream.

Another approach is proposed in [48]. Yuan et al. design a coarse-grain array to accelerate the arithmetic operations. The basic unit of the hardware accelerator is the Neural Element (NE) including 9 multiplication and 1 adding operation units. This basic unit is optimized to convolve 3x3 kernels. Figure 6 shows the coarse grain array formed by 16 NEs, which are arranged to form a Configuration Neural Block (CNB). To reconfigure this array two configurable routing units are used, namely Filter conncetions (FCs) and Input Connections (ICs). As their name suggest, these switching ressources are responsible to route kernel weights and input data to their desired location. Furthermore, 5 adding operation units are placed adding the output of multiple different NEs. In this way other kernel sizes can be supported from 1x1 to 12x12. Additionally, the overall architecture owns 2 CNBs to further increase the parallelism. Like the authors of [45] Yuan et al. provide a compiler taking trade-offs due to the computation to communication ratio and on-chip resources into account to optimize the routing. However, this architecture does not fully utilize the on-chip resources applied to other kernel sizes than 3x3 like 5x5 due to its coarse grained nature. Although the non-used processing elements can be turned off during execution and the smart arrangement and routing are producing a low degree of overhead, the circuit of the coarse grain array cannot be reconfigured as this architecture is designed as an ASIC implementation under a TSMC 65nm CMOS process. The ASIC is clocked by 100MHz and achieve a peak performance of $57,6GOP/s$ with a power consumption of $107mW$.

ASIC-based approaches offer great performance and low power capabilities; however, they lack flexibility and have a larger design flow process. The approaches based on this platform are highly customized for an application. Under this category, [49] introduced $Eyeriss$, accelerator for deep CNNs that aims for energy efficiency. The accelerator consists on an SRAM buffer that stores input image data, filter weights and partial sums to allow fast reuse of loaded data. This data is streamed to a spatial array of 14x12 processing engines (PE), which compute inner products between the image and filter weights. Each PE consists on a pipeline of three stages that computes the inner product of the input image and filter weights of a single row of the filter. The PE also contains local scratch pads that allow temporal reuse of the input image and filter weights to save energy. There is also another scratch pad in charge of storing partial sums generated for different images, channels or filters, also with the aim of reusing data and saving energy. To optimize data movement, the authors also propose a set of input Network on Chips (NoC), for filter, image and partial sum values, where a single buffer read is used by multiple PEs. This approach was implemented in a $65nm$ CMOS, achieving a frame rate $44.8fps$ and a core frequency of $250MHz$.

The work in [50] proposes an analog-digital hybrid architecture for CNNs targeting image recognition applications, focusing on high performance at low power consumption. The architecture consists on a pulse-width modulation circuit to compute the most common operations of a CNN and a digital memory to store intermediate results. Additionally, the design makes use of a time-sharing technique to execute the operations required by all the connections of the network with the restricted number of processing circuits available in the chip. This architecture was implemented with a $0.35\mu m$ CMOS pieces. The paper reports an execution time of $5ms$ for a network with 81 neurons and 1620 synapses, an operation performance of $2GOPS$ and a power consumption of $20mW$ for the PWM neuron circuits and $190mW$ for the digital circuit block.

The work in [51] proposes Yodann, an ASIC architecture for ultra-low power binary-weight CNN acceleration. In this work, a binary-weight CNN is chosen for implementation because limiting a CNN's weights to only two values (+1/-1) avoids the need of expensive operations such as multiplications, which can be replaced by simpler complement operations and multiplexers, thus reducing weight storage requirements. This also has the advantage of reducing I/O operations. Moreover, this approach implements also a latch-based standard cell memory (SCM) architecture with clock-gating, which provide better voltage scalability and energy efficiency than SRAMs, at the cost of a higher area consumption. The architecture was implemented using UMC $65nm$ standard cells using a voltage range of $0.6V - 1.2V$. The article reports a maximum frequency of $480MHz$ at $1.2V$ and $27.5MHz$ at $0.6V$ and an area of 1.3 MGE (Million Gate Equivalent).

Recently, in February 2017, the company ST Microelectronics published a System-on-Chip (SoC) design in FD-SOI 28nm accelerating CNNs on embedded devices. Desoli et al. [52] achieved a theoretical peak performance of $676GOP/s$ with a peak efficiency of $2.9TOPS/W$ (Tera Operations Per Second/ Watt). The interesting components of this architecture are the hardware convolutional accelerators supporting kernel kompression and the on-chip reconfigurable data-transfer fabric. The data-transfer is managed by 10 fully configurable DMAs. Additionally, a configurable stream switch guides 53 input and 40 ouitput streams to their desired locations like one the eight Convolution Accelerators (CAs). Hence, the CAs can be arbitrarily chained. Therefore, a configurable accelerator framework is used in order to configure the SoC during design-time. The CA is equipped with 4 stream interfaces, namely feature stream input, kernel stream input, intermediate data stream input and an output stream. The feature line buffer can store up to 12 channels with up to 512 pixels and provides 36 read ports fetching data in parallel. Moreover, up to 484 kernels values can be stored inside the kernel buffer. Convolution is done by 36x16x16bit overlapping and column-based fixed-point MACs able to convolve 4 kernels in parallel followed by an adder tree. This design is able to consistently reuse available hardware ressources due to its fully scalable configuration. It is worth to mention that Desoli et al. complete the SoC with a set of extensions like pheripherals, high-speed interfaces for imaging and a chip-to-chip multilink in order to offer a basic platform for sophisticated image processing and to connect several devices to a bigger accelerator.

In the same year, the Envision architecture was presented by Moons et al. The authors of [53] focus on increasing the energy efficiency of their CNN hardware accelerator with the help of subword-parallel Dynamic-Voltage-Accuracy-Frequency Scaling (DVAFS) enabling Envision to achieve 10TOPS/W in 28nm FDSOI. Therefore, Moons et al. extend the principle of DVAS with reusing inactive arithmetic cells at reduced precision. As a result, frequency and voltage of the processor can be significantly decreased compared to DVAS.

Although ASIC implementations offer greater performance capabilities in combination with a lower energy consumption they lack in terms of flexibility. While homogenous networks are great for ASIC implementations, executing heterogeneous ones owning different kernel sizes and feature maps often lead to an inefficient use of the hardware or parallelism possiblities. Thus, the application of FPGAs can overcome this problem. While the above described architectures aim to be realized in future as hard wired coprocessors, the utilization of the FPGA serves as a rapid prototyping platform. The development of new variants of CNNs is rapid and is improved due to their specific applications. Thus, the size and structure of the network also can be adjusted to specific applications. As mentioned earlier in this section, HLS is a promising way to accelerate the design time of hardware accelerators. Additionally, newer HLS tools like Vivado HLS provide a methodology to perform design space exploration with the help of tcl-scripts automatically. This offers great possibilities to create frameworks automatically generating bitstreams executable on reconfigurable devices. Solazzo et al. propose a web-based framework in [54] interfacing directly with Vivado HLS. Although HLS synthesis is not complicated, the synthesis time can be huge. Hence, the main contribution of [54] is to predict the resource utilization of a given network configuration. Unfortunately, no optimization methodologies are used. The C/C++ language was not designed taking parallelism into account, though. Hence, OpenCL is more native way to describe parallelism. Xilinx also provide a HLS tool called SDAccel focusing on the synthesis of OpenCL code. DiCecco et al. use this tool in [55] to add FPGA support to the Caffe deep learning framework. While OpenCL support in Caffe is already given DiCecco et al. designed their OpenCL implementations to be suitable to many architectures rather than only GPUs. While optimizations are CNN specific and can be easily performed by the SDAccel tool DiCecco et al. focusing on the integration and synchronization of FPGA accelerators in Caffe. Hence, Wang et al. describe in their work [56] methods to improve CNN accelerators with the help of SDAccel and OpenCL optimizing the pipelining structure and level of parallelism. All the approaches described in this section aim to maximize the performance of CNNs by explot-ing the level of parallelism and bandwidth for computing the feedforward path of CNNS. However, the resulting architectures heavily depend on the available target hardware ressouces and the desired application CNN. The less ressources are available, the harder is the task of keeping intermediate data on the on-chip memory avoiding bottlenecks. Furthermore, the paralellism level is dependent on the amount of feature maps, which have to be evaluated. The roofline-model and the optimization exploration, which was described regarding CNN in [41], is a good baseline for evaluating custom CNN accelerators. In combination with data quantification techniques, discussed in [44], sophisticated routing methods [39] and embedding methodologies into common deep learning frameworks [56], hardware implementations, esspecially on FPGAs, of CNNs could become a promosing alternative to GPU CNN acclerators not only applied on embedded devices.

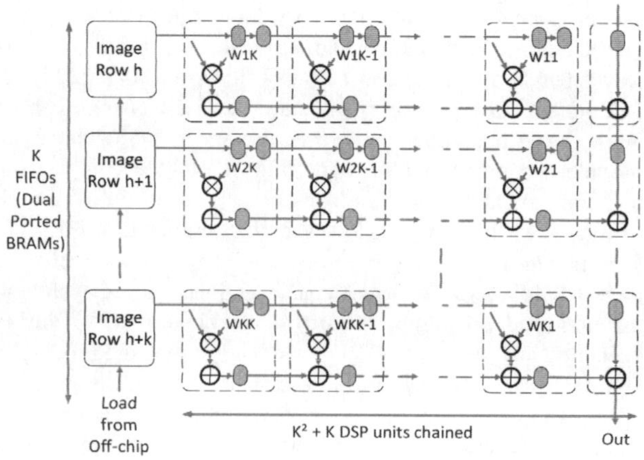

Fig. 5: A VPE array implementing the primitive 2D convolver unit by Sankaradas et al. [37].

V. Analysis of RNN Implementations on FPGAs

In general, similar to the optimizations regarding CNN implementations, two possibilities exist to increase the overall performance of RNNs regarding the inference phase on FP-GAs. However, due to the recursive structure of RNNs and the differences of the computations inside the neurons, the optimization has to be handled differently. On the one hand the computations, which must be done while passing the input through the network can be optimized. This includes adjusting

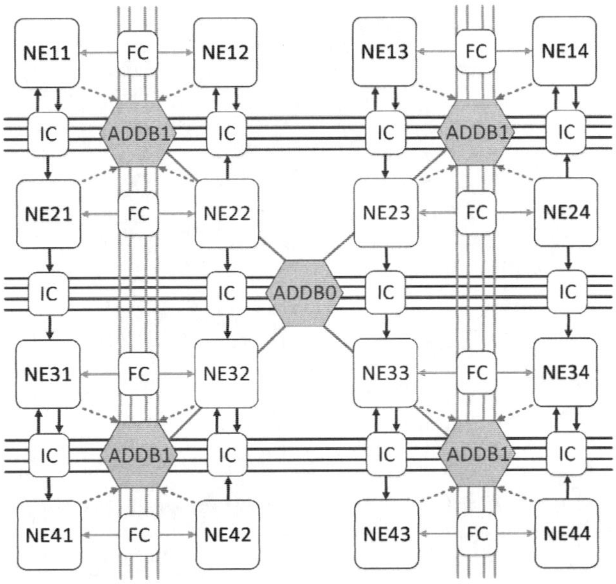

Fig. 6: Coarse grain array design to acclereate CNNs by Yuan et al. [48].

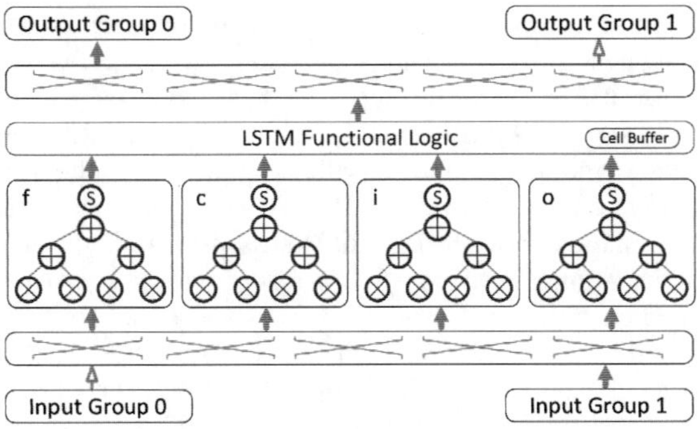

Fig. 7: Architecture of the accelerator for a LSTM-RNN proposed in [18].

the level of parallelism due to the hardware constraints, the choice of hardware accelerator module and approximations of computation, in case of an acceptable minimal loss of precision. On the other hand, the data communication, which includes weight parameters and inputs, between the FPGA and an external memory, like DRAM, can be optimized to improve the throughput. This is necessary because typically the FPGA on-chip-memory, BRAM or distributed memory, is too small to store all parameters of real-life RNNs. Thus, the developer of FPGA accelerators for RNNs have to consider both optimization paths. Moreover, to increase the overall performance both optimization paths must collaborate to avoid bottlenecks.

In [18], the authors focused on both optimization paths previously mentioned. Regarding the computation optimization, the authors profiled a typical LSTM-RNN inference structure and found out that the main bottleneck is caused by the computations, which mainly include floating point multiplication and addition, inside each LSTM gate. To optimize these operations, they split the computations in each gate into tiles, each of them carry out a portion of the inference process. Then, the execution among tiles is pipelined to optimize the throughput while the inner loops within each tile are unrolled and executed in parallel to improve the latency. The second most executed block of operations are the activation functions. These were replaced with a piecewise linear approximation of nonlinear function (PLAN), which was originally introduced by Amin et al. [57]. This approach consist of simple additions and shifting operations, which can be more efficiently implemented in hardware. This comes at a price of a small loss of accuracy, which can be ignored.

Regarding the optimization of communication requirements, the authors tackle the issue of irregular data access, which is caused by the transposition and tiling of the computation optimization described previously. This irregularity in the memory accesses causes a significant overhead on the communication between the DRAM and the FPGA. To solve this issue, the matrices used in the computations are modified offline in such a way that they can be accessed sequentially during the inference phase. Furthermore, 2 input buffers and 2 output sets of buffers working in a ping-pong fashion were added to further improve communication. Finally, a data dispatcher was added to maximize the the use of the bandwidth between the DRAM and the buffers.

To implement these optimization methods, they separated the computation scheme into four LSTM gate modules: the input, forget, cell and output. These models are shown in Figure 7. These modules receive tiled input vectors from the input buffers in parallel through a crossbar and carry out the inference process. The multiplications within this process are carried out in parallel within each LSTM gate module. Then, the results are summed up using an addition tree. the summed up results are delivered next to a *LSTM Functional Logic* module, which executes the remaining operations, such as element-wise multiplication, addition of gate vectors, activation, etc. Moreover, the current state of the LSTM cell is stored in a module called *Cell Buffer*. Finally, the complete results are sent to the output buffers through another crossbar. The Accelerator is designed with Vivado HLS and the system is implemented on a XILINX VC707 board with a Virtex7 FPGA chip. A DDR3 DRAM is used as external memory, which holds the parameters of the LSTM-RNN, as well as the inputs and outputs. A MicroBlaze processor is used to control the accelerator and to measure execution time. An AXI4 and an AXI4Lite are used for communication between the modules and to transfer commands, respectively. The evaluation shows that the system achieves a maximum performance of 7.26 GFLOP/s,

A different architecture is proposed by Chang et al. [58]. Like in the previously mentioned architecture, they focus on optimizing the operations of the LSTM inference process and the communication. The architecture of their approach is shown in Figure 8. This architecture has 3 LSTM gates, each of which carry out either an hyperbolic tangent or a logistic sigmoid function, and an element-wise multiplication module. Another similarity with the previous approach is the simplification of these functions, using piecewise linear approximation. This means, the functions where segmented into linear functions, i.e., $y = ax + b$, which are easier to be implemented on hardware. The values of each of these functions are stored offline in the Configuration Registers module. Each of these linear functions where implemented using a MAC operation and a comparator. In contrast to the previous design, Chang et al. [58] used fixed point 16-bit operations for MAC operations resulting in 32 bit values for further operations. While fixed-point computations are far more efficient for hardware implementations, a loss of accuracy has to be considered, which was denoted as a maximum of 7.1%. Furthermore, the gating computations are separated into two sequential steps. The input and cell gate computations are done in parallel as well as the output and forget gate computations. As a result, the output of the LSTM module is provided after 3 sequential steps. Thus, the coarse grained parallelism is not fully exploited. For communication optimization purposes, the authors of [58] use a combination of memory mapping and streaming interface. Therefore, four direct memory access (DMA) cores are used to access the external DRAM and reshape the data to be forwarded through 8 AXI4-Stream modules, which activity depends on the current routing, and are buffered with FIFOs. In comparison to the communication architecture presented by Guan et al. [18], the methodology is equal but the differences in implementation details are mainly arise because of the different coarse grained parallelism of the LSTM accelerator. The design is implemented on a Zedboard with Zynq 7020 FPGA from Xilinx. The architecture was tested with a character level language model, which, given a character from a text as input, it predicts the next character. The network consisted of 2 LSTM cells, each of which including 128 hidden units, and running with a frequency of $142MHz$. The performance was outlined to 264.4 million operations per second.

Lee et al. [30] used two LSTM-RNNs to build a speech recognition system. The general structure of the system is shown in Figure 9. The system uses a LSTM-RNN for acoustic modeling and another one for character-level modeling. The acoustic modeling LSTM-RNN analyzes the input speech and calculates the probability of occurrence of each character. The character-level modeling LSTM-RNN calculates the probability of the occurrence of each character given a previous one. Similarly, another language model calculates the probabilities at the word level. Finally, these results are combined using the N-best search algorithm.

Figure 10 shows the hardware architecture that implements this system. The architecture has a LSTM cell and an output tile, which are used intermittently for the acoustic modeling and for the character-level modeling operations, according to a control signal. The output of the LSTM cell is stored in a

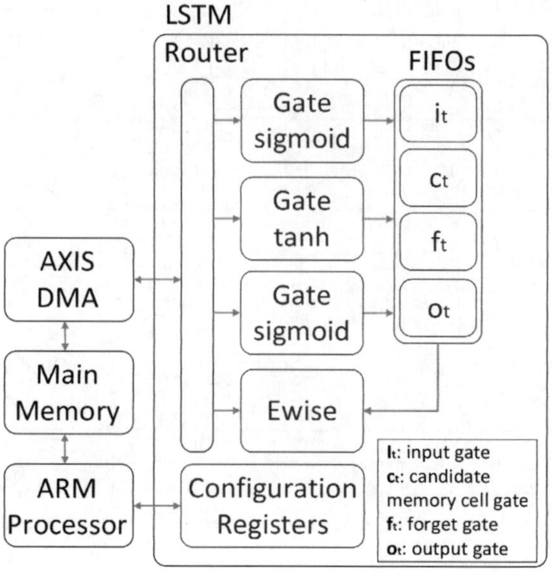

Fig. 8: Block diagram of the accelerator for a LSTM-RNN proposed in [58].

context memory, and is used in the next block of operations and by the N-best search algorithm.

In contrast to [58] and [18], the authors of [30] use a retrained based method to reduce the word-length of the weights. As a result, they achieve a quantification to 6 bits per weight. Due to this fact, for the desired speech recognition application all weight parameters can be stored on the on-chip-memory (BRAM) of the XC7Z045 FGPA device from Xilinx without loss of precision differences of retraining and hardware implemented inference computation. Without the requirement to optimize the communication from an external DRAM the focus of this work is the accelerator module optimization. Although the proposed LSTM accelerator module is separated into two different modules, the parallelism and task granularity differs from those proposed in [18] and [58]. All matrix-vector multiplications are computed inside one (PE) array, which consist of 512 PEs. The remaining computations including evaluating activation functions are done using an additional block called Extra Processing Unit (EPU). The outputs of the PE array are buffered and forwarded to the LSTM EPU. As mentioned above, the design benefits from a high level of fine-grained parallelism. However, the architecture is not comparable to the other design as no communication bottleneck has to be handled and the authors focus on the optimization of the whole speech recognition algorithm while considering real-time constraints for the desired application.

Besides, Ferreira et al. [59] follow a modular extensible architecture, they assume a similar reduction of communication complexity as assumed in [30]. A diagram of the architecture is shown in Figure 11. In contrast to [30] the word-length of the weights are 18 bits, which leads to a high

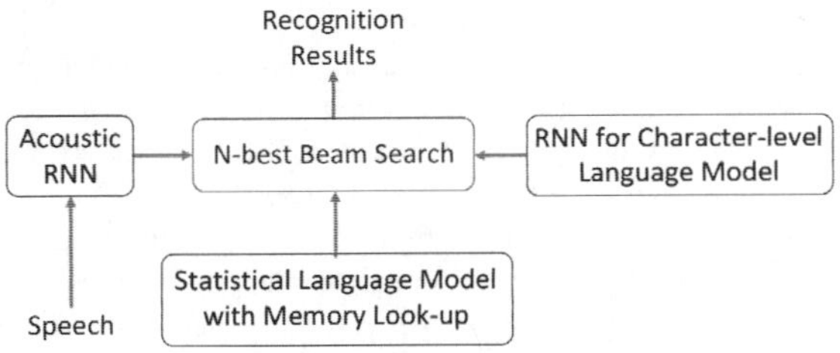

Fig. 9: Speech recognition system proposed in [30].

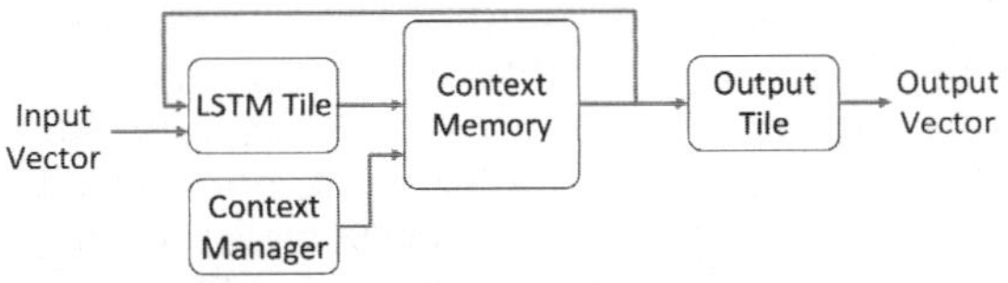

Fig. 10: Hardware architecture for the speech recognition system shown in Figure 8, as proposed in [30].

utilization of the DSP48E1 slices of the FPGA, and they are stored in LUTRAM. On the one hand, this distributed memory represents the fasted way of accessing the weights due to the physical closeness to the accelerator and the unlimited simultaneous port access to each LUTRAM array. In contrast BRAM supports a maximum of two port access. On the other hand, this method consumes a high amount of resources especially when the implemented network consists of many layers and LSTM-tiles. The architecture does not explore full parallelism in a coarse-grained manner. The matrix-vector multiplications are done in parallel for all four gates. Instead of directly implementing the activation functions $tanh()$ and $sigmoid()$, polynomial approximations where carried out, in order to find equivalent polynomials within an acceptable error range. The strategy Least Maximum Approximation was used to find the optimal polynomial for each activation funtion. Due to the negligible small amount of additional clock cycles needed for elementwise multiplication and polynomial approximations of $tanh()$ and $sigmoid()$, each of these computations where carried out in one single hardware module. The gate outputs are forwarded to a multiplexer and further routed to the desired hardware module. The design was implemented on a Xilinx XC 7Z020SoC device with different amounts of neurons per layer. The network size is not allowed to extend 31 neurons per layer due to the limited number of DSP-slices on the device. The frequency of the hardware accelerator was adjusted to the maximum with respect to the layer size. Thus, the design is capable achieving 4534.8 MOP/s, which is 17 times more than the performance reached in [58].

Han et al. [60] proposed a hardware accelerator for a speech recognition system based on LSTM-RNNs, which involves a compression method that significantly decreases the LSTM-RNN's size while keeping an acceptable accuracy. The compression method consists on pruning and quantization. The pruning is carried out by removing the weights from

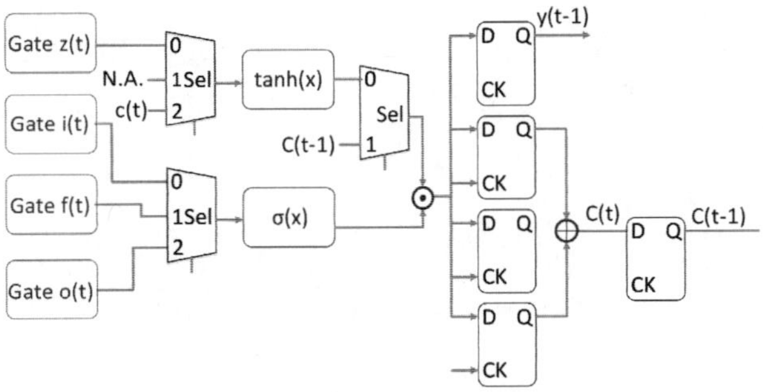

Fig. 11: Hardware architecture LSTM-RNN as proposed by Ferreira et al. [59].

the LSTM-RNN that do not contribute to the prediction accuracy. Moreover, the linear quantization strategy was used to generate weights represented by 12bit integers instead of 32 bit floating point values. Then, the compressed LSTM-RNN is implemented in hardware. A general diagram of the architecture is shown in Figure 12. Unlike the work presented in [30], where all weight parameters can be stored in on-chip memory due to a 6-bit quantization, the 12-bit quantization of this work made it necessary to store this data in external memory. Two 4GB DDR3 DRAMs where used for this purpose. Similar to [18], input and output buffers where used in a ping pong manner such that the communication and the computation are overlapped. Furthermore, this approach differentiates from the ones previously described by implementing modules, called channels, each of which can process a voice vector independently. Each channel consists of several Process Elements (PE), which carry out the inference process of the LSTM-RNN. Besides the usual challenges that implementing a LSTM-RNN on hardware implies, the pruning method used in the compression process introduces the problem of dealing with sparse matrices. To deal with this issue, a PE called Activation Vector Queue (ActQueue) is used to balance the workload among the rest of the PEs. The ActQueue PE consists of several FIFOs, which store elements from the input voice vector, and delivers the input elements to the PEs across all the channels, such that fast PEs are not blocked by slower ones. Furthermore, similarly to the approaches already described, linear approximations where used to implement the activation functions, and the matrix multiplication operations where carried out in parallel within a PE. The system was evaluated with a XILINX XCKU060 FPGA running at a frequency of $200MHz$ and compared against a software approach. The experimental results showed a throughput of $282GOP/s$

Li et al. [61] addressed the problematic of developing a proper model to approximate or evaluate the probabilities of finding out the next word in a sentence. They affirm that RNN is one of the best suited approaches to deal with this topic, on behalf of statistical methods such as n-gram finding or decision trees. They mentioned that, although RNN are more complex, need higher computation capabilities and long training times,

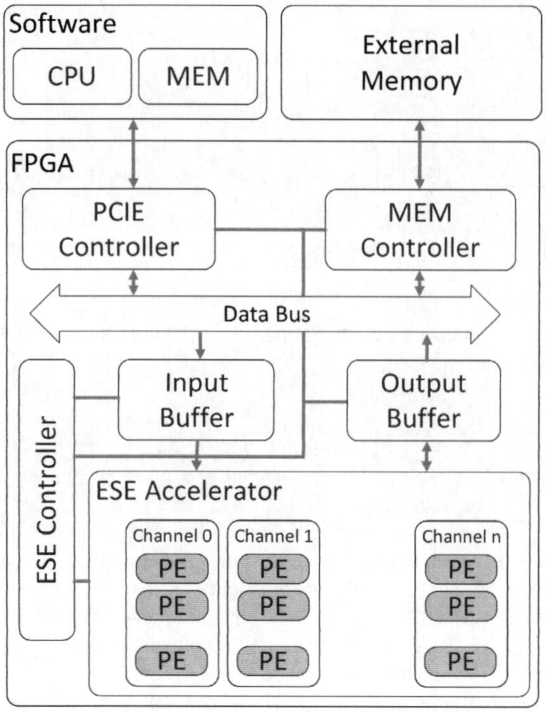

Fig. 12: Hardware accelerator for speech recognition system, with multiple channels for multiple voice vectors [60].

the results are more reliable since they can consider previous states and thus create a dependency model.

These computational shortcomings can be handled with the use of hardware approaches and hence they develop a model for FPGA acceleration. They delegate the starting and initialization of the weights and the acceleration system to the CPU of the host system. For the memory, they use an external memory, with 16 Dual Inline Memory (DIM) Modules and 1024 banks. These characteristics are profitable since the bank conflicts turn to be low. They also implement an Application Engine Hub (AEH) to manage the instructions from the host.

The PE are associated in major sets the computational Engines (CE). These CEs are separated into two classes with the only difference in the activation function. The first class is for the hidden layers, all PE in the hidden layers belong to this first class. The second class is dedicated to the output layer, and here the PEs are grouped in one of the many CE. The authors affirm that these characteristics are suited for expanding the number of PEs, depending on the requirements.

Previous approaches require the utilization of an on board-Block RAM, which the authors of [61] try to avoid in their approach. Therefore, they came up with the idea to utilize a hardware supported multithreading architecture, generating a thread for a defined matrix operation. The PEs are in charge of processing dedicated operations of a major task, that is, each task is separated in threads that are processed by the PEs.

As mentioned before, the CE is the manager of the memory accesses and can fetch information as needed or in a burst mode, in addition, this model has the advantage of data reuse by storing results either on a weight register or in a bias register. This is useful for the stage where the PEs are ready to start with the activation function processing.

Using these hardware configuration, Li et al. [61] affirm they obtain an improvement on the parallelism between layers presented on a previous paper and also the computation efficiency, in this matter, a fixed-point data conversion is used, under the premise that NN handle and correct the imprecisions of a truncation by themselves.

The authors also compared the performance with a multi-core CPU and a GPU. The CPU had 12 cores at a frequency of 2.3GHz, while the GPU 512 cores at 772MHz. The frequency for the FPGA was 150MHz. As expected, the GPU turned out to be the one with the lesser execution time, while the CPU the one that required more time. The energy analysis showed another perspective, where the FPGA was the one consuming less energy and the GPU turned second with a consumption level as high as almost 7 times the FPGA.

Renteria-Cedano et al. [62] investigate on an special type of NN: the Nonlinear Auto-Regressive Exogenous networks (NARX), which they state that they have been shown to converge much faster than other implementations of RNN. They implement the NARX network over an FPGA using only one hidden level, thus having a total of three layers, with the goal of linearizing microwave power amplifiers.

The authors present the hardware implementation where the PEs are able to carry out the operations necessary: multiply, add, accumulate and activation function. The flow starts when the information is provided to the PE, this process is according to its internal parameters, the multiplication afterwards is done in parallel. Finally, after the addition of the bias, the selected activation function, the hyperbolic tangent on a Taylor series implementation, takes place for those PE in the hidden layer. It is also important to mention that the authors used floating point for every operation and the general management of the NN is done according to Mealy type finite state Machine.

Another variation of a RNN is the Hopfield Network. Atencia et al. [63] recognize the benefits of implementing this type of network on FPGAs, since, as they mention, concurrency is an own characteristic of these networks and at the same time, they have a reduced number of neurons, which suits the capabilities of the state of the art for FPGAs at the time they developed their research. In this approach, a neuron consist of a RAM linked directly to a MAC, from this point the data is feed forwarded to a substractor, a multiplier, an accumulator and finally to the activation function before it is outputted and processed by a multiplexer. The weights for each neuron are calculated in an external software and stored in the neurons memory, these weights are then supplied as operands to a MAC together with a status value provided from the multiplexer. The next step is a bias substraction, its multiplication by the discretized value of the ordinary differential equation characteristic of Hopfield networks and the addition to a previous state value, finally the activation

TABLE I: COMPARISON OF IMPLEMENTATION APPROACHES

Approach	Device	Power [W]	Performance	Type
Sankaradas et al.[37]	Virtex-5	11	3.37 GMAC/s	CNN
Jin et al.[39]	Zynq-7000	4	40 GOP/s	CNN
Zhou et al.[40]	Virtex-7	n/a	3.75 GMAC/s	CNN
Zhang et al.[41]	Virtex-7	18.61	61.62 GFLOPS	CNN
Li et al.[46]	Virtex-7	30.2	565.94 GOP/s	CNN
Guo et al.[44]	Zynq 7020	3.5	n/a	CNN
Guan et al.[18]	VC707	20	7.26 GFLOP/s	RNN
Chang et al.[58]	Zynq 7020	2	0.264 GOP/s	RNN
Ferreira et al.[59]	Zynq 7020	2	4.538 GOP/s	RNN
Han et al.[60]	Kintex	41	282 GOP/s	RNN
	UltraScale	41	282 GOP/s	RNN
Li et al.[61]	Virtex-6	25	9. 6GOP/s	RNN

function is enforced with a LUT representing the tanh() function.

All the approaches described in this section aimed to maximize the performance of RNNs by parallelizing key operations of the inference phase of the network. Although the matrix operations carried out by RNNs are highly parallelizable with custom hardware architectures, there are still issues, which are still not solved entirely. The main issues we found were the representation of the RNN's parameters and the memory bottleneck, which are interrelated. For instance, [30] avoided the use of external memory by using 6 bit integers to represent the LSTM-RNN's parameters. While in that case the loss of accuracy brought by this quantization was deemed acceptable, this is highly dependent on the application and input data. Furthermore, whenever external memory was used, a special scheme had to be developed, such as ping-pong buffers, in order to minimize the bottleneck.

VI. Conclusion

As outlined in the previous sections, there are many possibilities to accelerate CNNs or RNNs with the help of hardware modules. Each of these hardware implementations have a significant speedup in comparison to a CPU implementation. From our perspective, there are several reasons making a fair comparison of all hardware architectures not possible. One of the reasons for that is, that the size of the networks mostly depends on the application as well as the real-time constraints. The analysis in Section IV and Section V focuses on benefits or deficits regarding the acceleration performance derived from architectural similarities and differences rather than comparing numbers. Table I summarizes the measurable dimensions of the CNN and RNN implementations on different FPGA architectures.

However, in our opinion, presenting only a comparison of quality metrics such as performance or throughput would not show a complete view of the advantages and drawbacks of each approach. For instance, the performance of almost all described hardware accelerators can be improved with simple approaches, like increasing the number of processing elements and bandwidth. Thus, an important influence factor of the FPGA prototypical architectures is the underlying platform. However, the FPGA technology and HLS support is improving rapidly. While the FPGA prototypical architectures and ASIC designs aim to low energy consumption on embedded devices reusing static processing blocks, future work should exploit the hardware reconfiguration capabilities of FPGAs in order to further increase flexibility needed regarding different layer types and sizes. It is also worth to mention that the combination of RNNs and CNNs, called RCNNs [64] (not to be confused with R-CNNs, which is Region based CNNs for object localization), is a promising approach improving the accuracy of object and scene detection. For example, the platform proposed in 2017 by Shin et al. [65] combines a CNN and a RNN in a single configurable processor to harness the advantages from both networks: the image recognition capabilities from the CNNs and the ability to recognize sequential dependencies between the data from the RNNs. This combination, however, brings new challenges, since their hardware requirements can be very different. For instance, the convolutional layers of CNNs require a large number of operations over a relatively small number of weights, while LSTM cells require a smaller number of operations over a much larger number of parameters.

Finally, in the industrial environment, is of relevance to mention that Google's Cloud Tensor Processing Unit (TPU)[66] is a viable alternative for accelerating NN implementations to those presented in this article. These TPUs are ASICs designed especially for machine learning applications, and according to Google, have been used successfully on different projects, e.g., Alpha Go or Street View.

Acknowledgment

This work was done under support of CONACyT (Grant 359472).

References

[1] J. Hoffmann, O. Navarro, F. Kästner, B. Janssen, and M. Hübner, "A survey on cnn and rnn implementations," in *PESARO 2017, The Seventh International Conference on Performance, Safety and Robustness in Complex Systems and Applications*, 2017.

[2] A. Krizhevsky, I. Sutskever, and G. E. Hinton, "Imagenet classification with deep convolutional neural networks," in *Advances in Neural Information Processing Systems 25*, F. Pereira, C. J. C. Burges, L. Bottou, and K. Q. Weinberger, Eds. Curran Associates, Inc., 2012, pp. 1097–1105.

[3] I. Goodfellow, Y. Bengio, and A. Courville, *Deep Learning*. MIT Press, 2016.

[4] W. Zhao, S. Du, and W. J. Emery, "Object-based convolutional neural network for high-resolution imagery classification," *IEEE Journal of Selected Topics in Applied Earth Observations and Remote Sensing*, vol. PP, no. 99, pp. 1–11, 2017.

[5] H. J. Jeong, M. J. Lee, and Y. G. Ha, "Integrated learning system for object recognition from images based on convolutional neural network," in *2016 International Conference on Computational Science and Computational Intelligence (CSCI)*, Dec 2016, pp. 824–828.

[6] T. He and J. Droppo, "Exploiting lstm structure in deep neural networks for speech recognition," in *2016 IEEE International Conference on Acoustics, Speech and Signal Processing (ICASSP)*, March 2016, pp. 5445–5449.

[7] Y. Jia, E. Shelhamer, J. Donahue, S. Karayev, J. Long, R. Girshick, S. Guadarrama, and T. Darrell, "Caffe: Convolutional architecture for fast feature embedding," in *Proceedings of the 22nd ACM international conference on Multimedia*. ACM, 2014, pp. 675–678.

[8] Theano Development Team, "Theano: A Python framework for fast computation of mathematical expressions," *arXiv e-prints*, vol. abs/1605.02688, May 2016.

[9] M. Abadi, A. Agarwal, P. Barham, E. Brevdo, Z. Chen, C. Citro, G. S. Corrado, A. Davis, J. Dean, M. Devin, S. Ghemawat, I. Goodfellow, A. Harp, G. Irving, M. Isard, Y. Jia, R. Jozefowicz, L. Kaiser, M. Kudlur, J. Levenberg, D. Mané, R. Monga, S. Moore, D. Murray, C. Olah, M. Schuster, J. Shlens, B. Steiner, I. Sutskever, K. Talwar, P. Tucker, V. Vanhoucke, V. Vasudevan, F. Viégas, O. Vinyals, P. Warden, M. Wattenberg, M. Wicke, Y. Yu, and X. Zheng, "TensorFlow: Large-scale machine learning on heterogeneous systems," 2015, software available from tensorflow.org.

[10] S. Chetlur, C. Woolley, P. Vandermersch, J. Cohen, J. Tran, B. Catanzaro, and E. Shelhamer, "cudnn: Efficient primitives for deep learning," *arXiv preprint arXiv:1410.0759*, 2014.

[11] S. Barrachina, M. Castillo, F. D. Igual, R. Mayo, and E. S. Quintana-Orti, "Evaluation and tuning of the level 3 cublas for graphics processors," in *2008 IEEE International Symposium on Parallel and Distributed Processing*, April 2008, pp. 1–8.

[12] Y. Sugomori, *Java Deep Learning Essentials.* Packt Publishing Ltd., 2016.

[13] A. Krizhevsky, I. Sutskever, and G. E. Hinton, "Imagenet classification with deep convolutional neural networks," Web site: http://papers.nips.cc/paper/4824-imagenet-classification-with-deep-convolutional-neural-networks.pdf [Last accessed: 24 September 2017], pp. 1097–1105, 2012.

[14] K. Simonyan and A. Zisserman, "Very deep convolutional networks for large-scale image recognition," *CoRR*, vol. abs/1409.1556, 2014. [Online]. Available: http://arxiv.org/abs/1409.1556

[15] C. Szegedy, W. Liu, Y. Jia, P. Sermanet, S. E. Reed, D. Anguelov, D. Erhan, V. Vanhoucke, and A. Rabinovich, "Going deeper with convolutions," Web site: http://dblp.uni-trier.de/rec/bib/journals/corr/SzegedyLJSRAEVR14[Last accessed: 21 September 2017], 2014.

[16] K. He, X. Zhang, S. Ren, and J. Sun, "Deep residual learning for image recognition," http://arxiv.org/abs/1512.03385 [Last accessed:7 June 2017], 2015.

[17] Y. Bengio, P. Simard, and P. Frasconi, "Learning long-term dependencies with gradient descent is difficult," *IEEE Transactions on Neural Networks*, vol. 5, no. 2, pp. 157–166, Mar 1994.

[18] Y. Guan, Z. Yuan, G. Sun, and J. Cong, "Fpga-based accelerator for long short-term memory recurrent neural networks," in *2017 22nd Asia and South Pacific Design Automation Conference (ASP-DAC)*, Jan 2017, pp. 629–634.

[19] S. Hochreiter and J. Schmidhuber, "Long short-term memory," *Neural Computation*, vol. 9, no. 8, pp. 1735–1780, Nov 1997.

[20] J. Chung, Ç. Gülçehre, K. Cho, and Y. Bengio, "Empirical evaluation of gated recurrent neural networks on sequence modeling," *CoRR*, vol. abs/1412.3555, 2014.

[21] J. Schmidhuber, "Deep learning in neural networks: An overview," *CoRR*, vol. abs/1404.7828, 2014.

[22] Z. C. Lipton, "A critical review of recurrent neural networks for sequence learning," Web site: http://arxiv.org/abs/1506.00019 [Last accessed: 12 September 2017], 2015.

[23] J. J. Hopfield, "Neural networks and physical systems with emergent collective computational abilities," *Proceedings of the National Academy of Sciences*, vol. 79, no. 8, pp. 2554–2558, 1982, accessed: 09 Jun 2017. [Online]. Available: http://www.pnas.org/content/79/8/2554.abstract

[24] L. C. Jain and L. R. Medsker, *Recurrent Neural Networks: Design and Applications.* CRC Press, Inc., 2001.

[25] Y. Bengio, R. D. Mori, G. Flammia, and R. Kompe, "Global optimization of a neural network-hidden markov model hybrid," *IEEE Transactions on Neural Networks*, vol. 3, no. 2, pp. 252–259, Mar 1992.

[26] R. Pascanu, T. Mikolov, and Y. Bengio, "On the difficulty of training Recurrent Neural Networks," http://adsabs.harvard.edu/abs/2012arXiv1211.5063P [Last accessed: 21 September 2017], Nov. 2012.

[27] M. Schuster and K. K. Paliwal, "Bidirectional recurrent neural networks," *IEEE Transactions on Signal Processing*, vol. 45, no. 11, pp. 2673–2681, Nov 1997.

[28] K. Cho, B. van Merrienboer, Ç. Gülçehre, F. Bougares, H. Schwenk, and Y. Bengio, "Learning phrase representations using RNN encoder-decoder for statistical machine translation," Web site: http://arxiv.org/abs/1406.1078 [Last accessed: 13 September 2017], 2014.

[29] A. K. Jain, D. L. Maskell, and S. A. Fahmy, "Are coarse-grained overlays ready for general purpose application acceleration on fpgas?" in *2016 IEEE 14th Intl Conf on Dependable, Autonomic and Secure Computing, 14th Intl Conf on Pervasive Intelligence and Computing, 2nd Intl Conf on Big Data Intelligence and Computing and Cyber Science and Technology Congress(DASC/PiCom/DataCom/CyberSciTech)*, Aug 2016, pp. 586–593.

[30] M. Lee, K. Hwang, J. Park, S. Choi, S. Shin, and W. Sung, "Fpga-based low-power speech recognition with recurrent neural networks," in *2016 IEEE International Workshop on Signal Processing Systems (SiPS)*, Oct 2016, pp. 230–235.

[31] M. Al Kadi, B. Janssen, and M. Huebner, "Fgpu: An simt-architecture for fpgas," Web site: http://doi.acm.org/10.1145/2847263.2847273 [Last accessed: 20 September 2017], New York, NY, USA, pp. 254–263, 2016.

[32] E. Nurvitadhi, J. Sim, D. Sheffield, A. Mishra, S. Krishnan, and D. Marr, "Accelerating recurrent neural networks in analytics servers: Comparison of fpga, cpu, gpu, and asic," in *2016 26th International Conference on Field Programmable Logic and Applications (FPL)*, Aug 2016, pp. 1–4.

[33] E. Nurvitadhi, G. Venkatesh, J. Sim, D. Marr, R. Huang, J. Ong Gee Hock, Y. T. Liew, K. Srivatsan, D. Moss, S. Subhaschandra, and G. Boudoukh, "Can fpgas beat gpus in accelerating next-generation deep neural networks?" in *Proceedings of the 2017 ACM/SIGDA International Symposium on Field-Programmable Gate Arrays*, ser. FPGA '17. New York, NY, USA: ACM, 2017, pp. 5–14.

[34] (2017, Sep.) Opencl 1.2 specification. version: 1.2. document revision: 19. Web site: http://www.khronos.org/registry/OpenCL/specs/opencl-1.2.pdf [Last accessed: 16 September 2017].

[35] (2017, Sep.) Stratix 10 gx/sx device overview. version: S10-overview 2016.10.31. Web site: https://www.altera.com/en_US/pdfs/literature/hb/stratix-10/s10-overview.pdf [Last accessed: 15 September 2017].

[36] (2017, Sep.) Ultrascale architecture and product data sheet: Overview. v2.11. Web site: http://arxiv.org/abs/1506.00019 [Last accessed: 12 September 2017]. [Online]. Available: https://www.xilinx.com/support/documentation/data_sheets/ds890-ultrascale-overview.pdf

[37] M. Sankaradas, V. Jakkula, S. Cadambi, S. Chakradhar, I. Durdanovic, E. Cosatto, and H. P. Graf, "A massively parallel coprocessor for convolutional neural networks," in *2009 20th IEEE International Conference on Application-specific Systems, Architectures and Processors*, July 2009, pp. 53–60.

[38] R. Doshi, K. W. Hung, L. Liang, and K. H. Chiu, "Deep learning neural networks optimization using hardware cost penalty," in *2016 IEEE International Symposium on Circuits and Systems (ISCAS)*, May 2016, pp. 1954–1957.

[39] J. Jin, V. Gokhale, A. Dundar, B. Krishnamurthy, B. Martini, and E. Culurciello, "An efficient implementation of deep convolutional neural networks on a mobile coprocessor," in *2014 IEEE 57th International Midwest Symposium on Circuits and Systems (MWSCAS)*, Aug 2014, pp. 133–136.

[40] Y. Zhou and J. Jiang, "An fpga-based accelerator implementation for deep convolutional neural networks," in *2015 4th International Conference on Computer Science and Network Technology (ICCSNT)*, vol. 01, Dec 2015, pp. 829–832.

[41] C. Zhang, P. Li, G. Sun, Y. Guan, B. Xiao, and J. Cong, "Optimizing fpga-based accelerator design for deep convolutional neural networks," in *Proceedings of the 2015 ACM/SIGDA International Symposium on Field-Programmable Gate Arrays*, ser. FPGA '15. New York, NY, USA: ACM, 2015, pp. 161–170.

[42] S. Williams, A. Waterman, and D. Patterson, "Roofline: An insightful visual performance model for multicore architectures," *Commun. ACM*, vol. 52, no. 4, pp. 65–76, Apr. 2009.

[43] H. Li, X. Fan, L. Jiao, W. Cao, X. Zhou, and L. Wang, "A high performance fpga-based accelerator for large-scale convolutional neural networks," in *2016 26th International Conference on Field Programmable Logic and Applications (FPL)*, Aug 2016, pp. 1–9.

[44] K. Guo, L. Sui, J. Qiu, J. Yu, J. Wang, S. Yao, S. Han, Y. Wang, and H. Yang, "Angel-eye: A complete design flow for mapping cnn onto embedded fpga," *IEEE Transactions on Computer-Aided Design of Integrated Circuits and Systems*, vol. PP, no. 99, pp. 1–1, 2017.

[45] J. Qiu, J. Wang, S. Yao, K. Guo, B. Li, E. Zhou, J. Yu, T. Tang, N. Xu, S. Song, Y. Wang, and H. Yang, "Going deeper with embedded fpga

platform for convolutional neural network," in *Proceedings of the 2016 ACM/SIGDA International Symposium on Field-Programmable Gate Arrays*, ser. FPGA '16. New York, NY, USA: ACM, 2016, pp. 26–35.

[46] N. Li, S. Takaki, Y. Tomiokay, and H. Kitazawa, "A multistage dataflow implementation of a deep convolutional neural network based on fpga for high-speed object recognition," in *2016 IEEE Southwest Symposium on Image Analysis and Interpretation (SSIAI)*, March 2016, pp. 165–168.

[47] A. Dundar, J. Jin, B. Martini, and E. Culurciello, "Embedded streaming deep neural networks accelerator with applications," *IEEE Transactions on Neural Networks and Learning Systems*, vol. PP, no. 99, pp. 1–12, 2016.

[48] Z. Yuan, Y. Liu, J. Yue, J. Li, and H. Yang, "Coral: Coarse-grained reconfigurable architecture for convolutional neural networks," in *2017 IEEE/ACM International Symposium on Low Power Electronics and Design (ISLPED)*, July 2017, pp. 1–6.

[49] Y.-H. Chen, T. Krishna, J. S. Emer, and V. Sze, "Eyeriss: An energy-efficient reconfigurable accelerator for deep convolutional neural networks," *IEEE Journal of Solid-State Circuits*, vol. 52, no. 1, pp. 127–138, 2017.

[50] K. Korekado, T. Morie, O. Nomura, H. Ando, T. Nakano, M. Matsugu, and A. Iwata, "A convolutional neural network vlsi for image recognition using merged/mixed analog-digital architecture," in *Knowledge-Based Intelligent Information and Engineering Systems*. Springer, 2003, pp. 169–176.

[51] R. Andri, L. Cavigelli, D. Rossi, and L. Benini, "Yodann: An architecture for ultra-low power binary-weight cnn acceleration," *IEEE Transactions on Computer-Aided Design of Integrated Circuits and Systems*, 2017.

[52] G. Desoli, N. Chawla, T. Boesch, S. p. Singh, E. Guidetti, F. D. Ambroggi, T. Majo, P. Zambotti, M. Ayodhyawasi, H. Singh, and N. Aggarwal, "14.1 a 2.9tops/w deep convolutional neural network soc in fd-soi 28nm for intelligent embedded systems," in *2017 IEEE International Solid-State Circuits Conference (ISSCC)*, Feb 2017, pp. 238–239.

[53] B. Moons, R. Uytterhoeven, W. Dehaene, and M. Verhelst, "14.5 envision: A 0.26-to-10tops/w subword-parallel dynamic-voltage-accuracy-frequency-scalable convolutional neural network processor in 28nm fdsoi," in *2017 IEEE International Solid-State Circuits Conference (ISSCC)*, Feb 2017, pp. 246–247.

[54] A. Solazzo, E. D. Sozzo, I. D. Rose, M. D. Silvestri, G. C. Durelli, and M. D. Santambrogio, "Hardware design automation of convolutional neural networks," in *2016 IEEE Computer Society Annual Symposium on VLSI (ISVLSI)*, July 2016, pp. 224–229.

[55] R. DiCecco, G. Lacey, J. Vasiljevic, P. Chow, G. Taylor, and S. Areibi, "Caffeinated fpgas: Fpga framework for convolutional neural networks," in *2016 International Conference on Field-Programmable Technology (FPT)*, Dec 2016, pp. 265–268.

[56] Z. Wang, F. Qiao, Z. Liu, Y. Shan, X. Zhou, L. Luo, and H. Yang, "Optimizing convolutional neural network on fpga under heterogeneous computing framework with opencl," in *2016 IEEE Region 10 Conference (TENCON)*, Nov 2016, pp. 3433–3438.

[57] H. Amin, K. M. Curtis, and B. R. Hayes-Gill, "Piecewise linear approximation applied to nonlinear function of a neural network," *IEE Proceedings - Circuits, Devices and Systems*, vol. 144, no. 6, pp. 313–317, Dec 1997.

[58] E. C. Andre Xian Ming Chang, Berin Martini, "Recurrent neural networks hardware implementation on fpga," in *arXiv preprint arXiv:1511.05552*, 2015.

[59] J. C. Ferreira and J. Fonseca, "An fpga implementation of a long short-term memory neural network," in *2016 International Conference on ReConFigurable Computing and FPGAs (ReConFig)*, Nov 2016, pp. 1–8.

[60] S. Han, J. Kang, H. Mao, Y. Hu, X. Li, Y. Li, D. Xie, H. Luo, S. Yao, Y. Wang *et al.*, "Ese: Efficient speech recognition engine with sparse lstm on fpga." in *FPGA*, 2017, pp. 75–84.

[61] S. Li, C. Wu, H. Li, B. Li, Y. Wang, and Q. Qiu, "Fpga acceleration of recurrent neural network based language model," in *2015 IEEE 23rd Annual International Symposium on Field-Programmable Custom Computing Machines*, May 2015, pp. 111–118.

[62] J. A. Renteria-Cedano, L. M. Aguilar-Lobo, J. R. Loo-Yau, and S. Ortega-Cisneros, "Implementation of a narx neural network in a fpga for modeling the inverse characteristics of power amplifiers," in *2014 IEEE 57th International Midwest Symposium on Circuits and Systems (MWSCAS)*, Aug 2014, pp. 209–212.

[63] M. Atencia, H. Boumeridja, G. Joya, F. Garca-Lagos, and F. Sandoval, "Fpga implementation of a systems identification module based upon hopfield networks," *Neurocomputing*, vol. 70, no. 16, pp. 2828 – 2835, 2007, neural Network Applications in Electrical Engineering Selected papers from the 3rd International Work-Conference on Artificial Neural Networks (IWANN 2005).

[64] M. Liang and X. Hu, "Recurrent convolutional neural network for object recognition," in *2015 IEEE Conference on Computer Vision and Pattern Recognition (CVPR)*, June 2015, pp. 3367–3375.

[65] D. Shin, J. Lee, J. Lee, and H. J. Yoo, "14.2 dnpu: An 8.1tops/w reconfigurable cnn-rnn processor for general-purpose deep neural networks," in *2017 IEEE International Solid-State Circuits Conference (ISSCC)*, Feb 2017, pp. 240–241.

[66] Google, "Google tpu alpha," Web site: https://cloud.google.com/tpu/ [Last accessed: 4 September 2017], Sept 2017.

A Model-Driven Approach for Configurable Evaluation of Traceability Information

Hendrik Bünder

itemis AG,
Bonn, Germany
Email: buender@itemis.de

***Abstract*—Requirement traceability is the ability to explicate and pursue the relations between all artifacts that specify, implement, test, or document a software solution. Besides being required by laws and regulations in safety-critical industries, the traceability information models can give insight on project progress and quality. Yet, only a few companies are utilizing this competitive advantage due to missing tool support. The paper introduces an integrated solution to define and execute company- or project-specific analysis statements written in a dedicated domain-specific language. First, the capabilities of the Traceability Analysis Language are demonstrated by defining coverage, impact and consistency analysis. Every analysis is defined as a rule expression that compares a customizable metric's value (aggregated from the traceability information model) against an individual threshold. The focus of the Traceability Analysis Language is to make the definition and execution of information aggregation and evaluation from a traceability information model configurable and thereby allow users to define their own analyses based on their regulatory, project-specific, or individual needs. Further, the analyses are applied to a model according to the Automotive Software Process Improvement and Capability Determination (A-SPICE) standard. Second, the underlying grammar, as well as the mechanisms to make data retrieval configurable, are explained. Finally, the paper reports on case study findings at a tier one automotive supplier company. The case study revealed that the possibility to introduce custom data retrieval functions is crucial in real-world scenarios. Further, the case study showed that the traceability analysis language supported the tier one automotive supplier in the process of being A-SPICE re-certified.**

Keywords*–*Traceability; Domain-Specific Language; Software Metrics; Model-driven Software Development; Xtext.

I. Introduction

The paper builds upon previous work [1] and elaborates on the specification of the query language, additional configuration options, and extended case study results. While the initial contribution was focusing on configurable analysis expressions utilizing the rule, metric and grammar language, this works extends the approach by introducing custom data retrieval functions. Additionally, the paper elaborates on the grammar of the query language. Finally, detailed findings from the case study at a tier one automotive supplier are explained. In addition to analyzing the runtime behavior of the analysis statements, the results of the case study include a detailed analysis of the different user groups, their information needs, and how the traceability analysis language (TAL) was utilized to satisfy these needs.

Traceability is the ability to describe and follow an artifact and all its linked artifacts through its whole life in forward and backward direction [2]. Although many companies create traceability information models for their software development activities either because they are obligated by regulations [3] or because it is prescribed by process maturity models, there is a lack of support for the analysis of such models [4].

On the one hand, recent research describes how to define and query traceability information models [5][6]. This is an essential prerequisite for retrieving specific trace information from a Traceability Information Model. However, far too little attention has been paid to taking advantage of further processing the gathered trace information. In particular, information retrieved from a traceability information model (TIM) can be aggregated in order to support software development and project management activities with a real-time overview of the state of development.

On the other hand, research has been done on defining relevant metrics for TIMs [7], but the corresponding data collection process is non-configurable. As a result, potential analyses are limited to predefined questions and cannot provide comprehensive answers to ad hoc or recurring information needs. For example, projects using an iterative software development approach might be interested in the achievement of objectives within each development phase, whereas other projects might focus on a comprehensive documentation along the process of creating and modifying software artifacts.

The approach presented in this paper fills the gap between both areas by introducing the Traceability Analysis Language. By defining coverage, impact, and consistency analyses for a model based on the Automotive Software Process Improvement and Capability Determination standard. Use cases for the Traceability Analysis Language features are exemplified. Analyses are specified as rule expressions that compare individual metrics to specified thresholds. The underlying metrics values are computed by evaluating metrics expressions that offer functionalities to aggregate results of a query statement.

The TAL comes with an interpreter implementation for each part of the language, so that rule, metric, and query expressions cannot only be defined, but can also be executed against a traceability information model. More specifically, the analysis language is based on a traceability metamodel defining the abstract artifact types that are relevant within the development process. All TAL expressions therefore target the structural characteristics of the TIM.

In addition to elaborating on potential use cases for the TAL, the paper reports on first industrial experience. The case study was executed at a tier one automotive supplier where the TAL was used in 5 projects. Further, the users where categorized in three groups and their specific traceability information needs were analyzed. The TAL, its interpreter, and the graphical user interface integration were tested with these user groups to meet their information requirements.

The contributions of this paper are threefold: first, it provides a domain-specific Traceability Analysis Language to define rules, metrics, and queries in a fully configurable and integrated way. Second, it demonstrates the feasibility of this work with a prototypical interpreter implementation for real-time evaluation of those trace analyses. In addition, it illustrates the TAL's capabilities in the context of the A-SPICE standard and reports on extended results from a case study in the automotive sector.

Having discussed related work in Section II, Section III presents the capabilities of the TAL by exemplifying impact, coverage, and consistency analyses. In Section IV the underlying grammar for rule, metrics, and query definitions and their expected runtime behavior are explained. Section V reports on extended findings from a case study conducted at a tier one automotive supplier. In Section VI, the language, the prototypical implementation, and case study results are discussed before the paper concludes in Section VII.

II. Related Work

Requirements traceability is essential for the verification of the progress and completeness of a software implementation [8]. While, e.g., in the aviation or medical industry traceability is prescribed by law [3], there are also process maturity models requesting a certain level of traceability [9].

Traceable artifacts such as *Software Requirement*, *Software Unit*, or *Test Specification*, and the links between those such as *details*, *implements*, and *tests* constitute the TIM [10]. Retrieving traceability information and establishing a TIM is beyond the scope of this paper and approaches for standardization such as [11] have already been researched.

In contrast to the high effort that is made to create and maintain a TIM, only a fraction of practitioners takes advantage of the inherent information [3]. However, Rempel and Mäder (2015) have shown that the number of related requirements or the average distance between related requirements have a positive correlation with the number of defects associated with this requirement. Traceability models not only ease maintenance tasks and the evolution of software systems [12] but can also support analyses in diverse fields of software engineering such as development practices, product quality, or productivity [13]. In addition, other model-driven domains, such as variability management in software product lines, benefit from traceability information [14].

Due to the lack of sophisticated tool support, these opportunities are often missed [4]. On the one hand, query languages for TIMs have been researched extensively, including Traceability Query Language (TQL) [5], Visual Trace Modeling Language (VTML) [6], and Traceability Representation Language (TRL) [15]. On the other hand, traceability tools mostly offer a predefined set of evaluations, often with simple tree or matrix views, e.g., [16]. Hence, especially company- or project-specific information regarding software quality and project progress cannot be retrieved and remains unused.

Our approach integrates both fields of research using a textual domain-specific language DSL [17] that is focused on describing customized rule, metric and query expressions. In contrast to the Traceability Metamodelling Language [18] defining a domain-specific configuration of traceable artifacts, the work builds on a model regarding the specification of type-safe expressions and for deriving the scope of available elements from concrete TIM instances.

III. An Integrated Traceability Analysis Language

The capabilities of the TAL will be demonstrated by defining analyses from the categories of coverage, impact and consistency analysis as introduced by the A-SPICE standard [19]. In addition to these rather static analyses, there are also traceability analyses focusing on data mining techniques as introduced by [13]. Even though some of these could be defined using the introduced domain-specific language, they remain out of scope of this paper.

A. Scenarios for Traceability Analyses

The first scenario focuses on measuring the impact of the alteration of one or more artifacts on the whole system [20]. Recent research has shown that artifacts with a high number of trace links are more likely to cause bugs when they are changed [7]. Moreover, the impact analysis can be a good basis for the estimation of the costs of changing a certain part of the software. This estimation then not only includes the costs of implementing the change itself, but also the effort needed to adjust and test the dependent components [21].

The second scenario appears to be the most common, since many TIM analyses are concerned with verifying that a certain path and subsequently a particular coverage is given, e.g., "*are all requirements covered by a test case*" or "*have all test cases a link to a positive test result*" [4]. In addition to verifying that certain paths are available within a TIM, coverage metrics are mostly concerned with the identification of missing paths [10].

The third use case describes the consistency between traceable artifacts. Besides ensuring that all requirements are implemented, consistency analyses should also ensure that there are no unrequested changes to the implementation [22]. Consistency is generally required between all artifacts within a TIM in accordance to the Traceability Information Configuration Model (TICM), so that all required trace links for the traced artifacts are available [19].

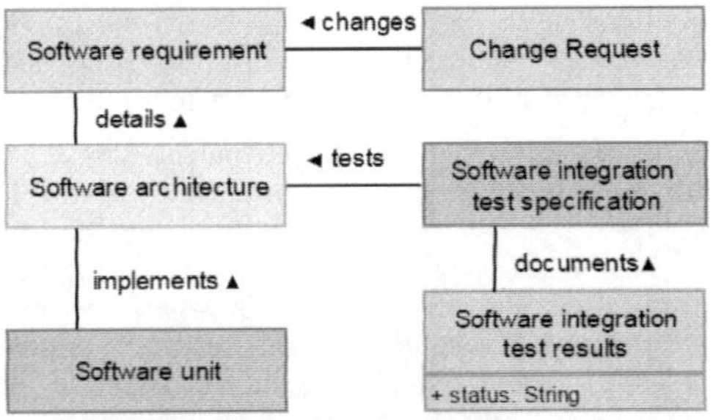

Figure 1. Traceability Information Configuration Model.

Figure 1 shows a simplified TICM based on the A-SPICE standard [19] that defines the traceable artifact types *Change Request, Software Requirement, Software Architecture, Software Unit, Software Integration Test Specification*, and *Software Integration Test Result*. Also, the link types *changes, details, implements, tests*, and *documents* are specified by the configuration model. The arrowheads in Figure 1 represent

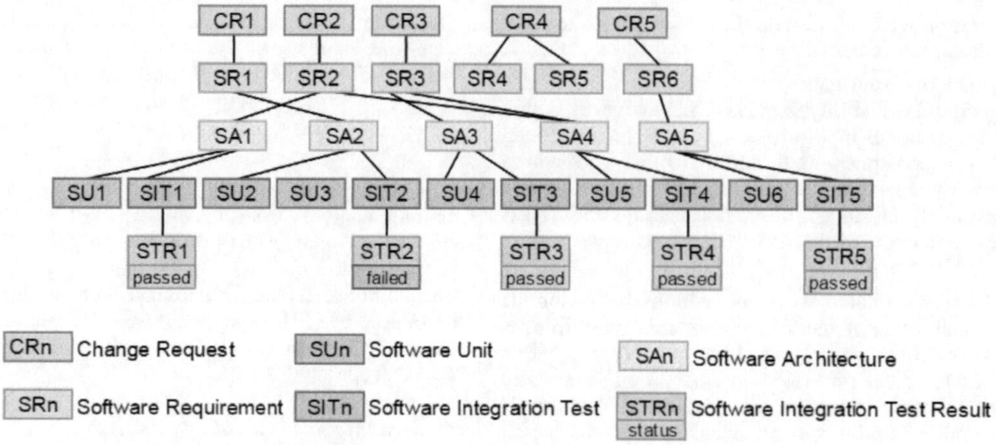

Figure 2. Sample Traceability Information Model.

the primary trace link direction, however, trace links can be traversed in both directions [23]. The traceable artifact *Software Integration Test Result* also defines a customizable attribute called "status" that holds the actual result.

Considering the triad of economic, technical, and social problem space, the flexibility to adapt to existing work practices increases the productivity of a traceability solution [24]. Therefore, configuration models provide the abstract description of traced artifact types in a company context. A TIM captures the concrete artifact representations and their relationships according to such a TICM and constitutes the basis for the analyses (cf. Section IV).

Figure 2 shows a traceability information model based on the sample TICM described above. The TIM contains multiple instances of the classes defined in the TICM that can be understood as proxies of the original artifacts. Those artifacts may be of different format, e.g., Word, Excel or Class files. Within the traceability software, adapters can be configured to parse an artifact's content and create a traceable proxy object in accordance to the TICM. In addition, the underlying traceability software product offers the possibility to enhance the proxy objects with customizable attributes. The *Software Integration Test Result* from Figure 1, for example, holds the actual result of the test case in the customizable attribute "status".

1) Impact Analysis: The impact analysis shown in Figure 3 checks the number of related requirements (NRR) [7] starting from every *Software Requirement* by using the aggregated results of a metric expression, which is based on a query. The analysis begins after the *rule* keyword that is followed by an arbitrary name. The right hand side of the equation specifies the severity of breaking the rule stated in the parentheses. In this case, a rule breach will lead to a warning message with the text in quotation marks. The most important part of the analysis is the comparison part that specifies the threshold, which in this case is a number of related requirements greater than 2. If the metrics' value is greater, the warning message will be returned as a result of the analysis.

The second component of the TAL expression is the metric expression that in this case, counts the related requirements. Each metric is introduced by the keyword *metric*, again followed

```
result relatedReqs =
  tracesFrom Software Requirement to Software Requirement
  collect(start.name ->srcRequirement,
          end.name    -> trgtRequirement)
metric NRR = count(relatedReqs.srcRequirement)
rule NRRWarning = warnIf(NRR>2, "A high number of related
     software requirements could provoke errors.")
```

Figure 3. Metric: Number of related requirements (NRR).

by an arbitrary name, which is used to reference a metric either from another metric or from a rule as shown in Figure 3. The expression uses the *count* function to compute the number of related requirements. The *count* function takes a column reference to count all rows that have the same value in the given column. In the metric expression shown above, all traces from one *Software Requirement* to a *Software Requirement* have the name of the source *Software Requirement* in their first column, so that the *count* function will count all traces per *Software Requirement*. As shown in Table I, the result of the metric evaluation is a tabular data structure with always two columns. The first holds the source artifact and the second column holds the evaluated metric value. For the given example, the first column holds the name of each *Software Requirement* and the second column contains the evaluated number of directly and indirectly referenced *Software Requirements*.

TABLE I. NRR METRIC: TABULAR RESULT STRUCTURE.

Software Requirement	*NRR*
SR1	0
SR2	2
SR3	2
SR4	1
SR5	1
SR6	1

Finally, the metric is based on a query expression that is used to retrieve information from the underlying TIM. The *tracesFrom... to...* function returns all paths between source and target artifact passed into the function as parameters. In comparison to expressing this statement in other query languages such as Structured Query Language (SQL), no knowledge about the potential paths between the source and target artifacts in the TIM is needed.

Figure 3 shows that the columns of the tabular result structure are defined in the brackets after the keyword *collect*. In the first column the name of the *Software Requirement* of each path is given and in the second column the name of each target *Software Requirement* is given. Both columns can contain the same artifacts multiple times, but the combination of each target with each source artifact is only contained once.

2) Coverage Analysis: Figure 4 shows a coverage analysis that is concerned with the number of related test case results per software requirement. In contrast to the analysis shown in Figure 3, it introduces two new concepts.

```
result tracesSwReqToTestResult =
  tracesFrom Software Requirement
  to         Software Integration Test Result
  collect(start.name-> name, count(1)-> tcrs)
  where(end.status = "passed")
  groupBy(name)
rule lowTC = warnIf(tracesSwReqToTestResult.tcrs < 2,
"Low number of test results!")
rule noTC = errorIf(tracesSwReqToTestResult.tcrs < 1,
  "No test results found!")
```

Figure 4. Software Requirement Test Result Coverage Analysis.

First, the analysis is not dependent on a metric expression, but directly bound to a query result. Since metric and query expression results are returned in the same tabular structure, rules can be applied to both. Second, the analysis shown in Figure 4 demonstrates the concept of a staggered analysis, i.e., one column or metric is referenced once from a warning and error rule, respectively. The rule interpreter will recognize this construct and will return the analysis result with the highest severity, e.g., when the error rule applies, the warning rule message is omitted. The rules shown above ensure that the test of each *Software Requirement* is documented by at least one test result. However, to fulfill the rule completely, each *Software Requirement* should be covered by two *Software Integration Tests* and subsequently two *Software Integration Test Results*.

TABLE II. COVERAGE ANALYSIS: TABULAR RESULT STRUCTURE.

Software Requirement	*Analysis Result*
SR1	No test results found!
SR2	Ok
SR3	Ok
SR4	No test results found!
SR5	No test results found!
SR6	Low number of test results!

Table II shows the result of the staggered analysis. The test coverage analysis returns an "Ok" message for two of the six *Software Requirements*, while one is marked with a warning message and the remaining three caused an error message.

The query expressions result is limited to *Software Integration Test Results* with status "passed" by evaluating the customizable attribute "status" using a *where* clause. Since the query language offers some functions to do basic aggregation, it is possible to bypass metric expressions in this case. In Figure 4 the aggregation is done by the *groupBy* and the *count* function. The second column specifies an aggregation function that counts all entries in a given column per row based on the column name passed as parameter. In general, the result of this function will be 1 per row since there is only one value per row and column but in combination with the "groupBy" function the number of aggregated values per cell is computed. The resulting tabular structure contains one row per *Software Requirement* with the respective name and the cumulated number of traces to different Software Integration Test Results as columns.

3) Consistency Analysis: The following will show two consistency analysis samples to verify that all *Software Requirements* are linked to at least one *Software Unit* and vice versa.

```
result consistetSrcTrgt =
  tracesFrom Software Requirement to Software Unit
  collect(start.name ->name, count(1)-> targets)
  groupBy(name)
rule notCoveredError = errorIf(swUnits<1, "The software
    requirement is not implemented.")
```

Figure 5. Consistency Analysis.

Figure 5 shows a consistency analysis composed of a rule and a query expression. The rule *notCoveredError* returns an error message if the number of traces between *Software Requirements* and *Software Units* is smaller than one, which means that the particular *Software Requirements* is not implemented.

TABLE III. CONSISTENCY ANALYSIS: SOFTWARE REQUIREMENT IMPLEMENTATION.

Name	*Analysis Result*
SR1	Ok
SR2	Ok
SR3	Ok
SR4	The Software Requirement is not implemented!
SR5	The Software Requirement is not implemented!
SR6	Ok

Table III shows the result of the analysis as defined in Figure 5. For "SR4" and "SR5" there is no trace to a *Software Unit* so that the analysis marks these two with an error message. To verify that all implemented *Software Units* are requested by a *Software Requirement*, the query can easily be altered by switching the parameters of the "tracesFrom... to..." function and by changing the error message. Table IV shows the result of the altered analysis revealing that "SU3" despite all others has not been requested.

TABLE IV. CONSISTENCY ANALYSIS: SOFTWARE UNIT REQUESTED.

Name	*Analysis Result*
SU1	Ok
SU2	Ok
SU3	The Software Requirement has not been requested!
SU4	Ok
SU5	Ok
SU6	Ok

These examples show that the language offers extensive support for retrieving and aggregating information in TIMs. The following sections will demonstrate how the TAL integrates with the traceability solution it is build upon, and how the different parts of the language are defined.

IV. COMPOSITION OF THE TRACEABILITY ANALYSIS LANGUAGE

The following focuses on the technical foundations of the TAL. After giving an overview over the modeling layers the paper continues on elaborating the grammar definitions of query, metrics and analysis language.

A. Modeling Layers

Figure 6 shows the integration between the different model layers referred to in this paper, starting from the *Eclipse Ecore Model* as shared meta meta model [25]. The Xtext framework, which is used to define the analysis language generates an instance of this model [26] to represent the *Analysis Language Meta Model* (ALMM). Individual queries, metrics, and rules are specified within a concrete instance, the *Analysis Language Model* (ALM), using the created domain-specific language. An interpreter was implemented using Xtend, a Java extension developed as part of the Xtext framework and specially designed to navigate and interact with the analysis language's Eclipse Ecore models [27].

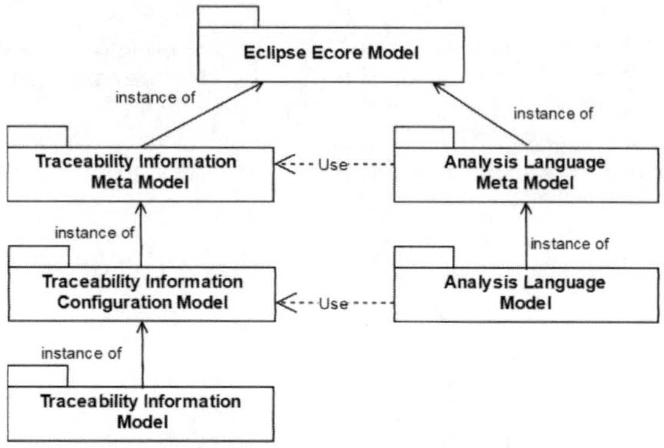

Figure 6. Conceptual Integration of Model Layers.

Likewise, the *Traceability Information Model* used in this paper contains the actual traceability information, for example the concrete software requirement *SR1*. It is again an instance of a formal abstract description, the so called TICM. The TICM describes traceable artifact types, e.g., *Software Requirement* or *Software Architecture*, and the available link types, e.g., *details*. This model itself is based on a proprietary *Traceability Information Meta Model* (TIMM) defining the basic traceability constructs such as an artifact type and link type. To structure the DSL, the TAL itself is hierarchically subdivided into three components, namely rule, metric, and query expressions.

B. Rule Grammar

Since a query result or a metric value alone delivers few insights into the quality or the progress of a project, rule expressions are the main part of the TAL. Only by comparing the metric value to a pre-defined threshold or another metrics' value information is exposed. The grammar contains rules for standard comparison operations, which are *equal, not equal, greater than, smaller than, greater or equals*, and *smaller or equals*. A rule expression can either return a warning or an error result after executing the comparison including an individual message. Since query and metrics result descriptions implement the same tabular result interface, rules can be applied to both. Accordingly, the result of an evaluated rule expression is also stored using the same tabular interface.

```
WarnIf = ID '=' 'warnIf(' RuleBody ')';
RuleBody = (MetricDefinition | ResultDeclaration '.' Column)
     Operator RuleAtomic ',' MESSAGE;
```

Figure 7. Rule Grammar.

The *RuleBody* rule shown in Figure 7 is the central part of the rule grammar. On the left side of the *Operator* a metric expression or a column from a query expression result can be referenced. The next part of the rule is the comparison *Operator* followed by a *RuleAtomic* value to compare the expression to. The *RuleAtomic* value is either a constant number or a reference to another metrics expression.

C. Metrics Grammar

Complimentary to recent research that focuses on specific traceability metrics and their meaningfulness [7], the approach described in this paper allows for the definition of individual metrics. An extended Backus-Naur form (EBNF)-like Xtext grammar defines the available features including arithmetic operations, operator precedence using parentheses, and the integration of query expressions. The metrics grammar of the TAL itself has two main components. One is the *ResultDeclaration* that encapsulates the result of a previously specified query. The other is an arbitrary number of metrics definitions that may aggregate query results or other metrics recursively.

```
MetricDefinition = 'metric' ID '=' MetricExpression;

MetricExpression = Term  { ('+' | '-') Term};
Term = Factor { ('*' | '/') Factor};
Factor = SumFunction | CountFunction | LengthFunction |
     DOUBLE | ColumnSelection | MetricDefinition | '('
     MetricExpression ')' ;
```

Figure 8. Grammar rules for metrics expressions.

Figure 8 shows a part of the metric grammar defining the support for the basic four arithmetic operations as well as the correct use of parentheses. Since the corresponding parser generated by Another Tool for Language Recognition (ANTLR) works top-down, the grammar must not be left recursive [28]. First, the rule *Factor* allows for the usage of constant double values. Second, metric expressions can contain pre-defined functions such as sum, length, or count to be applied to the results of a query. Third, columns from the result of a query can be referenced so that metric expressions per query expression result row can be computed. Finally, metric expressions can refer to other metric expressions to further aggregate already accumulated values. Thereby, interpreting metric expressions can be modularized to reuse intermediate metrics and to ensure maintainability.

The metrics grammar as part of the TAL defines arithmetic operations that aggregate the results of an interpreted query expression. The combination of a configurable query expressions with configurable metric definitions allows users to define their individual metrics.

D. Query Grammar

The analyses defined using metric and rule expressions depend on the result of a query that retrieves the raw data from the underlying TIM. Although there are many existing query languages available, a proprietary implementation is currently used because of three reasons.

First, the query language should reuse the types from TICM to enable live validation of analyses even before they are executed. The Xtext-based implementation offers easy mechanisms to satisfy this requirement, while others such as SQL are evaluated only at runtime. Second, some of the existing query languages such as SQL or Language Integrated

Query (LINQ) are too verbose (cf. Figure 11) or do not offer predefined functions to query graphs. Finally, other languages such as SEMMLE QL [29] or RASCAL [30] are focused on source code analyses and do not interact well with Eclipse Modeling Framework (EMF) models.

```
Query:
 ('result' ID)? QFeatureCall QCollect? QWhere? QGroupBy?;

QFeatureCall:
ID ( '(' (ID (',' ID)* )? ')')?;

QCollect:
'collect' '('QMemberFeatureCall(',' QMemberFeatureCall)*')';

QWhere:
 'where' '(' QCompareExpression (('AND'|'OR')
      QCompareExpression)* ')';

QGroupBy:
'groupBy' '('QMemberFeatureCall(',' QMemberFeatureCall)*')';

QMemberFeatureCall:
ID ('.' ID)* '->' ID;

QCompareExpression:
ID ('='|'!='|'<'|'>'|'>='|'<=') ID;
```

Figure 9. Query Language Grammar.

In Figure 9, a slightly simplified grammar of the Query language in Extended Backus-Naur Form (EBNF) is shown. The postfix operators "?" and "*" indicate optional and arbitrarily repeated features, respectively. "|" divides alternatives. Terminal symbols appear in single quotes. The grammar first shows the `Query` rule that may contain `QFeatureCall, QCollect, QWhere, QGroupBy` statements.

The `QFeatureCall` rule contains the ID of the function to be called followed by the expected parameters in parenthesis. While the grammar itself looks very simple, the real benefit comes from using the Xtext language workbench. During definition of a query expression, Xtexts ScopeProvider looks for functions that are visibile (or "in scope") for the analysis. The ProposalProvider takes the visible elements and creates a proposal for each function within the editor.

By default, the Traceability Analysis Language comes with pre-defined functions such as `tracesFromTo, artifactsWithoutTraceFromTo, or linkedArtifacts`. In addition, it is possible to implement company-, or project-specific functions. For such a function to be proposed in the editor, a certain interface has to implemented. Further, as Figure 10 shows, annotations are used to classify the function.

```
@FunctionType(priority = 200, type = ARTIFACT)
public Iterable<TVMDArtifact> notLinkedArtifacts(
 @ScopeSource(ALL_ARTIFACT_TYPES) @ScopeType(TYPE_INSTANCE)
     TVMCArtifactType type) {
  return ...
}
```

Figure 10. Sample Function. Returning all not linked artifacts.

First, the annotation in Figure 10 states the `priority` and the `type`. The `priority` parameter manages the execution in case of multiple function calls at a time. The `type` determines, which kind of elements are returned. A function may return instances of elements from the traceability configuration model, such as *Artifact* or *Link*. The latter annotation attribute is evaluated by Scope- and ProposalProvider in order to avoid invalid analysis statements. Second, the method itself has to return a typed iterable that contains the result of the graph traversal. Finally, every parameter of a function has to be detailed in order to enable rich user experience through the calculated scope and proposals. `ScopeSource` specifies if the particular parameter is either from the traceability configuration model or a query result that is further processed. `ScopeType` determines if a meta-model type or an instance of such is returned.

The defined interface, allows for custom functions to be seamlessly integrated into the existing set of query functions. The underlying framework can offer the same editor support as for pre-defined functions, because the custom functions are detailed in terms of parameters, return types, and priority.

After having explained the `QFeatureCall` and its underlying concepts, the following will demonstrate the remaining query grammar. The `QCollect` defines the columns of a query result and contains an arbitrary number of `QMemberFeatureCalls`. Each `QMemberFeatureCall` defines one column by calling methods on the `QFeatureCall` result (cf. Figure 5). After potentially defining a chain of method calls, the result can be assigned to a variable after the keyword —>.

The so defined columns can be re-used in the subsequent `QWhere` and `QGroupBy` statements. The where-clause filters the result of a function called through a `QFeatureCall`. After the keyword *where* an arbitrary number of `QComparisonExpressions` follow that support binary comparison operations. In order to filter based on multiple criteria the comparison statements can be combined with the logical operators `AND` and `OR`. In addition, the result can be further aggregated using `QGroupBy`. Following the keyword *groupBy* a list of attributes is stated as criteria for grouping the result. The query grammar includes many concepts and language support for data retrieval and aggregation. However, more specialized aggregations such as calculating averages or medians the metrics grammar was created.

The query expressions offer a powerful and well-integrated mechanism to retrieve information from a given TIM. Especially, the integration with the traceability information configuration model enables the reuse of already known terms such as the trace artifact type names. Furthermore, complex graph traversals are completely hidden from the user who only specifies the traceable source and target artifact based on the TICM. For example, the concise query of Figure 4 already requires a complex statement when expressed in SQL syntax (cf. Figure 11). If the graph traversal functions included in the TAL are not sufficient, custom functions can be implemented to do specific or more complex data retrieval.

```
SELECT r.name, count(u.id) AS tcrs
FROM SwRequirement r
INNER JOIN SwRequirement_SwArchitecture ra ON r.id=ra.r_id
INNER JOIN SwArchitecture a ON ra.a_id=a.id
INNER JOIN SwArchitecture_SwIntegrationTest ai
  ON a.id=ai.a_id
INNER JOIN SwIntegrationTest i ON ai.i_id=i.id
INNER JOIN SwIntegrationTest_SwIntegrationTestResult it
  ON i.id=it.i_id
INNER JOIN SwIntegrationTestResult t ON it.t_id=t.id
WHERE t.status='passed'
GROUP BY r.name;
```

Figure 11. SQL equivalent to query of Figure 4.

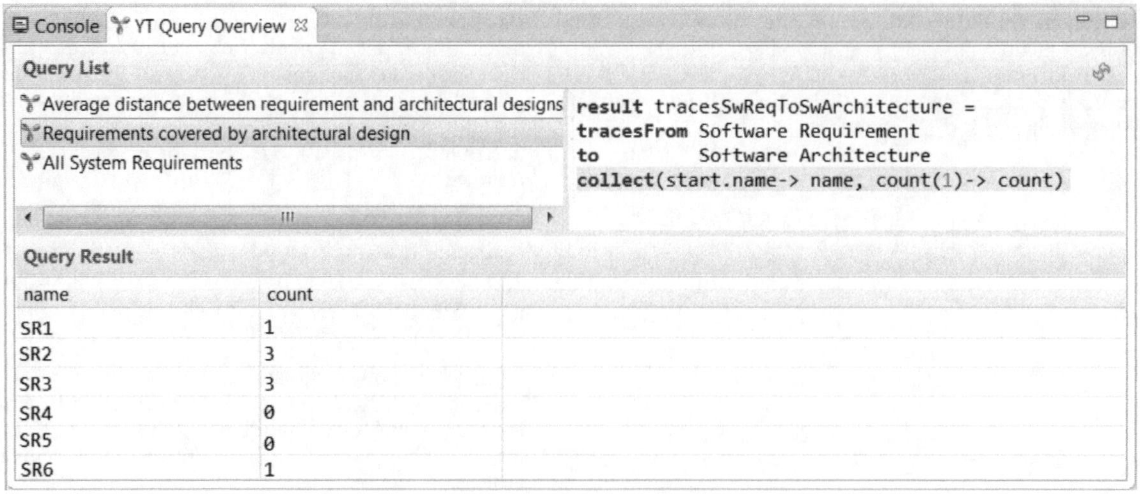

Figure 12. Screenshot of the analysis language interpreter.

E. Performance

Within the prototypical implementation, traceable artifacts from custom traceability information configuration models as shown in Figure 1 can be used for query, metrics, and rule definitions. Due to an efficient implementation used by the *tracesFrom... to...* function, analysis are re-executed immediately when an analysis is saved or can be triggered from a menu entry. The efficiency of the depth-first algorithm implementation was verified by interpreting expressions using TIMs ranging from 1,000 to 50,000 artificially created traceable artifacts. The underlying TICM was build according to the traceable artifact definitions of the A-SPICE standard [19].

TABLE V. DURATION OF TAL EVALUATION.

Artifacts	*Start Artifacts*	*Duration (in s)*
1,000	300	0.012
8,000	1,500	0.1
50,000	8,500	2.2

Table V shows the duration for interpreting the analysis expression from Figure 4 against TIMs of different sizes. The first column shows the overall number of traceable artifacts and links in the TIM. The second column gives the number of start artifacts for the depth-first algorithm implementation, i.e., the number of *Software Requirements* for the exemplary analysis expression. The third column contains the execution time on an Intel Core i7-4700MQ processor at 2.4 GHz and 16 GB RAM. As shown, executing expressions can be done efficiently even for large size models, sufficient for real-world applications to regular reporting and ad hoc analysis purposes.

The efficient implementation of the depth-first algorithm allows for re-execution on every save. However, it also add the constraints to all custom functions to be highly efficient. Additionally implemented functions with long execution times will have a negative effect on user experience and finally on the TAL at all.

V. CASE STUDY

Besides theoretical usage scenarios for the TAL, first experiences in real-world projects were gained with a tier one automotive supplier. The Traceability Analysis Language was used in five projects with TIMs ranging from 30,000 to 80,000 traceable artifacts defined in accordance to the Automotive SPICE standard.

To demonstrate the feasibility of the designed TAL and perform flexible evaluations of traceability information models, a prototype was developed. The analysis language is based on the aforementioned Xtext framework and integrated in the integrated development environment Eclipse using its plug-in mechanism [31]. The introduced interpreter evaluates rule, metric, and query expressions whenever the respective expression is modified and saved in the editor.

Currently, both components are integrated in Yakindu Traceability (YT) a software solution for creating, maintaining and analyzing traceability information models [32]. Therefore, the analysis language is configured to utilize the proprietary TIMM from which traceability information configuration models and concrete TIMs are defined. At runtime, the expression editor triggers the interpreter to request the current TIM from the underlying software solution and subsequently perform the given analysis.

The Eclipse view in Figure 12 shows the integration of the TAL into YT for creating and maintaining traceability information models. The view consist of three parts that all can be used individually in other views within an Eclipse application. First, the upper left part lists all available analyses in the current workspace. Second, on the upper right side the details of a selected analysis are shown in an embedded editor. The user can edit the expressions and is supported by syntax highlighting, code completion, and live validations. Finally, the bottom half of the view contains a dynamic table that lists the results from an executed analysis language expression. In Figure 12, the column headings "name" and "count" are defined from the query's *collect* statement. The values in the rows represent the values from the interpreted analysis expression. In this case the table shows the result of a coverage analysis showing all software requirements and the number of related software architecture artifacts.

At the tier one automotive supplier, multiple project roles used the Eclipse integrated TAL editor. The types of users can be divided into three groups, namely "power user", "direct user" and "indirect user". The main characteristic of power users is that they create queries. These might be used personally or shared with team members. Within the group of power users, there are two project roles involved. On the one hand, the process owners who are responsible for the traceability process within the automotive supplier company. Process owners define analyses that are used as basis for reports and quality gates throughout the process. On the other hand, there are experts from the YT vendor, which do consulting and customization. While process owners create analyses with the given functionality of the TAL, YT experts additionally develop and enhance YT itself. Although functions can be introduced by anyone, the case study has shown that it is done most efficiently by YT experts.

The second user group consists of so called direct users. They differ from power users by only using predefined analyses. Further, the user group consists of more project roles, namely architect, developer, and hardware tester. The case study has revealed that all three project roles have different requirements that need to be covered by the TAL. While architects are mainly concerned with analyzing the coverage between requirements, software architecture, and software units, developers use traceability data to ease development and maintenance tasks. Therefore, impact analyses play a superior role for developers, to estimate the impact of a particular change. Hardware testers have a very strong focus on coverage analysis in order to plan and execute testing tasks.

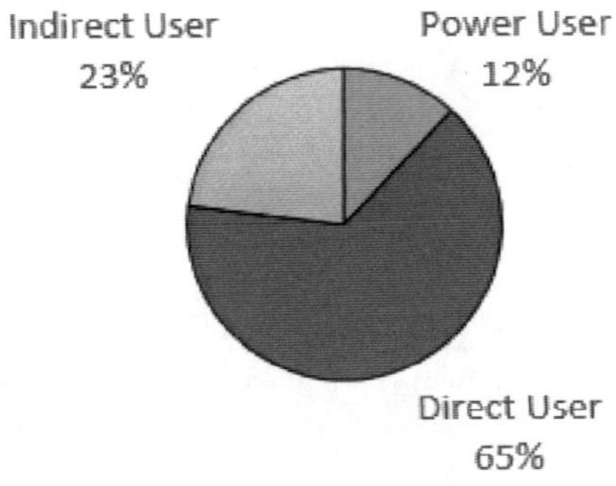

Figure 13. Users per user group.

The third group consists of users that do not interact directly with the TAL. It is therefore called indirect users. In addition to executing analyses within the Eclipse view, the underlying infrastructure is also used to aggregate data on a regular basis. This aggregated data is integrated into reports that are sent to different project roles such as requirements engineers or project managers. While the first two user groups use the TAL for short-term or immediate tasks, indirect users justify medium and long term decisions from the aggregated traceability analyses. Requirements engineers are responsible for a consistent implementation. Thus, they are interested in analyses such as "Are all requirements implemented?". In addition, project managers require information about the overall implementation and testing status of their project.

Within the case study, all three user groups were involved in using the TAL and the introduced editor. Based on the project role, different analyses were defined in order to satisfy the aforementioned information needs. The predefined analyses have replaced complex SQL statements that included up to seven joins to follow the links trough the traceability information model. Because the *tracesFrom... to...* function encapsulates the graph traversal, the analyses are more resilient to changes of the traceability configuration model.

While users were able to collect their data, especially the coverage analyses required by the hardware testers introduced some challenges. In contrast to the rather simple example in Section III-A2, the specification of requirement coverage as used by the tier one automotive supplier is more than two pages long. The extensive definition is due to the following two factors. First, compared to the sample TICM in Figure 1 the TICM contains more artifacts and links between them. Second, there are subsequently more ways to "cover" a requirement. However, not all paths through the traceability information model create valid coverage. Although it would have been possible to define the analysis statement using the existing TAL functionalities, it was decided to implement a custom function. Encapsulating the data aggregation and the majority of rules from the requirements coverage specification in a custom function increased the overall readability and maintainability of the analysis. Introducing a custom function minimized the length of the analysis statement by 85%.

Since other traceability solutions often struggle with performance issues, when it comes to large models, a main focus of the case study was on the runtime of analysis execution. The case study has shown that executing the far more complex real world functions including the custom function took nearly the same time as the aforementioned artificial analysis. Because the functions implement efficient graph traversal algorithms, they can be executed in real time. Therefore, the TAL solution can be integrated seamlessly.

The overall feedback from users involved in the case study was positive. They especially emphasized the easy to learn and powerful query language. Further, the traceability analysis language played an important role during an official A-SPICE Level 3 assessment. By using the TAL, all relevant data could be retrieved and reported in order to pass the assessment [33]. All in all, the TAL was used successfully on a daily basis as well as in a more official setting.

VI. Discussion

The discussion is divided into three parts. It starts with discussing different scenarios, in which the TAL could be applied. The second part elaborates on the findings of the case study executed at a tier one automotive supplier. Finally, the limitations of the introduced approach are explained.

A. *Applying the Analysis Language*

Defining and evaluating analysis statements with the prototypical implementation has shown that the approach is feasible to collect metrics for different kinds of traceability projects. The most basic metric expression reads like *the proportion of artifacts of type A that have no trace to artifacts of type*

B. Some generic scenarios focused on impact, coverage, and consistency analyses have been exemplified in Section III-A. However, there are more specific metrics that are applicable and reasonable for a particular industry sector, a specific project organization, or a certain development process as demonstrated by the case study.

In addition to the case study findings, industry-specific metrics, e.g., in the banking sector, could focus on the impact of a certain change request regarding coordination and test effort estimation. Project-specific management rules may for instance highlight components causing a high number of reported defects to indicate where to perform quality measures, e.g., code reviews. Moreover, the current progress of a software development project can be exposed by defining a staggered analysis relating design phase artifacts (e.g., *Software Requirements* that are not linked to a *Software Architecture*) and implementation artifacts (e.g., *Software Architectures* without trace to a *Software Unit*) in relation to the overall number of *Software Requirements*. Analysis expressions could also be specific to the software development process. In agile projects for example the velocity of an iteration could be combined with the number of bugs related to the delivered functionality. Thereby, it could be determined whether the number of bugs correlates with the scope of delivered functionality. These use cases emphasize the flexibility of the analysis language — in combination with an adaptable configuration model — for applying traceability analyses to a variety of domains, not necessarily bound to programming or software development in general. For example, a TIM for an academic paper may define traceable artifacts such as *authors*, *chapters*, and *references*. An analysis on such a paper could find all papers that cite a certain author or the average number of citations per chapter. It is therefore possible to execute analyses on other domains with graph-based structures that can benefit from traceability information.

B. Case Study

The case study executed at a tier one automotive supplier revealed that there are different user groups using the TAL. While nearly 80% of the users interact directly with the TAL editor, the remaining 20% use information gathered using the TAL. The reasons that only 12% of the users wrote queries are mainly organizational. On the one hand, traceability analysis results are used internally for reporting the project status or identifying change impacts. On the other hand, a sophisticated analysis capability is an important basis for external process audits such as A-SPICE level 3. In order to ensure high quality, error free queries, only a few well trained employees write and verify analysis definitions. After being verified, these analyses are shared with the different project teams and their results become binding. Although only power users directly use the TAL to define queries, the language statements need to be as readable as possible. Thereby, direct users can quickly understand the purpose of a particular analysis. While users from both groups have stated that TAL is easy to understand, additional research is required to support this claim.

Moreover, the case study has shown that YT experts were faster to implement custom functions. In addition, power users from the tier one automotive supplier showed no interest in writing custom functions. It has to be analyzed whether this is due to the fact that YT experts were available or because the custom function interface is to complex. Moreover, it has to be analyzed, what needs to be done to enable TAL users to specify their own analysis more easily.

In contrast to the aforementioned user groups, the interaction with the traceability information models has not changed for the indirect users. However, the underlying infrastructure to retrieve and aggregate the data has been changed. By introducing the TAL, complex SQL statements (cf. Figure 11) could be replaced by shorter analysis statements. Although the TAL definitions are less verbose, the impacts on the maintainability need to be studied. While the statements become shorter by hiding the complex graph traversal, the traversal algorithms need to be tested thoroughly. If an analysis result is wrong because of an error in the underlying traversal algorithm, failure detection and fixing becomes very difficult. During the early stages of the case study, every TAL analysis was cross-checked manually by a domain expert. The findings from this testing approach were two-fold: first, failures in the algorithm implementation or the analysis expressions were identified and fixed. Second, the TAL definitions revealed errorneous and inconsistent data in the traceability information model.

Since the concept provides that analyses are executed on every save, the underlying algorithms need to be very fast. The case study has shown that the execution times achieved with artificial models could be confirmed within an industry setting. Yet, both traceability configuration models are based on the A-SPICE standard. Therefore, additional research is required with other, more complex TICM.

In general all required information for the different user groups and project roles could be retrieved using the TAL. However, when managing and analyzing multiple versions of an artifact and its combination with others, as explained by software product line engineering, further investigation is required. Yet, the challenges are not solely within the analysis but also in the creation and maintenance of the underlying TIM.

C. Limitations

The approach presented in this paper is bound to limitations regarding both technical and organizational aspects. Regarding the impact of the developed DSL on software quality management practices, first investigations have taken place. However, more are needed to draw sustainable conclusions.

Although all analyses required by the participants could be satisfied, the case study at a tier one automotive supplier has shown that additional analysis capabilities are required. One main requirement is to evaluate, how much of an expected trace path is available in a certain TIM. If there is no complete path from a *System Requirement* to a *Software Integration Test Result*, it would be beneficial to show partial matches and to list missing artifacts such as a missing *Software Integration Test Result* or *Software Integration Test Specification*. Extending the result of an analysis in accordance to this requirement would enhance the information about the progress of a project.

From a language-user perspective, the big advantage of being free to configure any query, metric or rule expression is also a challenge. A language user has to be aware of the traceable artifacts and links in the TIM and how this trace information could be connected to extract reasonable measures. In addition, these analyses are safety critical and therefore need to be implemented and tested by domain experts. Moreover, the context-dependent choice of suitable metrics in terms of type, number, and thresholds is subject to further research. These limitations do not impede the value of this work, though. In fact, in combination with the discussed application scenarios they provide the foundation for future work.

VII. CONCLUSION

This work describes a textual domain-specific language to analyze existing traceability information models. The TAL is divided into query, metric, and rule parts that are all implemented with the state-of-the-art framework Xtext. The introduced approach goes beyond existing tool support for querying traceability information models. By closing the gap between information retrieval, metric definition, and result evaluation, the analysis capabilities are solid ground for project- or company-specific metrics. Since the proposed analysis language reuses the artifact-type names from the traceability information configuration model, the expressions are defined using well known terms. Additionally, the newly introduced custom functions ensured short and concise analysis statements.

On the one hand, the introduced approach is based on an Eclipse Ecore model and is thereby completely independent of the specific type of traced artifacts. On the other hand, it is well integrated into an existing TICM and IDE using Xtext and the Eclipse platform. All parts of the TAL are fully configurable regarding analysis expression, limit thresholds, and query statements in an integrated approach to close the gap between *querying* and *analyzing* traceability information models. Subsequently, measures for TIMs can be specific to a certain industry sector, a company, a project or even a role within a project. The scenarios described in Section III-A propose areas, in which configurable analyses provide benefits for project managers, quality managers, and developers. These claims were supported by findings from the conducted case study.

Using the implemented interpreter for real-time execution of expressions, first project experiences within the automotive industry have shown that the TAL analyses are evaluated efficiently and are more resilient than other approaches, e.g., SQL-based analyses. Further, it has been shown that the analysis statements are mainly created by a small group of users, while the majority consumes the results either directly within the TAL editor or indirectly through higher level reports. Therefore, it can be concluded that the language itself needs to offer powerful mechanisms to enable power users to write queries efficiently. Additionally, the language has to be easy to understand so that also direct users recognize the purpose of a query.

While all information needs could be satisfied by the TAL, there was one situation during the case study where a custom function was required. In general, it can be concluded that within every analysis statement the majority of data retrieval and aggregation should be done by the query functions. In addition to previous work, it has been shown that the approach benefits from the additional configuration options in the query language. By introducing custom functions for complex data retrieval, the TAL statements remained small and concise. Subsequently, the metrics and rule statements are used solely for final aggregation and presentation.

Future work could focus on further assessing the applicability in real world projects and defining a structured process to identify reasonable metrics for a specific setting. Such a process might not only support sophisticated traceability analyses but could also propose industry-proven metrics and thresholds. Additionally, it could be investigated, how many custom functions are required throughout different projects and whether there are any shared patterns between them. These patterns might motivate the extension of the standard query functions provided by the TAL.

Some advanced features such as metrics comparisons over time using TIM snapshots to further enhance the analysis are yet to be implemented. Moreover, creating traceability information models for software product lines remains a challenge, which also affects the analysis capabilities.

In addition to evaluating the metrics against static values, future work might also focus on utilizing statistical methods from the data mining field. Classification algorithms or association rules for example could be used to find patterns in traceability information models and thus gain additional insights from large-scale TIMs.

All in all, the paper has introduced a highly customizable approach to specify traceability analyses in order to utilize the extensive insight contained in traceability information models. In addition, the implemented interpreter was used successfully at a tier one automotive supplier to satisfy the information needs of different user groups.

REFERENCES

[1] H. Bünder, H. Kuchen, and C. Rieger, "A model-driven approach for evaluating traceability information," in SOFTENG 2017, The Third International Conference on Advances and Trends in Software Engineering. IARIA, 2017, pp. 59–65.

[2] O. C. Z. Gotel and C. W. Finkelstein, "An analysis of the requirements traceability problem," in Proceedings of IEEE International Conference on Requirements Engineering, 1994, pp. 94–101.

[3] J. Cleland-Huang, O. Gotel, J. Huffman Hayes, P. Mäder, and A. Zisman, "Software traceability: Trends and future directions," in Proceedings of the on Future of Software Engineering. ACM, 2014, pp. 55–69.

[4] E. Bouillon, P. Mäder, and I. Philippow, "A survey on usage scenarios for requirements traceability in practice," in Requirements Engineering: Foundation for Software Quality. Springer, 2013, pp. 158–173.

[5] J. I. Maletic and M. L. Collard, "Tql: A query language to support traceability," in ICSE Workshop on Traceability in Emerging Forms of Software Engineering, 2009, pp. 16–20.

[6] P. Mäder and J. Cleland-Huang, "A visual language for modeling and executing traceability queries," Software and Systems Modeling, vol. 12, no. 3, 2013, pp. 537–553.

[7] P. Rempel and P. Mäder, "Estimating the implementation risk of requirements in agile software development projects with traceability metrics," in Requirements Engineering: Foundation for Software Quality. Springer, 2015, pp. 81–97.

[8] M. Völter, DSL engineering: Designing, implementing and using domain-specific languages. CreateSpace Independent Publishing Platform, 2013.

[9] J. Cleland-Huang, M. Heimdahl, J. Huffman Hayes, R. Lutz, and P. Maeder, "Trace queries for safety requirements in high assurance systems," LNCS, vol. 7195, 2012, pp. 179–193.

[10] P. Mader, O. Gotel, and I. Philippow, "Getting back to basics: Promoting the use of a traceability information model in practice," 7th Intl. Workshop on Traceability in Emerging Forms of Software Engineering, 2013, pp. 21–25.

[11] A. Graf, N. Sasidharan, and Ö. Gürsoy, "Requirements, traceability and dsls in eclipse with the requirements interchange format (reqif)," in Second International Conference on Complex Systems Design & Management. Springer, 2012, pp. 187–199.

[12] P. Mäder and A. Egyed, "Do developers benefit from requirements traceability when evolving and maintaining a software system?" Empirical Softw. Eng., vol. 20, no. 2, 2015, pp. 413–441.

[13] A. Begel and T. Zimmermann, "Analyze this! 145 questions for data scientists in software engineering," in 36th International Conference on Software Engineering. ACM, 2014, pp. 12–23.

[14] N. Anquetil et al., "A model-driven traceability framework for software product lines," Software & Systems Modeling, vol. 9, no. 4, 2010, pp. 427–451.

[15] A. Marques, F. Ramalho, and W. L. Andrade, "Trl: A traceability representation language," in Proceedings of the 30th Annual ACM Symposium on Applied Computing. ACM, 2015, pp. 1358–1363.

[16] H. Schwarz, Universal traceability. Logos Verlag Berlin, 2012.

[17] M. Mernik, J. Heering, and A. M. Sloane, "When and how to develop domain-specific languages," ACM Comput. Surv., vol. 37, no. 4, 2005, pp. 316–344.

[18] N. Drivalos, D. S. Kolovos, R. F. Paige, and K. J. Fernandes, "Engineering a dsl for software traceability," in Software Language Engineering. Springer, 2009, vol. 5452, pp. 151–167.

[19] Automotive Special Interest Group, "Automotive spice process reference model," 2015, URL: http://automotivespice.com/fileadmin/software-download/Automotive_SPICE_PAM_30.pdf [retrieved: 14.8.2017].

[20] R. S. Arnold and S. A. Bohner, "Impact analysis-towards a framework for comparison," in ICSM, vol. 93, 1993, pp. 292–301.

[21] C. Ingram and S. Riddle, "Cost-benefits of traceability," in Software and Systems Traceability, J. Cleland-Huang, O. Gotel, and A. Zisman, Eds. Springer London, 2012, pp. 23–42.

[22] N. Kececi, J. Garbajosa, and P. Bourque, "Modeling functional requirements to support traceability analysis," in 2006 IEEE International Symposium on Industrial Electronics, vol. 4, 2006, pp. 3305–3310.

[23] J. Cleland-Huang, O. Gotel, and A. Zisman, Eds., Software and Systems Traceability. Springer London, 2012.

[24] H. U. Asuncion, F. François, and R. N. Taylor, "An end-to-end industrial software traceability tool," in 6th Joint Meeting of the European Software Engineering Conference and the ACM SIGSOFT Symposium on The Foundations of Software Engineering. ACM, 2007, pp. 115–124.

[25] R. C. Gronback, Eclipse Modeling Project: A Domain-Specific Language (DSL) Toolkit, 1st ed. Addison-Wesley Professional, 2009.

[26] The Eclipse Foundation, "Xtext documentation," 2017, URL: https://eclipse.org/Xtext/documentation/ [retrieved: 14.8.2017].

[27] ——, "Xtend modernized java," 2017, URL: http://eclipse.org/xtend/ [retrieved: 14.8.2017].

[28] L. Bettini, Implementing domain-specific languages with Xtext and Xtend. Packt Pub, 2013.

[29] M. Verbaere, E. Hajiyev, and O. d. Moor, "Improve software quality with SemmleCode: An eclipse plugin for semantic code search," in 22nd ACM SIGPLAN Conference on Object-oriented Programming Systems and Applications Companion. ACM, 2007, pp. 880–881.

[30] P. Klint, T. van der Storm, and J. Vinju, "Rascal: A domain specific language for source code analysis and manipulation," in 9th IEEE International Working Conference on Source Code Analysis and Manipulation. IEEE Computer Society, 2009, pp. 168–177.

[31] The Eclipse Foundation, "PDE/user guide," 2017, URL: http://wiki.eclipse.org/PDE/User_Guide [retrieved: 14.8.2017].

[32] itemis AG, "Yakindu traceability," 2017. [Online]. Available: https://www.itemis.com/en/yakindu/traceability/

[33] itemis AG, "Kostal finalises aspice assessment successfully with yakindu traceability," 2017, URL: https://www.itemis.com/en/yakindu/references/kostal/ [retrieved: 14.8.2017].

Accurate and Robust Skin Feature Extraction Scheme for Aging Estimation

Hyungjoon Kim, Jisoo Park, Eenjun Hwang
School of Electrical Engineering
Korea University
Anam-Dong, Seongbuk-Gu, Seoul, Republic Korea
E-mail: {hyungjun89, jisoo_park, ehwang04}@korea.ac.kr

Woogeol Kim
VC Smart Validation Team
LG Electronics
Pyeongtaek, Republic Korea
E-mail: woogeol.kim@lge.com

Abstract— **In this paper, we revise our method for skin feature extraction based on cell segmentation to improve its accuracy, efficiency and robustness that are very critical in the realistic skin condition analysis. In order to achieve such goals, we enhance the contrast of wrinkles on the skin by using the contrast limited adaptive histogram equalization (CLAHE) and highlight the depth of wrinkles by using the extended-minima transform. By performing watershed transform, we can segment the skin image into labelled skin cells and calculate various skin features from the labelled cells. We focus on two types of skin features that play a key role in assessing the degree of skin aging; cell features and wrinkle features. To evaluate the performance and robustness of our revised method, we collected skin images using three different types of microscopy cameras and extracted their cell and wrinkle features using the revised method. Through various experiments, we show that our revised method achieves 10% increase in the skin feature extraction accuracy and 50% decrease in the skin feature extraction time compared to our previous method.**

Keywords- Skin analysis; Feature extraction; Wrinkle feature; Contrast stretching; Microscopy image.

I. INTRODUCTION

In this paper, we reinforce the experimental part of our work [1] for skin feature extraction scheme. Various factors, such as exposure to sunlight or pollution, smoking and excessive drinking are known to accelerate the normal skin aging process and eventually lead to premature skin aging. Since skin is the outermost part of the human body, people have shown great interest in the beauty and health of their skin. This in return leads to diverse studies related to skin analysis, skin treatment, and skin aging. Usually, the degree of skin aging has been evaluated by dermatologists based on their personal experience or knowledge. This is because there is no standard method for quantitative and objective evaluation. If such method was available, then users would get consistent and quantitative information about their skin condition, and hence perform suitable treatment for their skin more effectively and conveniently.

In our previous work, we proposed a scheme for skin texture aging trend analysis based on diverse skin texture features such as texture length, width, depth, cell count and cell area. To extract such features, we cropped microscopy skin image, carried out histogram equalization, removed noise and then binarized the image using the Otsu threshold. After that, we segmented the skin texture into cells by using the watershed algorithm and calculated their features [2][3]. However, there are several problems in our previous work. Two serious problems among them are feature extraction time and feature extraction accuracy. The former is due to the fact that its feature extraction is pixel-based and hence all pixels in each cell should be considered. The latter is due to the fact that preprocessing steps in the previous work were optimized for a specific microscope camera. Hence, the feature extraction result might be not good when using other types of cameras.

In this paper, we modify some of the preprocessing steps and segmentation method in the previous work to improve the accuracy, efficiency and robustness of skin feature extraction. Figure 1 shows the overall steps to achieve that, which can be divided into preprocessing, cell segmentation and feature extraction. In the preprocessing, the original image is cropped to reduce the effect of vignetting. Then, contrast stretching is applied in order to enhance the intensity of wrinkles against skin. Denoising filters are applied to the image to reduce noise in the image. In the cell segmentation, extended-minima transform and watershed algorithm are used for cell-based segmentation. Each cell cluster is labeled, and the labeled information is utilized for calculating skin features. We extract five features from the skin image to analyze the skin condition.

The remainder of this paper is organized as follows. In Section II, we introduce several related works for skin analysis, wrinkle detection and cell segmentation. Detailed techniques for skin segmentation are described in Section III and skin feature extraction method is described in Section IV. We explain our experiment and conclude this paper in Section V.

II. RELATED WORKS

So far, medical analysis and diagnosis based on biometric images have been performed in the various domains. Skin analysis is one of the most popular and interesting tasks, since skin is the outermost part of the human body. Various methods for extracting diverse features from skin images and evaluating its condition quantitatively have been proposed.

As an effort to detect skin wrinkles, H. Tanaka et al. applied a cross-binarization method to digital skin image to get its binary image, and then, the short straight line matching method to detect wrinkles from the binary image and measure their length [4]. More specifically, for each base line in the

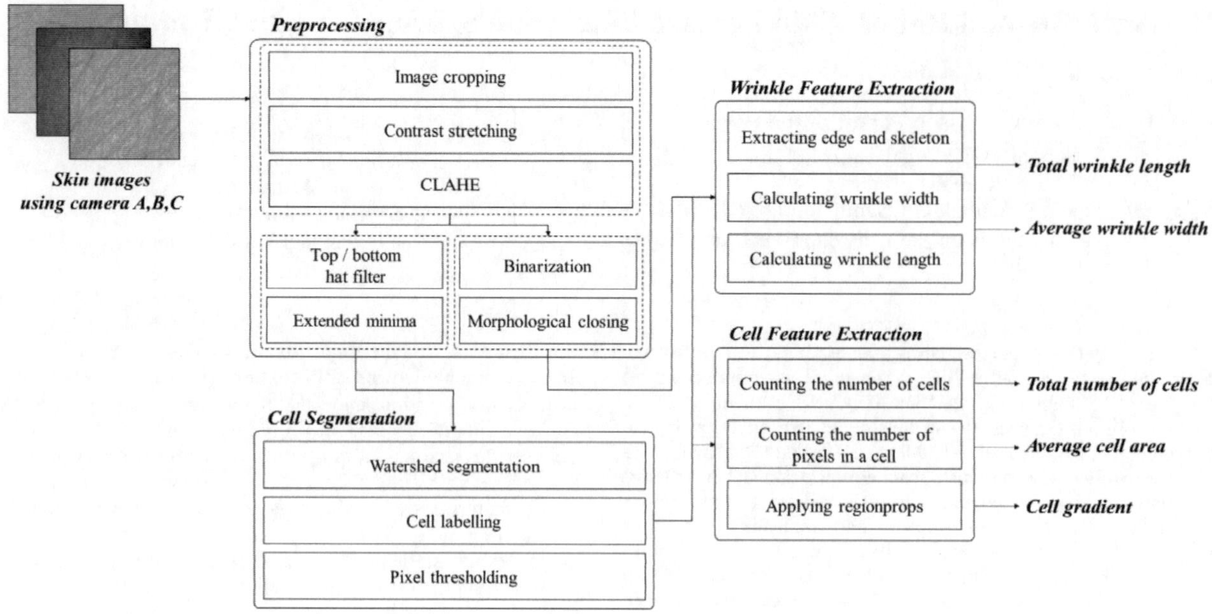

Figure 1. Overall scheme of skin feature extraction

cross-binarized image, if more than 70% of its pixels are marked black, then the line is considered a wrinkle. After that, they continue from the end of current base line to create a new base line. This repeats until the end of the wrinkle or the end of the image is reached. J. Ute et al. measured the topography of skin surface using an optical 3D device and showed that there is a significant dependency between skin surface topography and the age [5]. On the other hand, G. O. Cula et al. developed the automatic facial wrinkles detection algorithm based on estimating the orientation and frequency of the elongated spatial feature, captured via digital image filtering [6]. Recently Yow. Ai Ping et al. proposed the ASHIMA system framework and showed how to process HD-OCT (High-Definition Optical Coherence Tomography) skin images automatically to measure the epidermal thickness and skin surface topography [7]. H. Razalli et al. estimated human's age range based on facial wrinkle analysis [8]. They mentioned when fewer wrinkles are detected or extracted, it will consequently affect the process to estimate the correct age. To solve that, they proposed a new method to extract facial wrinkles in a face image using Hessian based filter (HBF) for age estimation. They tested their proposed method for FG-NET database and compared its performance with other methods.

One of the most popular algorithms for segmenting a skin microscope image into cells is watershed segmentation. Although it has been a long time since this algorithm was introduced, it is still widely used in various image processing applications. A. Das and D. Ghoshal segmented human skin region using watershed segmentation [9]. They converted RGB image into YCbCr color image, and then modified marker based watershed algorithm has been applied on Cr component for segmentation of human skin region. They compared their method with other algorithms. The methods were tested on FRI CVL Face Database. Z. JunXiong et al proposed a method for extracting features of jujube fruit wrinkle using the watershed segmentation [10]. They first converted original RGB image into gray scale image, and then, applied morphological reconstruction to remove noise. After that, they performed the H-minima extended transformation to label the foreground of jujube fruit images, and then segmented the labeled foreground regions using a distance transform-based watershed algorithm.

III. SKIN SEGMENTATION METHOD

A. Preprocessing

Direct image processing on microscope image or captured image might cause several problems if the image is in RGB (Red-Green-Blue) form. Usually, dealing with RGB image shows less accuracy than dealing with gray image. Other typical factors to decrease the accuracy are vignetting effect and noises. To avoid these problems, original images need to be converted into binary images through preprocessing. In this work, preprocessing consists of three steps: (i) the original image is cropped to reduce the effect of vignetting. (ii) Contrast stretching [11] is applied to make brightness difference between skin and wrinkle bigger. (iii) Adaptive histogram equalization is applied to the image. Figure 2 shows overall steps of preprocessing and their result on an example skin image.

1) Cropping

Due to the limitations of the camera and the interference of the light source, captured images may have a noise known as vignetting effect. Vignetting is a phenomenon where the

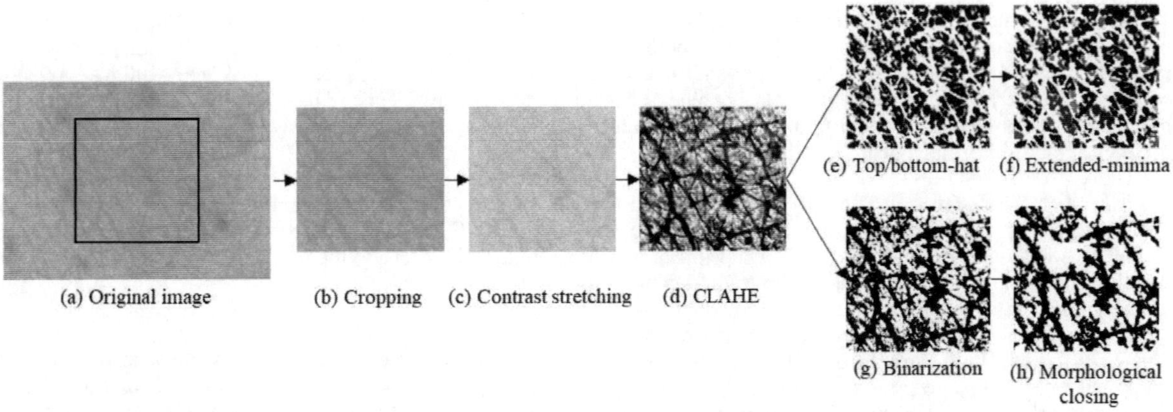

Figure 2. The example of overall preprocessing steps

outer edges of the images become dark due to the reduction of light at the periphery of camera lens, and as a result, the captured images have different color histogram distributions. An example of vignetting effect is shown in Figure 3, where we can see the dark area around the corner. In order to avoid such phenomenon, we cropped 300 by 300 pixels from the center of the image, which has the concentrated luminous source of the image. Figure 2 (b) shows the result of image cropping for an input image shown in Figure 2 (a), where the rectangle indicates the cropping size.

Figure 3. Example of vignetting effect

2) Contrast stretching

Accurate detection of skin wrinkles is very crucial in the skin analysis and the accuracy can be improved by clearly separating skin and wrinkle pixels in the image. However, original images often lack sufficient contrast depending on the conditions under which the image was photographed such as light source and shooting area. Insufficient contrast could make certain areas in the image have similar contrast even though they must be distinguished. This problem can be moderated by contrast stretching. Contrast stretching expands the dynamic range of the intensity levels so that it spans the color distance between skin and wrinkle. The equation of contrast stretching used in this paper is shown in Eq. (1).

$$V_{out} = \begin{cases} 0.6 \times V_{in} + 0.4, & V_{in} > \alpha \\ 0.25 \times V_{in}, & V_{in} < \beta \\ V_{in} = V_{in}, & Others \end{cases} \quad (1)$$

Here, V is a value in HSV domain and α and β are two constants calculated by Eq. (2). Other constants are obtained experimentally.

$$\alpha = \sqrt{\max(V) \times \min(V)} / V_{average}$$
$$\beta = \max(V) \times \sqrt{\max(V) \times \min(V)} \quad (2)$$

Figure 2 (c) shows the effect of contrast stretching for the cropped image. In the figure, we can see that the intensity of the skin pixels is reduced and the color distinction between skin and winkle becomes more prominent.

3) Contrast limited adaptive histogram equalization

Skin wrinkles can be detected using the watershed algorithm [12]. However, we observed that the algorithm couldn't detect all the wrinkles due to the lack of contrast. Hence, before we apply the watershed algorithm to the skin image, we need to enhance the intensity of winkles by using the contrast limited adaptive histogram equalization (CLAHE) method to the image [13]. Histogram equalization is a gray scale transformation used for contrast enhancement. It aims to get an image with uniformly distributed intensity levels over the whole intensity scale. In some case, the result of histogram equalization might be worse compared to the original image since the histogram of the resulting image becomes approximately flat. For instance, when high peaks in the histogram are caused by an uninteresting area, histogram equalization results in enhanced visibility of unwanted image area. This means that the local contrast requirement is not satisfied, and as a result, minor contrast differences are entirely ignored when the number of pixels falling in a particular gray range is relatively small.

An adaptive method to avoid this drawback is block-based processing of histogram equalization [14]. In this method, an image is divided into sub-images or blocks, and histogram equalization is performed on each sub-images or blocks. Then, blocking artifacts among neighboring blocks are minimized by filtering or bilinear interpolation.

The CLAHE method uses a clip limit to overcome the noise problem. That is, the amplification is limited by clipping the histogram at a predefined value before computing the Cumulative Distribution Function (CDF). The value at which the histogram is clipped, the so-called clip limit, depends on the normalization of the histogram and thereby on the size of the neighborhood region. The redistribution will push some bins over the clip limit again, resulting in an effective clip limit that is larger than the prescribed limit.

In our work, we need to remove hairs from the gray image. Hairs can be mistaken for wrinkles and hence they are the most critical and common noise in the wrinkle detection. Skin hairs are easily removed by a simple threshold filter. Figure 2 (d) shows the result of the CLAHE method.

4) Binarization

In order to measure the width of wrinkles, we need to detect the contour of wrinkles and their skeleton. The contour and skeleton can be obtained by performing canny edge detection and morphological thinning [15][16]. They are effectively working on the binary image. Hence, we apply Otsu threshold to the resulting image of CLAHE method to obtain its binary image [17]. Figure 2 (g) shows the result of binarization.

5) Denoise

Even though CLAHE images and binarized images are ready for feature extraction, there are still likely to have some noises due to the hardware limitation or environmental factors when taking pictures. To reduce the effect of such noises, we perform a denoise process. We apply different denoise process to the CLACHE and binarized images, In the case of CLAHE image, top-hat, bottom-hat filter is applied to remove noise. Figure 2 (e) shows the result after applying top, bottom-hat filter. After filtering, Extended-minima transform and watershed segmentation are performed for cell segmentation. In the case of binarized images, morphological closing is performed to remove noise. Figure 2 (h) shows the result of morphological closing.

6) Extended-minima transform

Even though watershed transform is widely used for image segmentation, it often suffers from the over-segmentation problem since regional minima or ultimate eroded points are employed for segmenting cells directly. One of the key factors that determine the accuracy of skin image segmentation by wrinkle cells is how much the minima points are extended. In this paper, we revise the extended-minima transform, which is the regional minima of the H-minima transform. Regional minima are connected components of pixels with a constant intensity value, and whose external boundary pixels have higher value.

In other words, the result of h-minimum operator is linked to the depth of the minima. In a skin image, wrinkle cells consist of some minima and maxima. Minima correspond to parts of low depth points and maxima correspond to high depth points. Therefore, using the extended-minima transform, we can increase the depth between wrinkle cell clusters. It can help the watershed transform to cluster the wrinkle cells. First, we extract minima from an image and extend the depth of the points. Figure 2 (h) shows the result after imposing the extended minima to the original gray scale image.

B. Segmentation processing

In this section, we describe how to segment a skin image into wrinkle cells using the extended-minima transform [18] and watershed transform. Watershed transform is one of the most widely used image segmentation techniques in image processing and we use it for segmenting a skin image into wrinkle cells. Especially, we perform the extended-minima transform before the watershed transform in order to increase the accuracy of finding wrinkle cells.

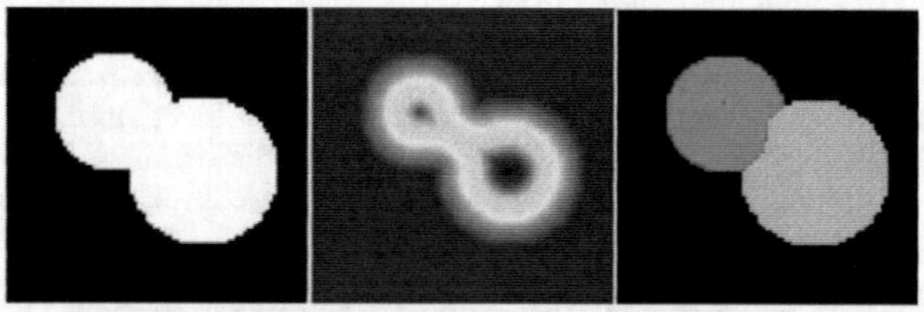

(a) Overlapping objects (b) Distances (c) Separated objects

Figure 4. Segmentation using watershed transform

1) Watershed segmentation

Image segmentation is a computer analysis of image objects to decide which pixel of the image belongs to which object. Basically, this is the process of separating objects from background, as well as from each other. Watershed transform is a powerful and well-known tool for performing image segmentation. Figure 4 shows how to segment two overlapping circles using the watershed transform.

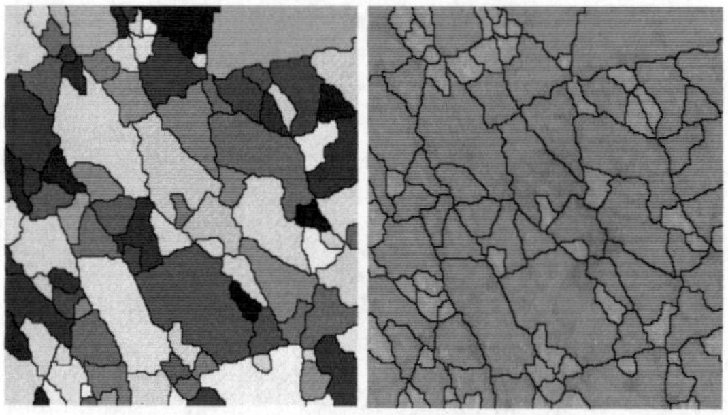

(a) Labeled image (b) Filtered image with valid cells

Figure 5. Labelling process

To segment them, an image distance to the background is computed. The maxima of the distance (i.e., the minima of the opposite of the distance) are chosen as markers, and the flooding of basins from such markers separates the two circles along a watershed line. We adapt these steps to our skin image, so that pixels of each wrinkle cell are clustered.

2) Cell labelling

Wrinkle cell labelling can be easily done by applying the watershed transform to the skin image. From the result of watershed transform, we can get a collection of wrinkle cells. Each cell contains the positions of the pixels in the cell which belong to same cluster. Figure 5 (a) shows an example of wrinkle cells labeling, where each cell is labeled using a different color.

3) Pixel thresholding

Sometimes, the segmentation result contains unexpected cells with very small size, which are usually noise or moles. Since they are not the regular wrinkle cells, they should be removed. We can calculate area of every labelled cell easily by counting the number of pixels in the cell. The threshold size by which we determine whether to remove the cell or not can be calculated by Eq. (3).

$$Threshold = \frac{\sum_i Area_i}{ScaleRatio \times n} \tag{3}$$

Here, $Area_i$ is the number of pixels in the ith cell and n is the total number of cells. Also, $ScaleRatio$ is defined by Eq. (4).

$$ScaleRatio = \frac{\max(Area) + \min(Area)}{mean(Area)} \tag{4}$$

Figure 5 (b) shows all the noisy cells detected by this method. We remove them by merging with their neighboring cell or enclosing cell.

IV. Skin Feature Extraction

A. Defining skin features

TABLE I. ASSUMPTIONS BASED ON COMMON KNOWLEDGE OF SKIN

1. Total wrinkle length decreases with age.
2. Wrinkle width increases with age.
3. Wrinkle depth increases with age.
4. Wrinkle cell area increases with age.
5. The number of cells decreases with age.
6. Diameter ratio of inscribed circle and circumscribed circle of a cell decreases with age.
7. Total length of lines connecting cross points of a cell increases with age.

We have developed algorithms for extracting various cell and wrinkle features from microscopy skin images. Our feature extraction method is based on the labeled image described so far. Before we describe our feature extraction scheme in detail, we first show several assumptions we made based on common knowledge of skin [2] in Table I.

In the table, the 6th assumption needs some explanation. Usually, each wrinkle cell has its own shape and the cell shape is getting distorted with aging. So, it might be helpful to evaluate how much a skin cell is distorted for skin aging estimation. In this paper, we represent the degree of distortion by the ratio of inscribed circle and circumscribed circle. Hence, if the cell's shape is very regular like regular polygon, the ratio approaches to 1. However, this method requires much processing time since it considers all the pixels in a cell. To alleviate this problem, we replace existing method with regionprops. This method considers how irregular a cell shape is based on the angle instead of the ratio of radius length. In other words, we consider the slope of principal horizontal axis as the distortion degree of a cell.

Finally, we define five skin features for skin aging estimation. They are cell count, average cell area, average cell gradient, total wrinkle length, and average wrinkle width. Cell count indicates how many cells are in the skin image. Average cell area indicates the average area of cells in the skin image. Cell gradient is what we described above,

The wrinkle itself is a very important clue for estimating the degree of skin aging. We use two wrinkle features in this work; the total wrinkle length and the average wrinkle width. We will describe detailed steps for extracting these features in the following.

B. Calculating skin features

In this section, we describe how to calculate five skin features. At first, the number of cells can be easily obtained by counting the number of labeled cells while excluding cells with invalid size as we described earlier.

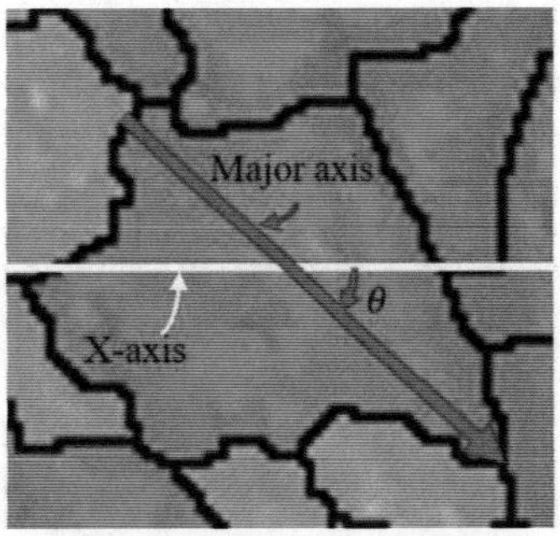

Figure 6. Example of calculating angle

The average cell area is also simply calculated by dividing the total number of pixels in the labeled cells by the number of cells which we obtained in the first place. In order to calculate the cell gradient, we used the regionprops function [19] which calculates a set of features for each labeled region.

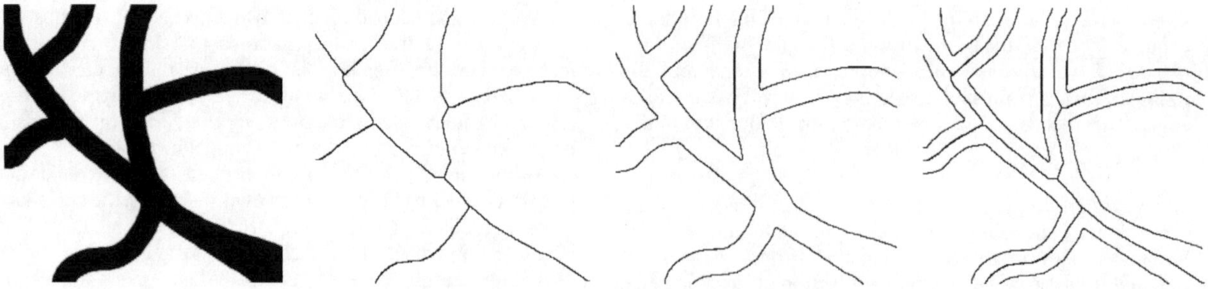

(a) A binary image (b) Its skeleton image (c) Contour image (d) Skeleton + contour

Figure 7. Extracting wrinkle skeleton and contour

One of the major features in the result of regionprops is the scalar angle value for each labeled region. It can be obtained by calculating the angle between the x-axis and the major axis of the ellipse that has the same second-moment as the region. Figure 6 illustrates how to calculate the angle. In the Figure, white line describes x-axis and red arrow shows a major axis. The angle between these two lines is calculated by regionprops method.

Total wrinkle length can be calculated using the line sieving method. This method first counts the pixels on the horizontal and vertical texture lines. It then counts the pixels along the diagonal line, and estimates the actual wrinkle length considering its slope. In the case of single pixel islands on the image, we simply count these islands and add the number to the total length.

To calculate average wrinkle width is a little complicated compared with other features. Figure 7 shows overall steps for to obtaining wrinkle width. We first apply morphological thinning on binary image. Thinning is a morphological operation that removes foreground in overall binary image. Figure 7 (b) shows the result of morphological thinning on the original image in Figure 7 (a). It consists of a set of 1x1 pixel points called skeleton. These pixels have specific direction, thus we can calculate each point's direction. In order to calculate the direction, we used Principal Component Analysis (PCA) algorithm [20]. PCA algorithm is a method of calculating Eigen value and Eigen vector by using all data's covariance and average.

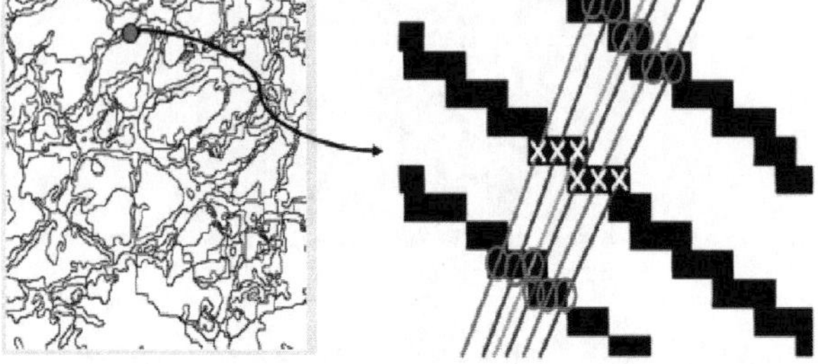

Figure 8. Calculating wrinkle width

Using this algorithm, we can get all of points on the skeleton's direction. Then, we can get a perpendicular line for each point. After calculating perpendicular lines, we can get the wrinkle contour by using canny edge detection. Figure 7 (c) shows the wrinkle contour detected by using canny edge detection. Finally, we can merge the skeleton and contour together as shown in Figure 7 (d). When aforementioned processes are done, we can calculate its wrinkle width. Figure 8 shows how to calculate average wrinkle thickness. The left image in the figure is merged image of wrinkle skeleton and contour as shown in Figure 7 (d). The right image magnifies a specific point of the image. In the figure, each white '×' is skeleton point, and the line passing the skeleton point is a normal line. The red circles indicate the intersection of line and wrinkle contour. The length between these two intersection points is the wrinkle thickness at that point.

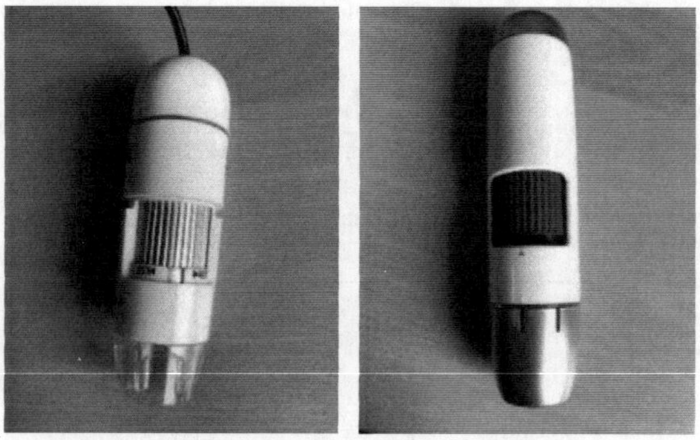

(a) Camera A (b) Camera B

(c) Camera C

Figure 9. Microscopy cameras compatible with smartphone

(a) Original cropped image (b) Ground truth (c) Removed skin area (d) Proposed method (e) Overlapping

Figure 10. Evaluation of cell detection accuracy

V. EXPERIMENTS

In order to evaluate the performance of our revised scheme, we performed several experiments based on the Matlab 2016a. To collect skin images, we used three different microscopy cameras shown in Figure 9, which are easily connected with smartphone. The reason we used different cameras is that images show quite different characteristics depending on the camera. Hence, to see the robustness of our method, we decided to test diverse cameras.

The scales of the cameras A, B, and C are 50X to 500X, 25X to 400X and 60X, respectively. In our previous work, we used the camera C only. We got approximately 300 face skin images and 60 hand skin images.

In our previous work, we evaluated the accuracy of our revised method by matching binary image pixel and cell contour [1]. In that case, we consider binary image as ground truth. However, sometimes binary image is not appropriate for use as ground truth. A typical case is when the original image contains various unexpected characteristics such as noise, mole, and light reflection. To solve this problem, we have made the ground truth manually. In the evaluation, we focused on two tasks: wrinkle line detection and cell detection. Numerical data for some of the experimental results are shown in Table II. More detailed analysis of the results is described in the next Section.

TABLE II. NUMERICAL DATA FOR EXPERIMENTAL RESULT

	Sub 1	*Sub 2*	*Sub 3*	*Sub 4*	*Sub 5*	*Sub 6*	...	*AVERAGE*
Face Wrinkle-CAMERA A-Revised method	96.512	97.11	97.362	94.912	95.334	96.112	...	96.520
Face Wrinkle-CAMERA A-Previous method	88.905	87.013	90.288	89.991	86.032	84.950	...	86.276
Face Wrinkle-CAMERA B-Revised method	95.748	96.869	97.390	97.938	96.381	96.920	...	96.837
Face Wrinkle-CAMERA B-Previous method	84.897	85.647	85.327	88.739	85.773	87.137	...	86.389
Face Wrinkle-CAMERA C-Revised method	95.720	96.801	95.147	94.510	94.490	96.400		95.912
Face Wrinkle-CAMERA C-Previous method	89.604	89.585	91.200	90.073	89.979	91.369	...	89.781
Hand Wrinkle-CAMERA A-Revised method	96.456	97.957	95.095	97.016	97.476	96.094	...	97.260
Hand Wrinkle-CAMERA A-Previous method	87.967	89.220	89.837	91.700	88.448	89.302	...	89.115
Hand Wrinkle-CAMERA B-Revised method	97.021	95.170	96.664	95.308	97.943	96.215	...	97.103
Hand Wrinkle-CAMERA B-Previous method	88.935	88.290	89.139	88.235	89.325	89.574	...	88.835
Hand Wrinkle-CAMERA C-Revised method	97.015	97.109	95.165	96.463	98.658	96.231	...	97.303
Hand Wrinkle-CAMERA C-Previous method	91.888	91.051	92.364	88.966	90.729	89.719	...	90.927
Face Wrinkle-CAMERA A-Revised method	98.520	97.437	97.991	95.554	96.143	96.340	...	96.612
Face Wrinkle-CAMERA A-Previous method	86.353	84.977	85.957	83.203	84.901	84.431	...	85.255
Face Wrinkle-CAMERA B-Revised method	94.966	97.051	96.825	96.576	95.209	97.670	...	96.543
Face Wrinkle-CAMERA B-Previous method	83.696	83.047	83.369	83.084	81.596	83.060	...	83.346
Face Wrinkle-CAMERA C-Revised method	96.304	96.156	95.979	96.601	95.132	98.099	...	97.135
Face Wrinkle-CAMERA C-Previous method	87.754	87.214	87.199	86.436	88.253	87.101	...	87.234
Hand Wrinkle-CAMERA A-Revised method	96.193	98.259	96.683	96.319	96.614	96.060	...	96.908
Hand Wrinkle-CAMERA A-Previous method	88.245	91.891	91.020	89.673	88.108	88.500	...	89.365
Hand Wrinkle-CAMERA B-Revised method	97.057	98.025	95.902	94.904	95.785	97.568	...	97.234
Hand Wrinkle-CAMERA B-Previous method	89.596	89.657	89.075	89.389	88.729	90.067	...	89.205
Hand Wrinkle-CAMERA C-Revised method	96.427	98.244	96.940	97.454	98.342	98.828	...	97.789
Hand Wrinkle-CAMERA C-Previous method	90.128	92.507	91.906	91.178	91.051	91.028	...	91.246

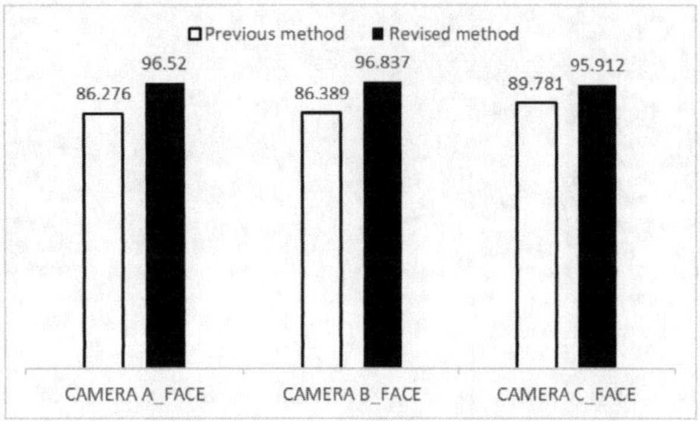

(a) Accuracy of face wrinkle line detection

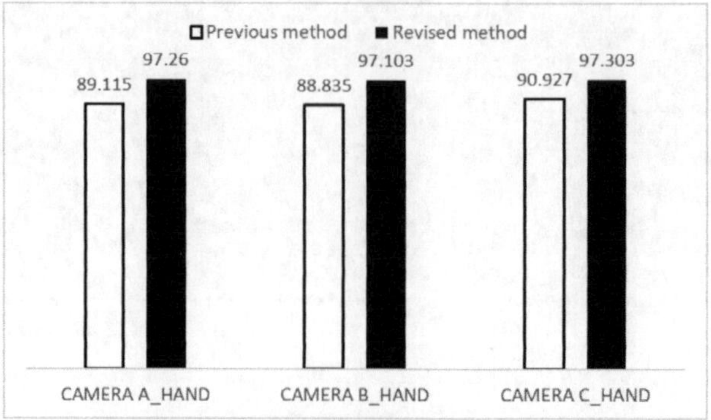

(b) Accuracy of hand wrinkle line detection

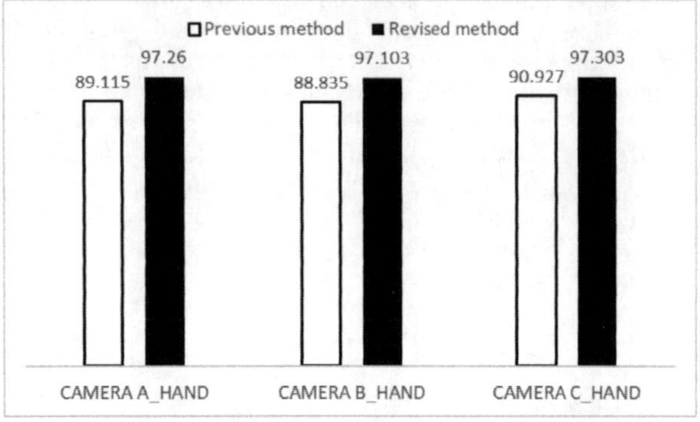

(c) Accuracy of face cell detection

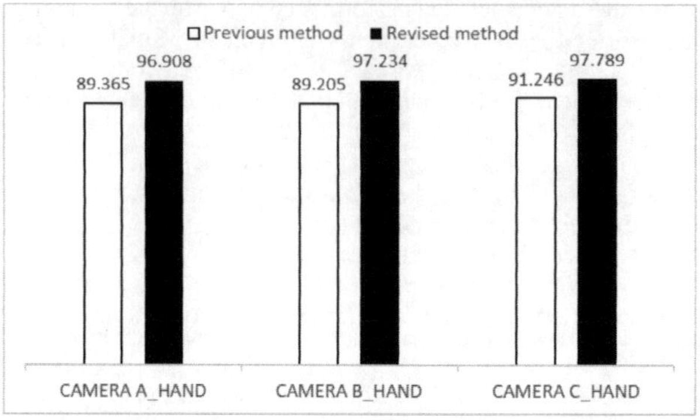

(d) Accuracy of hand cell detection

Figure 11. Accuracy comparison

A. Wrinkle line detection accuracy

To evaluate the accuracy of wrinkle detection, we made ground truth manually using all the images captured using three cameras. That is, we identified and marked cell boundaries (wrinkle) with eyes.

Figure 10 shows an example. Figure 10 (a) shows an original image of 300x300 pixel. Figure 10 (b) shows all the manually identified wrinkle lines on the skin image, and Figure 10 (c) shows only wrinkle lines. On the other hand, Figure 10 (d) shows all the wrinkle lines detected by our proposed method. The detection accuracy can be confirmed visually by overlapping Figure 10 (c) and Figure10 (d) as shown in Figure 10 (e) and quantitatively measured by using Eq. (5).

$$Accuracy = \frac{NWP \cap WP_{GT}}{NWP} \times 100 \qquad (5)$$

Here, NWP is the number of wrinkle pixels and WP_{GT} is the number of pixels on the wrinkle lines in the ground truth.

Basically, the equation counts those pixels that exist on both wrinkle lines, and then they are divided by the total number of pixels on the cell contour lines.

Figure 11 compares the accuracy of our previous method and revised method on the face and hand skin images. From the figure, we can see that our revised method achieved higher accuracy compared to the previous method.

Moreover, our revised method is more robust in hardware characteristics. For instance, Figure 12 shows the result of wrinkle detection on the facial and hand skin using three different cameras. As shown in the figure, our previous method showed different but poor performance depending on camera. However, our revised method showed good and consistent performance regardless of camera.

B. Cell detection

To evaluate the accuracy of cell detection, we used the same ground truth that we mentioned in the last section as follows. If the cell detected by our revised method has a similar location with some cell in the ground truth and the ratio of the cell pixels over the ground truth cell is more than

80%, we declare the cell correctly detected. The accuracy of cell detection is compared in Figure 11 (c) and (d). The accuracy is a little lower compared to the wrinkle detection accuracy. This is because in the case of cell detection, all pixels need to be matched

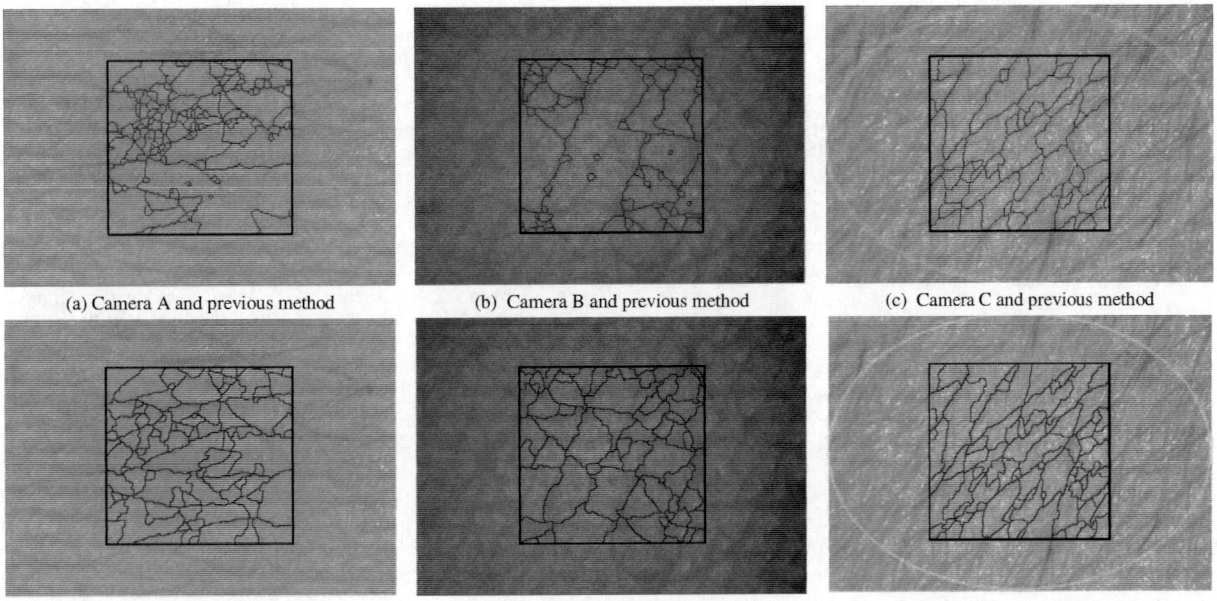

(a) Camera A and previous method (b) Camera B and previous method (c) Camera C and previous method

(d) Camera A and revised method (e) Camera B and revised method (f) Camera C and revised method

Figure 12. Robustness comparison

C. Execution time

Next, we compare the execution time of our previous and revised methods spent for cell detection. Here, total execution time consists of preprocessing time, cell segmentation time and feature extraction time. Figure 13 compares the execution time of previous method and revised method spent for analyzing one skin image. In the figure, both methods have very similar segmentation time since they use same segmentation method. But, we can see considerable reductions in the preprocessing time and feature extraction time. Especially, feature extraction time has been reduced to more than 1/3 by removing pixel-based computation. This reduction is very critical since feature extraction time occupies considerable part of total execution time. As a result, our revised method has reduced the execution time by half compared with the previous method.

VI. CONCLUSION

In this paper, we revised our method for skin feature extraction to improve its accuracy, efficiency and robustness. To improve the accuracy of skin cell detection, we enhanced the contrast of wrinkles on the skin by using the contrast limited adaptive histogram equalization (CLAHE) and highlighted the depth of wrinkles by using the extended-minima transform. In the experiments, we collected skin images using diverse cameras and measured the accuracy and execution time. The result shows that the performance has improved twice in terms of execution time and the accuracy also has improved by 10%. In addition, the performance was not affected much by the camera type, which shows the robustness of our method.

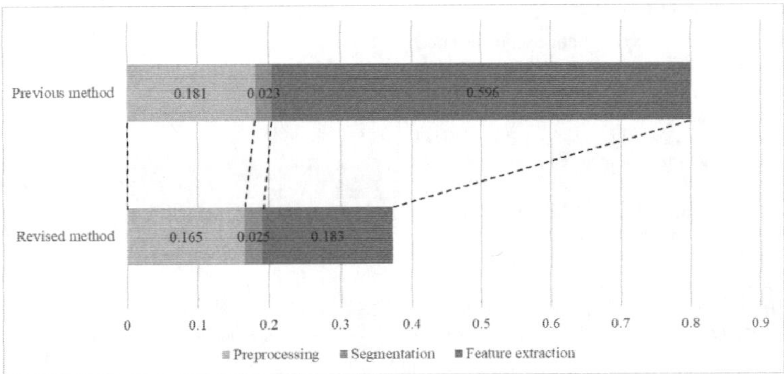

Figure 13. Comparison of excution time

ACKNOWLEDGEMENT

This work was supported by Institute for Information & communications Technology Promotion (IITP) grant funded by the Korea government (MSIP) (No. R0190-16-2012, High Performance Big Data Analytics Platform Performance Acceleration Technologies Development).

REFERENCES

[1] W. Kim, H. Kim, and E. Hwang, "Improving Feature Extraction Accuracy for Skin Analysis," The Ninth International Conferences on Advances in Multimedia, pp. 26-31, April 2017.

[2] Y. H. Choi, D. Kim, E. Hwang, and B. Kim, "Skin texture aging trend analysis using dermoscopy images," Skin Research and Technology, vol. 20, no. 4, pp. 486-497, 2014.

[3] Y.-H. Choi, Y.-S. Tak, S. Rho, and E. Hwang, "Skin feature extraction and processing model for statistical skin age estimation," Multimedia tools and applications, vol. 64, no. 2, pp. 227-247, 2013.

[4] H. Tanaka et al., "Quantitative evaluation of elderly skin based on digital image analysis," Skin research and technology, vol. 14, no. 2, pp. 192-200, 2008.

[5] U. Jacobi et al., "In vivo determination of skin surface topography using an optical 3D device," Skin Research and Technology, vol. 10, no. 4, pp. 207-214, 2004.

[6] G. O. Cula, P. R. Bargo, A. Nkengne, and N. Kollias, "Assessing facial wrinkles: automatic detection and quantification," Skin Research and Technology, vol. 19, no. 1, pp. e243-e251, 2013.

[7] A. P. Yow et al., "Automated in vivo 3D high-definition optical coherence tomography skin analysis system," in Engineering in Medicine and Biology Society (EMBC), 2016 IEEE 38th Annual International Conference of the, pp. 3895-3898, 2016.

[8] Razalli, et al., "Age Range Estimation Based on Facial Wrinkle Analysis Using Hessian Based Filter," Advanced Computer and Communication Engineering Technology, Springer International Publishing, pp. 759-769, 2016.

[9] A. Das and D. Ghoshal, "Human Skin Region Segmentation Based on Chrominance Component Using Modified Watershed Algorithm," Procedia Computer Science, 89, pp. 856-863, 2016.

[10] R. C. Gonzalez and R. E. Woods, "Digital Image Processing," Addison-Wesley, Third edition, 2008.

[11] Z. Junxiong, M. Qingqin, L. Wei, and X. Tingting, "Feature extraction of jujube fruit wrinkle based on the watershed segmentation," International Journal of Agricultural and Biological Engineering, vol. 10, no.4, pp.165-172, 2017

[12] L. J. Belaid and W. Mourou, "Image segmentation: a watershed transformation algorithm," Image Analysis & Stereology, vol. 28, no. 2, pp. 93-102, 2011.

[13] Pizer, et al., "Contrast-limited adaptive histogram equalization: speed and effectiveness," in Visualization in Biomedical Computing, Proceedings of the First Conference on, pp. 337-345, 1990.

[14] Y. C. Hum, K. W. Lai, and M. I. Mohamad Salim, "Multiobjectives bihistogram equalization for image contrast enhancement," Complexity, vol. 20, no. 2, pp. 22-36, 2014.

[15] J. Canny, "A computational approach to edge detection," IEEE Transactions on Pattern Analysis and Machine Intelligence, Vol. 8, No. 6, pp. 679-698, 1986.

[16] L. Lam, S. W. Lee, and C. Y. Suen, "Thinning Methodologies-A Comprehensive Survey," IEEE Transactions on Pattern Analysis and Machine Intelligence, Vol 14, Issue 9, pp. 879, 1992.

[17] N. Otsu, "A threshold selection method from gray-level histograms," Automatica, vol. 11, no. 285-296, pp. 23-27, 1975.

[18] P. Soille, Morphological image analysis: principles and applications. Springer Science & Business Media, 2013.

[19] A. Othmani, et al., "Region-based segmentation on depth images from a 3D reference surface for tree species recognition," Image Processing (ICIP), 2013 20th IEEE International Conference on. IEEE, pp. 3399-3402, 2013.

[20] S. Wold, K. Esbensen, and P. Geladi, "Principal component analysis," Chemometrics and intelligent laboratory systems, vol. 2, no. 1-3, pp. 37-52, 1987.

A Framework for Reproducible Evaluation of Semantic Storage Options

Jedrzej Rybicki* and Benedikt von St. Vieth§
Juelich Supercomputing Center (JSC)
Forschungszentrum Juelich GmbH, Germany
Email: *j.rybicki@fz-juelich.de, §b.von.st.vieth@fz-juelich.de

Abstract—**Despite the urgent need to conduct computer-driven experiments in a reproducible fashion, there is no widely-accepted, established approach to this problem. The rise of Open Data surely helps in understanding and verifying some of the research findings, but the true verification comes from a means to reproduce the original tests. This paper proposes a framework for conducting such reproducible experiments. It leverages Docker to facilitate exchange of, not just source code used in test trails but rather whole, ready-to-run experimental environments. The lightweight virtualization provided by Docker makes it very portable across a wide variety of hardware and software platforms. We explain the framework in detail, discuss its advantages as well as shortcomings, and assess how future-proof it is. The usability of the proposed framework was verified by conducting a reproducible evaluation of the possible storage options for semantic annotations. This use case emerged in the context of a particular distributed infrastructure, where users requested a possibility to annotate stored digital objects. There are many possible technologies that can be used to store semantic annotations. We evaluated performance and suitability of relational databases, document stores, and graph databases, to conclude that the graph database is the best candidate to efficiently handle the task. Although, it has also some limitations, which we will point out. By using the proposed framework in the aforementioned evaluation, we enable other researchers to repeat it, but also benchmark alternative technologies if required. Furthermore, the framework can be reused in an iterative process of performance tuning of the selected storage option, to quantify and verify the influence of particular configuration changes. The main output of this paper is a framework which allows to easily redo the evaluation of semantic storage options.**

Keywords–Deploying Linked Data; Reproducibility; Distributed Infrastructures; Benchmarking.

I. INTRODUCTION

This work is an extended version of our previous publication [1], it presents new experiments, new results, and a more detailed literature review.

Distributed research infrastructures like EUDAT (EUropean DATa [2]) provide generic services to manage research data in an efficient and cost-effective way. Since the research communities using the services advance over time, they are constantly expressing new requirements with respect to kinds of data and possible usages that the infrastructure should support. An example of a community requirement EUDAT, was confronted with, was the support for semantic annotations across its data management services.

Semantic annotations are a very powerful tool to work with data in a distributed environment. They extend the context of the data, and by that increase the data understandability. One can conjure the semantic annotations as a facility to add meta-data and comments to entities managed in the infrastructure. An example would be a keyword attached to a digital object, but more sophisticated cases are envisioned as well. We will explain the model in more detail later in this paper, but astute reader can imagine that efficient annotations handling should enable different types of search queries. It should be possible to retrieve all annotations for a given object, but also reverse lookups (i.e., localizing all data objects with given keyword in our example) will be used. The uptake of this new service will only happen if sufficient performance of both kind of queries can be granted.

This paper is focused on evaluating semantic storage options. We consider a technology to be a valid option for storing annotations if it allows for permanent storage and very basic retrieval operations as described above. There are a lot of products on the marked that advertise much more sophistication with respect to handling specific semantic operations but we wanted to remain generic and include broad range of products in our evaluation. There are many ways in which annotations can be stored. The EUDAT service plans to use the World Wide Web Consortium (W3C) Annotation Data Model [3]. As it is based on JavaScript Object Notation for Linked Data (JSON-LD [4]), an obvious approach would be to use document stores for the task. Such storages (also called document-oriented databases) are optimized to handle semi-structured data (called documents). The managed documents are usually in JSON format. Examples of document stores are MongoDB [5], CouchDB [6], or Elasticsearch [7].

Because annotations are attached to the data objects, the whole data set forms a graph with managed entities and annotating metadata as nodes and annotations as relations between them. Thus, we have included the graph database neo4j [8] into the evaluation of possible storage backends. Lastly, based on the feedback to the original conference paper describing our first results [1], we include relational database management system (RDBMS) MySQL [9] into our evaluation. Relational databases are mature technology, their operations are well understood, and they have high proliferation in distributed infrastructures. Therefore, they constitute an excellent reference point for the above mentioned (perhaps less known) alternatives.

Requirements submitted to EUDAT are analyzed from different view angles. One of them is the performance evaluation of candidate technologies. To this end, resource and service providers are constantly testing and benchmarking possible approaches and new technologies. Such evaluations, must adhere to scientific standards in terms of methodology, transparency, and reproducibility. This is absolutely necessary to make the transparent decisions whether or not a given requirement is implemented and how. Furthermore, such evaluation can be reused by other infrastructures and service providers. The trend to share the results subsumed under the term of Open Data [10] is an important first step in sharing the results. But much more beneficial would be to move the sharing beyond just the results and to make the programs and experimental setups sharable as well. Currently, there is no established solution for such a sharing. The paper includes the results we obtained and their discussion. But our overarching goal was to make the result reproducible, i.e., provide all the tools we used in our evaluations in such a form that an independent researcher can not only retrieve and analyze them but also redo the evaluation and obtain the same results (at least quantitatively). We limit ourselves to the software layers of the conducted experiments starting from the used operating system, libraries, up to the software used for generating the data, measuring the scalability and visualizing the results. This working definition of reproducibility we use across the paper lays somewhat between terms reproducibility and replicability as used in science philosophy.

In one of our previous papers [11], we have already shown that Docker [12] can be leveraged to provide on-demand instances of popular web services in the context of a distributed research infrastructure. Although, such seamless provisioning of services can be used to conduct reproducible research, there are more aspects to it. In this paper, we will exercise a whole workflow from testing, through result processing, up to visualization of the outcomes. We will use Docker and `docker-compose` [13] to conduct the steps in a transparent, sharable, and reproducible way. We will test our approach by evaluating storage options to handle semantic annotations. Based on our results, one can select a technology to best fit her particular use case. The selection of the technology is, however, only the first step towards a working solution. The software used to manage the data must be tuned to obtain best possible performance. Such a tuning is usually done in an iterative way, where the influence of each particular change in configuration on the overall performance is measured and evaluated. The reproducibility framework presented in this paper makes such iterative tests easier to run.

This paper is an extended version of a conference contribution [1]. It includes more experiments and a new possible technology candidate (MySQL). Beside providing more details on the our testing framework, we devoted an additional section to a discussion of functional suitability of the selected technologies. In particular, we elaborate on how the JSON-LD model can be stored in different backends. A new feature of our framework, which we describe in detail here, is the possibility to orchestrate all the experiments and run all the tests, process the results, and visualize the results in a fully automated fashion. This was a remaining step for seamless sharing of the complete experimental setups. We also include an assessment of how future-proof our solution is and a detailed review of the related work.

The rest of this paper is structured as follows. In Section II we will review the state of the art of both semantic storage options and reproducible evaluations in computer science and lay down our vision. Section III explains what semantic annotations are and discuss suitable storage options. Subsequently, we present the selected storage technologies in more detail and touch on the related subject of data modeling. Section V is devoted to the detailed experimental setup and we describe how our reproducibility framework is built and should be used. In particular, the section also discusses how future-proof the approach is. Section VI is presenting the results for the selected semantic storage options. Detailed discussion of the evaluation of the different storage options can be found in Section VII. We conclude the paper with a summary and an outlook on the future work.

II. Related Work

De Witte et al. [14] prepared a benchmark for evaluating triple stores to store Linked Data. Interestingly, they rely on official images available in the Amazon Web Services Cloud [15] to make the results of the evaluation more reproducible. In the later work of this authors also approaches of running the benchmarks with help of Jupyter Notebooks [16] resemble some similarities with our framework. In our work we concentrated more on semantic annotations (with different benchmarks) and did not include triple stores in our evaluations. Also our focus was on making the complete evaluation reproducible beyond particular cloud solutions.

Pacaci et al. [17] examined applicability of relational databases to store social-media-like graphs and compared their performance with graph database systems. Their results are similar to ours. The advantage of the graph database is very good visible for shortest-path queries. In terms of point queries, relational database systems perform better. Also in terms of the writing performance the results are pretty analogous. The relational database (PostgreSQL [18]) exhibited significantly better update performance and maintain up to an order of magnitude faster write throughput compared to their competitors. It should be mentioned that the experimental setup used there differs significantly. In the referred work, unlike our experiments, the whole database are loaded into memory. We believe that this is very beneficial for the relational databases as joins become much faster. The results surely speak for including relational databases in our evaluation.

Hernandez et al. [19] used Wikidata [20] knowledge-base to define a set of benchmarks for popular semantic storage solutions. The focus of the work lays on creating a benchmark with queries close to the observed in real life deployment. It would be interesting to combine the approach into the presented experimental framework to produce more meaningful results. With respect to benchmarks it is worth to mention one more effort. The Linked Data Benchmark Council (LDBC) [21] is a joint effort of academia and industry devoted to establishing benchmarks, benchmark practices, and benchmark results for graph data management software. It has developed two benchmarks: Social Network Benchmark [22] and Semantic Publishing Benchmark [23]. Even if the proposed benchmarks might not necessarily be the best indicators whether a selected technology can provide good performance when storing semantic annotations, they give a lot of useful hints in this regard. It would be also very interesting to incorporate this standardized benchmarks into our experimental framework, we might pursue this direction in the future. The final result should be a standardized set of benchmarks and a agreed-on framework for conducting reproducible experiments using the benchmarks.

There exists a body of work on reproducible research in computational science. Donoho et al. [24] provide an interesting philosophical background on the problem of reproducible research, underlining the potential credibility crisis lack of it can lead to. Finally, they describe their approach to reproducibility research in harmonic analysis. The approach are developed for different kinds of problems, and use different (discipline-specific) tools. Freire et al. [25] provides an overview of the state-of-the-art of reproducible research in the context of data management. Another example of a community defining standard practices for sharing computer code and programs is the publication of Eglen et al. [26], discussing the issue in the context of neuroscience. It might be expected that more and more research communities will undertake the effort of explicitly defining best practices and tools for reproducible experiments. Our work is parallel to such efforts. The proposed framework is not tailored to a specific community. It can, however, accommodate many community-specific tools and thus serve as a basis for the community specific standard testing procedures.

The problem of reproducibility is closely related to the idea of research collaboration. Chandy et al. [27] present how experiments can be conducted in a fully distributed fashion. Where both resources and researchers are spread across the world, yet still are able to conduct reproducible research. We believe that our work, conducted in context of a distributed, inter-disciplinary infrastructure offered by EUDAT, fits well in the authors' vision.

III. Semantic Annotations

Roughly speaking, the EUDAT distributed infrastructure is built to manage research data in form of digital objects (DOs). The objects are composed of bit streams and uniquely identified by persistent identifiers (PIDs) [28]. In some cases the objects also include metadata descriptions. The PIDs are offered by the ePIC system [29]. They can be used to reference the particular objects, for instance in scientific publications. The PID system constitutes an indirection layer that simplifies (future) access to the digital objects, also allowing to move the data between locations without invalidating publications referring to them.

On the other hand, PIDs are just opaque identifiers and on their own provide very little information about the DO they are pointing to, hence, they are not very well suited for browsing and searching through the EUDAT data repositories. Therefore, EUDAT is working on enabling semantic annotations for the objects stored in its distributed research infrastructure. Such annotations describe the DO they are pointing to, extend their context and thus have the potential to facilitate efficient search of data. The current approach is to use the W3C format for annotations. The W3C web annotation data format is pretty simple: Each annotation is a relation between a *body*, e.g., EUDAT data object, and *target*, e.g., metadata describing that object. A basic annotation, as proposed by W3C, is shown in Figure 1.

It is important to notice that both target and body objects in the annotation have unique identifiers. These are crucial from the user's perspective. It can be expect that the users will be interested to view a list of all annotations for a given body id, i.e., all metadata descriptions for a specific data object. Also, a reverse lookup producing all the data objects with specific tag (i.e., a retrieval by target id) represents important functionality. Those expected usage scenarios were used as major hints for our benchmarks. We use three kinds of operations to mesure suitability of a semantic storage option:

- creation of a new, non-existing annotation,

```
{
  "@context": "http://www.w3.org/ns/anno.jsonld",
  "id": "http://example.org/anno2",
  "type": "Annotation",
  "body": {
    "id": "http://example.org/analysis1.mp3",
    "format": "audio/mpeg",
    "language": "fr"
  },
  "target": {
    "id": "http://example.gov/patent1.pdf",
    "format": "application/pdf",
    "language": ["en", "ar"],
    "textDirection": "ltr",
    "processingLanguage": "en"
  }
}
```

Figure 1. A Basic Annotation in W3C Annotation Data Model Format (source: [3]).

- retrieval of an existing annotation by its target id,
- retrieval of an existing annotation by its body id.

All those operations are expected for the final service offering the storage and management of semantic annotations in EUDAT infrastructure. The ratio between the operations is not yet known, but it can be expected that retrieval will be more frequent than store operations. In the long term, more annotations will be read than written.

IV. Storage options

There are many options to store semantic annotations. One obvious approach would be to stick to the JSON-LD rendering as proposed by W3C, use it as the internal storing format, and find a storage backend that can support it. There are many NoSQL solutions (called document stores), which are optimized to manage JSON documents. MongoDB [5] is one of the most popular document stores on the market.

Another storage option we considered is based on the following observation. Annotated objects with annotating metadata form a graph (with annotations as edges). To account for this way of thinking, a graph database like neo4j [8] could be used as a storage backend.

Finally, we included a relational database representative MySQL [9] in our evaluation. It is a mature technology, familiar to both system administrators and users. Although its direct suitability will be discussed later, we believe that a traditional relational database can server very well, at least as a reference point for the remaining results.

For our experiments we used a very simplified form of annotations. We reduced them to just having a target, body id, and creation time. So they were in fact much simpler than the one presented on Figure 1, yet sufficiently complex to approximate the real-world usage. Thus, there were no problems in storing the annotations in the selected database backends. The question of the performance of the products will be discussed later. Firstly, we would like to discuss the suitability of the single products in terms of their functionality, i.e., whether or not they can handle more complex annotations.

The JSON-LD "internal representation of an annotation is the result of transforming a JSON syntactic structure into the core data structures suitable for direct processing: arrays, dictionaries, strings, numbers, booleans, and null" [4]. Modeling arrays and dictionaries in a relational database might be hard. Two obvious options are to store the content of an array as concatenated strings or store the content in a separate table and subsequently use joins to render the complete representation of an annotation. Former approach has its obvious limitations. String comparisons are costly, and for more sophisticated searching criterion, even more expensive regular expressions will have to be used. The later approach, comes at the cost of performance penalty of joins. Similarly, storing "internal" JSON objects, encapsulated in JSON-LD is not an easy task for a relational database. It would probably require to again use distinct tables for each of such an internal objects and rely on laborious joins to render the complete annotation object.

The relational databases require rigid database schema defining fields of single tables, whereas JSON-LD enables far-reaching flexibility in this regard. Some annotations might have fields that other annotations do not have. Depending on the application it might be possible to pre-define a set of annotation fields or again use joins to make the schema more flexible. As mentioned above, each join influence the performance in a negative way. It also makes the queries required to gather all the data from all tables more complex. For our experiments we have modeled annotations as a single table in the relational database. With a primary key composed of target and body id. Because we avoid joins, we obtain lower limit of the response times. Each join, required by more sophisticated models, would increase the response times.

MongoDB is a document store, which supports JSON natively and, therefore, it can handle JSON-LD without additional adaptation. It does not require (and in fact does not allow) to define an equivalent of a database schema. The JSON documents (i.e., annotations) stored in one database can differ significantly with respect to fields they contain. This high flexibility comes at a cost. Although, an explicit, up-front schema model is not required, an implicit model (at the query time) is still present. The application logic has to get to grips with potential heterogeneity of the records, for instance, when presenting the results to the users. Also the lack of a schema makes the definition of constrains and, thus reduction of redundancy, harder. Each document in the document store contains a complete annotation with both target and body objects. The most popular keywords will be stored many times. Such redundancy is relevant for the typical kind of queries the database would have to handle. For instance, to identify all the data objects marked with a given keyword, a full scan of the database would be required. Also, to avoid duplicates, a search would have to be conducted before a new item is inserted into the database. In our experiments, we don't create redundant annotations, the benchmarking program takes care of generating unique content, and we see no redundancy problems, which would occur in real-world applications.

The graph database we used in our experiments (neo4j) does not support JSON-LD natively, but it does not require a rigid schema either. It is possible to have graph nodes with a varying list of fields. At the same time, neo4j occupies a middle ground position with respect to defining constrains. It is possible, yet not mandatory, to define fields that each annotation has to have. It is also possible to define uniqueness constraints to ensure that no duplicates of annotations are stored. We have modeled annotations as two nodes connected by a single relation. In the labeled graph model that neo4j implements, it is possible to add properties to nodes and relations. Properties can be defined as lists and maps so there is no mismatch between JSON-LD and the neo4j model.

V. Experimental setup

To obtain meaningful benchmarking results it is important to minimize the number of "moving parts" and reduce the testing environment to components, which are absolutely necessary. In particular, we were not interested in the performance of the web interface that will be used to work with annotations or the performance penalty caused by its integration with other EUDAT services. Therefore, we have written a Python program with methods for generating annotations with unique body and target identifiers, and for storing and retrieving of the data. The methods use simple interfaces to access selected database stores: MongoDB, neo4j, and MySQL.

A. Docker

To enable easy reproducibility of the conducted tests, we have prepared a Docker-based environment. Docker [12] is a lightweight virtualization solution based on Linux Kernel features like *namespaces* and *cgroups* to isolate guests from the host system. Docker uses image templates to start containers (i.e., guest processes). Furthermore, Docker provides tools to easily exchange images via the public Docker Hub [30], or private on-site repositories. Docker introduces a notion of an official image, which is created and maintained by the provider of a given technology. There are official images for major Linux distributions, but also for popular content management systems and databases. It is possible (and common) to take such images as basis, modify them (e.g., by installing software, or changing their configuration), and publish them as new images in the Docker Hub. The images are built in a hierarchical fashion by applying a "write-on-modify" principle. Thus, it is possible to trace back all the changes done to a given image during the installation and configuration of the software it comprises. It is also possible to review the content of an image before running it. This significantly increases the mutual trust between Docker users and reduces security implications of running Docker containers.

One way of creating images, which we used in our work, is to create a `Dockerfile` describing all the steps required to setup the dependencies, install the software, and configure it. An example of such a `Dockerfile` is depicted in Figure 3. It is an image file of our testing program. Readers with some Debian/Ubuntu experience will recognize initial steps of installing, e.g., `python`, starting from the 3rd line of the file. A sequence of following `RUN` commands set up the python dependencies required by our testing program. The `CMD` directive is defining a command to run upon creation of a container. By default, it will run a bunch of tests against all the supported database backends. The command can be overwritten for each container created from this image. The `VOLUME` instruction states that `/results/` directory in the containers created from this image will store unique data (in our case results) and is not part of the image. As we will show later, upon creation of a container, it is possible to map the volume on any directory of the host machine.

```
mongo:
  image: mongo:3.4.5
neo:
  image: neo4j:3.2
  environment:
    - NEO4J_AUTH=none
mysql:
   image: mysql:5.7.18
   environment:
      - MYSQL_ROOT_PASSWORD=root
tester:
  build: .
  dockerfile: Dockerfile-tester
  links:
    - mongo
    - neo
    - mysql
```

Figure 2. An example of the `docker-compose` deployment descriptor for our experimental environment.

The Docker ecosystem embraces many tools, among them `docker-compose` [13], which is a tool for defining and running multi-container applications that we are going to use in our experiments. In our case we run the testing program and respective backends. The deployments for `docker-compose` are defined via `yaml` files, describing what containers should be started and how they are connected to each other. The deployment descriptor for our testing environment is depicted in Figure 2. It defines three containers for the storage backends, and how they should be created (by using official images). Finally, a container with our benchmarking program is defined. It is created from a `Dockerfile` (`Dockerfile-tester`) and is connected to the remaining containers. For Docker images it is possible to define explicit versions that shall be used. Usually also an image with a tag `latest` is available, and points to the most up-to-date version of the given product. As can be seen in Figure 2, we use explicit versions of the images.

There are many reason why we are using Docker as a basis of our framework. Firstly, due to the virtualization it is possible to run our test programs on almost any platform (regardless of the operating system it uses). The images also contain the dependencies and libraries required, so again the configuration of the host system may be neglected. The possibility to review all the changes done in a particular Docker image enables transparency and understandability of the obtained results. The Docker Hub facilitates an easy exchange of the Docker images containing programs used in the evaluations between researchers. Last but not least, by using Docker volumes, it is possible to separate data from the programs, in our case: results and processing tools.

B. Solution details

All technology providers we considered (MongoDB, neo4j, and MySQL) offer official images for their databases, which we used for our evaluation [31] [32] [33]. We created a Docker image for our testing program and prepared a `docker-compose`-based testing environment. The source code and the documentation is stored on GitHub [34], enabling the verification and repetition of the benchmarking. In fact, we plan to reuse this framework to do some further testing of different EUDAT-inspired use cases in the future. Given a system with a running Docker daemon and `docker-compose`, it is first required to build, and retrieve official images.

```
docker-compose build .
docker-compose pull
cd processor
docker build . -t processor && cd ..
cd visualizer
docker build . -t visualizer && cd ..
```

Starting the evaluation benchmark is done by merely issuing one command like:

```
docker-compose run \\
  --volume=/path/:/results/ \\
  --name exp1
  tester
```

The `--name` parameter of the above command is not strictly required, it attaches a user-defined name (`exp1`) to the particular experimental run, which is convenient for the further analysis. The `--volume` parameter maps the `/results/` directory from the container on `/path/` directory on the host system. Hence, it is possible to separate results for different experiments from each other. It only requires to map the container volume to different physical paths of the host.

Also, Docker images for processing of the results and visualizing them are provided. The first step transforms the results from the evaluation by using command:

```
docker run --volumes-from exp1 \\
  processor
```

The processing step is transforming raw results from the first step into a more human readable form. If multiple results for a given set of parameter are available, an average value with standard deviation is calculated.

The `--volumes-from` parameter is used to attach the storage volume with the data produced in the first step to the newly created Docker container. Please note that we are using the name assigned to the experiment in the previous step (`exp1`) rather than a physical path on the host system. It should be stressed that for a volume of a container to be used by different container, it is not required for the former to be running. In our case, at the time of processing of the results, the benchmarking program is no longer running. Docker maintains its volumes, unless they are explicitly deleted by the user. So there is some persistence of the volumes beyond the lifetime of single container (and experiment run).

Finally, the plots that we will present in the following section are created with help of `gnuplot` [35] and other tools embodied in a Docker image, which again uses volume with data from previous steps and can be run with following command:

```
docker run --volumes-from exp1 \\
  visualizer
```

To enable the sequential processing of the data, we internally agreed to store all the data (results, visualizations, etc.) in the same path defined as a Docker volume. Thanks to this contract, we can guarantee that data are not becoming part of the Docker images and thus will not hinder their

```
FROM ubuntu:latest
MAINTAINER j.rybicki@fz-juelich.de
RUN DBEIAN_FRONTEND=noninteractive apt-get update && \
   apt-get install python python-pip python-mysql.connector -y && \
   apt-get clean autoclean && \
   apt-get autoremove && \
   rm -rf /var/lib/{apt,dpkg,cache,log}
VOLUME /results/
RUN mkdir /app/
ADD . /app/
RUN pip install -r /app/requirements.txt && chmod +x /app/test.py
WORKDIR /results/
CMD sleep 10 && \
    /app/test.py dummy 10 1000 && \
    /app/test.py neo 10 1000 &&  \
    /app/test.py mongo 10 1000 && \
    /app/test.py sql 10 1000
```

Figure 3. Dockerfile of the Tester image.

reuse. Secondly, it is easily possible to extend the workflow by adding new steps or modify existing ones, for instance, if different types of visualization are required. It must be, however, safeguarded that the processing steps don't overlap their outputs, e.g., don't use the same file names to store the results.

C. Orchestration

Although it is hard to quantify, we found Docker tools pretty easy and intuitive to use. In fact, not much deep knowledge of Docker is required to just run the above commands. Nevertheless, our goal is to make the results highly and easily reproducible. We aim at ways of sharing complete, running, testing environment with all the dependencies required to repeat the tests.

Docker does not support the execution of workflows (i.e., subsequent commands). Thus, we had to search for alternatives. One solution would be to use scripts or programming languages to automate the execution of the commands. It is not an easy task to make the scripts understandable, adjustable, and really portable. It would require a lot of effort to create scripts for all the platforms on which prepared Docker can be deployed. Alternatively, the scripts could be encapsulated in a virtualization solution to enable cross-platform compatibility. In fact we already presented a lightweight virtualization solution, namely Docker.

It is possible to chain commands as mentioned before in a CMD directive of a new Docker container, which we call orchestrating container. It would not be, however, very beneficial to then create the testing environment in the container as this would substantially increase the virtualization overhead. Therefore, we propose a different solution. The orchestrating container could access the Docker interface of the host it is running on, use this interface to create the testing environment, run the tests, process the results, and produce the visualizations. An overview of this approach is depicted in Figure 4. The socket file used for communication between Docker client and Docker daemon can be injected into the orchestrating container and subsequently used by the Docker and docker-compose clients installed in the orchestrating container. After starting the container it will pull all required images from Docker Hub and afterwards run them in the proper order. Therefore, to execute the whole workflow, it is only required to issue just one command:

```
docker run \\
  -v /var/run/docker.sock:\\
  /var/run/docker.sock \\
  httpprincess/orchestrator:1.0
```

The main disadvantage of the solution is its lack of flexibility in terms of managing volumes. Volumes used for storing the results are mounted from the host machine and not from the orchestrating container. Thus, to change the location the /results/ volume is mapped on, one would have to manipulate docker-compose setup files confined in the orchestrator image or use the default location. It is still possible to refer to the volumes by using container names though. Also, to change the evaluation parameters it would be required to change the image. To this end, a feature of running Docker containers in an interactive way might be beneficial.

We expect that the provided orchestration container will be used to automate the parameter tuning or for just repeating the experiments we did. For more advance usages (like testing against different technologies), the orchestrator will provide hints on how to conduct the experiments and setup the testing environment, but the researcher will have to step in and make some changes anyhow.

D. Making the framework future-proof

Our main goal was to make the evaluation of the semantic storage options reproducible. It also means that the researchers wishing to repeat our experiments should be able to do so even in some distant future. In this section we would like to discuss how future-proof the presented solution is.

It is hard to predict changes in the technology landscape. The main corner stone of our framework is Docker. Although this technology is pretty new, it is based on Linux Kernel features available already for a longer period of time. It should be stressed that Docker (unlike typical virtualization technologies) does not include a Kernel in the containers but rather use the Kernel of the host system and rely on its features for process isolation. The Docker images we use as a basis for our images will become obsolete, but by publishing our Dockerfiles we enable the rebuilt of the

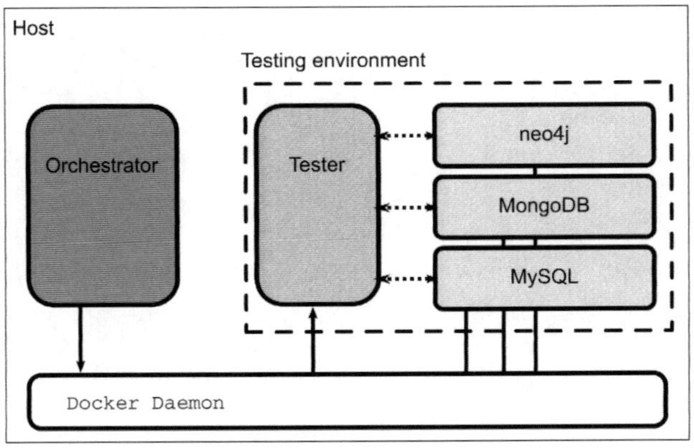

Figure 4. Schematic explanation of the orchestration solution.

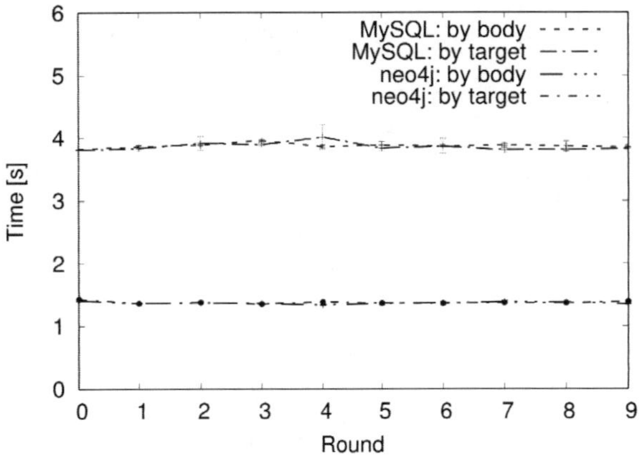

Figure 5. Difference between retrieval by target and by body for neo4j and MySQL ($reps = 10000$ records are added and retrieved in each round).

images with new versions. Using just the `Dockerfiles` to built the images, has some drawbacks. As can be seen in Figure 3, in the process of building the image, software from the official Linux distribution repository is retrieved and installed. When (in not so distant future) new versions of this software become available, the produced images will also be different. To circumvent this limitation we uploaded the images to the Docker Hub [36] [37] [38] [39]. It is no longer required to build the images, they can be retrieved from this repository with a `pull` command:

```
docker pull httpprincess/tester:1.0
```

Docker allows for tagging of the images with versions. Even if the images change in the future, and new version becomes available, it is still possible to retrieve old images. All the images used for the experiments presented in this paper were tagged as version `1.0`.

When discussing a more distant future we run into different kinds of issues. If Docker become obsolete, the availability of our source code [34], together with the respective `Dockerfiles` becomes important. Although the images cannot be built anymore (presuming there is no Docker), they still constitute a formal description of the installation and configuration process.

The future availability of the selected storage technologies is not in our hands, but this is the motivation for making the process of performance evaluation reproducible. The same tests can be run against new version of the products or (after some modifications) against similar products that will become available. As mentioned before, in the `docker-compose` file describing our testing environment, we use explicit versions of the official images of the storage technologies (rather than opting for `latest` images). As long as those versions are available in the Docker Hub, it would be possible to repeated our experiments.

VI. Results

All the tests were run on the same virtual machine with 16 VCPUs, 16 GB RAM, using Ubuntu 16.04 LTS. We used official Docker images for MongoDB in version 3.4.5, neo4j in version 3.2, and MySQL in version 5.7.8. The Docker daemon was running version 1.12.6, and `docker-compose` in version 1.14.0.

Our experiments are defined by three parameters:

1) $engine$: database engine (currently MongoDB, neo4j, and MySQL),
2) $rounds$: number of rounds,
3) $reps$: number of repetitions in each round.

The tests were divided into rounds and in each round all the previously defined database operations (see Section III) were conducted in the following order. Firstly, $reps$ number of records were created, subsequently random (with repetition) $reps$ annotations were retrieved by specifying existing $target.id$, finally $reps$ random annotations were fetched by $body.id$. We measured the time of each activity, that is the complete time to create records, time to retrieve all $reps$ record by target and body id. Three time measurements were made in each round. Please note, that no records were removed, i.e., for given $reps = 1000$, the database grown in each round by new 1000 records. If not stated differently, each experiment was repeated three times and the average value of response times with standard deviation were calculated for each round.

A. Retrieval scalability

Figure 5 presents the response times for retrieval of the annotations by target and by body. We only compare the results for neo4j and MySQL. As can be seen, for a given technology there is not much difference in the response times. Situation looks a little bit different for MongoDB, which is depicted separately in Figure 6 as the absolute values are much higher, and would make the previous plot less readable. There is a difference between body and target retrieval, yet the differences lay within the standard error value. For the reminder of this section (if not stated differently) only retrieval by the body id will be presented.

In Figure 7, Figure 8, and Figure 9, we depicted the retrieval scalability of each technology tested. For that we conducted three experiments with different values of $reps$ (1000, 5000, 10000), each had 10 rounds. Figure 7 shows

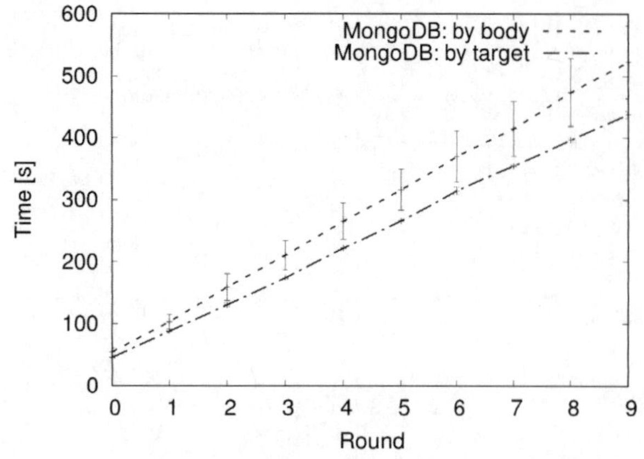

Figure 6. Difference between retrieval by target and by body for MongoDB ($reps$ = 10000 records are added and retrieved in each round).

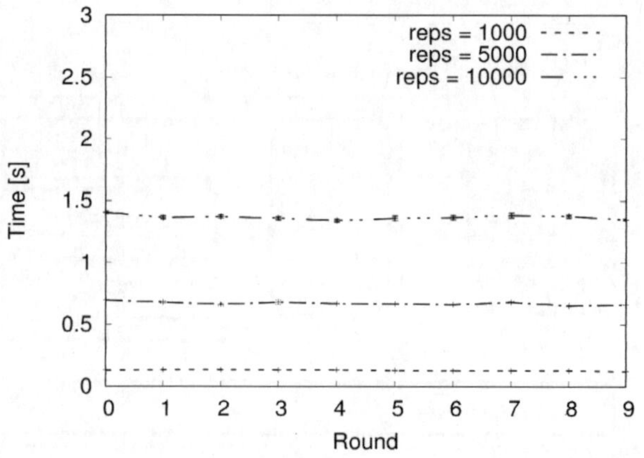

Figure 8. Retrieval scalability for neo4j ($reps$ new records are added, and $reps$ random records are retrieved in each round).

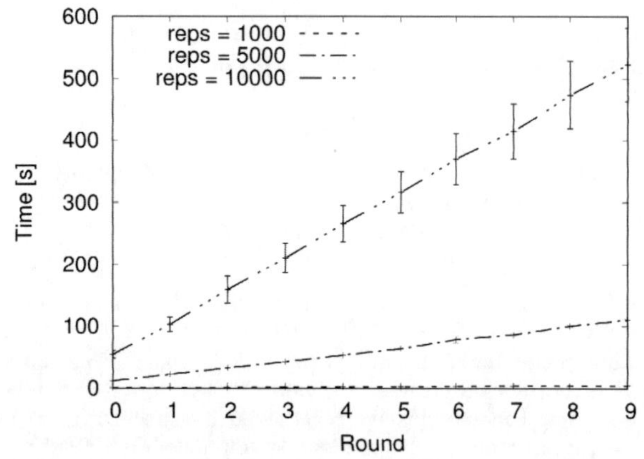

Figure 7. Retrieval scalability for MongoDB ($reps$ records are added, and $reps$ random records are retrieved in each round).

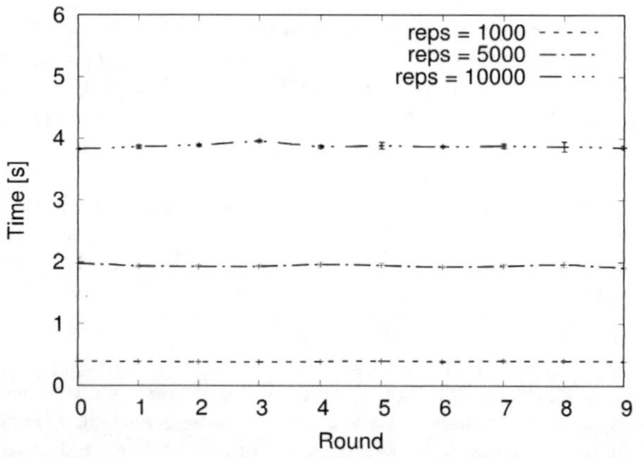

Figure 9. Retrieval scalability for MySQL ($reps$ new records are added, and $reps$ random records are retrieved in each round).

that the performance of MongoDB is dramatically decreasing with the increasing number of records in the store. Also, the absolute values achieved by MongoDB are not very good, to retrieve 10000 random annotations from a database with 90000 documents, almost eight minutes are required.

The retrieval times for the same amount of data from the neo4j database of the same size are much lower as can be seen in Figure 8 (please note that the y axis was scaled comparing to Figure 7). Also, the scalability of neo4j is much better, neo4j produces constant answer times regardless of the size of the database. For comparison with the MongoDB, time to retrieve 10000 random entities from a neo4j graph (regardless of its size), varies around $1.37s$. When comparing neo4j with MySQL (i.e., Figure 8 with Figure 9), one can see that neo4j is faster across the parameter range by roughly a factor of 3, but MySQL remains much faster than MongoDB.

B. Storing scalability

The situation is a little bit different for creation times. We depicted them in Figure 10 and Figure 11. This time MongoDB outperforms its competitors. Both neo4j and MySQL suffer under high variance in the query times. For higher value of $reps = 10000$, neo4j is clearly the slowest in creating new annotations. We believe that the main reason for this is the fact that neo4j is using the most sophisticated model for annotations. A creation of an annotation requires creation of two nodes in the graph (one for target and one for body) and an edge connecting them. Upon creation, neo4j is also verifying the uniqueness constrain for the created nodes. MySQL is storing the values for annotation in one table, and MongoDB does not verify the uniqueness. As stated above, in a more realistic scenarios, one would have to use multiple tables for storing annotations in MySQL, and run transactions to add new values. Also in case of MongoDB, firstly a laborious search across the database would be required to avoid duplicates. It would increase the query times by the amount depicted in Figure 7.

VII. Discussion

Our evaluation included three distinct classes of products: document store (MongoDB), relational database (MySQL),

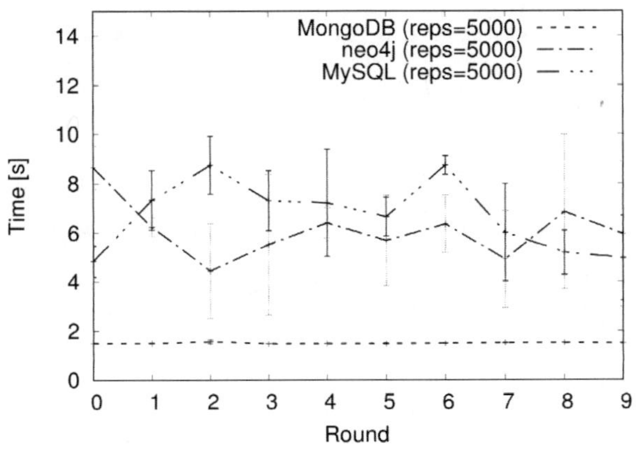

Figure 10. Comparison of creation scalability ($reps = 5000$ new records are added in each round).

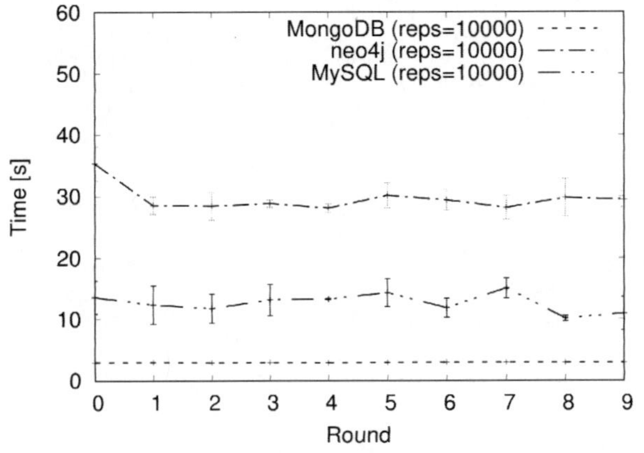

Figure 11. Comparison of creation scalability ($reps = 10000$ new records are added in each round).

and a native graph database (neo4j). The evaluation can be roughly split in two main experiments: storing and retrieving. In terms of retrieving of annotations the neo4j is a clear winner, followed by MySQL. The storing part was best handled by MongoDB, which displayed very good scalability. On the overall, we have two products that excel in one metric: neo4j in retrieval and MongoDB in storing. MySQL occupies the middle position in both dimensions.

We discussed the suitability of the products. We argued that neo4j might be best suited also for handling more sophisticated use cases than those in our tests. On the other hand, the results for MySQL would be probably degraded in case of more complicated (and thus more join-intensive) queries.

The final recommendation with respect to kind of storage that should be used to manage semantic annotations depends on the ratio between reads and writes the service has to handle. In most of the cases the reading would be the most dominant operation and then probably neo4j is the best option. In case of very write-intensive applications, MongoDB might be a better option. Also more complex deployments with both MongoDB and neo4j supporting respectively write and read operations (and synchronizing the storage in the background) are conceivable.

The evaluation was conducted with the help of the above described framework. It is hard to quantify how easy it is to use, but the actual deployment of the software and starting of experiments was done with help of Docker and took very little time and effort. We stick to our definition of reproducibility (see Section I) and exclude the influence of the hardware. We can, however, see that it has some influence on the results. A clear indicator for that is the variance of the measured values across test runs. We include the variance in the evaluation plots. The goal of the reproducible evaluation is not to obtain exactly the same curves on the plot, but rather quantitatively same results within given range of confidence intervals.

VIII. Conclusion and Future Work

In this paper, we have evaluated different options for storing semantic annotations. From these options native graph database seems to be the best general candidate technology, some specific use cases can be better off with other tested solutions.

Our main contribution is the framework for conducting the above described experiments in a reproducible fashion. This framework is based on a novel technology and allows a seamless exchange of not only code used for benchmarks but complete, ready-to-run experimental setups between the researchers. We implemented the framework in such a way that it is possible to reproduce our experiments, process the results, and produce plots by issuing just one command. Furthermore, by sharing both the source code of our testing scripts and formal Docker-based description of their installation, we allow researchers to reuse and adjust them to answer different research questions. We discussed how future-proof the framework is and, although, such predictions are always hard, we argued that the framework has some potential to better understand and repeat our experiments even in the future.

In our future work, it would be interesting to follow two directions. Firstly, incorporate more sophisticated benchmarks in our framework to validate our current recommendations with respect to the tested technologies. Such benchmarks could bring to surface currently hidden scalability and redundancy management problems we alluded to. Secondly, the application of the framework to other use cases and other technologies could cast some light on its extensibility. Such more extensive applications would also help in defining more robust ways of exchanging data between the steps of the workflow.

Acknowledgment

The work has been supported by EUDAT2020, funded by the European Union under the Horizon 2020 programme - DG CONNECT e-Infrastructures (Contract No. 654065).

References

[1] J. Rybicki and B. von St. Vieth, “Reproducible evaluation of semantic storage options,” in Proceedings of the 3rd IARIA International Conference on Big Data, Small Data, Linked Data and Open Data (ALLDATA ’17), Apr. 2017, pp. 26–29, ISBN: 978-1-61208-552-4, ISSN: 2519-8386.

[2] W. Gentzsch, D. Lecarpentier, and P. Wittenburg, "Big data in science and the EUDAT project," in Proceedings of the Service Research and Innovation Institute Global Conference, Apr. 2014, pp. 191–194, ISBN: 978-1-4799-5193-2, ISSN: 2166-0786.

[3] W3C Web Annotation Data Model. [Online]. Available: https://www.w3.org/TR/annotation-model/ [retrieved: Nov., 2017]

[4] A JSON-based Serialization for Linked Data. [Online]. Available: https://json-ld.org/ [retrieved: Nov., 2017]

[5] MongoDB. [Online]. Available: https://www.mongodb.com/ [retrieved: Nov., 2017]

[6] Apache CouchDB. [Online]. Available: https://couchdb.apache.org/ [retrieved: Nov., 2017]

[7] C. Gormley and Z. Tong, Elasticsearch: The Definitive Guide. O'Reilly Media, 2015, ISBN: 978-1-449-35854-9.

[8] J. Webber, "A programmatic introduction to Neo4j," in Proceedings of the 3rd ACM Annual Conference on Systems, Programming, and Applications: Software for Humanity (SPLASH '12), Oct. 2012, pp. 217–218, ISBN: 978-1-4503-1563-0.

[9] MySQL. [Online]. Available: https://www.mysql.com/ [retrieved: Nov., 2017]

[10] M. B. Gurstein, "Open data: Empowering the empowered or effective data use for everyone?" First Monday, vol. 16, no. 2, 2011, ISSN: 13960466.

[11] J. Rybicki and B. v. St. Vieth, "DARIAH Meta Hosting: Sharing software in a distributed infrastructure," in Proceedings of the 38th IEEE International Convention on Information and Communication Technology, Electronics and Microelectronics (MIPRO '15), May 2015, pp. 217–222, ISBN: 978-9-5323-3082-3.

[12] Docker. [Online]. Available: https://www.docker.com/ [retrieved: Nov., 2017]

[13] Docker Compose. [Online]. Available: https://docs.docker.com/-compose/ [retrieved: Nov., 2017]

[14] D. De Witte, L. De Vocht, R. Verborgh, K. Knecht, F. Pattyn, H. Constandt, E. Mannens, and R. Van de Walle, "Big linked data ETL benchmark on cloud commodity hardware," in Proceedings of the ACM International Workshop on Semantic Big Data (SBD '16), 2016, pp. 1–6, ISBN: 978-1-4503-4299-5.

[15] Amazon Web Services. [Online]. Available: https://aws.amazon.com/ [retrieved: Nov., 2017]

[16] Project Jupyter. [Online]. Available: http://jupyter.org/ [retrieved: Nov., 2017]

[17] A. Pacaci, A. Zhou, J. Lin, and M. T. Özsu, "Do we need specialized graph databases?: Benchmarking real-time social networking applications," in Proceedings of the Fifth International Workshop on Graph Data-management Experiences & Systems (GRADES '17), 2017, pp. 1–7, ISBN: 978-1-4503-5038-9.

[18] S. Riggs, G. Ciolli, and G. Bartolini, PostgreSQL Administration Cookbook, 9.5/9.6. Packt Publishing, 2017, ISBN: 978-1-785-88318-7.

[19] D. Hernández, A. Hogan, C. Riveros, C. Rojas, and E. Zerega, "Querying wikidata: Comparing SPARQL, relational and graph databases," in Proceedings of the 15th International Semantic Web Conference (ISWC '16), Oct. 2016, pp. 88–103, ISBN: 978-3-319-46546-3.

[20] Wikidata. [Online]. Available: https://www.wikidata.org/ [retrieved: Nov., 2017]

[21] Linked Data Benchmark Council (LDBC). [Online]. Available: http://www.ldbcouncil.org/ [retrieved: Nov., 2017]

[22] O. Erling, A. Averbuch, J. Larriba-Pey, H. Chafi, A. Gubichev, A. Prat, M.-D. Pham, and P. Boncz, "The LDBC social network benchmark: Interactive workload," in Proceedings of the ACM International Conference on Management of Data (SIGMOD '15), 2015, pp. 619–630, ISBN: 978-1-4503-2758-9.

[23] A. Iosup, T. Hegeman, W. L. Ngai, S. Heldens, A. Prat-Pérez, T. Manhardto, H. Chafio, M. Capotă, N. Sundaram, M. Anderson, I. G. Tănase, Y. Xia, L. Nai, and P. Boncz, "LDBC graphalytics: A benchmark for large-scale graph analysis on parallel and distributed platforms," Proceedings of the Very Large Data Base Endowment, vol. 9, no. 13, Sep. 2016, pp. 1317–1328.

[24] D. L. Donoho, A. Maleki, I. U. Rahman, M. Shahram, and V. Stodden, "Reproducible research in computational harmonic analysis," Computing in Science & Engineering, vol. 11, no. 1, 2009, pp. 8–18, ISSN: 1521-9615.

[25] J. Freire, P. Bonnet, and D. Shasha, "Computational reproducibility: State-of-the-art, challenges, and database research opportunities," in Proceedings of the ACM International Conference on Management of Data (SIGMOD '12), 2012, pp. 593–596, ISBN: 978-1-4503-1247-9.

[26] S. Eglen, B. Marwick, Y. Halchenko, M. Hanke, S. Sufi, P. Gleeson, R. A. Silver, A. Davison, L. Lanyon, M. Abrams et al., "Towards standard practices for sharing computer code and programs in neuroscience," Nature Neuroscience, vol. 20, no. 6, 2017, pp. 770–773, ISSN: 1097-6256.

[27] K. M. Chandy, J. Kiniry, A. Rifkin, and D. Zimmerman, "Webs of archived distributed computations for asynchronous collaboration," The Journal of Supercomputing, vol. 11, no. 2, 1997, pp. 101–118, ISSN: 1573-0484.

[28] R. Kahn and R. Wilensky, "A framework for distributed digital object services," International Journal on Digital Libraries, vol. 6, no. 2, Apr. 2006, pp. 115–123, ISSN: 1432-5012.

[29] ePIC Consortium. ePIC – persistent identifiers for eResearch. [Online]. Available: http://www.pidconsortium.eu/ [retrieved: Nov., 2017]

[30] Docker Hub. [Online]. Available: https://hub.docker.com/ [retrieved: Nov., 2017]

[31] Official Docker MongoDB Image. [Online]. Available: https://hub.-docker.com/_/mongo/ [retrieved: Nov., 2017]

[32] Official Docker neo4j Image. [Online]. Available: https://hub.docker.-com/_/neo4j/ [retrieved: Nov., 2017]

[33] Official Docker MySQL Image. [Online]. Available: https://hub.-docker.com/_/mysql/ [retrieved: Nov., 2017]

[34] J. Rybicki. Annotations scalablity: Source code reposiotry. [Online]. Available: https://github.com/httpPrincess/annotations-scalability [retrieved: Nov., 2017]

[35] Gnuplot. [Online]. Available: http://gnuplot.sourceforge.net/ [retrieved: Nov., 2017]

[36] J. Rybicki. Docker image for Tester. [Online]. Available: https://hub.docker.com/r/httpprincess/tester/ [retrieved: Nov., 2017]

[37] ——. Docker image for Results Processor. [Online]. Available: https://hub.docker.com/r/httpprincess/processor/ [retrieved: Nov., 2017]

[38] ——. Docker image for Orchestrator. [Online]. Available: https://hub.docker.com/r/httpprincess/orchestrator/ [retrieved: Nov., 2017]

[39] ——. Docker image for Results Visualizer. [Online]. Available: https://hub.docker.com/r/httpprincess/orchestrator/ [retrieved: Nov., 2017]

Empirical Evaluation of Data Visualizations by Non-Expert Users

Elena Ornig, Jolon Faichney, Bela Stantic
School of Information and Communication Technology
Griffith University
Gold Coast, Australia
email: elena.ornig@griffithuni.edu.au
email: {j.faichney, b.stantic}@griffith.edu.au

Abstract — **With the increased release of Open Government Data (OGD), several problems hinder the breakthrough of the Open Data agenda into the mainstream. One of these problems is the slow acceptance of OGD by non-expert end-users. They do not have the technical skills and prefer a *human-readable* format compared to the experts who demand *machine-readable* data. Recently, some OGD portals added interactive visualizations to ease the use of OGD by non-expert users. However, the question of human-usability or what makes it easier for non-experts to interact with OGD visualizations, remains open. With the aim to answer this question, we report results on the evaluation of OGD visualizations from the field experiment conducted with non-expert users. We discuss results and insights to inform designers and OGD providers.**

Keywords - data visualization; empirical evaluation; open government data; non-expert users.

I. INTRODUCTION

This paper is an extended version of [1]. In this paper we provide more detail on the conducted field experiment; explain how the Visualization Evaluation Design Constructor (VEDC) was applied and provide more detail about experiment results and observations, including informal comparisons with Data USA portal and an extension to the previous discussion.

The current number of released datasets is now over 18 million [2]. According to dataportal.org, there are 520 registered government portals [3]. On the International Open Government Dataset Search, there are 192 catalogs in 24 languages, representing 43 countries [4]. These numbers represent a growing supply of OGD for users. However, there are many barriers preventing OGD breakthrough into the mainstream [5]. One possible barrier, which we investigate, is the limited usability of open data.

A study on barriers to Open Data Agenda, found that the initial focus has been on the supply side, followed by a focus on data discovery and integration; only recently, with the increased development of data applications, the concern has been raised on the demand side [5]. Additionally, the desired format of the data is one that is machine-readable. The motivation is based on the principle of completeness so that the community has access to raw information from datasets [6].

A downside to this motivation is that it is only usable by a small percentage of the community, those with technical computer skills, such as computer programmers and data analysts, i.e. the experts in data creation, modification, and manipulation. The focus on machine-readability has limited the human-usability of open data. The users with a lack of technical skills, particularly *common citizens,* will find using OGD in the form of reports, visualizations and applications more usable [7]. On the other hand, *informed citizens* can view visualizations and analytical results [8].

Several studies addressed the question of OGD demand, its consumption and the lack of user's technical skills. Shadbolt et al. [8] listed several lessons that can form part of a roadmap to move away from raw government data to a Linked-data Web (LDW) that can be regularly consumed by citizens. Ding et al. [9] developed the Semantic Web-based Tetherless World Constellation (TWC) Linked Open Government Data (LOGD) portal to support LOGD production and consumption. They concluded that LOGD must provide service to a diverse set of stakeholders, including *average citizens*. The MIT Media Lab created the free software portal DataViva, as an information visualization engine, to make open government data more comprehensible for the *average user* [10].

Furthermore, the MIT Media Lab, in partnership with Deloitte and Datawheel, released "the most comprehensive website and visualization engine," Data USA, to make it easier to use OGD for people without technical skills [11]. Graves and Hendler [7] proposed use of visualizations to deal with a lack of technical expertise and developed a prototype tool to simplify the creation of visualization based on Open Data for non-expert users.

Though, none of these studies had provided a formal evaluation of human usability of OGD, they acknowledged the need for visualization [8], its potential to lower demand on technical expertise [7][9][11] and the need to evaluate how citizens can participate, and what makes it easier for them to consume OGD [7]. We characterize a *common citizen*, an *average user* or a *user without technical skills* as a non-expert user.

This paper is organized as follows. First, we investigate what stops non-expert users utilize OGD. Secondly, we evaluate what limits usability for non-expert citizens in using existing OGD visualizations incorporated into portals [1]. In Section II we provide an overview of the identified problems and challenges in visualization and its evaluation.

Next, motivated to better understand the complexity of visualization evaluation, we conceptualized the Evaluation Method Mapping (EMM) approach. This approach and how it was applied, is described in Section III. In order to access possible evaluation methods and techniques, we developed the Visualization Evaluation Design Constructor (VEDC). The VEDC is a framework that consists of four, essential for any evaluation, elements: general goals, evaluation methods, theoretical implications and practical aspects. The VEDC was applied to construct a task-based field experiment. The use of VEDC is also explained in Section III.

A formal experiment was conducted to evaluate the usability of three different visualizations: 1) TreeMap, which represents data in percentage terms; 2) Map, which represents the spatial distribution of variables, and 3) Stacked, which represents growth of a variable over a period of time. The results and findings are shown in Section IV. Furthermore, we discuss significance and implications of the results in Section V. Finally, Section VI contains our conclusions and offers directions for future work.

II. BACKGROUND

A. Multi-disciplinary fusion of Visualization

Visualization is an effective technique for the communication of data, due to our natural ability to understand patterns. Ware [12] provides a scientific explanation:

"The human visual system is a pattern seeker of enormous power and subtlety. The eye and the visual cortex of the brain form a massively parallel processor that provides the highest bandwidth channel into human cognitive centers."

Ware [12] views the role of visualization in cognitive systems as small but crucial and expanding. Though, Ware highlights several capabilities of information visualization, including its ability to help humans comprehend large amounts of data; he takes a view that all people have the same visual system, which can only perceive presented data in a particular way. Thus, he argues, if we can understand how we perceive data, we can build better visual displays. Shneiderman [13], from the field of Human Computer Interaction (HCI) views information visualization as a subfield. There is no strict formula for a successful interface but only a few basic approaches. The computer is seen as a 'tool' to extend the user's body, in order to create experience where the user is in control, confident and focused on their goal. This *optimal experience* is achieved through a balance when the interface is simple, not confusing, but at the same time—not boring.

Two decades ago, Butler, Almond, Bergeron, Brodlie, and Haber [14], in their discussion of the general understanding of visualization, asked if visualization is a general process or "a collection of unique, unrelated techniques?" They queried if the scope of the visualization reference model should include related domains: visual perception, computer-human interface and computer graphics? Who should use it—providers, developers or users? Would they use it to learn techniques, to evaluate systems, to design systems or to define standards? Since then, several visualization reference models and taxonomies of visualization techniques were developed, including: a data-oriented taxonomy by Card and Mackinlay [15] and a type-by-task taxonomy by Shneiderman [17]. Also, Khan and Khan [16] have published a collection of all visualization techniques, giving each a brief introduction to guide young researchers through their work in visualization.

A decade ago, Lengler and Eppler [18] overviewed the discipline of visualization studies and found it a highly unstructured domain of research in the context of applicable visualization methods. To provide assistance for researchers and practitioners, a user-centered periodic table of 100 visualization methods was created as a prototypical example based on Shneiderman's Visual Information-Seeking Mantra. In their table of visualization methods, they highlighted the fact that there is not necessarily one appropriate method but rather a few different methods that could be applied for a particular requirement. By using this table, a designer could see which methods are providing overview, overview *and* details on demand, and which methods are good at providing additional details.

They also categorized visualization methods according to cognitive processes: convergent and divergent thinking. For example, an area chart, which is a type of data visualization method and a data map, which is another type of information visualization method, can both be used to *overview* an entire collection of items (Shneiderman's design principle [17]). The treemap, an information visualization method, can be used for simultaneous *overview* and *detail* (Shneiderman's design principle [17]). These three methods of visualization are applicable to the cognitive process of convergent thinking. Lengler and Eppler [18] used several selection criteria before a specific method was included in the table: a method must be fully documented, must be put into practice in real-life, must illustrate complex issues, must be applicable by non-experts and previously evaluated.

These criteria reflect the underlining multi-disciplinary fusion of visualization in general, and the information visualization field, which originated from low level perception and statistics, and in modern times includes [19]: "color theory, visual cognition, visual grammars, interaction theory, visual analytics, and information theory." This inherited multi-disciplinary fusion causes a challenge for scientists to define a unified theory of visualization.

Traditionally, a general theory can be formulated through the process of eliminating or unifying competing and complementary theories, from determined domains [20]. In regards to data and information visualization, some possible theories were discussed by a group of scientists from Brown University in the US [20]. Demiralp [20] identified a need for specific and restricted theoretic models that would provide explicit methods for effective visualizations. He concludes that the question of how to measure and construct effective visualizations, in general, is an unsolved problem. Laidlaw [20] observed a controversy in identifying what defines a theory of visualization. Wijk [20] stated that the discipline of visualization is a technology and not a science.

In order to understand what works and does not work, there is a need to develop methods and techniques and a need for cross-cutting insights as a guide in searching for new visualization solutions. Ware [20] argued that the reason why visualization works is in its transformation of data, which creates visual patterns. These patterns, due to natural human perception skills, then help to solve problems. Since theory is based on generalized experimental results, then, in "the case of data visualization in large part this has to be the theory of perception" [20]. Thus, applied perception and distributed cognitive algorithms are all that is needed for the theory of visualization design. In addition, the panelists argued [20] that evaluating visualization with user studies is insufficient and inefficient when an inductive approach is used.

B. Evaluation challenges

However, the advantage of evaluating visualization has many different values for other researchers. Plaisant [21] sees evaluation value, particularly by *potential adopters* or *new users,* in the discoveries of the same data through new perspectives i.e. in answers to questions "you didn't know you had" and even possible changes in work practices. She argues that controlled experiments and usability studies help to recognize the tool's potential and limitations. Lam et al. [22] define evaluation as a complex science which aids in the detailed understanding of a tool or system and their supportive processes. This includes "exploratory data analysis and reasoning, communication through visualization or collaborative data analysis." They specified evaluation as an assessment of the visualizations themselves and contributed a new, scenario-based approach for the information visualization research community [22]. Carpendale [23] emphasized the importance of empirical research and called for more convincing evaluations to encourage wider adoption of information visualization tools.

Despite the difference in opinion on the benefit in evaluation of visualization and the existing lack of a unified theory, in terms of design principles, significant and well-established work has been done in the fields of data and information visualization and HCI.

Shneiderman [17], the inventor of treemap visualization, developed a type-by-task taxonomy to guide designers of advanced graphical user interfaces: *overview first* ("Gain an overview of the entire collection"); *zoom* ("Zoom in on items of interest") *and filter* ("filter out uninteresting items")*; then details-on-demand ("Select an item or group and get details when needed").* He defined these as basic principles, commonly known as the Visual Information Seeking Mantra. He used this mantra as a starting point to propose a type-by-task taxonomy (TTT) of information visualization, adding new tasks: *relate, history,* and *extract*. These seven tasks represent a high level of abstraction based on the user's problems, to be solved in seven data types: "1-, 2-, 3-dimensional data, temporal and multi-dimensional data, and tree and network data" for controlled exploration by users [17]. Shneiderman [14] also laid the philosophical foundation for designers to make systems comprehensible, the interfaces predictable and controllable, and the features understandable for the tasks. The design must amplify user's capabilities and make users feel like masters who can accomplish their tasks with pride.

To achieve this, the theory of visualization needs methodologies to integrate its rules into visualization software [19]. The designers of visualizations need a reminder that serving a human need is the purpose of technology [24]. Information visualization needs new evaluative methodologies for usability studies, with a learning-centered perspective [25]. The evaluators need improvement of usability testing. This will help to conduct more rigorous empirical research, where the methodology fits a proposed research question, a given situation and a research goal [23]. Plaisant [21] recommends evaluations where tools are matched with users, tasks, and real problems. She describes recorded observations of users as "the basis for refinement or redesigns, leading to better implementations, guidelines for designers and the refinement of theories."

Additionally, there are still ten major unsolved information visualization problems [25]. They are usability; understanding of elementary perceptual-cognitive tasks; prior knowledge in operating devices and domain knowledge to interpret content; education and training through accessible tutorials for the general public to promote awareness of the potential and problems of information visualization; quality metrics to enhance advances in evaluation and selection of visualizations; the enduring scalability problem; understanding interaction of insights and aesthetics; necessity to distinguish visualization processes with built-in trend identification mechanisms and without; algorithms resolving conflicting evidence; and the challenge of knowledge domain visualization (KDViz) [25]. These unsolved problems [25] add complexity to information visualization in general and its evaluation.

Finally, there is an important element in the process of evaluation—the human factor [16]. Since the evaluation of visualization is directly related to human-computer interaction and interaction with an interface to complete tasks, finding an appropriate sample of participants can be challenging [23]. In Graves and Handler's [7] paper which evaluated tools and visualization techniques for OGD visualization, the majority of users had some technical or domain expertise. In the papers that investigated multiple cases of evaluations, concern was raised on the overreliance on students [22][23]. The reasons are varied. In some cases, the expertise of the participants is necessary [23] and in some, it is simply difficult to find the intended users, have a large enough sample and conduct an effective empirical evaluation. The most challenging part is to relate [23] "a new set of results to previous research and to existing theory." In our case, we could not find any related formal evaluation of OGD interactive visualizations by non-expert users, nor could we confidently use one general theory.

However, to evaluate OGD visualizations, we identified our intended users. We found and adopted two simple arguments made by Barrence [10] and Hammer [27]: "There's not a lot of value for data without the right visualization," and "Open data has little value if people can't use it."

III. METHODOLOGY

Our overall approach was based on systematic investigation of what was clearly understood and what was not in the evaluation of visualizations. However, through our literature research, we realized that all problems surrounding OGD can be divided into two types: inherent and accumulated.

A. The Evaluation Method Mapping approach

The inherent types are interoperability, scalability, accessibility, integrity, reusability, integration, visualization, production, quality, and interaction. These are not new problems for researchers and some of these problems can be defined as general problems. These problems have already been investigated and their evaluation methods can be easily found through literature research.

The accumulated problems or the new problems are transparency, social barriers, cultural barriers, participation, technical barriers, legislative barriers, regulation, supply and demand, economic impact, cost of release, maintenance cost, management and resource allocation, which occurred recently with OGD release or are directly related to OGD. However, when both inherent and accumulated problems are broken down into specific issues, the similarities of these issues can be matched. Then, through the matching of issues, the methods of evaluation can be found much easier by viewing directly related sources. This is how we arrived at the idea to conceptualize the EMM approach and created the first version of a manually compiled repository (See Appendix A).

For example, Martin [5] investigated: implementation barriers and barriers to use in relation to the open data agenda. One of the found issues/barriers [5] is "limited interoperability between government ICT systems." If we look at the inherent general problem in our repository as shown in the Table I, we find a list of investigated specific issues, including "system interoperability."

Table I. Partial excerpt from Appendix A repository.

Accumulated Issues	Inherent problems with specific issues	Known evaluation methods	Source with links
Limited interoperability between government ICT systems	Interoperability (general problem) Specific issues: System interoperability	System Interoperability Framework	Authors and links to the source

These listed issues are directly related to the next column and its known evaluation methods, including practiced and proposed methods, models, frameworks, measures, metrics, and evaluation criteria. These methods are connected to the subsequent column, which provides a source of information and a link. If a researcher decides to proceed with evaluation, they will find actual links as shown in Appendix A (not shown in Table I for brevity). There, they can find the examples of methods and examples of how to collect and analyse data.

Initially, we used this repository to find methods for our evaluation of interactive visualizations. In the inherent problems of visualization is a list of 18 different known and investigated issues. It is easy to see the listed methods in the next column: high-dimensional data visualization analysis, practice of evaluating visualization, evaluation methods, user interface evaluation, simple visual prototypes and task sets based on a visual taxonomy, heuristic evaluation and an evaluation of several quality predictors for model simplification. For our empirical evaluation of interactive visualization techniques, we chose a field experiment, which is usually conducted in a realistic setting and allows an experimenter to have some degree of observation [23]. The provided sources of information revealed several challenges for information visualization empirical research: difficulty in finding the right focus, asking the right questions and working out sufficient and precise procedures for data collection.

B. The Visualization Evaluation Design Constructor

Further investigation uncovered that evaluation of information visualization is closely related to HCI evaluations, when tasks are based on interaction with an interface: overview, zoom, filter and getting necessary details [17]. Furthermore, it relates to the usability of a system, interface or device. Thus, the challenge is to understand results clearly in order to identify where the problem is: in the application, in a specific technique [23] or in the design of device.

To overcome these challenges, we obtained inspiration from Lam's et al. [22] suggestion to reflect on goals and questions prior to a decision of applying specific methods. As a result, we used meta-data analysis to generalize research questions into more generic groups These groups were further classified into general research goals based on their strategic orientation: problem-oriented, theory-oriented, product-oriented, process-oriented and user-oriented. On a higher, conceptual level, their complex interrelation allowed us to classify them based on their key strategic focus. Furthermore, by analyzing and generalizing theoretical implications [23] and practical aspects [22] of evaluation, we defined four essential elements common to all related fields. These are general goals, evaluation methods, theoretical implications, and practical aspects. Based on these elements we developed the VEDC framework as shown in Figure 1.

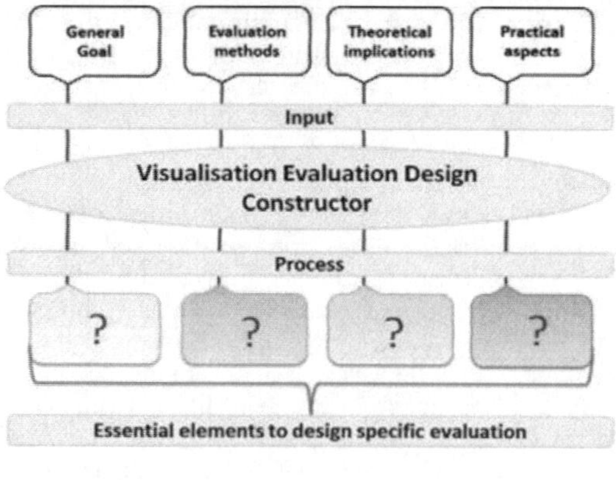

Figure 1. Visualization Evaluation Design Constructor (VEDC) framework.

The VEDC emphasizes the interconnectedness and interrelation of the essential elements for evaluation of any visualization. We argue that for any evaluation there are at least four essential elements: a general goal with a particular strategic focus, one evaluation method or combination of different methods, an underlying theory or a set of theories and subsequently, some practical aspects.

Our overall approach to this study is a combination of qualitative and quantitative approaches which complement one another [23] in order to find potential usability issues and inform designers [22]. The general goal was strategically focused on the user (user-oriented). Based on the general goal, we overviewed the literature related to the users' requirements, needs, wants, desires and user interaction with systems, devices, applications, interfaces and visualizations, and their evaluations [7][17][21][23][24].

This helped us to choose our method – a field experiment to obtain empirical evidence with an emphasis on realism [16][17][22][23]. The perception of data visualization [22], the choice of design [28], the Visual Information-Seeking Mantra principles of information visualization application design [17], and the usability test for use of data visualization tool [22] provided theoretical background. Subsequently, we could not avoid the consideration of practical aspects such as: procedures and techniques [21][22][23]; sample size [22][23][26]; data collection and analysis [21][22][23]; research ethics; and observer-experimenter-evaluator effects [21][22][23].

The VEDC was created to overview the Literature on the existing evaluations and their analysis. We view the VEDC framework as an advanced method for organizing literature related to evaluation research. The VEDC is currently limited but can be used as a guide (See Appendix B, C, D and E) with the existing four repositories of collected information and related sources.

Each repository has a set of the most common goals with related (most) common research questions (See Appendix B), a set of related evaluation methods with related possible theoretical implications (See Appendix C), a set of theoretical implications with direct relations to the theories (See Appendix D) and a set of practical aspects that could have implications on the research (See Appendix E).

The first repository has four strategically-oriented goals. Each goal has generically grouped problem question(s) directly related to the common research questions. These generic questions lead to the directly related existing sources of information. The information in the sources includes solutions and recommendations, helping to clarify research questions. Once the research question is clarified, the next step is to look for evaluation methods.

The second repository represents existing evaluation methods: a perception based evaluation, empirical studies, quantitative and qualitative evaluations, etc. Each method has information on possible known theoretical implications and specifically related descriptions of the existing methods. These are: a controlled user study, scenarios for understanding data analysis, quantitative experimental research, etc. The provided descriptions indicate what can be found in the existing sources of information.

The third repository classifies theoretical implications and existing theories under interrelated fields. They are: data visualization, information visualization, human-computer interaction, cognitive psychology, computer graphics, etc. The descriptions of theoretical implications lead directly to the existing sources of information.

The last repository defines practical implications in evaluations under general titles. These are: procedures and techniques, evaluators, participant's sample sizes, data, observer (or experimenter or evaluator) effect, tools for data collection and research ethics. Each general title has more specific descriptions. Each description leads to the existing source of information.

As an example, researchers can find how to compare heuristic evaluation and cognitive walkthrough, etc. The steps from one repository to another are not essential which makes the VEDC more flexible in use.

C. *Web-based field experiment*

Our overall method is based on a set of task-based experiments and observations.

To evaluate the usability of open data interactive visualization techniques, we performed a web-based field experiment using the DataViva [10] as a tool for interaction with visualizations. DataViva is a web portal for Brazil's open data developed in partnership with the MIT Media Lab [10]. Since starting this investigation, the MIT Media Lab has also launched the Data USA open data portal, which contains updated visualizations [11].

We evaluated Data USA informally in an attempt to compare our findings. The field experiment focused on three visualization techniques provided by DataViva: TreeMap, Map (data map), and Stacked (area chart). All three belong to the category of descriptive applications. Figures 2, 3 and 4 showing examples of these visualizations.

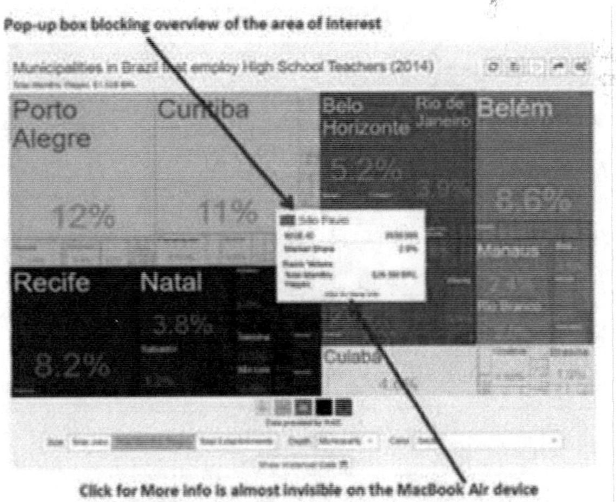

Figure 2. DataViva TreeMap visualization.

We engaged our users at 7 different locations around Gold Coast city, Australia, in public places where Wi-Fi access was freely available. To conduct the experiment, we used a MacBook Air laptop for internet access; DataViva website created specifically for OGD of Brazil to evaluate its visualizations; and software Debut as a tool for video and audio data collection. The software Debut allowed to capture audio and video recordings for every single task conducted by our participants in parallel with actual observations. Our goal was to test at least 10 participants as this is a suitable number according to Faulkner [26]. He showed that for usability testing, 10 users are sufficient enough, to find 80% of the problems.

To balance the control between observer and the users and to balance the trade-offs between generalization, precision, and realism [23], the experiment was broken down into two stages: a preliminary stage and a controlled-testing stage.

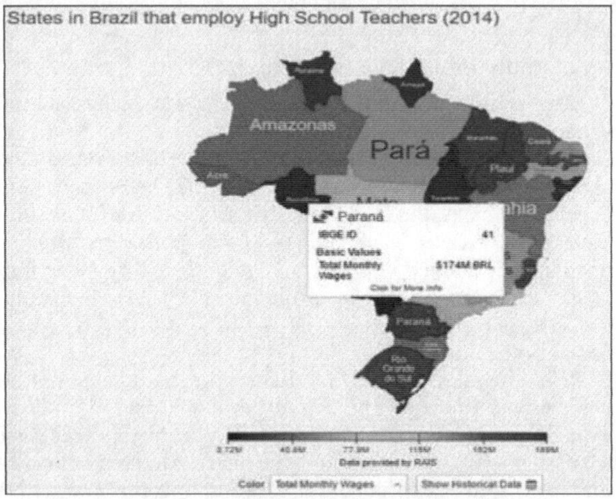

Figure 3. DataViva Map visualization.

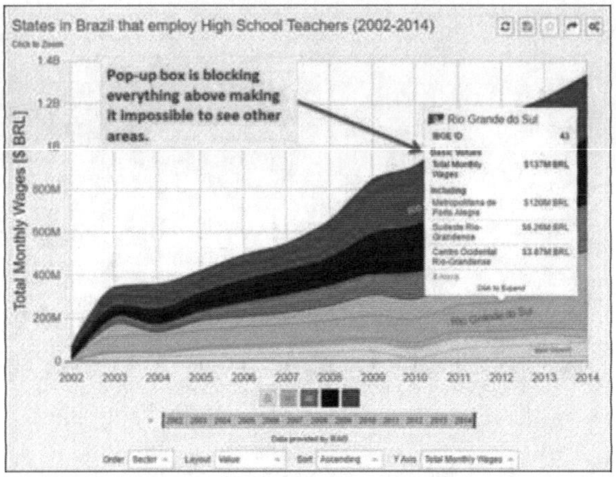

Figure 4. DataViva Stacked visualization.

The preliminary stage included presenting the participant with an information sheet about the study. This was followed by conversational questioning, to find out what stops non-expert users from using OGD. This stage was concluded with the formal signing of the consent form. The controlled-testing stage included 5 minutes of device and interface familiarization. This was followed by performance tasks designed as a motivational scenario based on an envisaged real situation. Tasks were designed to solve real problems with real data, in a real setting. This was designed in such a way, that the participants would always interact with a new interface, with every new task.

The user's interaction was captured with screen recording software and audio that were later analyzed to calculate completion time. We used an unenforced think-aloud protocol [23] to support the identification of possible usability issues. Specifically, for visualizations, the users were given 3 tasks to complete, each using a different visualization technique and a different task for that visualization.

The controlled tasks were designed on data about high-school teachers in Sao Paulo. The flow of all tasks mirrored Shneiderman's [17] visual mantra: overview first, zoom and filter, then detail-on-demand. Task 0 was designed to find a specific area to evaluate navigation through the DataViva web portal. The participants needed to start with the *Home page*, find *Occupations*, then find the *High School Teachers* page. On this page, they needed to find the *Preview* area for *Wages and Jobs* and then click on the *Municipality* under *WAGES BY* title to open a drop-down list of visualizations: TreeMap, Map and Stacked. It did not have a predicted completion time but it was measured later via video recordings. This task had three different possible paths, leading to the same information. Each path was mapped by the number of clicks: first – four, second – five and last – six, averaging at five clicks.

Tasks 1, 2 and 3 were designed to search for specific information in order to give a correct answer. The answers for Tasks 1, 2 and 3 were located in the listed visualizations. Task 1 required finding the total amount of jobs, where hierarchical data was graphically represented by TreeMap visualization, based on 2014 data. The correct answer was "7.08 k." The predicted time was 30 sec.

Task 2 required users to find the nominal wage growth, visually represented by Map (similar to choropleth/thematic or data map) visualization and based on 2014 data. The correct answer was 11%. The predicted time was 30 sec. Task 3 required users to find total monthly wages, visually represented by Stacked (similar to area chart/stacked area graph) visualization. It was based on the volume of an aggregated summary of 2012 data. The predicted time was 20 sec. The predicted time for Task 1, 2 and 3 included average download times.

This was followed by rating based on user's preferences to quantify user's subjective opinion for overall assessment of each single visualization interface. The participants' subjective judgments were turned into numbers, with the use of a rating scale: first choice = 1, second choice = 2 and the last choice = 3. Finally, the participants were asked a single open-ended question: "Why do you prefer this particular visualisation compare to others?

In addition, the experiment observer was provided with the designed templates to make observational notes of the participant behavior and to confirm the accuracy of the information found by participants in all tasks. These notes (qualitative data) were analysed and compared to the tasks' measured results (quantitative data) in order to obtain insights into the process of evaluation and the participant's interaction with visualizations.

IV. RESULTS

Our experiment sample was based on 12 users, selected randomly, at seven pre-defined locations with free access to the Internet via Wi-Fi, to achieve realism of a pre-defined scenario for a realistic setting, with realistic tasks and real users. The target number was 10. First, we knew [23] that with a realistic setting it would be difficult "to get a large enough participant sample."

Secondly, we were familiar with reported successes of usability tests to evaluate a data visualization tool with eight [22] or ten [26] participants. Thirdly, we were not generalizing our findings to make statistically significant statements. Also, the practical part of research was conducted by a novice investigator taking on the role of experimenter and observer [23]. However, we do understand that with only 12 participants there is a high rick of bias.

The participants average age was 54 years. As shown in Figure 5, 33% had a university degree, 42% had a college education and 25% were educated at TAFE (a technical training institution). 80% of the participants were female.

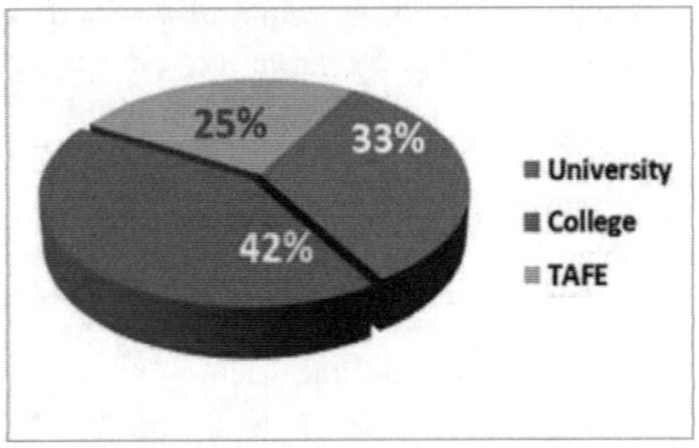

Figure 5. Distribution of participants occupations.

Their professional occupations were very diverse: an international shipping company accountant, a business consultant, the CFO of a mid-sized engineering company, a fashion designer (single operator), special needs teacher, administration clerk from a small company, administrator of small reselling company, retired real estate consultant, kitchen equipment installer, private college administrator, a retired construction worker and a retired nurse.

A. *Results from preliminary stage*

The time spent per participant to complete the tasks took on average 11 minutes, excluding 5 minutes given to participants to familiarize with the DataViva interface and the time spent to answer the open-ended question. More than 80 hours were spent on the preliminary stage by the novice investigator on approaching random people and conversing in order to select and sign up participants. This means that the time to find one suitable participant took considerable time.

At the preliminary stage, we approached participants with conversational questioning to find out what stops them from using OGD. The presented results reflect an analysis of the answers from the 12 selected participants. 83.2% of participants answered that they had never heard of OGD; did not know OGD existed; or what it meant. However, after their interaction with open data, 66.6% had expressed an interest to know more.

The average completion time for Task 0 (navigating from the home page to the visualization) was two minutes and ten seconds, and on average took 7 clicks. Only two participants were familiar with how to operate the laptop. 66% of participants failed to remember that one click is sufficient to select an item and 75% forgot to scroll with two fingers. Some users blamed their double-clicking habit on primarily using a mouse instead of a touch pad. It was our assumption that the participants were familiar with the Mac look-and-feel, but the majority were not. This wrong assumption might severely have influenced the results of our study.

However, the size of the Mac screen compared to often bigger sized displays of personal home computers is likely to had affected the visibility of the title *Explore our database*, which can be seen only when scrolled down. It was observed that more than 80% of participants did not use the *Get started* button, located in the middle of the screen or the *Search* option, located on the top bar of the *Home page*. As shown in Figure 6, only a few participants commented that they could not see it clearly or that the background image was too busy.

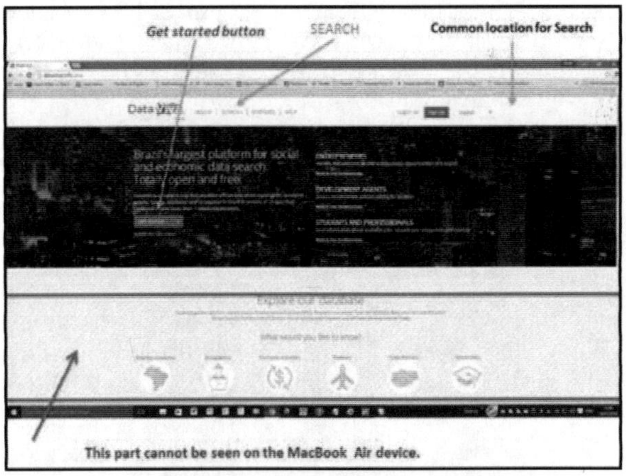

Figure 6. DataViva Home page.

B. *Results from Controlled-testing stage*

No user errors were recorded through Tasks 1, 2 and 3. The average time to complete each task as shown in Table II, was calculated and linked to ratings.

The Map visualization was the quickest, followed by Stacked, and then TreeMap. Participants were asked to rate the visualizations in order of preference. Figure 7 shows the results of the preferences rating. The participants then were asked open question: "Why do you prefer this particular visualisation compare to others?" Their comments were recorded, later analysed and compared with our observations.

Table II. Correlation between time performance and rating.

Visualizations	Average time per participant	Rating
Map	1 min	First
Stacked	1 min 13 sec	Second
TreeMap	1 min 19 sec	Last

The Map visualization was rated as the first choice, it was also the most frequent second choice; not one participant rated Map as their last choice. The ratings of TreeMap and Stacked were very similar. Stacked having one extra rating for second place and one less for the last. As a result, the order of preference for the participants was Map, Stacked, and TreeMap, as shown in Table II, which correlates with the time it took to complete each task.

Participants also provided reasons why they gave visualizations the particular rating. The Map visualization was chosen because it was perceived as a familiar shape, that of a geographic map, and easy to use. The Stacked visualization had contradictory perceptions. Some perceived it as easy to understand and clear. Others found it confusing and reported that it "didn't make sense." Participants that rated the TreeMap first, found it easy to find information. Those that rated it second stated that it was "not clear." Those that rated it last said it was confusing, busy, and more difficult to find information.

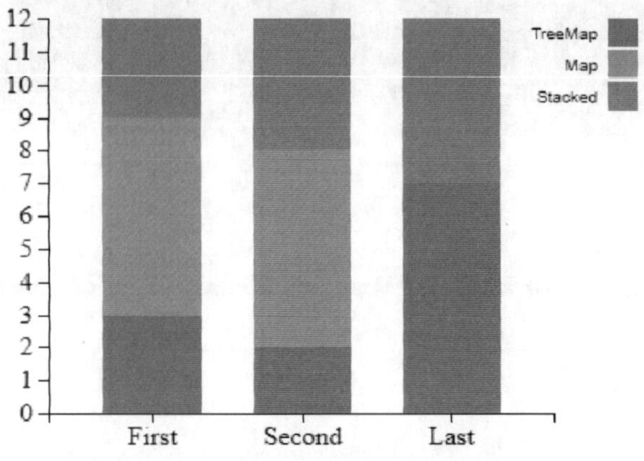

Figure 7. Rated preferences for each visualization type.

Through analysis of observational notes and recorded comments, the participants revealed their perceptions on shapes, sizes, color contrast, and features in the visual presentation of data. "Easy to find info," "I like TreeMap screen" and "The TreeMap was the easiest one" - were the most favorable comments for TreeMap visualization. The majority of participants complained: "Not clear enough" (in regards to color contrast), "… busy, visually it is busy" (too many areas), "… small to find and navigate" (in regards to headings), "confusing" (in regards to low contrast between headings and colored areas), "Boarders between small squares unclear," "Hard to read headings," and "more difficult" (to find information).

The recorded comments: "The Map is similar to the world map…" or "…map is easy to see" and similar comments, clearly demonstrated favorable preferences for Map visualization due to its shape familiarity.

With Stacked visualization, the perceptions were polarized: from "clear" to "confused." This was due to the inability of some of the participants to read the graph.

The popup box interference was the major reason for slowing down task completion in Tasks 1, 2 and 3. The recorded comments and observational notes confirmed this as a major issue for all three visualizations.

The results of the controlled-testing stage, which measured our participants' performance with three visualizations are conclusive even if they are not statistically significant to make generalizations. Furthermore, the performance results, shown in Table II, which are supported by their ratings of preferences shown in Figure 7. However, the participants' comments and our own observations of what had affected their performance gave us a more insightful picture revealing usability issues.

One might assume that these results reflect familiarity as a single contributor to the performance, supported by ratings. Though the familiar shape was perceived more favorably and more likely contributed to better performance, it was not the only factor.

The average downloading time for each visualization was calculated into the predicted performance time. The TreeMap and Stacked downloading time was between 7-8 seconds, more than twice longer than Map (about 3 seconds). Taking into consideration that the majority of participants were already getting frustrated with navigation, the slow downloading of TreeMap and Staked increased their negative perception.

The downloading time is a usability issue and more likely contributed to the negative perception of TreeMap and Stacked visualisations. This means that the familiarity of the Map shape was not necessarily the only factor for user's perception. Furthermore, shape and size of the display, color and color contrast, the size of text and the use of features are usability issues. They are meant to enhance usability of visualizations and not frustrate or confuse. However, according to participants' comments, the TreeMap and Stacked were perceived as confusing, cluttering (visually busy) and unclear. These contributors to usability are matters of display layout and the effectiveness of style.

The uncontrollable popup boxes, incorporated into each visualization, were a major usability issue. Users did not feel in control of this feature which appeared unexpectedly on the mouse rollover in each evaluated visualization. The details should have been given when they are needed. That is why they referred to as *details-on-demand* [17] appearing when one clicks on the selected item and not during the *overview*.

C. Data USA Comparison

MIT Media Lab also produced the Data USA portal. We overviewed the portal to see if it could be compared with our findings. From our perspective, the *Home page* of Data USA, as seen in Figure 8, is much clearer on where to start searching.

Figure 8. Data USA Home page.

In contrast, the DataViva *Home page* has the *Search* option in the header bar, the *Get started* button in the middle of the left side of the page, the *Explore our database* option and the additional several icons are located at the bottom of the page, as shown in Figure 6. This confused the participants, as there were too many options for the same outcome. With regards to visualizations, we found that the TreeMap on both portals looked almost identical, however geographical maps appear differently. We did not find stacked charts, only line charts.

V. Discussion

The goal of this investigation was strategically focused on users who had no technical skills in data creation, modification, and manipulation and no knowledge in data domain. Also, we realized that the majority of the participants were not familiar with the Mac look-and-feel and unaware that OGD existed. In addition, each participant had different cognitive limitations, age, gender and level of education.

These factors, including differences in external noise and lighting in various cafes and factors that we might not yet be aware of, had some effect on the participants' performance and perception. What then is the point to report the results from a field experiment which had a questionable number of sample size, diminishing its statistical significance?

The point is to learn and to inform about potential usability issues of mainstream applications for general users such as OGD portals with incorporated interactive visualisations.

First, for the concern that has been raised on the demand side of utilizing OGD by non-expert users. Only two participants had previously heard of open data. However, the majority of participants demonstrated their interest to know more about OGD. After completing their tasks, they asked what OGD represents, where to find existing portals, and how to use OGD for their benefit.

This indicates that if citizens were more aware of OGD it might increase their interest to utilize OGD potentially contributing to the increase of its demand [5]. Though this is not a statistically meaningful conclusion, it is a possible indicator on the issue of awareness that could be further investigated by OGD suppliers and developers.

Secondly, TreeMap is a very common visualization tool, often used in data journalism, however, we found that participants had the most trouble with it, both in terms of taking the longest time to complete the task, and also in response to the open question. This can be explained by non-expert users' unfamiliarity with TreeMap visualization compared with Map and Stacked.

Additionally, this visualization represents a significant amount of information in one space, increasing demand on the end-users to find specific information. The demand to find specific information, under constraint, could be a second explanation for difficulties experienced. If participants were asked to explore data at their own pace and interest, their opinion and overall experience with TreeMap visualization could have had a different outcome.

Furthermore, if we take into consideration that when TreeMap was first prototyped 27 years ago, it required training for effective use [21]. The current version, deployed in DataViva, was used by people without technical skills, for the first time. The 100% correct answers, found by participants in 1 min and 19 secs on average, without any preliminary demonstration gives us a different perspective.

The interactive choropleth map was first prototyped 24 years ago. At the time, novice users reported difficulties in even starting to use it, perceiving it as too complicated [21]. The modern version, the Map, deployed by DataViva, was perceived by our participants as the easiest to use. Though only one person used zooming, and none of the participants noticed a slider.

The stacked chart is a kind of area chart, which was first published in 1786 [28]. However, the average completion time for the task was more than three times over the predicted time. Several participants did not know how to read a chart. The majority had a substantial level of education and according to their professional occupations, one could assume they would understand how to navigate through a chart. Further analysis revealed that those who understood a chart, completed their task faster, compared to those who did not.

Also, there was confusion with the differences in the area sizes. The participants did not understand why some areas were too narrow, compared with others. None of them acknowledged the slider, but later, one participant, after completion of their last task asked what it was. When the experimenter explained, the participant commented that she had no idea that such a feature exists.

However, for TreeMap and Stacked, the slow time of downloading; the small size of visualization in contrast to the size of display; the difficulty of some users to see a contrast between neighboring areas; and the low contrast between headings and colored areas indicate that these are usability issues that could be improved by designers. These are well-known usability issues in conveying information.

The most significant usability problem with all three visualizations was a feature known as the tooltip plugin or more commonly known, as a popup box. With all three visualizations, the popup box was blocking the overview. Taking into consideration the extended principles for designers of data visualizations: *overview first, zoom* and *filter*; then *details-on-demand* [17], we demonstrated, as shown in Figure 2, 3 and 4, that this feature was blocking overview with details even before they were demanded by the users.

The problem with the feature is that it appears on a mouse rollover and cannot be controlled by the users [13]. Thus, this very useful feature is poorly implemented. As the user is navigating to interact with the visualization, the popup box occludes the area they want to interact with. We have provided possible solutions to the popup box issue for each of the visualizations, shown in Figures 9, 10 and 11. The solution is generally to display the popup box to the side or it should only appear [17] when the area of interest is clicked on. Overall, the usability issues with the DataViva interface might appear to be insignificant to designers, but it had a negative effect on the non-expert end-users. Also, our own experience in conducting this field experiment proved how difficult it is to find intended users, chose the right sample and conduct an effective empirical evaluation [23].

In summary, we assumed that if we could find and describe potential usability issues we could inform designers and help them to understand what can be improved to make interactive visualization more user friendly and easier to use.

Other usability issues were not new and are avoidable by designers if they would follow basic approaches for successful interfaces [13] and well-established design principles [17] for interactive visualizations.

VI. Conclusion and Future Work

The OGD movement is maturing with large quantities of data being released by governments around the world. The embracing of the open data agenda has not necessarily translated into uptake by OGD consumers. We propose that this is because of the focus on machine-readability rather than human-usability. Recent efforts are focusing on providing interactive visualizations of OGD to make it easier for non-expert users to get engaged with OGD.

In this paper, we evaluated three visualizations from one OGD portal, to identify strengths and weaknesses of visualization techniques, specifically for non-expert users, which currently has not been investigated in literature. Even though our participants were unfamiliar with OGD, after a short introduction they were able to answer the problems set before them, under 2 minutes on average. This demonstrates the advantage visualizations have over technical and raw data. This serves as a strong argument for OGD portals to provide visualizations to increase end-user uptake by non-expert users.

Comparing three different methods of OGD visualization, the clear preference was for Map visualization which represents data on a geographical map. The basis for Map being the greatest preference, both qualitatively and quantitatively, is more likely due to its shape familiarity to the non-expert user. Concrete concepts are quicker to grasp than abstract concepts. However, we cannot dismiss other usability factors that contributed to the performance of participants and their rating based on their perception.

The TreeMap and Stacked visualizations represented data more abstractly, which requires a greater conceptual leap for non-expert users to make. However, other usability issues did not help the ease of use. Therefore, to encourage end-user uptake of OGD, visualizations should be selected that are concrete and familiar to end-users, such as Map visualizations. The more abstract visualizations containing large amounts of information in one space, need to be simplified further. It is in line with the basic purpose of visually representing data, that insight must be represented as easily as possible [16].

Note that visualizations such as TreeMap have been designed to address many usability and visualization factors, however, we have found that for non-expert users, concreteness and familiarity are important factors. However, with resolved usability issues with TreeMap and Stacked, the overall perception by non-expert users could be much more positive.

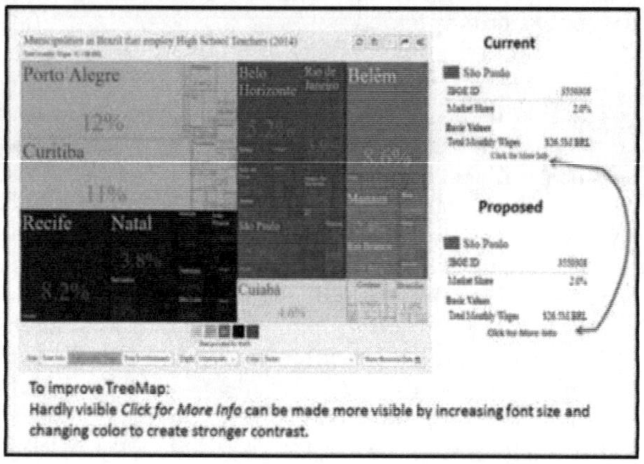

Figure 9. Non-occluding popup box for TreeMap visualization.

Our study also identified an issue with popups, where a simple and useful feature, when poorly implemented, can grossly impact the effectiveness of a visualization. This reinforces the need not just for visualizations, but for end-user testing to verify the effectiveness of the visualizations' features.

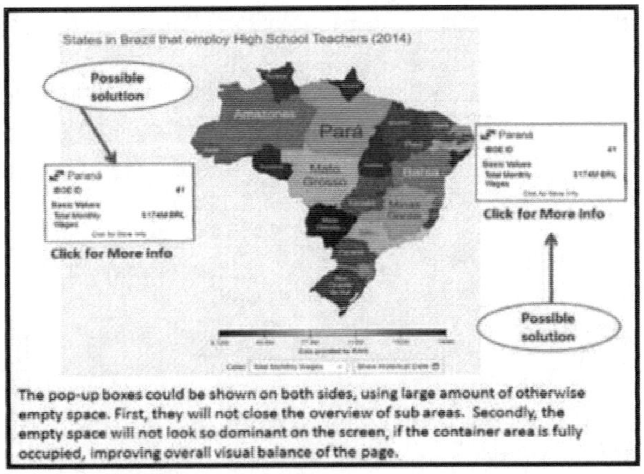

Figure 10. Non-occluding popup box for Map visualization.

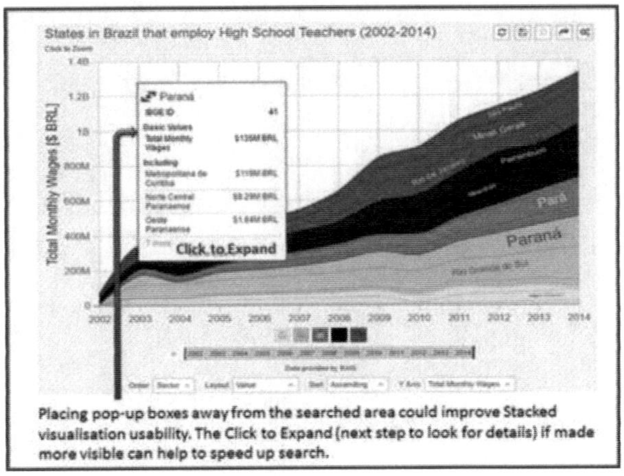

Figure 11. Non-occluding popup box for Stacked visualization.

Our study supports the argument for the need of an optimized visualization that is easy to use, with a comprehensible information visualization language. These usability issues should be tackled with the consideration of several fields, including the human factor [16]. What we observed is that users are primarily concerned with ease and simplicity of use, which supports the argument that usability is all about ease of use [13]. This also supports the argument that the value of data is in the right visualization [10] and if people cannot use open data, then it does not hold value for them [27].

Subsequently, if non-expert end-users will not use it, then the uptake of OGD would remain limited.

ACKNOWLEDGMENT

We would like to acknowledge all participants who greatly contributed their time and effort to support this project.

REFERENCES

[1] E. Ornig, J. Faichney and B. Stantic, "Empirical Evaluation of Open Government Data Visualisations," The Third International Conference on Big Data, Small Data, Linked Data and Open Data (ALLDATA 2017), Apr. 2017.

[2] data.world, "data.world Launches to Make the World's Data Easier to Find, Use, and Share." 11 July, 2016, retrieved: March, 2017. [Online]. Available: https://globenewswire.com/news-release/2016/07/11/855045/0/en/data-world-Launches-to-Make-the-World-s-Data-Easier-to-Find-Use-and-Share.html

[3] Data Portals, "A Comprehensive List of Open Data Portals from Around the World," retrieved: March, 2017. [Online]. Available: http://dataportals.org/

[4] Linking Open Government Data, "IOGDS Analytics," retrieved: March, 2017. [Online]. Available: https://logd.tw.rpi.edu/iogds_analytics_2

[5] C. Martin, "Barriers to the Open Government Data Agenda: Taking a Multi - Level Perspective," Policy & Internet, 6 (3), pp 217-240, 2014.

[6] Sunlight Foundation, "Ten principles for opening up government," August 11, 2010. Retrieved: July, 2017. [Online]. Available: http://sunlightfoundation.com/policy/documents/ten-opendata- principles/

[7] A. Graves and J. Hendler, (2014). "A study on the use of visualizations for Open Government Data," Information Polity: The International Journal Of Government & Democracy In The Information Age, 19(1/2), pp.73-91. doi:10.3233/IP-140333

[8] N. Shadbolt, K. O'Hara, T. Berners-Lee, N. Gibbins, H. Glaser and W. Hall, (2012). "Linked open government data: Lessons from data. gov. uk," IEEE Intelligent Systems, 27(3), pp. 16-24.

[9] L. Ding, T. Lebo, J, S. Erickson, D. DiFranzo, G. T. Williams, X. Li, J. Michaelis, A. Graves, J. G. Zheng, Z. Shangguan, J. Flores, D. L. Mcguinness and J. A. Hendler, "TWC LOGD: A Portal for Linked Open Government Data Ecosystems," Journal of Web Semantics, 9 (3), pp. 325-333, 2011.

[10] S. Ferro, "New MIT Media Lab Tool Lets Anyone Visualize Unwieldy Government Data," CO.DESIGN. [Online]. Available: https://www.fastcodesign.com/3022701/new-mit-media-lab-tool-lets-anyone-visualize-unwieldy-government-data

[11] S. Lohr, "Website Seeks to Make Government Data Easier to Sift Through," *The new York Times,* Technology, Apr., 2016. [Online] Available: https://www.nytimes.com/2016/04/05/technology/datausa-government-data.html?mcubz=0

[12] C. Ware, "Information visualization: Perception for design," Elsevier. Third edition, 2013.

[13] B. Shneiderman and B. B. Bederson, "The Craft of Information Visualization: Readings and Reflections," Morgan Kaufmann Publishers Inc., San Francisco, CA, USA, 2003. ISBN:1558609156

[14] D. M. Butler, C. James, R. Almond, D. Bergeron, K. W. Brodlie and R. B. Haber, 1993. "Visualization reference models," In Proceedings of the 4th conference on Visualization '93 (VIS '93), Dan Bergeron and Greg Nielson

(Eds.). IEEE Computer Society, Washington, DC, USA, pp. 337-342.

[15] S. K. Card, J. D. Mackinlay. "The Structure of the Information Visualization Design Space," Proceedings of IEEE Symposium on Information Visualization (InfoVis '97), Phoenix, Arizona, 92-99 Color Plate 125, 1997.

[16] M. Khan and S. S. Khan, "Data and Information Visualization Methods, and Interactive Mechanisms: A Survey," International Journal of computer Applications, vol. 34, no. 1, pp.1-12, November. 2011.

[17] B. Shneiderman, "The Eye Have It: A Task by Data Type Taxonomy for Information Visualizations," In Proceedings of 1996 IEEE Symposium on Visual Languages, Boulder, CO, USA. DOI: 10.1109/VL.1996.545307.

[18] R. Lengler and M. J. Eppler. 2007. "Towards a periodic table of visualization methods of management," In Proceedings of the IASTED International Conference on Graphics and Visualization in Engineering (GVE '07), ACTA Press, Anaheim, CA, USA, pp. 83-88.

[19] C. Ziemkiewicz, P. Kinnaird, R. Kosara, J. Mackinlay, B. Rogowitz, and J. S. Yi. 2010. "Visualization Theory: Putting the Pieces Together," 2014-10-13. [Online] Available: https://pdfs.semanticscholar.org/42f3/dc15a3d5577b42143be1b8d7eb91e16d9d82.pdf

[20] C. Demiralp, D. H. Laidlaw, J. J. Van Wijk, and C. Ware, "Theories of Visualization—Are There Any?" Brown University. Panel discussion. Sep, 2016.[Online]. Available: http://hci.stanford.edu/~cagatay/projects/vismodel/TheoriesOfVisualization-Vis11.pdf

[21] C. Plaisant, "The challenge of information visualization evaluation," In Proceedings of the working conference on Advanced visual interfaces (pp. 109-116). ACM, May, 2004.

[22] H. Lam, E. Bertini, P. Isenberg, C. Plaisant and S. Carpendale, "Empirical Studies in Information Visualization: Seven Scenarios," in IEEE Transactions on Visualization and Computer Graphics, vol. 18, no. 9, pp. 1520-1536, Sept. DOI=2012.doi: 10.1109/TVCG.2011.279, 2012.

[23] S. Carpendale, "Evaluating information visualizations," Information Visualization: Human-Centered Issues and Perspectives, vol. 4950, pp. 19-45, 2008

[24] B. Shneiderman, "A Grander Goal: A Thousand-fold Increase in Human Capabilities," Educom Review, 32, 6, 410. HCIL-97-23, Nov-Dec 1997. [Online]. Available from: http://hcil2.cs.umd.edu/trs/97-23/97-23.html

[25] C. Chen, "Top 10 Unsolved Information Visualization Problems," Ed. Theresa-Marie Rhyne. IEEE Computer Graphics and Applications, Volume: 25, Issue: 4, pp. 12-16. 11 July, 2005

[26] L. Faulkner, "Beyond the five-user assumption: Benefits of increased sample sizes in usability testing," Behavior Research Methods, Instruments and Computers, Volume: 35, Issue: 3, pp. 379-383, 2003

[27] C. Hammer, "Open Data Has Little Value If People Can't Use It." Harvard Business School Review, 29 Mar., 2013. Retrieved 20 Aug. 2016. [Online] Available: https://hbr.org/2013/03/open-data-has-little-value-if

[28] E. Tufte, "The Visual Display of Quantitative Information," Cheshire, Connecticut, pp. 13. 1983.

Appendix A - Evaluation Method Mapping (partial presentation).

Accumulated Issues	Inherent problems with specific issues	Known evaluation methods, measures, metrics, models, evaluation criteria, etc.	Source with links
Interoperability in an open data ecosystem	Interoperability (general problem)	Evaluation models Existing interoperability evaluation models, the similarities and differences in their philosophy and implementation, assessment process of the system.	Rezaei, R., Chiew, T. K., Lee, S. P., & Aliee, Z. S. (2014). Interoperability evaluation models: A systematic review. Computers in Industry, 65(1), 1. doi: 10.1016/j.compind.2013.09.001; http://www.sciencedirect.com/science/article/pii/S0166361513001887
Limited Interoperability between government ICT systems	Specific issues: Data exchange; Information exchange; Service exchange; System interoperability; Application interoperability; Infrastructure interoperability; Knowledge exchange; Network interoperability; Technical interoperability; Operational interoperability.	System Interoperability Framework e-Business inspired eHealth interoperability framework from an overall system perspective.	Craig E. Kuziemsky and Jens H. Weber-Jahnke, "An eBusiness-based Framework for eHealth Interoperability," Journal of Emerging Technologies in Web Intelligence, Vol. 1, No. 2, pp. 129-136, November 2009. doi:10.4304/jetwi.1.2.129-136 http://www.jetwi.us/uploadfile/2014/1226/20141226054221610.
Open standards of interoperability for open data end-users		Technical Interoperability Maturity Model The Information Systems; Interoperability Maturity Model (ISIMM); Interoperability of hardware, software, data, communication and physical interoperability for Government, including measures.	Staden, S. V., & Mbale, J. (2012). The information systems interoperability maturity model (ISIMM): Towards standardizing technical interoperability and assessment within government. International Journal of Information Engineering and Electronic Business, 4(5), 36-41. http://www.mecs-press.org/ijieeb/ijieeb-v4-n5/IJIEEB-V4-N5-5.pdf
		Conceptual Evaluation and Selection Framework The parts and forms of the evaluation framework; Interoperability levels; Activities of the evaluation process.	Mykkänen, J. A., & Tuomainen, M. P. (2008). An evaluation and selection framework for interoperability standards. Information and Software Technology, 50(3), 176-197. doi: 10.1016/j.infsof.2006.12.001 http://www.sciencedirect.com/science/article/pii/S0950584906001960
Identifying scalable solutions across government	Scalability (general problem) Specific issues: Operating system; Database server; Application server; Hardware performance;	Design and Evaluation Efficient parallel hash algorithms for processing large-scale data, including a theoretical analysis of different hashing; Frameworks and testing scalability.	Cheng, L., Kotoulas, S., Ward, T. E., & Theodoropoulos, G. (2014). Design and evaluation of parallel hashing over large-scale data. Paper presented at the 1-10. doi:10.1109/HiPC.2014.7116909
			Liu, H. H., & Books24x7, I. (2009). Software performance and scalability: A quantitative approach (1st ed.). Hoboken, N.J: John Wiley & Sons.
Government yet to improve technical accessibility of Open Data	Accessibility (general problem) Specific issues: Data accessibility; Website accessibility.	Potential improvements of UX research The products, dimensions of experience, and methodologies across a systematically selected sample of 51 publications from 2005-2009, reporting a total of 66 empirical studies.	Bargas-Avila, J.A., Hornbæk, K., 2011. Old wine in new bottles or novel challenges: a critical analysis of empirical studies of user experience. In: Proceedings of the SIGCHI Conference on Human Factors in Computing Systems CHI '11. ACM, New York, NY, USA. pp. 2689–2698. http://dl.acm.org/citation.cfm?id=1979336

Appendix B – VEDC: General goal based on strategic focus.

General goal	Generically grouped	Commonly encountered	Source of information https://www.researchgate.net/publication/310843052_Evaluation_of_Open_Government_Data_Visualisations
Problem oriented	What is the problem and how to solve it?	To identify a problem (potential or open)	Graves and Hendler [22], Chen [25], Bederson et al [28], P Plaisant [29], Teyseyre at al [30], Khan [31], Trochim [32], Shneiderman [33], Eliane [34], Ware [36], Heer [38], Carpendale [42], Dong [41], Ellis et al [43], Çağatay [45], Andrews [47], Faulkner [49], Hilbert et al [50].
		To identify its cause (issues and limitations)	Plaisant [29], Lam et al [23], Bederson et al [28], Teyseyre at al [30], Khan [31], Trochim [32], Shneiderman [33], Ware [36], Heer [38], Carpendale [42], Ellis et al [43], Goebel [46], Faulkner [49], Hilbert et al [50]
		To find solution	Lengler et al [26], Bederson et al [28], Teyseyre at al [30], Carpendale [42], Ellis et al [43], Çağatay [45], Andrews [47], Hilbert et al [50].
		To provide recommendations	Lam et al [23], Shneiderman [27], Carpendale [42], Andrews [47], Faulkner [49].
Theory oriented	How to test hypothesis?	To prove it	Lam et al [23], Graves and Hendler [22], Zhu [24], Bederson et al [28], Ware [36], Heer [38].
		To generate	Shneiderman [33], Eliane [34], Carpendale [42], Çağatay [45], Zhai [48].
Product oriented	How to develop new application? How to develop new system? How to develop new feature?	To evaluate design	Shneiderman [27], Lam et al [23], Zhu [24], Bederson et al [28], Plaisant [29], Eliane [43].
		To evaluate prototype	Graves and Hendler [22], Lam et al [23], Bederson et al [28], Plaisant [29], Teyseyre at al [30], Khan [31], Ware [36], Ellis et al [43], Hilbert et al [50], Shneiderman [51].
		To evaluate product	Lam et al [23], Bederson et al [28], Plaisant [29], Teyseyre at al [30], Trochim [32], Shneiderman [33], Ware [36], Carpendale [42], Ellis et al [43], Andrews [47], Zhai [48].
Process oriented	How to evaluate process?	Workflow process	Lam et al [23], Eliane [34], Carpendale [42]
		Data exploration	Lam et al [23], Shneiderman [27], Bederson et al [28], Plaisant [29], Teyseyre at al [30].
		Data analytics	Lam et al [23], Plaisant [29], Teyseyre at al [30], Khan [31], Shneiderman [33], Eliane [34].
		Descriptive process	Lam et al [23], Bederson et al [28], Plaisant [29], Teyseyre at al [30], Khan [31], Ware [36].
		Displaying data	Lam et al [23], Shneiderman [27], Bederson et al [28], Plaisant [29], Teyseyre at al [30],
User oriented	How to satisfy their requirements? How to satisfy their needs? How to satisfy their wants? Good interaction	Evaluate requirements	Bederson et al [28], Teyseyre at al [30], Khan [31], Çağatay [45], Hilbert et al [50].
		Evaluate needs	Bederson et al [28], Plaisant [29], Teyseyre at al [30], Khan [31], Trochim [32].
		Evaluate wants	Bederson et al [28], Shneiderman [33], Heer [38], Rogowitz [44], Hilbert et al [50].
		Evaluate interaction	Lam et al [23], Bederson et al [28], Plaisant [29], Teyseyre at al [30], Khan [31], Eliane [34].

Appendix C – VEDC: Evaluation Methods Repository (partial presentation).

Evaluation methods	Description	Source with links
A Perception-Based Evaluation Possible theoretical implication: Data Visualization; Computer Graphics; Perception theory.	A controlled user study to test against the following hypotheses: Projection performance is task-dependent; Certain projections perform better on certain types of tasks; Projection performance depends on the nature of the data; Subjects prefer projections with good segregation capability.	Etemadpour, Ronak, et al. "Perception-based evaluation of projection methods for multidimensional data visualization." IEEE transactions on visualization and computer graphics 21.1 (2015): 81-94. http://ieeexplore.ieee.org/abstract/document/6832613/
An evaluation for categorical data Possible theoretical implications: Information visualization; Data Visualization.	A task based performance evaluation: A method designed for categorical data; Approaches in the context of two basic data analysis tasks; Efficiency of the quantification approach.	Fernstad, Sara Johansson, and Jimmy Johansson. "A task based performance evaluation of visualization approaches for categorical data analysis." Information Visualisation (IV), 2011 15th International Conference on. IEEE, 2011. http://ieeexplore.ieee.org/abstract/document/6004026/
Nine common evaluation methods Possible theoretical implications: Information Visualization; Data Visualization; Visual cognition; Human-Computer Interaction (HCI).	Methods & Types of Evaluation: Classification of types to perform evaluation; Evaluation of information visualization techniques;	K. Andrews. Evaluation comes in many guises. In CHI workshop on BEyond time and errors: novel evaluation methods for Information Visualization (BELIV), pages 7–8, 2008. http://www.dis.uniroma1.it/beliv08/pospap/andrews.pdf
Multi-dimensional In-depth Long-term Case Studies (MILCs) Possible theoretical implications: Information Visualization; HCI; Visual cognition; Information theory; Visual perception; Color theory.	Strategies for evaluation: Evaluation methods; Multi-dimensional In-depth Long-term Case studies guidelines.	Shneiderman, Ben, and Catherine Plaisant. "Strategies for evaluating information visualization tools: multi-dimensional in-depth long-term case studies." Proceedings of the 2006 AVI workshop on BEyond time and errors: novel evaluation methods for information visualization. ACM, 2006. http://dl.acm.org/citation.cfm?id=1168158
User studies Possible theoretical implications: Data Visualization; Information visualization; Computer Graphics; Visual cognition; Perceptual psychology.	Why, how and when: Building experiments that include human participants.	Kosara, R., Healey, C. G., Interrante, V., Laidlaw, D. H., & Ware, C. (2003). Thoughts on user studies: Why, how, and when. IEEE Computer Graphics and Applications, 23(4), 20-25. https://pdfs.semanticscholar.org/d39b/f307f99188ff66404d2cda78590f3b24127c.pdf
Task and Insight methods Possible theoretical implications: Information Visualization; Data Visualization; Computer Graphics; Bioinformatics.	Empirical evaluation methods: Tasks benchmarking; Comparison of information visualization studies; The insight method's ability to confirm results of the task method.	North, Chris, Purvi Saraiya, and Karen Duca. "A comparison of benchmark task and insight evaluation methods for information visualization." Information Visualization 10.3 (2011): 162-181. http://journals.sagepub.com/doi/abs/10.1177/1473871611415989

Appendix D – VEDC: Theoretical Implications Repository (partial presentation).

Title	Theoretical implications to consider	Source with links
Data Visualization	Theory and practice in the design of data graphics; Graphical presentation of statistics.	Tufte, Edward R., and Glenn M. Schmieg. "The visual display of quantitative information." American Journal of Physics 53.11 (1985): 1117-1118. http://aapt.scitation.org/doi/abs/10.1119/1.14057
	How to model summarizes data; Three strategies for visualizing statistical models (includes case studies).	Wickham, Hadley, Dianne Cook, and Heike Hofmann. "Visualizing statistical models: removing the blindfold." Statistical Analysis and Data Mining: The ASA Data Science Journal 8.4 (2015): 203-225. http://onlinelibrary.wiley.com/doi/10.1002/sam.11271/full
	A new theoretical framework for data visualization approaches; Iterative stochastic matrix approximation for data visualization (includes a set of experiments).	Labiod, Lazhar, and Mohamed Nadif. "A unified framework for data visualization and coclustering." IEEE transactions on neural networks and learning systems 26.9 (2015): 2194-2199. http://ieeexplore.ieee.org/abstract/document/6945382/
Information Visualization	Information Visualization – theories and understanding	Ben Shneiderman and Benjamin B. Bederson. 2003. The Craft of Information Visualization: Readings and Reflections. Morgan Kaufmann Publishers Inc., San Francisco, CA, USA. Chapter 8., pp.349 - 351 http://dl.acm.org/citation.cfm?id=961853
	Theories of Visualization	Demiralp, Çağatay, David Laidlaw H., Jarke Van Wijk J., and Colin Ware. "Theories of Visualization—Are There Any?" Theories of Visualization—Are There Any? (n.d.) Brown University. Panel discussion. Web. 02 Sept. 2016. http://hci.stanford.edu/~cagatay/projects/vismodel/TheoriesOfVisualization-Vis11.pdf
	Different approaches to the theoretical foundations of Information Visualization: data-centric predictive theory, information theory, and scientific modeling.	Purchase, H. C., Andrienko, N., Jankun-Kelly, T. J., & Ward, M. Theoretical Foundations of Information Visualization. http://geoanalytics.net/and/papers/springer08a.pdf
Human-Computer Interaction	Design Theories, Methods and Tools	Kurosu, Masaaki, ed. Human-Computer Interaction Theories, Methods, and Tools: 16th International Conference, HCI International 2014, Heraklion, Crete, Greece, June 22-27, 2014, Proceedings. Vol. 8510. Springer, 2014. https://books.google.com.au/books?hl=en&lr=&id=D1m7BQAAQBAJ&oi=fnd&pg=PR6v
Information Theory	An information-theoretic framework for visualization	Chen, Min, and Heike Jänicke. "An information-theoretic framework for visualization." IEEE Transactions on Visualization and Computer Graphics. http://citeseerx.ist.psu.edu/viewdoc/summary?doi=10.1.1.372.5270
Color Theory	A theory of color combination (theoretical model): Dimensions of the color combinatorics model; Similarities between color percepts & examples of various order rhythms regarding colors. (visual appearance, texture, basic elements).	Hård, A., & Sivik, L. (2001). A theory of colors in combination? A descriptive model related to the NCS color-order system. Color Research & Application, 26(1), 4-28. doi:10.1002/1520-6378(200102)26:1<4: AID-COL3>3.0.CO;2-T http://onlinelibrary.wiley.com/doi/10.1002/1520-6378(200102)26:1%3C4::AID-COL3%3E3.0.CO;2-T/abstract http://www.lacambrecouleur.be/pdf/A_Theory_of_Colors_in_Combination.pdf

Appendix E – VEDC: Practical Aspects Repository (partial presentation).

Title	Description	Source with links
Procedures & Techniques	Heuristic evaluation compared to user testing	Doubleday, Ann, et al. "A comparison of usability techniques for evaluating design." Proceedings of the 2nd conference on Designing interactive systems: processes, practices, methods, and techniques. ACM, 1997. http://dl.acm.org/citation.cfm?id=263583
	What influences users' preferences?	De Angeli, A., Sutcliffe, A., & Hartmann, J. (2006). Interaction, usability and aesthetics: What influences users' preferences? 2006 271-280. doi:10.1145/1142405.1142446 http://dl.acm.org/citation.cfm?id=1142446
Sample Size	Why you only need to test with 5 users?	Nielsen, J. (2000, March). Why you only need to test with 5 users: Alertbox. Retrieved 3 Sept, 2016 from https://www.nngroup.com/articles/why-you-only-need-to-test-with-5-users/
	Why and when five test users aren't enough?	Woolrych, Alan, and Gilbert Cockton. "Why and when five test users aren't enough." Proceedings of IHM-HCI 2001 conference. Vol. 2. Eds.) (Cépaduès Editions, Toulouse, FR, 2001), 2001. https://www.researchgate.net/publication/200553185_Why_and_when_five_test_users_aren%27t_enough
	How many users do you need to test?	Lewis, James R. "Sample sizes for usability tests: mostly math, not magic." interactions 13.6 (2006): 29-33. http://dl.acm.org/citation.cfm?id=1167973
Evaluators	Non-expert's performance compares to experts.	Laidlaw, David H., et al. "Comparing 2D vector field visualization methods: A user study." IEEE Transactions on Visualization and Computer Graphics 11.1 (2005): 59-70.
	Domain experts	Brewer, Isaac, et al. "Collaborative geographic visualization: Enabling shared understanding of environmental processes." Information Visualization, 2000. InfoVis 2000. IEEE Symposium on. IEEE, 2000. http://ieeexplore.ieee.org/abstract/document/885102/
	Usability experts	Tory, Melanie, and Torsten Moller. "Evaluating visualizations: do expert reviews work?" IEEE computer graphics and applications 25.5 (2005): 8-11. https://pdfs.semanticscholar.org/21dc/f2a158b05f24b48a3624fee46e8cea6d53c6.pdf
Tools for Data Collection	Testing tools	Teixeira, Carlos, Bernardo Santos, and Ana Respicio. "Usability testing tools for web graphical interfaces." Informatica Dec. 2013: 435. Expanded Academic ASAP. Web. 3 Sept. 2016. http://www.informatica.si/index.php/informatica/article/viewFile/473/477
	Eye-tracking methods	Tarasewich, P. and Fillion, S. Discount Eye Tracking: The Enhanced Restricted Focus Viewer. Proc. AMCIS (2004). http://aisel.aisnet.org/cgi/viewcontent.cgi?article=1961&context=amcis2004
Observer Evaluator Effect	User experience and evaluator intervention	Held JE, Biers DW. Software usability testing: Do evaluator intervention and task structure make any difference? In Proceedings of the Human Factors and Ergonomics Society Annual Meeting 1992 Oct (Vol. 36, No. 16, pp. 1215-1219). Sage CA: Los Angeles, CA: SAGE Publications. http://journals.sagepub.com/doi/abs/10.1177/154193129203601607
	Observer accuracy in usability testing	Adriane M. Donkers, Jo W. Tombaugh, and Richard F. Dillon. 1992. Observer accuracy in usability testing: the effects of obviousness and prior knowledge of usability problems. In Posters and Short Talks of the 1992 SIGCHI Conference on Human Factors in Computing Systems (CHI '92). ACM, New York, NY, USA, 127-128. http://dx.doi.org/10.1145/1125021.1125116

Universal Design Mobile Interface Guidelines for Mobile Health and Wellness Apps for an Aging Population Including People Aging with Disabilities

Ljilja Ruzic, Christina N. Harrington, and Jon A. Sanford
The Center for Assistive Technology and Environmental Access (CATEA)
Georgia Institute of Technology
Atlanta, GA, USA
e-mail: ljilja@gatech.edu, cnh@gatech.edu, jon.sanford@design.gatech.edu

Abstract—**The usability of mobile interfaces for older adults is becoming more important as the population ages and their use of technology increases. Whereas a few design strategies have been developed to guide the design of the mobile interfaces for an aging population, these strategies and their related principles and guidelines are focused on either older adults or individuals with disabilities. The size of the population aging with disabilities is growing. However, there are no guidelines that include this end-user population. Adaptation and integration of the existing strategies were necessary to create an inclusive and comprehensive set of guidelines for interactive mobile interfaces for older adults that includes people aging with disabilities. The paper presents an overview of the Universal Design Mobile Interface Guidelines, UDMIG, for an aging population and individuals aging with disabilities, and the related evaluation checklist. UDMIG v.2.2 and the checklist were developed to ensure usability of future mobile technologies by older adults through a universal design strategy that accommodates all users to the greatest extent possible. Moreover, the paper details the application of the guidelines to the design of the mobile health and wellness self-management app for individuals aging with multiple sclerosis, MS Assistant. Additionally, it reports the results of an expert review with the purpose of evaluating the effectiveness of implementing UDMIG v.2.2 in the design of MS Assistant.**

Keywords-aging; aging with disabilities; design; evaluation; guidelines; mobile interfaces.

I. Introduction

This research paper is based on the previously reported contribution on the design and evaluation of mobile interfaces for an aging population [1].

Older adults encounter many barriers while interacting with mobile applications [2]-[5]. Lack of physical space (e.g., small touch and physical buttons), confusion with their location within the context, use of menus that require precise movements, use of small fonts, content placement, and use of large contents that require memory recall, are some of the barriers that lead to longer and less successful task completion [6][7].

The usability of mobile interfaces for older adults is becoming more important as the population ages and seniors' use of technology increases. To ensure usability of new technologies for older adults, a number of design strategies have been proposed. While these strategies may adequately address the usability issues for people experiencing the normal aging process, they do not address the increasing number of usability barriers experienced by people aging with disabilities, a user population that is also growing at a rapid pace [8][9].

To be inclusive of people aging with and into disability in the design of interactive mobile interfaces, the Universal Design Mobile Interface Guidelines (UDMIG), was developed. The UDMIG is a comprehensive set of usability guidelines based on four established design strategies for desktop and mobile user interfaces, including, Universal Design (UD), Design for Aging (DfA), Universal Usability (UU), and Handheld Mobile Device Interface Design (MID).

This paper describes the development of the UDMIG and its associated checklist to ensure usability of future mobile technologies by older adults through a universal design strategy that accommodates all users to the greatest extent possible. In addition, it details the application of the guidelines to the design of MS Assistant, a mobile health and wellness self-management app for individuals aging with multiple sclerosis.

This paper is organized into six sections. Section II provides a background of the four design strategies that formed the basis of the UDMIG. In addition, it describes the current evaluation tools used for the assessment of mobile touchscreen interfaces for an aging population. Section III describes the three prototypes of the mobile interface guidelines for an aging population and their refinement, to include individuals aging with disabilities in UDMIG v.2.2. Section IV identifies the specific design criteria derived from UDMIG v2.2, which should be applied to the development of the mobile applications for older adults with disabilities. Section V describes the development of MS Assistant, a mobile health management application for people with Multiple Sclerosis (MS) based on the design criteria. Section VI presents the results of an expert review to evaluate the effectiveness of implementing the UDMIG design criteria in the design of MS Assistant. Finally, Section VII provides a discussion of the current state of MS Assistant and proposes future work.

II. Background: Design for Aging

There are four widely accepted strategies that are applied to the design of desktop and mobile user interfaces that are relevant for the target population. These include UD, DfA, UU, and MID.

UD is the design everyday products that are usable by everyone (to the greatest extent possible). By doing so, UD facilitates usability, thereby eliminating physical barriers to usability (and inclusivity) that would be experienced by any individual, including older adults and people with disabilities [10][11]. The Principles of UD [12][13] consists of seven principles and twenty-nine guidelines. Although originally developed to apply to physical products, the Principles of UD are equally applicable to the design of digital technologies.

In contrast to UD, DfA [14] specifically addresses the specific functional limitations associated with aging and user interfaces. DfA identifies the factors that constrain the use of products and user interfaces by older adults, as well as aspects of human-computer interface design that accommodate older users with age-associated disabilities and limitations [15]. It has fifty-two design guidelines grouped into six categories that cover design of visual, auditory, and haptic presentation of information, input and output devices, and effective interface design.

UU is comprised of eight guidelines, called the Eight Golden Rules of Interface Design. Whereas UD was initially developed for the design of physical environments (e.g., buildings, spaces, products, graphics), UU is intended to support usability, inclusivity, and utility of information and communication technologies [16]. Based on UU, the MID [17] modified and extended the eight golden rules to provide general design guidance for the usability of mobile platforms (Table I).

TABLE I. DESIGN STRATEGIES, THEIR TARGET AUDIENCE AND DESIGN

Design Strategy	Target Audience	Target Design
UD	All Users	Physical Environments
DfA	Seniors	User interfaces
UU	All Users	ICT
MID	All Users	Mobile Interfaces

While each of the four design strategies is commonly used to guide the design of mobile interfaces, none are sufficiently comprehensive to ensure that mobile user interfaces will be usable by older adults. Clearly, the first three strategies, UD, DfA, and UU, which were developed prior to the proliferation of mobile interfaces, are not specific to this platform. In contrast, whereas the MID is the mobile platform-specific, DfA is the only population-specific (i.e., a focus on older adults) strategy. Moreover, it is also the only strategy that clearly links individuals' needs and abilities to design solutions. As such, it provides both an understanding of *what* the functional problems of older adults are and guidance on *how* design can be used to solve those issues. This person-environment (P-E) fit approach [18] not only provides an understanding of *why* interface design needs to be different to be usable by older adults but also the tools to create unique and innovative interfaces without relying on a rigid set of prescriptive rules.

With the lack of an aging-relevant set of usability guidelines for mobile interfaces, there is a similar lack of a comprehensive evaluation tool to assess the usability of mobile touchscreen interfaces for this population. Existing assessment tools were either designed for other scales of design (e.g., products, services, spaces, buildings), developed to support the design of web interfaces for individuals with disabilities, or created for an evaluation of user interfaces for the general population. Five tools, the UD Checklist, Universal Design Performance Measures for Products, Product Evaluation Countdown, Universal Design Assessment Protocol and GUDC Guidelines are intended to assess the physical environment based on the UD principles.

The *UD Checklist* [19][20] assesses design based on both UD principles and ranges of users' abilities (i.e., vision, hearing, speech, cognition, dexterity, communication, balance, stature, upper and lower body strength and mobility, lifespan) to indicate the degree to which the outcome met the criteria for each design principle and each type of ability, respectively. This tool was intended to evaluate architectural spaces. It does not assess the specific design features, and it only evaluates the proposed design, not actual designs in use. The *Universal Design Performance Measures for Products* [21] uses twenty-nine UD guidelines as performance measures, and the five-point rating scale from strongly disagree to strongly agree, with a choice of not applicable to identify strengths and weaknesses of a product. It is intended to evaluate the usability of products throughout their life cycle, develop usability testing and focus groups, and identify and promote UD features of products. The second version of this tool called the *Product Evaluation Countdown* [22], was developed for use by end-users with their ranges and levels of abilities to test the actual demands of products. *Universal Design Assessment Protocol* (UDAP) [11][23] assesses UD principles by ability as well as across the range of abilities, evaluating design at the level of each UD guideline, thus providing a more precise analysis. However, the tool proved to be very complex and impractical to quantify UD with its six hundred and twelve-cell matrix. The Global Universal Design Commission, Inc. (GUDC) created *GUDC Rating System* that covers design process, site and building elements, customer service, and facilities management, which is building-type specific [11].

In addition to UD-derived evaluation tools for the physical environment, the *Web Content Accessibility Guidelines (WCAG) 2.0 Checklist* was developed by the Web Accessibility Initiative (WAI) of the World Wide Web Consortium (W3C) [24] to evaluate the accessibility of web pages and HTML content for users with disabilities. However, the tool is neither specific to mobile devices nor does accessibility necessarily equate to usability. Finally, although a number of other evaluation checklists and frameworks for testing the usability of mobile apps have been proposed [25]-[28], these tools are intended for the general population and do not recognize a variety and ranges of limitations an aging population faces.

III. UNIVERSAL DESIGN MOBILE INTERFACE GUIDELINES, UDMIG

The first version of the guidelines, UDMIG v.1.0, which has been previously reported [29][30], was created by applying DfA, UU, and MIG to the seven Principles of UD. This version relied too much on principles and guidelines of universal design as the underlying basis for the UDMIG. As such, it failed to incorporate P-E interaction approach that was a unique contribution of DfA, contained inconsistent language and level of specificity, and needed further refinement.

A. UDMIG v.2.0

To overcome problems with UDMIG 1.0, UDMIG v.2.0 [31] was developed within a framework based on the P-E fit model [18] as an organizing principle (Fig. 1).

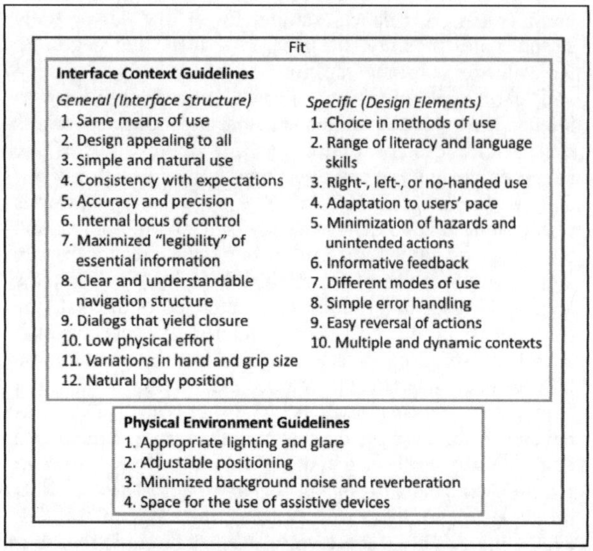

Figure 1. Structure of UDMIG v.2.0 based on P-E Model and its person, environment, and fit components.

The P-E fit approach [18] assesses the match or fit between a person's ability and the demands of the environment to promote healthy aging. Usability of mobile applications is achieved when there is a match between a person's ability and the design of the interface. In UDMIG v.2.0, the fit between the range of human abilities and the environment is manifested as a set of performance guidelines. These guidelines cover both the contextual environment of the interface and the physical environment in which the interface is used. For purposes of designing interfaces only guidelines specific to the interface environment, itself, were considered in the development of UDMIG. Moreover, the interface environment can be further differentiated by those guidelines that address the design of the interface structure (e.g., layout and navigation), as well as those that guide the design of the specific design elements (e.g., buttons and text) (Fig. 1).

B. UDMIG v.2.1

UDMIG v.2.0 failed to include the people aging with disabilities. Whereas data indicate that this is a growing population of potential users [8][9], the guidelines did not address the types of impairments and comorbidities experienced by these individuals.

To expand UDMIG v.2.0 to include individuals aging with disabilities, a study with people with multiple sclerosis (MS) was conducted [32]. MS was taken as an example of aging with disability. People with MS were chosen as an ideal end-user population as they represent a diverse user group that has symptoms that vary widely from an individual to an individual, but also within individuals over time. Moreover, MS presents with chronic symptoms that share many of the functional limitations associated with aging, including a decline in muscle strength, problems with balance, weakness, fatigue, reduced sensation, vision impairments, bowel and bladder dysfunction, cognitive impairment, pain, osteoporosis and sleep disturbances [33]-[36]. In addition, a majority of individuals diagnosed with MS experience major decline in their abilities due to the progression of MS after five years post-diagnosis [37]. Following this period, they need to learn how to cope with the functional limitations caused by the disease and how to age with MS.

The study [32] evaluated the usability of two health and wellness self-management mobile applications for individuals with MS and one health app for the general population. The three apps were evaluated by older adults and individuals with MS to identify the effectiveness of app attributes.

Study participants reported a number of additional recommendations for the design of mobile health and wellness applications:

- Navigation needs to be clear, intuitive, consistent, and easy to understand;
- Locating pages needs to be easy and intuitive;
- Task completion needs to be evident and bold so that users know they have accomplished their tasks and they can continue with the subsequent activities;
- Provide specific and clear instructions for every step of the actions;
- Font, buttons, and icons size (screen characters and targets) should be large enough to be usable by the end-users;
- Color contrast needs to be very high to allow for ease of use and legibility of information;
- Avoid use of scrolling and spinner.

This set of evidence-based design recommendations is intended to assist with the future development of health and wellness mobile interfaces for older adults, including people aging with disabilities.

The recommendations represent the most important design elements that need to be considered for the development of mobile interfaces for an aging population and present the main considerations when designing for this specific population.

Based on the results of the reported study [32], the design recommendations were used to prioritize UDMIG v. 2.1 as eight essential guidelines and the rest as optional/advisory guidelines. Among these eight essential design guidelines, six refer to the interface structure and two to the design elements. In addition, Same Means of Use guideline was added as the ninth mandatory guideline because it is the only UD principle that is essential to inclusivity and participation (Table II).

TABLE II. UDMIG V.2.1

Design Elements Guidelines	Interface Structure Guidelines
Essential Guidelines	
1. Accuracy and precision	1. Same means of use
2. Informative feedback	2. Clear and understandable navigation structure 3. Consistency with expectations 4. Simple and natural use 5. Dialogs that yield closure 6. Maximized "legibility" of essential information 7. Range of literacy and language skills
Advisory Guidelines	
3. Choice in methods of use 4. Minimization of hazards and unintended actions 5. Different modes of use 6. Easy reversal of actions	8. Internal locus of control 9. Adaptation to users' pace 10. Multiple and dynamic contexts 11. Design appealing to all 12. Right-, left- or no-handed use 13. Low physical effort 14. Variations in hand and grip size 15. Natural body position

These first nine design guidelines (i.e., the first two design elements guidelines and the first seven interface structure guidelines) should be used as the mandatory guidelines when designing for an aging population, including individuals aging with disabilities. The rest of UDMIG v.2.1 should be used as the recommended best practices.

IV. DESIGN CRITERIA FOR MOBILE APPS

Based on the UDMIG v.2.1, design criteria for a health and wellness self-monitoring mobile application for individuals aging with MS were developed. Each design guideline resulted in one or more corresponding design criteria, which were specified to be implemented in the app design.

UDMIG v.2.1 represent a set of performance guidelines. However, among the four founding design strategies, DfA is the only one that included prescriptive guidelines. Therefore, a number of design criteria are presented as prescriptive, and the majority as performance-based. Although the objective of both prescriptive and performance design criteria is to achieve usable design outcomes, they do so in very different ways. Prescriptive criteria focus on means and methods of achieving usability by dictating what must be done to achieve a usable outcome. This is largely achieved without specifying what the design of the outcome might look like. As a result, the more prescriptive design criteria are, the fewer design alternatives there are and therefore fewer ways to achieve a usable outcome. For example, DE guideline *Accuracy and Precision* provides a specific design criterion that the size of the buttons should be at least 16.5mm diagonally and 11.7mm square. In addition, it dictates the minimum contrast based on the WCAG 2.0 1.4.3 [24] level AA and level AAA. In contrast, performance design criteria focus on the product or results of the design process. Performance-based criteria suggest what the usable outcome should be without regard to how that outcome is achieved. As a result, performance design criteria provide greater flexibility in design outcomes by providing opportunities for designers to rely on their own interpretation and creativity to achieve a usable outcome. For example, IC guideline *Dialogs that yield closure* provides a design criterion that the related information should be grouped together and the most frequent operations should be highest on the menu structure. The later one focuses on the design outcome and leaves it up to the designer to determine what the related information is and how to group it, and what the most frequent operations within the design are.

A. Design Elements (DE) Guidelines and Criteria

Essential Guidelines

1. *Accuracy and precision*
   a. Size of the buttons is at least 16.5mm diagonally and 11.7mm square [38];
   b. Minimum contrast: the visual presentation of text and images of a text should have a contrast ratio of at least 4.5:1 (Level AA), preferably 7:1 (Level AAA) except for the following:
      i. Large Text: Large-scale text and images of large-scale text should have a contrast ratio of at least 3:1;
      ii. Incidental: Text or images of text that are part of an inactive user interface component, that are pure decoration, that are not visible to anyone, or that are part of a picture that contains significant other visual content, have no contrast requirement;
      iii. Logotypes: Text that is part of a logo or brand name has no minimum contrast requirement (WCAG 2.0 1.4.3) [24];
2. *Informative feedback*
   a. For every operator action, there is a system feedback, such as a beep when pressing a key or an error message for an invalid input value [16];

b. Provide a feedback about a confirmation of an activity and a current state [14][32];

c. For each icon provide a text description [38];

Advisory Guidelines

3. *Choice in methods of use*
   a. Provide an option to select or deselect all user preferences such as voice input (e.g., Siri, voice control) in Settings, available as accessibility features in iOS [11][17];
4. *Minimization of hazards and unintended actions*
   a. Provide text warnings as opposed to symbols and icons [14];
   b. Avoid short-duration menu displays [14];
   c. Frequent and important actions should be visible and easily accessible [11][14];
   d. Tap targets on touchscreens should be at least 16.5mm diagonally and 11.7mm square [38];
   e. Tap targets should be in colors that stand out, and arranged in linear order [30][39];
   f. Avoid use of attention-catching techniques, such as flashing and scrolling text and images in the periphery [14];
5. *Different modes of use*
   a. Use alternative interaction modes such as sound, vibration, and light [11];
   b. Provide both tactile/haptic and auditory feedback with keypads [14];
   c. Provide several alternative voices [17];
   d. Provide redundant visual presentation of essential information (e.g., color, icons, and text) [11];
6. *Easy reversal of actions*
   a. Provide "Are you sure?" prompts for important actions that can be disabled in Settings [11][14][30];
   b. If an error is made, the system should be able to detect the error and offer a prompt message for handling the error (e.g., if an entry for weight is skipped, provide a text message "Please enter a target weight") [16].

B. *Interface Context (IC) Guidelines and Criteria*

Essential Guidelines

1. *Same means of use*
   a. Eliminate specialized design and language [11];
   b. Provide one hardware and software application that allows individualized preferences [11][40];
2. *Clear and understandable navigation structure*
   a. Use the same design elements for the navigation from page to page, such as next and back buttons or similar [30] [32][39];
   b. Have navigation assistance (e.g., menu, instructions) for how to navigate to specific points in the system, which includes navigation to not only the home page, but also any relevant page [14];
   c. Provide specific, clear, and evident instructions for every step of the actions, and allow users to disable these instructions in Settings and on the instructions page [32];
   d. Provide more than one way to go to different pages while keeping the consistency [32];
3. *Consistency with expectations*
   a. Identical terminology is used in prompts, menus, and help screens [14];
   b. Consistent commands are employed throughout (e.g., Next, Back) [14];
   c. Ensure standardized format and keep consistent location of target items within (e.g., navigation buttons, Settings button, and error messages should always appear at the same location) [14];
   d. Provide the icon with the title of the current functional feature at the top navigation bar on every page;
4. *Simple and natural use*
   a. Frequent and important actions should be visible and easily accessible (e.g., Next and Back buttons on the lower left and right side, Home page button on the upper left corner) [14];
   b. Avoid use of the picker [32];
   c. Avoid scrolling text because it is difficult to process, especially horizontal formats; use a slow scrolling rate if it cannot be avoided [14][32];
5. *Dialogs that yield closure*
   a. Group related information and have most frequent operations highest on the menu structure [14];
   b. Indicate clearly on the middle of the top navigation bar where the user currently is at any point of time (e.g., diary, reports, games, symptoms) [14];
   c. After users save any data, provide the information that their records have been saved and secured [16][32];
   d. Make it clear how to navigate to all main points of the interface from the homepage (i.e., main functional features on the home page), and how to go back to homepage from any other page (i.e., home page button on every page) [32];
   e. Provide an obvious feedback (visual, audio, and/or tactile) when a target is selected [14];
   f. Make it clear which option is active (i.e., selected state) and what the consequences of an action are (i.e., by pressing the selected button and Next button the selected feature page will open) [14][32];

6. *Maximized "legibility" of essential information*
    a. Size of the buttons is at least 16.5mm diagonally and 11.7mm square [38];
    b. Whenever possible use 14-point and bigger serif or sans serif fonts (i.e., use Helvetica primarily, and use Arial and Times Roman as secondary options), and use at least 12-point when not [41];
    c. Avoid cursive and decorative fonts and use of all uppercase letters [14];
    d. Provide good structure (e.g., grammar) in spoken and written text [14];
    e. Provide video conferencing in addition to talking on a phone [14];
7. *Range of literacy and language skills*
    a. Avoid use of technical language [14];
    b. Keep reading level of text material at grade 10 or below [14];

Advisory Guidelines

8. *Internal locus of control*
    a. Provide a choice of linear vs. random access [30][39];
9. *Adaptation to users' pace*
    a. Profile provides personalization option for users' skill levels: novice to expert users [16][17];
10. *Multiple and dynamic contexts*
    a. Users can configure input and output to their needs and desires (e.g., text size, brightness) in Settings [17];
    b. Allow for a configuration of the context, such as environmental conditions (e.g., brightness, noise levels, weather), and presence of strangers and locations that restrict use of some app features (e.g., speech input and output in libraries) [17];
11. *Design appealing to all*
    a. Provide color palette that can be used by colorblind users [17];
12. *Right-, left- or no-handed use*
    a. Place main navigation buttons of equal importance accessible for both right- and left-handed users (e.g., Next and Back buttons at the lower left- and right-hand side) [39];
13. *Low physical effort*
    a. Avoid double-clicking and use single tap instead [14];
    b. Minimize steps (i.e., basic tasks) when possible [14];
14. *Variations in hand and grip size*
    a. If the targets are large enough (at least 16.5mm diagonally and 11.7mm square), a spacing between them can be zero [14][38];
    b. If targets are small, make spacing between them visible (e.g., 3mm) [14][38];
    c. If possible, place tap targets near the center or the bottom of the screen [38];
15. *Natural body position*
    a. Place main navigation buttons of equal importance at the bottom of the screen (e.g., Next and Back buttons at the lower left- and right-hand side) [39].

V. MS Assistant: A Mobile Health Management Application

Based on the UDMIG v. 2.2 design criteria, a mobile health and wellness app, *MS Assistant,* was developed to enhance health self-management for people with MS. The app was designed to provide eight functions, to allow for personalization, and to assist with medication adherence and other daily tasks with alert/reminder systems. These eight functions were selected based on the findings of a qualitative study [40], which was conducted to identify the specific needs for self-management of health and wellness among people with MS and to recognize the opportunities to meet those needs through mobile apps. A number of preferred functions were identified and grouped into eight categories (i.e., daily self-reporting of health and wellness, keeping and communicating health and wellness records, education, social support, alert and reminder systems, virtual reality games, telehealth, personalization).

Functions. The eight functions include diary, reports, MS friends, games, education, goals, vitals, and emergency.

Diary provides a comprehensive tool for understanding the disease on a daily basis and over time, and how best to manage it through everyday self-management tasks, such as mood, symptoms, energy level, activity, sleep length and quality, and diet.

Reports allows users to compile their health management data into useful reports that can be shared electronically with healthcare providers and caregivers.

MS Friends is a social support feature that connects users with other people with MS to share their experiences and everyday challenges.

Games features VR games that would enable users to perform real-world activities that they might find challenging. In addition, this feature has cognitive and classic games that help people with MS with cognitive functioning, and physical games, which help them with the balance.

Education provides the latest news and research about MS as well as health and wellness tips.

Goals enables users to set up their personal health and wellness goals to keep them motivated and inspired.

Vitals offers remote health and wellness monitoring through the Bluetooth connected devices, such as blood pressure monitoring devices, scales, sleep and activity trackers (e.g., Fitbit), and similar.

Emergency lets users place calls directly to their healthcare providers, caregivers, and 911.

Structure. MS Assistant provides two types of navigation: linear and random access. Linear interaction allows users to go through the pages by making or skipping a selection and pressing the Next button. Users can go through the whole interface in a linear fashion by using the Next and Back buttons on every page, which provides consistency and simplicity. After a selection is made, the Next button takes users to the following page of the interface. When the user taps on any button, the button changes to the selected colored background and white text that visually emphasizes the selection (Fig. 2). To change the selection, a user can tap the button again to deselect it.

For navigating through the pages, the user can tap on the Next and Back buttons located at the bottom corners of the screen (Fig. 2). For example, after tapping on the Diary button users are taken to the first Diary page where they can select the Mood. The selected state of the Mood button confirms the selection, and Next button takes users to the Symptoms page. Users are through all the Diary pages by tapping the Next buttons. After making the final selection on the Diet pages, users are taken to the Home Page. In addition, for the expert users and ones who prefer a direct selection, all of the functional features are accessible from the Home page. Moreover, every page has the Home and Back buttons to allow an easy random access. Back button takes users to the main Diary page and directly make selections.

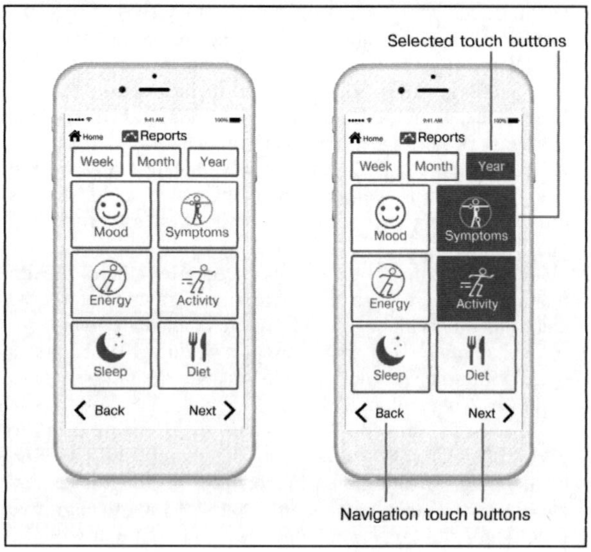

Figure 2. Linear interaction on the Reports page.

Design Decisions. Design decisions for MS Assistant were based on the UDMIG v.2.2 and corresponding design criteria.

A. *Design Elements (DE) Guidelines*

Essential Guidelines

1. Accuracy and precision

To facilitate the accuracy and precision required to accommodate different abilities, preferences, situations, contexts of use, ages, novice and expert users, and enhance users' experience, provided screen characters and targets are designed to be conspicuous and accessible (e.g., font size is at least 14-point and higher, the button size is at least 16.5mm diagonally and 11.7mm square [36]). In addition, every function is presented by its color of the touch buttons on the Home Page and throughout the app (Fig. 3a). The color scheme for the Home Page buttons (i.e., functional features) is chosen to pass the assessment against the WCAG 2.0 1.4.3 [20] color contrast success criteria. Contrast is maximized by using black on white text.

2. Informative feedback

When the user taps on any button to make a selection, the button changes to the selected state button with a colored background and white text that visually emphasize the selection. An error message shows up on the screen after the user creates an invalid input value. Top navigation bar provides information about the current functional feature by providing a title with an icon (e.g., Diary with its icon, Mood with its icon, etc.). After users finish all the tasks in the last section of the Diary, which is the Diet, they are taken to the Home page by tapping on the Next button.

Advisory Guidelines

3. Choice in methods of use

Different inputs and choices of input to accommodate variations in abilities, preferences, situations, and contexts of use are available in Settings as Input and Touch selections. For example, speech input through Siri and voice control is available for users.

4. Minimization of hazards and unintended actions

Text warnings, as opposed to symbols and icons, are provided in the form of prompts that can be disabled in Settings. Frequent and important actions are visible and easily accessible by placing the Home button on the navigation top bar and the Next and Back buttons on the bottom of the screen on every page (Fig. 3b).

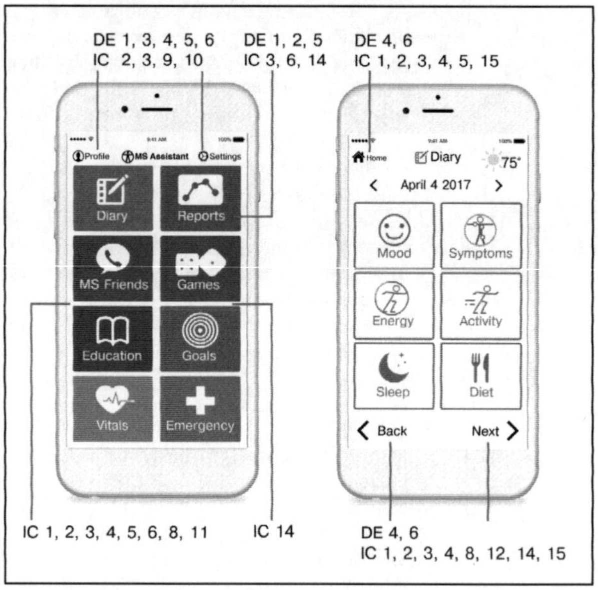

Figure 3. Homepage (3a) and Diary page (3b).

Short-duration menu displays are eliminated because of the slower processing speed of an aging population. Instead, after the user taps on any button, the button changes to the selected state that lasts until the user taps on the Next button or he or she decides to deselect it.

5. Different modes of use

Different modes (pictorial, verbal, tactile) for redundant presentation of essential information to accommodate different abilities, preferences, and contexts of use are available and can be selected and deselected in Settings as Output and Touch accommodations. For example, alternative interaction modes such as sound, vibration, and light, haptic and auditory feedback with keypads, and several alternative voices can be selected. In addition, all touchscreen buttons provide redundant visual cues through color, icons, and text. Because of the limitations of iPhone 6, vibration (haptic) feedback is not available for this version and can be turned on for the iPhone 7 version and above.

6. Easy reversal of actions

Fail-safe features are provided to minimize hazards and errors. The units of reversibility are a single action, a data entry, or a complete group of actions. For example, "Are you sure you want to send the reports to the selected contacts?" is a confirmation message after a user selects the reports and contacts, with reversion back to the contacts screen when users press "No" (Fig. 4b). Easy reversal of an action is provided through the option to cancel unwanted task in this prompt message if the list of contacts is wrong. Similarly, if a target weight is skipped in the Goals, a text message "Please enter a target weight" shows up to remind the user to fill out the weight.

B. *Interface Structure (IS) Guidelines*

Essential Guidelines

1. Same means of use

The design goal is one mobile health and wellness app for all users, rather than accessible design for people with disabilities. As a universally designed system, the app design avoids segregating or stigmatizing users and provides participation by providing the same hardware and software application that allows individualized preferences.

2. Clear and understandable navigation structure

Users can choose to have linear navigation using the same type of linear navigation (e.g., Next and Back buttons) on every page or they can go back to the Home page and use random access navigation to go directly to a function. Navigation assistance is provided with instructions for how to navigate to specific points in the system and the Home page button on every page. Specifically, every functional feature has an instruction page that explains the content and interactions. For those who no longer need instructions, they can be disabled on the Instructions page itself and in the Settings.

3. Consistency with expectations

Consistent sequences of actions are required in similar situations. For example, users make a selection by tapping the button when the selected state of the button appears and navigate to the next page by tapping the Next button on every page. Identical terminology is used in all screens, prompts, error messages, text messages, and information screens. Consistent commands are employed throughout the interface (e.g., Next and Back buttons, Homepage button). Moreover, names, titles, color schemes, screen appearances, "look and feel," standard layouts, fonts, and font sizes are consistent throughout the app. In addition, consistency with pre-existing expectations is provided. For example, Next button is placed on the right-hand side, the Back button is located on the left-hand side, and selection is made by tapping a button. Information is arranged consistent with its importance by having the icon and the title of the current functional feature at the top navigation bar together with the Home page button (Fig. 4a).

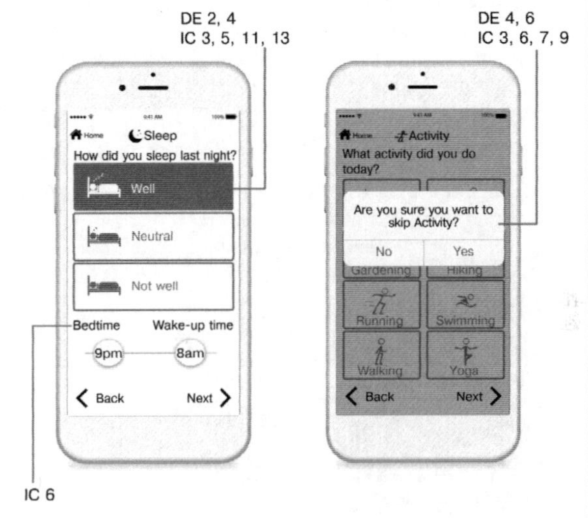

Figure 4. Sleep page (4a) and Activity page with "Are you sure?" prompt message (4b).

4. Simple and natural use

Complexity is eliminated by having simple screen designs that require a single task per screen (Fig. 5b). The Next and Back buttons are placed on the bottom of the page to allow for the natural use and navigation. Use of the scrolling is eliminated by having the single task on one screen. In addition, use of the picker is eliminated, and a slider, keypad, and buttons are used throughout the interface. Moreover, navigation is simple for novice users and those with cognitive limitations (linear navigation) as well as a for expert/advanced users (random access). Use of all attention-catching techniques is avoided.

5. Dialogs that yield closure

Screens are designed in a way that the related information is grouped, and the most frequent operations are placed highest on the menu structure. For example, on the Activity page, its icon and the title are highest on the screen and placed on the top navigation bar, start and end time is at the top of the page after the name of an activity, followed by the distance. The comments section is at the bottom of the screen. Related information is grouped, such that every functional feature has its own pages and colors that add to the differentiation between the selections. In addition, it is clear and simple to navigate to all main points of the interface from the Home page (e.g., Diary, Reports, MS Friends, Games, Education, Goals, Vitals, and Emergency), and to go back to Home page from any other page (e.g., Home page button, Next and Back buttons). It is clearly indicated which option is active by having the selected state of the tapped buttons, and what the consequences of an action are. For example, by tapping on the Next button after making a selection, the next page will open. An obvious visual feedback is provided when a target is selected together by changing the color of the button to a color of the outline of the selected button. A vibratory feedback was not possible to implement on iPhone 6, which is a major drawback of this model. However, it is highly recommended, and it is possible to implement it on iPhone 6s and iPhone 7 devices.

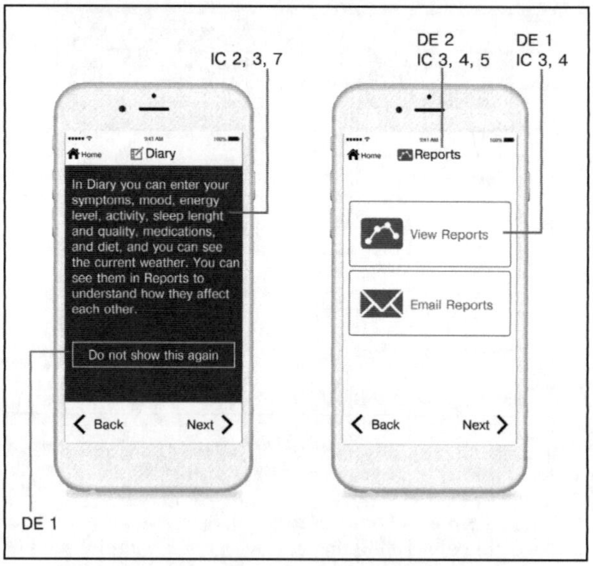

Figure 5. Diary Instructions page (5a) and Reports page (5b).

6. Maximized "legibility" of essential information

Screen characters and targets are designed to be conspicuous and accessible by designing the icons and buttons to be large enough to select easily. Helvetica 14-point font and bigger was the only font used.

7. Range of literacy and language skills

Research suggests that technical language might be difficult for older adults, as their educational attainment levels may be lower than that of younger adults [12]. Therefore, simple conversational language is used for all text material, and reading level of text material is kept at grade 10 or below (Fig. 5a).

Advisory Guidelines

8. *Internal locus of control*

The system should be designed such that users initiate actions rather than respond to them [14]. In addition, users can choose a navigation system and various preferences, such as linear vs. random access and novice vs. expert user navigation.

9. *Adaptation to users' pace*

The adaptable pace is provided in Settings and Profile to accommodate novice and expert users, different ages, abilities, preferences, situations, and contexts of use. Users can choose to navigate the app as novice or expert users, and they can personalize the app in the Settings. Pop-up menu durations are designed to be controlled by the user and require their confirmation (e.g., press "OK", "No", "Yes") to continue carrying out the commands.

10. Multiple and dynamic contexts

The Settings feature enables users to customize the input and output modalities to their needs and desires (e.g., text size, brightness) as well as the context, such as environmental conditions (e.g., brightness, noise levels, weather), presence of strangers and locations that restrict use of some app features (e.g., speech input and output in libraries) [39][40].

11. Design appealing to all

The app was designed to be appealing to all to enhance usability and marketability [14][15]. Color and its manipulation are important considerations for visual interfaces. MS Assistant has a color scheme that can be used by colorblind users.

12. *Right-, left- or no-handed use*

MS Assistant is designed to provide a right or left-handed access and use by having the main navigation buttons of equal importance at the lower left- and right-hand side (i.e., Next and Back buttons).

13. *Low physical effort*

The app is designed to minimize repetitive actions and sustained physical effort to provide ease of use, efficiency, comfort, and minimize fatigue [11] by using only single-tap [12] and by minimizing navigation steps.

14. *Variations in hand and grip size*

Large keys and appropriate inter-key spacing on a keypad are used to allow ease of use [12]. For the small targets (less than 16.5mm diagonally and 11.7mm square), a spacing between them is designed to be visible (e.g., 3mm) [12][36]. For the large targets, preferred is to provide the spacing between them although it can be zero. In addition, the tap targets are placed near the center or the bottom of the screen [36].

15. *Natural body position*

MS Assistant has the main navigation buttons at the bottom of the screen to provide comfort and minimize fatigue [37].

VI. Effectiveness of the Implementing the UDMIG v.2.2

For the purpose of evaluating the effectiveness of implementing UDMIG v.2.2 in the design of MS Assistant, we conducted an expert review to identify design elements that needed improvement to successfully apply the guidelines and recommend possible refinements.

A. Methods

Participants

Ten researchers and/or designers with experience in aging, accessibility, human-computer interaction, human factors, industrial design, universal design, and/or usability participated in the study. Inclusion criteria were individuals 18+ years of age who have more than three years of experience in one or more of the areas of expertise described above. Participants' expertise included accessibility (n=8), usability (n=8), aging (n=7), human factors (n=6), universal design (n=6), human-computer interaction (n=5), and industrial design (n=2) respectively. The mean number of years of their working experience was 13 years.

Experts rated their familiarity with user interface design for people with MS, dexterity, cognitive, and visual limitations on a scale of "not familiar" to "somewhat familiar" to "very familiar." For familiarity with interface design for people MS, 3 respondents were not familiar and 10 were somewhat familiar. Regarding the design of interfaces for individuals with dexterity limitations, 1 expert was not familiar (n=1), 5 were somewhat familiar and 4 were very familiar. For interface design for people with cognitive limitations, 8 experts were somewhat familiar and 2 very familiar. Finally, 3 participants were somewhat familiar and 7 were very familiar (n=7) with interface design for people with vision limitations.

Procedures

After signing the informed consent form approved by the Georgia Tech Institutional Review Board (IRB), experts completed a demographic questionnaire about their areas of expertise and a number of years they have worked in the field. Experts then performed directed tasks using MS Assistant without any training or assistance. They received a simple script that included entering health and wellness data (i.e., mood, symptoms and related difficulties, energy level, daily activity, sleep length and quality, and diet), emailing the reports, calling MS friend, finding virtual reality games, reading the MS news, setting up the weight goal, inputting the blood pressure, calling the healthcare provider, entering the personal information, and increasing the text size. Experts then used the UDMIG v.2.2 checklist to rate how well each guideline was implemented, identified design elements needing improvement, and provided recommendations for their refinement.

UDMIG v.2.2 Checklist

Prescriptive design guidelines and standards are easy to interpret and to objectively assess. Assessment of performance guidelines is multidimensional since it incorporates both activity and participation [11]. All performance-based guidelines are subject to interpretation by experts as well as end-users to a certain extent, which makes objective measurement slightly difficult. UDMIG v.2.2 Checklist rates agreement with achieving each of the design guidelines using the 5-point Likert scale where 1 = strongly disagree and 5 = strongly agree with each of the applicable design criteria. It is intended to be used by end-users and to assist designers to think about the needs of potential users who would interact with their mobile touchscreen applications.

The complete checklist used for this expert review has 50 items (i.e., design criteria). An example of the checklist based on some of the design criteria (e.g., one design criteria per guideline) used for the expert review is presented in Table III.

TABLE III. UDMIG V.2.2 CHECKLIST

Design Elements Guidelines	Interface Context Guidelines
This application provides…	
1. The button size of at least 16.5mm diagonally and 11.7mm square.	1. The same means of use for all users, by eliminating specialized design and signage.
2. Feedback about a confirmation of my activity and a current state.	2. The same design elements for the navigation from page to page (e.g., Next, Back Home page buttons).
3. Alternate methods of input and use, such as speech input.	3. Standardized format and keeps the consistent location of target items within (e.g., navigation buttons, and error messages).
4. Text warnings as opposed to symbols and icons.	4. Visible and easily accessible frequent and important actions (e.g., a location of Next, Back, Homepage button).
5. Different modes of feedback, such as sound, vibration, or light feedback.	5. A clear indication on the middle of the top navigation bar where the user currently is at any point in time (e.g., diary, reports, games).
6. Easy reversal of my actions if I make a mistake, such as "Are you sure you want to send the reports to the selected contacts?", with reversion back to the contacts screen when I press "No."	6. The minimum contrast between the background colors against the images and text based on WCAG 2.0 1.4.3 Level AA, and preferably Level AAA.
	7. Reading level of text material at grade 10 or below.
	8. A choice of linear vs. random access.
	9. Personalization option to change my skill level from a "novice" to an "expert" user.
	10. A configuration of the output to my needs and preferences (e.g., text size, brightness).
	11. An aesthetically plausible color scheme that can be used by colorblind users.
	12. Main navigation buttons of equal importance accessible for both right- and left-handed users (e.g., Next and Back buttons at the lower left- and right-hand side).
	13. Use of a single tap throughout the app instead of double-clicking.
	14. The spacing between the small targets visible (e.g., 3mm).
	15. Main navigation buttons of equal importance at the bottom of the screen (i.e., Next and Back buttons).

Data Analysis

Mean and standard deviation for the rating of each guideline were calculated, as well as the mean and standard deviation of ratings for each participant. 16 ratings for the participant number 8 were excluded because they skipped the page with ratings of the guidelines IC5d to IC13d.

B. Results

10 participants rated 50 items on the checklist. The total number of responses is 484, with 16 missing responses that were not used in the analyses.

The mean of all the ratings for design criteria per participant is within a range of 3.90 – 4.89. The design criteria DE6b (i.e., This app provides the system which can detect the error and offer a prompt message for handling it; if an entry for weight is skipped, provide a text message "Please enter a target weight") had the lowest mean of the ratings equal to 3.90. This was the only mean value lower than 4. Participants stated that the app provided a prompt message for handling an error. However, the prompt should "offer options to submit data without all responses submitted." Current prompts informed the users that they need to enter missing information and did not offer an option to skip certain fields. They made users fill out all the information on the page.

Out of a total of 484 responses, almost 70% (n=332) of the design criteria were rated as a 5. An additional one-quarter (n=126) were rated as a 4. The lowest rating for any criterion was 2 (n=6) and an additional 20 were rated as a 3.

Among the 10 participants, mean ratings ranged from 3.86 – 4.92. The participant with the lowest overall mean ratings (mean = 3.86) did not give a rating higher than 4 to any individual criterion with 44 rated as a 4 and 6 rated as 2 or 3.

In addition, participants identified specific usability issues with the design of some of the interface elements and structure, including navigation, labeling, scrolling while using a keyboard, color contrast, same means of use, page layout, and miscategorization. (Table IV).

Design of the elements of the user interface was the largest category with a total of 16 participants reporting usability problems in 3 subcategories. 8 participants stated that Profile and Settings should be redesigned to "stand out" and "look more prominent." Design in Adobe Illustrator presented in this paper followed the guidelines strictly and made a distinction between the name of the app, MS Assistant, and Profile and Settings buttons on the first page (Fig. 3). However, because of the limitations of iOS and the size of the top navigation bar, there was no space for the Profile and Settings icons because of the minimum font size dictated by the UDMIG v.2.2. Participants suggested that those two buttons should "look like buttons" with possibly adding a black border to them or a background color so that those look like the other buttons on the home page. In addition, 6 participants reported that top navigation bar icons that represent a title of the current page, including the weather icon, "look clickable" (Fig. 3b, Fig. 4, and Fig. 5). During the design phase, Adobe Illustrator prototypes made a clear distinction between the design of the home button and the title of the current page (e.g., Diary, Mood, Vitals, etc.). However, since the iOS limited the size of the top navigation bar and there was no compromise on the side of the font size, those two looked the same. Thus, the current title of the page looked "like a button." Participants recommended that "header should look different than the home button." Moreover, 2 participants commented that the design of the slider used on the symptoms, difficulties, and sleep pages probably needs redesign because of the problems with motor control in individuals with MS, and possible use of the stylus. 1 participant commented that the "numbers on the bottom should be on top of the slider."

TABLE IV. USABILITY PROBLEMS

Categories	Usability problems	Number of participants
Design of user interface elements	Profile, Settings not prominent	8
	Top navigation bar icons look like buttons	5
	Use of slider	3
Navigation	Having "to press on Next after a choice is made"	9
Labeling	Input, Output buttons	6
	Education button	5
	Speech button	4
	Emergency button	2
	Energized button	2
Lack of page scrolling while using a keyboard	Scrolling disabled	5
Color contrast	White on grey (instructions page)	2
	Green on grey (Do not show this again button in selected state)	1
Same means of use	Next, Back buttons	2
Page layout	Spacing between the top buttons and buttons below	2
	View Reports button is bellow Email Reports button	2
Miscategorization	Mood in Diary	1

9 participants reported problems with navigation due to having "to press on Next after a choice is made," which "was not clear at first." They either "expected to double click" or just click on the selection to open that particular page. However, all of them understood that this way of navigation is beneficial to an aging population that uses this app as a novice user.

Labeling was a category that included suggestions to rename "Input" and "Output" categories of Settings into a non-technical language (n=6). 4 of them thought that "Speech" should be renamed into "Audio" because it represents the settings for the sound coming from the device. Another suggestion was to rename "Education" into "Digest" or "Resources" because "News" category did not belong in there (n=5). It was not clear that a healthcare provider would be listed under Emergency functional feature (n=2), but there was no agreement on the alternative location for it. 1 participants suggested that it should be moved under Reports as an additional sub-feature named Contacts. The other participant stated they "didn't want to click because I thought it would call 911," but did not think any other location would be more suitable for it. Mood page had an "Energized" icon, which was confusing labeling to 2 participants because of Diary category "Energy level."

They suggested that "Anxious and Excited are missing" and that "Energized could be elsewhere."

Lack of page scrolling while using a keyboard was found problematic (n=5). Participants recommended to "add scrolling where additional input is needed." Scrolling was disabled throughout the interface because of the IC4c design criteria requirement.

Color contrast on the instructions pages with white on grey was not high enough to 2 participants, and "Do not show this again" button in a selected state with green text on grey background did not have high enough contrast to 1 participant.

Same means of use category has 2 participants who reported that "Next" and "Back" buttons look like a part of the specialized use and design.

Page layout category included a recommendation to move "View Reports" button above "Email Reports" button (n=2), and to increase the spacing between "Week", "Month", and "Year" buttons, and the other selection buttons on the Reports pages and between "Manual input" button and the rest of the screen on Vitals page (n=2).

Miscategorization was reported by 1 participants when they were not sure if Mood should be on Diary page.

VII. CONCLUSION

UDMIG v.2.2 and the related evaluation checklist were developed to ensure usability of future mobile applications by older adults, including individuals aging with disabilities. A universal design approach was used to accommodate all users to the greatest extent possible. Based on each UDMIG v.2.2 guideline and its design criteria, a representative statement with the 5-point Likert scale was created. The purpose of the checklist is to rate the agreement with each of the guidelines. It was developed for the end-users and usability experts to evaluate the usability and equitability of the mobile interfaces for an aging population.

The application of UDMIG v.2.2 to a mobile health and wellness app design was presented to illustrate and showcase the possible uses of the guidelines for a population of individuals aging with disabilities. eHealth mobile application for individuals aging with MS, MS Assistant was developed for this purpose. People with MS represent an ideal user group for application and evaluation of UDMIG v.2.2 and the checklist. They are a diverse user group with symptoms that vary widely from individual to individual and within an individual over time.

The study was conducted with the purpose to have expert evaluators rate the extent to which each guideline was implemented in the mobile app MS Assistant, to identify design elements that need improvement, and to suggest their possible improvements. Overall, this implementation of the guidelines to the design of the mobile app scored well. All mean values of the participants' ratings were equal to 4 or higher, except for the one equal to 3.86. The results of the study confirm that MS Assistant effectively implemented UDMIG v.2.2. There was a number of recommendations related to the minor usability problems found in the app.

The future work will require a refinement of the mobile app design based on those recommendations from the expert reviewers. Moreover, a usability testing of MS Assistant with individuals aging with MS will be conducted to assess the overall usability of the app to determine the effectiveness of UDMIG v.2.2 in producing a universally usable product. User outcome measures, such as a number of errors, completion time, and satisfaction ratings will be collected.

ACKNOWLEDGMENT

This research was supported by a grant from the National Institute on Disability, Independent Living, and Rehabilitation Research (NIDILRR grant number 90RE5016-01-00) under the auspices of The Rehabilitation Engineering Research Center on Technologies to Support Successful Aging with Disability (RERC TechSAge). NIDILRR is a Center within the Administration for Community Living (ACL), Department of Health and Human Services (HHS).

REFERENCES

[1] L. Ruzic, C. N. Harrington, and J. A. Sanford, "Design and Evaluation of Mobile Interfaces for an Agign Population," The Tenth International Conference on Advances in Computer-Human Interactions (ACHI2017), Mar. 2017.

[2] A. Holzinger, G. Searle, and A. Nischelwitzer, "On some aspects of improving mobile applications for the elderly," International Conference on Universal Access in Human-Computer Interaction (HCII2007), Springer, Jul. 2007, pp. 923-932.

[3] M. Ziefle, "The influence of user expertise and phone complexity on performance, ease of use and learnability of different mobile phones," Behaviour & Information Technology, vol. 21, pp. 303-311, Jan. 2002.

[4] M. Ziefle and S. Bay, "How older adults meet complexity: aging effects on the usability of different mobile phones," Behaviour & Information Technology, vol. 24, pp. 375-389, Sep. 2005.

[5] M. Ziefle, S. Bay, and A. Schwade, "On keys' meanings and modes: The impact of different key solutions on children's efficiency using a mobile phone," Behaviour & Information Technology, vol. 25, pp. 413-431, Sep. 2006.

[6] A. Chadwick-Dias, M. McNulty, and T. Tullis, "Web usability and age: how design changes can improve performance," Conference on Universal Usability (CUU 2003), Nov. 2003, pp. 30-37.

[7] S. A. Becker, "A study of web usability for older adults seeking online health resources," ACM Transactions on Computer-Human Interaction (TOCHI 2004), Dec. 2004, vol. 11, pp. 387-406.

[8] D. Sheets, "Aging with disabilities: ageism and more," Generations, vol. 29, pp. 37-41, 2005.

[9] G. Anderson, "Chronic Care: Making the Case for Ongoing Care," Partnership for Solutions, 2010.

[10] C. M. Law, J. S. Yi, Y. S. Choi, and J. A. Jacko, "A systematic examination of universal design resources: part 1, heuristic evaluation," Universal Access in the Information Society, vol. 7, pp. 31-54, Apr. 2008.

[11] J. A. Sanford, Universal Design as a Rehabilitation Strategy: Design for the Ages. New York, NY: Springer Publishing Company, 2012.

[12] B. R. Connell, Principles of Universal Design NC State University.[Online].Avalable:https://projects.ncsu.edu/ncsu/design/cud/about_ud/udprinciples.htm [Accessed: 20-Jan-2017].

[13] M. F. Story, "Maximizing Usability: The Principles of Universal Design," Assistive technology, vol. 10, pp. 4-12, 1998.

[14] A. D. Fisk, W. A. Rogers, N. Charness, S. J. Czaja, and J. Sharit, Designing for older adults: Principles and creative human factors approaches. Boca Raton, FL: CRC Press, Taylor & Francic Group, 2009.

[15] M. Zajicek, "Interface design for older adults," Proc. The 2001 EC/NSF Workshop on Universal Accessibility of Ubiquitous Computing: Providing for The Elderly (WUAUC'01), ACM, May 2001, pp. 60-65.

[16] B. Shneiderman and C. Plaisant, Designing the user interface: strategies for effective human-computer interaction. Pearson Education India, 2010.

[17] J. Gong, and P. Tarasewich, "Guidelines for handheld mobile device interface design," Proc. DSI 2004 Annual Meeting, Citeseer, Nov. 2004, pp. 3751-3756.

[18] M. P. Lawton and L. Nahemow, "Ecology and the aging process," The psychology of adult development and aging, pp. 619-674, 1973.

[19] G. Finkel and Y. Gold, "Actualizing universal design," Journal of Leisurability, vol. 26, pp. 25-30, 1999.

[20] The Executive Policy Committee, "Universal Design policy," vol.5, Dec. 2001.

[21] M. F. Story and J. L. Mueller, "Universal Design Performance Measures for Products to Support the Practice of Universal Design," Proc. Human Factors and Ergonomics Society Annual Meeting (HFES), SAGE Publications, Sep. 2004, pp. 1116-1120.

[22] E. Mpofu and T. Oakland, Rehabilitation and health assessment: applying ICF guidelines. Springer, 2010.

[23] J. Sanford, E. Mpofu, and T. Oakland, "Assessing universal design in the physical environment," Rehabilitation and Health Assessment, pp. 255-278, 2010.

[24] Web Content Accessibility Guidelines 2.0 Overview. [Online].Avalable:https://www.w3.org/WAI/intro/wcag.php [Accessed: 20-Jan-2017].

[25] M. de Sá and L. Carriço, "An evaluation framework for mobile user interfaces," 12th IFIP Conference on Human-Computer Interaction, Springer, Aug. 2009, pp. 708-721.

[26] Y. G. Ji, J. H. Park, C. Lee, and M. H. Yun, "A usability checklist for the usability evaluation of mobile phone user interface," International Journal of Human-Computer Interaction, vol. 20, pp. 207-231, Jul. 2006.

[27] J. Heo, D. H. Ham, S. Park, C. Song, and W. C. Yoon, "A framework for evaluating the usability of mobile phones based on multi-level, hierarchical model of usability factors," Interacting with Computers, vol. 21, pp. 263-275, Aug. 2009.

[28] D. H. Ham, J. Heo, P. Fossick, W. Wong, S. Park, C. Song, and M. Bradley, "Conceptual framework and models for identifying and organizing usability impact factors of mobile phones," Proc. The 18th Australia Conference on Computer-Human Interaction: Design: Activities, Artefacts and Environments (OZCHI '06), ACM, Nov. 2006, pp. 261-268.

[29] L. Kascak, C. B. Rébola, and J. Sanford, "Integrating Universal Design (UD) Principles and Mobile Design Guidelines to Improve Design of Mobile Health Applications for Older Adults," Proc. IEEE International Conference on Healthcare Informatics (ICHI 2014), IEEE Press, Sep. 2014, pp. 343-348.

[30] L. R. Kascak, E. Y. Liu, and J. A. Sanford, "Universal Design (UD) Guidelines for Interactive Mobile Voting Interfaces for Older Adults," Proc. 9th International Conference on Universal Access in Human-Computer Interaction (HCII2015), Springer, Aug. 2015, pp. 215-225.

[31] L. Ruzic and J. A. Sanford, "Universal design mobile interface guidelines (UDMIG) for an aging population," in CFP Mobile EHealth, Springer, in press.

[32] L. Ruzic and J. A. Sanford, "Usability of Mobile Consumer Applications for Individuals Aging with Multiple Sclerosis," 9th International Conference on Universal Access in Human-Computer Interaction (HCII2017), Springer, Jan. 2017, pp. 258-276.

[33] M. Stern, "Aging with multiple sclerosis," Physical medicine and rehabilitation clinics of North America, vol. 16, pp. 219-234, 2005.

[34] M. Stern, L. Sorkin, K. Milton, and K. Sperber, "Aging with multiple sclerosis," Physical medicine and rehabilitation clinics of North America, vol. 21, pp. 403-417, 2010.

[35] W. E. Fleming and C. P. Pollak, "Sleep disorders in multiple sclerosis," Seminars in Neurology, pp. 64-68, 2005.

[36] M. Finlayson, "Health and social profile of older adults with MS: Findings from three studies," International Journal of MS Care, vol. 4, pp. 139-151, 2002.

[37] E. E. Gulick, "Symptom and activities of daily living trajectory in multiple sclerosis: a 10-year study," Nursing Research, vol. 47, pp. 137-14, 1998.

[38] J. Johnson and K. Finn, Designing User Interfaces for an Aging Population: Towards Universal Design. Morgan Kaufmann, 2017.

[39] S. T. Lee, Y. E. Liu, L. Ruzic, and J. Sanford, "Universal design ballot interfaces on voting performance and satisfaction of voters with and without vision loss," Proc. The 2016 CHI Conference on Human Factors in Computing Systems (CHI2016), ACM, May 2016, pp. 4861-4871.

[40] L. Ruzic and J. A. Sanford, "Needs Assessment: Functional Features in Mobile Health and Wellness Self-Monitoring Applications for People with Multiple Sclerosis," Journal of Healthcare Informatics Research, 2017, in press.

[41] L. Kascak, C. B. Rébola, R. Braunstein, and J. A. Sanford, "Icon Design to Improve Communication of Health Information to Older Adults," Communication Design Quarterly Review, Vol. 2, pp. 6-32, Nov. 2013, doi:10.1145/2559866.2559867

[42] P. Tarasewich, "Designing mobile commerce applications," Communications of the ACM, Vol. 46, No. 2, pp. 57-60, Dec. 2003.

[43] H. Kim, J. Kim, Y. Lee, M. Chae, and Y. Choi, "An empirical study of the use contexts and usability problems in mobile Internet," Proc. The 35th Annual Hawaii International Conference on System Sciences (HICSS 2002), IEEE, Jan. 2002, pp. 1767-1776.

International Journal on Advances in Software, vol 10 no 3 & 4, year 2017, http://www.iariajournals.org/software/

Visualizations for Hierarchical Data: Analyzing User Behavior and Performance with Eye Tracking

Nicholas H. Müller*, Benny Liebold†, Daniel Pietschmann†, Peter Ohler†, and Paul Rosenthal‡

*Faculty of Computer Science and Business Information Systems,
University of Applied Sciences Würzburg-Schweinfurt, Würzburg, Germany
Email: nicholas.mueller@fhws.de

†Institute for Media Research, Chemnitz University of Technology, Chemnitz, Germany
Email: {benny.liebold, daniel.pietschmann, peter.ohler}@phil.tu-chemnitz.de

‡Institute of Computer Science, University of Rostock, Rostock, Germany
Email: research@paul-rosenthal.de

***Abstract*—Visualizing hierarchical structures is of great importance in many economic and scientific applications. Many different approaches have been developed and enhanced in the last decades. Each of them claims specific advantages over competing methods, usually referring to visual or structural properties. Although several user studies investigated the usefulness of specific approaches, for practitioners it often remains unclear what the practical advantages of the approaches are and in which contexts they are useful. In our user study, we systematically investigated the value of three frequently used visualization types for the intuitive understanding of hierarchical data: treemap, icicle plot, and nodelink. We measured user performance in terms of correctness and time and tracked eye movements for each participant. The results regarding the user performance revealed that nodelink and icicle plot performed well, whereas treemap only exceeded chance level in one easy task. Still, the analysis of eye-tracking measures suggests that treemaps draw visual attention better to relevant elements. However, treemap visualizations built up less influential visual gaze patterns, compared to nodelinks and icicle plots. Finally, implications for facilitating human intuition and problem solving strategies are discussed.**

***Keywords*–User Study; Hierarchy Visualization; Perception; Eye-tracking; Eye-gaze Patterns.**

I. Introduction

This paper is an extended version of a work, recently presented at the International Conference on Advances in Computer-Human Interactions (ACHI) [1]. First results of the reported study were already presented at the EuroVis Workshop on Reproducibility, Verification, and Validation in Visualization (EuroRV^3) [2]. In this paper, we report an extended and more thorough analysis, including the investigation of eye-gaze patterns. The main objective of the study was the research of visualizing hierarchical data, which has a long tradition going back to the drawings of medieval family trees. A wide research field with very different visualization approaches developed over the last three decades, investigating a multitude of different visualization properties and aiming at all kinds of different applications. However, despite this long tradition there are still new developments in the field through new applications and demands [3], [4], [5], [6].

A comprehensive overview over most of the proposed hierarchy visualization techniques is maintained by treevis.net [7], [8]. Every approach was published with several advantages in mind and was at the time of publication an advancement to the state of the art. However, apart from their professional experiences, practitioners have no objective benchmarks to decide, which new (or even older) visualization fits their needs best.

This issue becomes even more eminent considering the importance of hierarchical data structures in science [9], [10] and economy [11], [12], where visualizations can significantly influence large-scale decisions [13]. For example, Vliegen et al. [14] presented different applications of treemaps to business data. They found that in general there are too many parameters to set and tune in standard visualizations and concluded that users need custom solutions, specifically designed by visualization experts. Especially in this environment, where decisions can have drastic consequences and frequently have to be made in a short time frame, users need to understand the properties and shortcomings of visualizations to be aware of possible implications.

In this paper, we make a step towards studying which visualizations are intuitively understandable by non-experts. To this end, we investigate how different visualization techniques impact the users' understanding of the data. Since we treat visualizations as objectively as possible, our goal is not to show which visualization is superior, but to understand what problems and pitfalls arise when non-experts use different visualizations to solve typical tasks.

We restricted our study to static and non-interactive visualizations. Apart from being much easier to interpret, especially when analyzing problem solving patterns, they are highly relevant, since many practitioners mainly rely on static visualizations on paper or digital presentations to convey their data. In most cases, it would be just too cumbersome for non-visualization scientists or managers to run an interactive session with a visualization software just to understand their data and results of related scientists or competitors. Therefore, we also excluded all pure visualizations heavily relying on 3D metaphors. They always require at least basic interaction capabilities to produce meaningful results. Since Burch et al. [15] showed that radial techniques [16] for the visualization of hierarchies are understood less intuitively, we further restricted our study to linear visualization techniques. After a thorough analysis of several well-established reporting and analysis software packages, we decided to compare nodelinks, treemaps, and icicle plots, because they represent the most common visualization techniques.

In addition, we restrict our considerations to the area of visualizing hierarchical data with additional scalar dimension, which is highly relevant especially in the business environment. More precisely, the data consists of a rooted tree $T = (V, E, v_{\text{root}})$, where V is the non-empty set of data elements (nodes), E is a subset of $V \times V$ representing the hierarchy relations (edges), and $v_{\text{root}} \in V$ is the root node of the hierarchy. Additionally, a function $f : V \to \mathbb{R}^+$ is given, which assigns each node a specific positive value and respects the hierarchy. More precisely, the sum of function values of all children of a node is always smaller or equal than the function value of the node. One example for such data is a company structure with annual expenses.

In Sections III and IV, we present background about the tackled visualizations and the relations to cognitive science. We give a precise description of our study setup in Section V. In Section VI, we present a detailed analysis of the results of the user study with respect to participants' performance and eye-gaze data.

II. Related Work

General design rules for good visualizations have been intensively discussed in the last decades and are often based on the investigation of visual attention [17], [18] and the understanding of the human cognitive system. In this regard, the effects of colors in visualizations received much research attention, because they represent a particular powerful visual cue [19], [20], [21], [22]. A comprehensive overview about those design rules and general strategies was presented by Ware [23].

One of the most-used practical examples when visualizing hierarchies with an additional scalar component is the file system of computers. Stasko et al. [24] evaluated the two visualization techniques treemap [25] and sunburst [26] with respect to their capabilities for standard file-management tasks, like locating files or comparing file sizes. They measured user performance by logging their number of correct answers and their reaction times. They found that sunburst significantly outperforms the treemap representation, presumably because of the more explicit representation of hierarchy relations in sunburst.

In a very similar study, Bladh et al. [27] evaluated the usefulness of encoding the depth of nodes in a treemap using the third dimension in comparison to a traditional treemap visualization. Again, users had to complete typical file-management tasks. It turned out that both visualizations were not significantly different in most tasks, i. e., the third dimension did not result in a performance loss due to the additional navigational and cognitive efforts. However, users' performance was significantly better with the 3D visualization when having to identify the node with the highest depth in the hierarchy.

Wang et al. [28] had a similar experimental setting by comparing a standard file browser to rings [29] and treemap [25]. They evaluated the effectiveness of the methods based on complex questions, such as finding two similar directories or the most homogeneous directory. The users' performance was measured by assessing their answering time. Additionally, they were asked to rate the difficulty of each question with the respective visualization. In summary, the file explorer performed significantly worse than both other methods with no significant difference between rings and treemap.

Ziemkiewicz and Kosara [30] showed that the methaphoric presentation of tasks influences users' performance during the work with hierarchy visualizations. In our study, we followed this findings and extended the scope by formulating the tasks abstractly with respect to the hierarchy.

Borkin et al. [31] presented a new method for visualizing filesystem provenance data, which relies on a combination of a radial-based tree layout and a time-based node grouping. The system was evaluated with domain experts and compared to a state-of-the-art nodelink tool [32] by measuring accuracy and efficiency. Results show that the new tool outperforms the state of the art. A very interesting additional finding was that there was a significant gender effect in the state-of-the-art method, which was not the case for the proposed method.

Teets et al. [33] stressed the need for evaluation of the effectiveness of visualizations especially in the business environment. They analyzed a very specific application in the field of process monitoring, which was based on production data of a can factory. Their evaluation relied on cognitive fit theory, i. e., they investigated how good the visualizations and induced mental models fit to the problem solving strategies. They found no information loss when not displaying accurate values in a tabular fashion as well as a significantly faster solution time when using visual representations.

While most studies rely on user performance data in terms of the number of correct answers and reaction times, eye-tracking studies have been the exception. However, Burch et al. [15] investigated the impact of different layouts of nodelinks using eye-tracking. They used one question type and an explanatory task. The users were confronted with two different linear layouts with four different placements of the root node and a radial layout of the nodelink. Burch et al. assessed both eye-movements and performance data, allowing to systematically compare the results from different measurement approaches. The users performed much better with the axis-aligned layouts than with the circular one, which might be a result of the typically linear fashion of information display, the users are familiar with. In line with this argument, the traditional layout with the root node at the top performed best, which further emphasizes the role of individual experience with visualizations in understanding them intuitively and using them for problem solving.

A recent variation of the treemap design is the angular treemap [34] with the goal to enhance comprehension of hierarchy levels by rotating parts of the treemap. Liang et al. [35] conducted an experiment comparing traditional and angular treemaps. The study mainly investigated search tasks and measured completion time. While it turned out that the new design was significantly better, the flexible method needs several well-tuned parameters and, thus, should be set up by visualization experts to achieve comparable results.

III. Visualizations for Hierarchical Data

The need for visualization expertise is true for many new and sophisticated visualization techniques. However, there

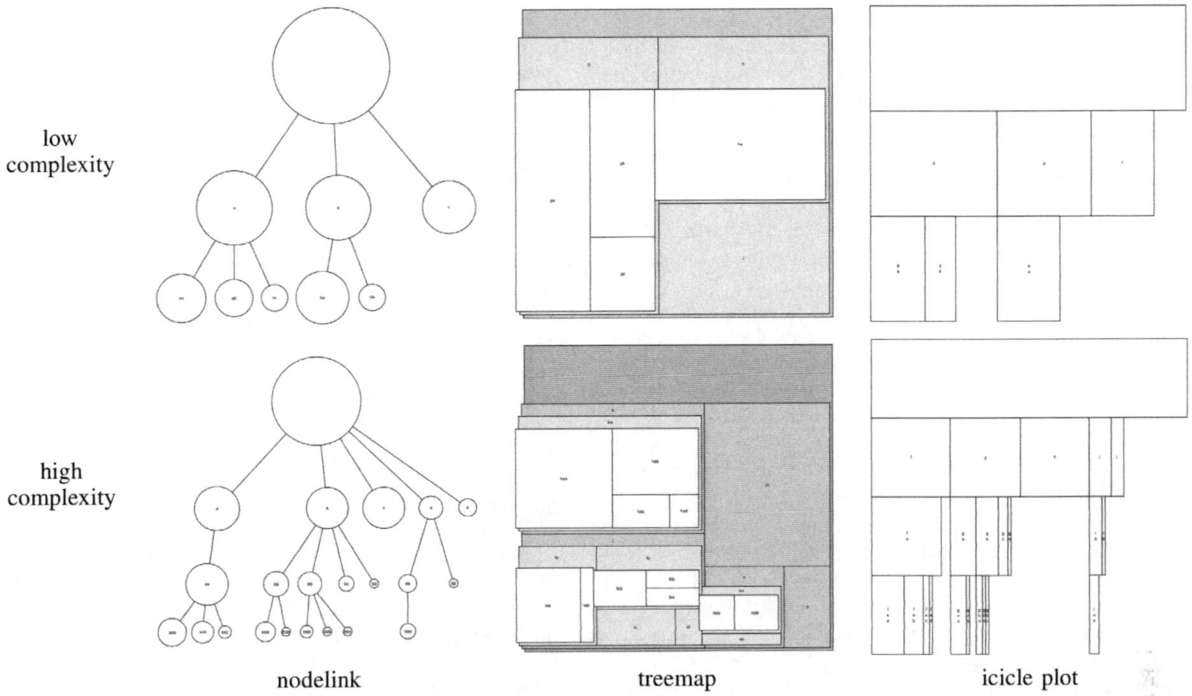

Figure 1. Example stimuli that where used for the user study. For each of the four questions, we presented three different visualization types (nodelink, treemap, icicle plot) of equivalent hierarchies with additional scalar values per node. In addition, we varied the complexity of the hierarchies, resulting in visualizations with low (height two, maximum three children per node) and high complexity (height three, maximum five children per node).

is an ever growing demand for easily usable and reliable visualization techniques for hierarchical data in practice that can be used without much prior knowledge. Therefore, we wanted to investigate the properties of three of the most-used and practice-relevant visualization techniques for hierarchies with additional scalar dimension. We intended to investigate these visualizations with respect to fast and accurate data comprehension for users with low visualization knowledge and only a short time of familiarization with the type of visualization. After elaborate inspection of the treevis repository [8] and several software packages for productive use [36], [37], [38], [39], we decided to compare nodelinks, treemaps, and icicle plots. Illustrations of the investigated visualization methods are given in Figure 1.

The use of nodelinks for drawing trees is very intuitive since it replicates the structure of botanical trees. Consequently, nodelinks have already been used for ages to represent hierarchies and the research on optimal drawing of nodelinks has a long tradition [40]. The strengths of the nodelink representation are its intuitiveness and clear representation [41]. However, many competing techniques produce less empty space and allow a more integrated visualization of the additional scalar dimension.

The concept of treemaps, as one of these presumably superior techniques, has been introduced by Johnson and Shneiderman [25]. Since then a lot of different modifications, additions, and enhancements were proposed [42], [43], [44], [45], still respecting the initial idea of maximizing screen space usage and implicit encoding of the hierarchy. These aspects are often referred to as the main advantages of the concept. Problematic properties, which are nowadays still constant topic of further research [46], are the inherent overplotting, problems with hierarchy perception, and complications with node distribution.

The icicle plot is another concept with a long tradition and was originally proposed by Kruskal and Landwehr [47] for the display of cluster hierarchies and based on the trees and castles of Kleiner and Hartigan [48]. Although it has been shown that users perform worse, when using radial layouts [15], icicle plots are used less often in practical applications [49], [50], [51] than their radial counterpart, the sunburst diagram [26], [52], [53], [54]. Sometimes not even the correct name for this linearized sunburst is used. Still, the icicle plot combines two strengths of nodelink and treemap, namely the intuitive top-down design and the implicit hierarchy encoding. In addition, it inherently features a one-dimensional encoding of the additional scalar dimension. On the other hand, the screen-space usage is less efficient compared to treemaps.

IV. Cognitive Processing of Visualizations

Assessing the effectiveness of visualizations, requires to distinguish between the visual search phase and the stage of central information processing. In the visual search phase, the user has to identify relevant elements of a visualization. During this process the user constantly reallocates the attention to different elements of a visualization. Following Schneider and Shiffrin [55], [56], this process can be characterized as an interplay of bottom-up (automatic) and top-down (controlled) attention allocation.

Our visual field can be considered as an assembly of

elements competing for our attention [57]. Bottom-up processes are triggered by elements, which stand out from their environment. A node of a visualization could for example be colored differently or have a different shape compared to other elements. This type of attention allocation is highly automated. Top-down attention, on the other hand, is moderated by the user's intention and previous knowledge. For example, when the user's goal is to compare two elements of a visualization, the user employs a strategy of visual search, during which the positions of all relevant entities are identified. The search process itself can be carried out both by chaotically searching for relevant elements (bottom-up) or deducting the relative position of an element from other elements through previous knowledge about the type of visualization (top-down) [58]. The first strategy is suited for users without any previous knowledge and its efficiency depends on the visualization's complexity. The latter strategy, however, can be employed by users, who understood the basic principles of a visualization, and should result in a more efficient use.

As we can only observe eye movements by users, we are usually not able to distinguish between bottom-up and top-down attention allocation. Both mechanisms directly impact which elements our eyes fixate. Additionally, the mere fact that users fixate an element of a visualization does not imply that this element is being processed centrally. Moreover, it does not even imply that the user is looking at the element, because attention can also be allocated towards elements outside of central vision [59]. Although we are not able to see elements as clearly when using peripheral vision, humans are still able to estimate object shape and size rather accurately when distributing visual attention over a larger area of the visual field. If, however, we were able to observe reoccurring patterns of eye-movements, both within users and between users, we can be sure that these patterns represent phases of top-down attention allocation. Visualizations that produce this kind of reoccurring patterns can be considered as an efficient means of data display. Thus, one important goal of the current study was to extend existing research by employing eye-tracking not only to count and compare fixations, but to investigate transitions between visualization elements as well as reoccurring fixation patterns.

When the relevant elements of a visualization are identified, the user enters the stage of central information processing. The success and the efficiency of a visualization depend both on user and visualization properties. User properties affecting visualization processing are most likely previous knowledge about the type of visualization, general intelligence components, especially those related to visual-spatial information processing, and possible impairments (e.g., color or stereo blindness). In terms of information processing, nearly all properties of a visualization, like color usage, descriptiveness, intuitiveness, alignment, or visual data preparation affect success and efficiency. In this paper, we assess indicators for both phases of visualization processing. While performance data allow the empirical investigation of the information processing phase, eye-tracking and reaction times enable the investigation of the visual search phase.

V. METHOD

We conducted a laboratory experiment, during which participants had to solve problems using different visualization techniques. For each participant, the performance in terms of accuracy and completion times as well as eye movements were recorded.

A. Stimulus Materials

We employed a $3 \times 4 \times 2$ within-subjects factor design with visualization type, task, and hierarchy complexity as independent variables.

1) Visualization Types: All hierarchies with additional positive scalar values per node were visualized using three different visualization types, illustrated in Figure 1. The nodelinks were generated using Reingold and Tilford's algorithm [40]. The additional scalar value per node was indicated by the area of each node's circle. As for all three different visualization types, each non-root node was annotated with an alphanumeric code to allow for unique identification by the users. The treemaps were generated using the squarified approach [44], again encoding each node's scalar value by area. To enhance the perception of different hierarchy levels, nodes were color coded in different grey scales and, following Bladh et al. [27], stacked in a 2.5D fashion. The icicle plots were generated in the top-down fashion that is used most often. Screen space was divided in rows of equal height, depending on the height of the hierarchy. The root node's width was set to the full width. For each node, all children were drawn below the node with a width proportional to the scalar values, respectively.

2) Tasks: We interviewed several researchers from different fields of economics and social sciences, who regularly deal with hierarchical data. In most cases, they seek to understand the hierarchical structure, which means understanding the relation between nodes, comparing the values of different nodes, or counting nodes or leaves of trees or subtrees. We identified four tasks, which are commonly performed when confronted with the given visualizations. From these tasks, three are hypothesized to favor one of the visualization types, respectively. For the fourth tasks, we could not find any strong indications on what visualization might be favored and added it as an exploratory task. In detail, the tasks were:

- T1: Count all leaf nodes of the hierarchy.
- T2: Count all nodes of the hierarchy.
- T3: Compare the combined area of two pairs of nodes within one level of the hierarchy.
- T4: Compare the combined area of two pairs of nodes across different levels of the hierarchy.

The tasks differ in difficulty: Counting leaves and nodes is less cognitive exertive than comparing the sizes of nodes. However, this does not affect our main goal, the analysis of differences between the visualization methods.

3) Hierarchy Complexities: As base data set we used two artificial hierarchies with different levels of complexity. The hierarchy with low complexity had height two and had a maximum of three children per node. In contrast, the height of the hierarchy with high complexity was three with a maximum number of five children per node. An illustration of the different complexities can be seen in Figure 1.

Since the hierarchy for all visualizations was initially equal per complexity level and question, it could have happened that participants remembered their choice from a different visualization and just replicated it. To overcome this problem, we slightly changed hierarchies (changed size of one node or added/removed one node/leaf) for each visualization of one complexity-task combination. Consequently, tasks and answers were not equal per visualization but still comparable in terms of difficulty. Participants were informed that similar hierarchies might not always result in the same answers.

B. Hypotheses

From a review of relevant literature and recommendations in software packages, we extracted several claims of what benefits the used visualizations should have. Together with the tailored questions, this resulted in the following hypotheses, which we wanted to check with our experiment.

H1: Task **T1** favors the treemap over both other visualization types.
Counting leaves on a treemap reduces the task to simply counting all non-occluded rectangles. Users have to traverse the whole hierarchy to count the leaves in both other visualizations.

H2: Task **T2** favors the nodelink over both other visualizations.
Counting nodes is reduced to simply counting all circles in the nodelink visualization, which are, even in contrast to the icicle plot, clearly distinguishable from background and auxiliary lines.

H3: Task **T3** favors the icicle plot over both other visualizations.
Comparing sizes of nodes within one level of the hierarchy should be easier when comparing lengths on one straight line using the icicle-plot visualization. In contrast, users have to sum up and compare areas of different proportions when using a treemap and, even more difficult, sum up differently-sized circular areas in the case of the nodelink.

H4: Treemap performs worst in the tasks **T1**, **T3**, and **T4** due to overplotting.

H5: When only varying hierarchy complexity, users perform better with the low complex hierarchy compared to high complexity.

C. Sample

We recruited $N = 69$ second year university students of the local communication studies program (age: $M = 21.09$, $SD = 2.40$, female = 53). The students were well-skilled in reading academic publications and working with statistical analyses and charts. Apart from their general experience, they had no specific knowledge in either of the presented visualization methods nor in visualization of hierarchies in general. They received study credit for their participation.

D. Procedure

To control for sequence effects, we generated two different pre-randomized sequences respecting a non-repetition restriction. Each participant was assigned to one of the sequences in which the combinations were presented, respectively. Both sequences did not differ in their performance ($t(67) = -0.238$, n.s.). The hierarchies were presented on a 19" computer screen with a resolution of 1280 × 1024 pixels via E-Prime 2.0. An SMI RED eye-tracker from SensoMotoric Instruments was installed below the screen and recorded eye movements at 50 Hz. The stimuli were presented at a head distance of about 700 mm. However, due to the contact-free setup, slight variations of the distance during the experiment were possible, which should not affect the results due to the within-subjects factor design, and the SMI hardware being able to compensate for movements. All participants were calibrated using a five point matrix according to the standard SMI RED setup procedure. Each event in E-Prime was logged within the eye-tracking data file, which allowed to synchronize stimulus presentation and eye-tracking data. In the first part of the instructions, the definition of a hierarchy, the difference between leaves and nodes, and the different types of visualizations were explained to the participants by showing examples. They also received a speed-accuracy instruction (i. e., "Please answer as quickly and accurately as you can!").

During the experiment, participants were first shown a textual description of the task (e. g., "How many leaves does the hierarchy have?") as well as the possible answers and then had to press a key to proceed. This allowed each participant to read and understand the task and the answers at her own pace. Next, the hierarchy visualization was presented in addition to the task and the answers. Participants then had to respond by pressing one of three answer keys, with one correct answer and two distractors, resulting in a chance level of $p = 0.33$. E-Prime automatically logged the participant's answer and completion time, i. e., the time of stimulus onset until the participant's response. In average, the response time for an item was M = 19.6 sec (SD = 5.9). This procedure allowed us to be able to judge users reaction times without the delay of having them typing in the correct number. First, all participants were shown a training sequence of the visualizations. Afterwards, all three visualizations in both the high and low complexity were presented. Nodes to be compared were named in the question before the visualization was shown and remained visible during the task until an answer was given. The whole procedure took less than 25 minutes per participant. After the computer test, participants filled out an electronic questionnaire with items concerning manipulation checks and demographic data.

VI. Results

We recruited undergraduate students from Chemnitz University of Technology, and therefore, conducted the study with a very homogeneous set of participants. Thus, demographic assessments did not show any correlations or other interesting variables regarding age, gender, or occupation. A plot of the participants' performance with respect to the independent variables is shown in Figure 2.

To test our hypotheses, we used a $3 \times 4 \times 2$ repeated measures ANOVA (analysis of variance) with participants' performance as dependent variable. Alpha levels for all calculations were set to $p < 0.05$. Due to the violation of the sphericity assumption, Greenhouse-Geisser-corrected dfs are reported, when necessary. We found a significant main effect for the type of visualization ($F(2, 136) = 53.77$, $p < 0.001$, $\eta^2_{\text{part}} = 0.442$). More specifically, performance was significantly lower when using treemap compared to nodelink and icicle plot, whereas the latter two did not differ significantly. Participants performed well above chance level with both nodelink ($M = 0.55$, $t(68) = 8.73$, $p < 0.001$) and icicle-plot visualizations ($M = 0.54$, $t(68) = 9.03$, $p < 0.001$). However, participants did not perform above chance when presented the

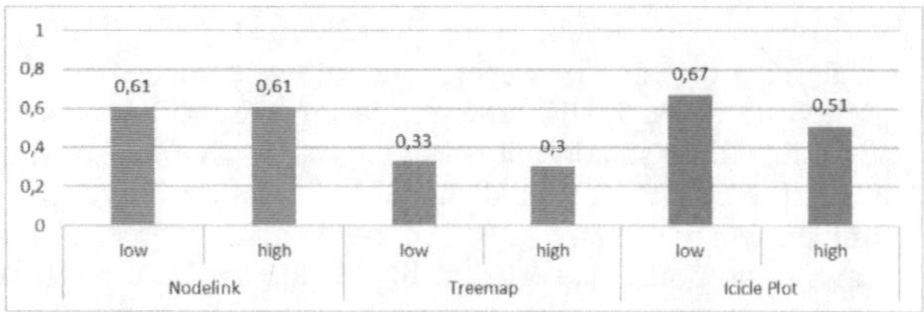

T1: Count Leaves

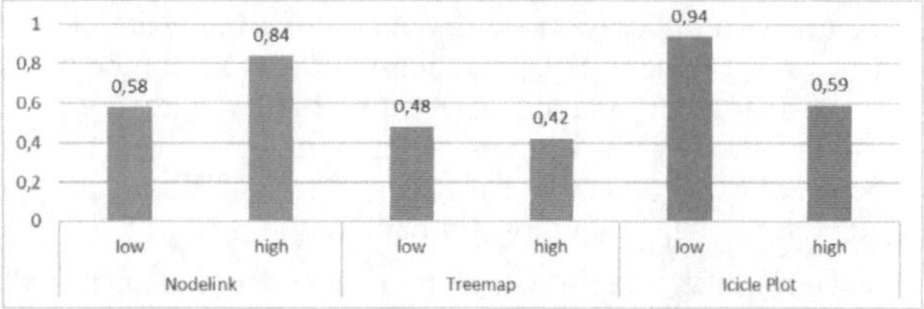

T2: Count Nodes

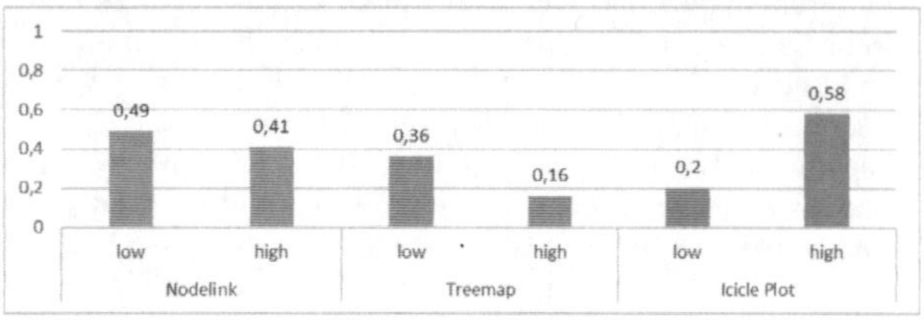

T3: Compare in Level

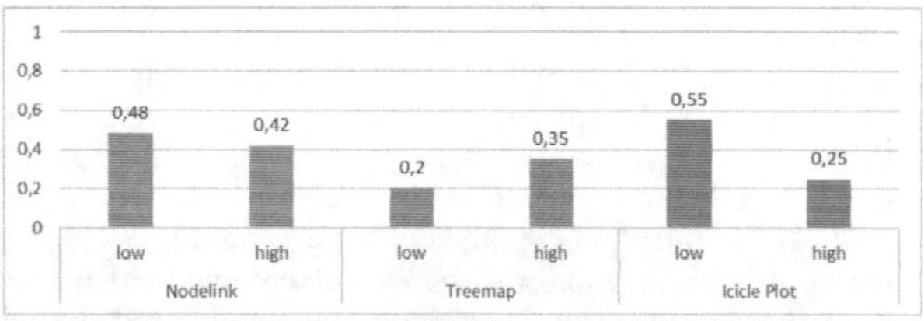

T4: Compare Between Levels

Figure 2. Plot of the average correctness of participants' answers to the four questions with respect to visualization type and hierarchy complexity. Chance level is at 0.33.

treemap ($M = 0.33$, $t(68) = -0.332$, n.s.). These first results validate hypothesis **H4**. Furthermore, we found that participants were able to perform above chance level only in task **T2** when using a treemap, i. e., counting nodes at low complexity ($M = 0.48$, $t(68) = 2.40$, $p < 0.05$). This discovery directly opposes hypothesis **H1** and lets the treemap stand out as the worst choice for all tasks. Even at its best performing task **T2**, nodelink and icicle plot performed significantly better ($F(1, 74) = 50.02$, $p < 0.001$, $\eta^2_{\text{part}} = 0.403$).

Results did not show a significant main effect for complexity of hierarchies, ($F(1, 68) = 2.607$, n.s.). Consequently it seems that, in the current setting, hypothesis **H5** can not be confirmed. However, revisiting the stimuli and analyzing the after-test feedback resulted in at least two possible factors influencing the results with respect to this hypothesis. One surprising fact is that participants performed significantly better with the complex nodelink compared to the less complex nodelink for task **T2**, counting nodes ($t(74) = -4.32$, $p < 0.001$, $\eta^2_{\text{part}} = 0.20$). It is apparent that some participants were uncertain if the root node is also counted as a node and, consequently, counted one node less. In the high complex stimulus, this was compensated, because, as all answering options were above their count, the participants simply chose the lowest possible answer, which was the right one. In the low complex stimulus, this strategy did not work, as indicated in Table I. Due to this occurrence, it is not possible to validate hypothesis **H2** although the performance of the nodelink is still significantly better than both other visualizations when only using the complex hierarchy ($F(1, 74) = 32.85$, $p < 0.001$, $\eta^2_{\text{part}} = 0.307$).

TABLE I. OBSERVED RELATIVE FREQUENCIES FOR TASK **T2** USING NODELINK REPRESENTATION. FOR LOW AND HIGH COMPLEX HIERARCHIES, THE CORRECT ANSWER IS RESPECTIVELY HIGHLIGHTED WITH GREY.

Answer	Low Compl.	Answer	High Compl.
7	6.8%	22	84.7%
8	34,7%	23	13.6%
9	58.5%	24	1.7%

We encountered another surprising result when we compared icicle plots of high and low complexity for task **T3**. Again, the less complex hierarchy is performing significantly worse than the complex hierarchy ($t(74) = -5.11$, $p < 0.001$). The performance is even significantly below chance level ($t(74) = -2.52$, $p < 0.05$), leading to the conclusion that the participants were confident in their (wrong) answers. After carefully inspecting the stimulus for the low complex hierarchy, illustrated in Figure 3, we assume that participants' confidence was based on a wrong assumption about the pictorial information. The Gestalt-laws [60] suggest certain cognitive grouping tendencies when confronted with images. Based on the Gestalt-laws of proximity, closure, and common region, the nodes da, db, and dc are perceived as belonging together. The task, however, asks to judge the combined size of the first two ($da + db$) against the other node and an "external one" ($dc+ea$). Due to this, we assume a misleading perception, which lets the participants underestimate the size of $da + db$. The cognitive process of "moving" area dc over to ea (or reverse) might be influenced by the distance between the two because of the impression that both nodes together (a gestalt) require more space due to the empty space between them. This overestimation could be the reason, why hypothesis **H3** cannot be supported, although in the high complex setting icicle plot performed, as predicted, significantly better than nodelink and treemap at **T3** ($F(1, 74) = 22.57$, $p < 0.001$, $\eta^2_{\text{part}} = 0.234$).

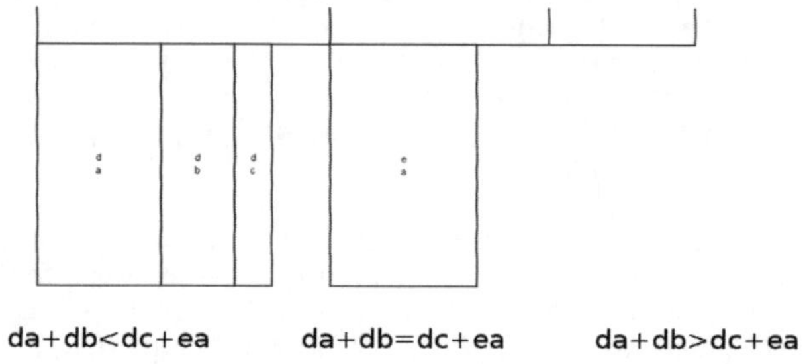

Figure 3. Close-up view of the stimulus for task **T3** using the low complex hierarchy and the icicle-plot visualization. The area $da + db$ is actually larger than $dc + ea$ but the latter is overestimated due to the empty space between both areas.

A. Heatmaps

Beyond looking into the participants' performance, we also recorded the eye-movement of all participants during the tasks. For the analysis, the areas of interest were defined with respect to each task of the study. Fixations were detected, based on 80 ms duration. After careful inspection of the heatmaps for each task, we decided to enlarge each area of interest by 20 pixels beyond the actual node to account for measurement error and peripheral vision when looking at rather small nodes (see for example Figure 6). As a first approach we analyzed the heatmaps of different tasks and visualizations and their evolution over time to gain insight into the participants' general search strategies and visual foci. The heatmaps were generated by accumulating fixations over a specified period of time and the calculation of the smoothed average density of fixations for each pixel. The resulting density function was color-coded in the range between minimum and maximum using the built-in color scheme of the eye-tracking software, depicted below:

In Figure 4, we illustrate the heatmaps for different subsequent periods of time for nodelink and icicle plot of the high complex hierarchy and task **T2**. The heatmaps suggest a top-down and left-right movement of participants' fixations, which is consistent with the top-down screen-space structure of the visualizations. This coincides with the expected gaze direction that is deeply rooted into cultural education. Eye-tracking research regarding reading and comprehension in Saudi-Arabia revealed fixation patterns from right to left [61], in contrast to the typical findings in western countries. Li and Briley [62], therefore, differentiate between a habitual eye movement and a situational one, which, on occasions, might be in conflict.

Since the participants for the presented study were all from Germany, we assume homogeneous habituated reading patterns: Since most of their reading materials in everyday life are dextrograde, a gaze movement pattern from left to right and top to bottom was to be expected. One of the most prominent indications for this habituated behavior is visible in the fixations on the answer options at the bottom of the screen moving from left to right on every visualization within this study.

A very similar habitual top-down pattern in the heatmaps is encountered when visualizing the same hierarchy with a treemap (Figure 5), although this visualization does not imply an inherent top-down screen-space structure. Because treemaps do not explicitly follow this structural order with several clearly distinct hierarchy levels, participants might have to reorient repeatedly and remember which elements were already processed. This discrepancy might be partially responsible for the participants' bad performance with treemaps. The same applies to task **T1** where participants again followed a top-down strategy, as illustrated in Figure 6.

Another interesting, but unexpected finding with respect to the treemap visualization was that participants' performance at **T3** with the complex hierarchy was significantly worse than chance level ($t(74) = -4.54$, $p < 0.001$). This again indicates that participants were confident in giving a wrong answer. When inspecting the respective heatmap for the whole task processing time (Figure 7), it becomes apparent that fixations concentrate mainly in the upper parts of the relevant regions.

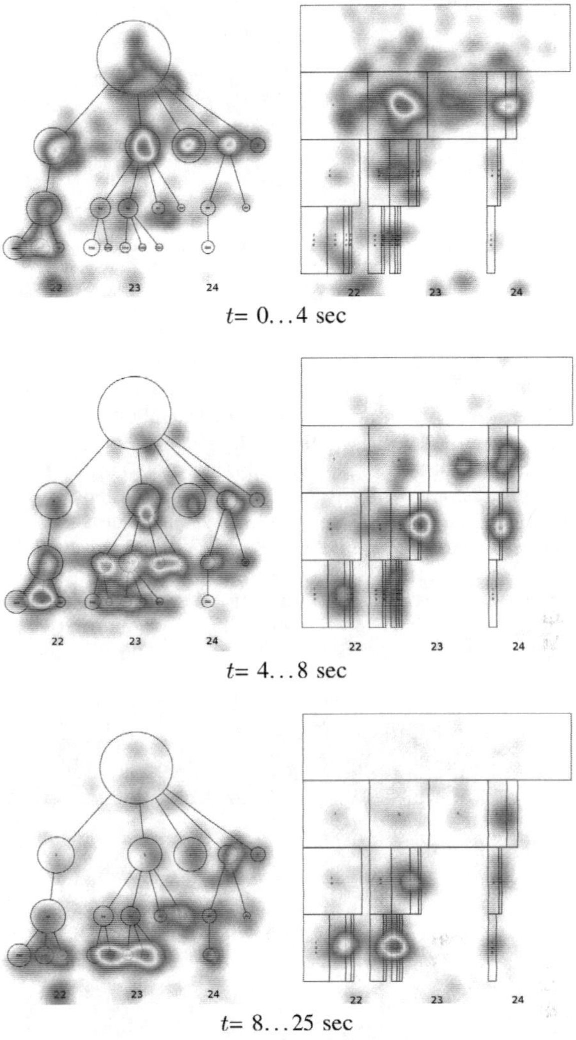

Figure 4. Accumulated heatmaps for the task **T2** and the complex hierarchy for three subsequent periods of time. Note the apparent top-down and left-right pattern of participants' gazes when counting the nodes of the hierarchy.

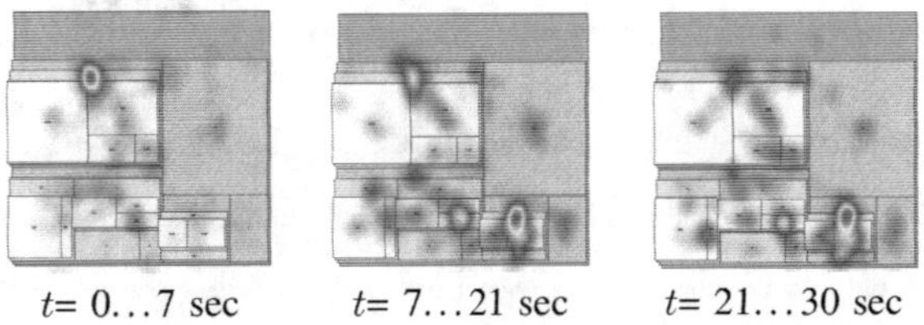

Figure 5. Accumulated heatmaps for the task **T2**, counting all nodes of the hierarchy, and the complex hierarchy. For three subsequent periods of time, we indicate the heatmaps of the treemap visualization. Although treemaps feature only limited top-down characteristics in screen space, the typical European pattern of top-down processing is apparent.

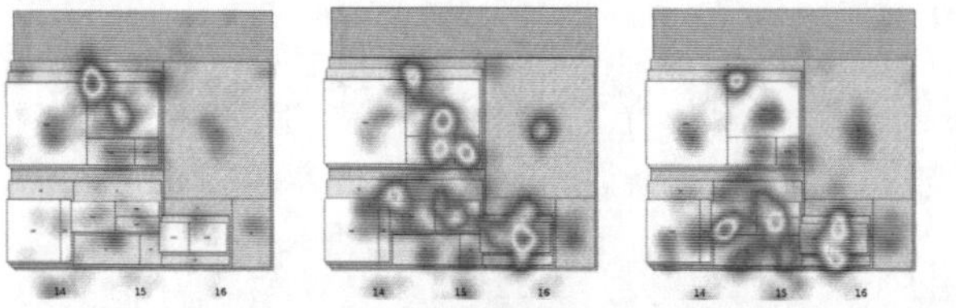

Figure 6. Accumulated heatmaps for the task **T1**, counting all leaves of the hierarchy, and the complex hierarchy. The heatmaps of the treemap visualization are depicted for three subsequent periods of time. Again, the top-down tendency of processing, although the screen space design of the treemap has no such component, is apparent.

Due to the self-occluding design of treemaps, these are the only parts of occluded regions that are directly observable. When only concentrating on the non-occluded parts the areas of nodes l and k are quite equal, although the area of node k is in fact much larger than the area of l. This might have, in combination with the very small area of node o and the relatively large, but mostly occluded area of n, led to the impression that the area of $l+n$ is smaller than the area of $k+o$. Thus, the participants might have followed a misconception of the treemap visualization. The same explanation can account for the significantly lower-than-chance performance of the less complex treemap at **T4** ($t = -2.52$; $p < 0.05$).

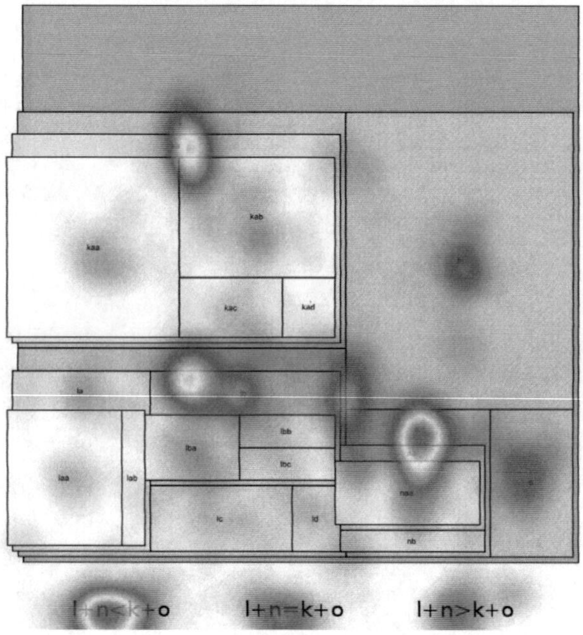

Figure 7. Accumulated heatmap for the whole time of **T3** using the treemap visualization for the complex hierarchy. Participants' fixations concentrated mainly on the upper, non-occluded, parts of the relevant regions, making it hard to correctly estimate the areas.

B. Odds Ratios

In addition to inspecting the heatmaps, we performed statistical analyses for the participants' fixations. When fixations in task-relevant areas of interest are succeeded by task-relevant fixations, the participant's visual attention remains at task-relevant nodes, which is an important feature of effective visualizations. For this, we computed odds ratios, which compare the odds of remaining at task-relevant nodes of two visualizations for each task. We first divided the chance of task-relevant fixations by the chance of irrelevant fixations after looking at relevant areas of interest. This gives us an odd of relevant follow-up fixations for each visualization. We then divided the odds of one visualization by the odds of another visualizations to get the respective odds ratio. This allows to compare two visualizations directly regarding their ability to keep users focused on relevant areas. We used the nodelink visualization as a baseline for the other two visualizations, because it is the most established one. Respective confidence intervals (95%) for the odds ratios allow comparisons of the suitability of a given visualization to promote fixations that remain within task-relevant areas. Odds ratios of around 1.0 indicate that the chance of hitting an important area of interest is not significantly different for both visualizations. Confidence intervals of different visualization combinations not overlapping with 1.0 indicate a significant difference between them. A plot of the different odds ratios and confidence intervals with respect to task and visualization type combinations is given in Figure 8.

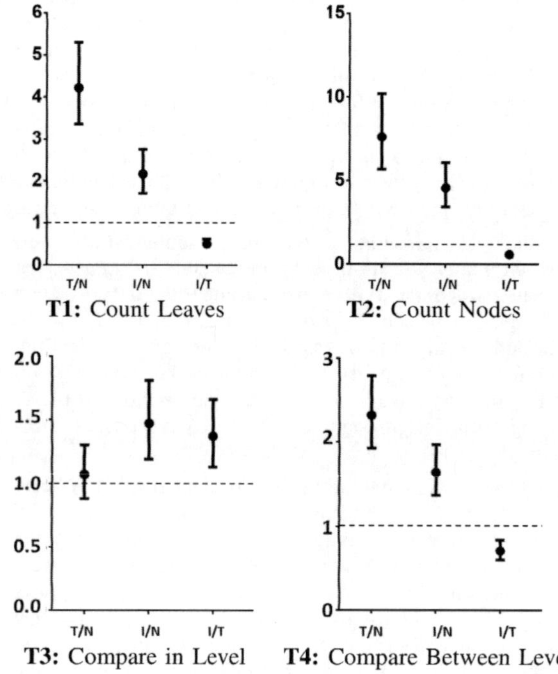

Figure 8. Plots of odds ratios and confidence intervals. For each task and combination of visualizations (N = nodelink, T = treemap, I = icicle plot), the respective odds ratio is indicated together with its 95% confidence interval.

T1 produced significant differences between all visualizations in their ability to draw user attention to task-relevant areas of interest. Within this particular task, the treemap visualization outperforms the other visualizations, regarding its chance to draw attention to task-relevant areas. The odds of looking at important areas of a treemap during the task are four times higher compared to a nodelink ($\Delta\text{odds}_{T/N} = 4.22$; CI: $[3.36, 5.30]$). Comparing icicle plots and treemaps also indi-

TABLE II. DESCRIPTIVE STATISTICS FOR IDENTIFIED PATTERNS. FOR EACH VISUALIZATION WE INDICATE THE NUMBER OF PATTERNS WITH RESPECT TO THE NUMBER OF INVOLVED EVENTS, THE TOTAL NUMBER OF OCCURRED PATTERNS, THE MEAN NUMBER OF OCCURRENCES FOR ALL PATTERNS WITH RESPECTIVE STANDARD DEVIATION, AND MEAN PROPORTION OF THE SESSION TIME IN SECONDS FOR EACH PATTERN WITH RESPECTIVE STANDARD DEVIATION.

Visualization	Number of Patterns According to Complexity			Total Number of Occurred Patterns	Mean Number of Occurrences per Pattern	Mean Proportion of Session Time per Pattern
	2 Events	3 Events	4 Events			
nodelink	7	6	0	1227	94.38 (22.63)	8.46 (5.17)
icicle plot	6	7	1	1643	123.07 (50.70)	5.29 (2.34)
treemap	5	4	0	1099	122.11 (69.61)	3.11 (1.45)

cates a one-to-two advantage for the treemap ($\Delta\text{odds}_{I/T} = 0.51$; CI: $[0.42, 0.63]$). Furthermore, the odds for the icicle-plot visualization are twice as high compared to the nodelink ($\Delta\text{odds}_{I/N} = 2.17$; CI: $[1.71, 2.75]$). These results can be explained by the ratio of relevant to irrelevant screen space, which is highest for the treemap and lowest for nodelink. However, the significant advantage of the icicle plot over the nodelink cannot be explained by the small difference in relevant screen space, but might be a result of the eye-trackers resolution.

T2 presents a similar pattern, but with overall higher odds ratios. The improvement in odds for treemap compared to icicle plot relative to nodelink, however, is only marginally significant. Still, both perform again better than the nodelink in keeping the participants' attention within task-relevant areas. However, when counting nodes, the ratio of relevant screen space to overall screen space is nearly one for the treemap and close to one for the icicle plot. Consequently, participants have only few chances to actually look at non task-relevant positions, directly explaining the very high odds.

The tasks of comparing the volume of two groups of areas **T3** and **T4** reveal rather different odds ratios. Within one level of the hierarchy there is almost no difference between the treemap and the nodelink visualization ($\Delta\text{odds}_{T/N} = 1.07$; CI: $[0.88, 1.3]$), but a slightly higher odds ratio for the icicle plot compared to nodelink ($\Delta\text{odds}_{I/N} = 1.47$; CI: $[1.19, 1.81]$) and the treemap ($\Delta\text{odds}_{I/T} = 1.37$; CI: $[1.13, 1.66]$). When looking at comparisons between different levels of hierarchy, however, both treemap ($\Delta\text{odds}_{T/N} = 2.32$; CI: $[1.93, 2.79]$) and icicle plot ($\Delta\text{odds}_{I/N} = 1.64$; CI: $[1.37, 1.97]$) again outperform the nodelink visualization. Additionally, the treemap is again significantly better than the icicle plot ($\Delta\text{odds}_{I/T} = 0.71$; CI: $[0.6, 0.84]$).

These results suggest that the treemap visualization is indeed effective in promoting task-relevant fixations due to its maximization of screen space. Additionally, the icicle plot performs better in guiding user gaze compared to nodelinks. However, these benefits in visual perception are not reflected in the user performance measure, because nodelinks still perform rather good compared to the visually more efficient visualization techniques. This could be seen as an indicator of the high relevance of previous experience with visualization techniques compared to their visual arrangement. Also, this finding suggests that the sometimes quoted principle of more efficient use of screen space automatically results in higher value of the visualization for the user.

C. Eye-gaze Patterns and Problem Solving Strategies

Another indicator of the visual efficiency of different visualizations is their ability to offer stable problem solving patterns. Following this approach, visually efficient and intuitive visualizations have benefits compared to other visualizations, because of their inherent design. This results in problem solving strategies that are interpersonally invariant. Less intuitive visualizations, however, provoke individualistic problem solving strategies, which highly depend on interpersonal differences and, thus, depend on the user's prior experience rather than intuitive understanding of the visualization. The ability to invoke interpersonally stable gaze patterns can be considered as an indicator of top-down attention allocation due to the visualization's affordances that is closely linked to problem solving, i. e. the user's eyes are guided by the intuitive understanding of the hierarchy's visualization.

In order to investigate, whether nodelinks, icicle plots, and treemaps lead to differences in the employed problem solving strategies, it is necessary to first identify these strategies. Interestingly, empirical research on problem solving only rarely examined behavioral data on a temporal scale. This is also true for eye-tracking data, which are usually analyzed using aggregated data, such as frequencies and durations, of single areas of interest. Because problem solving requires the user to gather information from multiple sources, which then have to be integrated, we added an additional layer into our analysis: Apart from analyzing single areas of interest, we identified repeating patterns of eye movements to investigate the involved problem solving processes.

Automated pattern detection software is able to detect patterns within observations that elude the human eye. To identify problem solving strategies of our participants, we used Theme 6 by PatternVision, which is based on the T-pattern analysis introduced by Magnuson [63] to analyze categorical data on a time scale. A T-pattern is defined by two events happening in significantly similar time intervals. We analyzed the hardest task (**T4**) and ran separate T-pattern analyses on the nodelink, icicle-plot, and treemap visualizations. The pattern search parameters were identical for all three analyses: We only analyzed task-relevant areas of interest to identify only patterns that are relevant to the problem solving process. The criterion for the pattern detection was set to $p < 0.005$ (significance levels for the time intervals) and univariate patterns (follow-up fixations within the same area of interest) were excluded from the analysis. Furthermore, we restricted the analysis to patterns being present in at least 50% of the sample. This way, the T-pattern analysis only identified patterns with a high degree of interpersonal stability. We identified 13 patterns for nodelink, 14 patterns for icicle plot and 9 patterns for treemap. The patterns involved mostly two or three events, only the icicle-plot visualization caused a significant pattern with four events, see Table II.

The identified patterns can be grouped into two categories:

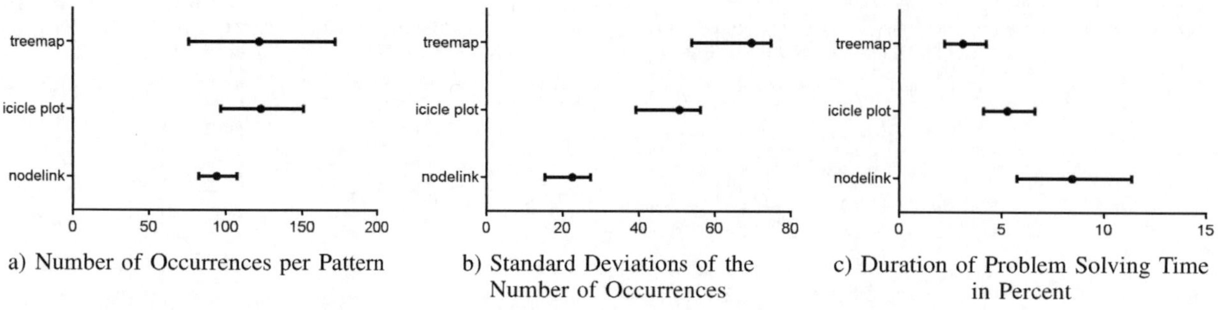

Figure 9. Bias corrected and bootstrapped 95% confidence intervals for three measures resulting from the pattern detection.

First, across all visualizations participants showed patterns containing nodes whose areas needed to be summed ($n = 17$). Interestingly the majority of these patterns ($n = 14$) involved only the group of nodes that is mentioned second in the task description, but rarely nodes of the other group ($n = 3$). Second, participants showed patterns comparing nodes between the two groups ($n = 19$). Only icicle plot elicited a pattern containing four events. Otherwise, the types of patterns appear to be evenly distributed between the three types of visualizations. Overall we found no evidence for effects of the type of visualization on the number of different pattern types (Fisher's exact test: $\chi^2(4) = 4.20$, n.s.). We also found no significant relation between the type of visualization and the number of identified patterns of different complexities (Fisher's exact test: $\chi^2(4) = 1.85$, n.s.).

To compare the properties of the identified patterns, we analyzed the number of occurrences of the patterns, see Figure 9 a), and the share of time devoted to each pattern between the types of visualization, see Figure 9 c). To test for effects of the type of visualization on both outcomes, we calculated two separate ANOVAs. The ANOVA on the number of occurrences revealed no significant effect of the type of visualization (Brown-Forsythe: $F(2, 16.55) = 1.20$, n.s.). The ANOVA on the share of time devoted to the identified patterns reveals a significant effect of the type of visualization (Brown-Forsythe: $F(2, 18.98) = 7.29, p < 0.01$). Planned contrasts indicate that nodelinks and icicle plots lead to significantly more time devoted to stable patterns compared to treemaps, ($t(1, 24.15) = 7.29$, $p < 0.01$, $\eta^2 = 0.38$). The difference between nodelink and icicle plot was marginally not significant, ($t(1, 16.43) = -2.03$, n.s., $\eta^2 = 0.13$).

The analysis of T-patterns within the eye gaze behavior of participants revealed no significant differences for the types of elicited gaze patterns. This might be a result of the low test power due to the low number of identified patterns. The test power could be raised easily by lowering the criterion of pattern distribution across the samples to a value below 50%, which would reveal a higher number of patterns. However, the resulting patterns would then represent more individualistic approaches to problem solving, which was not our focus of analysis. However, when we analyzed the parameters of the identified patterns, we found that although the number of occurrences of the patterns was not different between the three types of visualization, the standard deviations of the number of occurrences was most homogeneous for nodelinks. This could be interpreted as an indicator of the fact that users are already accustomed to work with nodelinks, because their required number of interpersonally stable pattern fixations is less dependent on the type of pattern than for icicle plot. Both visualizations should elicit patterns with similarly homogeneous occurrences, because both differ only slightly in their representation format and should, therefore, allow similar gaze patterns, yet their gaze pattern occurrences are significantly more heterogeneous.

A significant effect was found for the share of time devoted to the identified patterns. Nodelink and icicle plot elicited patterns with significantly more devoted time than treemap. This is both in line with our analysis of the performance data as well as the analysis of odds ratios to look at relevant elements and with our assumption that intuitive visualizations would produce interindividually stable gaze patterns, which are helpful for the process of problem solving. Overall, our data partially support our findings on the differences of nodelink, icicle plot, and treemap in their visual efficiency. Another approach to analyze identified patterns would be a qualitative comparison between patterns, which, however, is only feasible for more complex patterns, which again would shift the focus of analysis to individualistic problem solving approaches. For example, we identified a significant pattern containing 17 events for icicle plots, but it was only shared by three participants and occurred only once for each of them.

VII. Conclusions and Future Work

We presented a user study, which allowed us to analyze three of the most commonly used visualizations for hierarchical data with additional scalar dimension, namely nodelink, treemap, and icicle plot. These three visualization techniques of two hierarchy complexities (high, low) were tested at four tasks that are common for these types of visualizations. In addition to measuring completion time and correctness of responses, we analyzed the participants eye movements during problem solving. The statistical analysis of the participants' performance revealed that the treemap visualization performed worst. It barely exalted chance level and never performed better than fifty percent. For nodelink and icicle plot, our hypotheses were mostly supported due to well-known properties of both visualizations.

However, we also found some puzzling effects: The analysis of gaze heatmaps revealed that the 2.5D representation format of treemaps was possibly misleading participants during area judgments of occluded nodes. Additionally, we found that the use of icicle plots, with a better screen-space usage compared to nodelinks, might come along with the problem that areas might be judged differently simply because of their mutual distance, i. e., the sum of closely spaced nodes is perceived smaller than nodes with a higher distance. Further, we showed that participants used typical top-down and left-right gaze patterns during the counting tasks, which are better supported by the general structure of nodelinks and icicle plots.

A deeper analysis of the eye-tracking data enabled us to calculate the odds of continued visual attention at relevant nodes. Here, treemaps performed superior in most tasks, which can be seen as proof of its optimized screen-space usage. However, the user performance contradicts this finding: Optimized screen-space usage is no guarantee for good user performance. Interestingly, icicle plots outperformed nodelinks in both comparison tasks with respect to odds ratios, suggesting that icicle plots concentrate participants' attention to the relevant areas by omitting unimportant structures. Moreover, our data revealed that participants devote more time to stable problem solving strategies when using nodelink or icicle plot visualizations. In a future study, one could further investigate the users' problem solving strategies with the help of more complex tasks.

In sum, we were able to replicate several findings from earlier studies, especially about the problematic properties of treemaps. Visualization designers should be aware of the possible misinterpretation of areas of occluded areas. Also the correct identification of the number of inner nodes is often complicated by the occlusion problem. We enriched previous work by recording detailed eye-gaze data, allowing for in-depth inspection and interpretation of the users' processes. Our analyses revealed several pitfalls for visualization design as well as for visual user-study planning and execution, particularly dealing with the powerful Gestalt-laws. Those findings facilitate different directions for future analyses, for example if the choice of nodes' positions plays a crucial role for area perception or if area shape, circular or squared, is a significant factor for good counting, finding, or comparing performance. In general, it seems that classical visualizations are very efficient in most of the practice-oriented cases and that many of the well-known rules of thumb for visualizations have to be investigated much more in the future.

REFERENCES

[1] N. H. Müller, B. Liebold, D. Pietschmann, P. Ohler, and P. Rosenthal, "Hierarchy visualization designs and their impact on perception and problem solving strategies," in Proceedings of the International Conference on Advances in Computer-Human Interactions, 2017, pp. 93–101.

[2] ——, "Gaze into hierarchy: A practice-oriented eye tracking study," in Proceedings of the EuroVis Workshop on Reproducibility, Verification, and Validation in Visualization, 2013, pp. 9–10.

[3] D. Auber, C. Huet, A. Lambert, B. Renoust, A. Sallaberry, and A. Saulnier, "Gospermap: Using a gosper curve for laying out hierarchical data," IEEE Trans. Vis. Comput. Graphics, vol. 19, no. 11, 2013, pp. 1820–1832.

[4] E. Bakke, D. Karger, and R. Miller, "Automatic layout of structured hierarchical reports," IEEE Trans. Vis. Comput. Graphics, vol. 19, no. 12, 2013, pp. 2586–2595.

[5] J. Bernard, N. Wilhelm, B. Kruger, T. May, T. Schreck, and J. Kohlhammer, "Motionexplorer: Exploratory search in human motion capture data based on hierarchical aggregation," IEEE Trans. Vis. Comput. Graphics, vol. 19, no. 12, 2013, pp. 2257–2266.

[6] W. Dou, L. Yu, X. Wang, Z. Ma, and W. Ribarsky, "Hierarchicaltopics: Visually exploring large text collections using topic hierarchies," IEEE Trans. Vis. Comput. Graphics, vol. 19, no. 12, 2013, pp. 2002–2011.

[7] H. Schulz, "Treevis.net: A tree visualization reference," IEEE Computer Graphics and Applications, vol. 31, no. 6, 2011, pp. 11–15.

[8] H.-J. Schulz, S. Hadlak, and H. Schumann, "The design space of implicit hierarchy visualization: A survey," IEEE Trans. Vis. Comput. Graphics, vol. 17, no. 4, 2011, pp. 393–411.

[9] A. M. Cuadros, F. V. Paulovich, R. Minghim, and G. P. Telles, "Point placement by phylogenetic trees and its application to visual analysis of document collections," in Proceedings of the IEEE Symposium on Visual Analytics Science and Technology, W. Ribarsky and J. Dill, Eds. IEEE Computer Society, 2007, pp. 99–106.

[10] D. M. Kidd, "Geophylogenies and the map of life," Systematic Biology, vol. 59, no. 6, 2010, pp. 741–752.

[11] W. N. Dilla, D. J. Janvrin, and C. Jeffrey, "The impact of graphical displays of pro forma earnings information on professional and non-professional investors' earnings judgments," Behavioral Research in Accounting, vol. 25, no. 1, 2012, pp. 37–60.

[12] A. S. Kelton, R. R. Pennington, and B. M. Tuttle, "The effects of information presentation format on judgment and decision making: A review of the information systems research," Journal of Information Systems, vol. 24, no. 2, 2010, pp. 79–105.

[13] E. Tufte, The visual display of quantitative information, 2nd ed. Cheshire, Conn: Graphics Press, 2001.

[14] R. Vliegen, J. van Wijk, and E.-J. van der Linden, "Visualizing business data with generalized treemaps," IEEE Trans. Vis. Comput. Graphic, vol. 12, no. 5, 2006, pp. 789–796.

[15] M. Burch, N. Konevtsova, J. Heinrich, M. Hoeferlin, and D. Weiskopf, "Evaluation of traditional, orthogonal, and radial tree diagrams by an eye tracking study," IEEE Trans. Vis. Comput. Graphics, vol. 17, no. 12, 2011, pp. 2440–2448.

[16] G. Draper, Y. Livnat, and R. Riesenfeld, "A survey of radial methods for information visualization," IEEE Trans. Vis. Comput. Graphics, vol. 15, no. 5, 2009, pp. 759–776.

[17] C. G. Healey, K. S. Booth, and J. T. Enns, "High-speed visual estimation using preattentive processing," ACM Trans. Comput.-Hum. Interact., vol. 3, June 1996, pp. 107–135.

[18] C. G. Healey and J. Enns, "Attention and visual memory in visualization and computer graphics," IEEE Trans. Vis. Comput. Graphics, vol. 18, no. 7, 2012, pp. 1170–1188.

[19] C. Healey, "Choosing effective colours for data visualization," in Proceedings of IEEE Visualization, 1996, pp. 263–270.

[20] D. Keim, "Designing pixel-oriented visualization techniques: theory and applications," IEEE Trans. Visual. Comput. Graphics, vol. 6, no. 1, 2000, pp. 59–78.

[21] S. Lin, J. Fortuna, C. Kulkarni, M. Stone, and J. Heer, "Selecting semantically-resonant colors for data visualization," Computer Graphics Forum, vol. 32, no. 3pt4, 2013, pp. 401–410.

[22] M. Stone, "In color perception, size matters," IEEE Computer Graphics and Applications, vol. 32, no. 2, 2012, pp. 8–13.

[23] C. Ware, Information Visualization: Perception for Design. Morgan Kaufmann Publishers Inc., 2004.

[24] J. Stasko, R. Catrambone, M. Guzdial, and K. McDonald, "An evaluation of space-filling information visualizations for depicting hierarchical structures," International Journal of Human-Computer Studies, vol. 53, no. 5, 2000, pp. 663–694.

[25] B. Johnson and B. Shneiderman, "Tree-maps: a space-filling approach to the visualization of hierarchical information structures," in Proceedings of IEEE Visualization, 1991, pp. 284–291.

[26] K. Andrews and H. Heidegger, "Information slices: Visualising and exploring large hierarchies using cascading, semi-circular discs," in Proceedings of the IEEE Information Visualization Symposium, 1998, pp. 9–12.

[27] T. Bladh, D. Carr, and J. Scholl, "Extending tree-maps to three dimensions: A comparative study," in Computer Human Interaction, ser. Lecture Notes in Computer Science, M. Masoodian, S. Jones, and B. Rogers, Eds. Springer Berlin Heidelberg, 2004, vol. 3101, pp. 50–59.

[28] Y. Wang, S. T. Teoh, and K.-L. Ma, "Evaluating the effectiveness of tree visualization systems for knowledge discovery," in Proceedings of EuroVis, 2006, pp. 67–74.

[29] S. Teoh and M. Kwan-Liu, "Rings: A technique for visualizing large hierarchies," in Graph Drawing, ser. Lecture Notes in Computer Science, M. T. Goodrich and S. G. Kobourov, Eds. Springer Berlin Heidelberg, 2002, vol. 2528, pp. 268–275.

[30] C. Ziemkiewicz and R. Kosara, "The shaping of information by visual metaphors," IEEE Trans. Vis. Comput. Graphics, vol. 14, no. 6, 2008, pp. 1269–1276.

[31] M. Borkin, C. Yeh, M. Boyd, P. Macko, K. Gajos, M. Seltzer, and H. Pfister, "Evaluation of filesystem provenance visualization tools," IEEE Trans. Vis. Comput. Graphics, vol. 19, no. 12, 2013, pp. 2476–2485.

[32] P. Macko and M. I. Seltzer, "Provenance map orbiter: Interactive exploration of large provenance graphs," in Proceedings of the 3rd USENIX Workshop on the Theory and Practice of Provenance, 2011.

[33] J. Teets, D. Tegarden, and R. Russell, "Using cognitive fit theory to evaluate the effectiveness of information visualizations: An example using quality assurance data," IEEE Trans. Vis. Comput. Graphics, vol. 16, no. 5, 2010, pp. 841–853.

[34] J. Liang, Q. V. Nguyen, S. Simoff, and M. L. Huang, "Angular treemaps - a new technique for visualizing and emphasizing hierarchical structures," in Proceedings of the International Conference on Information Visualisation, 2012, pp. 74–80.

[35] J. Liang, M. L. Huang, and Q. V. Nguyen, "Perceptual user study for combined treemap," in Proceedings of the International Conference on Machine Learning and Applications, vol. 1, 2012, pp. 300–305.

[36] R. L. Sallam, C. Howson, C. J. Idoine, T. W. Oestreich, J. L. Richardson, and J. Tapadinhas, "Magic quadrant for business intelligence and analytics platforms," Gartner, 2017.

[37] P. Hand and N. Kharpate, Qlik Sense Cookbook. Packt Publishing, 2015.

[38] T. Lachev and E. Price, Applied Microsoft Power BI: Bring Your Data to Life!, 1st ed. Prologika Press, 2015.

[39] J. Stirrup, A. Nandeshwar, A. Ohmann, and M. Floyd, Tableau: Creating Interactive Data Visualizations. Packt Publishing, 2016.

[40] E. M. Reingold and J. Tilford, "Tidier drawings of trees," IEEE Trans. Software Eng., vol. SE-7, no. 2, 1981, pp. 223–228.

[41] C. Plaisant, J. Grosjean, and B. B. Bederson, "Spacetree: Supporting exploration in large node link tree, design evolution and empirical evaluation," in Proceedings of IEEE Information Visualization, 2002, pp. 57–64.

[42] M. Balzer and O. Deussen, "Voronoi treemaps," in Proceedings of the IEEE Symposium on Information Visualization, 2005, pp. 49–56.

[43] R. Blanch and E. Lecolinet, "Browsing zoomable treemaps: Structure-aware multi-scale navigation techniques," IEEE Trans. Vis. Comput. Graphics, vol. 13, no. 6, 2007, pp. 1248–1253.

[44] M. Bruls, K. Huizing, and J. van Wijk, "Squarified treemaps," in Proceedings of the Joint Eurographics and IEEE TCVG Symposium on Visualization, 1999, pp. 33–42.

[45] J. van Wijk and H. Van de Wetering, "Cushion treemaps: visualization of hierarchical information," in Proceedings of the IEEE Symposium on Information Visualization, 1999, pp. 73–78.

[46] S. Tak and A. Cockburn, "Enhanced spatial stability with hilbert and moore treemaps," IEEE Trans. Vis. Comput. Graphics, vol. 19, no. 1, 2013, pp. 141–148.

[47] J. B. Kruskal and J. M. Landwehr, "Icicle plots: Better displays for hierarchical clustering," The American Statistician, vol. 37, no. 2, 1983, pp. 162–168.

[48] B. Kleiner and J. A. Hartigan, "Representing points in many dimensions by trees and castles," Journal Am. Stat. Assoc., vol. 76, no. 374, 1981, pp. 260–269.

[49] F. Beck, M. Burch, C. Vehlow, S. Diehl, and D. Weiskopf, "Rapid serial visual presentation in dynamic graph visualization," in Proceedings of the IEEE Symposium on Visual Languages and Human-Centric Computing, 2012, pp. 185–192.

[50] C. Gouveia, J. Campos, and R. Abreu, "Using html5 visualizations in software fault localization," in Proceedings of the IEEE Working Conference on Software Visualization, 2013, pp. 1–10.

[51] J. Zhao, F. Chevalier, C. Collins, and R. Balakrishnan, "Facilitating discourse analysis with interactive visualization," IEEE Trans. Vis. Comput. Graphics, vol. 18, no. 12, 2012, pp. 2639–2648.

[52] S. Elsen, "Visgi: Visualizing git branches," in Proceedings of the IEEE Working Conference on Software Visualization, 2013, pp. 1–4.

[53] C. Rohrdantz, M. Hund, T. Mayer, B. Wälchli, and D. A. Keim, "The world's languages explorer: Visual analysis of language features in genealogical and areal contexts," Computer Graphics Forum, vol. 31, no. 3pt1, 2012, pp. 935–944.

[54] J. Stasko and E. Zhang, "Focus+context display and navigation techniques for enhancing radial, space-filling hierarchy visualizations," in Proceedings of IEEE Information Visualization, 2000, pp. 57–65.

[55] W. Schneider and R. M. Shiffrin, "Controlled and automatic human information processing: Detection, search, and attention," Psychological Review, vol. 84, no. 1, 1977, pp. 1–66.

[56] R. M. Shiffrin and W. Schneider, "Controlled and automatic human information processing: Perceptual learning, automatic attending and a general theory," Psychological Review, vol. 84, no. 1, 1977, pp. 127–190.

[57] R. Desimone and J. Duncan, "Neural mechanisms of selective visual attention," Annual Review of Neuroscience, vol. 18, no. 1, 1995, pp. 193–222.

[58] A. Torralba, A. Oliva, M. S. Castelhano, and J. M. Henderson, "Contextual guidance of eye movements and attention in real-world scenes: The role of global features in object search," Psychological Review, vol. 113, no. 4, 2006, pp. 766–786.

[59] J. Intriligator and P. Cavanagh, "The spatial resolution of visual attention," Cognitive Psychology, vol. 43, no. 3, 2001, pp. 171–216.

[60] J. Wagemans, J. H. Elder, M. Kubovy, S. E. Palmer, M. A. Peterson, M. Singh, and R. von der Heydt, "A century of gestalt psychology in visual perception: I. Perceptual grouping and figure-ground organization," Psychol Bull., vol. 138, no. 6, 2012, pp. 1172–1217.

[61] A. Al-Edaily, A. Al-Wabil, and Y. Al-Ohali, "Interactive screening for learning difficulties: Analyzing visual patterns of reading arabic scripts with eye tracking," in HCI International 2013 - Posters Extended Abstracts, ser. Communications in Computer and Information Science, C. Stephanidis, Ed. Springer Berlin Heidelberg, 2013, vol. 374, pp. 3–7.

[62] E. Li and D. Briley, "Attitudes shaped by eye movements: The reading direction effect," Advances in Consumer Research, vol. 39, 2011, pp. 666–667.

[63] M. Magnusson, "Discovering hidden time patterns in behavior: T-patterns and their detection," Behavior Research Methods, Instruments, & Computers, vol. 32, no. 1, 2000, pp. 93–110.

International Journal on Advances in Software, vol 10 no 3 & 4, year 2017, http://www.iariajournals.org/software/

Applying Information Flow Tracking to the Development Cycle

Thomas Lie and Pål Ellingsen
Department of Computing, Mathematics and Physics
Western Norway University of Applied Sciences
Bergen, Norway
Email: thomas.lie@student.hib.no, pal.ellingsen@hvl.no

***Abstract*—Information flow vulnerabilities such as Structured Query Language (SQL) Injection and Cross-Site Scripting are highly relevant issues in web applications. This article expands on a an earlier paper by the authors to investigate how to apply information flow tracking in the form of taint analysis to detect this domain of vulnerabilities in. Different types of taint analysis implementations exists and a challenge is how web application frameworks are handled by the taint analysis implementation. This technique is tested by a developing a prototype application for a company covering a genuine need. This application also functions as an artefact application in conducting taint analysis. Using this artefact, a proposed solution for integrating taint analysis in the process of developing Java EE web applications is tested. Analysing the results, it is shown that it is possible to integrate taint analysis in the development cycle, but it is also made clear that the technique must be improved to properly support its use in an automated build system.**

Keywords*–*Information flow tracking; taint analysis; iterative development; software security; injection attacks.

I. Introduction

A. Background

Web applications exposes its host system to the end-user. The nature of this exposure makes all web applications susceptible to security vulnerabilities in various ways. The Open Web Application Security Project (OWASP) periodically publishes a report that covers the ten most common security problems. Two of the top problems are information flow based, namely *Injection* and *Cross-Site Scripting*. Being information flow based means that untrusted data enters the application to eventually be executed as a part of a critical command. An example of a common injection vulnerability, SQL injection, is shown in Figure 1 as a snippet from a Java servlet [1].

```
String username = request.getParameter("username");
String password = request.getParameter("password");
Statement st = conn.createStatement();
String query = "SELECT * FROM users WHERE username='" +
               username + "' AND password='" + password + "'";
ResultSet rs = st.executeQuery(query);
```

Figure 1. Vulnerable code in a Java login servlet susceptible to SQL injection

The example is taken from a login servlet that gets two user submitted parameters, *username* and *password*, and uses them directly in a dynamic SQL query. The injection is accomplished if the WHERE clause can be evaluated true without providing a matching login credential. This can be done by adding *' OR '1'='1* in the *password* parameter because the OR condition will always evaluate true.

A way to detect information flow based security flaws is by performing *static taint analysis*. The idea is that variables that directly or indirectly can be modified by the user is identified as tainted. If a tainted variable is used to execute critical commands a potential security flaw is detected. In the example in Figure 1 the method *request.getParameter(...)* gets user input and the variable in which the data is stored is identified as a *source* in taint analysis. On the other side of the information flow is the method *st.executeQuery(query)*, which is an endpoint executing a critical command, identified as a *sink* in taint analysis.

In developing applications in general a popular approach to work by is to implement some kind of agile software development methodology. The main agile practice that this article is highlighting is *Iterative and Incremental development*. Being iterative means that the current state of the developed functionality is improved, adding quality to the code for a better product. Incremental development refers to breaking up the work into smaller pieces. The pieces are scheduled to be developed, usually in timeboxed cycles, and integrated in the software as they are finished. This could also be done as a response to new or changing requirements.

When using agile software development methodologies, a principle from the Agile Manifesto is worth mentioning, *deliver working software frequently*. This principle encourages to develop functionality in small time frames so that the customer frequently is presented the latest product increment. For the developers it is tempting to maximize the deliverance of functional requirements if the customer has not communicated an emphasis on non-functional requirements such as software security.

B. Problem Description

The main objective of this article is to study how to integrate static taint analysis in an iterative and incremental development process to detect information flow based security vulnerabilities in Java EE web applications. This integration was proposed by the authors in an earlier work [2], but in this paper, we apply the proposed principle to an actual development process.

A typical Java EE web application featuring several different components will be developed in order to attain practical experience using the technology. This application will be in use by a company in an industrial environment possibly accessed through the internet. Potential security flaws may expose confidential data through information flow security vulnerabilities.

Because of the principle of frequent delivery in agile software development methodologies, integrating security analysis should be as cheap as possible in regards to the process of analysis. The following aspects will be considered.

- Resources needed in form of preparing the application for analysis parameters before execution of the taint analysis
- Typically, how much time is needed to run the taint analysis for a considerable large web application
- Resources needed in order to interpret and respond to the taint analysis output

C. Article Outline

In the following, we want to study how taint analysis can be integrated in the development process, and how suitable the existing implementations are for this kind of integration. To carry out this study, we have applied the analysis to the development of a Java Enterprise Edition (Java EE) application throughout the development process. The outline of the rest of this paper is as follows. Section II describes the principles of taint analysis, other works related to this and state of the art. In Section III, the methodology used in this study is presented. Then, an actual implementation of the proposed method is demonstrated in Section IV. Based on this, the results and an analysis of these is presented in Section V. Finally, our findings are summed up in Section VI.

II. Theoretical Background

A. Software Development

When developing software, a common approach is to establish a *Software Development Life Cycle (SDLC)*. The SDLC's function is to cover all processes associated with the software developed. Different types of SDLC models exists. However, whether it being Waterfall, Agile or some other model the processes in the SDLC can be identified in five phases. The phases are named *Requirements*, *Design*, *Development*, *Test* and *Deployment* [3].

Developing software requires planning of both *functional requirements* and *non-functional requirements* in order to deliver an acceptable end product. The functional requirements refer to the functionality of the software whereas non-functional requirements refer to quality attributes, e.g., capacity, efficiency, performance, privacy and security.

Requirements phase addresses the gathering and analysis of requirements regarding the environment in which the software is operating in. Non-functional requirements based on security policies and standards and other relevant industry standards that affect the type of software developed are included in this phase.

Design phase is where the functional requirements of the software developed is planned based on the mapping of requirements in the first phase. This phase also includes architectural choices that determines the technologies used in the development of the software.

Development phase contains the actual coding of the software developed. Both functional requirements and non-functional requirements from the earlier planning phases are being addressed. A usual approach is to develop the functional requirements in small programs called units. These units is then tested for their functionality, called *Unit Testing*.

Test phase is where test cases are built based on requirements criteria from earlier phases. Both test cases for functional requirements and non-functional requirements are included. The test phase is iterative in nature meaning that the problems found would need to be addressed and fixed in the development phase. And when fixed, the system would need to go through the test phase once again.

Deployment phase is the final phase that exists to install the software and make it ready to run in its intended environment or released into the market. At this point both testing of functional requirements and non-functional requirements are finished [3].

B. Software Security

OWASP analyse data from software security firms and periodically publishes a report about the top 10 most common security vulnerabilities found in web applications. The data analysed covers over 500,000 vulnerabilities over thousands of applications making this list a well documented ranking of the most common vulnerabilities present in web applications today [1].

Two of the types of vulnerabilities at the top of the OWASP top 10 list are information flow based, namely *injection* and *cross-site scripting*. Being information flow based means that in order for an attacker to successfully exploit the type of vulnerability, untrusted data must enter the application. This untrusted data then bypasses the validation due to a poor validation routine or a complete lack of validation. When the untrusted data eventually reaches the critical command the attacker aimed for, the vulnerability is exploited.

In the category of injection based vulnerabilities resides numerous exploitable implementations such as queries for SQL, Lightweight Directory Access Protocol (LDAP), Xpath or NoSQL and command injection in form of operatings system commands or program arguments. Due to the widespread use of database access based on SQL in web applications, the most common injection vulnerability is therefore SQL injection. Two other types of information flow vulnerabilities that are worth briefly mentioning are *path traversal* and *HTTP response splitting*. Path traversal allows an attacker to access or control files that are not intended by the application. This can happen if the application fails to restrict access to the file system. Path traversal belongs in the category *insecure direct object references* in the OWASP top 10 [1] [4].

HTTP response splitting is a technique that involves splitting the HTTP response enabling an attacker to gain control over the second HTTP response. The HTTP response could be split if the application includes malicious data in the HTTP response header. Simply supplying a line break (CR and LF) in the malicious data splits the response. Implications includes

Figure 2. The Software Development Life Cycle [3].

web cache poisoning, cross-user defacements, page hijacking and cross-site scripting [4].

C. SQL Injection

SQL injection can be further broken down into different types of injection techniques. *Tautology* is a technique to bypass authentication and access data through the *WHERE* clause by making the query always evaluate to true. The SQL injection example shown in Figure 1 is an example using that technique. The following SQL query is a general SQL injection example of the tautology technique. [5].

*SELECT * FROM <tablename>WHERE userId = <id>and password = <wrongPassword>OR 1=1;*

A technique used in order to force the application to display an error message sent from the database is called *logically incorrect queries*. The idea is to make the SQL query fail in order to acquire information about the database structure such as table and column names. If the application does not withheld such error messages from the users an attacker could learn enough to forge an effectively targeted SQL injection to access or modify the desired data. In the following example SQL query an additional *query delineation (')* is added after the username parameter rendering the SQL query incorrect. In this specific case the error message would reveal the name of the password parameter [5].

*SELECT * FROM <tablename>WHERE username = <anyUsername>' and password = <anyPassword>;*

The next technique, named *union queries*, uses the *UNION* clause in order to acquire information from other tables in the database. In the following example an attacker needs a valid user and password pair. The attacker adds the extended query in the password field after the valid password. This example fetches the current user's credit card number [5].

*SELECT * FROM <tablename>WHERE userId = <id>and password = <rightPassword>UNION SELECT creditCardNumber FROM CreditCardTable;*

Piggy-backed queries is a technique to expand the number of SQL queries the DBMS would execute by using the *query delimiter (;)*. The first query is the former query, which will be executed normally and the following queries that are added by the attacker are also executed. Since an attacker could construct any SQL query, the possibilities for exploitation are extensive. Some outcomes could be adding, modifying or deleting data, performing denial of service and executing remote commands. In the following example an additional query is constructed deleting a table [5].

*SELECT * FROM <tablename>WHERE userId = <id>and password = <rightPassword>; DROP TABLE <tablename>;*

The preceding SQL query examples are the simplest SQL injection techniques. A couple of other techniques are also worth mentioning that are slightly more advanced. *Blind injection* could be used to acquire data if the application is hiding database error messages from the attacker. The concept is to query the database with queries evaluating true or false in order to slowly accumulate information by elimination. The prerequisite for this to work is to find a way to tell whether the query evaluates true or false. This could be done in e.g., a login context [5].

In case a way to tell if the evaluation is true or false is not found, the next technique could be applied, namely *timing attacks*. With the help of an if-then statement and the *WAITFOR* clause a delay could be set depending on how the query evaluates. E.g., a database delay for 5 seconds could be set if the query evaluates true and otherwise have no database delay. By observing the response a conclusion could be made in whether the query evaluated true or false [5].

D. Cross-Site Scripting

Cross-site scripting is a vulnerability that enables the attacker to get a user visiting an infected website to run malicious scripts. Some outcomes for the attacker is hijacking the user's session, redirecting to other websites and modifying the compromised website's presentation of its content. Three types of cross-site scripting attacks exists. *Non-persistent attacks* is the most common type and is an attack that is not stored persistently, but reflected to the victim immediately. An approach is that the attacker sends a URL to a vulnerable, but seemingly trustworthy, web page. The link contains a malicious script that will be executed if the victim clicks it. Consider the following example URL exploiting a web page search field susceptible to cross-site scripting because a lack of validating both user input and output. The user input is the search string and the output is what is outputted in the search results web page [5].

http://vulnerable.site/search.php?query=<script>alert(0)</script>

In this example the script is only triggering an alert box. This script could be crafted in order to steal the victim's cookies, session or other accessible information. The second variation of cross-site scripting is called *persistent attack*. Instead of crafting a malicious URL this technique goes hand in hand with injection in that the malicious script are stored persistently, e.g., in a database. The attacker first injects the malicious script in the vulnerable web site and the victim visits the web site serving the script at a later point in time. An example could be a message board where users posts messages accessible by other users [5].

The third cross-site scripting technique is called *DOM based cross-site scripting attack*. This approach is different in comparison to the other techniques in that it is a client side issue. The idea is to manipulate the Document Object Model (DOM) by injecting malicious data into the website, e.g., inserting a fake login form tricking the victim into submitting sensitive information. Web sites are vulnerable to this type of attacks because input are not validated and escaped properly.

A web site could have good validation routines server side, but since this type of attack opens for purely client side manipulation validation of input data client side is crucial [5].

E. Mapping Threats

In order to eliminate security flaws when developing a web application a crucial point is that the software developers need to have an idea of how the web application is vulnerable. An option is to use a *threat analysis*, which fits in the design phase of the SDLC. The analysis typically consists of three steps. The first step is to determine and categorize the system's possible threats. Then each threat are ranked by the expected security risk. Finally, a mitigation plan regarding the ranked list is laid out [3].

Another concept that can be used in threat analysis to identify threats is mapping the application's *attack surface*. An attack surface is defined as all possible entry points an attacker can use to attack the application. In a web application all web pages the attacker can access contributes to the attack surface. For the information flow based vulnerabilities included in the threat analysis a mitigation plan could contain specific design choices in order to counter these threats. However, additional initiatives should be included in the testing phase to make sure any developer mistakes are caught [3].

An approach in order to catch developer mistakes is to initiate a manual code review by security experts. This strategy, although usually highly effective, is both expensive and time consuming. Automatic detection of vulnerabilities in some form is the preferred way to go.

F. Methods for Detecting Vulnerabilities

Numerous approaches for detecting SQL injection and cross-site scripting are documented. Some of them are briefly described in the following paragraphs. *SQLUnitGen* is a tool to detect SQL injection vulnerabilities in Java applications. First, the tool traces input values that are used for a SQL query. Based on this analysis, test cases are generated in form of unit tests with attack input. Lastly, the test cases are executed and a test result summary showing vulnerable code locations are provided [6].

Fine-grained access control is more of a way of eliminating the possibility for SQL injection rather than detecting it. The concept is to restrict database access to information only the authenticated user is allowed to view. This is done by assigning a key to the user, which is required in order to successfully query the database. Access control are in fact moved from the application layer to the database layer. Any attempt to execute SQL injection cannot affect the data of different users. [7].

SQLCHECKER is a runtime checking algorithm implementation for preventing SQL injection. It checks whether an SQL query matches the established query grammar rules and the policy specifying permitted syntactic forms in regards to the external input used in the query. This means that any external input is not allowed to modify the syntactic structure of the SQL query. Meta-characters are applied to external input functioning as a secret key for identifying which data originated externally [8].

Brower-enforced embedded policies is a method for preventing cross-site scripting vulnerabilities. The concept is to include policies about which scripts are safe to run in the web application. Two types of policies are supported. A whitelisting policy provided by the web application as a list of valid hashes of safe scripts. Whenever a script is detected in the browser, it is passed to a hook function hashing it with a one-way hashing algorithm. Any script whose hash is not in the provided list is rejected [9].

The second policy, *DOM sandboxing*, is made to enable the use of unknown scripts. This could be a necessary evil for a web site for e.g., requiring scripts in third-party ads. Contrary to the first policy, this is a blacklisting policy. The web page structure is mapped and any occurrences of the *noexecute* keyword within an *<div>* or *<span>* element enables sandbox mode in that element disallowing running scripts [9].

The methods covered in the preceding paragraphs for both detecting and/or preventing SQL injection and cross-site scripting have one thing in common. All approaches present detection solutions limited to their respective vulnerability whether it being either SQL injection or cross-site scripting. Since both types of vulnerabilities belong to the same category of vulnerabilities, information flow vulnerabilities, a mutual approach is desirable to explore. Such approach should also be able to detect all forms of information flow vulnerabilities.

FindBugs is a popular static analysis tool for Java. It has a plugin architecture allowing convenient adding of bug detectors presently detecting both SQL injection and cross-site scripting. The bug detectors analyse the Java bytecode in order to detect occurrences of bug patterns. FindBugs states the following:

"Because its analysis is sometimes imprecise, FindBugs can report false warnings, which are warnings that do not indicate real errors. In practice, the rate of false warnings reported by FindBugs is less than 50% [10]."

Up to 50% false warnings may be acceptable if the goal of the analysis is just to get a general idea of where to do coding improvements in a development process. Having a much more precise analysis reporting none or low false warnings saves the developer's time. Therefore, finding a method with a much higher accuracy is preferable. The approach this article are looking into in order to detect information flow vulnerabilities is an approach called *taint analysis*.

G. Taint Analysis

Taint analysis resides within the domain of information flow analyses. Essentially this means that tracking how variables propagate throughout the application of analysis is the core idea. In order to detect information flow vulnerabilities entry points for external inputs in the application needs to be identified. The external inputs could be data from any source outside the application that is not trusted. In other words where there is a crossing in the application's established trust boundary. In a web application context this is typically user input fetched from a web page form, but would also include e.g., URL parameters, HTTP header data and cookies.

```
HashMap map = ...;
String id = request.getParameter("id"); //Source
User user = (User) map.get(id);
```

Figure 3. A tainted source variable containing an id to fetch data from a HashMap indirectly induces taint on an object [11]

In taint analysis the identified entry points are called *sources*. The sources are marked as tainted and the analysis tracks how these tainted variables propagate throughout the application. A tainted variable rarely exclusively resides in the original assigned variable and thus it propagates. This means that it affects variables other than its original assignment. This can happen directly or indirectly. Directly in that e.g., a tainted string object is assigned either fully or partly to a new object of some sort. An example of indirect propagation is that a tainted variable that contains an id is used to determine what data is assigned to a new variable, see Figure 3 [11].

Tainted variables in itself are not harmful for any applications. It is when a tainted variable is used in a critical operation without proper sanitization that vulnerabilities could be introduced. Sanitizing a variable means to remove data or format it in a way that it will not contain any data that could exploit the critical command in which it will be used. An example is that when querying a database with a tainted string it could open for SQL injection if the string contains characters that either changes the intended query or splits it into additional new queries. Proper sanitization would remove the unwanted characters eliminating the possibility of unintended queries and essentially preventing SQL injection.

Contrary to input data being assigned as sources, methods that executes critical operations are called *sinks* in taint analysis. When a tainted variable has the possibility to be used within a sink a successful taint analysis implementation would detect this as a vulnerability. Consider the SQL injection example in Figure 1 the method *request.getParameter(...)* reads input from the user. This input is stored in a string making it tainted. On the other side of the information flow is the method *st.executeQuery(query)*, which is a sink. When the tainted source string are used in the sink as part of the SQL query without sanitization an information flow vulnerability is evident.

Taint analysis can be divided into two approaches, *dynamic taint analysis* and *static taint analysis*. The dynamic taint analysis approach analyses the different executed paths in an application specific runtime environment. Tracking information flow between identified source memory addresses and sink memory addresses is generally how this kind of analysis is carried out. A potential vulnerability is detected if an information flow between a source memory address and a sink memory address is detected. Static taint analysis is a method that analyse the application source code. This means that ultimately all possible execution paths can be covered in this type of analysis whereas in a dynamic taint analysis context only those paths specifically included in the analysis are covered.

The concept of taint analysis has been around for several decades. The scripting programming language Perl introduced *taint mode* with Perl 3 in 1989. Taint mode is implemented as a native feature in Perl's interpreter and is enabled if the Perl script runs with the *-T* switch. When taint mode is enabled all strings that originates from outside the program are marked as tainted. If a critical operation is executed with a tainted string the program fails with an error. Examples of sinks are methods to write to files, executing shell commands and sending information over the network.

In order to enable the use of tainted strings in sinks, Perl taint mode policy is that the string needs to be untainted. This process consists of sanitizing the string by using regular expressions. Consider the use of regular expression in order to e.g., remove a trailing character. In this case the developer needs to be aware that doing this removes the taint from the string. The lack of further sanitizing of the tainted string renders it with an improper sanitization for safely being used in sinks.

The Perl taint mode implementation is a dynamic approach since the analysis tracks tainted strings in the program's runtime environment. Dynamic taint analysis has some variations in areas of use and Perl taint mode resides within the category *unknown vulnerability detection*. This is, as shown with the Perl taint mode example, simply detecting misuses of user input during execution with the goal being preventing code injection attacks [12].

Further, dynamic taint analysis can also be used in *test case generation* to automatically generate input to test applications. This is suitable for detecting how the behaviour of an application changes with different types of input. Such analysis could be desirable as a step in the development testing phase of a deployed application since this could also detect vulnerabilities that are implementation specific. Dynamic taint analysis can also be used as a *malware analysis* in revealing how information flows through a malicious software binary [12].

Taking this analysis one step further enables malicious software detection of e.g., keyloggers, packet sniffers and stealth backdoors. The concept being marking input from keyboard, network interface and hard disk as tainted and then tracking the taint propagation to generate a taint graph. By using the taint graph in automatically generating policies through profiling on a malicious software free system detection of anomalies are enabled. E.g., in the case of detecting keyloggers, the profile includes which modules that normally would access the keyboard input on a per application basis. When a keylogger is trying to access a specific profiled application this could be detected [13].

In both static and dynamic taint analysis implementations the precision of the analysis is important for it to be trustworthy. Generally, two outcomes can affect the analysis precision. The first scenario is when the analysis for some reason marks a variable as tainted that has not propagated from a tainted variable. This is called *over tainting* and leads to *false positives*, which means that the reported error is truly not an error. The second outcome is when the analysis misses an information flow from a source to a sink. Thus, the analysis does not report an error that actually is present. This is called *under tainting* and the term *false negative* describes the absent of an actual error [12].

Dynamic taint analysis has, as shown in previous paragraphs, several types of applications. However, static taint analysis may be a better fit for integration within the development process due to the direct analysis of source code. There are different ways to implement static taint analysis. Three of them, which are implementations for Java, are elaborated on in the following sections.

H. Taint Analysis for Java

The first implementation, *Taint Analysis for Java*, consists of two analysis phases. The first phase performs a pointer analysis and builds a call graph. Pointer analysis, also called points-to analysis, enables mapping of what objects a variable can point to. A call graph in this context is static, which means that it is an approximation of every possible way to run the program in regards to invoking methods. The paper describes an implementation of specific algorithms, but the analysis design is flexible in that using any set of desired algorithms are feasible [14].

The second phase takes the results of the first phase as input and uses a *hybrid thin slicing* algorithm to track tainted information flow. *Thin slicing* is a method to find all the relevant statements affecting the point of interest, which is called the seed. In comparison to a traditionally *program slicing* algorithm, thin slicing is lightweight in that it only includes the statements producing the value at the seed. This means that the statements that explain why producers affect the seed are excluded in a thin slice. [15].

Thin slicing works well with taint analysis because the statements most relevant to a tainted flow is captured. Hybrid thin slicing essentially produces a Hybrid System Dependence Graph (HSDG) consisting of nodes corresponding to load, call and store statements. The call statements represent source and sink methods. The HSDG has two types of edges, *direct edges* and *summary edges*, that represent data dependence. The data dependence information is computed in the first phase by the pointer analysis. Tainted flows are found by computing reachability in the HSDG from each source call statement adding the necessary data dependence edges on demand [14].

The way this implementation defines sources and sinks is through *security rules*. Security rules exist on the form (S1,S2,S3). S1 is a set of sources. A source is a method having a return value, which is considered tainted. S2 is a set of *sanitizers*. A sanitizer is a method that takes a tainted input as parameter and returns that parameter in a taint-free form. S3 is a set of sinks. Each sink is defined as a pair (m,P), where *m* is the method performing the security sensitive operation and *P* defines the parameters in *m* that are vulnerable when assigned with tainted data [14].

Taint Analysis for Java includes ways to incorporate web application frameworks in the analysis. External configuration files often define how the inner workings of a framework is laid out. Therefore a conservative approximation of possible behaviour is modelled. For the Apache Struts framework, which is an implementation of the Model View Controller (MVC) pattern, the *Action* and *Action Form* classes are specially treated. These classes contains *execute* methods taking an *ActionForm* instance as a parameter. This instance contains fields, which are populated by the framework based on user input meaning it should be considered tainted. Thus, the analysis implements a model treating the *Action* classes as entry points [14].

Refer to Section II-K1 for more information on the article describing Taint Analysis for Java.

I. Tainted Object Propagation Analysis

The second static taint analysis implementation is similar to Taint Analysis for Java in that it is based on pointer analysis and construction of a call graph, refer to Section II-H. However, this implementation depends on pointer analysis and call graph alone in detecting tainted flows. The analysis uses binary decision diagrams in the form of a tool called *bddbddb* (BDD-Based Deductive DataBase), which includes pointer analysis and a call graph representation [4].

Binary decision diagrams can be utilized in adding compression to a standard binary decision tree based on reduction rules. In the context of this analysis the compression of the representation of all paths in the call graph makes it possible to efficiently represent as many as 10^{14} contexts. This allows the analysis implementation to scale to applications consisting of almost 1000 classes [4].

In order to detect vulnerabilities, specific vulnerability patterns needs to be expressed by the user. A pattern consists of *source descriptors*, *sink descriptors* and *derivation descriptors*. Source descriptors specify where user input enters the application, e.g., HttpServletRequest.getParameter(String). Sink descriptors specify a critical command that can be executed, e.g., Connection.executeQuery(String). Lastly, derivation descriptors specify how an object can propagate within the application, e.g., through construction of strings with StringBuffer.append(String) [4].

Tainted Object Propagation Analysis does not implement any handling of web application frameworks. Refer to Section II-K2 for more information on the article describing Tainted Object Propagation Analysis.

J. Type-based Taint Analysis

The third implementation, Type-based Taint Analysis, differs from the preceding approaches in that a *type system* is the basis of the analysis. The implemented type system is called *SFlow*, which is a context-sensitive type system for secure information flow. SFlow has two basic type qualifiers, namely *tainted* and *safe*. Sources and sinks are identified in that methods and fields are annotated using these type qualifiers. A type system is a system that intends to prove that no type error can occur based on the rules established. This is done by assigning a type with each computed value in the type system and the flow of these values are then examined. This concept is called *subtyping* [11].

The subtyping hierarchy is defined as $safe <: tainted$. This means that a flow from tainted sources to safe sinks are disallowed. The other way around, assigning a safe variable to a tainted variable, is allowed. For an example of annotation, refer to Figure 1 where the source *request.getParameter(...)* would be annotated as tainted and the sink *st.executeQuery(query)* would be annotated as safe [11].

A third type qualifier, *poly*, is included in order to correctly propagate tainted and safe variables through object manipulation, e.g., with String methods *append* and *toString*. All object manipulation methods, such as String *append* and *toString*, would be annotated as poly. The poly qualifier in combination with viewpoint adaptation rules ensures that the implementation is context-sensitive. This means that parameters returned from such methods inherits the manipulated inbound parameter's type qualifier (tainted of safe). As a result the subtyping hierarchy becomes *safe* <: *poly* <: *tainted* [11].

Another benefit with the poly qualifier implementation is that tainted variables properly propagate in third-party libraries. As a result all application code is included in the analysis. Type-based Taint Analysis also supports web application frameworks in the same way as regular Java API is supported, namely by annotating the relevant fields and methods. An example is that for the Apache Struts framework the *Action* class containing the *execute* method is what needs to be annotated. This method takes an *ActionForm* instance as a parameter that contains fields, which are populated by the framework based on tainted user input. Simply annotating the *ActionForm* parameter as tainted would include the framework in the analysis [11].

Type inference implies identifying a valid typing based on the subtyping rules defined in the SFlow type system. A succeeded inference means that there are no flows from sources to sinks. If the type inference fails, a type error is evident meaning that a flow from a tainted source to a safe sink is present. Refer to Section II-K3 for more information on the article describing Type-based Taint Analysis [11].

K. Related Work

In choosing which articles to be included as related work, the emphasis is on articles describing practical taint analysis implementations backed by analysis results. Theoretical implementations can be a good starting points in expanding a research topic. But since the main goal of this article is to study how taint analysis can be integrated in a development process an actual working taint analysis implementation is preferable.

1) TAJ: Effective Taint Analysis of Web Applications : This paper describes the design and implementation of a static Taint Analysis for Java (TAJ). The use of pointer analysis and the construction of a call graph is the first step in the analysis. Further, a hybrid thin slicing algorithm is used to create a Hybrid System Dependence Graph (HSDG). Finally, computation of reachability in the HSDG is conducted in order to find tainted flows. Scalability is built in enabling analysis of applications of any size with the help of a set of techniques designed to produce useful results given limited time and space. Techniques included are priority-driven call graph construction and using bounds on other parts of the analysis, e.g., to limit the size of a slice in the hybrid thin slicing algorithm [14].

TAJ was designed to support a commercial product, IBM Rational AppScan Developer Edition (AppScan DE), and has therefore undergone extensive evaluation. 22 different applications that mostly make use of web frameworks are analysed using 5 different variations of the thin slicing algorithm. This was done in order to identify an efficient compromise on performance and the number of false positives present because the analysis introduces a high percentage of false positives. However, few false negatives are reported by the analysis [14].

2) Finding Security Vulnerabilities in Java Applications with Static Analysis : This paper proposes a static taint analysis implementation based on a context-sensitive pointer analysis. Based on the pointer analysis a call graph is generated. The paper describes the class of information flow vulnerabilities as the tainted object propagation problem. Users need to provide a specification of which methods that can lead to a vulnerability in the form of different types of descriptors. The specifications are automatically translated into static analysers. Results of the analysis are presented as a plugin for Eclipse IDE enabling examination of each vulnerability found [4].

It is reported that this analysis scales to programs of almost 1000 classes. Further, the analysis is done at the bytecode-level meaning that the approach can be applied to other forms of bytecode, e.g., enabling the analysis of C# code. There is no information on how this analysis can include other web application frameworks other than the standard Java EE implementation [4].

The analysis was run on nine popular open-source applications resulting in 29 detected vulnerabilities. Two of the vulnerabilities resided in widely-used Java libraries. Further, the analysis yielded 12 false positives, however, all false positives came from one of the nine applications. The authors concluded that their approach yields very few false positives [4].

3) Type-based Taint Analysis for Java Web Applications : This paper presents a type-based taint analysis approach. SFlow, a context-sensitive type system for secure information flow is implemented in a checking framework that the authors has built in previous work. This framework infers and checks object ownership and reference immutability. Users need to annotate sources and sinks, and the analysis runs without further input from the user reporting either a concrete typing or type errors indicating information flow vulnerabilities [11].

The taint analysis approach handles reflection, libraries and frameworks effectively. Handling reflection is possible because SFlow does not require abstraction of heap objects, as the flow is tracked through subtyping. Both libraries and frameworks are also handled through subtyping together with the fact that the analysis is modular. This means that it can analyse any given set of classes. If the set contains an unknown callee, e.g., a library method with unknown source code, both source and sink information flow are correctly tracked through subtyping [11].

Evaluations that are performed on 13 relatively large Java web applications have shown both precision and scalability. It has zero false positives for most of the applications and about 15% false positives on average. An indirect comparison with TAJ, [14], and F4F, [16], was done in that both implementations are included in the commercial tool AppScan Source. In addition, another commercial tool was also included in the comparison, Fortify SCA [11].

AppScan Source and Fortify SCA detect respectively 50% and 61% of all vulnerabilities, while SFlow detects 100%. The precision is 74% for AppScan Source, 81% for Fortify SCA and 76% for the SFlow implementation. Precision P is defined in the following way where T indicates the number of true positives meaning the correct detections, and F being the number of false positives [11].

$$P = \frac{T}{T+F}$$

4) F4F: Taint Analysis of Framework-based Web Applications : This paper describes F4F (Framework For Frameworks), which is a framework for conveniently adding support to framework-based web applications in taint analysis. Since framework implementations extensively use reflection, conducting static taint analysis are often unable to detect vulnerabilities correctly. F4F presents a way to generate a specification of a program's framework-specific behaviours and integrate this specification into the taint analysis engine without changes to the underlying analysis engine. [16].

The approach F4F uses is to utilize the Web Application Framework Language (WAFL) in order to generate specifications. Futher, a helper tool, WAFL2Java, translates the WAFL specifications to Java code for use with the taint analysis implementation. A higher-level API for generating WAFL specifications is also implemented easing the process of writing WAFL generators. WAFL specification support is added to the taint analysis implementation ACTARUS, which is an improved version of TAJ, refer to Section II-H and II-K1. TAJ includes a built-in framework support that is not included in ACTARUS. However, the combination of ACTARUS and F4F discovers more framework-related issues than TAJ [16].

F4F is evaluated by analysing nine subject programs. The set of programs exercises four supported frameworks. Eight use Struts, three use Spring, five use Tiles and six use EL. F4F detected 525 new vulnerabilities compared to ACTARUS taint analysis without F4F support. The number of more vulnerabilities detected per program ranged from 1.1X-14.9X with a harmonic mean of 2.10X. A manual inspection of the new vulnerabilities detected revealed that many were exploitable or reflected bad security practice [16].

5) Related Work Conclusion: Three practical implementations of taint analysis are included as related work. The analysis methods for those implementations are described in detail in Section II-H, II-I and II-J. Other variations of taint analysis implementations exists, however, limiting to these three implementations covers the most important methodologies present in the domain of taint analysis implementations. Also, these implementations are crafted specifically for Java in order to fit with analysis in the context of Java EE web application development. Taint analysis implementations exists for numerous programming languages, especially for the C/C++ programming language.

In addition to the taint analysis implementation articles an article describing the use of taint analysis in framework-based web applications is presented. The Java EE web application implementation is in itself a framework and it can also be extended by third-party framework implementations. Frameworks introduce a layer of added complexity and it appears to be a challenge to properly cover frameworks in static taint analysis implementations. With this in mind and an overview of different taint analysis implementations the course is set in deciding the methodology.

III. METHODOLOGY

Taking a brief look at the core of the problem description, refer to Section I-B, it is stating that this article will study how to integrate static taint analysis in Java EE web applications. Refer to Section II-F briefly stating some proposed methods for detecting information flow vulnerabilities, static taint analysis is explored in this article. Both because this type of analysis embraces the detection of the whole domain of information flow vulnerabilities. And that it may have significantly fewer false warnings in comparison to e.g., analyses depending on code patterns such as the FindBugs static analysis tool. The research approach regarding the problem description is to carry out a case study in two main parts.

The first part is to develop a prototype Java EE web application of an acceptable size so that it is not too small in regards to performing taint analysis on it. This means that the prototype application should preferably have multiple modules interacting with external processes, i.e., at a minimum implementing a database connection. Further the user interaction would naturally be done through a website utilizing specific Java EE technologies.

For this type of article, why is such a development of a prototype application necessary? One could simply argue that using an open source Java EE web application as the artefact for performing taint analysis is equally sufficient. However a clear advantage is that when developing a new application the developer gains an exceptional understanding of all the inner workings of the application. E.g., knowing exactly which technologies are used, how the application should function and also be aware of all system critical commands implemented in the application.

The goal of the last part in the case study is to architect a solution to the taint analysis implementation. Many aspects regarding this implementation would need to be clarified. Based on the experiences with the implementation of taint analysis in the specific prototype application general conclusions regarding the problem description would be drawn.

Section II-G describes different approaches implementing static taint analysis and thus is the basis in choosing the analysis method. The first two implementations described are not freely available for use. However if one of those approaches had been in any way superior to the third alternative, Type-based Taint Analysis, an effort to acquire the implementation might have been worth it. The choice of analysis method is as implied the Type-based Taint Analysis. This choice is convenient in that the analysis platform is available as an open source project.

Type-based Taint Analysis also looks promising due to how web application frameworks are handled. Analysing frameworks are especially relevant in Java EE web applications, e.g., in form of the Java Server Faces (JSF) framework managing the application's front-end. Based on how the article are describing this analysis method it would seem that the implementation is feasible as an integrated step in in a Java EE web application development context, refer to Section II-K3.

IV. Prototype Application Development

In this chapter a description of the prototype application is given. Additionally, an overview of the development process for the prototype application is covered. Security aspects in form of the prototype application's attack surface is also discussed.

A. Existing System

The prototype application is an application that is going to replace a standalone SMS alarm system used at Findus' food plant in Tønsberg, Norway. Currently, this SMS alarm system is used to notify personnel of irregularities affecting the production environment.

Two main applications of alarms are set up. The first application covers fire and gas alarms. Fire alarms are of course mandatory in any industrial building. However, gas alarms are present because the cooling systems are using hazardous coolants. Both alarms are prior notification alarms. This means that when detectors are sensing increased levels of either smoke/heat or gaseous particles respectively, alarms are delivered to the desired people. This could in some situations buy some time for investigating and reacting before the actual alarm is activated triggering a call for the fire department.

The other application of the SMS alarm system is to manually notify personnel, e.g., the supervisor or technical assistance, of incidents regarding the process machines. These types of alarms are mainly triggered by mechanical push buttons located near critical places such as vegetable cutters, conveyor belts and transport pumps.

B. Limitations

The standalone system is limited in how alarms are connected. It does not support any kind of communication buses. This means that every alarm needs to be electrically connected resulting in a strict limitation to the number of alarms possible. This has greatly prevented expansion of the system. The system supports both digital and analogue alarm inputs limited to 20 digital and 8 analogue. Digital alarms are typically connected to either a manual push button or a relay output from e.g., a fire alarm system.

Analogue alarms could be anything providing a measurement such as a temperature sensor or a level indicator. Contrary to a digital alarm triggering an alarm based on a binary signal, an analogue alarm needs a set point indicating when an alarm should trigger. Additionally, information whether the alarm area of the analogue signal should be triggered above or below the set point is also required. All 20 digital alarm inputs are used, however, at the present time no analogue alarms are in use.

Apart from the limited number of digital inputs the main limitation is the connectivity process. Electrically connecting alarm signals are expensive. Both because it is a time consuming task to physically connect an alarm signal to the alarm system and expensive in regards to the cost of cables and the occupation of a relay output.

Another limitation greatly preventing expansion is that the alarm system has its phone book filled up. The alarm system supports a maximum of 8 phone numbers. This means that only 8 individuals has the possibility to receive alarm messages. Further, no way of customizing the format of the alarm message is possible. The alarm text simply shows the alarm input number and a customizable alarm name consisting of maximum 12 characters. Finally, it is worth mentioning that the configuration of the alarm system is a cumbersome process. Two possible approaches are supported. Either through sending SMS command messages or connecting a computer to the system's serial configuration interface.

C. The New Alarm System Architecture

This section covers the initial planning phase for developing the new SMS alarm system ideally countering the limitations of the existing system by choosing an appropriate architecture.

D. Available Resources

In order to develop the SMS alarm system an initial assessment of Findus' existing resources and infrastructure are mapped. This kind of mapping is done to be able to design a system with the ability to utilize the available resources reducing cost and overall complexity. Refer to Section IV-B stating that the main limitation of the original alarm system is the alarm input connectivity.

A look at how information from process machines is accessed reveals that the use of a Supervisory Control and Data Acquisition (SCADA) system is in place. This system monitors and controls the process machines over Ethernet network connectivity. This is possible because the process machines are controlled by Siemens S7 Programmable Logic Controllers (PLCs) equipped with Hilscher netLINK NL 50-MPI adapters. This adapter enables Ethernet connection to the process machines by acting as an Multi-Point Interface (MPI) node on the PLC's MPI network.

Utilizing the same process machine Ethernet communication as the SCADA system would eliminate both the limitations regarding the maximum number of alarm inputs and the expensive connectivity process. When it comes to running the new SMS alarm system there is currently free server capacity within the technical network, where also the SCADA system resides.

E. Sending SMS Alarm Messages

The utilization of existing process machine Ethernet communication and server capacity goes a long way. However, the process of sending the SMS alarm messages needs a solution. Two options are possible. Either using an external SMS messaging service provider or sending SMS messages with the help of a standalone GSM modem. An SMS messaging service provider would be the easy solution simply requiring a subscription and an implementation of the service's SMS message Application Programming Interface (API). The GSM modem approach requires a dedicated SIM card with an active subscription and a complete implementation of the GSM modem communication in the new alarm system application.

Even though less work is needed with an SMS messaging service provider it comes with some disadvantages. It would

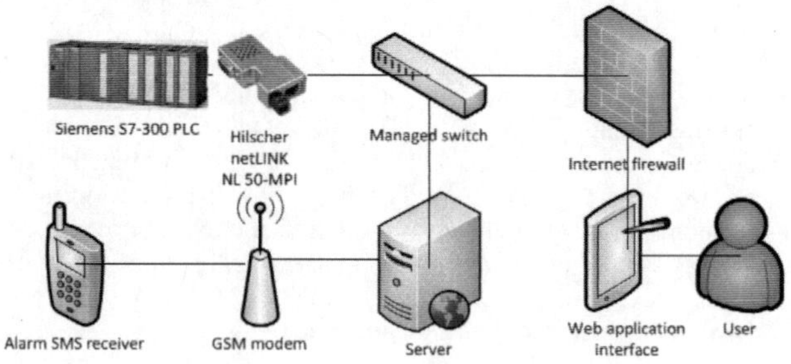

Figure 4. Architectural sketch of the components in the new SMS alarm system

require an internet connection at all times and would also introduce an external dependency. Some risks regarding this dependency is service downtime and delays reducing the quality of the alarm SMS messages. An option in eliminating these risks is to implement a failover routine to a second SMS messaging service provider. This will lead to another disadvantage: increasing the system's complexity. And since GSM modems are available at an inexpensive price, the GSM modem approach is preferable.

F. Architectural Sketch

The initial planning phase leads to an overview of the different components the new SMS alarm system should consist of. See Figure 4 for an architectural sketch of the component composition. Two more concepts are added in addition to the components established in the preceding sections. The first concept is a user and a web application interface that represents that the configuration of the SMS alarm system would be done with a web application implementation. The second concept is the alarm SMS receiver, which typically is a mobile phone exactly like it is done in the original alarm system.

G. Development Technology Choices

Technologies chosen need to be able to meet the architectural design requirements established for the application. The framework chosen for developing the prototype application is Java EE with the Java Server Faces (JSF) user interface framework. By choosing a web application framework it is easy to implement web pages for configuring the prototype application. The goal for this implementation is to eliminate the limitation regarding the cumbersome process of configuring the original alarm system, refer to Section IV-B.

The IDE that will be used is Eclipse and the Java project for the prototype application is managed by Maven build system. An advantage with using Maven build system is that it contains a definition file for defining which libraries that should be included in the Java project. Building the application will automatically download these dependencies from the Maven repository. By using such a system it is straightforward to deploy the application elsewhere, e.g., to a production server.

H. Development of the Prototype Application

Although a fully-fledged SDLC methodology was not followed given the in this project, several concepts were integrated in the SDLC in order to ensure deliverance of an acceptable end product. Concepts derived from the agile manifesto core value *customer collaboration over contract negotiation* were embraced. Initially, this means that the design choices and functionality of the prototype application were discussed and determined through periodic communication with the industial partner.

Further, enabling development of the prototype application iteratively and incrementally was done by embracing continuous delivery. This means that the functionality was split up and developed in smaller tasks and delivered in predefined iteration cycles of e.g., two weeks. When developing in this way a common approach is to have a test server, called a continuous integration server, for deployment. The test server is a temporary server that is as similar as possible to the production server. For the prototype application this means that access to a PLC and connection to a GSM modem was provided.

The continuous integration tool chosen is Jenkins. This is a tool for use on a continuous integration server and it was installed on the test server. It was configured to automatically deploy the prototype application to Apache Tomcat, which is the Java servlet container used. This works by pushing code to a version control system, such as Git. When Jenkins detects a change in the Git repository, the source code is pulled, built and deployed on the test server.

Additionally, the Jenkins plugin SonarQube was set up to automatically run on every build. This plugin includes various code checking tools in order to improve the code quality by suggesting changes. FindBugs, briefly mentioned in Section II-F, is one of the tools included in SonarQube.

In order to establish the course of how the development of the prototype application was conducted user stories was the main tool used. This is a tool derived form the agile SDLC methodology and is a brief description of a requirement stating the desired feature. In other words splitting up functionality into smaller manageable pieces fitting well in a continuous delivery context. The functionality stated in the user stories originated from collaboration with the customer.

Finally, a concept also used is sprints. Each sprint is a defined period of time in order to complete a set of user stories. The time frame of each sprint was defined to two weeks. The application was developed in six sprints and had a total of ten user stories defined. A brief description of the main modules are provided in the following sections.

The prototype application can roughly be divided into the following main modules.

- Communication with PLCs
- Sending triggered alarm SMS messages
- GUI for configuration of parameters

I. Communication with PLCs

The application communicates with the configured PLCs through Ethernet in the same way the SCADA system does. All PLC parameters that are configured for acquiring are fetched and stored in a database residing on the same server as the prototype application is running. The parameter update interval is customizable and it is set to one second as the default setting. It is worth noting that the PLC communication is conducted unencrypted on a dedicated VLAN on the technical network. Encrypted communication is not supported by the MPI to Ethernet adapters currently in use.

J. Sending Triggered Alarm SMS Messages

This module is twofold in that first a determination if an alarm is triggered are carried out and secondly if an alarm triggers an alarm SMS message are sent. There are different settings for each configured alarm defining the respective alarm rule. Based on a comparison of the last and current parameter value in light of the current alarm rule a decision about whether or not the alarm triggered is made. On triggering of an alarm, an SMS message is sent to the assigned phone numbers for that alarm in particular. This is done using the GSM modem connected serially to the server.

K. Interface for Configuration of Parameters

The application's parameters are customizable using web pages as the interface and the database as parameter storage. The main functionality in the interface is the possibility to define which PLC variables to retrieve, phone numbers to be used, definition of alarm triggers based on PLC variables available and mapping of the defined phone numbers to the specified alarm triggers. Further, application specific parameters is also included, such as alarm trigger check interval, PLC variable update interval and default alarm message.

The GUI also includes monitoring of the PLC variables fetched including a time stamp, logging of sent alarm messages and the health status of the GSM modem in form of the GSM signal quality. An utility for sending custom SMS messages is also added to the interface. This is done in order to have a convenient way of notifying users of special events, e.g., system downtime.

Lastly, it is worth mentioning that the GUI is implemented with a basic built in login routine provided by the application server, Apache Tomcat. All interactions with the configuration web pages is also strictly enforced to always use encrypted transport protocols, namely Secure Socets Layer (SSL).

L. Prototype Application's Attack Surface

Analysing potential areas in the prototype application that has a possibility of introducing vulnerabilities is advantageous in that an awareness in those areas are raised. Preferably this awareness could lead to implementing measures countering potential vulnerabilities. A method in doing this is to conduct a mapping of the attack surface, refer to Section II-B.

In order to map the prototype application's attack surface knowledge of what features the application has implemented is required. For the prototype application a look at all the system critical operations is the first step. These operations could be seen as the attack target in the application and are covered in the following list.

- PLC communication to acquire process machine data
- GSM modem for sending alarm SMS messages
- Database connection for storing process machine data, sent SMS messages and all configuration parameters on the configuration web pages

The listed attack targets can ultimately be exploited in different ways. Both the PLC communication and the database connection can pose vulnerable to information leakage and data manipulation, while the GSM modem could be hijacked. The next step is to analyse the different entry points that contributes to the total attack surface. It is the entry points that enables a potential attacker to reach the critical operations. The following list contains possible entry points.

- All configuration web pages
- The server hosting the prototype application and the database
- VLAN where PLC communication is conducted

In the following subsections aspects around each mapped entry point are discussed. This includes thoughts about how the application is vulnerable and suggested countermeasures.

M. Configuration Web Pages

The prototype application is developed for the possibility of being accessed through the internet. Being accessible through the internet contributes to this entry point being highly exposed. With this consideration in mind security measures such as a login system and the use of encrypted transport protocols are implemented in the application.

The login system used is basic authentication, a login implementation included in Apache Tomcat. For this prototype application login credentials are simply statically added to the configuration file *tomcat-users.xml*. Accessing any of the configuration web pages renders a pop-up dialogue requiring a valid user name and password combination.

Possible weaknesses that can lead to a vulnerable system for this login implementation is brute force attacks, eavesdropping the login credentials and social engineering. In order to counter brute force attacks Apache Tomcat has an option to restrict access after a number of unsuccessful login attempts. The default settings when implementing this feature is that the user is locked for 300 seconds after 5 unsuccessful login attempts. As for eavesdropping the login credentials this can be possible if a third party has access to the communication data. Countering this is done by restricting the communication for the prototype application to always use an encrypted transport protocol.

Having taken these technical considerations a last threat cannot easily be avoided, namely social engineering. The number of possible entry points increase proportionally with the amount of users having access to the system. That being said, as this topic is slightly out of scope of this article, apart from being aware that this adds to the attack surface no consideration on this point is taken.

N. Application and Database Server

The prototype application and its database server is hosted locally on a server owned and maintained by the company itself. The entry points regarding this server is by gaining access to the server locally and through one of the VLANs on the local network that it uses. With self-maintained servers patching routines for fixing new vulnerabilities is important in order to make these entry points the least possible accessible.

A special threat regarding the prototype application that is worth mentioning is the GSM modem. With access to the server comes direct access to the GSM modem enabling an attacker to abuse any features possible by the GSM modem.

O. PLC Communication

The PLC communication could be accessed either through the server or the dedicated PLC communication Virtual Local Area Network (VLAN). The threat in conjunction with these entry points is the acquisition of information about the company's processes through the PLC communication. Further, if the attacker has the possibility to transmit custom network packets on the PLC communication VLAN the attacker would also have the ability to write data to the PLCs. This means essentially to have full control of the process machines in the company.

Since the communication with the PLCs are currently conducted unencrypted and with no means of authentication countermeasures for this entry point are limited to securing the PLC communication VLAN in the best possible way.

V. Analysis and Assessment

A. Role of the Prototype Application

The prototype application would ideally be developed in iterations with an integrated taint analysis implementation as a part of the static analysis step. However, the application was fully developed before the taint analysis implementation was set up. This means that the taint analysis is carried out after all development iterations are finished.

As a result the experiences that would have been acquired conducting taint analysis in the developing phase are absent. Since the prototype application is limited in size with a moderate number of iterations conducting taint analysis at the end of the development are considered adequate in order to draw a conclusion. The bigger the application the more value of frequent analysis. This is because the issues found earlier in a big application environment would contribute knowledge to prevent making the same mistakes over and over as the application progress. Thus saving developer resources.

B. Type-based Taint Analysis Implementation

Refer to Section III stating that the type-based taint analysis approach is used in this article. This implementation is called SFlow, refer to Section II-J for a brief overview of the concepts. SFlow is made open source using the Apache License (version 2.0), available at *github.com/proganalysis/type-inference*. It is built as a compiler plugin to *The Checker Framework*. This framework enhances Java's type system in order to detect a broader domain of errors at compile time. In addition to command-line usage The Checker Framework is also available as a plugin supporting various build systems and IDEs. Two popular IDEs worth mentioning in this regard are IntelliJ and Eclipse [11].

```
package javax.servlet;
import checkers.inference.sflow.quals.*;

public interface ServletRequest {
    /*@Tainted*/ String getParameter(String arg0);
    ...
}
```

Figure 5. Annotation example identifying a method for getting a Java servlet parameter as source

In a typical development environment the use of a continuous integration tool is common practise. This tool includes automated building of the application and running any desired plugins, e.g., static source code analyses. An example for such a tool for Java web applications is Jenkins. Integrating taint analysis in the continuous integration tool and/or the developer IDE is crucial for successfully conducting taint analysis without needless overhead. In this regard SFlow looks promising.

However, in order to enable analysis with SFlow an integration with build systems and IDEs is not sufficient alone. SFlow also requires some preparations in identifying which fields and methods are considered sources and sinks to actually detect information flow errors. The Checker Framework is designed to use annotations in order to identify fields and methods in Java classes of interest.

C. Annotating Sources and Sinks with SFlow

Two approaches in annotating Java classes exists, a manual and an automatic approach. The manual approach is that the developer adds an annotation on each field or method of interest. This is a cumbersome and time consuming task with too much overhead for the developer. In addition such task is prone to errors. The automatic approach is to compile an annotated Java Development Kit (JDK), which is added to the Java classpath of the SFlow analysis.

This JDK includes libraries the project uses with sources and sinks annotated. This way the annotation process becomes a one time event and any involvement of the developers is avoided. However, all new libraries implemented that introduces new methods for entry points (sources) or executing system critical commands (sinks) would need to be annotated and included in the annotated JDK in order to detect errors for their implementations. At present time SFlow comes with support for some of the Java EE classes containing sources and sinks such as the *getParameter* method in the *javax.servlet.ServletRequest* class and the *executeQuery* method in the *java.sql.Statement* class, see Figure 1 as an usage example [11].

Annotating sources and sinks is done respectively with the annotations */*@Tainted*/* and */*@Safe*/*. Notice that for a standard Java compiler this additions to the code is unnoticed since they are in fact commented out. The idea is that any annotations specific to The Checker Framework would not brake a standard Java compilation. See Figure 5 and 6 for examples of how annotations are defined for sources and sinks respectively.

Additionally, the SFlow annotated JDK comes with annotations for the Apache Struts Framework and the Spring Framework. To be able to analyse the prototype application

```
package java.sql;
import checkers.inference.sflow.quals.*;

public interface Statement extends Wrapper {
    ResultSet executeQuery(/*@Safe*/ String arg0) throws SQLException;
    ...
}
```

Figure 6. Annotation example identifying a method for executing an SQL query as sink

fully, libraries and relevant Java EE classes missing from the annotated JDK needs to be included. In order to map which annotations are missing a look at the application's attack surface is a good indication, refer to Section IV-L. From this knowledge the annotated JDK needs to include the methods regarding PLC communication, GSM modem communication and the configuration web pages.

Regarding the PLC communication standard Java classes are used for sending and receiving data on a socket, namely the *write* method in the *java.io.DataOutputStream* class and the *read* method in the *java.io.BufferedInputStream* class. SFlow includes annotations on methods for file read and write, but does not annotate read and write methods on a socket. Although the potential for vulnerabilities maybe lower working with a socket, the fact that this opens for untrusted data that can be forged by an attacker cannot be fully avoided. Also depending on the application, external system critical commands could be evident when writing to a socket.

As for the GSM modem communication the Java Simple Serial Connector (jSSC) library is used to communicate serially with it. Data fetched could be malicious and would need to be annotated as a source and commands would need to be regarded as system critical and annotated as sinks. Similar to working with a socket the need for annotation is considered a task of lower priority.

The configuration web pages includes interactions with users and are the most obvious place to make sure of having proper annotations making this the highest priority to implement. Therefore, an attempt to annotate the Java Expression Language (EL) implementation were made. Expression Language enables the JSF user interface to interact with Java Beans. In other words it acts as a communication bridge between the front-end and the back-end for fetching user input and presenting data to the user.

An attempt to annotate the *setValue* method in the *BeanELResolver* class was made. This method takes three parameters in addition to the EL context parameter; *base*, *property* and *val*. Base is the Java Bean, property is the name of the variable to manipulate in the Java Bean and val is the user supplied data to be assigned to that variable. See Figure 7 for the annotation. Having annotated this method and compiled it into the annotated JDK, a crafted example that would be found as a vulnerability by the analysis was made in order to check if the annotation was working correctly. The analysis however did not report any vulnerabilities. Further research needs to be done in finding out how to properly annotate the JSF user interface interaction with Java Beans.

In order to prepare an application for type-based taint analysis, annotations needs to be included and compiled in the annotated JDK based on what technologies and libraries are

```
package javax.el;
import checkers.inference.sflow.quals.Tainted;

public class BeanELResolver extends ELResolver {
    public void setValue(ELContext context, Object base, Object property,
                                /*@Tainted*/ Object val) throws ... {
        throw new RuntimeException("skeleton method");
    }
    ...
}
```

Figure 7. An attempt to annotate the *setValue* method in the *BeanELResolver* class for defining user input as source from the configuration web pages

```
package databeans;

import java.io.Serializable;
import javax.faces.bean.ManagedBean;
import javax.faces.bean.SessionScoped;
import javax.validation.constraints.Size;
import org.hibernate.validator.constraints.NotEmpty;

@ManagedBean
@SessionScoped
public class DatastoreBean implements Serializable {

    private static final long serialVersionUID = 1L;

    @NotEmpty(message = "Please write a name...")
    @Size(max=255, message = "Please write a name of max 255 characters...")
    private /*@checkers.inference.sflow.quals.Tainted*/ String name;
    ...
}
```

Figure 8. Manually annotated variable in the Java Bean used to store which PLC data variables that should be fetched by the prototype application

implemented in the application. At the present time the SFlow annotated JDK supports a limited variety of technologies and libraries. Thus, in general requiring relatively much annotation work depending on the size of the application.

D. Analysis Results

Since a successful annotation for the JSF user interface interaction with Java Beans is yet to be done analysis results for the prototype application is non-existing. However as a simulated test the variables in the Java Beans that are user manipulatable were manually annotated. See Figure 8 for an example of a manually annotated variable in the Java Bean that is used to store which PLC data variables that should be fetched. The user provided variables are stored in the database.

The taint analysis detected no errors due to how the prototype application is managing SQL queries. Namely with SQL query parametrization. This means that an SQL query is set up with a predefined structure taking exactly the defined data types as parameters, see Figure 9. This predefined structure makes it impossible to split a query in multiple queries or add more parameters than intended in the query. Thus, making this approach a good practise countering SQL injection and the analysis rightfully did not detect this as an information flow vulnerability.

In order to detect a vulnerability with the taint analysis implementation the SQL query was temporary changed to the standard *executeQuery* method displayed in Figure 1. SFlow then reported the type error shown in Figure 10. The first code reference in the type error text refers to line 385 in *Database.java*. This is where the string variable used in the SQL query, named *sql*, is first initialised. Next, a reference to line 387 in *Database.java* is made. This refers to where the safe method is used with the tainted variable, which in this case is *statement.executeQuery(sql)*. Finally, the type error text reports which class the safe method originates from. In this case it is the *java.sql.Statement* class.

```
public boolean addEntryInDatastore(String name, int plcId, int datablockNumber,
                                   int startAddress, int dataType) {
    if (connectDB()) {
        try {
            preparedStatement = connection.prepareStatement("INSERT INTO sms_alarm_system.variables
                (name, plc_id, datablockNumber, startAddress, dataType) VALUES (?, ?, ?, ?, ?)");
            preparedStatement.setString(1, name);
            preparedStatement.setInt(2, plcId);
            preparedStatement.setInt(3, datablockNumber);
            preparedStatement.setInt(4, startAddress);
            preparedStatement.setInt(5, dataType);
            preparedStatement.executeUpdate();
        } catch (Exception e) {
            LOGGER.log(Level.SEVERE, e.toString(), e);
            close();
            return false;
        } finally {
            close();
        }
    } else {
        return false;
    }
    return true;
}
```

Figure 9. SQL query with parametrization used in the prototype application to store connection information of a PLC data variable that should be fetched in the prototype application

```
SUB-7466: Database.java:385(23543):VAR_sql{@Tainted} <:
(23573:#CONSTANT#Database.java:387:(callsite)statement.executeQuery(sql)
{@Poly @Safe @Tainted} =m=> zLIB:java.sql.Statement:0(23572):PAR_arg0{@Safe})
```

Figure 10. SFlow type error showing that there is an information flow vulnerability in line 387 in *Database.java* in the *executeQuery* method

The type error identifies the tainted variable and the code location of it first being initialised as well as the location of the safe method using the tainted variable. This information is sufficient for a developer in order to understand where to start the work of countering the type error. For the SQL query example the obvious countermeasure is to switch to the SQL query parametrization approach. However, if SQL query parametrization is not a possibility, or for other kinds of type errors, a look at where the tainted variable first originated from may be necessary. In this case the developer would need to research the path of the tainted variable. This could take a lot of valuable time if the application is big. It would have been advantageous if the type error text also stated the code location in where the tainted variable originated.

E. Integrating Taint Analysis in the SDLC

Considering modern development practises are team based, and in fact multi-team based on big projects, it is important to include this observation in assessing if static taint analysis can efficiently integrate in the SDLC. An agile development methodology including an iterative and incremental workflow leads to developing a piece of software in numerous modules. Being able to properly test both a single module and a set of modules for detecting information flow vulnerabilities is preferable.

According to *Type-based Taint Analysis for Java Web Applications* technical report the taint analysis implementation is modular meaning that a whole program is not necessary for analysis. This is promising considering the modern development practice described in the previous paragraph. Additionally, the taint analysis implementation should be included in the development phase along with other testing activities, refer to Section II-A describing the different phases in the SDLC [11].

In addition to the development phase, the testing phase could include static taint analysis. However, the reason to avoid integration within the testing phase is that anything added to that phase adds unnecessary overhead. Even if overhead running the analysis is eliminated by making it fully automated, a system for countering the output in form of requested fixes for the next development phase iteration needs some resources. Also, a known concept is that the earlier vulnerabilities are found in the SDLC the cheaper it is to get them fixed. The aim is therefore to craft a solution to integrate static taint analysis into the development phase.

Some methods for detecting and/or preventing information flow vulnerabilities are listed in Section II-F. Most of the methods focus exclusively on either SQL injection or cross-site scripting rendering detection of other information flow attacks uncovered. Although FindBugs is an example of a static analysis covering most, if not all, the information flow vulnerabilities its detecting algorithm is prone to have a high percentage of false positives. The choice of type-based taint analysis in the form of SFlow is done because it could detect a high number of vulnerabilities and also have a low number of false positives. Refer to Section II-J showing that a comparison of SFlow and two commercial security testing tools shows that SFlow detects a significantly higher number of vulnerabilities.

Refer to the preceding sections stating that a working implementation of SFlow is set up. Although the attempt to add the Java EE JSF framework to the SFlow annotated JDK was not successful, results exists by doing a manual annotation. A challenge with this implementation is to properly annotate external libraries, e.g., frameworks, in order to enable a working analysis without developer intervention. Manual annotations is not an option because in addition to creating extra work for the developer it is prone to errors. For SFlow to be a successful security analysis tool the annotation process needs to improve.

One approach in changing the annotation process is to take a concept from the paper *F4F: Taint Analysis of Framework-based Web Application*, refer to Section II-K4. This paper describes a framework as a solution for adding web application frameworks to a taint analysis implementation. In a similar way a framework for adding annotations to the SFlow annotated JDK could be developed easing the work of figuring out how to conduct the process of annotation. This framework could also include verification routines for testing that the annotations are working correctly [16].

Another change SFlow must undergo is the way the analysis is conducted. In its current form SFlow exists as a manual command-line tool. For this tool to exist in the development phase without unnecessary overhead an automatic integration of the analysis is required. Therefore, integrating SFlow as a plugin in an IDE by utilizing this support by The Checker Framework could be a good solution. This would make the taint analysis convenient and seamless for the developer enabling analysis whenever the developer builds the application and/or desires to run it. However, deciding if the integration is not creating too much overhead for the developer boils down to the running time of the taint analysis implementation.

Results from the *Type-based Taint Analysis for Java Web Applications* technical report states that analysing 13 relatively large application resulted in running times of less than four minutes for all applications except one. The analysis ran on a server with Intel Xeon X3460 2.8GHz CPU and 8GB RAM. As for the smaller prototype application the running time is about 30 seconds on a laptop with Intel Core i5-3210M 2.5GHz CPU and 6GB RAM [11].

Even though the running time of the taint analysis is done within minutes and may not introduce a significant overhead for the developer running the analysis in the background, implementation in a different way could be advantageous. This solution is to incorporate taint analysis in a continuous integration tool, e.g., Jenkins, by integrating SFlow in the build system it uses, e.g., Maven. By doing this, the taint analysis will automatically run on every build. The errors will then show up as compiler errors and warnings in the continuous integration tool for the developers to address.

SFlow needs to undergo at least two significant changes in order to become a powerful taint analysis security tool for integration in the development phase in the SDLC. First, the annotation process for adding web application frameworks and external libraries must become more user-friendly in order to be practical. As suggested, a solution to this would be to develop a framework for easing the annotation process. And secondly, the analysis should be integrated either in the developer's IDE, or preferably within the build system of the continuous integration tool.

VI. Conclusion

Information flow vulnerabilities can occur when applications handle untrusted data. SQL injection and cross-site scripting are the most common information flow vulnerabilities. There are numerous methods presented in countering these vulnerabilities. One method, static taint analysis, looks promising in that it has the ability to cover detection of all kinds of information flow vulnerabilities. Out of three static taint analysis implementations, Type-based taint analysis was chosen as the preferred implementation. This approach looked promising in the way web application frameworks are handled. The implementation is also freely available as an open-source project. A proposed solution in integrating this taint analysis approach in an iterative and incremental development process was presented.

The proposed solution used the developed prototype application as a manageable sized concept application for implementing taint analysis. Annotations of sources and sinks are needed to detect information flow vulnerabilities. Some libraries are already annotated in the taint analysis implementation, referred to as the annotated JDK. To properly analyse an application all libraries containing sources and sinks in a developed application needs to be included in the annotated JDK.

The development of the prototype application gave a good technical understanding of the inner workings of the application. This was advantageous in order to identify what needed to be annotated. The approach of mapping the attack surface of the prototype application turned out to be an effective way to identify the libraries containing sources and sinks.

Three main areas was identified: PLC communication, GSM modem communication and the configuration web pages. The configuration web pages was considered the highest priority and an attempt to annotate the *BeanELResolver* class was made. This class is used for communication between the JSF user interface and the Java beans. However, the annotation attempt was unsuccessful and more research is required in how to get the annotation working properly.

In order to obtain taint analysis results a Java bean in the prototype application was manually annotated. Changing the SQL query method from the safer parametrized method to the unsafe dynamic method was necessary in order to detect a type error with the taint analysis. The type error contains information about the code location of the tainted variable's initialization, the code location of the sink this variable is used in and from what class the sink method originates. It would also have been preferable if the type error contained information of the code location of the source variable. This could save valuable time for the developer investigating the type error.

Preparing the taint analysis implementation for analysis is mostly about making sure the libraries that are used are included in the annotated JDK and are also working properly. The experiences with annotation indicates that this is not a straight forward process and could need much resources in order to get it right. A framework for easing the process of annotation including verification that the annotation works correctly is proposed as a solution to this challenge.

Multiple approaches in conducting the taint analysis are possible. Running the taint analysis manually in command line, integrating it in the developer's IDE and integrating it in the continuous integration tool are all possibilities. The latter suggestion is proposed as the most effective solution; implementing taint analysis in the continuous integration tool's build system. This is considered an effective approach because an analysis could take several minutes to complete depending on application size. Also, processes done automatically and by an external instance will not be a distraction for the developer. When to counter any detected type errors is then up to when the developer monitors the notifications given in the continuous integration tool.

Considering the prototype application was finished without having a proper taint analysis implementation ready for testing, this proposition would need more research in order to draw a finite conclusion in how this actually will work in an iterative and incremental development process.

VII. Further Work

In order to support Java EE web applications using JSF user interface, the next step in the taint analysis implementation is to get the annotation of the *BeanELResolver* class to work. Either this is just an annotation task or it may reveal other fundamental challenges, e.g., how the taint analysis processes the Java beans variables in conjunction with the *BeanELResolver* class.

Further work also includes more research in the area of how it is best to integrate taint analysis in a development process. The proposed solution of integrating the analysis in a continuous integration tool's build system is worth exploring. An actual proof-of-concept implementation could be using Jenkins continuous integration tool with the Maven build system.

The nature of the cumbersome annotation work presently leads to the taint analysis implementation being for the enthusiast only. A course worth researching, as suggested, is to develop a framework for easing the process of annotating. A suggestion for even further work is to make the taint analysis implementation mainstream. An extension of the taint analysis implementation is possible because it is released as an open-source application. Developers could then contribute to the taint analysis implementation by providing working annotations of frameworks and libraries.

Such a project would contribute a working out-of-the box taint analysis tool that supports a large number of popular frameworks and external libraries for others to easily include in their development processes reducing the number of implemented information flow vulnerabilities.

REFERENCES

[1] T. Lie and P. Ellingsen, "Integrating static taint analysis in an iterative software development life cycle," in Proceedings of SOFTENG 2017, The Third International Conference on Advances and Trends in Software Engineering. International Academy, Research and Industry Association (IARIA), 2017.

[2] OWASP Foundation, "OWASP top 10 - 2013: The ten most critical web application security risks," 2013, Accessed: 2017-04-13. [Online]. Available: https://www.owasp.org/images/f/f8/OWASP_Top_10_-_2013.pdf

[3] M. S. Merkow and L. Raghavan, Secure and Resilient Software Development. CRC Press, 2010.

[4] V. B. Livshits and M. S. Lam, "Finding security vulnerabilities in java applications with static analysis." in Usenix Proceedings of the 14th Conference on USENIX Security Symposium, vol. 2013, 2005, pp. 271–286.

[5] A. K. Baranwal, "Approaches to detect sql injection and xss in web applications," Term Survey paper-EECE 571b, University of British Columbia, 2012.

[6] Y. Shin, L. Williams, and T. Xie, "Sqlunitgen: Test case generation for sql injection detection," North Carolina State University, Raleigh Technical report, NCSU CSC TR, vol. 21, 2006, p. 2006.

[7] A. Roichman and E. Gudes, "Fine-grained access control to web databases," in Proceedings of the 12th ACM symposium on Access control models and technologies. ACM, 2007, pp. 31–40.

[8] Z. Su and G. Wassermann, "The essence of command injection attacks in web applications," in ACM SIGPLAN Notices, vol. 41, no. 1. ACM, 2006, pp. 372–382.

[9] T. Jim, N. Swamy, and M. Hicks, "Defeating script injection attacks with browser-enforced embedded policies," in Proceedings of the 16th international conference on World Wide Web. ACM, 2007, pp. 601–610.

[10] The FindBugs Project, "Findbugs," 2015, Accessed: 2017-04-13. [Online]. Available: http://findbugs.sourceforge.net/

[11] W. Huang, Y. Dong, and A. Milanova, "Type-based taint analysis for java web applications," in International Conference on Fundamental Approaches to Software Engineering. Springer, 2014, pp. 140–154.

[12] E. J. Schwartz, T. Avgerinos, and D. Brumley, "All you ever wanted to know about dynamic taint analysis and forward symbolic execution (but might have been afraid to ask)," in 2010 IEEE Symposium on Security and Privacy. IEEE, 2010, pp. 317–331.

[13] H. Yin and D. Song, "Whole-system fine-grained taint analysis for automatic malware detection and analysis," 2007, Accessed: 2017-04-13. [Online]. Available: http://bitblaze.cs.berkeley.edu/papers/malware-detect.pdf

[14] O. Tripp, M. Pistoia, S. J. Fink, M. Sridharan, and O. Weisman, "Taj: effective taint analysis of web applications," in ACM Sigplan Notices, vol. 44, no. 6. ACM, 2009, pp. 87–97.

[15] M. Sridharan, S. J. Fink, and R. Bodik, "Thin slicing," ACM SIGPLAN Notices, vol. 42, no. 6, 2007, pp. 112–122.

[16] M. Sridharan, S. Artzi, M. Pistoia, S. Guarnieri, O. Tripp, and R. Berg, "F4F: taint analysis of framework-based web applications," ACM SIGPLAN Notices, vol. 46, no. 10, 2011, pp. 1053–1068.

Compositing Ground Penetrating Radar Scans of Differing Frequencies for Better Depth Perception

Roger Tilley, Hamid R. Sadjadpour, Farid Dowla
Department of Electrical Engineering
University of California, Santa Cruz
Santa Cruz, CA. 95064
Email: {rtvax, hamid, dowla} @soe.ucsc.edu

Abstract— **Methods developed to reduce interference in a noisy environment, be it radar target responses or effective communications in the presence of noise for mobile phone users, are vital in delivering a clear usable signal. The methods used to render a cleaner signal can also be used to combine signals of various frequencies. Ground Penetrating Radar (GPR) scans over the same area are no exception. This paper explores using an optimization problem solver, the Expectation Maximization (EM) Algorithm, to define the weights to use to combine multiple GPR scans at different frequencies over the same target area. This approach exploits the Gaussian Mixture Model (GMM) feature of the EM algorithm to produce a cleaner image at depth. Our method demonstrates a measured improvement toward producing a cleaner image.**

Keywords-Ground Penetrating Radar; Expectation Maximization; Gaussian Mixture Model; Maximum Likelihood parameter estimation; Finite Difference Time Domain Method, GprMax.

I. INTRODUCTION

Ground Penetrating Radar (GPR) scans are used to illuminate objects in various terrain types at different depths. The frequency scan that best illuminates an object is different at each depth. Higher frequency scans image objects closer to the surface in great detail while lower frequencies image objects deeper with less fidelity. Assuming GPR radar scans at different frequencies over the same terrain can be treated like sub-components of a square wave, where the summation of sub-components determines a crisp square wave; then, adding the scans together should form an improved image of the terrain being scanned with higher resolution to a lower depth [1]; a byproduct of the summation. Just simply adding each scan together, as demonstrated in this paper, has been shown not to be sufficient for the GPR case but does suffice for square wave, triangle wave, and sawtooth wave cases. For GPR scans, a weighted version of each scan presents the best solution to this problem [2]. Employing.an optimization problem solver to determine the weight applied to each scan is the first use of this method to develop an optimal weighted combination of GPR frequency scans. In the literature, other methods have been proposed to solve this problem with varying success; all with a very similar approach to each other. Methods by Dougherty et al. [3], Booth et al. [4], and Bancroft [5] all discussed ways to weight each signal used to combine individual frequency traces of GPR scans. Absent from these works are optimization problem solvers such as the Expectation Maximization (EM) Algorithm [6]. We have chosen to investigate using the data mixture feature of the EM Algorithm to develop optimal weights.

In this paper, we describe the EM algorithm and its data mixture feature, as it relates to GPR scans of different frequencies, and compare the results with the methods of Dougherty et al. [3], Booth et al. [4], and Bancroft [5]. This paper is organized as follows. In Section II, we discuss work related to the multi-frequency GPR mixture process. In Section III, the EM Algorithm data mixture process is described. In Section IV, the Maximum-Likelihood (ML) Estimation process and its relationship to the EM Algorithm data mixture process [6][7] is described. In Section V, we present an EM Algorithm Test Case. Section VI, briefly, describes the methods of Dougherty et al. [3]. in developing signal weights. Section VII, the methods examined by Booth et al. [4] are discussed. In Section VIII, the methods proposed by Bancroft [5] are discussed. In Section IX, we demonstrate that computer modeling can be used to substitute for real data. In Section X, we present results of simulated GPR scan examples using the software GprMax [8], comparing EM Algorithm data mixture method with methods of Dougherty et al. [3], Booth et al. [4], and Bancroft [5]. In Section XI, we draw some conclusions and discuss possible future work.

II. RELATED WORK

A search of the relevant literature uncovered only a few publications on compositing of GPR signals. The earliest works found discussed GPR time-slice analysis, GPR overlay analysis and GPR isosurface rendering, all similar in approach; mostly by archaeologists. The general approach was to illuminate the strongest reflections at a specified time or depth with a color or shading. Assemble the information by layers of depth or time and display the completed result. [9].

Dougherty et al. [3] was the earliest work found, which attempted to combine GPR signal traces for site characterization and bandwidth enhancement. Their research involved real data taken from a former lumber mill waste site near Boise, Idaho. Part of the focus was on developing a method to simulate the direct arrival pulse to ultimately subtract from the traces. An additional paper focus was on enhancing the GPR response by summing the traces of differing frequencies. The latter part of the paper, focused on establishing proof of bandwidth enhancement through summation. Some success was noted but, equally weighting and summing the traces only marginally enhanced the results. Bandwidth enhancement was confirmed after trace summation using correlation.

The results of Dougherty et al. [3] were re-affirmed in two publications both authored by Booth et al. [2][4]. They successfully repeated the enhancement of the spectral bandwidth by compositing; adding to the compositing method, shifts to align trace direct arrival peaks and an adjustment to trace weights before summing. The scan weights were adjusted to enhance the magnitude of the higher frequency scans while de-emphasizing the magnitude of lower frequency scans. Booth et al. [2] used data sets from glacial deposits near Guelph, Ontario, Canada for the first publication. The second publication [4], focused on attempting to find the best method to combine GPR frequency scans. GPR data sets from the Waterloo Moraine in Ontario, Canada were analyzed. Several methods to combine multiple frequencies were documented. Weighting factors were developed from trace averaged amplitude spectra, as well as time invariant weighting factors output from a least-squares analysis, were evaluated. The time invariant weight methods developed, attempted to match the compositing results to an idealized amplitude spectrum. Improvements over Dougherty et al. [3]. were realized.

Bancroft [5] continued the work by studying previous compositing methods by Dougherty et al. [3]. and Booth et al. [4]. Bancroft [5] introduced additional methods to compute weights for use in compositing GPR frequencies. One introduced method Bancroft [5] named the double ramp summation method, where one ramp suppresses a frequency's energy over time while a second ramp introduces an adjacent frequency's energy over time. The ramp length was arbitrarily defined but, based on the wavelength of the GPR frequency of interest. The start time for each ramp was a calculated value based on the GPR frequency of interest. Bancroft's [5] other method was called Amplitude Envelope Equalization. The weights used in this ramp summation technique were developed as a ratio of the average envelope of GPR frequencies. Improvements over Booth et al. [4] were not dramatic for the cases presented.

The "state of the art" or related work to date has focused on mathematically defining the weights for each frequency by equal weighting, by the value needed to equalize the spectra of GPR frequencies, through ramp summation, or by a least-squares process to match an idealized amplitude spectrum. Optimization problem solving methods have yet to be explored. Our previous work [1] addresses the problem as a clustering mixture model problem, well suited for EM methods.

III. Expectation Maximization Algorithm

The EM Algorithm is used to solve many types of problems. One type is to group like items contained in complex mixtures; another type is to solve incomplete data problems by performing Maximum Likelihood (ML) parameter estimation. A third type is to determine the membership weights of data points in a cluster within a finite Gaussian Mixture Model (GMM) [10][11]. This third feature is what will be exploited to combine multiple GPR frequency scans into a composite wave. Other mathematical distributions can represent the data set created by GPR scans, but we used a Gaussian distribution because it is often used when the distribution of the real-valued random variables is unknown.

We can define a finite mixture model f(x;θ) of K components as mixtures of a Gaussian function as:

$$f(\underline{x};\theta) = \sum_{k=1}^{K} \alpha_k p_k(\underline{x}|\,\theta_k), \qquad (1)$$

Where:

- $p_k(\underline{x}|\theta_k)$ are K mixture components with a distribution defined over $p(\underline{x}|\theta_k)$ with parameters $\theta_k = \{\underline{\mu}_k, C_k\}$ (mean, covariance)
- $p_k(\underline{x}|\theta_k) =$
$$\frac{1}{(2\pi)^{d/2}|C_k|^{1/2}} e^{-\frac{1}{2}(\underline{x}-\underline{\mu_k})^T C_k^{-1}(\underline{x}-\underline{\mu_k})} \qquad (2)$$
- α_k are K mixture weights, where $\sum_{k=1}^{K} \alpha_k = 1$.
- $\{\underline{x_i}, \dots\dots, \underline{x_n}\}$ Data set for a mixture component in d dimensional space.

There are 2 steps in each iteration of the EM Algorithm, the Expectation step (E-step) and the Maximization step (M-step). The E-Step computes the conditional expectation of the group membership weights ($w_{ik}'s$) for $\underline{x_i}'s$, adding unobservable data given θ_k. The M-Step computes new parameter values $(\alpha_k, \underline{\mu}_k, C_k)$ to maximize the finite mixture model using the membership weights. The E-Step and M-Step are repeated until a stopping criterion is reached (convergence). Convergence is indicated by the log-likelihood of $f(\underline{x};\theta)$ not changing substantially from one iteration to the next.

E-Step –

$$w_{ik} = \frac{p_k(\underline{x_i}|\theta_k) * \alpha_k}{\sum_{m=1}^{K} p_m(\underline{x_i}|\theta_m) * \alpha_m} \qquad (3)$$

for $1 \le k \le K,\ 1 \le i \le N;$

with constraint $\sum_{k=1}^{K} w_{ik} = 1$

M-Step –

$$N_k = \sum_{i=1}^{N} w_{ik} \quad (4)$$

$$\alpha_k^{new} = \frac{N_k}{N}, \text{ for } 1 \leq k \leq K \quad (5)$$

$$\underline{\mu}_k^{new} = \left(\frac{1}{N_k}\right) \sum_{i=1}^{N} w_{ik} * \underline{x}_i \quad (6)$$

for $1 \leq k \leq K$

$$C_k^{new} =$$

$$\left(\frac{1}{N_k}\right) \sum_{i=1}^{N} w_{ik} * \left(\underline{x}_i - \underline{\mu}_k^{new}\right)\left(\underline{x}_i - \underline{\mu}_k^{new}\right)^T \quad (7)$$

Convergence (log likelihood of $f(\underline{x};\theta)$) –

$$\text{Log}\, l(\vartheta) =$$

$$\sum_{i=1}^{N} \log f(\underline{x}_i;\theta) =$$

$$\sum_{i=1}^{N} \left(\log \sum_{k=1}^{K} \alpha_k p_k(\underline{x}_i|\theta_k)\right) \quad (8)$$

These equations that make up the EM Algorithm were implemented in MATLAB. The variables 'k' and 'x' represent the different scanning frequencies and GPR trace scans, respectively. Each trace, at a frequency and transmitter (Tx)/receiver (Rx) position, are analyzed and combined for all frequencies using the EM Algorithm before moving on to the next position. Described below are the EM GMM process steps.

Expectation Maximization Gaussian Mixture Model process:

1. Initialize algorithm parameters; weights (mixture and group membership), mean, covariance, for each trace.
2. Expectation step – estimate parameters.
3. Maximization step – maximize estimated parameters.
4. Check for convergence – log likelihood of mixture model.
5. Repeat steps 2 – 4 until change from iteration to iteration is below or equal a defined value.
6. Combine traces with defined mixture weights.

IV. Maximum Likelihood Estimation Process and the EM Relationship

Maximum Likelihood Estimation (MLE) can provide a good estimate of an unknown parameter, which maximizes the probability of getting the data we observed (likelihood). A simple example is as follows. Given a random sample X_1, X_2, …, X_n, independent and identically distributed (i.i.d.) with a probability density function $f(x_i, \theta)$, where θ is the unknown parameter to be estimated; the joint probability density function (PDF) can be labeled as L(θ).

$$L(\theta) = P(X_1 = x_1, X_2 = x_2, \ldots, X_n = x_n) = f(x_1;\theta) * f(x_2;\theta) \ldots f(x_n;\theta) = \prod_{i=1}^{n} f(x_i;\theta) \quad (9)$$

Assuming the probability density function is Gaussian with known variance σ^2 and unknown mean, μ, then, the likelihood equation becomes the following:

$$L(\mu) = \prod_{i=1}^{n} f(x_i;\mu,\sigma^2) = \sigma^{-n}(2\pi)^{-n/2}\exp\left(-\frac{1}{2\sigma^2}\sum_{i=1}^{n}(x_i-\mu)^2\right) \quad (10)$$

To solve for the mean, μ, we take the partial derivative of the log likelihood equation with respect to (w.r.t.) the mean, μ, and set the result equal to 0 to solve the resultant equation for the variable μ. Taking a second partial derivative of the log likelihood w.r.t. μ and returning a negative value verifies that the parameter μ does indeed represent the maximum value for the likelihood function.

$$\text{Log}\,(L(\mu)) = -n\log(\sigma) - \frac{n}{2}\log(2\pi) - \sum_{i=1}^{n}\frac{(x_i-\mu)^2}{2\sigma} \quad (11)$$

$$\frac{\partial}{\partial\mu}(\log(L(u))) = -2(-1)\sum_{i=1}^{n}\frac{(x_i-\mu)}{2\sigma^2} = 0 \quad (12)$$

$$\text{Solve for } \mu; \qquad \mu = \frac{\sum_{i=1}^{n} x_i}{n} \quad (13)$$

The process can be repeated for the variance should it not be known. The MLE process becomes hard if there are at least two sets of data where only one set is partially observed (hidden) or when estimating mixture parameters is necessary.

A mixture distribution has a PDF of the form $f(x) = \sum_{k=1}^{K}\alpha_k f(x;\theta_k)$, where there are K number of components in the mixture model and for each k, there is a PDF, $f(x;\theta_k)$ as well as a weight α_k and a complete observed data set x. Other assumed constraints are $\sum_k \alpha_k = 1$ and $\alpha_k \geq 0$ for all k. The joint PDF takes on the form with n observed data for each k:

$$L(x|\alpha,\theta_k) = \prod_{i=1}^{n}\sum_{k=1}^{K}\alpha_k f(x_i;\,\theta_k) \quad (14)$$

The log of the likelihood equation yields the following:

$$\text{Log}\left(\left(L(x|\alpha,\theta_k)\right)\right) = \sum_{i=1}^{n} log \sum_{k=1}^{K}\alpha_k f(x_i;\theta_k) \quad (15)$$

Solving this weighted MLE equation using MLE is challenging because of the log of sums and the challenge to determine what value to start with for the weight associated with an individual distribution α_k. There may be many local maxima that are less than the global maximum that are available. Choosing the weight value that arrives at the global maximum for the log likelihood is not likely in short order.

The EM algorithm provides a means to estimate the weights and guarantee convergence of the likelihood equation [6][7] to a non-decreasing local maximum with each completion of all steps of the algorithm. The EM algorithm reduces the MLE optimization problem to a sequence of simpler optimization sub-problems that are each guaranteed to converge.

Another way to describe the MLE process and the EM algorithm relationship is through this example of 2 different coins tossed [12]. Two coins each tossed 10 times with the result of Heads or Tails recorded as well as, which coin produced the recorded values for 5 sets of 10 tosses. All information is known therefore the calculation of the probability of Heads (θ_A) for coin A and the calculation of Heads (θ_B) for coin B are straight forward.

$$\theta_A = \frac{\#of\ heads\ using\ coin\ A}{Total\ \#\ of\ coin\ flips\ for\ coin\ A} \quad (16)$$

$$\theta_B = \frac{\#of\ heads\ using\ coin\ B}{Total\ \#\ of\ coin\ flips\ for\ coin\ B} \quad (17)$$

Restructuring the problem such that the coin that was used, for any of the 5 sets of 10-coin tosses, is unknown. The approach of calculating with hidden data, which coin, involves an iterative scheme where a guess is made to determine, which coin was used for each of the 5 sets; then, calculating the MLE as before; repeating this process until convergence. Many local maxima are found before the global maximum is determined. Each local maximum reached in the interim is not necessarily larger than the previous outcome. Changing the initial guess can change the order of the outcome.

The EM process for this example is implemented such that the probability of start values is calculated using existing data (Expectation Step). The following step is to recalculate the model parameters then, calculate the maxima for that set of parameters using an MLE process (Maximization Step). The EM process is repeated until a global maximum is reached. The EM process creates a simpler optimization sub-problem at each iteration that is guaranteed to converge and has been shown to have an increasing maximum value for each cycle (E-Step, M-Step). A set of equations as shown below represent the EM solution given initial values of θ_A and θ_B.

Expectation Step

$$p(A)_i = \frac{\theta_A{}^{NH}(1-\theta_A)^{NH}}{\theta_A{}^{NH}(1-\theta_A)^{NH} + \theta_B{}^{NH}(1-\theta_B)^{NH}} \quad (18)$$

$$p(B)_i = \frac{\theta_B{}^{NH}(1-\theta_B)^{NH}}{\theta_A{}^{NH}(1-\theta_A)^{NH} + \theta_B{}^{NH}(1-\theta_B)^{NH}} \quad (19)$$

where: NH is the number of heads in set *i* of 5 sets of 10 tossed coins, x_i;
$p(A)_i$ – probability of heads for coin A in set *i*;
$p(B)_i$ – probability of heads for coin B in set *i*

Maximization Step

$$\theta_A = \frac{\sum_{i=1}^{5} p(A)_i}{\sum_{i=1}^{5} p(A)_i + \sum_{i=1}^{5} p(B)_i} \quad (20)$$

$$\theta_B = \frac{\sum_{i=1}^{5} p(B)_i}{\sum_{i=1}^{5} p(A)_i + \sum_{i=1}^{5} p(B)_i} \quad (21)$$

The EM algorithm provides a workable solution to a very hard problem when hidden or incomplete data exists. It incorporates the MLE process only after reducing the model to a form, which is guaranteed to converge. Combining GPR frequency scans have an aspect that the actual weight values for each frequency are unknown or hidden. The way the EM algorithm accomplishes workable solutions to hidden or incomplete data sets, distinguishes it from other optimization problem solvers, thus making it a featured candidate to provide a viable solution for combining multiple GPR frequency scans.

V. EXPECTATION MAXIMIZATION TEST CASE

As an EM GMM test case, we constructed a series of six sine waves (50, 150, 250, 350, 450 and 550 Hz) noted in Figures 1-3, which when weighted properly, sum to the square wave of Figure 4. Figure 5, demonstrates the result determined by the EM GMM as compared to the desired result. The apparent error can be attributed to at least two conditions; to machine round off errors of the computer used and to the group membership weights, w_{ik} and/or mixture weights, α_k each constrained to sum to one. The weights normally sum to greater than one depending on the number of signals added together. Even when the weights for sine wave to square wave construction are scaled to a maximum value of one; they still do not match up to the EM GMM generated weights. Despite this limitation, the mixed success

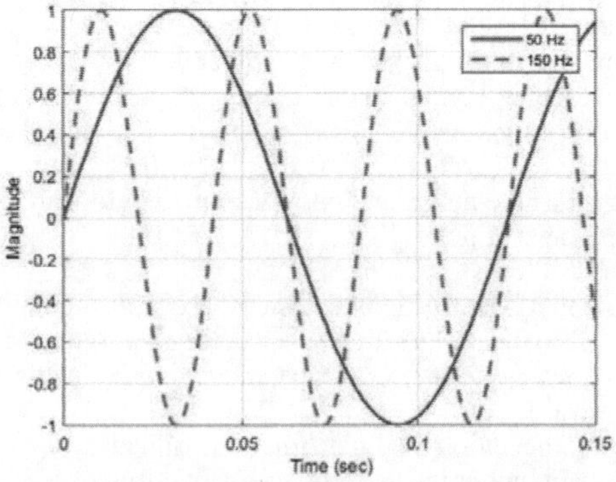

Figure 1. Sine wave frequencies 50-150 Hz.

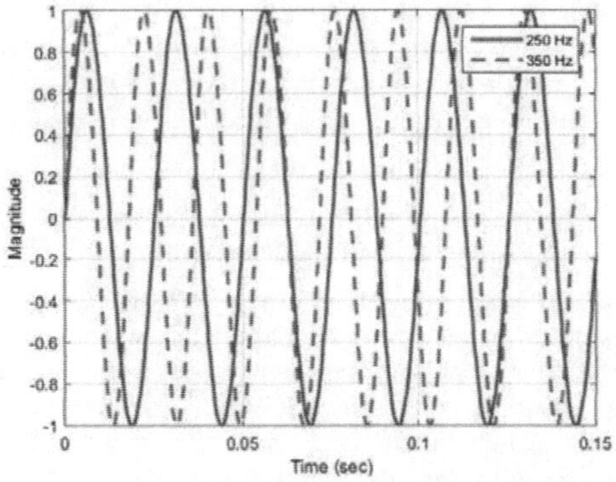

Figure 2. Sine wave frequencies 250, 350Hz.

of adding arbitrary frequencies together bolsters our idea to use the EM GMM method on multiple GPR scans. The GPR frequencies to choose for the analyses are simply the frequencies needed to span the depth and detail the GPR user wishes to achieve. As a reminder, low frequencies image deep with low resolution where as high frequencies image with great detail in a shallow area.

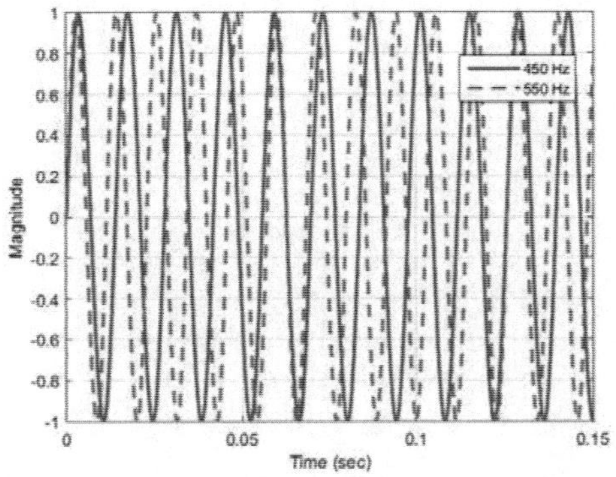

Figure 3. Sine wave frequencies, 450-550 Hz.

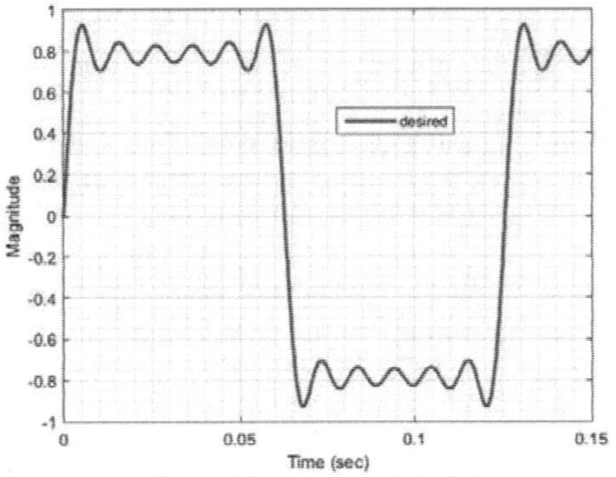

Figure 4. Square wave desired signal.

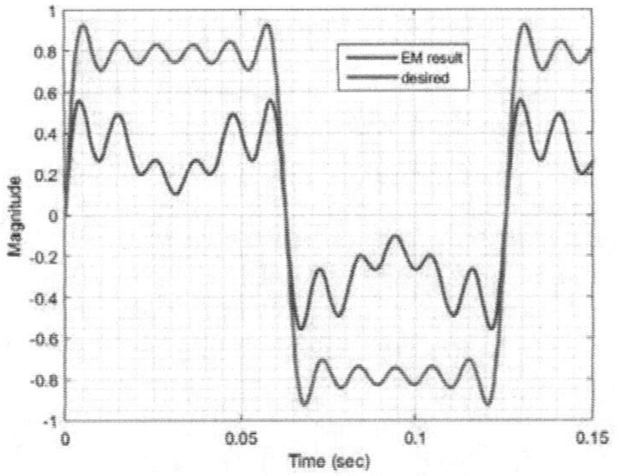

Figure 5. EM algorithm result with desired signal.

VI. DOUGHERTY ET AL. PROCESS

Dougherty et al. [3]. collected GPR data from a former lumber mill waste site near Boise, Idaho. He sought to enhance the original GPR data through air wave/direct arrival wave removal, and bandwidth enhancement. They first aligned each trace by the direct arrival pulse in each trace then, removed DC shifts; the low frequency "wow" component, followed by scaling each trace by the L2 norm of the direct arrival pulse. The traces were summed and the resultant direct arrival estimate was then, subtracted from each trace removing the direct arrival signal. An exponential gain recovery function was applied to each trace. Equal weighting was applied to each trace with the direct arrival signal removed as each frequency was summed. Dougherty et al. [3] demonstrated some clarity of shallow reflections due to direct wave removal. They achieved resolution and continuity of reflection enhancement by summing the frequencies. Spectral bandwidth was increased as well. However, the resultant signal was overwhelmed by the lower frequencies in the summation.

Dougherty et al. [3] process steps are as follows:

1. Align each trace by direct arrival.
2. Remove DC shift.
3. Remove low frequency (wow).
4. Scale each trace by L2 norm of direct arrival pulse.
5. Sum traces to form estimate of direct arrival signal.
6. Subtract estimate from each trace.
7. Apply exponential gain recovery function
8. Apply equal weighting to each trace.
9. Sum each trace all frequencies.

VII. BOOTH ET AL. PROCESS

Booth et al. [4], using real data acquired at a site on the Waterloo Moraine (an accumulation of glacial debris) in Ontario, Canada, examine five methods of achieving an increased bandwidth and thus a more approximate delta function through evaluating composite synthetic GPR wavelets; with a few method variations. The simple summation of [3] was examined, as one method. A second method, examined a scaled summation approach where the maximum value of each frequency spectra was determined and the spectrums equalized. The values used to equalize the spectra provided the signal weighting prior to summation. A third method, involved shifting traces such that the main peaks of the direct arrival pulses were aligned with the dominant peak then, the scaled summation of method two was applied. Method three provided the best result for increased spectral bandwidth, thus the best delta function, and GPR resolution for synthetic wavelets. Booth et al. [4] repeated the above analyses with GPR traces with one change. The time-shifting of traces was changed to align the first break of each trace at 0 ns. Then method two was applied, averaging the frequency spectra of each trace for one frequency then, determining the frequency weight;

repeating for all frequencies. This process was given the name of dominant frequency amplitude equalization (DFAE). As a final discussion, another weighting method was examined where the weighting factors were obtained from a least squares analysis, Optimal Spectral Whitening (OSW) that attempts to match the summed result to a defined optimal amplitude spectrum. The defined optimal spectrum determines over what set of frequencies the frequency data sets would be enhanced. A time-varying Fourier transformation of each data set must be performed prior to implementing the least square analysis.

The OSW process determined a time window to operate on by choosing the longest wavelet period of the GPR scanned frequencies. A frequency spectrum was produced for each time window of each trace. The spectra for a scan frequency were averaged together, and a magnitude was determined for each scanned frequency over the time-window spectra. The magnitude determined became a row in the OSW matrix. The process continues for each scan frequency for that time-window resulting in an over-determined linear system. Then solving the over-determined linear system for the frequency weights using a defined desired spectral amplitude. The desired spectral amplitude is usually defined as identical values (constant), one for each scan frequency. The OSW process is complete with the combining of traces for that time window with the computed weights.

Booth et al. [4] process steps are as follows:

Method 2 –

1. Determine frequency spectrum of each wavelet.
2. Equalize spectra for all frequencies; the magnitude needed to equalize spectra determines the weight for that frequency. (method 3 variation – average the frequency spectra of each trace for one frequency then, determining the weight; repeating for all frequencies).
3. Sum each wavelet of all frequencies with appropriate weight for that frequency.

Method 3 –

1. Shift all traces such that main peaks of Direct Arrival Signal are aligned. (variation – align the first break of each trace to 0 ns).
2. Continue by applying the steps of method 2.

DFAE – method 4

1. Remove DC shift.
2. Remove low frequency (wow).
3. Shift all traces to first break of Direct Arrival.
4. Remove direct signal (mute-ramping from 0% to 100% at chosen mute time).
5. Determine frequency spectrum of each trace.
6. Average spectrum for ensemble estimate.
7. Equalize ensemble spectra for all frequencies; the magnitude needed to equalize spectra determines the weight for that frequency.
8. Sum each trace of all frequencies with appropriate weight for that frequency.

OSW – method 5

1. Remove DC shift.
2. Remove low frequency (wow).
3. Shift all traces to first break of Direct Arrival.
4. Remove direct signal (mute- mute-ramping from 0% to 100% at chosen mute time).
5. Average traces for each frequency.
6. Compute spectra of average trace for each frequency.
7. Determine magnitude at scan frequencies for each spectra; becomes a row in OSW matrix "A". One row for each frequency.
8. Determine idealized frequency spectra vector "S"; vector usually set to value of one for each scan frequency.
9. Determine weights by solving matrix equation $W = (A^T * A)^{-1} * A^T * S$.
10. Combine weighted frequency traces; $sum = traces * W$.
11. Repeat steps 6 -10 for all analysis time windows over the GPR reflection Profile. Time window should be greater than the longest wavelet period to be sampled.

VIII. Bancroft Process

Bancroft [5], using real data from Santa Rosa Island, Florida, discusses the findings of Dougherty et al. [3] and the methods described by Booth et al. [4], while defining other methods to determine the weighting factors. One method uses a ramped summation method where the higher frequency data was suppressed by the same amount that the lower frequency data was enhanced over the two-way transit time of a GPR scan. Bancroft [5] discussed this double ramped summation technique using linear or Butterworth function ramps. To determine the ramp length for each frequency, Bancroft [5] multiplied the wavelength period of a frequency by an arbitrary number of 15 for 15 wave periods. For the double ramped method two adjacent frequencies were used; one frequency that was being enhanced and one frequency that was suppressed. The ramp length was determined by the frequency that was being suppressed. The 15th wave period was used as the ramp length. The start time was determined by examining the amplitude envelope of a trace. The amplitude envelope was calculated by taking the absolute value of the Hilbert transformation of a single trace. The minimum value of the log of the averaged amplitude envelope for all traces of one frequency determines the suppression start time for that frequency.

Another method discussed was called the Amplitude Envelope Equalization (AEE) technique. Without Automatic Gain Control (AGC) applied to each frequency data set, a set of multipliers were calculated as the ratio of the average envelope value of the lowest frequency and the average envelope value of the other frequency data sets. The weights or multipliers determined this way were applied to AGC processed frequency data sets over the portion of time that each frequency was to be enhanced. Determining the portion of time a ratio is applied was calculated by finding the minimum value of the log of the amplitude envelope (envelope computed without AGC applied); indicating the time where the suppression of that particular frequency data begins. This point was defined as data too attenuated to provide useful information. The average amplitude value of one frequency was determined by averaging the envelopes of all traces at one frequency. The weights established by this averaging method were used in conjunction with the double ramped summation method described earlier.

Bancroft [5] also suggests an alternative subjective method to determine the weighting through visual inspection of each frequency data set; but there was much less clarity as to how this was done and how experienced the reviewer must be.

Bancroft [5] process steps are as follows:

1. Clip data prior to first arrival.
2. Remove low frequency (wow).
3. Automatic gain control gain.
4. Bandpass filter.
5. Determine length of decreasing ramp in nanoseconds beginning with highest frequency.
6. Determine amplitude envelope of all traces (without AGC) of one frequency and average them. Repeat for all frequencies.
7. Determine the suppression start time by finding the minimum value of the log of the amplitude envelope.
8. Process traces adding them using the ramp summation technique.

Amplitude Envelope Equalization Technique -

1. Clip data prior to first arrival.
2. Remove low frequency (wow).
3. Automatic gain control gain.
4. Bandpass filter.
5. Determine length of decreasing ramp in nanoseconds beginning with highest frequency.
6. Determine amplitude envelope of all traces (without AGC) of one frequency and average them. Repeat for all frequencies.
7. Determine the suppression start time by finding the minimum value of the log of the amplitude envelope.
8. Determine the AEE multipliers as a ratio of the average envelope of the lowest frequency data set and the average envelope of the other frequency data sets.
9. Apply the AEE multipliers to the ramped summation technique.

IX. Computer Modeling Verification

Computer model verification that GprMax delivers reasonably accurate simulated GPR scans is presented in reference [13]. In the reference, target objects were buried on a test site called "The Forest Lodge", located near Greenville, California in the Northern Sierra about 60 miles (96.56 kilometers) north of Lake Tahoe. The objects were metal (tin) roofing sheets approximately 1.83 meters (6 feet) long by 66 centimeters (26 inches) wide by 1.27 millimeters (0.05 inches) in depth. There were 8 sheets in total buried at depths of 0.5 meters (1.64 feet), 1.0 meters (3.28 feet), 1.5 meters (4.92 feet), 2.0 meters (6.56 feet), 2.75 meters (9.02 feet), 3.0 meters (9.84 feet), 3.5 meters (11.48 feet) and 4.0 meters (13.12 feet), roughly 1.83 meters (6 feet) apart. The soil content appeared to be a mixture of clay and sand, though a geological survey was not conducted. Figure 6 shows the tin sheets before burial. A MALA Imaging Radar Array System (MIRA), a multi-static radar by MALA GeoScience Corporation, was used to scan the Forest Lodge site. This radar consisted of 9 Tx's and 8 Rx's, constructed such that each receiver collected a signal from 2 adjacent transmitters at different times, constructing 2 channels received by one receiver. This radar's center frequency was set at 200 MHz providing 16 channels of data cutting a 2-meter swath over targets of interest to create a 3-D image. The results shown in Figure 7 depict only 5 of the 8 roofing sheets clearly, in a stair step fashion as they were buried. For the 3-D model of Figure 8 a dry sand medium was used for the analysis. Figure 9 and Figure 10 show two 2-D slices of the results of a 200 MHz analysis using the GprMax modeling program. Actual and model results

Figure 6. Target GPR imaging objects, tin roofing sheets, were buried at various depths. The experiments provided ground truth GPR data for hardware to software comparison.

compare favorably though the simulation shows all 8 sheets, 5 of them well. My argument that software analysis can be used successfully to study actual GPR received data is strengthened. Using a mixture of clay and sand as the medium in the model we believe would show a better fit; target reflections would be attenuated more. This could be achieved by adjusting the permittivity, affecting the velocity through the medium, and adjusting the conductivity, affecting signal attenuation. This success of actual data verses model data comparison, supports the use of computer simulation for accurate results and shall be used in the remaining analyses within this paper.

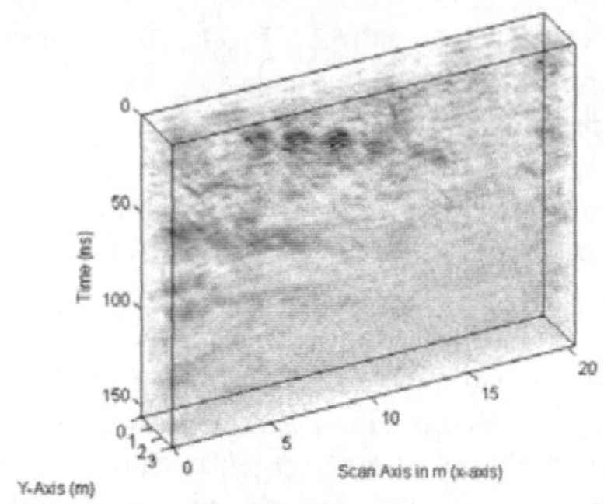

Figure 7. Processed 3-D data scanned by MALA MIRA radar over the Forest Lodge test site of buried tin sheets of known depth. 5 of the 8 roofing sheets are visible in a stair step fashion.

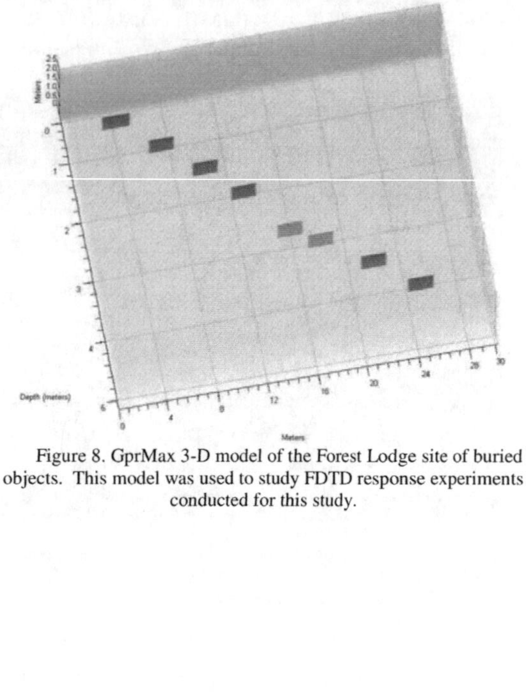

Figure 8. GprMax 3-D model of the Forest Lodge site of buried objects. This model was used to study FDTD response experiments conducted for this study.

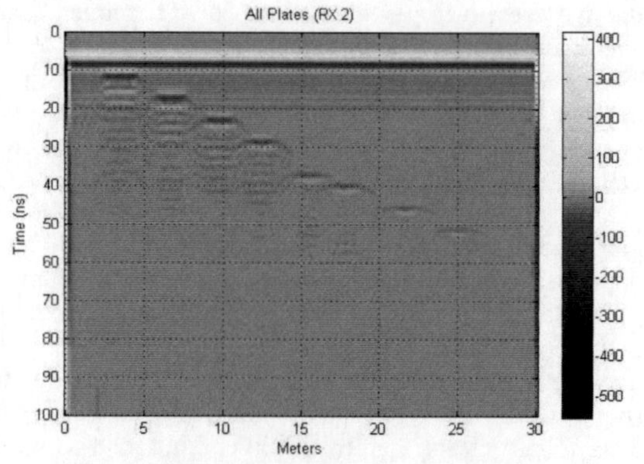

Figure 9.

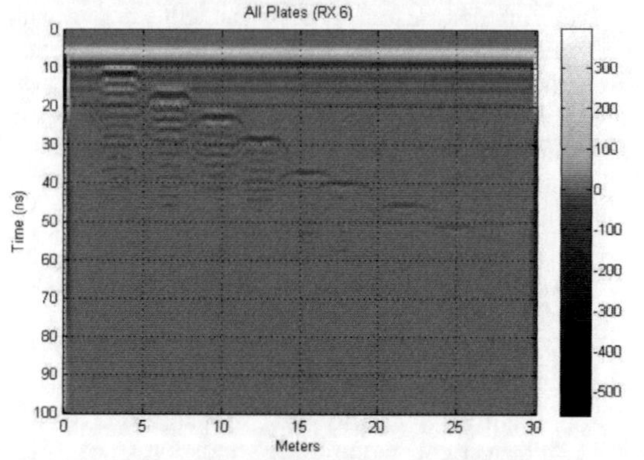

Figure 10.

Figure 9 and Figure 10 FDTD Analysis results at 200 MHz for two 2-D slices of the 3-D analysis results. All 8 of the simulated buried tin sheets are shown.

X. GPR SCAN RESULTS

To determine the capability of the EM GMM problem solver, a fictional area was defined using a Finite Difference Time Domain (FDTD) [14][15][16] modeling software package to produce GPR scans simulating real GPR scans. A Proprietary package in development, similar in operation to the popular GprMax software program by A. Giannopoulos [8] using the Transmission-Line Matrix (TLM) methods, as well as the GprMax software package were used to model a defined space. The FDTD method provides a solution to Maxwell's equations expressed in differential form. Whereas the TLM method provides a solution by simulating the propagation of electric and magnetic fields by voltage and current pulses in interconnected transmission lines [17]. Only 2-D analyses were performed.

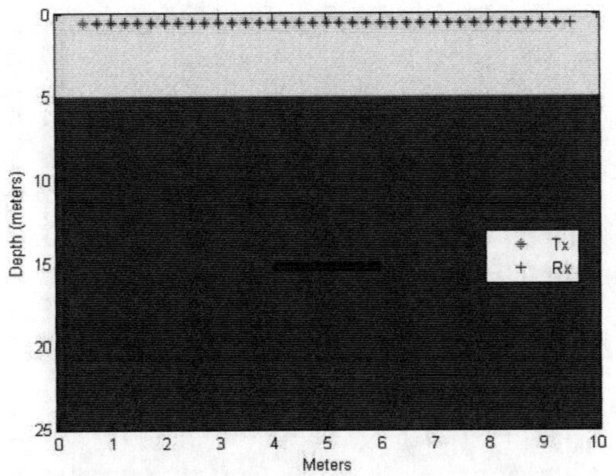

Figure 11. Defined Space with buried target at 15 meters depth and Tx's & Rx's 5 meters above ground.

The defined space modeled consisted of a Transmitter (Tx) and Receiver (Rx) suspended 5 meters above ground in air with a target (perfect electrical conductor) buried 10 meters below ground in a moist-sand medium with a relative permittivity (ε_r) of 9.0 and an electrical conductivity of 0.001 mS/m (Test Case 1 - TC1). The target is 2 meters in length and 0.5 meters in depth. The transmitter and receiver were moved along the length of the defined space as shown in Figure 11 for a total of 36 scans at 0.25 meters per step. The Tx starts at 0.5 meters ending at 9.5 meters, and the Rx starts at 0.75 meters ending at 9.75 meters, well within the defined space of 10 meters in length by 25 meters in depth. Each scan is 425 ns long, capable of receiving a reflected signal approximately 24 meters below Tx's and Rx's in moist-sand and air, with a minimum grid space of 200 points in x-direction, (Δx – 0.05 meters), and 500 points in y-direction, (Δy – 0.05 meters).

Simulated GPR scans were repeated for 20, 30, 50, 100, 500 and 900 MHz frequencies. A 2-D display for each frequency result is shown in Figures 12-19. In each case the object is correctly identified at approximately 10 meters below ground, approximately 15 meters below Tx's and Rx's or approximately 240 ns from the direct arrival signal (black line on plot); the two-way travel time for the radar signal. An individual trace by trace display is shown in Figure 17 and Figure 19, to better depict the target return signal. Arrow 1 in Figure 12 shows the direct arrival signal and ground bounce (radar return from the ground). Arrow 2 in Figure 12 denotes the target reflection at depth. In the 30MHz trace result (Figure 13), the target is indicated by arrow 3. The remaining unlabeled arrows indicate the target reflection at depth for the indicated scan frequency. Of interest, is the line length in frequency scans 100 MHz and below indicating the target, representing limited if not non-existent edge detection. For this analysis, the test area length is less than half the depth (25 meters depth by 10 meters length), more like a bore hole, contributing to the limited target edge detection. Arrow 4 (Figure 19) exhibits better edge detection.

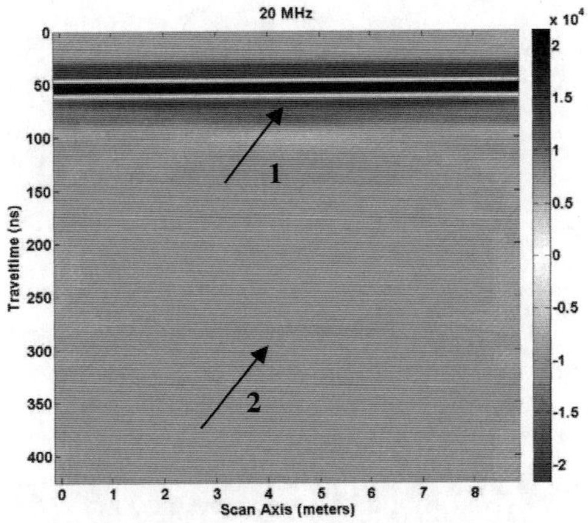

Figure 12. 2-D GPR scans 20MHz.

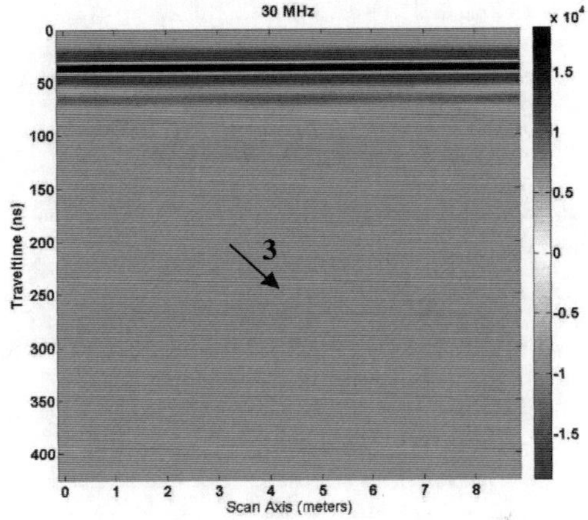

Figure 13. 2-D GPR scan 30MHz.

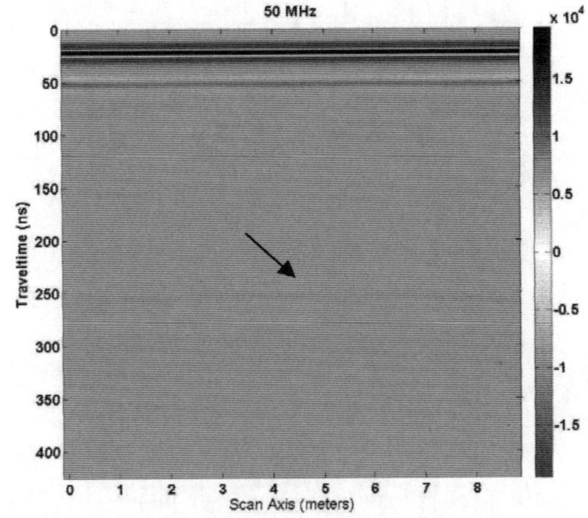

Figure 14. 2-D GPR scan 50MHz.

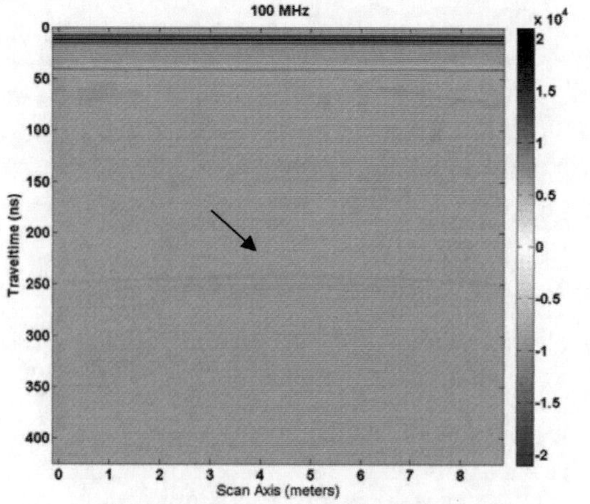

Figure 15. 2-D GPR scan 100MHz.

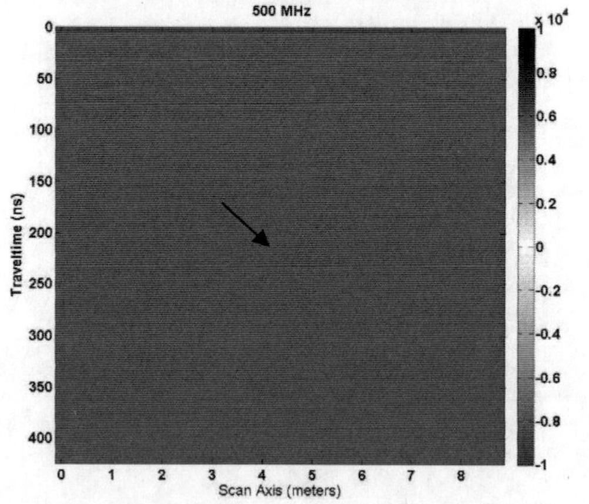

Figure 16. GPR scan 500MHz.

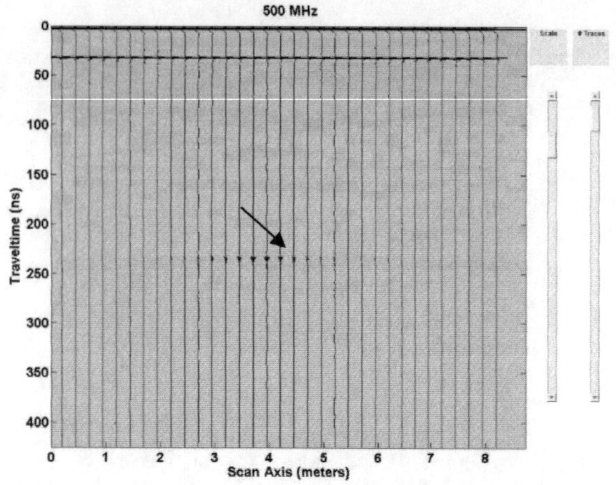

Figure 17. GPR scan 500MHz (individual traces).

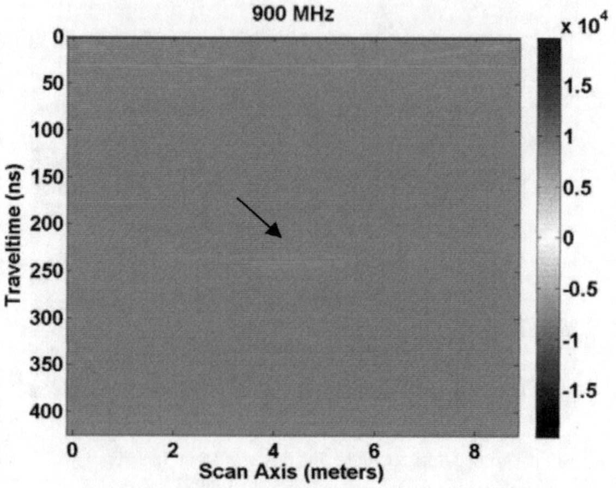

Figure 18. GPR scan 900MHz (normal 2 D image display).

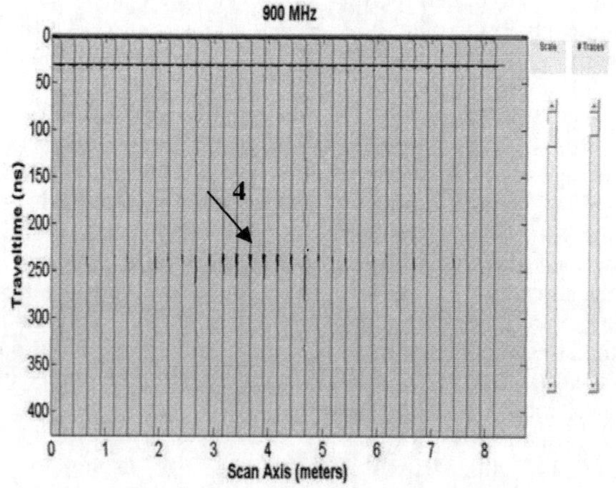

Figure. 19. GPR scan 900MHz (individual traces).

In all the simulated GPR scan results, as the frequency is increased, the area where the target exists is more pronounced. The opposite occurs as the scan frequency is lowered.

Figure 20 shows the result of adding each of the frequencies together having removed the direct arrival signal and scaling each signal max value to the same magnitude. A broad area of target reflection is shown from approximately 240 ns to 320 ns in depth (two-way travel time); a very rough indication of target depth. The direct arrival signal was removed by subtracting a GPR scan without a target from a scan with a target, for each frequency.

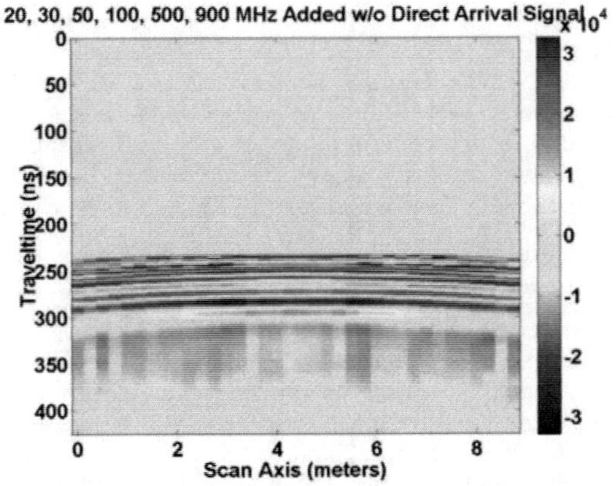

Figure 20. Sum of frequency signals with direct arrival and ground bounce signals removed.

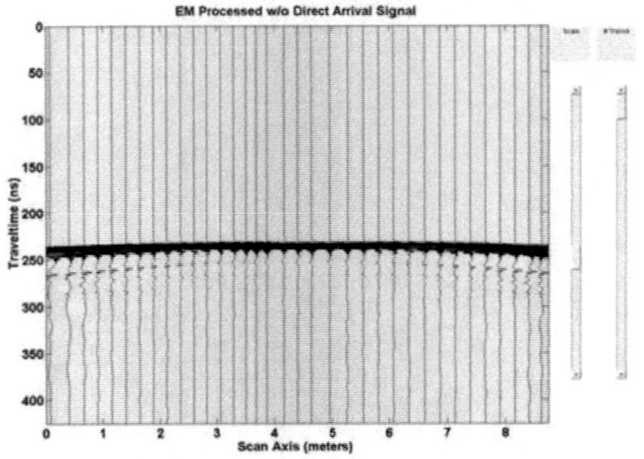

Figure 22. EM processed signal traces with Direct Arrival and ground bounce signals removed.

Figure 21 and Figure 22 show the same signals combined using the EM algorithm to determine the weight of each signal. Figure 22 shows the EM processed individual signal traces. The area that is being scanned is more like a bore hole, twice as deep as its width. This accounts for the broad reverse "u-shaped" area that begins at target depth. The existence of lower frequencies in the sum broadens the output result.

Figure 23 shows the results of applying the Dougherty et al. [3] approach to the same test area. The target depth is correctly identified but the depth indication is slightly less crisp than the EM algorithm case. The EM case depicts a thinner line in depth. It appears the delta depth issue (less crisp) is the result of the lower frequencies in the sum. However, the Dougherty et al. [3] approach shows better edge detection. The width of the target is better defined though still wider than the defined area but less than the EM GMM case. For the Dougherty et al. [3] case, part of the Direct Arrival/Ground bounce signal is visible due to the method used to remove them from each frequency scan.

For the same test area, applying the Booth et al. [4] OSW approach with one time-window results in the output shown in Figure 24. Again, the target depth is correctly identified but like the Dougherty et al. [3] method the depth indication is quite broad. The delta time depth indication is larger than the EM and Dougherty et al. [3] methods, (Figure 21 and Figure 23). Similar to the EM method, the width in scan axis length is large; edge detection is not well defined. The thickest part of the trace indicates the test target.

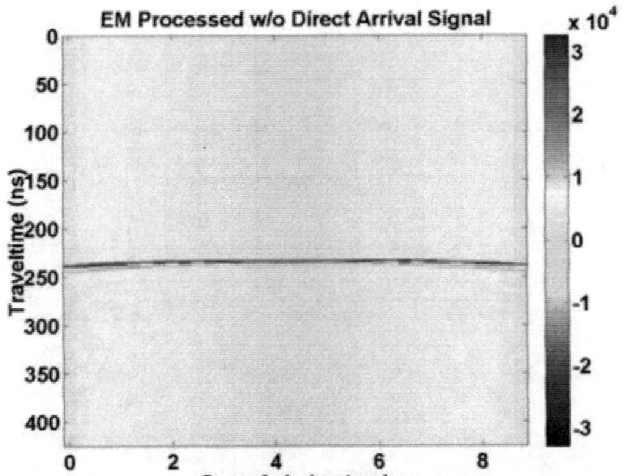

Figure 21. EM sum of frequency signals with Direct Arrival and ground bounce signals removed.

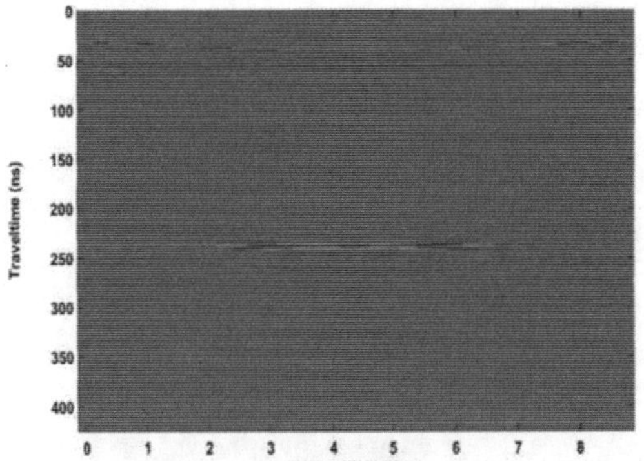

Figure 23. Dougherty et al. [3] standard response for TC1.

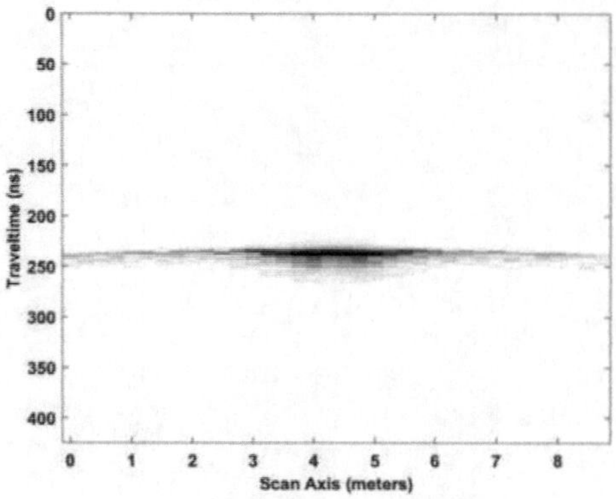

Figure 24. Booth et al. [4] response for TC1.

Figure 25 demonstrates the AEE method of Bancroft [5]. The target depth is correctly identified and the depth indication is like that of the EM method, sharp but slightly broader in depth. This is about the same as the Dougherty et al. [3] method, and smaller than the Booth et al. [4] method. Target edge detection is more like Booth et al. [4] where the thickest part of the GPR result indicates the test target. Like the EM method the GPR reflection covers a wide area (0 to 9 meters) in scan axis length. How much of this response is due to the bore hole effect of the target area is unknown at this time. We applied a modified AEE method consisting of calculated multipliers only and not the ramped summation because the calculated start and end of each ramp conflicted with each other, which is not the case for the scan frequencies chosen by Bancroft [5].

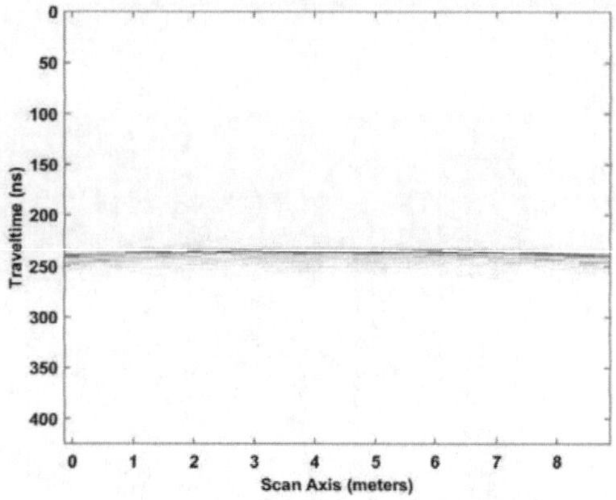

Figure 25. Output from Amplitude Envelope Equalization method of Bancroft [5] for TC1.

For test case 1, the test area definition poses a problem as to the effect of the bore hole like definition of the target area, on the outcome of the scan response. Of concern, is whether a less than crisp edge detection or the addition of large magnitude lower frequencies, are making the depth indicators broad. By exercising a more complicated test area with broader scan area we attempted to address these concerns.

The second defined area consists of an area 30 meters in length and 25 meters in depth with little or no space above ground, (0.15 meters), for the Tx and Rx used (Test Case 2 – TC2). They are swept along the scan axis length starting at 0.5 meters (Tx) and ending at 24.85 meters with spacing between the Tx and Rx the same as before (0.25 meters), as shown in Figure 26. The number of GPR scans is 145. The electrical conductivity of the ground is the same as before but the relative permittivity (ε_r) is 3.0 for dry sand. Each scan is 550 ns long, capable of receiving a reflected signal approximately 48 meters below Tx's and Rx's in dry sand, with a minimum grid space of 150 points in x direction, (Δx – 0.2 meters), and 2500 points in the y direction, (Δy - 0.01 meters). Simulated burial in the ground at 8 different levels (4.565, 6.065, 8.565, 10.065, 12.815, 14.065, 16.565 and 18.065 meters) are sheets of corrugated aluminum, modeled as perfect electrical conductors for ease of computation. Each sheet is approximately 2 meters in length and 0.1 meters in depth. The GPR scanning frequencies are the same as before. The result for the EM method, shown in Figure 27, identifies 8 targets at very close to the correct depth (approximately 50, 70, 100, 116, 148, 160, 190 and 208 ns for two-way travel time at a velocity in the medium of 0.1732 m/ns for the defined relative permittivity) with edges depicted reliably but with less fidelity as one descends in depth. Figure 28 displays the individual GPR traces instead of the image response.

Applying the Dougherty et al. [3] method to this second test area produces the GPR response shown in Figure 29. Note that not all plates are depicted. Only 5 and barely 6 of the 8 are designated. Where the plates end in width is tolerably detectable; edges are noted but not clearly. The result is poorer than the EM processed response of Figure 27; direct arrival signal removed by subtraction as before.

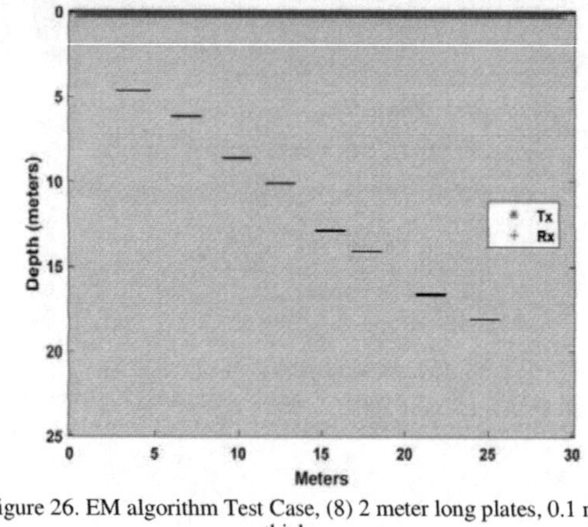

Figure 26. EM algorithm Test Case, (8) 2 meter long plates, 0.1 meter thick.

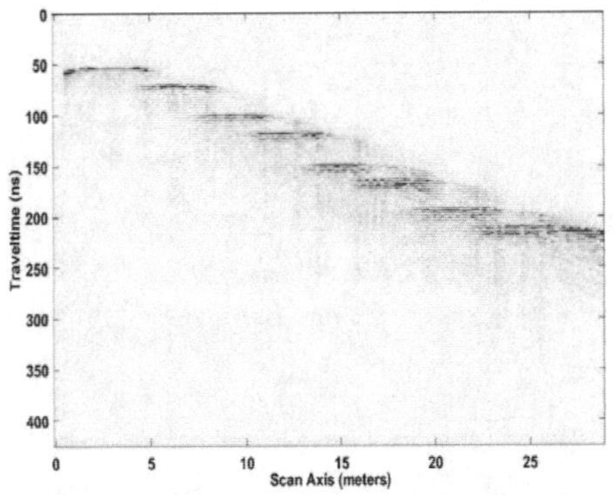

Figure 27. GPR scan result for complex structure.

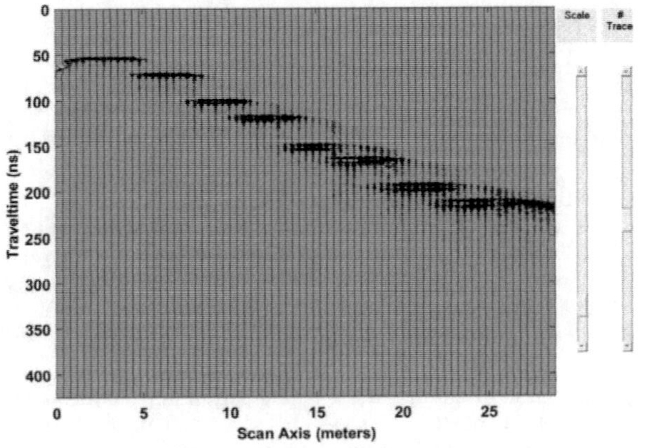

Figure 28. EM processed signal traces for complex structure.

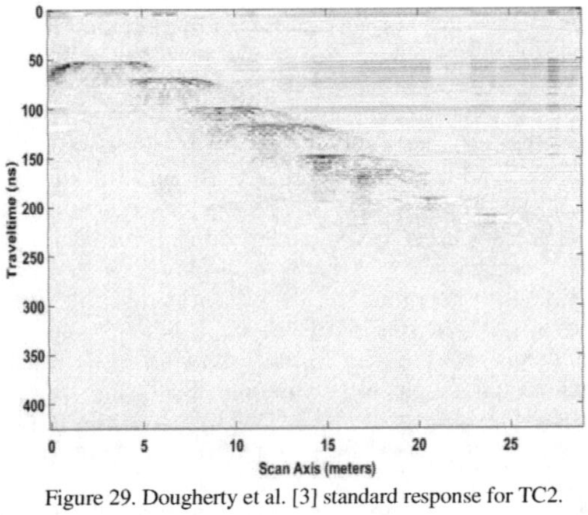

Figure 29. Dougherty et al. [3] standard response for TC2.

Figure 30 shows the GPR response of the Booth et al. [4] OSW method with one time-window applied to this second test area. The ground bounce (shown as a straight line at approximately 50 ns in Figure 30) is still present in the image because the mute feature had to balance between removing the direct arrival/ground bounce signal and not removing the reflection of the first plate at a depth of approximately 50 ns two-way travel time. Again only a few plates are detectable. Easily shown are the first 4 plates and barely plates 5 and 6 of the 8 plates in the test area. Comparing the result to the EM method, the Booth et al. [4] method falls short at depth. Edge detection is poorer than the EM method but comparable to the Dougherty et al. [3] method.

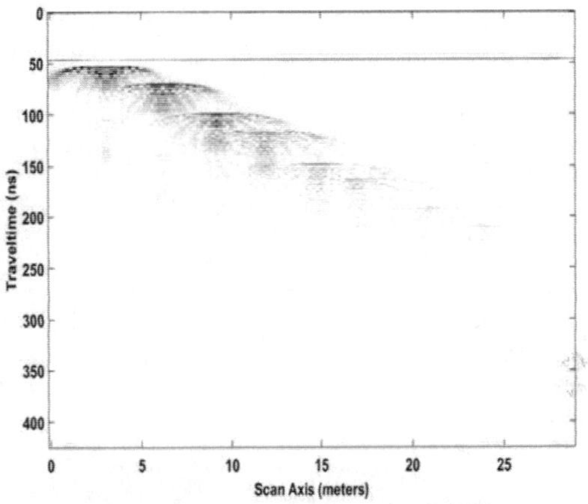

Figure 30. Booth et al. [4] response for TC2.

Figure 31 depicts the result of employing the AEE Bancroft [5] method on test area 2. Like Booth et al. [4] and Dougherty et al. [3] before, not all buried plates are illuminated. Of the 8 plates, 4 are depicted with a possibility of 3 more. Added under plates at 50 ns and 75 ns in depth are "ghost" plates at 100 ns and 150 ns. There were no targets buried at these two points. Edge detection is better than Booth et al. [4] and Dougherty et al. [3] and on par with the EM algorithm. Again, only the calculated AEE multipliers were used due to the same ramp start and end conflict issue.

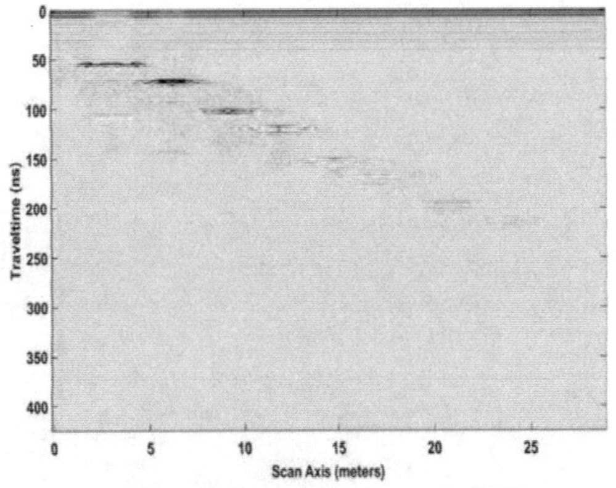

Figure 31. Bancroft [5] response for TC2.

For this more complicated test case, the EM algorithm has performed the best in terms of revealing the 8 buried plates. Edge detection is still not great but tolerable for the EM method for both test cases and the Bancroft method for the second test case. The larger scan area does address the bore hole effect question of wider scan axis length reducing wide reflection traces. The dimensions of the scan area does affect the width of the scan axis reflections. The ability to achieve crisp edge detection has not changed much however.

The previous test cases modeled were all in homogenous material either moist sand or dry sand. Of interest to be modeled were objects placed in a non-homogenous material; layered like what could appear in nature. As an additional test case (TC3), a model area was created with dry sand, clay, concrete, granite, and limestone with relative permittivity of material noted in Figure 32. Sheets of corrugated aluminum, modeled as perfect electrical conductors were buried as noted in the previous test case. The result (Figure 33) for the EM method on this test case mirrors that of the previous homogeneous medium case. There are a few subtle changes (coloration differences – the concrete buried object, plate 6, has a lighter color for example), which coincide with material the aluminum sheets (perfect electrical conductors) are buried in. Figure 34 shows the individual GPR traces.

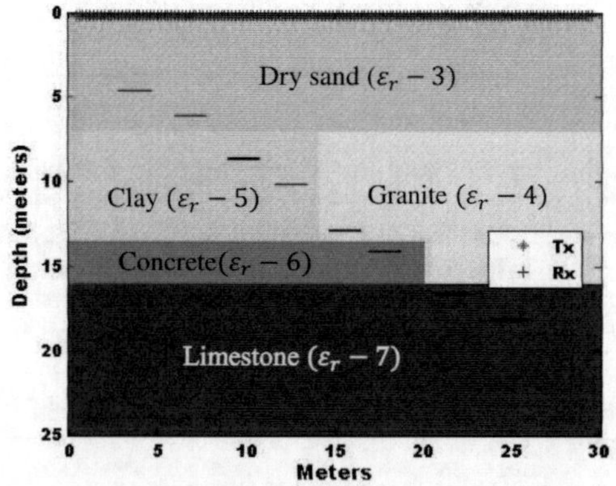

Figure 32. Test Case Area 3 (8) 2 meter long plates, 0.1 meter in depth.

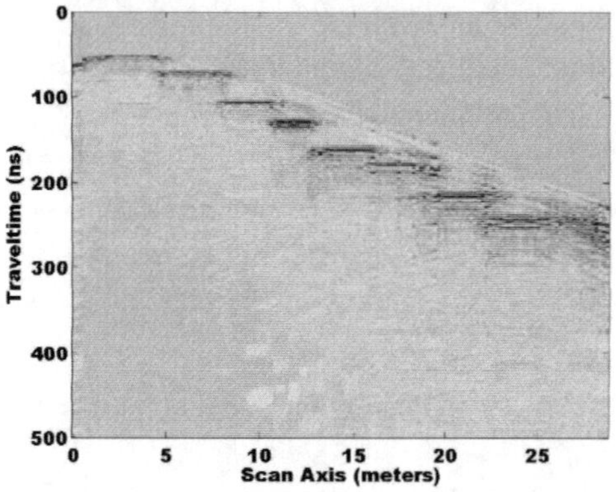

Figure 33. EM Algorithm GPR scan result for TC3 (8) Plates shown

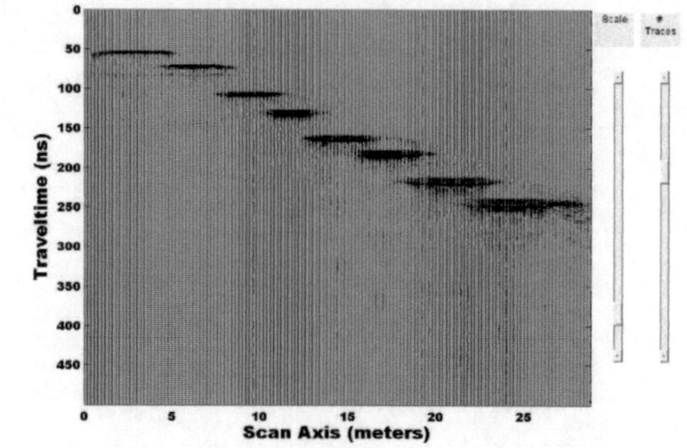

Figure 34. EM Algorithm GPR Scan result showing individual traces for TC3.

XI. CONCLUSION AND FUTURE WORK

In this paper, we have explored using the Expectation Maximization Gaussian Mixture Model, an optimization problem solver, to define weights to combine multiple GPR frequency scans over the same area to improve image resolution to a lower depth. First, we looked at using the EM GMM method to combine multiple frequency sine waves to form a square wave by defining the best set of weights for the square wave frequency harmonics presented. Though not without problems, the process performs reasonably well in forming a square wave combining the multiple frequencies. The value of the mixture weights summing to one is an issue to look at; but they are defined that way in the EM GMM algorithm. Actual multiple sine wave mixture weight values are different but similar in magnitude. Though not ideal, there was enough success to pursue using the EM GMM technique on GPR scans over the same area at different frequencies, the first use of this technique on GPR scans of multiple frequencies. We explored whether the Maximum Likelihood Estimation process would be more fitting for our analyses. In exploring this technique, we were reminded that the MLE process, though workable, presents problems when hidden or incomplete data exists [6][7]. The resultant likelihood equation does not have a closed form solution or a single global maximum and becomes very hard to solve. Whereas the EM Algorithm provides a well-structured solution by creating a set of simpler optimization sub-problems, from the MLE process, that are guaranteed to converge and produce local maxima at each iteration that increase until a global maximum is reached.

In considering the EM GMM case for GPR signals we encountered several other methods, in the literature, that attempted to combine scans of various frequencies over the same target area. Methods by Dougherty et al. [3], Booth et al. [4] and Bancroft [5] were compared to our EM GMM method [18] as a way to judge how well our method performed compared to solutions found in the literature. Because we lacked the equipment hardware to perform field experiments, a well-known computer program was used to model simulated target areas. The targets were perfect electrical conductors and the media used well-defined permittivity values. The scan results demonstrated the effectiveness of the software program GprMax [8]. The connection between actual and simulated results were detailed in reference [13] and discussed here briefly. The GprMax [8] results were determined to be an accurate depiction of field experiments. We found that in comparing our EM GMM process with Dougherty et al. [3], Booth et al. [4] and Bancroft [5], our process faired the best in recognizing images at depths down to 20 meters in moist sand and dry sand media. As a final test, we performed an experiment with the same targets positioned this time in several media types that varied with depth from the surface. In this non-homogenous experiment, we used dry sand first then, clay and granite, concrete and finally limestone as the final layer. The result was the same as without such division in media types.

Our results uncovered problem areas in need of future study. The edge detection ability, how to reliably remove the direct wave/ground bounce without removing the reflected radar response from the target, and how to best align GPR trace starting points across frequencies, are a few examples. Solving the alignment problem appears to reduce the thickness in depth of the GPR scan results. Of interest in a future project would be the result of using the EM GMM method in finding tunnels in a realistic clutter environment.

APPENDIX A

A.1 GPR BASICS

Ground Penetrating Radar method provides a way to map sub-surface artifacts or structures using radio waves. GPR modes in practice consist of reflection, velocity sounding (common mid-point) mode and trans-illumination. The most common mode is the reflection mode where a GPR radio wave from a transmitter at or above the ground surface, propagates through a medium to a buried target, reflecting the radar wave back to a receiving antenna. The velocity sounding or common mid-point mode provides a method to determine the velocity of the radio wave in a medium by setting a transmitter and receiver at a specified distance apart; instituting a scan then, moving both transmitter and receiver a distance further apart, repeating the process several times. The result provides a way to calculate the velocity through the medium that the radio waves have encountered. Trans-illumination is used for Bore holes in two ways; One, a transmitter (Tx) and receiver (Rx) are moved in unison from one position to another beginning at the surface of a bore hole then, lower on either side of the area of interest; scanning is across the area of interest. Two, only one transmitter is used and several receivers are placed at various positions in depth. Figure 1A depicts these modes. Antenna orientation, polarization and the available power verses the loss mechanisms determined by the radar range equation are of interest but beyond the scope of this paper.

Of interest in the reflection mode method are the signal arrival types, the theoretical resolution of a GPR system, and what item is the major contributor to the velocity in a medium. The signal arrival types are the direct air wave, critically refracted air wave, direct ground wave, and reflected wave. The theoretical resolution is proportional to ¼ of the velocity in a medium divided by the frequency of the radio wave (i.e. the wavelength in a medium divided by 4; $Theoretical\ resolution = \left(\lambda = \frac{V}{f}\right)/4$). The velocity in a medium is proportional to the speed of light in a vacuum divided by the square root of the relative permittivity of the medium making permittivity the major influence on the velocity in a medium.

$$Velocity = (c/(\sqrt{\varepsilon_r})) * 1e^{-9}\text{meters/ns} \qquad (1A)$$

c = speed of light ($3e^8$ meters/sec)

ε_r – relative permittivity

Permittivity is defined as a measure of how an electric field is affected and affects a dielectric medium. Figure 2A and Figure 3A. depict the signal arrival types, and equations governing time, depth and velocity measurements.

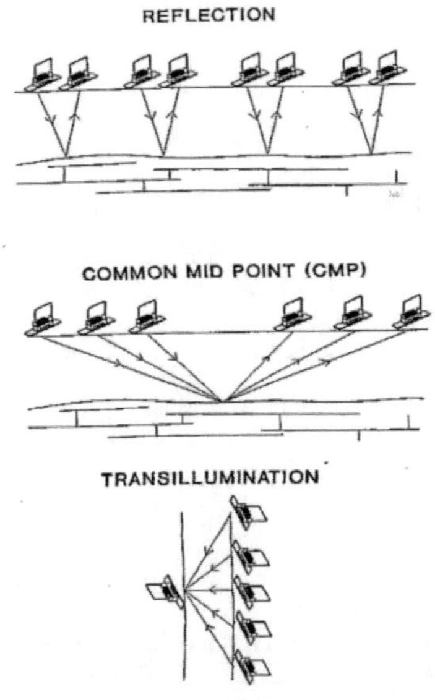

Figure 1A. GPR Scanning Modes [19].

Typically, short radar pulses are transmitted into the medium. The most common pulses used are the "Ricker Pulse" (second derivative of a Gaussian pulse) or the first derivative of a Gaussian pulse (a Monocycle) (Figure 4A).

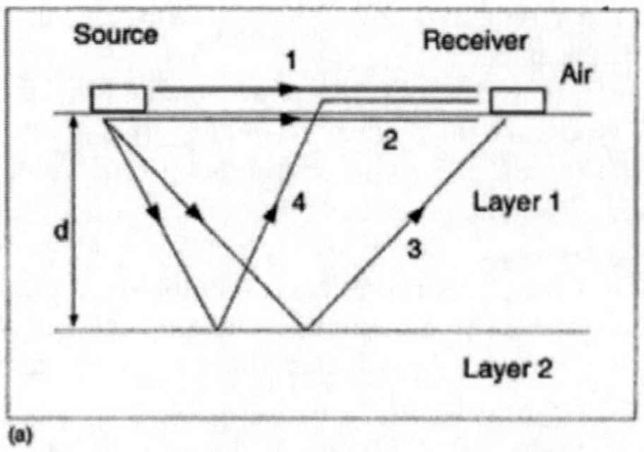

Figure 2A. GPR Arrival Types [20].

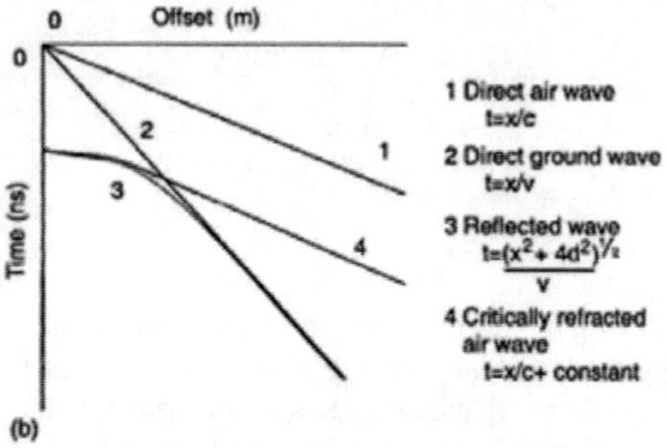

Figure 3A. Simple CMP plot w/equations for Arrival Types [20].

Most equipment manufacturers do not divulge their transmit pulse type; but the "Ricker" Pulse is assumed. Figures 5A-8A show plots of typical reflected signals received without a buried target at various frequencies. Each Tx/Rx is 5 meters above the ground (dry sand) in air. Shown are the direct arrival signal and the ground bounce. Note as the frequency increases, the direct arrival gets sharper and the ground bounce is better defined though the time of the return signal occurs is the same.

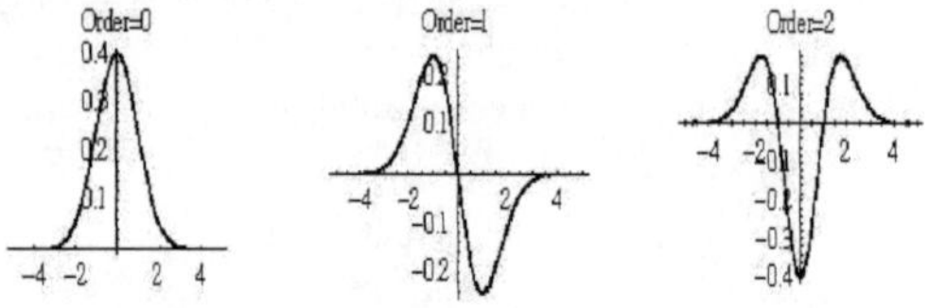

Figure 4A. Gaussian, 1st derivative (Monocycle), 2nd derivative (Ricker)(normally GPR response signals for Monocycle and Ricker are inverted) [21].

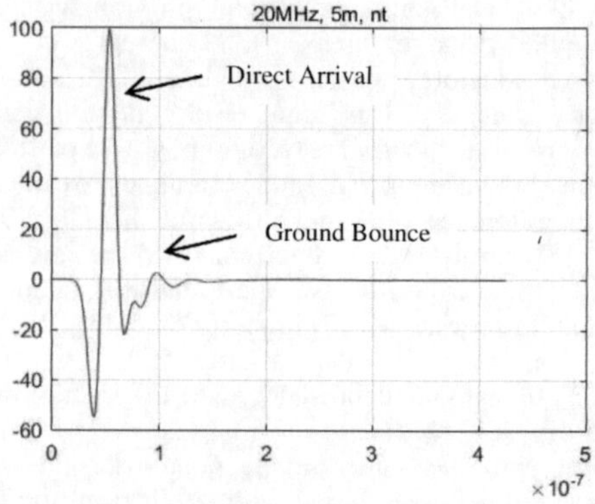

Figure 5A. Direct arrival and ground bounce, 20MHz.

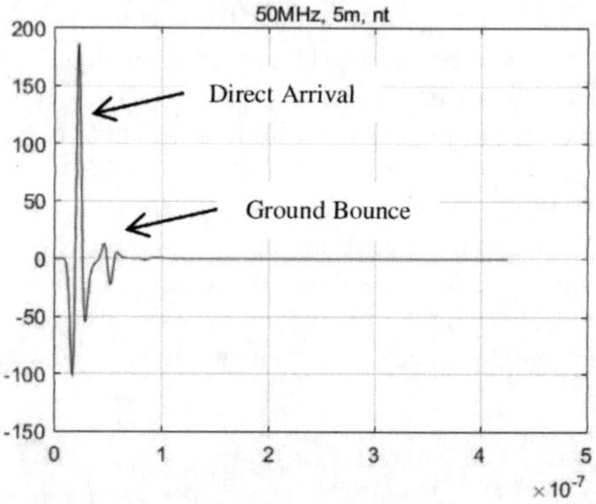

Figure 6A. Direct arrival and ground bounce, 50MHz.

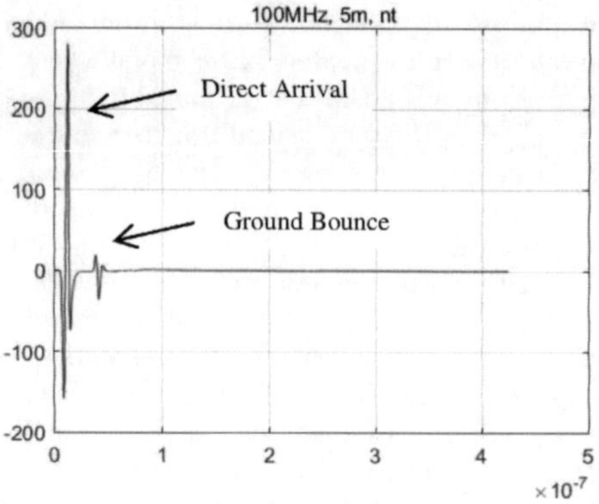

Figure 7A. Direct arrival and ground bounce, 100MHz.

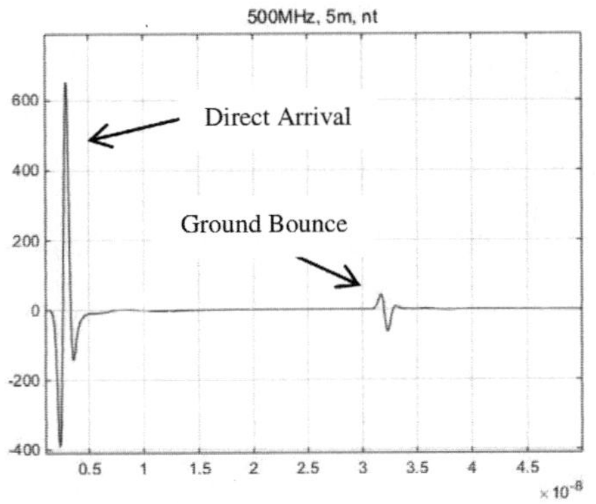

Figure 8A. Direct arrival and ground bounce, 500MHz.

Several methods exist to calculate the velocity of a radio wave in a medium. The two most popular are derived from the common mid-point (CMP) mode. Figure 3A depicts the first method, a simple plot of the CMP results with equations. Figure 9A depicts the second method, the (time2 – Tx/Rx separation2) analysis method named (t^2-x^2) where the slope of the plot is equal to 1/(velocity squared). With simple manipulation of the result, the velocity in a medium can be determined.

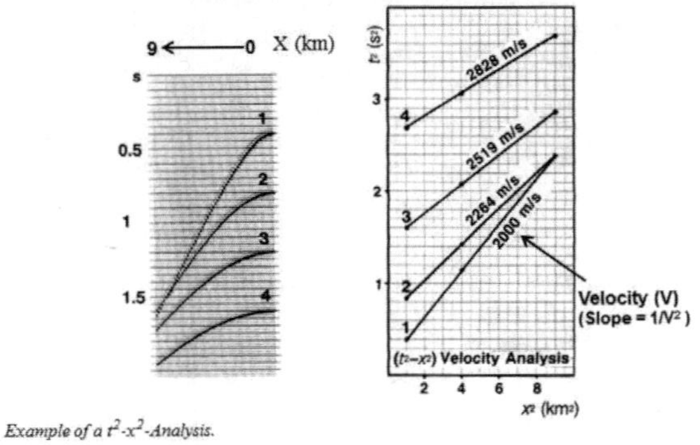

Figure 9A. Shows $t^2 - x^2\ Analysis$ (s⇔t) [22].

A.2 Modeling Basics

The top 2 methods used to model GPR analysis are the Transmission-Line Matrix (TLM) method and the Finite Difference Time Domain (FDTD) method [15]. Both methods provide a solution to Maxwell's equation subject to geometry, initial conditions, and boundaries of a problem. The TLM method [17] is implemented as an electrical network model solution to an electromagnetic field problem. Transmission lines are interconnected at regular intervals to form TLM nodes. The propagation of electric and magnetic fields are simulated by voltage and current pulses. The model space step defines the distance between TLM adjacent nodes. The time step represents the time, which a pulse takes to travel from one TLM node to the next.

The FDTD method provides a solution to Maxwell's equations expressed in differential form. The partial derivatives in Maxwell equations are discretized using central difference techniques resulting in difference equations, which are solved by an iterative process. Included in the difference equations are the model space step and time step.

A.3 Two-Way-Travel-Time (TWTT)

Figure 10A and Figure 11A demonstrate the GPR trace of the example in Figure 6 at 20 and 50 Mhz. The target is 10 meters below the ground and 15 meters from the Tx's and Rx's. There are 2 mediums the radar signal travels through, free space (Tx/Rx to ground) and moist sand (ground to target). The velocities for the 2 mediums are 0.3 m/ns (free space) and 0.1 m/ns (moist sand). To determine the distance to the target from the Tx/Rx from Figure 7A, the mediums and the velocity through the mediums alone the following occurs.

$$TWTT = \frac{2*distance\ Tx/Rx\ to\ target}{Velocity\ through\ the\ media} \quad (2A)$$

TWTT = 280 ns - 40 ns =240 ns, from Figure 7A.

Medium 1 – free space, velocity 0.3 m/ns, distance to ground from Tx/Rx is 5 meters

TWTT (1)= (2 * 5 meters)/(0.3 m/ns)≈33 ns

Medium 2 – moist sand, velocity 0.1 m/ns, distance to target from ground is:

d = (0.1 m/ns * (240 ns - 33 ns))/2 ≈10.35 meters.

Total calculated distance (d) from Tx/Rx to target is 15.35 meters (5 meters + 10.35 meters); close to the defined 15-meter distance, but accurate because true distance from Tx/Rx to target is at an angle, which is longer than the perpendicular distance.

A.4 Velocity Through a Medium and Penetration Depth [23]

The velocity is dependent on a material's relative permittivity. The higher the relative permittivity of a medium, the lower the velocity is through the medium. When the relative permittivity of a medium is known the calculated velocity through the medium can be calculated using equation 1A.

Example: free-space has a permittivity (ε_r) = 1,
$Velocity = [\,3e + 8/Sqrt(1) * 1e - 9]$ m/ns.
V = 0.3 m/ns.

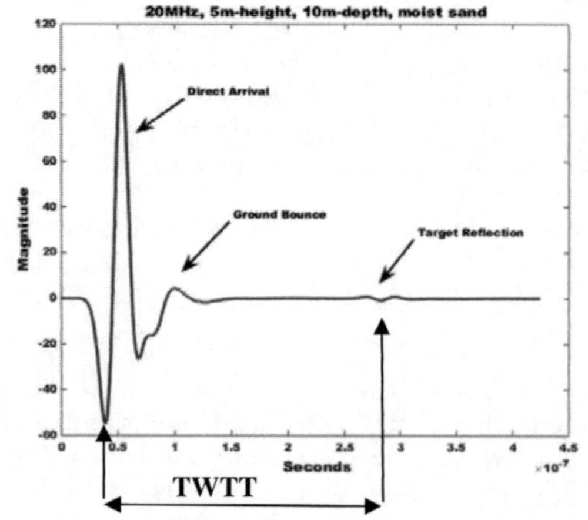

Figure 10A. GPR trace depicting Two-way-transit-time for a target at 20MHz.

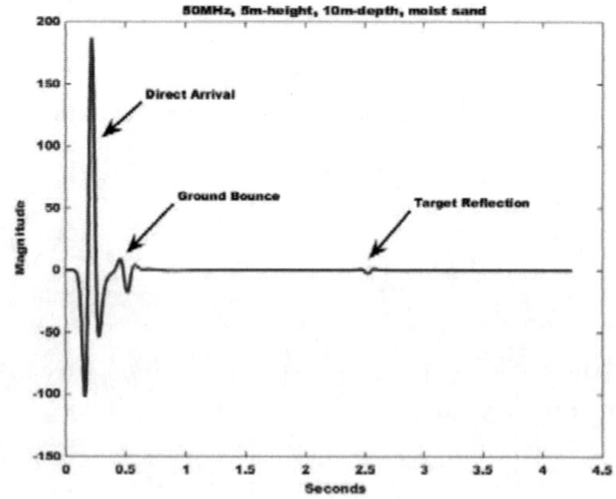

Figure 11A. GPR trace depicting Two-way-transit-time for same target of Figure 10A at 50 MHz.

As the electrical conductivity, (units Siemens/meter), increases the penetration depth decreases, determining how deep an electrical signal will penetrate. Higher frequencies reduce the depth penetration but increase image resolution. Table 1 lists a few nominal values for permittivity and conductivity.

TABLE 1 (MEDIUM AND VELOCITY VALUES)

Medium	ε_r	Velocity (m/ns)	Conductivity (mS/m)
concrete	6	0.1225	0.01
clay	5	0.1342	2
dry-sand	3	0.1732	0.01
granite	4	0.1500	0.01
limestone	7	0.1134	0.5

ACKNOWLEDGMENT

This work was performed under the auspices of Sandia National Laboratories a multimission laboratory managed and operated by National Technology and Engineering Solutions of Sandia, LLC, a wholly owned subsidiary of Honeywell International, Inc. for the U.S. Department of Energy's National Nuclear Security Administration under contract DE-NA-0003525.

REFERENCES

[1] R. Tilley, H. Sadjadpour, and F. Dowla, "Combining Ground Penetrating Radar Scans of Differing Frequencies Through Signal Processing," The Ninth International Conference on Advanced Geographic Information Systems, Applications, and Services, GEOProcessing 2017, Nice, France, Mar 2017, pp. 32-38, ISBN:978-1-61208-539-5.

[2] A. L. Endres, A. Booth, and T. Murray, "Multiple Frequency Compositing of Spatially Coincident GPR Data Sets," Proceedings of the Tenth International Conference on Ground Penetrating Radar, 2004, Delft, The Netherlands, June 2004, pp. 271-274, ISBN: 90-9017959-3.

[3] M. E. Dougherty, P. Michaels, J. R. Pelton, and L. M. Liberty, "Enhancement of Ground Penetrating Radar Data Through Signal Processing," Symposium on the Application of Geophysics to Engineering and Environmental Problems 1994, pp. 1021-1028, Jan 1994, DOI 10.4133/1.2922053.

[4] A. D. Booth, A. L. Endres, and T. Murray, "Spectral Bandwidth Enhancement of GPR Profiling Data Using Multiple-Frequency Compositing," Journal of Applied Geophysics, vol 67, pp. 88-97, Jan 2009, DOI 10.1016/j.jappgeo.2008.09.015.

[5] S. W. Bancroft, "Optimizing the Imaging of Multiple Frequency GPR Datasets using composite Radargrams: An Example from Santa Rosa Island, Florida," PhD dissertation, University of South Florida, 2010.

[6] A. P. Dempster, N.M. Laird and D.B. Rubin, "Maximum Likelihood from Incomplete Data via the EM Algorithm," Journal of the Royal Statistical society, Series B (Methodological) 39(1): pp. 1-38, 1977, JSTOR 2984875.MR0501537.

[7] C. R. Shalizi, "Advanced Data Analysis from an Elementary Point of View," Book Draft from Lecture Notes for Course 36-402 at Carnegie Mellon University, Chapters 19.1-19.2.2, January 2017,

http://www.stat.cmu.edu/~cshalizi/ADAfaEPoV/ADAfaEPoV.pdf, 2017.11.23.

[8] A. Giannopoulos, "Modelling Ground Penetrating Radar by GprMax," Construction and Building Materials, vol. 19, pp. 755-762, Dec 2005, DOI 10.1016/j.conbuildmat.2005.06.007.

[9] J. A. Pena, T. Teixido, "Cover Surfaces as a New Technique for 3-D Image Enhancement, Archaelogical Applications," Repositorio Institucional de la Universidad de Granada, Spain, 2012, http://hdl.handle.net/10481/22949, 2017.11.23.

[10] Padhraic Smyth, "The EM Algorithm for Gaussian Mixtures, Probabilistic Learning: Theory and Algorithms, CS274A," University of California, Irvine, Department of Computer Science, Lecture Note 4.

[11] J. J. Verbeek, N. Vlassis, and B. Kröse, "Efficient Greedy Learning of Gaussian Mixtures," The 13th Belgian-Dutch Conference on Artificial Intelligence (BNAIC'01),pp. 251-258, 2001, INRIA-00321510.

[12] C. Do, S. Batzoglou, "What is the Expectation Maximization Algorithm," Nature Biotechnology vol. 26, Issue 8, pp. 897-899, 2008, DOI 10.1038/NTBL1406.

[13] R. Tilley, F. Dowla, F. Nekoogar, and H. Sadjadpour, "GPR Imaging for Deeply Buried Objects: A comparative Study based on FDTD models and Field Experiments," Selected Papers Presented at MODSIM World 2011 Conference and Expo; pp. 45-51, Mar. 2012; (NASA/CP-2012-217326); (SEE 20130008625) .

[14] A. P. Annan, "Electromagnetic Principles of Ground Penetrating Radar," in Ground Penetrating Radar Theory and Applications, M. J. Harry, Ed., ed Amsterdam: Elsevier, pp. 1-40, 2009, ISBN: 978-0-444-53348-7.

[15] A. Tavlove, "Review of the formulation and Applications of the Finite-Difference Time-Domain Method for Numerical Modeling of Electromagnetic-Wave Interactions with Arbitrary Structures," Wave Motion, vol. 10, pp. 547-582, Dec 1988, DOI 10.1016/0165-2125(88)90012-1.

[16] N. Blindow, D. Eisenburger, B. Illich, H. Petzold, and T. Richter, "Ground Penetrating Radar," in Environmental Geology, Ed. Springer Berlin Heidelberg, pp. 283-235, 2008, DOI 10.1007/978-3-540-74671-3_10.

[17] C. Christopoulos, "The Transmission-Line Modeling (TLM) Method in Electromagnetics," Synthesis Lectures on Computational Electromagnetics, vol. 1, Issue 1, pp. 1-132, Morgan & Claypool Publishers, 2006, DOI 10.2200/S00027ED1V01Y200605CEM1007.

[18] R. Tilley, H. Sadjadpour, and F. Dowla, "Extending Ground Penetrating Radar Imaging Capabilities Through Signal Processing," Proceedings of the 2nd World Congress on Civil, Structural, and Environmental Engineering (CSEE'17), Barcelona, Spain, April 2017, ISSN 2371-5294, DOI 10.11159/icgre17.194.

[19] A. P. Annan, and S.W. Cosway, "Ground Penetrating Radar Design," Proceedings of the Symposium on the Application of Geophysics to Engineering and Environmental Problems (SAGEEP), vol 2, pp. 329-351, 1992, DOI 10.4133/1.2921946.

[20] J. van der Kruk, E. C. Slob, and J. T. Fokkema, "Background of ground-penetrating radar measurements," Journal of Geologie en Mijnbouw, vol. 77, Issue 2, pp. 177-188, 1998, DOI 10.1023/A:103546619639.

[21] B. M. ter Haar Romeny, "Front-End Vision and Multi-Scale Image Analysis: Multi-Scale Computer Vision Theory and Applications written in Mathematica," Springer Publishers, 2008, ISBN 978-1-4020-1507-6.

[22] J. van der Kruk, "Reflection Seismic I," Lecture Series in WS 2004/2005, Institut für Geophysik ETH Zürich, http://www.wgeosoft.ch/Document/Reflection_ETHZ.pdf, 2017.11.23.

[23] H. M. Jol, editor, "Ground Penetrating Radar Theory and Applications," Elsevier Science, 2009, ISBN: 978-0-444-53348-7.

Designing Microservice-Based Applications by Using a Domain-Driven Design Approach

Benjamin Hippchen, Pascal Giessler, Roland Heinz Steinegger,
Michael Schneider and Sebastian Abeck

Research Group Cooperation & Management (C&M)
Karlsruhe Institute of Technology (KIT)
Zirkel 2, 76131 Karlsruhe, Germany
(benjamin.hippchen | pascal.giessler | steinegger | abeck)@kit.edu,
michael.schneider5@student.kit.edu

***Abstract*—The current trend of building web applications using microservice architectures is based on the domain-driven design concept. Among practitioners, domain-driven design is a widely accepted approach to building applications. Applying and extending the concepts and tasks of domain-driven design is challenging because it lacks a software development process description and classification within existing software development process approaches. For these reasons, this paper provides a brief overview of domain-driven design-based software development activities and their classification into a well-known software development process.**

Keywords–Domain-driven design; behavior-driven development; domain model; microservices; API;

I. Introduction

This article is an extended version of [1], which was published at SOFTENG 2017. Our former article presents an overview of activities for building microservice-based applications by using a domain-driven design (DDD) approach. In addition, we discuss the elicitation of requirements, align the hexagonal architecture for microservices into the field of software architecture and discuss testing and implementing the different layers of microservices. By considering application requirements, we tackle limitations described in our previous article. Microservice architectures have evolved into a popular method for building multiplatform applications over the past few years. A well-known example is Netflix, who offers applications for several platforms, including mobile devices, smart TVs and gaming consoles [2]. Service-oriented architectures are the foundation of microservice architectures, but microservices have unique properties [3]. A microservice is autonomous and provides a limited set of (business) functions. In service-oriented architectures, designing services and selecting boundaries are fundamental problems.

The traditional approach, as discussed by Erl [4], suggests a technical and functional separation of services. In contrast, according to Evans [5], DDD provides the key concepts required to compartmentalize microservices [2]. The DDD approach provides a means of representing the real world in the architecture, for instance, by using bounded contexts representing organizational units [6], and also identifies and focuses on the core domain; both of these characteristics lead to improved software architecture quality [7]. In microservice architectures, these bounded contexts are used to arrange and identify microservices [2]. Using DDD is a critical success factor in building microservice-based applications [2].

When applying DDD to the development of microservice-based applications, several problems may arise, depending on the level of experience of the development team. Domain-driven design offers principles, patterns, activities, and examples of how to build a domain model, which is its core artifact. However, it neither provides a detailed and systematic development process for applying these principles and patterns nor does it classify them into the field of software engineering. Classifying the activities, introduced by DDD, into the activities of a software development process could improve the applicability. Further, the classification of the patterns and principles into software architecture concepts, such as architecture perspectives and its requirements, supports software architects in designing microservice architectures.

In addition, there are no clear guidelines regarding how to derive the basic web application programming interfaces (web APIs) that act as a service contract between microservices and the application. The importance of a service contract is described by Erl [4]. From the business perspective, the web APIs also have strategic value; therefore, the development team must design it in a manner that emphasizes quality [8].

Furthermore, applications and, in particular, user interfaces, are often not considered or only considered superficially during the process of designing service-oriented architectures [2][4]. However, the application can play a major role when building the underlying microservices. Domain-driven design emphasizes that the application is necessary to determine the underlying domain logic of microservices; the user interface is important to consider when designing specific web APIs for the UI when using the backends for frontends (BFF) pattern [2]. When designing microservices within the software-as-a-service (SaaS) context, there is no graphical user interface; instead, there is a technical one. The target group shifts from end users to external companies or independent developers who can benefit from the capabilities of the offered service. For this reason, a web API has to be designed in such a manner that it can map as many possible use cases for a particular domain as possible. The resulting set of use cases represents the requirements that must be handled by the web API and the microservices.

We experienced these challenges when establishing a software development process based on DDD to build SmartCampus, a service-oriented web application. During the process we could not find literature that addressed these problems. Thus, we classify DDD activities within the field of software engineering, arrange the components of a microservice-based application according to the layers of DDD and describe the activities necessary in building microservice-based applications. We apply these activities in an agile software development process used to build parts of the SmartCampus application and discuss both the results and limitations. Further, we combined the application of DDD with behavior-driven development (BDD). The gap of the requirement specification on the application level, which we discussed in our previous article, is tackled through the "living documentation" [9]. So, DDD provides the core of the application and BDD specifies the access to it. BDD also helps to test the application from a user's point of view and to test the domain model at the same time.

This article is structured as follows: In Section II, DDD, BDD and microservice architecture, including a general introduction to software architecture and development and other related concepts, are introduced. Section III classifies DDD, BDD and microservices and introduces the software development activities required in building microservice-based applications according to the requirements of DDD. In the next section, a case study demonstrates the application of these activities within a software development process, including artifacts. The limitations discovered while applying the activities are described in Section V. A conclusion regarding the activities and possible future areas of inquiry is presented in Section VI.

II. Foundation and Related Work

This section provides an overview of model-driven engineering (an approach that is similar to DDD), DDD itself, traditional software engineering activities (which are used to classify DDD activites), BDD for requirements elicitation, software architecture in general (as the foundation being the foundation for classifying microservice architecture) and microservice architecture.

A. Model-Driven Engineering and Model-Driven Architecture

Schmidt [10] describes Model-Driven Engineering (MDE) as an approach that is used to effectively express domains in models. The Object Management Group (OMG) introduced their framework model-driven architecture (MDA) [11] to support the implementation of MDE. MDA identifies three steps necessary in moving from the abstract design to the implementation of an application. Three models are created by carrying out these steps: 1) computation independent model (CIM) provides domain concepts without taking technological aspects into consideration, 2) platform independent model (PIM) enriches the CIM with computational aspects; and 3) platform specific model (PSM) enriches the PIM with the aspects of implementation that are specific to a particular technological platform.

Using a model-driven approach, models become the primary artifacts in the development of applications. Thus, a clear understanding of the model and modeling language is necessary for an effective use. Metamodels are used to define the possibilities about what the model language can express [12]. In case of the Unified Modeling Language (UML), OMG defined the Meta-Object Facility (MOF) as the basis for all metamodels [12]. Defining model languages with this framework, a four-layer metamodeling architecture is applied: 1) M0 designates the real world object, that will be model, 2) M1 denotes the model, which represents M0, 3) M2 defines a metamodel for limiting the modeling possibilities from M1, 4) M3 represents the meta-metamodel, which specifies the modeling language for metamodels. Since MDA is a model-driven appraoch, it sticks to the four-layer architecture from MOF.

B. Software Engineering Activities and Domain-Driven Design

Brügge et al. [13] describe a widely accepted software engineering approach in the context of object-orientation. We use their concepts to classify the activities we identified to build microservice-based applications using DDD. This object-oriented approach works well when small teams build applications that span a several domains. [13] offers an overview of the activities that take place during software development: requirements elicitation, analysis, systems design, object design, implementation, and testing. (These activities are discussed further in the article's introduction of the development activities.)

DDD is an approach that is used in application development where the domain model is the central artifact. Software architects and developers use the domain model as main source for software design and development. Furthermore, DDD focuses on the business logic of the customer's domain and neglects technical aspects of the application. Evans introduced this approach in the book "Domain-Driven Design: Tackling Complexity in the Hearth of Software" and identified the essential principles, activities, and patterns required when using DDD [5].

A domain model that conforms to Evans' DDD approach contains everything that is necessary to understand the domain [5]. This approach goes beyond the traditional understanding of a domain model, which is connected to a formalized model using the UML [14]. To distinguish between the two concepts, following Fairbanks [15], we use the term information model which corresponds to a CIM. It is a part of the domain model and consists out of concepts, relationships, and constraints. In order to support downstream implementation, Evans adds implementation specific details to the model. The resulting domain model corresponds to a PIM. In case of DDD, the modeling language of the domain model is not specified by an metamodel—like the CIM and PIM in MDA. A metamodel would be contradictory to the "everything is allowed in the domain model" philosophy of Evans. The comparison of the domain model to a CIM and PIM only reflects the evolution of the domain model and states nothing about the modeling language. As a result, the systematic approach of MDA cannot be applied to DDD's domain models.

In Evans' approach to DDD, the central principle is to align the desired application with the domain model. The domain model shapes the "*ubiquitous language*" that is used among the team members and functions as a tool used to achieve this goal.

C. Requirements Elicitation with Behavior-Driven Development

The requirement elicitation activity described by Brügge [13] could be carried out in various ways. With DDD, requirements are gathered and stated in the domain model [5]. Regarding the layered architecture of DDD (see Section II-B), just requirements of the domain layer are covered. So, there is a lack of specifications for the other layers.

With BDD the requirement elicitation is carried out by the developers and application users themselves [9]; there is a difference between users and domain experts. BDD builds on an informal and executable requirement specification for the intended application. Both, users and developers, are exploring the requirements of the application, sharpening their picture of the application and establishing a shared understanding. The idea of BDD is based on test-driven development (TDD) and its automated acceptance tests [9], which determine the correctness of the application [16]. Furthermore, BDD emphasizes the understanding of the user's domain. BDD uses the ubiquitous language known from DDD [9].

The philosophy behind BDD is a requirement elicitation from outside-in [9]. North characterizes "*code-by-example*" in the context of BDD [17]. The most visible behavior is elicited first; then it is implemented. During the implementation, new details are discovered, which will also be stated as requirements. In BDD, requirements are stated as features, which are further divided into scenarios [9]. The language Gherkin is usually used to describe these artifacts formally. Each scenario is written in common speech and is refined in steps. Each step starts with a predefined (Gherkin) keyword, which is necessary to execute the tests in later stages. Through the binding of BDD features to implementation and testing activities, the requirement specification must be kept up-to-date; it becomes a "living documentation" [9].

D. Microservice Architectures

Vogel et al. provide a comprehensive framework for the area of software architecture [18], which is used to classify microservices and DDD. Their architecture framework has six dimensions: 1) architectures and architecture disciplines, 2) architecture perspectives, 3) architecture requirements, 4) architecture means, 5) organizations and individuals and 6) architecture methods. The essential terms used in describing an architecture are: systems, which consist of software and hardware building blocks; a software building block can be a functional, technical or platform building block. Building blocks can also consist of other building blocks and may require them. The authors also introduce the concept of architecture views; their definition is influenced by the IEEE [19]. Architecture views are part of the documentation that describes the architecture. Each view is motivated by stakeholders' concerns. These concerns specify the viewpoints on the architecture and, thus, specify the views.

Newman provides a comprehensive overview of microservices and related topics from an industry perspective [2]. He defines a microservice as a "small, autonomous service" that does one thing well; and adds that the term "small" is difficult to define. In contrast to services in a service-oriented architecture according to Erl [4], the single purpose principle results in microservices having similar sizes within an architecture [3]. Two mapping studies regarding microservices and microservice architecture reveal that a gap in the literature regarding these topics exists [20][21].

Regarding the structure of a microservice based application, Vernon introduces the hexagonal architecture in the context of DDD [22]. Initially, the corresponding architecture pattern was postulated by Cockburn in [23]. In the resulting architecture by applying this pattern, the concerns of a microservice are separated into several layers, see Figure 1. According to Cockburn, the hexagonal architecture consists out of the domain model, application services and adapters with ports. Each side of the hexagon stands for a particular port, although, in practice, there could be more than six distinct ports. Using these ports, the microservice can upstream or downstream information with clients. For consuming microservices, the client has to use one of the exposed ports and its corresponding adapter. The adapters work like an anti corruption layer. Highly relying on the dependency inversion principle (DIP) from Martin [24], the domain model as the core and hence the business logic is independent of the surrounding application services and adapters. The layer dependencies are applied from the outside to inside. (Further relevant information is discussed during the section of this article that classifies microservice architectures.)

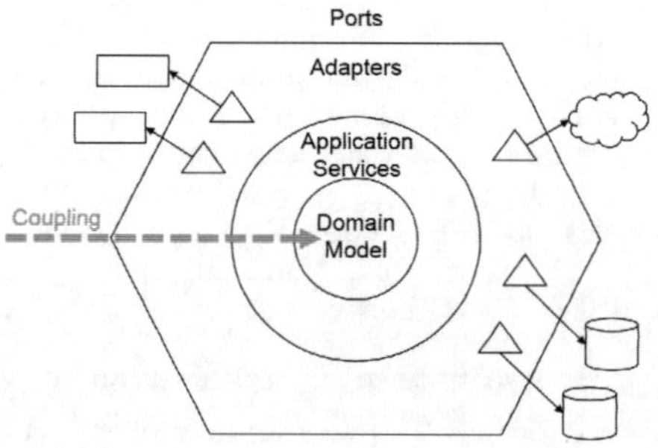

Figure 1. The hexagonal architecture pattern from Cockburn [23]

III. Process

This section classifies the activities involved in DDD and concepts related to microservice architectures; furthermore, the software development activities involved in building microservice-based applications using DDD are introduced. The activities discussed can be applied to various software process models. However, DDD requires that one constantly scrutinizes and adjusts the understanding of the domain. Thus, agile software development processes are most suitable.

A. Classification

We identify specifications, that are missing when just applying DDD to build a microservice-based application, by classifying DDD and microservice architecture using the software architecture concepts of Vogel et al. [18]. We divide the classification process into two parts: first, we discuss the architecture perspective and second the architecture requirements.

Concerning the architecture perspective, software architecture can be divided into macro- and micro-architecture; it can further be divided into organization, system and building block level. The organization and system levels form the macro-architecture whereas the building block level can be assigned either to the macro or micro-architecture, depending on what is required for the concrete architecture. [18] Despite their names, microservice architecture and the domain model describe the macro-architecture. A microservice is a functional or technical software building block that requires a platform to run on. Neither DDD nor microservices limit the underlying platform. When using DDD, microservices are structured according to the organizational units using bounded contexts from the domain model [2][22]. The domain objects within a bounded context specify the core architecture of a microservice.

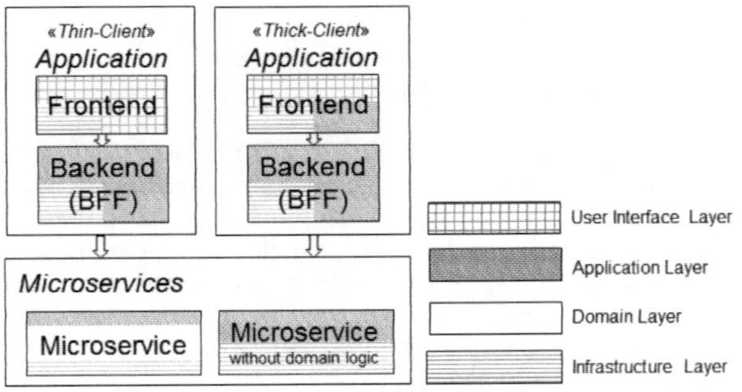

Figure 2. Software building blocks and their layers in a microservice-based application

Domain-driven design requires a layered architecture to separate the domain from other concerns [5]. Evans suggests a four-layered architecture, consisting of the user interface, application, domain, and infrastructure layers. Figure 2 shows the distribution of these layers among the software building blocks of microservice-based applications. On the highest abstraction level, microservice-based applications can be divided into applications and microservices. The application consists of a frontend, which is either thick or thin (meaning that it contains application logic or not), and its backend, which provides the application logic. The backend uses the microservices to access the domain layer or general infrastructure functionality. Each microservice has an application layer on top. The application layer translates requests into either the domain or infrastructure layers. Infrastructure logic *may* be part of each software building block. In our approach, we applied the layer distribution following Miller's approach [25].

In a layered architecture, higher layers can communicate with lower layers. Figure 3 depicts the layered architecture's communication paths applied to the above-mentioned software building blocks [25]. The frontend should not directly call the microservices; we emphasize this by using dashed arrows.

The layering from Figure 2 shows that the layering introduced by DDD is also applied to the microservice architecture. Going into the implementation of a microservice, the sequence of the layers changes. The underlying structure of the microservices is defined through the hexagonal architecture pattern by Cockburn [23]. Having a more accurate look at the building blocks of the microservices, we are using an onion architecture introduced by Palermo

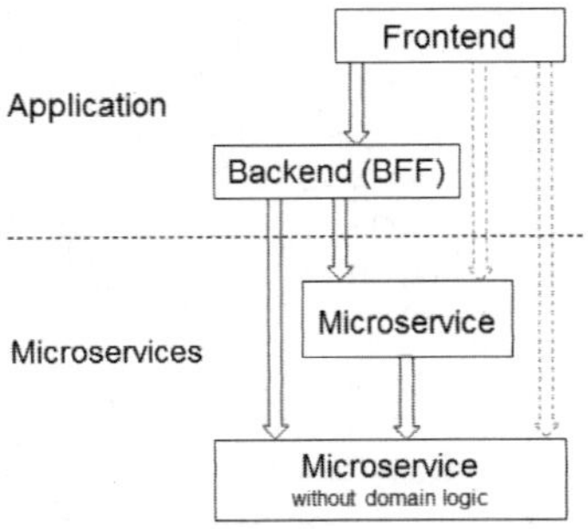

Figure 3. Communication between software building blocks

[26] with minimal adoptions as shown in Figure 4. The onion architecture builds on the hexagonal architecture. Vernon states that the hexagonal architecture and the onion architecture are the same [22]. On the outer layer of the onion architecture, we find the infrastructure as well as the exposed interface as fine-grained building blocks. The infrastructure part of the layer provides technical functionality for the operation of the service such as database access. The exposed user interfaces focuses on the provisioning of the underlying business domain that can be used by clients for interaction. Like in the hexagonal architecture, the adapter pattern is used on this layer. In addition, the onion architecture adds a new layer, the so-called domain services. Domain services represent behavior that cannot be mapped to domain objects [5][22]. For instance, this is the case if the behavior is spread over multiple domain objects to form a business workflow. This way, the domain services are tightly coupled with the domain objects; together, they build the whole domain. In [26], Palermo also puts the interface definition of the repository on this layer. But, in our opinion, this approach would mix the domain-specific layer with technical aspects. That is why we add the so-called glue layer that acts as a link layer between the application and domain. The from DDD known repositories or factories are put into this layer. The heart of the onion architecture is represented by the domain objects.

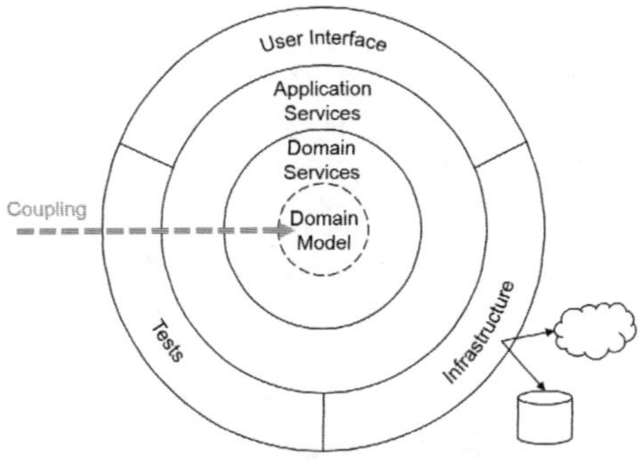

Figure 4. Our adapted onion architecture based on Palermo [26]

The layered architecture is applied to the whole application and divides it into horizontally-divided layers. Meanwhile, the onion architecture is applied to the microservice building blocks from Figure 3 and divides them in a vertical manner. Going back to DDD, a microservice is defined through a single bounded context in the customer's domain [2]. Considering the microservice architecture as an onion makes it more suitable with the concept of bounded contexts. Every microservice has to work autonomously, which is intended with the layering of the onion architecture.

Concerning architecture requirements, the decision to build microservice-based applications is taken at the organizational level (see the classification of service-oriented applications in [18]). Along with a microservice architecture, the organization should choose a protocol that allows all of the microservices within the organization to communicate; e.g., using representational state transfer (REST) over hypertext transfer protocol (HTTP) with a set of guidelines or an event bus. The platform running the microservices (e.g., Docker), the database technologies, the implementation of identity and access management etc. *might* also be organizational requirements; when building a microservice architecture the software architects have to decide, whether or not these concerns should be homogenous. We could not identify any requirements concerning the system or building block levels that are based on DDD or the microservice approach.

Some specification is still missing. The domain model specifies the functional view on the domain but does not consider technical aspects [5]. Thus, in addition to the domain model, there is a need for artifacts that describe the microservice architecture, including technical microservices and platform architecture. Furthermore, assuming that the domain model describes the architecture of the domain layer, the user interface, application, and infrastructure layer are not specified. Translating this into the context of the software building blocks, the frontend and backend may require specification. The decision to add further artifacts could be based on the risks involved in the application, as discussed by Fairbanks [15]. In case of the application layer, we started using BDD as an approach for eliciting requirements as features from the application users. The features could also be used for testing the domain layer. Further, we decided to add a user interface (UI)/user experience (UX) design, which specifies both the user interface and the user's interaction. Thus, this artifact specifies the frontend and backend.

B. Activity Overview

Next, we are introducing the activities involved in building microservice-based applications. These activities facilitate the development of applications within similar domains, e.g., an application that offers information on points of interest, an application navigating from and to points of interest and an application that enables the management of points of interest. We align our activities with the traditional software development activities described by Brügge et al. [13]. Therefore, the activities end after testing, and we do not discuss deployment and/or maintenance. Artifacts associated to deployment and maintenance, such as a deployment diagram or a platform description, are not discussed. Figure 5 depicts the three activities and their interrelations: *requirements elicitation and analysis*, *design* and *implementation and testing*.

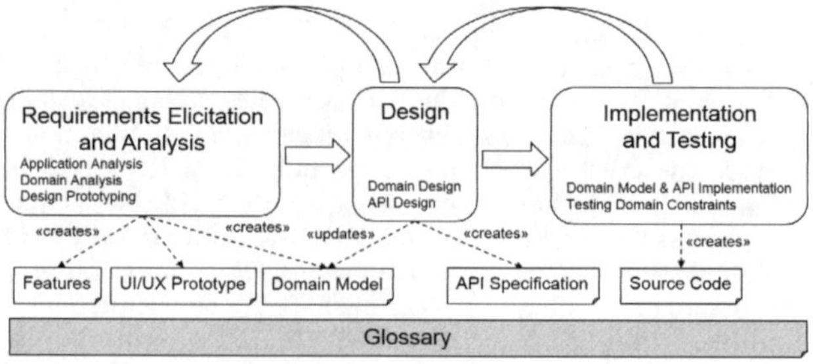

Figure 5. Overview of the activities used in building microservice-based applications

During the *requirements elicitation and analysis*, three sub-activities take place: first, the application requirements are stated in features with and from users by following the BDD approach; second, the information model, as part of the domain model, is created by "crunching knowledge" with domain experts; third, a prototype is designed and is discussed with both the user and customer. As all activities are closely related (when discussing prototypes, the knowledge of the domain gets deeper, when discovering the information model, terms or workflows might change, and while eliciting requirements, the goal of the application is sharpened), we combined them into a single activity.

The *design* is comprised of the sub-activities involved in designing the domain and the APIs of the microservices. Based on the UI/UX design and further discussions with the domain experts, the information model is refined, e.g., design decisions are made, and design patterns from DDD are applied. Domain design is comparable to the system design activity discussed by Brügge et al. [13]. The system is divided into subsystems that, according to Conway's Law [6], can be realized by individual teams using bounded contexts. Domain design results in a domain model that must be bound to the implementation artifacts. As the microservices offer access to the domain model and translate from the application layer to the domain layer, both the UI/UX design (representing the user interface layer and the application layer) as well as the domain model (representing the domain layer of DDD) are used to design the web APIs of the microservices. If using a BFF, its web API is designed, too. This activity can be assigned to the object design activity discussed by Brügge et al. [13].

After this preliminary work, the microservices are *implemented and tested*. The web APIs describe the microservices' entry points. These entry points and their application logic are implemented and tested, as the microservices' domain model. The features from the application analysis are used to test the application. In particular, they are used to test the constraints defined in the domain model, such as multiplicities or directed associations.

The ubiquitous language is central to the use of DDD, therefore, we introduced a glossary to capture the domain terms. Each term of the ubiquitous language is listed and described by a few sentences. We see the glossary as a cross-sectional artifact. It is created and updated in each activity of Figure 5. Maintaining the glossary takes effort, but the benefits outweigh this effort.

Evans states that developing a "*deep model*", with which

to facilitate software development requires "*exploration and experimentation*" [5]. Thus, in order to gain insights into the domain across the whole software development activities, software developers must be open-minded. The knowledge gained will probably lead to changes being made to the artifacts created in the previous phases. Therefore, a process of iteration and returning to previous phases is possible in each phase; in other words, it is very common for developers to switch between phases and activities. Of course, experienced developers may make fewer mistakes and discover insights earlier, but hidden knowledge and misunderstandings are common. In the following sections, the phases are explained in more detail.

C. Requirements Elicitation and Analysis

The first activity deals with the understanding of the application and the needs of the users. Three non-chronological ordered activities take place in this phase, namely the analysis of the application, exploration of the domain and the design of a prototype. These activities influence each other to a significant degree; terms from the application features and the domain model are used in the prototype, while new insights may result in changes being made to them. We see a strong connection between the process of eliciting the application requirements, developing the domain model and design prototyping that arise due to the specifications that are not captured during the domain modeling process. Every domain concept displayed in the design prototype must be modeled in the domain model and vice versa. In addition, the domain concepts must be used by the application features. Small iterations during the analysis phase are required to ensure that all artifacts are consistent.

1) Application Analysis: Specifying the Application with BDD: The functionality of the application depends on the needs of the user. Therefore, we see a comprehensive requirement elicitation with the users. By applying BDD to elicit requirements, the users are fully involved [9]. Requirements are stated in features (see Section II-C) and scenarios. Each feature is created by developers, users or both. A developer explores the intended application while discussing and creating features with users. BDD also emphasizes that users are able to create features on their own. Both, developer and user, features have to be considered equal for the implementation activity. This activity is resulting into a comprehensive requirement specification, which is executable for automated application testing. Regarding the layered architecture from DDD, the application layer from our intended application is specified.

By using BDD, our approach starts with the creation of features by the developers and users. Both are discussing and simultaneously creating the features. We noticed an improvement in quality and accuracy, if developers and users are collaborating during feature creation. BDD emphasizes an "*outside-in*" approach for the elicitation of application requirements [9]. The most visible behavior is stated as a feature and implemented subsequently. During implementation, developers will discover more details, which have to be discussed with the users. Either an existing feature is adjusted or a new feature is created. Afterward, the features are implemented step-by-step. North calls this "*code-by-example*" in a presentation at London's QCon 2009 [17].

During discussions and feature-writing, the synergy with DDD gets visible. The ubiquitous language is established and sharpened while talking about the features. Developers get insights about the relevant domain concepts. In addition, BDD emphasizes a "*living documentation*", which is achieved by the strong binding of features, implementation and testing [9][27]. This living documentation requires a continuous adoption of features; they need to be up-to-date in every phase of the project. The living documentation leads to a meaningful requirement specification.

The application analysis using BDD is resulting into a requirement specification, which consists of informal features and scenarios. The informal character makes it possible for users and developers to validate the correctness. The "for everybody" readable features provide an up-to-date source of knowledge, which enables that the functionality is implemented properly and works as intended. Developers can use the features as guidance during the implementation and as a main artifact for writing tests.

2) Domain Analysis: Exploring the Domain with DDD: Without a complete understanding of the domain, building applications that satisfy the requirements is difficult. In our approach, we focus on Evans' book "Domain-Driven Design: Tackling Complexity in the Heart of Software" in order to understand the needs and, thus, the domain through modeling [5]. Creating a comprehensive domain model in this phase even requires experienced domain modelers to acquire new knowledge. After this activity, we are left with a domain model that is the equivalent of an information model (see Section II-B). UML class diagram syntax is used to describe concepts and their relationships, constraints, etc. [15][28]. Also, this information model corresponds to a CIM. CIM is well known from the MDA [29][30].

According to DDD, collaboration with customers is essential to the exploration process and, in particular, the modeling of the domain. Thus, the permanently recurring activity, in DDD is knowledge crunching [5]. The development team simultaneously holds discussions with customers while carrying out the modeling process and creating the domain model. Conforming to the pattern *Hands-On Modelers*, every team member involved in the software development process should also participate in the domain-modeling process in order to promote creativity [5]. In addition, the "*ubiquitous language*" is established, which is the cross-team language. As Vernon [22] suggests, we create a glossary to record the terms of the domain that are part of ubiquitios language. The process, by which the domain model is developed, is influenced to a great degree by exploration and experimentation [5]. It is far better to implement a domain model that is not completly satisfactory than to repeatedly refine the domain model without actually implementing it [5]. Using the DDD approach requires an iterative process that takes into account principles taken from the agile development processes, such as short time to market. Especially the domain model needs to be adapted iteratively.

Complex domains automatically lead to a complex domain model; this complexity may make it difficult for readers to understand the domain model. As a result, it is necessary to split the model into multiple diagrams [25], which enables the modeler to model different aspects of the domain. Dynamic behaviors, such as workflows, are concepts that are relevant to the domain. We adopted the architectural view concept (see Section III-A) from software architecture [18] by introducing "*domain views*", which guides the modeler to model different aspects of the domain. The concept is designed to split the domain model into multiple diagrams. Furthermore, it simplifies and structures the modeling activity. We see the need for a more guided modeling activity to support less experienced modelers.

Figure 6 displays the building blocks of the domain view concept and their relations. DDD is always based on an application and each artifact is aligned with the desired functionalities. Thus, the domain model belongs to the application and is only valid for the specific application. The domain model consists of mulitple domain views, which contains the domain objects. A domain view is assigned to a specific domain view type. This domain view type is used to determine the domain objects and identify the possible representation with UML diagrams. A type of a domain view is specified through one or more stakeholders. Each stakeholder describes the system from their respective viewpoints; stakeholders have one or more interests. Evans states, that for representing domain knowledge every possible diagram is allowed for modeling the domain model as long as it is supporting the understanding of the domain concept [5]. In our approach, we limited the possible representations with a set of UML diagrams. Each domain view type has its own set.

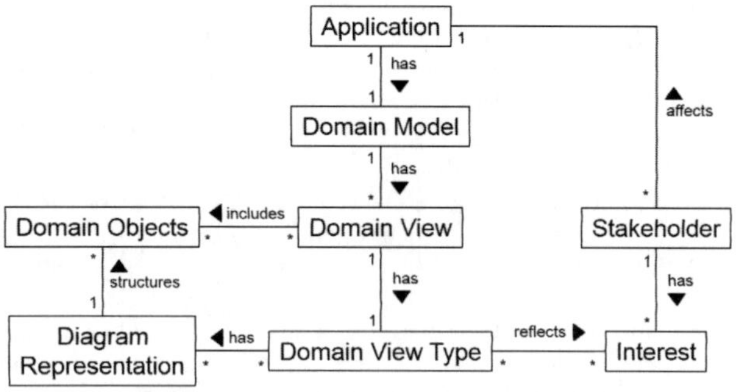

Figure 6. Building blocks of the domain view concept

We created two domain view types. First, the "*relation view*" models domain objects and their real world relationships with each other. This domain view type addresses the static behavior of the domain. Second, the "*process view*" represents the dynamic behavior of the domain. Domain objects and interactions are used to model processes of the domain.

The relation between the interest of a stakeholder and domain view type (see Figure 6) makes it possible to determine the right persons for the discussion of the domain view contents. Thus, during knowledge crunching, we were able to identify modelers and domain experts. Stakeholders have different interests and affect the structure of the domain view content. In addition to the domain expert, we defined developers, software architects, security architects and API designers as stakeholders. The API designer as a stakeholder emphasizes the development of microservice-based applications.

The result of exploring the domain is a domain model, which contains concepts that are relevant to the application (also called the "*domain knowledge*") [5]. Domain-driven design emphasizes the focus on the core domain. Implementing this domain has the highest priority [5]; the best developers are assigned.

3) Design Prototyping: By means of knowledge crunching, we obtain a complete understanding of the domain considered. The requirements of an application are use case-specific and function as indicators of the domain logic that must be modeled in the domain model. Based on BDD and the discussion with the stakeholders, each identified feature will be represented in the so-called design prototype. A prototype is an efficient means of testing new design concepts and determining their efficiency [31]. The design prototype is specialized, as it focuses on the application's UI and the UX. Since the customer primarily interacts with the UI, it is also an ideal artifact for further discussions with customers regarding the domain model. Further benefits of using a prototype can be found in [31]. Similarly to knowledge crunching, design prototyping is an iterative activity. Each iteration involves a brain-storming session that focuses on design ideas, taking into account the given boundary conditions, realization of the previously chosen design ideas and presentation and review of the resulting design prototype. As part of the review process, feedback from the customer will be collected and analyzed in order to identify the design changes necessary for the next iteration. The design prototyping process is completed when the prototype satisfies all of the customer's needs.

D. Design Phase

Two activities take place during the design phase: domain and API design. These activities require the domain model and the UI/UX design created during the previous phase. After the design phase, both the domain model and the API specifications will be ready to implement.

1) Domain Design: From Computational to PIM: An important DDD concept is the binding of the domain to the process of implementation [5]. The domain model is the core artifact required in achieving this domain-layer goal. During the analysis phase, a CIM is created as a part of the domain model. First, this model is divided into bounded contexts, and, second, these bounded contexts are extended and refined, e.g., by applying design patterns to satisfy the application's requirements. These activities were based on the examples provided by Evans and Vernon [5][22].

The organizational structure is used to divide the information model into bounded contexts. Due to its importance, this task requires experience and several iterations [22][32]. The process of division is closely linked to the division of the development teams, as each works on a bounded context [2]. Thus, intermediate results should be discussed with the domain experts and other team members. The result is a context map that depicts the relationship between the bounded contexts.

The next steps are mainly carried out by the development teams that are responsible for each bounded context. The goal of the next activity is to refine and extend the domain model according to the application's requirements. Both BDD features and UI/UX design are the main source considered when it comes to determining the application's requirements.

In all likelihood, the domain objects in the information model will already be marked with stereotypes that indicate their type, e.g., aggregate root, value object, entity or domain event. Some services might be identified during the analysis phase. Domain objects that lack a stereotype should be addressed first, meaning that a stereotype should be added. Next, the design patterns repository, factory and domain service are added according to the application's requirements. For example, if there is a need to display a domain object in the UI, a repository may be added, or, if there is a complex aggregate root, a factory could be added [5]. During the entire design process, the domain experts and other sources of information should be involved (this is referred to continuous knowledge crunching). After applying the design patterns, the domain model is ready to be implemented.

2) API Design: Deriving the Web API from the PIM: Microservices provide their implemented business functions via web APIs [2]. A web API can be seen as a specialization of a traditional API, which is why we extend the definition offered by Gebhart et al. slightly further: an API is "a contract prescribing how to interact with the underlying system [over the Web]," [33, p. 139]. From a business perspective, a web API can be seen as a highly valuable asset [8][34] that can also serve as a solution for digital transformation [33].

A web API can be used to coordinate microservices in the mapping of a complex business workflow onto the area of microservices or to offer business functionality to third-party developers [33]. To facilitate the reuse and discovery of existing microservice functions, the exposed web APIs should be designed with care. According to Newman [2], Jacobsen [34] and Mulloy [35], web APIs should adhere to the following informal quality criteria: 1) they should be easy to understand, learn and use from a service consumer's point of view, 2) they should be abstracted from a particular technology, 3) they should be consistent in look and feel and 4) they should be robust in terms of evolution.

To address these challenges, it is necessary to develop a systematic approach for deriving the web API from its underlying domain model. First, we decided to build web APIs in a resource-oriented manner that can be positioned on the second level of the Richardson maturity model [36]; we do not pursue the hypermedia approach suggested by Fielding [37] to reduce complexity when building microservice-based applications. Second, we have identified resources and sub-resources from the underlying PIM by examining the relationships between the domain objects. For the identification, we have created heuristics based on a UML class diagram that allows us to derive resource candidates systematically. The derived resources are then categorized in different types of resources according to Tilkov [38] and Rathod et al. [39]. Based on the resulting categorized set of resources, we have added URIs so that each resource can be addressed over the web without ambiguity. For the URI structure, we have followed several conventions to improve the discoverability and ensure the consistency in the context of our microservice landscape. The used conventions are listed as linguistic patterns and established best practices in this area [40]. Afterward, we have investigated the possible interactions of each of the identified resource types regarding their life cycle and mapped them subsequently to the modeled behavior of the domain. In addition, the interactions that will be exposed by the web API has to be also aligned with the BDD features, domain model, and UI/UX design; that is why the domain views (see Section III-C2) play a significant role. Nonetheless, the interactions should not be limited to the different use cases to ensure a high reusability. This fact is of particular importance when choosing an appropriate API strategy. Up to this point, we have made no technology decisions; the resulting model can be seen as a PIM. With the selection of an appropriate application protocol such as HTTP or Constrained Application Protocol (CoAP), we transform the PIM to a PSM.

The result of this design approach was finally structured according to the specifications of OpenAPI, which has the goal of "defining a standard, language-agnostic interface to REST APIs, which allows both humans and computers to discover and understand the capabilities of the service without access to source code, documentation, or through network traffic inspection" [41]. In addition to this, we have extracted our guidelines for designing resource-oriented APIs in the form of a checklist in [40].

3) API Design: Deriving the Web API for BFF from the Design Prototype: A BFF is a pattern that is commonly used to avoid so-called chatty APIs [2]. Chatty APIs often result in the service consumer having to make a large number of requests in order to obtain the required information [35, p. 30f]. This is mainly due the fact that the domain information or logic required is spread over multiple microservices and primarily designed for reusability, rather than a specific use case in the form of a concrete application. In addition, BFFs allow a development team to focus on the UI and UX-specific requirements of an application by not restricting themselves to the microservices' exposed web APIs. When using DDD, additional application logic can be required, such as data transformation, caching or orchestration, which may be implemented at the BFF level or at the application layer [5]. For this reason, the BFF can be seen as part of the UI [2].

In our approach, the UI and UX specific requirements are represented using a design prototype that resulted from the analysis phase (see Section III-C3). Similarly to Section III-D2, we decided to adopt a resource-oriented style for the BFF web API and applied the same web API guidelines. The use of other solutions, such as a method-oriented approach, is also possible. For deriving the web API, we considered each view regarding the represented information as well as the interaction elements used for data manipulation. This approach allowed us to build resources, their representations and the necessary operations. The resulting web API is highly linked to the UI and must be connected to the underlying domain represented by microservices. Since both the domain model and the design prototype were designed using *ubiquitous language*, the required microservices can be identified with a minimum of effort and orchestrated on the application layer in order to fulfill the requirements specified by the BFF web API derived previously.

E. Implementation and Testing

The features, domain model and specification of the web API enabled the development team to implement the application. This section discusses the implementation and testing of the microservices. We do not discuss the implementation of the UI/UX design, as the focus of this study is on DDD and building microservices. However, the implementation and testing of the BFF, as the connection between the front-end and the microservices, are discussed. Furthermore, we discuss the use of BDD features for testing the domain model.

1) Implementation: Developing the Microservice: First, we focus on implementing and testing the microservices. Using the specified API, each bounded context is implemented as a microservice. A development project, e.g., a Maven or Gradle project that includes source code, necessary dependencies, and build instructions, is created and pushed into the version control repository. We recommend offering the API specification as part of the microservice; it is added to the repository and delivered through its web interface. Using this approach, changes to the API can be pushed to the repository together with their implementation. In addition, the API specification can also be delivered at runtime when offering a dedicated endpoint. This could, for example, be useful when having a dedicated API management system or a central service registry.

Domain-driven design highly recommends the use of continuous integration [5]; thus, the continuous integration pipeline was also configured. In addition to that, we have also added continous inspection that checks our latest build artifact against our test cases, coding guidelines or common issues from the Open Web Application Security Project (OWASP). Vernon [22] describes how to implement REST resources separating the application from the domain layer. The web API describes entry points to the microservice; they can be implemented in a straightforward manner. In order to separate application-specific parts from those that are domain specific, e.g., the usage of REST, logic at the entry points should be application specific. Thus, a microservice should have an application layer on top. Typically, this layer is implemented as an anti-corruption layer; a design pattern used to achieve a clean separation of application and domain-terms [22]. Additionally, by preventing the use of domain objects as input parameters,—the Spring framework offers this functionality by using the Jackson framework [42]—, the coupling of domain objects and the web API is reduced. Thus, some minor changes to the domain model will not influence the implementation of the interface [22]. Again, the whole architecture of the microservice is illustrated in Figure 4.

The domain layer is implemented according to the domain model. Thus, when using an object-oriented programming language, the domain objects in the bounded context are mapped to classes. Constraints, such as multiplicities and domain logic, are implemented in the domain object. If a domain object from another microservice is used, a reference to the object is saved, e.g., by using its identifier [22][43]. Implemented domain objects are intelligent objects that ensure the constraints within the domain. To make sure that the constraints are correctly implemented, development approaches such as test-driven development [16] or even behavior-driven development [44] are good choices in order for achieving this. But, constraints can be distributed among the domain model; thus, constraints might be overseen. Separating the tester and the developer of the functionality, pair-programming and reviews can help to overcome this problem.

Besides the application and domain layers, the infrastructure layer is also part of the microservice. This layer contains the functionality used to access databases, log events, enforce authorization, cache results, discover services, etc.—in other words, everything that supports the application and domain layers. Apparent is the support for domain repositories. If a microservice has a repository, the infrastructure layer must offer access to a database.

Last, we discuss the implementation of the UI's backend. The backend is an application of the BFF pattern. Therefore, a main goal is to offer a facade that conceals the microservice architecture; implementation can be kept simple. Its web API is implemented according to the API specification. In our case, the specification is oriented to the microservice web API's specification; thus, the request can be directly forwarded to the microservice.

Depending on the specification, the frontend may be required to support further functionality; e.g., authentication and access control may be implemented in the UI's backend.

2) Testing: Using BDD for Verifying the Correctness of the Domain Model: In our approach, we use BDD for eliciting the requirement specification of the desired application. Thus, features are the main source of knowledge for developing and testing. These features are executable and intended to test the functionality of the application. Applying the code-by-example approach leads to an test-driven development activity. First, the most visible behavior of the application is stated as features. Afterwards, the development team implements the functionality until the feature passes the tests. During implementation, the development team will further explore the application requirements, add more features and implement them subsequently. Repeating this procedure over and over again leads to the intended application. The implementation is driven from the outside to the inside.

In consideration of the onion architecture of microservices, BDD starts with the specification of the outer layer and moves into the domain model during implementation. The domain model is getting the second source of knowledge. Through this refinement of the features the ubiquitous language and the domain knowledge appear; this makes the BDD testing effective [9]. Due to that, we see a strong synergy between BDD and DDD. North states that both approaches supports each other [17]. BDD enables modelers and domain experts to be more effective while knowledge crunching. The discussions are structured along the specified features. DDD helps the development team and the users to structure the discussion about the application requirements. Without a shared understanding of the domain concepts, the eliciting is impaired.

Domain concepts within the DDD domain model are tested through scenarios from the BDD features. The link between the domain model and the scenarios is the ubiquitous language. Furthermore, the domain model specifies the functionality of the domain objects. Thus, the usage of domain objects is indirectly limited; that helps developers and users to write correct features. Also dynamic behavior of the domain model, e.g., sequence diagrams in the process views (see Section III-C2), are tested. Through this limitation, we encountered the problem in the case study, that users desires functionality, which does not fit to the domain concepts.

IV. CASE STUDY: THESIS ADMINISTRATION

In our case study, we attempted to modernize the thesis administration process within the Department of Informatics at the Karlsruhe Institute of Technology. Our goal was to create an application based on microservices and to offer it to the university through the service-oriented platform SmartCampus [45] that we developed in our research group. To execute the project, we chose Scrum as our software development process.

A. Eliciting the User Requirements

Following our approach, we began by eliciting the user-requirements with BDD. First, we identified users of the intended application. We focused on students and members of the examination committee, which are responsible for the coordination of exams; we chose a few contact persons from each group. After that, we started several discussions to elicit the most visible behavior, which we subsequently stated as BDD features. For each discovered feature, we developed scenarios as shown in Figure 7. These were easy to understand for our application users by following the "for everyone" readable approach. Therefore, we were able to further discuss our features and sharpen our understanding of the intended application.

Furthermore, we got some first impressions about the domain through the revealed domain logic in our scenarios; the guidance for exploring the domain with DDD.

Scenario: Assigning a student to a thesis offer
  Given an approved thesis offer
  When a student is assigned to a thesis
  And the student accepts the assignment to the thesis
  Then the student is assigned to the thesis
  And the thesis offer is no longer available for any further assignments

Figure 7. Extracted scenario of a feature regarding the assignment of a student to a thesis

In addition, the specified scenarios allowed us to implement tests before starting with the implementation of the application. If a test fails after the implementation of the feature, or after changing parts of the code, we know that the application-requirements are not fulfilled.

B. Crunching the Information Model

Following the approach further, we began eliciting domain knowledge through knowledge crunching. After we identified the domain experts (members of the Main Examination Committee), we began to discuss the domain. We soon noticed that the thesis is one of the main concepts in this domain. Thus, we first explored the concept of the thesis by interviewing domain experts. Beyond the concepts and relationships we also noticed constraints regarding the thesis. We included these constraints in the information model. Figure 8 shows a section of our crunched information model. We placed the *Thesis* in the center of the model to reflect its central position within the core domain.

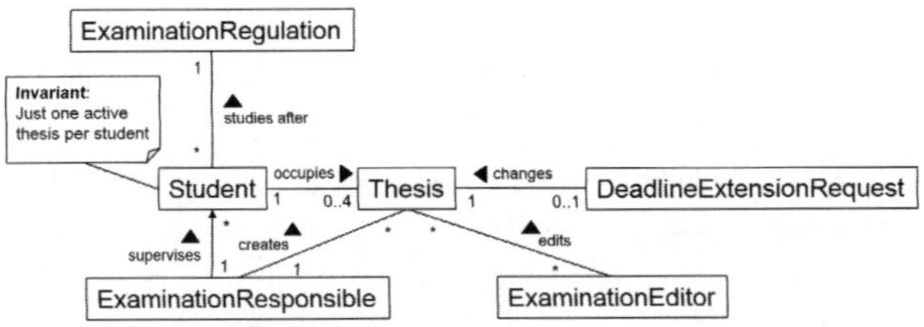

Figure 8. Section of the information model, showing concepts in the thesis domain

Further discussions regarding the concept of the thesis provided us with information about states that a thesis can demonstrate. At this point, we adopted the domain view approach. We modeled a finite automaton in order to determine our understanding of this concept and discuss it with the domain experts, as shown in Figure 9. The diagram supports the process of understanding, without the use of typical UML elements.

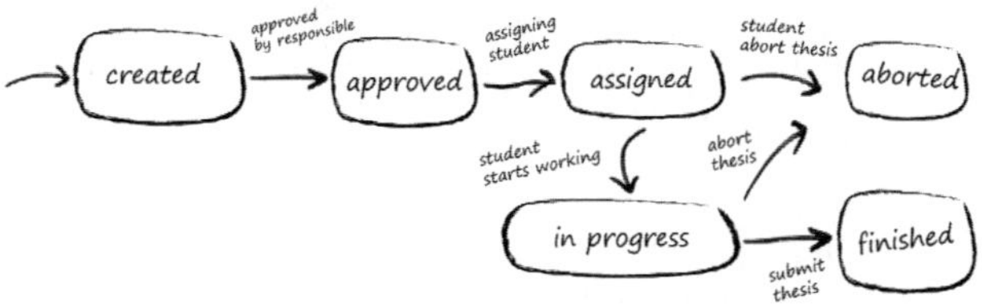

Figure 9. Finite automaton sketches the possible thesis states

After discussions with the domain experts, we had developed our desired information model and were thus able to transform it into a PIM.

C. Creating the Design Prototype

Beyond crunching the information model, we started the design prototyping process and sketched each identified use case. Figure 10 shows the information page of a specific thesis. This prototype was used to validate the elicited domain knowledge.

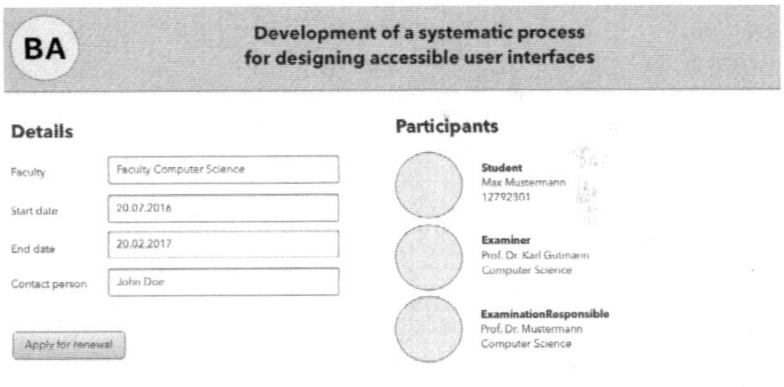

Figure 10. Early phase of a mockup for visualizing thesis details

D. Enriching the Information Model

After eliciting the domain knowledge and creating a design prototype, we were able to enrich our information model with implementation details. We mainly focused on using DDD concepts such as bounded context, entities, value objects or repositories [5]. At first, accordingly to Conway's Law [6], we structured the domain into bounded contexts, thus dividing the thesis administration domain into microservices. Having done this, we were able to create a context map that represented the composition of the bounded contexts (see Figure 11).

Thereafter, we began to identify entities and value objects and made a decision regarding persistence within our intended

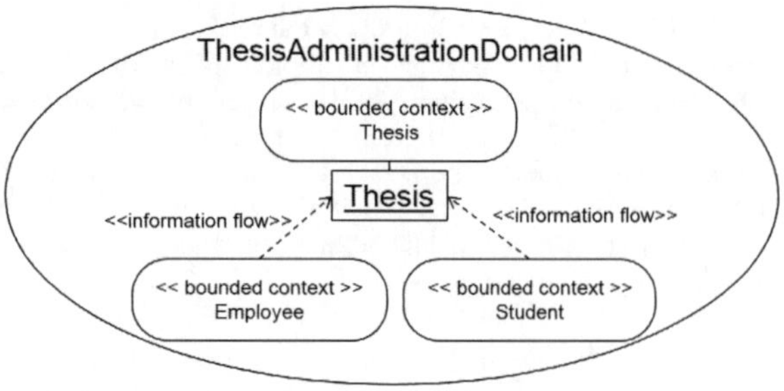

Figure 11. Context map representing the bounded contexts of the thesis administration domain

application through repositories. When applying the patterns, we took into account the application's requirements. For example, we decided that the domain object "Student" in Figure 12 did not require a repository, as it does not need to be globally accessible.

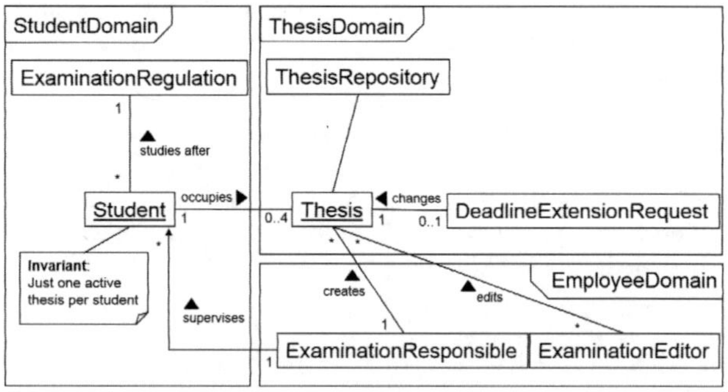

Figure 12. Thesis-specific section of the domain model, including DDD concepts

E. Design and Implementation of the API Specification

The API specification was designed with reference to the domain model and the design of the UI/UX. Figure 13 depicts how a single thesis resource and its attributes can be accessed. The attributes are mainly influenced by the information modeled in the design prototype.

F. Implementing the Microservice

During the implementation phase, the domain objects in the bounded context were mapped to the source code. As mentioned in Section III-A, a onion architecture is used to separate domain, application and infrastructure logic within a microservice. We used Java and the Spring framework to implement the microservices. In another project, we have also used the classic Java Enterprise Edition (JEE) approach so our implementation phase can be considered independent from the chosen implementation technology.

Java packages were used to separate the domain, application and infrastructure layers as shown in Figure 14. The Spring framework supported the developers to focus

Figure 13. OpenAPI specification of displaying a single thesis using SwaggerUI

Figure 14. Package structure and classes of the Java implementation

on the domain layer, because it has the concepts of DDD in mind. We used several annotations named according to DDD concepts. Also, we used the *data transfer object (DTO)* pattern from Fowler in the application layer [46]. The DTOs define the input and output structure of requests and enable to use the serialization functionality of Spring. The DTO has to be aligned with the representations defined in the OpenAPI specification in Section III-D2.

The source code of the thesis controller in Figure 16 shows the usage of Spring annotations and the DTO pattern. The entry point to the application is defined by the *RestController* annotation at Line 1). Each request to the path

```
1  @RestController("/theses")
2  public class ThesisController {
3   private ThesisRepository thesisRepository;
4   @Autowired
5    public ThesisController(ThesisRepository
        thesisRepository) {
6     this.thesisRepository = thesisRepository;
7    }
8    @RequestMapping(method=PUT)
9    public ThesisDto create(ThesisDto thesisDto) {
10    try {
11          Thesis thesis = new Thesis(thesisDto.
              getTitle(), /* ... */);
12          this.thesisRepository.save(thesis);
13     } catch (Exception ex) {
14          handleException(ex);
15     }
16          return new ThesisDto(thesis);
17     }
18     // ...
19 }
```

Figure 15. Part of the ThesisController

"*/theses*" relative to the application's path is handled by the *ThesisController*. By using dependency injection offered by Spring, interfaces and their implementation could be seperated. E.g., the implementation of the *ThesisRepository* is not part of the application layer. Instead, the infrastructure layer contains the implementing class *ThesisMongoRepository*, which uses, in this case, the NoSQL database Mongo DB as its persistence technology. Spring injects this implementation in the constructor of the *ThesisController*, because of the *Autowired* annotation (see Lines 4) to 7)). Starting at Line 8), a method for receiving and processing the thesis creation requests is implemented. The *RequestMapping* annotation with the parameter *PUT* makes Spring forward HTTP PUT requests to this method. Spring serializes the request body into a *ThesisDto* object. A thesis domain object is created by using the information encapsulated by this DTO. Afterward, the thesis domain object is persisted using the *ThesisRepository*. The *handleException* method handles exceptions and makes Spring respond with an *ErrorDto* object according to our API style guidelines (see [40]).

```
1  public Thesis(String title, Date startDate, Date
       endDate, UUID examinationEditorId, UUID
      exam /* ... */) throws ValidationException {
2   super();
3   setTitle(title);
4   setStartDate(startDate);
5   // ...
6  }
7  public void setTitle(String title) throws
      ValidationException {
8   if ((title != null) && (title.length() >
       MIN_TITLE_LENGTH)) {
9     this.title = title;
10  } else {
11   throw new ValidationException(/* ... */);
12  }
```

Figure 16. Part of the Thesis domain object

Domain objects shall always be valid and, thus, never contain information that is not consistent with the domain model. Therefore, the creation and manipulation of domain objects has to be handled with care. In our simple implementation, we decided to handle validation on our own and did not use a framework. The creation of the thesis domain object is depicted as a source code example in Figure 16. The constructor expects all attributes that are needed for a valid thesis. As an alternative, the factory pattern [47] could be applied to reduce the complexity of the constructor. The parameters are forwarded to the setters of the attribute starting from Line 3. The validation is implemented in the setters according to the domain model. As an alternative, one can use a dedicated method for verifying the invariants of a domain object before creating or updating it. In our source code example, the title must not be null and must have more than MIN_TITLE_LENGTH characters. If the validation fails, the setters, as well as the constructor, throw a *ValidationException* (Line 11)). The controller on the application layer can handle this exception and translate it for the requesting client. In our case, just the first failing validation is communicated to the application layer. The factory pattern could improve the implementation. A *ThesisFactory* might offer a method, which communciates a summary of validation problems.

G. Synergy between our Approach and Scrum

It turned out that our approach worked well with Scrum. We considered Scrum artifacts during each activity and attempted to directly create them. In addition, Scrum's iterative approach proved a good fit for our activities. This corresponds with the DDD principle of exploration and experimentation discussed by Evans [5].

In addition to our original article [1], we added features to describe user requirements. These improved the activity of writing items for the Product Backlog. BDD features and Scrum user stories are quite similar, because both describe the user's view on the application. Thus, through the combination of features and the design prototype, we could easily fill the Product Backlog. Furthermore, the activities of our approach can be used to refine the Items for the Spring Backlog. The interconnection of feautres, models and source code simplified the changes in the Backlog after each iteration.

V. Limitations

The activities we introduced provide an overview of the activities that take place when applying DDD in building microservice-based applications. These activities represent a first step towards a complete process that includes all of the required artifacts. Our research indicated that several topics require further investigation and more detailed descriptions; for example, it is quite difficult to systematize the design of the domain model according to DDD. Best practices could be identified and added to the process description to support the performance of this activity.

During the case study, we received useful feedback from the software development team. In Section III-A on classification, we discussed concerns regarding the specification that are not covered by the artifacts. We used the UI/UX design in addition to DDD and the microservice approach to provide the missing specification for the user interface and application layer; however, the development team still had problems implementing the application layer. At this point, we discovered that the application layer is still not fully specified. To further solve this problem, we added BDD to our process. With BDD the development team was able to specify the overall application and capture the functionality. It is likely, that there are more specification artifacts that must be identified, but the introduction of BDD helped us applying DDD for building microservice-based applications. Using the Spring framework, which supports developers in several ways, much of the infrastructure layer source code is supplied. Thus, these specifications are unnecessary.

While discussing the implementation process and testing activities, we noted that the implementation of a domain model created according to DDD is (slightly) bound to object-oriented programming languages. This is due to the fact that the concepts and diagrams introduced in [5] have object-oriented programming in mind. The use of a functional programming language might require a different set of patterns and diagrams; as such, the process identified in this article is also somewhat bound to implementation using an object-oriented language.

According to our domain view concept, the domain model consists out of multiple diagrams, which underlie one or more predefined representation styles. Mostly we used to the UML for the representation of domain model content. This use of UML suggests that we also have a underlying modeling language—or metamodel—for our domain model, but that would contradict Evans' premise "everything is allowed in the domain model". Introducing a modeling language for domain modeling would allow a systematic approach for deriving a web-API from the domain model.

VI. Conclusion and Future Work

Domain-driven design offers key concepts and steps for building applications that are based on a microservice architecture. However, the concepts lack links to existing software engineering knowledge. We classified both with reference to software architecture concepts and software development activities. In addition, we provided an overview of software development activities and artifacts used in building microservice-based applications, expanding on existing DDD literature. Using a case study, we demonstrated the application of these activities in an agile software development process, by building a thesis management application as part of the SmartCampus platform; we also provided examples of the artifacts that resulted. The overview of activities and their classification represents a first step towards a complete process for developing such web applications; we also described its limitations and discussed the missing artifacts. However, the application of DDD is still challenging and requires further investigations. The concept of domain views seems as a step forward but the concept is not yet mature; it lacks a well definition of its application and benefits.

Domain-driven design is about focusing on the domain, including its concepts, their relationships and business logic. Microservice architectures are about arranging and dividing distributed software building blocks. We identified a missing requirement specification and absent artifacts during the process of classification and the case study. We will further refine the activities towards a software development process to identify a sufficient set of artifacts.

The focus of DDD is the domain and its specification within a domain model. The other layers of the layered architecture are not provided through the domain model. For providing the application layer, we introduced BDD to our approach. The behavior of the application was stated in the form of plain text features. Furthermore, these features could be used to automatically test the application. In consideration of the architecture of our microservices, BDD tests each layer of the onion architecture. In case of our approach, we only described the testing activity of the domain model. Our research in this topic is not completed yet, so further research activities will concern the application of DDD in combination with BDD.

A major advantage offered by the use of DDD and microservices is the ability to reuse existing functions. Identity and access management are domains (almost) every application requires; thus, we will investigate building a knowledge repository and enriching the activities and artifacts so that the models and functionality used in this domain can be reused by other applications. In addition to this research topic, we will continue to focus on how we can systematically derive web APIs for microservices while bearing in mind quality requirements such as potential for future evolution. The web API also plays a significant role in discovering and reusing microservices in the context of a microservice landscape.

Applying the concept of the domain views on the modeling activities of DDD supports modelers and domain experts. Based on the definition of domain view types, modelers are more guided while modeling the domain. Nevertheless, cutting the domain model into multiple diagrams with domain views still requires much experience. The identification of the cutting edges of the domain model depends on the purpose of the application and the design decisions of the development team. In further investigations, we are going to extend the domain view concept to provide better support for modelers.

Acknowledgment

We are very thankful to Pascal Burkhardt for his contributions, both through discussions and the input he provided regarding his projects, as well as to Philip Hoyer for providing his opinions during our discussions. Furthermore, we would like to thank the following members of the development team and domain experts for participating in the case study: Florian Beuer, Lukas Bach, Anne Sielemann, Johanna Thiemich, Rainer Schlund, Niko Benkler, Adis Heric, Pablo Castro, Mark Pollmann, Iona Gheta, Johannes Theuerkorn and David Schneiter.

References

[1] R. Steinegger, P. Giessler, B. Hippchen, and S. Abeck, "Overview of a Domain-Driven Design Approach to Build Microservice-Based Applications," in SOFTENG: The Third International Conference on Advances and Trends in Software Engineering, April 2017.

[2] S. Newman, Building Microservices, 1st ed. O'Reilly Media, Inc., 2015.

[3] M. Richards, Microservices vs. Service-Oriented Architecture. O'Reilly Media, Inc., 2015.

[4] T. Erl, SOA Principles of Service Design (The Prentice Hall Service-Oriented Computing Series from Thomas Erl). Upper Saddle River, NJ, USA: Prentice Hall PTR, 2007.

[5] E. Evans, Domain-Driven Design: Tackling Complexity in the Heart of Software. Addison-Wesley Professional, 2003.

[6] M. E. Conway, "How do Committees Invent," Datamation, vol. 14, no. 4, 1968, pp. 28–31.

[7] E. Landre, H. Wesenberg, and H. Rønneberg, "Architectural Improvement by Use of Strategic Level Domain-driven Design," in Companion to the 21st ACM SIGPLAN Symposium on Object-oriented Programming Systems, Languages, and Applications, ser. OOPSLA '06. ACM, 2006, pp. 809–814, URL: http://doi.acm.org/10.1145/1176617.1176728 [retrieved: 2017.11.30].

[8] B. Iyer and M. Subramaniam, "The Strategic Value of APIs," January 2015, URL: https://hbr.org/2015/01/the-strategic-value-of-apis [retrieved: 2017.11.30].

[9] M. Wynne and A. Hellesoy, The Cucumber Book: Behaviour-Driven Development for Testers and Developers. Pragmatic Bookshelf, 2012.

[10] D. C. Schmidt, "Model-Driven Engineering," Computer-IEEE Computer Society, vol. 39, no. 2, 2006, p. 25.

[11] A. G. Kleppe, J. Warmer, W. Bast, and M. Explained, "The Model Driven Architecture: Practice and Promise," 2003.

[12] E. Seidewitz, "What Models Mean," IEEE Software, vol. 20, no. 5, 2003, pp. 26–32.

[13] B. Bruegge and A. H. Dutoit, Object-Oriented Software Engineering Using UML, Patterns and Java-(Required). Prentice Hall, 2004.

[14] I. Jacobson, G. Booch, and J. Rumbaugh, The Unified Software Development Process. Addison-wesley Reading, 1999, vol. 1.

[15] G. Fairbanks, Just Enough Software Architecture: A Risk-Driven Approach. Marshall & Brainerd, 2010.

[16] K. Beck, Test-Driven Development: By Example. Addison-Wesley Professional, 2003.

[17] D. North. BDD & DDD. QCon London 2009. URL: https://www.infoq.com/presentations/bdd-and-ddd [retrieved: 2017.11.30]. (2009)

[18] O. Vogel, I. Arnold, A. Chughtai, and T. Kehrer, Software Architecture: A Comprehensive Framework and Guide for Practitioners. Springer Berlin Heidelberg, 2011, URL: http://dx.doi.org/10.1007/978-3-642-19736-9 [retrieved: 2017.11.30].

[19] I. A. W. Group et al., "IEEE Recommended Practice for Architectural Description," IEEE Std, vol. 1471, 1998.

[20] N. Alshuqayran, N. Ali, and R. Evans, "A systematic mapping study in microservice architecture," in Service-Oriented Computing and Applications (SOCA), 2016 IEEE 9th International Conference on. IEEE, 2016, pp. 44–51.

[21] C. Pahl and P. Jamshidi, "Microservices: A Systematic Mapping Study," in Proceedings of the 6th International Conference on Cloud Computing and Services Science, 2016, pp. 137–146.

[22] V. Vernon, Implementing Domain-Driven Design. Addison-Wesley, 2013.

[23] A. Cockburn, "The Pattern: Ports and Adapters," 2005, URL: http://alistair.cockburn.us/Hexagonal+architecture [retrieved: 2017.11.30].

[24] R. C. Martin, Agile Software Development: Principles, Patterns, and Practices. Prentice Hall, 2002.

[25] S. Millett, Patterns, Principles and Practices of Domain-Driven Design. John Wiley & Sons, 2015.

[26] J. Palermo, "The Onion Architecture," URL: http://jeffreypalermo.com/blog/the-onion-architecture-part-1/ [retrieved: 2017.11.30].

[27] G. Adzic, Specification by Example: How Successful Teams Deliver the Right Software, 1st ed. Greenwich, CT, USA: Manning Publications Co., 2011.

[28] Y. T. Lee, "Information Modeling: From Design to Implementation," in Proceedings of the Second World Manufacturing Congress. Citeseer, 1999, pp. 315–321.

[29] J. Osis, E. Asnina, and A. Grave, "Formal Computation Independent Model of the Problem Domain Within the MDA." in ISIM. Citeseer, 2007.

[30] T. Stahl, M. Voelter, and K. Czarnecki, Model-Driven Software Development: Technology, Engineering, Management. John Wiley & Sons, 2006.

[31] J. Arnowitz, M. Arent, and N. Berger, Effective Prototyping for Software Makers. San Francisco, CA, USA: Morgan Kaufmann Publishers Inc., 2006.

[32] E. Evans, "Tackling Complexity in the Heart of Software," January 2016, Domain-Driven Design Europe 2016, URL: https://dddeurope.com/2016/eric-evans.html [retrieved: 2017.11.30].

[33] M. Gebhart, P. Giessler, and S. Abeck, "Challenges of the Digital Transformation in Software Engineering," ICSEA 2016 : The Eleventh International Conference on Software Engineering Advances, 2016, pp. 136–141.

[34] D. Jacobson, G. Brail, and D. Woods, APIs: A Strategy Guide. O'Reilly Media, Inc., 2011.

[35] B. Mulloy, "Web API Design - Crafting Interfaces that Developers Love," March 2012, URL: http://pages.apigee.com/rs/apigee/images/api-design-ebook-2012-03.pdf [retrieved: 2017.11.30].

[36] J. Webber, S. Parastatidis, and I. Robinson, REST in Practice: Hypermedia and Systems Architecture, 1st ed. O'Reilly Media, Inc., 2010.

[37] R. T. Fielding, "Architectural Styles and the Design of Network-Based Software Architectures," Ph.D. dissertation, University of California, Irvine, 2000.

[38] S. Tilkov, M. Eigenbrodt, S. Schreier, and O. Wolf, REST und HTTP: Entwicklung und Integration nach dem Architekturstil des Web. dpunkt, 2015, URL: https://books.google.de/books?id=pJF-ngEACAAJ [retrieved: 2017.11.30].

[39] D. M. Rathod, S. M. Parikh, and B. V. Buddhadev, "Structural and Behavioral Modeling of RESTful Web Service Interface Using UML," in 2013 International Conference on Intelligent Systems and Signal Processing (ISSP), March 2013, pp. 28–33.

[40] P. Giessler, M. Gebhart, D. Sarancin, R. Steinegger, and S. Abeck, "Best Practices for the Design of RESTful Web Services," International Conferences of Software Advances (ICSEA), 2015, URL: http://www.thinkmind.org/download.php?articleid=icsea_2015_15_10_10016 [retrieved: 2017.11.30].

[41] OpenAPI, "The OpenAPI Specification (fka The Swagger Specification)," 2017, URL: https://github.com/OAI/OpenAPI-Specification [retrieved: 2017.11.30].

[42] FasterXML, LLC , "Jackson JSON Processor Wiki," 2017, URL: http://wiki.fasterxml.com/JacksonHome [retrieved: 2017.11.30].

[43] O. Gierke, "DDD & REST - Domain Driven APIs for the Web," November 2016, SpringOne Platform, URL: https://www.infoq.com/presentations/ddd-rest [retrieved: 2017.11.30].

[44] D. North, "Behavior Modification: The Evolution of Behavior-Driven Development," Better Software, vol. 8, no. 3, 2006.

[45] R. Steinegger, J. Schäfer, M. Vogler, and S. Abeck, "Attack Surface Reduction for Web Services Based on Authorization Patterns," The Eighth International Conference on Emerging Security Information, Systems and Technologies (SECURWARE 2014), 2014, pp. 194–201.

[46] M. Fowler, Patterns of Enterprise Application Architecture. Addison-Wesley Longman Publishing Co., Inc., 2002.

[47] J. Vlissides, R. Helm, R. Johnson, and E. Gamma, "Design Patterns: Elements of Reusable Object-Oriented Software," Reading: Addison-Wesley, vol. 49, no. 120, 1995, p. 11.

State-of-the-Art Overview on 3D Model Representations and Transformations in the Context of Computer-Aided Design

Christoph Schinko[1,2], Andreas Riffnaller-Schiefer[1], Ulrich Krispel[1,2], Eva Eggeling[1,2], and Torsten Ullrich[1,2]

[1]Institute of Computer Graphics and Knowledge Visualization, Graz University of Technology &
[2]Fraunhofer Austria Research GmbH, Inffeldgasse 16c, 8010 Graz, Austria

{ christoph.schinko, ulrich.krispel, eva.eggeling, torsten.ullrich } @fraunhofer.at,
a.schiefer@cgv.tugraz.at

***Abstract*—Within a virtual world, either in virtual reality or in a simulation environment, the digital counterparts of real objects are described by mathematical and computational models. Depending on the purpose, the field of application, and the used toolchain a wide variety of model representations is established. As a consequence, conversion methods and transformation algorithms are becoming increasingly important. This article gives a state of the art overview on model representations and on the most important transformation techniques.**

Keywords–3D Model Representations; 3D Transformations; Computer-Aided Design

I. Introduction

Many different ways of model descriptions are available, tailored to the requirements in their respective areas of research. In the context of Computer-Aided Design (CAD), the model description and representation of a digital counterpart of a real object is called a shape description. An overview on shape descriptions and their transformations has been presented at the ninth International Conferences on Advances in Multimedia. This article is based on the corresponding conference contribution "3D Model Representations and Transformations in the Context of Computer-Aided Design: a State-of-the-Art Overview" [1] and gives a more detailed state of the art overview on shape representations and on the most important model transformation techniques.

At this point, it is important to emphasize that there are differences in the process of shape perception between human beings and computers. Two important aspects have to be mentioned in this context. On the one hand, there are sensory differences. In their natural surrounding, human beings can rely on their five senses to perceive a shape. Consequently, it is often a combination of these senses that makes up the sensation of a shape. While computers can be fitted with many different sensors, adding up to far more different senses compared to human beings, it usually boils down to a specific sensor being used to perceive a shape. The reason for that circumstance is directly related to the second aspect in this context – the reasoning itself. The human brain is yet to find a matching rival in the world of computer science. While computers are programmed to outperform the human brain in various, but rather specific tasks like number crunching, the computer is no thinking machine. Interdisciplinary developments in all fields of computer science over the recent years bring us ever closer to creating the thinking machine. However, especially for a computer, the task of shape classification heavily depends on the underlying description. Even after successfully classifying shapes, a computer is yet not aware of the meaning of shape, as discussed by Sven Havemann et al. in their work [2]. For the description of shape, it is important to be aware of these differences, even if shape classification is not in the context of this article.

The following two Sections describe the model representations (Section II) and the transformation techniques (Section III). The model representations include point sets (Section II-A), polygonal representations (Section II-B), parametric surfaces (Section II-C), subdivision surfaces (Section II-D), implicit surfaces (Section II-E), volumetric surfaces (Section II-F), and generative models (Section II-G). The description of transformation techniques gives a general overview and outlines important algorithms: level-of-detail techniques (Section III-A), marching cubes (Section III-B), random sample consensus (Section III-C), midsurfaces & isogeometry (Section III-D), parametric subdivision surfaces (Section III-E), and semantic enrichment (Section III-F). The final conclusion summarizes the state-of-art overview and shows open questions for future research directions (Section IV).

II. Model Representations

In dictionaries, shapes are described by words forming a textual definition:

> **bowl** a rather deep, round dish or basin, used chiefly for holding liquids, food, etc.
>
> Dictionary.com

From a computer science point of view, this definition is of a rather abstract nature representing a difficult basis for creating detectors. A computer program relies on more formal, mathematical definitions. For a human being, this description is sufficient enough to easily recognize the described shape when seeing it. The precondition for this accomplishment of the human brain is a basic understanding of the terms and definitions used in the description. Bootstrapping of the basic concepts on a textual basis alone is hardly possible. All available senses are used to create a mental image of the surrounding environment, making it possible to establish a connection between sensory input and concepts of shapes. With this connection available, a single sensory input is enough for the brain to be made aware of the related concepts. As an example, the human visual system is capable of identifying and categorizing objects. Not only real-world objects, but also schematic drawings, pictures, paintings, etc. can serve as input. The description itself can also be available in the form of an image. This form of information is often found in biology, e.g., for describing animal or plant species.

Representation and description of shapes and objects in images is one of the basic methods to describe image content. However, similar to textual descriptions, image-based descriptions are a rather informal definition of shape, thus representing a difficult basis for creating algorithmic detectors. This is due to the loss of one dimension of object information when projecting a real-world object onto the 2D image plane. Shape information in images is often also affected by noise, distortion and occlusion. As a result, the shape extracted from the image only partially represents the real-world object.

In the context of CAD and Computer-Aided Manufacturing, a shape model has to be complete and has to comprehend all needed information. For these purposes, volumetric and boundary-/surface-based representations are used.

A. Point Sets

Points are a basic primitive to describe the surface of a shape [3]. A point set is a list of points defined in a coordinate system. While points are not the primitive of choice when using 3D modeling software to create shapes, they are widely used by 3D scanners due to the nature of their measurements. A point set is the outcome when measuring a large number of points on an object's surface.

Figure 1. A laser scan of a soup bowl has been the basis of this point cloud. The data set has been processed (cleansed and resampled) and consists of 62 500 points.

The data set in Figure 1 shows a point cloud of a soup bowl consisting of 62 500 points. High resolution scans of larger objects require special techniques and/or out-of-core approaches due to the huge amount of data. For rendering approaches of point sets, the literature survey by Markus Gross and Hanspeter Pfister offers in-depth explanation [4]. The creation of another shape representation from point set data is called shape reconstruction.

B. Polygonal Faces

A very common representation to describe a shape's surface is to use a mesh of polygonal faces. The accuracy of the representation heavily depends on the shape's outline and is directly affected by the number of faces. A cylinder, for example, cannot be accurately represented by planar faces – it can only be approximated. Curved surfaces, in general, cannot be represented exactly, whereas objects having planar boundaries obviously can be. This limitation is often outweighed by its advantages in the field of CAD:

- Computer graphics hardware is tailored towards processing polygonal faces – especially triangles. This is the reason why many of the other shape representations are converted into polygonal meshes prior to rendering.
- A lot of tools and algorithms exist to create, process and display polygonal objects [5], [6].

The data structures for storing polygonal meshes are numerous. In a very simple form, a list of coordinates (x,y,z) representing the vertices of the polygons can be used. The de-facto standard data interface between CAD software and machines (e.g., milling machines, 3D printers, etc.) is the stereolithography file format (STL). It simply consists of a triangle list specifying its vertices. An illustrative STL-example is shown in Figure 2.

Figure 2. The laser scan of the "soup bowl" example (see Figure 1) is the input of a surface reconstruction algorithm, which returns a triangle mesh.

While this data structure is sufficient for some manufacturing purposes, it may not satisfy the needs of a 3D modeler for editing. More sophisticated data structures reproducing hierarchical structures (groups, edges, vertices) and adding additional attributes like normals, colors and texture coordinates provide a remedy. The problem of traversing a mesh can be tackled by introducing vertex-, face- and half-edge-iterators. They are typically, but not exclusively, used in combination with the concept of half-edges. The idea is to represent an edge between two vertices by two half-edges of opposite direction (see Figure 3).

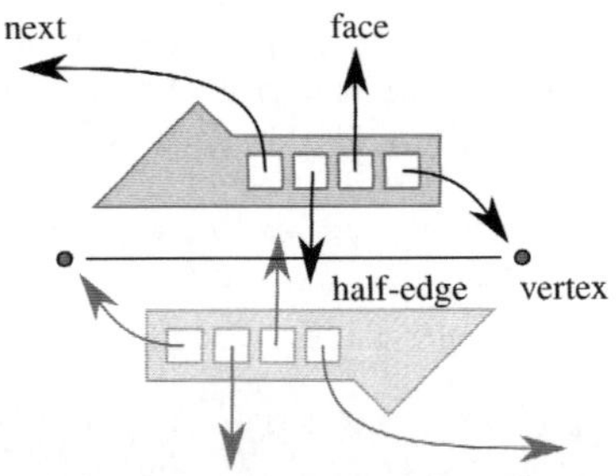

Figure 3. The half-edge data structure stores four references to (i) an associated vertex and (ii) an associated face. Furthermore, the half-edge data structure has (iii) a reference to its edge mate and (iv) to the next half-edge of the same face in counter-clockwise direction.

A half-edge is a directed edge with references to its opposite half-edge, its incident face, vertex and next half-edge. By defining operations using this data structure, it is possible to conveniently traverse a mesh [7].

C. Parametric Surface Representations

A parametric representation of a shape's surface is defined by a vector-valued parametrization function $f : \Omega \to S$ mapping a 2D parameter domain $\Omega \subset \mathbb{R}^2$ to the surface $S = f(\Omega) \subset \mathbb{R}^3$. This representation is a general way to specify a surface. The approximation theorem by Karl Weierstrass states, that finding an explicit formulation with a single function approximating a more complex function (shape) can be achieved by using polynomials.

Weierstrass Approximation Theorem Let f be a continuous real-valued function on the closed interval $[a, b]$. Then f can be uniformly approximated by polynomials.

A constructive proof of the theorem is given by Sergi Bernstein through his work on Bernstein polynomials. As any surface can be approximated by polynomials, the concept of polynomial surface patches has gained currency in the CAD domain [8], [9]. The idea is to split the function domain into smaller regions. Each surface patch, henceforth called patch, is described by a distinct parametric function approximating the local geometry of the patch. To obtain a good overall approximation of the surface, it is necessary to carefully chose the layout of the patches (form, size, number) and to deal with possible discontinuities on patch borders depending on the representation [10].

1. Bézier Surfaces

A Bézier surface is a two-dimensional surface in 3D generated from the Cartesian product of two Bézier curves [11]. A Bézier surface of degree (m, n) is defined as a parametric function

$$f(u, v) = \sum_{i=0}^{m} \sum_{j=0}^{n} \mathbf{b}_{ij} B_i^m(u) B_j^n(v).$$

It is evaluated over the unit square $(u, v) \in [0, 1] \times [0, 1]$ with the control points $\mathbf{b}_{ij} \in \mathbb{R}^3$ and two Bernstein polynomials $B_j^n(v)$. A Bernstein polynomial is defined by

$$B_i^n(t) = \binom{n}{i} t^i (1-t)^{n-i}$$

of degree n for $t \in [0, 1]$.

In CAD, Bézier surfaces are often used in the form of bicubic Bézier patches, i.e., a set of 4×4 points represents the control mesh and is responsible for the shape of the surface as illustrated in Figure 4.

In all cases, Bézier curves and the corresponding Bézier surfaces have important properties:

- Bézier curves and surfaces fulfill the partition of unity property as
$$\sum_{i=0}^{n} B_i^n(u) = 1.$$
Thus the relationship between a Bézier curve / surface and its control mesh is invariant under affine transformations.
- A Bézier curve / surface is contained within the convex hull of its control mesh. Furthermore, the start and end points (of a curve) resp. the four corner points (of a surface) are interpolated by the Bézier curve / surface.
- A Bézier surface exhibits four boundary curves being Bézier curves themselves and their control points are the boundary points of the control mesh.
- The control points do not exert local control alone. Moving a single control point affects the whole surface. Geometric continuity (e.g., G^1, G^2) between patches can only be achieved by satisfying constraints on the control points' positions.

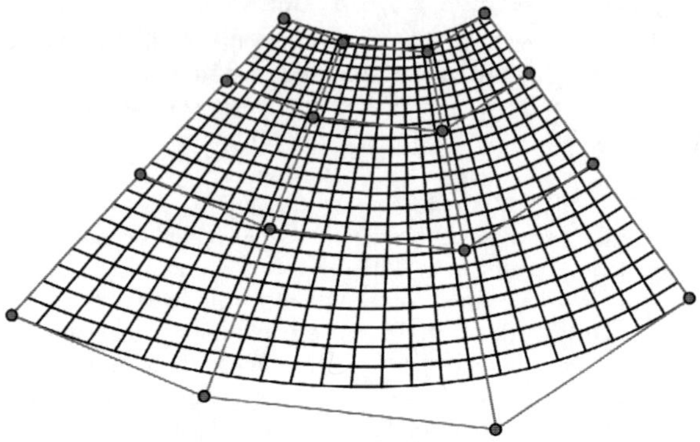

Figure 4. A tensor product surface is based on a curve representation. Consequently, this Bézier surface shares many properties (end point interpolation, convex hull property, etc.) with its corresponding curve type. A negative aspect of tensor product surfaces is the limitation to strictly rectangular topology (control mesh in red).

2. Rational Bézier Surfaces

The idea behind rational Bézier surfaces is to add adjustable weights to extend the design space of shapes [12]. In contrast to a Bézier surface, which can only approximate spheres and cylinders, the rational Bézier Surfaces can describe them exactly – a very important property in CAD. A rational Bézier surface of degree (m, n) is defined with the control points $\mathbf{b}_{ij} \in \mathbb{R}^3$, the weights $w_{ij} \in \mathbb{R}$, and the Bernstein polynomials $B_i^n(u)$ as

$$\begin{aligned} f(u, v) &= \sum_{i=0}^{m} \sum_{j=0}^{n} \begin{pmatrix} w_{ij}\mathbf{b}_{ij} \\ w_{ij} \end{pmatrix} B_i^m(u)\, B_j^n(v) \\ &= \frac{\sum_{i=0}^{m} \sum_{j=0}^{n} w_{ij}\, \mathbf{b}_{ij}\, B_i^m(u)\, B_j^n(v)}{\sum_{i=0}^{m} \sum_{j=0}^{n} w_{ij}\, B_i^m(u)\, B_j^n(v)}. \end{aligned}$$

Rational Bézier surfaces are a special case of non-uniform, ration B-spline (NURBS) surfaces, which are a generalization of B-spline Surfaces.

3. B-spline Surfaces

B-spline surfaces exhibit advantages when joining patches under continuity requirements. Let $m, n, k, l \in \mathbb{N}$ with $m \geq k$ and $n \geq l$. Then, a B-spline surface of degree (k, l) is defined as

$$f(u,v) = \sum_{i=0}^{m} \sum_{j=0}^{n} \mathbf{d}_{ij}\, N_i^k(u)\, N_j^l(v),$$

with the basis functions

$$N_i^0(t) = \begin{cases} 1, & \text{if } t_i \leq t < t_{i+1} \\ 0, & \text{otherwise} \end{cases}$$

and

$$N_i^r(t) = \frac{t - t_i}{t_{i+r} - t_i} N_i^{r-1}(t) + \frac{t_{i+1+r} - t}{t_{i+1+r} - t_{i+1}} N_{i+1}^{r-1}(t)$$

for $1 \leq r \leq n$ and a non-decreasing sequence of knots, a so-called knot vector,

$$T = \{t_0 \leq \cdots \leq t_n \leq \cdots \leq t_{n+m+1}\}.$$

It can be evaluated over $(u, v) \in [u_k, u_{m+1}[\times[v_l, v_{n+1}[$ with the control points $\mathbf{d}_{ij} \in \mathbb{R}^3$ and the polynomials $N_i^k(u)$ and $N_j^l(v)$. The control points $\mathbf{d}_{ij}$ forming the control polygon are called *de Boor* points.

In computer graphics, B-spline surfaces are typically used in the form of bi-cubic B-spline patches. A single cubic B-spline curve segment is defined by four control points, as a consequence, 4×4 control points define a bi-cubic B-spline patch segment. By choosing appropriate knot vectors, a B-spline surface can become a Bézier surface. B-splines with knots t_i satisfying the conditions

$$t_0 = 0$$

and

$$t_{i+1} = t_i \quad \text{or} \quad t_{i+1} = t_i + 1,$$

for $i = 0, \ldots, n+m$ are called uniform B-splines.

B-spline curves and surface satisfy properties similar to Bézier curves and surfaces [11]:

1) The relationship between a B-spline curve / surface and its control mesh is invariant under affine transformations.
2) A B-spline surface is contained within the convex hull of its control mesh: $f(u, v) \in$ convex hull $\{d_{kl} | i \leq k \leq i + m, j \leq l \leq j + n\}$.
3) In contrast to Bézier surfaces, the control points exert local control; i.e., if a control point is moved, only the local neighborhood is affected and
4) a B-spline surface can become a Bézier surface by choosing appropriate knot vectors.

Higher order geometric continuity (e.g., G^1, G^2) at borders of combined B-spline patches can be achieved by satisfying constraints on boundary control points and by appropriate choice of knot vectors.

4. NURBS Surfaces

The combination of rational Bézier techniques and B-spline techniques leads to non-uniform, rational B-splines, NURBS for short [13]:

Let $m, n, k, l \in \mathbb{N}$ with $m \geq l$ and $n \geq k$. Additionally, let

$$\mathbf{u} = (u_0, \ldots, u_{m+k+1})^T$$

and

$$\mathbf{v} = (v_0, \ldots, v_{n+l+1})^T$$

be two knot vectors and

$$w_{00}, \ldots, w_{mn} \in \mathbb{R},$$

$$\mathbf{d}_{00}, \ldots, \mathbf{d}_{mn} \in \mathbb{R}^3.$$

Then, a non-uniform, rational B-spline (NURBS) surface of degree (k, l) is defined as

$$\begin{aligned} f(u,v) &= \sum_{i=0}^{m} \sum_{j=0}^{n} \left(\frac{w_{ij} \mathbf{b}_{ij}}{w_{ij}} \right) N_i^k(u)\, N_j^l(v) \\ &= \frac{\sum_{i=0}^{m} \sum_{j=0}^{n} w_{ij}\, \mathbf{b}_{ij}\, N_i^k(u)\, N_j^l(v)}{\sum_{i=0}^{m} \sum_{j=0}^{n} w_{ij}\, N_i^k(u)\, N_j^l(v)}. \end{aligned}$$

over $(u, v) \in [u_l, u_{m+1}[\times[v_k, v_{n+1}[$ with the polynomials $N_i^k(u)$ and $N_j^l(v)$, the knot vectors $\mathbf{u}$ and $\mathbf{v}$, the control points $\mathbf{d}_{ij}$ with weights $w_{00}, \ldots, w_{mn}$. Similar to B-spline patches, NURBS surfaces are commonly used in computer graphics in the form of bi-cubic NURBS patches.

B-spline surfaces and Bézier surfaces are special cases of NURBS surfaces [14]. If all weights are equal, a NURBS surface becomes a B-spline surface. Additionally, when all knot vectors are chosen appropriately, the B-spline surface becomes a Bézier surface.

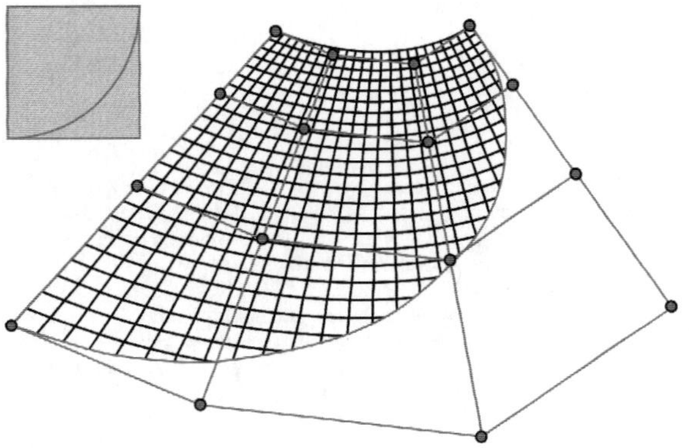

Figure 5. A trimmed Bézier / B-spline / NURBS surface consists of a parameter domain (upper left) and a set of control points. Furthermore, a closed curve (blue) within the parameter domain separates the domain into two parts: a valid part and an invalid part. The final surface in 3D only consists of those points whose parameters are valid [15].

A common way to model arbitrarily complex smooth surfaces is to use a mesh of bi-cubic NURBS patches. Regular meshes consisting of bi-cubic patches formed by vertices of valence four can be seen as connected planar graphs. A direct consequence of the Euler characteristic for connected planar graphs with the aforementioned properties is that such meshes must be topologically equivalent to an infinite plane, a torus, or an infinite cylinder – all other shapes cannot be constructed unless using trimming or stitching as illustrated in Figure 5. The resulting surfaces offer precise feature control at the cost of computational complexity due to trimming and stitching [16].

D. Subdivision Surfaces

Subdivision surfaces are the generalization of spline surfaces to arbitrary topology. Instead of evaluating the surface itself, the refinement of the control polygon represents the subdivision surface. There are many different subdivision schemes, e.g., Catmull-Clark [17], Doo-Sabin [18], Loop [19], Kobbelt [20], etc.

The subdivision scheme presented by Edwin Catmull and Jim Clark is a generalization of bicubic B-spline surfaces to arbitrary topology [17]. The set of 4×4 control points $\mathbf{p}_{ij}$ forms the starting mesh for an iterative refinement process where each step results in a finer mesh. One iteration of such a subdivision process is shown in Figure 6.

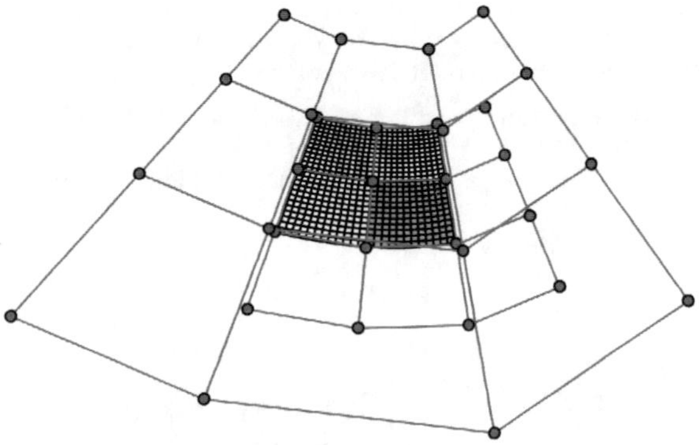

Figure 6. The Catmull-Clark subdivision scheme is based on the idea to describe a subpatch of a bicubic B-spline patch by a bicubic B-spline patch. The starting point is a bicubic patch (red), which generates a surface (wireframe in black), if evaluated over the domain $(u, v) \in [0, 1] \times [0, 1]$. Then the subsurface belonging to $[0, 1/2] \times [0, 1/2]$ is inspected and its corresponding control mesh (blue) is determined. The correspondences between the original mesh (red) and its subdivided version (blue) are the B-spline refinement rules. The Catmull-Clark subdivision scheme generalizes theses rules to arbitrary meshes.

Subdivision surfaces are invariant under affine transformations. They offer the benefit of being easy to implement and computationally efficient. Only the local neighborhood is used for the computation of new points. A major advantage of subdivision surfaces is their repeated refinement process – level-of-detail algorithms are always "included" by design.

Most commonly-used subdivision schemes, like those mentioned previously, only support non-rational surfaces of low degree, i.e., quadratic or cubic, with an uniform parameterization. This limits their use in the context of CAD. For example, due to the missing rational representation, conic sections like cylinders cannot be exactly represented by such surfaces. Also, a non-uniform parameterization is often required, e.g., to define Bézier-like interpolating boundaries, as is commonly done with NURBS surfaces. And higher degree surfaces provide additional advantages like higher continuity for smooth surfaces or improved convergence in the context of analysis.

Ideally, a CAD surface representation would provide the precise control of NURBS without the need for trimming and stitching. To achieve this, Cashman et al. [21] extended the Catmull-Clark subdivision scheme to non-uniform, higher degree, and rational surfaces. This subdivision scheme is compatible with odd degree NURBS in regular regions, away from extraordinary vertices with a valence other than four, but generalizes to arbitrary topology control meshes. It therefore combines the advantages of NURBS and subdivision surfaces in a single surface representation.

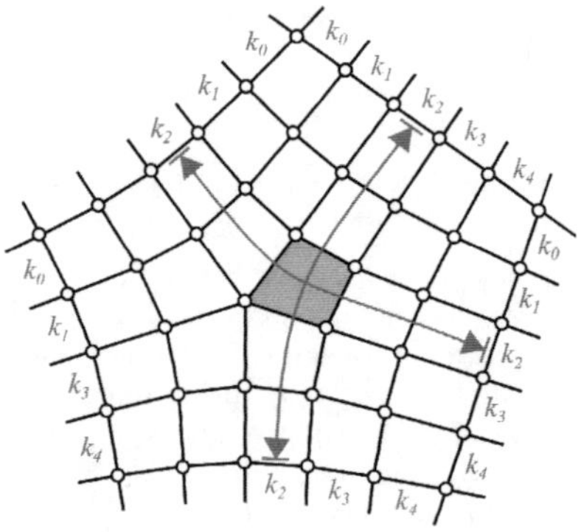

Figure 7. For the NURBS compatible subdivision scheme, the two local knot vectors, indicated by arrows, defining the parameterization of a face (shaded in gray) are derived from the knot spacings k associated with each edge of the control mesh.

Similar to rational Bézier surfaces or NURBS, each control point of a NURBS compatible subdivision surface gets an additional weight to provide a rational representation. To allow for a non-uniform parameterization, a knot spacing k is associated with each edge in the control mesh, defining the interval between two knot values in the knot vector. Knot spacings are required to be equal on opposite edges of a quadrilateral face. Therefore, a knot spacing is always defined for a strip of faces, similar to NURBS. This definition leads to each face of the control mesh having two associated local knot vectors $\mathbf{u}$ and $\mathbf{v}$, visualized as two colored arrows in Figure 7.

Subdivision is then performed in two stages. During the initial refine stage, edges and faces are split according to the subdivision rules [21], which depend on the valence of control points and the local knot vector. The refinement is followed by multiple smoothing steps, depending on the degree of the surface, in which all control points are moved to their new, updated position. This results in a smooth surface that is equivalent to the corresponding NURBS surface for regular regions of the control mesh and is at least C^1 continuous in all other regions.

E. Implicit Surface Representations

In contrast to the parametric surface representations described above, implicit surfaces, are defined as isosurfaces by a function $\mathbb{R}^3 \to \mathbb{R}$ [22]. Therefore, similar to voxels, a surface is only indirectly specified. A simple 3D example of an implicit surface is the following definition of a torus with major radius R and minor radius r

$$f(x, y, z) = (x^2 + y^2 + z^2 + R^2 - r^2)^2 - 4R^2(x^2 + y^2) = 0.$$

Inside and outside of the surface is defined by $f(x, y, z) < 0$, respectively $f(x, y, z) > 0$. While a parametric description of the torus exists, many implicit surfaces do not have a closed, parametric form. In terms of expressiveness, implicit surfaces are more powerful than parametric surfaces [23].

Drawbacks of implicit surfaces are the inherent difficulty of describing sharp features (unless trimming is used) or finding points on the surface. However, this representation has several advantages. Efficient checks whether a point is inside a shape or not are possible. Since the surface is not represented explicitly, topology changes are easily possible. Surface intersections, as well as boolean set operations (the basis of constructive solid geometry) can also be implemented efficiently. Using implicit functions the operations of constructive solid geometry can be mapped to simple, mathematical terms:

If $g_1, g_2, \ldots, g_n$ are implicit functions, then the CSG operations are:

- **union**
$$\bigcup_{i=1,\ldots,n} g_i(p) = \min_{i=1,\ldots,n} g_i(p)$$
- **intersection**
$$\bigcap_{i=1,\ldots,n} g_i(p) = \max_{i=1,\ldots,n} g_i(p)$$

For a smooth blending Alexander A. Pasko and Vladimir V. Savchenko [24] suggest the blending function [25]

$$\bigcup_{i=1,\ldots,n} (g_1, g_2) = \frac{1}{1+\alpha}\left(g_1 + g_2 - \sqrt{g_1^2 + g_2^2 - 2\alpha g_1 g_2}\right).$$

Implicit surfaces can be described in algebraic form (see the example of the torus), as a sum of spherical basis functions (so called blobby models), as convolution surfaces (skeletons), procedurally, as variational functions, or by using samples. The latter approach directly relates to volumetric shape descriptions.

F. Volumetric Shape Descriptions

Volumetric approaches can be used to indirectly describe a shape's surface. In contrast to surface-based descriptions, they define the surface to be a boundary between the interior and the exterior of a shape. However, the idea behind these approaches is not so much a description of a shape's surface, but a description of the entire volume. Such representations are frequently used in visualization and analysis of medical and scientific data.

1. Voxels

Data sets originating from measurements do not have continuous values and are limited to the points in space where measurements have been collected. It is very common that data points form a uniform regular grid. Such data points in 3D are known as voxels, a name related to their 2D counterparts: the pixels. Since a voxel represents only a single point in a grid, the space between voxels is not represented. Depending on the area of application, the data point can be multi-dimensional, e.g., a vector of density and color. Due to the fact that position and size of a voxel are pre-defined, voxels are good at representing regularly sampled spaces. The approximation of free-form shapes suffers from this inherent property. Figure 8 illustrates the approximation artifacts of a free-form shape represented by voxels.

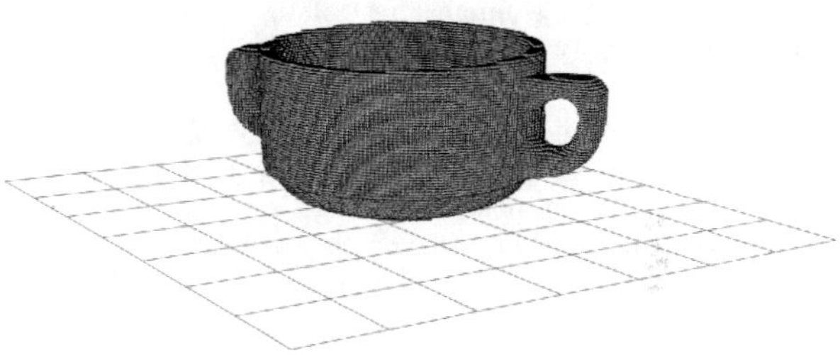

Figure 8. The "voxelized" soup bowl data set shows the typical approximation artifacts of a grid-based representation.

Voxel representations do not suffer from numerical instabilities as they are typically defined on an integer grid. A major drawback of voxel representations is the amount of data needed for storage. For example, a $512 \times 512 \times 512$ voxel grid storing 32-bit floating point values occupies 512MB of memory. Depending on the intended use, the memory footprint may be too high and it may appear rather coarse.

Typical use cases are the visualization and analysis of medical data (medical imaging) acquired from sources like computed tomography (CT), magnetic resonance imaging (MRI), or 3D ultrasonography.

2. Convex Polytopes

Shapes can be described as geometric objects with flat sides – so called polytopes. They are defined in any dimension as n-dimensional polytopes or n-polytopes. Two-dimensional polygons are called 2-polytopes and three-dimensional polytopes are called 3-polytopes. A special case of a polytope is a convex polytope having the additional property of being a convex set of points in n-dimensional space $\mathbb{R}^n$, respectively in n-dimensional Euclidean space $\mathbb{E}^n$. Convex polytopes can be defined over their convex hull, or by the intersection of half-spaces.

Branko Grünbaum and Geoffrey C. Shephard define a convex polytope as the convex hull of any finite set of points in Euclidean space $\mathbb{E}^n$ $(n \geq 1)$ [26]. A set $S \subseteq \mathbb{E}^n$ is convex, if for any pair of points $\mathbf{x}, \mathbf{y} \in S$, the line segment

$$\lambda \cdot \mathbf{x} + (1 - \lambda) \cdot \mathbf{y}$$

with $0 \leq \lambda \leq 1$, lies entirely in S. For any set S, the smallest convex set containing S is called the convex hull of S. A definition relying on the convex hull of a set of points is called a vertex representation.

Convex polytopes can also be defined as the intersection of a finite number of half-spaces [27]. Because of the fact that the intersection of arbitrary half-spaces need not be bounded, this property must be explicitly required. An algebraic formulation for convex polytopes consists of the set of bounded solutions to a system of linear inequalities. Hence, a closed convex polytope can be written as a system of linear inequalities.

$$\begin{aligned} a_{11}\mathbf{x}_1 + a_{12}\mathbf{x}_2 + \cdots + a_{1n}\mathbf{x}_n &\leq b_1 \\ a_{21}\mathbf{x}_1 + a_{22}\mathbf{x}_2 + \cdots + a_{2n}\mathbf{x}_n &\leq b_2 \\ \vdots \quad\quad \vdots \quad\quad\quad & \vdots \quad \vdots \\ a_{m1}\mathbf{x}_1 + a_{m2}\mathbf{x}_2 + \cdots + a_{mn}\mathbf{x}_n &\leq b_m \end{aligned}$$

with m defining the number of half-spaces of the polytope. Open convex polytopes are defined similarly with strict inequalities instead of non-strict ones [28].

A limitation of convex polytopes is the inherent restriction to represent convex geometry only. The representation of non-convex geometry is possible through composition of convex polytopes. Topologically, convex polytopes are homeomorphic to a closed ball.

Convex polytopes are a subject of mathematical study since ancient Greek times. There is a number of special polytopes in three-dimensional space admitting a particularly high degree of symmetry – the so-called Platonic solids, tetrahedron, hexahedron, octahedron, dodecahedron and icosahedron. They are bounded by congruent regular polygonal faces exhibiting a consistent vertex valance over all vertices.

3. Constructive Solid Geometry

Constructive solid geometry (CSG) is a technique to create complex shapes out of primitive objects. These CSG primitives typically consist of cuboids, cylinders, prisms, pyramids, spheres and cones. Complex geometry is created by instantiation, transformation, and combination of the primitives. They are combined by using regularized boolean set operations like union, difference and intersection that are included in the representation. A CSG object is represented as a tree with inner nodes representing operators and primitives in the leaves.

In order to determine the shape described by a CSG tree, all operations have to be evaluated bottom-up until the root node is evaluated. Depending on the representation of the leaf geometry, this task can vary in complexity. Some implementations rely on representations that require the creation of a combined shape for the evaluation of the CSG tree, others do not create a combined representation. In that sense, CSG is not as much a representation as it is a set of operations that need to be implemented for the underlying shape representation [29].

As a consequence, CSG can also be performed on other shapes and shape representations. Two different approaches can be used to evaluate CSG objects: object-space approaches and image-space approaches. The main difference between the two approaches is that object-space approaches create shapes, while image-space approaches "only" create correct images.

Object-space CSG approaches using primitives described implicitly can be calculated accurately. Performing CSG on other shape representations (like polygonal meshes) typically introduces accuracy problems, due to the finite precision of floating-point numbers. A common representation used for CSG operations are binary space partitioning (BSP) trees. BSP is a method for subdividing a space into convex cells yielding a tree data structure. This data structure can be used to perform CSG operations using tree-merging as described by Bruce Naylor et al. [30]. The algorithm is relying on accurate information of inside and outside of a shape (or, in case of planes, above and below).

G. Generative Shape Descriptions & Design Automation

Algorithmic shape descriptions are also called generative, procedural, or parametric descriptions. However, there are differences between the three terms. Parametric descriptions are loop-computable programs (the functions it can compute are the primitive recursive functions), and therefore they always terminate [31]. On the other hand, procedural descriptions offer additional features (like arbitrary recursion), are structured in procedures, and are not guaranteed to terminate. Compared to procedural descriptions, generative descriptions are a more general term, including, for example, functional languages.

In this context, algorithmic descriptions are henceforth referred to as generative descriptions. The process of creating such descriptions is referred to as generative modeling and design automation. In contrast to many other descriptions, which are only describing a shape's appearance, generative shape descriptions represent inherent rules related to the structure of a shape. In simple terms, it is a computer program for the construction of the shape. It typically produces a surface-based or volumetric shape description for further use. In the article "Modeling Procedural Knowledge – A Generative Modeler for Cultural Heritage" [32] by Christoph Schinko et al., the authors state that all objects with well-organized structures and repetitive forms can be described in such a way. Many researchers enforce the creation of generative descriptions due to its many advantages [33].

Its strength lies in the compact description compared to conventional approaches, which does not depend on the counter of primitives but on the model's complexity itself [34]. Particularly large scale models and scenes – such as plants, buildings, cities, and landscapes – can be described efficiently. Generative descriptions make complex models manageable as they allow identifying a shape's high-level parameters.

Another advantage is the included expert knowledge within an object description, e.g., classification schemes used in architecture, archaeology, civil engineering, etc. can be mapped to procedures. For a specific object only its type and its instantiation parameters have to be identified. This identification is required by digital library services: markup, indexing, and retrieval [35]. The importance of semantic meta data becomes obvious in the context of electronic product data management, product lifecycle management, data exchange and storage or, more general, of digital libraries.

A disadvantage of generative shape descriptions is their dependency to (1.) a programming language, in which the shape is implemented and to (2.) a primitive geometry representation (point sets, meshes, etc.), which is the return type of the implemented shape function. As a consequence, generative descriptions can be realized in many different ways [33] and the conversion between different kinds of generative descriptions relies on translation techniques developed in the field of compiler construction [36].

Generative descriptions have been developed in order to generate highly complex shapes based on a set of formal construction rules. They represent a whole family of shapes, not just a single shape. A specific exemplar is obtained by defining a set of parameters, or a sequence of processing steps: Shape design becomes rule design [37].

Because such descriptions already belong to a specific class of shapes, there is no need for detectors. However, with a generative description at hand, it is interesting to enrich other descriptions and representations. What is the best generative description of one or several given instances of an object class? This question is regarded as the inverse modeling problem [38].

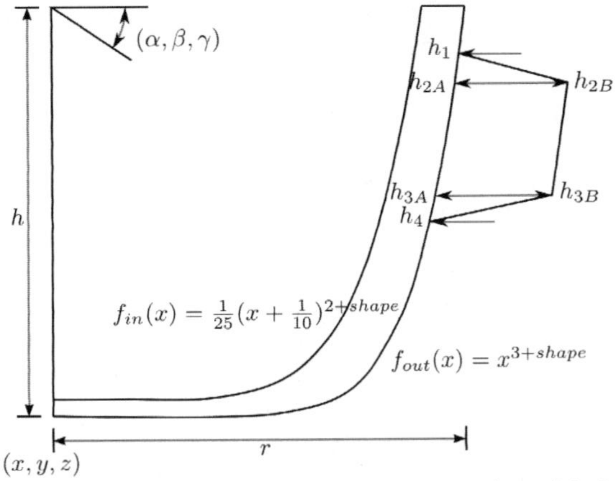

Figure 9. The generative model takes several parameters: (x, y, z) is the base point of the bowl and (α, β, γ) define its orientation. Its shape is defined by an inner f_{in} and outer f_{out} shape function with one free parameter $shape$. These functions are rotated around the cup's main axis and scaled with the parameters r and h. The handles are defined via control points of a Bézier curve.

In order to continue the example of the soup bowl mentioned before, Figure 9 sketches an automated design of a bowl. The generative model is implemented as a function M that takes several parameters $\mathbf{x} = (x_0, \ldots, x_n)$ and which returns a 3D model of a bowl. Automatic fitting routines [38] are able to register the generative design with the STL input data set (see Figure 2) and to determine the optimal input parameters (see Figure 10).

In detail, the registration algorithm converts the STL input data set into a point cloud P. For each instance of the generative model description $M(\mathbf{x})$; i.e., for each evaluation of a specific parameter set $\mathbf{x}$, the geometric distance $d(M(\mathbf{x}), P)$ between the two 3D models is calculated [39]. An optimization algorithm minimizes this distance d by evaluating different parameter sets $\mathbf{x}_1, \mathbf{x}_2, \ldots$ i.e., it minimizes the error function

$$f(\mathbf{x}) = d(M(\mathbf{x}), P) \stackrel{!}{=} \min_{\mathbf{x}} . \qquad (1)$$

As the parameter domain may be a mixture of discrete and continuous spaces, the optimization routine should be able to handle both; for example using the combination of an evolution strategy with an integrated gradient approach [40].

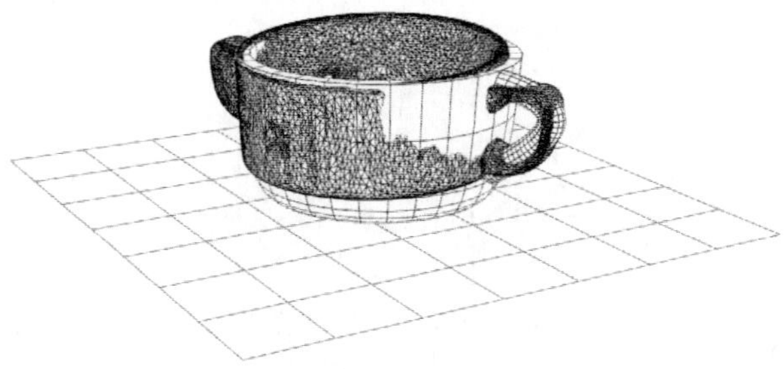

Figure 10. The "generative" soup bowl represents an ideal soup bowl. It is a "clean" quad mesh; in contrast to the "noisy" triangle mesh, which is the input of the generative fitting routine. The fitting calculates the optimal parameters so that the generative soup bowl fits its noisy counterpart. Showing input and output data in the same visualization outlines the quality of the fitting process.

III. Model Transformation

In a product life cycle, the digital counterpart of a future, real-world object has to pass several stages of a multi-step pipeline. First sketches of a product are represented in a different representation than the final CAD production-ready data set. Furthermore, virtual product tests and simulations require special purpose model representation as well. As a consequence, each transformation between two possible model representations has a field of application. For the presented representations Table I lists the conversion methods and algorithms. Furthermore, the following paragraphs describe the conversion ideas that have a wide-spread field of applications.

A. Level-of-Detail Techniques

Managing level of detail is at once a very current and a very old topic in computer graphics. As early as 1976 James Clark described the benefits of representing objects within a scene at several resolutions. Recent years have seen many algorithms, papers, and software tools devoted to generating and managing such multiresolution representations of objects automatically [70].

The idea of "Level of Detail", or LOD for short, is an important topic in computer graphics as it is one of the key optimization strategies that would help 3D graphical programs, such as modeling software to run faster and reliably rendered across all the new and old hardware.

B. Marching Cubes

Marching cubes is a computer graphics algorithm by William E. Lorensen and Harvey E. Cline for extracting a polygonal mesh of an isosurface from a three-dimensional discrete scalar field.

The algorithm proceeds through the scalar field, taking eight neighbor locations at a time (thus forming an imaginary cube), then determining the polygon(s) needed to represent the part of the isosurface that passes through this cube. The individual polygons are then fused into the desired surface.

This is done by creating an index to a precalculated array of 256 possible polygon configurations ($2^8 = 256$) within the cube, by treating each of the 8 scalar values as a bit in an 8-bit integer. If the scalar's value is higher than the iso-value (i.e., it is inside the surface) then the appropriate bit is set to one, while if it is lower (outside), it is set to zero. The final value, after all eight scalars are checked, is the actual index to the polygon indices array.

Finally, each vertex of the generated polygons is placed on the appropriate position along the cube's edge by linearly interpolating the two scalar values that are connected by that edge.

The gradient of the scalar field at each grid point is also the normal vector of a hypothetical isosurface passing from that point. Therefore, it is reasonable to interpolate these normals along the edges of each cube to find the normals of the generated vertices, which are essential for shading the resulting mesh with some illumination model.

C. Random Sample Consensus

A simple and elegant conceptual framework to estimate parameters is the Random Sample Consensus (RANSAC) paradigm by Martin A. Fischler and Robert C. Bolles [71]. This technique is capable of extracting a variety of different models out of unstructured, noisy, sparse, and incomplete data. In the context of computer-aided design it is often used to fit geometric primitives such as planes, spheres, etc. to a point cloud [72].

RANSAC-based algorithms proceed by randomly taking (ideally few) samples, calculating the free parameters of a model (for example the four parameters of a plane). Then all samples of the input data set "vote", whether they agree with the hypothesis (if they are close enough to the suggested plane). This procedure is repeated a few times, and the hypothesis with the highest acceptance rate wins by "consensus". Samples, which agreed to a hypothesis, can be removed from the input data set and the process can be started again, basically until no samples remain.

The number of iterations, which are needed until a "good" hypothesis is found, can be determined stochastically. Let the input data set consist of $(r + s)$ elements, of which r belong to a model, which shall be identified. If n samples are needed to generate a model instance, the probability that k randomly chosen samples belong to this model is distributed hypergeometrically; that means $P(X = k)$ can be calculated via the formula

$$P(X = k) = \frac{\binom{r}{k}\binom{s}{n-k}}{\binom{r+s}{n}}.$$

Therefore, the probability that at least one sample does not belong to this model is $1 - P(X = n)$. If the process of model generation and testing is done in j times, the probability that always at least one sample does not belong to the current model is $(1 - P(X = n))^j$. If p is the probability that the RANSAC algorithm returns the correct result, the probability of a failure is $1 - p$. The probability of such a failure is described by the term $(1 - P(X = n))^j$. Therefore, this term has to equal $1-p$. Solving the resulting equation for j returns the expected number of needed iterations:

$$j = \frac{\ln(1-p)}{\ln\left(1 - \frac{\binom{r}{n}}{\binom{r+s}{n}}\right)}$$

For example, if 20% of all points belong to a plane and the remaining points are distributed randomly, then the noise is at a level of 80%. In this case, the algorithm will need 373 iterations to detect this plane with a probability $p = 0.95$; respectively 574 iterations to ensure a probability of $p = 0.99$.

D. Midsurfaces & Isogeometry

Thin objects such as papers or metal sheets often appear in various contexts. Non-zero structural thickness is a factor that influences their dynamic movements. Nevertheless, those objects are often abstracted as two-dimensional entities, so-called thin shells. The simulation of 3D solids has been studied for a long time. Since thin shells are special cases of 3D solids, one may apply the techniques developed for 3D solids to the simulation of thin shells. Unfortunately, this approach does not produce satisfactory results; modeling thin shells as 3D elastic solids requires very fine FEM meshes to correctly capture the global bending behavior.

A thin shell is a 3D elastic solid, of which one dimension is small with respect to the others. This particular geometry covers a wide range of engineering designs common in the automotive and aerospace industries, but also in everyday life in the form of, e.g., objects made of metal sheet or thin plastic materials. For analysis this geometry is formulated in terms of the middle surface / midsurface of the shell.

The creation of a thin shell representation of an arbitrary object is an open question. Nevertheless, approaches to identify pairs of opposite patches, which can be merged to a single patch, and volume thinning techniques [73], [74] often lead to sufficient results.

As typical product development consists of several stages – mainly design in CAD system and analysis / simulation in computer aided engineering (CAE) systems – CAD models often have to be converted and transformed.

Isogeometric analysis (IGA) refers to analysis based directly on the geometry representation used in CAD. It therefore avoids transforming the designed geometry into an approximated simulation mesh for analysis. Isogeometric analysis was introduced by Hughes et al. [75] for NURBS based surfaces, but has also been successfully applied to other surface representations like subdivision surfaces [76], [77]. With IGA, the same basis functions used to define the CAD geometry are also used to represent the simulation geometry and the fields of unknowns for analysis. Because isogeometric analysis does not require the creation of a separate simulation mesh, it bridges the gap between CAD and CAE and facilitates an ideal integration of modeling and analysis.

While the main focus of IGA is to more closely link design and analysis in engineering, this technique is also used in other fields; for example, physics-based modeling tools based on IGA have been integrated into a modeling application [78]. The designed subdivision geometry is directly used to compute deformations based on an isogeometric thin shell analysis. The results are immediately available in the modeling application. Another example are soft-body deformations for virtual reality environments [79], which are computed interactively based on isogeometric analysis of the subdivision surfaces used for visualization.

E. Parametric Subdivision Surfaces

As subdivision surfaces are defined by an iterative refinement algorithm, they generally cannot be directly evaluated as a parametric surface. While regular regions often define a known parametric surface, like bi-cubic B-splines in the case of Catmull-Clark subdivision, this does not apply to irregular regions near extraordinary vertices.

How to exactly evaluate irregular regions of a subdivision surface at arbitrary parameter values has been shown by Stam, first for Catmull-Clark [59] and later also for Loop subdivision [60]. The evaluation is based on a set of eigenbasis functions, derived from the subdivision matrix of the particular subdivision scheme. This idea has also been extended to the higher degree NURBS compatible subdivision scheme [77]. These approaches therefore provide a parametric mapping of parameter values to points on the subdivision surface.

Another approach to convert a subdivision surface to an approximate parametric surface is to extract regular B-spline patches from the subdivision surface. For example, while regular regions of a Catmull-Clark surface can be directly mapped to bi-cubic B-spline patches, irregular regions need to be approximated to get C^1 continuous patches [61].

F. Semantic Enrichment

The problem of extracting semantic information from 3D data can be formulated simply as *What is the point?* [80] A-priori it is not clear whether a given point of a laser-scanned 3D scene, for example, belongs to a wall, to a door, or to the ground [81]. To answer this question is called semantic enrichment and it is always an act of interpretation [2].

The idea of generalized documents is to treat multimedia data, in particular 3D data sets, just like ordinary text documents, so that they can be inserted into a digital library. For any digital library to be able to handle a given media type, it must be integrated with the generic services that a digital library provides, namely markup, indexing, and retrieval. This defines a digital library in terms of the function it provides [82], [83]. Like any library, it contains meta-information for all data sets. In the simplest case, the metadata are of the Dublin Core type (title, creator/author, and time of creation, etc.) [84]. This is insufficient for large databases with a huge number of 3D objects, because of their versatility and rich structure. Scanned models are used in raw data collections, for documentation archival, virtual reconstruction, historical data analysis, and for high-quality visualization for dissemination purposes [85]. Navigating and browsing through the geometric models must be possible not only in 3D, but also on the semantic level. The need for higher-level semantic information becomes immediately clear when considering typical questions users might want to ask when a large database of 3D objects is available.

- How many different types of chairs are stored in the library?
- I want to compare the noses of all these statues, can you extract them?
- ...

These questions cannot be answered, if the library simply treats 3D objects as binary large objects (BLOB) as it is done quite often. For a heap of geometric primitives without semantics, it is hard – if not impossible – to realize the mandatory services required by a digital library, especially in the context of electronic data exchange, storage and retrieval.

In the context of CAD, the processes of markup, indexing, and retrieval are a challenge with many open problems [86], [87].

IV. Conclusion

Model representations and their transformation into each other have been a challenge in the past and will remain a future challenge as well. The search for a comprehensive model representation combining the advantages of the various, different approaches is still on-going.

Especially the semantic question remains unanswered. Adding semantics to shapes is an important, if not the vital, step towards the great vision of visual computing: To not only capture reality by sampling the world with 2D and 3D acquisition devices, but also to represent reality within a computer in a meaningful, ideally even in an editable form. Qualitative leaps can only be expected, if this open problem is solved, and the semantic gap is eventually closed in a reliable and sustainable way.

Acknowledgment

The authors gratefully acknowledge the support of the Austrian Research Promotion Agency, the Forschungsförderungsgesellschaft (FFG) for the research project AEDA (K-Projekt "Advanced Engineering Design Automation").

TABLE I. TRANSFORMATION BETWEEN MODEL REPRESENTATIONS.

Model Transformation from\to	*Point Sets*	*Polygonal Faces*	*Parametric Surfaces*	*Subdivision Surfaces*	*Implicit Surfaces*	*Volumetric Shapes*	*Generative Shapes*
Point Sets		Poisson Reconstruction [41], [42]	Surface Fitting and Regression [10]	Surface Fitting [43]	Surface Fitting [44], Gaussian Density Computation [45]	Direct Evaluation [46], Gaussian Density Computation [45]	Generative Fitting [38]
Polygonal Faces	Monte Carlo Sampling [47], [48]	Mesh Processing [5]	Surface Fitting [49]	Surface Fitting [50], [51]	Variational Inter- polation [52]	Scan-line Filling [53]	Generative Fitting [38]
Parametric Surfaces	Monte Carlo Sampling [47], [48]	Triangulation [11], [13]	Conversion [12], [11]	Extended Subdivision Surfaces [54], NURBS-compatible Subdivision [21], Conversion [55]	Spherical Coordinates [56]	Forward Differencing [53]	Inverse (Procedural) Modeling [37]
Subdivision Surfaces	Monte Carlo Sampling [47], [48]	Evaluation [57], Tesselation [58]	Exact Evaluation [59], [60], Patching [61], Extended Subdivision Surfaces [54]			Evaluation [57] / Tesselation [58] with Forward Differencing [53]	Inverse (Procedural) Modeling [62]
Implicit Surfaces	Point Evaluation [63]	Marching Cubes [64], [65]	Spherical coordinate [56]	Interpolation [66]		Voxelization [67]	Inverse (Procedural) Modeling [68]
Volumetric Shapes	Point Sampling / Iso-Surface-Extraction [69]	Marching Cubes [64]	via polygonal faces representation (marching cubes [64])	via polygonal faces representation (marching cubes [64])	via polygonal faces representation (marching cubes [64])		Generative Fitting [38], Inverse (Procedural) Modeling [68]
Generative Shapes	Evaluation [33]	Evaluation [33]	Evaluation [33]	Evaluation [33]	Evaluation [33]	Evaluation [33]	Euclides [36]

REFERENCES

[1] C. Schinko, U. Krispel, E. Eggeling, and T. Ullrich, "3d model representations and transformations in the context of computer-aided design: a state-of-the-art overview," Proceedings of the International Conference on Advances in Multimedia (MMedia), vol. 9, 2017, pp. 10–15.

[2] S. Havemann, T. Ullrich, and D. W. Fellner, "The Meaning of Shape and some Techniques to Extract It," Multimedia Information Extraction, vol. 1, 2012, pp. 81–98.

[3] M. Zwicker, M. Pauly, O. Knoll, and M. Gross, "Pointshop 3D: an interactive system for point-based surface editing," Proceedings of 2002 ACM Siggraph, vol. 21, 2002, pp. 322–329.

[4] M. Gross and H. Pfister, Point-Based Graphics. San Francisco, California, USA: Morgan Kaufmann Publishers Inc., 2007.

[5] M. Botsch, L. Kobbelt, and M. Pauly, Polygon Mesh Processing. Natick, Massachusetts, USA: AK Peters, 2010.

[6] M. Attene, D. Giorgi, M. Ferri, and B. Falcidieno, "On converting sets of tetrahedra to combinatorial and pl manifolds," Computer Aided Geometric Design, vol. 26, 2009, pp. 850–864.

[7] M. Botsch, S. Steinberg, S. Bischoff, and L. Kobbelt, "Openmesh – a generic and efficient polygon mesh data structure," Proceedings of OpenSG Symposium, vol. 1, 2002, pp. 1–5.

[8] G. Farin, Curves and Surfaces for Computer Aided Geometric Design, G. Farin, Ed. Academic Press Professional, Inc., 1990.

[9] H. Pottmann and S. Leopoldseder, "Geometries for CAGD," Handbook of 3D Modeling, G. Farin, J. Hoschek, and M.-S. Kim (editors), vol. 1, 2002, pp. 43–73.

[10] J. Hoschek and D. Lasser, Grundlagen der Geometrischen Datenverarbeitung (english: Fundamentals of Computer Aided Geometric Design), J. Hoschek and D. Lasser, Eds. Teubner, 1989.

[11] H. Prautzsch, W. Boehm, and M. Paluszny, Bézier and B-Spline Techniques, H. Prautzsch, W. Boehm, and M. Paluszny, Eds. Springer, 2002.

[12] G. Aumann and K. Spitzmüller, Computerorientierte Geometrie (english: Computer-Oriented Geometry), G. Aumann and K. Spitzmüller, Eds. BI-Wissenschafts-Verlag, 1993.

[13] L. Piegl and W. Tiller, The NURBS book, L. Piegl and W. Tiller, Eds. Springer-Verlag New York, Inc., 1997.

[14] J. Fisher, J. Lowther, and C.-K. Shene, "If you know b-splines well, you also know NURBS!" Proceedings of the 35th SIGCSE technical symposium on Computer science education, vol. 35, 2004, pp. 343–347.

[15] B. Hamann and P.-Y. Tsai, "A tessellation algorithm for the representation of trimmed NURBS surfaces with arbitrary trimming curves." Computer Aided Design, vol. 28, 1996, pp. 461–472.

[16] G. Farin, NURBS for Curve and Surface Design from Projective Geometry to Practical Use, G. Farin, Ed. AK Peters, Ltd., 1999.

[17] E. Catmull and J. Clark, "Recursively generated B-spline surfaces on arbitrary topological meshes," Computer-Aided Design, vol. 10, 1978, pp. 350–355.

[18] D. Doo and M. Sabin, "Behavior of Recursive Division Surfaces near Extraordinary Points," Computer Aided Design, vol. 10, no. 6, 1978, pp. 356–360.

[19] C. Loop, "Smooth Subdivision Surfaces Based on Triangles," Master's Thesis, University of Utah, USA, vol. 1, 1987, pp. 1–74.

[20] L. Kobbelt, "Interpolatory Subdivision on Open Quadrilateral Nets with Arbitrary Topology," Computer Graphics Forum, vol. 15, no. 3, 1996, pp. 409–420.

[21] T. J. Cashman, U. H. Augsdörfer, N. A. Dodgson, and M. A. Sabin, "Nurbs with extraordinary points: High-degree, non-uniform, rational subdivision schemes," ACM Transactions on Graphics, vol. 28, no. 3, Jul. 2009, pp. 46:1–46:9.

[22] E. Sultanow, "Implizite Flächen (english: Implicit surfaces)," Technical Report at Hasso-Plattner-Institut, vol. 1, 2004, pp. 1–11.

[23] A. Knoll, Y. Hijazi, C. Hansen, I. Wald, and H. Hagen, "Interactive Ray Tracing of Arbitrary Implicits with SIMD Interval Arithmetic," Proceedings of IEEE Symposium on Interactive Ray Tracing, vol. 7, 2007, pp. 11–18.

[24] A. A. Pasko and V. V. Savchenko, "Blending Operations for the Functionally Based Constructive Geometry," Set-theoretic Solid Modeling: Techniques and Applications / Information Geometers, vol. 94, 1994, pp. 151–161.

[25] G. I. Pasko, A. A. Pasko, and T. L. Kunii, "Bounded Blending for Function-Based Shape Modeling," IEEE Computer Graphics and Applications, vol. 25, 2005, pp. 36–45.

[26] B. Grünbaum and G. C. Shephard, "Convex polytopes," Bull. Lond. Math. Soc., vol. 1, 1969, pp. 257–300.

[27] U. Krispel, T. Ullrich, and D. W. Fellner, "Fast and Exact Plane-Based Representation for Polygonal Meshes," Proceeding of the International Conference on Computer Graphics, Visualization, Computer Vision and Image Processing, vol. 8, 2014, pp. 189–196.

[28] W. Thaller, U. Krispel, R. Zmugg, S. Havemann, and D. W. Fellner, "Shape Grammars on Convex Polyhedra," Computers & Graphics, vol. 37, 2013, pp. 707–717.

[29] Y. Hijazi, A. Knoll, M. Schott, A. Kensler, C. Hansen, and H. Hagen, "CSG Operations of Arbitrary Primitives with Interval Arithmetic and Real-Time Ray Casting," Scientific Visualization: Advanced Concepts, vol. 978-3-939897-19-4, 2010, pp. 78–89.

[30] B. Naylor, J. Amanatides, and W. Thibault, "Merging bsp trees yields polyhedral set operations," ACM Transactions on Graphics, vol. 24, no. 4, 1990, pp. 115–124.

[31] U. Schöning, Theoretische Informatik - kurz gefasst, 5th ed. Heidelberg: Spektrum Akademischer Verlag, 2008.

[32] C. Schinko, M. Strobl, T. Ullrich, and D. W. Fellner, "Modeling Procedural Knowledge – a generative modeler for cultural heritage," Proceedings of EUROMED 2010 - Lecture Notes on Computer Science, vol. 6436, 2010, pp. 153–165.

[33] U. Krispel, C. Schinko, and T. Ullrich, "A Survey of Algorithmic Shapes," Remote Sensing, vol. 7, 2015, pp. 12 763–12 792.

[34] R. Berndt, D. W. Fellner, and S. Havemann, "Generative 3D Models: a Key to More Information within less Bandwidth at Higher Quality," Proceeding of the 10th International Conference on 3D Web Technology, vol. 1, 2005, pp. 111–121.

[35] D. W. Fellner and S. Havemann, "Striving for an adequate vocabulary: Next generation metadata," Proceedings of the 29th Annual Conference of the German Classification Society, vol. 29, 2005, pp. 13–20.

[36] C. Schinko, M. Strobl, T. Ullrich, and D. W. Fellner, "Scripting technology for generative modeling," International Journal on Advances in Software, vol. 4, no. 3-4, 2011, pp. 308–326.

[37] U. Krispel, C. Schinko, and T. Ullrich, "The Rules Behind – Tutorial on Generative Modeling," Proceedings of Symposium on Geometry Processing / Graduate School, vol. 12, 2014, pp. 21–249.

[38] T. Ullrich and D. W. Fellner, "Generative Object Definition and Semantic Recognition," Proceedings of the Eurographics Workshop on 3D Object Retrieval, vol. 4, 2011, pp. 1–8.

[39] T. Ullrich, V. Settgast, U. Krispel, C. Fünfzig, and D. W. Fellner, "Distance Calculation between a Point and a Subdivision Surface," Proceedings of 2007 Vision, Modeling and Visualization (VMV), vol. 1, 2007, pp. 161–169.

[40] T. Ullrich, V. Settgast, and D. W. Fellner, "Semantic Fitting and Reconstruction," Journal on Computing and Cultural Heritage, vol. 1, no. 2, 2008, pp. 1201–1220.

[41] M. Kazhdan, M. Bolitho, and H. Hoppe, "Poisson surface reconstruction," Symposium on Geometry Processing, vol. 4, 2006, pp. 61–70.

[42] R. B. Rusu and S. Cousins, "3d is here: Point cloud library (pcl)," IEEE International Conference on Robotics and Automation (ICRA), vol. 28, May 9-13 2011, pp. 1–4.

[43] K.-S. D. Cheng, W. Wang, H. Qin, K.-Y. K. Wong, H. Yang, and Y. Liu, "Fitting Subdivision Surfaces to Unorganized Point Data using SDM," Proceedings of 12th Pacific Conference on Computer Graphics and Applications, vol. 1, 2004, pp. 16–24.

[44] P. Keller, O. Kreylos, E. S. Cowgill, L. H. Kellogg, and M. Hering-Bertram, "Construction of implicit surfaces from point clouds using a feature-based approach," Dagstuhl Publishing, vol. 2, 2011, pp. 129–143.

[45] R. Preiner, O. Mattausch, M. Arikan, R. Pajarola, and M. Wimmer,

"Continuous projection for fast l1 reconstruction," ACM Transactions on Graphics, vol. 20, no. 9, 2014, pp. 1280–1292.

[46] S. Muraki, "Volumetric shape description of range data using 'blobby model'," SIGGRAPH Comput. Graph., vol. 25, no. 4, Jul. 1991, pp. 227–235.

[47] P. Cignoni, M. Callieri, M. Corsini, M. Dellepiane, F. Ganovelli, and G. Ranzuglia, "Meshlab: an open-source mesh processing tool," Eurographics Italian Chapter Conference, vol. 3, 2008, pp. 129–136.

[48] D. P. Kroese, T. Brereton, T. Taimre, and Z. I. Botev, "Why the monte carlo method is so important today," Wires – Computational Statistics, vol. 6, 2014, pp. 386–392.

[49] W. Ma and J. P. Kruth, "Nurbs curve and surface fitting for reverse engineering," The International Journal of Advanced Manufacturing Technology, vol. 14, no. 12, 1998, pp. 918–927.

[50] X. Ma, S. Keates, Y. Jiang, and J. Kosinka, "Subdivision surface fitting to a dense mesh using ridges and umbilics," Computer Aided Geometric Design, vol. 32, 2015, pp. 5–21.

[51] D. Panozzo, M. Tarini, N. Pietroni, P. Cignoni, and E. Puppo, "Automatic construction of quad-based subdivision surfaces using fitmaps," IEEE Transactions on Visualization & Computer Graphics, vol. 17, no. undefined, 2011, pp. 1510–1520.

[52] G. Yngve and G. Turk, "Robust creation of implicit surfaces from polygonal meshes," IEEE Transactions on Visualization and Computer Graphics, vol. 8, no. 4, 2002, pp. 346–359.

[53] A. Kaufman, "Efficient algorithms for 3d scan-conversion of parametric curves, surfaces, and volumes," Proceedings of the annual conference on computer graphics and interactive techniques, vol. 14, 1987, pp. 171–179.

[54] K. Mueller, L. Reusche, and D. W. Fellner, "Acm transactions on graphics," Extended subdivision surfaces: Building a bridge between NURBS and Catmull-Clark surfaces, vol. 25, 2006, pp. 268–292.

[55] J. Shen, J. kosinka, M. Sabin, and N. Dodgson, "Computer aided geometric design," Converting a CAD model into a non-uniform subdivision surface, vol. 48, 2016, pp. 17–35.

[56] C. Ünsalan and A. Erçil, "Conversions between parametric and implicit forms using polar/spherical coordinate representations," Computer Vision and Image Understanding, vol. 81, no. 1, 2001, pp. 1–25.

[57] W. Ma, "Subdivision surfaces for cad: an overview," Computer-Aided Design, vol. 37, no. 7, 2005, pp. 693–709.

[58] K. Müller and S. Havemann, "Subdivision surface tesselation on the fly using a versatile mesh data structure," Computer Graphics Forum, vol. 19, 2000, pp. 151–159.

[59] J. Stam, "Exact evaluation of Catmull-Clark subdivision surfaces at arbitrary parameter values," Proceedings of the annual conference on computer graphics and interactive techniques, vol. 25, 1998, pp. 395–404.

[60] ——, "Evaluation of Loop subdivision surfaces," Proceedings of the annual conference on computer graphics and interactive techniques (Course Notes), vol. 26, 1999, pp. 1–15.

[61] J. Peters, "Patching Catmull-Clark meshes," Proceedings of the Annual Conference on Computer Graphics and Interactive Techniques, vol. 27, 2000, pp. 255–258.

[62] C. Schinko, U. Krispel, T. Ullrich, and D. W. Fellner, "Built by Algorithms – State of the Art Report on Procedural Modeling," Proceeding of the International Workshop on 3D Virtual Reconstruction and Visualization of Complex Architectures (3D-ARCH), vol. 6, 2015, pp. 469–479.

[63] P. Ning and J. Bloomenthal, "An evaluation of implicit surface tilers," IEEE Computer Graphics and Applications, vol. 13, no. 6, 1993, pp. 33–41.

[64] T. S. Newman and H. Yi, "A survey of the marching cubes algorithm," Computers & Graphics, vol. 30, 2006, pp. 854–879.

[65] L. P. Kobbelt, M. Botsch, U. Schwanecke, and H.-P. Seidel, "Feature sensitive surface extraction from volume data," International Conference on Computer Graphics and Interactive Techniques, vol. 28, 2001, pp. 57–66.

[66] X. Jin, H. Sun, and Q. Peng, "Subdivision interpolating implicit surfaces," Computers & Graphics, vol. 27, no. 5, 2003, pp. 763–772.

[67] N. Stolte and A. Kaufman, "Novel techniques for robust voxelization and visualization of implicit surfaces," Graphical Models, vol. 63, no. 6, 2001, pp. 387–412.

[68] C. Schinko, U. Krispel, and T. Ullrich, "Know the Rules – Tutorial on Procedural Modeling," Proceedings of the International Joint Conference on Computer Vision, Imaging and Computer Graphics Theory and Applications (GRAPP Tutorial Notes), vol. 10, 2015, p. 27ff.

[69] R. U. Lobello, F. Dupont, and F. Denis, "Out-of-core adaptive isosurface extraction from binary volume data," Graphical Models, vol. 76, 2014, pp. 593–608.

[70] D. Luebke, M. Reddy, J. D. Cohen, A. Varshney, B. Watson, and R. Huebner, Level of Detail for 3D Graphics, 1st ed. Heidelberg, Germany: Morgan Kaufmann, 2002.

[71] M. A. Fischler and R. C. Bolles, "Random sample consensus: a paradigm for model fitting with applications to image analysis and automated cartography," Communications of the ACM, vol. 24, no. 6, 1981, pp. 381–395.

[72] R. Schnabel, R. Wahl, and R. Klein, "Efficient RANSAC for Point-Cloud Shape Detection," Computer Graphics Forum, vol. 26, no. 2, 2007, pp. 214–226.

[73] T. Itoh, Y. Yamaguchi, and K. Koyamada, "Fast isosurface generation using the volume thinning algorithm," IEEE Transactions on Visualization and Computer Graphics, vol. 7, 2001, pp. 32–46.

[74] T. Fujimori, Y. Kobayashi, and H. Suzuki, "Separated medial surface extraction from ct data of machine parts," Proceedings of the international conference on Geometric Modeling and Processing (GMP), vol. 4, 2006, pp. 313–324.

[75] T. J. R. Hughes, J. Cottrell, and Y. Bazilevs, "Isogeometric analysis: CAD, finite elements, NURBS, exact geometry and mesh refinement," Computer Methods in Applied Mechanics and Engineering, vol. 194, 2005, pp. 4135–4195.

[76] F. Cirak, M. Ortiz, and P. Schröder, "Subdivision surfaces: A new paradigm for thin-shell finite element analysis," International Journal for Numerical Methods in Engineering, vol. 47, no. 12, 2000, pp. 2039–2072.

[77] A. Riffnaller-Schiefer, U. H. Augsdörfer, and D. W. Fellner, "Isogeometric shell analysis with NURBS compatible subdivision surfaces," Applied Mathematics and Computation, vol. 272, 2016, pp. 139–147.

[78] ——, "Isogeometric analysis for modelling and design," Proceedings of EUROGRAPHICS – Short Papers, vol. 34, 2015, pp. 17–20.

[79] ——, "Interactive physics-based deformation for virtual worlds," Proceedings of the International Conference on Cyberworlds, 2017 (to appear).

[80] S. Biasotti, B. Falcidieno, D. Giorgi, and M. Spagnuolo, Mathematical Tools for Shape Analysis and Description. Morgan & Claypool Publishers, 2014.

[81] M. Attene, F. Robbiano, M. Spagnuolo, and B. Falcidieno, "Characterization of 3d shape parts for semantic annotation," Computer-Aided Design, vol. 41, 2009, pp. 756–763.

[82] D. W. Fellner, "Graphics Content in Digital Libraries: Old Problems, Recent Solutions, Future Demands," Journal of Universal Computer Science, vol. 7, 2001, pp. 400–409.

[83] D. W. Fellner, D. Saupe, and H. Krottmaier, "3D Documents," IEEE Computer Graphics and Applications, vol. 27, no. 4, 2007, pp. 20–21.

[84] Dublin Core Metadata Initiative, "Dublin Core Metadata Initiative," http://dublincore.org/ [retrieved: Feb. 2017], 1995.

[85] V. Settgast, T. Ullrich, and D. W. Fellner, "Information Technology for Cultural Heritage," IEEE Potentials, vol. 26, no. 4, 2007, pp. 38–43.

[86] C. Schinko, T. Vosgien, T. Prante, T. Schreck, and T. Ullrich, "Search & retrieval in cad databases – a user-centric state-of-the-art overview," Proceedings of the International Joint Conference on Computer Vision, Imaging and Computer Graphics Theory and Applications (GRAPP 2017), vol. 12, 2017, pp. 306–313.

[87] H. Laga, M. Mortara, and M. Spagnuolo, "Geometry and context for semantic correspondences and functionality recognition in man-made 3d shapes," ACM Transactions on Graphics, vol. 32, 2013, p. 150ff.

International Journal on Advances in Software, vol 10 no 3 & 4, year 2017, http://www.iariajournals.org/software/

Measurement-based Cost Estimation Method for Multi-Table Join Operation in an In-Memory Database

Tsuyoshi Tanaka* and Hiroshi Ishikawa†

Faculty of System Design, Tokyo Metropolitan University, Tokyo, Japan
Email: *tanaka-tsuyoshi@ed.tmu.ac.jp and †ishikawa-hiroshi@tmu.ac.jp

***Abstract*—Non-volatile memory is applied not only to storage subsystems but also to the main memory to improve performance and increase capacity. In the near future, some in-memory database systems will use a non-volatile main memory as a durable medium instead of the existing storage devices, such as hard disk drives or solid-state drives. For such in-memory database systems, the cost of memory access instead of I/O processing decreases, and the CPU cost increases relative to the most suitable access path selected for a database query. Therefore, a high-precision cost calculation method for query execution is required. In particular, when the database system cannot select the proper join method, the query execution time increases. Accordingly, a database join operation cost model using statistical information measured by a performance monitor embedded in the CPU is proposed and the accuracy of estimating the change point of join methods is evaluated. The results show that the proposed method can improve the accuracy of cost calculations to more than 90% compared to the conventional method. In conclusion, the in-memory database system using the proposed cost calculation method can select the best join method.**

Index Terms*—*Non-volatile memory; In-memory database systems; Query optimization; Query execution cost.

I. INTRODUCTION

This paper is the extended work of a paper presented at the MMEDIA 2017 conference [1]. Improving the performance and expanding the capacity of the non-volatile memory (NVM) is applicable to both high-speed disk drives and main memory units. Intel and Micron developed a NVM called 3D Xpoint memory [2] for such use. An NVM is implemented as a byte-addressable memory and assigned as part of the main memory space. An application programming interface (API) [3] [4] for accessing the NVM was proposed to make the development of applications easier. Roughly speaking, the API provides two types of access methods to the NVM from the software. The first is the "load/store type," which is the same method used to access the conventional main memory from user applications. The other is the "read/write type," which is the method used by existing input/output (I/O) devices, such as hard disk drives (HDDs) or solid-state drives (SSD), through operating system (OS) calls such as read/write functions. There are two types of implementations of in-memory databases through the application of a NVM to the main memory. The load/store type must be implemented using array structures or list structures on a main memory address area, such as the durable media of the database (Figure 1(c)). The read/write type can be easily applied to the existing database management system (DBMS) because the database files stored on disk drives (Figure 1(a)) are moved to files on the NVM defined by the API for the NVM (Figure 1(b)). When accessing the database, the performance of the load/store type is better than the read/write type because the DBMS directly accesses the database without any I/O device emulation operation. Database administration operations (e.g., system configuration, backup, etc.) do not have to be changed, which means that it is easy for the administrators to introduce the in-memory database system.

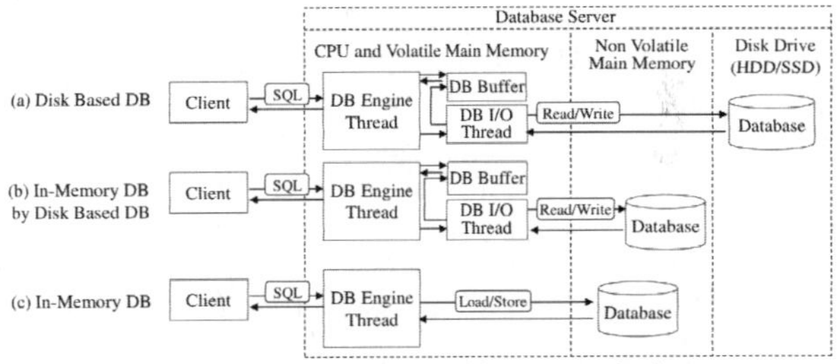

Fig. 1. Disk-based database and in-memory database

The DBMS encounters a problem when preparing for the execution of a query. In general, the DBMS performs several steps prior to query execution. First, it analyzes the query. Second, it creates multiple execution plans. Third, it estimates the query processing cost for each execution plan. Finally, it selects the minimum-cost execution plan from the plurality of candidates. For example, when the DBMS joins two tables, such as the R table and S table shown in Figure 2(a), it generates the execution plan (Figure 2(b)) that minimizes the number of rows to be referenced. At this time, the execution time depends on the join method that the DBMS selects. The DBMS estimates the cost of each join method using statistical information from the database, and chooses the method with the lowest cost. In general, the cost of a join operation is a function of the ratio of the extracted records to all the records. Hereafter, we refer to this ratio as the selectivity. In Figure 2, the selectivity is determined by condition x for column R.C in Figure 2(c). In Figure 2(c), two cost functions intersect at X_{cross}. Join method 2 must be chosen from the left side of X_{cross}, and join method 1 should be chosen from the right side of X_{cross}. If the DBMS cannot estimate the selectivity X_{cross} accurately, it will choose the wrong join method.

On the other hand, the query execution cost ($cost$) is generally expressed as the sum of the central processing unit

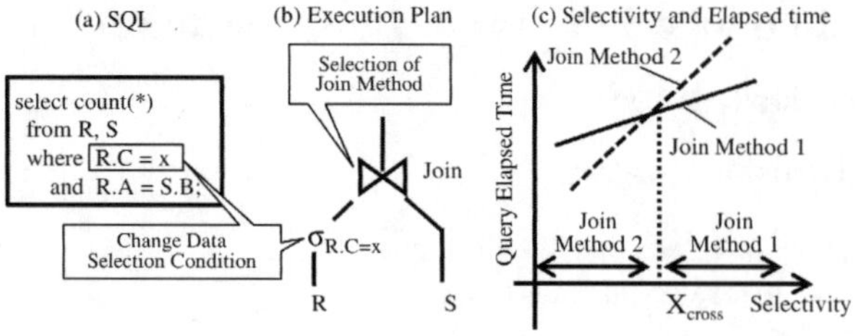

Fig. 2. Cost estimation problem for the selection of join methods

(CPU) cost (cpu_cost) and the I/O cost (io_cost) [5] [6]. The CPU cost is the CPU time, while the I/O cost is the latency when accessing the disk drive:

$$cost = cpu\_cost + io\_cost \tag{1}$$

For example, the cost formula for MySQL is given below [7]. The cost of scanning a table R is given by

$$table\_scan\_cost(\mathrm{R}) = record(\mathrm{R}) \times CPR + page(\mathrm{R}) \times CPIO \tag{2}$$

where $record(\mathrm{R})$ is the number of records of table R, CPR is the CPU cost per record, $page(\mathrm{R})$ is the number of pages of table R, and $CPIO$ is the I/O cost per page stored record for DBMS access. When table R (inner table) and table S (outer table) are joined, the cost of a join operation is given by

$$table\_join\_cost(\mathrm{R},\mathrm{S}) = table\_scan\_cost(\mathrm{R}) + record(R) \times selectivity \times records\_per\_key(\mathrm{S}) \times (CPIO + CPR) \tag{3}$$

where $selectivity$ is the selectivity ratio given by the distribution of attributes, and the selection conditions, such as a where-clause definition in SQL and $records\_per\_key(\mathrm{S})$, are the number of join keys specified by table S's records. Here, $CPR = 0.2$ and $CPIO = 1$ are the default defined values. However, this cost model was established under the condition that I/O performance is the bottleneck of the query execution time. A further improvement in disk performance increases the CPU cost relative to the I/O cost. If the I/O cost itself ultimately disappears with a native in-memory database (Figure 1(c)), then it becomes necessary to accurately predict the CPU cost.

To improve the accuracy of CPU processing cost prediction, the estimation of CPU processing time must become more accurate than with the conventional method mentioned above. In general, the CPU processing time can be predicted by the product of the number of executed instructions and the latency until an instruction is completed. To estimate the latency with high accuracy, it is necessary to consider the hardware structure, such as instruction execution parallelism, cache miss ratio, and memory hierarchy. These problems cannot be solved by the software algorithm alone. In order to improve the accuracy of cost calculation, we focused on constructing a CPU operation model by considering the CPU architecture [1].

In general, two approaches exist for query cost calculation: white-box analysis [8] and black-box analysis [9]. In the white-box analytic approach, the cost calculation model for a single DBMS system is the sum of CPU cost and I/O cost. These cost calculation models are functions of the number of records accessed by DBMS. The black-box analysis approach does not compute the sum by using each operation cost like accessing records of tables, accessing I/O, etc., but calculates the cost using multiple regression, which analyzes the objective variable with the information that the user of the database ordinarily obtains (explanatory variable such as the cardinality of the table). In most of the open source and commercial DBMSs, the white-box analysis approach is used because of the ease of understanding the models. This study adopts the white-box analysis approach for the same reason. The black-box analysis approach can easily deal with any DBMS because it does not use DBMS-dependent information. However, its estimation accuracy worsens in cases where the value of cost is small [9]. Therefore, this study aims to calculate an accurate cost when the cost value is small, by modeling the CPU activities.

In this study, we propose a method based on statistical information on CPU operations to improve the accuracy of CPU cost estimation for in-memory databases applied to existing DBMSs (Figure 1(b)). Our method can be easily applied to native in-memory databases (Figure 1(c)). Our contribution can be summarized as follows:

- First, we propose a method for modeling CPU cycles and estimating the join operation cost for a database. While considering the CPU pipeline architecture, we classify the CPU cycles into three components: a pipeline stall cycle caused by instruction cache misses, a pipeline stall cycle caused by branch misprediction, and an access cycle of data caches or main memory. Using this classification, we propose a CPU cycle modeling method that can express the total CPU execution time. In addition, to estimate the processing time of the join operation of a database, we decompose the pattern of join processing into four parts and estimate the join operation cost using a combination of these parts (Section II).
- Second, we analyze the trends or characteristics of the measured results for the join operation by using a performance monitor embedded in the CPU and determine the cost estimation formulas (Section III).
- Finally, we verify the accuracy of the proposed CPU cost estimation formulas by comparing the actual CPU processing cycle and conventional CPU cost estimation formula of MySQL (Section IV).

II. Proposed CPU Cost Model

In this section, we first analyze the CPU pipeline architecture and categorize pipeline events. Second, we propose the CPU operation cycle estimation method, which can express whole CPU process cycles by considering the categorized events. Third, we categorize join operations of the DBMS and divide the join operation into several parts. We propose an estimation model based on a combination of these parts. Finally, we create the CPU cost formulas for estimating each part of the join operation using statistical information measured by the performance monitor embedded in the CPU, and then combine these join part formulas to obtain the complete CPU cost estimation formula.

A. Model of CPU Operation Time

We chose the Intel Nehalem processor as a typical model of a CPU for application to the database server because all of the processors developed after Nehalem, namely Sandy Bridge, Haswell, and Skylake, are based on the pipeline architecture of Nehalem. Partial enhancements, such as additional cache for micro-operations (μOPs), increased reorder buffer entries, and increased instruction execution units, were added to the successor CPUs of Nehalem.

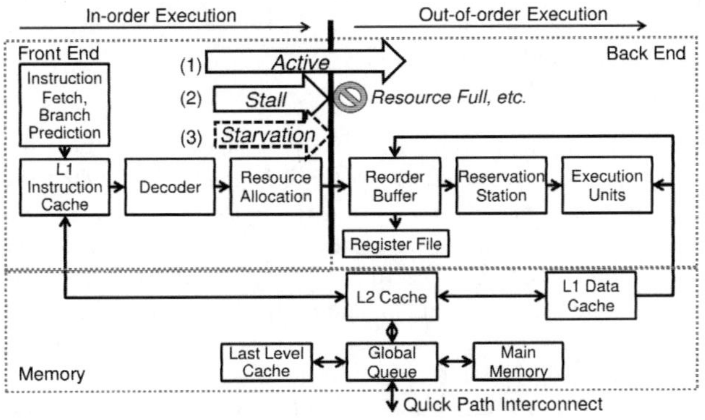

Fig. 3. Focus point of the CPU pipeline

The pipeline is composed of a front-end and back-end, as shown in Figure 3 [10]. The front-end fetches instructions from the L1 instruction cache (L1I) and decodes them into μOPs in-order. The term "in-order" means that a subsequent instruction cannot override the preceding instructions in the pipeline. After decoding the instructions, the front-end issues the μOPs to the back-end. Conversely, the back-end executes the μOPs in execution units that are out-of-order. The back-end can execute the μOPs in a different order than that issued by the front-end to improve the throughput of operating μOPs. An L1I miss causes the pipeline of the front-end to stall until the missing instruction is fetched from the lower level cache or main memory. A branch prediction miss causes a dozen cycles of the instructions executed speculatively to be flashed, and the front-end cannot issue μOPs. Such a condition is referred to as an *instruction-starvation state* (Figure 3(3)). There are cases in which the μOP issued in the front-end is not executed because of the saturation of the reorder buffer or reservation station in the back-end, or the data dependency of the preceding instructions. We refer to this state as a *stall state* (Figure 3(2)). In addition, we refer to the state in which the μOPs are issued without an *instruction-starvation state* or a *stall state* as an *active state*.

A summary of the notations related to CPU cost calculation to be used later in the study is presented in Table I before creating the CPU cost calculation model.

In this study, we focus on the boundary between the front-end and back-end in the CPU pipeline (Figure 3) to model the overall operation of the CPU. The μOPs are issued from front-end to back-end, and are stored in buffers, i.e., the reorder buffer and reservation station. The buffers allow us to change the processing order of μOPs from in-order to out-of-order across the boundary. The CPU-embedded performance monitor can measure events such as the saturation of buffers, de-queues from buffers by the completion of μOPs, and the existence of μOPs to issue to the back-end [10]. Any CPU cycle situation can be modeled by the performance monitor to analyze these events. Therefore, we propose a measurement-based estimation of the query execution cost. The *active state* is estimated from the number of events in which the μOP is issued without delay in the back-end buffer. The back-end buffer holds the μOPs until the execution of the μOPs is completed, and the μOPs are deleted from the buffer. The *stall state* is estimated from the number of events for which the buffer cannot receive μOPs. The *starvation state* is inferred from the event count where there are no μOPs to be issued to the back-end buffer. The total CPU cycle is composed of the *active state*, *stall state*, and *starvation state* cycles. Therefore, the following equation can be obtained:

$$C_{Total} = C_{Active} + C_{Stall} + C_{Starvation} \tag{4}$$

The cycles per instruction (CPI) metric, which refers to the number of CPU clock cycles per instruction, is widely used for evaluating the CPU processing efficiency [11]. CPI is calculated as the product of the number of references to the memory and the latency of the memory access. Latency is the delay time when fetching an instruction or data from memory. CPI is given by

$$CPI = CPI0 + \{\sum_{i=2}^{LLC} (H_{Li} \times L_{Li} \times BF_{Li}) + (H_{MM} \times L_{MM} \times BF_{MM})\} \tag{5}$$

where LLC denotes last level cache and means the lowest cache in the cache memory hierarchy; the blocking factor [11] is a correction coefficient for concealing the latency by executing instructions in parallel. The second term on the right-hand side of (5) is the product of the number of memory references, latency, and blocking factor, i.e., the *stall state*. The product of the second term on the right-hand side of (5) and the number of instructions I is the pipeline stall cycle (C_{Stall}):

$$C_{Stall} = \sum_{Li=L2}^{LLC} (M_{Li} \times L_{Li} \times BF_{Li}) + (M_{MM} \times L_{MM} \times BF_{MM}) \tag{6}$$

$$C_{Total} = CPI \times I = CPI0 \times I + C_{Stall} \tag{7}$$

From (5)–(7), we can show that $CPI0$ includes the *active state* and *starvation state*.

TABLE I. NOTATIONS FOR THE CPU COST CALCULATION MODEL

Symbol		Description
I		Number of instructions to complete a query
I_{Load}		Number of load instructions
CPI		Cycle per instruction (CPI)
$CPI0$		Cycle per instruction (CPI) on the condition that all of instructions and data are stored in L1 cache
M_{events}		Number of events
	events	**Description**
	MM	References of instructions and data to main memory
	MMI	References of instructions to main memory
	MMD	References of data to main memory
	Li	References of instructions and data to Li cache
	LiI	References of instructions to Li cache
	MP	Branch mispredictions
	$LMMI$	References of instructions to local main memory
	$LMMD$	References of data to local main memory
	$LLLCI$	References of instructions to local LLC
	$LLLCD$	References of data to local LLC
	$RLLCI$	References of instructions to remote LLC
	$RLLCD$	References of data to remote LLC
L_{memory}		Latency of cache memory or main memory
	memory	**Description**
	MM	Main memory
	Li	Li Cache
	MP	Recovering latency from a branch misprediction
	LMM	Local main memory
	$LLLC$	Local LLC
	$RLLC$	Remote LLC
BF_{events}		Blocking factor of $events$
	events	**Description**
	MM	References of instructions and data to main memory
	MMI	References of instructions to main memory
	MMD	References of data to main memory
	Li	References of instructions and data to Li cache
	LiI	References of instructions to Li cache
	LiD	References of data to Li cache
	MP	Branch misprediction and instruction cache miss occur simultaneously
H_{memory}		Ratio of $memory$ references to instructions ($H_{memory} = M_{mememory}/I$)
	memory	**Description**
	MM	References to main memory
	Li	References to Li cache memory
	LiI	References of instructions to Li cache
	LiD	References of data to Li cache
C_{state}		CPU cycles in $state$ during executing a query
	state	**Description**
	$Total$	Total of all states
	$Active$	Not occurring stall
	$Stall$	Stall of CPU pipeline
	$Starvation$	Starvation of instructions to issue
	$ICacheMiss$	CPU cycles from occurrence of L1I miss until the acquisition of an instruction from other cache or the main memory
	$DCacheAcc$	CPU cycles in *active state*
	MP	Total CPU cycles when recovering from branch mispredictions
C_{join_state}		CPU cycles of $join$ in $state$
	join	**Description**
	NLJ	Nested Loop Join
	$Build$	Build phase of Hash Join
	$Probe$	Probe phase of Hash Join
	$CmdBld$	Combination build phase
	$CmdPrb$	Combination probe phase
	state	**Description**
	$ICacheMiss$	CPU cycles from occurrence of L1I miss until the acquisition of an instruction from other cache or the main memory
	$DCacheAcc$	CPU cycles in *active state*
	MP	Total CPU cycles when recovering from branch mispredictions
$RC_{I\_total(n)}$		Total number of accessed records in n inner tables and entries of indexes
P		Selectivity of the tables for join
P_O		Selectivity of the outer table
P_{Ik}		Selectivity of the inner table$k$
R_O		Number of records in outer table
R_{Ik}		Number of records in inner table k ($k = 1, 2, \cdots$)
$R_{I\_total(n)}$		Total number of accessed records in n inner tables
$RC_{I\_total(n)}$		Total number of accessed records in n inner tables and entries of indexes

$$CPI0 \times I = C_{Active} + C_{Starvation} \quad (8)$$

The *starvation state* is mainly caused by instruction cache misses or branch mispredictions, and can be classified as the number of CPU cycles from the occurrence of one of these events until the acquisition of the next instruction to be executed.

$$C_{Starvation} = C_{ICacheMiss} + M_{MP} \times L_{MP} \times BF_{MP} \quad (9)$$

$$C_{ICacheMiss} = \sum_{Li=L2}^{LLC} (M_{LiI} \times L_{Li} \times BF_{LiI}) + (M_{MMI} \times L_{MM} \times BF_{MMI}) \quad (10)$$

Here, BF is a correction coefficient for considering that both branch misprediction and instruction cache miss occur simultaneously. $ICacheMiss$ is expressed as 10 by modifying 6 because the operations after instruction cache misses and data cache misses are the same. Only the terms relating to branch misprediction are defined.

$$C_{MP} = M_{MP} \times L_{MP} \times BF_{MP} \quad (11)$$

According to previous research [12], the CPI of the decision support system benchmark is 1.5–2.5. In general, when the CPI is 1, this means that one instruction is completed in one cycle; thus the instructions are executed sequentially in query execution. In addition, because the indices and tables of the database are usually implemented with list or tree structures, the next reference address becomes clear only after the stored data that the pointer refers to is read out. In particular, the characteristics of such a memory reference in the list structure are applied to a benchmark program for measuring memory latency [13]. Therefore, the *stall state* occurs because the operation of the stalled instruction waits for the preceding data reference processing to be completed. From the viewpoint of memory reference, the *active state* can be considered as an L1 data cache (L1D) reference, and the *stall state* can be considered as a reference to a cache level lower than L1 or a main memory reference. Therefore, the CPU cycles in the *active state* and *stall state* can be integrated as $C_{DCacheAcc}$

$$C_{DCacheAcc} = C_{Active} + C_{Stall} \quad (12)$$

$$C_{DCacheAcc} = \sum_{Li=L1}^{LLC} (M_{LiD} \times L_{Li} \times BF_{LiD}) + (M_{MMD} \times L_{MM} \times BF_{MMD}) \quad (13)$$

where (6) and (13) use the same symbols for both the latency and blocking factor for convenience, but the contents are different.

From the above discussion, the total number of CPU cycles is calculated using

$$C_{Total} = C_{DCacheAcc} + C_{ICacheMiss} + C_{MP} \quad (14)$$

In this study, each term on the right-hand side of (14) uses statistical information obtained from actual measurements.

B. DBMS Operation Model

DBMS queries perform operations including selection, projection, and join. Queries performing the join operation depend on the join method chosen by the DBMS's optimizer. The optimizer selects the join method to minimize the operating cost of the join operation. The cost depends on the selectivity of records defined by the clause of the SQL and the statistics of the attribute value of the database. Most DBMSs calculate the statistics during data loading to the database. This study focuses on cost estimation for the optimization of join operations. There are three basic joins: nested loop join (NLJ), hash join (HJ), and sort-merge join (SMJ).

NLJ searches records from the inner table every time it reads one record from the outer table. The generalized operation model of NLJ is shown in Figure 4. The process involves tracing multiple tables and indices from the point of view of memory access, which means repeatedly traversing linked lists. Therefore, NLJ can be regarded as searching between the outer table and the huge internal table created by tracing multiple tables in the same way as loop expansion by a compiler. Moreover, it is possible to calculate the cost of NLJ for multiple tables using the cost estimation function with two typical NLJs (Figure 4(a)), which is a function of the number of total records to be referenced in the multitable join. NLJ and HJ are regarded as part of our proposed cost estimation method. In this work, we do not examine SMJ because it is possible to apply the proposed method using the steps from the other join methods, specifically dividing parts into sorting and merging operations and then calculating the measured statistical values for each model. Figure 4 also shows that HJ is decomposed into a build phase (Figure 4(b-1)) and a probe phase (Figure 4(b-2)) because each operation of HJ is executed sequentially and can be modeled separately in the cost calculation formula based on measurement results.

When more than three tables are joined, the DBMS optimizer chooses a combination of different join methods for executing a query. Figure 5 shows a combination of HJ and NLJ. The first table to operate a join is called the "outer table," while the other tables are called "inner table." In addition, the inner tables are called "inner table1" and "inner table2" according to the joining order. A combination of different join methods is divided into an HJ build phase (Figure 5 (c-1)). The cost model of (c-1) is the same as (b-1). However, the cost model of (c-2) is different from the one mentioned above. It is presumed that the HJ probe phase and NLJ cannot be divided because the DBMS repeatedly searches one record in table Y using the hash table X, and searches table Z by NLJ. The (c-1) phase is called the "combination build phase" and the (c-2) phase is called the "combination probe phase."

C. Cost Calculation Formula

Before considering the cost calculation formulas, we define the inputs and outputs as listed in Table II. The information input into the cost calculation formulas is recorded in the database for management as statistical information, and is collected generally by the DBMS when storing or updating

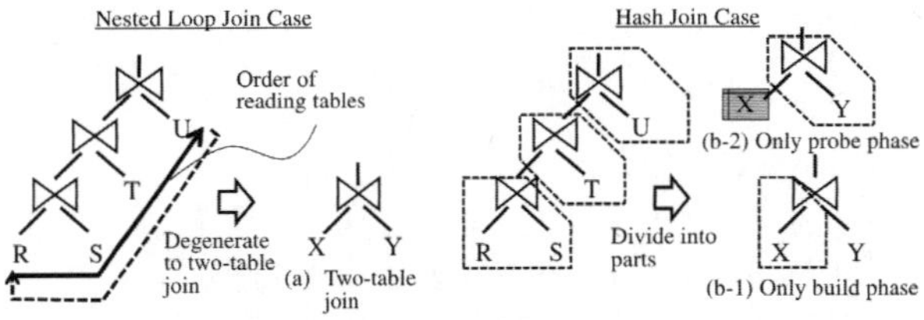

Fig. 4. Degradation and split cost calculation method

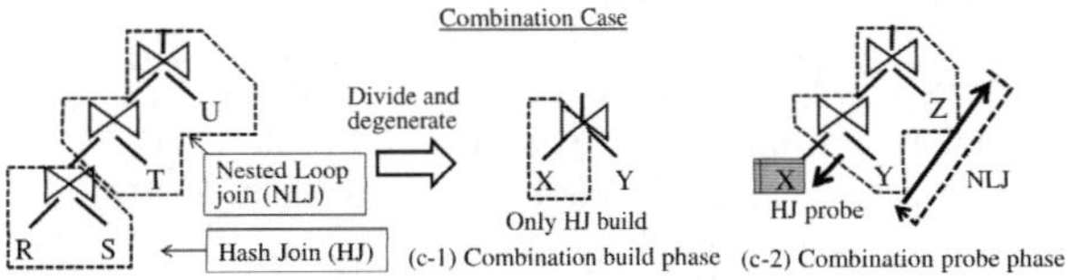

Fig. 5. NLJ after HJ Case

the record. Information regarding memory latency and I/O response time is also required. This information can be measured with a simple benchmark program [13].

TABLE II. PARAMETER LIST FOR COST CALCULATION

Input	Selectivity of outer table to join and number of records of tables
Output	Calculated cost expressed by number of CPU cycles
Parameters of cost calculation formulas	*Static information*: Memory latency and I/O response time *Information obtained from measurement*: Relational formula between the input information and number of CPU cycles of the events on the right-hand side of (14) (e.g., slope and intercept if the input information and the number of cycles of the event of interest can be linearly approximated.)

In this section, we derive the cost calculation formulas (14) for NLJ, HJ, and a combination of NLJ and HJ, where each element of (14) is obtained as a function of the selectivity and number of records in the joining tables. The cost formula of NLJ

$$\begin{aligned} C_{NLJ\_Total}(P,P_{Ik},R_O,R_{Ik}) &= C_{NLJ\_ICacheMiss}(P_O,P_{Ik},R_O,R_{Ik}) \\ &+ C_{NLJ\_MP}(P_O,P_{Ik},R_O,R_{Ik}) \\ &+ C_{NLJ\_DCacheAcc}(P_O,P_{Ik},R_O,R_{Ik}) \end{aligned} \quad (15)$$

is obtained by combining (10), (11), (13), and (14). The cost related to each element of the instruction cache miss, branch misprediction, and data reference are expressed as

$$\begin{aligned} C_{NLJ\_ICacheMiss}(P_O,P_{Ik},R_O,R_{Ik}) &= M_{L2I}(P_O,P_{Ik},R_O,R_{Ik}) \times L_{L2} \times BF_{L2I} \\ &+ M_{LLCI}(P_O,P_{Ik},R_O,R_{Ik}) \times L_{LLC} \times BF_{LLCI} \\ &+ M_{MMI}(P_O,P_{Ik},R_O,R_{Ik}) \times L_{MM} \times BF_{MMI} \end{aligned} \quad (16)$$

$$C_{NLJ\_MP}(P_O,P_{Ik},R_O,R_{Ik}) = M_{MP}(P_O,P_{Ik},R_O,R_{Ik}) \times L_{MP} \times BF_{MP}(P_O,R_O,R_{Ik}) \quad (17)$$

$$C_{NLJ\_DCacheAcc}(P_O,P_{Ik},R_O,R_{Ik}) = M_{L1D}(P_O,P_{Ik},R_O,R_{Ik}) \times L_{L1} \times BF_{L2D}(P_O,P_{Ik},R_O,R_{Ik}) + M_{L2D}(P,R_O,R_{Ik}) \times L_{L2} \times BF_{L2D}(P_O,P_{Ik},R_O,R_{Ik}) + M_{LLCD}(P,R_O,R_{Ik}) \times L_{LLC} \times BF_{LLCD}(P_O,P_{Ik},R_O,R_{Ik}) + M_{MMD}(P,R_O,R_{Ik}) \times L_{MM} \times BF_{MM}(P_O,P_{Ik},R_O,R_{Ik}) \quad (18)$$

The structure of the cost calculation formulas is basically a product-sum formula of the number of occurrences of the event, its latency, and the correction coefficient. The number of data references from the L1D cache, L2 cache, LLC cache, main memory (M_{L1D}, M_{L2}, M_{LLC}, and M_{MM}), number of branch mispredictions (M_{MP}), and blocking factor BF are expressed as a function of the selectivity P_O, P_{Ik}, and the number of rows of the table R_O, R_{Ik}. The cost of the instruction reference $C_{NLJ\_ICacheMiss}$ does not include L1I hits because it means the L1I cache miss penalty. However, the cost of the data reference $C_{NLJ\_DCacheAcc}$ includes L1D hits because the data reference includes all of the data access.

The cost calculation formula of HJ is obtained in the same way as that of NLJ with selectivity P

$$C_{Phase\_Total}(P,R) = C_{Phase\_ICacheMiss}(P,R) + C_{Phase\_MP}(P,R) + C_{Phase\_DCacheAcc}(P,R) \quad (19)$$

$$C_{Phase\_ICacheMiss}(P,R) = M_{L2I}(P,R) \times L_{L2} \times BF_{L2I}(P,R) + M_{LLCI}(P,R) \times L_{LLC} \times BF_{LLCI}(P,R) + M_{MMI}(P,R) \times L_{MM} \times BF_{MMI}(P,R) \quad (20)$$

$$C_{Phase\_MP}(P,R) = M_{MP}(P,R) \times L_{MP} \times BF_{MP}(P,R) \quad (21)$$

$$C_{Phase\_DCacheAcc}(P,R) = M_{L1D}(P,R) \times L_{L1} \times BF_{L2D}(P,R) + M_{L2D}(P,R) \times L_{L2} \times BF_{L2D}(P,R) + M_{LLCD}(P,R) \times L_{LLC} \times BF_{LLCD}(P,R) + M_{MMD}(P,R) \times L_{MM} \times BF_{MMD}(P,R) \quad (22)$$

where

$$\{Phase, P, R\} = \begin{cases} \{Build, P_O, R_O\} & \text{build phase} \\ \{Probe, P_{Ik}, R_I\} & \text{probe phase} \end{cases}$$

In the build phase, the cache and main memory references, branch misprediction, and blocking factor are expressed as functions of selectivity P and the number of records of the outer table (R_O). In the probe phase, these are expressed as functions of selectivity P and the number of records of the inner table (R_{Ik}). For a combination case like Figure 5(c-1), the cost formula of the combination build phase can be created with reference to the cost formula of the HJ build phase.

$$C_{CmbBld\_Total}(P_O,R_O) = C_{CmbBld\_ICacheMiss}(P_O,R_O) + C_{CmbBld\_MP}(P_O,R_O) + C_{CmbBld\_DCacheAcc}(P_O,R_O) \quad (23)$$

$$C_{CmbBld\_ICacheMiss}(P_O,R_O) = M_{L2I}(P_O,R_O) \times L_{L2} \times BF_{L2I}(P_O,R_O) + M_{LLCI}(P_O,R_O) \times L_{LLC} \times BF_{LLCI}(P_O,R_O) + M_{MMI}(P_O,R_O) \times L_{MM} \times BF_{MMI}(P_O,R_O) \quad (24)$$

$$C_{CmbBld\_MP}(P_O,R_O) = M_{MP}(P_O,R_O) \times L_{MP} \times BF_{MP}(P_O,R_O) \quad (25)$$

$$C_{CmbBld\_DCacheAcc}(P_O,R_O) = M_{L1D}(P_O,R_O) \times L_{L1} \times BF_{L2D}(P_O,R_O) + M_{L2D}(P_O,R_O) \times L_{L2} \times BF_{L2D}(P_O,R_O) + M_{LLCD}(P_O,R_O) \times L_{LLC} \times BF_{LLCD}(P_O,R_O) + M_{MMD}(P_O,R_O) \times L_{MM} \times BF_{MMD}(P_O,R_O) \quad (26)$$

$$C_{CmbPrb\_Total}(P_O,P_{Ik},R_O,R_{Ik}) = C_{CmbPrb\_ICacheMiss}(P_O,P_{Ik},R_O,R_{Ik}) + C_{CmbPrb\_MP}(P_O,P_{Ik},R_O,R_{Ik}) + C_{CmbPrb\_DCacheAcc}(P_O,P_{Ik},R_O,R_{Ik}) \quad (27)$$

For a combination case like Figure 5(c-2), the cost formula of the combination build phase can be created with reference to the cost formula of NLJ.

$$C_{CmbPrb\_ICacheMiss}(P_O,P_{Ik},R_O,R_{Ik}) = M_{L2I}(P_O,P_{Ik},R_O,R_{Ik}) \times L_{L2} \times BF_{L2I} + M_{LLCI}(P_O,P_{Ik},R_O,R_{Ik}) \times L_{LLC} \times BF_{LLCI} + M_{MMI}(P_O,P_{Ik},R_O,R_{Ik}) \times L_{MM} \times BF_{MMI} \quad (28)$$

$$C_{CmbPrb\_MP}(P_O,P_{Ik},R_O,R_{Ik}) = M_{MP}(P_O,P_{Ik},R_O,R_{Ik}) \times L_{MP} \times BF_{MP}(P_O,R_O,R_{Ik}) \quad (29)$$

$$C_{CmbPrb\_DCacheAcc}(P_O,P_{Ik},R_O,R_{Ik}) = M_{L1D}(P_O,P_{Ik},R_O,R_{Ik}) \times L_{L1} \times BF_{L2D}(P_O,P_{Ik},R_O,R_{Ik}) + M_{L2D}(P,R_O,R_{Ik}) \times L_{L2} \times BF_{L2D}(P_O,P_{Ik},R_O,R_{Ik}) + M_{LLCD}(P,R_O,R_{Ik}) \times L_{LLC} \times BF_{LLCD}(P_O,P_{Ik},R_O,R_{Ik}) + M_{MMD}(P,R_O,R_{Ik}) \times L_{MM} \times BF_{MM}(P_O,P_{Ik},R_O,R_{Ik}) \quad (30)$$

The aim of this study is to improve the accuracy of the CPU cost calculation. Therefore, we use a method to statistically obtain the parameters of the calculation formula from measured values using the performance monitor. One of the parameters, memory latency, depends on the hardware configuration, which includes the number of CPUs, the slot position in which the main memory modules are installed, and other factors. According to J. L. Lo et al. [14], the memory access concentration is low when executing analytic queries, such as the TPC-H benchmark, and does not increase the memory latency.

III. Evaluation of Parameters Obtained for the Cost Formula

To obtain the parameters in Table II, actual measurements were made. The measurement environment is listed in Table III. We used Westmere CPUs as they have the same architecture as Nehalem. The servers are equipped with two CPUs. The main memory is connected to each CPU. The memory connected to one CPU is called the local memory, while the other is called the remote memory. In general, such a memory architecture is known as non-uniform memory access (NUMA). The latencies of the local and remote memory are different. In this study, main memory modules are installed in only one CPU to simplify the examination of measurement results. An NVM Flash SSD was used as a disk device to store the database to improve the experimental efficiency. We used the open-source MariaDB [15] as the DBMS as it supports multithreading and asynchronous I/O, can utilize the latest hardware characteristics, and supports multiple join methods. Specifically, the NLJ supported by MariaDB is a block NLJ, which is an improvement of the NLJ. However, under the conditions of the query and index used in this study, it behaves like the general NLJ. The version of MariaDB used in this study does not select the effective join method automatically; it is specified based on the configuration parameters.

TABLE III. EVALUATION ENVIRONMENT

CPU	Xeon L5630 2.13 GHz 4-core, LLC 12 MB [Westmere-EP]) ×2
Memory	DDR3 12 GB (4 GB ×3) physically attached to only one CPU
Disk (DB)	PCIe NVMe Flash SSD 800 GB ×1 (Note: maximum throughput suppressed by server's PCIe I/F(ver.1.0a), about 1/4 of max throughput)
Disk (OS)	SAS 10,000 rpm 600 GB, RAID5 (4 Data + 1 Parity)
OS	CentOS 6.6 (x64)
DBMS	MariaDB 10.1.8 with InnoDB storage engine (Note: storage engine's buffer cache size is scaled to be 1 TB if database size is SF 100 TB.)

The query to be evaluated and its measurement conditions are shown in Figure 6. In the SQL statement, we modified Query 3 of TPC-H for an evaluation of two-table join and extracted only join processing (Figure 6(a)). The order of joining tables is shown in Figure 6(b). This query execution plan is generated by Mariadb. The database size is scale factor (SF) 5 defined in the TPC-H specification. SF5 means that the total size of the database is 5 GB. In order to apply the proposed technology to the actual system, we used small-scale data to minimize the measurement time. The indices of the database are created on the primary keys and the foreign keys are defined in the specification of TPC-H [16].

We changed the search conditions of the query against the c_acctbal column of the outer table in order to change the selectivity of the data to be referenced (Figure 6(c)). As for NLJ, the selectivity and number of records of the inner table were changed (Figure 6(c) and (d)). The purpose of changing the selectivity is to change the total number of records accessed by the DBMS. The purpose of changing the number of records of the inner table is to change the number of records that have the same key as the record selected from the outer table. This means changing the length of the linked lists that have the key to join with the inner table. As for HJ, only the outer table was accessed in the build phase, and the number of records of the outer table was changed (Figure 6(e)). In the probe phase, only the inner table was accessed, and the number of records of the inner table was changed (Figure 6(d)). In order to accurately measure the CPU events of the build phase, the empty inner table (Figure 6(f)) was used for joining with the outer table. In order to measure CPU events without affecting DBMS behavior, the CPU events that occurred during the probe phase are measured as follows:

$$\begin{aligned}&(\textit{Number of CPU events during probe phase})\\&=(\textit{Number of CPU events during total query execution})\\&\quad-(\textit{Number of CPU events during build phase})\end{aligned} \tag{31}$$

For the combination case, the query and its measurement conditions are shown in Figure 7. This query is based on Query 3 of TPC-H. The order of joining tables is shown in Figure 7(b). This query execution plan is generated by Mariadb. The search condition and selectivity of the outer table are shown in Figure 7(c). This condition is used for modeling Figure 5(c-1). In addition, the search condition and those of the inner tables are shown in Figure 7(d). This condition for the inner table1 and the inner table2 was used for modeling Figure 5(c-2). The search condition (e) in Figure 7 was introduced to accurately measure instructions, LOAD instructions, and branch mispredictions because we found that these events were more highly affected than other events through our preliminary experiment.

The CPU performance counter data was collected using Intel® Vtune™ Amplifier XE. We refer to Levinthal (2009) [10] for a description of the content of those counters. The measured data is mainly related to the number of accesses to the cache and main memory, the state of the pipeline such as the number of stall cycles, and the number of cache hits or misses. All of the counters and the methods of preprocessing them are presented in Table B.I and B.II in Appendix B.

It is necessary to analyze not only CPU time but also I/O operation time to estimate the whole execution time of a query (1). We measured the I/O count and response time using systemtap and constructed the I/O cost calculation formulas by analyzing the relation between I/O and the selectivity or number of records.

IV. Measurement Results and Cost Calculation Formulas

In this study, we investigate the relationships between selectivity, number of instructions, number of events related to memory reference, and number of branch mispredictions. For NLJ, the number of instructions and number of memory

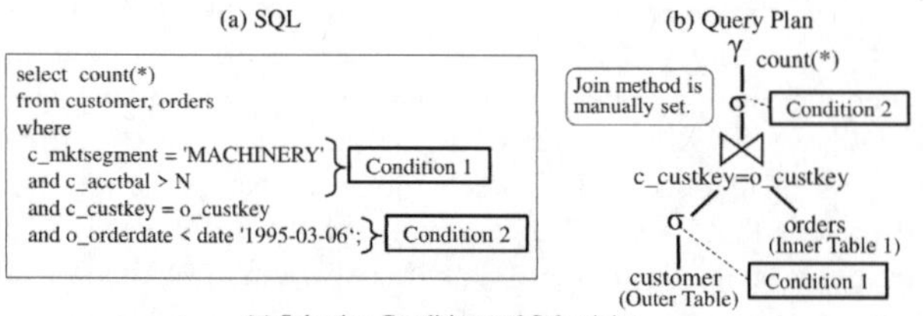

(c) Selection Condition and Selectivity

N	9998	9978	9798	9200	9000
Selectivity P_O (Condition 1)	3.62×10^{-05}	4.00×10^{-04}	3.67×10^{-03}	1.45×10^{-02}	1.82×10^{-02}

(d) Condition of Inner Table

Number of Records in Inner Table	7,500,000	5,625,000	3,750,000	1,875,000

(e) Condition of Outer Table

Number of Records in Outer Table	750,000	562,500	375,000	187,500

(f) Condition of Inner Table for Measuring Build Phase

Number of Records in Inner Table	7,500,000	5,625,000	3,750,000	1,875,000
Number of Records in Outer Table	0			

Fig. 6. Target query of measurement and cost estimation for two-table join

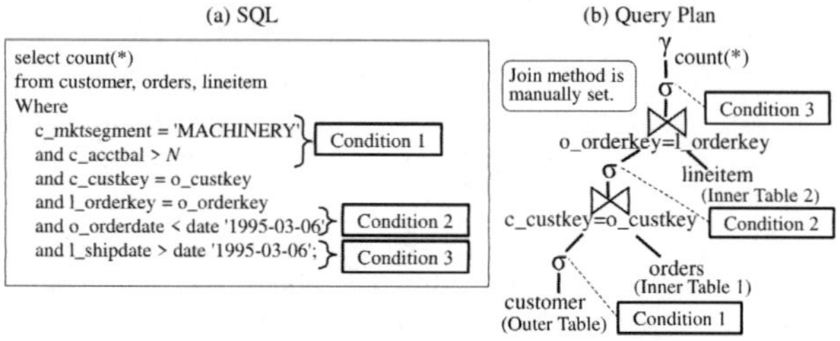

(c) Selection Condition and Selectivity

N	9998	9978	9798	9200	9000
Selectivity P_O (Condition 1)	3.62×10^{-5}	4.00×10^{-4}	3.67×10^{-3}	1.45×10^{-2}	1.82×10^{-2}
Selectivity P_{II} (Condition 2)	0.482	0.482	0.482	0.482	0.482

(d) Condition of Combination Probe phase

Number of Records in Inner Table1	7,500,000	5,625,000	3,750,000	1,875,000
Number of Records in Inner Table2	37,500,000			

(e) Condition of Combination Probe phase for Instruction, LOAD Instruction and Branch Misprediction Events

Number of Records in Inner Table1	7,500,000	5,625,000	3,750,000	1,875,000
Number of Records in Inner Table2	52,500,000			
	37,500,000			
	22,500,000			

Fig. 7. Target query of measurement and cost estimation for three-table join

references are expected to increase because the number of records accessed by the DBMS increases in proportion to the increase in selectivity. Based on the assumptions, we now analyze the measurement results and create formulas using linear regression. For HJ, all of the records of the outer table and inner table were accessed in both the build phase and probe phase. The cost formulas were assumed to not have selectivity as a variable; we analyzed the measurement results based on this assumption. For the combination of HJ and NLJ, the combination build phase was considered to be the same as the build phase of HJ. We investigated the relationships between the number of selected records from the outer table, number of records in the inner tables, and number of CPU events.

The CPU cost calculation formulas were obtained through the following steps. First, the number of instructions, references of each cache memory, and main memory and branch mispredictions were analyzed using regression analysis, and the regression models were created. In addition, the relationship between the sum of the product of the references to each memory and its latency, and $C_{ICacheMiss}$ (10) and $C_{DCacheAcc}$ (13) were modeled. Here, C_{MP} (11) was obtained from the product of the number of pipeline stages of the front-end, which is 12 in Nehalem, and the number of mispredictions from the measurement results. Each value of memory latency is referred from [10] [17]. The number of disk I/O was modeled using the measured I/O access count and I/O response time. Finally, the cost calculation formulas were evaluated from the viewpoint of the accuracy of intersection of the two join methods (X_{cross} in Figure 2) with the conventional method.

Figure 8(1) shows the relationship between the number of records the DBMS accessed and load instructions. Figure 8(7) shows the relationship between the total number of accessed records and number of instructions. The number of records is the product of the number of outer table records, number of inner table records, and selectivity. The dotted line is the linear regression line, and its slope and intercept are listed in Table IV. The coefficient of determination (R^2) is near 1 and the P value on the F test is less than 0.05. Therefore, the linear regression model is highly accurate. The slope and intercept were used to create the cost calculation model. Figures 8(2) and (8) show the relationship between the number of instructions executed by the DBMS and the number of L1 cache hits. Figures 8(3)–(6) and (9)–(12) show the relationships between the number of accesses to L2, LLC, and main memory, and the number of cache misses of the upper-level cache. These relationships can be linearly approximated because each R^2 is near 1 and each P value is less than 0.05 in Table IV. In this work, a two-CPU server was used and the LLC and main memory were connected to each CPU. The LLC and main memory of the CPU on which DBMS threads are running are called the *local LLC* and *local main memory*. The others are called *remote LLC* and *remote main memory*. The upper-level cache is the local LLC. There are no references to the remote main memory because the main memory is connected to only one CPU in our experimental environment. Figure 8(13) shows the relationship between the number of records accessed for the join operation and the branch misprediction cycles C_{MP}. Figure 8(14) shows the relationship between the product of the number of instruction accesses and latency, and the L1I miss cycles (miss penalty), $C_{ICacheMiss}$. Figure 8(15) shows the relationship between the products of the number of data accesses and latency, and the data cache and main memory access, $C_{DCacheAcc}$. Each graph can also be approximated by a regression line because each R^2 is near 1 and each P value is less than 0.05 in Table IV.

Figures 9(a1)–(a15), (b1)–(b15) and Figures 10(1)–(15) show the tendency of instructions, cache or main memory accesses, branch misprediction cycles, instruction cache miss cycles, and data cache access cycles. These events tend to be similar to those of the NLJ. The dotted line is the linear regression line, and its slope and intercept are shown in Table IV and Table V. The coefficient of determination (R^2) is near 1 and the P value on the F test is less than 0.05.

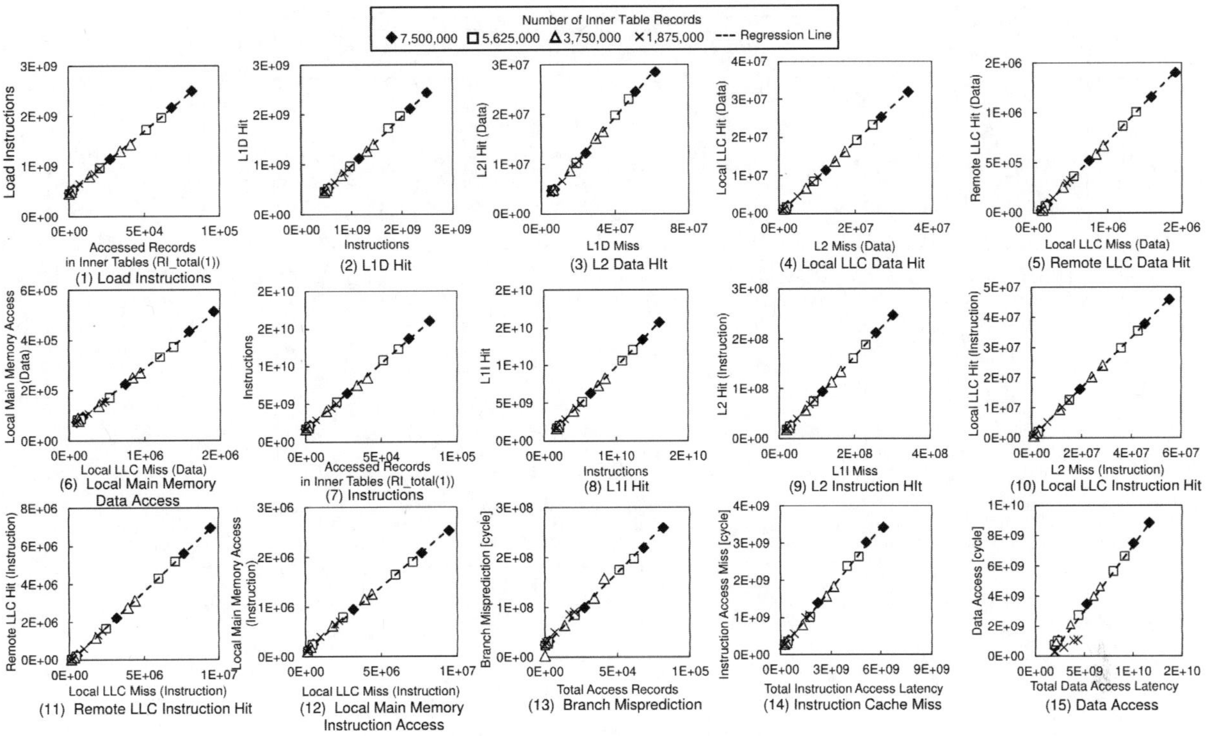

Fig. 8. CPU event count on executing NLJ

Therefore, the linear regression model is highly accurate. The slope and intercept are used for creating the cost calculation model.

In particular, the slope of the regression line in Figures 8(2)–(5) and (9)–(11); Figures 9(a2)–(a5), (a9)–(a11), (b2)–(b5), and (b9)–(b11); and Figures 10(2)–(5) and (9)–(11) represents the cache hit rate because the definition of cache hit rate is the quotient of the number of cache hits and number of cache references, and the upper-level cache miss becomes the lower-level cache reference.

In this study, the number of cache hits is chosen as an explanatory variable, as shown in Figure 11(a), which is the same graph as that in Figure 8(8). In general, the cache hit ratio is more often used for modeling CPU memory access than the number of cache hits. However, the cache hit ratio graph (Figure 11(b)) has a hyperbolic shape. The CPU cost calculation function should be simple in order to apply a simple formula to the actual DBMS. In addition, the reason why the cache hit ratio graph has a hyperbolic shape is explained by the following expressions (32) and (33).

The regression line of Figure 11(a) is

$$M_{L1I} = A \times I + B, \tag{32}$$

where A and B are the slope and intercept of a linear regression on the two table join in Figure 6, respectively. The cache hit ratio is obtained by dividing the number of cache hits by that of instructions. Therefore, the cache hit ratio (33) is obtained by dividing both sides of (32) by I.

$$(L1I\ Hit\ Ratio) = A + \frac{B}{I}, \tag{33}$$

In order to apply the two-table join calculation model to three or more tables, it is necessary to estimate the total number of accessed records in the inner tables (Figure 4(a), Figure 5 (c-1)). As shown in Figure 12, the number of accessed records in inner table1 is $R_{I0} \times P_{I0} \times rsk_0$ where rsk_0 is ratio of R_{I1} to R_{I0} (34). If $R_{I1} < R_{I0}$, then $rsk_0 = 1$ because the number of accessed records in inner table1 is as large as the references from the outer table. The number of references from inner table1 to inner table2 is $R_{I0} \times P_{I0} \times rsk_0 \times P_{I1} \times rsk_1$. Therefore, the total number of accessed records in the inner tables is $(R_{I0} \times P_{I0} \times rsk_0) + (R_{I0} \times P_{I0} \times rsk_0 \times P_{I1} \times rsk_1)$. Based on the above, we introduce rsk and $R_{I\_total}(n)$, which are written as (34) and (35).

$$rsk_i = \begin{cases} \dfrac{R_{Ii}}{R_{I(i-1)}} & R_{Ii} \geq R_{I(i-1)} \text{ where } R_{I0} = R_O \\ 1 & R_{Ii} < R_{I(i-1)} \end{cases} \tag{34}$$

$$R_{I\_total(n)} = R_O \times \sum_{j=1}^{n} \prod_{i=0}^{j-1} (rsk_i \times P_{Ii}) \tag{35}$$

where n of $R_{I\_total}(n)$ means the number of inner tables to join.

In the combination probe phase, multiple inner tables are traversed with the key of the records in the hash table.

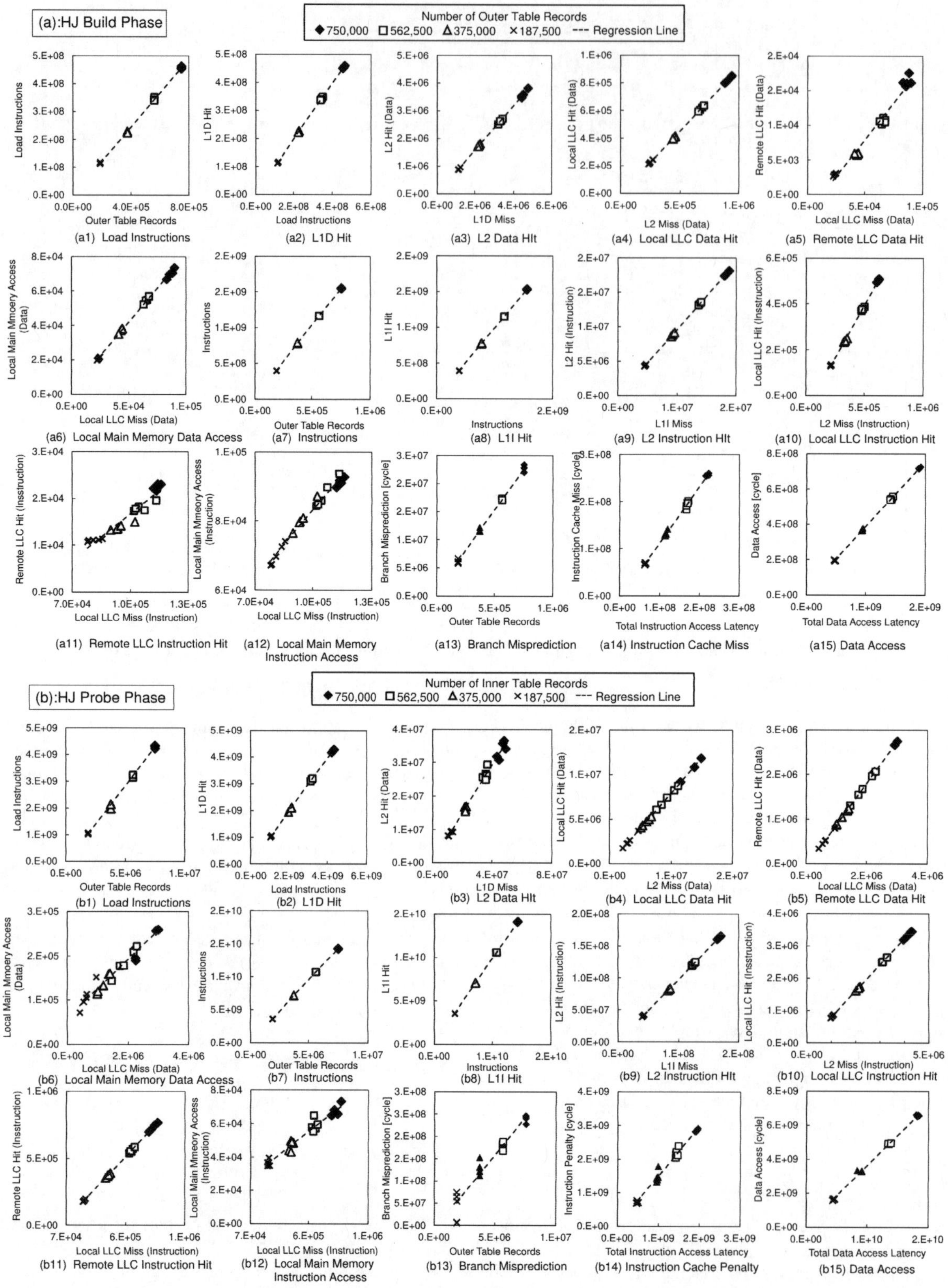

Fig. 9. CPU event count on executing HJ: (a) build phase, (b) probe phase)

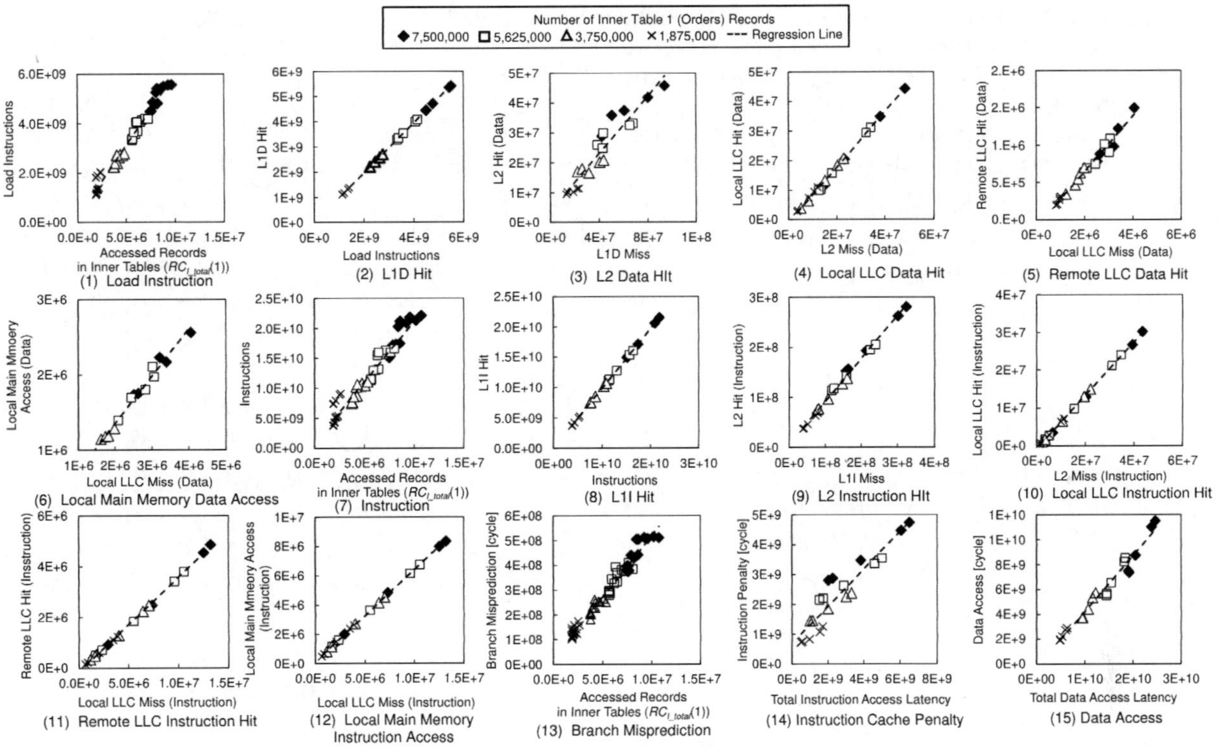

Fig. 10. CPU event count on combination probe phase

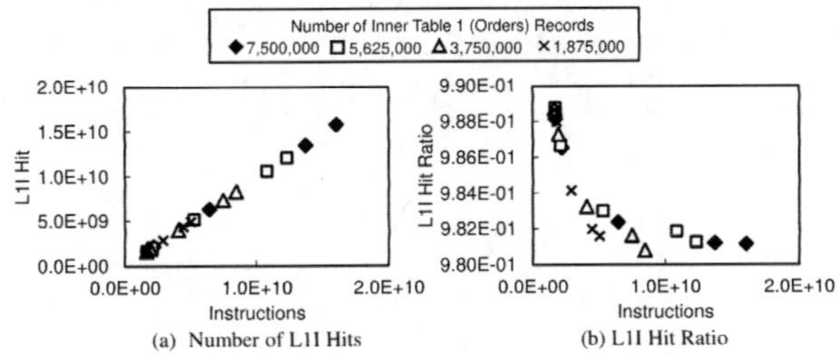

Fig. 11. Problem of modeling cache hit ratio

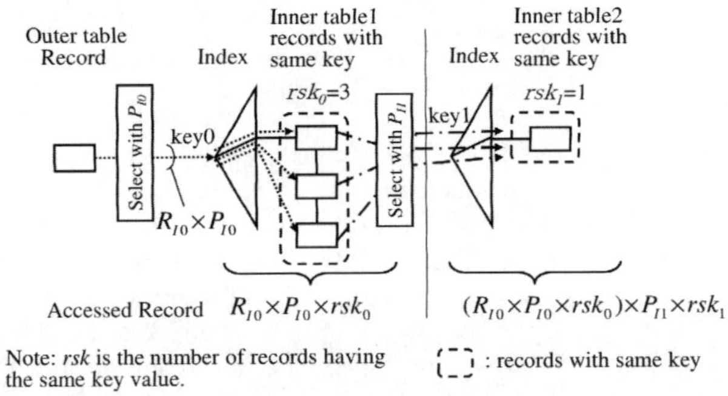

Fig. 12. Simple example of number of records having the same key value (rsk)

The number of instructions, LOAD instructions, and branch mispredictions are proportional to the number of inner table records accessed by the DBMS. However, the number of these events also depends on the number of entries in the hash table. It is necessary to obtain the sum of these two kinds of records with different properties. In general, the height of the index is approximately 3 to 4 as more than 100 records are registered in each node of the B+ tree. When the cost calculation equations are a function of only the accessed records in the inner tables, the traversing records among nodes and inside nodes can be considered as constant and omitted from the cost calculation model. However, in order to consider the scan of the hash table at the same time, it is necessary to consider both index height and records having the same key. Therefore, in the combination probe phase, $RC_{I\_total}(n)$ was introduced to construct a cost calculation formula. $RC_{I\_total}(n)$ is given by (36) as follows:

$$RC_{I\_total(n)} = R_O \times \left\{ \sum_{j=1}^{n} \prod_{i=0}^{j-1} (rsk_i \times P_{Ii}) \times \left(log_t(R_{Ii}) + \frac{rsk_i + 1}{2} \right) + 1 \right\} \quad (36)$$

where t is the number of entries stored in an index page. t is 100 because the B+ tree index stores more than 100 records in an index page.

The number of instructions, LOAD instructions, and branch mispredictions in the NLJ and combination probe phase are proportional to the number of referenced records in the inner tables (Figure 8(1)(7)(13) and Figure 10(1)(7)(13)).

Based on the above considerations, the formula for calculating the cost of the join methods is

$$I = A1 \times R + B1 \tag{37}$$

$$M_{L1I} = A2 \times I + B2 \tag{38}$$

$$M_{L2I} = A3 \times (I - M_{L1I}) + B3 \tag{39}$$

$$M_{LLLCI} = A4 \times (I - M_{L1I} - M_{L2I}) + B4 \tag{40}$$

$$M_{RLLCI} = A5 \times (I - M_{L1I} - M_{L2I} - M_{LLLCI}) + B5 \tag{41}$$

$$M_{LMMI} = A6 \times (I - M_{L1I} - M_{L2I} - M_{LLLCI}) + B6 \tag{42}$$

$$I_{Load} = A7 \times R + B7 \tag{43}$$

$$M_{L1D} = A8 \times I_{Load} + B8 \tag{44}$$

$$M_{L2D} = A9 \times (I - M_{L1D}) + B9 \tag{45}$$

$$M_{LLLCD} = A10 \times (I - M_{L1D} - M_{L2D}) + B10 \tag{46}$$

$$M_{RLLCD} = A11 \times (I - M_{L1D} - M_{L2D} - M_{LLLCD}) + B11 \tag{47}$$

$$M_{LMMD} = A12 \times (I - M_{L1D} - M_{L2D} - M_{LLLCD}) + B12 \tag{48}$$

$$\begin{aligned} C_{ICacheMiss} = {} & A13 \times (M_{L2I} \times L_{L2} + M_{LLLCI} \times L_{LLLC} \\ & + M_{RLLCI} \times L_{RLLC} + M_{LMMI} \times L_{LMM}) + B13 \end{aligned} \tag{49}$$

$$\begin{aligned} C_{DCacheAcc} = {} & A14 \times (M_{L1D} \times L_{L1} + M_{L2D} \times L_{L2} \\ & + M_{LLLCD} \times L_{LLLC} + M_{RLLCD} \times L_{RLLC} \\ & + M_{LMMD} \times L_{LMM}) + B14 \end{aligned} \tag{50}$$

$$C_{MP} = A15 \times R + B15 \tag{51}$$

where

$$R = \begin{cases} R_{I\_total(n)} & \text{NLJ} \\ R_O & \text{HJ build phase and combination build phase} \\ R_I & \text{HJ probe phase} \\ RC_{I\_total(n)} & \text{Combination probe phase} \end{cases}$$

The cost calculation formulas ((14), (37)–(51)) can become the following single formula by focusing on R ((52), (53), (54)). This formula suggests that our approach means estimating an accurate unit CPU cost per accessed record.

$$C_{Total} = \alpha \times R + \beta \tag{52}$$

where

$$\begin{aligned} \alpha = {} & A1 \times A13 \times (L_{L2} \times A3 \times (1 - A2) \\ & + L_{LLLC} \times A4 \times (1 - A3 - A2 + A2 \times A3) \\ & + L_{RLLC} \times A5 \times (1 - A2 - A3 + A2 \times A3 - A4 + A3 \times A4 \\ & + A2 \times A4 - A2 \times A3 \times A4) \\ & + L_{LMM} \times A6 \times (1 - A2 - A3 + A2 \times A3 - A4 + A3 \times A4 \\ & + A2 \times A4 - A2 \times A3 \times A4)) \\ & + A7 \times A14 \times (L_{L1} \times A8 + A14 \times L_{L2} \times (A9 - A8 \times A9) \\ & + L_{LLLC} \times A10 \times (1 - A9 - A8 + A8 \times A9) \\ & + L_{RLLC} \times A11 \times (1 - A8 - A9 + A8 \times A9 - A10 + A9 \times A10 \\ & + A8 \times A10 - A8 \times A9 \times A10) \\ & + L_{LMM} \times A12 \times (1 - A8 - A9 + A8 \times A9 - A10 + A9 \times A10 \\ & + A8 \times A10 - A8 \times A9 \times A10)) + A15 \end{aligned} \tag{53}$$

$$\begin{aligned} \beta = {} & A13 \times (L_{L2} \times (-A3 \times B2 + B3) \\ & + L_{LLLC} \times (-A4 \times B2 + A3 \times A4 \times B2 - A4 \times B3 + B4) \\ & + L_{RLLC} \times (-A5 \times B2 + A3 \times A5 \times B2 - A5 \times B3 \\ & + A4 \times A5 \times B2 - A3 \times A4 \times A5 \times B2 + A4 \times A5 \times B3 \\ & - A5 \times B4 + B5) \\ & + L_{LMM} \times (-A6 \times B2 + A3 \times A6 \times B2 - A6 \times B3 + A4 \\ & \times A6 \times B2 - A3 \times A4 \times A6 \times B2 + A4 \times A6 \times B3 - A6 \times B4 \\ & + B5)) + A14 \times (L_{L1} \times B8 + L_{L2} \times (-A9 \times B8 + B9) \\ & + L_{LLLC} \times (-A10 \times B8 + A9 \times A10 \times B8 - A10 \times B9 + B10) \\ & + L_{RLLC} \times (-A11 \times B8 + A9 \times A11 \times B8 - A11 \times B9 \\ & + A10 \times A11 \times B8 - A9 \times A10 \times A11 \times B8 + A10 \times A11 \times B9 \\ & - A11 \times B10 + B11) \\ & + L_{LMM} \times (-A12 \times B8 + A9 \times A12 \times B8 - A12 \times B9 \\ & + A10 \times A12 \times B8 - A9 \times A10 \times A12 \times B8 + A10 \times A12 \times B9 \\ & - A12 \times B10 + B11)) + B13 + B14 + B15 \end{aligned} \tag{54}$$

Table IV lists the definitions of the parameters given in (37)–(51) for NLJ and HJ. In the case of NLJ, the calculation formula of the number of disk I/Os was created using the regression line shown in Figure 13(a). The measured I/O response time ($io\_responcetime$) was 154 μs. The I/O cost of NLJ is as follows:

$$io\_cost = (A16 \times R_O \times R_{I1} \times P_O + B16) \times io\_responce\_time \tag{55}$$

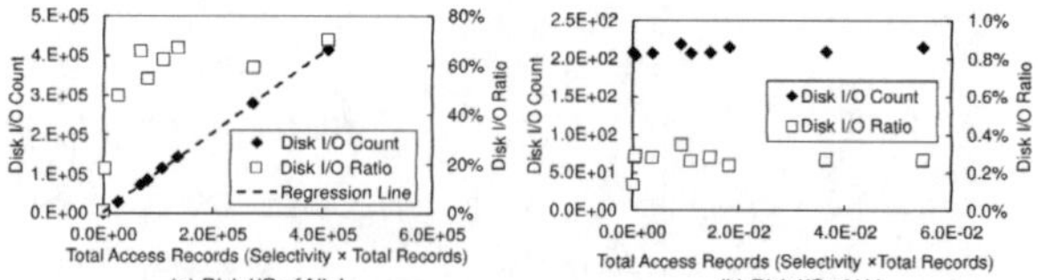

(a) Disk I/O of NLJ (b) Disk I/O of HJ

Fig. 13. Number of disk I/O and disk I/O processing time during NLJ and HJ

However, in the case of HJ, the ratio of the processing time of disk I/O and the query execution time of HJ was less than 1% in Figure 13(b). The cost calculation formula is composed of only the CPU cost and disk I/O cost. In order to apply in-memory databases (Figure 1(b)), it is sufficient to change the disk I/O latency to the latency of the memory based disk.

In the combination probe phase, the calculation formula for the number of disk I/Os was created using the multiple regression line shown in Figure 14. The I/O cost of combination probe phase is as follows:

$$io\_cost = (A17 \times R_{I1} \times P_{I1} + A18 \times R_{I1} \times \sum_{i=1}^{n} rsk_i + B17) \times io\_responce\_time \quad (56)$$

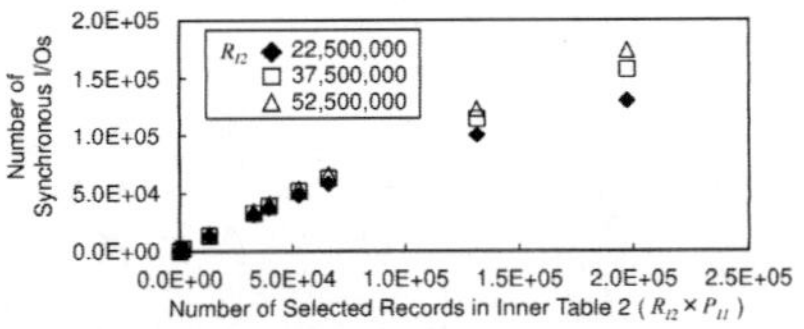

Fig. 14. Number of synchronous disk I/O count during combination probe phase

The regression models for the combination join are also expressed by the same equations, (37)–(51), as the two-table NLJ and HJ. Table V lists the definitions of the parameters.

TABLE IV. SLOPE AND INTERCEPT OF THE REGRESSION MODELS

Type		Slope (Regression Coefficient)		Intercept (Regression Constant)	R^2	P value on F test	Reference
NLJ	A1	1.745×10^5	B1	1.64×10^9	9.99×10^{-1}	1.30×10^{-29}	Figure 8(1)
	A2	9.80×10^{-1}	B2	1.26×10^7	1.00	2.18×10^{-58}	Figure 8(2)
	A3	8.08×10^{-1}	B3	2.68×10^6	1.00	2.91×10^{-40}	Figure 8(3)
	A4	8.32×10^{-1}	B4	5.23×10^4	1.00	3.93×10^{-39}	Figure 8(4)
	A5	7.43×10^{-1}	B5	-1.18×10^5	1.00	3.77×10^{-34}	Figure 8(5)
	A6	2.58×10^{-1}	B6	1.18×10^5	9.98×10^{-1}	7.05×10^{-26}	Figure 8(6)
	A7	2.46×10^4	B7	4.63×10^8	9.99×10^{-1}	5.97×10^{-31}	Figure 8(7)
	A8	9.72×10^{-1}	B8	7.05×10^6	1.00	3.85×10^{-53}	Figure 8(8)
	A9	4.34×10^{-1}	B9	1.95×10^6	9.99×10^{-1}	5.17×10^{-28}	Figure 8(9)
	A10	9.44×10^{-1}	B10	-2.87×10^4	1.00	2.06×10^{-44}	Figure 810)
	A11	7.61×10^{-1}	B11	-4.84×10^4	1.00	2.80×10^{-35}	Figure 8(11)
	A12	2.39×10^{-1}	B12	4.84×10^4	9.98×10^{-1}	3.10×10^{-26}	Figure 8(12)
	A13	5.45×10^{-1}	B13	1.41×10^8	9.98×10^{-1}	1.21×10^{-25}	Figure 8(13)
	A14	8.59×10^{-1}	B14	-1.25×10^9	9.67×10^{-1}	9.00×10^{-15}	Figure 8(14)
	A15	2.90×10^3	B15	2.40×10^7	9.90×10^{-1}	1.35×10^{-19}	Figure 8(15)
HJ Build	A1	2.05×10^3	B1	1.58×10^7	1.00	4.21×10^{-40}	Figure 9(a1)
	A2	9.88×10^{-1}	B2	2.53×10^5	1.00	2.19×10^{-61}	Figure 9(a2)
	A3	9.71×10^{-1}	B3	-7.48×10^4	1.00	1.79×10^{-49}	Figure 9(a3)
	A4	9.19×10^{-1}	B4	-6.57×10^4	9.99×10^{-1}	7.76×10^{-31}	Figure 9(a4)
	A5	3.32×10^{-1}	B5	-1.64×10^4	9.29×10^{-1}	8.38×10^{-12}	Figure 9(a5)
	A6	6.68×10^{-1}	B6	1.64×10^4	9.82×10^{-1}	4.49×10^{-17}	Figure 9(a6)
	A7	6.10×10^2	B7	2.85×10^5	9.99×10^{-1}	4.46×10^{-30}	Figure 9(a7)
	A8	9.90×10^{-1}	B8	-1.89×10^3	1.00	1.05×10^{-57}	Figure 9(a8)
	A9	8.03×10^{-1}	B9	-2.39×10^4	1.00	6.00×10^{-33}	Figure 9(a9)
	A10	9.04×10^{-1}	B10	1.58×10^2	1.00	8.94×10^{-46}	Figure 9(a10)
	A11	2.13×10^{-1}	B11	-2.74×10^3	9.80×10^{-1}	1.13×10^{-16}	Figure 9(a11)
	A12	7.87×10^{-1}	B12	2.74×10^3	9.98×10^{-1}	8.16×10^{-27}	Figure 9(a12)
	A13	1.20	B13	-8.24×10^6	9.98×10^{-1}	2.14×10^{-25}	Figure 9(a13)
	A14	3.69×10^{-1}	B14	2.02×10^7	1.00	6.83×10^{-32}	Figure 9(a14)
	A15	2.94×10^1	B15	6.41×10^5	9.97×10^{-1}	2.86×10^{-24}	Figure 9(a15)
HJ Probe	A1	1.90×10^3	B1	2.33×10^7	1.00	3.46×10^{-46}	Figure 9(b1)
	A2	9.88×10^{-1}	B2	3.88×10^5	1.00	3.69×10^{-62}	Figure 9(b2)
	A3	9.75×10^{-1}	B3	-1.76×10^4	1.00	6.81×10^{-52}	Figure 9(b3)
	A4	8.13×10^{-1}	B4	-2.44×10^4	1.00	1.12×10^{-41}	Figure 9(b4)
	A5	9.46×10^{-1}	B5	-2.44×10^4	1.00	8.30×10^{-36}	Figure 9(b5)
	A6	5.45×10^{-2}	B6	2.44×10^4	9.56×10^{-1}	1.15×10^{-13}	Figure 9(b6)
	A7	5.76×10^2	B7	-3.57×10^7	9.99×10^{-1}	6.14×10^{-27}	Figure 9(b7)
	A8	9.89×10^{-1}	B8	-3.89×10^5	1.00	6.68×10^{-54}	Figure 9 (b8)
	A9	7.29×10^{-1}	B9	1.58×10^5	9.88×10^{-1}	7.30×10^{-19}	Figure 9(b9)
	A10	7.95×10^{-1}	B10	2.81×10^4	1.00	5.98×10^{-33}	Figure 9 (b10)
	A11	9.34×10^{-1}	B11	-6.04×10^4	1.00	7.79×10^{-34}	Figure 9 (b11)
	A12	6.60×10^{-2}	B12	6.04×10^4	9.52×10^{-1}	2.69×10^{-13}	Figure 9(b12)
	A13	1.48	B13	2.87×10^{07}	9.87×10^{-1}	1.40×10^{-18}	Figure 9(b13)
	A14	3.58×10^{-1}	B14	6.61×10^7	9.98×10^{-1}	1.75×10^{-25}	Figure 9(b14)
	A15	3.45×10^1	B15	-1.39×10^7	9.35×10^{-1}	3.77×10^{-12}	Figure 9(b15)
NLJ (I/O)	A16	1.02	B16	2.52×10^3	1.00	1.85×10^{-15}	Figure 13(a)
HJ (I/O)	A16	0.000	B16	0.000	N/A	N/A	N/A

To evaluate the cost calculation formulas, we used a larger TPC-H database than the database used for measurement (SF100), and chose a combination of the following two tables, *customer* and *orders*, *supplier* and *lineitem*, and *part* and *lineitem*. In addition, in order to evaluate the join of more

TABLE V. SLOPE AND INTERCEPT OF THE REGRESSION MODELS IN COMBINATION PROBE PHASE

Type		Slope (Regression Coefficient)		Intercept (Regression Constant)	R^2	P value on F test	Reference
Probe	A1	2.01×10^3	B1	9.80×10^8	9.42×10^{-1}	1.63×10^{-37}	Figure 10(1)
	A2	9.86×10^{-1}	B16	1.79×10^7	1.00	1.11×10^{-44}	Figure 10(2)
	A3	8.53×10^{-1}	B3	6.58×10^6	9.94×10^{-1}	2.79×10^{-21}	Figure 10(3)
	A4	7.06×10^{-1}	B4	-6.80×10^5	9.99×10^{-1}	3.12×10^{-29}	Figure 10(4)
	A5	3.74×10^{-1}	B5	-1.58×10^5	9.99×10^{-1}	3.51×10^{-28}	Figure 10(5)
	A6	6.26×10^{-1}	B6	1.58×10^5	1.00	3.21×10^{-32}	Figure 10(6)
	A7	5.76×10^2	B7	2.31×10^8	9.75×10^{-1}	2.78×10^{-48}	Figure 10(7)
	A8	9.86×10^{-1}	B8	1.83×10^6	1.00	1.75×10^{-41}	Figure 10(8)
	A9	4.79×10^{-1}	B9	3.97×10^6	9.00×10^{-1}	2.03×10^{-10}	Figure 10(9)
	A10	9.36×10^{-1}	B10	-9.55×10^5	9.97×10^{-1}	7.85×10^{-25}	Figure 1010)
	A11	3.70×10^{-1}	B11	-9.15×10^4	9.75×10^{-1}	6.97×10^{-16}	Figure 10(11)
	A12	6.30×10^{-1}	B12	9.15×10^4	9.91×10^{-1}	5.74×10^{-12}	Figure 10(12)
	A13	6.25×10^{-1}	B13	6.85×10^8	8.75×10^{-1}	1.51×10^{-9}	Figure 10(13)
	A14	4.49×10^{-1}	B14	-2.66×10^8	9.72×10^{-1}	2.16×10^{-15}	Figure 10(14)
	A15	4.93×10^1	B15	2.62×10^7	9.70×10^{-1}	1.03×10^{-45}	Figure 10(15)
Probe (I/O)	A17	7.84×10^{-1}	B17	-3.24×10^{-4}	9.77×10^{-1}	7.43×10^{-21}	N/A
	A18	2.43×10^3					N/A

than two tables, the following combinations were chosen: (*customer*, *orders*, *lineitem*), (*supplier*, *lineitem*, *part*, *orders*, *customer*), and (*part*, *lineitem*, *supplier*, *orders*, *customer*). In the five-table join case, the STRAIGHT_JOIN query hint was used to keep the join order of tables. Detailed measurement conditions are shown in Appendix A. The parameter setting of the cost calculation formulas was generated from the measurement values when joining *customer* and *orders*, whose size is SF5. For the join cases of three or more tables, the measurement values under joining *customer*, *orders*, and *lineitem* were used. The I/O processing time was added to allow comparison with the query execution time. The proposed cost calculation method was compared with the measured query execution time and conventional method (2)(3). The conventional method is expressed as the sum of the CPU cost and the I/O cost as mentioned in Section I. Each cost is calculated as the product of the number of records and the manually defined processing unit cost of CPU or I/O. The conventional method and proposed method followed the execution plan generated by MariaDB. In our measurement environment, the HJ execution plan for joining more than two tables is the combination case (Figure 5). We evaluated whether the selectivity where the join method is switched can be estimated accurately. However, because the conventional method does not support HJ, single-table scans of the outer and inner tables were used. Moreover, MariaDB, as used in this experiment, cannot use the function to automatically select the join method, and only the join method set by the user was selected. The goal of this study is to accurately find the intersection point of the NLJ and HJ graphs. As a result, in all of the cases evaluated, the proposed method was able to find the intersection point with an accuracy of one significant figure or better compared to the conventional method (Figure 15 and Figure 16). The improvement ratios of the proposed method and conventional method are shown in Table VI. The second and third rows indicate the difference between the intersection point (selectivity) of the measured result and that of the conventional method or proposed method. The improvement ratio was obtained by dividing the difference between the intersection selectivity of the conventional method

TABLE VI. IMPROVEMENT RATIO FOR ESTIMATING INTERSECTION OF NLJ AND HJ

Join tables	C-O	P-L	S-L	C-O-L	S-L-P-O-C	P-L-S-O-C
Conventional method	1.5×10^{-2}	3.5×10^{-3}	2.2×10^{-3}	7.5×10^{-3}	8.9×10^{-2}	2.2×10^{-5}
Proposed method	1.3×10^{-4}	3.2×10^{-4}	1.9×10^{-4}	8.8×10^{-5}	3.0×10^{-4}	2.2×10^{-7}
Improvement ratio	99%	91%	91%	99%	97%	99%

Note: C: Customer, O: Orders, L: Lineitem, P: Part, S: Supplier

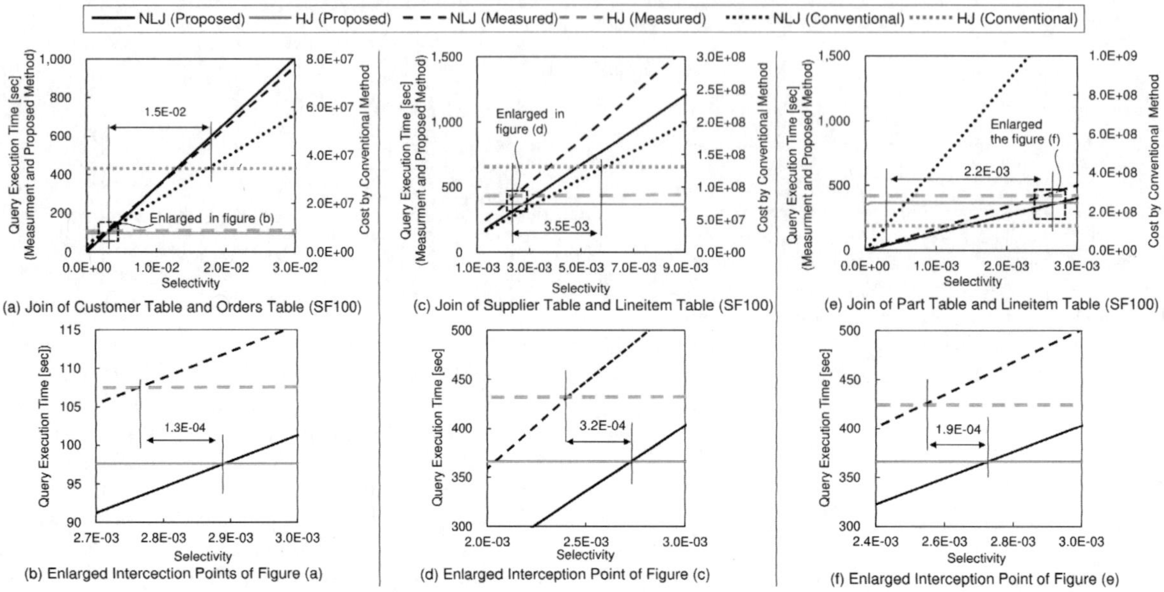

Fig. 15. Cost Comparison of measured, proposed cost model, and conventional cost model results for joining two tables

and that of the proposed method by that of the conventional method. Table VI shows that the proposed method improved the accuracy of selecting the proper join method by 90% or more.

V. DISCUSSION

In the acquisition of measurement data for constructing the cost calculation formula, because the type of counters that the hardware monitor can collect at one time is limited to four, it is necessary to perform measurements several times to obtain an accurate measurement of 40 events. Therefore, a certain amount of time must be allocated for measurement. For example, it took approximately 5 h and 30 min to perform the measurements in this study. From the perspective of allocating time for measurement, and given the fact that the CPU cost calculation formula does not need to be changed unless there is a change in hardware configuration or DBMS join operation codes, it is appropriate to create the proposed CPU cost calculation formula when integrating or updating a system. With regard to the use of the cost calculation formula, the proposed CPU cost formula was used in the optimization process to be executed before executing a query. The CPU cost of executing the query was calculated from the number of records to be searched. As shown in references [18] [19], in a general DBMS, the histograms representing the relationship between the attribute value and appearance frequency are automatically acquired when inserting or updating records. From the histogram and condition of the clause of the query, it is possible to estimate the number of records accessed by the DBMS. In this way, the CPU costs can be calculated with only the data already acquired by the DBMS; hence, the costs can be calculated by the cost calculation formula before query execution.

The combination join case modeled in this study was the two or more tables join case, as shown in Figure 5. Theoretically, there is a case in which HJ is assigned after NLJ. In the case where HJ was executed after NLJ (Figure 17), the cost model (d-1) was the same as (a), and the cost model (d-3) was the same as (b-2). The cost model of (d-2) was required because building the hash table from temporary table X was not covered in the other case. Most of the join cases seem to be classified as in Figures 4, 5, and 17, and creating the cost models (a), (b-1), (b-2), (c-2), and (d-2) can support most of the join cases. However, the NLJ–HJ case cannot be implemented in our measurement environment. This problem can be solved by using a different DBMS.

We proposed a cost calculation method for an in-memory DBMS using a disk-based DBMS. The calculation formulas were created using the data measured by the CPU-embedded performance monitor. The results reveal that the proposed method can estimate the intersection point of the join methods more accurately than the conventional method. We used TPC-

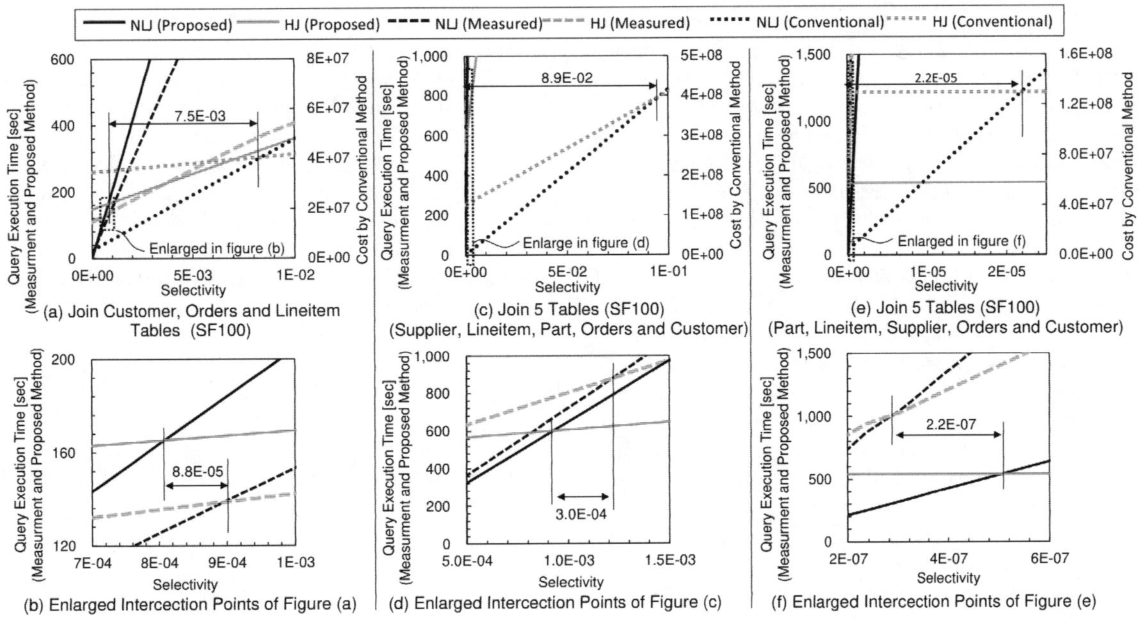

Fig. 16. Cost Comparison of measured, proposed cost model, and conventional cost model results for joining three or more tables

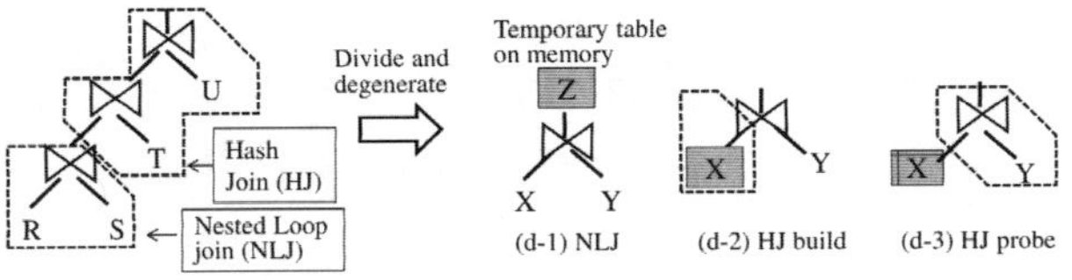

Fig. 17. NLJ after HJ Case

H for measuring CPU activities. TPC-H has the advantage of making it easy to analyze the evaluation results because the data distribution is uniform. However, the actual data is skewed in terms of the distribution of keys. The premise of the technique proposed in this study is the accuracy of selectivity, i.e., even if the distribution of data varies, if the selectivity is the same, then the same measurement results are obtained. Because a general DBMS acquires attribute values and their distribution in a database is in the form of a histogram when loading data to the database, the prerequisites for applying the proposed technique are considered to be satisfactory. However, it is necessary to develop a technique to derive histogram information and input it as an input parameter of the cost formulas.

As this technique sets parameters based on actual measurements, it is difficult to deal with various patterns, such as the presence or absence of indices and complex queries. Although we have focused on the operation of all CPU cycles, it is necessary for practical use to simplify the model by omitting some parameters. For the collection of statistical data, it is conceivable that actual measurements can be performed at the time of initial installation and parameter setting. However, when the DBMS code is modified, it is difficult to change in real time; hence, a separate complementary technology is required. As a breakthrough measure, it is possible to reduce both the amount of data to be verified and the measurement points.

In this study, only the cost model for join operations was proposed. However, the query operation includes not only join but also filter, group-by, and sorting operations. These operations are difficult to execute by using only a query. However, part of the query can be extracted by taking the difference between queries, similar to our approach for modeling the HJ probe phase (31).

VI. Related Work

Evaluation of the CPU performance using the performance monitor for behavior analysis of a DBMS has long been conducted. In particular, in the evaluation of the benchmark TPC-D for decision support systems, the L1 miss and processing delay owing to the L2 cache occupy a large part of the CPI components, and are important in terms of performance. However, these are only used for bottleneck analysis [20].

The query execution cost calculation approaches include the white-box analysis [8] and the black-box analysis [9]. In the white-box analytic approach, the cost calculation model for a single server is composed of CPU cost and I/O cost. Based on these approaches, there are some cost calculation methods. One is the product of a unit cost and the number of accessed records [5] [6]. Another is to estimate cost from the execution time of several evaluation queries [8]. With the black box-model analysis approach, a multiple regression is performed using parameters that the DBMS user can refer easily, such as the cardinality of tables. Our approach combines both characteristics.

From a different viewpoint, there exist the macro-level and micro-level approaches. The macro-level approach is suitable for a heterogeneous DBMS system because it is composed of different DBMSs (open source or commercial DBMSs) and cost is calculated based on the processing time of commonly executable queries. Our approach is a micro-level one. It is created from measurement results of CPU events while executing a query. The micro-level approach can create an accurate model by considering the CPU operation, but it cannot be applied to different DBMS.

Our cost calculation model uses the statistic information of the CPU measured under a static environment. However, multiple applications are executed on a real production system. The cost model of a multiple-application environment is based on multiple regression models and it uses sample-query execution time and statistical calibration methods [21] [22]. Applying these methods to our approach will help achieve a more accurate model.

Another study on the micro-level approach is the method that applies a CPI measurement and focuses on a memory reference for cost calculations (5) of an in-memory database [23] [24]. This research targeted a DBMS that use the load/store type memory access (Figure 1(c)). In this work, the number of cache hits or main memory accesses was predicted from the data access pattern of the database, and the cost was calculated as the product of the number of cache hits or main memory accesses and the memory latency. The modeling of *CPI0*, which is the state where all data exist in the L1 cache, and modeling of instruction cache misses have not been considered in previous studies. Although not explicitly mentioned in the literature, it was presumed that it was impossible to reproduce and measure the state in which all instructions and data were on the L1 cache, which is the definition of *CPI0*, using methods such as a CPU-embedded performance monitor.

In our research, the performance of queries was considered as a function of selectivity. Kester *et al.* [25] used not only selectivity but also the concurrency of queries in the execution to calculate the query execution cost. When many queries are executed simultaneously in a cloud computing system, hardware resources (e.g., memory bandwidth, disk bandwidth, etc.) will become scarce. In this case, the hardware resource utilization is affected by query performance. Our proposed method can support concurrency by introducing the queuing theory in the memory latency and I/O latency model.

VII. Conclusions and Future Work

In this study, we proposed a cost calculation method for an in-memory DBMS using a disk-based DBMS. We focused on a CPU pipeline architecture and classified the CPU cycles into three types based on the operational characteristics of the front-end and back-end. The calculation formulas were created using data measured by the CPU-embedded performance monitor. In the evaluation of the two-table join, three-table join, and five-table join, the difference in selectivity corresponding to the intersection points of NLJ and HJ, between the proposed method and measurements, was increased in more than 90% from the conventional method. This means that the cost formulas can model the actual join operation with high accuracy. By applying the proposed cost calculation formulas, the proper join method can be selected and the risk of unexpected query execution delay for users of the DBMS can be reduced. In the future, we will evaluate different generation of CPUs and analyze how the differences in CPU architecture affect the cost formulas. We will also implement a DBMS that automatically distinguishes CPU differences from the analysis results and automatically corrects the parameters for cost calculation or the calculation model itself.

Appendix A
Queries for Evaluating Cost Calculation Formulas

The Queries used for evaluation of the proposed cost calculation formulas are shown in Figure A.1, A.2, A.3, and A.4.

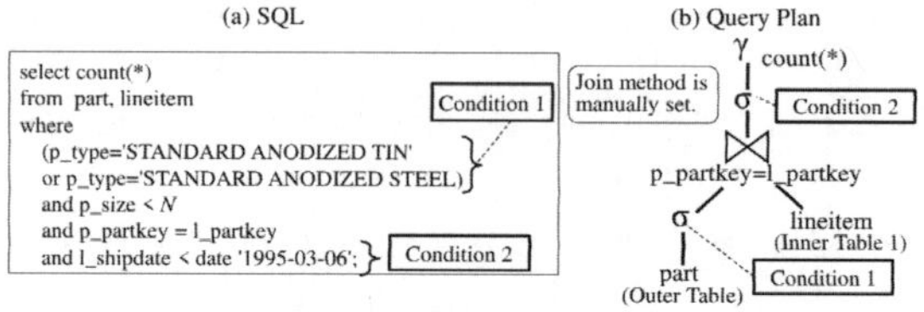

(c) Selection Condition and Selectivity

N	6	8	10	20	30	40	50
Selectivity P_O (Condition 1)	1.33×10^{-3}	1.87×10^{-3}	2.40×10^{-3}	5.07×10^{-3}	7.73×10^{-3}	1.04×10^{-2}	1.31×10^{-2}

Fig. A.1. Target query of cost estimation for part and lineitem join

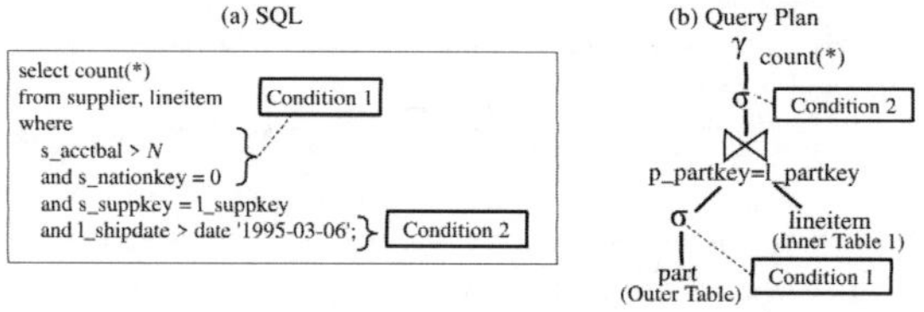

(c) Selection Condition and Selectivity

N	9998	9978	9798	9200	9000	8000	7000
Selectivity P_O (Condition 1)	7.24×10^{-6}	8.00×10^{-5}	7.35×10^{-4}	2.91×10^{-3}	3.64×10^{-3}	7.27×10^{-3}	1.09×10^{-2}

Fig. A.2. Target query of cost estimation for supplier and lineitem join

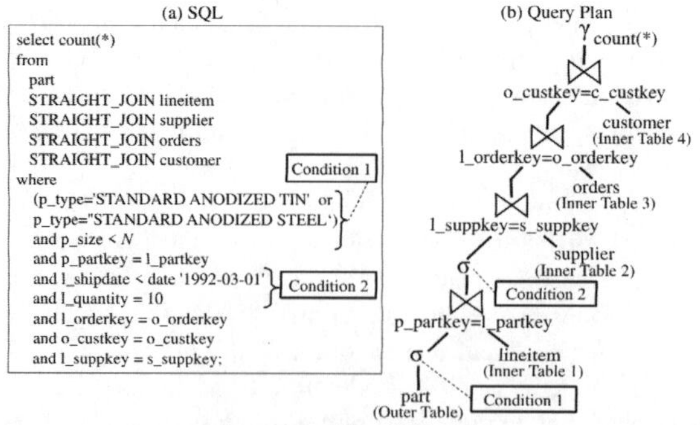

(c) Selection Condition and Selectivity

N	6	8	10	20	30	40	50
Selectivity P_O (Condition 1)	1.33×10^{-3}	1.87×10^{-3}	2.40×10^{-3}	5.07×10^{-3}	7.73×10^{-3}	1.04×10^{-2}	1.31×10^{-2}

Fig. A.3. Target query of cost estimation for part, lineitem, supplier, orders, and customer join

(a) SQL

```
select count(*)
from
   supplier
   STRAIGHT_JOIN lineitem
   STRAIGHT_JOIN part
   STRAIGHT_JOIN orders
   STRAIGHT_JOIN customer
where
   s_acctbal > 9998          } Condition 1
   and s_nationkey = 0       }
   and s_suppkey = l_suppkey
   and l_shipdate > date '1995-03-06' } Condition 2
   and l_partkey = p_partkey
   and l_orderkey = o_orderkey
   and o_custkey = c_custkey;
```

(b) Query Plan

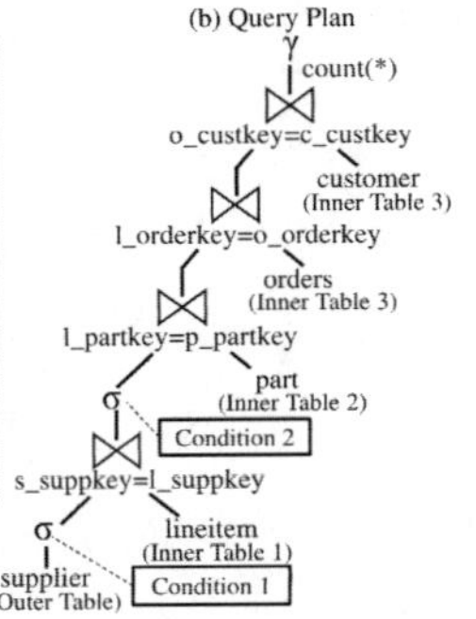

(c) Selection Condition and Selectivity

N	9998	9978	9798	9200	9000	8000	7000
Selectivity P_O (Condition 1)	7.24×10^{-6}	8.00×10^{-5}	7.35×10^{-4}	2.91×10^{-3}	3.64×10^{-3}	7.27×10^{-3}	1.09×10^{-2}

Fig. A.4. Target query of cost estimation for supplier, lineitem, part, orders and customer join

APPENDIX B
MEASURED CPU COUNTERS

The list of CPU counters for modeling the CPU cost calculation are shown in Table B.I. The constants and intermediate variable for modeling cost calculation formulas are shown in Table B.II. The column of "Symbol" means variables in the cost calculation formulas.

TABLE B.I. Lists of CPU Counters to Measure and Preprocess

No.	Counter Name
$E1$	CPU_CLK_UNHALTED.THREAD
$E2$	INST_RETIRED.ANY
$E3$	BR_MISP_EXEC.ANY
$E4$	DTLB_MISSES.ANY
$E5$	ITLB_MISS_RETIRED
$E6$	L1I.CYCLES_STALLED
$E7$	L1I.HITS
$E8$	L1I.MISSES
$E9$	L2_RQSTS.IFETCH_HIT
$E10$	L2_RQSTS.IFETCH_MISS
$E11$	MEM_INST_RETIRED.LOADS
$E12$	MEM_LOAD_RETIRED.HIT_LFB
$E13$	MEM_LOAD_RETIRED.L1D_HIT
$E14$	MEM_LOAD_RETIRED.L2_HIT
$E15$	MEM_LOAD_RETIRED.LLC_MISS
$E16$	MEM_LOAD_RETIRED.LLC_UNSHARED_HIT
$E17$	MEM_LOAD_RETIRED.OTHER_CORE_L2_HIT_HITM
$E18$	OFFCORE_RESPONSE.DATA_IFETCH.LOCAL_CACHE_1
$E19$	OFFCORE_RESPONSE.DATA_IFETCH.LOCAL_DRAM _AND_REMOTE_CACHE_HIT_0
$E20$	OFFCORE_RESPONSE.DATA_IFETCH.OTHER_LOCAL _DRAM_1
$E21$	OFFCORE_RESPONSE.DATA_IFETCH.REMOTE_CACHE _HITM_0
$E22$	OFFCORE_RESPONSE.DATA_IFETCH.REMOTE_DRAM_1
$E23$	OFFCORE_RESPONSE.DATA_IN.LOCAL_DRAM_AND _REMOTE_CACHE_HIT_0
$E24$	OFFCORE_RESPONSE.DATA_IN.OTHER_LOCAL_DRAM_0
$E25$	OFFCORE_RESPONSE.DATA_IN.REMOTE_CACHE_HITM_0
$E26$	OFFCORE_RESPONSE.DATA_IN.REMOTE_DRAM_1
$E27$	RESOURCE_STALLS.ANY
$E28$	RESOURCE_STALLS.LOAD
$E29$	RESOURCE_STALLS.ROB_FULL
$E30$	RESOURCE_STALLS.RS_FULL
$E31$	RESOURCE_STALLS.STORE
$E32$	UOPS_ISSUED.ANY
$E33$	UOPS_ISSUED.CORE_STALL_CYCLES
$E34$	UOPS_ISSUED.CYCLES_ALL_THREADS
$E35$	UOPS_ISSUED.FUSED
$E36$	UOPS_RETIRED.ANY

REFERENCES

[1] T. Tanaka and H. Ishikawa, "Measurement-based cost estimation method of a join operation for an in-memory database," in *MMEDIA 2017, The Ninth International Conferences on Advances in Multimedia*. Venice, Italy: IARIA, April 2017, pp. 57–66.

[2] A. Foong and F. Hady, "Storage as fast as rest of the system," in *2016 IEEE 8th International Memory Workshop (IMW)*, May 2016, pp. 1–4.

[3] A. Rudoff, "Programming models to enable persistent memory," Storage Developer Conference, SNIA, Santa Clara, CA, USA, September, 2012, https://www.snia.org/sites/default/orig/SDC2012/presentations/Solid_State/AndyRudoff_Program_Models.pdf [retrieved: March, 2017].

[4] ——, "The impact of the NVM programming model," Storage Developer Conference, SNIA, Santa Clara, CA, USA, September, 2013, https://www.snia.org/sites/default/files/files2/files2/SDC2013/presentations/GeneralSession/AndyRudoff_Impact_NVM.pdf [retrieved: March, 2017].

[5] P. G. Selinger, M. M. Astrahan, D. D. Chamberlin, R. A. Lorie, and T. G. Price, "Access path selection in a relational database management system," in *Proceedings of the 1979 ACM SIGMOD International Conference on Management of Data*, ser. SIGMOD '79. New York, NY, USA: ACM, 1979, pp. 23–34. [Online]. Available: http://doi.acm.org/10.1145/582095.582099

[6] W. Wu *et al.*, "Predicting query execution time: Are optimizer cost models really unusable?" in *Data Engineering (ICDE), 2013 IEEE 29th International Conference on*, April 2013, pp. 1081–1092.

[7] O. Sandsta, "Mysql Cost Model," http://www.slideshare.net/olavsa/mysql-optimizer-cost-model [retrieved: March, 2017], October 2014.

[8] W. Du, R. Krishnamurthy, and M.-C. Shan, "Query optimization in a heterogeneous dbms," in *VLDB*, vol. 92, 1992, pp. 277–291.

[9] Q. Zhu and P.-A. Larson, "Building regression cost models for multidatabase systems," in *Proceedings of the Fourth International Conference on on Parallel and Distributed Information Systems*, ser. DIS '96. Washington, DC, USA: IEEE Computer Society, 1996, pp. 220–231. [Online]. Available: http://dl.acm.org/citation.cfm?id=382006.383210

[10] D. Levinthal, "Performance analysis guide for intel core i7 processor and intel xeon 5500 processors," *Intel Performance Analysis Guide*, vol. 30, p. 18, 2009.

[11] P. Apparao, R. Iyer, and D. Newell, "Towards modeling & analysis of consolidated CMP servers," *SIGARCH Comput. Archit. News*, vol. 36, no. 2, pp. 38–45, May 2008. [Online]. Available: http://doi.acm.org/10.1145/1399972.1399980

[12] N. Hardavellas *et al.*, "Database servers on chip multiprocessors: Limitations and opportunities," in *Proceedings of the Biennial Conference on Innovative Data Systems Research (CIDR)*, Asilomar, CA, USA, January 2007, pp. 79–87.

[13] L. McVoy *et al.*, "lmbench: Portable tools for performance analysis." in *USENIX annual technical conference*, San Diego, CA, USA, 1996, pp. 279–294.

[14] J. L. Lo *et al.*, "An analysis of database workload performance on simultaneous multithreaded processors," in *ACM SIGARCH Computer Architecture News*, vol. 26, no. 3. IEEE Computer Society, 1998, pp. 39–50.

[15] (2017) The MariaDB foundation - ensuring continuity and open collaboration in the mariadb ecosystem. [Online]. Available: https://mariadb.org/

[16] "TPC BENCHMARK™ H (decision support) standard specification revision 2.17.1, Transaction Processing Performance council (TPC)," http://www.tpc.org/tpc_documents_current_versions/pdf/tpch2.17.1.pdf [retrieved: March, 2017], 2014.

[17] (2017) 7-Zip LZMA Benchmark. [Online]. Available: http://www.7-cpu.com/

[18] A. Aboulnaga *et al.*, "Automated statistics collection in DB2 UDB," in *Proceedings of the Thirtieth International Conference on Very Large Data Bases - Volume 30*, ser. VLDB '04. VLDB Endowment, 2004, pp. 1158–1169. [Online]. Available: http://dl.acm.org/citation.cfm?id=1316689.1316788

[19] I. Babae, "Engine-independent persistent statistics with histograms in MariaDB," Percona Live MySQL Conference and Expo 2013, April, 2013, https://www.percona.com/live/london-2013/sites/default/files/slides/uc2013-EIPS-final.pdf [retrieved: March, 2017].

TABLE B.II. Lists of Constants and Intermediate Variable

No.	Symbol	Events	Value
$E37$	—	CPU frequency [GHz] (Xeon L5630)	2.13
$E38$	L_{L1}	L1I Latency [cycle]	4
$E39$	L_{L1}	L1D Latency [cycle]	4
$E40$	L_{L2}	L2 Latency [cycle]	10
$E41$	L_{LLLC}	Local LLC Latency [cycle]	40
$E42$	L_{RLLC}	Remote LLC Latency [cycle]	200
$E43$	L_{LMM}	Local Main Memory Latency [cycle]	$E41 + 67[ns] \times E37$
$E44$	—	Remote Main Memory Latency [cycle]	$E41 + 105[ns] \times E37$
$E45$	L_{MP}	Branchmiss prediction cycle	15
No.	**Symbol**	**Events**	**Calculation Formula for Preprocessing**
$E46$	I_{Load}	LOAD instruction	E11
$E47$	M_{L1D}	L1D Hit (data)	$E46 \times E13/(E12 + E13 + E14 + E15 + E16 + E17)$
$E48$	—	L1D Miss (data)	$E46 - E47$
$E49$	M_{L2D}	L2 Hit (data)	$E46 \times ((1 - (E13/(E12 + E13 + E14 + E15 + E16 + E17))) \times (E14/(E14 + E15 + E16 + E17)))$
$E50$	—	L2 Miss (data)	$E48 - E49$
$E51$	M_{LLLCD}	LLC Hit (data)	$E46 \times ((1 - (E13/(E12 + E13 + E14 + E15 + E16 + E17))) \times (1 - (E14/(E14 + E15 + E16 + E17))) \times ((E16 + E17)/(E15 + E16 + E17)))$
$E52$	—	LLC Miss (data)	$E50 - E51$
$E53$	M_{RLLCD}	Remote LLC Hit (data)	$E46 \times ((1 - (E13/(E12 + E13 + E14 + E15 + E16 + E17))) \times (1 - (E14/(E14 + E15 + E16 + E17))) \times (1 - ((E16 + E17)/(E16 + E17 + E15))) \times ((E23 + E25)/(E23 + E24 + E25 + E26)))$
$E54$	M_{LMMD}	Local Main Memory (data)	$E46 \times ((1 - (E13/(E12 + E13 + E14 + E15 + E16 + E17))) \times (1 - (E14/(E14 + E15 + E16 + E17))) \times (1 - ((E16 + E17)/(E16 + E17 + E15))) \times (E24/(E23 + E24 + E25 + E26)))$
$E55$	—	Remote Main Memory (data)	$E46 \times ((1 - (E13/(E12 + E13 + E14 + E15 + E16 + E17))) \times (1 - (E14/(E14 + E15 + E16 + E17))) \times (1 - ((E16 + E17)/(E16 + E17 + E15))) \times (E26/(E23 + E24 + E25 + E26)))$
$E56$	—	Total Data Access Latency	$E47 \times E39 + E49 \times E40 + E51 \times E41 + E54 \times E43 + E55 \times E44 + E53 \times E42$
$E57$	I	Instruction	$E2 + E3$
$E58$	M_{L1I}	L1I Hit (instruction)	$E57 - E8$
$E59$	—	L1I Miss (instruction)	$E57 - E58$
$E60$	M_{L2I}	L2 Hit (instruction)	$E8 - E10$
$E61$	—	L2 Miiss (instruction)	$E59 - E60$
$E62$	M_{LLLCI}	Local LLC Hit (instruction)	$E10 \times ((E18/(E18 + E19 + E21 + E20 + E22)))$
$E63$	—	Local LLC Miss (instruction)	$E61 - E62$
$E64$	M_{RLLCD}	Remote LLC Hit (instruction)	$E57 \times ((E10/E57) \times (((E19 + E21)/(E18 + E19 + E20 + E21 + E22))))$
$E65$	M_{LMMD}	Local Main Memory (instruction)	$E10 \times ((E20/(E18 + E19 + E20 + E21 + E22))))$
$E66$	—	Remote Main Memory (instruction)	$(E33 - E27) \times ((E10/E57) \times (E22/(E18 + E19 + E20 + E21 + E22)))$
$E67$	—	Total Instruction Access Latency	$E60 \times E40 + E62 \times E41 + E64 \times E42 + E65 \times E43 + E66 \times E44$
$E68$	$C_{DCacheAcc}$	Data Access	$E27 + E34$
$E69$	C_{MP}	Branch Mispredition Penalty	$E3 \times E45$
$E70$	$C_{ICacheMiss}$	Instruction Penalty	$E33 - E27 - E69$

[20] A. Ailamaki, D. J. DeWitt, M. D. Hill, and D. A. Wood, "DBMSs on a modern processor: Where does time go?" in *VLDB" 99, Proceedings of 25th International Conference on Very Large Data Bases, September 7-10, 1999, Edinburgh, Scotland, UK*, no. DIAS-CONF-1999-001, 1999, pp. 266–277.

[21] A. Rahal, Q. Zhu, and P.-A. Larson, "Evolutionary techniques for updating query cost models in a dynamic multidatabase environment," *The VLDB Journal*, vol. 13, no. 2, pp. 162–176, May 2004. [Online]. Available: http://dx.doi.org/10.1007/s00778-003-0110-4

[22] Q. Zhu, S. Motheramgari, and Y. Sun, "Cost estimation for large queries via fractional analysis and probabilistic approach in dynamic multidatabase environments," in *Proceedings of the 11th International Conference on Database and Expert Systems Applications*, ser. DEXA '00. London, UK, UK: Springer-Verlag, 2000, pp. 509–525. [Online]. Available: http://dl.acm.org/citation.cfm?id=648313.755672

[23] S. Manegold, P. A. Boncz, and M. L. Kersten, "Optimizing database architecture for the new bottleneck: memory access," *The VLDB Journal*, vol. 9, no. 3, pp. 231–246, 2000.

[24] S. Manegold, P. Boncz, and M. L. Kersten, "Generic database cost models for hierarchical memory systems," in *Proceedings of the 28th international conference on Very Large Data Bases*. VLDB Endowment, 2002, pp. 191–202.

[25] M. S. Kester, M. Athanassoulis, and S. Idreos, "Access path selection in main-memory optimized data systems: Should I scan or should I probe?" in *Proceedings of the 2017 ACM International Conference on Management of Data*, ser. SIGMOD '17. New York, NY, USA: ACM, 2017, pp. 715–730. [Online]. Available: http://doi.acm.org/10.1145/3035918.3064049

Effects of an Apriori-based Data-mining Algorithm for Detecting Type 3 Clones

Yoshihisa Udagawa
Computer Science Department, Faculty of Engineering,
Tokyo Polytechnic University
Atsugi-city, Kanagawa, Japan
e-mail: udagawa@cs.t-kougei.ac.jp

***Abstract*—A code clone is a fragment of source code that appears at least twice in software source code. Code clones introduce difficulties in software maintenance because an error in one fragment is reproduced in code clones. It is significant to detect every code clones for making software maintenance easy and reliable.**

This paper describes software clone detection techniques using an *Apriori*-based sequential data mining algorithm. The *Apriori*-based algorithm is used because it is designed to find all frequent items that occur no less than a user-specified threshold named the minimum support (minSup). Since clones are slightly modified by adding, removing, or changing source code in general, the algorithm for detecting code clones has to deal with both match and mismatch portions of source code. The essential idea of the proposed approach is a combination of a partial string match using the longest-common-subsequence (LCS) and an *Apriori*-based algorithm for finding frequent sequences.

Generally, *Apriori*-based algorithms extract vast numbers of frequent sequences especially when the minSup is small, creating an obstacle to the detection of code clones. The novelties of our approach include pruning processes that depend on characteristics of a programming language, techniques to reduce the number of frequent sequences, and functions to control repetitive subsequences. We evaluate the effectiveness of the proposed algorithm based on experimental results using the source code of the *Java SDK SWING* graphics package. The results show that the proposed sequential data mining algorithm maintains the performance at a practical level until the minSup reaches two. This paper also shows some mined sequences and source code to demonstrate that the proposed algorithm works from short sequences to long ones.

Keywords*—*Code clone;* Apriori-*based algorithm; Maximal frequent sequence; Longest common subsequence(LCS) algorithm; Java source code.

I. Introduction

Two or more fragments of source code that are identical or similar to each other are named code clones. Programmers can reuse software code to speed up development, especially when similar functionality is already implemented in programs. Code clones are very common in large software, because they can significantly reduce programming effort and shorten programming time. However, code clones are believed to be harmful in the quality management across the software life cycle, especially in the maintenance phase. Code clones complicate software maintenance, because an error in a cloned fragment is reproduced in every copy. In other words, if there are many code clones in software source code, and a bug is found in one code clone, a programmer must check and update all of its instances consistently.

Techniques detecting similar code patterns including code clones help programmers understand the software code with less pain. Accumulated code patterns can lead to programming knowledge about a particular application. Techniques to detect code clones can be an essential part of programming knowledge extraction. The programming knowledge can enhance the performance of a project team enabling to provide high-quality software on schedule.

Since code clones are a set of similar fragments that appear at least twice in source code, the problem of finding code clones is essentially the detection of a set of string sequences that partially match and appear at least twice. The previous studies of Udagawa [1][2] propose a sequential data mining algorithm for string sequences based on an *Apriori* principle [3]. This paper enhances the previous studies through applying the algorithm to a large scale software, i.e., the *Java SDK SWING* graphics package.

A number of approaches have been developed to detect code clones based on textual similarity, three types of cloned code have been identified [4]. Type 1 is an exact copy without modification, with the exception of layout and comments. Type 2 is a slightly different copy typically resulting from renaming of variables or constants. Type 3 is a copy with further modifications typically resulting from adding, removing, or changing code units. Since Type-3 clones are generated by modifying original code units, there are mismatch portions of code when the clones and its original code units are compared. The mismatch portion is referred to as a "gap" in this paper.

Research on Type 3 clones has been conducted in recent decades, because there are substantially more significant clones of Type 3 than those of Types 1 or 2 in software for industrial applications. Our approach also focuses on finding Type 3 clones.

The following issues have to be addressed in finding this type of clone.

(1) How to handle gaps in pattern matching.
There are many algorithms that are tailored to handle gaps in similarity measures, such as sequence alignment,

dynamic pattern matching, tree-based matching, and graph-based matching techniques [4][5].

(2) How to find frequently occurring patterns.
The detection of frequently occurring patterns in a set of sequence data has been researched thoroughly, as reported in the sequential pattern-mining literature [3][6]-[10]. There are several studies [11]-[13] using an *Apriori*-based algorithm to discover code clones in source code.

Code clones are defined as a set of syntactically and/or semantically similar fragments of source code [4][5]. Since source code consists of a sequence of statements, finding clone code can be achieved by finding similar sequences that occur at least twice. *Apriori*-based sequential pattern-mining algorithms are worth studying, because they are especially designed to detect a set of frequently occurring sequences. The algorithms take a positive integer threshold set by a user called "minimum support" or "minSup" for short. The choice of minSup controls the level of frequency [3][10].

In previous studies [1][2], Udagawa shows that repeated structures in a method adversely affect the performance, especially when the minSup is two or three using *Java SDK 1.8.0_101 awt* [1] and *Apache Struts 2.5.2 Core* [2]. This paper builds on those studies using the large-scale software *Java SDK 1.8.0_101 SWING* and analyzes to what extent the minSup affects the number of retrieved sequences and time performance. For this purpose, the proposed *Apriori*-based sequential mining algorithm is properly revised to deal with the repeated structures in a method.

The contributions of this paper are as follows:

(I) design and implementation of a code transformation parser that extracts code matching statements, including control statements and typed method calls;

(II) design and implementation of a sequential data-mining algorithm that maintains performance at a practical level until the threshold minSup reaches two;

(III) evaluation of the proposed algorithm using the *Java SDK 1.8.0_101 SWING* graphics package with respect to a minSup of two to ten and a gap size of zero to three. In addition to time performance, the number of mined sequences is analyzed for each length of sequences showing that the number of repeated structures in a method accounts for a large part of the mined sequences, especially in the case when the minSup is two.

The remainder of the paper is organized as follows. After presenting some basic definitions and terminology on frequent sequence mining techniques in Section II, we gave an overview of the proposed approach in Section III. Section IV describes the proposed algorithm for discovering clone candidates using an *Apriori*-based maximal frequent sequence mining technique. Section V presents the experimental results using the *Java SDK 1.8.0_101 SWING* package with some mined sequences and source code. Section VI presents some of the most related work. Section VII concludes the paper with our plans for future work.

II. BASIC DEFINITIONS

Definition 1 (sequence and sequence database). A sequence is an enumerated collection of items in which repetitions are allowed. A sequence database is a set of the sequences. Formally, they are defined as follows.

Let I = { $i_1, i_2, \ldots, i_h$ } be a set of items (symbols). A sequence s_x is an ordered list of items $s_x = x_{j1} \rightarrow x_{j2} \rightarrow \ldots \rightarrow x_{jn}$ such that $x_{jk} \subseteq I$ $(1 \leq jk \leq h)$. A sequence database (SDB) is a set of sequences SDB = $\langle s_1, s_2, \ldots, s_p \rangle$ having sequence identifiers (SIDs) 1, 2, …, p.

Definition 2 (sequence containment). The notion of containment between two sequences is a key concept to characterize matching of the sequences. The sequence containment is defined by the identical or match items that are consecutively paired between two sequences. The concept of sequence containment is formalized as follows.

A sequence $s_a = a_1 \rightarrow a_2 \rightarrow \ldots \rightarrow a_n$ is said to be contained in a sequence $s_b = b_1 \rightarrow b_2 \rightarrow \ldots \rightarrow b_m$ $(n \leq m)$ iff there exists a strictly increasing sequence of integers q taken from [1, n], $1 \leq q[1] < q[2] < \ldots < q[n] \leq m$ such that $a_1 = b_{q[1]}$, $a_2 = b_{q[2]}$, …, $a_n = b_{q[n]}$ (denoted as $s_a \sqsubseteq s_b$).

Definition 3 (gapped sequence containment). A gap is a non-identical or mismatch item that consists either or both of the sequences. The concept of a gapped sequence containment is essential for detecting Type-3 clones because they are generated through modifications of adding, removing, or changing code units that cause gaps between two sequences. The gapped sequence containment is formally defined using a threshold, i.e., maxGap, that specifies the maximum length of non-identical or mismatch items.

Let maxGap be a threshold set by a user. A sequence $s_a = a_1 \rightarrow a_2 \rightarrow \ldots \rightarrow a_n$ is said to be contained in a sequence $s_b = b_1 \rightarrow b_2 \rightarrow \ldots \rightarrow b_m$ with respect to maxGap iff $a_1 = b_{q[1]}$, $a_2 = b_{q[2]}$, …, $a_n = b_{q[n]}$ and $q[j]-q[j-1]-1 \leq maxGap$ for all $2 \leq j \leq n$.

Definition 4 (prefix and postfix with respect to maxGap). A sequence can be divided into two subsequences, i.e., prefix and postfix, according to the concept of the gapped sequence containment.

A sequence $s_a = a_1 \rightarrow a_2 \rightarrow \ldots \rightarrow a_n$ is called a prefix of a sequence $s_b = b_1 \rightarrow b_2 \rightarrow \ldots \rightarrow b_m$ $(n \leq m)$ iff s_a is a gapped sequence containment of s_b with maxGap. A subsequence $s'_b = b_{n+1} \rightarrow \ldots \rightarrow b_m$ is called a postfix of s_b with respect to prefix s_a, denoted as $s_b = s_a \rightarrow s'_b$.

Definition 5 (support count with respect to maxGap). The support count of a sequence is defined by the number of its occurrences that appear in a sequence database. Since gaps in a sequence increase the chance of matching, the support count depends on maxGap.

Given a value of maxGap, the support count of a sequence s_b in a sequence database SDB with respect to maxGap is defined as the number of sequences $s \in$ SDB such that s_b is a gapped sequence containment of s with respect to maxGap and is denoted by $sup_{maxGap}(s_b)$.

Definition 6 (multi-occurrence mode and single-occurrence mode). Given a value of maxGap and a sequence $s_b = b_1 \rightarrow b_2 \rightarrow \ldots \rightarrow b_m$ with a prefix s_a, the sequence s_b has a support of $sup_{maxGap}(s_b)$ that is greater than zero.

When the prefix s_a is contained in a postfix of s_b, i.e., $s'_b = b_{n+1} \rightarrow \ldots \rightarrow b_m$, the support is calculated as $sup_{maxGap}(s_b) + 1$.

This calculation is applied recursively for each postfix of s_b to determine the support number. The support number calculated recursively is referred to as the support number in *multi-occurrence mode* in this paper. This mode is critical when dealing with long sequences, such as nucleotide DNA sequences [6][7], and periodically repeated patterns over time [8]. The support number without the calculation of the postfix of s_b is referred to as the support number in *single-occurrence mode*. The algorithm proposed in the paper supports both of these modes.

Definition 7 (frequent sequences with maxGap). Let maxGap and minSup be thresholds set by a user. A sequence s_b is referred to as a frequent sequence with respect to maxGap iff $sup_{maxGap}(s_b) \geq minSup$. The problem of sequence mining on a sequence database SDB is to discover all frequent sequences for given integers maxGap and minSup.

Definition 8 (closed frequent sequence). A closed frequent sequence is defined to be a frequent sequence for which there exists no super sequence that has the same support count as the original sequence [10][14].

Definition 9 (maximal frequent sequence). A maximal frequent sequence is defined to be a frequent sequence for which none of its immediate super sequences are frequent [9][10]. The maximal frequent sequence is valuable, because it provides the most compact representation of frequent sequences [14].

The closed frequent sequence is widely used when a system is designed to generate an association rule [10] that is inferred from a support number of a frequent sequence.

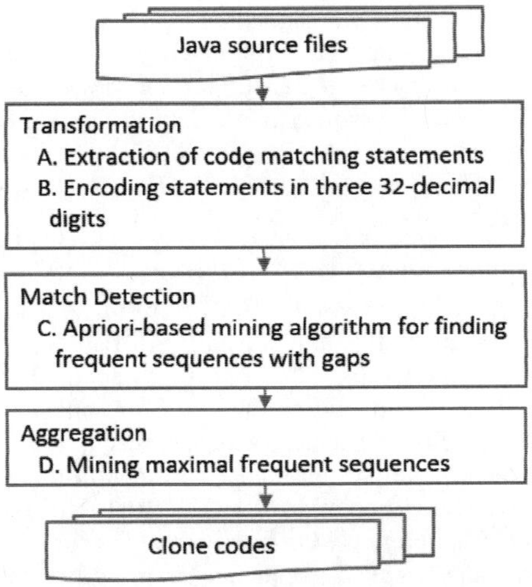

Figure 1. Overview of the proposed approach

III. Overview of Proposed Approach

Fig. 1 provides an overview of the proposed approach. According to the terminology in the survey [4], our approach can be summarized in three steps, transformation, match detection, and aggregation.

A. *Extraction of code matching statements*

Under the assumption that method calls and control statements characterize a program, the proposed parser extracts them in a *Java* program. Generally, the instance method is preceded by a variable whose type refers to a class object to which the method belongs. The proposed parser traces a type declaration of a variable and translates a variable identifier to its data type or class identifier as follows. The translation allows us to deal with Type 2 clones.

<variable>.<method identifier>

is translated into

<data type>.<method identifier> or

<class identifier>.<method identifier>.

The parser extracts control statements with various levels of nesting. A block is represented by the "{" and "}" symbols. Thus, the number of "{" symbols indicate the number of nesting levels. The following *Java* keywords for 15 control statements are processed by the proposed parser;

if, else if, else, switch, while, do, for, break, continue, return, throw, synchronized, try, catch, finally.

We selected the *Java SDK 1.8.0_101 SWING* package as the target of our study. The total number of lines is 372,186, qualifying the *SWING* package as a kind of large-scale software in the industry.

Fig. 2 shows an example of the extracted structure of the *paintContentBorderBottomEdge(Graphics g, int tabP, int sIndex, int x, int y, int w, int h)* method in the *BasicTabbedPaneUI.java* file of the *javax.swing.plaf.basic* package. The three numbers preceded by the # symbol are the numbers of comments, blank lines, and code lines, respectively. Fig. 3 shows the source code of the *paintContentBorderBottomEdge()* method whose matching statements are shown in Fig. 2.

```
BasicTabbedPaneUI::paintContentBorderBottomEdge
        (Graphics g, int tabP, int sIndex, int x, int y, int w, int h)
#               5       0       24
{
getTabBounds()
g.setColor()
        if{
        g.drawLine()
        g.setColor()
        g.drawLine()
        }
        else{
        g.drawLine()
        g.setColor()
        g.drawLine()
                if{
                g.setColor()
                g.drawLine()
                g.setColor()
                g.drawLine()
                }
        }
}
```

Figure 2. Example of an extracted structure

```
protected void paintContentBorderBottomEdge(Graphics g,
                                           int tabPlacement,
                                           int selectedIndex,
                                           int x, int y, int w, int h) {
    Rectangle selRect = selectedIndex < 0? null :
                           getTabBounds(selectedIndex, calcRect);
    g.setColor(shadow);
    // Draw unbroken line if tabs are not on BOTTOM, OR
    // selected tab is not in run adjacent to content, OR
    // selected tab is not visible (SCROLL_TAB_LAYOUT)
    //
    if (tabPlacement != BOTTOM || selectedIndex < 0 ||
        (selRect.y - 1 > h) ||
        (selRect.x < x || selRect.x > x + w)) {
        g.drawLine(x+1, y+h-2, x+w-2, y+h-2);
        g.setColor(darkShadow);
        g.drawLine(x, y+h-1, x+w-1, y+h-1);
    } else {
        // Break line to show visual connection to selected tab
        g.drawLine(x+1, y+h-2, selRect.x - 1, y+h-2);
        g.setColor(darkShadow);
        g.drawLine(x, y+h-1, selRect.x - 1, y+h-1);
        if (selRect.x + selRect.width < x + w - 2) {
            g.setColor(shadow);
            g.drawLine(selRect.x + selRect.width, y+h-2, x+w-2, y+h-2);
            g.setColor(darkShadow);
            g.drawLine(selRect.x + selRect.width, y+h-1, x+w-1, y+h-1);
        }
    }
}
```

Figure 3. Source code corresponding to Fig. 2

In this study, we deal only with *Java*. However, a slight modification of the parser allows us to apply the proposed approach to other languages such as C/C++ and Visual Basic.

B. *Encoding statements in three base-32 digits*

The conventional longest-common-subsequence (LCS) algorithm [15] takes two given strings as input and returns values depending on the number of matching characters of the strings. Because the length of statements in program code differs, the conventional LCS algorithm does not work effectively. In other words, for short statements, such as *if* and *try* statements, the LCS algorithm returns small LCS values for matching. For long statements, such as *synchronized* statements or a long method identifier, the LCS algorithm returns large LCS values.

We have developed an encoder that converts a statement to three base-32 digits (to cope with 32,768 identifiers), resulting in a fair base for a similarity metric in clone detection. Fig. 4 shows the encoded statements that correspond to the matching statements shown in Fig. 2. Fig. 5 shows a portion of the mapping table between three base-32 digits and the matching statements extracted from the original source files.

```
BasicTabbedPaneUI::paintContentBorderBottomEdge(Graph
ics g:int tabPlacement:int selectedIndex:int x:int y:int w:int
h)→001→4F2→07F→002→07G→07F→07G→005→009
→07G→07F→07G→002→07F→07G→07F→07G→005→
005→005
```

Figure 4. Encoded statements corresponding to Fig. 2

001, {	...
002, if{	07D, g.getColor()
...	07E, g.translate()
005, }	07F, g.setColor()
006, return	07G, g.drawLine()
007, putValue()	07H, Border.paintBorder()
008, this()	07I, Border.getBorderInsets()
009, else{	07J, g.drawRect()
...	...

Figure 5. Mapping table between three base-32 digits and a code matching statement used to encode statements in Fig. 4

C. *Apriori-based mining algorithm for finding frequent sequences with gaps*

We have developed a mining algorithm to find frequent sequences based on the *Apriori* principle [3][10], i.e., *if an itemset is frequent, then all of its subsets must be frequent.*

Frequent sequence mining is essentially different from itemset mining, because a subsequence can repeat not only in different sequences but also within each sequence. For example, given two sequences C→C→A and B→C→A→B →A→C→A, there are three occurrences of the subsequence C→A. The repetitions within a sequence [6]-[8] are critical when dealing with long sequences such as protein sequences, stock exchange rates, or customer purchase histories.

Note that the proposed algorithm is implemented to run in two modes, i.e., *multi-occurrence mode* to find all subsequences included in a given sequence, and *single-occurrence mode* to find a subsequence in a given sequence even if there exist several subsequences. As described in Section V, the multi-occurrence mode detects so many code matchings that it has an adverse effect on performance, especially when the minSup is two, and the maxGap is one to three.

The LCS algorithm is also tailored to match three base-32 digits as a unit. That algorithm can match two given sequences even if there is a "gap." Given two sequences of matching strings S1 and S2, let |lcs| be the length of their longest common subsequence, and let |common (S1, S2)| be the common length of S1 and S2 from a back trace algorithm. The "gap size" gs is defined as gs = |common (S1, S2)| – |lcs|.

D. *Mining maximal frequent sequences*

Frequent sequence mining tends to result in a very large number of sequential patterns, creating difficulty for users in analyzing the results. Closed and maximal frequent sequences are two representations for alleviating this drawback. A closed frequent sequence needs to be used in the case in which a system under consideration is designed to deal with an association rule [3][10][14] that plays an important role in knowledge discovery.

A maximal frequent sequence is a sequence that is frequent in a sequence database and that is not contained in any other longer frequent sequences. Maximal frequent sequences comprise a subset of the closed frequent sequences. Such a sequence is representative in the sense that all sequential patterns can be derived from it. Because we are interested only in finding a set of frequent sequences that are representative of a code clone, we developed an algorithm to discover the maximal frequent sequences.

IV. PROPOSED FREQUENT SEQUENCE MINING ALGORITHM

We have developed two algorithms for detecting code clones with gaps. The first is for mining frequent sequences, and the second is for extracting the maximal frequent sequences from a set of frequent sequences.

A. *Proposed Frequent Sequence Mining Algorithm*

The proposed approach is based on frequent sequence mining. A subsequence is considered frequent when it occurs no less than a user-specified minimum support threshold (i.e., minSup) in a sequence database. Note that a subsequence is not necessarily contiguous in an original sequence since the proposed algorithm deals with Type-3 clones.

We assume that a sequence is "a list of items," whereas several algorithms for sequential pattern mining [6]-[9] deal with a kind of sequence that consists of "a list of sets of items." Our assumption is reasonable, because we focus on detecting code clones that consist of "a list of statements." In addition, the assumption simplifies the implementation of the proposed algorithm, enabling it to achieve high performance as described in Section V.

The proposed frequent sequence-mining algorithm contains two methods, GProbe (Fig. 6) and Retrieve_Cand (Fig. 7). It follows the key idea behind the *Apriori* principle;

if a sequence S in a sequence database appears N times, so does every subsequence R of S at least.

The algorithm takes two arguments, minSup and maxGap (the allowable maximal number of gaps).

Fig. 6 shows the pseudocode of the algorithm GProbe. The algorithm takes two arguments, minSup and maxGap (the allowable maximal number of gaps). Let S_k be the set of frequent sequences of size k, and C_k the set of pairs of candidate sequences with frequency k. Let $CSyn_k$ be the set of gap-synonyms of a candidate sequence $c \in C_k$. The gap-synonym of a candidate sequence c is a sequence that matches c with no more than maxGap gaps.

- The algorithm initializes $k = 1$ and ANS = Φ. S_1 is initialized to hold 15 control statements of *Java*, based on the assumption that an important code clone is preceded by at least one control statement (lines 2 and 3).
- Next, the algorithm iteratively generates candidate k-sequences using the frequent (k–1)-sequences found in the previous iteration (line 5). Candidate generation is implemented using the function, Retrieve_Cand (S_k), which is described in Fig. 7.
- Then, the algorithm eliminates all candidate sequences whose support counts are less than minSup (line 8).
- If the support count of a candidate sequence *c* satisfies the minSup condition, then *c* is merged into ANS, which always contains all frequent sequences discovered thus far (line 9).
- S_k is reconstructed by merging *c* and its gap-synonym $CSyn_k$ (line 10).
- The algorithm terminates when there are no new frequent sequences generated, i.e., $S_k = \Phi$ (line 13).

```
1  GProbe()
2  k= 1;  ANS= Φ;
3  S1 = { 15 control statements of Java };
4  repeat
5      Ck, CSynk = Retrieve_Cand(Sk);
6      k= k+1;  Sk= Φ;
7      for each element c in Ck
8          if ( frequency of c >= minSup ){
9              ANS= ANS U { c };
10             Sk= Sk U { c } U CSynk;
11         }
12     end for
13 until Sk = Φ;
```

Figure 6. Pseudocode of the algorithm to find frequent sequences

Briefly, the Retrieve_Cand(S_k) method in Fig. 7 works as follows:

- C and CSyn are initialized to empty (line 2).
- The three *for* loops examine all possible matches between a sequence s_k in S_k and sequences in a sequence database (lines 3, 4, and 5).
- The LCS algorithm is executed to compute the match and gap counts (line 6).
- The *if* statement screens a sequence based on the match and gap counts (line 7).
- If a sequence s_k satisfies the match- and gap-count conditions, then a sequence s_{k+1}, i.e., a sequence s_k extended by one statement of program code, is merged into the candidate sequences C (line 8). Line 8 also implies counting the frequency of a sequence s_{k+1}.
- A gap-synonym of the candidate sequence s_{k+1} is maintained (line 9).
- The Retrieve_Cand (S_k) method returns C and CSyn as the results of execution for S_k (line 15).

```
1  Retrieve_Cand(Sk);
2  C = Φ;  CSyn = Φ;
3  for each element sk in Sk
4      for each element t in the sequence database
5          for each position p that sk matches in t
6              Compute the LCS between sk and t at position p ;
7              if ( match count >= k & gap count <= maxGap ){
8                  C = C U { sk+1 };  // put element sk+1 and count frequency.
9                  CSyn = CSyn U { sk+1' };  // sk+1' (≠ sk+1) is a sequence that
10                     // matches with sk+1 under minSup and maxGap conditions.
11             }
12         end for
13     end for
14 end for
15 return C, CSyn
```

Figure 7. Pseudocode of the algorithm for retrieving candidate sequences for the next repetition

B. Extracting Frequent Sequences

In our approach, we assume that a program structure is represented as a sequence of statements preceded by a class-method ID. Each statement is encoded as three base-32 digits to enable the LCS algorithm to work correctly, regardless of the length of the original program statement.

The proposed algorithm is illustrated for the given sample sequence database in Fig. 8. MTHD# is an abbreviated notation for a class-method ID.

```
MTHD1→005→003
MTHD2→005→00A→003→003
MTHD3→005→003→00F→006→005→003
MTHD4→005→006→003→005→00C
```

Figure 8. Example sequence database

Fig. 9 shows the result for the frequent sequences in the multi-occurrence mode for a gap of zero and a minSup of two, which can be expressed as a minSup of 50% since the total number of sequences is 4. "005" is a frequent sequence with a minSup count of six, because "005" occurs once in the first and second sequences and twice in the third and fourth sequences. The proposed algorithm maintains an ID-List, which indicates the positions at which a frequent sequence appears in a sequence database. The ID-List for "005" is 1|2|3+3|4+4.

Similarly, 005→003→ is a frequent sequence with a minSup count of three, i.e., the ID-List for 005→003→ is 1|3+3.

```
005→         N=6 (1|2|3+3|4+4)
005→003→     N=3 (1|3+3)
```

Figure 9. Result of the frequent sequences (gap, 0; minSup, 2)

Fig. 10 shows the result of the frequent sequences for a gap of one and minSup of two. "005" is a frequent sequence with a minSup count of six, which is the same in the case of a gap of zero.

Similarly, 005→003→ is a frequent sequence with a minSup count of five. In addition to the consecutive sequence 005→003→, the proposed algorithm detects gapped sequences. In the case of 005→003→, the algorithm detects 005→00A→003→ in the second sequence and 005→006→003→ in the fourth sequence. Thus, the ID-List for 005→003→ is 1|2|3+3|4.

```
005→         N=6 (1|2|3+3|4+4)
005→003→     N=5 (1|2|3+3|4)
```

Figure 10. Result of the frequent sequences (gap, 1; minSup, 2).

Fig. 11 shows the result of the frequent sequences for a gap of two and a minSup of two. In addition to 005→ and 005→003→, 005→006→ is detected as a frequent sequence because 005→003→00F→006→ in the third sequence matches 005→006→ with a gap of two, and 005→006→ in the fourth sequence with a gap of zero. Thus, the ID-List for 005→006→ is 3|4.

```
005→         N=6 (1|2|3+3|4+4)
005→003→     N=5 (1|2|3+3|4)
005→006→     N=2 (3|4)
```

Figure 11. Result of the frequent sequences (gap, 2; minSup, 2)

C. Extracting Maximal Frequent Sequences

A frequent sequence is defined to be a maximal frequent sequence if it has no super (or longer) sequence that is a frequent sequence. Such a sequence is representative, because it can be used to recover all frequent sequences. Several algorithms for finding the maximal frequent sequences and/or itemsets use sophisticated search and pruning techniques to reduce the number of sequence and/or item set candidates during the mining process [9].

However, we wish to compare the effects of a maximal frequent sequence with those of a frequent sequence; therefore, the proposed algorithm first mines a set of frequent sequences and then extracts the maximal frequent sequences.

Screening maximal frequent sequences from frequent sequences with a gap of zero is fairly simple. Given a set of frequent sequences Fs, the set of maximal frequent sequences MaxFs is defined by the following formula:

$$MaxFs = \{x \in Fs \mid \forall y \in Fs\ (x \not\subset y) \land (|x| + 1 = |y|)\}.$$

$x \not\subset y$ says that a sequence x is not included in a sequence y. Since a gap has length zero, the length of the immediate super sequence is $|x| + 1$.

The proposed algorithm is described using the sample sequence database in Fig. 12.

```
001→
002→
003→
004→
001→002→
004→003→
001→002→004→
004→002→003→001→
001→008→002→055→004→
```

Figure 12. Example frequent sequences

Fig. 13 shows a set of maximal frequent sequences. The frequent sequence 001→ is not a maximal frequent sequence, because there is a frequent sequence 001→002→ that includes a sequence 001 and whose length is two. In the same manner, we see that the sequences 002→, 003→, and 004→ are not maximal frequent sequences. 001→002→ is not a maximal frequent sequence, because the sequence 001→002→004→ includes 001→002→.

On the other hand, the sequence 004→003→ is a maximal frequent sequence, because there are no frequent sequences that exactly include this sequence. In the same manner, we see that the sequences 001→002→004→, 004→002→003→001→ and 001→008→ 002→055→004→ are maximal frequent sequences.

```
004→003→
001→002→004→
004→002→003→001→
001→008→002→055→004→
```

Figure 13. Result of maximal frequent sequences (gap, 0)

Now, we extend the definition of maximal frequent sequences for gaps greater than zero. Let maxGap be the maximal gap under consideration.

$$\mathrm{MaxFs}_{\mathrm{maxGap}} = \{ x \in \mathrm{Fs} \mid \forall y \in \mathrm{Fs}\ (x \not\subset_{\mathrm{maxGap}} y) \wedge |x| + 1 + \mathrm{maxGap} = |y| \}$$

$x \not\subset_{\mathrm{maxGap}} y$ says that a sequence x is not included in a sequence y under the gap constraint maxGap.

Fig. 14 shows a set of maximal frequent sequences for a maxGap of one. 004→003→ is not a maximal frequent sequence because 004→003→ is included in the sequence 004→002→003→001→ for a maxGap of one.

```
001→002→004→
004→002→003→001→
001→008→002→055→004→
```

Figure 14. Result of maximal frequent sequences (gap, 1)

Fig. 15 shows a set of maximal frequent sequences for a maxGap of two. In this case, 001→002→004→ is not a maximal frequent sequence, because 001→002→004→ is included in 001→008→002→055→004→ for a maxGap of two.

```
004→002→003→001→
001→008→002→055→004→
```

Figure 15. Result of maximal frequent sequences (gap, 2)

V. EXPERIMENTAL RESULTS

This section presents a statistical evaluation of experimental results. *Java* provides a wide range of functions including GUI, network, security, image and sound programming. Among them, *Java SDK 1.8.0_101 SWING* is a set of program components that provide the capability to process image data in various formats, to create graphical user interface (GUI) components, to handle events generated from a user, and to paint graphics of various shapes, etc. Because GUI components such as buttons, text fields, etc., and events such as mouse action, keystroke handling, etc., share functional commonalities, the *SWIMG* package is expected to include various code clones.

The source code of *Java SDK 1.8.0_101 SWING* package is input to the proposed parser to extract matching statements, i.e., method calls and control statements. Then, they are encoded to translate matching statements to three base-32 digits, making match detection successful. A statement sequence is generated for each method.

The total number of source code lines is 372,186. The extracted statement sequences comprise 9,234 lines that roughly correspond to the number of methods calls. The number of extracted unique IDs is 6,310. Since method calls in *Java* source code are preceded by a data type and/or a class identifier, the methods with the same method signatures that are defined in different classes are treated as distinguished ones. The method calls preceded by a data type and/or a class identifier allow *Java* to implement the overriding of methods that play an important role in object-oriented programming.

We performed the experiments using the following PC environment:

CPU: Intel Core i7-6700 (3.40 GHz)
Main memory: 8 GB
OS: Windows 10 HOME 64 Bit
Programming Language: *Java 1.8.0_101*.

The experiments are performed for minSup of two to ten, and maxGap of zero to three. minSup of two means that all possible clones are detected, if a code clone is defined as a fragment of source code that appears at least twice in the package. maxGap of zero means identical or un-gapped sequence matching. Comparison with the results of experiments on maxGap of zero to three shows the functionality and performance of the proposed algorithm.

A. *Numbers of Retrieved Frequent Sequences*

Fig. 16 compares the number of retrieved frequent sequences with respect to maxGap (zero to three) and minSup (two to ten). For comparison, Fig. 16 shows the number of retrieved frequent itemsets of the *Java* implementation of the *Apriori* algorithm [16]. The proposed algorithm for a maxGap of zero is comparable to the *Apriori* algorithm for a minSup of five to ten. The *Apriori* algorithm fails to generate frequent itemsets for a minSup of two, because it never completes the process within six hours.

As expected, the number of retrieved frequent sequences increases as maxGap increases and minSup decreases. The proposed algorithm can find frequent sequences that occur at least twice (minSup of two) in the sequence database, which is necessary for finding all possible code clones. One of the important findings of the experiment is that the effect of repetitions within a sequence becomes conspicuous when the minSup equals two. A detailed analysis of the retrieved frequent sequences is discussed in Subsection "*C. Sequence Length Analysis w.r.t minSup and maxGap.*"

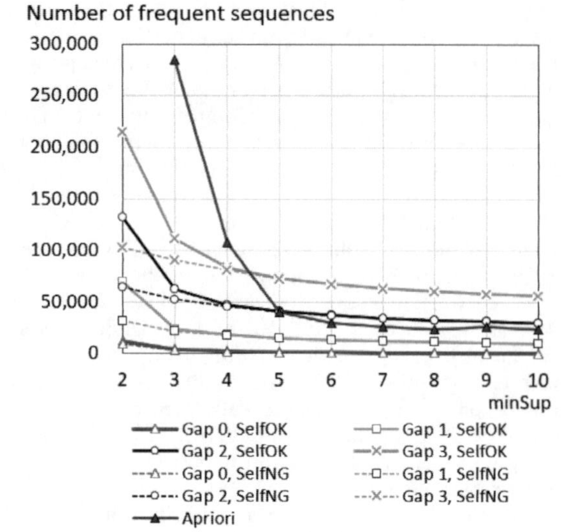

Figure 16. Numbers of retrieved frequent sequences (gap size, 0 and 1–3; minSup, 2–10) and frequent itemsets for the *Apriori* algorithm

Fig. 17 shows the ratio of the number of maximal frequent sequences to the number of frequent sequences. In most of the cases, the ratio decreases as minSup values decrease. This can be explained by the fact that decreasing minSup values probably have a negative effect on the relevance of frequent sequences. Thus, redundant frequent sequences are likely mined as minSup values decrease, resulting in the low ratio of the number of maximal frequent sequences to the number of frequent sequences.

The ratios are generally smaller in the multi-occurrence mode than in the single-occurrence mode. This might be because the single-occurrence mode suppresses extraction of frequent subsequences caused by repetitions within a sequence.

The results show that the gap size affects the ratio by approximately 8.0% for a minSup of two.

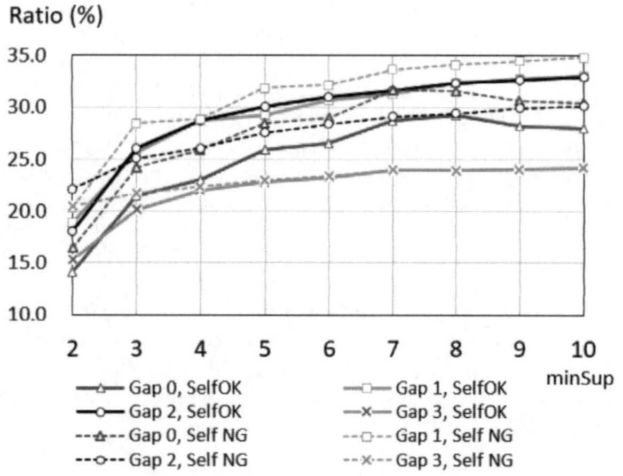

Figure 17. Ratio of the number of maximal frequent sequences to the number of frequent sequences (gap size, 0 and 1–3; minSup, 2–10)

B. *Time Analysis*

Fig. 18 shows the elapsed time in seconds for retrieving frequent sequences for a minSup of two to ten. The proposed algorithm for a maxGap of zero is comparable to the *Apriori* algorithm for a minSup of three to ten as for performance. However, the *Apriori* algorithm fails to find frequent itemsets for a minSup of two within six hours.

The proposed algorithm can retrieve frequent sequences fairly efficiently. For example, it takes 1,437 seconds to identify 31,825 frequent sequences for a maxGap of one and a minSup of two in the single-occurrence mode. Note that elapsed time increases as maxGap increases. This tendency is obvious especially for a minSup of two and three for a maxGap of zero to two, and a minSup of two to six for a maxGap of three. As for differences between the multi-and single-occurrence modes, the ratios of elapsed time range from 1.27 (for a maxGap of zero) to 3.06 (for a maxGap of one). Some reasons for performance degradation are analyzed in the next subsection.

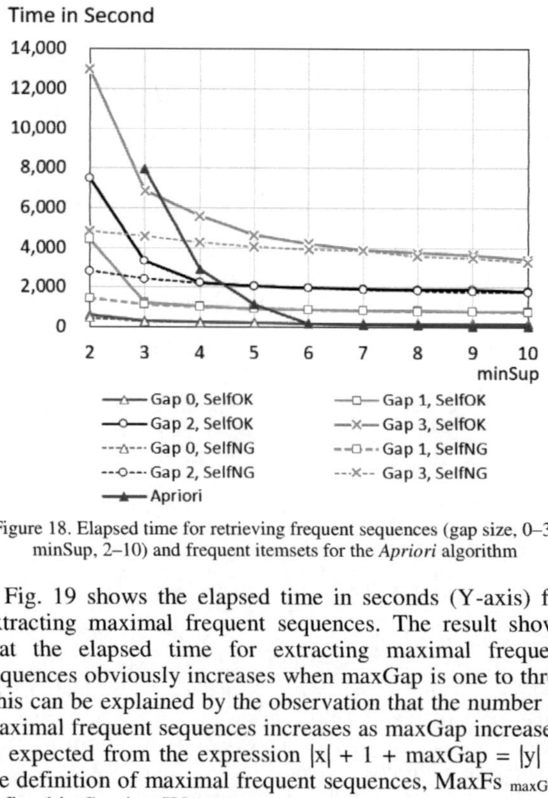

Figure 18. Elapsed time for retrieving frequent sequences (gap size, 0–3; minSup, 2–10) and frequent itemsets for the *Apriori* algorithm

Fig. 19 shows the elapsed time in seconds (Y-axis) for extracting maximal frequent sequences. The result shows that the elapsed time for extracting maximal frequent sequences obviously increases when maxGap is one to three. This can be explained by the observation that the number of maximal frequent sequences increases as maxGap increases, as expected from the expression |x| + 1 + maxGap = |y| in the definition of maximal frequent sequences, MaxFs $_{maxGap}$, defined in Section IV.

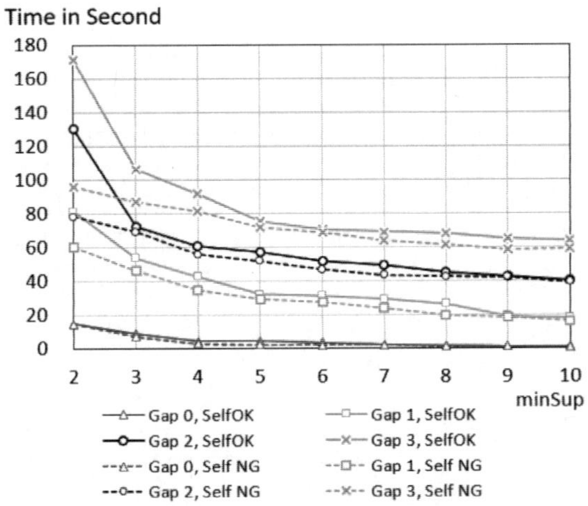

Figure 19. Elapsed time for extracting maximal frequent sequences

C. Sequence Length Analysis w.r.t minSup and maxGap

Fig. 20 shows the number of retrieved maximal frequent sequences the first time for each minSup for a maxGap of zero to three. For example, S2-S3 in Fig. 20 indicates the difference between the results of a minSup of two and those of a minSup of three. The vertical axis of Fig. 20 for S2-S3 indicates the number of maximal frequent sequences that is found the first time when the minSup is two.

The numbers are mostly affected by the modes of the proposed algorithm, i.e., multiple or single occurrences with a minSup of two. The ratios of the number of sequences in multi-occurrence to single-occurrence modes for a minSup of two are 1.3 (for a maxGap of zero), 3.3 (for a maxGap of one), 4.4 (for a maxGap of two), and 5.4 (for a maxGap of three).

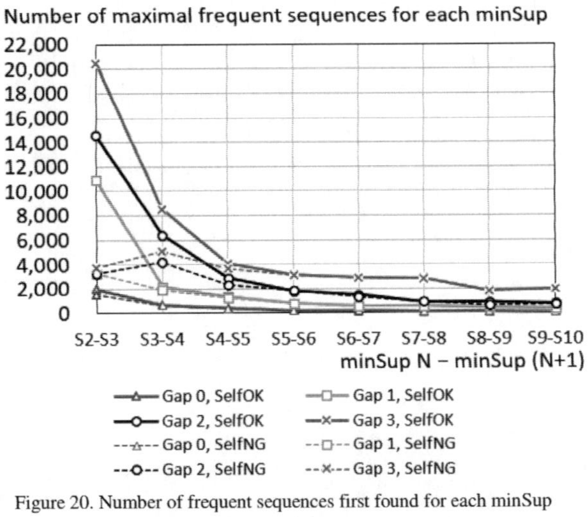

Figure 20. Number of frequent sequences first found for each minSup

Fig. 21 shows the number of maximal frequent sequences for each sequence length (two to 30) in the multi-occurrence mode and a maxGap of three with a minSup ranging from two to five. The maximum length of a sequence is 150 in the multi-occurrence mode. Note that Fig. 21 omits the results on sequences of length 31–150. The number of maximal frequent sequences for each length reaches a peak around a sequence length of eight to ten for each minSup of two to five. This suggests that code clones of length eight to ten occur most frequently.

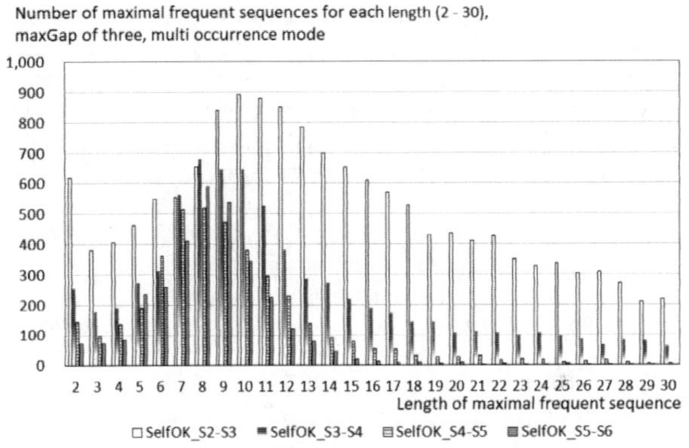

Figure 21. Number of retrieved sequences for each length in multi occurrence mode and a maxGap of three

Fig. 22 shows the number of maximal frequent sequences for each length in the single-occurrence mode. The maximum length of the sequences is 54 in the single-occurrence mode. The number of sequences is substantially decreased owing to the suppression of repetitive subsequences, analyzed in the following section.

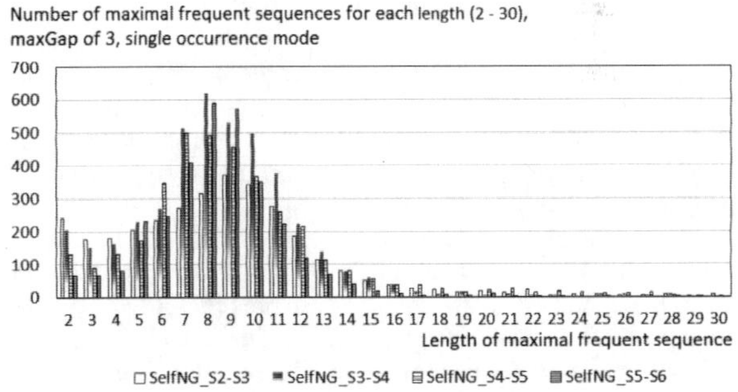

Figure 22. Number of retrieved sequences for each length in single-occurrence mode and a maxGap of three

D. Source Code Findings

TABLE I shows two sample sequences that include key sequences repetitively. The subsequences in bold and underlined text indicate the key sequences.

The first sequence in TABLE I includes the key sequence 002→4NM→002→4MI→005→005→ twice. The sequence is mined only in multi-occurrence mode with a minSup of two and with gap of one. The second sequence in TABLE I includes the key sequence 065→04Q→4HU→4HV →4HV→065→04Q→ three times. The first subsequence **04Q→4HU→4HV →4HV→***065→04Q→* matches the key sequence with gap of one, i.e., the first 065→ is mismatched. In the second subsequence, *065→04Q→* appears as the heads of the second subsequence, i.e., *065→04Q→*4HU→ 4HV→4HV →065→04Q→, which fully matches the key sequence. The third subsequence follows after the second subsequence sharing *065→04Q→* at the top of the third subsequence.

The results of the experiments show that there are many repetitive subsequences of statements in a method. Since these repetitive subsequences are found in a method, programmers are expected to find them easily in the screen of a program editor. Based on this observation, it can be safely said that the single-occurrence mode is preferable to clone mining from the programmer's point of view.

TABLE I. SAMPLE SEQUENCES INCLUDE KEY SEQUENCE REPETITIVELY

No.	Method signiture and statement sequences
1	Handler::repaintDropLocation(JTable.DropLocation loc)→001→002→006→005→**002→4MH→002→4MI→005→**006→005→**002→4NM→002→4MI→005 →005→**002→4NM→002→4MI→005→005→005
2	ScrollableTabSupport::updateView()→001→4G9→4GF→4HS→4HM→4HN→4HT→002→04P→04Q→04Q→002→005→065→04Q→04Q→002→005→065→005→005→4GB→04P→**04Q→4HU→4HV→4HV→***065→04Q→***4HU→4HV→4HV→***065→04Q→***4HU→4HV→4HV→065→04Q→*00M→4HU→4HV→4HV→005→005

TABLE II shows a sample set of methods that include the key sequence 002→07F→07J→07F→07G→07G→ in single-occurrence mode with gap of two. Actually, 07F, 07G, and 07J are symbols for the methods *setColor(), drawLine(),* and *drawRect()*, respectively. All of these methods are concerned with paint graphics.

The third and fourth methods are fairly said to be code clones, because their entire statement sequences are completely matched, and they are defined in the same *BasicTabbedPaneUI.java* file. The third method in TABLE II, i.e., the *paintContentBorderBottomEdge()* method, is the method shown in Figs. 2 and 3.

The other methods cannot be safely said to be clones, because they are defined in different files, and they are partially matched with the key sequence. However, the sequence patterns of *setColor(), drawLine(),* and *drawRect()* are informative to programmers for implementing paint graphics. The proposed mining algorithm can serve to find all of the related sequence patterns within a specified gap, viz., maxGap. In addition, these methods are worth checking in the event of bug fixes.

TABLE II. SAMPLE SET OF METHODS

No.	Method signiture and statement sequences
1	SwatchPanel::paintComponent(Graphics g) →001→07F→07S→000→000→0GU→07F→002→005→009→005→07S→07F→07G→07G→**002→07F→07G→07G→**07G→07G→07G→07G→005→005→005→005
2	RolloverButtonBorder::paintBorder(Component c, Graphics g, int x, int y, int w, int h) →001→2PO→2PP→002→005→002→07D→07E→**002→07F→07J→07F→07G→07G →**005→009→07F→07J→07F→07G→07G→005→07E→07F→005→005
3	BasicTabbedPaneUI::paintContentBorderBottomEdge(Graphics g, int tabP, int sIndex, int x, int y, int w, int h) →001→4F2→07F→002→07G→07F→07G→005→009→07G→07F→07G→**002→07F→07G→07F→07G→**005→005→005
4	BasicTabbedPaneUI::paintContentBorderRightEdge(Graphics g, int tabP, int sIndex, int x, int y, int w, int h) →001→4F2→07F→002→07G→07F→07G→005→009→07G→07F→07G**→002→07F→07G→07F→07G→**005→005→005
5	MetalComboBoxUI::paintCurrentValueBackground(Graphics g, Rectangle bounds, boolean hasFocus) →001→**002→07F→07J→07F→**07J→002→07F→32T→002→07S→005→002→07S→005→005→005→018→074→005→005
6	Handler::paintDraggedArea(Graphics g, int rMin, int rMac, TableColumn draggedColumn, int distance) →001→29D→4MH→4MH→2C2→07F→07S→07F→07S→**002→07F→07G→07G→**005 →000→4MH→3J9→002→07F→4MH→07G→005→005→005
7	ToolBarBorder::paintBorder(Comp c, Graphics g, int x, int y, int w, int h) →001→002→006→005→07E→002→002→5AL→002→5AM→005→009→5AM→005→005→009→5AL→5AM→005→005→**002→07F→07G→07F→07G→**005→07E→005
8	MetalPropertyListener::paintTrack(Graphics g) →001→002→5LQ→006→005→5LR→5BD→07E→002→5LO→005→009→002→005→009→5LP→5LP→005→005→**002→07F→07J→07F→07G→07G→**07F→07G→07G→005→009→07F→07J→005→002→002→002→005→009→005→005→009→002→005→009→005→005→**002→07F→07G→07G→**07F→07S→005→009→07F→07S→005→005 →07E→005

TABLE III shows a pair of methods that share a rather long key sequence:
1T2→1SB→1T3→002→1T4→05Q→002→1T5→005→0 BC→005→005→015→1T6→002→1T7→005→005→017 →005→017→005→017→005→002→015→005→017→0 05→005→002→17K→005→1SD→002→006→005→.

The length of the key sequence is 37. This epitomizes the effectiveness of a minSup of two, because there are only two methods that share this key sequence in the *Java SDK 1.8.0_101 SWING* package. Though their statement sequences are not fully matched, they are considered to be clones, because they are defined in the same *Java* file and they share a large amount of functionality.

TABLE III. METHODS SHARING A KEY SEQUENCE OF LENGTH 37

No.	Method signiture and statement sequences
1	JOptionPane::showInternalOptionDialog(Component parentComponent, Object message, String title, int optionType, int messageType, Icon icon, Object[] options, Object initialValue) →001→1S5→1T1→0RO→1SG→**1T2→1SB→1T3→002→1T4→05Q→002→1T5→005→0BC→005→005→015→1T6→002→1T7→005→005→017→005→017→005→017→005→002→015→005→017→005→005→1SH→002→17K→005→002→006→005→**002→002→006→005→006→005→000→002→006→005→005→006→005
2	JOptionPane::showInternalInputDialog(Component parentComponent, Object message, String title, int messageType, Icon icon, Object[] selectionValues, Object initialSelectionValue) →001→1S5→1T1→0RO→1S6→1S7→1S8→**1T2→1SB→1T3→002→1T4→05Q→002→1T5→005→0BC→005→005→015→1T6→002→1T7→005→005→017→005→017→005→017→005→002→015→005→017→005→005→002→17K→005→1SD→002→006→005→**006→005

TABLE IV shows a pair of methods that share the longest key sequence of length 54 in single-occurrence mode with a minSup of two and with gap of zero. 001→ is not a component of the key sequence, because 001→ corresponds to the statement "{" that is not a control statement and thus is excluded from the statement at the initialization process of the proposed algorithm. Though they are defined in the different *Java* files, they are considered to be code clones, because they have entirely the same statement sequences in the same context of similar *SWING* components, i.e., Button and Label.

TABLE IV. METHODS SHARING THE LONGEST KEY SEQUENCE OF LENGTH 54

No.	Method signiture and statement sequences
1	AccessibleAbstractButton::getAfterIndex(int part, int index)→ 001→**002→006→005→04P→04Q→002→006→005→015→006→005→017→006→005→04Q→015→01G→04R→04S→04T→002→006→005→04T→002→006→005→006→005→017→006→005→04Q→015→01G→04U→04S→04T→002→006→005→04T→002→006→005→006→005→017→006→005→00M→006→005→005**
2	AccessibleJLabel::getAfterIndex(int par, int index)→ 001→**002→006→005→04P→04Q→002→006→005→015→006→005→017→006→005→04Q→015→01G→04R→04S→04T→002→006→005→04T→002→006→005→006→005→017→006→005→04Q→015→01G→04U→04S→04T→002→006→005→04T→002→006→005→006→005→017→006→005→00M→006→005→005**

Fig. 23 shows the source code of the *getAfterIndex()* method in the *javax/swing/AbstractButton.java* file. It is somewhat surprising that the two methods share not only the statements corresponding to the key sequence, but also every character of the comments.

```
/**
 * Returns the String after a given index.
 *
 * @param part the AccessibleText.CHARACTER, AccessibleText.WORD,
 * or AccessibleText.SENTENCE to retrieve
 * @param index an index within the text &gt;= 0
 * @return the letter, word, or sentence, null for an invalid
 * index or part
 * @since 1.3
 */
public String getAfterIndex(int part, int index) {
    if (index < 0 || index >= getCharCount()) {
        return null;
    }
    switch (part) {
    case AccessibleText.CHARACTER:
        if (index+1 >= getCharCount()) {
            return null;
        }
        try {
            return getText(index+1, 1);
        } catch (BadLocationException e) {
            return null;
        }
    case AccessibleText.WORD:
        try {
            String s = getText(0, getCharCount());
            BreakIterator words = BreakIterator.getWordInstance(getLocale());
            words.setText(s);
            int start = words.following(index);
            if (start == BreakIterator.DONE || start >= s.length()) {
                return null;
            }
            int end = words.following(start);
            if (end == BreakIterator.DONE || end >= s.length()) {
                return null;
            }
            return s.substring(start, end);
        } catch (BadLocationException e) {
            return null;
        }
    case AccessibleText.SENTENCE:
        try {
            String s = getText(0, getCharCount());
            BreakIterator sentence =
                BreakIterator.getSentenceInstance(getLocale());
            sentence.setText(s);
            int start = sentence.following(index);
            if (start == BreakIterator.DONE || start > s.length()) {
                return null;
            }
            int end = sentence.following(start);
            if (end == BreakIterator.DONE || end > s.length()) {
                return null;
            }
            return s.substring(start, end);
        } catch (BadLocationException e) {
            return null;
        }
    default:
        return null;
    }
}
```

Figure 23. Source code of *getAfterIndex()* method

VI. RELATED WORK

Zhu and Wu [6] propose an *Apriori*-like algorithm to mine a set of gap-constrained sequential patterns that can be found in a long sequence, such as stock exchange rates, DNA, and protein sequences. Ding et al. [7] discuss an algorithm for mining repetitive gapped subsequences and apply the proposed algorithm to program execution traces. Kiran et al. [8] propose a model for mining periodic-frequent patterns that occur at regular intervals or gaps in long sequences. Fournier-Viger et al. [9] discuss the importance of maximal sequential pattern mining and propose an efficient algorithm for finding the maximal patterns.

Wahler et al. [11] propose a method for detecting clones of Types 1 and 2 that are represented as abstract syntax trees in the Extensible Markup Language (XML) by applying a frequent itemset mining technique. Their tool uses the *Apriori* algorithm to identify features as frequent itemsets in large numbers of software program statements. They devise an efficient link structure and a hash table for achieving efficiency in practical applications.

Li et al. [12] propose a tool, CP-Miner, which uses the closed frequent patterns mining technique [10][14] to detect frequent subsequences including statements with gaps. CP-Miner shows that a frequent subsequence mining technique can avert redundant comparisons, leading to improved time performance.

El-Matarawy et al. [13] propose a clone detection technique based on sequential pattern mining. Their method treats source code lines as transactions and statements as items. Their algorithm is applied to discover frequent itemsets in the source code that exceed a given frequency threshold, viz., minSup. Finally, their method finds the maximum frequent sequential patterns [9][10][14] of code clone sequences.

Their approach deals with each program statements including variable declaration, arithmetic calculation, etc, to detect code clones. Each non-reserved word in the source code is replaced by the same letter "X". In addition, any data types are replaced by the same letter "T". Thus the identity of the statements seem to be greatly lessen. They don't discuss the effect of the transformation of replacing by the same letters in their experiments. In this study, because we extract method calls preceded by a data type and/or a class identifier, the matching statements extracted from source code reserve full identity of them. The method calls with a data type and/or a class identifier code enable the overriding of methods that is essential in *Java* as an object-oriented programming language. The results of experiments, Fig. 23 for instance, show that identified method calls and control statements provides sufficient information for detecting code clones.

As for calculation of gaps, El-Matarawy et al. don't clearly describe processes and parameters on gaps. According to the paper [13], their *Apriori*-based algorithm generates candidate code clones of length i+1 by using Cartesian product of $CC_i \times F$, where CC_i is a set of code clones of length i, and F is a set of frequent statements of length one. Then, the dedicated check process examines the presence of code clones, which seems to handle gaps. In this study, we use an LCS algorithm for systematic handling of gaps of similar sequences as described in Section IV.

Accurate detection of near-miss intentional clones (NICAD) [17] is a text-based code clone detection technique. NICAD uses a parser that extracts functions and performs pretty-printing to standardize code format and an LCS algorithm [15] to compare potential clones with gaps. Unlike an *Apriori*-based approach, NICAD compares each potential clone with all of the others. Regarding LCS, Iliopoulos and Rahman [18] introduce the idea of a gap constraint in LCS to address the problem of extracting multiple sequence alignments in DNA sequences.

Murakami et al. [19] propose a token-based method. Their method detects gapped code clones using a well-known local sequence-alignment algorithm, the Smith-Waterman algorithm [20]. They discuss a sophisticated backtracking algorithm tailored for code clone detection.

VII. Conclusions and Future Work

In this paper, we presented an attempt to identify Type 3 code clones. Our approach consists of four steps, extraction of code matching statements, encoding statements in base-32 digits, detecting frequent sequences with gaps, and mining the maximal frequent sequences. The paper deals primarily with the last two steps.

Experiments using *Java SDK 1.8.0_101 SWING* package source code show that the proposed algorithm works successfully for finding clones with respect to a maxGap of zero through three and a minSup of two through ten.

As long as code clones are defined syntactically as similar code segments that occur at least twice, the proposed algorithm achieves 100% recall and 100% precision [13] as a result of the nature of *Aprior*-based data mining with a minSup of two.

In this study, all matching statements, i.e., control statements and typed method calls, are treated equally because we focus on the detection of code clones. In practice, however, each statements should be weighted to reflect their relative importance from the programmer's point of view.

Future work is planned to develop functions to cluster code clones according to the weighted parameters set to each matching statements. The functions aim at providing practical guidance and insights to facilitate understanding and maintenance of large scale software.

ACKNOWLEDGMENT

The authors would like to thank the anonymous reviewers for their invaluable feedback. This research is supported by the JSPS KAKENHI under grant number 16K00161.

References

[1] Y. Udagawa, "On the Effect of Minimum Support and Maximum Gap for Code Clone Detection — An Approach Using Apriori-based Algorithm —", Proc. 3rd international Conference on Advances and Trends in Software Engineering (SOFTENG 2017), April 23 - 27, 2017, pp. 66-73.

[2] Y. Udagawa, "Maximal Frequent Sequence Mining for Finding Software Clones," Proc. 18th International Conference on Information Integration and Web-based Applications & Services (iiWAS 2016), Nov. 2016, pp. 28-35.

[3] R. Agrawal, T. Imielinski, and A. Swami "Mining association rules between sets of items in large databases," Proc. ACM SIGMOD International Conference on Management of Data, June 1993, pp. 207-216.

[4] C. K. Roy and J. R. Cordy "A survey on software clone detection research," Queen's Technical Report:541 Queen's Uni-versity at Kingston, Ontario, Canada, Sep. 2007, pp. 1-115.

[5] A. Sheneamer and J. Kalita. "A survey of software clone detection techniques," International Journal of Computer Applications, vol.v137, issue 10, Mar. 2016, pp. 1-21.

[6] X. Zhu, and X. Wu "Mining complex patterns across sequences with gap requirements," Proc. 20th International Joint Conference on Artifical Intelligence(IJCAI'07), Jan. 2007, pp. 2934-2940.

[7] B. Ding, D. Lo, J. Han,and S-C. Khoo "Efficient Mining of Closed Repetitive Gapped Subsequences from a Sequence Database," Proc. 25th IEEE International Conference on Data Engineering (ICDE 2009), March 2009, pp. 1024-1035.

[8] R. U. Kiran, M. Kitsuregawa, and P. K. Reddy "Efficient discovery of periodic-frequent patterns in very large databases," Journal of Systems and Software, vol. 112, issue C, Feb. 2016, pp. 110-121.

[9] P. Fournier-Viger, C-W. Wu, A. Gomariz, and V. S-M. Tseng "VMSP: Efficient Vertical Mining of Maximal Sequential Patterns," Proc. 27th Canadian Conference on Artificial Intelligence (AI 2014), May 2014, pp. 83-94.

[10] P-N. Tan, M. Steinbach, and V. Kumar "Introduction to Data Mining," Addison-Wesley, March 2006.

[11] V. Wahler, D. Seipel, J. Wolff, and G. Fischer "Clone detection in source code by frequent itemset techniques," Proc. IEEE International Workshop on Source Code Analysis and Manipulation, Oct. 2004, pp. 128-135.

[12] Z. Li, S. Lu, S. Myagmar, and Y. Zhou "CP-Miner: A tool for finding copy-paste and related bugs in operating system code," Proc. 6th Symposium on Operating System Design and Implementation, Dec, 2004, pp. 289-302.

[13] A. El-Matarawy, M. El-Ramly, and R. Bahgat "Code clone detection using sequential pattern mining," International Journal of Computer Applications, vol. 127, issue 2, Oct. 2015, pp. 10-18.

[14] R. Verma, "Compact Representation of Frequent Itemset," http://www.hypertextbookshop.com/dataminingbook/public_version/contents/chapters/chapter002/section004/blue/page001.html, 2009.

[15] J. Hunt, W. and Szymanski, T. G. "A fast algorithm for computing longest common subsequences," Comm. ACM, vol. 20, issue.5, May 1977, pp. 350-353.

[16] M. Monperrus, N. Magnus, and S. Yibin "Java implementation of the Apriori algorithm for mining frequent itemsets," GitHub, Inc., https://gist.github.com/monperrus/7157717, 2010.

[17] C. K. Roy and J. R. Cordy "NICAD: Accurate detection of near-miss intentional clons using flexible pretty-printing and code normalization," Proc. 16th IEEE International Conference on Program Comprehension, June 2008, pp. 172-181.

[18] C. S. Iliopoulos and M. S. Rahman "Algorithms for computing variants of the longest common subsequence problem," Theoretical Computer Science vol. 395, issues 2–3, May 2008, pp. 255–267.

[19] H. Murakami, K. Hotta, Y. Higo, H. Igaki, and S.Kusumoto "Gapped code detection with lightweight source code analysis," Proc. IEEE 21st International Conference on Program Comprehension (ICPC), May 2013, pp. 93-102.

[20] "Smith–Waterman algorithm," https://en.wikipedia.org/wiki/Smith%E2%80%93Waterman_algorithm, Aug. 2016.

A New Approach for Vehicles Detection in Low Altitude Aerial Images based on Edge Density

Antonio J. R. Neves, Manuel Camarneiro and Lucas Cozinheiro

DETI/IEETA, University of Aveiro,
3810-193 Aveiro, Portugal
Email: {an, mcamarneiro, lucas.cozinheiro}@ua.pt

Abstract—**Drones and Computer Vision are both important research topics nowadays. Combining these two technologies enables having different perspectives of a scene and capturing them with digital cameras onboard drones. Incorporating onboard processing of the acquired images might provide extremely useful information from different scenarios, allowing the drones to perform autonomously with applications in several contexts. In this paper, we present algorithms to process images captured by drones over parking lots in order to detect parked vehicles and further estimate occupancy rates or cars parked in a wrong place. As far as we know, low altitude image processing is still an open problem in the computer vision community. Experimental tests with the developed algorithms were performed in different parking lots across the University of Aveiro Campus under different lighting conditions to check their accuracy and processing requirements. Detailed experimental results are presented in this paper and an image database was produced in order to allow future experiments by other researchers. The obtained results presented in this paper demonstrate the effectiveness of the proposed approaches.**

Keywords–Drones; Image processing; object detection.

I. Introduction

This manuscript is an extended version of the original paper presented at the Second International Conference on Advances in Signal, Image and Video Processing, SIGNAL 2017 [1]. This extended version provides a deep overview about the proposed algorithms for car detection on low altitude images and more experimental results using these algorithms.

Recent drones are equipped with digital cameras and are very prospective for a variety of commercial uses such as aerial photography, surveillance, etc. However, in order to deploy autonomous drones, it is necessary to include onboard smart computer vision systems and autopilot capabilities. In the application of aerial imaging, object detection and tracking are essential to capturing key objects in a scene. Object detection and tracking are classic problems in computer vision. However, there are more challenges with drones due to top-down view angles and real-time constraints. Additionally, a challenging problem is the strong weight and area constraint of embedded hardware that limits the drones to run computation intensive algorithms, such as deep learning, with limited hardware resource.

Solutions using drones and computer vision are not restricted to security. There is a huge number of possible areas where these devices might be useful [3] [5]. Although, only a few commercial drones are able to perform some basic image processing on the acquired images. There is still a long way to go through on scientific research about this technology combination. Lately, a few commercial solutions are available for applications in agriculture mainly used to monitor plants growth, watering levels and fruit maturation. Some prototypes are also being tested for save and rescue tasks or fast mail delivery.

Before the proliferation of drones, monitoring vehicles from aerial imagery was already possible, making use of pictures either taken from satellite or from manned aircrafts. For this kind of images there are several approaches regarding algorithms to detect and locate cars. This is often associated with high altitude or satellite imagery [4] [7]. Even though, as this project was intended to process images obtained in lower altitude flights (about 10 meters from the ground), most of the published work does not apply. Thus, the solution was to create algorithms from scratch for parking lots with three different types of pavement, given as inputs the altitude of the drone and the parking zone location in relation to the main road.

The experimental results presented on this work are based on images captured using a Cheerson CX-20 and a Parrot Bebop 2 [2] flying on a selected path over some of the University of Aveiro parking lots spread across the Campus as shown in Figure 1.

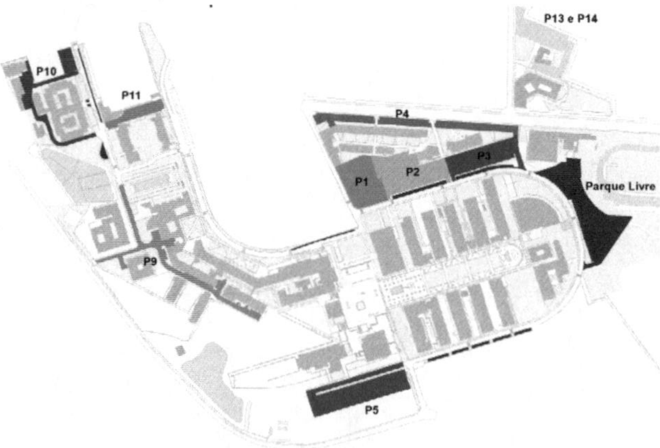

Figure 1. University of Aveiro Parking Lots.

Images were captured over some parking lots taking into consideration the type of pavement. Images were obtained either from pavements built exclusively on tar (Figure 2), on block pavement (Figure 3) and both (Figure 4). Algorithms were further developed to detect parked vehicles over each type of pavement identified before.

Figure 2. Tar Parking Lot.

Figure 3. Block Pavement Parking Lot.

Figure 4. Mixed Pavement Parking Lot.

The algorithms were tested on an external computer used for development but were also adapted for further tests in single boards in order to determine the possibility of having image processing onboard while the drone moves over the parking lots. Without local processing, this solution would either depend on a fast and heavy data transfer link, for captured images to be processed in a remote server, or take a longer time gap since the drone is sent to capture images, returns and delivers data acquired on its base station for further processing and analysis.

In this paper we present experimental results showing the effectiveness of the proposed approach, both in terms of detection ratio, as well as in terms of processing time.

The paper is organised as follows: Sections II and III introduce respectively Drones and relevant related work. Sections IV to VI detail the proposed solution from an overview on Low Altitude Vehicle Detection, to our solution Pavement and Vehicle Detection. Section VII is reserved for experimental results, while finally, in Section VIII, we draw some conclusions.

II. Drones

Unmanned Aerial Vehicles (UAV) or commonly denominated Drones are aircrafts able to fly without a human pilot on board and can either be remote controlled or simply fly autonomously. UAV were firstly developed for military purposes but quickly became popular. By the end of the last century some people already managed to control small aircrafts remotely but brushless motors and new batteries brought some more efficiency to these models, allowing them to operate only on electric power and quickly lead to further research in this area.

Different designs came up alongside scaled planes and helicopters but multicopters stood out. Multicopters or Multirotors are in fact rotorcrafts with 2 or more motors, combining the features of a regular helicopter - vertical take-off and landing and hovering capability - with the stability obtained by the extra motors. The quadrotor or quadcopter soon appears as a stable model, as well as efficient and easy to control, which makes it the most usual UAV flying these days. It is composed by a X-shaped body with 2 opposite propellers rotating clockwise and 2 other rotating counterclockwise illustrated in Figure 5.

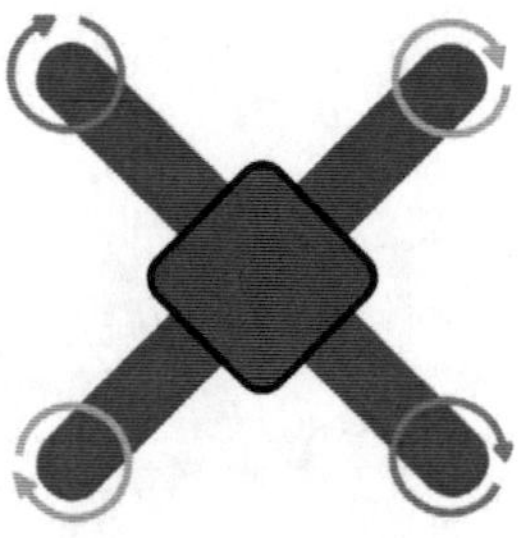

Figure 5. Quadcopter scheme.

A. *Used Drones - Cheerson*

Quanum Nova or Cheerson CX-20 is a commercial drone with an open-source ArduPilot Mega (APM) flight controller assembled in a fragile plastic frame presented in Figure 6.

Besides the customisation possibilities offered by the flight controller it also features a GPS module supporting path planning (pre programmed route from a smartphone) and a 2D stabilised gimbal for cameras. Stability is evident after some flying tests remotely controlled. Controlling range is also considerable. Nevertheless, a First Person View System(FPV)

Figure 6. Cheerson CX-20.

on board is missing - this shows up to be very important while flying for image acquisition. This drone also has some failsafe options and in case the pilot is not able to land, he can still touch two buttons making it return to the take off position. GPS accuracy is not disappointing, still it misses the target by 3 to 5 meters.

Quanum Nova is very versatile for aerial imagery solutions due to its stability, strength and design, which enables fixing and transporting a large diversity of action cameras and stabilisation gimbals onboard. Even though installing telemetry and activating pre defined paths is difficult and makes it harder to get it completely autonomous and able to repeat some footage over the same parking zones. Flight time goes up to 15 minutes but it is significantly reduced if using a camera and specially a stabilisation gimbal, which also compromises image acquisition over some big parking lots.

B. Used Drones - Bebop

The second UAV operated was Parrot Bebop2, which is a small sized quadcopter with a built-in panoramic camera (Figure 7).

Figure 7. Bebop 2.

It is controlled over Wi-Fi and does not require a specific remote. Any smartphone or tablet (having Parrot application installed) will be quickly transmitting all the instructions needed to determine the tasks of the Bebop. Range is not great but as it is possible to upload a well defined path, range is not a constraint. At a first look it seems small and fragile but it proved to be quite resistant to strong winds. It is also extremely easy to pilot since it takes off and lands automatically while keeping steady in case of no remote input.

In the smartphone or tablet it is possible to watch real time images obtained by the camera (FPV) and also have sensorial information such as altitude, speed or temperature. These features are crucial while obtaining images from parking lots since they enable visual feedback in real time and consequently allow the pilot to correct the position of the drone. The built-in camera is the only limitation of this drone when compared to Quanum Nova. Rotation is not available but Parrot software performs some lens and movement correction to obtain an image less distorted and almost perpendicular to the ground.

Camera and image processing onboard play an important role in the whole sensorial system since they are responsible for calculating drone speed. Taking images every 16 milliseconds Parrot software computes ground displacement and from it estimates drone speed. Despite having a battery similar to the ones used in Quanum Nova, flight times are almost doubled. Significant power losses caused by camera stabilisation drives (what happened in Quanum Nova) were eliminated and its light weight roughly contributes for a longer battery life.

III. RELATED WORK

Before the proliferation of drones, monitoring vehicles from aerial imagery was already possible, making use of pictures either taken from satellite or from manned aircraft. For this kind of images there are several approaches regarding CV algorithms to detect and extract cars position.

Jae-Young Choi and Young-Kyu Yang developed algorithms to detect vehicles in high altitude aerial images [4].

They started by finding small blobs which size should correspond to a car, using mean shift clustering algorithm. By choosing a radius interval, maximum and minimum car size, they could find regions of interest in the image.

After that, assuming the rectangular shape of the car, they evaluated the shape formed by the edges inside each blob.

Finally, merging blobs overlapped would eliminate vehicles counted more than once, happening when windshield and car color don not match.

Two images where this algorithm was applied are presented in Figure 8 alongside detection results.

Evaluation criteria	Left image	Right image
Number of detection	63	129
False alarms	5	11
False negative alarms	12	16
Detection rate (%)	84.0	88.9
Accuracy rate (%)	92.1	91.5

Figure 8. Choi Vehicle Detection Results [4].

Tuermer also published some work on algorithms for vehicle detection on aerial images obtained from regular piloted aircrafts [7]. Images are captured at a minimum altitude of 1000m with high resolution cameras. Still in the best cases each pixel represent a 15cm square on the ground.

Developed algorithm consisted of three main parts:

- Pre processing: Smoothing image and applying region growing technique on pixels with similar RGB values (color information). This separates interest zones to be further processed.
- Calculate histogram of Oriented Gradients (hOG) for each interest region created before.
- Decide if interest area is a vehicle using cascade classifiers.

After processing and evaluating some training image sets, algorithm was tested achieving about 80 percent of confidence on detected vehicles. In Figure 9 a sequence detection using Tuermer's solution is presented.

The two presented examples were chosen to illustrate some of the best techniques proposed for vehicle detection in high altitude images. Although there are several other approaches none of them are applicable to this project. No recent investigation in this area was found and all approaches assume high altitude images and ignore if the car is in a parking place or moving in the road.

In this paper the main objective is achieving fast image processing for low altitude images and aims to detect only parked vehicles, a new algorithm was written from scratch.

IV. Car Detection in Low Altitude Images

To evaluate parking lots capacity the first mandatory task is image acquisition. Assuming the drone is correctly positioned regarding the road, a frame should be captured and sent to the image processing unit. Once there, the image might need to be corrected in case of heavy distortion effects. After this, the algorithm should try to detect vehicles, compare them with others detected in previous images to check if they were already counted, and finally update the counter. This repetitive pipeline is presented in a circular graphic in Figure 10.

Vehicle detection is obviously a decisive part of software but a broad range of cars might appear in a parking lot. Features like color, size or shape may vary from one to another making it harder to create a global solution capable of detecting them all based only on these features. At the same time, it is necessary to ensure that detected objects are effectively vehicles, distinguishing them from similar objects that might appear.

Distinguishing pavement from other objects placed above the ground could be a possible solution. Even though, this sets up another challenge. Homogeneous gray concrete or tar might be easily discarded using a color filter threshold. Nevertheless, the same technique will not work in a park built in block pavement.

Taking into consideration all the challenges presented above, the global algorithm for car detection based on edge density analysis is divided into three main parts:

- Road Detection - Different types of pavement will look completely different from an aerial perspective, but it is crucial to detect the central road of the parking lot in order to determine the parking places which are distributed on the sides of the road.
- Select Zones where vehicles are expected to be parked - After having the road segmented, it is possible to estimate its width, comparing it to the parking places size, thus confining the searching window.
- Vehicle Detection- Analyse features like color and edge density on the regions of interest in order to detect if there are parked vehicles there.

Figure 9. Tuermer Vehicle Detection Results [7].

The most important modules of the proposed algorithm are represented in Figure 11.

V. PAVEMENT DETECTION

As stated before parking lots are built over different types of pavement which directly affects the chosen image process-

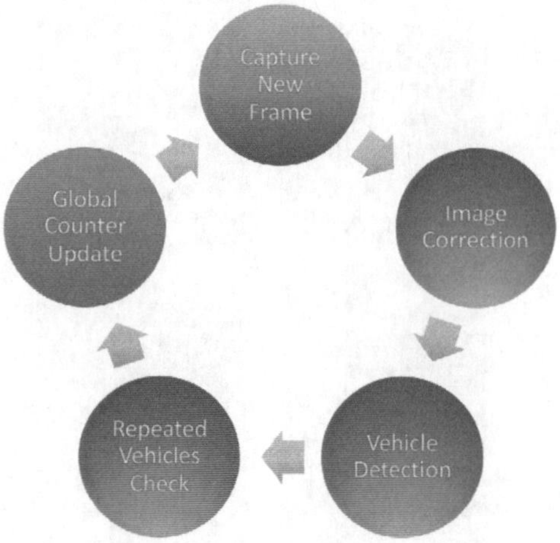

Figure 10. Global Solution Pipeline.

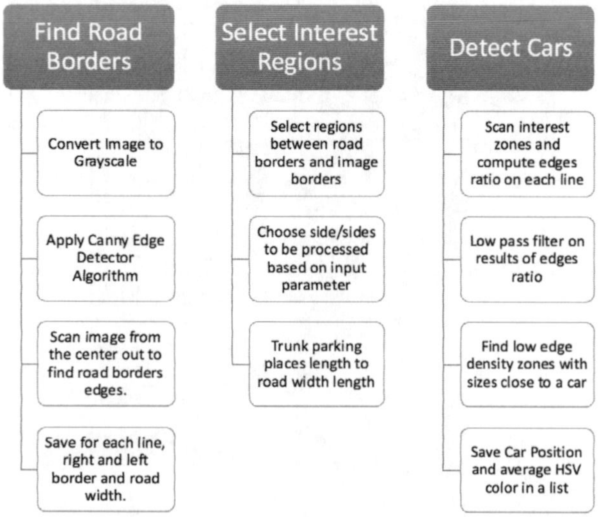

Figure 11. Main modules of the proposed Vehicle Detection Algorithm.

ing method. In order to turn the algorithm suitable for the three different types found in the University parking lots different approaches were used.

A. *Block Pavement Detection*

Canny Edge Detector algorithm [6] was used as a fast and optimized method to perform gradient computations and retrieve the most important edges for each acquired image. Figure 12 shows a fine mesh, which corresponds to the edges of each small block that composes the pavement. Cars, on the other hand, are found in zones of low edge concentration.

It would be possible to simply cluster regions with low edge density and compare their size to the expected car size (which estimation would depend on the altitude of the drone). Even though this would give space to detection errors, either by

Figure 12. At the top, an image of a Block Pavement Parking. On the bottom the corresponding gradient Image.

including more than one car in a single cluster or by analysing uninteresting zones in the surrounding areas. Some gardens or sidewalks, for instance, feature smooth surfaces making it harder to distinguish them from parked vehicles.

The solution was finding the road borders to further estimate parking places position. After applying a color filter and Hough lines detector to locate the grids along the road, it is possible to establish the interest regions, on the left, right, or both sides of the road (Figures 13 and 14).

Figure 13. On the left, the image acquired by the drone, on the right the road borders detected.

Figure 14. Road is removed as well as unwanted lateral zones. The length of the parking places is very close to access the width of the road, thus interest region is trunked as presented.

B. *Tar Pavement Detection*

Images obtained over tar pavement are smoother and lack of edges when compared to blocks pavement presented before. Despite that fact, it is still possible to reuse the logic from the last algorithm, detecting the road using the limit lines and trunking the interest regions.

Figure 15. On the left, the image acquired by the drone, on the right the road borders detected.

As tar is homogeneous either in texture as in colour, checking if a low edge density zone is free or occupied can be done using color matching, making sure it is different from the tar found in the road (Figure 16).

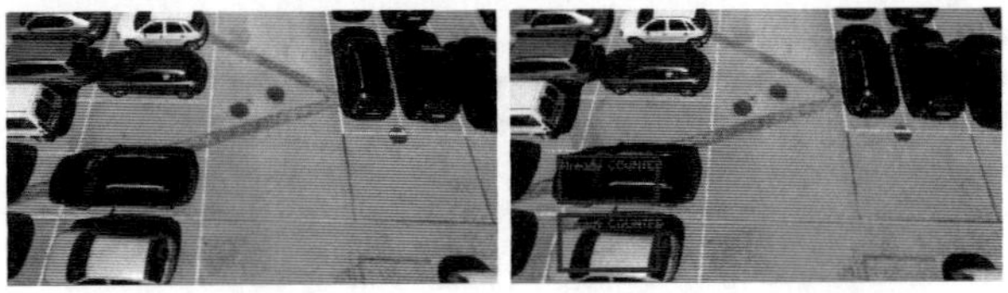

Figure 16. On the left, the image acquired by the drone, on the right the vehicle detection on tar parkings.

C. Mixed Pavement

Most of the studied parking lots are built on both tar (used in the access road) and blocks with different configurations (used in parking places). The algorithm developed for this type of pavement slightly differs from the others, given the impossibility of detecting road based on color filters.

In this case, road limits are determined using the same notion of edge density. Tar zones are not expected to have high gradient values thus road might be easily detected. Further vehicle detection is performed as explained for the block pavement, as well as vehicle repetition check (see Figures 17 and 18).

Figure 17. Road detection in mixed pavement parking lots. Raster scan window used to evaluate edge density is variable and affects processing times and road detection accuracy.

VI. VEHICLE DETECTION

Having the road segmented and a valid estimation of the regions corresponding to parking places, edge density analysis may now be performed for each one of these regions.

Figure 18. Vehicle detection in mixed pavement parking lots.

A. Edge Density Analysis

This analysis is done across the Y axis of the image (from the top to the bottom), evaluating the ratio of pixels which do not belong to edges. As vehicles often display some edges (dividing the doors from the roof for example) and considering them could be a reason for the algorithm to detect a division between two distinct cars. To eliminate this issue first step consisted in setting a minimum distance between cars, and the second step consists in reducing noise interference, visible in high frequency signal plotted. To achieve it a low pass filter is applied and the result is shown in Figure 4.21. Figure 19 was the picture used for the edge density analysis, where it is expected to find two significant low edge density peaks, corresponding to the cars on the right side of the image. Computed data is then plotted (Figure 20) and a lower pass filter is applied (Figure 21).

Figure 19. Sample image where edge density analysis is performed.

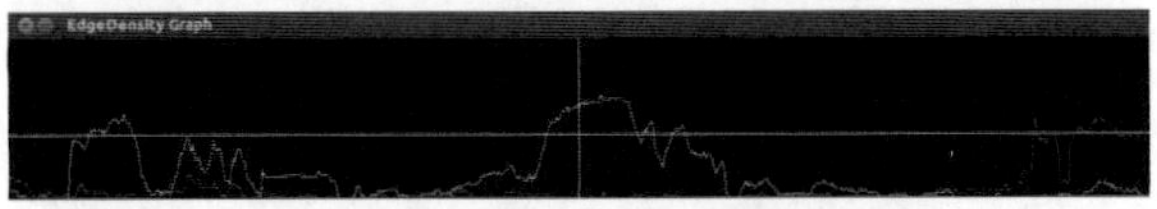

Figure 20. Green line peaks represent low edge concentration along the right region of interest, while red line represents the same analysis on the left side of the road.

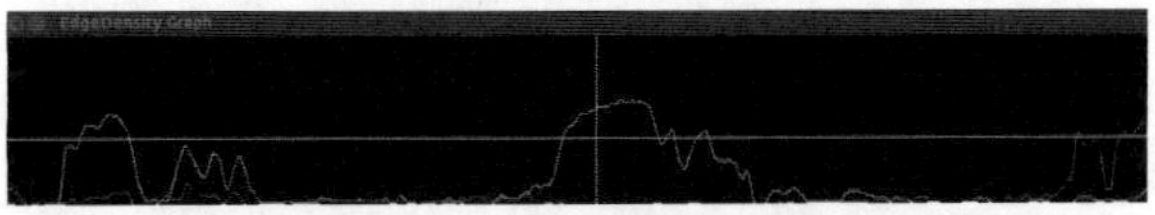

Figure 21. Edge density graph after application of a low pass filter. Noise reduction is noticeable.

The expected size of the vehicle is now compared with the size of detected stains according to their position on the image.

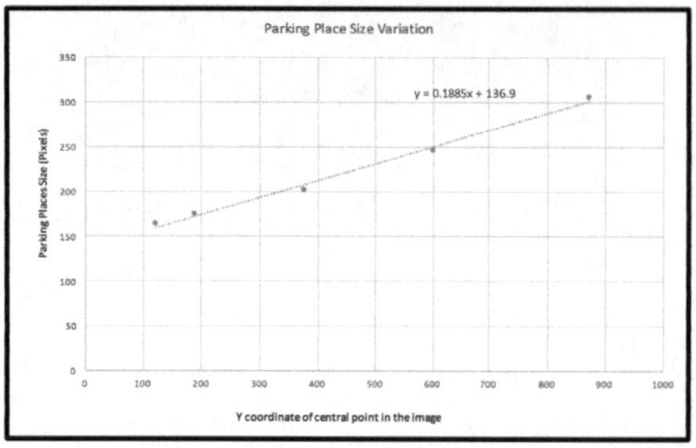

Figure 22. The area occupied by similar parked vehicles varies across the image with the distance from them to the camera.

Objects on the top (lower Y values) appear smaller due to the perspective introduced by the Drone used for image acquiring, still the vehicle size varies almost linearly. As the tilt angle of the camera is kept approximately constant throughout the flight, this linear variation is the same for all acquired images. This allows the computation of the expected vehicle size according to its location within the image. Even though, on the top of the image with such a small expected vehicle size, it might be difficult to distinguish and split two or more cars parked next to each other. To solve this issue the algorithm analyses only the lower half of the image where vehicle representation is more evident. In case of having a car right in the middle of the picture the algorithm keeps looking on the upper part of the image for the end of this low edge density region.

B. Repeated Vehicles Check

Despite the drone is moving with an almost constant speed, it is not possible to capture images without any overlay, meaning that the same vehicle might be present in more than one frame. To avoid double counting, it is required storing color, size and position features of vehicles detected in the last frame to compare them with the vehicles detected at the moment (Figure 23).

Figure 23. New and Repeated Vehicles Detected

VII. EXPERIMENTAL RESULTS

This section presents important values measured and analysed for the studied solutions. These are related to detection accuracy and processing times. Tests were applied on sample videos captured over different parking lots: two on tar pavement, two on block pavement and four on mixed pavement (block and tar).

All tests were performed using an Unix distribution (Ubuntu 14.04.3) installed on a computer with an Intel Core i5-3340M CPU @ 2.70GHz 4 processor with 4Gb RAM. Images captured were recorded as video and split into frames considering only one frame each half a second. A splitting tool was also developed to read each frame of the video and save images every 500 milliseconds in a specific directory previously defined.

Car detection accuracy is evaluated frame by frame comparing manual annotation of the number of cars depicted with detection boxes drawn by the algorithm.

It is crucial to choose a suitable edge detection method since these operations are performed every time a new image is processed. It is important to ensure some points regarding the chosen method:

- Detects low edge concentration over the road pavement (in case the road is made of tar)
- Creates high edge density zones over block pavement, contrasting with uniform surfaces on vehicles.
- Takes a short period of time to compute all the edges in an image.

Choosing the most suitable values enables accurate detection of homogeneous regions as shown in some examples presented in Figure 27.

It is now evident that Canny is an optimised edge detection method, possible to adapt to different situations by conveniently adjusting its parameters. It also features less processing requisites when compared to Sobel making it the best method and the one used for the rest of the algorithm tests.

Finding road limits composes a crucial step in the pipeline of the algorithm since this is performed in every park and is essencial to the location of interest zones. It is not relevant to have high accuracy in this procedure as the main goal is to eliminate the major region of the image representing road. It is not decisive to remove every single pixel from the road and preserve all other pixels, what is mandatory is the task to be quickly executed in every frame captured. Even though, road detection methods are distinct for different parking lots and different solutions should be developed for different pavement types.

On the other hand, vehicle detection based on low concentration of edges over the interest regions should be as accurate as possible and is applicable with only a few parameters adjustments to all studied parking lots. The following sections will detail results obtained for each type of parking lot studied.

Parking Lots in homogeneous kind of pavement are perhaps the most simple to deal with. Higher detection rates are then most likely to happen in P1 (Table I and Figure 25).

The block pavement revealed to be a difficult background to extract vehicles from. Despite edge density zones concept being easier to imagine in this situation, region segmentation

Figure 24. Sliding window influence on road detection.

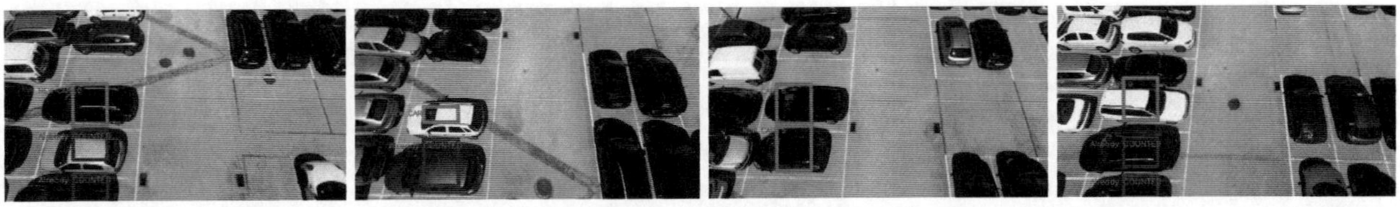

Figure 25. Cars detected on tar parking lot P1.

Figure 26. Cars detected on block pavement parking lot P5.

Figure 27. Two different edge detection algorithms tested with different parameters. From left to right, top to bottom: Canny Min=10, Max=50, Sobel X=1, Y=1, Canny Min=2, Max=200, Sobel X=2, Y=2.

TABLE I. RESULTS FOR TAR PARKING LOT.

Parking Lot	Parked Cars	Counted Cars	Repeated Counting	False Positives	Undetected Cars	Detection Rate
P1	17	17	0	0	0	100%

is not easy as there are some homogeneous surfaces in the parking lot borders.

The technique used to detect road borders in the parking lot P5 is based on the grids detection, as referred before. This is very tricky since there is no color differentiation between pavement and grids, all that changes is edges density. Hough Lines detector keeps being used to determine border lines and, as expected, it increases processing time. In Table II detection results are presented while some detection examples are presented in Figure 26.

TABLE II. RESULTS FOR BLOCK PARKING LOT.

Parking Lot	Parked Cars	Counted Cars	Repeated Counting	False Positives	Undetected Cars	Detection Rate
P5	61	61	2	0	2	97%
P5	78	78	1	1	2	97%

In the parking lots 2 and 3, the pavement is mixed. An homogeneous tar surface is found on the road, while the rest is made on block pavement.

Road detection is made based on a sliding window, which runs from the image center to its borders. This window might not move pixel by pixel, it may, for instance, jump 10 pixels every step saving some processing time. On its turn, window size might also be increased, loosing some definition on the road border found but improving the performance of the algorithm.

To evaluate this, several experiments were made in P2 in order to find a good relation between road borders detection accuracy and processing requisites as shown in Figure 24 and Table V.

Since the goal is the development of fully autonomous drones, we tested the developed algorithms on several single-boards (Raspberry Pi 2 Model B, IGEPv2 DM3730 and EPIA-P910) in order to decide what could be the best hardware solution, considering not only processing capacity but also properties like weight and power consumption . Eight random

TABLE III. DETAILED PROCESSING TIME FOR BLOCK PARKING LOT USING A RASPBERRY PI 2 MODEL B.

Frame	1	2	3	4	5	6	7	8
Open Time (RGB)	128	125	131	127	130	127	129	127
Gray	36	22	22	22	22	22	22	22
HSV	135	129	131	133	129	127	134	128
Find road	494	478	498	481	491	483	490	481
Car analysis	226	223	234	227	216	224	218	215
Cars found	1	1	2	2	1	1	1	1
Cars on image	1	1	2	2	1	1	1	1
%	100%	100%	100%	100%	100%	100%	100%	100%
TOTAL (ms)	1073	1030	1069	1042	1041	1035	1044	1025
				% AVG	100%			

TABLE IV. DETAILED PROCESSING TIME FOR MIXED PAVEMENT PARKING LOT USING A RASPBERRY PI 2 MODEL B.

Frame	1	2	3	4	5	6	7	8
Open Time (RGB)	141	144	142	146	140	144	137	145
Gray	36	22	23	23	22	22	22	22
HSV	138	128	130	127	128	130	128	129
Find road	431	430	422	428	421	427	422	420
Canny	284	278	272	281	284	280	277	271
Car analysis	226	225	223	218	222	225	245	237
Cars found	1	1	1	1	1	1	2	2
Cars on image	1	1	1	2	1	1	2	2
%	100%	100%	100%	50%	100%	100%	100%	100%
TOTAL (ms)	1309	1280	1265	1276	1269	1280	1284	1276
				% AVG	94%			

TABLE V. RESULTS FOR MIXED PARKING LOTS.

Parking Lot	Parked Cars	Counted Cars	Repeated Counting	False Positives	Undetected Cars	Detection Rate
P2	46	45	0	1	2	96%
P2	20	20	0	0	0	100%
P3	39	39	0	1	1	97%
P3	24	23	0	0	1	96%

images acquired were chosen and analysed on the singleboard. Processing times for each step of the algorithm detailed before are presented in Tables III and IV. The processing times obviously increase when running the developed algorithms on these single boards. However, we observe that it is possible to reduce the speed of the drone because the images acquired continuously have a considerable repetition of information. With this in mind, and evaluating the experimental results obtained, we consider that Raspberry Pi 2 reaches reasonable values for onboard processing.

VIII. CONCLUSION

The algorithms presented in this paper showed promising results for the detection of vehicles on low altitude images acquired by Drones, being a solution for parking lots management.

The developed algorithms fulfilled the low processing requirements, which enables the algorithms to process images every second and allows the drone to move at a reasonable speed; the accuracy associated to vehicle detection and counting is also high. Furthermore, results obtained for tests made in three different types of pavement indicated a versatile solution, adaptable to several contexts achieving good performances with slight parameter adjustments from park to park.

As future work, we are developing algorithms for boats detection on water and the preliminaries results were also satisfactory. We think this work can provide an interesting contribution to our future smart cities, as a starting point for monitoring of objects of interest using drones. Moreover, we are optimising the presented algorithms to be used onboard of the drone in order to have a fully autonomous solution.

REFERENCES

[1] A. J. R. Neves, M. Camarneiro and L. Cozinheiro. "Vehicle Detection on Low Altitude Images Based on Edge Density," Proc. of the Second International Conference on Advances in Signal, Image and Video Processing, SIGNAL 2017, pp. 3337.

[2] www.parrot.com/us/Drones/Parrot-Bebop-2, Bebop 2 drone, retrieved April, 2017.

[3] www.amazon.com/b?node=8037720011, Amazon prime air, retrieved April, 2017.

[4] J.-Y Choi and Y.-K. Yang, "Vehicle detection in aerial images," Technical report, College of IT, Kyungwon University, 2009.

[5] dailytech.com, Flying rescue drone prototype to provide lifesaving aid to swimmers, retrieved April, 2017.

[6] R. Maini and H. Aggrwal, "Study and comparison of various image edge detection techniques," Technical report, Punjabi University, India, 2009.

[7] S. Tuermer, J. Leitloff, P. Reinartz and U. Stilla, "Automatic vehicle detection in aerial image sequences of urban areas using 3D HOG features," Technical report, Technische Universitaet Muenchen, German Aerospace Center, 2010.

Algorithms for Face Detection on Infrared Thermal Images

Ricardo Ribeiro
DETI/IEETA
University of Aveiro
3810-193 Aveiro, Portugal
Email: rfribeiro@ua.pt

António J. R. Neves
DETI/IEETA
University of Aveiro
3810-193 Aveiro, Portugal
Email: an@ua.pt

Abstract*—Face detection on digital images is an area with immense practical potential which includes a wide range of commercial and research applications, and it continues to be one of the most active research areas on computer vision. Even after several decades of intense research, the state-of-the-art in this topic continues to improve, benefiting from advances in a wide range of different fields. In an attempt to overcome some of the limitations in face detection using visible light, the use of thermal imaging has emerged as a particularly promising research direction. This is possible because nowadays the infrared sensors have reached a new technological level. In this work we propose several methods for face detection on infrared thermal images. The well known algorithm developed by Paul Viola and Michael Jones, using Haar feature-based cascade classifiers, is used to compare the traditional algorithms developed for visible light images when applied to thermal imaging. Moreover, we present three algorithms for face detection, using image segmentation a pre-processing step to obtain a binary image. Our first approach is based on the use of an edge detection algorithm applied to the binary image. The face detection is based on the analysis of the obtained contours. As a second approach, the use of a template matching method searches and try to find the best location of a template image with the shape of human head in the binary image. In a third approach, a matching algorithm is used. This algorithm correlates a template with the distance transform of the edge image. This algorithm incorporates edge orientation information resulting in the reduction of false detection and the cost variation is limited. We performed tests taking into consideration different environments. Two of them were events at the University of Aveiro with the objective to simulate real environments, were several images were recorded while people were looking to posters. Some other laboratory tests were performed with image captured processed in real time. The results show that the proposed methods have promising outcome, but the second method is the most suitable for the performed experiments.

Keywords–Face detection; Infrared images; Image processing; Robotics; Object detection.

I. Introduction

This manuscript is an extended version of the original paper presented at the Second International Conference on Advances in Signal, Image and Video Processing, SIGNAL 2017 [1]. This extended version provides a deep overview on thermal cameras, includes more detailed information about the proposed algorithms for face detection on thermal images and more experimental results using these algorithms. As far as we know, there is limited research on this topic so we believe this work is an important contribution to the field.

In this work, we propose algorithms for face detection using thermal infrared cameras. The main goals of this work are the use of these type of sensors in service robots and in monitoring people attention, taking into consideration of the temperature of the face over time. We are also working on emotional analysis through thermal images.

Infrared thermal cameras, also called thermographic cameras or simply thermal cameras, are used to capture radiation from the electromagnetic spectrum that the human eyes cannot see. This radiation called by infrared radiation was discovered in 1800, by William Herschel (1738-1822) [2].

Since infrared radiation was discovered, the infrared technology is in constant development. This radiation has been used in many applications in different scientific areas, for example medicine, astronomy, military, computer vision, among others. The development of the first infrared cameras began with an infrared line scanner. These line scanners were built for military requirements in the late 1940s. In the early 1950s, infrared thermal viewers took one hour to produce a single image [3].

The infrared radiation is captured by the sensor and converted to a thermal image. Figure 1 shows an thermal image complemented with an image in the visual spectrum from the same scene (typically a Red, Green and Blue - RGB - image).

(a) Thermal image (b) RGB image

Figure 1. An example of a thermal image and the same scene acquired by a RGB camera.

Thermal cameras are becoming a common tool for a wide range of science applications. A survey providing an overview of the current applications is presented in [4]. These applications began in the military field but were increasingly expanded into other fields due to the lower cost, resolution and quality increase of the image, being more accessible for academic applications, industrial, research, agricultural, security, personal use, among others applications. In robotics, for computer vision, thermal image analysis and processing is in constant development, being used more often in systems for detection, recognition and tracking of objects, humans, among others.

This paper is organized as follows. An introductory section that provides a brief introduction to the paper and presents the objective. In Section II, we provide concepts and a literature review of relevant content of this work. Infrared thermal radiation is discussed, as well as the nature of infrared thermal cameras. Also in this section, we describe some related work. In Section III, we present in detail the proposed algorithms for face detection on infrared thermal images. In Section IV, we provide experimental results of the tests performed in different environments, conditions and scenes. Finally, a summary of work done, comparison of the algorithms, concluding remarks and our future work are made in Section V.

II. Thermal Images

The infrared radiation is often referred as thermal radiation, due to all objects with a temperature above absolute zero emit infrared radiation [4]. In the electromagnetic spectrum, the infrared spectral region is located from the wavelengths of 0.7 to 1000 micrometers (μm), as can be seen in Figure 2.

The infrared band lies below of the red light of the visible spectrum. This wavelength band is often subdivided into different spectral regions depending on the characteristics of this radiation in each region. Figure 2 also shows this different regions that are [5][6]:

- **Near-infrared (NIR, wavelength 0.7-1.4 μm)** - Used in fiber optic telecommunications and night vision devices.
- **Short-wavelength infrared (SWIR, wavelength 1.4-3 μm)** - Used in long distance telecommunications.
- **Mid-wavelength infrared (MWIR, wavelength 3-8 μm)** - Used in military application like guided missile technology. Sometimes called thermal infrared.
- **Long-wavelength infrared (LWIR, wavelength 8-15 μm)** - Used in thermal imaging that uses sensors to obtain images of objects. It is based on thermal emissions. This subdivision is also called the thermal infrared.
- **Far-infrared (FIR, wavelength 15-1000 μm)** - Used in military and astronomy applications.

For infrared or thermal imaging not all subdivisions of the infrared spectrum are used, only a small part called thermal infrared. Figure 3 shows an expanded view of this small region.

According to [7], commercial cameras are available for three spectral ranges that are defined for thermography. These three ranges are: the long-wave (LW) region between 7 to 14 μm, the mid-wave (MW) region between 3 to 5 μm and short-wave (SW) region between 0.9 to 1.7 μm. The reason of the restriction to these wavelengths are the physics of detectors, the transmission properties of the atmosphere and considerations of the amount of thermal radiation to be expected. The thermal motion of charged particles in matter generate the thermal radiation.

As previously stated, every object that has a temperature above of 0 K (-273.15 °C) emits thermal radiation in a different wavelength depending on the temperature and material properties. A blackbody is a perfect emitter of thermal radiation. As definition "a blackbody allows all incident radiation to pass into it (no reflected energy) and internally absorbs all the incident radiation (no energy transmitted through the body). This is true for radiation of all wavelengths and for all angles of incidence. Hence the blackbody is a perfect absorber for all incident radiation" [8].

Planck's law in general says that every physical body emits electromagnetic radiation. Due to its dependence on temperature, Planck radiation is considered thermal radiation. Figure 4 shows the spectral nature of Planck's law, where the emissive power of a blackbody at several temperatures is related with the wavelength.

The concept of emissivity is important to understand the thermal radiation emissions of a physical body. In a simple way, two objects with different emissivities at the same physical temperature will not have the same temperature in a thermal image. The emissivity also depends on the temperature of the surface as well as wavelength and angle. Kirchhoff's law states that the emissivity of a ideal blackbody is 1, this means that a blackbody absorbs all the radiation.

Figure 5 shows a thermal image with a Leslie's cube and the respective visible spectrum image in grayscale. All faces of the cube are at the same temperature. In grayscale image the face that has been painted black has more emissivity than the polished face. So the polished face of the cube emits less thermal radiation than the black face and reflects the radiation emitted by the hand. The polished faces are composed of shiny metal, such as aluminium, that are metals with low emissivity. The emissivity of the polished face of the images of the left is higher than the polished face of the right images and the white painted surface is nearly as emissive as a black surface.

Leslie's cube is used to demonstrate and measure the variations in emissivities for different materials.

The transmission of radiation in the atmosphere is not the same in all wavelengths due to the existence of several gases that absorb some radiation. Molecules of the atmosphere, as CO_2 and H_2O, are able to absorb infrared radiation. This radiation is not transmitted in some wavelength around 2.7 μm (H_2O and CO_2), around 4.2 μm (CO_2), between 5.5 and 7 μm (H_2O) and above 14 μm (H_2O, CO_2). This absorption defines the wavelength that the thermal cameras are sensitive. Figure 6 illustrates this absorption over these wavelengths and demonstrates that CO_2 and H_2O dominate attenuation of the infrared radiation.

Michael Vollmer and Klaus-Peter Mollmann have a book "Infrared Thermal Imaging: Fundamentals, Research and Applications" [7] that explains, among of others, physical principles and laws for infrared or thermal radiation.

A. Infrared Thermal Cameras

Nowadays, infrared cameras are scanning devices that capture one point or one row of an image at a time, or use a staring array. This array uses a two-dimensional focal plane array (FPA) where all image elements are captured at the same time with each detector element in the array [4]. The FPA techonology is the most used in infrared detectors. Infrared cameras also include optical lens, electronic circuits, possibly a cooler for the detector or a shutter and software for processing and displaying images to store and transmit captured data in addition to the FPA detector. A simple diagram of an infrared camera is represented in Figure 7.

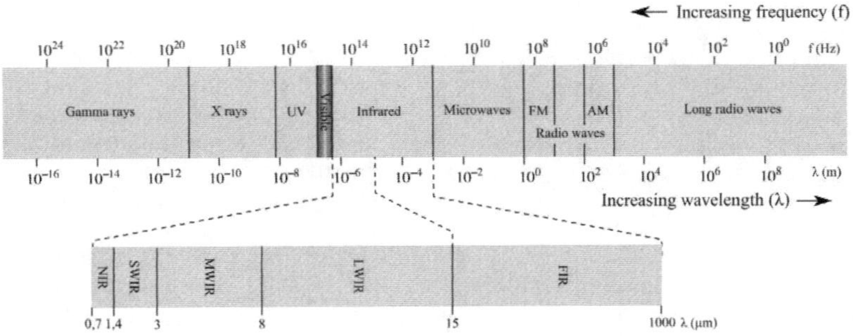

Figure 2. Electromagnetic spectrum with different divisions of infrared spectrum [4].

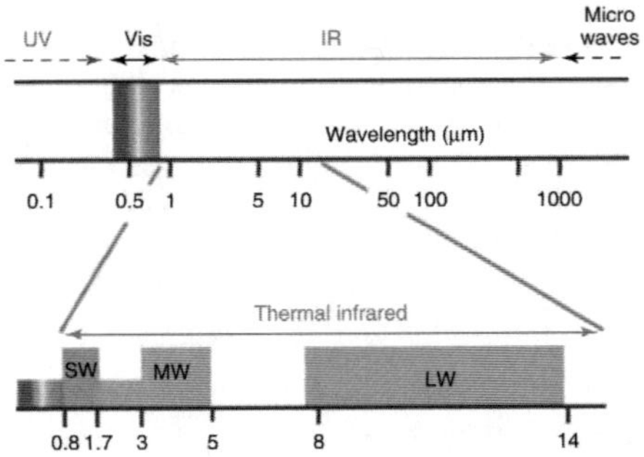

Figure 3. Infrared and adjacent spectral regions with expanded view of thermal infrared region [7].

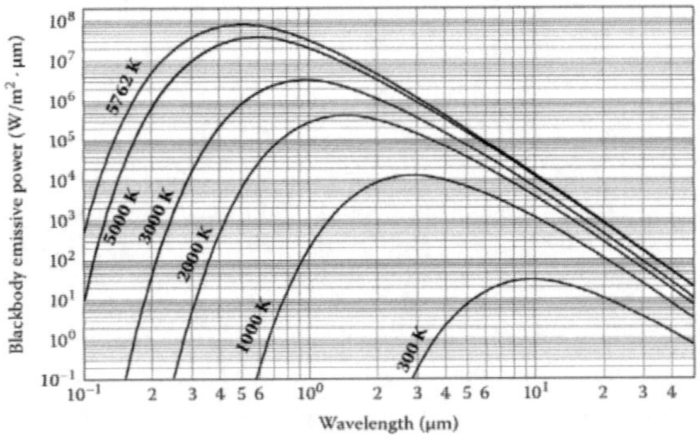

Figure 4. Emissive power of a blackbody according to wavelength at several temperatures [8].

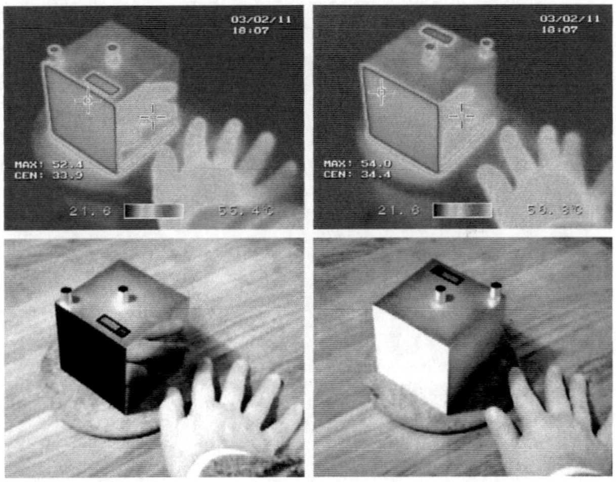

Figure 5. Leslei's cube with four faces at the same temperature represented in thermal and grayscale image [9].

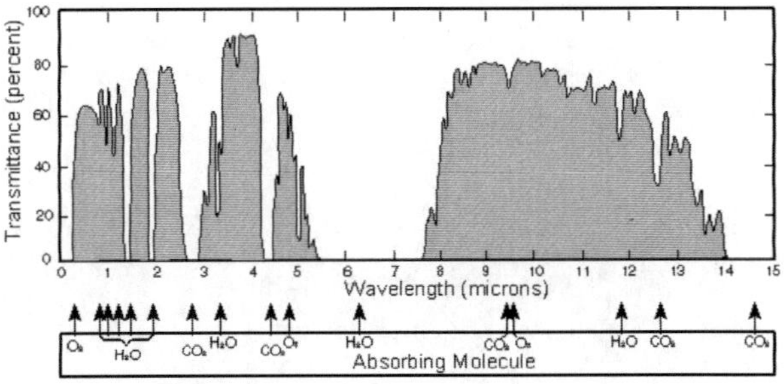

Figure 6. Atmospheric transmission in different infrared wavelengths [10].

Thermal cameras are generally divided into two types: cooled or uncooled. Cooled infrared detectors normally operate in a wavelength of 2 to 5.6 μm range that corresponds to the SWIR and MWIR band [11]. These detectors are called photon detectors or quantum detectors and convert the absorbed infrared radiation directly into a change of the electronic energy distribution in a semiconductor by changing the free charge carrier concentration [4]. Cooled thermal cameras have typical operating temperature of around 77 kelvins (K). Detectors without cooling are not sensitive to the infrared radiation, being flooded or blinded by their own radiation [11]. A camera with these type of detectors has a high sensitivity and can deliver hundreds of high-definition (HD) resolution frames per second.

Uncooled cameras are usually composed of thermal detectors. Thermal detectors convert the absorbed infrared radiation into thermal energy causing a rise in the detector tempera-

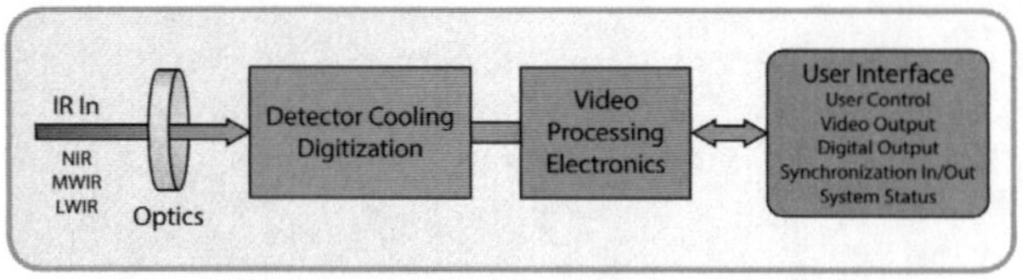

Figure 7. Simplified block diagram of an infrared camera [11].

ture. Most infrared cameras of this type have microbolometer detectors. Microbolometer FPAs are thermal sensors and can be created from metal or semiconductor material. Figure 8 shows the basic anatomy of a typical microbolometer pixel. Uncooled infrared detectors operate in a wavelength of 8 to 14 μm range, the LWIR band. These detectors have lower sensitivity and slower response time than cooled detectors but in compensation they are smaller, silent and low cost. In this work, the infrared thermal camera used is uncooled and uses microbolometers that are the most used in commercial infrared cameras [12].

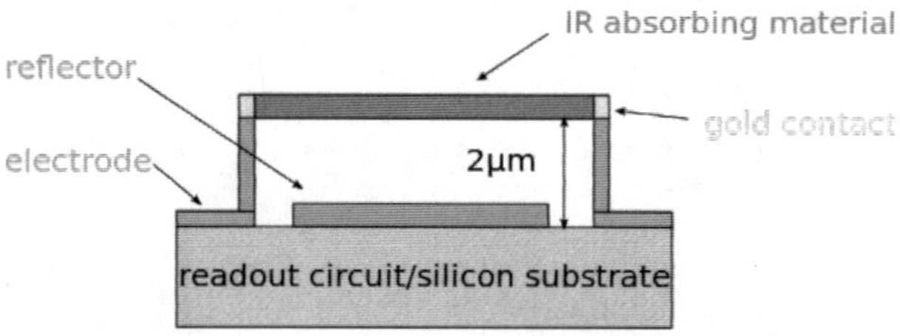

Figure 8. Cross-sectional view of a microbolometer [13].

The output data of a thermal camera is typically an image in grayscale with depth form 8 to 16 bit per pixel. Radiometric cameras usually provide output data in a raw 16-bit intensity value. These cameras are considered calibrated if they can measure temperatures through the output data. Some cameras also have a mode to visualize the output data in pseudo colors, 24 bit per pixel, due to the details of an image being more perceptible by the human eye to color images than grayscale images. Figure 9 shows an image captured by an infrared thermal camera using different colorizations.

(a) Gray *(b) Iron* *(c) Rainbow*

Figure 9. Thermal images in grayscale(a) and pseudo color (b)(c) [14].

B. Related Works

In color or RGB cameras, the colors and visibility of the scene depend on an energy source, such as the sun or artificial light. The captured RGB images depend on the illumination, with changing intensity, color balance, direction and among others, which sometimes affects image processing in some applications. Furthermore, nothing can be captured in total darkness.

Thermal cameras are advantageous in many applications due to their ability to capture invisible radiation seeing in total darkness, their robustness to illumination changes and shadow effects, and less intrusion on privacy [15]. Thereby they do not depend on any external energy source. The human body emits infrared radiation in the form of heat and its temperature tends to remain constant. Generally, the part of the human body, which is not covered, is the face and it stands out from the background. These cameras, when calibrated, are advantageous in temperature measurement compared to point-based methods since temperatures over a large area can be compared, although contact methods are more efficient [14]. In this work, the thermal camera used is not calibrated, so it is not possible to know the exact temperature in the region of interest.

Some algorithms for face detection using color or grayscale images currently have a very high efficiency rate but it is not possible to use them directly in the thermal images. Using these algorithms may result in some problems regarding thermal imaging, that can reduce this efficiency significantly, such as occlusion of the face with objects that emit infrared radiation, the uniform temperature in the face, objects with the shape and same temperature of the face, the face away from the camera, among others. For this reason, only one feature-based algorithm is used, Haar Cascade [16]. The Opencv library provides utilities and functions to use the Haar Cascade algorithm and training cascade classifiers to use in thermal imaging for face detection. This algorithm has an efficient feature selection, a scale and location invariant detector [16]. The face detection in this work is represented on a shape of a bounding box obtaining not only the face, but also some background noise that can affect the detected face for future work.

Comparing with visible light cameras, thermal cameras have a considerable higher cost. For example, a thermal camera with low resolution 80×60, such as the camera used in this work, costs hundreds of euros and increasing the resolution comes with a higher prices of many thousands of euros. These cameras need more training than visual cameras for correct usage. The emissivity and reflectivity of different materials and the impact of the atmosphere affects the captured thermal image. In order to provide accurate measurements of temperature, these cameras need to be calibrated according to the physical principles, which is a complex process.

The face is one of the zones of the human body that is more suitable for the body temperature extraction and posteriorly the emotion analysis. The face detection in this work is represented on a shape of a bounding box obtaining the face and also some surrounding background noise that can affect the detected face for the next modules. The temperature measurement and emotional analysis of the face is being developed, not being included in this current work.

III. Proposed Approach

In this section, different algorithms and methods for face detection are described. The goal is to implement the algorithms on a real-time application. Therefore, these algorithms will be tested on a real-time system. The development of this work is made in C++ programming language, through the

OpenCV library, which is an open source computer vision and machine learning software library.

The resources used for the acquisition of the thermal image and the way of how the image is generated are also described in this section. Figure 10 shows a block diagram with the process from the incidence of infrared radiation on the thermal camera to the detection represented in the image to be displayed, using the proposed algorithms. The first two blocks are part of the integrated camera module. In order to receive the data, the Serial Peripheral Interface (SPI) port of Raspberry Pi is configured. The large block encompasses all the steps for data processing, obtaining the thermal image. This image is processed by the proposed algorithms and it is displayed with face detection in shape of a rectangle. In the next section, each block of the diagram is described in detail.

A. Image Acquisition

The acquisition of the thermal image is made in real-time. This image acquisition process is based on a developing project by the company Pure Engineering [17]. A FLIR LEPTON Long Wave Infrared (50 shutterless) camera module is used, with a focal plane array of 80×60 active pixels [18]. This camera is a non-radiometric version. This camera is also not calibrated, therefore it is not possible to obtain temperature values of each pixel. The output value also changes with the temperature value of the infrared sensor of the camera and the temperature of the scene. It is also used a Raspberry Pi 3 model B for communication, such as SPI communication, and image processing. This camera also supports a command and control interface (CCI) hosted on a Two-Wire Interface (TWI) similar to Inter-Integrated Circuit (I2C) for software interface [18].

The incident infrared radiation passes through the lens assembly and it is focused from the scene onto an 80×60 array of thermal detectors (microbolometers), which integrate the complete FPA. The serial stream from the FPA is received by a system on a chip (SoC) device, which provides signal processing and output formatting. The data is sent via the Lepton Video over Serial Peripheral Interface (VoSPI) protocol to the Raspberry Pi. When the camera is turned on, the SPI port of the Raspberry Pi must be opened for communication, in order to receive the data sent by the camera. It is needed to set the SPI mode, the bit per word and the SPI bus speed, so that there is no communication failure and data is received correctly through the SPI port selected.

Through the VoSPI, the output data are received in an 14-bits data. To be able to display a visible thermal image, this data is converted into an image matrix arranged in an 8-bits data with one channel provided by OpenCV. In the 14-bits data, each pixel can assume a wide range of values and this range corresponds to temperature values between -10 °C to +65 °C. As in this case it is only important the temperature of the scene captured by the camera, the data received has to be filtered.

The process of converting the 14-bits data into 8-bits data starts with the conditioning of the data, searching for the maximum and minimum values of the frame pixels received. Generally, in an 8-bits image with one channel the pixel values are between 0 and 255. In this image, the minimum value corresponds to 0 and the maximum value to 255. The columns and rows of each pixel are calculated and it is created the visible thermal image. The first image of Figure 1 shows a thermal image obtained. Darker areas correspond to colder regions in the scene. This thermal image is the input image for the proposed algorithms.

B. Haar Cascades

Haar Cascades is a machine learning approach, using Viola and Jones algorithm [16], for visual object detection where a cascade function is trained from positive images (images of faces) and negative images (images without faces). The performance of the trained classifier will be better, as more images are used.

Haar Cascades is one of the algorithms implemented by OpenCV library. This algorithm was studied by Mekyska et al. [19] showing a machine learning approach for face detection and it requires a high number of images of the object to be detected for the cascade training. A similar study was made in this work, but the results of the face detection are considered of low accuracy in a first stage, as it can be seen in [1]. In this paper, these results were improved by training a new cascade classifier, using face annotations. The thermal images with faces that were used for the cascade training can be obtained on the online dataset [20]. The results of the cascade training for Haar Cascade are shown in the results section.

C. Implementation Details

As far as we know, face detection on thermal images did not received too much attention on computer vision as the counterpart on visible light images. There are some possible ways of using some functionalities of the OpenCV library.

Figure 11 shows an approach for thermal image pre-processing before the different face detection algorithms is applied. Thermal image is, on a first stage, segmented and filtered with morphological operators in order to obtain a binary image for the later use of the three algorithms proposed for face detection using thermal image segmentation. The algorithms Template Matching and Chamfer Matching use, in addition to the binary image, a template for recognizing this pattern in the thermal image.

Segmentation uses the Otsus method that is a thresholding binarization method [21] and filtering is performed using morphological operators, such as dilation, erosion, opening and closing [22]. In this work, the following algorithms are developed/adapted and implemented:

- **Face Contours** - Acquisition and filtering of the contours in order to obtain the longest contour in the binary image and detect the face through it [23].
- **Template Matching** - Technique for finding areas of an image that match to a template image [24].
- **Chamfer Matching** - Technique to find the best alignment between two edge maps [25].

1) Segmentation and Filtering: The thermal image obtained goes through a pre-processing in order to create a binary image. Before being segmented, the thermal image is processed using Gaussian blur [26] to reduce image noise and smooth the image. Then Otsus method is used. Otsus method is a parameterless global thresholding binarization method [21]. This method involves iterating through all the possible threshold values, assuming that the image contains two classes

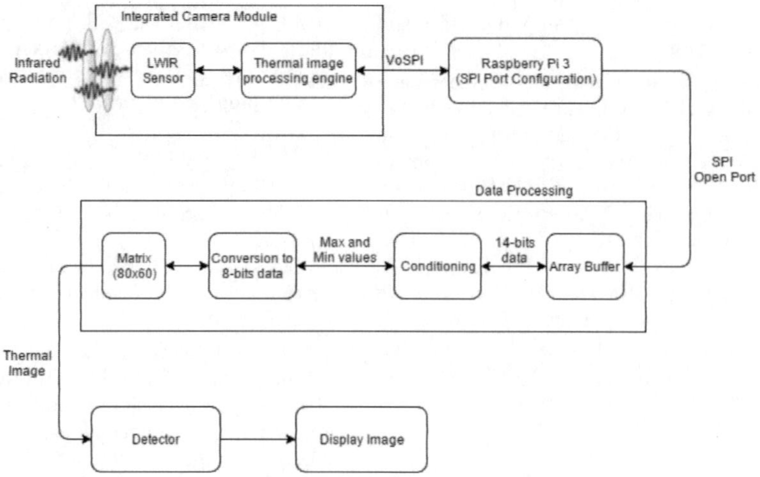

Figure 10. Processing of the infrared radiation emitted by the scene until the image is displayed.

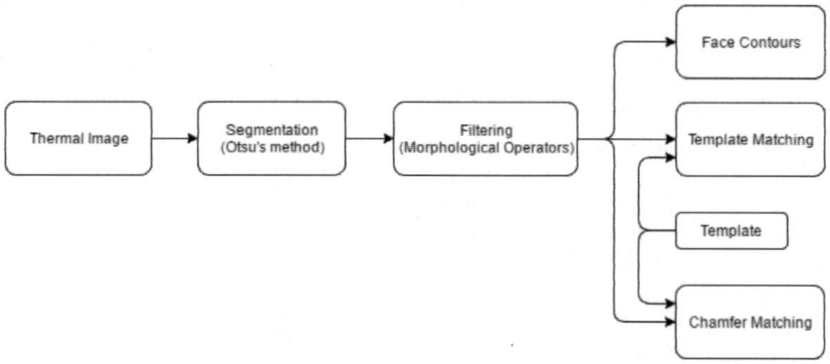

Figure 11. Thermal image processing approach to be used by the algorithms.

of pixels following bi-modal histogram (foreground pixels and background pixels) and calculating the optimum threshold separating the two classes, i.e., the pixels that either fall in foreground or background. The aim is to find the threshold value where the sum of foreground and background spreads is at its minimum [27].

The binary image generated using this method may still contain small black parts that are not relevant for face detection using the proposed algorithms. So this image is filtered with morphological operators in order to remove this noise. The word morphology concerns shapes: in mathematical morphology we process images according to shape, by treating both as sets of points. In this way, morphological operators define local transformations that change pixel values that are represented as sets. The ways in which pixel values are changed is formalized by the definition of the hit or miss transformation [26]. The two basic morphological operators are Erosion and Dilation. The variant forms are Opening and Closing. In this paper, these transformations are used in order to obtain a clean and uniform binary image.

2) Face Contours: Through the binary image an edges map is created, using the Canny edge detector algorithm [28], where the contours are found [23]. The Canny algorithm is one of the most popular edge detection technique that obtains structural information from the image and reduces the data to be processed. Among the edge detection techniques, Canny edges detection algorithm performs better under different scenarios and under noisy conditions [29].

The edges image does not contain any information about the edges as entities in themselves. The next step is to assemble the edge pixels into contours [30]. These contours are filtered in order to obtain just the contour of the larger area. Due to the contour of having some parts of the human body that are not relevant for face detection, for example neck and shoulders, the highest point of the contour is found. This point matches to the highest point on the face. Starting at this point, the two points that correspond to the largest width of the face are found. The detection of the face is made with this two points and the highest point in the face contour.

3) Template Matching: Template Matching is one of many techniques that uses a template to search and find the best match of this template, in an image. This is usually made by "sliding" a template with a similar pattern to the one or more that it is trying to find, across the image in horizontal scan and at each pixel, it calculates the distance between the template and the region of interest.

There are different matching methods to perform the template matching technique. The method Normalized Cross-

Correlation (NCC) is used, which according to [24] remains a viable choice for some if not all applications. According to [31], considering the image f with size M_x x M_y at the point (x, y), the intensity value of the image f is $f(x, y)$. The template t has a size of N_x x N_y. A common way to calculate the position (u_{pos}, v_{pos}) of the template t in the image f is to evaluate the NCC value γ at each point (u, v), which has been shifted by u steps in the x direction and by v steps in the y direction. The following equation gives a basic definition for the NCC [31]:

$$\gamma = \frac{\sum_{x,y}\left(f(x,y) - \overline{f}_{u,v}\right)\left(t(x-u, y-u) - \overline{t}\right)}{\sqrt{\sum_{x,y}\left(f(x,y) - \overline{f}_{u,v}\right)^2 \sum_{x,y}\left(t(x-u, y-u) - \overline{t}\right)^2}} \quad (1)$$

Where $\overline{f}_{u,v}$ is the mean value of $f(x, y)$ within the area of the template t shifted to (u, v). With similar notation $\overline{t}$ is the mean value of the template. Due to this normalization, $\gamma(x, y)$ is independent to changes in brightness or contrast of the image, which are related to the mean value and the standard deviation. In template matching, the position of the template in an image is determined by searching the maximum of $\gamma(x, y)$ [31].

Authors of [32] use an Image Pyramid to perform the template matching for objects with different sizes. In this work image pyramid is used to detect faces of different scales increasing the performance of the template matching. Due to the image captured by the camera being small in resolution, the pyramid image is created from a template with approximately the size of the image. Each level of the pyramid is generated downsizing the original template. Figure 12 shows the original template, that will be used, in the first image followed by images of some levels of the pyramid created. A good template is needed to obtain better results in the template matching.

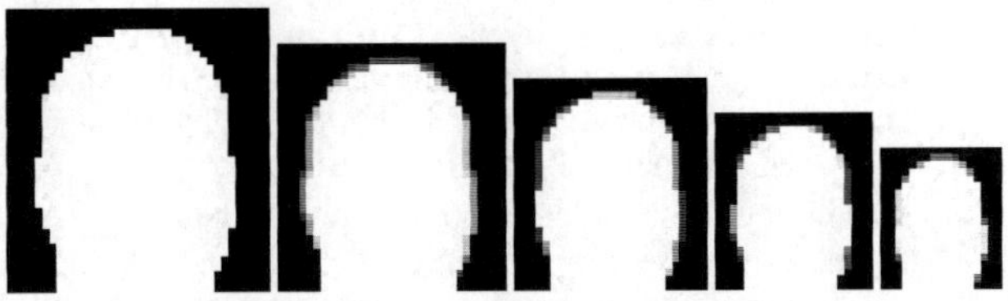

Figure 12. Example of the template in different scales.

4) Chamfer Matching: The Chamfer Matching algorithm lies in shape matching using the edges maps and the respective Distance Transform [33] of a query image and a template image. The edges maps are created using the Canny edge detector algorithm [28] for simplicity and accuracy.

According to [25], the edge map of the query image is considered as $U = u_i$ and the edge map of the template as $V = v_j$, where u_i and v_j are the points of the edges of the image and the template, respectively. The distance transform is applied, creating an image where each pixel value denotes the distance to the nearest point of U. The Distance Transform algorithm computes an approximation of the Euclidean distance.

To increase the efficiency, the matching cost can be computed via a distance transform image $DT_V(x) = min_{v_j \in V} \mid x - v_j \mid$, which specifies the distance from each pixel to the nearest edge pixel in V. The chamfer distance $d_{CM}(U, V)$ is determined by the average of distances between each point $u_i \in U$, and its nearest edge in V, as in the following equation

$$d_{CM}(U, V) = \frac{1}{n} \sum_{u_i \in U} DT_V(u_i) \quad (2)$$

where $n = \mid U \mid$.

In [25], to improve robustness, several variants of chamfer matching have been introduced by incorporating edge orientation information into the matching cost. The better match between image and template is the location of the minimal chamfer distance. In this case, the used template is considered to be matched at locations where the chamfer distance is below a defined threshold. To improve the detection for faces with different sizes, not only one template is used. The original template is resized in different scales, as shown in Figure 12.

IV. Experimental Results

The infrared thermal camera used, presented in Figure 13, is a long-wavelength infrared (LWIR) camera module. This camera is connected to a Raspberry Pi 3 single board to be used as processing device.

Figure 13. FLIR Lepton thermal camera module with breakout board [1].

In this section, the experimental results to verify the effectiveness of the implemented algorithms are present. In order to compare and analyze results, the variables precision and recall are calculated for an understanding and measure of relevance [34]. Figure 14 represents how to the calculation of precision and recall are made.

Using the Haar Cascades algorithm, tests were performed using captured images at the University of Aveiro event, "Teaching Day". The other algorithms were tested using images from another event organized by the Department of Electronics, Telecommunications and Informatics (DETI) of the University of Aveiro, called "Students & Teachers @deti 2017". Since the goal is the real time use, the proposed algorithms were tested under controlled conditions over time. The thermal images obtained in 8-bit grayscale in the image acquisition process were used as input and subsequently processed in each proposed algorithm. Examples of this type of images is represented in Figure 15.

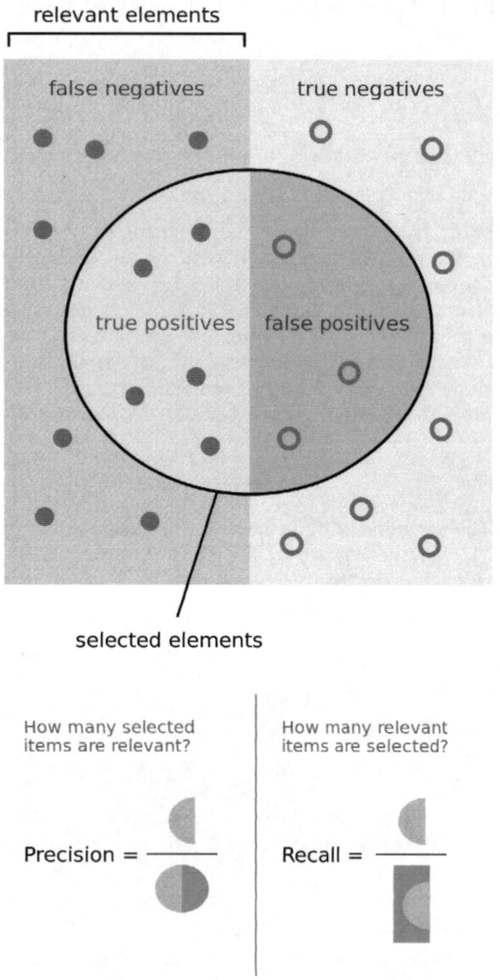

Figure 14. Precision and Recall [35].

Figure 15. Examples of images captured in Teaching Day.

A. Haar Cascades

In this work, the well-known traditional Viola-Jones algorithm for images of the visible spectrum was tested in thermal images using the same cascade classifiers for frontal face detection used for color images in order to show that this algorithm needs a well-trained classifier for the desired situation. Although it is intended to detect faces in both images, the image type is a very important factor to be considered. In visible images, the image is created based on the intensity of the primary colors, such as Red, Blue and Green, and the set of these colors generate a RGB image. In the case of the thermal image, the image is generated based on the emitted infrared radiation in the form of heat.

In [1] the Haar Cascade algorithm was used for a simple test. Figure 16 shows the preliminary example of face detection using HaarCascade. In this work, new tests were performed using the classifier use in [1] and improving this classifier in order to obtain better results.

Figure 16. Face detected using Haar Cascades [1].

1) Teaching Day: At the University of Aveiro, there are initiatives that have been carried out in the last years, of critical and shared debate around teaching and learning, such as Teaching Day. In the course of this work, it was carried out the 5th edition of the Teaching Day with the theme "Technology at the service of learning: opportunities and constraints".

In the Teaching Day, students and teachers share practices and experiences of using technologies in the classroom and beyond, reflecting together the multiple ways in which technology contributes to new ways of being, teaching and learning, as well as of communicating and experiencing.

During the presentation of posters, the thermal camera used in this work was capturing frames of people who stopped to read the posters. Thousands of images were captured during this day. These images were chosen in order to reduce the number of data to be analyzed, this is, some repeated images without people for face detection were eliminated. The total of images that were used in the tests were 8130 images. Figure 15 shows some examples of images captured during the Teaching Day. In all these images there are as many faces as images. Since the camera captures low resolution images, some of these faces appear as a few pixels less than 20×20. The classifiers provided by Opencv library were trained for an input pattern size of 20×20 or 24×24 in [36]. There are more or less 1602 frontal faces that can be detected. The faces were counted manually, seeing each frame of these images. Only faces that have a dimension of approximately equal to or greater than 20×20 pixels have been counted, because the classifiers were trained for an input pattern of this size.

The first test using the Haar Cascade algorithm was made with these classifiers. The Opencv library provides three different classifiers for frontal face detection on visible light images but only two of the three classifiers were used, which were trained for an input pattern size of 20×20. The other classifier was trained for an input pattern size of 24×24. According to [36], 20×20 is the optimal input pattern size for frontal face detection. Table I shows the number of detections, the number of false positives, the precision and recall of the detection of the classifier (a) and (b). Examples of the face detection using theses classifiers are shown in Figure 17. The last image of each row is considered as false positive.

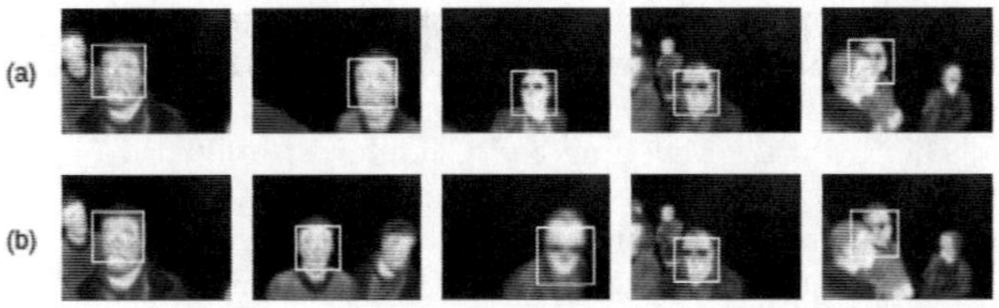

Figure 17. Examples of detection using classifiers (a) and (b) trained for visible light images.

Using cascade classifiers for visible light images in thermal images, the recall of the detection is very low. This means that the algorithm using these classifiers returns almost none of the faces present in the images. Therefore it is not possible to use this algorithm directly in thermal image. In order to improve the results, it was made a Haar Cascade training for face detection in thermal images.

With the purpose of demonstrating that using a machine learning for training a new classifier, it is possible to improve the face detection using thermal images. The OpenCV library provides an easy way for creating training samples from positive and negative images. It also provides the tool for training classifiers through these samples. Before creating the samples, the positive and negative thermal images were collected .

The dataset used, in this attempt of training classifiers for face detection on thermal images, is OTCBVS Benchmark Dataset Collection [37]. This dataset provides among of thermal images that can be used as positive and negative images. For positive images, the Terravic Facial IR Database [20] is used, that has thermal images of faces. There are images of 18 different faces with variations, such as rotation of the face, images captured indoor and outdoor, people with glasses and hat. For the training of the classifiers not all the images of the database were used, being selected only 1154 positive images. Figure 18 shows examples of these positive images. 757 negative images were collected from other database of the OTCBVS Benchmark Dataset Collection [37] and thermal images on the web. An example of these negative images are shown in Figure 19.

The second test using the Haar Cascade algorithm was made with the classifier trained in the previous section. In this test, the thermal images captured during the Teaching Day presented in Figure 15 were used. Face detection is unstable since it does not detect the face if the image does not contain the neck and shoulders of the person. For this reason, the number of faces increase to 4173, being the size 20×20 for the whole face, neck and shoulders. Examples of the face detection using the trained classifier are presented in Figure 20. In last row of the figure with false positive detections are presented. The number of detections are 5049 and 2251 of

Figure 18. Examples of positive images.

Figure 19. Examples of negative images.

these detections contain a face (true positives). The other 2798 detections are false positives. Therefore, the calculated precision and recall are 44.6% and 53.9%, respectively.

The study presented on [19] used the Viola and Jones algorithm [16] applied to thermal image. The results of this study show that in order to obtain a good accuracy, a large amount of training data is needed. In this study, the positive images only contain the face and not other members of the human body. However, the results of the study made in [19] have better performance comparing with the results presented in this first stage.

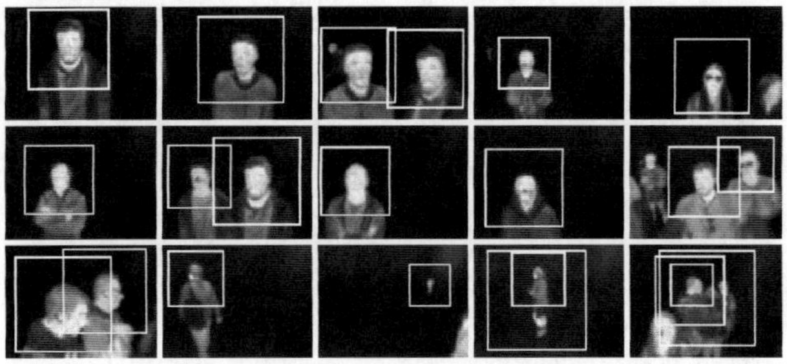

Figure 20. Examples of the detection using Haar Cascade algorithm with the trained classifier for thermal images.

In other to attempt improving the performance of the detection, the positive images of the Figure 18 were edited and cropped to train a classifier with positive images containing only faces. Figure 21 shows examples of this new positive images. The parameters used in this training are the same of the previous training by changing only the positive images. 5770 samples with window size of 20×20 were also created.

For this test, there are more or less 1602 faces that can be

TABLE I. Results of the test using classifiers trained in [36] for frontal face detection.

Cascade Classifiers	Number of Faces	Number of Detections	False Positives	Precision (%)	Recall (%)
a	1602	17	3	82.4	0.8
b	1602	16	1	93.8	0.9

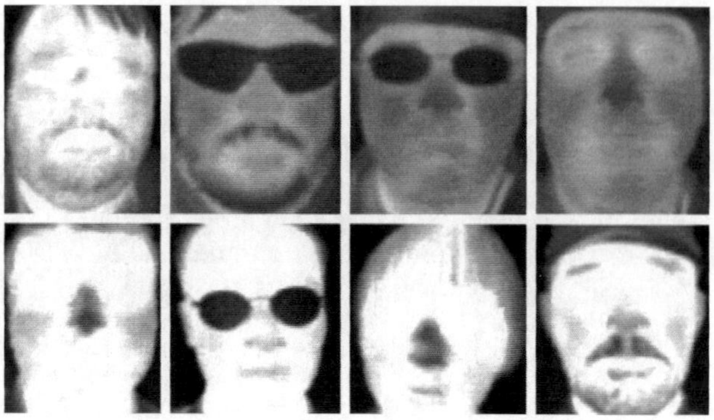

Figure 21. Examples of positive images containing only faces.

detected. Examples of the face detection using the improved classifier are presented in Figure 22. Results of images with false positives detection are presented in the last row of the figure. 3829 possible faces were detected, but only 1464 corresponded to true positive. Consequently, the number of false positives is 2375. The precision and recall are 38.1% and 91.4%, respectively.

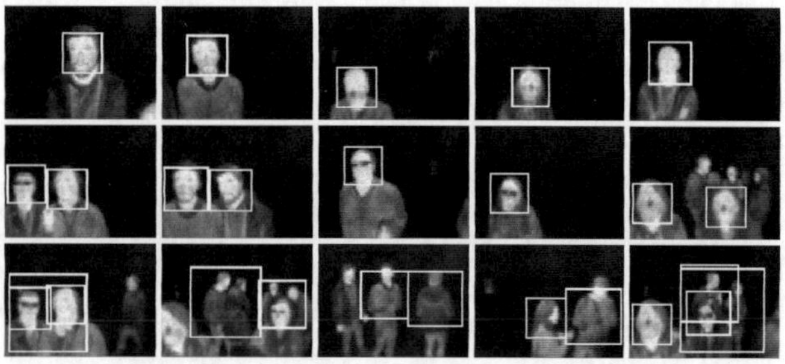

Figure 22. Examples of the detection using Haar Cascade algorithm with the improved classifier for thermal images.

For the purpose of better understanding the results of all tests performed using the Haar Cascade algorithm, Table II presents the results for face detection of each classifier used. In this table, the cascade classifiers are represented by letters, being the letters "a" and "b" for the classifiers trained by [36], "c" and "d" the first and last classifiers trained in this paper. The results shows that the training made to improve the first training detects most of the faces in the images. Although it has a lower precision than the first training, the detection only contains the face and not other members of the human body.

B. Proposed Methods for Face Detection

In this section, experimental results are presented using a pre-processing of the thermal images for the three proposed algorithms. The Face Contours algorithm is an algorithm, using the contours of the resulting binary image, made for single detection that helps to understand how the detection of edges and the manipulation of theses contours in an image works. The Template Matching and Chamfer Matching involve other concepts besides the detection of edges and contours. These algorithms use a template by searching the binary image for this pattern, calculating errors or distances to find the best match.

One of the tests using Template Matching and Chamfer Matching algorithms was made using images captured in the event "Students & Teachers @deti 2017". The first test using Face Contours algorithm was made with images captured for single face detection.

1) Students & Teachers @deti 2017: Students & teachers @deti is an open day of DETI of the University of Aveiro, where the students show their project work and the teachers show their research and development (R&D) activities. In this day, it is shown, to the whole academic community (students, teachers) and business companies, the work developed in the department during the academic year.

The work developed in this work was exhibited in this event. It was taken the initiative to capture thermal images during this event, in order to test these images with the proposed algorithms. 18072 thermal images were captured and 2935 of these images were selected. In order to reduce the data to be processed, some repeated images were removed. Examples of images captured during this event are shown in Figure 23. These images were used in the next sections to test the proposed algorithms.

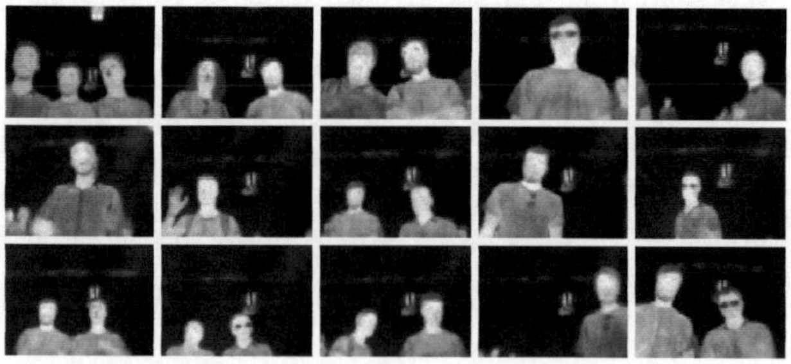

Figure 23. Examples of images captured in the event students & teachers @deti.

2) Pre-Processing: Preliminary results have been presented in [1] as shown in Figure 24(b) and Figure 24(c) an example of the segmentation obtained in this type of images and the use of morphological operators, respectively.

The next algorithms use a binary image similar to that shown in Figure 24(c) as the input image. Using the thermal images captured in the event "Students & Teachers @deti

TABLE II. Results of all tests made in this work using the Haar Cascade algorithm.

Cascade Classifiers	Windows Size	Number of Faces	Number of Detections	True Positives	False Positives	Precision (%)	Recall (%)
a	20x20	1602	17	14	3	82.4	0.8
b	20x20	1602	16	15	1	93.8	0.9
c	20x20	4173	5049	2251	2798	44,6	53.9
d	20x20	1602	3839	1464	2375	38.1	91.4

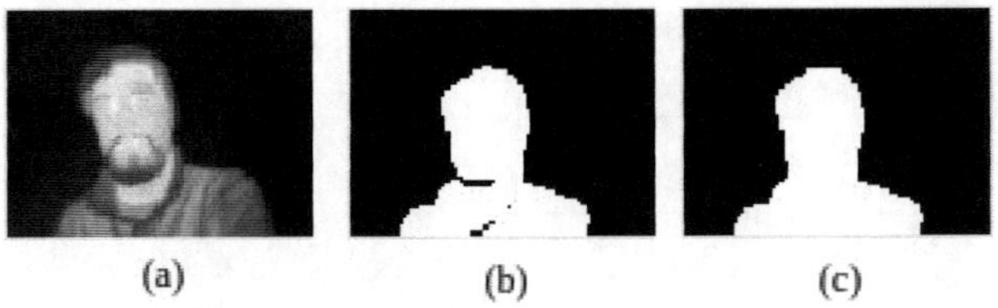

Figure 24. Thermal image(a) followed by segmentation(b) and the morphological operation(c) [1].

2017", examples of pre-processing results of the thermal images of Figure 23 are shown in Figure 25.

Figure 25. Examples of binary images using images captured in the event.

3) Face Contours: The first results obtained using this algorithm are presented in [1]. Figure 26 shows the preliminary example of face detection using this algorithm.

This algorithm was developed for single face detection, therefore the images of Figure 23 are not used for this test. Figure 27 shows the sequence of images processed by this algorithm, from image capture to final face detection. These results can be influenced if the contours of the face are discontinued for some reason. This algorithm is not developed for multiple face detection as can be seen in the last row of the Figure 27.

4) Template Matching: Figure 28 shows some examples of the tests performed previously in [1]. Using the images of Figure 23, a test was made for this algorithm. When using template matching algorithm a good template is needed. Figure 12 shows the used template in different scales. This algorithm slides the template over the binary images of Figure 25. Figure 29 shows some examples of the face detection using this algorithm. The last row of this figure represents examples with false positive detections.

5) Chamfer Matching: This algorithm uses the same template of the Template Matching algorithm shown in Figure 12, but it is converted to an edge using the Canny edge detector algorithm to be used later in the construction of the matching cost image. Examples of distance transform image are shown in Figure 30. Preliminary results using Chamfer Matching have been presented in [1]. Figure 31 shows examples of face detection of previously performed tests. Some results applying the Chamfer Matching are shown in Figure 32. Examples of false positive detections are shown in the last row of the figure.

Table III shows the results of the algorithms, Template Matching and Chamfer Matching, that used images of the Figure 23. These two algorithms are capable to detect multiple faces in a thermal image. Comparing the both results, Template Matching is the algorithm that has more precision and recall. This means that Template Matching can detect more faces than fake faces on all detected faces and detects most of the faces in the images.

C. Real-Time Results

In order to test and compare the performance of the different algorithms proposed over time, a test was made within a controlled environment. This environment was a classroom where students work on their computers. The thermal camera was placed in front of a students with a constant background and without movement. The student's face was at a distance of about 50 to 100 centimeters from the camera. During the test, the student acts normally working on his computer and talking to other students in the classroom, varying the pose and the rotation of the face, not constantly looking towards the camera. The test duration for each algorithm was approximately 20 minutes in a total of 80 minutes. The captured thermal images was limited to a frame rate of 2 frames per second.

Figure 33 shows examples of the face detection of these tests using the four algorithms implemented in this work, Haar Cascade, Face Contours, Template Matching and Chamfer Matching, respectively from left to right of this figure. The two last rows of the Figure 33 shows examples of false positives and bad detections.

The results of the test over the time can be seen in Table IV. Analyzing this table, the precision of the algorithms is very similar but the Haar Cascade is the one that has less precision and recall. Face Contours algorithm has the best results for this test. This algorithm for application of single face detection has a good performance, having some limitations, such as the contours discontinuation of the face or a background with objects at the same temperature as the face.

Comparing Template Matching and Chamfer Matching, the number of false positives is practically the same but the number of faces and frames in 20 minutes of the test is lower, due to the processing time of the Chamfer Matching algorithm. Table V shows the average of the processing time of the

Figure 26. Some examples of face detection in different conditions using contour detection [1].

TABLE III. Results of the test using thermal images of the event with multiples detection.

Proposed Algorithms	Number of Faces	Number of Detections	True Positives	False Positives	Precision (%)	Recall (%)
Template Matching	3229	3535	2770	765	78.4	85.8
Chamfer Matching	3229	3361	1810	1551	53.9	56.1

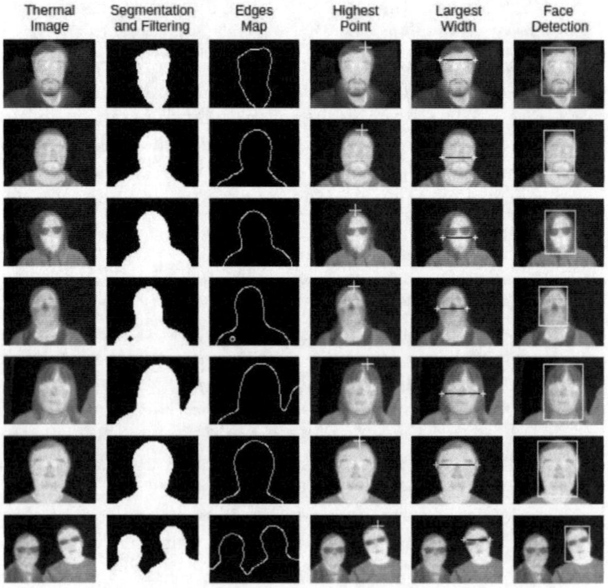

Figure 27. Examples of the results using Face Contours algorithm.

test for each algorithm. Chamfer Matching has the highest processing time, being almost 3 times slower comparing with others algorithms. This algorithm involves several steps, which require more processing time, for example distance transform and edge orientation.

V. Conclusions

In this paper we present a study regarding the development and adaptation of several algorithms for face detection in thermal images. Face detection on thermal imaging is a possible approach to overcome the challenges on face detection in visible light images, even after decades of active research.

Despite the thermal camera used is not calibrated, being impossible to know the exact temperature in the region of interest, the detection results were satisfactory and opens new directions on this field. As future work, we intend to improve the implemented algorithms for face detection and develop algorithms for calibration of this type of sensors, in order to measure absolute temperatures.

In terms of experimental results, Haar Cascade using Viola and Jones algorithm has better performance and accuracy based on [19]. However, this algorithm needs a large amount of data and time for training to obtain good results. Face detection in thermal image using Haar Cascade can be improved using one of the proposed methods for image segmentation and create several thermal images that contain only the face for training database in order to obtain better detection. The use of classifiers for visible light images in thermal images is not at all possible, due to infrared thermal cameras using sensors to create an image from the emitted radiation of the scene in the form of heat and the RGB cameras use sensors for captures intensity of light. The last trained classifier has better results than the other classifiers used in this work.

Face detection through thermal imaging using segmentation has a good accuracy in single face detection. For multiple detections, the results show that the better used algorithm is Template Matching. Comparing the algorithms used in this paper, Template Matching is the most suitable. Although Face contours and Haar Cascade have a processing time similar to Template Matching, the Haar Cascade has a lower recall, detecting more false positives and Face Contours has the disadvantage of not detecting multiple faces. Chamfer Matching has a similar detection to Template Matching for single detection but the processing time of this algorithm is almost 3 times slower and the detection performance, when applied to multiple face detection, decreases significantly.

Finally, we are also working on image registration algorithms, for the simultaneous use of these cameras and RGB cameras, in order to obtain a multimodal detection system.

Acknowledgment

This work was partially supported by national funds through the FCT - Foundation for Science and Technology, and by european funds through FEDER, under the COMPETE 2020 and Portugal 2020 programs, in the context of the projects UID/CEC/00127/2013.

References

[1] R. F. Ribeiro, J. M. Fernandes, and A. J. Neves, "Face detection on infrared thermal image," in Proc. SIGNAL, 2017, pp. 38–42.

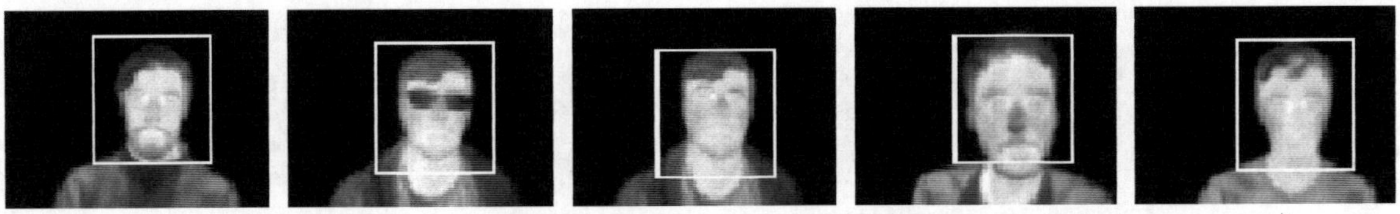

Figure 28. Some examples of face detection in different conditions using Template Matching [1].

TABLE IV. Results of the test in a classroom for proposed algorithms.

Proposed Algorithms	Number of Faces	Number of Detections	True Positives	False Positives	Precision (%)	Recall (%)
Haar Cascade	2035	1530	1465	65	95.8	72.0
Face Contours	1981	1965	1960	5	99.7	99.2
Template Matching	2026	1819	1817	2	99.9	89.7
Chamfer Matching	1614	1323	1320	3	99.8	81.8

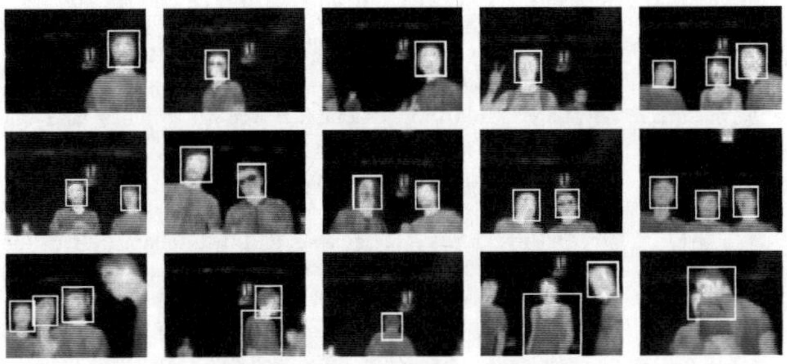

Figure 29. Face detection based on Template Matching.

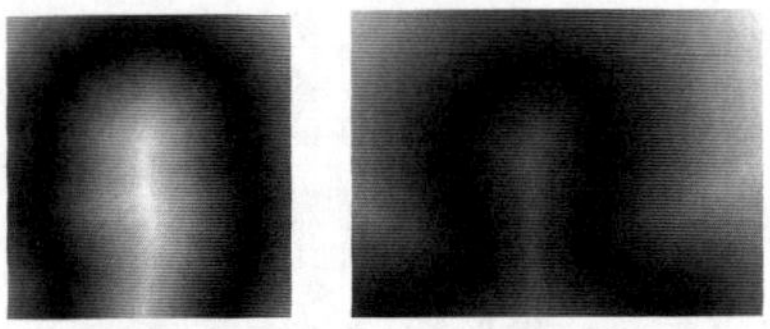

Figure 30. Example of Distance Transform image of template(a) and query image(b) [1].

TABLE V. Processing time of each proposed algorithm.

Proposed Algorithms	Number of Frames	Average Processing Time (ms)
Haar Cascade	2035	87.92
Face Contours	1981	90.11
Template Matching	2027	90.41
Chamfer Matching	1616	242.93

[2] M. Rowan-Robinson, Night vision: Exploring the infrared universe. Cambridge University Press, 2013.

[3] H. Kaplan, Practical applications of infrared thermal sensing and imaging equipment. SPIE press, 2007, vol. 75.

[4] R. Gade and T. B. Moeslund, "Thermal cameras and applications: A survey," Machine vision and applications, vol. 25, no. 1, 2014, pp. 245–262.

[5] J. Byrnes, Unexploded ordnance detection and mitigation. Springer Science & Business Media, 2008.

[6] B. MikaélA, Infrared Radiation: A Handbook for Applications. Springer Science & Business Media, 2013.

[7] M. Vollmer and K.-P. Möllmann, "Fundamentals of infrared thermal imaging," Infrared Thermal Imaging: Fundamentals, Research and Applications, 2010, pp. 1–72.

[8] J. R. Howell, M. P. Menguc, and R. Siegel, Thermal radiation heat transfer. CRC press, 2010.

[9] P. Kuiper, "Lesliescube — Wikipedia, the free encyclopedia," 2011, [accessed November 22, 2017]. [Online]. Available: https://en.wikipedia.org/wiki/Emissivity#/media/File:LesliesCube.png

[10] Wikipedia, "Atmospheric windows in the infrared — Wikipedia, the free encyclopedia."

[11] FLIR Systems, AB, "The ultimate infrared handbook for r&d professionals." [accessed November 22, 2017]. [Online]. Available: http://www.flirmedia.com/

[12] A. Schaufelbuhl, N. Schneeberger, U. Munch, M. Waelti, O. Paul, O. Brand, H. Baltes, C. Menolfi, Q. Huang, E. Doering et al., "Uncooled low-cost thermal imager based on micromachined cmos integrated sensor array," Journal of Microelectromechanical systems, vol. 10, no. 4, 2001, pp. 503–510.

[13] FeuRenard, "Very generalized view of the layers of a microbolometer — Wikipedia, the free encyclopedia," 2016, [accessed November 22, 2017]. [Online]. Available: https://commons.wikimedia.org

[14] A. Berg, "Detection and tracking in thermal infrared imagery," Ph.D. dissertation, Linköping University Electronic Press, 2016.

[15] A. Berg, J. Ahlberg, and M. Felsberg, "A thermal object tracking benchmark," in Advanced Video and Signal Based Surveillance (AVSS), 2015 12th IEEE International Conference on. IEEE, 2015, pp. 1–6.

[16] P. Viola and M. Jones, "Rapid object detection using a boosted cascade of simple features," in Computer Vision and Pattern Recognition, 2001. CVPR 2001. Proceedings of the 2001 IEEE Computer Society Conference on, vol. 1. IEEE, 2001, pp. I–I.

[17] Pure Engineering LLC, "Flir lepton breakout board," [accessed November 22, 2017]. [Online]. Available: http://www.pureengineering.com/projects/lepton

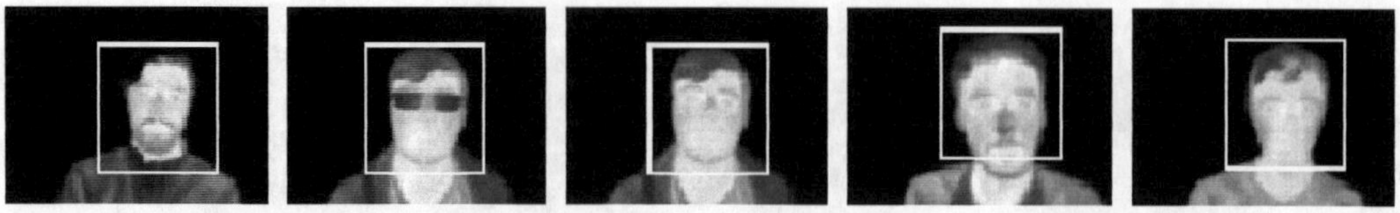

Figure 31. Some examples of face detection in different conditions using Chamfer Matching [1].

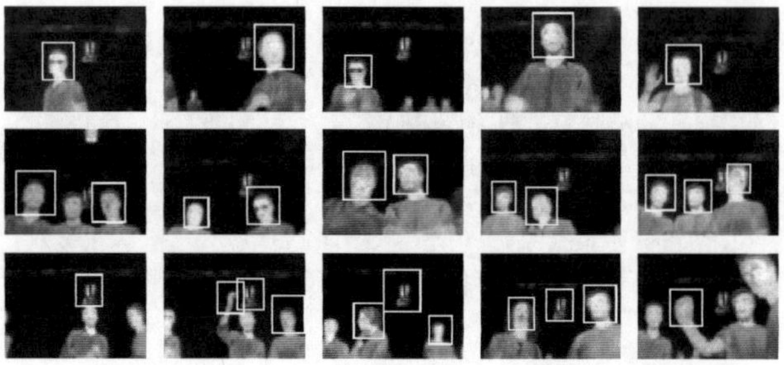

Figure 32. Examples of the face detection using Chamfer Matching algorithm.

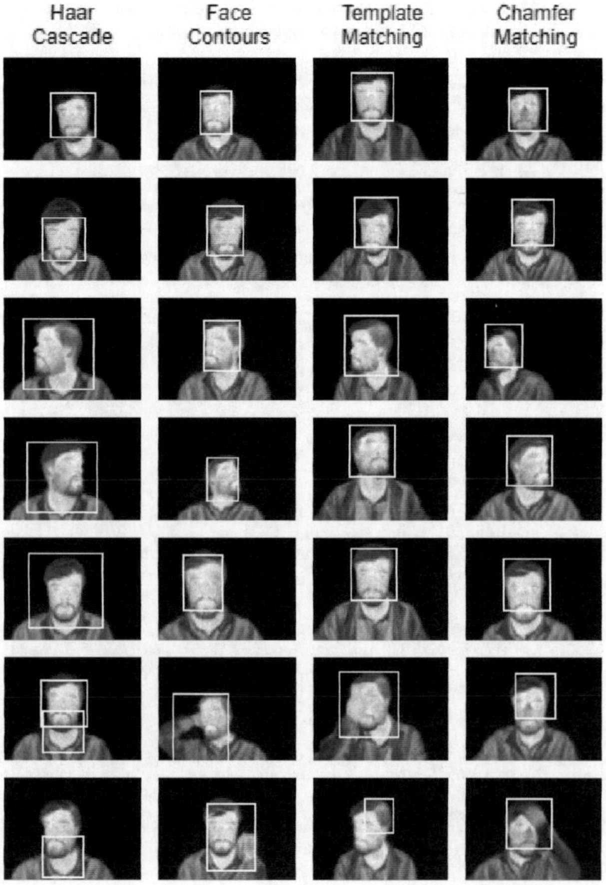

Figure 33. Examples of the face detection of the four implemented algorithms.

[18] FLIR, "Flir lepton long wave infrared (lwir) datasheet," 2016, [accessed November 22, 2017]. [Online]. Available: http://www.flir.com

[19] J. Mekyska, V. Espinosa-Duró, and M. Faundez-Zanuy, "Face segmentation: A comparison between visible and thermal images," in Security Technology (ICCST), 2010 IEEE International Carnahan Conference on. IEEE, 2010, pp. 185–189.

[20] Roland Miezianko, Terravic Research Infrared Database, "Dataset 04: Terravic facial infrared database," [accessed November 22, 2017]. [Online]. Available: http://vcipl-okstate.org/pbvs/bench/Data/04/download.html

[21] R. F. Moghaddam and M. Cheriet, "Adotsu: An adaptive and parameterless generalization of otsu's method for document image binarization," Pattern Recognition, vol. 45, no. 6, 2012, pp. 2419–2431.

[22] H. J. Heijmans, "Connected morphological operators for binary images," Computer Vision and Image Understanding, vol. 73, no. 1, 1999, pp. 99–120.

[23] S. Suzuki et al., "Topological structural analysis of digitized binary images by border following," Computer vision, graphics, and image processing, vol. 30, no. 1, 1985, pp. 32–46.

[24] J. P. Lewis, "Fast normalized cross-correlation," in Vision interface, vol. 10, no. 1, 1995, pp. 120–123.

[25] M.-Y. Liu, O. Tuzel, A. Veeraraghavan, and R. Chellappa, "Fast directional chamfer matching," in Computer Vision and Pattern Recognition (CVPR), 2010 IEEE Conference on. IEEE, 2010, pp. 1696–1703.

[26] M. S. Nixon and A. S. Aguado, Feature extraction & image processing for computer vision. Academic Press, 2012.

[27] N. Otsu, "A threshold selection method from gray-level histograms," IEEE transactions on systems, man, and cybernetics, vol. 9, no. 1, 1979, pp. 62–66.

[28] J. Canny, "A computational approach to edge detection," IEEE Transactions on pattern analysis and machine intelligence, no. 6, 1986, pp. 679–698.

[29] R. Maini and H. Aggarwal, "Study and comparison of various image edge detection techniques," International journal of image processing (IJIP), vol. 3, no. 1, 2009, pp. 1–11.

[30] A. Kaehler and G. Bradski, Learning OpenCV 3: Computer Vision in C++ with the OpenCV Library. " O'Reilly Media, Inc.", 2016.

[31] K. Briechle and U. D. Hanebeck, "Template matching using fast normalized cross correlation," in Proc. SPIE, vol. 4387, 2001.

[32] L. Ferreira, A. Neves, A. Pereira, E. Pedrosa, and J. Cunha, "Human detection and tracking using a kinect camera for an autonomous service robot," Advances in Aritificial Intelligence-Local Proceedings, EPIA, 2013, pp. 276–288.

[33] G. Borgefors, "Distance transformations in digital images," Computer vision, graphics, and image processing, vol. 34, no. 3, 1986, pp. 344–371.

[34] D. M. Powers, "Evaluation: From precision, recall and f-measure to roc., informedness, markedness & correlation," Journal of Machine Learning Technologies, vol. 2, no. 1, 2011, pp. 37–63.

[35] Walber, "Precision and recall — Wikipedia, the free encyclopedia," 2014, [accessed November 22, 2017]. [Online]. Available: https://commons.wikimedia.org/wiki/File%3APrecisionrecall.svg

[36] R. Lienhart, A. Kuranov, and V. Pisarevsky, "Empirical analysis of detection cascades of boosted classifiers for rapid object detection," Pattern Recognition, 2003, pp. 297–304.

[37] IEEE OTCBVS WS Series Bench, "Otcbvs benchmark dataset collection," [accessed November 22, 2017]. [Online]. Available: http://vcipl-okstate.org/pbvs/bench/index.html

CitySense: Combining Geolocated Data for Urban Area Profiling

Danae Pla Karidi, Harry Nakos, Alexandros Efentakis, Yannis Stavrakas
IMIS, Athena RC
email: {danae, xnakos, efentakis, yannis}@imis.athena-innovation.gr

Abstract—**Social networks, available open data and massive online APIs provide huge amounts of data about our surrounding location, especially for cities and urban areas. Unfortunately, most previous applications and research usually focused on one kind of data over the other, thus presenting a biased and partial view of each location in question, hence partially negating the benefits of such approaches. To remedy this, we developed the CitySense framework that simultaneously combines data from administrative sources (e.g., public agencies), massive Point of Interest APIs (Google Places, Foursquare) and social microblogs (Twitter) to provide a unified view of all available information about an urban area, in an intuitive and easy to use web-application platform. This work describes the engineering and design challenges of such an effort and how these different and divergent sources of information may be combined to provide an accurate and diverse visualization for our use-case, the urban area of Chicago, USA.**

Keywords- Social networks; Crowdsourcing; Open data; Geographic visualization.

I. Introduction and Motivation

The emergence of social networks, microblogging platforms, check-in applications and smartphone / Global Positioning System (GPS) devices in recent years has generated vast amounts of data regarding the location of users. To exploit this vastly growing data, recent research has focused on utilizing the geographic aspect of this information for statistical profiling of geographical areas [1], event detection, sentiment analysis of users, place-name disambiguation [2][3], identification of popular hotspots and their temporal variation, identifying and visualizing the typical movement pattern of users throughout the day [4][5], as well as improving existing city maps [6][7]. However, volunteered geographic information (VGI) contributed by online users is imprecise and inaccurate by design and it should, thus, be used with extra caution for critical applications.

Likewise, the increasing necessity for efficient location-based services and effective online advertising drove leading web providers (e.g., Google, Here, Bing, Foursquare) to store and offer Point of Interest (PoI) information to their users, usually through the use of online Application Programming Interfaces (APIs). Such an approach has several benefits, since the users not only have access to information about their nearby PoIs but they may also provide (or view) reviews or notify their friends of their current whereabouts. The same web services also allow shop-owners and enterprises to advertise their stores and the services they offer. However, as any commercial offering there are limitations on the use of those APIs, thus providing users with a very locally-limited view of the existing city infrastructure that cannot be directly used to extract additional information for city-scale areas.

On a separate front, the open data movement argued that citizens should have access to the data collected by government agencies, since they are the ones funding data collection through their taxes. A second strong supporting argument is that public access to government data helps individuals and enterprises to create apps that boost the economy and provide better services to the citizens, at no additional cost. Some countries and cities have openly released such data, which provide another alternative view of urban areas. Although this open data is official, curated, of excellent quality and impossible to collect by individuals, it has the obvious disadvantage that it cannot be real-time, it is usually not available through APIs and most importantly it may be updated at very infrequent intervals (e.g., census data), therefore at risk of being rather outdated.

Overall, the aforementioned three sources of information, i.e., volunteered geographic information, online PoI data and official open data each have their own strengths and weaknesses, regarding accuracy, update-rate, ease of use and availability. Likewise, applications or research that utilize and rely on only one of those types of data offer a biased and imprecise view of reality that could potentially be misleading. To remedy this, this work proposes the *CitySense* framework [1] that utilizes open data from administrative sources, online PoI APIs and social microblogs (tweets) to provide a unified view of our use-case, the urban area of Chicago. The main innovation and focus of the paper is to show how disparate datasets of various origins can be combined to provide a more complete picture of a geographical area. The corresponding web application [48] may be viewed with any modern web browser (Chrome, Firefox). Our emphasis is on how to efficiently spatially aggregate, visualize and present the end-user with an aesthetically pleasing and intuitive view of available raw data for any of these three sources, with minimum intervention, so that the end-user could freely interpret this information at his own will. As such, the CitySense application could be easily extended with additional features with minimal effort. Moreover, the CitySense Database is designed for the efficient storage and retrieval of the data acquired from the three above-mentioned sources. Overall, CitySense is a dynamic urban area viewer that integrates various datasets related to an urban area, providing a rich visualization of a city's life.

As a motivating example, consider a newcomer to the city, who has to search for a house in an unfamiliar area. She has to answer some questions, in order to narrow down and locate the neighborhoods to search. These questions may involve criteria like education facilities (''Where are the most popular residential neighborhoods having high level educational facilities?'') and security (''Where is the downtown area with the lowest criminality measures?''). As another example, consider a tour operator that needs to track the tourist activity in a city, in order to offer improved tour packages and services. However, monitoring massive tourist activity using traditional methods would require lots of efforts, examination of many updating sources, hence huge costs and time involving off-line on-the-spot observation.

The central idea behind our approach is described in [1], where we presented the CitySense framework. In this paper, we extend that work by providing a deeper description of CityProfiler, the subsystem responsible for data collection, and a thorough description of the CitySense Database design and schema.

The outline of this work is as follows. Section II presents related work. Section III describes the objectives, the architecture and the web-based application of CitySense. Section IV describes the CitySense technical challenges. Section V describes the CitySense Database design. Finally, Section VI gives conclusions and directions for future work.

II. RELATED WORK

In recent years, as data from location sharing systems are constantly increasing, researchers have proposed a wide variety of "urban sensing" methods, based on location data derived from all kinds of sources: social media posts and check-ins, cellphone activity, taxicab records, demographic data, etc. Scientists combined social sciences, computer science and data mining tools, in order to derive useful knowledge regarding the life of cities. Cranshaw et al. [8] tried to reveal the dynamics of a city based on social media activity, while in [9][10], authors characterized sub-regions of cities by mining significant patterns extracted from geo-tagged tweets. Frias-Martinez et al. [11] focused on deriving land uses and points of interest in a specific urban area based on tweeting patterns and Noulas et al. [12] analyzed user check-in dynamics, to mine meaningful spatio-temporal patterns for urban spaces analysis. Much work has been done in the field of using social media textual and semantic content for urban analysis purposes. For example, Pozdnoukhov et al. [13] conducted real-time spatial analysis of the topical content of streaming tweets. Moreover, Noulas et al. [14] proposed the comparison of urban neighborhoods by using semantic information attached to places that people check in, while Kling et al. [15] applied a probabilistic topic model to obtain a decomposition of the stream of digital traces into a set of urban topics related to various activities of the citizens using Foursquare and Twitter data. Grabovitch-Zuyev et al. [16] studied the correlation between textual content and geospatial locations in tweets and Kamath et al. [17] used the spatio-temporal propagation of hashtags to characterize locations. Prediction methodologies have widely used geo-tagged social content. For example, Kinsella et al. [18] created language models of locations extracted from geotagged Twitter data, in order to predict the location of an individual tweet, in [19]-[22], the authors aimed to model friendship between users by analyzing their location trails and Cheng et al. [23] estimated a Twitter user's city-level location based purely on the content of the user's tweets. Moreover, researchers have focused on trend and event detection by detecting correlations between topics and locations [24][25]. Lately, many works have been published focusing on urban mobility patterns. For example, Veloso et al. [26] analyzed the taxicab trajectory records in Lisbon to explore the distribution relationship between pick-up locations and drop-off locations. In [27], the authors explored real-time analytical methodologies for spatio-temporal data of citizens' daily travel patterns in urban environment. The authors of [28]-[32] used the moving trajectory data of mobile phone users to study city dynamics and human mobility, while the authors of [33]-[36] analyzed the human mobility using social media data. Another field connected to urban analysis is the geodemographic classifications, which represent small area classifications that provide summary indicators of the social, economic and demographic characteristics of neighborhoods [37]. In the area of location demographics and socio-economic prediction and correlation, researchers have proposed a variety of methods based on geo-tagged social media data [38]-[40].

A wide variety of applications that describe the life of urban areas have been developed so far. For example, EvenTweet [41] is a framework to detect localized events in real-time from a Twitter stream and to track the evolution of such events over time. Moreover, the "One million Tweet Map" [42] is a web app that displays the last million tweets over the world map in real-time. Every second the map is updated, dropping twenty of the earliest tweets and plotting out the latest twenty keeping the number of tweets hovering at 1,000,000, showing clustered tweets in regions around the world, while users are able to zoom in or out on the map, and cause the re-aggregation of the clusters. Furthermore, the "tweepsmap" [43] application provides users with efficient geo-targeted twitter analytics and management and "trendsmap" [44] and "tweetmap" [45] shows the geo located latest trends from Twitter on a map. In Urban Census Demographics visualization field, the "Mapping America: Every City, Every Block" [46] enables users to browse local data from the Census Bureau's American Community Survey, based on samples from 2005 to 2009. Finally, "Social Explorer" [47] provides map based tools for visual exploration of demographic information, including the U.S. Census, American Community Survey, United Kingdom Census, Canadian Census, Eurostat, FBI Uniformed Crime Report, American election results, Religious Congregation Membership Study, World Development Indicators.

Although those works provide thorough insights in some aspects of life in an urban area, they fail to provide an integrated and global view of the city and to enable the user

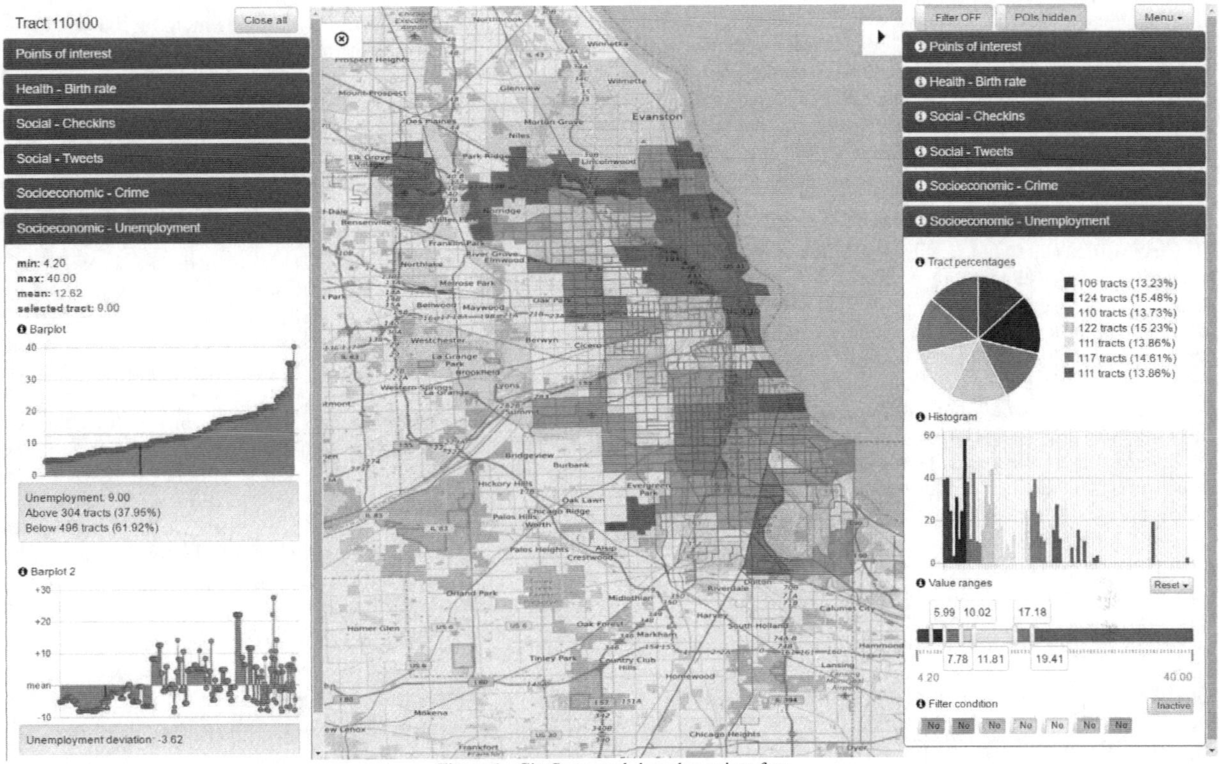

Figure 1. CitySense web-based user interface

to interactively answer questions by combining datasets. CitySense aims to fill these gaps by integrating multiple data sources and providing an interactive user interface supporting filters, multiple view options and drill down abilities.

III. BROWSING INTEGRATED CITY DATA

In this section, we present an overview of CitySense. We also discuss the objectives and present the features of the application.

A. Objectives and Architecture

CitySense is a dynamic urban area viewer, that integrates various datasets related to an urban area and provides a rich visualization of a city's life. The application can answer questions at many levels by exploiting the variety of datasets referring to a city and joining disparate data sources in an easy way. Users can view several aspects of city life statically or over time, for the whole city or for each part, mixing data sources to uncover patterns and information that would not be obvious from just observing the datasets.

The CitySense application [48] aims to provide a fast and easy way to:

- combine disparate data sources regarding various city aspects,
- filter data and drill down through a map-based visualization environment, and
- answer questions, explore and discover valuable information to convey the sense of the city.

The system architecture is presented in Figure 2 and includes the front-end Web-based Application of CitySense, the Data Infrastructure and Refresher units, the GeoServer that is discussed in Section IV-C and the CityProfiler subsystem (the dotted box in Figure 2) that was developed to collect the data related to the city from the data sources and is presented in detail in Section III-B.

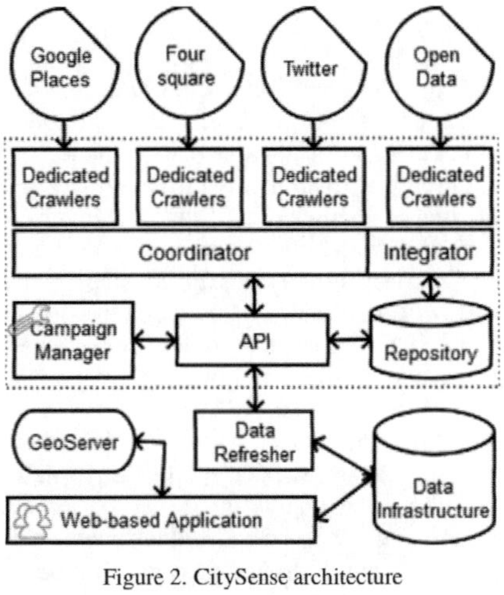

Figure 2. CitySense architecture

A screenshot of the CitySense web-based user interface is shown in Figure 1. The city of Chicago was selected for the pilot application, due to the amount and quality of official census data that are available. An additional reason is that Chicago's residents are exhibiting strong social media activity; moreover, a sufficient number of Points of Interest (PoIs) is available as well.

B. Harvesting Data with CityProfiler

CityProfiler (included in the dotted box in Figure 2) is a subsystem of CitySense, responsible for collecting data related to an urban area from diverse sources. Its basic functionality is to collect all available PoIs and tweets that come from the city and to store them in a repository together with relevant metadata.

Specifically, PoI data are extracted using Google Places and Foursquare APIs. Social Media data containing geospatial information are available via the Twitter API. The diversity of these sources raised the need for developing specific modules, called crawlers, to handle each data source. PoI crawlers collect PoI information using two methods. The first (general) method requires the selection of a geographic area and a PoI category, and returns a list of PoIs in the area belonging to this category. The second (special) method requires the selection of a PoI using a unique identifier and returns additional PoI information (name, address, phone number, opening hours, rating, etc.). In any case, the first (general) method returns the unique identifier of each PoI contained in the response list. This identifier can be used by the second (special) method to obtain more information about that PoI. The data obtained by the second method are stored in the repository.

In the case of the collection of geo-located tweets and check-ins, the corresponding crawler uses a method that requires the selection of a geographic area, and returns a list of geo-located tweets and check-ins, which have been posted from this area. Specifically, the crawler employs the Twitter Streaming API that provides real-time streaming data. Hence, the crawler has to collect geo-located tweets and check-ins dynamically. This is achieved by using the Twitter Streaming API in a sliding time window. Finally, the data obtained are stored in the repository.

Specifically, Google Places Crawler took 48 hours to complete the Chicago PoI collection. The 184,392 PoIs collected and stored in the database are depicted in Figure 3i. Meanwhile, the Foursquare Crawler had collected and stored 93,893 PoIs that are depicted in Figure 3ii. Figure 3iii depicts the complete PoI collection, from both Google Places and Foursquare Crawlers. Finally, Figure 3iv depicts the locations of 10,286 geo-located tweets (shown as blue dots) and 1,310 check-ins (shown as orange dots) that were collected by Social Media Crawler within these 48 hours.

CityProfiler provides an API and a GUI through which applications and users, respectively, can define and perform new collection campaigns. Each campaign, which is defined by certain parameters, results in an independent collection. These parameters control the individual crawlers that gather data through available APIs, and are the following:

- Crawling Duration: defines the duration of the campaign.
- Crawler Selection: selects which of the available crawlers (corresponding to distinct data sources like Foursquare, Google Maps, Facebook, Twitter, etc.) will participate in the campaign.
- Crawling Location: defines a crawling location by setting a point on the map and a range around it.
- Category Selection: selects target PoI categories and optionally keywords for the crawling to be based on. Keywords are used to narrow crawling, when the PoI category employed is deemed too broad (e.g., keyword "high school" is used when crawling Google Places for high schools, since "school" is the only applicable category). Category Selection can also collect all PoIs in a location, regardless of their category.
- Crawling Frequency Selection: some of the collected data need a systematic update, because of the changes that might occur to PoIs (e.g., a coffee shop might become a bar or new PoIs might show up). CityProfiler can perform repetitive campaigns with large duration in which multiple collections can be performed using the same parameters. Frequency Selection defines, therefore, how often the campaign should automatically restart.

Figure 3i. Chicago Google Places PoIs

Figure 3ii. Chicago Foursquare PoIs

Figure 3iii. Chicago Google Places and Foursquare PoIs

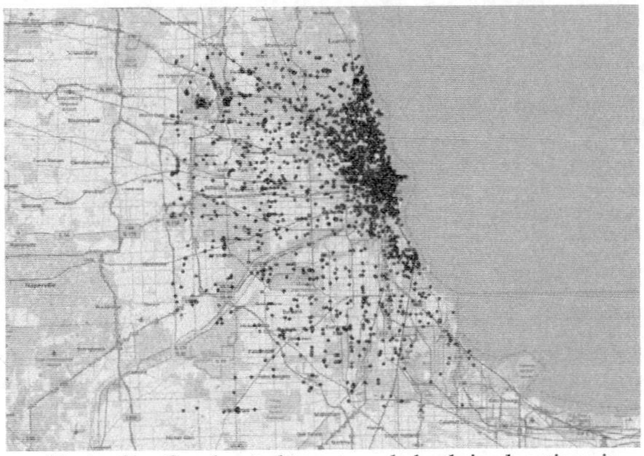

Figure 3iv. Geo-located tweets and check-ins locations in Chicago

CityProfiler is able to perform multiple campaigns in parallel, therefore there is a need of a Coordinator (see Figure 2) to control the crawlers and manage the campaigns. Moreover, CityProfiler manages resources in an intelligent way ensuring that all the restrictions imposed by the sources are met (e.g., maximum number of requests per time period), and that overlapping requests are avoided. Retrieved data are cleaned to exclude duplicates, and are temporarily stored in a repository.

C. *Data Preprocessing and Integration*

CitySense aims to shed light on the life of a city by exploiting three types of data: Points of Interest, Social Media and Open Census Data. PoI and Social Media Data are generated constantly by users and services. Therefore, we collect and update them in a regular and automatic way using CityProfiler, as discussed in Section III-B. Unlike these types of data, Open Census Data are generated by diverse sources (local authorities) at unpredictable time intervals. Moreover, they are published in various data formats (CSV, tab delimited, etc.). Therefore, Open Census Data require a case-dependent preprocessing and integration procedure keeping pace with their publication and taking into account the variety of data sources and formats. Finally, the diverse nature of these datasets requires a special integration regarding the aspect of time as well.

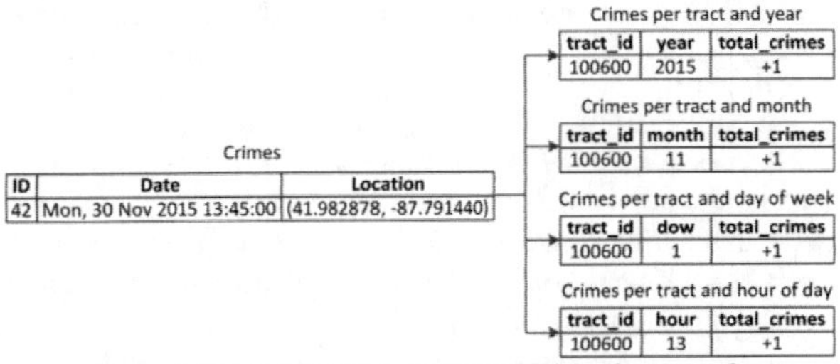

Figure 4. Crime data preprocessing and integration example

An example of the preprocessing and integration transformation regarding Crime data is presented in Figure 4. On the left side of the figure, we observe a single row of crime data that was downloaded in CSV format. This row represents a crime incident and contains its time and location. On the right side of the figure, we observe how this crime is represented in our database. Specifically, it is assigned to a tract (a specific geographical partition of the city) based on its location. The specific crime instance is represented by increasing the counter (total_crimes) in four tables, each representing a different time granularity: per year, month, day of week and hour of day.

D. *CitySense Features and Design*

Figure 1 shows CitySense web-based user interface. The central element of the visualization is the map of Chicago, which is divided in smaller sections, called tracts. Tracts are existing administrative divisions already used by the Chicago city government departments. Chicago contains 801 tracts and each of them describes a small area that is considered to be relatively uniform and corresponds ideally to about 1200 households (2000-4000 residents). Tract boundaries are always visible (blue line) on the map and when an individual tract is chosen its boundaries are highlighted with a red border line.

On the two sides of the map, CitySense provides two complementary views of Chicago. The first view appears on the right side and provides functions regarding the city as a whole. Hence, users can define visualization and filter options and observe the results both on the coloring of the city map and on distribution charts. The second view, is on the left side, and provides charts concerning only the selected tract, dark-highlighted on the map. This view, which appears when a tract is selected, helps users drill down to observe the special characteristics of each tract and to compare it with the city's overview. These views can be active concurrently, enabling users to observe different datasets in a general level and in tract level at the same time.

Both views provide visualizations and charts tailored to the corresponding dataset. For example, as shown in Figure 1, map coloring and charts visualize the Unemployment dataset.

To select a dataset, the user has to select a *data drawer*. Data drawers (dark rectangles) can be accessed concurrently in both views and represent the available datasets, e.g., "Points of Interest", "Health - Birth rate", "Social – Tweets", etc. According to the type of the particular dataset (see Section IV-A) each data drawer can contain different UI elements like pie charts, histograms, color range sliders and implement suitable functionality like value-based map coloring, temporal and combined filtering and superimposed PoI information.

The map coloring is based on user adjustable color range sliders that are available in each data drawer. Such a slider is presented in Figure 5 (top). After the color ranges are adjusted, users can define one or more colors as filtering parameters for combining various datasets. In other words, CitySense combines datasets (data drawers) by filtering the tracts based on their color. A color filtering slider, where only the violet color (leftmost) is defined as filtering condition, is shown in Figure 5 (bottom).

The tracts that satisfy the conditions set in all data drawers are colored grey on the map. Figure 6 shows the filter output for Social-Tweets and Socioeconomic-Crime datasets.

Certain datasets are visualized based on temporal aspects (per month/day/hour). The temporal functions described here are shown in Figure 7. Thus, users can select the time granularity, e.g., month of year, day of week, hour of day to adjust the charts and map coloring accordingly. Additionally, users can color the map or view the tract charts based on a specific month, day, or two-hour interval.

Finally, the CitySense application enables the user to see superimposed PoI information on the map at any moment. The user can select one or more categories (Food, Residence, Outdoors & Recreation, etc.) and the corresponding PoIs appear on the map as shown in Figure 8.

Figure 5. Coloring and filtering color slider

Figure 6. Filtered map

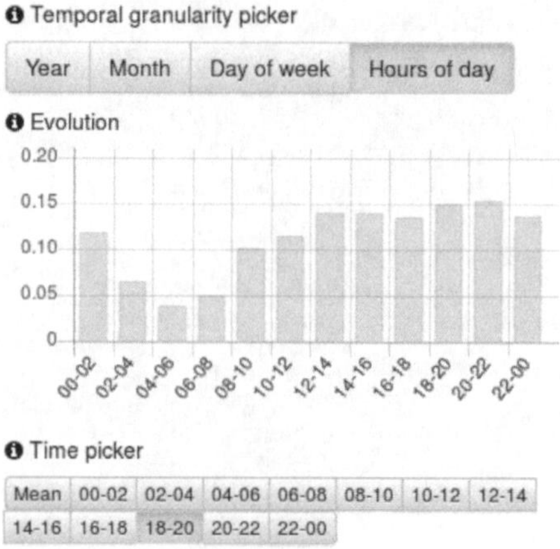

Figure 7. Temporal pickers

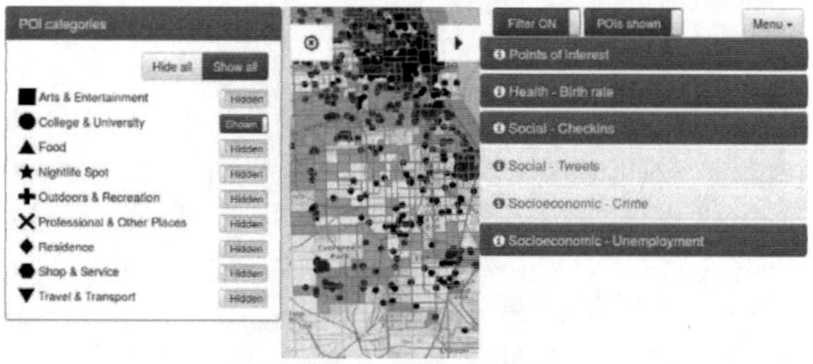

Figure 8. Filtered map with PoIs

IV. TECHNICAL CHALLENGES

In this section, we present in detail the technical challenges of the CitySense application.

A. *Organizing Disparate Datasets*

In order to convey the sense of a city CitySense must integrate and visualize a variety of datasets. The data sources that are integrated consist of demographic, social media and PoI data. The diverse nature of these datasets requires a different integration manipulation regarding the aspect of time. As we show in Table 1:

- Open Census Data can be visualized both in a static (overtime) or in a temporal way (per month/ day/hour). For instance, Health and Unemployment data are visualized statically and Crime data temporally.
- Social Media Data can be visualized in a static, temporal or dynamic way, although they are produced and gathered dynamically (real time). The feature of real time dynamic visualization of social media data is currently being developed.
- Point of Interest Data are visualized in a static way.

TABLE I. DIVERSITY OF DATASET VISUALIZATION REGARDING TIME

	static	temporal	dynamic
Open Census Data	✓	✓	
Social Media Data	✓	✓	✓ ongoing development
Point of Interest Data	✓		

The above organization of data helped to overcome their diversity and provide coherent visualization and treatment within the application.

A related problem is that of the initialization of the user-adjustable color range sliders. Our goal was to provide a reasonable use of map coloring to help users draw conclusions about the city. Therefore, we provided two options for initialization. The first, the value-based initialization option, breaks the slider based on equidistant values. However, this approach is sensitive to data with extreme outlier values or extreme concentration in certain ranges. The second option provides a percentage-based initialization, hence breaks the slider based on equal distribution percentages. However, this approach is sensitive to having many tracts with almost equal values. As an example, Figure 9 shows the value-based initialization for crime data.

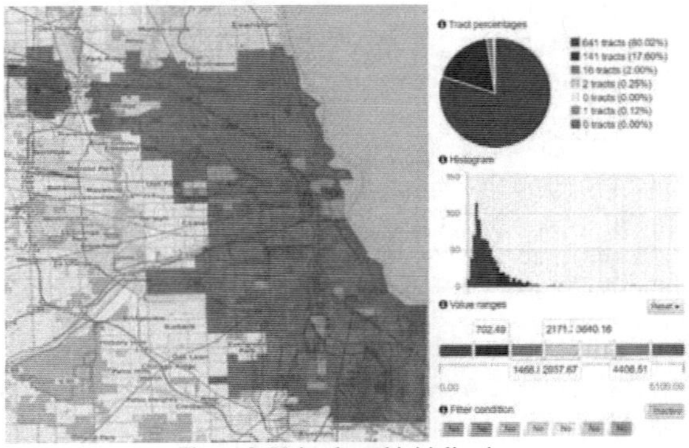

Figure 9. Value-based initialization

As we can observe in the histogram shown in Figure 8 (right), the crime data mainly occupy a small value range, between 0 and 1468, resulting in the almost two-colored map (violet and indigo – colors may not be visible on printed document) of Figure 9 (left). To address this issue, we use the percentage-based initialization, which is presented in Figure 10.

The resulting map coloring shown in Figure 10 (left) is obviously improved. However, as we can observe in the tract percentages shown in Figure 10 (right), the crime data distributions are not equally divided, because some tracts have almost equal values with respect to the range step and, therefore, cannot be equally classified.

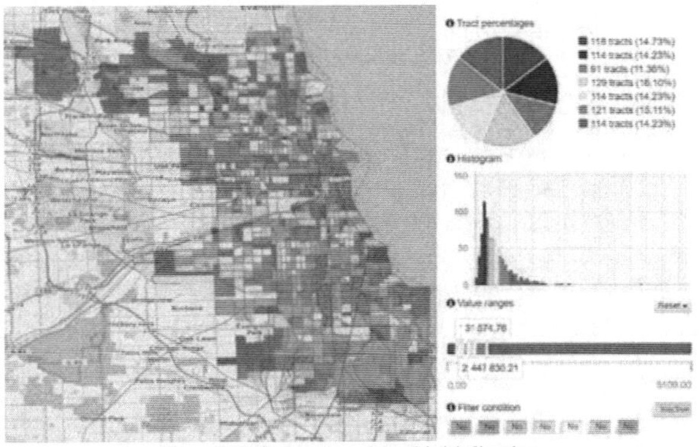

Figure 10. Percentage-based initialization

B. *Acquiring Data of an Area*

CityProfiler gathers PoI data from an urban area by performing calls to API services like Google Places and Foursquare, which set restrictions and constraints. A naïve crawling of PoIs, in terms of a whole city, would not be able to collect the entire amount of PoIs, but only a small portion of it as dictated by the rules imposed by the source. CitySense deals with this issue by breaking the area to smaller parts in advance. Specifically, the city is divided in squares of longitude and latitude of 0.03 degrees before the PoI crawling. In case this method doesn't gather all the PoIs, then recursion is used.

Additionally, CityProfiler collects real-time social data from the city. In order to achieve this, CityProfiler performs a real-time crawling of tweets with Twitter Streaming API, using a location box, which encompasses the city as filter parameter. Only the geo-located tweets (that are posted along with their latitude and longitude) are collected. In order to collect social check-ins and the PoIs that they were posted at, CityProfiler performs a call to Foursquare API every time a tweet contains a Swarm (mobile app that allows users to share their location within their social network) link. This way, the application collects temporal information concerning geo-located tweets, including their hashtags and check-ins posted at city PoIs.

C. *Implementation and Efficiency Issues*

Several implementation decisions had to be made, so that the application would run efficiently. The application needed to be lightweight with respect to memory and processing power consumption, as well as responsive with respect to the end-user experience.

At certain parts of the application a large number of geometries, namely tens of thousands of PoIs, needs to appear on the screen simultaneously. The option of handling each geometry as a separate entity and drawing it on the map separately would require much memory and processing power especially when zooming in and out the map. The approach employed is based on drawing relevant geometries as one image layer containing all geometries. GeoServer (shown in Figure 2) is leveraged for generating and serving image layers. For additional efficiency, the built-in caching functionality of image layers by GeoServer is utilized. This way subsequent requests may use already generated image layers.

The application's requirements involve aggregate queries on data, spanning the geospatial and temporal dimensions. Such queries take much time, if performed on raw data, resulting in degradation of responsiveness for the end-user. In order to avoid costly operations during runtime, a preprocessing stage is employed. The database design for preprocessed data was driven by the critical use cases available to the end-user via the UI. As an example, the user is able to query for check-in data, aggregated per tract, pertaining to a specific PoI category and a specific day of week. Raw check-in data contain the geographic coordinates of the PoI, the category of the PoI, as well as the date and time of the check-in, across two tables. Tract geometries are stored in a separate table as well. Such a query cannot be executed instantaneously. During the preprocessing stage, the coordinates of the PoIs are mapped to the intersecting tracts, the days of week are extracted from date and time, and aggregation per tract and day of week is performed. The preprocessing results are stored in database tables. This way efficient querying for check-ins, in a specific PoI category, on a specific day of week, is achieved. Separate tables are employed to deal with different time granularity aspects of the temporal dimension, i.e., there exist separate tables for years, months, days of week, hours of day. Another optimization measure in the same direction is the delegation of heavy computations to the initialization stage of application services. This has an effect on the start-up time of the application, but speeds up requests during runtime.

The application currently encompasses a relatively small number of datasets, so data handling is manageable using PostgreSQL database system, as described in Section V. If the datasets grow in number, a data warehouse can be used to facilitate data management and efficient processing of aggregate queries.

D. Adapting to Other Cities

One of our primary concerns during the development of the CitySense framework was adaptability of the framework to other cities. Adaptation of CitySense to another city is comprised of three major tasks, partitioning of the city area, integration of Open Census Data and implementation of the relevant access methods, and specialization of the front-end according to the available city data.

1) City Area Partitioning

CitySense is essentially parametric with respect to the attributes that define the city of interest, namely a bounding rectangle that encloses the city and a partitioning scheme for the city. The partitioning scheme may in theory consist of an arbitrary set of polygons that collectively cover the whole city. Choosing a partitioning scheme is, nevertheless, not that straightforward. In order to effectively choose a partitioning scheme, official administrative partitioning schemes should be looked into (e.g., community areas, ZIP codes, census tracts), focusing on partitioning schemes used in Open Census Data of interest. Disregarding such partitioning schemes and employing an arbitrary one could result in Open Census Data of interest rendered either useless or hard to map to the employed partitioning scheme. Should the official partitioning scheme be considered too fine-grained, grouping could be applied to the small partitions, in order to acquire a more coarse-grained partitioning scheme to use. Should the official partitioning scheme be too coarse-grained, segmentation of the large partitions into smaller ones would result in a more fine-grained partitioning scheme to use.

2) Open Census Data Integration and Access

Open Census Data is the most cumbersome type of data to integrate into CitySense. While CityProfiler data are the same, irrespective of the city of interest, Open Census Data could be vastly different, even among different types of Open Census Data for the same city. Open Census Data could be stored in database tables or files. As long as data transfer from the back-end to the front-end is of the same form, regardless of the type of data, all underlying implementation details have no other constraints. Open Census Data will often make use of a specific partitioning scheme that will generally diverge from the partitioning scheme applied to the city. Such data will need to be mapped to the employed partitioning scheme. There is no recipe for universally handling this issue, hence the aforementioned suggestion to let Open Census Data drive the choice of a partitioning scheme for the city. Open Census Data with temporal and/or categorical dimensions should be stored in a way that will facilitate efficient data retrieval based on corresponding parameters. The methods that implement data access should also support temporal and/or categorical parameters, if should such dimensions exist for a specific type of Open Census Data. While parameters are specific to each type of Open Census Data, the response from the back-end should always be of the same form, so that all response data can be treated uniformly by the front-end.

3) Front-end Specialization

Specialization of the front-end in order to support the city data available by the back-end is the final task in the process of CitySense adaptation. Each dataset is represented by a data drawer both in the left and the right sidebar. All datasets follow the same protocol with respect to the data sent by the back-end. The only thing that needs to be specialized per dataset is the data picker, in case that one exists for a specific dataset. The data picker is used to navigate categorically and/or temporally within the dataset. The data picker parameters will be transformed to request parameters that are received by the back-end. The back-end response will follow the data transfer protocol. The data drawer, therefore, needs no other specialization before it can display the received data.

E. Linear Prediction Model

Very often the datasets are not independent of each other. For example, infant mortality is very likely to be income-related, and is increased in areas with low income. One way to predict values of a variable (response) based on the corresponding values of other variables (predictors) is to find a suitable linear model based on the method of least squares. There are two reasons for constructing such models:

- They can provide an "exploratory analysis" of data. Through comparing the predicted values with the actual it is possible that correlations between variables can be explored, e.g., crimes are associated with income and unemployment.
- They can provide an estimation of a missing value for a tract, since this value can be inferred based on the values of predictors for this tract.

The CitySense application supports the construction of linear models for any of the available datasets. As an example, we consider crime data. From the application menu, we can create linear models (select "New model fit"), regarding crime as response and any combination of predictors. As an example, consider Crime as response, with predictors the Income, the Unemployment, the Checkins and the Points of Interest. The result of the model (the prediction for the crime values), which are shown in Figure 11, when compared with the actual data for crime, confirms the association of crime with the specific predictors.

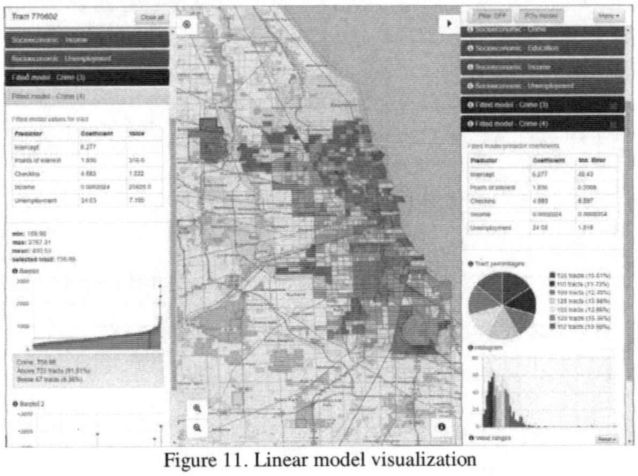

Figure 11. Linear model visualization

Moreover, before the model construction, there was no crime value for the upper left tract in the dataset. As we observe in Figure 11, the same tract has a value and appears in red color. Since this tract is selected (red outline), the data for that tract as derived from the linear model are shown in the left tray.

V. CITYSENSE DATABASE

The diverse and complex nature of the data used in CitySense application poses considerable challenges in data handling and storage. Thus, data come in many different formats and comprise varying content. Therefore, CitySense Database was designed with a flexible structure that can accommodate the diverse styles of the data.

A. Database Requirements

In order to meet the requirements of the application, we opted to use a relational database, which allows the application to immediately retrieve the necessary information based on several criteria. The efficient organization of information regarding PoI, Open Census, and Social Media data, requires a database that can adapt to their diverse nature. Specifically:

- Points of Interest require the storage of accompanying features such as name and location. The tract where the PoI is located is also stored, in order to achieve efficient aggregation based on tracts. At the same time, it is necessary to store the PoI category that each PoI belongs to (Arts & Entertainment, Food, etc.), so that aggregation based on categories is possible as well. Finally, Points of Interest have no need for separate time information, since they are considered static in time.
- Open Census Data comprise both static and temporal data. For example, demographic data, socio-economic indicators, and health indicators are presented as static data and, therefore, temporal information storage is not required for them. On the other hand, crime data require the storage of information about crime distribution over time (per month, day of week, etc.).
- Social Media Data, namely tweets and check-ins, are essentially temporal data. It is, therefore, necessary to store the information on their distribution over time. Besides spatial information storage, which is necessary for both tweets and check-ins, our system also needs to store the associated PoI category for check-ins. This is needed for check-in aggregation per PoI category.

B. Database Design and Schema

The main goal of the CitySense project is to exploit as much data as possible for a particular area, in order to have a realistic depiction of its "trace" on multiple levels. Therefore, the database presented here is designed to meet all the requirements of CitySense application, and also to be flexible to adapt to future requirements and store new data that may arise. The corresponding ER diagram of the database is presented in Figure 12.

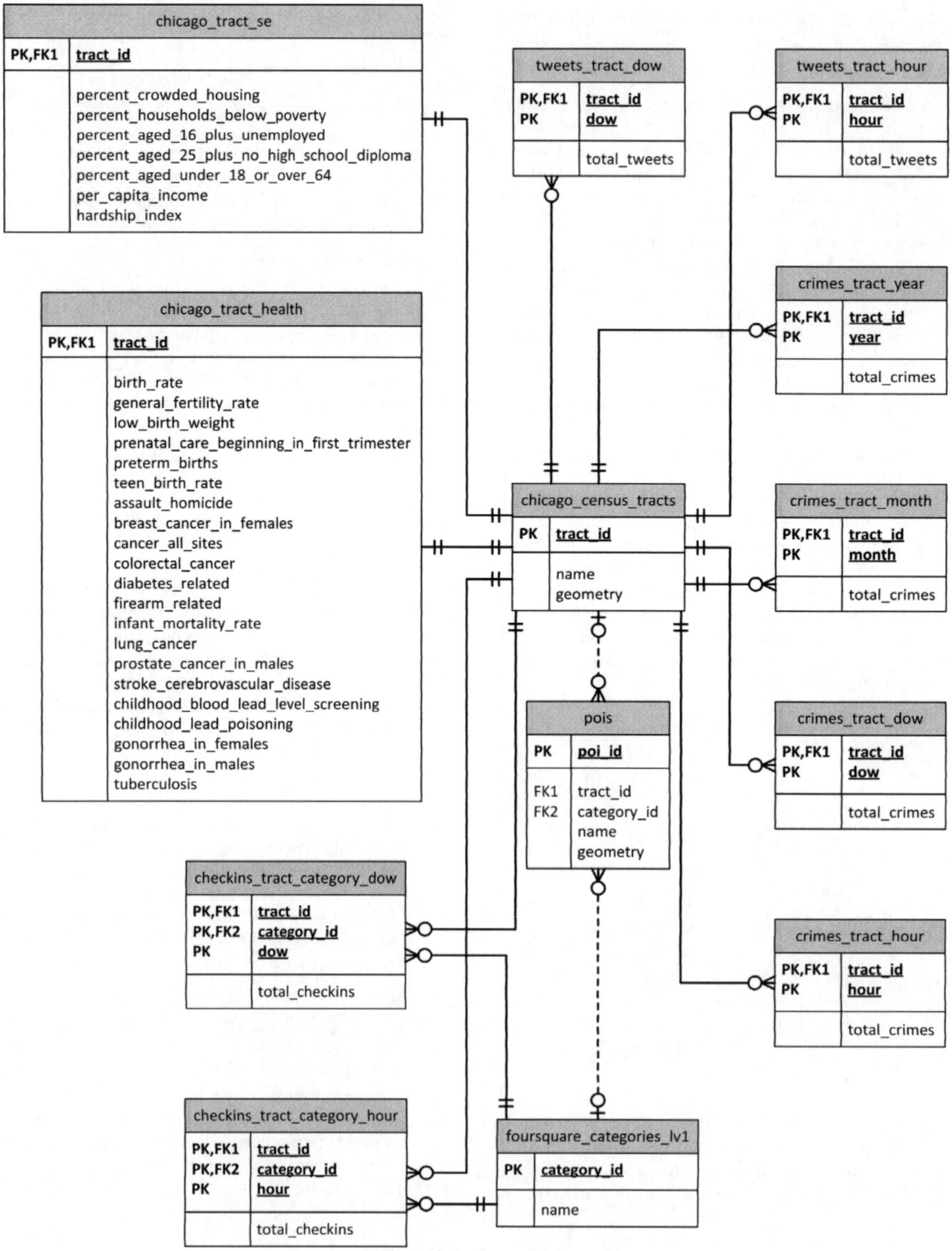

Figure 12. Database schema

The following is a detailed description of all the tables forming the database:

- **chicago_census_tracts:** The table contains all Chicago tracts that the application supports. More specifically, it contains the tract unique identifier, tract name, and polygon geometry that encompasses the tract.
- **chicago_tract_se:** The table is used to store the socio-economic indicator data used by the application. More specifically, it contains the per capita income, poverty rates, unemployment rate, etc., per tract.
- **chicago_tract_health:** The table is used to store the health indicator data used by the application. More specifically, it contains indicators of infant mortality, premature births, fertility, etc., per tract.
- **crimes_tract_year:** The table contains the crime data that the application uses. The table stores the number of crimes per tract at a yearly time breakdown.
- **crimes_tract_month:** The table contains the crime data that the application uses. The table stores the number of crimes per tract at a monthly time breakdown.
- **crimes_tract_dow:** The table contains the crime data that the application uses. The table stores the number of crimes per tract and day of week.
- **crimes_tract_hour:** The table contains the crime data that the application uses. The table stores the number of crimes per tract and time of day.
- **tweets_tract_dow:** The table contains the geo-located tweets data that the application uses. The table stores the number of tweets per tract and day of week.
- **tweets_tract_hour:** The table contains the geo-located tweets data that the application uses. The table stores the number of tweets per tract and time of day.
- **foursquare_categories_lv1:** The table is used to store the PoI categories that the application uses. The information stored consists of the unique identifier of the PoI category and the category name.
- **pois:** The table is used to store the Points of Interest that the application uses. The information stored consists of the unique identifier of the point of interest, its name, the point geometry that pinpoints the PoI's location, as well as its category and the tract in which the PoI is located.
- **checkins_tract_category_dow:** The table contains the data of the geolocated tweets that represent check-ins at some point of interest. The table stores the number of check-ins per tract, PoI category, and day of week.
- **checkins_tract_category_hour:** The table contains the data of the geolocated tweets that represent check-ins at some point of interest. The table stores the number of check-ins per tract, PoI category, and time of day.

The application is using a PostgreSQL database system. PostgreSQL is an open source relational database management system. To manage spatial information in an efficient way, we used the PostGIS extension of PostgreSQL, the official spatial extension of PostgreSQL. PostGIS is a software library that adds support for geographic objects (polygons, points) to PostgreSQL databases.

VI. CONCLUSION AND FUTURE WORK

In this work, we presented CitySense, a dynamic urban area viewer that provides a rich visualization of city's life, by integrating disparate datasets. The application helps answer questions and reveals several aspects of city life that would not be obvious from just observing the datasets. In order to accomplish that, we developed special data collection and managing tools, rich visualization and filtering functions and dealt with several technical challenges. Currently, we are developing the feature of dynamic visualization of social media data (tweet posts, check-ins and hashtags). The support for dynamic datasets could be used to cover city power consumption and traffic data in the future. Another future target concerns the incorporation of road network information into our system. Users could calculate the actual distance between PoIs, by exploiting special road network based functions provided by CitySense. Finally, as more and more data is integrated through CitySense, the problem of scalability will arise. Therefore, a cloud data infrastructure is considered to fit CitySense's future data storing and managing needs.

ACKNOWLEDGMENT

This work was partially supported by the "Research Programs for Excellence 2014-2016 – CitySense".

REFERENCES

[1] D. Pla Karidi, H. Nakos, A. Efentakis, and Y. Stavrakas, "CitySense: Retrieving, Visualizing and Combining Datasets on Urban Areas," Proceedings of the the Ninth International Conference on Advances in Databases, Knowledge, and Data Applications, DBKDA 2017.

[2] A. Crooks, D. Pfoser, A. Jenkins, A. Croitoru, A. Stefanidis, D. Smith, S. Karagiorgou, A. Efentakis, and G. Lamprianidis, "Crowdsourcing urban form and function," International Journal of Geographical Information Science 29.5, pp. 720-741, 2015.

[3] E. Drymonas, A. Efentakis, and D. Pfoser, "Opinion mapping travelblogs," In Proceedings of Terra Cognita workshop in conjunction with the 10th International Semantic Web Conference 2011, pp. 23-36.

[4] A. Efentakis, S. Brakatsoulas, N. Grivas, G. Lamprianidis, K. Patroumpas., and D. Pfoser, "Towards a flexible and scalable fleet management service," In Proceedings of the Sixth ACM SIGSPATIAL International Workshop on Computational Transportation Science, p. 79, 2013.

[5] A. Efentakis, N. Grivas, G. Lamprianidis, G. Magenschab, and D. Pfoser, "Isochrones, traffic and DEMOgraphics," In Proceedings of the 21st ACM SIGSPATIAL International Conference on Advances in Geographic Information Systems, pp. 548-551, 2013.

[6] A. Efentakis, S. Brakatsoulas, N. Grivas, and D. Pfoser, "Crowdsourcing turning restrictions for OpenStreetMap," In EDBT/ICDT Workshops, pp. 355-362, 2014.

[7] A. Efentakis, N. Grivas, D. Pfoser, and Y. Vassiliou, "Crowdsourcing turning-restrictions from map-matched trajectories," Information Systems, 64, pp. 221-236, 2017.

[8] J. Cranshaw, R. Schwartz, J. Hong, and N. Sadeh, "The livehoods project: Utilizing social media to understand the dynamics of a city," Association for the Advancement of Artificial Intelligence, 2012.

[9] S. Wakamiya, R. Lee, and K. Sumiya, "Crowd-sourced urban life monitoring: urban area characterization based crowd behavioral patterns from twitter," In Proceedings of the 6th International Conference on Ubiquitous Information Management and Communication, p. 26, 2012.

[10] R. Lee, S. Wakamiya, and K. Sumiya, "Urban area characterization based on crowd behavioral lifelogs over Twitter," Personal and ubiquitous computing, 17(4), pp. 605-620, 2013.

[11] V. Frias-Martinez, V. Soto, H. Hohwald, and E. Frias-Martinez, "Characterizing urban landscapes using geolocated tweets," International Confernece on Social Computing (SocialCom), pp. 239-248, 2012.

[12] A. Noulas, S. Scellato, C. Mascolo, and M. Pontil, "An Empirical Study of Geographic User Activity Patterns in Foursquare," International Conference on Web And Social Media (ICWSM), pp. 70-573, 2012.

[13] A. Pozdnoukhov and C. Kaiser, "Space-time dynamics of topics in streaming text," In Proceedings of the 3rd ACM SIGSPATIAL International Workshop on Location-Based Social Networks, pp. 1-8, 2011.

[14] A. Noulas, S. Scellato, C. Mascolo, and M. Pontil, "Exploiting Semantic Annotations for Clustering Geographic Areas and Users in Location-based Social Networks," The Social Mobile Web, 11(2), 2011.

[15] F. Kling and A. Pozdnoukhov, "When a city tells a story: urban topic analysis," In Proceedings of the 20th International Conference On Advances in Geographic Information Systems, pp. 482-485, 2012.

[16] I. Grabovitch-Zuyev, Y. Kanza, E. Kravi, and B. Pat, "On the correlation between textual content and geospatial locations in microblogs," In Proceedings of Workshop on Managing and Mining Enriched Geo-Spatial Data, p. 3, 2014.

[17] K. Kamath., J. Caverlee, K. Lee, and Z. Cheng, "Spatio-temporal dynamics of online memes: a study of geo-tagged tweets," In Proceedings of the 22nd International Conference on World Wide Web, pp. 667-678, 2013.

[18] S. Kinsella, V. Murdock, and N. O'Hare, "I'm eating a sandwich in Glasgow: modeling locations with tweets," In Proceedings of the 3rd international workshop on Search and mining user-generated contents, pp. 61-68, 2011.

[19] J. Cranshaw, E. Toch, J. Hong, A. Kittur, and N. Sadeh, "Bridging the gap between physical location and online social networks," In Proceedings of the 12th ACM International Conference On Ubiquitous Computing, pp. 119-128, 2010.

[20] D. Crandall, L. Backstrom, D. Cosley, S. Suri, D. Huttenlocher, and J. Kleinberg, "Inferring social ties from geographic coincidences," Proceedings of the National Academy of Sciences, 107(52), 2010.

[21] E. Cho, S. Myers, and J. Leskovec, "Friendship and mobility: user movement in location-based social networks," In Proceedings of the 17th ACM SIGKDD International Conference on Knowledge Discovery and Data Mining, pp. 1082-1090, 2011.

[22] L. Backstrom, E. Sun, and C. Marlow, "Find me if you can: improving geographical prediction with social and spatial proximity," In Proceedings of the 19th International Conference on World Wide Web, pp. 61-70, 2010.

[23] Z. Cheng, J. Caverlee, and K. Lee, "You are where you tweet: a content-based approach to geo-locating twitter users," In Proceedings of the 19th ACM International Conference on Information and Knowledge Management, pp. 759-768, 2010.

[24] C. Budak, T. Georgiou, D. Agrawal, and A. El Abbadi, "Geoscope: Online detection of geo-correlated information trends in social networks," Proceedings of the VLDB Endowment, 7(4), pp. 229-240, 2013.

[25] R. Lee and K. Sumiya, "Measuring geographical regularities of crowd behaviors for Twitter-based geo-social event detection," In Proceedings of the 2nd ACM SIGSPATIAL International Workshop on Location Based Social Networks, pp. 1-10 ,2010.

[26] M. Veloso, S. Phithakkitnukoon, and C. Bento, "Sensing urban mobility with taxi flow," In Proceedings of the 3rd ACM SIGSPATIAL International Workshop on Location-Based Social Networks, pp. 41-44, 2011.

[27] L. Liu, A. Biderman, and C. Ratti, "Urban mobility landscape: Real time monitoring of urban mobility patterns," In Proceedings of the 11th International Conference on Computers in Urban Planning and Urban Management, pp. 1-16, 2009.

[28] C. Ratti, D. Frenchman, R. Pulselli, and S. Williams, "Mobile landscapes: using location data from cell phones for urban analysis," Environment and Planning B: Planning and Design, 33(5), pp. 727-748, 2006.

[29] J. Reades, F. Calabrese, A. Sevtsuk, and C. Ratti, "Cellular census: Explorations in urban data collection," IEEE Pervasive Computing, 6(3), 2007.

[30] M. Gonzalez, C. Hidalgo, and A. Barabasi, "Understanding individual human mobility patterns," Nature, 453(7196), pp. 779-782, 2008.

[31] F. Calabrese, M. Diao, G. Di Lorenzo, J. Ferreira, and C. Ratti, "Understanding individual mobility patterns from urban sensing data: A mobile phone trace example," Transportation research part C: Emerging Technologies, 26, pp. 301-313, 2013.

[32] D. Taniar and J. Goh, "On mining movement pattern from mobile users." International Journal of Distributed Sensor Networks, 3(1), pp. 69-86, 2007.

[33] A. Chua, E. Marcheggiani, L. Servillo, and A. Moere, "Flowsampler: Visual analysis of urban flows in geolocated social media data," In International Conference on Social Informatics, pp. 5-17, 2014.

[34] J. L. Toole, C. Herrera-Yaqüe, C. M. Schneider, and M González, "Coupling human mobility and social ties," Journal of The Royal Society Interface, 12(105), 2015.

[35] B. Hawelka, I. Sitko, E. Beinat, S. Sobolevsky, P. Kazakopoulos, and C. Ratti, "Geo-located Twitter as proxy for global mobility patterns," Cartography and Geographic Information Science, 41(3), pp. 260-271, 2014.

[36] Z. Cheng, J. Caverlee, K. Lee, and D. Z. Sui, "Exploring millions of footprints in location sharing services," International Conference on Web And Social Media (ICWSM), pp. 81-88, 2011.

[37] R. Harris, P. Sleight, and R. Webber, "Geodemographics, GIS and Neighbourhood Targeting," Journal of Direct, Data and Digital Marketing Practice, 8, pp. 364-368, 2007.

[38] P. A. Longley and M. Adnan, "Geo-temporal Twitter demographics," International Journal of Geographical Information Science, 30(2), pp. 369-389, 2016.

[39] D. Hristova, M. J. Williams, M. Musolesi, P. Panzarasa, and C. Mascolo, "Measuring urban social diversity using interconnected geo-social networks," In Proceedings of the 25th International Conference on World Wide Web, pp. 21-30, 2016.

[40] A. Llorente, M. Garcia-Herranz, M. Cebrian, and E. Moro, "Social media fingerprints of unemployment," PloS one 10(5), 2015.

[41] H. Abdelhaq, C. Sengstock, and M. Gertz, "Eventweet: Online localized event detection from twitter," Proceedings of the VLDB Endowment, 6(12), pp. 1326-1329, 2013.

[42] The one million tweet map, retrieved on April 8 2017 from http://onemilliontweetmap.com

[43] Tweepsmap, retrieved on April 8 2017 from https://tweepsmap.com

[44] Trendsmap Realtime Local Twitter Trends, retrieved on April 8 2017 from http://trendsmap.com

[45] MapD Tweetmap, retrieved on April 8 2017 from https://www.mapd.com/demos/tweetmap

[46] Mapping America: Every City, Every Block, retrieved on April 8 2017 from http://www.nytimes.com/projects/census/2010/explorer.html

[47] Social Explorer, retrieved on April 8 2017 from https://www.socialexplorer.com/explore/maps

[48] CitySense, retrieved on April 8 2017 from http://citysense.imis.athena-innovation.gr:8080/citysense/

A Non-Linear Method to Interpolate Binary Images Using Location and Neighborhood Adaptive Rules

Pullat Joy Prabhakaran
International Institute of Information Technology – Bangalore
Electronic city, Bangalore, India 560100
e-mail: joy@iiitb.ac.in

Palanganda Ganapathy Poonacha
International Institute of Information Technology – Bangalore
Electronic city, Bangalore, India 560100
e-mail: poonacha.pg@iiitb.ac.in

Abstract— **In this paper, we propose a new zooming technique for binary images, using location and neighborhood adaptive, non-linear interpolation rules. These rules are inspired by the way an artist would draw an enlarged image. Using simple examples, we show that the output generated by popular interpolation techniques is very different from what a human does. Our rules are based on such observations for simple objects, and they try to mimic what an artist does. Using these rules, we interpolate complex images and demonstrate the impact. We compare our method with bicubic interpolation and show that our method gives better visual quality. We also show that, on an average, our method results in higher PSNR and a lower MPSNR. The SSIM of the output images are nearly the same for both methods. Our method overcomes a number of problems associated with known interpolation techniques, such as blurring and thickening of edges. Our method uses a set of sixteen rules in five categories. Each pixel in the interpolated image is computed by a chosen rule. The choice depends on the location of the pixel and the content in the neighborhood. The size of the neighborhood varies. Some rules can be influenced by distant pixels in the input and can impact distant pixels in the output. We present examples showing the effectiveness of our method. The results are visually appealing. We show that lines and dots, with single pixel thickness, retain their thickness. Inclined lines and solids don't develop as much jaggedness as happens with bicubic interpolation. Similarly, curves are also relatively smoother.**

Keywords- resolution; interpolation; binary-image; thinnes; location-adaptive; neighborhood-adaptiv; corner; slope.

I. Introduction

When High Resolution (HR) images are created by interpolating Low Resolution (LR) images, unpleasant artifacts are seen. Interpolation artifacts are errors introduced into the HR image by the interpolation process. In [1], we proposed an interpolation method for binary images that generated visually appealing images. Popular methods like nearest neighbor, bilinear and bicubic [2] interpolation, generate more unpleasant artifacts like smoothing of edges and pixelation. Figure 1 shows the artifacts that are created when a dot and a line are interpolated using bicubic interpolation and Average of Nearest Neighbors (ANN) [3] interpolation. For clarity, the image shown is magnified by a factor of 8, and some of the unchanging regions have been removed. The interpolation is by a factor of 2. Figure 1B and 1D show the outputs of bicubic and ANN interpolation, respectively. Interpolation introduces artifacts and these are the intermediate shades of gray. To bring this out clearly, the new shades have been assigned colors in Figure 1C and 1E. Different colors represent different magnitudes of gray. The specific colors have no significance here. We see that more pixels are distorted by bicubic interpolation.

It can be seen that these kinds of errors will not be introduced by an artist. Also, a human can identify and eliminate many of the errors caused by popular interpolation methods. Our method tries to encapsulate some of the things that we feel an artist does to enlarge images.

Interpolation artifacts are most likely to arise at object edges, on lines and curves that are one pixel thick, on inclined and curved solids or object intersections. Popular interpolation methods cause more unwanted artifacts in the case of binary image zooming.

A large number of interpolation methods are available in the literature [1]–[15]. Some of these, like Nearest Neighbor, Bilinear and Bicubic [2] methods, use surface fitting techniques with pre-defined constraints. These methods often create undesirable artifacts in the output. Many methods have been proposed to minimize such artifacts. In [4], an orientation constraint is computed for each pixel to be generated. The pixel value is computed as a function of this constraint and the four surrounding neighbors. In an earlier work [3], we proposed an interpolation method called Average of Nearest Neighbors (ANN). This was based on the idea that each pixel in the interpolated image should be generated by using all the available nearest neighbors in the original image and none of the other pixels.

In [5], curvature of the low resolution image is evaluated and this curvature information is interpolated using bilinear interpolation. The interpolated curvature information is used as a driving constraint to interpolate the complete image. In [6], the image is first interpolated using bilinear interpolation. As a second step, the quality is improved using a fourth order Partial Differential Equation (PDE) based method. A directional bicubic scheme is proposed in [7]. Here, the strongest edge in each 7x7 neighborhood is detected. If the edge strength is greater than a threshold, a one-dimensional bicubic interpolation is done along the edge. Our method shares some similarities with [7] because it also tries to find and preserves local edges.

In [8] and [9], a two-step super resolution process is studied. In the first step, the low resolution image is interpolated using Bicubic interpolation. Then, the HR image is further processed to improve the quality at the edges. In [8], the gradient profile of the LR image is used as a driving

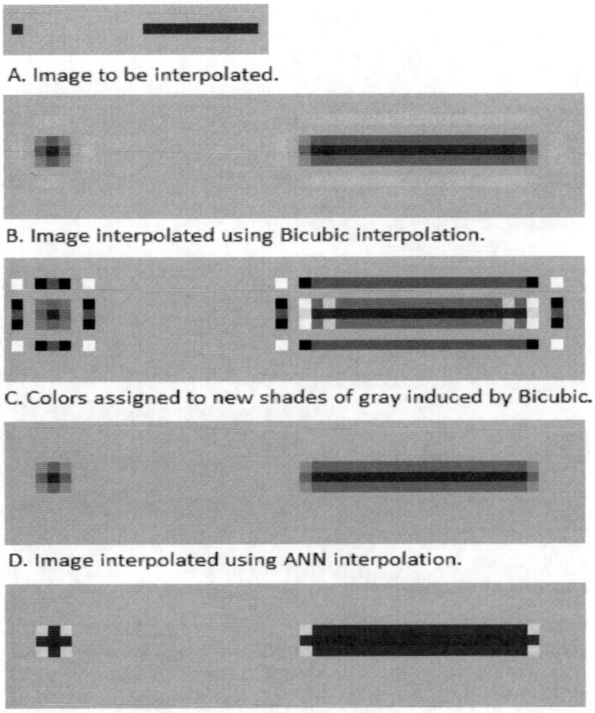

A. Image to be interpolated.

B. Image interpolated using Bicubic interpolation.

C. Colors assigned to new shades of gray induced by Bicubic.

D. Image interpolated using ANN interpolation.

E. Colors assigned to new shades of gray induced by ANN.

Figure 1. Impact of interpolation by different methods. The input dot and line are one pixel thick. The original image has two shades of gray. Interpolation introduces pixels in shades of gray that were not present in the original. In C and E, the shades introduced by interpolation are shown in different colors for better visibility.

gradient prior to change the gradient profile of the interpolated image. This process makes the edges sharper. In [9], this idea is extended by splitting the feature space into multiple subspaces and generating multiple priors.

In some scenarios, a frame from a video sequence needs to be interpolated. In [10] and [11], techniques to use information from adjacent frames to improve quality are discussed. The former uses an adaptive Wiener filter while the later uses Delaunay triangulation.

A machine learning based approach is discussed in [12]. Unknown pixels in the interpolated image are generated using the training data set that best matches the region near the pixel. The patch around the unknown pixel is matched with patches in the training set. Using the best matched stored patch, the pixel is assigned a value. The algorithm to do the matching takes into account the LR patch and the neighboring patches. A training based method that incorporates an explicit noise model is used to expand binary text images in [13].

In [14], edges are found as a first step. The edges are used to compute unknown pixels using cubic spline. In [15], unknown pixels are assigned the value of the neighbor that is closest to the value got by bilinear interpolation.

In this paper, we propose a Location and Neighborhood Adaptive (LNA) interpolation for binary images to be scaled by a factor of 2. Qualitatively, we show that the method generates visually pleasing images. For quantitative evaluation, we have compared LNA with bicubic interpolation using three standard metrics. These are Peak Signal to Noise Ratio (PSNR), Modified PSNR (MPSNR) and Structural Similarity (SSIM) index. PSNR represents a measure of the peak error while MPSNR is PSNR computed after applying a low pass filter. SSIM tries to measure the perceptual difference between two images.

PSNR is computed as:

$$\mathrm{PSNR} = 10\log_{10}\frac{\mathrm{Max}^2}{\mathrm{MSE}}$$

Where Max is the maximum possible value of each pixel and has the value 1 in our examples of binary images.

MPSNR is computed by passing the images being compared through a low pass filter, and then finding the PSNR of the filtered images. We have used a nine point, mean filter for our computations.

SSIM is computed as follows:

$$\mathrm{SSIM}(x,y) = \frac{(2\mu_x\mu_y + c_1)(2\sigma_{xy} + c_2)}{(\mu_x^2 + \mu_y^2 + c_1)(\sigma_x^2 + \sigma_y^2 + c_2)}$$

where x and y are two windows of equal size, μ_x and μ_y are the averages of the values in x and y, σ_x and σ_y their variances and σ_{xy} the covariance of x and y. c_1 and c_2 are constants of value $(0.01 * L)^2$ and $(0.03 * L)^2$ respectively, where L is the maximum value of a pixel magnitude. For our samples, the value of L is 1.

SSIM index can be computed for different windows. We have divided the test images into equal blocks of size 8x8 and computed SSIM index for each block. The average of all the block indices is the SSIM index of the image.

To explain the LNA method and also to demonstrate some of its features, we have used a few synthetic images that we have created. To validate the method, we have used sixteen commonly used test images. These images are from USC [16], Kodak [17] and Hlevkin [18].

The rest of this paper is organized as follows. Section II explains the LNA process and gives an overview. Section III describes the interpolation process and the five categories of rules. Subsections A to E, in Section III, describe the categories and associated rules. Experimental results are given in Section IV. Conclusions and suggestions for further extensions are given in Section V.

II. THE LNA APPROACH TO INTERPOLATION

LNA comprises of a set of rules. The rules try to mimic what an artist would do to define each pixel in the interpolated image. The outputs of a few popular interpolation techniques are shown in Figure 1. We see that the output is different from what an artist is likely to generate. Some of these differences are because, in Figure 1, the algorithms were allowed to generate pixels in grayscale, i.e., each pixel could take any one of 256 shades of gray. In Figure 2, we restrict the input and output to binary, i.e., each

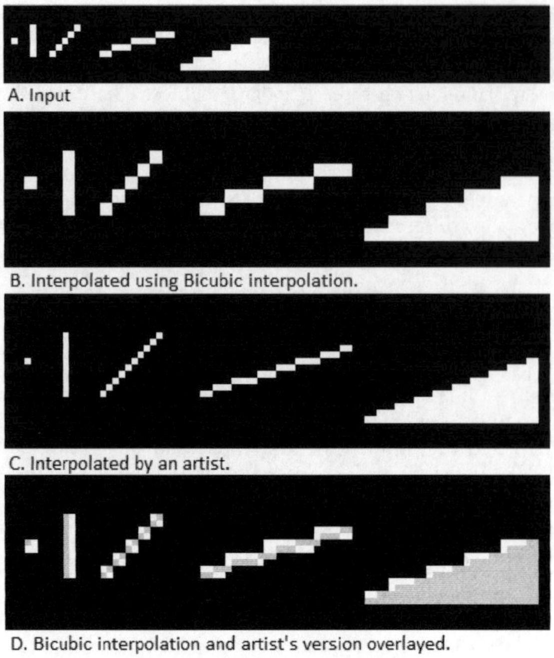

Figure 2. A comparison of simple figures interpolated using bicubic interpolation and interpolated by an artist.

pixel can take one of two possible values. Figure 2 shows the difference in result when a simple binary image is interpolated using bicubic interpolation and when an artist enlarges it.

Figure 2D overlays the results of the interpolation and the exact differences are seen. The artist has retained thin features as thin. As a result, the dot has remained a single pixel in HR and the line has retained single pixel thickness. Similarly, slopes are better formed when an artist enlarges an image.

The rules of LNA try to mimic the interpolation process of the artist. The rules required to interpolate a typical color image with three color planes or a typical grayscale image with 256 gray shades are very complex. In this paper, we demonstrate the effectiveness of the LNA approach for binary images. The rules for binary images cannot be directly extended to grayscale or color images.

The method consists of a set of sixteen rules, grouped into five categories. The rules are of widely varying complexities. The choice of rule to assign value to a pixel depends on its location and the content in the neighborhood. The size of the neighborhood is dynamic and depends on the content. Some rules can be influenced by distant pixels in the input, and some rules can influence distant pixels in the output. This can be seen in Rules 14 and 16, described in the next section.

If the neighborhood meets certain conditions, our method implicitly tries to detect if an unknown pixel is part of an edge, a line or a corner. Based on this, it applies appropriate rules. To maintain smoothness of lines and edges, it both adds and deletes pixels in the foreground color when

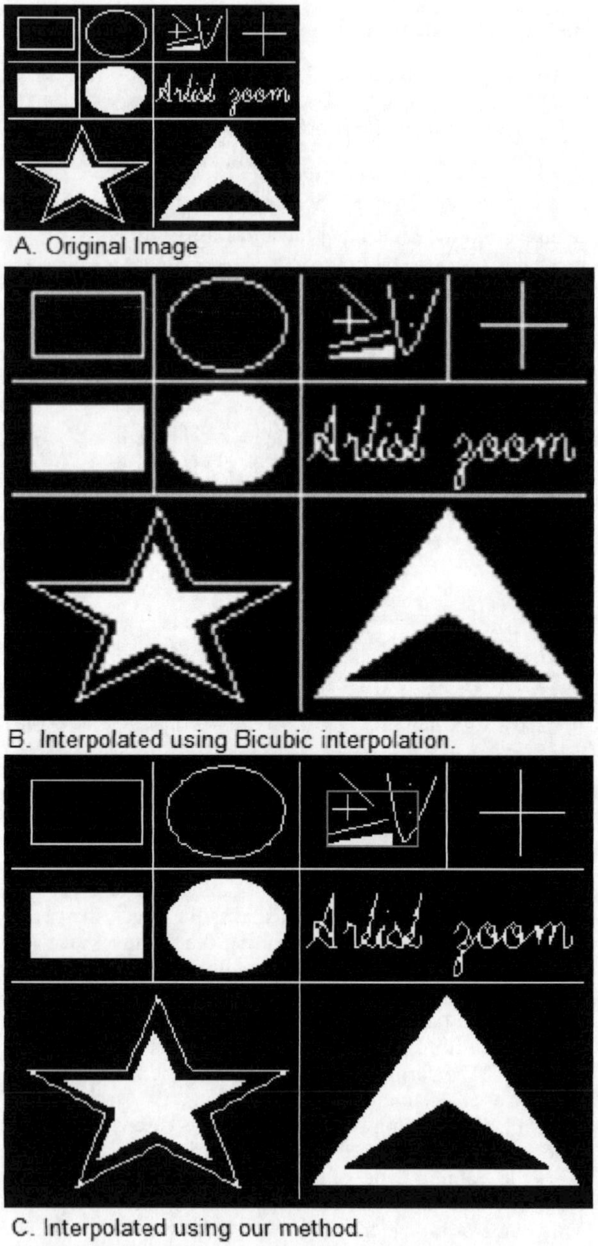

Figure 3. Comparison of our method with bicubic interpolation.

compared with simple pixel replication. The deletion ensures that smoothing does not cause extra thickening.

The interpolation process and individual rules are explained in Section III. The explanation is with reference to simple geometric figures. In Section IV we show that by applying the same rules to binary versions of standard test images like Lena, Baboon, Monarch and Barbara, we get good visual results.

Figure 3A shows the image used to explain our method. Figure 3B shows the image, interpolated using bicubic interpolation. The bicubic interpolation is done using Matlab. Figure 3C shows the same image, magnified using our method. As can be seen, the bicubic interpolation introduces more distortion than our method. The region in Figure 3C, shown in the red box, will be used to explain our method.

III. THE INTERPOLATION PROCESS

LNA categorizes unknown pixels in the HR canvas based on their locations. This is shown in Figure 4. The circles in the image represent individual pixels. At the start of the interpolation process, all these pixels are unknown. We categorize the pixels as O, H, V and D. Pixels on the even rows and even columns are of type O. The O pixels are what would be retained if the HR image is decimated by subsampling, using a scale factor of 2. Pixels on even rows and odd columns are of type H. Pixels on the odd rows and even columns are of type V. Pixels on odd rows and odd columns are of type D. Every pixel in the image falls into one of these categories.

Our method comprises of a set of rules and a decision tree to choose the rule for each pixel. Figure 5 shows a high level flowchart of the interpolation process. The first part depicts the initial setup. It starts with the LR image being read in. After this, a two pixel wide empty margin is added on all four sides of the LR image. This makes it possible for LNA to process the boundary pixels in the LR image without having additional logic to handle boundary conditions. After the interpolation process, this empty margin is stripped from the interpolated HR image.

After the margin is added, an empty HR canvas, with twice the height and width of the LR image (including the empty margin), is created. Then, a four pixel wide margin is created in the canvas by setting all the pixels in this margin to background color. This ends the setup process.

After setup, the HR canvas is scanned pixel by pixel. The scan starts at the top left corner (0, 0), and ends at the bottom right. We refer to the pixel at the current scan location as the current pixel. The first two decision boxes in the flowchart control the scan.

The third decision box checks if the current pixel has already been assigned a value. This can happen if it is a part of the empty margin, or if the current pixel was assigned a value when the scan was at an earlier pixel. The latter is possible because LNA can assign values to multiple pixels in a single iteration. So, if the current pixel has already been assigned a value, the scan continues to the next location.

The next three checks are to see if the current pixel is an 'O' pixel, 'H' pixel or 'V' pixel. The 'O' pixel is assigned a value using the one rule in Category 1. This does not depend on the neighborhood.

Some rules used to define ‘H’, ‘V’ and ‘D’ pixels, use multiple pixels in the neighborhood to decide the value of a single pixel. The number of pixels a rule considers and the locations of the pixels considered, depend on the values of the pixels, i.e., the image content. The logic used to choose the relevant neighborhood for a rule is explained along with the rules in the subsections III A to III E.

The 'H' pixel is assigned a value using Category 2 rules. An 'H' pixel has two immediate LR neighbors, one on the left and other to the right. Category 2 rules use the LR neighbors, and, under certain conditions, may use a bigger neighborhood. This is discussed in the next section when we discuss individual rules.

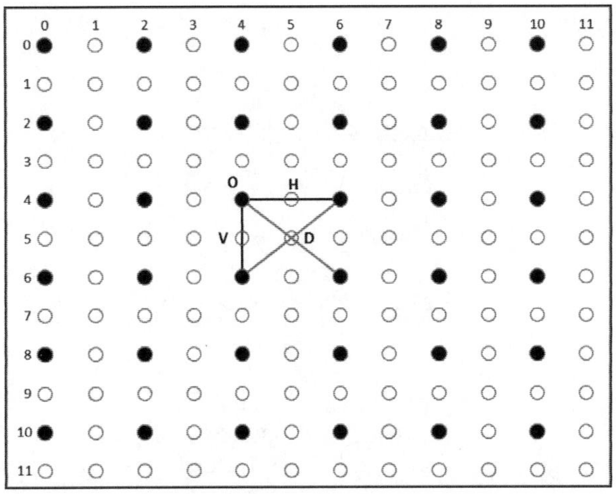

Figure 4. A representation of the HR image showing the types of pixels that need to be generated through interpolation.

The 'V' pixel is assigned a value using Category 3 rules. These are similar to Category 2 rules. The only difference is that a 'V' pixel has LR neighbors above and below.

If the current pixel is not of type 'O', 'H' or 'V', it is a 'D' pixel. These are assigned values using Category 4 rules. Some of the Category 4 rules assign values to pixels that are not in the current scan location. This is shown as the next step in the flow chart. If this path is not taken, there is a possibility that the neighborhood is such that Category 5 rules are to be applied. This is the next step shown.

After the rules pertaining to the current pixel and its neighborhood are applied, the scan moves to the next pixel and the process gets repeated. Once the scan completes, the margin that was added in the beginning is removed and the HR image is stored.

In all the examples, we have used a white foreground and black background.

In the interpolation process, we say that a pixel in the LR image is horizontally thin if its immediate horizontal neighbors, on the left and right, are of different magnitude from it. Similarly, we say that a pixel is vertically thin if the pixel's immediate vertical neighbors, above and below, are of different magnitude from it.

Some rules can assign values to pixels ahead of the current scan location. Some rules can override or pre-empt other rules, depending on the neighborhood conditions.

Depending on the neighborhood of the pixel, one of the rules in the chosen category is invoked. The rules, in each category, have an order of precedence. If one rule is applied, the rules with lower precedence are not considered. In the following subsections, the rules are described in the order of their decreasing precedence.

Category 5 has one rule and it can change values assigned by other rules.

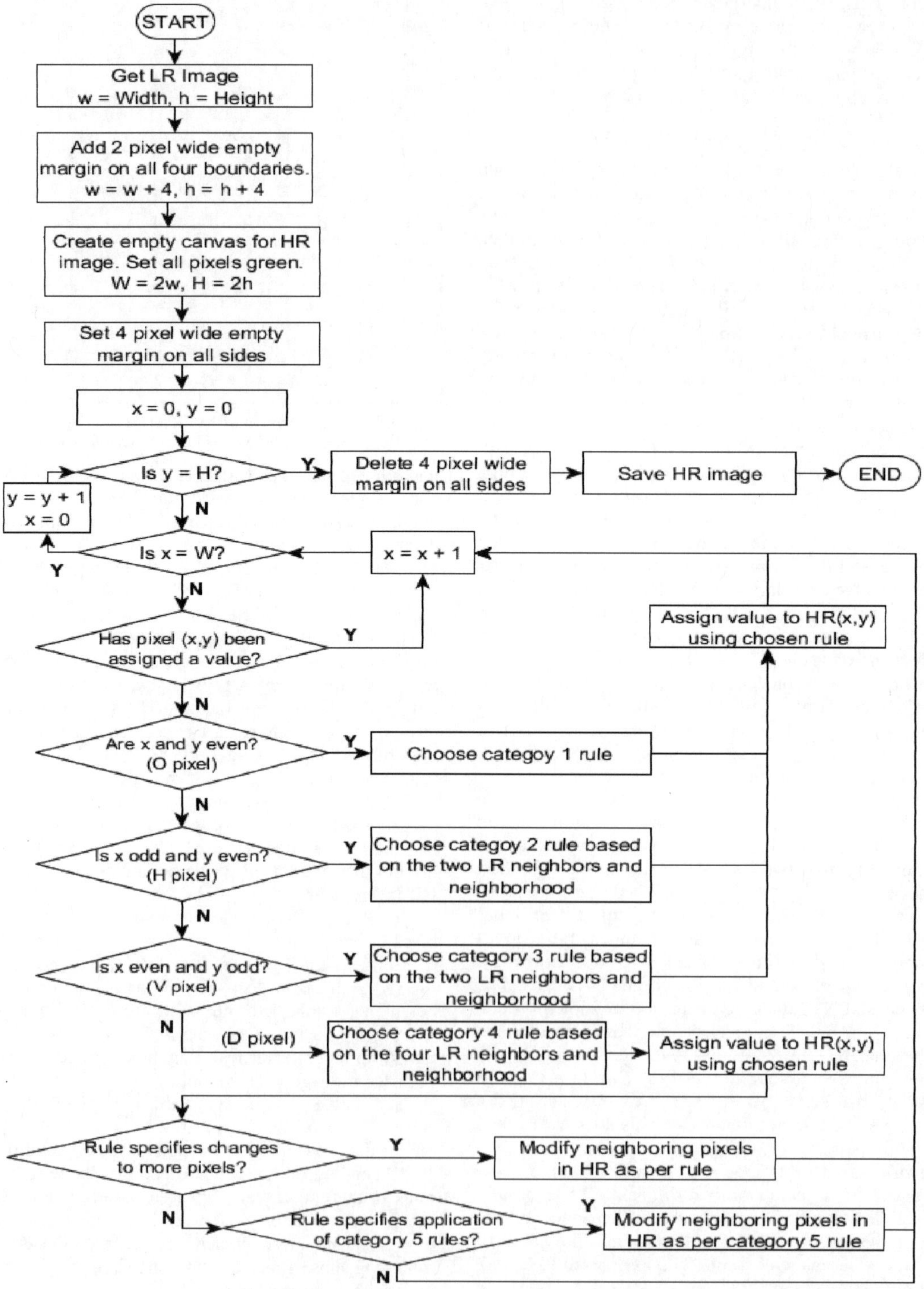

Figure 5. High level flowchart of the LNA process flow and decision tree.

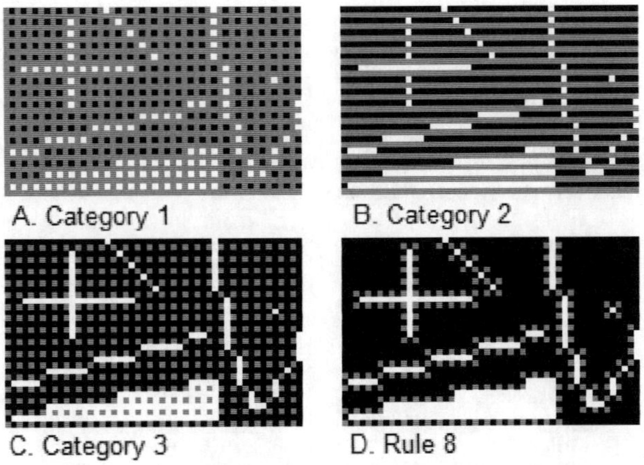

Figure 6. Impact of different rules. The captions show the additional category of rules or specific rule applied.

The method is implemented as a single pass. It starts at the top left corner and scans through the image, row by row. For each pixel, it chooses the appropriate rule and applies it.

We describe the method as a set of rules. Corresponding to each rule or a group of rules, we have a figure showing impact of the rule or group of rules. For example, Figure 6A represents the output if only Category 1 rules are applied and Figure 6B shows the output if both Category 1 and Category 2 rules are applied. The change from Figure 6A to Figure 6B is the impact of the Category 2 rules.

A. *Category 1 rule*

This category has one rule and applies to all pixels of the type O. In Figure 4, these pixels are shown as filled, black circles. The rule maps all pixels in the LR image to the HR image.

1) Rule 1: Assign the value of the pixel at location (x, y) in the original image (LR) to the pixel at location (2x,2y) in the interpolated (HR) image.

For example, pixels at locations (4,4) and (6,4) in the HR image are assigned values of pixels at locations (2,2) and (3,2) respectively in the LR image. Figure 6A shows the enlarged portion of the HR canvas and it depicts how the empty canvas gets partially populated.

B. *Category 2 rules*

The three rules in this category apply to unknown pixels of the type H. H pixels have a known horizontal neighbor each on the left and right. In Figure 4, the neighbors of pixel H are shown connected to it by black lines. The values of these neighbors are known because they are the values in the LR image.

1) Rule 2: If the neighbors on the left and right are equal, assign the value of the neighbors to the unknown pixel.

2) Rule 3: If the neighbors on the left and right differ and if only one of them is horizontally thin, assign the value of the pixel that is not thin to the unknown pixel.

3) Rule 4: If none of the preceding rules assigned a value to the unknown pixel, set it to the background color.

Figure 6B is generated by applying Rules 1 to 4. The changes from Figure 6A are caused by the category 2 rules. We see that the horizontal lines, in both colors, have become better formed. We also see that unknown pixels on either side of known pixels, in a vertical line in the foreground color, have been set to the background color.

C. *Category 3 rules*

These rules are similar to the category 2 rules but apply to unknown pixels of the type V. Such pixels have vertical neighbors with known magnitudes. In Figure 4, the neighbors of pixel V are shown connected to it by black lines. Here we will use the concept of vertical thinness that was defined earlier.

1) Rule 5: If the neighbors above and below are equal, assign their value to the unknown pixel.

2) Rule 6: If the neighbors above and below differ and if only one of them is vertically thin, assign the value of the pixel that is not thin to the unknown pixel.

3) Rule 7: If none of the preceding rules assigned a value to the unknown pixel, set it to the background color.

Figure 6C shows the impact of these rules. The changes from Figure 6B to Figure 6C are caused by the category 3 rules. We see that the vertical lines have become well-formed and more unknown pixels near horizontal lines have been assigned values.

D. *Category 4 rules*

The eight rules in this category apply to the unknown pixels of the type D. Such pixels have four diagonal neighbors whose magnitudes are known. In Figure 4, the four neighbors of pixel D are shown connected to it by red lines. Unlike the rules in the preceding categories, some of the rules here impact more than one pixel. However, they do not change any pixel that was assigned value by Rule 1.

1) Rule 8: If all four diagonal neighbors are equal, assign the value of the neighbors to the unknown pixel.

Figure 6D is generated by applying Rules 1 to 8. The change from Figure 6C to Figure 6D is caused by Rule 8. We see that most of the unknown pixels have been resolved and solids are well-formed. Most of the unknown pixels that remain are at the edges.

2) Rule 9: If all four neighbors are not equal and diagonally opposite neighbors are equal, then attempt to resolve as follows. If one and only one diagonal pair is both horizontally and vertically thin, then assign its value to the unknown pixel. Else, if all neighbors are horizontally and vertically thin, then assign it the foreground color.

Figure 7A shows the impact of this rule. We see that the diagonal lines are better formed. Unknown pixels adjacent to the diagonal line and also at its end remain unresolved.

3) Rule 10: If all four neighbors are not equal but the diagonally opposite neighbors are equal and the two diagonally opposite pixels in the foreground color are end points of two horizontal or two vertical line segments, assign the foreground color to the unknown pixel. After doing this, apply Rule 16.

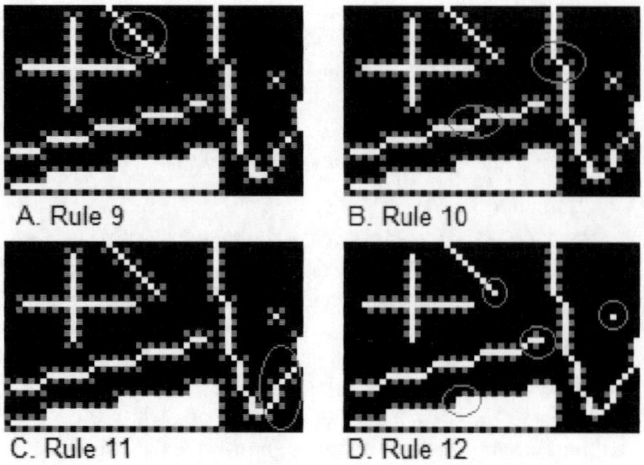

Figure 7. Impact of applying Rules 9-12. The captions show the additional rule and the red call outs show its impact.

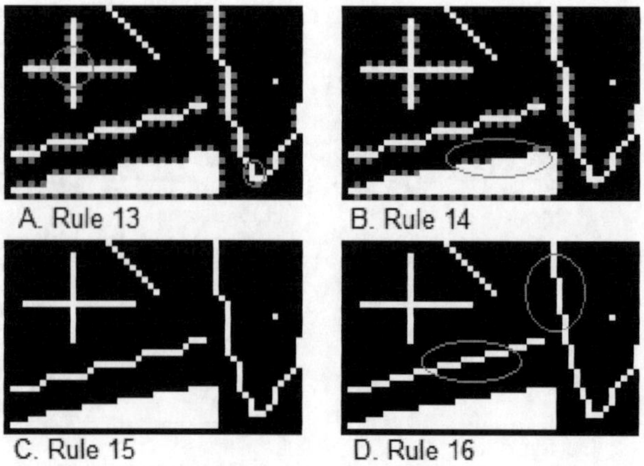

Figure 8. Impact of Rules 13-16. The captions show the additional rule and the red call outs show its impact.

Figure 7B shows the impact of this rule. This rule connects line segments forming longer lines or curves.

4) Rule 11: If diagonally opposite neighbors are equal and the preceding rules did not resolve the unknown pixel, assign it the foreground color.

Figure 7C shows the impact is similar to that of Rule 10.

5) Rule 12: If the unknown pixel has three diagonal neighbors of the background color, set it to the background color.

This rule makes corners of solids and dots better formed. The impact can be seen in Figure 7D.

The next three rules use the following definitions. These are applicable when only three neighbors are equal to the foreground color. These pixels form two perpendicular segments. Each of these has a length of two pixels or is part of a longer segment. The lengths are from the LR image.

Corner: If both the perpendicular arms have a length of two or if both of them are parts of longer segments.

Slope: If one perpendicular arm is of length two and the other is part of a longer segment.

Well-formed slope: If the longer arm of a slope does not have any adjacent pixel, on the same side as the shorter arm, having the foreground color.

6) Rule 13: If the unknown pixel has three neighbors that are a part of a corner, set it to the background color.

Figure 8A shows the impact of this rule. The corners formed by intersecting segments become better formed.

7) Rule 14: If three neighbors are part of a slope, set the unknown pixel to the foreground color. If the slope is well-formed, extend the unknown pixel in the direction of the longer arm by the length of the longer arm in the original image. Flag the extension to prevent overwriting.

Figure 8B shows the impact of the rule. Rule 14 differs from the preceding rules as it can impact pixels far removed from the unknown pixel. It makes inclines smoother, as seen on the inclined edge of the solid element in the figure.

This smoothness in the feature is achieved by converting each step like feature into two steps. This makes transitions smaller. This rule can impact pixels about half way across in the image, in either horizontal or vertical directions. The new step drawn is always on an odd numbered row or column. So it does not change any pixel that was assigned a value from the original image by Rule 1.

8) Rule 15: If none of the preceding rules assigned a value to the unknown pixel, set it to the background color.

Figure 8C shows the impact of this rule. After Rule 15 is applied, no pixel remains unknown.

E. Category 5 rule

Category 5 has one rule. It is categorized separately because of its unique behavior. It is invoked whenever Rule 10 is applied. If Rule 10 assigns a value to the unknown pixel, two of the diagonal neighbors of the pixel are end points of two horizontal or two vertical segments in the foreground color.

1) Rule 16: Draw two segments from the unknown pixel, parallel to the two segments whose endpoints are diagonal neighbors. The length of the new segments should be half the lengths of the corresponding segments in the original image. Set the pixels corresponding to the two original segments that are now adjacent to the new segments, to the background color. Flag all the impacted pixels so that they are not changed later when subsequent pixels are considered.

Figure 8D shows the impact of Rule 16. It is the only rule that changes pixels that were assigned values by Rule 1. Rule 16 helps better interpolate inclined lines where the inclination is not 45 degrees. The impact is seen on curves also because curves are formed using segments and points.

Figure 9 shows another comparison of our method with bicubic interpolation. The differences are clearly visible and the output of LNA is more pleasing.

IV. Experimental Results

In this section we compare LNA with bicubic interpolation, with some recently reported work and with the ideal reference for simple geometric figures. We compare the computation time and interpolation quality. The comparisons are for standard test images and also simple geometric

Figure 9. Comparison of zooming. The first image is the input; the second is generated by our method and the third by bicubic interpolation.

shapes. The experiments are on a general purpose computer. Since the execution time for the same process and inputs vary, the experiment is done ten times and the minimum and average time taken is shown. To evaluate the output, we examine visual quality as well as three standard metrics namely PSNR, MPSNR and SSIM. The experiments are performed on 16 different test images from standard sources.

A. Computation time

Table I shows the execution time for LNA and bicubic interpolation. The time shown is from ten executions. The time was measured on a computer with an Intel i5-3210M CPU @ 2.50GHz, 4.00 GB RAM and 64 bit Windows 8. The bicubic and LNA interpolations were implemented using Visual C++ in Visual Studio 2010. While measuring time, no other user processes were running. The results show that LNA is faster.

B. Visual comparison between LNA and bicubic interpolation

In Figures 10 and 11, we compare the outputs when standard test images are interpolated. The figures shown are Lena, Baboon, Barbara and Monarch. Only a portion of the original images are shown in the figures. This is to ensure that the artifacts are clearly visible. The figures show the portion of the original, low-resolution, color image and its binary version in the first row. The second row shows the output of bicubic interpolation and the third row the output of LNA interpolation.

The original color images were converted to grayscale using the formula:

GRAY = 0.2989 * R + 0.5870 * G + 0.1140 * B

The R (red), G (green) and B (blue) values were in the range 0 to 255 and the resultant GRAY value also is in the same range. The binary image was generated by setting all pixels with grayscale value greater than 127 to white and the rest to black.

The figures clearly show the sharp edges that LNA is able to generate. In these images, the notion of foreground color and background color is difficult to define. Because of this, in certain situations, some of the rules in LNA do not

TABLE I. COMPARISON OF EXECUTION TIME

	Time in milliseconds			
	Bicubic		*LNA*	
	Min	*Ave*	*Min*	*Ave*
lena	38.0	47.1	28.6	36.8
baboon	37.3	43.0	29.8	34.9
peppers	36.2	42.6	27.7	32.4
airplane	39.4	47.1	27.0	33.9
house	9.5	15.9	7.8	11.4
splash	35.6	42.0	30.8	41.3
jellybeans	8.8	11.7	6.9	9.5
car	36.2	42.8	29.2	39.4
sailboat	37.2	45.0	27.2	37.7
san_diego	38.0	41.3	28.7	33.8
earth	36.5	39.8	27.7	34.2
kodim23	53.1	62.7	40.3	49.0
tree	10.2	16.0	7.2	12.2
monarch	54.8	62.5	41.0	51.5
barbara	56.6	70.2	44.3	54.8
goldhill	56.2	63.9	43.7	51.7
Average	**40.3**	**43.4**	**34.0**	**35.3**

perform the intended function fully. In spite of this, the visual quality is better than bicubic interpolation. The difference between the outputs generated by bicubic and LNA interpolation can be clearly seen at the edges, inclined lines and curves. We can also see that fine features are retained by LNA. This is particularly noticeable in the Monarch and Barbara images in Figure 11.

C. PSNR and MPSNR

When a reference image is available, PSNR and Modified PSNR (MPSNR) are often used as measures of interpolation quality. Table II shows the PSNR and MPSNR of sixteen standard test images, after they were interpolated using LNA and bicubic interpolation.

The data in Table II is for the complete test image, and not portions of the image, as shown in Figures 10 and 11.

We see that LNA gives better PSNR, while bicubic interpolation gives better MPSNR.

It should be noted that some of the LNA rules, like rule 16, reduce PSNR. However, as seen in Figures 10 and 11, this results in better visual quality.

D. SSIM

Table II also shows the SSIM index of sixteen standard test images after they were interpolated. We see that the SSIM index, for both LNA and bicubic interpolation, is similar.

Figure 10. Comparison using Lena and Baboon. Row 1: Original and binary version. Row 2: Output of bicubic. Row 3: Output of LNA.

Figure 11. Comparison using Monarch and Barbara. Row 1: Original and binary version. Row 2: Output of bicubic. Row 3: Output of LNA.

TABLE II. COMPARISON OF LNA AND BICUBIC INTERPOLATION USING PSNR, MPSNR AND SSIM

			PSNR in dB		MPSNR in dB		SSIM Index	
	Height	*Width*	*Bicubic*	*LNA*	*Bicubic*	*LNA*	*Bicubic*	*LNA*
lena	512	512	14.26	14.63	21.64	21.33	0.84	0.84
baboon	512	512	8.73	8.75	16.2	15.14	0.55	0.53
peppers	512	512	15.21	15.59	22.34	22.05	0.85	0.86
airplane	512	512	15.76	15.53	22.93	21.64	0.89	0.88
house	256	256	11.22	13.07	17.8	19.62	0.71	0.74
splash	512	512	20.58	21.73	27.48	28.19	0.95	0.95
jellybeans	256	256	15.63	15.61	22.55	21.78	0.89	0.88
car	512	512	13.13	12.76	20.5	18.92	0.81	0.81
sailboat	512	512	14.79	14.84	22.15	21.24	0.82	0.82
san_diego	512	512	9.69	9.9	17.3	16.57	0.58	0.56
earth	512	512	13.67	13.34	21.34	19.73	0.79	0.77
kodim23	512	768	17.48	17.71	25.13	24.37	0.91	0.92
tree	256	256	12.84	12.97	19.94	19.2	0.79	0.78
monarch	512	768	16.28	16.64	23.7	23.34	0.89	0.89
barbara	576	720	11.61	11.77	19.16	18.64	0.77	0.77
goldhill	576	720	14.18	15.12	21.06	21.54	0.82	0.83
Average			**14.07**	**14.37**	**21.33**	**20.83**	**0.80**	**0.80**

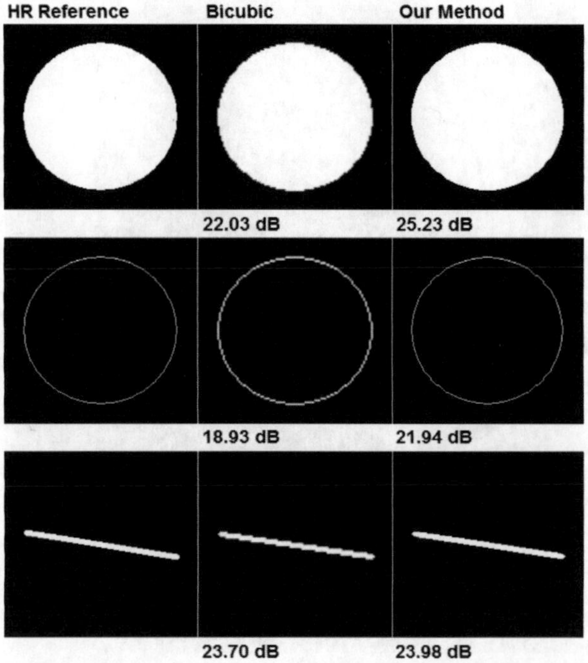

Figure 12. Comparison in Decibel (dB) of interpolation with ideal.reference.

E. *PSNR comparison using ideal reference*

In this section, we evaluate our method using geometric shapes. This allows us to specify the desired result of interpolation and generate reference images in HR for comparison.

The reference HR images, for a scale factor of two, are defined as follows. For a line thickness of one, a line of length l in LR should produce a line length 2l in HR, a circle of radius r should produce a circle of radius 2r and a rectangle of dimension h x w should produce a rectangle of size 2h x 2w. Each of the interpolated images should retain a line thickness of one pixel.

If the source image has thickness, then the thickness is also to be doubled. A line of n pixel thickness and length l, should produce a line of thickness 2n and length 2l, if n > 1.

The input images and reference images were drawn using Visual C++. Lines, rectangles and circles were drawn using the LineTo, Ellipse and Rectangle functions in the CDC class. Line thickness was set using the CreatePen function in the CPen class.

Figure 12 shows the comparison of LNA with bicubic interpolation. In the figure, the first test case is a filled circle. The reference image was drawn as a filled circle of radius 80. The input to bicubic interpolation and to our method was a filled circle of radius 40. The same approach was used to generate reference images for other shapes also. The Bicubic interpolation was done using Matlab.

TABLE III. COMPARISON OF PSNR AND MPSNR

	Thickness		PSNR in dB		MPSNR in dB	
	LR	*HR*	*Our method*	*Bicubic*	*Our method*	*Bicubic*
Rectangle	1	1	match	22.98	match	27.33
Circle	1	1	21.94	18.93	36	24.33
Line - 45 degree	1	1	46.02	26.54	56.16	31.92
Line - 10 degree	1	1	24.35	23.11	35.43	27.98
Rectangle	3	6	22.37	21.10	27.57	25.13
Circle	3	6	21.46	19.96	29.19	25.27
Line - 45 degree	3	6	25.19	27.40	32.14	34.68
Line - 10 degree	3	6	23.98	23.70	30.09	28.12
Filled Rectangle	NA	NA	match	26.49	match	30.85
Filled Circle	NA	NA	25.23	22.03	33	26.76

TABLE IV. COMPARISON OF OUR METHOD WITH OTHER METHODS

	Percentage of PSNR (dB) improvement over Bicubic				
	Our Method		*CIM [5]*	*Gradient Orientation [14]*	*NNV [15]*
	PSNR	MPSNR			
Lena	2.59	12.90	2.35	0.92	
Peppers	2.50	14.12	1.09		1.71

Table III shows the comparison for more simple images using both PSNR and MPSNR. We see good PSNR improvement by both measures. Table III also shows a PSNR decrease for a three pixel thick line at 45 degrees. In Figure 13, this image is analyzed. The figure shows a portion of the image, marked in red, magnified 8 times. In the magnified region, a set of colored squares with the same size as a pixel, have been shown just below the line. Using these pixels to help count, we see that the reference line is 8 pixels wide along the x axis, while our method has generated a line of width 7 pixels. This happens because, in many situations, our method assigns the background color when other rules don't resolve an unknown pixel. This biases images towards thinness and the bias is of one pixel. This helps the image look sharp but the difference in thickness is reflected in the lower PSNR.

F. *Comparison with some similar, recent work*

A direct comparison of our method with results available in [1]-[15] is difficult because our method is only formulated for binary images. To do a comparison, we converted two of the commonly used images, Lena and Peppers, to binary and used these as the reference images. We decimated these images by a factor of 2 and then interpolated them back to original size. We compared the interpolated images with the reference. The results are shown in Table II. The results have to be viewed keeping in mind the fact that the input for our experiments is binary while the input to the other methods is a grayscale image.

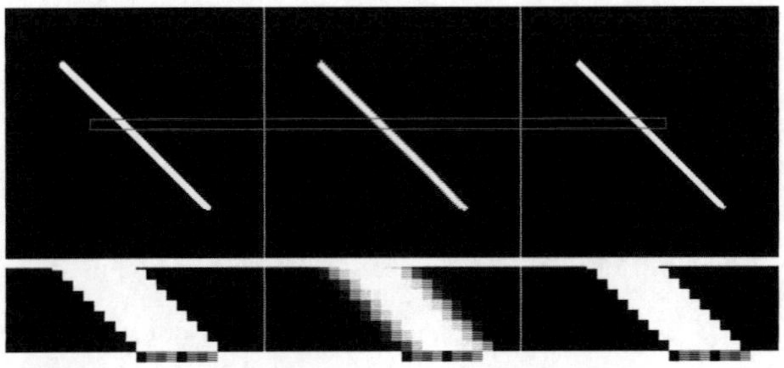

Figure 13. Magnified comparison of the outputs of interpolation.

In [13], a text super-resolution is considered. Here the input is binary. It uses text images for training. It achieves an improvement between 0% and 19% in Mean Square Error (MSE), when compared with pixel replication. The results are for different text symbols. Our method improved MSE by 5.7% for Lena and 2.1% for Peppers.

G. *Analysis of the results*

The results presented in this section show that LNA is computationally more efficient than bicubic interpolation. The amount of processing required in LNA depends on the image content.

Visual comparison shows that LNA generates visually pleasing output. This is true for the geometric shapes and also the standard test images. This is because LNA is designed to maintain sharpness and to generate smooth lines in the interpolated image.

Quantitative quality comparison shows that LNA is better in terms of PSNR while bicubic is better in terms of MPSNR. This is because LNA is designed to keep features sharp and so, on an average, the error in pixels is lower. This reflects in the higher PSNR. LNA is inferior in terms of MPSNR because it is computed after passing the images through a low pass filter. This blurs the image edges. LNA is designed to keep the edges sharp and so when the PSNR is computed after filtering both the reference and target, the result is inferior.

V. CONCLUSIONS

To generate visually pleasing, magnified images, we have proposed a new technique for binary images. It uses non-linear zooming rules that are Location and Neighborhood Adaptive (LNA). These rules are inspired by the way an artist would enlarge an image. The method overcomes a number of problems, such as blurring and thickening of edges that are associated with known interpolation techniques. The results are visually appealing. Lines and dots, with single pixel thickness, retain their thickness. Inclined lines, curves and solids look much better compared to other interpolation methods.

In LNA, some rules need the foreground color as an input. Some other rules assign a default color because the method could not determine a pixel's color based on the inputs it considered. Furthermore, a study is required to improve these rules. Studies are required to analyze the possibility of using larger neighborhoods as input, to further improve the quality of interpolation.

A consequence of LNA is that it may change relative sizes of some objects. Objects without thickness remain without thickness while those with thickness, increase in thickness. So, if an object is formed using both these kinds of components, the change in relative thickness becomes visible. Also, a study is required to devise mechanisms to scale all components of an object consistently.

In the future, a study is needed to extend this method to grayscale and color images. A solution that is usable could probably be built by working with ranges of color values, and using functions to specify values for unknown pixels.

REFERENCES

[1] P. J. Prabhakaran, and P. G. Poonacha, "A Novel Location and Neighborhood Adaptive Method for Binary Image Interpolation," SIGNAL 2017: The Second International Conference on Advances in Signal, Image and Video Processing, pp. 14-20, 2017.

[2] W. H. Press, S. A. Teukolsky, W. T. Vetterling, and B. P. Flannery, Numerical Recipes in C, 2nd ed. Cambridge University Press, pp. 125-127, 1992.

[3] P. J. Prabhakaran and P. G. Poonacha, "A new decimation and interpolation algorithm and an efficient lossless compression technique for images," Communications (NCC), 2015 Twenty First National Conference on, pp. 1-6, 2015.

[4] H. Jiang and C. Moloney, "A new direction adaptive scheme for image interpolation," International Conference on Image Processing, Vol. 3, pp. 369-372, 2002.

[5] H. Kim, Y. Cha, and S. Kim, "Curvature Interpolation Method for Image Zooming," IEEE Transactions on Image Processing, Vol. 20, No. 7, pp. 1895-1903, July 2011.

[6] R. Gao, J. P. Song, and X. C. Tai, "Image zooming algorithm based on partial differential equations technique," International Journal of Numerical Analysis and Modelling, Vol. 6, No. 2, pp. 284-292, 2009.

[7] L. Jing, Z. Gan, and X. Zhu, "Directional Bicubic Interpolation-A New Method of Image Super-Resolution," 3rd International Conference on Multimedia Technology (ICMT-13). Atlantis Press, pp. 470-477, November 2013.

[8] J. Sun, Z. Xu, and H. Y. Shum, "Image super-resolution using gradient profile prior," 2008 IEEE Conference on Computer Vision and Pattern Recognition, Anchorage, AK, pp. 1-8, 2008.

[9] C. Y. Yang and M. H. Yang, "Fast Direct Super-Resolution by Simple Functions," 2013 IEEE International Conference on Computer Vision, Sydney, NSW, pp. 561-568, 2013.

[10] R. Hardie, "A fast image super-resolution algorithm using an adaptive Wiener filter," IEEE Transactions on Image Processing, Vol. 16, No. 12, pp. 2953-2964, 2007.

[11] S. Lerttrattanapanich and N. K. Bost, "High resolution image formation from low resolution frames using delaunay triangulation," IEEE Transaction on Image Processing, Vol. 11, No. 12, pp. 1427-1441, 2002.

[12] W. T. Freeman, T. R. Jones, and E. C. Pasztor, "Example-Based Super-Resolution," IEEE Comput. Graph. Appl. 22, 2, pp. 56-65, 2002.

[13] G. Dalley, B. Freeman, and J. Marks, "Single-frame text super-resolution: a Bayesian approach," Image Processing, 2004. ICIP '04. 2004 International Conference on, 2004, Vol. 5, pp. 3295-3298, 2004.

[14] S. Ousguine, F. Essannouni, L. Essannouni, and D. Aboutajdine, "A new image interpolation using gradient-orientation and cubic spline interpolation," ISSR-Journals, vol. 5, no. 3, 2014.

[15] O. Rukundo and C. Hanqiang, "Nearest Neighbor Value Interpolation," in 2014 International Conference on Computer Vision Theory and Applications (VISAPP), 2012.

[16] The University of Southern California – Signal and Image Processing Institute (USC-SIPI) image database. "http://sipi.usc.edu/database/database.php". [Online; accessed 31-July-2017].

[17] Kodak lossless true color image suite. http://r0k.us/graphics/kodak/". [Online; accessed 31-July-2017].

[18] Index of testimages. "http://www.hlevkin.com/TestImages/". [Online; accessed 31-July-2017].

WaveletTrie: a Compressed Self-Indexed Data Structure Supporting Efficient Database Operations

Stefan Böttcher, Rita Hartel, Jonas Manuel
Department of Computer Science,
University of Paderborn,
Paderborn, Germany
email: stb@uni-paderborn.de, rst@uni-paderborn.de, jmanuel@live.uni-paderborn.de

Abstract—**An indexed compressed sequence of strings is a representation of a string sequence that on the one hand is more space efficient than the original sequence, but on the other hand supports more efficient operations on these strings. Whenever an indexed compressed sequence of strings supports efficient evaluation of typical database operations, like searching for exact matches or prefixes, range queries, computing the union or the intersection of sets of strings, or data modifications, databases can strongly benefit from storing their table columns in form of an indexed compressed sequence. In this paper, we show how to extend the data structure of the Wavelet Trie to an indexed compressed sequence of strings that supports efficient operations on column oriented databases. Therefore, we present algorithms for executing database operations like union, intersection, and range-queries on string sequences represented by an extended Wavelet Trie. Furthermore, in our evaluation, we show that performing these typical database operations on the extended Wavelet Trie is faster than simulating these operations on gzip- or bzip2-compressed data.**

Keywords—Column-oriented database management systems; compression; compressed indexed sequences of strings.

I. INTRODUCTION

The work presented in this paper extends the ideas presented in [1] at DBKDA 2017.

Column-oriented DataBase Management Systems (DBMS) organize their data tables within column stores, each containing an ordered sequence of entries. This data organization technique is preferable, especially when used for read-intensive applications like data warehouses, where in order to analyze the data, queries and aggregates have to be evaluated on sequences of similar data contained in a single column [2]. A second advantage of column-oriented data stores is that they can be compressed stronger than row oriented data stores, as each column and therefore each contiguous sequence of data contains data from the same domain and thus contains less entropy.

As long as main-memory availability is a run-time bottleneck, data compression is beneficial to virtually "enhance" the capacity of the main-memory, i.e., column-oriented data stores can benefit from storing their string columns in form of *compressed indexed sequences of strings*. A major challenge when using a compressed data structure for a string column is to support typical database operations in efficient time without full decompression of the compressed data structure.

This paper is organized as follows. In Section III, we introduce the basic concepts used in the following sections. In Section IV, we explain different operations on the Wavelet Trie and discuss how to implement them. In Section V, we show an extensive performance evaluation, in which we compare the performance of these operations on the Wavelet Trie with the performance of the gzip and bzip2 (de)compression.

II. RELATED WORK

Column stores like, for instance, C-STORE [2], Vertica [3], or SAP HANA [4] typically rely on combinations of compression techniques like Run-Length Encoding, Delta Encoding, or dictionary-based approaches. These compression techniques do not contain a self-index, but have to occupy additional space to store an index that allows for efficient operations like, for instance the evaluation of range queries. When main-memory availability is the major runtime bottleneck, we consider this to be a disadvantage.

In contrast, the Wavelet Tree [5] is a self-index data structure, and it can be regarded as an enhancement of variable length encodings (e.g., Huffman [6], Hu-Tucker [7]). The Wavelet Tree rearranges the encoded string S in form of a tree and thereby allows for random access to S. Variations of the Wavelet Tree use the tree topology to enhance Fibonacci encoded data [8] or Elias and Rice variable length encoded data [9]. In [10] an n-ary Wavelet Tree is used instead of a binary Wavelet Tree (e.g., a 128-ary Wavelet Tree by using bytes instead of bits in each node of the Wavelet Tree). A pruned form of the Wavelet Tree is the Skeleton Huffman tree [11] leading to a more compressed representation. Although avoiding the need for an additional index, Wavelet Trees have the disadvantage that common prefixes in multiple strings are stored multiple times.

This disadvantage is avoided by the Wavelet Trie [12][13], which is a self-index, i.e., avoids the storage of extra index structures, and can be regarded as a generalization of the Wavelet Tree for string sequences S and the Patricia Trie [14]. The Wavelet Trie rearranges a sequence S of encoded strings $s_1,\ldots,s_n$ in form of a tree thereby storing common prefixes of $s_1,\ldots,s_n$ only once, and it allows for random access to each s_i of S. That is why in this paper, we use a Wavelet Trie to store compressed indexed sequences of strings.

Wavelet Tries support the following basic operations that are used within column-oriented DBMS: the operations *access(n)* that returns the n-th string of a given column and that is used for example when finding values of the same database tuple contained in other columns, or *search(s)/searchPrefix(s)* that searches for all positions within the current column that contain a string value s (or that contain a string value having the prefix s). Beside these elementary search operations, Wavelet Tries support elementary data manipulation operations on the compressed data format as, e.g., to insert a string at a given position, to append a string, or to delete a string from the sequence.

[12] and [13] introduce the concept of the Wavelet Trie and discuss the complexity of the following operations, which are executed on the Wavelet Trie encoding a given string sequence:

- Access(pos) returns the pos-th string of the string sequence
- Rank(s, pos)/RankPrefix(s, pos) return the number of occurrences of string s (or strings starting with the prefix s) up to position pos in the string sequence
- Select(s, i)/SelectPrefix(s, i) returns the position of the i-th string s (or string starting with prefix s) of the string sequence
- Insert(s, pos) simulate on the Wavelet Trie an insertion of the string s before position pos into the string sequence
- Append(s) simulate on the Wavelet Trie an appending of the string s to the end of the string sequence
- Delete(pos) simulate on the Wavelet Trie a deletion of the string at position pos of the string sequence

Although this is sufficient to support the most elementary database operations in column stores, in order to support more enhanced data analysis, efficient query processing should go beyond these elementary operations. Hereby, the main challenge is to support efficient complex read operations like intersection, union, and range queries on column stores without decompression of large parts of the compressed data.

Our goal is that these operations on compressed data are executed not only with a smaller main-memory footprint, but also faster on compressed data compared to a decompress-read approach that first decompresses the data before a read operation (or write operation) is done.

Our first contribution is to extend the Wavelet Trie [12][13] published in 2012 by Grossi and Gupta by concepts and efficient implementations of enhanced database operations (intersection, union, and range queries).

When standard string compressors like gzip or bzip2 are used for compressing sequences of strings stored in a database table column, such a compressed sequence of strings has to be decompressed, before a database operation can even be executed. That is why our second contribution is an evaluation, comparing the performance of database operations on our extended Wavelet Trie with the decompression time needed by bzip2 or by gzip for a compressed sequence of strings. We show that performing typical operations on string sequences like searching for exact matches or prefixes, range queries, or update operations like insertion or deletion, or operations on two string sequences like merge or intersection, directly on the Wavelet Trie is faster than simulating these operations on bzip2- and gzip-compressed data.

III. Preprocessing and Basic Concepts

In this section, we introduce the basic concepts used in the remainder of this paper.

A. Preprocessing

In order to allow a space-efficient storage of a string sequence SS, the Wavelet Trie requires the strings of the string sequence to be pairwise prefix-free, i.e., no string $st_i \in SS$ is allowed to be a prefix of another string $st_j \in SS$. The requirement that SS has to be a prefix-free sequence, is not a critical restriction, as a prefix-free set of strings can be easily constructed for any set SS as follows. A special terminal symbol that is lexicographically smaller than each character occurring in each string $st_i \in SS$ is appended to each string $st_i \in SS$. For example, in Figure 1, we added the symbol '\$' to the end of each string, thereby yielding a prefix free sequence, although the previously given string sequence (rob, romulus, robert) is not prefix free, as 'rob' is a prefix of 'robert'.

Furthermore, before we use the Wavelet Trie to store a sequence $SS=(st_1,\dots,st_n)$ of strings, we apply the Hu-Tucker algorithm [7] to all characters of all $st_i \in SS$, i.e., we encode each character c of each $st_i \in SS$ by its Hu-Tucker code ht(c). Thereby, we get a sequence $S=(s_1,\dots,s_n)$ of bit-strings, where s_i is the Hu-Tucker code of st_i, yielding a lexicographic Huffman code for the bit-strings s_i, i.e., $s_i <_{lexi} s_j \Leftrightarrow st_i <_{lexi} st_j$, where $<_{lexi}$ denotes "less than in lexicographical order".

In order to search for a string st in SS, we apply the same Hu-Tucker codes to the characters of st, yielding a bit-string s that we can search for in the Wavelet Trie.

For example, for the string sequence SS=(rob\$, romulus\$, robert\$), and its Hu-Tucker codes listed in Table 1, we get the sequence
$S=(s_1, s_2, s_3)$ of bit-strings with
s_1 = 101 100 0100 00,
s_2 = 101 100 0111 111 0110 111 1100 00, and
s_3 = 101 100 0100 0101 101 1101 00.

TABLE I. Hu-Tucker codes of our examples

char c	code(c)	char c	code(c)
\$	00	**o**	100
b	0100	**r**	101
e	0101	**s**	1100
l	0110	**t**	1101
m	0111	**u**	111

Whenever we describe operations that work on two Wavelet Tries, we assume that both Wavelet Tries are based on the same Hu-Tucker-Encoding.

After the preprocessing steps, we construct the Wavelet Trie according to the construction method given in the Wavelet Trie definition of the following section.

In order to keep the following definition and the construction principle of the Wavelet Trie simple, we assume that the string sequence SS represented by the Wavelet Trie always consists of at least two different strings, i.e., $st_i \in SS$, $st_j \in SS$, and $st_i \neq st_j$. As a consequence, also SS's Hu-Tucker encoded sequence $S=(s_1,\ldots,s_n)$ of bit-strings contains at least two different bit-strings. Whenever this is not the case, we could simply store the size of S externally, or add a binary string s_{new}, $s_{new} \neq s_i$, $i \in \{1,\ldots,n\}$ to the end of the sequence S, such that our Wavelet Trie represents a bit-string sequence S that consists of at least two different bit-strings.

B. Basic Concepts

Similarly to [12][13], we define the Wavelet Trie as follows:

Definition (Wavelet Trie): Let S be a non-empty sequence of bit-strings, $S=(s_1,\ldots, s_n)$, $s_i \in \{0,1\}^*$, whose underlying bit-string set $S_{set}=\{s_1,\ldots,s_n\}$ is pair-wise prefix-free. The Wavelet Trie of S, denoted WT(S), is a binary tree, which is built recursively as follows:

(i) If the bit-string set S_{set} of S consists of a single bit-string element only, i.e., $s_1 = \ldots = s_n$, the Wavelet Trie is a single node labeled with $\alpha = s_1 = \ldots = s_n$ and $\beta=\varepsilon$, i.e., β is an empty bit-vector.

(ii) Otherwise, WT(S), the Wavelet Trie of S is a binary tree whose root node is labeled with two bit-vectors, α and β, and whose children (respectively labeled with 0 and 1) are $WT(S_{\alpha 0})$ and $WT(S_{\alpha 1})$, the Wavelet Tries of sequences $S_{\alpha 0}$ and $S_{\alpha 1}$ of bit-strings, where α, β, $S_{\alpha 0}$, and $S_{\alpha 1}$ are defined as follows. α is the longest common prefix of the bit-strings s_i contained in S. For any $1 \leq i \leq n$, we then can write $s_i = \alpha b_i \gamma_i$, where b_i is a single bit. We then define the sequences $S_{\alpha 0} = (\gamma_i \mid \alpha 0 \gamma_i \in S)$ and $S_{\alpha 1} = (\gamma_i \mid \alpha 1 \gamma_i \in S)$ of bit-strings, i.e., the first sequence contains suffixes γ_i of $s_i \in S$ such that s_i begins with $\alpha 0$ and the second sequence contains suffixes γ_i of $s_i \in S$ such that s_i begins with $\alpha 1$. Finally, the bitvector $\beta = (b_i \mid \alpha b_i \gamma_i \in S)$ collects all the bits b_i that discriminate for a given $s_i = \alpha b_i \gamma_i$, whether the suffix γ_i is in $S_{\alpha 0}$ or is in $S_{\alpha 1}$.

Example: Continuing the previous example, Figure 1 shows the Wavelet Trie representing the sequence $S=(s_1, s_2, s_3)$ of bit-strings

s_1 = 101 100 01 0 0 0 0,

s_2 = 101 100 01 1 1 111 0110 111 1100 00,

s_3 = 101 100 01 0 0 0 1 01 101 1101 00.

representing the strings of the sequence SS= (rob\$, romulus\$, robert\$). The characters are shown in Figure 1 only for the purpose of illustration, but are not contained in the Wavelet Trie. All three bit-strings s_1, s_2, s_3 share the common prefix α = 101 100 01 and differ in the next bit b_i, which is 0 for s_1 and for s_3, but 1 for s_2. The bit-string sequence $S_{\alpha 0} = (\gamma_1, \gamma_3)$ containing the suffixes γ_1 and γ_3 of s_1 and s_3 is represented by the left sub-tree of the Wavelet Trie's root node, and the bit-string sequence $S_{\alpha 1} = (\gamma_2)$ is represented by the right child. Continuing with the left subtree of the Wavelet Trie's root node, γ_1 and γ_3 share the common prefix 00 and differ in the next bit, such that here we get a new bit-vector α=00 and a new bit-vector β that contains only two bits, one for s_1, the other for s_3. All leaf nodes contain the common bit-vector α and an empty bit-vector β, as they represent a bit-string set containing a single element only.

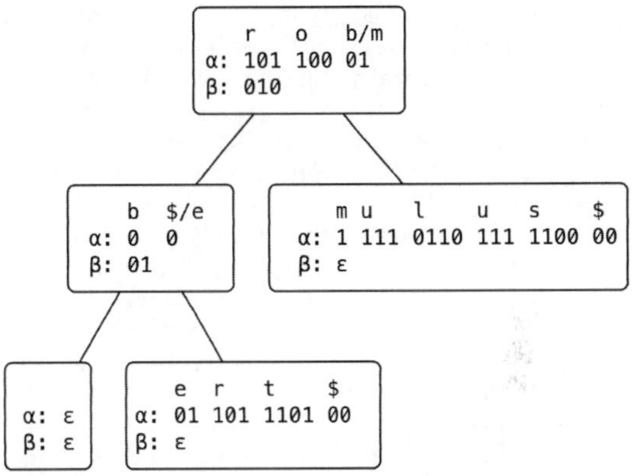

Figure 1. Wavelet Trie representing the bit-string sequence (101 100 01 0 0 0 0, 101 100 01 1 1 111 0110 111 1100 00, 101 100 01 0 0 0 1 01 101 1101 00)

Remarks: If the whole Wavelet Trie consisted of a single node only, this node would be a leaf node having a bit-vector α, but having an empty bit-vector β, i.e., we could not derive the size of the sequence S represented by the leaf node. That is why we required S to contain at least two different bit-strings $s_i,s_j \in S$ with $s_i \neq s_j$. Given this requirement, in the following, we can assume that the whole Wavelet Trie considered always consists of more than one node.

If we reach a leaf node of the Wavelet Trie, i.e., the sequence represented by that leaf node has a bit-string set containing a single element only, we know the size n of the sequence by counting the number of bits within the β bit-vector of the leaf's parent node.

IV. Database Operations on top of the Wavelet Trie

In the following sections, we denote the left child of a Wavelet Trie node also as its 0-child, and the right child of a Wavelet Trie node also as its 1-child.

For the following operations, we assume that they are methods of an object of type WaveletTrie and that they can directly access the object variables α, β, and size. The size of a Wavelet Trie wt is $|\beta|$, i.e., the number of bits of β if wt is an inner node, and for a leaf node, it is the number of 0-bits in wt's parent node p, if wt is p's left child, and the number of 1-bits in wt's parent node p, if wt is p's right child.

A. Search/Query Operations

Let S=(s_1,..., s_n) be a given bit-string sequence that is represented by a Wavelet Trie wt having the root node wt.root, and let s be a given bit-string that we search for in S. The *search(s)* operation applied to wt.root returns a list of all the positions i in S of those bit-strings s_i that are equal to s. Similarly, the *searchPrefix(s)* operation applied to wt.root returns a list of the positions i in S of all those bit-strings s_i that have a prefix s.

For example, assume, we want to search for robert$ in the string sequence SS_2=(rob$, romulus$, robert$, robert$, romulus$, robert$), and we use the same Hu-Tucker coding as before. We search for the bit-string 101 100 0100 0101 101 1101 00 corresponding to robert$ in the Wavelet Trie corresponding to SS_2 (c.f. Figure 3), and we get the result position list [3,4,6].

In order to search for all matching positions in the Wavelet Trie, the function *search(s)* (c.f. Code 1) recursively traverses down the tree representing the Wavelet Trie, until we have found all bits of the binary string s, and bottom-up "translates" all matching positions into matching positions in the Wavelet Trie's root node.

In more detail, the search works as follows: Let n be the current node having a bit-vector α, a bit-vector β, and (if n is not the Wavelet Trie's root node) having a parent node pa, such that n is the b-child of pa and β of pa contains k b-bits. Assume that we search for all positions where a given bit-string s occurs.

```
1 Function search(BitString s):
2 if s=α and isLeaf then
3    return [1,...,size];
4 else if α.isPrefixOf(s) and !isLeaf then
5    Bit b = α.getFirstDifferentBit(s);
6    γ = s.getSuffix(α);
7    [p1,...,pm] = getChild(b).search(γ);
8    return β.select(b, [p1,...,pm]);
9 return ∅;
```

Code 1. Search for all exact occurrences of a word

The search has to distinguish 3 cases:

1. If we have found all bits of s and we have reached the end of the α of a leaf node (line 2), we have reached an exact match. For the leaf node representing the exact match, we return a vector [1,...,size] (line 3), where size is the number of bit-strings represented by that leaf, i.e., each position in [1,...,size] is a matching position for s in this leaf node.

2. If s≠α, α is a prefix of s and n is no leaf node (lines 4-8), s is of the form s=αbγ (lines 5-6) with a potentially empty γ. In this case, we perform the search operation for the bit-string γ on n's b-child (c.f. Figure 2), resulting in a list of matching positions [p_1,...,p_m] in the current node's b-child (c.f. line 7). These positions are then (line 8) translated into matching positions of the current node as described below.

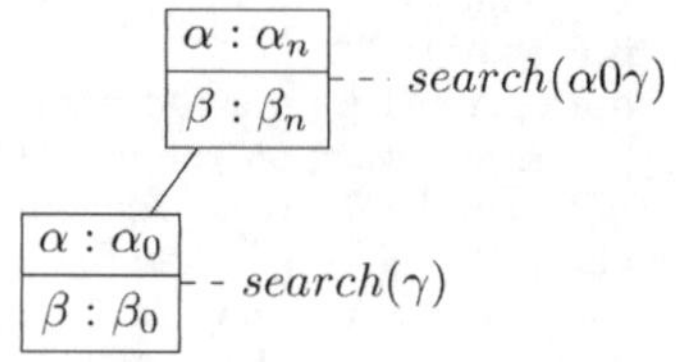

Figure 2. Search operation, if α is a prefix of search string s.

3. If none of the above cases matches, the Wavelet Trie does not contain a binary string matching the search criteria, and we return an empty list of positions (line 9).

In order to determine the exact matching positions in S, matching positions in the Wavelet Trie's nodes are computed bottom-up, i.e., we start in the matching leaf node and "translate" matching positions in a Wavelet Trie node n to matching positions in n's parent node pa (line 8).

Hereby, the method β.select(b, [p_1,..., p_m]), called in line 8 of Code 1, is implemented as shown in Code 2, where β.select(b,p_i) returns the position of the p_i^{th} b-bit in the bit-vector β.

```
Function select(Bit b, [p1,...,pm]):
   return [select(b,p1),...,select(b,pm)];
```

Code 2. Auxiliary method β.select(b, [p_1,..., p_m])

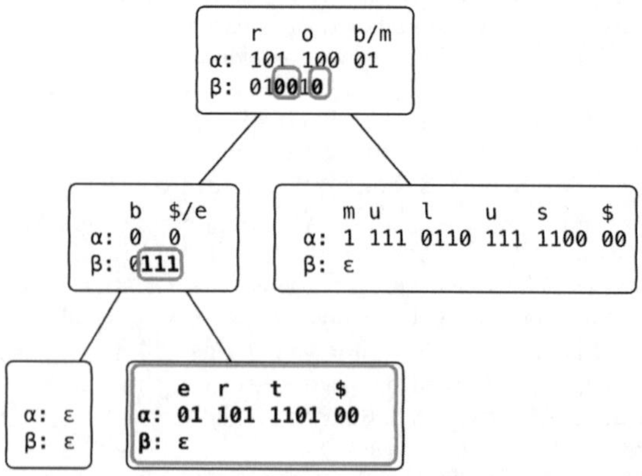

Figure 3. Search for "robert$".

Example: Figure 3 shows a slightly modified version of the Wavelet Trie of Figure 1 that represents the string sequence SS_2=(rob$, romulus$, robert$, robert$, romulus$, robert$). In order to search for all occurrences of "robert$", i.e., of the binary string s = 101 100 01 0 0 0101 101 1101 00, we start with the root node. As α = 101 100 01 is a prefix of s, and the next bit b in s is 0, we continue to search for the remaining substring s_L = 0 0101 101 1101 00 of s within the left child of the root node. Here, α = 0 0 is again a prefix of s1, and the next bit b of s_L is 1. Therefore, we continue to search for the remaining substring s_{LR} = 01 101 1101 00 of s_L in the right child node. As now, $\alpha = s_{LR}$, and the current node is a leaf node, all strings represented by this leaf node are matches. From the leaf's parent's ß-bit-vector, we know that our leaf node represents 3 occurrences of s, thus, we return the list of positions [1, 2, 3] from the leaf node to its parent. Recursive execution returns to the previous call of this method executed for the leaf' parent, i.e., the left child of the root. As the leaf is the right child of its parent and here, the 1st, 2nd, and 3rd 1-bits occur at positions 2, 3, and 4 in β, we return [2, 3, 4]. Similarly, when execution returns from its left child to the root node, the 2nd, 3rd, and 4th 0-bits occur at positions 3,4, and 6 in β. Therefore, the final result is that the strings on positions [3, 4, 6] are equal to the search string 'robert$'.

Similarly, if we do not want to search for exact matches, but for prefixes, i.e., we search for all positions of binary strings starting with the given prefix s, we just have to slightly modify our algorithm:

If we have found all bits of s on the current path in the Wavelet Trie, we do not care, whether or not we have reached a leaf node, and translate the current positions into positions of the Wavelet Trie's root node. That is, the code for searchPrefix() is as follows:

```
Function searchPrefix(BitString s):
if s=α or s.isPrefixOf(α) then
   return [1,...,size];
else if α.isPrefixOf(s) and !isLeaf then
   Bit b = α.getFirstDifferentBit(s);
   γ = s.getSuffix(α);
   [p₁,...,pₘ] = getChild(b).search(γ);
   return β.select(b, [p₁,...,pₘ]);
return ∅;
```

Code 3. Search for all strings that start with a given prefix

B. Between/Range Queries (less than, greater than)

The operation between(s_L,s_H) returns a list of positions of strings $s_i \in S$, such that $s_L \leq_{lexi} s_i \leq_{lexi} s_H$. Similarly, the operation lessThan(s) returns a list of positions of bit-strings s_i, such that $s_i \leq_{lexi}$ s, and the operation greaterThan(s) returns a list of positions of bit-strings s_i, such that $s_i \geq_{lexi}$ s.

For example, assume, we want to search for all strings greater than robb$ in the string sequence SS_2=(rob$, romulus$, robert$, robert$, romulus$, robert$), and we use the same Hu-Tucker coding as before. We search for all bit-strings that are greater than the bit-string 101 100 0100 0100 00 corresponding to robb$ in the Wavelet Trie corresponding to SS_2 (c.f. Figure 4), and we get the result position list [2,5,3,4,6] corresponding to the positions of either one of the strings robert$ or one of the strings romulus$.

In this section, we explain how to implement the operation greaterThan(s). To adapt this operation in order to implement between(s_L,s_H) or lessThan(s) is quite straightforward.

Let the current node n be a node with labels α and β.

```
1 Function greaterThan(BitVector s):
2 if α>=s then
3   return [1...size];
4 else if α.isPrefixOf(s) then
5   if not isLeaf then
6     Bit b = α.getFirstDifferentBit(b);
7     λ = s.getSuffix(α);
8     if b=1 then
9       [p₁,...,pₘ] = getChild(1)
                    .greaterThan(λ));
10      return β.select(1, [p₁,...,pₘ]);
11    else
12      [p₁,...,pₘ] = getChild(0)
                    .greaterThan(λ));
13      return
14      β.select(0, [p₁,...,pₘ]) ⊕
15      β.select(1, [1,...,rank(1,|β|]);
16 else return ∅;
```

Code 4. Search for positions of all words greater than a given string

If α≥s (which includes the case that s is a prefix of α, i.e., α=sbδ with a potentially empty δ), we know that all bit-strings represented by the Wavelet Trie rooted in n are greater than or equal to s, i.e., we return the list of positions [1, ..., size] (lines 2-3).

In the other case, if α is a prefix of s, i.e., s= αbλ (lines 4-16), we have to consider the value of b and get two sub-cases.

Lines 8-10 treat the sub-case b=1. Here, all remaining bit-strings represented by the Wavelet Trie rooted in n's 0-child start with a 0-bit and therefore cannot be greater than the remaining search bit-string 1λ of s, i.e., only n's 1-child can represent greater remaining bit-strings. As the 1-bit of the remaining search bit-string 1λ is consumed while search moves to n's 1-child, we have to apply the operation greaterThan(λ) only to n's 1-child (line 9) with the remaining search bit-string λ, and translate the matching positions $[p_1,...,p_m]$ within n's 1-child's β-vector into matching positions wihtin n's β-vector (line 10).

Lines 11-15 treat the other sub-case, b=0:

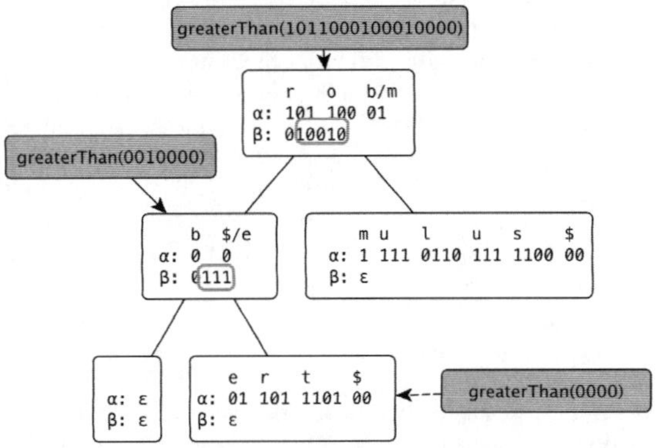

Figure 4. Search for strings greater than "robb$"

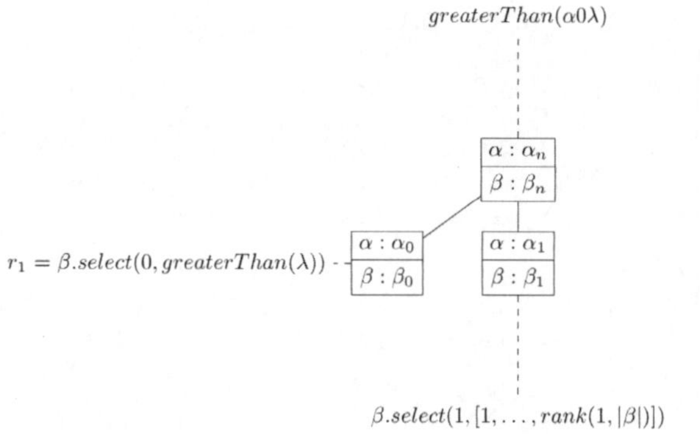

Figure 5. greaterThan if α is a prefix of search string s.

Here, the returned result list $r_1 \oplus r_2$ of matching positions wihtin n's β-vector consists of two sub-lists r_1 (line 14) and r_2 (line 15), which are computed as follows. We search for the positions $[p_1,...,p_m]$ of remaining bit-strings greater than λ within n's 0-child (line 12) and translate these positions into positions of n's β bit-vector (line 14) to get r_1 However, as all remaining bit-strings represented by the Wavelet Trie rooted in n's 1-child start with a 1-bit and are therefore greater than the remaining search bit-string 0λ of s, each 1-bit of n's β bit-vector represents a match to our search. That is why we also return the positions of all 1-bits in β in line 15 of Code 4, i.e., $r_2 = \beta.select(1,[1,\ldots,rank(1, |\beta|])$. This is also illustrated in Figure 5. Finally, we return $r=r_1 \oplus r_2$ (lines 13-15).

In the last case, α<s and α is not a prefix of s, no string represented by this Wavelet Trie rooted in n can be greater than or equal to s, i.e., we return the empty list (line 16).

Example: Figure 4 shows the search for all strings greater than the binary string s = 101 100 0100 0100 00 (="robb$") within the string sequence SS_2=(rob$, romulus$, robert$, robert$, romulus$, robert$). We compare s with α of the Wavelet Trie's root. As α is a prefix of s and the next bit after α in s is 0, we select all 1-bits of β (positions 2 and 5) and compute greaterThan applied to the remaining bit-string s_L = 0 0100 00 and the left child of the root. Again α is a prefix of s_L, but this time, the next bit after α in s is 1, so we continue with the right child and the remaining bit-string s_{LR} = 0000 and compute greaterThan(0000). As $\alpha > s_{LR}$ for s_{LR} = 0000, we return positions [1, 2, 3], which correspond to the 1st, 2nd, and 3rd 1-bit of the β bit-vector of its parent, i.e., to the positions [2, 3, 4]. The positions [2, 3, 4] correspond to the 2nd, 3rd, and 4th 0-bit of the β bit-vector of the root, i.e., to positions [3, 4, 6]. So the final result are the positions [2, 5] ⊕ [3, 4, 6] = [2, 5, 3, 4, 6].

Note that we can similarly create a new Wavelet Trie that consists of all bit-strings greater than s, if we first copy the Wavelet Trie, and then, using the list $[p_1,\ldots, p_m]$ of result positions returned by greaterThan(s), for deleting all strings at a position $p_i \in [p_1,\ldots, p_m]$ from the copy of the Wavelet Trie. Note that the algorithm for deleting a string at a given position is explained in the following section, Section C. Of course, we do not need to search first and delete in a second pass, but can nest both operations by deleting the bits while propagating the positions up to the root node.

C. Delete

This operation deletes the binary string s_{pos} at position pos from the Wavelet Trie.

For example, assume, we want to delete the 3rd string from string sequence SS=(rob$, romulus$, robert$), and we use the same Hu-Tucker coding as before. We delete the binary string 101 100 0100 0101 101 1101 00 corresponding to robert$ from the Wavelet Trie corresponding to SS (c.f. Figure 7). As a consequence, we have to *collapse* the left child of the root, i.e., to combine it with its remaining single child into a single node.

```
1 Function delete (int pos):
2 if not isLeaf then
3    boolean b = β.getBit(pos);
4    int rank = β.delete(pos);
5    if β.hasOnly(1-b) then
6       collapse(1-b);
7    else
8       getChild(b).delete(rank);
```

Code 5. Delete word from WaveletTrie

In order to delete the binary string s_{pos} at position pos from the current node n (initially the root node), we delete the bit b at position pos from β (Code 5, line 4). If β afterwards still contains 0-bits and 1-bits and n's b-child is not a leaf node, we continue to delete the bit at position rank(b,pos) from the β-vector of n's b-child (lines 7-8).

If β contains either only 0-bits or only 1-bits (i.e., β=0* or β=1*, in general β=b*), we have to collapse the current node with its b-child n_b and thereby delete its (1-b)-child (lines 5-6).

Figure 6 shows the state before and after collapsing the node for b=0. To collapse a node n with its b-child n_b means the following: Let n_0 be the 0-child of n_b and n_1 be the 1-child of n_b. Let furthermore α_b and β_b be the labels of node n_b. Then the new labels of node n are $\alpha=\alpha_n b \alpha_b$ and $\beta=\beta_b$. Furthermore, n_0 becomes the new 0-child of n and n_1 becomes the new 1-child of n.

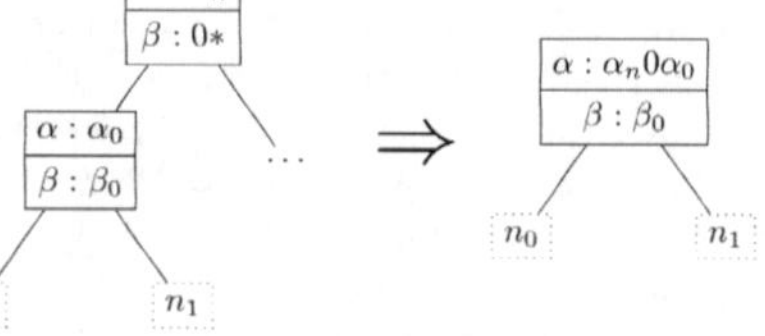

Figure 6. Before and after collapsing the node.

Example: Figure 7 shows the process of deleting the string s=101 100 0100 0101 101 1101 00 (=robert$) at position 3 from the WaveletTrie. In the root, we delete the 3rd bit, which is a 0-bit. We compute its rank within β. As it is the second 0-bit, the rank is two. We continue with deleting the second bit of the left child. As it is the single 1-bit, we can delete the right child. As the node now only has a left child and no right child, we finally collapse it with its left child.

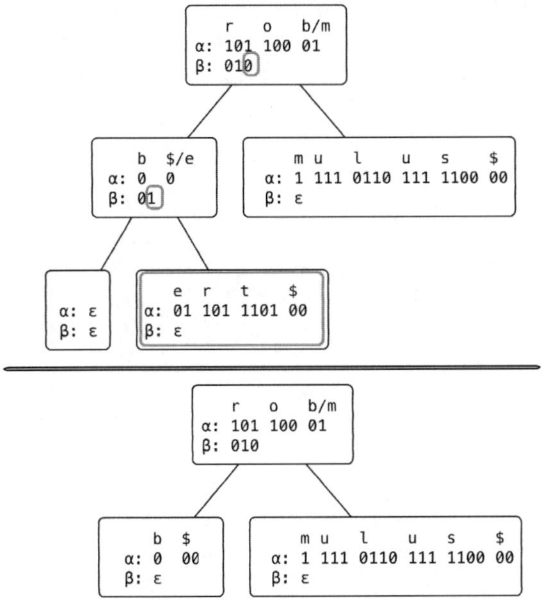

Figure 7. Deleting the 3rd string

D. Insert/Append

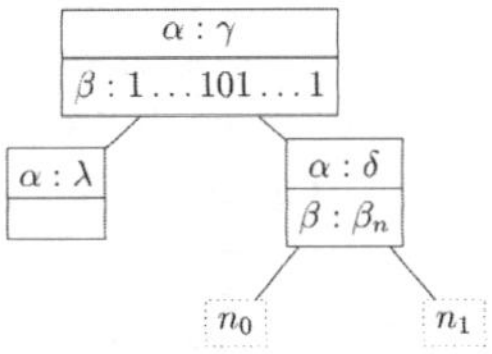

Figure 8. Result of insert operation if s and α_n have a common prefix.

This operation inserts a binary string s into the Wavelet Trie representing a string sequence $S=(s_1,\ldots,s_n)$ at position pos (or appends it to the end, if pos>n). Note that this operation is only defined if the set $S_{set} \cup \{s\}$ is prefix free.

For example, assume, we want to insert the string romulus$ (bit-string s=101 100 01 1 1 111 0110 111 1100 00) at position 2 into the string sequence SS_3=(rob$, robert$), and we use the same Hu-Tucker coding as before. We insert s into the Wavelet Trie corresponding to SS_3 (c.f. Figure 9), thereby splitting the previous root into the new root representing the common binary sub-string 101 100 01 of all three binary strings and a new 0-child representing the remaining common binary sub-string 00 of the binary strings of SS_3.

```
1 Function insert (int pos, BitVector s):
2 if αn = s then
3     return;
4 if αn.isPrefixOf(s) then
5     boolean b =αn.getFirstDifferentBit(s);
6     int rank = βn.insert(pos, b);
7     δ = s.getSuffix(αn);
8     getChild(b).insert(rank, δ);
9 else
10    BitVector γ = αn.getCommonPrefix(s);
11    boolean b = γ.getFirstDifferentBit(s);
12    BitVector δ  = αn.getSuffix(γ);
13    BitVector λ = s.getSuffix(γ);
14    α = γ;
15    BitVector β =BitVector(1-b, |βn|);
16    β.insert(pos, b);
17    setChild(b, WaveletTrie(λ));
18    setChild(b, WaveletTrie(δ, βn,
19                        child 0 , child 1 ));
```

Code 6. Append or insert a word to WaveletTrie at position pos

Code 6 summarizes the implementation of the insert operation. We consider the current node n of the Wavelet Trie (initially the root node) having the labels α_n and β_n and the binary string s to be inserted at position pos. As we require the Wavelet Trie before and after the insertion to be prefix free, we know that s must not be a prefix of α_n.

If α_n=s (lines 2-3), n must be a leaf node of the Wavelet Trie (as otherwise the Wavelet Trie would not be prefix free after the insertion). As the size of the leaf node is stored in the β-bit-vector of its parent, the insertion is completed and we do not need to do anything else.

If α_n is a prefix of s (lines 4-8), i.e., $s=\alpha_n b\delta$, where b is a bit, we insert bit b at position pos into β_n(line 6) and remember its rank, and insert the binary string δ into the b-child of n at the position remembered in that rank, i.e., rank(b,pos) (line 8).

Otherwise (lines 9-19), let γ be the common prefix of α_n and s (line 10) and let us assume w.l.o.g. that $\alpha_n=\gamma 1\delta$ (line 12) and $s=\gamma 0\lambda$ (line 13). This scenario is illustrated in Figure 8. Note that γ might even be an empty binary string. Let n_0 be the 0-child of n, and let n_1 be the 1-child of the current node. In this case, we change n into a node with α=γ (line 14), and β consists of $|\beta_n|$ 1-bits (line 15) and one 0-bit at position pos (line 16). The new 0-child of n is a node n' with α=λ (line 17). The new 1-child of n is a node n'' with α=δ and $\beta=\beta_n$(line 18). n'' gets n_0 as 0-child and n_1 as 1-child (line 19). Figure 8 shows this case after having inserted s into α_n.

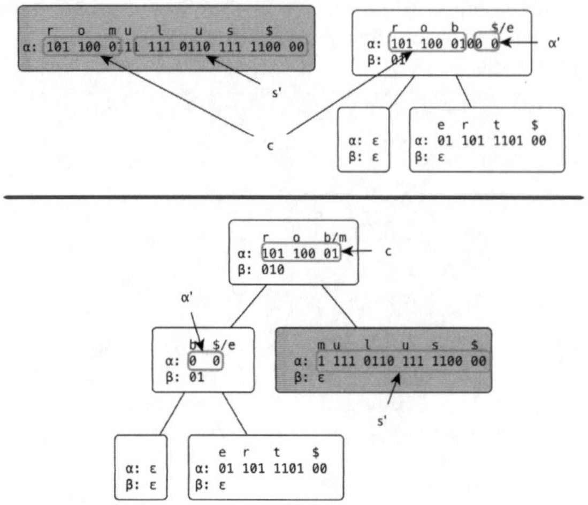

Figure 9. Inserting "romulus$" into the WaveletTrie

Example: Figure 9 shows the process of inserting the string s=101 100 0111 111 0110 111 1100 00 (=romulus$) as second string into the Wavelet Trie representing the string sequence SS_3=(rob$, robert$). We split s into the common prefix of s and α c=101 100 01, the next bit b=1, and the suffix s'=1 111 0110 111 1100 00 . And we split α into c, the next bit b'=0 and the suffix α'=00. The α-bitvector of the new root is α=c, β consists of 2 bits b'=0 representing the existing Wavelet Trie, in which we insert the bit b=1 at position 2. The left child of the new root becomes a node with α= α' and the beta of the left child is a copy of β=01. Furthermore, the two children of the left child are copies of the two child nodes of the previous root of the existing Wavelet Trie. The right child of the new root node becomes a new node with α=s' and β=ε.

E. Merge/Append + Union

This operation simulates the insertion of one string sequence SS_2 at a given position pos into another string sequence SS_1 on two Wavelet Tries t_1 representing SS_1 and t_2 representing SS_2. Note that this operation is only defined if the set $s_1 \cup s_2$ is prefix free.

For example, if we merge a copy of the Wavelet Trie in Figure 1 representing the string sequence SS= (rob$, romulus$, robert$) at position 2 into another copy of that Wavelet Trie, we get a new Wavelet Trie that represents the string sequence (rob$, romulus$, rob$, romulus$, robert$, robert$)

Let n_1 be the current node of t_1, i.e., the given Wavelet Trie, and n_2 be the current node of t_2, i.e., the Wavelet Trie to be merged or appended, where n_1 has the labels α_1 and β_1 and n_2 has the labels α_2 and β_2.

If $\alpha_1=\alpha_2$ and n_1 and n_2 are leaf nodes, nothing has to be done, and the operation is finished (lines 3-4).

Note that if $\alpha_1=\alpha_2$, the cases that n_1 is a leaf node, but n_2 is not a leaf node, and vice versa, cannot occur for the following reason. If $\alpha_1=\alpha_2$ and at least one node, n_1 or n_2 is not a leaf, also the other node must not be a leaf (line 5), because otherwise, $s_1 \cup s_2$ would not be prefix-free. Then, we insert β_2 at position pos into β_1 (line 6), merge the 0-child of n_2 at position β_1.rank(0,pos) into the 0-child of n_1 (line 7) and merge the 1-child of n_2 at position β_1.rank(1,pos) into the 1-child of n_1 (line 8).

```
1  Function merge(int pos, WaveletTrie t):
2  if t.α= α then
3    if isLeaf and t.isLeaf then
4      return;
5    /*neither the current node nor t
                 is a leaf node */
6    Rank r = β.insert(pos, t.β);
7    getChild(0).merge(r(0),t.getChild(0);
8    getChild(1).merge(r(1),t.getChild(1);
9  if α.isPrefixOf(t.α) then
10   Bit b = α.getFirstDifferentBit(t.α);
11   for i in 1..|t. β| do
12     Rank r = β.insert(pos, b);
13   t.α = t.α.getSuffix(α);
14   getChild(b).merge(r(b),t);
15 else if t.α.isPrefixOf(α) then
16   Bit b = t. α.getFirstDifferentBit(α);
17   WaveletTrie tmp = WaveletTrie
        (α.getSuffix(t.α), β,getChildren());
18   α = t.α;
19   β = BitVector(b, |tmp|);
20   Rank r = β.insert(pos, t.β);
21   tmp.merge(r(b),t.getChild(b));
22   setChild(b,tmp);
23   setChild(1-b,t.getChild(1-b));
24 else
25   BitVector γ = α.getCommonPrefix(t.α);
26   Bit b = γ.getFirstDifferentBit(t.α);
27   WaveletTrie t1 = WaveletTrie
     (t.α.getSuffix(γ),t.β,t.getChildren());
28   WaveletTrie t2 = WaveletTrie
        (t.α.getSuffix(γ),β,getChildren());
29   α = γ;
30   β = BitVector(1-b, | β|);
31   for i in 1..|t. β| do
32     β.insert(pos, b);
33   setChild(b,t1);
34   setChild(1-b,t2);
```

Code 7. Merge two Wavelet Tries

If α_1 is a prefix of α_2, i.e., $\alpha_2=\alpha_1 b\delta$ (lines 9-14), we insert b $|\beta_2|$ times at position pos into β_1 (lines 10-12). We change α_2 into δ (line 13) and merge n_2 into the b-child of n_1 at position β_1.rank(b,pos) (line 14).

If α_2 is a prefix of α_1, i.e., $\alpha_1=\alpha_2 b\lambda$ (lines 15-23), we create a new node n with labels $\alpha=\alpha_2$ (line 18) and β consisting of $|\beta_1|$ bits b, in which we insert β_2 at position pos (lines 19-20). The b-child of the node n is then the result of merging the b-child of n_2 at position β_1.rank(b,pos) into a node with labels α=γ and $\beta=\beta_1$, having the children of n_1 as children (lines 17, 22). The (1-b)-child of the node n is the (1-b)-child of n_2 (line 23).

Otherwise, α_1 and α_2 share a common prefix (lines 25-34). Let γ be the common prefix of α_1 and α_2, and let us assume w.l.o.g. that $\alpha_1=\gamma 1\delta$ and $\alpha_2=\gamma 0\lambda$ (c.f. Figure 10). Then, we modify the current node n by setting the label $\alpha=\gamma$ (line 29) and β to a bit-vector consisting of $|\beta_1|$ bits 1, in which we insert $|\beta_2|$ bits 0 at position pos (lines 30-32). The 0-child of node n is then a node with $\alpha=\lambda$ and $\beta=\beta_2$ having the children of n_2 as child nodes (lines 28,34), and the 1-child of node n is a node with $\alpha=\delta$ and $\beta=\beta_1$ having the children of n_1 as child nodes (lines 27,33).

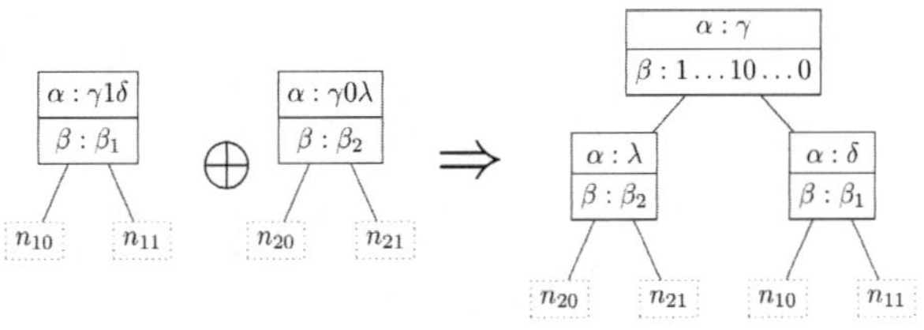

Figure 10. Appending t_1 and t_2 if α_1 and α_2 share a common prefix.

F. Intersection

This operation (c.f. Code 8) computes the set-intersection of two Wavelet Tries t_1 and t_2, i.e., it computes a Wavelet Trie that represents a lexicographically ordered list of all bit-strings s that occur in both, t_1 and in t_2.

Let n_1 be the current node of t_1 and n_2 be the current node of t_2, where n_1 has the labels α_1 and β_1 and n_2 has the labels α_2 and β_2.

If $\alpha_1=\alpha_2$ and n_1 and n_2 are leaf nodes, we can return n_1 as resulting Wavelet Trie (lines 3-4), as n_1 represents the intersection.

If $\alpha_1=\alpha_2$ and n_1 and n_2 are inner nodes, we compute the result node r_0 of the intersection of the 0-child of n_1 and of the 0-child of n_2 (line 6) and the result node r_1 of the intersection of the 1-child of n_1 and of the 1-child of n_2 (line 7). If both, the intersection of the 0-children of n_1 and n_2 and the intersection of the 1-children of n_1 and n_2 are empty (line 8), we return that the intersection of n_1 and n_2 is empty. Otherwise (lines 10-14), we return a new node n, with $\alpha=\alpha_1$, β consists of $|r_0|$ 0 bits followed by $|r_1|$ 1 bits, and n has r_0 as 0-child and has r_1 as 1-child. Note that by using this order of 0-bits and 1-bits in n's β-vector, we get the intersection in lexicographical order. If only one of the intersections is empty, we collapse the new node with the child representing the non-empty intersection (lines 10-11).

Let now either α_1 be a prefix of α_2 (lines 15-16) or vice versa (lines 17-18). Let us assume w.l.o.g. that α_2 is a prefix of α_1, i.e., $\alpha_1=\alpha_2 b\gamma$ (c.f. Figure 11). In this case, we change α_1 into $\alpha_1=\gamma$ and intersect this new node with the b-child of n_2 (line 4a). If the intersection does not return an empty node (line 5a), the β of the result node contains only bits b (i.e., only 1 bits or only 0 bits) as it does not have a (1-b)-child. Therefore, we collapse it with its single child node b-child n_b and thereby delete its (1-b)-child (lines 7a-10a).

```
1 Function intersection(WaveletTrie t1,
                         WaveletTrie t2):
2 if t1.α= t2.α then
3   if t1.isLeaf and t2.isLeaf then
4     return t1
5   else if not t1.isLeaf and
          not t2.isLeaf then
6     WaveletTrie r0 = intersection
       (t1.getChild(0), t2.getChild(0));
7     WaveletTrie r1 = intersection
       (t1.getChild(1),t2.getChild(1));
8     if r1=∅ and r2=∅ then return ∅;
9     else
10      res = WaveletTrie(t1.α,-,r0,r1);
11      if r0 = ∅ then res.collapse(1);
12      if r1 = ∅ then res.collapse(0);
13      res.β = 1^|r0| 0^|r1|;
14      return res;
15 if t1.α isPrefixOf t2.α then
16   return intersectionPrefix(t1,t2);
17 else if t2.α isPrefixOf t1.α then
18   return intersectionPrefix(t2,t1);
19 else return ∅;

1a Function intersectionPrefix(
     WaveletTrie pre, WaveletTrie other):
2a Bit b = pre.α.getFirstDifferentBit
                             (other.α);
3a other.α= other.α.getSuffix(pre.α);
4a WaveletTrie res_b =
     intersection(pre.getChild(b),other);
5a if res_b = ∅ then return ∅;
6a else
7a   res. α = pre. α;
8a   res.setChild(b,res_b);
9a   res.collaps(b);
10a  return res;
```

Code 8. Compute the intersection of two Wavelet Tries

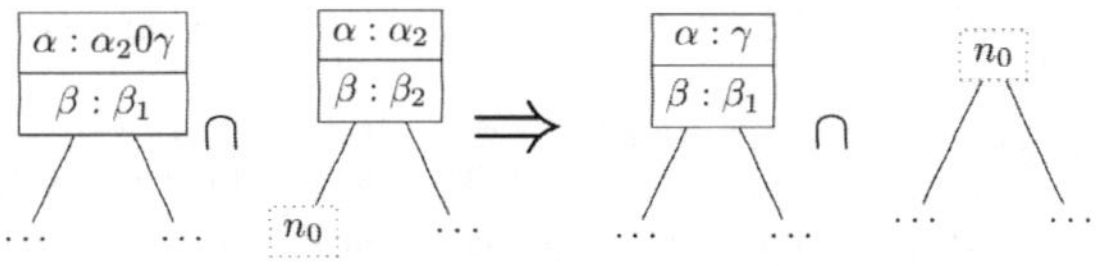

Figure 11. Intersection if α_2 is a prefix of α .

In all other cases, the intersection is empty (line 19). This includes the case that neither α_1 is a prefix of α_2 nor α_2 is a prefix of α_1 nor $\alpha_1=\alpha_2$ and the case that $\alpha_1=\alpha_2$ and exactly one node of n1, n2 is a leaf node and the other is an inner node.

V. Evaluation

To evaluate our implementation of the Wavelet Trie, we want to compare it with an approach that supports all the desired operations and provides a compression of the string sequences.

A natural approach to compare our implementation of the Wavelet Trie with is the approach to compress string sequences with a standard compressor like gzip or bzip2, to decompress them on demand, and to do the desired operations on the decompressed string sequence.

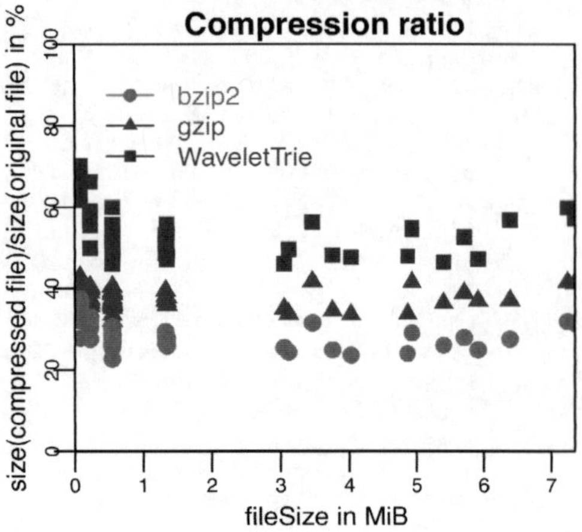

Figure 12. Compression ratio.

We did not compare our implementation with delta-encoding as delta-encoding has the following disadvantage. Delta-encoding cannot support any of the range queries, i.e., our prefix search (III.A), Between, LessThan, and GreaterThan (III.B), because equal strings are encoded different, depending on the previous string. Even intersection (III.F) is not supported. Therefore, delta-encoding does not meet our requirements.

The dictionary-based approach, assigning a segregated Huffman code to each entry results in a bit sequence that supports alphabetical comparisons. Run-length encoding compressing longer bit sequences also supports alphabetical comparisons. Both approaches are orthogonal and compatible to our approach, i.e., can be combined with it. As therefore, a performance comparison with dictionary-based approaches or with RLE is not useful, we have compared our approach with the powerful and widely use compressors gzip und bzip2.

We ran our tests on Mac OS X 10.5.5, 2.9 GHz Intel Core i7 with 8 GB 1600 MHz DDR3 running Java 1.8.0_45.

To evaluate rather text-centric operations, we used 114 texts of the project Gutenberg [15] with file sizes from 78 kB up to 7.3 MB to build a heterogeneous corpus. In order to simulate database operations of a column-oriented database, we used author information extracted from DBLP [16]. Out of these information, we generated lists consisting of 2500 up to 100000 authors.

In all time measurements, we performed 10 redundant runs and computed the average CPU time for all these runs.

A. Compression and Decompression

When evaluating the pure compression and decompression of Wavelet Trie, gzip and bzip2, we get the result that bzip compresses strongest while Wavelet Trie compresses worst (c.f. Figure 12), and that gzip compresses and decompresses fastest while Wavelet Trie compresses and decompresses slowest (c.f. Figure 13).

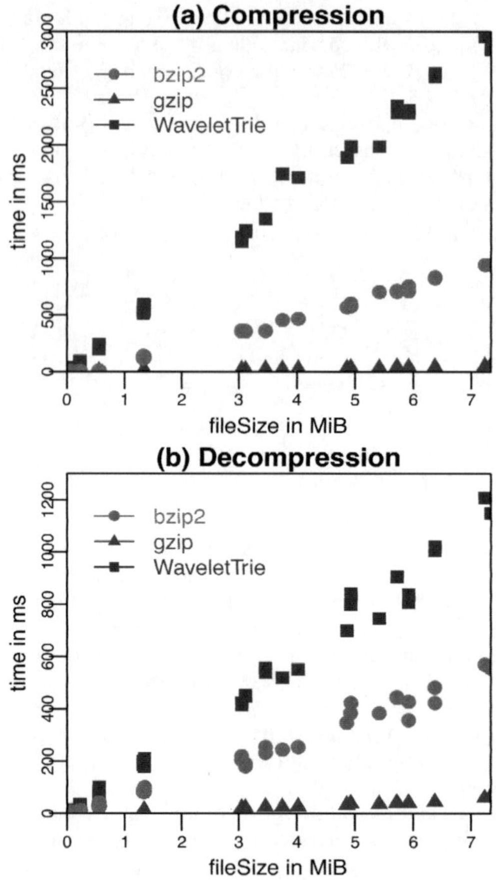

Figure 13. Compression and decompression time.

The main difference between the Wavelet Trie and the generic compressors is that the Wavelet Trie supports many operations on the compressed data, while gzip and bzip2 require to at least decompress the compressed data first, and for some operations to recompress the modified data afterwards. This means, there are a lot of applications that do not require the Wavelet Trie to decompress, as the concerning operations can be evaluated on the compressed data directly. We show the benefit of using the Wavelet Trie in the following subsections, in which we evaluate the performance of the different operations.

B. Search and searchPrefix

Figure 14 shows the search times for (a) a single word and (b) all words starting with a given prefix directly in the Wavelet Trie compared to the time needed for the pure decompression of bzip2 and gzip.

We searched within our Gutenberg corpus for all positions of the word 'file', which is contained in each file, and for all positions of words starting with the prefix 'e'. Although the times for bzip2 and for gzip comprise only the pure decompression, i.e., no search operation is performed on the decompressed bzip2 or the decompressed gzip file, the search directly on the Wavelet Trie is faster than the pure decompression times of bzip2 and of gzip.

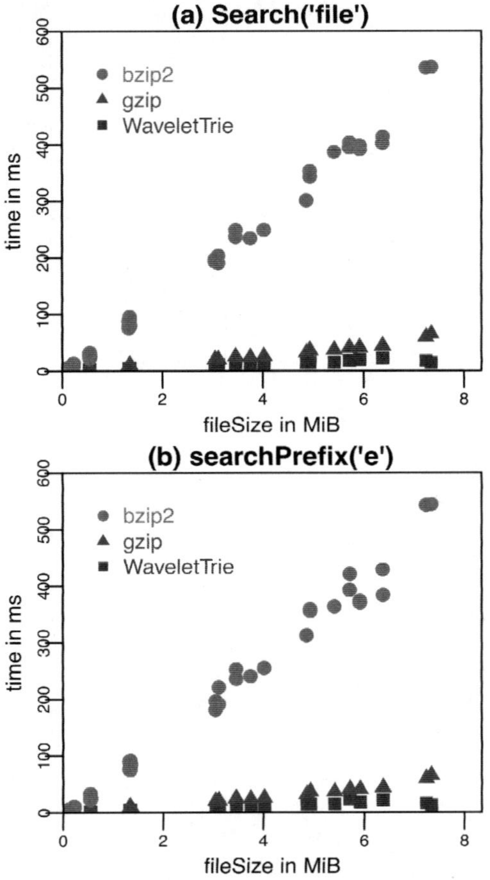

Figure 14. Search times for words in the Wavelet Trie compared to pure decompression time of bzip2 and of gzip.

C. Range queries

Figure 15 shows the results of comparing the search times (a) for words greater than 'e' but less than 'f' and (b) for words greater than 'identification' and less than 'identifier' directly on the Wavelet Trie with the pure decompression time of bzip 2 and gzip. These operations were again evaluated on the Gutenberg corpus. Although the times for bzip2 and for gzip comprise only the pure decompression, i.e., no search operation is performed, the search directly on the Wavelet Trie is faster than the pure decompression times of bzip2 and of gzip. The more specific the search query is, and thus the smaller the search result, the better is the performance benefit of the Wavelet Trie compared to bzip2 and gzip.

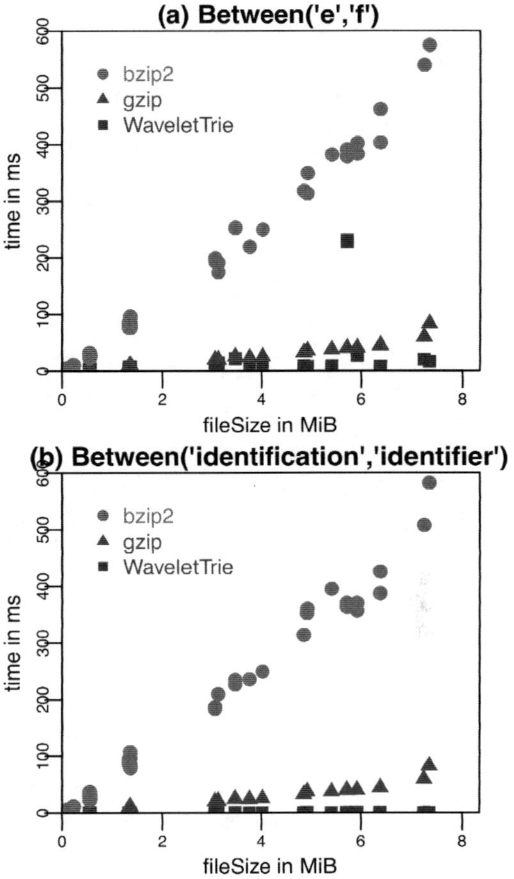

Figure 15. Range queries on the Wavelet Trie compared to pure decompression time of bzip2 and gzip.

D. Insert and Delete

As a first operation, we compared the insert and the delete operation directly on the Wavelet Trie with the pure decompression time of bzip2 and of gzip. We performed these operations on the documents of our Gutenberg corpus. Figure 16 shows the results. The insertion of the word 'database', which does not occur in any of the documents, as 50th word is faster than the pure decompression of bzip2 and as fast as the pure decompression of gzip. The same holds for the deletion of the 50th word.

Note that the decompression times for bzip2 and gzip neither contain the time needed to insert (or to delete respectively) a string nor the time needed to recompress the modified results.

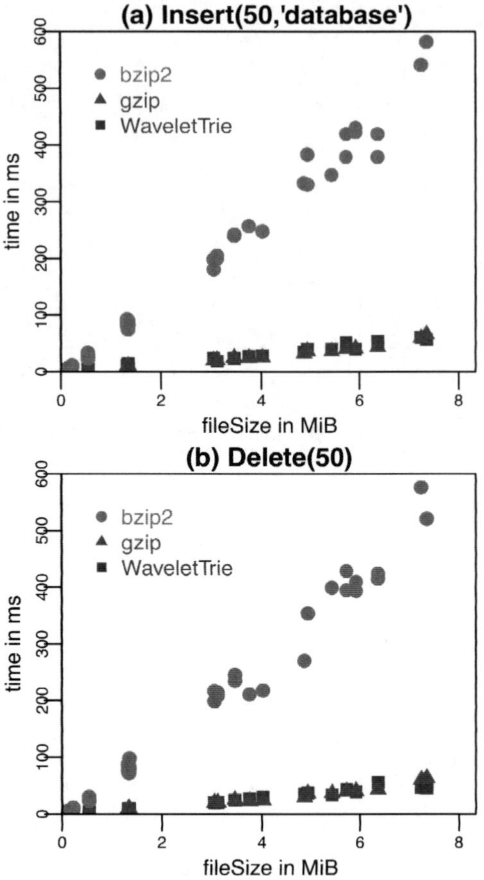

Figure 16. (a) Insertion and (b) Deletion in the Wavelet Trie compared to bzip2 and gzip decompression time.

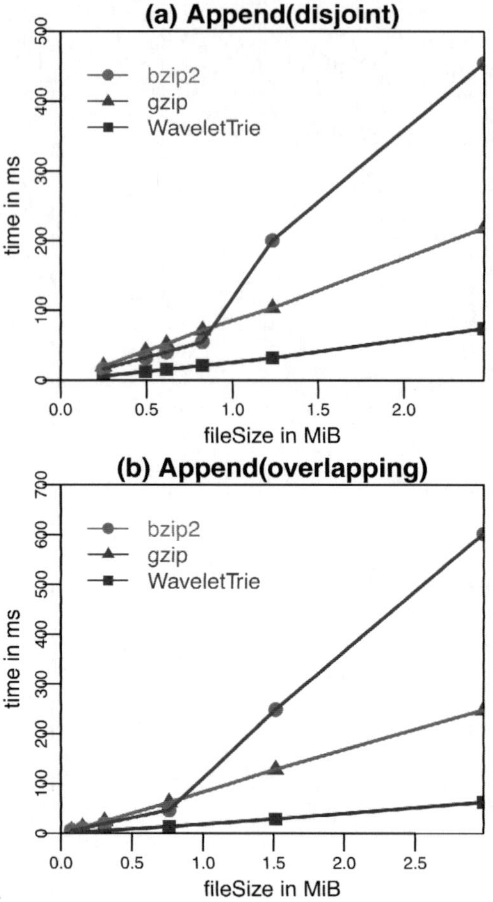

Figure 17. Comparison of the time to append two lists for Wavelet Trie, bzip2 and gzip.

E. Merge/Union

Finally, we evaluated the time to append one list to another list (c.f. Figure 17) and the time to insert a list at position 50 into a second one (c.f. Figure 18).

We performed both tests for disjoint lists as well as for lists that overlap in 50% of the entries. Again, we compared the time with the sequence of decompression and recompressing the concatenated list by using either bzip2 or gzip, i.e., we did not perform any merge or append operation for bzip2 or gzip. In both cases and for both operations, this operation on the Wavelet Trie is faster than the simulation of this operation for bzip2 and for gzip. The benefit of the Wavelet Trie in comparison to bzip2 and gzip is bigger for append operations than for the merge operation that inserts one list at a given position into the second one.

F. Intersection

The following tests were performed on our dblp author corpus. Figure 19 shows the results of comparing the intersection operation on two author lists with the sequence of decompression and recompressing the result list of the intersection using bzip2 and gzip. We computed the result list of the intersection prior to the test runs, i.e., the time needed to compute the intersection was not measured. We used two different sets of lists: the first is duplicate-free, whereas, in the second set, 50% of the list entries of the second list occur also in the first list. If the lists are completely disjoint, the intersection computed directly on the Wavelet Trie is faster than the sequence of decompression and recompression for bzip2 and as fast as this sequence of operations for gzip. If there is a large overlapping of the lists, gzip is faster than the Wavelet Trie, which still is faster than bzip2. Note that we did not perform any intersection operation for gzip and bzip2 compressed data.

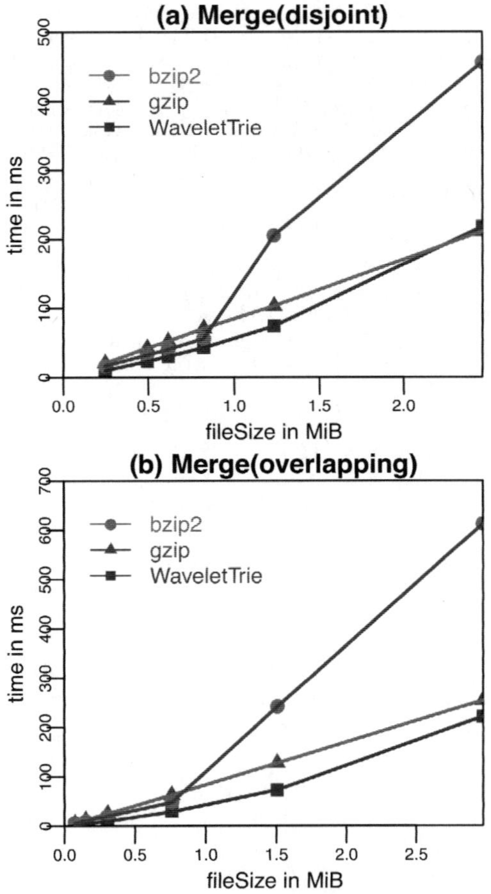

Figure 18. Comparison of the time to merge a list into another one for Wavelet Trie, bzip2 and gzip.

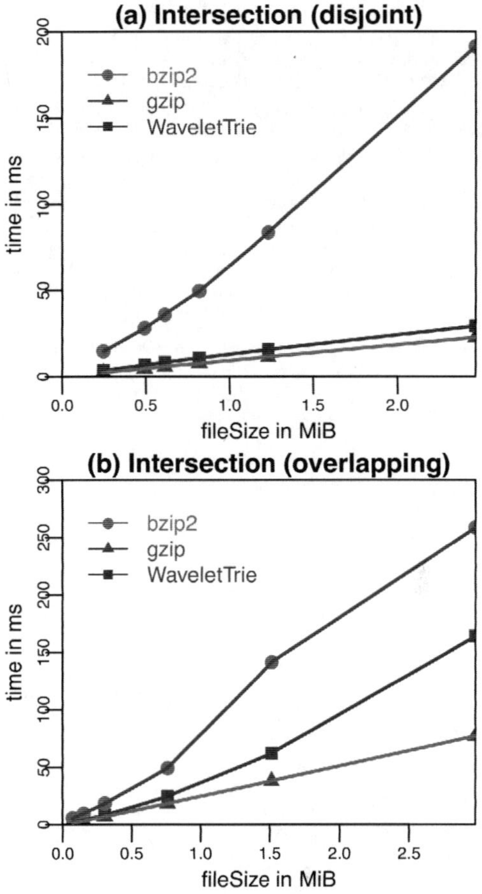

Figure 19. Computing the intersection directly on the Wavelet Trie compared to decompression, list concatenation and recompression time of bzip2 and gzip.

VI. CONCLUSION

In this paper, we presented and evaluated an extension of the Wavelet Trie [12][13] that allows to represent compressed indexed sequences of strings. As our evaluations have shown, operations like insertion, deletion, search queries, range queries, intersection and union can be performed on the compressed data as fast as or even faster than the simulation of these operations with the help of generic compressors like bzip2 or gzip. We therefore believe that the Wavelet Trie is a good approach to be used, e.g., in column-oriented main-memory databases to enhance the storage or memory capacity at the same time as the search performance.

REFERENCES

[1] S. Böttcher, R. Hartel, and J. Manuel, "A Column-Oriented Text Database API Implemented on Top of Wavelet Tries," in DBKDA 2017, The Ninth International Conference on Advances in Databases, Knowledge, and Data Applications, 2017, pp. 54–60.

[2] M. Stonebraker et al., "C-Store: A Column-oriented DBMS," in Proceedings of the 31st International Conference on Very Large Data Bases, Trondheim, Norway, August 30 - September 2, 2005, 2005, pp. 553–564.

[3] A. Lamb et al., "The Vertica Analytic Database: C-Store 7 Years Later," Proc. VLDB Endowment, vol. 5, no. 12, pp. 1790–1801, 2012.

[4] F. Färber et al., "SAP HANA Database - Data Management for Modern Business Applications," ACM Sigmod Rec., vol. 40, no. 4, pp. 45–51, 2012.

[5] R. Grossi, A. Gupta, and J. S. Vitter, "High-order entropy-compressed text indexes," in SODA '03 Proceedings of the fourteenth annual ACM-SIAM symposium on Discrete algorithms, 2003, vol. 39, no. 1, pp. 841–850.

[6] D. A. Huffman, "A Method for the Construction of

Minimum-Redundancy Codes," in Proceedings of the IRE, 1952, vol. 40, no. 9, pp. 1098–1101.

[7] T. C. Hu and A. C. Tucker, "Optimal Computer Search Trees and Variable-Length Alphabetical Codes," SIAM J. Appl. Math., vol. 21, no. 4, pp. 514–532, 1971.

[8] S. T. Klein and D. Shapira, "Random Access to Fibonacci Codes," Stringology, 2014, pp. 96–109, 2014.

[9] M. Külekci, "Enhanced variable-length codes: Improved compression with efficient random access," in Proc. Data Compression Conference DCC–2014, 2014, pp. 362–371.

[10] N. R. Brisaboa, A. Fariña, S. Ladra, and G. Navarro, "Reorganizing Compressed Text," in Proceedings of the 31st Annual International ACM SIGIR Conference on Research and Development in Information Retrieval, 2008, pp. 139–146.

[11] J. Herzberg, S. T. Klein, and D. Shapira, "Enhanced Direct Access to Huffman Encoded Files," in Data Compression Conference, 2015, p. 447.

[12] R. Grossi and G. Ottaviano, "The Wavelet Trie: Maintaining an Indexed Sequence of Strings in Compressed Space," *CoRR*, 2012. [Online]. Available: http://arxiv.org/abs/1204.3581. [Accessed: Nov, 2017].

[13] R. Grossi and G. Ottaviano, "The Wavelet Trie: Maintaining an Indexed Sequence of Strings in Compressed Space," in Proceedings of the 31st ACM SIGMOD-SIGACT-SIGART Symposium on Principles of Database Systems, PODS 2012, Scottsdale, AZ, USA, May 20-24, 2012, 2012, pp. 203–214.

[14] D. R. Morrison, "PATRICIA---Practical Algorithm To Retrieve Information Coded in Alphanumeric," J. ACM, vol. 15, no. 4, pp. 514–534, 1968.

[15] "Project Gutenberg," 2015. [Online]. Available: http://www.gutenberg.org/. [Accessed: Nov, 2017].

[16] "DBLP: computer science Bibliography." [Online]. Available: http://dblp.uni-trier.de. [Accessed: Nov, 2017].

iaria journals

www.iariajournals.org

International Journal On Advances in Intelligent Systems

issn: 1942-2679

International Journal On Advances in Internet Technology

issn: 1942-2652

International Journal On Advances in Life Sciences

issn: 1942-2660

International Journal On Advances in Networks and Services

issn: 1942-2644

International Journal On Advances in Security

issn: 1942-2636

International Journal On Advances in Software

issn: 1942-2628

International Journal On Advances in Systems and Measurements

issn: 1942-261x

International Journal On Advances in Telecommunications

issn: 1942-2601

**International Academy, Research,
and Industry Association (IARIA)**
412 Derby Way
Wilmington, DE 19810

ISBN 978-1-5108-5652-3
9 781510 856523

CURRAN ASSOCIATES INC.
proceedings.com

International Journal on Advances in Systems and Measurements

2017 Volume 10 Number 3&4

ISSN: 1942-261x

IARIA